The Rough Guide to

Egypt

There are more than one hundred and fifty Rough Guide titles
covering destinations from Amsterdam to Zimbabwe

Forthcoming titles include
Alaska • Copenhagen • Ibiza & Formentera • Iceland

Rough Guide Reference Series
Classical Music • Country Music • Drum 'n' bass • English Football
European Football • House • The Internet • Jazz • Music USA • Opera
Reggae • Rock Music • Techno • Unexplained Phenomena • World Music

Rough Guide Phrasebooks
Czech • Dutch • Egyptian Arabic • European Languages • French • German
Greek • Hindi & Urdu • Hungarian • Indonesian • Italian • Japanese
Mandarin Chinese • Mexican Spanish • Polish • Portuguese • Russian
Spanish • Swahili • Thai • Turkish • Vietnamese

Rough Guides on the Internet
www.roughguides.com

ROUGH GUIDE CREDITS

Text editor: Cameron Wilson
Series editor: Mark Ellingham
Editorial: Martin Dunford, Jonathan Buckley, Jo Mead, Kate Berens, Amanda Tomlin, Ann-Marie Shaw, Paul Gray, Helena Smith, Judith Bamber, Orla Duane, Olivia Eccleshall, Ruth Blackmore, Sophie Martin, Geoff Howard, Claire Saunders, Gavin Thomas, Alexander Mark Rogers, Polly Thomas, Joe Staines, Lisa Nellis, Andrew Tomičić, Claire Fogg, Richard Lim, Duncan Clark, Peter Buckley (UK); Andrew Rosenberg, Mary Beth Maioli, Don Bapst, Stephen Timblin (US)
Production: Susanne Hillen, Andy Hilliard, Link Hall, Helen Ostick, Julia Bovis, Michelle Draycott,

Katie Pringle, Robert Evers, Niamh Hatton, Mike Hancock, Robert McKinlay
Cartography: Melissa Baker, Maxine Repath, Nichola Goodliffe, Ed Wright
Picture research: Louise Boulton, Sharon Martins
Online editors: Kelly Cross (US)
Finance: John Fisher, Gary Singh, Edward Downey, Mark Hall, Tim Bill
Marketing & Publicity: Richard Trillo, Niki Smith, David Wearn, Jemima Broadbridge (UK); Jean-Marie Kelly, Myra Campolo, Simon Carloss (US)
Administration: Tania Hummel, Charlotte Marriott, Demelza Dallow

ACKNOWLEDGEMENTS

The author would like to thank the following people in Egypt for their hospitality, help and friendship: Enric, Hassan, Tayeb, Gamal, Hagg Ibrahim and Mr Magdy in Luxor; Farag in Hurghada; Salah Mohammed and Ahmed Soufry in Cairo; Dawn in Alex; Grassi in the oases. Also to the outstanding tourist officials: Omar Ahmed (Dakhla); Nahed Gad (Cairo); Mahdi Hweity (Siwa); Shoukri Saad (Aswan); Salwa Abu Zaid (Alexandria); General Hanafi and Colonel Hafiez of the tourist police.

This edition, like the previous ones, is dedicated to Gagou with love.

Jessica would like to thank Giampaolo Aiello and Karim Nur at Anemone Dive Centre, Ali Awartani, Hossam Helmy and Heshem Mostafa Kamal at Red Sea Diving Safari, Amr Hsaken Shell in Suez, Khaled Liston, Ehab Nammar at Sinainet, Nikki Priestley, Emad Raghab, Walid Ramadan and Sherif Pacha from Geographic

Adventures, Rod Rotundi, and Ibrahim Saad Awad-Allah and Eid Muhammed from Hammata.

The editor would like to thank: Simon, Jessica and Charles for their sterling efforts in updating the guide, and particularly Charles for putting up with endless queries; Sharon Martins for sifting through hundreds of photos; Stephen Townshend and Nick Thomson for help with Basics; Anne Hegarty and Gillian Armstrong for proofing; Helen Ostick for typesetting; *Rough Guides* cartographers Maxine Repath and Ed Wright and also Mandy Muggridge (GeoGraphics Services) for wrestling with the maps.

Many thanks also to all those **readers** of the previous edition of the Egypt guide who wrote in with tips, ideas and stories; your input was greatly appreciated by our team of updaters, and helped us to make this edition even better.

PUBLISHING INFORMATION

This fourth edition published June 2000 by
  Rough Guides Ltd, 62–70 Shorts Gardens,
  London, WC2H 9AH. Reprinted January 2001.
Distributed by the Penguin Group:
Penguin Books Ltd, 27 Wrights Lane, London W8 5TZ
Penguin Putnam, Inc. 375 Hudson Street, NY 10014,
  USA
Penguin Books Australia Ltd, 487 Maroondah Highway,
  PO Box 257, Ringwood, Victoria 3134, Australia
Penguin Books Canada Ltd, 10 Alcorn Avenue, Toronto,
  Ontario, Canada M4V 1E4
Penguin Books (NZ) Ltd, 182–190 Wairau Road,
  Auckland 10, New Zealand
Typeset in Linotron Univers and Century Old Style to an
  original design by Andrew Oliver.
Printed in England by Clays Ltd, St Ives PLC.
Illustrations in Part One and Part Three by Edward Briant.

Illustrations on p.1 & p.645 by Henry Iles
© Dan Richardson, 2000
No part of this book may be reproduced in any form
  without permission from the publisher except for the
  quotation of brief passages in reviews.
720pp – Includes index
A catalogue record for this book is available from the
  British Library
ISBN 1-85828-522-4

The publishers and authors have done their best to
  ensure the accuracy and currency of all the information
  in *The Rough Guide to Egypt*, however, they can accept
  no responsibility for any loss, injury, or inconvenience
  sustained by any traveller as a result of information or
  advice contained in the guide.

The Rough Guide to

Egypt

written and researched by

Dan Richardson

with additional contributions by

Simon Foster, Jessica Jacobs and Charles Young

ROUGH
GUIDES

THE ROUGH GUIDES

TRAVEL GUIDES • PHRASEBOOKS • MUSIC AND REFERENCE GUIDES

 We set out to do something different when the first Rough Guide was published in 1982. Mark Ellingham, just out of university, was travelling in Greece. He brought along the popular guides of the day, but found they were all lacking in some way. They were either strong on ruins and museums but went on for pages without mentioning a beach or taverna. Or they were so conscious of the need to save money that they lost sight of Greece's cultural and historical significance. Also, none of the books told him anything about Greece's contemporary life – its politics, its culture, its people, and how they lived.

So with no job in prospect, Mark decided to write his own guidebook, one which aimed to provide practical information that was second to none, detailing the best beaches and the hottest clubs and restaurants, while also giving hard-hitting accounts of every sight, both famous and obscure, and providing up-to-the-minute information on contemporary culture. It was a guide that encouraged independent travellers to find the best of Greece, and was a great success, getting shortlisted for the Thomas Cook travel guide award, and encouraging Mark,

along with three friends, to expand the series.

The Rough Guide list grew rapidly and the letters flooded in, indicating a much broader readership than had been anticipated, but one which uniformly appreciated the Rough Guide mix of practical detail and humour, irreverence and enthusiasm. Things haven't changed. The same four friends who began the series are still the caretakers of the Rough Guide mission today: to provide the most reliable, up-to-date and entertaining information to independent-minded travellers of all ages, on all budgets.

We now publish more than 150 titles and have offices in London and New York. The travel guides are written and researched by a dedicated team of more than 100 authors, based in Britain, Europe, the USA and Australia. We have also created a unique series of phrasebooks to accompany the travel series, along with an acclaimed series of music guides, and a best-selling pocket guide to the Internet and World Wide Web. We also publish comprehensive travel information on our Web site:

www.roughguides.com

HELP US UPDATE

We've gone to a lot of effort to ensure that the fourth edition of *The Rough Guide to* Egypt is accurate and up-to-date. However, things change — places get "discovered", opening hours are notoriously fickle, restaurants and rooms raise prices or lower standards. If you feel we've got it wrong or left something out, we'd like to know, and if you can remember the address, the price, the time, the phone number, so much the better.

We'll credit all contributions, and send a copy of the next edition (or any other Rough Guide if you prefer) for the best letters. Please mark letters: "Rough Guide Egypt Update" and send to:

Rough Guides, 62–70 Shorts Gardens, London WC2H 9AH, or Rough Guides, 4th Floor, 345 Hudson St, New York, NY 10014.

Or send email to: mail@roughguides.co.uk
Online updates about this book can be found on Rough Guides' Web site at www.roughguides.com

THE AUTHOR

Dan Richardson was born in England in 1958. Before joining Rough Guides in 1984, he worked as a sailor on the Red Sea and as a commodities dealer in Peru. Since then he has travelled extensively in Egypt and Eastern Europe. While in St Petersburg, he met his future wife, Anna; they now have a daughter, Sonia.

CONTENTS

Introduction xi

• CHAPTER 3: THE WESTERN DESERT OASES

• CHAPTER 4: ALEXANDRIA AND THE MEDITERRANEAN COAST

• CHAPTER 5: THE DELTA

• CHAPTER 6: THE CANAL ZONE

• CHAPTER 7: SINAI

● CHAPTER 8: THE RED SEA COAST & EASTERN DESERT   611–643

PART THREE CONTEXTS   645

LIST OF MAPS

MAP SYMBOLS

━━	Railway		🪦	Tomb
═══	Main road		Ⓜ	Metro station
───	Minor road		◉	Hotel
- - - -	Path		ℂ	Telephone
───	River		✉	Post office
━ ━ ━	Chapter division boundary		ⓘ	Information point
━ ■ ━ ■	International boundary		■	Building
⋔⋔	Cliff face		✠	Church
▦	Desert/beach		⛪	Monastery
✈	Airport		[†]	Christian cemetery
🌴	Oasis/palm tree		✡	Synagogue
🔱	Viewpoint		☪	Mosque
♦	Point of interest			Muslim cemetery
╱╲	Mountain range		▦	Park
▲	Mountain peak		▦	National park
△	Pyramid			Delta
⌂	Cave		⟦↰⟧	Coral reef
▤	Temple			

INTRODUCTION

E gypt is the oldest tourist destination on earth. Ancient Greeks and Romans started the trend, coming to goggle at the cyclopean scale of the Pyramids and the Colossi of Thebes. At the onset of colonial times, Napoleon and the British in turn looted Egypt's treasures to fill their national museums, sparking off a trickle of Grand Tourists that, by the 1860s, had grown into a flood of travellers, packaged for their Nile cruises and Egyptological lectures by the enterprising Thomas Cook.

Today, the attractions of the country are little different. The focus of most visits remains the great monuments of the Nile Valley, combined with a few days spent exploring the souks, mosques and *madrassas* of Islamic Cairo. However, possibilities for Egyptian travel also encompass snorkelling and diving along the Red Sea coasts, remote oases and camel trips into the mountains of Sinai, or visits to the Coptic monasteries of the Eastern Desert.

The land itself is a freak of nature, whose lifeblood is the River Nile. From the Sudanese border to the shores of the Mediterranean, the Nile Valley and its Delta are flanked by arid wastes, the latter as empty as the former are teeming with people. This stark duality between fertility and desolation is fundamental to Egypt's character and has shaped its development since prehistoric times, imparting continuity to diverse cultures and peoples over five millennia. It is a sense of permanence and timelessness that is buttressed by religion, which pervades every aspect of life. Although the pagan cults of ancient Egypt are as moribund as its legacy of mummies and temples, their ancient fertility rites and processions of boats still hold their place in the celebrations of Islam and Christianity.

The result is a multi-layered culture, which seems to accord equal respect to ancient and modern. The peasants (*fellaheen*) of the Nile and Bedouin tribes of the desert live much as their ancestors did a thousand years ago. Other communities include the Nubians of the far south, and the Coptic Christians, who trace their ancestry back to pharaonic times. What unites them is a love of their homeland, extended family ties, dignity, warmth and hospitality towards strangers. Though most visitors are drawn to Egypt by its monuments, the enduring memory is likely to be of its people and their way of life.

Regions and highlights

Each of the regions is discussed in its own chapter introduction; what follows is merely the briefest outline of the main attractions.

Most visitors arrive at **Cairo**. A seething megalopolis, its chief sightseeing appeal lies in its **bazaars** and medieval **mosques**, though there is scarcely less fascination in its juxtapositions of medieval and modern life, with fortified gates, villas and skyscrapers interwoven by flyovers whose traffic may be halted by herds of camels. The immensity and diversity of this "Mother of Cities" is as staggering as anything you'll encounter in Egypt, while just outside Cairo are the first of the **pyramids** that range across the desert to the edge of the Fayoum, among them the unsurpassable trio at **Giza** and the vast necropolis of **Saqqara**. Besides all this, there are superb **museums** devoted to Ancient, Coptic and Islamic Egypt, and enough **entertainments** to occupy weeks of your time.

However, the principal tourist lure remains, as ever, the **Nile Valley**, with its **ancient monuments** and timeless river vistas – felucca sailboat **cruises** being a great way to combine the two. The town of **Luxor** is synonymous with the magnificent temples of

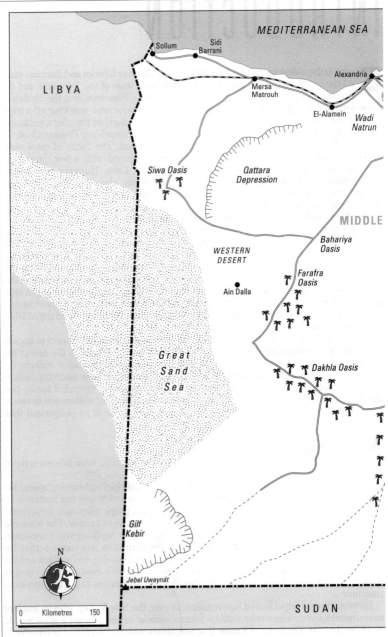

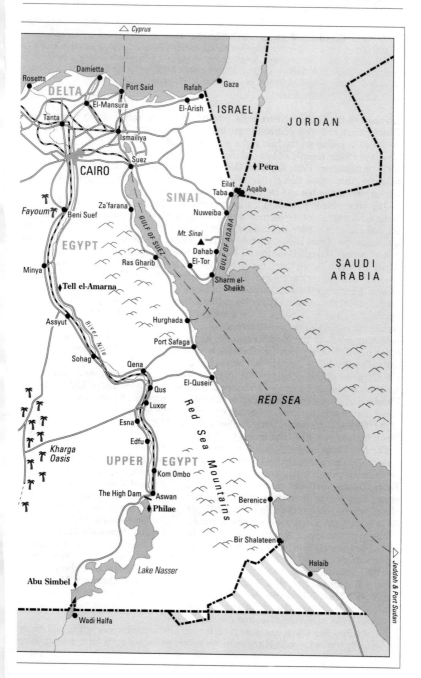

The **Arab Republic of Egypt** (*El-Gumhorriya Masr al-Arabiya*) covers an area of 1,002,000 square kilometres – roughly twice the size of France, or about equal to Texas – of which 96.4 percent is desert. Its population of over 60 million is twice that of the next most populous Arab country (Morocco) and makes a quarter of the total population of the Arab world. Sixty-five percent of Egyptians work on the land.

Karnak and the **Theban Necropolis**, which includes the **Valley of the Kings** where Tutankhamun and other pharaohs were buried. **Aswan**, Egypt's southernmost city, has the loveliest setting on the Nile and a languorous ambience. From here, you can visit the island **Philae temple of Isis** and the rock-hewn colossi at **Abu Simbel**. Other sites not to be missed are **Edfu** and **Kom Ombo** (between Luxor and Aswan) and – for those willing to chance their luck on the fringes of potentially risky Middle Egypt – the amazing temples of **Abydos** and **Dendara** (north of Luxor).

Only accessible to tourists in the last two decades, the **Western Desert Oases** are scattered across a vast, awesomely desolate region. **Siwa**, out towards the Libyan border, has a unique culture and history, limpid pools and bags of charm. Another option is to follow the "Great Desert Circuit" (starting from Cairo or Assyut) through the four "inner" oases. Though **Bahariya** and **Farafra** hold the most appeal, with the lovely **White Desert** between them, the larger oases of **Dakhla** and **Kharga** also have their rewards once you escape their modernized "capitals". And for those equipped to make serious desert expeditions, there's the challenge of entering the **Great Sand Sea** or tracing part of the infamous **Forty Days Road**. By way of contrast to these deep-desert locations are the quasi-oases of the **Fayoum** and **Wadi Natrun**, with their diverse ancient ruins and **Coptic monasteries**.

Moving north to the **Mediterranean**, Egypt's second city, **Alexandria**, boasts a string of beaches to which Cairenes flock in summer, and excellent seafood restaurants. Despite being founded by Alexander the Great and lost to the Romans by Cleopatra, the city today betrays little of its ancient glory; however, the ongoing underwater excavation of **Cleopatra's Palace** and (possibly) the legendary **Lighthouse of Pharos** may once more bring an air of majesty to Alexandria. Famous too for its decadence during colonial times, romantics can still indulge here in a nostalgic exploration of the "Capital of Memory", while further along the Mediterranean coast lie the World War II battlefield of **El-Alamein** and the Egyptian holiday resort of **Mersa Matrouh**.

The Nile **Delta**, east of Alexandria, musters few archeological monuments given its major role in ancient Egyptian history, and is largely overlooked by tourists. However, for those interested in Egyptian culture, the Delta hosts colourful religious **festivals** at **Tanta**, **Zagazig** and other towns. Further east lies the **Canal Zone**, dominated by the Suez Canal and its three cities. **Port Said** and **Ismailiya** are pleasant, albeit sleepy places, where you can get a feel of "real Egypt" without tripping over other tourists. **Suez** is grim, but a vital transport nexus between Cairo, Sinai and the Red Sea Coast.

Edged by coral reefs teeming with tropical fish, the **Sinai Peninsula** offers superb **diving** and **snorkelling**, and palmy **beaches** where women can swim unmolested. Resorts along the Gulf of Aqaba are varied enough to suit everyone, whether you're into the upmarket hotels of **Sharm el-Sheikh**, **Na'ama Bay** or **Taba**, or cheap, simple living at **Dahab** and **Nuweiba**. From there it's easy to visit **St Catherine's Monastery** and **Mount Sinai** (where Moses received the Ten Commandments) in the mountainous interior. With more time, cash and stamina, you can also embark on **jeep safaris** or **camel treks** to remote oases and spectacular wadis.

Egypt's **Red Sea Coast** has more reefs further offshore, with snorkelling and diving traditionally centred around **Hurghada**, while barely-touched reefs further south from

Port Safaga to **Mersa Allam** beckon serious diving enthusiasts. Inland, the mountainous **Eastern Desert** harbours the Coptic **Monasteries of St Paul** and **St Anthony**, Roman quarries and other antiquities, and dramatic rockscapes seen by few apart from the nomadic Bedouin.

When to go

Deciding on the best time for a visit involves striking a balance between climatic and tourist factors. Egypt's traditional season runs from **late November to late February**, when the Nile Valley is balmy, although Cairo can be overcast and chilly. However, at these times, particularly during the peak months of December and January, the major Nile resorts of Luxor and Aswan get unpleasantly crowded. This winter season is also the busiest period for the Sinai resorts, while Hurghada is active year round.

With this in mind, **March or April** are good compromise options, offering decent climate and fewer visitors. In **May and June** the heat is still tolerable but, after that, Egyptians rich enough to do so migrate to Alex and the coastal resorts. From **July to September** the south and desert are ferociously hot and sightseeing is best limited to early morning or evening – though August still sees droves of backpackers. **October into early November** is perhaps the best time of all, with easily manageable climate and crowds.

Weather and tourism apart, the **Islamic religious calendar** and its related festivals can have an effect on your travel. The most important factor is **Ramadan**, the month of daytime fasting, which can be problematic for eating and transport, though the festive evenings do much to compensate. See "Public Holidays and Moulids" in the Basics chapter for details of its timing.

MINIMUM/MAXIMUM TEMPERATURES °C (°F)						
	Jan	March	May	July	Sept	Nov
Alexandria *Mediterranean*	11/18 (51/65)	13/21 (55/70)	18/26 (64/79)	23/29 (73/85)	23/30 (73/86)	17/25 (62/77)
Aswan *Southern Nile Valley*	10/23 (50/74)	14/31 (58/87)	23/39 (74/103)	26/41 (79/106)	24/39 (75/103)	17/31 (62/87)
Cairo *Northern Nile Valley*	8/18 (47/65)	11/24 (52/75)	17/33 (63/91)	21/36 (70/96)	20/32 (68/90)	14/26 (58/78)
Dakhla *Western Desert*	5/21 (41/70)	8/28 (47/82)	20/37 (68/99)	23/40 (74/104)	21/36 (70/96)	12/28 (53/82)
Hurghada *Red Sea Coast*	10/21 (50/70)	12/23 (61/74)	21/30 (70/86)	25/32 (77/90)	23/30 (74/86)	15/25 (59/77)

Note that these are *average* daily maximum/minimum temperatures. Summer peaks in Aswan, Hurghada or Sinai, for example, can hit the 120°s F (low 50°s C) in hot years. The dryness of the air and absence of cloud cover makes for drastic fluctuations, though they do also make the heat tolerably un-sticky outside Cairo and the Delta.

The Mediterranean Coast can be windy and wet during wintertime.

PART ONE

THE

BASICS

KALABSHA TEMPLE

BASICS

GETTING THERE FROM BRITAIN AND IRELAND

The simplest way of getting to Egypt from Britain and Ireland is to fly. From London, there are regular direct scheduled flights to Cairo, Alexandria and Luxor, and highly competitive charters to Luxor, Hurghada (Red Sea) and Sharm el-Sheikh (Sinai). At the time of writing, there were no direct flights to Egypt from Ireland: you need connecting transport to London, or you can fly on a European airline via their "home" airport on the Continent.

If you're pushed for time, or want to make things easier, buying a package holiday makes a lot of sense. There are still some amazing bargains to be had amongst the basic Luxor-plus-Cairo or Luxor-only packages, although prices are beginning to rise now that the security situation seems to have stabilized. Besides these, many smaller independent operators feature felucca trips on the Nile, diving holidays on the Red Sea, or camel trekking in Sinai.

Alternatively, for anyone wanting to take in Egypt as part of wider travels in the Mediterranean or the Middle East, InterRail passes offer a cheap and flexible way to get there. For information on travelling on from Israel and Jordan, see p.16.

FLIGHTS

Flying direct to Cairo from London, you have a choice of **scheduled flights** on EgyptAir or British Airways, both of which fly daily from Heathrow. Fares vary according to the time of year (the most expensive being around Christmas) but depend more on the type of ticket – flexibility and duration being the main factors. BA currently charge £459 for a low-season return flight to Cairo (7-day advance-purchase, minimum 7-day stay, maximum 1 month, no refund or alterations), although discount agents may sell the same ticket for as little as £280. EgyptAir charges from £262 for a similar ticket, and also offers direct flights to Luxor from both Manchester (summer only) and Heathrow for the same price.

Most other major **European airlines** can sell you flights to Egypt (almost always Cairo) travelling via their own "home" airport on the Continent. Standards vary enormously from classy KLM, Lufthansa and Air France to tatty TAROM – most of the others fall somewhere in between. At the top end of the scale, prices are much the same as those of BA; at the other end you can pay well under £300 for a Pex or **Apex** fare. Apex tickets must be purchased three weeks in advance and are valid for a minimum stay of eight days up to a maximum of six months.

If the city near the "home" airport is interesting, consider breaking the journey for a **stopover** there; if not, you'll want to spend as little time as possible in the airport (Bucharest and Athens are the worst) – a factor that might determine your choice of airline. Addresses of airlines and agents are listed on pp.4 & 5.

You'll generally get the best deals on flights through **discount agencies** or student/youth travel specialists like **Campus Travel** or **STA Travel** (who have a dedicated Africa desk at their London Euston Road branch), which offer return flights to Cairo for £240–330. In addition to the recommended discount agents listed overleaf, useful **sources for finding a flight** are classified advertisements in the travel sections of newspapers like *The Independent* and *The Guardian* (Saturday editions), *The Sunday Times* or – in London – *Time Out* and *The Evening Standard*. High-street travel agents are also worth a look for deals on package holidays and charter flights. On the **Internet**, *www.cheapflights.com*, *www.lastminute.com* and *www.deckchair.com* are all worth a look, as are the Web sites of companies listed below, which often show special offers and last-minute deals.

It's also possible to get flight-only deals on **charter flights** – often for less than £200.

AIRLINES

Aer Lingus, 40 O'Connell St, Dublin 1 (☎01/844 4777); 2 Academy St, Cork (☎021/327 155); 136 O'Connell St, Limerick (☎061/474 239); *www.aerlingus.ie*. Several flights a day to London for connections on to Cairo.

Air France, 10 Warwick St, London W1R 5RA (☎0845/084 5111, *www.airfrance.com*). Flies to Cairo via Paris. Flight consolidators like Soliman Travel or Tradewings give reasonable fares; booking direct with Air France is much more expensive.

Air Malta, 314 Upper Richmond Rd, London SW15 6TU (☎020/8785 3177, *www.airmalta.com*). Flies to Cairo via Valletta.

Balkan-Bulgarian Airways, 322 Regent St, London W1R 5AG (☎020/7637 7637). Flies weekly to Cairo via Sofia. Can be good value.

British Airways, 156 Regent St, London W1R 6LB; 146 New St, Birmingham B2 4HN; 19–21 St Mary's Gate, Market St, Manchester M1 1PU; 64 Gordon St, Glasgow G1 3RS; 32 Frederick St, Edinburgh EH2 2JR (all enquiries ☎0345/222 111, *www.britishairways.com*). Flies London to Cairo direct, five times weekly.

British Midland, Belfast airport (☎0345/554 554); Dublin airport (☎01/283 8883); *www.iflybritishmidland.com*. For budget flights to London.

CSA, 72 Margaret St, London W1N 8HA (☎020/7255 1898); Manchester (☎0161/489 0241); Dublin (☎01/814 4626); *www.csa.cz*. Flies to Cairo via Prague. Cheap returns offer the chance to stop over in the Czech capital.

EgyptAir, 296 Regent St, London W1R 6PH (☎020/7734 2395, *www.egyptair.com*). Flies London to Cairo direct. No alcohol served on flights, though if you take your own they'll supply mixers.

El Al, UK House, 180 Oxford St, London W1N 0EL (☎020/7957 4100, *www.elal.com*). Flies to Cairo via Tel Aviv. Expensive.

KLM, ticket office at Heathrow Airport, Terminal 4 (☎08705/074 074, *www.klm.uk.com*). Flies to Cairo via Amsterdam. Usually expensive, but offers the convenience of flights from numerous regional British airports.

Lufthansa, 7/8 Conduit St, London W1R 9TG (all enquiries ☎0345/737 747, *www.lufthansa.com*). Flies to Cairo or Alex, via Frankfurt, from London, Birmingham and Manchester.

Malév, 1st floor, 22–25a Sackville St, London W1X 1ED (☎020/7439 0577, *www.malev.hu*). Flies to Cairo via Budapest. Malév is one of the better Eastern European airlines.

Olympic Airways, 11 Conduit St, London W1 0LP (☎020/7409 3400); Franklin House, 140–142 Pembroke Rd, Ballsbridge, Dublin 4 (☎01/608 0090); *www.olympicairways.gr*. Flies to Cairo via Athens. Worth checking for competitive fares, particularly from Dublin.

Ryanair, Phoenix House, Conyngham Rd, Dublin 8 (☎01/609 7800, *www.ryanair.ie*). Budget flights to London Stansted from Dublin, Cork, Kerry, Knock and Derry.

TAROM, 27 New Cavendish St, London W1N 7RL (☎020/7224 3693). Flies to Cairo via Bucharest. Unpredictable, with awful food and one of the worst airports in Europe, but may offer rock-bottom prices.

Turkish Airlines, 125 Pall Mall, London SW1Y 5EA (☎020/7499 4499, *www.turkishairlines.co*). Flies to Cairo via Istanbul.

Another advantage is that they fly direct to destinations other than Cairo – to Luxor, Hurghada or Sharm el-Sheikh – and may depart from regional airports as well as from London. Various operators offer special one-off flight deals: check out Kuoni, Hayes and Jarvis, Thomas Cook and Goldenjoy (see p.6 for addresses). At present, the cheapest flight-only deals to Sharm el-Sheikh are offered by the dive companies; these are usually not advertised, so approach the company direct. Generally bargains are advertised on Teletext and the Internet, in newspapers and magazines, and at high-street travel agents.

From **Ireland**, there are no direct flights to Egypt; the best option is to book a flight or package departing from Britain – either through your local travel agent or via the Internet – and get there on a budget flight. Return fares Dublin–London cost IR£80–140; try Ryanair, Aer Lingus or British Midland. Olympic Airways can get you to Cairo from Ireland for IR£429, but you'll still fly via London, with a second stop in Athens.

PACKAGES, ADVENTURE HOLIDAYS AND INCLUSIVE TOURS

Tour operators to Egypt come in many shapes and sizes. **Mainstream operators** offer traditional

DISCOUNT AGENTS IN BRITAIN AND IRELAND

Airline Network, Network House, Navigation Village, Riversway, Preston, Lancashire PR2 2YP (☎0870/241 0011, www.airnet.co.uk). New discount flights consolidator.

Air Tickets Direct ☎0990/320 321, www.booking.airtickets.co.uk. Telephone and Internet bookings only.

Flightline Essex ☎0800/036 0777, www.flightline.co.uk. Telephone and Internet discount flights consolidator.

North South Travel, Moulsham Mill Centre, Parkway, Chelmsford, Essex CM2 7PX (☎01245/608 291, brenda@nstravel.demon.co.uk). Friendly, competitive flight agent offering discounted fares – profits are used to support projects in the developing world.

Soliman Travel, 113 Earl's Court Rd, London SW5 9RL (☎020/7244 6855, www.solimantravel.co.uk). Well-established flight consolidators for scheduled flights.

STA Travel, 86 Old Brompton Rd, London SW7 3LH; 117 Euston Rd, London NW1 2SX; 38 Store St, London WC1E 7BZ; 11 Goodge St, London W1P 1FE (London branches ☎020/7361 6262); 38 North St, Brighton (☎01273/728 282); 25 Queens Rd, Bristol BS8 1QE (☎0117/929 4399); 38 Sidney St, Cambridge CB2 3HX (☎01223/366 966); 75 Deansgate, Manchester M3 2BW (☎0161/834 0668); 88 Vicar Lane, Leeds LS1 7JH (☎0113/244 9212); 78 Bold Street, Liverpool L1 4HR (☎0151/707 1123); 9 St Mary's Place, Newcastle-upon-Tyne NE1 7PG (☎0191/233 2111); 36 George St, Oxford OX1 2OJ (☎01865/792 800); 27 Forrest Rd, Edinburgh EH1 2QH (☎0131/226 7747); 184 Byres Rd, Glasgow G1 1JH (☎0141/338 6000); 30 Upper Kirkgate, Aberdeen AB10 1BE (☎0122/465 8222); branches also on university campuses in London, Birmingham, Bristol, Canterbury, Cardiff, Coventry, Durham, Glasgow, Leeds, Loughborough, Nottingham, Sheffield and Warwick; www.statravel.co.uk. Worldwide specialists in low-cost flights and tours for students and under-26s.

Tradewings, Morley House, Room 31/36, 320 Regent St, London W1R 5AG (☎020/7631 1840, www.travelshoppe.com). Flight consolidator for Balkan-Bulgarian Airlines.

Trailfinders, 194 Kensington High St, London W8 7RG (☎020/7938 3939); 1 Threadneedle St, London EC2R 8JX (☎020/7628 7628); 42–50 Earl's Court Rd, London W8 6FT (☎020/7938 3366); 58 Deansgate, Manchester M3 2FF (☎0161/839 6969); 254–284 Sauchiehall St, Glasgow G2 3EH (☎0141/353 2224); 22–24 The Priory Queensway, Birmingham B4 6BS (☎0121/236 1234); 48 Corn St, Bristol BS1 1HQ (☎0117/929 9000); 4/5 Dawson St, Dublin 2 (☎01/677 7888); www.trailfinders.co.uk. One of the best-informed agents for independent travellers.

Usit Campus, 52 Grosvenor Gardens, London SW1W 0AG (Europe ☎020/7730 3402, North America 7730 2101, worldwide 7730 8111); 541 Bristol Rd, Selly Oak, Birmingham B29 6AU (☎0121/414 1848); 61 Ditchling Rd, Brighton BN1 4SD (☎01273/570 226); 37–39 Queen's Rd, Clifton, Bristol BS8 1QE (☎0117/929 2494); 5 Emmanuel St, Cambridge CB1 1NE (☎01223/324 283); 53 Forest Rd, Edinburgh EH1 2QP (☎0131/225 6111, telesales 668 3303); 122 George St, Glasgow G1 1RF (☎0141/553 1818); 166 Deansgate, Manchester M3 3FE (☎0161/833 2046, telesales 273 1721); 105–106 St Aldates, Oxford OX1 1DO (☎01865/242 067); national call centre ☎0870/240 1010; www.usitcampus.co.uk, www.usit.ie (for Ireland and N.Ireland). Student/youth travel specialists, with branches all over Britain and Ireland.

---

tours and cruises, as well as **flight-plus-hotel packages** to Luxor, Aswan and elsewhere which can cost little more than a flight – for example, seven nights in Luxor for around £250 (often less if booked at the last minute) – and share the same advantage of varied departure and destination points (again check out the Internet, newspapers, etc – see above).

Other tour operators include small, independent **adventure holiday companies** priding themselves on modest-sized groups, adventurous itineraries or special interest activities – for all of which Egypt offers a lot of scope; and **diving holiday specialists**, who arrange trips to the Red Sea centres around Hurghada or Sharm el-Sheikh, usually inclusive of rental equipment and dives. All **prices quoted** in the box overleaf are inclusive of flights, unless otherwise stated.

BY TRAIN AND FERRY

Travelling **overland by train from Britain to Egypt** only makes sense if you intend to visit

BRITISH AND IRISH TOUR OPERATORS

MAINSTREAM OPERATORS

Bales Worldwide, Bales House, Junction Rd, Dorking, Surrey RH4 (☎01306/732 700; tailor-mades ☎01306/732 718, www.balesworldwide.com). Does 9- to 14-day Nile cruises (£599–1499); also offers 9-day (£699) and 14-day (£998) tours based in first-class hotels in Cairo, Luxor and Aswan.

British Airways Holidays, Astral Towers, Betts Way, London Rd, Crawley, Sussex RH10 2XA (☎0870/242 4245, www.baholidays.co.uk). Seven nights in Luxor from £439; 7-day Nile cruises from £575; and a Cairo–Alexandria package from £565.

Cruise Classified, 31 Crawford Place, London W1H 1HY (☎020/7723 6773). One-week cruises between Luxor and Aswan (from £499) as well as scheduled and charter flights.

Goldenjoy, 36 Mill Lane, London NW6 1NR (☎020/7794 9767, www.goldenjoy.co.uk). Seven nights in Luxor (from £399), Aswan (£479), or cruising the Nile (£419). Diving holidays at Sharm el-Sheikh or Hurghada are detailed in a separate sports brochure.

Hayes and Jarvis, Hayes House, 152 King St, London W6 0QU (☎020/8748 5050). Mostly 7-night packages: in Luxor from £255; cruising the Nile from £429; on the beach at Sharm el-Sheikh from £299; or Hurghada from £285. They also do a "Mystical Egypt Tour" from £975.

Joe Walsh Tours, 69 Upper O'Connell St, Dublin 2 (☎01/872 5536). 7-night Nile cruises (from IR£590) and 16-night Cairo–Luxor–Aswan cruises (IR£845–1345).

Kuoni, Kuoni House, Dorking, Surrey RH5 4AZ (☎01306/743 000, www.kuoni.co.uk). Experienced operator offering a wide variety of packages, including seven days in Sharm el-Sheikh from £369 (dive packages from £119 extra), and an add-on to Petra (three days, from £350).

Peltours, Sovereign House, 11/19 Ballards Lane, London N3 1UX (☎020/8343 0590, www.peltours.com). Does a deluxe 7-day Cairo/Nile cruise package from £1195, four days in Cairo for £429 or seven days for £599.

Soliman Travel, 162 Hammersmith Rd, London W6 7JP (☎020/8563 9119, www.solimantravel.co.uk). One of the longest-established tour operators with a large range of packages and tailor-mades mainly in five-star accommodation. Nile cruises from £399; seven nights in Luxor from £327; 7-night diving holidays in Hurghada or Sharm el-Sheikh from £490 with dive courses available at £20/day; and 3-night city breaks to Alex or Cairo for £350–370.

Somak Holidays, Somak House, Harrovian Village, Bessborough Rd, Harrow-on-the-Hill, Middlesex HA1 3EX (☎020/8423 3000, www.somak.co.uk). Offers cut-price flights to Luxor from £220, a 7-night Luxor package from £299, plus Nile cruises from £475.

Swan Hellenic, 77 New Oxford St, London WC1A 1PP (☎020/7800 2200, www.swanhellenic.com). Upmarket cruises that include Egypt as part of an itinerary called "Spring in the Holy Land"; cruise takes in Cairo, Luxor and Aswan, as well as Petra and Jerusalem (from £3195).

Thomas Cook, 45 Berkeley St, London W1X 5AE and high streets across London and the UK (nationwide ☎0990/666 222; Flights Direct ☎0990/101 520, www.tch.thomascook.com). Thomas Cook more or less created tourism in Egypt with his first escorted tour in 1869, and the country remains a speciality. They offer 10- to 15-day Nile cruises (£795–1295); a Red Sea tour including Petra in Jordan (from £1295); 4 days in Cairo (from £399); a week in Luxor (from £349); or twin-centre deals featuring Aswan and Sharm el-Sheikh or Cairo and Hurghada.

Thomson Direct reservations ☎0990/502399, brochures ☎01509/238 238. Part of Thomson Holidays; pick up a Thomson brochure from any high-street travel agent or ring the brochure-line to check out available deals.

other countries en route. The two most obvious **approaches** are via Greece, then by ferry to Haifa in Israel either from Piraeus in Greece (the port of Athens) or Limassol in Cyprus (which can only be reached by car ferry from Piraeus in the first place), and overland from there; or through Turkey, Syria, Jordan and Israel (see "Getting There from Israel and Jordan", p.16). Ferry services to Haifa have been much reduced in recent years – presently there are two services from Piraeus weekly, with fares starting at £141 per person. Viamare Travel, Graphic House, 2 Sumatra

Voyages Jules Verne, 21 Dorset Square, London NW1 6QG (☎020/7616 1000, *www.vjv.co.uk*). Seven-night Cairo/Nile cruises and four-night Cairo city-break (both from £595).

ADVENTURE HOLIDAY COMPANIES

Collette Pearson Travel, 64 South William St, Dublin 2 (☎01/677 1029, *cptravel@indigo.ie*). Agent for Exodus (see below).

Exodus, 9 Weir Rd, London SW12 0LT (☎020/8675 5550, *www.exodustravels.co.uk*). Their 14-day "Egyptian Discoverer" tour features a Nile cruise from Aswan to Luxor, a day in Hurghada and two nights in Cairo (from £825).

Explore Worldwide, 1 Frederick St, Aldershot, Hampshire GU11 1LQ (☎01252/319448, *www.explore.co.uk*). Highly respected small groups operator with several Egyptian programmes, including a 15-day Nile Valley and Red Sea tour with four days on a felucca (from £640); a 17-day Nubian Nile and Sinai package from £649; and a 16-day tour of the Nile and Western Desert from £700.

Guerba Expeditions, Wessex House, 40 Station Rd, Westbury, Wiltshire BA13 3JN (☎01373/826 611). Long-established Africa-overland experts with a variety of Egyptian tours, such as nine days in Cairo, Luxor and Aswan from £640, and a 14-day "Nile and Beyond" tour that includes a camel safari in Sinai, from £700.

High Places, The Globecentre, Penistone Rd, Sheffield S6 3AE (☎0114/275 7500, *www.highplaces.co.uk*). Does a two-week camel trek from Nuweiba to St Catherine's Monastery from £750.

Imaginative Traveller, 14 Barley Mow Passage, Chiswick, London W4 4PH (☎020/8742 8612, *www.imaginative-traveller.com*). Offers sixteen tours of Egypt, including 10-day Nile Valley and Red Sea trips (from £350); eight days in Alexandria and Siwa Oasis (from £250); and 7-day dive packages at Hurghada (from £245, £50 extra for course). These prices do not include flights.

Maxwells Travel, D'Olier Chambers, 1 Hawkins St, Dublin 2 (☎01/677 9479). Agent for Explore Worldwide (see above).

Top Deck, 131–135 Earl's Court Rd, London SW5 9RH (☎020/7370 4555). Youth-oriented tours favoured by Australians and New Zealanders include the 15-day felucca, Red Sea and Sinai "Pharaoh's Footsteps", from £459 (excluding flight).

DIVE HOLIDAY COMPANIES

Crusader Travel, 57 Church St, Twickenham, Middlesex TW1 3NR (☎020/8892 7606). Experienced, specialist agent for diving holidays, which helps clients shop around the tour operators.

Destination Red Sea, 125 East Barnet Rd, New Barnet, Herts EN4 9RF (☎020/8440 9900). PADI courses at Sharm el-Sheikh (from £499); and dive safaris in the "Red Sea Triangle" of Sinai, Eilat and Aqaba (from £699).

Explorer Tours, 223 Copper Mill Rd, Wraysbury, Middlesex TW19 9NW (☎01753/681999). PADI courses from £498 and 8-day jeep safaris in the Sinai from £595.

Oonasdivers, 23 Enys Rd, Eastbourne BN21 2DG (☎01323/648924, *www.oonasdivers.com*). PADI courses (from £630), and Red Sea safaris as far south as Ras Banas (from £610).

Regal Holidays, 22 High St, Sutton, Ely, Cambridgeshire CB6 2RB (☎01353/778096, *www.regal-diving.co.uk*). Various dive packages at Hurghada, Safaga and Sharm el-Sheikh (from £369 for seven days); plus safaris out of Hurghada, Sharm or Mersa Allam (from £599). Flies from Gatwick.

Scuba Way, 128a Church Rd, Hove, East Sussex BN3 2EA (☎01273/746261, *scubaway @compuserve.com*). 6-day packages for qualified divers (£399–580 depending on accommodation), based at Hurghada or Sharm el-Sheikh, plus basic PADI courses (£175–205 extra).

Rd, London NW6 1PU (☎020/7431 4560, *ferries@viamare.com*), is the British agent for most of the ferry companies. There are no longer any direct **ferries** from Greece or Cyprus to Egypt except for two cruise boats from Limassol in Cyprus to Port Said, whose passengers travel on a group visa and must return to Limassol after two days.

The cheapest way to cover both of these routes is to get an **InterRail** pass (*www.interrail.net/*), which covers train travel in Europe (excluding the country of purchase) and offers discounts on various ferries for a set period. The passes are available to **all ages**, and cover 26 countries that are grouped together into different zones. Under-26s pay £220 for a month for two zones (zones D and G include the Balkans, Greece and Turkey), £245 for three and £275 for all zones. For over-26s prices start at £269 a month for two zones or £349 for all zones. In Britain, passes are available through main train stations and most travel agents; in Ireland through USIT Campus.

Officially, you need to have been resident in Europe for at least six months to buy an InterRail pass (in practice, agents aren't always fussy about this). Vacationing **North Americans or Australians and New Zealanders** can buy a **Eurail pass instead (see p.12 or p.15).**

GETTING THERE FROM THE US AND CANADA

The volume of North American travellers to Egypt is not great – and this is reflected in a relative dearth of flights. Other than on EgyptAir and TWA, which fly direct to Cairo from New York (11hr) and Los Angeles (15hr), you'll have to transit via Europe or Israel. North American travel agents can arrange flights with no problem, or – if you're heading to London – you can arrange connections yourself (see the previous "Getting There from Britain and Ireland" section). If you are travelling to Israel or Jordan first, see p.16 for information on how to move on to Egypt.

SHOPPING FOR TICKETS

Barring special offers, the cheapest of the airlines' published fares is usually an **Apex** ticket, although this will carry certain restrictions: you have to book – and pay – at least 21 days before departure, spend at least seven days abroad (maximum stay 3 months), and you tend to get penalized if you change your schedule. Some airlines also issue **Special Apex** tickets to people younger than 24, often extending the maximum stay to a year. Many airlines offer youth or student fares to **under-25s** – a passport or driving licence is sufficient proof of age – though these tickets are subject to availability and can have eccentric booking conditions. It's worth remembering that most cheap return fares involve spending at least one Saturday night away and that many will only give a percentage refund if you need to cancel or alter your journey, so make sure you check the restrictions carefully before buying a ticket.

You can normally cut costs further by going through a **specialist flight agent** – either a **consolidator**, who buys up blocks of tickets from the airlines and sells them at a discount, or a **discount agent**, who in addition to dealing with discounted flights may also offer special student and youth fares and a range of other travel-related services such as travel insurance, rail passes, car rental, tours and the like. Bear in mind, though, that penalties for changing your plans can be stiff. Remember too that these companies make their money by dealing in bulk – don't expect them to answer lots of questions. Some agents specialize in **charter flights**, which may be cheaper than anything available on a scheduled route, but again departure dates are fixed and withdrawal penalties are high (check the refund policy). If you travel a lot, **discount travel clubs** are another option – the annual membership fee may be worth it for benefits such as cut-price air tickets and car rental.

AIRLINES

Air Canada (in Canada ☎1-888/247-2262; in US ☎1-800/776-3000, *www.aircanada.ca*). Flights from most major Canadian cities with connections to Cairo on one of the European carriers.

Air France (in US ☎1-800/237-2747; in Canada ☎1-800/667-2747, *www.airfrance.com*). Daily flights from NY, Miami, Atlanta, Boston, Chicago, Washington DC, Houston, San Francisco, LA, Toronto and Montréal to Paris with connections to Cairo.

Alitalia (in US ☎1-800/223-5730; in Canada ☎1-800/361-8336, *www.alitalia.com*). From NY, Boston, Miami, Chicago, LA, San Francisco, Toronto or Montréal to Cairo, via Milan or Rome.

British Airways (in US ☎1-800/247-9297; in Canada ☎1-800/668-1059, *www.britishairways.com*). Daily flights from most major North American cities to Cairo via London.

EgyptAir (☎1-800/334-6787, *www.egyptair.eg*). Direct flights from NY to Cairo daily except Monday and Wednesday; LA to Cairo (via NY) every Thursday and Saturday.

El Al (☎1-800/223-6700, *www.elal.com*). NY (daily except Friday) and Montréal (two flights weekly) to Cairo via Tel Aviv. Flights from Boston, Miami, Chicago, Washington DC, LA and Toronto routed through NY or Montréal.

Lufthansa (in US ☎1-800/645-3880; in Canada ☎1-800/563-5954, *www.lufthansa.com*). Daily flights to Cairo from NY (JFK), Newark, Boston, Philadelphia, Miami, Atlanta, Houston, Dallas, Chicago, Detroit, San Francisco, LA and Washington DC via Frankfurt.

Northwest/KLM (in US ☎1-800/447-4747; in Canada ☎1-800/361-5073, *www.nwa.com*). Daily flights to Cairo from NY, Boston, Chicago, Detroit, Minneapolis, Atlanta, Houston, Washington DC, San Francisco, LA and Seattle via Amsterdam.

Royal Jordanian (☎1-800/223-0470 or 212/949-0050, *www.rja.jo.com*). NY to Cairo via Amman every Tuesday, Wednesday, Saturday and Sunday.

SwissAir (in US ☎1-800/221-4750; in Canada ☎1-800/267-9477, *www.swissair.com*). NY, Boston, Chicago, Atlanta, Washington DC, LA, Toronto and Montréal via Zurich daily except Saturday.

TWA (☎1-800/892-4141, *www.twa.com*). Direct flights (Monday through Friday) from NY and LA to Cairo.

United Airlines (☎1-800/538-2929, *www.ual.com*). Flights from Washington DC, Chicago, LA or San Francisco to Frankfurt, linking with other airlines for the Cairo leg.

Don't automatically assume that tickets purchased through a travel specialist will be cheapest – once you get a quote, check with the airlines and you may turn up an even better deal. Be advised also that the pool of travel companies is swimming with sharks – exercise caution and never deal with a company that demands cash up front or refuses to accept payment by credit card.

Regardless of where you buy your ticket, **fares** will depend on the season: they are highest from June through the end of August, drop during the "shoulder" seasons – April, May, September and October – and you'll get the best prices during the low season, November to March (excluding Christmas and New Year, when prices are hiked up and seats are at a premium). Note also that flying at weekends may add around US/CAN$50 to the round-trip fare; price ranges quoted below are for Apex tickets and assume midweek travel.

Unfortunately, the likelihod of finding a **courier flight** (where you shepherd a parcel through customs in exchange for a heavily discounted ticket) is virtually nil for travel between North America and Egypt. However, if Egypt is only one stop on a longer journey, you might want to consider buying a **Round-the-World (RTW)** ticket. Some travel agents can sell you an "off-the-shelf" RTW ticket; others will tailor one according to your needs, but this is apt to be more expensive. A couple of off-the-shelf RTW itineraries are: San Francisco–Taipei–Bangkok–Cairo–Amsterdam–New York for US$1350; Atlanta–Tokyo–Hong Kong–Bangkok–Cairo–Zurich–London–New York for US$2050.

High Adventure Travel has a Web site that allows you to construct your own RTW itinerary (see box p.10).

FLIGHTS TO CAIRO

EgyptAir and **TWA** offer direct flights to Cairo from **New York** and **Los Angeles** (via NY), though they don't come especially cheap. Both airlines have five flights a week from NY, while TWA flies five times weekly from LA and EgyptAir

DISCOUNT FLIGHT AGENTS, TRAVEL CLUBS & CONSOLIDATORS

Airtech, 588 Broadway, Suite 204, New York, NY 10012 (☎1-800/575-TECH or 212/219-7000, *www.airtech.com*). Standby seat broker; also deals in consolidator fares.

Cheap Tickets, Inc. Offices nationwide (☎1-800/377-1000 or 212/570-1179, *www.cheaptickets.com*). Travel store dealing in discounted fares.

Council Travel, 205 E 42nd St, New York, NY 10017 (☎1-800/226-8624 or 212/822-2700, *www.counciltravel.com*). Branches also in many other US cities. Student/budget travel agency.

Educational Travel Center, 438 N Frances St, Madison, WI 53703 (☎1-800/747-5551 or 608/256-5551, *www.edtravel.com*). Student/youth and consolidator fares.

High Adventure Travel, 442 Post St, 4th Floor, San Francisco, CA 94102 (☎1-800/350 0612 or 415/912 5600, *www.airtreks.com*). RTW tickets. Web site features interactive database that lets you build and price your own RTW itinerary.

International Gay and Lesbian Travel Association (☎1-800/448-8550, *www.iglta.org*). Trade group with lists of gay-owned or gay-friendly travel agents, accommodation and other travel businesses.

Mister Cheaps (formerly Now Voyager), 74 Varick St, Suite 307, New York, NY 10013 (☎1-888/37-CHEAPS or 212/431-1616, *www.mistercheaps.com*). Consolidator.

Skylink, 265 Madison Ave, 5th Floor, New York, NY 10016 (☎1-800/892-0027, *www.pltravel.com*). Branches also in Chicago, LA, Montréal, Toronto and Washington DC. Consolidator.

STA Travel, 10 Downing St, New York, NY 10014 (☎1-800/777-0112 or 212/627-3111, *www.statravel.com*). Other branches in LA, San Francisco, Miami, Chicago, Seattle, Philadelphia, Washington DC and Boston. Worldwide discount travel firm specializing in student/youth fares, student IDs, travel insurance, car rental, rail passes etc.

TFI Tours International, 34 W 32nd St, New York, NY 10001 (☎1-800/745-8000 or 212/736-1140). Consolidator.

Travac Tours, 989 6th Ave, New York, NY 10018 (☎1-800/872-8800 or 212/563-3303, *www.thetravelsite.com*). Consolidator and charter broker.

Travel Avenue, 10 S Riverside Plaza, Suite 1404, Chicago, IL 60606 (☎1-800/333-3335 or 312/876-6866, *www.travelavenue.com*). Full-service travel agent that offers discounts in the form of rebates.

Travel CUTS (Canada), 187 College St, Toronto, ON M5T 1P7 (☎1-800/667-2887 or 416/979-2406, *www.travelcuts.com*); other branches nationwide. Canadian student travel organization specializing in student fares, IDs and other travel services.

Travelers Advantage, 311 W Superior St, Chicago, IL 60610 (☎1-800/255-0200, *www.travelersadvantage.com*). Travel club offering discounts on airfares, car rental and accommodation plus special packages from their own travel agency; annual membership fee US$59.95.

UniTravel, 11737 Administration Drive, Suite 120, St Louis, MO 63146 (☎1-800/325-2222 or 314/569-2501, *www.flightsforless.com*). Consolidator.

Worldtrek Travel, 111 Water St, New Haven, CT 06511 (☎1-800/243-1723 or 203/772-0470, *www.worldtek.com*). Discount travel agency.

Worldwide Discount Travel Club, 1674 Meridian Ave, Miami Beach, FL 33139 (☎305/534-2082). Travel club with discounts on package holidays only; no flight-only sales. Annual membership fee.

---

twice weekly. Apex round-trip fares from NY start at US$760 (low season), $830 (shoulder) and $1400 (high). With a connection from the midwest you can expect to pay around $200 extra. From LA, TWA fares start at $1190 low season, $1325 shoulder and $1800 high, with EgyptAir fares from $999/1099/1299 respectively.

If you are travelling to Cairo from the US **via Europe or Israel**, there's a much wider range of departure points and airlines to choose from.

Ticket prices with most airlines are much the same as the fare for a direct flight from New York (see above). Their flights are routed via their hub cities, so you should check that you won't have to wait overnight for your onward connection. Middle Eastern airlines such as Royal Jordanian can also offer competitive prices.

It's also worth checking discount agents such as STA, who can probably find a round-trip fare from New York for as little as US$650 in low sea-

TOUR OPERATORS

MAINSTREAM TOURS

Abercrombie & Kent, 1520 Kensington Rd, Suite 212, Oak Brook, IL 60521 (☎1-800-323-7308, *www.abercrombiekent.com*). Specializes in 11- to 14-day tours lead by expert Egyptologists; also create custom packages.

Contiki Tours, 2300 E Katella Ave, Suite 450, Anaheim, CA 92806 (☎1-800/CONTIKI, *www.contiki.com*). Travel specialists for 18–35-year-olds.

Cox and Kings, 25 Davis Blvd, Tampa, FA 33606 (☎1-800-999-1758, *www.zenonet.com/cox-kings*). Upmarket customized tour operator.

Esplanade Tours, 581 Boylston St, Boston, MA 02116 (☎1-800/426-5492, *www.esplanade-tours.com*). Various city breaks (flight/hotel) to Cairo, Luxor and Aswan plus 7-night Nile cruise on five-star deluxe vessel.

Globus and Cosmos, 5301 South Federal Circle, Littleton, CO 80123 (☎1-800/851-0728, *www.globusandcosmos.com*). Various fully escorted tours to Egypt.

Homeric Tours, 55 East 59th St, New York, NY 10022 (☎1-800/223-5570,

www.homerictours.com). Deluxe package tours of eight to fifteen days visiting Cairo, Aswan, Luxor, Hurghada and Sharm el-Sheikh, along with five-star Nile cruises. All-inclusive tours, US$1759–2269 per person. Greece and Israel extensions available.

Isram World of Travel, 630 Third Ave, New York, NY 10017 (☎1-800/223-7460, *www.isram.com*). Offers 9- to 14-day tours; specializes in Nile cruises.

Maupintour, 1421 Research park Drive, Lawrence, KA 66049 (☎1-800/255-4266, *www.maupintour.com*). Offers 10- to 21-day tours to Egypt, including Nile cruises and trips to the Red Sea.

Megatrails, 1828 2nd Ave, New York, NY 10128 (☎1-800/547-1211). Escorted package tours including Cairo, the Pyramids and Nile cruises.

Saga Holidays, 222 Berkeley St, Boston, MA 02116 (☎1-800/343-0273, *www.sagaholidays.com*). Specialists in group travel for seniors. 14-night Egypt and the Nile coach tour and cruise. From US$3499 (including flight).

ADVENTURE AND SPECIALIST TOURS

Adventure Center, 1311 63rd St, Suite 200, Emeryville, CA 94608 (☎1-800/227-8747 or 510/654-1879, *www.adventurecenter.com*). Diverse itineraries for small groups, including a Nile cruise, Red Sea diving, temples, the Pyramids and more.

Adventure Travel Company, 381 King St West, Toronto, ON M5V 1K1 (☎1-800/667-2887, *www.travelcuts.com*). Tour division of the Canadian discount travel company Travel CUTS.

Adventures Abroad, 2148-20800 Westminster Hwy, Richmond, BC V6V 2W3 (☎1-800/665-3998, *www.adventures-abroad.com*). Canadian-based company offering small group tours to Egypt or combined with Israel, Jordan, Syria etc. Activities include camel rides, trekking and felucca cruises.

Archeological Tours, 271 Madison Ave, Suite 904, New York, NY 10016 (☎212/986-3054, *www.archeologicaltoursinc.com*). Specialize in small group, archeological/historical educational tours with renowned Egyptologist.

Insight International Tours, 745 Atlantic Avenue, Suite 720, Boston, MA 02111

(☎1-800/582-8380, *www.insightvacations.com*). Cultural tours to Egypt. Also tours including Egypt, Israel and Jordan.

Overseas Adventure Travel, 347 Congress St, Boston, MA 02210 (☎1-800/955-1925, *www.oattravel.com*). Distinctive cultural and educational odysseys led by expert Egyptologists. The 15-day "Eternal Nile" tour includes Pyramid visits, a Nile cruise, and a camel ride in the desert.

Travcoa, 2350 S.E. Bristol St, Newport Beach, CA 92660 (☎1-800/992-2003, *www.travcoa@travcoa.com*). All-inclusive deluxe-accommodation tours led by experienced guides and prominent lecturers, who discuss history, politics, arts, etc. Offers several tours, including 13-day "Classic Egypt", 18-day "Egypt Adventure", plus extensions to Israel.

Wilderness Travel, 1102 Ninth St, Berkeley, CA 94710-1211 (☎1-800/368-2794, *www.wildernesstravel.com*). Offers small group, 16-day cultural and archeological expeditions (US$3200 excluding flight) with expert guide from the Pyramids to the mountains of Sinai.

son, $1180 in high season. Those with access to the Internet might also want to check out *www.bestfares.com* or *www.priceline.com*.

From **Canada** there are no direct flights to Cairo, but many of the European carriers operate services via their hub cities from **Toronto** and **Montréal** (from around CAN$2100 in low season; $2300 in high season). Air Canada can get you to Cairo (via a connection to a European carrier) from other parts of the country, but fares can be high; you're better off booking a separate flight to one of the "gateway" Canadian cities first and travelling on from there.

El Al offers a fare of CAN$2300 (no seasonal variation) from Toronto. Ringing around discount agents may get you fares as low as CAN$1050/1350 (low/high season) from Montréal or Toronto, CAN$1350/1650 from the west coast.

PACKAGE HOLIDAYS

There are many tour operators (see the box opposite) offering special **packages** to Egypt or custom independent tours. Most package holidays concentrate on Cairo and the Pyramids (often with an experienced Egyptologist as the guide), or a Nile Valley cruise; there are also plenty of others that take in more of the country or offer specialist activities – for example, archeological trips or diving safaris. Check the Sunday travel sections of papers such as the *New York Times* and *Los Angeles Times* for special travel deals.

EURAIL PASSES

If you are planning to visit a number of European countries en route to Egypt, it is a good idea to buy a **Eurail pass** to cover your train travel – these can only be purchased before leaving home. However, as there are no longer any ferries from Greece or Cyprus direct to Egypt – see "Getting There from Britain and Ireland" – and as Eurail passes do not cover the Balkans or Turkey, they are only viable for those who wish to travel through southern Europe and Israel to get to Egypt.

The best-known is the **Eurail Youthpass** (for under-26s), which costs US$388 for 15 days, $499 for 21 days, $623 for one month and $882 for two months; if you're 26 or over you'll have to buy a first-class **Eurail** pass, which costs US$554/718/890/1260 in the same increments. You stand a better chance of getting your money's worth out of a **Eurail Flexipass**, which is good for a certain number of travel days in a two-month period. This, too, comes in under-26/first-class versions: 10 days US$255/654; 15 days US$599/862. These passes can be bought from Rail Europe (226 Westchester Ave, White Plains, NY 10604; ☎1-800/438-7245, *www.raileurope.com*), the official Eurail agent in North America; from ScanTours (3439 Wade St, Los Angeles, CA 90066-1533; ☎1-800/223-7226, *www.scantours.com*) and from many regular travel agents, especially youth and student specialists (see listings on p.10).

GETTING THERE FROM AUSTRALIA & NEW ZEALAND

Most Australians and New Zealanders visit Egypt as an extension of a European trip, usually buying a flight to London, plus an add-on fare to Cairo. However, you might want to consider taking in Egypt as a stopover on a Round-the-World (RTW) ticket, or take advantage of some very reasonable budget fares to Cairo from Asia. If you are planning to travel on to Egypt from Israel or Jordan, see p.16.

Whatever route you decide on, all fares vary with the seasons; for most airlines, low season is mid-January to February 28 and October to November 15, and high from mid-May to August 31 and December 1 to mid-January (shoulder seasons cover the rest of the year). The prices quoted below are the fares published by the airlines. However, carriers regularly offer special promotions of up to 20 percent off the published price; and discount agents (see box below) can usually give a further ten percent reduction. If you shop around, you can expect to pay up to A/NZ$500–600 less than the published price at any time of year.

If you are travelling to **London** first, ticket prices are "common rated" (identical fare from dif-

---

DISCOUNT AGENTS

Accent on Travel, 545 Queen St, Brisbane (☎07/3832 1777).

Anywhere Travel, 345 Anzac Parade, Kingsford, Sydney (☎02/9663 0411, *anywhere @ozemail.com.au*).

Budget Travel, 16 Fort St, Auckland; other branches around the city (☎09/366 0061 or 0-800/808 040).

Destinations Unlimited, Level 7, FAI Building, 220 Queen St, Auckland (☎09/373 4033).

Flight Centres, Gateway Quayside, 1 Macquarie Place, Sydney (☎02/9241 2422); 19 Bourke St, Melbourne (☎03/9650 2899); plus other branches nationwide (☎13 1600 for nearest branch); National Bank Towers, 205–225 Queen St, Auckland (☎09/309 6171), and other branches countrywide (nearest branch ☎0-800/FLIGHTS); *www.flightcentre.com.au.*

Harvey World Travel, 631 Princes Highway, Kogarah, Sydney (☎02/9567 6099); branches nationwide.

Northern Gateway, 22 Cavenagh St, Darwin (☎08/8941 1394, *oztravel@norgate.com.au*).

STA Travel, 855 George St, Sydney (☎02/9212 1255); 208 Swanston St, Melbourne (☎03/9639 0599); other offices in state capitals and major universities (☎13 1776 for nearest branch; fastfare telesales ☎1-300/360 960); *traveller@ statravelaus.com.au; www.statravel.com.au.*

Travellers' Centre, 10 High St, Auckland (☎09/309 0458; fastfare telesales ☎09/366 6673; toll-free ☎0800/874 773) and other offices countrywide.

Thomas Cook, 175 Pitt St, Sydney (☎02/9231 2877); 257 Collins St, Melbourne (☎03/9282 0222); branches in other state capitals (☎13 1771 for nearest branch, or toll-free ☎1-800/063 913); 191 Queen St, Auckland (☎09/379 3920); *www.thomascook.com.au.*

Topdeck Travel, 65 Grenfell St, Adelaide (☎08/8232 7222).

Travel Direct Pty Ltd, Level 3, 349 Queen St, Brisbane (☎07/3221 4933).

Travel Shop, Suite 13, 890 Canning Hwy, Perth (☎08/9316 3888 or 1-800/108 108).

Tymtro Travel, Level 3, 355 Bulwara Rd, Sydney (☎1-300/652 969).

AIRLINES

Aeroflot, Level 24, 44 Market St, Sydney (☎02/9262 2233, *www.aeroflot.org*). No NZ office. Flies to London via Moscow from Sydney.

Air New Zealand, 5 Elizabeth St, Sydney (☎02/9223 4666); Cnr Customs & Queen streets, Auckland (☎09/336 2424); *www.airnz.com*. Flies to London from Auckland via LA and from east coast Australian cities via Auckland and LA.

British Airways, Level 19, AAP Centre, 259 George St, Sydney (☎02/9258 3200); 154 Queen St, Auckland (☎09/356 8690); *www.british-airways.com*. Flies to Cairo via Singapore/Bangkok and London, from major Australian cities.

Cathay Pacific, Level 8, 8 Spring St, Sydney (☎13 1747); Level 11, Arthur Andersen Tower, 205–209 Queen St, Auckland (☎09/379 0861); *www.cathaypacific.com*. Flights to London via Hong Kong from major Australian cities and Auckland.

EgyptAir, Level 16, 150 Pitt St, Sydney (☎02/9232 6677, *www.egyptair.com.eg*). No NZ office. Flies to Cairo via Singapore from east coast Australian cities.

Garuda Indonesia, 55 Hunter St, Sydney (☎02/9334 9900); Level 10, Westpac Tower, 120 Albert St, Auckland (☎09/366 1855). Flies to London via Denpasar from the main Australian and New Zealand cities.

Gulf Air, 403 George St, Sydney (☎02/9244 2199, *www.gulfairco.com*). No NZ office. Flights to Cairo via Singapore and Bahrain from east coast Australian cities.

Japan Airlines, Level 14, Darling Park, 201 Sussex St, Sydney (☎02/9272 1100); Level 12, Westpac Tower, 120 Albert St, Auckland (☎09/379 3202); *www.jal.co.jp*. Flies from Sydney, Brisbane, Cairns and Auckland to London via Osaka/Tokyo.

KLM, Level 13, 115 Pitt St, Sydney (☎1-300/303 747, *www.klm.com*). No NZ office. Flies to Cairo via Singapore and Amsterdam from Sydney.

Malaysia Airlines, 16 Spring St, Sydney (☎13 2627); Level 12, Swanson Centre, 12–26 Swanson St, Auckland (☎09/373 2741); *www.malaysiaair.com*. Flies from east coast Australian cities and Auckland to London via Kuala Lumpur.

Qantas, Chifley Square, 70 Hunter St, Sydney (☎02/9691 3636); 191 Queen St, Auckland (☎09/357 8900); *www.qantas.com.au*. Flies to London via Bangkok/Singapore from major Australian and New Zealand cities.

Royal Brunei Airlines, 25 Mary St, Brisbane (☎07/3221 7757, *www.bruneiair.com*). No NZ office. Flights from Brisbane, Darwin and Perth to London via Brunei.

Singapore Airlines, 17–19 Bridge St, Sydney (☎13 1011); Level 10, Westpac Plaza Building, cnr Customs and Albert streets, Auckland (☎09/379 3209); *www.singaporeair.com*. Flies to London via Singapore from major Australian and New Zealand cities.

Thai Airways, 75–77 Pitt St, Sydney (☎02/9844 0999); Level 1, Kensington Swan Building, 22 Fanshawe St, Auckland (☎09/377 3886); *www.thaiair.com*. Flies to London via Bangkok from Sydney, Melbourne, Brisbane, Perth and Auckland.

ferent departure points) for **Sydney**, **Melbourne** and **Brisbane**; in low season you can expect to pay around A$1600. From **Auckland**, low-season fares are around NZ$2400 (add on NZ$150–350 from Christchurch). For the final leg from London you can either arrange a flight once there (see "Getting There from Britain and Ireland"), or buy an add-on fare before you leave: in low season this will cost A$1015/NZ$1110, about A/NZ$100 more in high season. (If you want to travel on from Britain by train, see p.7 for information on Eurail passes.)

Via Asia, all flights to London involve a stop in the carrier's hub city. Fares vary considerably depending on the airline; the cheapest currently on offer are with Garuda: from **Sydney**, **Melbourne**, **Brisbane** and **Cairns**, fares start at around A$1350 (low season) and A$1900 (high season), and from **Auckland** at around NZ$1800 and NZ$2150. Mid-range fares are available on Japan Airlines, Malaysia Airlines, Thai Airways and Royal Brunei: around A$1700/NZ$2100 in low season and A$2200/NZ$2750 in high season. At the expensive end, tickets with Qantas, Cathay Pacific and Singapore cost between A$2399/NZ$3000 and A$2999/NZ$3750.

At present the only **RTW** fare from Australia and New Zealand that takes in Cairo is Qantas/British Airways' "Global Explorer", which allows six free stopovers worldwide for

A$2499/NZ$3120 in low season, A$2950/NZ$3690 in high.

PACKAGE HOLIDAYS

So far as **package holidays** go, many Australians and New Zealanders either sign up with a tour in Britain (see pp.6–7), or book a "land only" tour – which excludes the flight costs – and book their flight separately. There are however a few companies that organize flight-and-tour packages: see below for details (all offer land-only deals unless otherwise stated).

EURAIL PASSES

Eurail passes, which can only be purchased before leaving home, are a good idea if you are planning to visit a number of European countries on your way to Egypt. The following is a brief run-through of the passes and how much they cost;

for more information on possible routes, see "Getting There from North America".

The **Eurail Youthpass** (for under-26s) costs A$615/NZ$768 for 15 days (there are also 1- and 2-month versions); if you're 26 or over you'll have to buy a first-class **Eurail** pass, which costs A$880/NZ$1100 for the 15-day option. You'll probably find a **Eurail Flexipass** is better value, as it is good for a certain number of travel days in a two-month period; a 10-day pass costs A$725/NZ$906 for under-26s and A$1040/NZ$1300 for those 26 and over (you can also get a 15-day version). These passes can be bought from CIT, Level 2, 123 Clarence St, Sydney (☎02/9267 1255, *www.cittravel.com.au*), and branches in Melbourne, Adelaide, Brisbane and Perth (there is no NZ office – enquiries and reservations via Australian offices); and from travel agents, especially youth and student specialists such as STA (see listings above).

AGENTS FOR PACKAGE TOUR OPERATORS

Adventure World, 73 Walker St, North Sydney (☎1-800/221 931); also outlets in Brisbane, Melbourne, Adelaide and Perth; 101 Great South Rd, Remuera, Auckland (☎0-880/654 954, *www.adventureworld.com.au*). Agents for Explore Worldwide's 17-day escorted tour from Cairo to Luxor by bus, train, felucca and donkey, taking in the Valley of the Kings and the Pyramids. Price (A$1880/NZ$2350) includes accommodation, transport and some meals.

Allways PADI Travel, 168 High St, Ashburton, Melbourne (☎03/9885 5700 or 1-800/259 297). Eight-day dive trip exploring wrecks and coral reefs around Sharm el-Sheikh and Ras Mohammed from aboard the *Colona 5*. Price (A$3560/NZ$4450) includes return air fares from east coast Australia and 7 nights at sea, including all meals and two dives a day.

Made Easy Tours, PO Box 5020 Kenmore East, Brisbane (☎1-800/673 337). Offers a variety of packages ranging from sightseeing in Alexandria and Aswan to Nile cruises for inde-

pendent travellers or groups. Tours start from A$330/NZ$410 for 3 days with accommodation and meals.

Peregrine Adventures, 258 Lonsdale St, Melbourne (☎03/9663 8611, *www.peregrine.net.au*); also outlets in Brisbane, Sydney, Adelaide and Perth. Gecko's Adventures, Peregrine's low-cost touring arm, has a variety of accommodation and transport deals, including 15 days in Cairo, Luxor, Aswan and the Red Sea Coast (A$950/$NZ1190) and 14 days from Cairo to the Sinai peninsula, Luxor and Aswan (A$1395/$NZ1750). Also offers combined packages involving Egypt, Jordan and Israel.

Wiltrans/Maupintour, Level 10, 189 Kent St, Sydney (☎02/9255 0899). Luxury 10- to 17-day historical tours guided by Egyptologists, including Nile cruises, the Pyramids, camel rides and desert treks. Prices start from around A$3070/NZ$3840 for accommodation, transport and meals; optional 5-day extensions from A$1290/NZ$1610.

GETTING THERE FROM ISRAEL AND JORDAN

If your travels include Israel or Jordan, moving on to Egypt is fairly straightforward. You can either fly – from Tel Aviv or Amman to Cairo – or, more cheaply, use one of the many bus and ferry services. From Israel the quickest checkpoint for Cairo is the divided border town of Rafah, near the Mediterranean coast; for the resort towns of the Sinai peninsula, head for Taba (near Eilat). If you are travelling from Jordan, you can either go by ferry from Aqaba to the Sinai peninsula and then continue your journey by bus; or take the fast catamaran service that runs to Sinai's main resort, Sharm el-Sheikh, and on to Hurghada on the Red Sea Coast. See p.18 for details of Egyptian and Sinai-only visas and for addresses of Egyptian consulates in Israel and Jordan.

FROM ISRAEL

Entering Egypt via Rafah, you're subject to an **Israeli departure tax** of NIS108 (£16/US$26) and an **Egyptian entry tax** of £E7 (£1.50/US$2.50). Entering via Taba, both departure and entry taxes are slightly cheaper (NIS67 and £E17 respectively).

Most people crossing over at **Rafah** are travelling from Tel Aviv or Jerusalem to Cairo on one of the direct bus services between those cities. One-way (US$30–35) and return tickets (US$45–60) are available from several agencies; see the box opposite. It's best to book (and confirm return journeys) at least three days in advance. Many companies will also get your visa for you, which costs an extra NIS50 and takes between two and four days. **Beware** of bus companies trying to charge you for non-existent taxes; some even try

to claim that police escorts from Rafah to Cairo are an added expense.

Attempting to reach Rafah under your own steam involves travelling through the Palestinian-controlled Gaza Strip and changing *sherut* (*service*) taxis at several points. As the Israelis can seal off the Gaza Strip to Palestinians at short notice, this method is not recommended. Once at the border (open daily 24hr), the Egyptian guards will examine your passport and visa (which cannot be issued here), and demand the entry tax. The exchange office on the Egyptian side is open 24 hours. Rafah and nearby El-Arish in themselves have little to offer apart from bus and *service* taxi connections to Cairo.

Taba makes a fine jumping-off point for the Sinai coast resorts, St Catherine's Monastery or Cairo. Israeli travel agents again sell tickets on through buses **from Eilat** across the border into Sinai or on to Cairo; Mazada Tours also runs an express midnight service **from Tel Aviv**. However, local transport into Egypt is fairly simple to organize yourself. From Eilat, a taxi (NIS15) or a much cheaper #15 bus (which doesn't run on *Shabbat*) will get you to the Israeli checkpoint at Taba for an exit stamp; you then walk for 15 minutes across no-man's-land to the Egyptian side, where proceedings are similar to those at Rafah, except that **Sinai-only visas** can be obtained on the spot. If you're carrying any Israeli shekels, the bank at the *Taba Hilton,* a few banks in Sharm el-Sheikh and the Forex bureaux in Cairo are the only places in Egypt where you can legally exchange them. However, Israeli shekels are now common currency in the Sinai as far south as Dahab and many businesses will accept them at an exchange rate of NIS1 to £E1.

Travelling on from Taba (see p.568), there is one bus daily for Dahab and Sharm el-Sheikh (at 3pm; £E10 and £E15); four to Nuweiba (6.30am, 9am, 2pm and 3pm; £E10) and two to Cairo (8.30am and 1pm; £E65 and £E75). **Taxis** take full advantage of the fact that there's no bus to St Catherine's, and also demand premium rates for Nuweiba or places further down the Gulf of Aqaba. **Service taxis** are a bit cheaper, with per person rates £E30 to Nuweiba or Tarabin, £E50 to Dahab and £E75 to Sharm el-Sheikh. Prices for both drop immediately before the bus departs, and soar once it has departed.

ISRAELI BUS OPERATORS

Galilee Tours, 12 Shalom Aleichem St, Tel Aviv (☎03/516-2255); 3 Hillel St, Jerusalem (☎02/258-866); other offices in Eilat and Tiberias.

Marhagi Travel and Tourism, 139 Ibn Givrol St, Tel Aviv (☎03/604-1811, fax 604-2884).

Mazada Tours, 141 Ibn Givrol St, Tel Aviv (☎03/544-4454); 9 Koresh St, Jerusalem (☎02/623-5777, fax 625-5454).

ISRAELI TOUR OPERATORS

ISSTA (Israel Students Travel Company), 5 Yoel Salomon St, Nahalat Shiva'a, Jerusalem (☎02/624-3177, fax 624-2996).

Neot Ha Kikar Touring Company, 78 Ben-Yehuda St, Tel Aviv (☎03/522-8161); 36 Keren Ha-Yesod St, Jerusalem (☎02/636-494);

Hatmarim Blvd, Eilat (☎07/371-329). Specializes in Sinai treks.

SPNI (Society for the Protection of Nature in Israel), 19 Hasharon St, Tel Aviv (☎03/638-8674, fax 688-3940, *www.spni.org.il*). Organizes 4-day tours to the Sinai fron US$295.

You are not allowed to drive **rented cars** across the Israeli–Egyptian border.

FROM JORDAN

Starting out at Amman, it's best to buy combined bus and ferry tickets to Nuweiba from a travel agent. The **ferries** run between the Jordanian port of **Aqaba** and **Nuweiba** in Sinai; they should be trouble-free. If you haven't bought a through ticket from Amman, ferry tickets can be purchased from any agent in Aqaba; a first-class single currently costs US$32. Arrive two hours beforehand to go through customs and pay depar-

ture tax (JD6). Boats are supposed to sail at 11am and 4.30pm, and take three hours, but rarely do. On arrival in Nuweiba you can obtain a Sinai-only visa. See p.588 for information on Nuweiba itself, and on travelling in the opposite direction, towards Aqaba.

Alternatively, there's the catamaran service, which runs once a day (though schedules may change). The service takes only one hour to travel from Aqaba to Nuweiba (where Sinai-only visas are available at the port), so the expense of a one-way ticket (US$42) might be justified if you are in a hurry to move on from Sinai.

VISAS AND RED TAPE

Bureaucracy has flourished in Egypt for five thousand years, pervading most aspects of life. Nasser's promise of a civil service job for every graduate has led to a vastly over-staffed, inefficient administration, which you'll come up against when obtaining trav-el permits or visa extensions, and which may well defeat you if you try to do anything more complicated. Rules change from place to place and individual bureaucrats may interpret them differently, or introduce new regulations, or simply be obstructive through caprice. Remain patient and good-humoured no matter what.

PASSPORTS AND VISAS

All visitors to Egypt must hold **passports** that are valid for at least **six months** beyond the pro-posed date of entry to the country. Almost all Europeans, plus all North Americans and Australians and New Zealanders, must also obtain **tourist visas** (see below).

TOURIST VISAS

Regular tourist visas are available from Egyptian consulates abroad (see opposite), or on the spot at Cairo, Luxor and Hurghada air-ports. The process is generally painless and cheaper than getting one through a consulate, but bear in mind that visas issued at the airport are only valid for one month. You *cannot* get them at overland border crossings, or at Aswan, Suez or Nuweiba (apart from Sinai-only visas – see below). From an embassy or consulate the

single-visit and multiple-entry types of visa entitle you to stay in Egypt for three months; the latter allows you to go in and out of the country three times within this period. Don't be misled by statements on the application form that it is "valid for six months"; this simply means that it must be used within that period (validated from the day of issue).

Visa applications can be made in person or by post. Applying in person, you can normally get a visa the same day in Britain, North America, Australia, Israel or Jordan. Always turn up early in the day and expect to pay in cash – postal applications take between seven working days and six weeks to process. When returning the form, you need to include a regis-tered or recorded SAE, your passport, one photo, and a postal or money order (not a per-sonal cheque).

The **cost** varies according to your nationality, and from place to place. Getting a standard visa on arrival costs US$15, irrespective of your nationality. **At home**, Britons pay £15 (£18 for multiple-entry), US citizens US$15, Canadians (who must get one before they leave) pay CAN$48, Australians and New Zealanders A$35/NZ$45. **In Israel**, US, German and Scandinavian nationals are charged NIS50, most other nationalities NIS60. **In Jordan**, visa charges are higher in Aqaba than in Amman. Some consulates may demand that you pay in US$ instead of local currency, or ask you to sup-ply extra photos (and maybe glue to stick them down!). It's wise to allow for all these eventuali-ties.

If you don't mind being limited to Sinai, you can obtain special **Sinai-only visas** (US$10) at Taba on the Israeli–Egyptian border, St Catherine's Monastery or Sharm el-Sheikh air-port, or the seaports at Sharm el-Sheikh and Nuweiba. Valid for fourteen days only, this visa restricts you to the Aqaba coast down to Sharm el-Sheikh, and the vicinity of St Catherine's; it is **not valid** for Ras Mohammed, the mountains around St Catherine's (except for Mount Sinai), or any other part of Egypt. It can't be extended, and there's no period of grace for overstaying. Note that neither regular nor Sinai-only visas are avail-able at Rafah, the other crossing between Israel and Egypt.

EGYPTIAN EMBASSIES AND CONSULATES ABROAD

For visa applications in person, submit your passport and application in the morning and collect the visa the same afternoon (applications cannot be submitted then). An up-to-date list of Egyptian embassies can be found at *www.embassyworld.com.embassy/egypt1.htm*

Australia: 1 Darwin Ave, Yarralumla, ACT (☎02/6273 4437); 112 Glenmore Rd, Paddington, Sydney, NSW 2021 (☎02/9332 3388); Level 9, 124 Exhibition St, Melbourne, VIC 3000 (☎03/9654 8869).

Britain: 2 Lowndes St, London SW1X 9ET (☎020/7235 9777, *www.egypt-embassy.org.uk*). Mon–Fri 9.30am–12.30pm.

Canada: 454 Laurier Ave, E Ottawa, ON K1N 6R3 (☎613/234-4958); 1 Place Ville Marie, Suite 2617, Montréal, Quebec H3B 4S3 (☎514/866-8455). Both Mon–Fri 9.30am–1pm.

Ireland: 12 Clyde Rd, Dublin 4 (☎01/606 566)

Israel: 54 Basel St, Tel Aviv (☎03/546-5151); 68 Afrat St, Bna Betkha, Eilat (☎059/597-6115). In Tel Aviv Mon–Thurs & Sun 9–11am; in Eilat

Mon–Thurs & Sun 9–11am & 1–1.30pm, Fri 9–10am & 11am–noon.

Jordan: Jebel Amman, Amman (☎06/641 375); Sharia al-Istiqlal, Aqaba (☎03/316171). In Amman daily except Fri 9am–3pm; in Aqaba daily except Fri 9am–2pm.

New Zealand: *there is no Egyptian embassy or consulate in New Zealand; contact one of the consulates in Australia.*

US: 3521 International Court NW, Washington, DC 20008 (☎202/895-5400); 1110 Second Ave, New York, NY 10022 (☎212/759-7120); 3001 Pacific Ave, San Francisco, CA 94115 (☎415/346-9700); 500 N Michigan Ave, Suite 1900, Chicago, IL 60611 (☎312/828-9162); 1990 Post Oak Blvd, Suite 2180, Houston, TX 77056 (☎713/961-4915). All Mon–Fri 10.30am–12.30pm.

ISRAELI PASSPORT STAMPS

Most Arab countries except Egypt and Jordan will deny entry to anyone whose **passport shows evidence of a visit to Israel** – however, you still may encounter hostility from bureaucrats. Although Israeli immigration officials are happy to give you an entry stamp on a separate piece of paper if you ask first, an Egyptian entry stamp at Taba or Rafah in the Sinai will give you away – and the Egyptians insist on stamping your passport. So if you are travelling around the Middle East, be sure to visit Israel *after* you have been to Syria, Lebanon, or wherever.

PASSPORT PRECAUTIONS

Once **in Egypt**, you should always carry your passport with you: you'll need it to register at hotels, change money, collect mail, and possibly to show at police checkpoints. If you're travelling for any length of time, you may find it worthwhile to **register with your embassy** on arrival in Cairo, which will help speed things up if you lose your passport. At the least, it's a wise precaution to **photocopy** the pages recording your particulars and keep them separately. If you are travelling to areas of the country that require permits, spare sets of photocopies are useful for producing with your application.

OVERSTAYING AND EXTENSIONS

Tourists who **overstay** their (regular) visa are allowed a fifteen-day period of grace in which to renew it. After this, they're fined £E60 unless they can present a letter of apology from their embassy (which may in itself cost £E25).

One-month **visa extensions** are obtainable from the Mugamma in Cairo (see p.236) or offices in Alexandria, Luxor, Aswan, Suez, Sharm el-Sheikh, Mersa Matrouh and Ismailiya (addresses are detailed under their respective entries). Depending on the whim of the official, you may have to produce exchange receipts proving that you've cashed US$180 during the last month.

TRAVEL PERMITS

You can travel without restriction through most areas of Egypt. However, **special travel permits** are required for the Red Sea Coast beyond Mersa Allam and – depending on relations with Libya – between Mersa Matrouh and the border. Other border areas may also become problematic, so if you're thinking of visiting such areas, check beforehand. For travel permits (or information), contact the Ministry of the Interior in Cairo (see p.236); the process can take from five to fourteen days.

You'll have to supply one or two photos, and pay £E12–40. Procedures vary slightly from office to office, but shouldn't take longer than an hour.

Visitors anticipating an extended stay may apply for a **tourist residence visa**, valid for up to six months at a time. Applications are made to the same offices as for ordinary extensions.

CUSTOMS

Egyptian **customs** allow you to bring in 200 cigarettes (or 250g of tobacco) and one litre of **alcohol**. It's worth bearing in mind that Cairo and Luxor airports have **duty-free shops** for arriving passengers before *and* after customs. At the duty-free shop in the arrivals hall they will ask to see your ticket, but won't enquire whether you've already stocked up.

Though personal effects and cameras are exempt from duty, items such as electronic equipment and video cameras should be declared and listed on a Form D. If you lose them during your visit, they will be assumed "sold" when you come to leave and (unless you have police documentation of theft) you will have to pay 100 percent duty. On items with a high resale value (for example, laptop computers or video cameras) you may be required to pay a deposit against possible duty charges, which is refundable on departure. If customs insists on impounding goods, get a receipt and contact your consulate.

COSTS AND MONEY

Once you've arrived, Egypt is an inexpensive and good-value destination – except perhaps for Sinai and Hurghada, which are pricier than other parts of the country. As a rule, though, providing you avoid luxury hotels or tourist-only services, costs for food, accommodation and transport are low by European standards. The rate of exchange currently stands at about five Egyptian pounds to one pound sterling, and just over three Egyptian pounds to one US dollar.

SOME BASIC COSTS

Accommodation ranges from about £3–6 (US$5–10) a night for a double room in a basic, unclassified hotel to £80–150 (US$130–250) in Egypt's most luxurious establishments. On a limited budget, you can expect to get a decent double room in a one- or two-star hotel for £5–10 (US$8–16). The occasional splurge in a three-star hotel, with a pool, will cost £20–60 (US$36–100) for a double room off season, or £80–100 (US$120–160) at peak periods. To some extent, all these costs are affected by **where you are and when**. Though low-budget options exist, the cost of hotels is higher in Cairo, Sinai and Hurghada throughout the year; in Alexandria during the summer; and in Luxor and Aswan over winter.

The price of a **meal** reflects a similar span, but the basic Egyptian staple of *fuul* and *taamiya* (beans and felafel) or *kushari* (noodles, rice and lentils with hot sauce) can be had in a local eatery for about 30p (50¢). Egyptian pizzas, chicken or kebabs cost about £1–2 (US$1.60–3), and European-style meals in restaurants from around £4 (US$6).

Locally manufactured **drinks** are reasonably cheap – a bottle of Stella beer costing about £1 (US$1.65), native spirits or wines under £4 (US$6) – but imported booze is more expensive than back home in hotels and restaurants, which are generally the only outlets serving alcohol (though you can buy it cheaply in duty-free shops). Everyday items tend to be pricier in Sinai, Hurghada and the desert oases, where goods have to be trucked in from distant centres.

Unless you take domestic flights or rely heavily on private taxis, **transport** is likewise cheap. You can rent a car for £38/US$60 a day, including petrol (which costs less per litre than mineral water). The cost of buses, trains and collective taxis is generally absurdly low. For instance, the 885km train ride from Cairo to Aswan costs £13/US$20 for 1st class, £7/US$12 for air-conditioned 2nd class, and about £2/US$3 in 3rd class.

HIDDEN COSTS

Hidden costs in Egypt are fourfold. Most restaurant and hotel bills are liable to a **service charge** plus local taxes (Luxor and Hurghada have the highest), which increase the final cost by 17–25 percent (unless already included in the price, or irrelevant, as in really cheap hotels and cafés). Visiting the Pyramids and the monuments of the Nile Valley entails spending a lot on **site tickets** (ranging from £1–5/US$2–8), unless you have a student card (see below) entitling you to a fifty percent discount (which many non-students obtain in Cairo, see p.237). The custodians of tombs and temples and the medieval mosques of Islamic Cairo also expect to be tipped. For more on admission prices, see p.60.

A harder aspect to come to terms with is that you'll be confronted with real **poverty**. As a tourist, you're not going to solve any problems, but with an average Egyptian's wage at around £E120 a month (roughly £24/US$40), even a small tip can make a difference to individual family life. For Egyptians, giving money and goods to the needy is a natural act – and a requirement of Islam. As a presumed-rich *khawaga* (the Egyptian term for a foreigner), you will be expected to be liberal with **baksheesh**, which can be divided into three main varieties.

The most common is **tipping**: a small reward for a small service, which can encompass anyone from a waiter or lift operator to someone who unlocks a tomb or museum room at one of the ancient sites. The sums involved should be paltry – between 50pt and £E1– and you needn't feel railroaded into giving more; but try to strike a balance between defending your own wallet and acquiescing gracefully when appropriate. There's little point in spoiling your mood and offending people over trifling sums.

A second common type is more expensive: rewarding the **bending of rules** – many of which seem to have been designed for just that purpose. Examples might include letting you into an archeo-

logical site after hours (or into a vaguely restricted area), finding you a sleeper on a train when the carriages are "full", and so on. This should not be confused with bribery, which is a more serious business with its own etiquette and risks – best not entered into.

The last kind of *baksheesh* is simply alms giving. The disabled are traditional recipients of such gifts, and it seems right to join locals in giving out small change. Children, however, are a different case, pressing their demands only on tourists. If someone offers some genuine help and asks for an *alum* (pen), it seems fair enough, but to yield to every request perhaps encourages a cycle of dependency Egypt could do without.

If giving *baksheesh* in **foreign currency**, give notes rather than coins (which are useless to Egyptians).

YOUTH AND STUDENT DISCOUNTS

Full-time students are eligible for the **International Student ID Card (ISIC)**, which entitles the bearer to special air, rail and bus fares and discounts at museums, theatres and other attractions. For Americans there's also a health benefit, providing up to US$3000 in emergency medical coverage and US$100 a day for up to 60 days hospital care, plus a 24-hour hotline to call in the event of a medical, legal or financial emergency. The card costs £6 in Britain, £8 in Ireland, US$20 in the US, CAN$16 in Canada, A$15 in Australia and NZ$20 in New Zealand. You can also buy an ISIC card at the Medical Scientific Centre in Cairo for £E18 – but you still require a valid student ID card or proof of student status (see p.237 for further details). It may be possible to buy a card without presenting any student ID at some of the budget hotels in Cairo, but this is an unofficial practice which has been cracked down on in recent years. The ISIC card entitles to you to a fifty percent discount on most of Egypt's museums and sites and a thirty percent discount on rail fares. An alternative available to anyone under 26 is the **Go-25 card**, which costs £E15 and entitles holders to the same discounts (within Egypt) as the ISIC card. This card is also available from the Medical Scientific Centre in Cairo (see above).

PRICES AND INFLATION

Most of the **prices** in this book are given in local currency (see below). The main exceptions to this rule – airfares, top-flight accommodation and special packages – are reckoned in US$, although most are actually payable in Egyptian pounds backed by an exchange receipt.

Both of these price indications will certainly change, so costs quoted in this guide can't be taken for granted. However, the cost for tourists in real terms shouldn't rise so much compared to local prices, and might even decrease if your own currency is riding high.

Although Egyptian **inflation** is currently running at around seven percent, it's unevenly distributed. Prices for luxury goods and services (ie most things in the private sector) rise faster than the cost of public transport, petrol and basic foodstuffs, which is held down by subsidies that the government dare not abolish.

MONEY

Egypt's basic unit of **currency** is the **Egyptian pound** (called a *ginay* in Arabic, and written as £E or LE). It is pegged to the US$ at a rate of US$1=£E3.41, while floating against other hard currencies, whose exchange rates fluctuate.

It's easy to distinguish between **£E notes** since they bear Arabic numerals on one side, Western numerals on the other, and are colour coded: £E1 (brown), £E5 (blue), £E10 (red), £E20 (green), £E50 (red), £E100 (green). The £E50 has been suspect since forgeries came to light, while the £E100 is never used in everyday life.

The Egyptian pound is divided into 100 **piastres**, called *irsh* in Arabic and written as ↶ (abbreviated by Westerners to pt). There are 10pt, 25pt and 50pt notes, and variously sized **coins** to the value of 5pt, 10pt, 20pt, 25pt and 50pt; some 25pt coins have a hole in the middle.

Many of the notes in circulation are so ragged that merchants refuse them. Trying to palm off (and avoid receiving) decrepit notes can add spice to minor transactions, or be a real nuisance. Conversely, many vendors won't accept high denomination notes (£E20 upwards) due to a shortage of **change**. While some offer sweets in lieu of coins, others round prices up. Try to hoard coins for tips, fares and small purchases.

CARRYING YOUR MONEY

Arriving in Egypt, it is useful to have at least three days' survival money in **cash**. US dollars, English pounds, French francs and German Deutschmarks are easy to exchange almost anywhere – though due to **forgeries**, banks are often unwilling to

accept US$100 notes issued before 1992, or in less than mint condition. Aside from ordinary spending, hard cash (usually US$) may be required for visas, border taxes and suchlike. **Do not bring** New Zealand dollars, Irish punts, Scottish or Northern Irish pounds, which are not accepted by banks. Israeli shekels can only be changed at the Taba border crossing, or at Forex bureaux in Cairo.

The rest of your money should, ideally, be spread around different forms and currencies for the sake of security. You may wish to carry the bulk of it in a well-known brand of **travellers' cheque**, with **credit cards** and/or **Eurocheques** for backup. It is worth bearing in mind, however, that a number of banks now have **ATM** facilities, which enable you to draw directly from your bank account (see below). It therefore may not be necessary to carry too big a wad of traveller's cheques, or even a credit card. Note too that by taking cash in one currency and cheques in another, you can choose to exchange whichever offers the better rate.

American Express, Barclays, Citibank and Bank of America **travellers' cheques** are accepted by most banks and exchange offices. Thomas Cook cheques are usually good, though they may present problems in untouristed places – and, like Amex in Egypt, have a reputation for delaying refunds. Any other brand will prove more trouble than it's worth. **Eurocheques** backed by a Eurocard can be cashed at most branches of the Banque Misr, but Euro-travellers' cheques are not recommended. Cashing International Girocheques at major post offices entails an incredible rigmarole.

CREDIT CARDS AND CASH CARDS

Credit cards are accepted at major hotels, top-flight restaurants, some shops and airline offices, but virtually nowhere else. American Express, MasterCard and Visa are the likeliest to be accepted. Beware of people making extra copies of the receipt, to fraudulently bill you later; insist that the transaction is done before your eyes. **Cash advances** on Visa and MasterCard can be obtained at most branches of the Banque Misr, while American Express cardholders can cash personal cheques at the main Amex branches (see below).

In Cairo, Alexandria, Luxor, Hurghada and an increasing number of towns throughout Egypt, branches of the Banque Misr, The National Bank of Egypt and The Egyptian British Bank have **automated teller machines (ATMs)** that allow you to draw cash using Visa, MasterCard, Plus or Cirrus **cash cards** – though the machines do have an annoying habit of swallowing your card. The ATMs are usually situated outside the banks, inside airports and some shopping centres, so you can use them at any time. Be warned, however, that Cirrus charges US$5 for each withdrawal, and others may charge more – check with your card-issuer before leaving. The Egyptian British Bank ATMs also accept cards showing Electron, Express Net, Global Access, Electro Bank and Marine Machine.

BANKS AND EXCHANGE

Exchange rates at the main **Egyptian banks** (Bank of Alexandria, Banque Misr, Banque du Caire and National Bank of Egypt) and **Forex bureaux** (the generic term for private exchanges) vary enough to make a difference to people changing a lot of money at once, or bent on saving every penny – but not enough to worry about otherwise. In most towns there isn't much choice anyway; Forex bureaux are largely confined to Cairo, Alexandria and the Canal Cities. As a rule of thumb, Forex offer the best rates for cash, but may not take travellers' cheques; the transaction is also faster than in banks, where forms are passed among a bevy of clerks and counters.

This extended transaction is less likely at **foreign banks** (found only in Cairo and Alexandria) or branches **in hotels**, but there are plenty of exceptions in practice. If you're carrying **American Express** or **Thomas Cook** travellers' cheques (or cash) it's often quicker to do business at their own local branches (see overleaf).

Since the Egyptian pound was floated and a crackdown on moneychangers instituted, the **black market** for hard currency has withered. The fractional difference between the black market and official exchange rates offers zero incentive to deal with (possible) rip-off artists or *agents provocateurs*. That said, you might find it expedient to change some cash unofficially in the Sinai or the desert oases, where banks are thin on the ground and the risk factor is lower.

BANK OPENING HOURS, COMMISSION AND RECEIPTS

Opening hours for Egyptian banks are generally Monday to Thursday 8.30am–2pm, plus an evening shift (5–8pm in winter, 6–9pm in summer); some also open similar hours on Saturday, and from 10am to noon on Sunday (details are given as relevant in the text). Most foreign banks are open from 8.30am to 1pm Monday to Thursday, and sometimes on Sunday. For arriving visitors, the banks at Cairo Airport and the border crossings from Israel are open 24 hours daily, and those at ports open whenever a ship docks.

Commission is not generally charged on straight exchanges, but there might be 30pt stamp duty, which you can either pay on the spot or have them deduct from what you're owed. It's vital to ensure that you get a **postage stamp** if you're going to use the **exchange receipt** for transactions such as buying an airline ticket, since it's not deemed valid without one. Even if you're not planning to use them, it's wise to **keep all receipts** until you leave Egypt.

Rather than going through the hassle of **re-exchanging Egyptian pounds** into hard currency, it's better to spend it all before leaving (you *can't* use it at Cairo Airport's duty-free shop, but can in the café). While minor sums may not incur any forfeit, exchanging large amounts back into hard currency entails a "deduction" of £E30 per day from the sum total of your exchange receipts; what remains is eligible for conversion.

AMERICAN EXPRESS AND THOMAS COOK

American Express has several offices in Cairo and branches in Alexandria, Luxor, Aswan and Ismailiya. All of them can hold client mail and cash Amex travellers' cheques, paying out in Egyptian pounds. Money may be wired to any branch, most of which also allow Amex cardholders to buy travellers' cheques, or cash personal cheques. Green cardholders may draw up to US$1000 each week (US$200 in cash, the rest in travellers' cheques); for gold cardholders the limit is US$5000 (the first US$500 in cash).

Amex's old-established rival, **Thomas Cook**, will cash most brands of travellers' cheque, and sell their own cheques (in whatever hard currency you buy them with). Like Amex, they can also receive money wired from abroad (see below).

WIRING MONEY FROM ABROAD

If you run out of money and don't have a cash card, it's possible to wire money from abroad. One way is a straight **bank-to-bank transfer**. First, you need to find an Egyptian bank that is prepared to accept a wire; then write or fax your own home

AMERICAN EXPRESS OFFICES

Cairo (downtown): 15 Sharia Qasr el-Nil (☎02/574-7991, fax 578-4003; *Nile Hilton* (☎02/578-5001, fax 578-5003).

(Heliopolis): 72 Sharia Omar Ibn el Khattab (☎02/290-9158, fax 290-9157).

Alexandria: 34 El Moaskar El Romani, Roushdy (☎03/541-0177, fax 545-7363).

Luxor: c/o *Winter Palace Hotel* (☎ & fax 095/372-862).

Aswan: c/o *Old Cataract Hotel* (☎ & fax 097/302-909).

Ismailiya: c/o Menatours, 12 Sharia Sultan Hussein (☎064/324-361).

THOMAS COOK OFFICES

Cairo (downtown): 17 Sharia Mahmoud Bassiouny (☎02/574-3955, fax 576-2750); also at the new airport (☎02/265-2122, fax 291-6378) as well as the *Semiramis Intercontinental* and *Mena Palace* hotels.

(Mohandiseen): 10 26th July St (☎02/346-7187, fax 303-4530).

Alexandria: 15 Midan Saad Zaghloul (☎03/484-7830, fax 483-5118).

Luxor: c/o *Winter Palace Hotel* (☎095/372-402, fax 372-862).

Aswan: 59 Corniche el-Nil (☎097/304-011, fax 306-209).

Port Said: 43 Sharia el-Gumhorriya (☎066/227-559, fax 236-111).

Hurghada: 8 Sharia El Sheraton (☎ & fax 065/443-500).

Sharm el-Sheikh: Gafy Mall, Gafy Land (☎ & fax 062/601-808).

bank, giving your own account number, the name and address of the recipient bank, and a routing number; you'll also need to specify the form of ID that the recipient bank will accept before paying out your money.

If this proves too difficult or slow, enquire at American Express in Cairo about the **American Express MoneyGram Service**, which provides a ten-minute delivery. For Americans a third method is to have someone back home cable you money via **Western Union** (☎1-800/325-6000), which has branches in most capital cities and all major towns in the US, and can send money to Cairo, Luxor and Sharm el-Sheikh in Egypt. Wiring US$1000 to Europe will cost around US$75.

HEALTH AND INSURANCE

In Britain, travellers who call the "**Health Line**" (☎01891/224 100) run by **Masta** – the Medical Advisory Service for Travellers Abroad – can receive the latest detailed health advice by return post. In the US, you can get advice by phone from the **US Centers for Disease Control** (☎1-888/232-3228 or 404/332-4559, *www.cdc.gov*). In Australia and New Zealand, contact the **Travellers' Medical and Vaccination Centres**. Australia: Sydney (☎02/9221 7133), Melbourne (☎03/9602 5788), Adelaide (☎08/8267 3544), Brisbane (☎07/3221 9066), Perth (☎08/9321 1977), Canberra (☎02/6257 7156), Darwin (☎08/8981 2907) and Hobart (☎03/6223 7577). New Zealand: Auckland (☎09/373 3531), Christchurch (☎03/379 4000) and Wellington (☎04/473 0991).

Despite the potential health hazards of travel in Egypt, the majority of visitors experience nothing worse than a bout or two of diarrhoea. For minor health complaints, a visit to a pharmacy is likely to be sufficient. Egyptian pharmacists are well trained and dispense a wide range of drugs, including many normally on prescription in Europe. If they feel you need a full diagnosis, they can usually recommend a doctor – sometimes working on the premises. Most doctors speak English or French.

Although the change of diet and climate accounts for most health problems, **individual responses** vary. While some people adapt quickly to the heat and consume local food with impunity, others get sick and stay poorly (children and the elderly are likely to suffer the worst effects). If you're here for a week or two only, it makes sense to be cautious, but longer-staying visitors might prefer to get ill early, acclimatize, and worry less thereafter – a lot depends on your constitution. Bearing this in mind, take whatever precautions seem appropriate.

PREVENTATIVE MEDICINE

Although visitors to Egypt are not required to have **inoculations** unless coming from an infected area, you should always be up to date with **polio** and **tetanus**. It's also worth being vaccinated against **typhoid**, which occasionally flares up in parts of Egypt – although the **cholera** shot is generally acknowledged to be worthless. If you're hoping to visit southern Egypt, Sudan or

sub-Saharan Africa, a vaccination against **meningitis** is essential.

While not an issue for most tourists, visitors planning to stay a long time in Egypt or the Middle East should consider vaccination against **hepatitis**. The new shot for Hepatitis A (Havrix monodose) is expensive at about £50 (though your doctor may provide it free), but with a booster a year later it lasts for ten years. Hepatitis B is only transmitted through body fluids, so immunization is only really necessary for medical workers. Though all these vaccinations can be obtained in Cairo (see p.240), it is vital to ensure that any injections are done with sterile needles. If necessary, supply your own disposable syringe, sold at pharmacies.

Other precautions are fairly obvious, though whether all of them are justified is debatable. Guard against **heatstroke** (see below) and **food poisoning**. Rare meat and raw shellfish top the danger list, which descends via creamy sauces down to salads, juices, raw fruit and vegetables – and if slavishly followed would prevent you from eating most of what's on offer. Visitors who insist on washing everything (and only cleaning their teeth) in mineral water are overreacting. Just use common sense, and accustom your stomach gradually to Egyptian cooking. Asking for dishes to be served very hot (*sukhna awi*) will reduce the risk of catching anything. Take prompt care of **cuts and skin irritations**, since flies can quickly spread infections. Anthisan cream (available abroad) is good for bites, swellings and rashes.

PHARMACIES, DOCTORS AND HOSPITALS

Pharmacies, found in every town, form the advance guard of Egypt's health service. Pharmacists usually speak English, and can dispense most drugs without a prescription. Private **doctors** are equally common, but charge for consultations: expect to pay about £E50 (roughly £10/US$16) a session, excluding the price of any drugs you are prescribed. If you get seriously ill, private **hospitals** are generally preferable to public sector ones. Those attached to universities are usually well equipped and competent, but small-town hospitals are often abysmal. Many hospitals (*mustashfa*) require a **deposit** of around £E200. Normally you must pay this on admission; a delayed payment by your insurance company is not acceptable. Despite several good hospitals in Cairo and Alexandria, Egypt is basically no country in which to fall seriously ill.

HEALTH HAZARDS

The **tap water** in Egyptian towns and cities is heavily chlorinated and mostly safe to drink, but unpalatable and rough on tender stomachs. In rural areas, Sinai campsites and desert resthouses there's a fair risk of contaminated water.

Consequently, most tourists stick to **bottled mineral water**, which is widely available, tastes better, and won't upset sensitive tums. However, excessive fear of tap water is unjustified, and hard to sustain in practice if you're here for long. Once your guts have adjusted, it's usually okay to drink it without further purification (Halazone tablets, iodine crystals, or by boiling).

What you should avoid is any contact with stagnant water that might harbour **bilharzia** (schistosomiasis) flukes. Irrigation **canals** and the slower stretches of the **River Nile** are notoriously infested with these minute worms, which breed in the blood vessels of the abdomen and liver (the main symptom is blood in the urine). Don't drink or swim there, walk barefoot in the mud, or even on grass that's wet with Nile water. But it's okay to bathe in the saline pools of the desert oases.

HEAT AND DUST

Many visitors experience problems with Egypt's intense **heat**, particularly in the south. Because sweat evaporates immediately in the dry atmosphere, you can easily become dehydrated without realizing it. **Dehydration** is exacerbated by both alcohol and caffeine. Drink plenty of other fluids (at least three litres per day; twice as much if you're exerting yourself) and take a bit of extra salt with your food. Wear a hat and loose-fitting clothes (not synthetic fabrics), and a high-factor sunscreen to protect yourself from **sunburn**, especially during summer. Try to avoid going out in the middle of the day and wear a T-shirt when snorkelling, as the sun burns you even quicker in the water.

Heat exhaustion – signified by headaches, dizziness and nausea – is treated by resting in a cool place and drinking plenty of water or juice with a pinch of salt. An intense headache, heightened body temperature, flushed skin and the cessation of sweating are symptoms of **heatstroke**, which can be fatal if not treated *immediately*. The whole body must be cooled by immersion in tepid water, or the application of wet towels. Seek medical assistance.

Less seriously, visitors from cooler climates may suffer from **prickly heat**, an itchy rash caused by excessive perspiration trapped beneath the skin. Wearing loose clothing, keeping cool and bathing often will help relieve the symptoms until your body acclimatizes.

In non-air-conditioned environments, you might employ the traditional Egyptian method of sprinkling water on the ground to cool the surrounding area by evaporation – it also levels the dust.

Desert **dust** – or grit and smog in Cairo – may cause your **eyes** to itch and water. **Contact lens-users** should wear glasses instead, at least part of the time. If ordinary eye drops don't help, try antihistamine decongestant eye drops such as Vernacel, Vascon-A or Optihist. Persistent irritation may indicate **trachoma**, a contagious infection which is easily cured by antibiotics at an early stage, but eventually causes blindness if left untreated. Its prevalence in Egypt explains the number of older folk with cloudy eyes, and the ophthalmologists in every town.

Spending time in the desert, you might find that your **sinuses** get painfully irritated by windborne dust. Covering your nose and mouth with a scarf helps prevent this, while olbas oil or a nasal decongestant spray (available at pharmacies) can relieve the symptoms.

DIARRHOEA AND WORSE . . .

Almost every visitor to Egypt gets **diarrhoea** at some stage. Unless you're stricken by cramps, the best initial treatment is to simply adapt your diet. Fresh orange juice, lemon or lime juice may settle your stomach, or you could try bananas, or live yoghurt (if you can find it). Avoid other fruit and dairy produce, and keep your bodily fluids topped up by drinking plenty of bottled water (perhaps mixed with a rehydration sachet). If things don't improve after 24 hours – or if you have an enteric-type attack with cramps or vomiting – resort to Imodium or Lomotil, being sure not to exceed the recommended dose. Avoid Enterovioform, which is still available in Egypt despite being suspected of damaging the optic nerve. Don't give any of these quite powerful drugs to children.

If symptoms persist longer than a few days, or if you develop a fever or pass blood in your faeces, get medical help immediately, since diarrhoea can also be a symptom of serious infection. Accompanied by vomiting and fever, it may indicate **typhoid**, which responds well to antibiotics. Rarer is **cholera**, which requires urgent treatment with antibiotics and rehydration fluids; it is marked by a sudden onset of acute diarrhoea and cramps. Except for the "rice-water shits" typical of cholera, similar symptoms occur with bacilliary **dysentery**, which is treated with antibiotics. Amoebic dysentery is harder to shift and can cause permanent damage if untreated. The normal remedy is Metronidazole (Flagyl), which should only be taken under medical supervision.

RABIES AND MALARIA

Rabies is endemic in Egypt, where many wild animals and bats (sometimes found in temples and tombs) carry the disease. Avoid touching *any* strange animal, wild or domestic. Treatment must be given between exposure to the disease and the onset of symptoms; once these appear, rabies is invariably fatal. If you think you've been exposed, return home and seek help immediately. To err on the side of caution, consider having a rabies jab before coming to Egypt. It doesn't confer any protection, but fewer injections will be required should you become infected and need treatment.

Currently resurgent throughout Africa, **malaria**, spread by the anopheles mosquito, could become a problem in Egypt in the future, but isn't currently a threat. Consult your doctor, or enquire at a Medical Advisory Service (see box p.25) for latest information on malaria risk and prevention. The first signs of infection are muscular soreness and a low fever; four to eight days later, the characteristic bouts of chills and fever appear.

MOSQUITOES AND BUGS

Besides the risk of malaria, **mosquitoes** can make your life a misery. Horribly ubiquitous over the summer, these blood-sucking pests are never entirely absent – even in Cairo, despite locals' assertions to the contrary. The only solution is total war, using fans, mosquito coils, rub-on repellent, and perhaps a plug-in Ezalo device, sold at pharmacies. You can also reputedly make yourself less attractive to mosquitoes by taking Vitamin B-12 tablets, starting before you leave home. After two weeks of 50mg per day, your blood begins to smell bad to them. However, the best guarantee of a bite-less night's sleep is to bring a mosquito net with long tapes, to pin above your bed. Mosquitoes favour shady, damp areas, and anywhere around dusk.

Equally loathsome – and widespread – are **flies**, which transmit various diseases. Only insecticide spray or air-conditioning offers any protection. Some cheap hotels harbour fleas, scabies, mites, giant roaches and **other bugs**. Consult a pharmacist if you find yourself with a persistent skin irritation.

SCORPIONS AND SNAKES

The **danger** from scorpions and snakes is minimal, as most species are nocturnal, hide during the heat of the day, and generally avoid people. However, you shouldn't go barefoot, turn over rocks or stick your hands into dark crevices anywhere off the beaten track. Whereas the sting of larger, darker **scorpions** is no worse than a bad wasp sting, the venom of the pale, slender-clawed *Buthridae* is highly toxic. If stung, cold-pack the affected area and get to a doctor.

Egypt has two main types of poisonous snakes. **Vipers** vary in colour from sandy to reddish (or sometimes grey) and leave two fang punctures. The carpet viper, Egypt's deadliest snake, has a light X on its head. **Cobras** are recognizable by their distinctive hood and bite mark (a single row of teeth plus fang holes). The smaller Egyptian cobra (coloured sandy olive) is found throughout the country; the longer black-necked cobra (which can spit its venom up to three metres) only in the south. All snakebites should be washed immediately. Stay calm, as panicking sends the venom through your bloodstream more quickly, and get immediate medical help.

AIDS

Despite a TV campaign, the level of **AIDS** awareness is low, and most Egyptians still perceive it as a Western problem. The few cases reported in Egypt are almost certainly the tip of an iceberg, as prostitution and homosexuality are so clandestine, and few Egyptian men take any precautions. As throughout the world, the need for extreme caution, and safe sex, cannot be overstressed. Likewise, be absolutely sure that any injections, tattooing or acupuncture is done with sterile instruments. Pharmacies in cities plus a few shops in Hurghada and Sinai are the only places in Egypt to sell **condoms** (*kabout*) – either Egyptian-made *Tops* (liable to rip) or US imports (thick and short). It's best to bring your own.

WOMEN'S HEALTH

Travelling in the heat and taking antibiotics for an upset stomach, you are liable to **vaginal infections** even if you wash regularly with mild soap, wear cotton underwear and loose clothing. Yeast infections are treatable with Nystatin pessaries (available at pharmacies); "one-shot" Canesten pessaries (bring some from home if you're prone to thrush); or douches of a weak solution of vinegar or lemon juice. Sea bathing can also help. Trichomonas is usually treated with Flagyl, under medical supervision.

Sanitary protection is available from pharmacies in cities and tourist resorts, but seldom anywhere else, so it's wise to bring a supply for your trip.

Bring your own **contraceptives**, since the only forms widely available in Egypt are old-fashioned, high-dosage pills; the coil; and not too trusty condoms (see above). Cap-users should pack a spare, and enough spermicide and pessaries. If you're on the pill, beware that persistent diarrhoea can render it ineffective.

TRAVEL INSURANCE

Travel insurance can buy you peace of mind as well as save you money. Before you purchase any insurance, however, check what you have already. North Americans, in particular, may find themselves covered for medical expenses and loss of or damage to valuables while abroad (see below). Some credit cards, too, offer insurance benefits if you use them to pay for tickets, though the level of coverage may be less than adequate.

If you are travelling for any real length of time, however, additional or specific travel insurance is reassuring. Most **policies** are quite comprehensive, covering not just medical costs but also loss or theft of baggage and money; and in real trouble they should get you home. If you are diving, be sure that your policy covers you for this: treatment in a recompresssion chamber can cost US$1000 a day.

BRITISH AND IRISH COVER

Most travel agents and tour operators will offer you insurance when you book your flight or holiday, and some will insist you take it. These policies are usually reasonable value, though as ever, you should check the small print. If you feel the cover is inadequate (for example, if you are intending to do any dangerous sports such as diving), or you want to compare prices, any British travel agent, insurance broker or bank should be able to help – in Ireland travel agents are the best places to go. If you have a good "all risks" home insurance policy, it may well cover your possessions against loss or theft even when overseas, and many private medical schemes also cover you when abroad – make sure you know the procedure and carry their helpline number.

Nearly all insurance policies work by **reimbursing you** once you return home, so be sure to keep all your receipts from doctors and pharmacists. Any thefts should be reported immediately to the nearest police station and a police report obtained; no report, no refund. If you have had to undergo serious medical treatment, with major hospital bills, contact your consulate. They can normally arrange for an insurance company, or possibly relatives, to cover the fees, pending a claim.

In **Britain**, travel insurance schemes cost around £30 for eight to twelve days worldwide cover (including medical, lost luggage, cancellation etc); medical-only policies are about twenty percent cheaper. Policies issued by Campus Travel or STA (see p.5 for details), Liverpool Victoria (Frizzell House, County Gates, Bournemouth, Dorset BH1 2NF, ☎0800/680 690), Endsleigh Insurance (97–107 Southampton Row, London WC1B 4AG, ☎020/7436 4451), or Columbus Travel Insurance (17 Devonshire Square, London EC2M 4SQ, ☎020/7375 0011, *www.columbusdirect.co.uk*) are all good value – though do shop around and check the small print. In **Ireland** travel specialists such as Usit (see p.5 for details) offer good deals; their policies cost around IR£30 for six to ten days worldwide.

In both Britain and Ireland discounts are sometimes offered to **students** of any age and anyone under 26.

NORTH AMERICAN COVER

Before buying an insurance policy, check that you're not already covered. **Canadian provincial health plans** typically provide some overseas medical coverage, although they are unlikely to pick up the full tab in the event of a mishap. Holders of official **student/teacher/youth cards** (see p.21) are entitled to accident coverage and hospital inpatient benefits – the annual membership is far less than the cost of comparable insurance. **Students** may also find that their student health coverage extends during the vacations and for one term beyond the date of last enrollment. Bank and credit cards (particularly American Express) often provide certain levels of medical or other insurance, and travel insurance may also be included if you use a major credit or charge card to pay for your trip. **Homeowners' or renters'** insurance often covers theft or loss of documents, money and valuables while overseas.

After exhausting the possibilities above, you might want to contact a specialist **travel insurance** company; your travel agent can usually recommend one, or see the box below.

Travel insurance **policies** vary: some are comprehensive while others cover only certain risks (accidents, illnesses, delayed or lost luggage, cancelled flights, etc). In particular, ask whether the policy pays medical costs up front or reimburses you later, and whether it provides for medical evacuation to your home country. For policies that include lost or stolen luggage, check exactly what is and isn't covered, and make sure the per-article limit will cover your most valuable possession.

Most North American travel policies apply only to items lost, stolen or damaged while in the custody of an identifiable, responsible third party – hotel porter, airline, luggage consignment, etc. Even in these cases you will have to contact the local police within a certain time limit to have a complete report made out so that your insurer can process the claim.

The best **premiums** are usually to be had through student/youth travel agencies – STA policies, for example, cost US$55 for 15 days, $105 for a month, $180 for two months, then $55 per month for any additional period. If you're planning to do any dangerous sports (diving etc), be sure to ask whether these activities are covered: some companies levy a surcharge.

AUSTRALIAN AND NEW ZEALAND COVER

Travel insurance is put together by airlines and travel agent groups in conjunction with insurance companies. They are all comparable in premium and coverage. A typical policy for Egypt will cost around A$189/NZ$235 for one month, A$295/NZ$370 for two and A$380/NZ$475 for three. Certain adventure sports such as hang-gliding and mountaineering with ropes are not covered, and you should check the policy carefully to be sure you're covered for activities like bungee jumping and scuba diving.

TRAVEL INSURANCE COMPANIES IN NORTH AMERICA

Most travel agents will arrange travel insurance at no extra charge. The following insurance companies can be called directly.

Access America (☎1-800/284-8300, *www.acessamerica.com*).

Carefree Travel Insurance (☎1-800/323-3149).

Desjardins Travel Insurance – Canada only (☎1-800/463-7830, *www.avdl.com*).

STA Travel (☎1-800/777-0112 or 212/627-3111, *www.statravel.com*).

Travel Guard (☎1-800/826-1300, *www.noelgroup.com*).

Travel Insurance Services (☎1-800/937-1387, *www.travelinsure.com*).

AFTA, Level 3, 309 Pitt St, Sydney (☎02/9264 3299).

Cover More, Level 3, 60 Miller St, North Sydney (☎02/9202 8000).

Ready Plan, Level 7, 333 Kent St, Sydney (☎02/9650 5700); 141–147 Walker St, Dandenong, Victoria (☎03/9771 4000); Level 10, 63 Albert St, Auckland (☎09/300 5333).

INFORMATION AND MAPS

Besides this book, readily available sources of information include the Egyptian Tourist Authority (which has offices abroad and in Egypt), the Internet, travel agencies, hotels and local, often self-appointed, guides (see the section following).

TOURIST OFFICES

The **Egyptian Tourist Authority** (sometimes abbreviated as EGAPT) maintains general information offices in several countries (see below), where you can pick up a range of pamphlets. However, most are simply intended to whet your appetite, and few hard facts can be gained from offices abroad.

In Egypt itself, you'll get a variable response from **local tourist offices** (addresses are given throughout the guide). The most knowledgeable and helpful ones are in Aswan, Luxor, Alexandria, and the oases of Siwa and Dakhla. Staff in Cairo are also well informed, but may need prodding. Elsewhere, most provincial offices are good for a dated brochure, if nothing else.

TRAVEL AGENCIES AND HOTELS

Found in towns and cities, **travel agencies** can advise on (and book) transport, accommodation and excursions. Just remember that they are in business for themselves, so their advice may not be exactly unbiased.

The most ubiquitous agency is **Misr Travel**, the state-run tourist company, which operates hotels, buses and limos, and can make bookings for most things. Their main office is in Cairo (1 Sharia Talaat Harb, ☎02/393-0010). Misr Travel is also represented in London (2nd floor, 308 Langham House, Regent St, W1R 5AL, ☎020/7255 1087), New York (630 Fifth Ave, Suite 1460, New York, NY 10011, ☎1-800/223-4978 or 212/582-9210) and Sydney (see box below). **American Express** and **Thomas Cook** (see p.24) offer various services besides currency exchange.

Receptionists at **hotels** can also be a source of information, and maybe practical assistance. In Luxor, Hurghada and some of the Western Desert oases, most pensions double as information exchanges and all-round "fixers"; likewise, campsites and backpackers' hotels in Sinai.

MAP OUTLETS

BRITAIN

Daunt Books, 83 Marylebone High St, London W1M 3DE (☎020/7224 2295, fax 7224 6893); 193 Haverstock Hill, NW3 4QL (☎020/7794 4006).

Blackwell's Map and Travel Shop, 53 Broad St, Oxford OX1 3BQ (☎01865/792 792, bookshop@blackwell.co.uk).

Heffers Map and Travel, 3rd Floor, 19 Sidney St, Cambridge, CB2 3HL (☎01223/568467, www.heffers.co.uk).

James Thin Melven's Bookshop, 29 Union St, Inverness IV1 1QA (☎01463/233 500, www.jthin.co.uk).

John Smith and Sons, 57–61 St Vincent St, Glasgow G2 5TB (☎0141/221 7472, fax 248 4412, www.johnsmith.co.uk).

The Map Shop, 30a Belvoir St, Leicester LE1 6QH (☎0116/247 1400).

National Map Centre, 22–24 Caxton St, London SW17H 0QU (☎020/7222 2466, www.mapsworld.com).

Newcastle Map Centre, 55 Grey St, Newcastle-upon-Tyne NE1 6EF (☎0191/261 5622, nmc@enterprise.net).

Stanfords, 12–14 Long Acre, London WC2E 9LP (☎020/7836 1321, sales@stanfords.co.uk). Other branches in London are located at 52 Grosvenor Gardens (☎020/7730 1314), and 156 Regent St (☎020/7434 4744).

The Travel Bookshop, 13–15 Blenheim Crescent, London W11 2EE (☎020/7229 5260, www.thetravelbookshop.co.uk).

Waterstone's, 91 Deansgate, Manchester M3 2BW (☎0161/837 3000, fax 835 1534, www.waterstones-manchester-deansgate.co.uk).

IRELAND

Easons Bookshop, 40 O'Connell St, Dublin 1 (☎01/873 3811).

Fred Hanna's Bookshop, 27–29 Nassau St, Dublin 2 (☎01/677 1255).

Hodges Figgis Bookshop, 56–58 Dawson St, Dublin 2 (☎01/677 4754).

Waterstones, Queens Bldg, 8 Royal Ave, Belfast BT1 1DA (☎028/9024 7355); 7 Dawson St, Dublin 2 (☎01/679 1415); 69 Patrick St, Cork (☎021/276 522).

US AND CANADA

Book Passage, 51 Tamal Vista Blvd, Corte Madera, CA 94925 (☎1-800/999-7909 or 415/927-0960, www.bookpassaga.com).

The Complete Traveler Bookstore, 199 Madison Ave, New York, NY 10016 (☎212/685-9007).

Elliott Bay Book Company, 101 S Main St, Seattle, WA 98104 (☎1-800/962-5311 or 206/624-6600, www.elliottbaybook.com).

International Travel Maps & Books, 552 Seymour St, Vancouver, BC V6B 3J5 (☎604/687-3320, www.itmb.com).

Map Link Inc., 30 S La Patera Lane, Unit 5, Santa Barbara, CA 93117 (☎805/692-6777, www.maplink.com).

The Map Store Inc., 1636 I St NW, Washington, DC 20006 (☎1-800/544-2659 or 202/628-2608).

Open Air Books and Maps, 25 Toronto St, Toronto, ON M5C 2R1 (☎1-800/360-9185 or 416/363-0719).

Phileas Fogg's Books & Maps, 87 Stanford Shopping Center, Palo Alto, CA 94304 (☎1-800/533-FOGG, www.foggs.com).

Rand McNally, 444 N Michigan Ave, Chicago, IL 60611 (☎312/321-1751); 150 E 52nd St, New York, NY 10022 (☎212/758-7488); 595 Market St, San Francisco, CA 94105 (☎415/777-3131); 1201 Connecticut Ave NW, Washington, DC 20003 (☎202/223-6751).

Sierra Club Bookstore, 6014 College Ave, Oakland, CA 94618 (☎510/658-7470, www.sierraclubbookstore.com).

Travel Books & Language Center, 4437 Wisconsin Ave, Washington, DC 20016 (☎1-800/220-2665, www.travelbks.com).

Ulysses Travel Bookshop, 4176 St-Denis, Montréal, Quebec H2W 2M5 (☎514/843-9447, www.ulysses.ca).

TOURIST PUBLICATIONS

A series of **regional tourist booklets** under the generic heading *"Night & Day"* are sporadically available free of charge at tourist offices and hotels. Currently there are four, covering Cairo, Alexandria, Upper Egypt and the Red Sea, and the Canal Zone. Each contains a dubious map, notes on local sites and listings of hotels, restaurants, agencies and banks – usually years out of date.

The best guide to **what's on** is the monthly magazine *Egypt Today*, which lists activities, entertainment and exhibitions in Cairo and Alexandria, and events in Luxor and Aswan. Its feature articles cover diverse aspects of Egyptian culture and travel in Egypt. It's sold in Cairo and Alexandria. Selected events are also listed in the daily *Egyptian Gazette*, which is more widely available (see also p.56).

MAPS

The best **general map of Egypt**, published by Freytag & Berndt (1:1,000,000), is available in Cairo, Luxor and Aswan, and good map shops abroad. The more common Bartholomew map (1:1,000,000) is less detailed and way out of date. If the former is unavailable, Kümmerly & Frey (1:950,000) makes a decent substitute. Michelin map #154 covers Egypt and the Sudan: the latter is excellent, but the Egypt section is nothing special. Mobil's *Motoring Guide to Egypt* (sold at Mobil stations around the country) contains **road maps** and a number of town plans, but is really only worthwhile if you're planning to do a lot of motoring.

Taken together, several local **city plans** cover Cairo in comprehensive detail (see p.71). Elsewhere, however, coverage is poor or non-existent. Aside from fairly crude maps of Alexandria, Luxor, Aswan and Port Said, and photocopied handouts in Mersa Matrouh and Siwa Oasis, there are no town plans to be had. Those in this book are as good as any.

Full-blown desert expeditions require **special maps**. The best Egyptian ones are published by the Geological Survey and Mining Authority in Cairo (3 Sharia Salah Salem, Abbassiya; Mon–Thurs & Sun 8am–3pm). Alternatively, buy some *Tactical Pilotage Charts* (available from specialist map shops – see below) before leaving home. These include: Sinai (*TPC H-5A*), Siwa, the Qattara Depression and Bahariya Oasis (*TPC H-4B*), Farafra and Dakhla Oasis (*TPC H-4C*), Kharga Oasis (*TPC H-5D*) and the Darb al-Arba'in Desert (*TPC J-5A*).

ATTITUDES AND BEHAVIOUR

If you want to get the most from a trip to Egypt, it is vital not to assume that anyone who approaches you expects to profit from the encounter. Too many tourists do, and end up making little contact with an extraordinarily friendly people.

Behaviour and attitude on your part are important. If some Egyptians treat tourists with contempt, it has much to do with the way the latter behave. It helps everyone if you can avoid rudeness or aggressive behaviour in response to insistent offers or demands. And be aware, too, of the importance of dress: shorts are socially acceptable only at beach resorts (and for women only in private resorts or along the Aqaba coast); shirts (for both sexes) should cover your shoulders. Many tourists ignore these conventions, unaware of how it demeans them in the eyes of the Egyptians.

Photography needs to be undertaken with care. If you are obviously taking a photograph of someone, ask their permission – especially in the more remote, rural regions where you can cause genuine offence. You may also find people stop you from taking photos that show Egypt in a "poor" or "backward" light. On a more positive front, taking a photograph of (and later sending it to) someone you've struck up a friendship with, or exchanging photographs, is often – in the towns at least – greatly appreciated. As ever, be wary of photographing anything militarily sensitive (bridges, train stations, dams, etc). When **invited to a home**, it's normal to take your shoes off before entering the reception rooms. It is customary to take a gift: sweet pastries (or tea and sugar in rural areas) are always acceptable. At a communal meal, never use the left hand unless others are doing so.

FROM A WOMAN'S PERSPECTIVE

The biggest problem **women travellers** face in Egypt is the perceptions that Egyptian men have. Unless accompanied by husbands, women tourists are seen as loose, willing to have sex at the most casual opportunity, and – in Egyptian social terms – virtually on a par with prostitutes. While Hollywood films are partly to blame for this view, the root cause is the vast disparity between social norms in Islamic and Western countries.

Many women visitors do a range of things that no respectable Egyptian woman would consider: dressing "immodestly", showing shoulders and cleavage; sharing rooms with men to whom they are not married; drinking alcohol in bars or restaurants; smoking; even travelling alone on public transport, without a relative as an escort. Though some Egyptians know enough about Western ways to realize that this doesn't signify a prostitute (as it would for an Egyptian woman), most are ready to think the worst. Tales of affairs with tourists, and the scandalous Russians of Hurghada, are common currency among Egyptian males.

Without compromising your freedom too greatly, there are a few steps you can take to **improve your image**. Most important and obvious is **dress**: *loose* opaque clothes that cover all "immodest" areas (thighs, upper arms, chest) and hide your contours are a big help, and essential if you are travelling alone or in rural areas (where covering long hair is also advisable). On public transport (buses, trains, *service* taxis), try to sit with other women – who may often invite you to do so. On the Cairo metro and trams in Alexandria there are carriages reserved for women. If you're **travelling with a man**, wearing a wedding ring confers respectability, and asserting that you're married is better than admitting to be "just friends".

As anywhere, looking confident and knowing where you're going is a major help in avoiding hassle. Problems – most commonly hissing or groping – tend to come in **downtown Cairo** and in the public **beach resorts** (except Sinai's Aqaba coast, or Red Sea holiday villages, which are more or less the only places where you'll feel happy about sunbathing). In the **oases**, where attractions include open-air springs and hot pools, it's okay to bathe – but do so in at least a T-shirt and leggings: oasis people are among the most conservative in the country.

Your **reaction to harassment** is down to you. Some women find that verbal hassle is best ignored, while others may prefer to use an Egyptian brush-off like *khalás* (finished) or *úsqut* (be quiet). If you get groped, the best response is to yell *áram!* (evil!) or *sibnee le wadi* (don't touch me), which will shame any assailant in public, and may attract help. Groping an Egyptian woman would be judged totally unacceptable behaviour, so there's no reason why you should put up with it, either. Some women find that it occasionally helps to clout gropers, if only to make themselves feel better.

Conversely, enough foreign women have relationships with Egyptian men to justify a warning about **gigolos**. Every year, dozens of women are persuaded to invest money in Egypt and then find themselves powerless when things go wrong. Unless married to the man, they have *no* rights under Egyptian law, and are liable to be charged with prostitution. Even a marriage contract doesn't help much, as local lawyers are so corrupt.

On the positive side, **spending time with Egyptian women** can be a delight, if someone decides to take you under their wing. The difficulty in getting to know women is that fewer women than men speak English, and that you won't run into women in cafés or tourist facilities. However, public transport can be good meeting ground, as can shops and, best of all, local schools (Egypt has a high proportion of women teachers).

TRAVELLERS WITH DISABILITIES

Disability is common in Egypt; many conditions that would be treatable in the West, such as cataracts, cause permanent disabilities here because people can't afford the treatment. Disabled people are unlikely to get jobs (though there is a tradition of blind singers and preachers), so the choice is usually between staying at home being looked after by your family, and going out on the streets to beg for alms. For the disabled traveller, this has its advantages; disability and disfigurement do not get the same embarrassed reaction from Egyptians that they do from able-bodied Westerners. Disability carries no stigma, it is simply God's will, to be accepted and made light of – as Egyptians say, *Allah karim* (God is generous).

On the other hand, you'll be lucky to see a wheelchair or a disabled toilet, and the streets are full of all sorts of obstacles that would be hard for a blind or wheelchair-bound tourist to negotiate independently. Recently constructed hotels and other tourist facilities tend to be wheelchair-friendly, but few other places have ramps, which are intended for moving baggage rather than people, if they exist at all. If you walk with difficulty, you will find street obstacles and steep stairs hard going. Queuing, and the heat, will take it out of you if you have a condition that makes you tire quickly. A light, folding camp-stool could be invaluable if you have limited walking or standing power.

The **monuments** are a mix of the accessible and the impossible. Most of the major temples are built on relatively level sites, with a few steps here and there – manoeuvrable in a wheelchair or with sticks if you have an able-bodied helper. Your frustrations are likely to be with the tombs, which are almost always a struggle to reach – often sited halfway up cliffs, or down steep flights of steps. In the Valley of the Kings, for example, the only really straightforward tomb is that of Ramses VI. The Pyramids of Giza are accessible to viewing but not entry; Saqqara is difficult, being so sandy.

Cairo itself is bad news, especially Islamic Cairo, with its narrow, uneven alleys and heavy traffic, but with a car and helper, you could still see the Citadel and other major monuments. There's a lift in the Egyptian Antiquities Museum. Some **diving centres** in Sinai and Hurghada accept disabled students on their courses, and the hotels in these resorts tend to be wheelchair-friendly.

Taxis are easily affordable and quite adaptable; if you rent one for the day, the driver is certain to help you in and out, and perhaps even around the sites you visit. If you employ a guide, they may well also be prepared to help you with steps and other obstacles.

PLANNING A HOLIDAY

There are **organized tours and holidays** specifically for people with disabilities; see the box opposite for contacts – who will be able to put

CONTACTS FOR TRAVELLERS WITH DISABILITES

BRITAIN AND IRELAND

Disability Action Group, 2 Annadale Ave, Belfast BT7 3JH (☎028/9049 1011, hq@disabilityaction.org, www.disabilityaction.org). A good source of general information and advice for disabled travellers.

Holiday Care Service, 2nd Floor, Imperial Building, Victoria Rd, Horley, Surrey RH6 7PZ (☎01293/774 535, fax 784 647, minicom ☎01293/776 943). Provides free lists of accessible accommodation abroad. Information on financial help for holidays available.

Irish Wheelchair Association, Blackheath Drive, Clontarf, Dublin 3 (☎01/833 8241, info@iwa.ie). A national voluntary organization working with people with disabilities, and with related services for holidaymakers.

Misr Travel (see p.30 for details). Can be helpful with transport and accommodation arrangements.

RADAR (Royal Association for Disability and Rehabilitation), 12 City Forum, 250 City Rd, London EC1 V 8A (☎020/7250 3222, minicom ☎020/7250 4119, www.radar.org.uk). A good source of advice on holidays and travel abroad.

Tripscope, The Courtyard, Evelyn Rd, London W4 5JL (☎020/8994 9294, fax 8994 3618, minicom and local rate calls in the UK ☎08457/585 641, tripscope@cableinet.co.uk). A national telephone information service offering free advice on UK and international transport for those with a mobility problem.

US AND CANADA

Flying Wheels Travel Service, 143 W Bridge St, Owatonna, MN 55060 (☎1-800/535-6790, www.thq@ll.net). Operates tours for disabled travellers.

Jewish Rehabilitation Hospital, 3205 Place Alton Goldbloom, Chomedey Laval, Quebec H7V 1R2 (☎450/688-9550 ext226). Advice for disabled travellers.

Misr Travel (see p.30 for details).

Mobility International USA, PO Box 10767, Eugene, OR 97440 (voice and TDD: ☎541/343-1284). Information and referral services, access guides, tours and exchange programmes. Annual membership US$35 (includes half-yearly newsletter).

Society for the Advancement of Travel for the Handicapped (SATH), 347 Fifth Ave, New York, NY 10016 (☎212/447-7284, www.sath.org). Non-profit travel-industry referral service that passes queries on to its members as appropriate.

Travel Information Service ☎215/456-9600. Telephone information and referral service.

Twin Peaks Press, Box 129, Vancouver, WA 98666 (☎1-800/637-2256 or 360/694-2462). Publisher of the Directory of Travel Agencies for the Disabled, listing more than 370 agencies worldwide; Travel for the Disabled; and the Directory of Accessible Van Rentals and Wheelchair Vagabond, loaded with personal tips.

AUSTRALIA AND NEW ZEALAND

Australian Council for the Rehabilitation of the Disabled (ACROD), PO Box 60, Curtin, ACT 2605 (☎02/6282 4333); 24 Cabarita Rd, Cabarita NSW 2137 (☎02/9743 2699).

Disability Resource Centre, 60 Bennett St, Palmerston North, New Zealand (☎06/952 0011).

EGYPT

ETAMS Tours, 13 Sharia Qasr el-Nil, Cairo (☎02/345-0761). Specializes in custom-made tours for disabled individuals and groups.

Misr Travel (see p.30 for details).

Peace Tourism, 4 Sharia Ismail Sabry, Heliopolis, Cairo (☎02/355-1813). Can offer the same sort of assistance as Misr Travel.

you in touch with any specialists for trips to Egypt – and tour operators. If you want to be more independent, it's important to become an authority on where you must be self-reliant and where you may expect help, especially regarding transport and accommodation. It is also vital to be honest – with travel agencies, insurance companies and travel companions.

People with a pre-existing medical condition are sometimes excluded from travel **insurance policies**, so read the small print carefully. To make your journey simpler, ask your travel agent to notify airlines or bus companies, who can cope

better if they are expecting you, with, for example, a wheelchair provided at airports, and staff primed to help. A **medical certificate** of your fitness to travel, provided by your doctor, is also extremely useful; some airlines or insurance companies may insist on it.

Make sure that you have extra supplies of drugs – carried with you if you fly – and a prescription including the generic name in case of emergency. It's also a good idea to carry spares of any clothing or equipment that might be hard to find; if there's an association representing people with your disability, contact them early in the planning process.

SECURITY, POLICE AND CONSULATES

Since 1992, Egypt's image as a safe country to visit has been shattered by a wave of terrorism, which has scared many tourists away. The 1997 Luxor massacre dealt tourism a massive blow, and even now tourist numbers are twenty percent below their 1996 levels. Egyptians complain that most fears are wildly exaggerated, given that life continues as normal, muggings are unheard of and cities feel unintimidating at night. In the event, most visitors experience no trouble at all, and soon become as relaxed as the locals.

PETTY CRIME

While relatively few in number, **pickpockets** are skilled and concentrate on tourists. Most operate

in Cairo, notably in queues and on the crowded buses to the Pyramids. To play safe, keep your valuables in a **money belt** or a pouch under your shirt (leather or cotton materials are preferable to nylon, which can irritate in the heat). Overall, though, **casual theft** is more of a problem. Campsites, hostels and cheap hotels often have poor security, making it unwise to leave valuables there. At most places, you can deposit them at the reception (always get a receipt for cash).

If you are **driving**, it goes without saying you should not leave anything you cannot afford to lose visible or accessible in your car.

TERRORISM

The level of **terrorism** in Egypt has been reduced, following a crackdown on Islamic extremists and a ceasefire signed in March 1999 by the terrorist group responsible for many of the attacks on tourists. Although security forces and government officials are the prime targets for terrorists, tourists have reason to feel threatened, as Islamic radicals have shot at trains and tour buses, and even detonated a bomb inside one of the Pyramids. The worst **incidents** have been the killing of 17 Greek tourists in Cairo in April 1996, and the Luxor massacre of 1997 in which more than sixty people died. The situation is far from bad enough to warrant staying away altogether, but it's still a good idea to follow the news (as tourist attacks are often in response to Israeli actions), and also heed any travel advisory bulletins issued by your own government.

Aside from the (small) risk of riding through Middle Egypt on the train, it is easy to **avoid trouble spots**: the latest rundown of areas considered unsafe can be obtained from government advice lines in Britain (☎0374/500-926) and the US (☎202/647-5225), or from consulates in Cairo.

With the object of safeguarding tourists, certain **travel restrictions** have been imposed on foreigners (see box on p.258). In Cairo, Luxor and Aswan, railway clerks have been told not to sell tickets for any **trains** up or down the Nile Valley except on those services designated for tourists, which have plainclothes guards riding shotgun. Tourist buses between Cairo and Israel, and from Aswan to Luxor or Abu Simbel (if operating), must travel in a **convoy** (*kol*) with a police escort. Perversely, there is no formal ban on visiting "risky" areas, but the local police will certainly keep a close eye on you, and may insist on accompanying you to sites like Abydos or Dendara.

Another wise move is to **respect local customs** (in public, anyway). The less you stand out and cause offence, the smaller the chance of attracting any hostility. By going with the swim of society, you'll gain a measure of protection. There are also armed police everywhere, whose mission includes keeping an eye on your safety, but as their usual response to trouble is to let rip with Kalashnikovs, this is a somewhat mixed blessing. In the event of **real trouble**, hit the deck or get off the streets *immediately*.

THE POLICE

Egypt has a plethora of police forces whose high profile in Cairo (which has more cops per thousand citizens than any other capital in the world) and at checkpoints on trunk roads strikes first-time visitors as a sign of recent trouble, although it has actually been the rule since the 1960s. Whereas Egyptians fear police brutality, foreign visitors are usually treated with kid gloves and given the benefit of the doubt unless drugs or espionage are suspected.

The **Municipal Police** handle all crimes, and have a monopoly on law and order in smaller towns. Their uniform (khaki in winter, tan or white in summer) resembles that of the **Traffic Police**, who wear striped cuffs. Both get involved in accidents and can render assistance in emergencies. However, relatively few officers speak anything but Arabic.

If you've got a problem or need to report a crime, always go to the **Tourist Police**. The ordinary ranks wear the regular khaki police uniform with a "Tourist Police" armband; officers wear black uniforms in winter and white in summer. Found at tourist sites, museums, airports, stations and ports, they are supposedly trained to help tourists in distress, and speak a foreign language (usually English). In practice, the odds of getting such an officer are fifty-fifty – but it's worth trying them first. The more senior the officer, the better the chance.

The fourth conspicuous force is the **Central Security** police (dressed all in black and armed with Kalashnikovs), who guard embassies, banks and highways. Though normally genial enough, this largely conscript force will shift rapidly from tear gas to live rounds when ordered to crush demonstrations or civil unrest. If you find yourself getting caught up in anything, clear out quick. Ordinarily, though, they are nothing to worry about.

To guard vital utilities, there are also Electricity, Airport and **River Police** forces; the last is responsible for overseeing felucca journeys between Aswan and Luxor, though the formalities are usually handled by the captain of the boat rather than the passengers.

All of these forces deploy **plainclothes agents** who hang around near government buildings and crowded places, dressed as vendors or peasants – hence their nickname, the "Galabiyya Police". Aside from the sport of spotting agents in Cairo (where they dress quite snappily), tourists needn't think about them – though in hotels or bars, you might be disconcerted to find yourself chatting with a guy who suddenly announces that he's a cop. There are lots of them around.

Finally, there is **Military Intelligence**, which is only relevant to travellers who wish to visit remote parts of the Western Desert or go down beyond Mersa Allam on the Red Sea Coast, for which you need permission (details in the text). Their offices in Mersa Matrouh and the oases are signposted in English and quite tourist-friendly, whereas in Sinai they have secret agents stationed in Dahab, Nuweiba, Na'ama Bay and Sharm el-Sheikh, whose brief includes watching Israeli tourists, and locals who visit Israel.

Addresses and phone numbers of local police stations appear in the text.

FOREIGN CONSULATES IN EGYPT

If you do find yourself in trouble – or simply need a visa – there are **consulates** for most nationalities in **Cairo** (see p.237). Britain and several other European countries also maintain consulates in **Alexandria** (p.505) and **Port Said** (p.550). Consulates can advise on legal matters and replace missing passports, but are unsympathetic towards drug offenders and will not make loans to penniless travellers (though they will repatriate you as a last resort).

GETTING AROUND

Egyptian public transport is, on the whole, pretty good. There is an efficient rail network linking the Nile Valley, Delta and Canal Zone, and elsewhere you can travel easily enough by bus or collective (*service*) taxi. On the Nile you can indulge in feluccas or cruise boats, and in the desert there's the chance to test your camel-riding prowess. For the hurried, EgyptAir and Air Sinai also provide a network of flights.

TRAINS

Covering a limited network of routes, **trains** are best used for long hauls between the major cities, when air-conditioned services offer a comfier alternative to buses and taxis. For shorter journeys, however, trains are slower and less reliable. There's a crucial distinction between relatively fast **air-conditioned (A/C) trains** (including **wagons-lits** services) and the snail-like **non-A/C local-stop services**. For reasons of security, the authorities want tourists to use only specially designated A/C trains between Cairo and Upper Egypt, so railway clerks have been instructed not to sell tickets for other trains (see p.37). Most tourists abide by this but, if you have good reasons not to, it's possible to get an Egyptian to buy your ticket, or simply board a non-A/C train without a ticket, or buy one from the conductor.

Students with ISIC cards get 30 percent reductions on all fares except sleepers and *wagons-lits*.

A/C TRAINS

Air-conditioned trains nearly always have two classes of carriage. The most comfortable option is **1st class** (*daraga oola*), which has A/C, waiter service, reclining armchairs and no standing in the aisles. Unfortunately for those trying to sleep, they also screen videos until midnight. Air-conditioned **2nd class superior** (*daraga tania mumtaaza*) is less plush and more crowded – but at two-thirds of the price of 1st class it's a real bargain. Occasionally A/C trains will be 1st or 2nd class only.

Travelling between Cairo, Luxor and Aswan, foreigners are only allowed to use two "**tourist trains**", whose compartments are guarded by plainclothes cops toting Uzis. Trains have been fired upon around Minya and Qena on several occasions, but the odds of this happening to the train that you're on are pretty remote.

The regular **sleepers** attached to some services along the Nile Valley used to be an economical way of travelling overnight to Luxor or Aswan, but tourists may now only use the far costlier *wagons-lits* (see below). If you baulk at this, one alternative is to travel in an ordinary 1st or A/C 2nd class carriage, which should be comfortable enough to allow sleeping on an overnight journey, at a fraction of the cost of a *wagons-lits*.

Seats are **reservable** up to seven days in advance. There is occasional double booking but a little *baksheesh* to the conductor usually sorts out any problem. One common difficulty is that **return bookings** can't be arranged at the point of origin, so if you're travelling back to Cairo from Aswan/Luxor (or vice versa), it's best to book a seat the day you arrive. Most **travel agencies** sell 1st class tickets for a small commission, saving you from having to queue.

To give an idea of **fares**, a 1st class ticket from Cairo to Aswan costs about £13/US$20; A/C 2nd class £7/US$12.

NON-A/C TRAINS

Non-air-conditioned trains divide into **ordinary 2nd class** (*daraga tania aadia*), which has padded bench seating, and **3rd class** (*daraga talata*), which is just wooden benches and open doors and windows for ventilation. Both classes are invariably crowded, the rolling stock is ancient and often filthy, and schedules fanciful. Few foreigners use them, and the only reason to do so for a long journey is to save money. Over short distances, however, some might enjoy the funky disorder, with peasants and vendors getting on and off at every stop.

There is no advance booking for seats on these services and you needn't queue for a ticket at the station. You simply walk on and buy a ticket from the conductor, paying a small penalty fee (about 20p/30¢).

WAGONS-LITS

The ban on using regular sleepers persuades many tourists to cough up for snazzier *wagons-lits*; these may comprise an entire train, or be limited to a couple of carriages tacked on to a regular service. However, *wagons-lits* are also shot at quite often and are probably best avoided. If you do decide to book one, the fare is a hefty sum (currently £E315 – £63/US$95 – per person from Cairo to Luxor or Aswan) for anyone on a low budget – though still cheaper than a flight. Passengers get a comfortable two-bed cabin, with a sink; breakfast in bed; a dining car, bar and sometimes a disco.

Booking of *wagons-lits* is best done through branches of Thomas Cook or American Express, or in Cairo through the cash-only reservations centre (daily 9am–3pm; ☎574-9474) to the south of Ramses station, or at the *Helnan Shepheard Hotel* (see p.85).

BUSES

Inter-city **buses** are an inexpensive way to travel, and often preferable to trains. Besides being quicker for short trips along the Nile Valley, buses serve areas beyond the rail network, such as Sinai, the oases, Abu Simbel and Hurghada. Travelling in Egypt for any length of time, you are likely to make considerable use of the various networks.

BUS SERVICES

Egypt's bus network is divided between three main operators, based in Cairo. The **Upper Egypt Bus Company** serves all points along the Nile Valley, the Fayoum and inner oases, and the Red Sea Coast as far down as El-Quesir. Company buses are dark green, or tan on the desert routes. Sinai and the Canal Zone are covered by the **East Delta Bus Company**, whose livery is green and yellow. The **West Delta Bus Company**'s blue vehicles serve Alexandria, Mersa Matrouh, Siwa Oasis and the Nile Delta.

On most routes there's a choice between **air-conditioned** (A/C) buses – which are usually new(ish) and fast – and **non-A/C** ones, generally old rattletraps. The former are invariably more expensive, but whether their A/C actually works depends on the bus company and the route. While West Delta's services to Alex are reliable, you can't say the same for their buses from Alex to Siwa, or the Upper Egypt Bus Company's services between Assyut and Kharga Oasis.

Key routes (from Cairo to Alexandria, Luxor, Aswan and Hurghada) are also covered by the **Superjet** company, whose A/C buses have toilets, videos and expensive snacks. Their red, black and gold livery explains their nickname, the "Golden Arrows" or "Golden Rockets". Superjet is a subsidiary of the **Arab Union Transport Company**, which operates international services to Libya, Jordan, Kuwait and Saudi Arabia.

TERMINALS AND BOOKINGS

Though most towns have a single bus depot for all destinations, cities such as Cairo, Alexandria, Port Said and Ismailiya have several **terminals** (detailed in the guide). English- or French-speaking staff are fairly common at the larger ones, but rare in the provinces. **Schedules** – usually posted in Arabic only – change frequently, so information in this guide should be verified in person. Hotels in Sinai and the oases, and the tourist offices in Luxor and Aswan can also supply information.

At city terminals, **tickets** are normally sold from kiosks, up to 24 hours in advance for A/C or long-haul services. In the provinces, tickets may only be available an hour or so before departure, or on the bus itself in the case of through-services, which are often standing-room only when they arrive. Passengers on A/C services are usually assigned a seat (the number is written in Arabic on your ticket), but seats on "local" buses are taken willy-nilly.

SERVICE TAXIS

Collective **service taxis** are one of the best features of Egyptian transport. They operate on a wide variety of routes, are generally quicker than buses and trains, and fares are very reasonable. On the downside, maniacal driving on congested roads calls for strong nerves and a certain fatalism. Accidents are not uncommon.

The taxis are usually big **Peugeot saloons** carrying seven passengers or **minibuses** seating a dozen people. Most business is along specific routes, with more or less non-stop departures throughout the day on the main ones, while cross-desert traffic is restricted to early morning and late afternoon. You just show up at the terminal (locations are detailed, city by city, in the guide) and ask for a *service* to your destination. As soon as the requisite number of people (or less, if you're willing to pay extra) are assembled, the taxi sets off. As fewer people travel after dark in winter, you might have to wait a while for a ride to a distant town; catching a *service* to somewhere nearer, and then another one to your final destination, could be quicker.

On established routes *service* taxis keep to **fixed fares** for each passenger (detailed in the guide). You can ascertain current rates by asking at your hotel (or the tourist office), or observing what Egyptians pay at the end of the journey.

Alternatively, you can **charter a whole taxi** for yourself or a group – useful for day excursions or on odd routes. You will have to bargain hard to get a fair price (see entries in the guide).

CITY TRANSPORT

Most Egyptian towns are small enough to cover on foot, especially if you stay in a hotel near the centre. In larger cities, however, local transport is definitely useful. Learn to recognize Arabic numerals and you can take full advantage of the cheap **buses, minibuses and trams** that cover most of Alexandria and Cairo (which also has river taxis and an excellent metro). Bus and tram routes are detailed under individual entries in the guide.

Founded in 1934, the **Brooke Hospital for Animals** now has clinics in Cairo, Luxor, Aswan, Edfu and Alexandria, and pilot schemes in Jordan, India and Pakistan. They provide free treatment for any animal brought to the clinic, and rescue abandoned ones. Tourists are asked to help by admonishing drivers who gallop their horses, and not travelling more than four to a carriage. Boycotting the worst offenders may work, but it would be wrong to judge all owners of neglected animals harshly, for many simply can't afford to take their horse off the streets. Tourists are welcome to visit the Brooke clinics in Egypt. Donations can be sent to the Brooke Hospital for Animals, Broadmead House, 21 Panton St, London SW1Y 4DR (☎020/7930 0210).

Equally ubiquitous are four-seater **taxis** (black and white in Cairo, black and yellow in Alex), which often pick up extra passengers heading in the same direction. As meters are rarely used (or work), the trick is to know the fare and pay on arrival, rather than ask or haggle at the beginning. Above all, don't confuse these cabs with larger *special* taxis (usually Peugeot 504s or Mercedes), which cost three times more and prey on tourists. If you do rent a *special*, establish the price – and bargain it down – before you get in. The section on Cairo taxis (p.78) contains some more advice.

You will also come across **caleches** – horse-drawn buggies, also known as **hantours**. These are primarily tourist transport, and you'll be accosted by drivers in Alexandria, a few parts of Cairo, and most of all in Luxor and Aswan. Fares are high by local taxi standards and, despite supposed tariffs set by the local councils, are in practice entirely negotiable. In a few small towns, mostly in Middle Egypt, *caleches* remain part of local city transport. Ask locals the price of fares before climbing on board, or simply pay what you see fit at the end. Some of the horses and buggies are in pristine condition; others painful to behold. Tourists can help by boycotting drivers who abuse their animals, and by contributing to the Brooke Hospital for Animals (see box).

DRIVING, BIKING AND HITCHING

Driving in Egypt is not for the faint-hearted or inexperienced motorist. Cities, highways, backroads and *pistes* each pose a challenge to drivers' skills and nerve. Pedestrians and carts seem blithely indifferent to heavy traffic. Though accidents are less frequent than you'd think, the crumpled wrecks alongside highways are a constant reminder of the hazards of motoring.

Although driving on the right is pretty much universal, other **rules of the road** vary. Traffic **in cities** is relentless and anarchic, with vehicles weaving to and fro between lanes, signalling by horn. Two beeps means "I'm alongside and about to overtake". A single long blast warns "I can't (won't) stop and I'm coming through!" Extending your hand, fingers raised and tips together, is the signal for "Watch out, don't pass now"; spreading your fingers and flipping them forwards indicates "Go ahead". Although the car in front usually has right of way, buses and trams always take precedence.

On country roads – including the two-lane east and west bank "highways" along the Nile Valley – trucks and cars routinely overtake in the face of incoming traffic. The passing car usually flashes its lights as a warning, but not always. Most roads are bumpy, with deep potholes and all manner of traffic, including donkey carts and camels. Beware, especially, of children darting into the road. If you injure someone, relatives may take revenge on the spot. Avoid driving **after dark**, when Egyptians drive without lights, only flashing them on to high beam when they see another car approaching. Wandering pedestrians and animals, obstructions and sand drifts present extra hazards. During spring, flash floods can wash away roads in Sinai. On **pistes** (rough, unpaved tracks in the desert or mountains) there are special problems. You need a good deal of driving and mechanical confidence – and shouldn't attempt such routes if you don't feel your car's up to scratch. **Desert driving** is covered in detail on p.412.

Police checkpoints – signposted in English as "Traffic Stations" – occur on the approach roads to towns and along major trunk routes. Foreign motorists are usually waved through, but you might be asked to show your passport or driving licence. In Middle Egypt the checkpoints are militarized, and Egyptian vehicles may be searched for weapons.

The official **speed limit** outside towns is 90km per hour (100km on the Cairo–Alexandria Desert Road), but on certain stretches it can be as low as 30km per hour. Road signs are similar to those in Europe. The **minimum age** for driving in Egypt is 25 years; the **maximum age** limit is 70 years.

CAR RENTAL

Renting **a car** pays obvious dividends if you are pushed for time or plan to visit remote sites (you cannot bring rented cars across the border), but whether you'd want to drive yourself is another matter (see above) – it's not much more expensive to hire a car and driver.

Any branch of Misr Travel, and numerous local tour agencies, can fix you up with a **car and driver**. An alternative is simply to negotiate with local taxi drivers (see previous page).

For a **self-drive car**, visitors can make arrangements abroad through Hertz, Avis or Budget, or directly with local car rental compa-

---

MOTORING ORGANIZATIONS

American Automobile Association (AAA)
Each state has its own club – check the phone book for local addresses and phone numbers. The AAA can refer members to overseas auto associations and also provide international drivers' licences and *carnets de passage* (for those planning to transport cars across certain international boundaries).

Australian Automobile Association, 216 Northbourne Ave, Canberra ACT 2601 (☎02/6247 7311).

Automobile and Touring Club of Egypt, Cairo head office: 10 Sharia Qasr el-Nil; or its representatives at the harbours of Alexandria, Port Said, Suez or Nuweiba.

Automobile Association, Fanum House, Basingstoke, Hants RG21 2EA (☎01256/201 123); 36 Wellington Place, Belfast (☎028/9023 2131).

Canadian Automobile Association (CAA).
Each region has its own club – check the phone book for local addresses and phone numbers.

Irish Automobile Association, 23 Suffolk Rd, Dublin (☎01/667 9481); Cork (☎021/276 922).

New Zealand Automobile Association, Level 17, AA Centre, 99 Albert St, Auckland (☎09/377 4660).

Royal Automobile Club, PO Box 100, RAC House, 7 Brighton Rd, South Croydon CR2 6XW (☎020/8686 0088); 79 Chichester St, Belfast (☎028/9023 2640).

nies in Egypt (addresses given where relevant in the guide). It's worth shopping around for the best deal, since rates and terms vary considerably. At the cheaper end of the market, you can get a car with unlimited mileage for about US$60/£38 a day. To rent a vehicle you must have an International Driving Licence (obtainable from motoring organizations, see below) and be at least 25 years old. Most companies require a hefty deposit, and not all accept credit cards.

Before making a reservation, be sure to find out if you can pick up the car in one city and return it in another. Generally, this is only possible with cars from Hertz, Avis or Budget, found in the main cities and tourist centres. And before setting out, make sure the car comes with spare tyre, tool kit and full documentation – including insurance cover, which is compulsory issue with all rentals.

MOTORBIKES AND BIKES

Motorcycling could be a good way to travel around Egypt, but the red tape involved in bringing your own bike is diabolical (ask your national motoring organization and the Egyptian consulate for details). It's difficult to rent a machine except in Luxor or Hurghada. Bikers should be especially wary of potholes, sand and rocks, besides other traffic on the roads.

Useful for getting around small towns and reaching sites or beaches in the vicinity, **bicycles** can be rented in Luxor, Aswan, Hurghada, Siwa Oasis and other places for a modest sum. Cycling in big cities or over long distances is not advisable. Traffic is murderous, the heat brutal, and foreign cyclists are sometimes stoned by children (particularly in the Delta). If you're determined to cycle the **Nile Valley**, the new east bank expressway that runs down as far as Aswan is the safer route.

Most towns have a wealth of **general repair shops**, well used to servicing local bikes and mopeds. Though unlikely to have the correct spare parts for your make of bike, they can usually sort out some kind of temporary solution.

PETROL AND BREAKDOWNS

Petrol (*benzene*) stations are plentiful in larger towns but few and far between in rural and desert areas. Always fill your tank to the limit. Replace oil/air filters regularly, lest impurities in the petrol, and Egypt's ubiquitous dust, clog up the engine.

Egyptian **mechanics** are usually excellent at coping with breakdowns, and all medium-sized towns have garages (most with a range of spare parts for French, German and Japanese cars). But be aware that if you break down miles from anywhere you'll probably end up paying a lot to get a lorry to tow you back.

If you are driving your own vehicle, there is also the problem of having to re-export any car that you bring into the country (even a wreck). You can't just write off a car; you'll have to take it out of Egypt with you.

VEHICLE INSURANCE

All car-rental agreements must be sold along with third-party liability insurance, by law. Though accident and damage insurance should be included in the package, always make sure. In the case of an **accident**, get a written report from the police and from the doctor who first treats any injuries, without which your insurance may not cover the costs. Reports are written in Arabic.

Driving your own vehicle, you will need to take out **Egyptian insurance**. Policies are sold by the Al-Shark, Misr and National insurance companies; offices are found in most towns and at border crossings. Premiums vary according to the size, horsepower and value of the vehicle.

HITCHING

Hitching is largely confined to areas with minimal public transport (where anything that moves is considered fair game) or trunk routes (where hopefuls wait by the roadside for passing service taxis or scheduled buses). Since you'll probably end up paying anyway, there's no point in hitching unless you have to. Indeed, foreigners who hitch where proper transport is available may inspire contempt rather than sympathy. As few tourists have their own car in Egypt, you can't expect much help from that quarter, either. Women should never hitch without a male companion.

In the countryside and the desert, where buses may be sporadic or non-existent, it is standard practice for **lorries** (*camions*) and **pick-up trucks** (*bijous*) to carry and charge passengers. You may be asked to pay a little more than the locals, or have to bargain over a price, but it's straightforward enough. Getting rides from tractors is another possibility in rural areas.

Also noteworthy are **pilgrim convoys**, bound for the monasteries of Wadi Natrun, St Paul or St Anthony, or remoter sites to celebrate a festival such as the moulid of St Damyanah (p.531) or Sheikh al-Shazli (p.641).

FLIGHTS

Egyptian domestic air fares are average by international standards, but probably too expensive for most low-budget travellers. In general, it's only worth flying if your time is very limited, or for the

view – the Nile Valley and Sinai look amazing from the air.

EgyptAir, the national airline, enjoys a monopoly so it has no incentive to offer discounts. **Air Sinai** was specially created to serve the Sinai and Israel, in order to protect EgyptAir from the withdrawal of landing rights in other Arab countries, but is really just the same outfit under another name. Details of flights and the addresses of local offices appear in the text.

Fares are calculated in US$ but payable in Egyptian currency, backed by an exchange receipt. As a rough guide to prices, a one-way 2nd class ticket from Cairo to Luxor costs about US$70 (£44). In the winter season, you would be lucky to get any kind of flight between Cairo and Luxor, Aswan, Abu Simbel or St Catherine's Monastery, without booking at least a week ahead. Always reconfirm 72 hours prior to the journey, as overbooking is commonplace.

NILE CRUISES, FELUCCAS, FERRIES AND CATAMARANS

The colonial tradition of **Nile cruises**, familiar from films and novels, has spawned an industry deploying 240 steamers. Before the 1997 Luxor massacre, most cruise boats were booked months in advance by tour companies and it was difficult for individuals to make bookings in Egypt – but right now, it's much easier.

There are also some excellent cut-price offers available. Package deals cost as little as £350/US$560 for a week's cruise (see the "Getting There" sections for tour company details); while in Egypt you can arrange a four-day trip on the spot for around £115/US$180 (all prices are per person, in a twin cabin). Prices escalate dramatically with the luxury quotient. Most boats start off in Luxor, sailing down to Aswan, with stops at Esna, Edfu and Kom Ombo, over three to five days – longer cruises may also include Dendara or Philae, and begin or end in Cairo.

If you're looking for a cruise in Egypt, shop around and don't necessarily go for the cheapest deal – some boats leave a lot to be desired in terms of hygiene and living conditions. The luxurious boats with swimming pools can be wonderful, but you need to pick with care. If at all possible, try to look around the vessel first. The best deals are available from local agents (or directly from the boats) in Luxor and Aswan. The

Dive safaris are the boom tourist industry in Hurghada and Sinai (where they are called "Liveaboards"). Private charter boats take divers to remote reefs, on trips lasting from several days to two or three weeks. Most are pre-booked by groups, which may not welcome individuals joining them at the last moment, so it's better (and cheaper) to buy a package deal at home (see the "Gettiing There" sections for lists of operators). Read the Sinai and Red Sea Coast chapters for an idea of the dive sites on offer.

most reliable cruises are generally those sold in association with package holidays.

Feluccas, the lateen-sailed boats used on the Nile since antiquity, still serve as transport along many stretches of the river. Favoured by tourists for sunset cruises, they allow you to experience the changing moods and scenery of the Nile while lolling in blissful indolence.

Many visitors opt for longer **felucca cruises**, stopping at the temples between Luxor and Aswan – heading downriver from Aswan is the most popular route. While it's easy to arrange a cruise yourself (see p.392), several tour operators also offer packages.

Local **ferries** cross the Nile and the Suez Canal at various points (specified as relevant in the guide). They are generally cheap, battered and crowded. There are also smarter tourist ferries between Luxor and the West Bank, but it's more fun to use the ordinary boats.

Long-distance services are confined to the Red Sea and the Gulf of Aqaba, where the slow boats of yore have largely been superseded by a deluxe high-speed **catamaran** that zips over from Hurghada to Sharm el-Sheikh four days a week, in just ninety minutes. The US$33 (£22) fare isn't much more than is charged by the last of the old boats (which take over five hours), and is worth it to avoid the long overland journey via Suez, which requires the best part of a day. The catamaran also runs to the Jordanian port of Aqaba, and takes diving groups to various destinations.

HORSES, DONKEYS AND CAMELS

Around the Pyramids and the major Nile sites, donkeys, horses and camels are all available for rental. **Horses** are fun if you want to ride across stretches of sand between the Pyramids or gallop in the desert in Sinai. **Donkeys** are best used for visiting the Theban Necropolis, where they traverse mountains that you'd never cross on foot, and enliven the trip no end. Elsewhere they have less appeal, but you might rent a *caretta* (donkey-drawn taxi cart) to explore the pools and ruins in Siwa Oasis. The Arabic word for donkey is *humár* (plural *hameer*); a donkey-guide is called a *hámar*.

Camels (or, technically, dromedaries) make for pretty rigorous but exhilarating riding, and you'll probably want to try them at least once. They are good for short rides around Aswan, to the monastery of St Simeon, for example, but where they really come into their own is in Sinai or the Western Desert oases, where you can go trekking up wadis or across dunes that horses could never cope with. Trips – lasting anything from a half-day to a week – are easily enough arranged with local operators, or as part of "adventure holiday" packages before you set off.

Camel riding is a real art, which gets a little easier on the body with experience. The mounting is done for you but be sure to hold onto the pommel of the saddle as the camel raises itself in a triple-jerk manoeuvre. Once on, you have a choice of riding it like a horse or cocking a leg around the pommel, as the Bedouin do. Be sure to use a lot of padding around the pommel: what begins as a minor irritation can end up leaving your skin rubbed raw.

Beware also of being palmed off with a male (bull) camel that's in heat – they can be quite vicious. Bad signs are an inflated mouth sac, aggressive behaviour towards its mates, and lots of noise and slobbering. When enraged, camels can launch a fierce attack – they've been known to grip someone's neck and shake them like a rag doll, or crush the bones in a leg.

ACCOMMODATION

The main tourist centres offer a broad spectrum of accommodation, with everything from luxury palaces – familiar from movies such as *Death on the Nile* – to homely pensions and flea-ridden dives. Even in high season, in Cairo, Sinai or the Nile Valley, you should be able to find something in your preferred range. Elsewhere, the choice is generally more limited, with only basic lodgings available in most of the desert oases.

HOTELS

Egyptian hotels are loosely categorized into **star ratings**, ranging from five-star deluxe class down to one-star. Below this range, there are also unclassified hotels and pensions, some of them tailored to foreign backpackers, others mostly used by Egyptians.

Standards vary within any given category or price band – and from room to room in many places. The categorizations tend to have more meaning in the higher bands; once you're down to one or two stars, the differences are almost negligible.

Deluxe hotels are almost exclusively modern and chain-owned (*Sofitel, Mövenpick, Hilton,* etc), with swimming pools, bars, restaurants, air-conditioning and all the usual international facilities. **Four-star** hotels can be more characterful, including some famous (and reconditioned) names from the old tradition of Egyptian tourism: places like the *Old Cataract* in Aswan and the

Winter Palace in Luxor. Again, all hotels in this class are air-conditioned, with a pool, café and restaurant, etc. They merge into **three-star** hotels, among which there is again the odd gem, though most are 1970s-style towers, now becoming a little shabby. Facilities like plumbing and air-conditioning get a lot less reliable, too.

Down on the **two- and one-star** level, you rarely get air-conditioning, though better places will supply fans, and old-style buildings with balconies, high ceilings and louvred windows are well designed to cope with the heat. Conversely, these places can be distinctly chilly in winter, as they scarcely ever have any form of heating.

Some of the cheaper hotels are classified as **pensions**, which makes little difference in terms of facilities, but tends to signify family ownership and a friendlier ambience. Cairo, in particular, has some wonderful pensions.

At the cheap end of the scale, in the most popular tourist towns, like Luxor and Hurghada, you also get **"student hotels"**, specifically aimed at backpackers. They are often quite well run and equipped, if a bit cramped.

BOOKING AND CHARGES

Bookings for the **four- and five-star hotels** are best made through the central reservations office of the chain owning the hotel, or by fax. Simply turning up at a ritzy hotel, or even phoning ahead, you may find a reluctance to book you in, with staff perhaps claiming the hotel is full. Many rely on tour groups for their business and are not very interested in individual travellers. You may alternatively prefer to book as part of a package, through one of the many companies detailed in the "Getting There" sections. Package tourists get greatly **reduced rates**, while modest **discounts** may also be available to independent travellers who book from abroad – at *Sheraton* hotels, for instance (Britain: ☎0800/353 535; US & Canada: ☎1-800/334-8484).

At **mid-range hotels**, it is worth trying to book ahead if you want to stay in a particular place in **Cairo, Alex, Aswan or Luxor**. Elsewhere – and at all the **cheaper hotels** – most people just turn up. Phoning may itself prove unrewarding (see p.54).

ACCOMMODATION PRICE CODES

All the establishments listed in this book have been graded according to the categories listed below.

Prices given are for the **cheapest double room** in each establishment in high season (winter in Upper Egypt and Sinai, summer in Alexandria), including **tax**. Bear in mind, however, that Cairo is generally more expensive for accommodation of all types than most other places in Egypt; thus, a category ① place in Cairo may be pretty dire, while a room in Siwa Oasis at the same price may be quite comfortable. For places that offer **dorm beds**, rates per person are given in £E.

For the purposes of ready reckoning, we have taken the exchange rate as *roughly* US$1 = £E3; £1 = £E5. Please note that most hotels in categories ⑧ and ⑨ quote rates in US$, but will accept payment in £E.

① **under £E20/US$7**. This could be a fleapit in Cairo, a bed in a spartan resthouse in the Western Desert, or a room in a no-star hotel in Luxor or Hurghada. Electricity is certain, hot water less so.

② **£E20–30/US$7–10**. The rate for a basic room year-round in Cairo, or during peak times in Luxor, Aswan or Alexandria. No-star pensions and "student hotels" are generally a better deal than the bleak official youth hostels in most parts of Egypt, but as singles are rare, solo travellers may have to share with strangers or pay for a double room. Facilities are shared, with a good chance of hot water.

③ **£E30–45/US$10–15**. An average one-star hotel, containing a mixture of rooms with shared and private facilities, and in most cases comfortable enough for a shortish stay.

④ **£E45–65/US$15–20**. Mostly two-star hotels, with the odd three-star place: the facilities may amount to no more than in the previous category, or be considerably better, depending on the age and location of the hotel. Hotels in this category in Luxor and Hurghada will probably have a restaurant.

⑤ **£E65–100/US$20–35**. Largely three-star places, some rather aged, but there are many new ones in Hurghada, Luxor and Aswan. Rooms should have A/C, a phone, TV and fridge. There's certain to be a restaurant on the premises, and possibly a disco.

⑥ **£E100–150/US$35–50**. Posher three-star places, which in Luxor, Sinai or Hurghada could well have a pool.

⑦ **£E150–300/US$50–100**. The border line between three- and four-star hotels, where you can usually take a pool and A/C for granted, although the odd place with neither may charge such rates for half- or full-board accommodation.

⑧ **US$100–200/£E300–600**. At this level, prices are posted in US$, and you're talking somewhere pretty classy, like a top-flight chain-hotel or holiday village. There are scores along the Red Sea coasts, where the deal may include half-board.

⑨ **US$200/£E600 upwards**. The ritziest chain hotels and holiday villages, including such extravagances as the Agatha Christie suite of the *Old Cataract* in Aswan (US$500 a night).

Most hotels levy a **service charge** (12 percent) plus **local taxes** (2–15 percent) on top of their quoted rates. **Breakfast** is generally obligatory and may or may not be included in the room rate. It's not usually anything to get excited about. **Extra charges** most commonly turn up at mid-range hotels, which may add on a few pounds for a fan or air-conditioning, or a TV that doesn't work. (Even if it does, there's almost nothing worth watching on Egyptian channels.) Throughout this book we have indicated prices according to the system outlined in the box above.

HOTEL TOUTS

"Fishing" for guests (as Egyptians call it) is common practice in the main tourist centres, where new arrivals are approached by hotel touts at train and bus stations, airports and docks. Though some actually work in the hotel they're touting, most are simply hustling for commissions and quite prepared to use trickery to deliver clients to "their" establishment – swearing that other places are full, or closed, or whatever. In some cases, the hotel being touted may be agreeable, or even the best deal going; all too often, however, it's the grotty or overpriced places that depend on touts.

By studying the hotel listings and town plans in this book, you should be able to detect most scams. Advice for travellers flying into Cairo appears on p.73.

YOUTH HOSTELS

Egypt's **youth hostels** are cheap but their drawbacks are considerable. A daytime lock-out and night-time curfew are universal practice; so, too, is segregating the sexes and (usually) foreigners and Egyptians (which you might appreciate when riotous groups are in residence). The most salubrious hostels are in Cairo, Sharm el-Sheikh and Ismailiya. These, however, are far from where the action is, as are grungier places in Alexandria, Mersa Matrouh, Luxor, Assyut and Sohag. Only Aswan's hostel is smack in the centre.

It seems to be up to individual hostels whether you need an **Hostelling International (HI) card**, and their rulings change constantly. If admitted, non-HI members are usually charged £E1–3 extra per night, and may be granted automatic membership after six days. For more information, contact the Egyptian Youth Hostel Association in Cairo (see below for details). Addresses for all hostels appear in the text.

Also worth noting are a couple of **YMCA hostels**, which admit anyone. The one in Port Said is nothing special, but the YMCA in Assyut is positively luxurious and excellent value – not that any tourists are likely to visit Assyut.

RESTHOUSES

Chiefly found in the Western Desert oases, government **resthouses** offer basic triple-bed rooms and cold showers for about £1 per person. Guests may have to share with strangers unless they're willing to pay for beds to be kept unoccupied. Aside from tourists making the "Great Desert Circuit", resthouses are mostly used by truckers.

One of the resthouses in Dakhla Oasis offers hot springs and a pool. You can't rely on the outlying resthouses in Kharga Oasis, which are virtually derelict.

CAMPSITES

Egypt is not established camping territory. Such campsites as there are in the country tend to be **on the coast**, often shadeless and with few facilities, catering for holidaying Egyptian families. You'd have to be desperate to stay at these places.

Rather better are the occasional **campsites attached to hotels**, which may offer ready-pitched tents with camp beds, plus use of the hotel shower and toilet facilities. As for **camping wild**, you should always check with the authorities about any coastal site – some beaches are mined, others patrolled by the military. In the oases it's less of a problem, though any land near water will belong to someone: so again ask permission.

YOUTH HOSTEL ASSOCIATIONS

Australia Australian Youth Hostel Association, 422 Kent St, Sydney (☎02/9261 1111, *www.yha.au*). Annual membership A$47.

Canada Hostelling International/Canadian Hostelling Association, Suite 400, 205 Catherine St, Ottawa, ON K2P 1C3 (☎1-800/663-5777 or 613/237-7884, *www.hostellingintl.ca*). Annual membership CAN$25.

Egypt Egyptian Youth Hostel Association, 1 Sharia el-Ibrahimy, Cairo (☎02/354-0527). Annual membership £E24.

England and Wales Youth Hostel Association (YHA), Trevelyan House, 8 St Stephen's Hill, St Albans, Herts AL1 2DY (☎01727/845 047, *www.yha.org.uk*). London membership desk and booking office: 14 Southampton St, London WC2 7HY (☎020/7836 8541). Annual membership £11.

Ireland Youth Hostel Association of Northern Ireland, 22 Donegall Rd, Belfast BT12 5JN (☎028/9032 4733, *www.hini.org.uk*). Annual membership £8. An Oige, 61 Mountjoy St, Dublin 7 (☎01/830 4555, *www.irelandyha.org*). Annual membership IR£10.

New Zealand Youth Hostels Association of New Zealand, PO Box 436, Christchurch 1 (☎03/379 9970, *www.yha.org.nz*). Annual membership NZ$40.

Scotland Scottish Youth Hostel Association, 7 Glebe Crescent, Stirling FK8 2JA (☎01786/891 400, *www.syha.org.uk*). Annual membership £6.

US Hostelling International-American Youth Hostels (HI-AYH), 733 15th St NW, Suite 840, Washington, DC 20005 (☎202/783-6161, *www.hiayh.org*). Annual membership US$25.

EATING AND DRINKING

Egyptian food combines elements of Lebanese, Turkish, Syrian, Greek and French cuisines, modified to suit local conditions and tastes. Dishes tend to be simple and wholesome, made only with fresh ingredients, and therefore vary with the seasons. Nubian cooking, found in southern Egypt, is spicier than food in the north; in Alexandria, Mediterranean influences prevail. Cairo offers every kind of cuisine in the world.

Eating out falls into two camps. At a local level, there are cafés and diners, and loads of street stalls, which sell one or two simple dishes. More formally and expensively, restaurants cater to middle-class Egyptians and tourists. The latter have menus (most cafés don't) offering a broader range of dishes, and sometimes specializing in foreign cuisine. They will also invariably add a service charge and taxes to your bill, which usually increases the total by 17 percent. You are also expected to tip – conventions for which are byzantine. Basically, you tip in proportion to the size of the bill; below ten percent in expensive places, more where the sums involved are trifling. In juice bars and diners, customers simply put 10–25pt on a plate by the exit.

CAFÉS AND STREET FOOD

The staples of the Egyptian diet are bread ('*aish*, which also means "life"), *fuul* and *taamiya*. **Bread** is eaten with all meals and snacks and comes either as pitta-type '*aish shamsi* (sun-raised bread made from white flour) or '*aish baladi* (made from coarse wholewheat flour).

Native beans or **fuul** (pronounced "fool") can be prepared in several ways. Boiled and mashed

with tomatoes, onions and spices, they constitute *fuul madammes*, which are often served with a chopped boiled egg for breakfast. A similar mixture stuffed into '*aish baladi* constitutes the pitta-bread sandwiches sold on the street.

Deep-fried patties of green beans mixed with spices are called **taamiya** (or sometimes **felafel**, the name of their Israeli equivalent) and are again served in pitta bread, often with a snatch of salad, pickles and **tahina** (a sauce made from sesame paste, *tahini*).

A common appetizer is **torshi**, a mixture of pickled radishes, turnips, gherkins and carrots; luridly coloured, it is something of an acquired taste, as are pickled lemons, another favourite.

Another cheap café perennial is **makarona**, a clump of macaroni baked into a cake with minced lamb and tomato sauce inside. It's rather bland but very filling. Similarly common is **kushari**, which is a mixture of noodles, rice, macaroni, lentils and onions, in a spicy tomato sauce (another sauce, made of garlic, is optional). These are sold in tiled stand-up diners, also called *kushari*.

More elaborate, and pricier, are **fatir**, which can be either sweet or savoury. These are a cross between pizza and pancake, consisting of flaky filo pastry stuffed either with white cheese, peppers, mince, egg, onion and olives, or with raisins, jams, curds or just a dusting of icing sugar. They are served at café-like establishments known as *fatatri*.

Most **sandwiches** are small rolls with a minute portion of *basturma* (pastrami) or cheese. Other favourites include: grilled liver (*kibda*) with spicy green peppers and onions; tiny shrimps; and *mokh* (crumbed sheep's brains).

Lastly, there are **shawarma** – slices of marinated lamb, stuffed into pitta bread and garnished with salad and *tahina* – which are usually superior to the doner kebabs sold abroad, though foreigners often assume they are the same.

On the **hygiene** front, while cafés and tiled eateries with running water are generally safe, street grub is highly suspect unless it's peelable or hot.

RESTAURANT MEALS

The classic Egyptian restaurant or café meal is either a lamb **kebab** or **kofta** (spiced mince patties), accompanied or preceded by a couple of dips. The dips usually comprise **hummus** (made from chickpeas), *tahina* and **babaghanoush** (*tahina* with aubergine).

In a basic place, this is likely to be all that's on offer, save for a bit of salad (usually lettuce and tomato based), *fuul* and bread. However, you may also find other grilled meats. **Chicken** (*firakh*, pronounced "frakh" in Upper Egypt) is a standard, both in cafés and as take-away food from spit-roast stands. **Pigeon** (*hamam*) is common too, most often served with *freek* (spicy wheat) stuffing. There's not much meat on a pigeon, so it's best to order a couple each. In slightly fancier places, you may also encounter pigeon in a **tajine** or *ta'gell*, stewed with onions, tomatoes and rice in an earthenware pot.

More expensive restaurants feature these same dishes, plus a few that are more elaborate. Some may precede main courses with a larger selection of dips, plus olives, stuffed vine leaves and so on – a selection known, as in Greek, as **mezzes**. Soups, too, are occasionally featured, most famously **molukhiyya**, which is made from stewing Jew's mallow in chicken stock – a lot tastier than its disconcertingly slimy appearance suggests. Two common main dishes are **mahshi**, comprising stuffed vegetables (tomatoes, aubergines, etc), and **torly**, a mixed vegetable casserole with chunks of lamb, or occasionally beef (which in reality may be donkey, water buffalo or camel meat).

Fish (*samak*) is featured on restaurant menus in Alexandria, Aswan, the Red Sea Coast and Sinai. It is invariably grilled, served with salad and chips, and usually very tasty. There are many types, ranging from snapper to Nile perch; you're usually invited to pick your own fish from the ice box and it'll then be priced by weight. You may also find squid (*calamari*), shrimps (*gambari*) and octopus (*kaborya*).

One confusion you'll often run up against is the notion that **pasta**, **rice**, **chips** (French fries) and even **crisps** (potato chips) are interchangeable. Order rice and you'll get chips, and your querying of the matter will be regarded as inexplicable.

VEGETARIAN EATING

Most Egyptians eat vegetables most of the time – meat and fish are seen as luxuries. However, the concept of **vegetarianism** is totally incomprehensible to most people, and you'll be hard pushed to exclude meat stock from your diet. If you do get across the idea that you "don't eat

meat", you're as likely as not to be offered chicken or fish as a substitute.

CHEESE, CAKES, NUTS AND FRUIT

You can supplement regular cooked meals with a variety of fare available from corner shops, delicatessens, patisseries and street stalls.

There are two main types of Egyptian **cheese**: *gibna beyda* (white cheese), which tastes like Greek feta, and *gibna rumi* (Roman cheese), a hard, sharp yellow cheese. For breakfast you will often be given imported processed cheeses such as *La Vache qui Rit* ("The Laughing Cow" – a popular nickname for President Mubarak).

Nut shops (*ma'la*) are a high-street perennial, offering all kinds of peanuts (*fuul sudani*) and edible seeds. *Lib abyad* and *lib asmar* are varieties of pumpkin seeds, *lib battikh* come from watermelon, and chickpeas (*hummus*) are roasted and sugar-coated or dried and salted; all of these are sold by weight. Most nut shops also stock candies and mineral water.

Cakes are available at patisseries (some of which are attached to quite flash cafés) or from street stalls. The classics will be familiar to anyone who has travelled in Greece or Turkey: *baklava* (filo pastry soaked in honey and nuts) – called *basbousa* in Upper Egypt; *katif* (similar but with shredded wheat); and a variety of milk- or cornflour-based puddings, like *mahallabiyya* (sweet rice or cornflour, topped with pistachio nuts) and most famously *Umm Ali* (corn cake soaked in milk, sugar, coconut and cinnamon and served hot).

Fruits in Egypt are seasonal and wonderful. In winter there are oranges, bananas and pomegranates, followed by strawberries in March. In summer you get mangoes, melons, peaches, plums and grapes, plus a brief season (Aug–Sept) of prickly pears (cactus fruit). Fresh dates are harvested in late autumn. Only apples are imported, and thus expensive. All are readily available at street stalls, or can be drunk as juices at juice bars (see below).

DRINKS

As a predominantly Muslim country, Egypt gives alcohol a low profile. Drinks consist primarily of tea, coffee, fruit juices and familiar brands of soft drinks. Invitations to drink tea (*shurub shai?*) are as much a part of life in Egypt as they are in Britain, although the drink itself is served quite differently. Many Egyptian men accompany it with a *sheesha* (see below).

GLOSSARY OF EGYPTIAN FOOD AND DRINK

BASICS

'Aish	Bread	Firakh	Chicken	Shurba	Soup
Zibda	Butter	Zeit	Oil	Izzaza	Bottle
Beyd	Eggs	Zeitun	Olives	Kubbaya	Glass
Samak	Fish	Filfil	Pepper	Showka	Fork
Gibna	Cheese	Melh	Salt	Sikkeena	Knife
Gibna rumi	Yellow cheese	Sukkar	Sugar	Mala'a	Spoon
Gibna beyda	White cheese	Skhudaar	Vegetables	Tarabeyza	Table
Murabba	Jam	Salata	Salad	Garson	Waiter
'Asal	Honey	Fawakih	Fruit	Lista/menoo	Menu
Lahma	Meat	Zabadi	Yoghurt	Il-hisab	The bill

DRINKS

Shai	Tea	Saada	no sugar	'Asir	Fruit juice
Shai bi-na'ana	Tea with mint	Ahwa fransawi	Nescafe or	'Asir burtu'an	Orange juice
Shai bi-laban	Tea with milk		filter coffee	'Asir limoon	Lemon juice
Laban	Milk	Mayya	Water	'Asir manga	Mango juice
Ahwa	Turkish coffee	Mayya	Mineral water	Karkaday	Hibiscus juice
Ziyaada	very sweet	ma'adaniyya		Tamar hindi	Tamarind juice
Mazboot	medium	Beera	Beer	'Asab	Sugar cane
'Ariha	little sugar	Nibeet	Wine		juice

SOUPS, SALADS AND VEGETABLES

Shurba	Soup	Fasuliyya	Beans
Shurbit firakh	Chicken soup	Gazar	Carrots
Shurbit 'adas	Lentil soup	Bamya	Okra (ladies' fingers)
Shurbit khudaar	Vegetable soup	Bisilla	Peas
Salata	Salad	Batatis	Potatoes
Salatit khiyaar	Cucumber salad	Ruz	Rice
Salatit tamatim	Tomato salad	Torshi	Pickled vegetables
Salatit khadra	Mixed green salad	Baytingan	Aubergines
Basal	Onion		

MAIN DISHES

Kofta	Mincemeat flavoured with spices and onions, grilled on a skewer	Lahm dani	Lamb
		Kibda	Liver
Kebab	Chunks of meat, usually lamb, grilled with onions and tomatoes	Kalewi	Kidney
		Mukh	(Sheep) brains
Molukhiyya	Spinach-tasting dish made by stewing the leafy vegetable with meat or chicken broth and garlic	Dik rumi	Turkey
		Samak mashwi	Grilled fish served with salad, bread and dips
Firakh	Chicken grilled or stewed and served with vegetables	Gambari	Prawns
Hamam mashwi	Grilled pigeon	Calamari	Squid

APPETIZERS AND FAST FOOD

Fuul	Fava beans served with oil and lemon, sometimes also with onions, meat, eggs or tomato sauce	Kushari	Mixture of noodles, lentils and rice, topped with fried onions and a spicy tomato sauce
Taamiya	Balls of deep-fried mashed chickpeas and spices	Shakshouka	Chopped meat and tomato sauce, cooked with an egg on top
Shawarma	Slivers of pressed, spit-roasted lamb, served in pitta bread	Makarona	Macaroni "cake" baked in a white sauce or mincemeat gravy
Tahina	Sesame seed paste mixed with spices, garlic and lemon, eaten with pitta bread	Mahshi	Literally "stuffed", variety of vegetables (peppers, tomatoes, aubergines, courgettes) filled with mincemeat and/or rice, herbs and pine nuts
Hummus	Chickpea paste mixed with tahina, garlic and lemon, sometimes served with pine nuts and/or meat	Wara einab	Vine leaves filled as above and flavoured with lemon juice
Babaghanoush	Paste of mashed aubergines and tahina	Fatir	Sort of pancake/pizza made of layers of flaky filo pastry with sweet or savoury fillings

DESSERTS, SWEETS, FRUITS AND NUTS

Mahallabiyya	Sweet rice or cornflour pudding, topped with pistachios	Tuffah	Apples
		Mishmish	Apricots
		Mohz	Bananas
Balila	Milk dish with nuts, raisins and wheat	Balah	Dates
		Tin	Figs
Baklava	Flaky filo pastry, honey and nuts	Tin shawqi	Cactus fruit
Basbousa	Pastry of semolina, honey and nuts	Shammam	Melon
		Battikh	Watermelon
Umm (or Om) Ali	Corn cake soaked in milk, sugar, raisins, coconut and cinnamon, served hot	Farawla	Strawberries
		Fuul sudani	Peanuts
		Lib battikh	Watermelon seeds
Gelati, ays kriml	Ice cream	Loz	Almonds
'Ishta	Cream		

SOME PHRASES

Ayyzeen il-menu min fadlak	We'd like the menu please	. . . taza	. . . fresh
		. . . lahm	. . . meat
Sukkar aleel	With little sugar	. . . mistiwi kwaiyis	. . . cooked enough
Ihna ayyzeen . . .	We'd like to have . . .	. . . beyd	. . . eggs
Bidoon sukkar	Without sugar	Da laziz aawi	This is very tasty
Ey da?	What is this?	Iddini/iddina . . .	Give me/us . . .
Ma talabtish di	I didn't order this	Il-hisab, min	The bill, please
Ihna mush ayyzeen da	We don't want this	. . . taba'	. . . a plate
Da mish . .	This is not . . .	fadlak (m)/ fadlik (f). . . futa	. . . a napkin
Ana makulsh . . .	I can't/don't eat . . .	Shokran	Thank you

TEA, COFFEE AND KARKADAY

Egypt's national beverage, **tea** (shai), is generally made by boiling the leaves, and served black and sugared to taste – though posher cafés use tea-bags and may supply milk (ask for shai bi-laban). A glass of mint tea (shai bia na'ana) is refreshing when the weather is hot. You may also enjoy **herbal teas** like helba (a bright yellow infusion of fenugreek), yasoon (aniseed) or 'irfa (cinnamon).

Coffee (ahwa) is traditionally of the "Turkish" kind, served in tiny cups or glasses and pre-sugared as customers specify: saada (unsugared), 'ariha (slightly sweetened), mazboot (medium sweet) or ziyaada (syrupy). In some places you can also get it spiced with cardamom seeds (ahwa mahaweka). Most middle-class or tourist establishments also serve **European-style** coffee, made from Nescafé (or, worse, Misrcafé, an inferior local brand) rather than the real thing; with the option of having it with milk (ahwa bi-laban). Increasingly, however, five-star hotels and other upmarket places are investing in espresso machines.

Beverages are widely consumed in traditional **coffee houses** or **tearooms** (called ahwa), which are exclusively male territory. Foreign women won't be turned away but may feel uneasy, especially if unaccompanied by a man. For a more relaxed tea or coffee, try one of the middle-class places (in larger towns), which are often attached to patisseries, and where Egyptian women may also be found.

A third drink, characteristic of Egypt, is **karkaday** (or karkade), a deep-red infusion of hibiscus flowers. Most popular in Luxor and Aswan, it is equally refreshing drunk hot or cold. Elsewhere, alas, they tend to use dehydrated extract instead of real hibiscus, so it doesn't taste so good.

On cold winter evenings you might enjoy **sahleb**, a thick, creamy drink made from arrow-root, with cinnamon and nuts sprinkled on top. In hot weather Egyptians imbibe **rayeb** (soured milk), which is something of an acquired taste.

FRUIT JUICES AND SOFT DRINKS

Every main street has a couple of stand-up **juice bars**, recognizable by their displays of fruit. Normally, you order and pay at the cash desk before exchanging a plastic token for your drink at the counter.

Juices made from seasonal fruit include bur-tu'an (orange), mohz (banana; with milk mohz bi-laban), manga (mango), farawla (strawberry), gazar (carrot), asiir rumi (pomegranate), subia (coconut) and 'asab (the sickly-sweet, creamy light-green juice of crushed sugar cane). You can also order blends; nus w nus (literally "half and half") usually refers to carrot and orange juice, but other combinations can be specified.

Street vendors also ladle out iced asiir limoon (strong, sweet lemonade), bitter-sweet liquorice-water, and deliciously refreshing tamar hindi (tamarind).

Western-style **soft drinks**, including Coca-Cola, Fanta and 7-Up (called "Seven"), are available everywhere. Normally drunk on the spot, you'll have to pay a deposit on the bottle to take one away.

MINERAL WATER

Bottled **mineral water** (mayya ma'adaniyya) is widely available, particularly Baraka ("Blessing"; the company is owned by Nestlé); the brand Siwa (from the oasis of the same name) is less widely distributed. The former comes in 1.5-litre, one-litre and half-litre bottles. If tourists request water, it is assumed that they mean mineral water unless they specifically ask for **tap water** (mayya baladi), which is safe to drink in major towns and cities, but too chlorinated for the average visitor's palate; people with sensitive stomachs should definitely stick to bottled water. When buying mineral water, it is wise to check that the seal is intact; unsuspecting tourists may be palmed off with tap water – a favourite trick in the backpackers' resort of Dahab.

ALCOHOL

Alcohol can be obtained in most parts of Egypt, but the range of outlets is limited. In the Western Desert oases or Middle Egypt its sale is severely restricted or entirely prohibited. As a rule of thumb, hotels or Greek restaurants are the places

---

The **sheesha**, or waterpipe, is inseparable from Egyptian café society. It takes a special kind of tobacco mixed with molasses, which has a distinctive taste and aroma. Posh coffee houses may also stock apple-flavoured tobacco and provide disposable plastic mouthpieces for their clients' waterpipes. A sheesha is normally shared among friends, but you can decline to partake without causing offence. The term "hubbly bubbly" only refers to a waterpipe used for smoking hashish.

to try; if you can't see anyone drinking it, there's none to be had. When you do manage to locate a drink, keep in mind that the hot, dry climate makes for dehydration, and agonizing hangovers can easily result from overindulgence. Public drunkenness is totally unacceptable in Egypt. In deference to the non-drinking Muslim majority, the sale of alcohol is prohibited on the Prophet Mohammed's birthday and the first and last days of Ramadan (if not during the whole month).

Beer, whose consumption goes back to pharaonic times, is the most widely available form of alcohol. Native Stella beer is a light lager in half-litre bottles, which is okay if it hasn't sat in the sun for too long (some claim that the brown glass bottles are better than the green ones). To check that it hasn't gone flat, invert the bottle before opening and look for a fizzy head. Stella retails in most places for £E5–6, though discos may charge as much as £E10. Stella Export, with a blue rather than yellow label, is pricier (£E9–15) and comes in smaller bottles. Marzen, a dark bock beer, appears briefly in the spring; Aswali is a dark beer produced in Aswan. Imported beer, which is the most expensive (£E15–20), only appears in bars, flash hotels and restaurants. There is also Birrel, a non-alcoholic beer.

A half-dozen or so **Egyptian wines** are produced near Alexandria. Since an Englishwoman died after drinking a bottle spiked with methanol in 1996, many tourists won't touch them. Even discounting such fears, none is especially good, though they're drinkable with a meal. The most commonly found are Omar Khayyam (an awful dry red), Cru des Ptolémées (a poor dry white), and Rubis d'Egypte (an acceptable rosé). A new range of wines called Obélisque emerged in 1999, whose Rouge des Pharoahs is pretty good, though the rosé is less so and the white positively sickly. In most restaurants all these wines retail for about £E32 a bottle.

For serious drinking, Egyptians get stuck into spirits, mixed with beer. The favoured tipple is **brandy**, known by the slang name of *jaz* (literally, "bottle"), which comes under three labels: Ahmar (the cheapest), Maa'tak (the best) and Vin (the most common). **Zibib** is similar to Greek ouzo, but drunk neat. Avoid vile Egyptian-made **gin** and **whisky**, whose labels are designed to resemble famous Western brands. Imported spirits are sold at **duty-free shops** in the main resorts for modest sums (Johnny Walker Red Label US$12; Stolichnaya vodka US$7). Beware of Egyptians conning you into buying them duty-free liquor for resale on the **black market** (see p.234).

COMMUNICATIONS: POST, PHONES AND THE MEDIA

Post office hours are generally daily except Fri 8am–2pm (Ramadan 9am–3pm), though central offices may stay open until 8pm.

Almost invariably, offices are closed on Fridays. Airmail letters between Western Europe and Egypt generally take around a week to ten days, two to three weeks to North America or Australasia. Sending mail from Egypt, it speeds up the delivery if you get someone to write the name of the country in Arabic. As a rule, around fifteen percent of one's correspondence (in either direction) never arrives; letters containing photos or other items are especially prone to go astray.

It's best to send letters from a major city or hotel; blue **mailboxes** are for overseas airmail, red ones for domestic post. Airmail (*bariid gawwi*) **stamps** can be purchased at post offices, hotel shops and postcard stands, which may charge 5pt above the normal rate (80pt for a postcard/letter to anywhere in the world). **Registered mail**, costing 15–30pt extra, can be sent from any post office. Selected post offices in the main cities also offer an **Express Mail Service** (48hr to Europe or the US, which costs £E37–48 for letters under 100 grammes). **Private courier firms** such as Federal Express or DHL are limited to a few cities, and a lot more expensive.

To **send a parcel**, take it unsealed to a major post office for customs inspection, weighing and wrapping. The procedure – explained in detail in the Cairo section (p.240) – is much the same throughout Egypt.

POSTE RESTANTE

Receiving letters **poste restante** is a bit of a lottery, since post office workers don't always file letters under the initials you might expect. Ask for all your initials to be checked (including *M* for Mr, Ms, etc), and, if you're half expecting anything, suggest other letters as well. To have mail sent to you, it should be addressed (preferably with your surname underlined and/or highlighted) to *Poste Restante* at the central post office. To pick up mail, you'll need your passport.

A better option is to have mail sent to a major **hotel** (anything with three or more stars should be reliable) or **c/o American Express** (branches in Cairo, Alexandria, Luxor and Aswan; see p.24 for addresses). The latter service is officially only for Amex travellers' cheque- or cardholders. Note that **parcels** sent c/o American Express will be held at the post office (in the case of Cairo, at the branch on Sharia Mohammed Farid).

PHONES

All towns and cities have at least one 24-hour **telephone and telegraph office** (*maktab el-telephonat*, or *centraal*) for calling long-distance and abroad. Many of these feature orange direct-dial phones that take phonecards (£E15, £E20 or £E30), enabling you to avoid the old system of booking calls through the exchange. This involves giving the number to a clerk and paying for the call in advance, either for a set amount of time or £E30–40 for an open line, and settling the bill afterwards. Expect to queue and hang around a while. It's also possible to book (and prepay) a call that is routed through to your hotel or some other number. Alternatively, you can **make calls through a hotel** with a trunk or direct international line (most places with three or more stars

have them), which entails paying up to 100 percent above the normal rate. Always ascertain the rate first.

Regular **phone boxes** really only serve for local calls, which cost 10pt (though some kiosks only accept the old 5pt coins). You can also make local calls on semi-public phones owned by shopkeepers or hoteliers, who charge 25–50pt. **Phonecard booths** (Menatel or Nile Phone) are becoming increasingly common – shops which sell the cards usually display both companies' signs. Menatel (£E5, £E10, £E20 & £E40 cards) and Nile (£E5, £E10, £E15 & £E30 cards) both charge 25pt for a 3-minute local call and 20–60pt a minute for national, mobile and pager calls; international rates vary according to distance.

DIALLING

Overloaded exchanges and antiquated equipment make **local calls** a hit-and-miss affair, especially during peak hours. Even dialling slowly, you'll often get a wrong number. The **ringing tone** is similar to the one used in Britain; the **engaged tone** consists of two-second bursts of tone separated by one second's silence. A persistent whine or silence indicates that the number is unobtainable, or the local exchange is overloaded.

Long-distance calls within Egypt must be prefixed by a two- or three-digit area code number (listed under the appropriate chapters in this book) and are best made from a phonecard kiosk or arranged through your hotel or a telephone office.

International calls can be made using phonecards at Menatel and Nile kiosks or using the orange direct-dial phones at telephone and telegraph offices and other locations. Although using a phonecard may be easier, it remains slightly cheaper to go to a telephone office, where calls are booked and paid for in advance, and can either be taken in a booth or directed to an outside number such as a hotel. From Cairo, a three-minute call to the British Isles costs £E21 during peak hours (8am–8pm local time), to North America £E24 and to Australasia £E30; outside peak time all are around 25 percent less.

Direct dialling involves punching 00 for an international line, then the country code: Australia (61), US/Canada (1), Britain (44), Ireland (353), and finally the subscriber number, leaving out the initial digit of its local code. Select locations in Cairo also boast special phones for direct dialling to a specific country: **USADirect phones**

at American Express on Sharia Qasr el-Nil, and in the *Marriott, Ramses Hilton* and *SemiRamis* hotels; and **BT Direct phones** in the British Airways office on Midan Tahrir. These are the only phones in Egypt to allow **credit card and collect calls**, although Americans with an AT&T card can use it to call abroad from any major Egyptian city: dial ☎02/510-0200 and give the operator your international card number. The call will be billed to your (US) home address and charged as if it were made from the US.

CALLING EGYPT FROM ABROAD

Phoning Egypt from abroad, dial the international code (00 in Britain, Ireland and New Zealand; 011 in the US; 0011 in Australia); then 20 (for Egypt) followed by the **area code** minus the initial 0, and finally the **subscriber number**.

TELEGRAMS AND FAXES

Telegrams can be sent from any telephone office and are charged for per word (including the address).

Most hotels with three or more stars have **fax machines**, making this the best way to reserve a room from abroad. The procedure is the same as for phoning from abroad (see above); individual fax numbers appear in the text. Faxes can be sent from (and received at) certain telephone offices in the main cities; you can also have them sent to American Express offices, who'll hold them like client mail but won't notify the recipient. See p.241 for details of fax points in Cairo.

EGYPT ON THE INTERNET

There is currently an Internet boom in Egypt, both in terms of access and in the number of Egyptian Web sites. New servers are constantly being added to cope with demand, even as competing Web sites merge or disappear altogether – we've listed those that look most likely to survive. The biggest index of Egyptian sites is at *ce.eng.usf/pharos/home.html*. **Internet access** is available in almost all the main tourist destinations, with Internet cafés sprouting everywhere and hotels providing computers for guests to use. The charge for access is roughly £E10–15 an hour, although five-star hotels may charge up to £E60 an hour.

Egypt Tourism Net
www.tourism.egnet.net
Government-run tourism site with a database that includes hotels, embassies, airlines and car-rental agencies. Although mainly listing five-star establishments, it does include some budget places and could be useful if you're looking for accommodation outside of the main tourist centres.

The Official Ministry of Tourism Site
touregypt.net/
Pretty similar to Egypt Tourism Net, though snazzier and more high-tech with its virtual dive centre, discussion groups and "virtual Khan el-Khalili", which escorts you through Cairo's famous bazaar.

The Egyptian State Information Service Site
www.sis.gov.eg
As well as letting you down-load the Egyptian National Anthem, this site gives information on festivals and special events happening in Egypt. It also has a rundown on the history, culture, media and politics of the country – though it's hardly impartial.

Guardian's Egypt
guardians.net/egypt/gardcont.htm
Non-commercial site run by an American Egypt enthusiast, and a good one to visit for information on Ancient Egypt and the latest archeological finds. Masses of links, including to the Supreme Council of Antiquities and many of the museums that have Egyptian collections.

Essential Egyptology
www.newton.cam.uk/egypt
If you're serious about Egyptology, this site from the Newton Institute in Cambridge has helpful academic articles and links.

Egypt Sphinx Pyramids
www.nauticom.net/users.ata/egypt.html
This site takes you through the various theories of who built Egypt's most famous monuments – from Atlantis-dwellers to Martians.

The Egyptian Press
www.worldwidenews.com/egypt.htm
Links you up to all the Egyptian publications that have Web sites, with the advantage that you can read articles – including those critical of the Egyptian government – before the censors get to them.

Egypt Today
www.egypttoday.com
One of the best monthly English-language magazines, with news, arts and culture sections and an especially good listings page.

Human & Constitutional Rights in Egypt
www.hrcr.org/national/c_f/egypt.html

A Web page that shows you something of what life can at times be like for the ordinary Egyptian, including material that you won't find in the tourist brochures. Links to a wide range of sites about human rights abuses, women's issues and torture in Egypt.

THE MEDIA

As for other means of staying in touch, various British, US, French and German **newspapers** are available in Cairo, Alexandria, Luxor and Aswan, as are *Newsweek* and *Time* magazines. Elsewhere, however, you'll be lucky to find even the *Egyptian Gazette* (see below).

If you have a short-wave radio, you can pick up the **BBC World Service**, which is broadcast on 639KHz at 8.45am–noon, 3–5pm and 7–9pm; and on 1320KHz from 9pm to 3am (all local time). Reception is best in the north. The **Voice of America** broadcasts 24 hours on numerous frequencies on the AM (medium wave) or short wavebands. Both services carry news on the hour. In Cairo, FM95 broadcasts English-language news daily at 7.30am, 2.30pm and 8pm.

EGYPTIAN TV

Egypt has a plethora of terrestrial **television** channels, all state-controlled. Football or Koranic recitations account for the bulk of programming, so it's not worth paying extra for a TV set in your hotel room unless it receives cable or satellite TV – and even then, chances are that half the channels will be Turkish, Kuwaiti, or something equally dull.

Channels 1 and 2 both screen American films (generally after 10pm or during Ramadan between midnight and 4.30am) and **Nile TV**, in Cairo, also has news in English and French. In addition to these, some hotels receive **satellite channels** like *BBC World*, *CNN*, *Star Plus*, *Prime Sports*, *EuroNews* or *MTV*. Daily TV **schedules** appear in the *Egyptian Gazette*, whose Monday edition lists all the movies for the forthcoming week.

THE EGYPTIAN PRESS

The **Egyptian press** encompasses a range of daily papers and weekly magazines, chiefly published in English, French or Arabic.

The **English-language** *Egyptian Gazette* (on Saturday, the *Egyptian Mail*) carries agency reports, articles on Middle Eastern affairs, and tourist features. For more serious journalism, look out for the English edition of *Al-Ahram* (see below). There are also a couple of regional English-language journals: the informative weekly *Middle East Times* and the Saudi *Arab News*. The **French-language** counterparts of the *Egyptian Gazette/Egyptian Mail* are *Le Journal d'Egypte* and *Le Progrès Egyptien*; there is also a French edition of *Al-Ahram*, called *Hebdo*. All of them are fairly bland and heavily censored.

There's more diversity of opinion **in Arabic**. Egypt's oldest newspaper, *Al-Ahram* ("The Pyramids"), reflects official thinking, but less slavishly than *Mayo*, the organ of the ruling National Democratic Party. Other dailies with a party affiliation include *Al-Wafd* ("The Delegation"; conservative); *Al-Ahly* ("The Nation"; socialist); and *Al-Da'wa* ("The Call"; the journal of the Muslim Brotherhood). The left-wing *Al-Shaab* ("The People") is Egypt's most provocative paper; its editor and journalists are regularly jailed for exposing corruption.

PUBLIC HOLIDAYS AND MOULIDS

Egypt abounds in holidays and festivals of all kinds, both Muslim and Christian, national and local. Coming across a local moulid can be one of the most enjoyable experiences Egypt has to offer, with the chance to witness music, dancing and other entertainments.

Even if you're not interested in such festivals, it's important to be aware of **Ramadan**, when all Muslims (which means 90 percent of Egyptians) observe a total fast from sunrise to sunset for a month. This can pose big problems for travellers but the celebratory evenings are again good times to hear music and to share in hospitality.

ISLAMIC HOLIDAYS

Most Islamic holidays and festivals follow the Islamic calendar. This is lunar-based, so dates vary each year in relation to the Western calendar. You may find it useful to get hold of an annual prayer calendar from a local Islamic cultural centre in your own country.

The twelve **months** are *Moharrem* (30 days), *Safar* (29 days), *Rabi al-Awwal* (30 days), *Rabi el-Tani* (29 days), *Gumad al-Awwal* (30 days), *Gumad el-Tani* (29 days), *Ragab* (30 days), *Sha'ban* (29 days), *Ramadan* (30 days), *Shawwal* (29 days), *Zoul Qiddah* (30 days) and *Zoul Hagga* (29 days – or 30 days in leap years).

See overleaf for the estimated **starting dates of Moharrem** (which begins on *Ras el-Sana el-Hegira*) for the next three years. Note that a day in the Islamic calendar begins at sundown, as a consequence of which Islamic festivals start on the evening before you'd expect.

RAMADAN

Ramadan, in a sense, parallels the Christian Lent. The ninth month of the Islamic calendar, it commemorates the time in which the Koran was revealed to Mohammed. In contrast to the Christian West, though, the Muslim world observes the fast rigorously.

What **the fast** involves is abstention from food, drink and smoking during daylight hours, and abstinence from sex throughout the month. Strict Muslims will even refrain from swallowing, lest they "drink" their own saliva.

With all opening times and transport schedules going haywire, and most local cafés and restaurants closing during the day (or remaining open, but not selling food), Ramadan is in many respects a bad time to travel. (We have given the Ramadan opening times where available throughout the text.) It is certainly no time to try camel trekking in the Sinai – no guide would undertake the work – and it is probably safer to travel by bus during the mornings only, as drivers will be fasting, too. (Airline pilots are forbidden to observe the fast.)

But there is a compensation in witnessing and becoming absorbed in the pattern of the fast. At sunset, signalled by the sounding of a siren and the lighting of lamps on the minarets, an amazing calm and sense of well-being fall on the streets, as everyone eats *fuul* and *taamiya* and, in the cities at least, gets down to a night of celebration and entertainment. Throughout the evening, urban cafés – and main squares – provide venues for live music and singing, while in small towns and poorer quarters of big cities, you will often come across ritualized *zikrs* – trance-like chanting and swaying.

If you are a **non-Muslim** outsider you are not expected to observe Ramadan, but it is good to be sensitive about not breaking the fast (particularly smoking) in public. In fact, the best way to experience Ramadan – and to benefit from its naturally purifying rhythms – is to enter into it. You may not be able to last without an occasional glass of water, and you'll probably breakfast later than sunrise, but it is worth an attempt.

OTHER ISLAMIC HOLIDAYS

At the end of Ramadan comes the feast of **Eid al-Fitr**, a climax to the festivities in Cairo, though

RAMADAN AND ISLAMIC HOLIDAYS

Islamic religious holidays are calculated on the lunar calendar, so their dates rotate throughout the seasons (as does Ramadan's). Exact dates in the lunar calendar are impossible to predict – local Islamic centres can supply the current year's calendar only – but approximate dates for the next three years are:

	2000	2001	2002
Ramadan	Nov 27	Nov 16	Nov 5
Eid al-Fitr	Dec 27	Dec 16	Dec 5
Eid al-Adha	March 17	March 6	Feb 23
Ras el-Sana el-Hegira	April 6	March 26	March 15
Moulid al-Nabi	June 14	June 3	May 23

PUBLIC HOLIDAYS

January 1	New Year's Day	**October 6**	Armed Forces Day
April 25	Liberation Day	**October 23**	Suez Day
May 1	Labour Day	**December 23**	Victory Day
July 23	Revolution Day		

observed more privately in the villages. Equally important in the Muslim calendar is **Eid al-Adha** (aka *Corban Bairam* – the Great Feast), which celebrates the willingness of Ibrahim (Abraham) to obey God and sacrifice his son. The *Eid al-Adha* is followed, about three weeks later, by **Ras el-Sana el-Hegira**, the first day of the month of Moharrem, which marks the Muslim new year.

Both *eids* are traditional family gatherings. At the *Eid al-Adha* every household that can afford it will slaughter a sheep. You see them tethered everywhere, even on rooftops, for weeks prior to the event. The slaughtering is often done on the streets.

The fourth main religious holiday is the **Moulid al-Nabi**, the Prophet Mohammed's birthday. This is widely observed, with processions in many towns and cities.

MOULIDS

Moulids are the equivalent of medieval European saints' fairs: popular events combining piety, fun and commerce. Their ostensible aim is to obtain blessing (*baraka*) from the saint, but the social and cultural dimensions are equally important. Moulids are an opportunity for people to escape the monotony of their hard-working lives in several days of festivities, and for friends and families from different villages to meet. Farming problems are discussed, as well as family matters – and marriage – as people sing, dance, eat and pray together.

The largest events draw crowds of over a million, with companies of *mawladiya* (literally, "moulid people") running stalls and rides, and music blaring into the small hours. Smaller, rural moulids tend to be heavier on the practical devotion, with people bringing their children or livestock for blessing, or the sick to be cured.

DATES ...

With the exception of the *Moulid al-Nabi* (the Prophet's Birthday – see previous page), which is celebrated throughout Egypt, most moulids are localized affairs, usually centred around the mosque or tomb (*qubba*) of a holy man or woman. Most are scheduled according to the Islamic calendar, so dates vary from year to year when reckoned by the Western calendar.

To complicate matters further, certain moulids start (or finish) on a particular day (eg a Tuesday in a given month), rather than on any specific date. However, a minority of festivals occur at the same time every year, generally following the local harvest. If you're planning to attend a moulid, it's wise to verify the (approximate) dates given in this guide by asking local people or the tourist office.

... AND SPECTACLES

At the heart of every moulid is at least one **zikr** – a gathering of worshippers who chant and sway for hours, striving to attain a trance-like state of oneness with God.

Frequently, the *zikr* participants belong to one of the **Sufi brotherhoods**, which are differentiated by coloured banners, sashes or turbans, and named after their founding sheikh. The current incumbent of this office may lead them in a **zaffa** (parade) through town, and in olden times would ride a horse over his followers – a custom known as "the Treading", nowadays only practised in the Luxor region.

Luxor's own festival features a parade of boats; elsewhere, the procession may be led by camels or floats. Accompanying all this are **traditional entertainments**: mock stick fights, conjurers, acrobats and snake charmers; horses trained to dance to music; and, sometimes, belly dancers. Music and singing are a feature of every mould and locals often bring tape recorders to provide sounds for the rest of the year. If you are lucky enough to catch one of the major events, you'll get the chance to witness Egyptian popular culture at its richest.

The largest moulids are in Cairo, Tanta and Luxor. **Cairo** hosts three lengthy festivals in honour of El-Hussein, Saiyida Zeinab and the Imam al-Shafi'i (held during the months of *Rabi el-Tani*, *Ragab* and *Sha'ban*, respectively), plus numerous smaller festivals (see p.220). Following the cotton harvest in October, the Moulid of El-Bedawi in **Tanta** starts a cycle of lesser **Nile Delta festivals** that runs well into November (see p.524). Equally spectacular is the Moulid of Abu el-Haggag in **Luxor**, held during the month of *Sha'ban* (p.312).

Egypt's Christian Coptic minority often attend Islamic moulids – and vice versa. **Coptic moulids** share some of the social and market functions of their Islamic counterparts, and, similarly, at their core is the celebration of a saint's name-day. As you'd expect, the major Christian events of the year are also celebrated.

The dates of **Christmas** (January 6/7), **Epiphany** (January 19) and the **Annunciation** (March 21) are as specified in the Julian calendar used by the Orthodox Church, but **Easter** and its related feast days are reckoned according to the solar Coptic calendar, and therefore differ from both the Orthodox and Western dates by up to one month.

Major **saints' day events** include the Moulid of St Damyanah (May 15–20), the Feast of the Apostles Peter and Paul (July 12), and various moulids of the Virgin and St George during August. Many of these are held at monasteries in Middle Egypt, the Delta and the Red Sea Hills.

Lastly, a Coptic festival (of pharaonic origin) celebrated by all Egyptians is the **Sham el-Nessim**, a coming-of-spring festival which provides the excuse for mass picnics. Its name literally means "Sniffing the Breeze".

MONUMENTS AND SITES

The price of admission to Egypt's monuments skyrocketed in the 1990s, and entry costs now form a significant part of travel expenses. At major sites like the Theban Necropolis you could spend £20/US$30, taking into account such costly one-offs as Tutankhamun's tomb and the tomb of Nefertari – not to mention extra charges for the right to take photos inside tombs, or use a video camera. However, visitors qualify for 50 percent reductions on the price of admission tickets (but not photo permits) if they can present an ISIC student card or Go-25 card (see p.21).

GUIDES

Official **guides** can be engaged through branches of Misr Travel, American Express and Thomas Cook, local tourist offices and large hotels. You can also hire them on the spot at the Antiquities Museum in Cairo and the Pyramids of Giza. They normally charge a fixed hourly rate, which can be shared among a group of people, though obviously a group would be expected to make some additional tip.

Such professional guides can be useful at **major sites**, like the Valley of the Kings, where they will be able to ease your way through queues at the tombs. If you feel intimidated by the culture, too, you might welcome an intermediary for the first couple of days' sightseeing. In general, however, there's no special need to employ anyone: they tend to have enough work already with tour groups.

Far more common are **local, self-appointed guides**, who fall into two main categories. At ancient sites, there are always plenty of hangers-on, who will offer to show you "secret tombs" or "special reliefs", or just present themselves in tombs or temples, with palms outstretched. They don't have a lot to offer you, and encouragement makes life more difficult for everyone following. You can usually get rid of them by reading aloud from a guidebook.

The other kind – most often encountered in a small town or village – are people who genuinely want to help out foreigners, and maybe practise their English at the same time. They are often teenagers. Services offered could be escorting you from one taxi depot to another, or showing you the route to the souks or to a local site. The majority of people you meet this way don't expect money – children included – and you could risk offence by offering. If people want money from you for such activities, they won't be shy about asking.

An official version of this kind of guiding is offered by members of the **Tourist Friends Association**, who often approach lost-looking foreigners at bus and train stations, and will swiftly produce their identity cards. They are generally students, very friendly and helpful, and not on the make. Be courteous even if you don't want their help.

ANCIENT MONUMENTS

Egypt's **ancient sites and monuments** are maintained by the **Egyptian Antiquities Organization** (**EAO**). Most are kept open on a daily basis, with caretakers on hand to unlock tombs and point you towards the salient features. Local opening hours are detailed in individual entries; for a few hints on *baksheesh*, see p.21.

If you're a committed Egyptologist and want to visit sites that are under excavation or closed for repairs, you may want to contact the local branch of the EAO for a **special permit**. This is usually quite routine and you'll just be given a scrawled note in Arabic to show to the guards on site. A few sites – such as the Dahshur Pyramids – are in areas under military control, and require permission from the army; details are given in the text where appropriate.

MOSQUES AND MONASTERIES

Most of the **mosques** and their attached **madrassas** (Islamic colleges) that you'll want to visit are in Cairo, and, with the exception of the El-Hussein and Saiyida Zeinab mosques, are classified as "historic monuments". They are open routinely to non-Muslim visitors, although anyone not worshipping should avoid prayer times, especially the main service at noon on Friday. Elsewhere in the country, mosques are not used to seeing tourists and locals may object to your presence. Tread with care and if at all possible ask someone to take you in.

At all mosques, **dress** is important. Shorts (or short skirts) and exposed shoulders are out, and in some places women may be asked to cover their hair (a scarf might be provided). Above all, remember to remove your **shoes** upon entering the precinct. They will either be held by a shoe custodian (small *baksheesh* expected) or you can just leave them outside the door, or carry them in by hand (if you do this, place the soles together, as they are considered unclean).

Egyptian monasteries (which are Coptic, save for Greek Orthodox St Catherine's, in Sinai) admit visitors at all times except during the Lenten or other fasts (local fasts are detailed in the guide where appropriate). Similar rules of dress etiquette to those for mosques apply, though unless you go into the church itself you don't need to remove your shoes.

WORKING AND STUDYING IN EGYPT

Cairo offers work possibilities for teaching English as a foreign language, journalism or modelling, while the American University in Cairo (AUC) is a rewarding if expensive place to study Arabic, Middle Eastern affairs or Egyptology. To a lesser extent, opportunities to teach or study also exist in Alexandria. Elsewhere, you might find work as a tour rep or salesperson at one of the main resorts, as a diving instructor in Hurghada or Sinai, or a belly dancer in a hotel nightclub.

TEACHING ENGLISH

Teaching in Egypt largely means working in Cairo or Alexandria, where there are many private language schools, generally catering to adults. There's quite a big market for people wanting to learn both conversational and business English. Try contacting one of the following:

British Council, 192 Corniche el-Nil, Aguza, Cairo (☎02/344-8445); 9 Sharia Al-Batalassa, Alexandria (☎03/482-0199, *hala.Rizk@eg.britcoun.org*). An RSA TEFL certificate is required for jobs at the British Council, who recruit most of their staff in Britain (head office: 10 Spring Gardens, London SW1; ☎020/7930 8466). Vacancies do occur locally from time to time, however. Pays good rates.

International Language Institute (ILI), 2 Sharia Mohammed Bayoumi, Heliopolis, Cairo (☎02/418-9212, email: *ili@ritsec3.com.eg*). Affiliated to International House. ILI require an RSA TEFL certificate and a university degree. High turnover of staff, so a good chance of work. Rates are slightly lower than at the British Council.

JOURNALISM

Cairo has been the launch pad for several journalistic careers, for it is easy to place work with the local English-language media. **Egypt Today** takes travel articles and photos, while the **Egyptian Gazette** may need subeditors from time to time. International press agencies may also accept material and possibly employ stringers.

ACTING AND MODELLING

Westerners are often required as **extras** in Egyptian films, TV shows or advertisements. You aren't expected to be a professional model, nor are you paid like one: this is simply a day-to-day job for any face that fits, for about £E40–50 a day. You can make contact with agents at the *New Sun Café* in Cairo (see p.208). Women should keep their wits about them – and preferably a male escort.

DIVING INSTRUCTORS

Divers with Divemaster or Instructor certificates can often find work with **diving centres** in Hurghada or Sinai, which may also take on less qualified staff and let them learn on the job, at reduced rates of pay or in return for free tuition. Dive centres commonly turn a blind eye to the lack of a work permit, or might procure one for a valued worker. As with language schools, you should be wary about surrendering your passport, and ask other foreigners working in the same job about the potential drawbacks.

BELLYDANCING

Foreign bellydancers are much in demand in nightclubs in Cairo, Alexandria, Luxor and Hurghada. The work can be well paid, but you have to be careful: financial or sexual exploitation are real hazards. Aside from work, many foreign dancers come to Egypt to improve their art, or buy costumes. Finding a teacher is surprisingly difficult, as there are no schools as such; instruction takes place in people's homes and the addresses are hard to obtain. If you're interested, start mak-

ing enquiries at the specialist shops in Cairo's Khan el-Khalili bazaar, where you can buy costumes, music tapes and videos of top performers (see p.230).

TOURISM

Though most jobs in the tourism field are restricted to Egyptian nationals, and locally based companies usually insist on a work permit, you can sometimes fix up a season's work with a foreign tour operator abroad as a rep or tour guide. See the lists on p.6 and p.11 for companies to approach.

In Sinai, Hurghada and Luxor there may be a demand for people with foreign languages to sell dive courses or work on hotel reception desks. The most useful languages to have are German, French, Italian, Japanese or Russian (the last only in Hurghada). Ask around dive centres or upmarket hotels if you're interested.

STUDYING

The **American University in Cairo** (113 Sharia Qasr al-Aini, near Midan Tahrir; ☎02/355-2965, *www2.aucegypt.ed*) offers year-abroad and non-degree programmes, a summer school and intensive Arabic courses. A full year's tuition costs roughly US$12,000. US citizens may apply to the Stafford Loan Program; contact the Office of Admissions, 420 Fifth Ave, 3rd Floor, New York, NY 10018-2729 (☎212/730-8800, *www.aucegypt.edu*). For one-month courses, it is less expensive to **study Arabic** at the **British Council** (£E400) or **ILI** (£E350); see "Teaching English", above, for addresses.

Foreign students may also attend one- or two-term programmes at three **Egyptian universities**: Cairo, Ain Shams and Al-Azhar. These are valid for transferable credits at most American and some British universities. In the US, contact the **Egyptian Cultural and Educational Bureau**, 1303 New Hampshire Ave NW, Washington, DC 20036 (☎202/296-3888), or **AmidEast**, 1730 M St NW Suite 1100, Washington, DC 20036 (☎202/776-9600).

DIRECTORY

ABU AND UMM Literally "father of" and "mother of", Abu and Umm are used both as honorific titles and also figuratively as a nickname, picking out the salient characteristic or a person or object. They can also be used metaphorically, as in "The Mother of Battles".

ADDRESSES The words for street (*sharia*), avenue (*tariq*) and square (*midan*) always precede the name. Whole blocks often share a single street number, which may be in Arabic numerals (see also p.685).

CHILDREN evoke a warm response, which makes travelling with them easier than one might expect. Most hotels can supply an extra bed and breakfast (which should be supplemented for variety), while baby food and disposable nappies are available at pharmacies and stores in all large towns. Children of any age should enjoy camel and felucca rides, snorkelling and (a few of) the great monuments. All the main resorts have discos and sports facilities. From an adult minder's standpoint, most hazards can be minimized or avoided by taking due precautions. Children (especially young ones) are more susceptible than adults to heatstroke, dehydration and tummy upsets. Traffic is obviously dangerous, and stray animals (possible disease carriers), fenced-off beaches (probably mined – see below) and poisonous fish and coral in the Red Sea (see Chapter Seven) are also potential hazards.

CIGARETTES Almost the entire adult male population of Egypt smokes, and offering cigarettes around is common practice. The most popular brand is Cleopatra (£E1.50; £E1.60 in a crush-proof pack). Locally produced versions of Marlboro, Rothmans and Camel have a much higher tar content than their equivalents at home; the genuine article can be found in duty-free shops. Matches are *kibreet*; a cigarette lighter is a *wallah*.

DRUGS Unlike under President Sadat (who smoked dope himself), Egypt now has draconian anti-drugs laws that make **hanging or life imprisonment** mandatory for convicted smugglers and dealers (which could be interpreted to mean somebody caught with a few sachets of the stuff). Mere possession or use merits a severe prison sentence and a heavy fine (plus legal costs, upwards of US$1000). Despite this, *bango* (marijuana) is still consumed by Egyptians who can afford it, and by tourists in Dahab, Luxor, Aswan, Hurghada and Cairo. Providing it's done *discreetly*, the police usually turn a blind eye where tourists are concerned.

ELECTRICITY The current in Egypt is 220V, 50Hz. North American travellers with appliances designed for 110V should bring a converter. Most sockets are for round-pronged plugs, so you'll also need an adapter. Brief power cuts are quite common in Egypt.

FOOTBALL (*futbol*) is Egypt's national sport. The two Cairo-based rivals, Ahly and Zamalek, are the major teams and contributed most of the country's 1998 squad which won the Cup of Nations as well as the Arabic Super-Cup. Clashes between the two teams can be intense – and occasionally have led to rioting – but games are in general relaxed. Should their team win, thousands of jubilant supporters drive around Cairo honking horns and waving flags attached to lances – beware of being run over or impaled. Two other teams currently on the rise are Ismaily and Masry, while Santa Katerina is a team composed entirely of Sinai Bedouin who train by running up Mount Sinai twice a day. You can find detailed information about all aspects of Egyptian football at *www.angelfire.com/ak/EgyptianSports/*

GAY ATTITUDES Male homosexuality is common in Egypt, but attitudes towards it are schizophrenic. No Egyptian will declare himself gay –

USEFUL THINGS TO BRING

● **Alarm clock**. Vital for early-morning buses.

● **Clothes**. Keep both practicality and sensitivity in mind. As emphasized in "From a Woman's Perspective", Egypt is a deeply conservative nation; the more modest your dress the less hassle you will attract.

On the practicalities front, bear in mind that northern Egypt can be cold and damp in the winter, while the desert gets freezing at night, even in the spring and autumn. A warm sweater is invaluable. So, too, are a solid pair of shoes: burst pipes are commonplace, and wandering around muddy streets in sodden sandals is a miserable experience.

● **Cool bottle**. Keeps juice or water at a refreshing temperature on those long desert journeys.

● **Earplugs**. Help muffle the noise of videos on long-distance buses and trains, if you're trying to sleep.

● **Film**. Kodak and Fuji film is available in most towns and major resorts, but it may well be pretty old stock. It's best to bring adequate supplies.

For photography in dark alleyways, tombs and hidden corners, fast film (400–800 ASA) is useful. If you're looking for good landscape photographs, slow film (and/or getting out of bed early) is a must. See notes on behaviour on p.33.

● **Plug**. If you like your water to fill a basin, it is worth remembering to pack an omnisize plug: few hotels (even relatively upmarket ones) supply such equipment.

● **Sleeping bag**. A decent bag is invaluable if you're planning to sleep out in the desert in spring or autumn, or in any low-budget hotel over winter. In the summer, a sheet sleeping bag is handy if you're staying at cheaper hotels.

● **Snaps** of your family, home town, football team (or whatever) help bridge the language barrier. Locals will proudly show you their own.

● **Torch**. For exploring dark tombs, and use during power cuts.

● **Water-boiler**. Plug-in models, sold in Egypt, are good for making your own hot drinks.

---

which has connotations of femininity and weakness – and the dominant partner may well not consider himself to be indulging in a homosexual act. Rather, it is tacitly accepted as an outlet for urges that can't otherwise be satisfied: few men can afford marriage until their thirties, and boys have no other way of gaining sexual experience. Despite this, people are mindful that homosexuality is condemned in the Koran and the Bible, and reject the idea of Egypt as a "gay destination" (although male prostitution is an open secret in Luxor and Aswan).

In practice, this means that men travelling alone are liable to be propositioned (whatever their sexual orientation), but actively seeking partners can cause offence and lead to trouble. Egyptian law prohibits any "shameless or unnatural act" with a person of the same sex, and reserves even harsher penalties for cases involving the corruption of minors – while local citizens may take the law into their own hands in such cases. So far as propositions go, the crucial phrase to remember is "*Anna (mish) elk*" – "I'm (not) gay".

As emphasized under "Health", AIDS is a real threat in Egypt, despite the minuscule number of reported cases. There is some awareness of AIDS amongst Egyptians but most are steadfast in seeing it as a "disease for foreigners" and the concept, let alone the practice, of "safe sex" has yet to emerge.

There is no public perception of lesbianism.

LAUNDRY In Egypt no one goes to the laundry: if they don't do their own, they send it out to a *mahwagi*. Wherever you are staying, there will either be an in-house *mahwagi*, or one close by to call on. Some low-budget hotels in Luxor, Aswan and Hurghada allow guests to use their washing machine for a small charge, or gratis. You can buy washing powder at most pharmacies. Dry cleaners are confined to Cairo, Aswan and Hurghada.

MINEFIELDS still exist from World War II along the Mediterranean coast, and from Israeli conflicts in the interior of Sinai and along the Red Sea Coast. Do not take any risks in venturing into fenced-off territory, unless local people go there often.

SPELLINGS Arabic is notoriously hard to transliterate into Roman script. The existence of several systems, and the popular familiarity of certain spellings, make consistency a nightmare. Egyptians themselves employ English spelling loosely; basically, you get accustomed to different variations on the same Arabic name.

TIME is two hours ahead of GMT and seven hours ahead of EST, and a more elastic concept than Westerners are used to. In practice, "five minutes" often means an hour or more; *bahdeen* ("later") the next day; and *bukkra* ("tomorrow") an indefinite wait for something that may never happen. Besides hinting that it won't, *inshallah* ("God willing") can be a polite way of backing away from unwanted commitments – a game which foreigners can also play. Remember, too, that Western abruptness strikes Egyptians as rude; never begrudge the time it takes to say *Salaam aleikum*, or return a greeting.

TOILETS Public ones are almost always filthy, and there's never any toilet paper (though someone may sell it outside). They're usually known as *Toileta*, and marked with WC and Men and Women signs. Expect squat toilets in bus stations, resthouses and fleapit hotels; on sit-down toilets, beware of pranging yourself on the nozzle of the curly waterpipe, intended to assist the ablutions of devout Muslims, to whom toilet paper is anathema. Though it's wise to carry toilet paper (£E1.50 per double roll in pharmacies) at all times, paper tissues, sold on the streets (50pt), will serve at a pinch.

METRIC WEIGHTS AND MEASURES

1 ounce = 28.3 grammes	1 inch = 2.54 centimetres (cm)
1 pound = 454 grammes	1 foot = 0.3 metres (m)
2.2 pounds = 1 kilogramme (kg)	1 yard = 0.91m
1 pint = 0.47 litres	1.09 yards = 1m
1 quart = 0.94 litres	1 mile = 1.61 kilometres (km)
1 gallon = 3.87 litres	0.62 miles = 1km

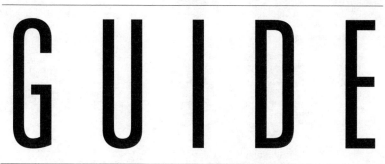

PART TWO

THE

GUIDE

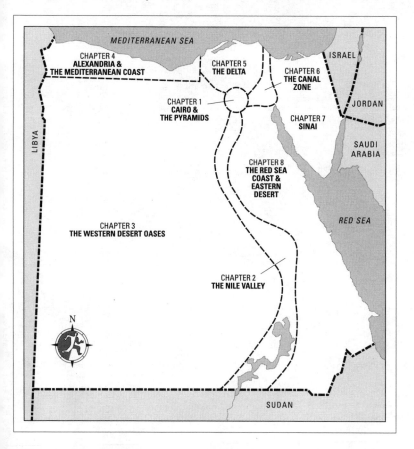

MEDITERRANEAN SEA

ISRAEL

CHAPTER 4
**ALEXANDRIA &
THE MEDITERRANEAN COAST**

CHAPTER 5
THE DELTA

CHAPTER 6
**THE CANAL
ZONE**

CHAPTER 1
**CAIRO &
THE PYRAMIDS**

JORDAN

CHAPTER 7
SINAI

SAUDI
ARABIA

CHAPTER 8
**THE RED SEA
COAST &
EASTERN
DESERT**

LIBYA

RED SEA

CHAPTER 3
THE WESTERN DESERT OASES

CHAPTER 2
THE NILE VALLEY

N

SUDAN

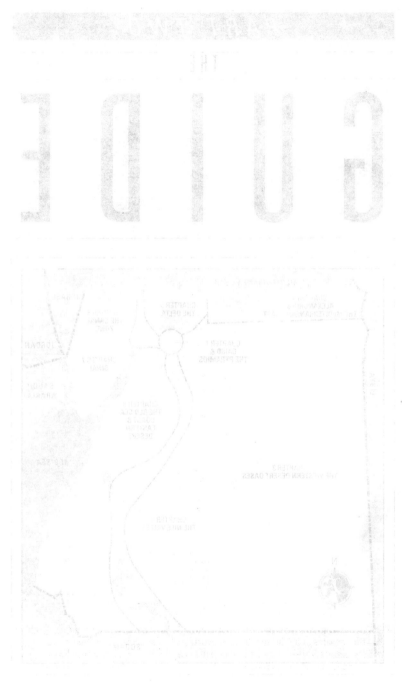

CHAPTER ONE

CAIRO AND THE PYRAMIDS

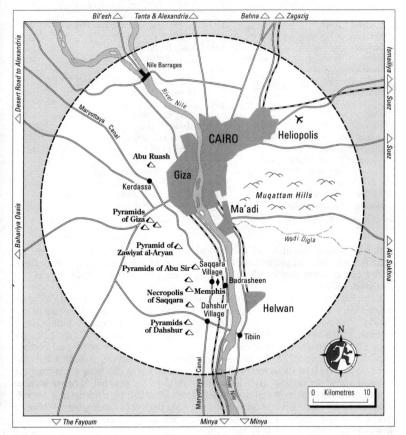

The twin streams of Egypt's history converge just below the Delta at **Cairo**, where the greatest city in the Islamic world sprawls across the Nile towards the **Pyramids**, those supreme monuments of antiquity. Every visitor to Egypt comes here, to reel at the Pyramids' baleful mass and the seething immensity of Cairo, with its bazaars, mosques and Citadel and extraordinary Antiquities Museum. It's equally impossible not to find yourself carried away by the streetlife, where medieval trades and customs coexist with a modern, cosmopolitan mix of Arab, African and European influences.

Cairo has been the largest city in Africa and the Middle East ever since the Mongols wasted Imperial Baghdad in 1258. Acknowledged as *Umm Dunya* or "**Mother of the World**" by medieval Arabs, and as Great Cairo by nineteenth-century Europeans, it remains, in Jan Morris's words, "one of the half-dozen supercapitals – capitals that are bigger than themselves or their countries . . . the focus of a whole culture, an ideology or a historical moment". As Egypt has been a prize for conquerors from Alexander the Great to Rommel, so Cairo has been a fulcrum of power in the Arab world from the Crusades unto the present day. The *ulema* of its thousand-year-old Al-Azhar Mosque (for centuries the foremost centre of Islamic intellectual life) remains the ultimate religious authority for millions of Sunni Muslims, from Jakarta to Birmingham. Wherever Arabic is spoken, Cairo's cultural magnetism is felt. Every strand of Egyptian society knits and unravels in this febrile megalopolis.

Egyptians have two names for the city, one ancient and popular, the other Islamic and official. The foremost is **Masr**, meaning both the capital and the land of Egypt – an ur-city that endlessly renews itself and dominates the nation, an idea rooted in pharaonic civilization. (For Egyptians abroad, "Masr" refers to their homeland; within its borders it means the capital.) Whereas *Masr* is timeless, the city's other name, **Al-Qahira** (The Conqueror), is linked to an event: the Fatimid conquest that made this the capital of an Islamic empire stretching from the Atlantic to the Hindu Kush. The name is rarely used in everyday speech.

Both archetypes still resonate and in monumental terms are symbolized by two dramatic **landmarks**: the **Pyramids of Giza** at the edge of the Western Desert and the great **Mosque of Mohammed Ali** – the modernizer of Islamic Egypt – which broods atop the Citadel. Between these two monuments sprawls a vast city, the colour of sand and ashes, of diverse worlds and time zones, and gross inequities. All is subsumed into an organism that somehow thrives in the terminal ward: medieval slums and Art Deco suburbs, garbage-pickers and marbled malls, donkey carts and limos, piousness and "the oaths of men exaggerating in the name of God". Cairo lives by its own contradictions.

This is a city, as Morris put it, "almost overwhelmed by its own fertility". Its **population** is today estimated at around eighteen million and is swollen by a further million commuters from the Delta and a thousand new migrants every day. Today, one third of Cairene households lack running water; a quarter of them have no sewers, either. Up to three million people reside in squatted cemeteries – the famous **Cities of the Dead**. The amount of green space per citizen has been calculated at thirteen square centimetres, not enough to cover a child's palm. Whereas earlier travellers noted that Cairo's air smelt "like hot bricks", visitors now find throat-rasping air **pollution**, chiefly caused

A BRIEF HISTORICAL OUTLINE

Cairo reveals its history in a succession of sights and quarters and it's in the descriptions of these areas that we've provided the relevant background. What follows is the briefest of outlines, with page references for the main accounts.

Cairo is an agglomeration of half a dozen cities, the earliest of which came into existence 2500 years *after* ancient **Memphis**, the first capital of pharaonic Egypt, was founded (c.3100 BC) across the river and to the south. During the heyday of the Old Kingdom, vast necropolises developed along the desert's edge as the pharaohs erected ever greater funerary monuments, from the first Step Pyramid at **Saqqara** to the unsurpassable **Pyramids of Giza** (for more on this part of the history, see p.181). Meanwhile, across the Nile, there flourished a sister-city of priests and solar cults known to posterity as **Ancient Heliopolis** (see p.179).

It took centuries of Persian, Greek and Roman rule to efface both cities, by which time a new fortified town had developed on the opposite bank. **Babylon-in-Egypt** was the beginning of the tale of cities that culminates in modern Cairo, the first chapter of which is described under "Old Cairo" (see p.149). Oppressed by foreign overlords, Babylon's citizens almost welcomed the army of Islam that conquered Egypt in 641. For strategic and spiritual reasons, their general, Amr, chose to found a new settlement beyond the walls of Babylon – **Fustat**, the "City of the Tent" (see "Old Cairo", p.161), which evolved into a sophisticated metropolis while Europe was in the Dark Ages.

Under successive dynasties of *khalifs* who ruled the Islamic Empire from Iraq, three more cities were founded, each to the northeast of the previous one, which itself was either spurned or devastated. When the schismatic Fatimids won the khalifate in 969, they created an entirely new walled city – **Al-Qahira** – beyond this teeming, half-derelict conurbation. **Fatimid Cairo** formed the nucleus of the later, vastly expanded and consolidated capital that Salah al-Din (Saladin) left to the Ayyubid dynasty in 1193. But their reliance on imported slave-warriors caused power to ebb to these Mamlukes, ushering in a new era.

Mamluke Cairo encompassed all the previous cities, Salah al-Din's Citadel (where the sultans dwelt), the northern port of Bulaq and vast cemeteries and rubbish tips beyond the city walls. Mamluke sultans like Beybars, Qalaoun, Barquq and Qaitbey erected mosques, mausoleums and caravanserais that still ennoble what is now called "Islamic Cairo". The like-named section of this chapter relates their stories, the Turkish takeover, the decline of **Ottoman Cairo** and the rise of Mohammed Ali, who began the modernization of the city. Under Ismail, the most profligate of his successors, a new, increasingly **European Cairo** arose beside the Nile (see "Central Cairo", p.91). By 1920, the city's area was six times greater than that of medieval Cairo, and since then its residential suburbs have expanded relentlessly, swallowing up farmland and desert. The emergence of this **Greater Cairo** is charted under "Gezira and the West Bank" and "The northern suburbs".

by traffic. Cairo out-pollutes LA every day of the week: breathing the atmosphere downtown is reputedly akin to smoking thirty cigarettes a day.

Cairo's genius is to humanize these inescapable realities with **social rituals**. The rarity of public violence owes less to the armed police on every corner than to the *dowshah*. When conflicts arise crowds gather, restrain both parties, encourage them to rant, sympathize with their grievances and then finally urge: *"Maalesh, maalesh"* (Let it be forgiven). Everyday life is sweetened by flowery gestures and salutations; misfortunes evoke thanks for Allah's dispensation (after all, things could be worse!). Even the poorest can be respected for piety; in the mosque, millionaire and beggar kneel side by side.

Extended-family values and neighbourly intervention prevail throughout the *baladi* quarters or **urban villages** where millions of first- and second-generation rural migrants live, whilst arcane structures underpin life in Islamic Cairo. On a city-wide basis, the colonial distinction between "native quarters" and *ifrangi* (foreign) districts has given way to a dynamic stasis between rich and poor, westernization and traditionalism, complacency and desperation. The city's tolerance has recently been further strained by natural and man-made calamities. In October 1992, up to a thousand people died in an **earthquake**, when shoddily built high-rises and hovels collapsed across the city. Its image took a worse battering abroad after the shooting of seventeen Greek tourists in 1996 and the firebombing of a German tour bus a year later – although the tourists now seem to be making a cautious return. Every year its polarities intensify, safety margins narrow and statistics make gloomier reading. The abyss beckons in prognoses of **future trends**, yet Cairo confounds doom sayers by dancing on the edge.

Arrival, orientation and information

Setting foot in a big city can be a daunting experience, but you needn't worry about Cairo. Being overcharged by a taxi driver and spending your first night in a second-rate hotel is the worst that can happen to newcomers. Hustlers might try to lure you into overpriced perfume shops, but elaborate swindles are rare and robbery with violence is unheard of.

Cairo International Airport has two main terminals, roughly 3km apart. **Terminal 1** (known as the old airport) is used by Egyptian carriers, El Al and most Arab, African and Eastern European airlines. Western European and US airlines use **Terminal 2** (aka the new airport). For airport information call ☎291-4255. You'll find 24-hour currency exchange as well as ATMs that accept Visa, Plus, Cirrus and MasterCard at both terminals.

If you're flying in from abroad, be sure to fill out the **customs declaration** on arrival (see p.20). Emerging from customs, you'll be waylaid by taxi drivers who'll swear that they're the only way of **getting into town**. Usually, this isn't so, but you might prefer going by **taxi** anyway. Egyptians pay £E10–15, but as a newly arrived foreigner, you'd do well to bargain the fare down to £E25; many drivers start by quoting £E50. Another ploy of the taxi drivers is to swear blind the hotel you want to go to is closed, full or a terrible place. They then take you to another hotel where they pick up a hefty commission, which will be quietly added to the cost of your room.

On one side of Terminal 1's forecourt is the parking area for **buses** (25pt) and **minibuses** (50pt) into the centre. Bus #400 leaves roughly every half-hour by day, hourly late at night or early in the morning, terminating by Midan Tahrir in downtown Cairo, as does minibus #27 (which runs until midnight). There is another 24-hour service – bus #948 – to Midan Ataba, on the northern edge of downtown. Terminal 2 is linked to the centre by two 24-hour buses: #949 to Tahrir and #948 to Ataba. The airport terminals are connected by a free EgyptAir **shuttle bus**, running all through the night. Besides the above options, there's a **limousine taxi service** next to Terminal 1's Masr Travel stand; prices are fixed and posted, though higher than regular taxi rates.

Buses from Israel, Jordan and Sinai usually wind up at the **Sinai Bus Terminal** (aka Abbassiya Station), 4km from the centre. Taxis outside grossly overcharge newcomers and try to inveigle them into hotels: resist them – Cairenes would feel generous if they paid £E5 for a black-and-white cab, or £E1.50 per person for a full seven-seater "special" taxi into the centre from here. Alternatively, cross the street (Sharia Ramses) outside the station and from the bus stop 20m to your right you can catch minibuses or buses to Midan Ramses and Midan Tahrir (see p.81 for bus numbers); or turn left outside the station and walk 300m on past the flyover to the hospital, where you have an even wider choice of buses and minibuses to Ramses, Tahrir and Ataba. The tickets on nearly all of the buses and minibuses plying these routes cost 25–50pt.

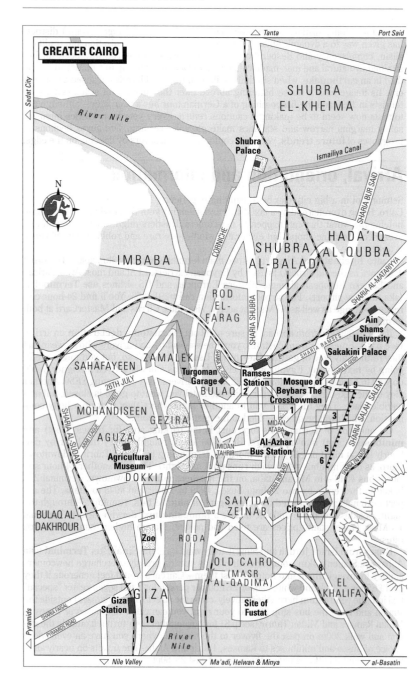

GREATER CAIRO

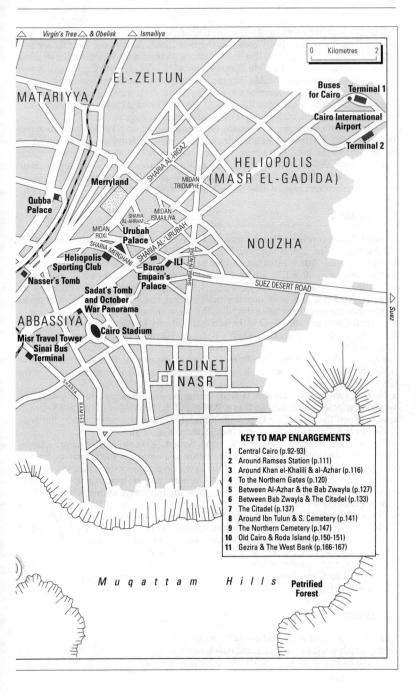

△ Virgin's Tree △ & Obelisk   △ Ismailiya

0   Kilometres   2

EL-ZEITUN

MATARIYYA

Buses
for Cairo   Terminal 1

Cairo International
Airport

Terminal 2

HELIOPOLIS
(MASŔ EL-GADIDA)

Merryland

MIDAN
TRIOMPHE

Qubba
Palace

SHARIA AL-HIGAZ

SHARIA
AL-AHRAM

MIDAN
ISMAILIYA

MIDAN
ROXI

Urubah
Palace

SHARIA AL-'URUBAH

NOUZHA

SHARIA MERGHANI

Heliopolis
Sporting Club

Baron
Empain's
Palace

ILI

SHARIA EN-NOZHA

Nasser's Tomb

Sadat's Tomb
and October
War Panorama

SUEZ DESERT ROAD

△ Suez

ABBASSIYA

Misr Travel Tower

Sinai Bus
Terminal

Cairo Stadium

MEDINET
NASR

SHARIA RAMSES

KEY TO MAP ENLARGEMENTS

1   Central Cairo (p.92-93)
2   Around Ramses Station (p.111)
3   Around Khan el-Khalili & al-Azhar (p.116)
4   To the Northern Gates (p.120)
5   Between Al-Azhar & the Bab Zwayla (p.127)
6   Between Bab Zwayla & The Citadel (p.133)
7   The Citadel (p.137)
8   Around Ibn Tulun & S. Cemetery (p.141)
9   The Northern Cemetery (p.147)
10   Old Cairo & Roda Island (p.150-151)
11   Gezira & The West Bank (p.166-167)

M u q a t t a m   H i l l s   Petrified
Forest

The bus terminal known as **Turgoman Garage**, in Bulaq, is where you're most likely to end up if you're arriving from elsewhere in Egypt. As it's only recently opened, transport from Turgoman into downtown Cairo is somewhat disorganized; the simplest option is to take a taxi (£E1.50 to Midan Ramses, £E2–3 to central Cairo), unless you fancy walking the 600m to Midan Ramses and catching a bus from there. Buses or *service* taxis from the Canal Zone or the Red Sea Coast drop passengers at the **Koulali Terminal** off Midan Ramses or the **Ahmed Helmi Terminal** behind Ramses Station; buses from Hurghada may drop you on Ramses Square, right outside.

All **trains** into Cairo stop at **Ramses Station** (see map on p.111 for the station and bus terminals). There are hotels nearby, but the neighbourhood is so grotty that most visitors prefer to head downtown by metro (Mubarak Station is beneath Midan Ramses), taxi (£E3–5), or a bus along Sharia Ramses. Alternatively, it's a twenty-minute walk down Sharia Ramses, taking a left at Sharia Emad el-Din or Sharia Orabi, into the main downtown area, where most of the budget hotels are located.

Orientation

Greater Cairo consists of two metropolitan governorates: **Cairo**, on the east bank of the Nile, and **Giza**, across the river. The **River Nile** (*Bahr el-Nil*, or simply *El-Nil*) is the prerequisite of their existence and fundamental to basic orientation. Bear in mind that it flows northwards through the city, so that "downriver" means north, and "upriver" south, a reversal of the usual associations. The city's waterfront is dominated by the **islands** of Gezira and Roda and the **bridges** that connect them to the **Corniche** (embankment) on either side of the Nile. There are four major divisions of the city:

● **Central Cairo** spreads inland to the east of the islands. Its **downtown** area – between Ezbekiya Gardens and **Midan Tahrir** – bears the stamp of Western planning, as does **Garden City**, the embassy quarter further south. At the northern end of central Cairo (beyond the downtown area) lies **Ramses Station**, the city's main train terminal. Most of the banks, airlines, cheap hotels and tourist restaurants lie within this swathe of the city.

● Further east sprawls **Islamic Cairo**, encompassing **Khan el-Khalili** bazaar, the Gamaliya quarter within the **Northern Walls**, and the labyrinthine Darb al-Ahmar district between the **Bab Zwayla** and the **Citadel**. Beyond the latter spread the eerie **Cities of the Dead** – the Northern and Southern Cemeteries.

● The Southern Cemetery and the populous **Saiyida Zeinab** quarter merge into the rubbish tips and wasteland bordering the **ruins of Fustat** and the **Coptic quarter** of **Old Cairo**, further to the south. From there, a ribbon of development follows the metro out to **Ma'adi**, Cairo's plushest residential suburb, and **Helwan**, the city's heaviest industrial centre. Except for stylish **Heliopolis**, the **northern suburbs** likewise hold little appeal for visitors.

● Across the river on the **west bank**, the residential neighbourhoods of **Aguza** and **Dokki** aren't as smart as nearby **Mohandiseen** or the high-rise northern end of **Gezira** island, known as **Zamalek**. The **Imbaba** district, just to the northeast, was once notable for its weekly **camel market**, but this has now moved slightly further out to Bil'esh. The dusty expanse of **Giza** (which lends its name to the west bank urban zone) is enlivened by **Cairo Zoo** and the nightclub-infested **Pyramids Road** leading to the **Pyramids of Giza**.

Information

Cairo's downtown **tourist office**, at 5 Sharia Adly (daily 9am–8pm; ☎391-3454), can supply a rather useless free map and out-of-date brochures, but little in the way of hard facts unless you speak to Laboudi, the older man who works there in the afternoons.

He is a font of knowledge and can provide reliable help with booking accommodation and tours. There are also tourist offices at both airport terminals: Terminal 1 (daily 8am–9pm; ☎291-4255 ext 2223); Terminal 2 (open 24hr; ☎291-4277). Tourist information is also available at Ramses Station (daily 8am–9pm; ☎579-0767) and the Giza Pyramids (daily 8am–5pm; ☎383-8823).

Should the need arise, an alleyway to the left of the Sharia Adly office gives access to the headquarters of the **tourist police** (open 24hr; ☎392-3642). Whether they're helpful or a waste of time largely depends on whom you encounter. Other tourist police stations can be found at Ramses Station (☎579-0767), the new airport (☎247-2584), the Giza Pyramids (☎335-1862), Khan el-Khalili (☎590-4827) and the Manial Palace (☎363-6707).

Maps and addresses

Cairo's more interesting areas are mapped in detail alongside their descriptions in this chapter. These **maps** – and the general plan on pp.74–75 – should suffice for most sightseeing needs, although for an overview of the city they can't match that provided by the grey-and-red *City Map of Cairo*, or the *Cairo Tourist Map*, sold at most tourist bookshops. The free "souvenir" map issued by the tourist office conveys the city's general layout, but can't be relied upon for navigation. Of more use for longer stays are *Cairo: A Practical Guide* (sadly unrevised since 1996), which also contains a useful set of maps; and the weighty *Cairo A–Z* (equally out of date); both cost £E30–50. At Lehnert & Landrock (44 Sharia Sherif), you can buy *Naguib Amin*'s detailed maps of Downtown/Garden City; Mohandiseen/Dokki/Giza; Zamalek; Heliopolis; Islamic Cairo; and Memphis/Saqqara – for around £E4.50 each.

It helps to memorize a few **geographical terms**. *Sharia* means "street" and always precedes the name (for example, Sharia Talaat Harb); narrower thoroughfares may be termed *Darb, Haret, Sikket* or *Zuqaq*, instead of Sharia. *Midan* denotes a square or open space. *Bab* signifies a medieval gate, after which certain quarters are named (for example, Bab el-Khalq); *Kubri* a bridge; and *Souk* a market. However, some of these words have more than one English transliteration (for example, *Sharia* is also spelt *Sharic* and *Chareh*), or may be inconsistently transliterated. **Street names** are posted in English (or French) and Arabic in central Cairo and Zamalek; almost everywhere else in Arabic only, or not at all. The same goes for **numbers**, rendered in Western and Arabic numerals (see p.685), or just the latter; a single number may denote a whole block with several entrance passageways – something to remember when you're following up addresses.

Don't expect **Cairenes** themselves to relate to maps; they comprehend their city differently. That said, however, people are remarkably helpful to visitors, going out of their way to steer them in the right direction; offer profuse thanks, but never *baksheesh*, which will offend in this situation.

CAIRO TELEPHONE CODE

Calling (or faxing) Cairo from outside Egypt, the **international access code** is ☎202; for direct dialling from another part of the country the **Cairo/Giza area code** is ☎02.

City transport

Getting around Cairo is relatively straightforward; Midan Tahrir is the main transport hub, with several other terminals in the centre connecting up the city (see "Buses" p.80). The metro is simple to use, and taxis inexpensive once you understand their system. Familiarize yourself with Arabic numerals (see "Language" in Contexts chapter) and you can also use buses and minibuses, which reach most parts of the city.

Since everyone drives like participants in the Paris–Dakar Rally, you might as well resign yourself to this. Accidents are surprisingly rare, all things considered. The streets are busy from 8am to midnight, and, unless you enjoy sweltering in traffic jams, it's best to try and avoid travelling during **rush hours** (7–10am & 4–7pm), when the streets are choked. An additional cause of confusion at the moment is the extensive drilling operations related to the Cairo Wastewater Project, which impede traffic at many points around the city.

The metro

Cairo's **metro** (the first in the Arab world) works like nothing else in the city: pristine and efficient, with a well-enforced ban on littering and smoking. Trains run every few minutes from 6am to midnight; outside of the rush hours (as above) they're no more over-crowded than in other cities around the world. The front carriage of each train is reserved for women, worth keeping in mind if you're a lone female traveller.

Stations are signposted with a large "M"; signs and route maps appear in Arabic and English. **Tickets** are purchased in the station (50pt for up to two stops; 80pt from the centre to anywhere; £E1.20 from one end of the line to the other); twin sets of booths cater for passengers heading in opposite directions, with separate queues for either sex. Hang onto your ticket to get through the automatic barriers at the other end. Travelling without a ticket will result in a fine (£E5).

The red metro line connects the northeastern suburb of **El-Marg** with the southern industrial district of **Helwan** (via Mubarak, Sadat, Saad Zaghoul, Saiyida Zeinab, Mar Girgis and Maadi), with the green line running from **Shobra** in the north to **Giza** (via Mubarak, Ataba, Sadat and Gezira). The yellow **Salah Salim** to **Imbaba** line (via Al-Azhar, Ataba and Zamalek) may open some time in 2000, and an extension of the green line from Giza to Fazal is under construction.

Taxis

The city has three kinds of taxi: **black-and-white cabs**, **service taxis** and **"specials"**. Though each requires different handling, some general rules apply. Firstly, choose the right sort of taxi. Secondly, try to discover the fare in advance (see below for a general guideline to fares); never start by asking how much. Third, don't expect drivers to

---

USEFUL METRO STATIONS

From a tourist's standpoint, there are seven **crucial stations**
(listed here from north to south):

MUBARAK, beneath Midan Ramses, is for reaching or leaving Ramses Station.

NASSER, two stops on, leads onto 26th July Street near the top end of Talaat Harb (take the High Court exit).

SADAT, the most used (and useful) station, is set beneath Midan Tahrir, and doubles as a pedestrian underpass.

SAIYIDA ZEINAB, two stops beyond, lies midway between that quarter and the northern end of Roda Island.

EL-MALEK EL-SALEH, the next stop, can usefully serve for exploring parts of Old Cairo.

MARI GIRGIS is the most useful stop for Coptic Cairo and Amr's Mosque.

GEZIRA/OPERA connects directly into the Opera Complex in south Gezira.

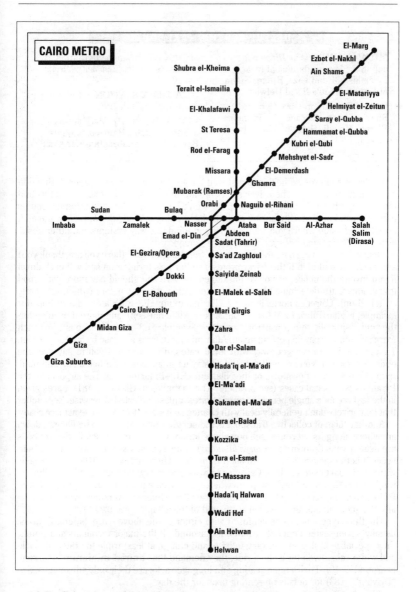

CAIRO METRO

El-Marg
Ezbet el-Nakhl
Ain Shams
El-Matariyya
Helmiyat el-Zeitun
Saray el-Qubba
Hammamat el-Qubba
Kubri el-Qubi
Mehshyet el-Sadr
El-Demerdash
Ghamra

Shubra el-Kheima
Terait el-Ismailia
El-Khalafawi
St Teresa
Rod el-Farag
Missara
Mubarak (Ramses)
Orabi
Naguib el-Rihani

Imbaba Sudan Zamalek Bulaq Nasser Ataba Bur Said Al-Azhar Salah Salim (Dirasa)

Emad el-Din
Abdeen
Sadat (Tahrir)
El-Gezira/Opera
Sa'ad Zaghloul
Dokki
Saiyida Zeinab
El-Bahouth
El-Malek el-Saleh
Cairo University
Mari Girgis
Midan Giza
Zahra
Giza
Dar el-Salam
Giza Suburbs
Hada'iq el-Ma'adi
El-Ma'adi
Sakanet el-Ma'adi
Tura el-Balad
Kozzika
Tura el-Esmet
El-Massara
Hada'iq Halwan
Wadi Hof
Ain Helwan
Helwan

speak English or know the location of every street. Identify a major landmark or thoroughfare in the vicinity and state that instead. If your destination is obscure or hard to pronounce, get it written down in Arabic. The best kind to use are four-seater **black-and-white taxis** (Fiats or Ladas), which often carry passengers collectively. Pick a major thoroughfare with traffic heading in the right direction, stand on the kerb, and wave and holler out your destination (for example, "Mohandiseen") as one approaches;

USEFUL SERVICE TAXI ROUTES	
MIDAN TAHRIR (*Nile Hilton* bus terminal) to the **Pyramids**, **Faisal** (near the Pyramids), **Midan Giza**, **Bulaq**, **Bulaq al-Dakrour**, **Ma'adi** and **Helwan**.	**MIDAN ATABA** to the **Pyramids**, **Sharia Sudan** (via Zamalek), **Dirasa** (via Al-Azhar).
RAMSES to **Midan Giza**, **Pyramids**, **Sharia Sudan** (via Zamalek), **Imbala**, **Waraq**, **Ma'adi**, **Helwan**, **Dirasa** (via Al-Azhar).	**GIZA TRAIN STATION** to Badrasheen (for Saqqara), **Dahshur**.
	PYRAMIDS ROAD (Maryotteya Canal) to **Tahrir**, **Ataba**, **Ramses**, **Saqqara**, **Badrasheen**, **Shabramant** (for Abu Sir).

if the driver's interested he'll stop and wait for you to run over. State your destination again, in more detail. If the driver starts talking money, say "*maalesh*" (forget it) and look for another cab; otherwise jump in. Don't be alarmed by the circuitous routes taken to avoid bottlenecks, nor by other people getting in along the way. Near the end, direct him to stop where you want (bearing in mind one-way systems and other obstacles) with "*hina/hinak kwayes*" (here/there's okay).

Ideally, you just hand over the money with "*itfuddel, shukran*" (here you are, thank you) and that's the end of it. If the driver protests, either he's trying it on and will back down if you invoke the police, or you've misjudged the fare and should pay more with good grace. **Fares** are determined by market rates rather than by meters (which are rarely switched on). Cairenes normally pay a £E1 minimum; £E3–5 for a downtown hop (for example, Midan Tahrir to Al-Azhar, Zamalek or Mohandiseen); and more if heading further out, especially to a prosperous area (for example £E8–10 to Heliopolis). For each extra person, you pay 25 percent again. After midnight, fares increase by 50–100 percent. Though foreigners can get away with **local rates**, drivers expect you to pay over the odds, especially if you are well dressed or staying in an expensive hotel: say £E5 minimum, £E5–8 across downtown or the Nile, and £E10–15 further out. The airport and the Pyramids are special cases (see p.73 and "The Pyramids of Giza"on p.181). Fares given in the text are for a single person at **tourist rates**, unless indicated otherwise. Remember that taxi drivers don't generally deal with change so it's best to have the exact fare ready.

Another form of collective transport is the **service taxi**, which can be flagged down anywhere along its set route (see box above for some of the most useful). *Service* taxis are usually vans (known as *arrabeya bil nafar*) or microbuses; *service* (pronounced "serveece") is the generic term for all such transport. There are some 60,000 *service* taxis which transport over a million Cairenes to work every day, causing appalling pollution, traffic jams (because they'll stop anywhere) and accidents. Fares range from 25pt to £E1 per person, according to the distance travelled. (Inter-city versions, which are usually Peugeot saloons, are covered at the end of this chapter; see p.247.)

The third type – not to be confused with either of the above – are **"special" taxis**, usually seven-seater Peugeot 504s. Found around all the major terminals and hotels, they specialize in fleecing unwary tourists and charge at least triple the rates of black-and-white cabs. Even for a short ride, they demand the **"tourist minimum"** (currently around £E10). Their ample seating and luggage racks are their only advantages. See "Driving" (p.83) for details on renting taxis for the day.

Buses

Cairo's **buses** are battered, exhaust-spewing workhorses, active from 5.30am to 12.30am daily (6.30am–6.30pm & 7.30pm–2am during Ramadan). Fares are cheap enough to be affordable by everyone, so buses are usually full, and overflow during the 7–10am and 4–7pm rush hours, when passengers hang from doorways or each other

BUS AND MINIBUS DESTINATIONS

DOWNTOWN: TERMINAL:	Midan Tahrir	Abdel Mouneem Riyad	Midan Ramses	Midan Ataba
DESTINATION				
Al-Azhar (Midan el-Hussein)	#186, #815, #904, minibus #77, #102	#63	#307, #961, minibus #10	#64
Amr Mosque (Coptic Cairo)	#93//, #134, #135, minibus #53	#93//, #134, #135, minibus#53	#93, #134, #135, minibus#53	#94, #831
Citadel	#174, #194, #235 #609, #811, minibus #54	#173, #811, minibus #53	#235, #811, minibus #54	#81, #69, minibus #57
Heliopolis *	#356 (A/C), #400, #949, minibus #27	#500, minibus #21, #35	#400, #500, #949, minibus #21, #27, #35	#500, #948, minibus #21, #35
Mohandiseen	#99 (to Sharia al-Sudan near Midan Lubnan), #194 (to Midan Nasr, Arab League St), minibus #76 (to Midan Bulaq)	#99, #173, minibus #73	#70 & many microbuses	#17 (to Midan Nasr, Arab League St), #19, #615 & minibus #76 (to Sharia al-Sudan near Midan Lubnan)
Pyramids of Giza	#30, #108, #356 & #357 (both A/C to the Sphinx), 900, #997, minibus ##183 (50pts to the Sphinx)	#913, #924, #356 & #357 (both A/C to the Sphinx)	#30, #958	minibus #183
Terminal 1 Old Airport	#400, minibus #27	#400, minibus #27	#400, minibus #27	#948 (24hr), minibus #27
Terminal 2 New Airport	#400, #949 (24hr)	#949 (24hr)	#949 (24hr)	#948 (24hr)
Sinai bus station	#39, #400, #949, minibus #27 & #35	#203	–	#176, #401, minibus #10
Zamalek	#13, minibus #49 (to Sharia Gubalaya, #71 (to 26th July St)	–	minibus #72	minibus #75
Other useful destinations	#214 to Manashi (for Bil'esh Camel Market)	–	#987 to Badra-sheen (for Saqqara), minibus #68 Sakakini Palace or to Bab Zwayla and the Blue Mosque	#401 to the Muqattam Hills

* Some of these go to Midan Roxi, some to Midan Ismailiya, some to both.

BUS NUMBERS IN ARABIC

13	١٣	63	٦٣	93//	٩٣//	400	٤٠٠	904	٩٠٤
17//	١٧/	64	٦٤	99(/)	٩٩(/)	401	٤٠١	913	٩١٣
21	٢١	65	٦٥	108	١٠٨	404	٤٠٤	924	٩٢٤
24	٢٤	66	٦٦	134/	١٣٤	500	٥٠٠	945/	٩٤٥/
27	٢٧	68	٦٨	135	١٣٥	609	٦٠٩	948	٩٤٨
30	٣٠	69	٦٩	174	١٧٤	611	٦١١	949	٩٤٩
33	٣٣	71	٧١	186	١٨٦	710	٧١٠	958	٩٥٨
35	٣٥	72(/)	٧٢(/)	194	١٩٤	811	٨١١	983	٩٨٣
50	٥٠	73	٧٣	210	٢١٠	814	٨١٤	987	٩٨٧
53	٥٣	76	٧٦	214	٢١٤	815	٨١٥	997	٩٩٧
54	٥٤	77	٧٧	235	٢٣٥	888	٨٨٨	998	٩٩٨
57	٥٧	83	٨٣	307	٣٠٧	900	٩٠٠		

and clamber in and out through windows. Though many foreigners are deterred from using buses by the risk of pickpockets and gropers, there's no denying that the network reaches virtually everywhere.

Buses are painted blue-and-white or red-and-white (the former being slightly more comfortable and more expensive), with **route numbers** in Arabic on the front, side and back. Those with slashed numbers (for example, #13/) may follow different routes from buses with the same number unslashed. Aside from the numbered bays on Midan Tahrir, few **stops** are clearly signposted (look for metal shelters, plaques on lampposts or crowds waiting), and buses generally slow down instead of halting, compelling passengers to board and disembark on the run. Except at terminals, you must enter through the rear door (which is often removed to facilitate access); at official stops, you're supposed to exit from the front. Conductors sell **tickets** (the flat fare on most routes is 25pt, or 50pt on longer routes) from behind a crush-bar by the rear door. The front of the bus is usually less crowded, so it's worth squeezing your way forwards; start edging towards the exit well before your destination.

New blue-and-white **A/C buses** are now being introduced on some routes for those who want to travel in comfort and avoid the crowds (flat fare £E2). At the moment, they serve only prosperous suburbs such as Heliopolis and Medinet Nasr and tourist sites like the Pyramids, but other routes will be added.

Most buses start from (or pass through) at least one of the city-centre **terminals** at Midan Tahrir, Abdel Mouneem Riyad (behind the Antiquities Museum), Midan Falaki (east of Tahrir and omitted from the destinations box on p.81 as nearly all buses from here pass through Tahrir), Midan Ramses and Midan Ataba. Write the number(s) in Arabic to show to enquiry booths or bystanders, who'll point you towards the right lane. At each of these locations, there are several bus stops, and where exactly you pick up your bus will depend on which direction it is going in, and whether it starts at the terminal or is simply passing through. In particular, note that there are two separate bus stations at Midan Ataba (one in the northern corner of the square on Sharia Clot Bey, the other in Ezbekiya Gardens opposite the Puppet Theatre) and at Abdel Mouneem Riyad (one behind the Antiquities Museum, the other right by the river). If possible, ask the conductor "*Rayih . . .?*"(are you going to . . .?) to make sure. At the time of writing, Midan Tahrir was being redeveloped and its future seems uncertain; if the buses listed under Midan Tahrir do move to another terminal in the next year or two, they will almost certainly leave from Abdel Mouneem Riyad.

Minibuses

During the early 1980s, the Cairo governorate introduced orange-and-white **minibuses** along many of the existing bus routes. Besides making better headway through traffic and actually halting at stops, they are far more comfortable and never crowded, as standing is not permitted. Tickets (25–50pt – prohibitively expensive for many Cairenes) are bought from the driver. Minibuses should not be confused with *service* taxis (usually smaller microbuses, see p.80). There are minibus **terminals** alongside the big bus stations in Midan Tahrir (by the *Nile Hilton* and near Arab League/Omar Makram Mosque) and Midan Ataba, and minibuses usually use the same bus stops as ordinary buses.

Trams and river-taxis
As the metro and minibus systems expand, Cairo's original **tram network** (built in colonial times) is being phased out. Although the Heliopolis tram system remains in use throughout that area (see "The northern suburbs", p.174, for details), we've given less attention to other lines. Other routes still in use include: Saiyida Zeinab along Sharia Bur Said to Mattoreya; from Midan Ataba along Sharia el-Geish to El Wayli in Abbssiya; and from Dirasa along Sharia Saleh Salem to Heliopolis and Medinet Nasr – but it's wise to check in advance that they are still running. Like buses, they are cheap and battered, with standing room only; their Arabic route numbers are posted above the driver's cab.

The most relaxing way to reach Old Cairo is by river-taxi. **River-taxis** (aka water-buses) leave from the Maspero Dock outside the Television Building, 600m north of the Antiquities Museum. Boats run every thirty to forty minutes to Old Cairo via Giza and Roda (the frequency may be slightly different during Ramadan); you can buy tickets (25pt flat fee) at the dock. On Fridays and Sundays, they also run up to the Nile Barrages at Qanatir (£E1.50 each way; see "Excursions from Cairo", p.242).

Driving
The only thing scarier than **driving in Cairo** is cycling, which is tantamount to suicide. Dashes, crawls and finely judged evasions are the order of the day; donkey carts and jaywalkers trust in motorists' swift reactions. Any collision draws a crowd. Minor dents are often settled by on-the-spot payoffs, but should injury occur, it's wise to involve a cop right away. Multistorey car parks, such as the one on Midan Ataba, are ignored as motorists park bumper-to-bumper along every kerb, leaving their handbrakes off so vehicles can be shifted by the local *minairdy* (whom they tip 25pt–£E1). Given all this, it's no surprise that few foreigners drive in Cairo.

To rent a car you must be at least 25 years old and have an International Driving Licence, held for at least a year. At last count, the cheapest of the big agencies was Budget (head office: 5 Sharia el-Makrizi, Zamalek, ☎340-0070; Cairo Airport ☎ 265-2395), which has Suzuki Swifts at US$50 per day, plus US$7 daily collision waiver, 12 percent tax and US20¢ per kilometre up to a maximum of 100km. A less expensive Egyptian company, Thrifty Egypt Limousine (central reservations ☎012/216-0531, with branches at the new airport and big hotels), offers the same car at about 20 percent less. Hertz, Avis and Europcar (all with offices at the airport and also found in most of the big hotels) are worth trying too.

Many of these agencies offer the preferable and reasonably priced option of **rented cars with drivers**. Average rates for a driver are around US$15 for a ten-hour day, plus US$2 for each extra hour of driving time. For overnight trips, you'll also be expected to pay about US$15 per night for his expenses and trouble. For shorter jaunts, consider renting a chauffeur-driven Mercedes from Misr Limousine (☎285-6124; desks at major hotels), or Europcar (☎347-4712), both of which charge by the hour.

Walking
The one advantage of Cairo's density is that many places of interest are within **walking** distance of Midan Tahrir or other transport ganglions. You can walk across downtown

Cairo from Tahrir to Midan Ataba in fifteen to thirty minutes; the same again brings you to Khan el-Khalili in the heart of Islamic Cairo. Starting from here or the Citadel, you can make fascinating walks through the medieval quarter, which doesn't suit other methods of exploration.

Arguably, walking is the only way to experience the city's pulsating streetlife. Though pavements are congested with vendors and pedestrians, they weave gracefully around each other, in contrast with the bullish jostlings of Western capitals. The commonest irritants are rubbish, noxious fumes and puddles, uneven pavements and gaping drains; in poorer quarters, the last two may not even exist. Women travellers must also reckon with gropers, who strike chiefly along Talaat Harb and around the Khan. Close proximity to a male escort confers some immunity, but the best solution is to develop an instant response (see "From a woman's perspective", p.33).

To make faster headway you can walk along the edge of the road – obviously, always facing oncoming traffic. **Traffic** is heavy from 8am to midnight, and ceases for a few hours before dawn. Its daytime flow only diminishes during Ramadan celebrations, major football matches, and the midday prayer on Fridays, when many side streets are carpeted over and used as outdoor mosques.

At all times, **crossing the road** takes boldness. Drivers will slow down to give people time to dart across, but dithering or freezing midway confuses them and increases the risk of an accident. A prolonged horn burst indicates that the driver can't or won't stop. Remember that motorists obey police signals rather than traffic lights, which were only installed in the 1980s and have yet to acquire any real local credibility.

Accommodation

Cairo is packed with **accommodation** to suit every tourist's taste and budget. When tourism is at its normal level, most hotels are busy or full throughout December and January, while the cheaper ones are flooded with backpackers over the summer. Although, given time, this pattern will doubtless reassert itself, at present you can be certain of a vacancy almost anywhere. Consequently, **hotel touts** compete more fiercely than ever. At the airport they masquerade as blazered "tourist officials" and are keen to book you into the most expensive hotel that will wash (say, £E75/US$25 a night for backpackers); downtown, they're more likely touting budget hotels. Taxi drivers are also in on the game and may claim a split from both parties. Yet **finding a room** needn't be traumatic if you take control of the situation. Officials can telephone about vacancies on your behalf from the airport, or you can simply hail a taxi and begin visiting downtown hotels (all the deluxe downtown hotels, except the *El-Gezirah Sheraton*, are marked on the map of Central Cairo on p.92; the mid-range and cheaper downtown places are keyed to the map.

ACCOMMODATION PRICE CODES

Throughout the guide, hotels and pensions are graded on a scale of ① to ⑨, indicating the price (including tax) of the **cheapest double room** in each establishment in high season (for places that offer **dorm beds**, rates per person are given in £E). Please note that most hotels in categories ⑧ and ⑨ quote rates in US$, but will accept payment in £E. For a full explanation of the following categories, see p.46. The price bands to which these codes refer are as follows:

① under £E20/US$7	④ £E45–65/US$15–20	⑦ £E150–300/US$50–100
② £E20–30/US$7–10	⑤ £E65–100/US$20–35	⑧ US$100–200/£E300–600
③ £E30–45/US$10–15	⑥ £E100–150/US$35–50	⑨ US$200/£E600 upwards

Hotels and pensions

Cairo's hotels reflect the city's diversity: deluxe chains overlooking the Nile; functional high-rises; colonial piles and homely pensions with the same raddled facades as bug-infested flophouses. **Standards** vary within any given price range or star rating – and from room to room in many places. Try to inspect the facilities (A/C denotes air-conditioning) before checking in. Also establish the price and any service tax or extra charges (which should be posted in reception) at the outset. Guests at deluxe hotels or certain budget places such as the *Ismailia House, New Palace, Sun, Magic*, and the *Pensione Roma* can avail themselves of **laundry services** charged at piece rates. In budget places, prices should be around £E1 for trousers, 50pt for shirts and 25pt for underwear. Elsewhere, hotel receptionists or building janitors can probably put you in touch with the local *makwagi*, who does washing and ironing also at piece rates.

Hotels with three or more stars require payment in US$, or Egyptian currency backed by an exchange receipt. Officially, rates are the same all year, with an annual rise in early October.

Deluxe and four-star hotels – city-wide

All the international chains are represented in Cairo, which has over thirty hotels with a four- or five-star (deluxe) rating. Though package tourists may get hefty reductions, the regular rates for such places start at around US$150 for a double. Our **city-wide selection** boasts fine locations, superlative facilities or splendid decor; none of the deluxe or four-star hotels include breakfast in their price.

El-Gezirah Sheraton (☎341-1333, fax 341-3640, *gzsher@rite.com*). Overlooking the Nile from the southern end of Gezira Island, with Lebanese, Chinese and Italian/Egyptian restaurants, the *El-Samar* restaurant-nightclub (currently closed for renovation), a casino, bank and the expensive *le Disco* nightclub. ⑧.

Helnan Shepheard Hotel (☎355-3800, fax 355-7284, *reshs@helnan.com*). Across the road from the *Semiramis*, this is the five-star, Nile-side version of the famous nineteenth-century establishment that stood on Midan Opera. Rooms on the quieter side facing the Muqattam Hills are cheaper. ⑧.

Hotel Meridien-Le Caire (☎362-1717, fax 362-1927). French-managed pile at the northern tip of Roda Island, commanding a superb river view and incorporating health club, pool, various cafés, bars and restaurants, including one open 24hr. ⑧.

Cairo Marriott, Sharia Saraya el-Gezira, off 26th July St, Zamalek (☎340-8888, fax 340-6667, *marriott@link.com.eg*). Modern guest rooms built around the lavish palace constructed to house Empress Eugénie. Offers fine restaurants and bars, a casino, nightclub and pool; non-residents can drink or dine in the khedival salons and billiard room. ⑧.

Mena House Oberoi (☎383-3222, fax 383-7777, *obmhobc@oberoi.com.eg*). Set in lush grounds near the Giza Pyramids, this one-time khedival hunting lodge witnessed Roosevelt and Churchill initiate the D-Day plan, and the formal signing of the peace treaty between Israel and Egypt. Its renovated arabesque halls and nineteenth-century rooms are delightful; the modern Mena Gardens annexe isn't. Facilities include the *Moghul* restaurant (the best Indian restaurant in Egypt), pool, golf course and tennis courts. ⑨.

Nile Hilton (☎578-0444, fax 578-0475, *nhilton@brainy1.ie-eg.com*). Sited between Midan Tahrir and the Nile, this refurbished 1950s building is one of the first landmarks you'll get to recognize in Cairo. In addition to the hotel, it contains a range of cafés and restaurants: the *Taverne du Champs de Mars, Ibis Café, BBQ Garden* and *Rotisserie Belvedere*. River-facing doubles cost more than rooms overlooking Tahrir. Winter nightclub on the roof; during summer, action revolves around the pool. ⑧.

Ramses Hilton (☎574-4400, fax 575-7152). Just north of the Antiquities Museum, this is Cairo's tallest hotel, with 3-storey atrium and glass elevator, pool, bars, restaurants and a casino open to non-residents. Rooms are luxurious to a fault. ⑧.

Semiramis Intercontinental (☎355-7171, fax 356-3020, *cairo@interconti.com*). Sited just south of Midan Tahrir, this hotel has elegant rooms with every facility, including Internet access and some with Nile views. There's also a gym, pool, Al-Rashid nightclub and a host of restaurants offering every type of cuisine. ⑨.

Mid-range and cheap places: hotels and pensions

The mid-range of the budget spectrum chiefly consists of **three-star hotels** whose rooms have private bathrooms and A/C, perhaps also fridges, phones and TV. If facilities fall short of what's advertised (and charged for), you're entitled to raise a stink. However, a couple of places in the centre are (more or less) refurbished colonial edifices whose old-world charm makes up for any lack of modern gadgetry.

Budget travellers usually go for the **cheap hotels and pensions** on the upper floors of downtown office buildings. Designed to exclude sunlight and circulate air during summer, the unheated ones can be damp and draughty in winter. During the summer, bedbugs and mosquitoes may infest seedier places where hot water (or any water at all) is often lacking. By way of compensation, some feature Art Deco rooms with sweeping balconies, and all can provide bottled water, tea and soft drinks. Most are reached from street level via an alleyway and/or lobby serving the entire building; many are locked at midnight, so if you arrive late at night you'll have to roust the doorman (*bowab*) who will probably expect some modest *baksheesh* for his trouble. Riding the elevators can feel like playing Russian roulette, but we've never heard of a serious accident.

The following rundown is by no means exhaustive, focusing as it does on places that are cheap, agreeable, or conveniently located (a few combine all these assets) – or bad enough to merit a warning. Note that accommodation in the areas around Midan Tahrir and Midan Talaat Harb, although convenient for the Antiquities Museum and downtown, is a honey-pot for every type of tout and con artist in Cairo. Notices in all the hotels in this area give due warning, but the constant harassment can give you a bad impression of the Egyptian people.

The hotels are listed according to location, the areas corresponding to descriptive sections (and maps) in this chapter; the downtown ones are all shown on the map on p.92, mostly keyed in by number. Breakfast is included in the price unless otherwise stated.

DOWNTOWN – BETWEEN TAHRIR AND EZBEKIYA

Talaat Harb, Mahmoud Bassiouni and Qasr el-Nil streets offer the widest range of budget hotels. A few are excellent, or really squalid; the majority fall somewhere in between. Richer tourists can choose between comfortable modern hotels or a number of vintage establishments redolent of pre-war high society.

Ambassador (1), 31 26th July St, opposite the law courts (☎578-3225, fax 574-3263). A deluxe place with spacious rooms on the 8th, 9th and 10th floors that give fine views over downtown Cairo and as far as the Citadel. Modern conveniences include satellite TV and a minibar in each room, and there's a 24hr restaurant, bar and a coffee shop. ⑦.

Amin (2), 38 Midan Falaki (☎393-3813). Reasonable rooms with fans; it's worth paying £E5 more for a room with private bathroom and constant hot water – the shared facilities aren't so clean. Near the footbridge leading to Bab al-Luq market. Breakfast not included. ③.

Anglo-Swiss (3), 14 Sharia Champollion (☎575-1497). Faded 1930s-style pension with a piano, library, spiral staircase and dining room. Cramped singles, but roomier doubles; hot water 7am–noon and 8–11pm in shared bathrooms. ③.

Berlin Hotel (4), Sharia El-Shawarby 2 (☎ & fax 395-7502, *berlinhotelcairo@hotmail.com*). Small hotel on the 4th floor, just off Qasr el-Nil, with lofty double and triple rooms that have optional A/C (£E20 extra), as well as dorm beds for £E15. All rooms have Art Deco fittings, mahogany floors and shower-cabins. Services include sauna, massage, communal kitchen, Internet access (£E12/hr), fax and an Internet telephone (£E3 per min anywhere in the world). ④.

Carlton (5), 21 26th July St (☎575-5022, fax 575-5323). Built in 1935 and creaking with wood-panelled period charm, albeit slightly worn around the edges. Modern facilities include A/C and TV with satellite reception in every room. Has a restaurant on the seventh floor and a very pleasant rooftop garden with coffee shop. ⑤.

Cleopatra Palace (6), 2 Sharia el-Bustan (☎575-9900, fax 575-9807). Three-star block with kitsch 1970s decor, an Egyptian restaurant, bar, nightclub, plus A/C rooms with baths and phones. ⑦.

Cosmopolitan (7), off Qasr el-Nil (☎392-3956, fax 393-3531). Refurbished, this monumental Art Nouveau building has a Grecian restaurant, Olde-English bar, bank and international calls facility. All rooms have A/C and private baths. Amex, MasterCard and Visa accepted. ⑦.

Crown (8), 9 Sharia Emad el-Din (☎591-8374). Salubrious and roomy, with hot water in shared bathrooms on 4th floor. Sufferers of bad backs will appreciate the firmness of the beds, but be aware that the singles can be a bit grubby. Breakfast not included. Twenty percent off for *Rough Guide* readers. ②.

Dahab Hotel (9), 26 Sharia Mahmoud Basiony (☎579-9104). A Dahab tourist camp transported to a downtown roof, this place has tiny, ultra-basic rooms – £E5 extra for a fan – and lots of backpackers (dorm beds £E10). Plenty of vegetation makes it a pleasant hang-out and facilities include a communal kitchen, laundry service, and 24-hour hot water. Plans are afoot for an Internet café. ②.

Garden City House (10), 26 Sharia Kamal al-Din Salah (☎354-4969 or 354-4126). Faded, rather noisy 1930s pension on the 3rd floor, on the edge of the Garden City, behind the *Semiramis*, with Nile views from some rooms. Half-board only and seriously overpriced. ⑥.

Grand (11), 17 26th July St (☎575-7700, fax 575-7593). Art Deco edifice with original lifts and furniture, a fountain, *Valley of the Kings* restaurant and a coffee shop – entrance in the alley off Sharia Talaat Harb. Most rooms have private baths, balconies, A/C and satellite TV. If you book in advance, they will not only collect you from the airport but also arrange a speedy route through customs and immigration. ⑥.

Hotel Claridge (12), 41 Sharia Talaat Harb (☎393-7776). Very noisy location over 26th July St. Some rooms nice, others grotty; private and shared bathrooms. ④.

Hotel Minerva (13), 39 Sharia Talaat Harb (☎392-0600). Clean, pleasant rooms with polished wood floors; most bathrooms are shared, but have proper bathtubs. Rooms with own bath cost £E4 extra. ②.

Hotel des Roses (14), 33 Sharia Talaat Harb (☎393-8022). An Art Deco hostelry; some rooms refurbished with their own bathrooms. A juddering lift ride to the top floor. ②.

Hotel Select (15), beside the synagogue on Sharia Adly (☎393-3707). Simple, mostly triple rooms and hot-water bathrooms, 8 floors up. Operates almost like a hostel, charging a rate per person (£E20), rather than for the room. ③.

Ismailia House (16), 1 Midan Tahrir (☎356-3122). Advance booking is advisable for this cool, clean and cheerful 7th-floor haven, with singles, doubles, triples, dorm beds (£E15), 24-hr hot water and MTV. The Tahrir-facing rooms are noisy all night. ③.

Lotus (17), 12 Sharia Talaat Harb (☎575-0627, fax 575-4270). Reception on the 7th floor, reached via an arcade signposted *Malév*. Clean, with friendly staff, a restaurant and a bar. Some rooms with A/C and private baths. Hot water 6–10am and 6–10pm. ⑤.

Magic Hotel (18), 10 El Bustan St, a quiet street near Midan El Tahrir (☎ & fax 579-5918, *magichotel@hotmail.com*). Very helpful and welcoming place with clean and comfortable rooms. Has a plush satellite TV lounge with all the international channels and Internet access at £E10 per hour. Call beforehand and someone will pick you up from the airport. Dorm beds £E20. ③.

New (19), 21 Sharia Adly (☎392-7065 or 392-7066, fax 392-9555). A reasonable mid-range place with comfortable, carpeted rooms, most with en-suite shower and toilet. ⑤.

New Palace Hotel (20), 17 Solimanel Halibi St (☎575-1322, fax 290-0101, *newpalacehotel @hotmail.com*). Staffed by friendly rogues – who are adept at extracting high prices for just about everything – this hotel has large, high-ceilinged rooms and is located near Midan Orabi, away from the main tourist areas. The rooftop garden is a pleasant meeting place, and other facilities include a pool table and Internet access at £E15 per hour. Ignore the hard sell on their Nile Valley package trip; it's far cheaper to do it independently. Dorm beds £E10; rooms with A/C available. ③.

Odeon Palace (21), 6 Sharia Abdel Hamid Said (☎776-637, fax 767-971). Modern three-star tower with restaurant and 24-hour roof garden bar, just off Sharia Talaat Harb; breakfast not included. ⑥.

Orient Palace (22), 14 26th July St (☎393-9375). Clean and friendly, with the cheapest singles (£E12) in town. On the 10th floor, with a rooftop café. ③.

Oxford (23), 32 Sharia Talaat Harb (☎575-8173); **Golden Hotel (24)**, 13 Sharia Talaat Harb (☎392-2659). Duo of grubby dives on central Sharia Talaat Harb, both pretty undesirable nowadays – though they were once legendary travellers' hotels. The *Oxford* has featured regularly in the crime pages of the local press for various illegal activities, including drug dealing and prostitution; frankly, it's not worth braving the bedbugs and filth just for a bit of underground history; breakfast not included. ②–③.

Pensione Roma (25), 169 Sharia Mohammed Farid – entrance around the side of the Gattegno department store (☎391-1088 or 391-1340). The stylish 1940s ambience, immaculately maintained by Madame Cressaty, comes highly recommended and reservations are essential (call at 9am or the night before). Constant hot water, shared and private bathrooms; laundry service. ④.

Sultan (☎772-258), **Hotel Safary** (☎575-0752), and **Venice Hotel** (☎575-1477, *jastar99 @hotmail.com*) **(26)**, 4 Sharia Tawfiqia. Dorm-only ultra-cheapies in a building opening onto a colourful market near Midan Orabi. All are very friendly, and offer hot water and use of kitchen facilities. *Safary* is popular with Japanese backpackers, despite being the least appealing of the three. Dorm beds £E5–7.

Sun (27), 9th floor, 2 Sharia Talaat Harb, take the left-hand lift (☎578-1786, fax 579-5849). Related to the *Ismailia* (see above), this central hotel is popular with backpackers and offers the same good-value facilities and friendly atmosphere. Sells beer. Dorms £E15. ③.

Tulip (28), 3 Midan Talaat Harb (☎393-9433, fax 361-1995). Decent old-style place facing *Groppi's*. The singles, doubles and triples – with and without private baths – have firm mattresses. Also has a restaurant/bar. ③.

Windsor (29), 19 Sharia Alfi Bey (☎591-5810, fax 921-621, *wdoss@link.com*). Agreeably faded vintage colonial comfort, bags of character – and the nicest bar in Cairo – make it worth a splurge. The patron's father, Ramses Wissa Wassef, founded Harraniyya's weaving school (see opposite). All rooms except the very cheapest have private bathroom, A/C and satellite TV. Fifteen percent discount for *Rough Guide* readers. ⑥.

DOWNTOWN – NEARER RAMSES STATION

Arriving late or leaving early from one of the terminals around Midan Ramses, the following places commend themselves despite their grim surroundings. Like some quieter hotels a bit nearer the centre, they're marked on the map on p.111. Avoid five total pits which aren't: the *Nobel, Ramses, Cairo Palace, Everest* and *Africa House*.

Big Ben, 33 Sharia Emad el-Din (☎590-8881). Singles, doubles and triples with fans, soft beds and a few with private bath – some even have balconies with a view of the mosque next door. Take the left-hand elevator in the foyer to the 9th floor; breakfast not included. ③.

Fontana, off Midan Ramses (☎ & fax 592-2145). Comfortable, with mod cons and a swimming pool, which makes the cost tolerable. Bar, restaurant, patisserie, and discos or belly dancing some nights. ⑤.

New Cecil, 29 Sharia Emad el-Din (☎591-3859). Clean-ish, with fans and shared hot-water bathrooms. On the 4th floor. ②.

Venus Hotel, 38 Sharia Ramses (☎575-0496, fax 336-7852). The best budget option near Ramses, the rooms are clean and comfortable although there's no A/C. There is, however, a comfortable TV lounge and they also store luggage, have a laundry service and even give a twenty percent discount to students. Also has triples and quads. ③.

Victoria, 66 Sharia el-Gumhorriya (☎589-2291, fax 591-3008). A 1930s hotel once frequented by George Bernard Shaw. The large recently renovated A/C rooms (many with mahogany furniture), bar and restaurant make this currently the best deal in town. Bank and hairdresser on the premises; international calls. Takes Amex, MasterCard and Visa. ⑥.

ISLAMIC CAIRO

Islamic Cairo rubs shoulders with its medieval past: noises, smells and insects penetrate one's room, while outside the quarter's values and customs demand recognition. Excluding numerous bug-ridden dives around Saiyida Zeinab and Khan el-Khalili, three hotels are worth considering. The *New Rich* is on the downtown plan on p.92; the other two are marked on the "Khan el-Khalili and Al-Azhar" map (p.116).

El-Hussein (☎591-8089 or 591-8664, fax 591-8479). Entered via a passage into *Fishawi's*, the hotel's balcony rooms overlooking the square are harangued by Cairo's loudest muezzins, while the upper floors shake from wedding parties in its rooftop restaurant (great views, awful food). Sleep is impossible during festivals, when the square bops all night. Pleasant singles and doubles, but it's worth paying £E20 extra for a private bathroom. Fine for women alone. Reservations advisable. ④.

New Rich (30), 74 Sharia Abdel Aziz, off Midan Ataba (☎390-0145, fax 390-6390). Roughly midway between downtown and Islamic Cairo. A/C singles and doubles with private or shared baths. ④.

Radwan (☎590-7561, fax 592-5287). Just across the Muski from the *El-Hussein*, so equally noisy, but with smaller rooms and less character. Singles, doubles and triples with shared or private baths. Sporadic hot water. Not advisable for women alone. ④.

ZAMALEK

The northern half of Gezira Island is quieter and fresher than central Cairo, except along 26th July Street, where buses and *service* taxis shuttle between downtown and the west bank, with an elevated roadway for through traffic. All the following hotels are keyed to the map on p.166. Besides its *Cairo Marriott* and *Gezirah Sheraton* (see p.85), the island has a few modern **three-star hotels** like the *President* at 22 Sharia Taha Hussein (☎340-0652, fax 341-1752; ⑥); *Horus House* at 21 Sharia Ismail Muhammed (☎340-3034, fax 340-3182; breakfast not included; ⑥); and the slightly seedier *Hotel Longchamps* (same address; ☎340-2311; ⑥), plus the two **cheaper options** following:

El-Nil Zamalek, Midan Sidki, off Sharia Aziz Abaza (☎340-1846, fax 340-0220). Spacious modern rooms with bath, phone, TV and A/C, and maybe a balcony overlooking the Nile. ⑤.

Mayfair, 9 Sharia Aziz Osman (☎340-7315, fax 341-1018). Quiet location near the French embassy with a pleasant terrace and garden access. Refurbished rooms with carpet and balcony are better value than the cheaper, grubbier ones – although these too are now being renovated. The entrance lobby is an Art Deco classic. Ten percent discount for *Rough Guide* readers. Recommended. ③.

Hostels and camping

Hostelling and camping offer meagre rewards by comparison with downtown hotels, and any gains in clean air or seclusion tend to be negated by the extra travel involved in sightseeing from an outlying base.

That said, the **HI youth hostel** near the El-Gama'a Bridge on Roda Island (☎364-0729, fax 368-4107; see map on p.150) is readily accessible by #83 minibus from Tahrir. Bus #8, #803, #900 and #904 also run nearby, or you can catch a river-taxi to the Giza University stop and walk back across the bridge. There is a choice between three-person dorms or cheaper six-person ones (£E10–12 or £E8–10; breakfast included) and it's open year-round. Non-HI members pay £E4 extra, or can take out monthly membership for £E24. Reception closes at midnight but they usually open the doors for you after that – though it's probably best to check this beforehand.

Salma Camping in Harraniyya, outside Giza (☎384-9152), attracts tourists with camper-vans or bikes. Camping or caravanning, it costs £E10 per person, including free hot showers with no extra tent or vehicle charge. Alternatively, you can rent a hut: £E30 for a small two-person cabin, £E40 for a four-person cabin (communal showers); breakfast is not included. Despite its bar-buffet and delightful garden, the site's distance from everywhere but the Wissa Wassef School (next door) is bound to cause difficulties. It's reached by turning off Pyramids Road towards Saqqara at Maryotteya Canal (1km before the pyramids), and then after 4km taking a signposted turn-off at Harraniyya village; continue for 100m, and the site is about 100m away on your right. Buses and *service* taxis run from town to the turn-off along Pyramids Road, from where you can catch regular *service* taxis to the Harraniyya turn-off.

Long stays and flat-hunting

Should you decide to stay a while, it's worth remembering that many hotels reduce their rates by ten percent after fifteen days' occupation. Depending on demand for rooms and your rapport with the management, it may be possible to negotiate further discounts for **long stays at pensions**. Unfortunately, the smart *Anglo-Swiss* and *Roma* are less open to persuasion than dives like the *Oxford*, which allows long-stay residents to customize their rooms and cook on the premises.

In the longer term it's better **to rent a flat**; a base with a phone makes working or socializing in Cairo a lot easier. Given the range of localities and amenities, expect to look at half a dozen places before settling on one. Check the small ads in *Cairo Today*, the *Maadi Messenger, British Community News, Egyptian Gazette* and *Community Times*; and notice boards at English-language institutes and cultural centres (see p.239), the American University, and at the Sunny Supermarket, 11 Sharia el-Aziz Osman, Zamalek (☎342-1121). Foreigners working or studying in Cairo often seek flat-mates or want to sublet during temporary absences. With luck, you can move into a fully furnished flat with little ado. As a general guide to **prices**, you can rent a flat in the centre for around £E400 per month per person, or a houseboat for two moored on the Nile at Aguza for £E750.

Another way involves using a *simsar* (flat agent), who can be found in any neigh-bourhood by making enquiries at local shops and cafés. Unless you spend a long, fruit-less day together, he's only paid when you settle on a place; ten percent of your first month's rent is the normal charge. Flat agencies in Ma'adi levy the same commission on both tenant and landlord. Additional "key money" is illegal, but often demanded.

Before agreeing to **sign a lease**, **check** plumbing, water pressure, sockets, lighting, phone, stove and water-heater (*buta* gas cylinders need changing), and ask if power or water cuts are regular occurrences. Also determine whether utilities (phone, gas, elec-tricity) and services (the *bowab*, garbage collector) are included in the rent, and paid up to date when you move in (ask to see receipts if necessary). All the flat's contents should be accurately noted on an inventory, and the responsibility for repairs and the size of the deposit established. A flat without a phone isn't likely to acquire one, what-ever the landlord promises.

Cairo's **residential neighbourhoods** range from smart Western enclaves to coun-trified *baladi* quarters. Quietly spacious **Ma'adi**, thirty minutes by metro from the cen-tre, is home to most of Egypt's American community, and mega-wealthy natives. **Zamalek**, favoured by embassies and European expats, is likewise costly, but always has vacancies. Another focus for the foreign community is **Heliopolis**, a self-contained suburb where palatial Art Deco flats jostle with air-conditioned high-rises. Rents here are lower than in downtown Cairo, where few flats are available at any price unless you move into **Bulaq** or plumb the Qasr al-Aini side of **Garden City**.

Across the Nile, middle-class **Dokki** merges into *baladi* market quarters, while **Mohandiseen** parades blocks of flats and shopping centres along its shiny boulevards. Single males with a grasp of Arabic and Egyptian ways might enjoy living in **baladi quarters** (Islamic Cairo, Bulaq, Imbaba), which are cheap and cheerful, unhygienic and noisy. Foreigners are expected to contribute to the incessant drama of local life and do (verbal) battle when necessary – personal privacy doesn't exist in these urban villages.

THE CITY

With so much to see (and overlook, initially), you can spend weeks in **CAIRO** and merely scratch the surface. But as visitors soon realize, there are lots of reasons why people don't stay for long. The city's density, climate and pollution conspire against it, and the culture shock is equally wearing. Tourists unfamiliar with Arab ways can take little for granted, regular visitors expect to be baffled, and not even Cairenes compre-hend the whole metropolis. The downside weighs especially on newcomers, since it's the main tourist sites that generate most friction. A day at Khan el-Khalili bazaar can feel like a course in sales resistance and *baksheesh* evasion. Generally, however, Cairenes are the warmest, best-natured city dwellers going. They have to be to live in such a pressure cooker without exploding. Their sly wit and prying render pretension and secrecy impotent; their spirited ingenuity transcends horrendous conditions.

Potential riots are defused by tolerance and custom; a web of ties resists alienation. Once you have something of the measure of this, Cairo feels an altogether different and more enjoyable place.

Central Cairo

Most people prefer to get accustomed to **central Cairo** before tackling the older, Islamic quarters, for even in this Westernized downtown area known as *wust al-Balad*, the culture shock can be profound. Beyond the sanctuary of the luxury hotels beside the Nile, crowds and traffic jostle for space in the fume-laden air; whistling cops direct weaving taxis and limousines, donkey carts and buses; office workers rub shoulders with *baladi* folk, Nubians and soldiers. The pavements and shadowy lobbies of cavernous Art Deco or Empire-style apartment buildings are a lifetime's world for many vendors and doormen – both major contributors to Cairo's grapevine. Above the crumbling pediments and hoardings, pigeon lofts and extra rooms spread across the rooftops – a spacious alternative to the streets below, forming a city above the city centre.

The area is essentially a lopsided triangle, bounded by **Ramses Station**, **Midan Ataba** and **Garden City**, and for the most part it's compact enough to explore on foot. Only the Ramses quarter and the further reaches of Garden City are sufficiently distant to justify using transport. At the heart of central Cairo is the broad, bustling expanse of **Midan Tahrir** (for an account of the square, see p.103); aside from being the city's main transport terminal, Tahrir's most famous landmark is the domed **Museum of Egyptian Antiquities**, which houses the finest collection of its kind in the world.

CAIRO'S MUSEUMS

Although Cairo has over a dozen museums, most visitors limit themselves to the big three, devoted respectively to **Egyptian Antiquities** (see below), **Coptic** (see p.154) and **Islamic Art** (see p.129). Of these, the Antiquities Museum is the most popular and by far the largest, necessitating at least two visits to do it any kind of justice. The Coptic and Islamic Art museums can each comfortably be seen in a couple of hours and make fitting adjuncts to exploration of their quarters of the city.

On a practical note, unless you're planning to buy a photo permit, it's best to leave your **camera** at the hotel. Otherwise you'll have to check it in at the entrance to all three main museums, a process which occasionally leads to the wrong camera being returned to the wrong owner. For the smaller museums, given temporary closures and erratic opening hours, it's worth telephoning the distant ones before setting out.

The Museum of Egyptian Antiquities

At the northern end of Midan Tahrir, the **Museum of Egyptian Antiquities** (daily 9am–5pm; during Ramadan 9am–3pm; £E20, students £E10, camera £E10, camcorder £E100; no flashes or tripods) feels almost as archaic as the civilization it records. Founded in 1858 by Auguste Mariette, who excavated the Serapeum at Saqqara and several major temples in Upper Egypt (and was later buried in the museum grounds), it has long since outgrown its present building, which now scarcely provides warehouse space for the pharaonic artefacts. Allowing one minute for each, it would take about nine months to view its 136,000 exhibits. Forty thousand more items lie crated in the basement, where many have sunk into the soft ground, necessitating excavations

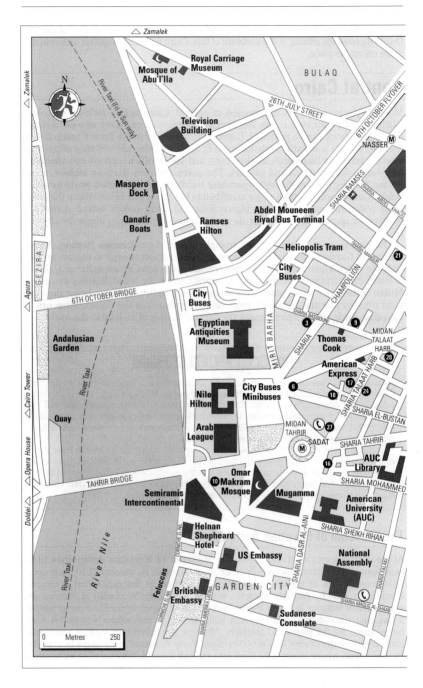

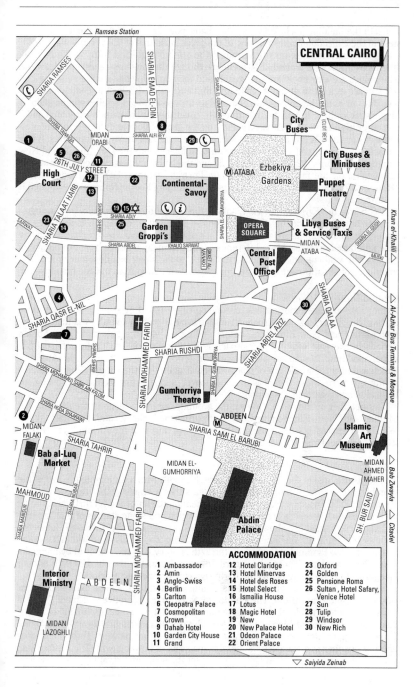

△ Ramses Station

CENTRAL CAIRO

SHARIA RAMSES

SHARIA EMAD EL-DIN

SHARIA TEWFIK

26TH JULY STREET

SHARIA ALFI BEY

MIDAN ORABI

High Court

SHARIA TALAAT HARB

SHARIA SHERIF

Garden Groppi's

SHARIA ADLY

SHARIA ABDEL

KHALIG SARWAT

SARWAT

Continental-Savoy

SHARIA EL-GUMHORRIYA

SHARIA EL-GUMHORRIYA

SHARIA EL-GUMHORRIYA

SIKKET AL MANAKH

OPERA SQUARE

Central Post Office

City Buses

City Buses & Minibuses

M ATABA   Ezbekiya Gardens

Puppet Theatre

Libya Buses & Service Taxis

MIDAN ATABA

SHARIA EL-GEISH

SHARIA DALAA

MUSKI

Khan el-Khalili ▷

△ Al-Azhar Bus Terminal & Mosque

SHARIA QASR EL-NIL

SHARIA MOHAMMED SABRI AIN KALOUM

SHARIA MOHAMMED FARID

SHARIA RUSHDI

SHARIA EL-GUMHORRIYA

SHARIA ABDEL AZIZ

Gumhorriya Theatre

SHARIA HODA SHAARAWI

MIDAN FALAKI

SHARIA TAHRIR

ABDEEN M

SHARIA SAMI EL BARUBI

MIDAN EL-GUMHORRIYA

Islamic Art Museum

MIDAN AHMED MAHER

▷ Bab Zwayla

▷ Citadel

Bab al-Luq Market

SHARIA NUBAR

MAHMOUD

SHARIA MANSUR

Interior Ministry

A B D E E N

SHARIA MOHAMMED FARID

MIDAN LAZOGHLI

Abdin Palace

SH. BUR SAID

▽ Saiyida Zeinab

ACCOMMODATION

1	Ambassador	12	Hotel Claridge	23	Oxford
2	Amin	13	Hotel Minervas	24	Golden
3	Anglo-Swiss	14	Hotel des Roses	25	Pensione Roma
4	Berlin	15	Hotel Select	26	Sultan , Hotel Safary,
5	Carlton	16	Ismailia House		Venice Hotel
6	Cleopatra Palace	17	Lotus	27	Sun
7	Cosmopolitan	18	Magic Hotel	28	Tulip
8	Crown	19	New	29	Windsor
9	Dahab Hotel	20	New Palace Hotel	30	New Rich
10	Garden City House	21	Odeon Palace		
11	Grand	22	Orient Palace		

beneath the building itself. Yet for all the chaos, poor lighting and captioning, the richness of the collection makes this one of the great museums of the world.

On entering the museum you'll probably be offered a **guided tour**, which generally lasts two hours (at around £E50 an hour), though the museum deserves at least six. The guides are extremely knowledgeable and they do help you to make sense of it all – if you are in a small group it really isn't that expensive. It's best to come on successive days or at the beginning and end of your trip, so as to get a fuller appreciation. A single visit of three to four hours suffices to cover the Tutankhamun exhibition and a few other **highlights**. The Amarna gallery on the ground floor and the selection of masterpieces on the other are all impressive, but everyone has their own favourites. A reasonable shortlist might include the cream of statuary from the Old, Middle and New Kingdoms (**Rooms 42, 32, 22 and 12**) and the Nubian funerary cache (**Room 44**) downstairs; on the first floor, the Fayoum Portraits (**Room 14**) and model figures (**Rooms 37, 32 and 27**), and, of course, the Mummy Room (**Room 56**) – though it costs extra.

A Guide to the Egyptian Museum, sold at the bookshop, lists exhibits by **catalogue** number but doesn't identify their location, so unless you're keen to look things up (labels on most exhibits are perfunctory) it's of little practical use. Exhibits are in any case numbered on at least two different systems, so many exhibits have two numbers. Should you want running commentary, it's easy to tag along behind a tour group. The first-floor **café-restaurant** is entered via the souvenir shop from outside the museum.

Ground floor

Exhibits are arranged more or less chronologically, so that by starting at the entrance and walking in a clockwise direction round the outer galleries you'll pass through the Old, Middle and New Kingdoms, before ending up with the Late and Greco-Roman periods in the east wing. This approach is historically and artistically coherent but rather plodding. A snappier alternative is to proceed instead through the Atrium – which samples the whole era of pharaonic civilization – to the superb Amarna gallery in the northern wing; then backtrack to cover sections that sound interesting, or instead head upstairs to Tutankhamun.

To suit either option, we've covered the ground floor in six sections: the Atrium, Old, Middle and New Kingdom galleries, the Amarna gallery, and the East Wing. Whichever approach you decide on, it's worth starting with the Atrium foyer (**Room 43**), where the dynastic saga begins.

THE ROTUNDA AND ATRIUM

The **Rotunda**, inside the museum entrance, kicks off with a highlighted "piece of the month" and **monumental sculptures** from various eras, notably three colossi of Ramses II (XIX Dynasty) and a statue of Amenhotep, son of the XVIII Dynasty royal architect Hapu. Also here are sixteen small wooden and stone statues of a 24th-century BC official named Ipy, showing him at various stages in his life. Just to the left of the door as you enter sits the limestone **statue of King Zoser**, installed within its *serdab* beside his Step Pyramid at Saqqara in the 27th century BC, and removed by archeologists 4600 years later. Those who regard Zoser's reign as the start of the Old Kingdom categorize the preceding era as the Early Dynastic or **Archaic Period**.

The actual forging of dynastic rule is commemorated by a famous exhibit in **Room 43**, as you enter the Atrium. The **Palette of Narmer**, a decorative version of the slate palettes used to grind kohl, records the unification of the Two Lands (c.3100 BC) by a ruler called Narmer or Menes. One side of the palette depicts him wearing the White Crown of Upper Egypt, smiting an enemy with a mace, while a falcon (Horus) ensnares another prisoner and tramples the heraldic papyrus of Lower Egypt. The reverse face shows him wearing their Red Crown to inspect the slain, and ravaging a fortress as a

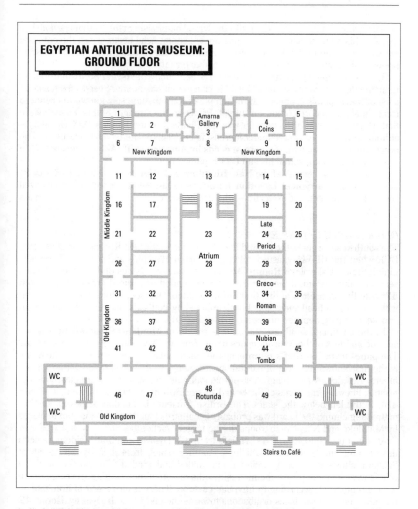

EGYPTIAN ANTIQUITIES MUSEUM: GROUND FLOOR

1
2
Amarna Gallery 3
4 Coins
5
6
7
New Kingdom
8
9
New Kingdom
10
11
12
13
14
15
Middle Kingdom
16
17
18
19
20
21
22
23
24
Late Period
25
26
27
Atrium 28
29
30
31
32
33
Greco-34 Roman
35
Old Kingdom
36
37
38
39
40
41
42
43
Nubian 44 Tombs
45
WC
46
47
48 Rotunda
49
50
WC
WC
Old Kingdom
WC
Stairs to Café

bull; dividing these tableaux are mythical beasts with entwined necks, restrained from conflict by bearded men, an arcane symbol of his political achievement. Two XII Dynasty **funerary barques** from the pyramid of Senusert III at Dahshur stand on either side of the room.

Room 33 holds **pyramidions** (pyramid capstones) from Dahshur, and more sarcophagi from the New Kingdom. Overshadowing those of Tuthmosis I and Queen Hatshepsut (before she became pharaoh), the **sarcophagus of Merneptah** is surmounted by a figure of the king as Osiris and protectively embraced from within by a relief of Nut, the sky goddess. But Merneptah's bid for immortality failed: when discovered at Tanis in 1939, his sarcophagus held the coffin of Psusennes, a XXI Dynasty ruler whose gold-sheathed mummy now lies upstairs.

At the centre of the Atrium is a **painted floor from the royal palace at Amarna** (XVIII Dynasty). A river brimming with ducks and fish is framed by reeds where waterfowl and cows amble, a fine example of the lyrical naturalism of the Amarna period. For more of this revolutionary epoch in pharaonic history, head upstairs past the **colossal statues of Amenophis III, Queen Tiy and their three daughters**, which serenely presage Akhenaten and Nefertiti in the northern wing.

But first you must pass through **Room 13**, containing the **Israel Stele** on the right. Its name derives from the boast "Israel is crushed, it has no more seed", from among a list of Merneptah's conquests at the temple of Karnak – the sole known reference to Israel in all the records of ancient Egypt. Partly on the strength of this, many believe that Merneptah, son of Ramses II, was the Pharaoh of the Exodus (XIX Dynasty) – although this view has come under increasing criticism of late (see box on p.159). The other side carries an earlier record of deeds by Amenophis III (Akhenaten's father) in the service of Amun, whom his son later repudiated.

The hall beyond is part of the **New Kingdom galleries**. Straight ahead (**Room 8**) lies a **model of a typical Egyptian house**, as excavated at Amarna, the short-lived capital of Akhenaten and Nefertiti – who are honoured with their own gallery across the hall.

OLD KINGDOM GALLERIES

The southwest corner of the ground floor is devoted to the **Old Kingdom** (c.2700–2181 BC), when the III–VI dynasties ruled Egypt from Memphis and built the Pyramids. Lining the central aisle of **Rooms 46–47** are funerary statues of deceased VIPs and servants (the custom of burying live retainers ended with the II Dynasty). In **Room 47**, note the **statuettes** of the dwarf Khnum-hotep, Overseer of the Wardrobe, a man with a deformed head and a hunchback afflicted by Pott's disease (Case B), and *shabti* (worker) figures, depicted preparing food (Case D).

To the north and south are three **slate triads of Menkaure flanked by Hathor** and the goddess of the Aphroditopolis nome, from the Mycenius valley temple at Giza. The **panel from Userkaf's temple**, by the fourth pillar on the north side of the room, is the first known example of natural scenes being used as decoration within a royal funerary edifice. A pied kingfisher, purple gallinule and sacred ibis are clearly recognizable; likewise fragments of the **beard of the Sphinx** at the end of the hall (**Room 48**), to the left below the stairs. The British Museum in London possesses another metre-long chunk; the beard was probably five metres long before it was shot to pieces by Mamluke and Napoleonic troops during target practice.

At the entrance to **Room 41**, reliefs from a V Dynasty tomb at Maidum depict a desert hunt and other rural activities. Another panel, from a V Dynasty tomb at Saqqara, shows grain being weighed out, milled and graded. The women on these reliefs wear long chemises, the men loincloths or sometimes nothing (revealing them to be circumcized, according to Egyptian custom). There is also a pair of **lion tables**, probably used for sacrifices or libations towards the end of the II Dynasty. **Room 42** boasts a superb **statue of Chephren**, his head embraced by Horus. Carved from black diorite, whose white marbling emphasizes the sinews of his knee and clenched fist, the statue comes from Chephren's valley temple at Giza. Equally arresting is the wooden **statue of Ka-aper**, a plump figure with an introspective gaze, which Arab diggers at Saqqara called "Sheikh al-Balad" because it resembled their own village headman. The **statue of a scribe**, poised for notation with an open scroll across his knees, is also memorable.

On the left-hand side of **Room 31**, six **wooden panels** from the tomb of Hesy-Re portray this senior scribe of the III Dynasty, who was also a dentist – the earliest known to history. On the wall are sandstone reliefs from Wadi Maraghah, near the ancient turquoise mines of Sinai. Twin limestone **statues of Ra-Nufer** signify his dual role as Memphite high priest of Ptah and Sokar; aside from their wigs and kilts, they look virtually identical. Both were created in the royal workshops, possibly by the same artist.

Room 32 is dominated by life-size seated statues of Prince Rahotep and Princess Nefert, from their *mastaba* at Maidum (IV Dynasty). His skin is painted brick-red, hers a creamy yellow – a distinction common in Egyptian art. Nefert wears a wig and diadem and swathes herself in a diaphanous wrap; the prince is simply clad in a waist cloth. Look out for the tableaux of the dwarf Seneb and his family. Embraced by his wife, this Overseer of the Wardrobe seems contented; his naked children hold their fingers to their lips. Nearby hangs a perfectly observed, vividly stylized mural, known as the Maidum Geese (III/IV Dynasty). Although the heyday of the Old Kingdom is poorly represented by a statue of Ti, its twilight era boasts the first known metal sculptures (c.2300 BC): two statues of Pepi I and his son, made by hammering sheets of copper over wooden armatures.

MIDDLE KINGDOM GALLERIES

With Room 26 you enter the Middle Kingdom, when centralized authority was restored and pyramid-building resumed under the XII Dynasty (c.1991–1786 BC). A relic of the previous era of civil wars (termed the First Intermediate Period) sits on the right, glum-faced. Endowed with hulking feet to suggest power, and black skin, crossed arms and a curly beard to link it to Osiris, the statue of Mentuhotpe Nebhepetre was buried near his funerary shrine at Deir el-Bahri and discovered by Howard Carter – whose horse fell through the roof. If the Mummy of Dagi were still around, it could use the pair of "eyes" carved inside its sarcophagus to espy two statues of Queen Nofret wearing a sheath dress and a Hathor wig, by the entrance to Room 21.

The statuettes at the back of Room 22 are striking for the uncharacteristic expressiveness of their faces. Also in the room are likenesses of Amenemhat III and Senusert I, but your attention is grabbed by the burial chamber of Harhotpe from Deir el-Bahri, covered inside with pictorial objects, charms and texts. Surrounding the chamber are ten limestone statues of Senusert from his pyramid complex at Lisht, stiffly formal in contrast to his cedarwood figure in the case to your right as you enter the room. The sides of these statues' thrones bear variations of the *sema-tawy* symbol of unification: Hapy the Nile-god, or Horus and Seth, entwining the heraldic plants of the Two Lands.

This basic imperative of statecraft might explain the unique double statue of Amenemhat III in Room 16. Personified as the Nile god bringing his people fish on trays, the dual figures may represent Upper and Lower Egypt, or the living king and his deified *ka*. Five lion-headed sphinxes with human faces watch your exit from the Middle Kingdom; the anarchic Second Intermediate Period and the Hyksos invasion go uncommemorated.

NEW KINGDOM GALLERIES

With Room 11 you pass into the New Kingdom, an era of renewed pharaonic power and imperial expansion under the XVIII and XIX dynasties (c.1567-1200 BC). Egypt's African and Asian empires were forged by Tuthmosis III, who had long been frustrated while his unwarlike stepmother, Hatshepsut, ruled as pharaoh. From one of the Osiride pillars of her great temple at Deir el-Bahri comes a commanding crowned head of Hatshepsut, while in Room 12 you'll find a grey schist statue of Tuthmosis III, and other masterpieces of XVIII Dynasty art. The Hathor Shrine from Tuthmosis III's ruined temple at Deir el-Bahri contains a statue of the goddess in her bovine form, emerging reborn from a papyrus swamp. Tuthmosis stands beneath her cow's head, and is suckled as an infant in the fresco behind Hathor's statue, overshadowed by a star-spangled ceiling. To the right of the shrine is a block statue of Hatshepsut's vizier, Senenmut, and her daughter Neferure: the trio's relationship has inspired much speculation. From the same period comes a section of the Deir el-Bahri "Punt reliefs" (in the second niche on the left), showing the obese Queen of Punt and her donkey, observed by Hatshepsut during her expedition to that fabled land.

By the left-hand wall, two **statues** of a man named **Amenhotep** portray him as a young scribe of humble birth, and as an octogenarian priest, honoured for his direction of massive works like the Colossi of Memnon. Between Amenhotep's figures stands a grey granite **statue of Tutankhamun as Khonsu** (with the side lock of youth), removed from the temple of the moon-god at Karnak.

Before turning the corner into the northern wing, you encounter two **lion-headed statues of Sekhmet**, found at Karnak. **Sphinxes** with the heads of Hatshepsut and her family dominate the central aisle of **Rooms 6** and **7**. Some of the reliefs along the southern wall come from the Tomb of Maya at Saqqara, which was uncovered last century but subsequently lost until its rediscovery in 1986. From **Room 8**, most visitors check out the Amarna gallery (see below) before walking through the cast of statues and sarcophagi in **Room 9**. Many of the ancient **coins** in **Room 4** bear the head of Alexander the Great.

To the left of the stairs, in **Room 10**, note the relief on a block from Ramses II's temple at Memphis, which shows him subjugating Egypt's foes. In a motif repeated on dozens of temple pylons, the king grabs the hair of a Libyan, Nubian and Syrian, and wields an axe. Ramessid pharaohs who never fought a battle were especially keen on such **reliefs**. The room ends with a pun: a statue of Ramses II as a child, finger in mouth, holding a plant while protected by the sun-god *Re* or *Ra*, which combines with the word for child (*mes*) and the word for the plant (*sw*) to form his name. From Room 10 you can follow the New Kingdom into the east wing (covered below), or climb the stairs to the Tutankhamun galleries on the upper floor.

THE AMARNA GALLERY

Room 3 focuses on the **Amarna period**: a break with centuries of tradition which barely outlasted the reign of Pharaoh Akhenaten (c.1379–1362 BC) and Queen Nefertiti. Rejecting Amun and the other deities of Thebes, they decreed the supremacy of a single god, the Aten; built a new capital at Amarna in Middle Egypt to escape the old bureaucracy; and left enigmatic works of art that provoke a reaction.

Staring down from the walls are four **colossi of Akhenaten**, whose attenuated skull and face, flaring lips and nostrils, rounded thighs and belly are suggestive of a hermaphrodite or a primeval earth goddess. Because these characteristics are carried over to the figures of his wife and daughters on certain **steles** (in the left-hand niche and the cases in front of it) and tomb reliefs, it has been argued that the Amarna style pandered to some physical abnormality in Akhenaten (or the royal family) – the captions hint at perversions. Others retort that the exquisite **head of Nefertiti**, in Berlin, proves that it was just a stylistic device. Another feature of Amarna art was its note of intimacy: a **stele of the royal family** (numbered #167) portrays Akhenaten dandling their eldest daughter, Meritaten, whilst Nefertiti cradles her sisters. For the first time in Egyptian art, breakfast was depicted. The Amarna focus on this world rather than the afterlife infused traditional subjects with new vitality – witness the freer brush strokes on the fragments of a **marsh scene**. The **Amarna Letters** (Case A) record pleas for troops to aid the pharaoh's vassals in Palestine, the impact of his death, and Nefertiti's search for allies against those who pressed Tutankhamun to reverse the Amarna revolution. Originally baked into earthen "envelopes" for delivery, these cuneiform tablets were stored in the Foreign Office archives at Amarna.

The carnelian, gold and glass-inlaid **coffin** back in **Room 8** is usually ascribed to Smenkhkare, who ruled alongside Akhenaten in his final years and is variously identified as the pharaoh's son-in-law, brother or lover – or as Nefertiti herself (see p.268).

THE EAST WING

As an inducement to follow the New Kingdom into the east wing, **Room 15** has a sexy statue of the wife of Nakht Min (Case 195). Inside **Room 14** is a huge alabaster **stat-**

ue of Seti I, whose sensitive facial modelling recalls Nefertiti's head. Originally, it would have worn a *nemset* headdress like the one on Tutankhamun's funerary mask. More striking, however, is the restored pink granite triple statue of Ramses III being crowned by Horus and Set, representing order and chaos respectively.

Waning with the XX Dynasty and expiring with the XXI, the New Kingdom was followed by the so-called **Late Period** of mostly foreign rulers. **Room 25** contains a granite **head of Taharqa**, the XXV Dynasty Nubian king who conquered Thebes and is mentioned in the Bible (II Kings 19:9). From the same period comes an alabaster **statue of Amenirdis the Elder**, whom the pharaoh made divine votaress of Amun to watch over the Theban priesthood (**Room 30**). Dressed as a New Kingdom queen, Amenirdis wears a falcon headdress crowned with *uraei*, originally topped by a Hathor crown bearing a solar disc and horns. Of the diverse **statues of deities** in **Room 24**, it's Taweret (or Tweri), the pregnant-hippopotamus goddess of childbirth, that most visitors remember.

Rooms 34 and **35** cover the **Greco-Roman Period** (332 BC onwards), when Classical art engaged with Ancient Egyptian symbolism. The meld of styles is typified by the bizarre **statues** (especially that of Alexander II at the threshold of the room) **and sarcophagi** in **Room 49**. Even if you decide to skip the rest of the wing, it's worth visiting **Room 44**, devoted to **artefacts from royal Nubian tombs** south of Abu Simbel. The burial of Blemmye royalty involved the strangulation of servants and butchery of horses. An equine skeleton, saddlery, crowns and weaponry were unearthed in graves at Qustul and Ballana, where the Blemmye still worshipped Isis and Horus long after Egypt had become Christian.

First floor

The upper floor is dominated by the Tutankhamun galleries, which occupy the best part of two wings. Once you've seen Tut's treasures, everything but the Mummy Room and the display of masterpieces seems lacklustre – even though the other galleries feature artefacts just as fine as those downstairs. Come back another day and check them out.

TUTANKHAMUN GALLERIES

The funerary impedimenta of the boy-king **Tutankhamun** numbers 1700 items and fills a dozen rooms. Given the brevity of his reign (1361–1352 BC) and the paucity of his tomb in the Valley of the Kings, one's mind boggles at the treasure that must have been stashed with great pharaohs like Ramses or Seti. Tutankhamun merely fronted the Theban counter-revolution that effaced Amarna and restored the cult of Amun and its priesthood to their former primacy. However, the influence of Amarna is apparent in some of the **exhibits**, which are laid out roughly as they were packed into his tomb: chests and statues (**Room 45**) preceding furniture (**Rooms 40, 35, 30, 25, 20, 15 and 10**), shrines (**Rooms 9–7**) and gold appurtenances (**Room 3**). Adjacent to this are jewellery (**Room 4**) and other treasures from diverse tombs (**Rooms 2 and 13**). Most visitors make a beeline for the last four (2, 3 and 4 close fifteen minutes early), ignoring the sequence just outlined. If that includes you, skip ahead through the following rundown.

When Carter's team penetrated the sealed corridor in 1922 they found an antechamber stuffed with caskets and detritus ransacked by robbers, and two life-size **ka statues of Tutankhamun**, whose black skin symbolized his rebirth. Pass between these into **Room 45** to see a **shrine of Anubis**, carried in his cortege: the protector of the dead as a vigilant jackal with gilded ears and silver claws. To ensure quality of afterlife, Tut also packed an ebony and ivory **gaming set** for playing *senet* (a game similar to draughts), and a host of **shabti figures** to fulfil any tasks the gods might set him. The king's clothes and unguents were stored in two magnificent **chests**. On the lid and

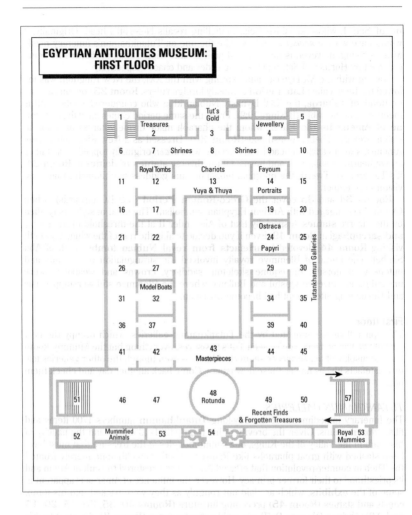

EGYPTIAN ANTIQUITIES MUSEUM: FIRST FLOOR

sides of the "Painted Chest", he is depicted hunting ostriches and antelopes and devastating ranks of Syrians in his war chariot, larger than life; the end panels show him trampling other foes in the guise of the sphinx. By contrast, the lid of the "Inlaid Chest" in **Room 40** bears a gentle, Amarna-style vignette of Ankhesenamun (daughter of Nefertiti and Akhenaten) offering lotus, papyrus and mandrake to her husband, framed by poppies, pomegranates and cornflowers. Note the **Amarna toilet seat** in the corridor and the **statues of Tutankhamun hunting with a harpoon** between **Rooms 35 and 30**. The **golden shrine** covered in repoussé scenes of conjugal harmony once held statues of Tut and his wife Ankhesenamun that were stolen in antiquity.

Next come **thrones and chairs (Rooms 30, 25 and 20)**. On the back rest of the gilded throne with winged-serpent arms and clawed feet, the royal couple relax in the rays of the Aten, their names given in the Amarna form – dating it to the time when

Tutankhamun still observed the Amarna heresy. The "ecclesiastical throne"(the prototype for episcopal thrones of the Christian Church) is exquisitely inlaid with ebony and gold, but looks uncomfortable. More typical of pharaonic design are the wooden *Heb* chair and footstools, and a commode that wouldn't look amiss at Harrods. **Room 30** features a **gilded trumpet** (last played in 1939) and **"Prisoners' Canes"**, whose ebony (Nubian) and ivory (Asian) inlaid figures symbolize the unity of north and south.

From ivory headrests in **Room 10**, it's a natural progression to **gilded beds** dedicated to the gods whose animal forms are carved on their bedposts (**Room 15**). Similar figures protect the golden **canopic chest** that held the jars containing the pharaoh's viscera (**Room 9**). Ranged along **Rooms 7 and 8** are four boxy **gilded shrines**, which fitted one inside another like Russian dolls, enclosing Tutankhamun's sarcophagus.

The always packed-out **Room 3** contains **Tutankhamun's gold**, some of which may be on tour abroad. Assuming it's in Cairo, the centrepiece is his haunting **funerary mask**, wearing a *nemset* headdress inlaid with lapis lazuli, quartz and obsidian. His mummiform **coffin**, adorned with the same materials, comes a close second; hands clasped in the Osiride position, the figure is protected by the cloisonné feathers of Wadjet, Nekhbet, Isis and Nephthys. On Tutankhamun's mummy (which remains in his tomb at the Valley of the Kings) were placed scores of **amulets**, a cloisonné **corselet** spangled with glass and carnelian, gem-encrusted **pectorals** and a pair of golden **sandals** – all displayed here.

The **Jewellery Room** next door is equally overpowering. A VI Dynasty golden **head of a falcon** (once attached to a copper body) from Hieraconpolis rates as the star attraction, but there's stiff competition from the **crown and necklaces of Princess Khnumyt** and the **diadem and pectorals of Princess Set-Hathor**. Buried near the latter at Dahshur were the **amethyst belt and anklet of Mereret**, another XII Dynasty princess. The ceremonial **axe of Ahmosis**, commemorating his expulsion of the Hyksos from Egypt, was buried in the tomb of his mother, Queen Ahhotep. From the same cache (found by Mariette in 1859) came a hinged bracelet of lapis lazuli and the bizarre **golden flies** of the Order of Valour – bug-eyed decorations for bravery.

Room 2 displays two royal caches. The **furniture of Queen Hetepheres** has been expertly reconstructed from heaps of gold and rotten wood. As the wife of Snofru and mother of Cheops, she was buried near her son's pyramid at Giza with a sedan chair, gold vessels and a canopied bed. From the XXI–XXII Dynasty, when northern Egypt was ruled from the Delta, comes the **Treasure of Tanis**. Of the three royal caches unearthed by Montet in 1939, the richest was that of Psusennes I, whose electrum coffin was found inside the sarcophagus of Merneptah (see downstairs). His gold necklace is made from rows of discs, in the New Kingdom style.

Between **Room 8** and the Atrium stand two wooden **chariots**, found in the antechamber of Tutankhamun's tomb. Intended for state occasions, their gilded stucco reliefs show Asiatics and Nubians in bondage; pharaonic war chariots were lighter and stronger. The finest **objects from the tomb of Yuya and Thuya (Room 13)** are Thuya's gem-inlaid gilded mask, their mummiform coffins and statues of the couple. As parents of Queen Tiy (wife of Amenophis III), they were buried in the Valley of the Kings; their tomb was found intact in the late nineteenth century.

Having finished with Tut, you can either head down the western wing to the Mummy Room, or tackle the other galleries (see below).

MUMMIES

The southern end of the museum's upper floor harbours two rooms full of mummies. **Room 53** exhibits **mummified animals and birds** from necropolises across Egypt, evincing the strength of animal cults towards the end of the pagan era, when devotees embalmed everything from bulls to mice and fish.

Modern Egyptians regard these relics of ancestral superstition with equanimity, but the exhibition of human remains offended many – hence Sadat's closure of the famous **Mummy Room** (previously Room 52) in 1981. Since then, the Egyptian Museum and the Getty Institute have been working to restore the badly decomposed royal mummies. The results of their work are now displayed in Room 56, where you have to buy another ticket (£E40, students £E20; closes twenty minutes early) to see them. Altogether eleven royal mummies are displayed here (clearly labelled and arranged chronologically anticlockwise around the room), including the mortal remains of some of the most famous pharaohs, in particular the great conquerors of the XIX Dynasty, Seti I and his son Ramses II, the latter looking rather slighter in the flesh than the massive statue of him outside the train station. Also here is Ramses's son, Merneptah, whom many believe to be the pharaoh of the Biblical exodus (see box p.159). Unless you have a keen interest in mummies, it's probably not worth the high price you have to pay to see them – a reaction echoed by many readers' letters.

All the mummies are kept in sealed cases at controlled humidity, and most of them look remarkably peaceful – Tuthmosis II and Tuthmosis IV could almost be sleeping – and many still have hair. Queen Henuttawi's curly locks and handsome face suggest Nubian origin. In deference to the deceased, no photography or guiding are allowed, and the low hum of *sotto voce* chatter is only broken by the attendant periodically calling for "Silence, please! The mummies were found in the royal cache at Deir el-Bahri (see p.348) and in a spare chamber in the tomb of Amenophis II (see p.345), where they had been reburied during the XXI Dynasty to protect them from grave robbers. For a description of the mummification process, see p.336; and for a graphic demonstration of the hollowness of a mummy, take a look up Ramses V's right nostril – from this angle you'll be able to see straight out though the hole in his skull.

THE OTHER GALLERIES

To view the other galleries in approximate chronological order you should start at **Room 43** (overlooking the Atrium) and proceed in a clockwise direction, as on the ground floor. However, since most visitors wander in from Tut's galleries, we've described the western and eastern wings from that standpoint.

Starting with the **western wing**, notice the "**Heart Scarabs**" that were placed upon the throats of mummies, bearing a spell that implored the deceased's heart not to bear witness against him or her during the Judgement of Osiris (**Room 6**). **Room 12**'s hoard of **objects from XVIII Dynasty royal tombs** includes the mummies of a child and a gazelle (Case I); priestly wigs and wig boxes (Case L); two leopards from the funerary cache of Amenophis II; and the chariot of Tuthmosis IV. **Room 17** holds the **contents of private tombs**, notably that of Sennedjem, from the Workmen's village near the Valley of the Kings. With skills honed on royal tombs, Sennedjem carved himself a stylish vault; its door depicts him playing *senet*. The sarcophagus of his son Khonsu carries a design showing the lions of Today and Yesterday supporting the rising sun, while Anubis embalms his mummy under the protection of Isis and Nephthys.

While the corridor displays **canopic chests and coffins**, the inner rooms feature **Middle Kingdom models**. From Meketre's tomb at Thebes come marvellous domestic figures and tableaux: a woman carrying wine jars on her head, peasants netting fish from reed boats, and cattle being driven past an estate-owner (**Room 27**). Compare the fully crewed model boats in Case F of **Room 32** with the unmanned solar barques for voyaging through eternity, in Case E. In the corridor outside stands an unusual *ka* statue of Pharaoh Hor, mounted on a sliding base to signify his posthumous wanderings. Model-soldier buffs will delight in the phalanxes of Nubian archers and Egyptian pikemen from the tomb of Prince Mesehti at Assyut, in **Room 37**.

The museum's **southern wing** is best seen at a trot. The middle section contains a **model of a funerary complex** showing how the pyramids and their temples related to the Nile (**Room 48**), and the square **leather funerary tent** of an XXI Dynasty queen (by the southeast stairway). More striking are two exhibitions in the central section: **recent finds and forgotten treasures**, which are showcased outside **Room 54**; and a **selection of masterpieces** nearer the Atrium. The latter includes a panel of blue faïence tiles from Zoser's burial hall at Saqqara; a stone head of Queen Tiy that prefigures the Amarna style; and "dancing dwarves" modelled on equatorial pygmies (in the same case).

If approached from the north, the **eastern wing** begins with **Room 14**, containing a couple of mummies and the superbly lifelike "**Fayoum Portraits**" found by Petrie at Hawara. Painted in encaustic (pigments mixed into molten wax) while their sitters were alive, the portraits were glued onto Greco-Roman mummies (100–250 AD). The staggering diversity of Egypt's pantheon by the late pagan era is suggested by the **statues of deities** in **Room 19**. Next door and the room after are devoted to **ostraca and papyri**. Ostraca were limestone flakes or potshards, on which were scratched sketches or ephemeral writing; papyrus was used for finished artwork and lasting **manuscripts**. Besides the *Book of the Dead* (**Room 24**) and the *Book of AmDuat* (depicting the Weighing of the Heart ceremony), note the *Satirical Papyrus*, showing mice being served by cats in a parody of offerings to the gods. **Room 29** also displays a scribe's writing kit and an artist's paints and brushes. Although the **miscellaneous and everyday objects** in **Rooms 39 and 34** are hardly thrilling, it's worth popping into **Room 44** to see the faïence panels from the palaces of Ramses II and III.

Midan Tahrir and around

The centre of modern Cairo is a concrete assertion of national pride, which threatens to burst as it pumps traffic around the city. Created on the site of Britain's Qasr el-Nil Barracks after the 1952 revolution, **Midan Tahrir** (Liberation Square) embodies the drawbacks of subsequent political trends. During the 1960s, two bureaucratic monoliths and several transport depots responsible for much of Egypt and all of Greater Cairo were concentrated here, as Nasser adopted Soviet-style centralization. A decade later, Sadat rejected his mentor's "Arab Socialism" in favour of an *Infitah* (Open Door) to Western capitalism, causing private car ownership to soar almost as fast as Cairo's population. Impending gridlock was only averted by digging a metro; in spite of which, buses and roads are still grossly overcrowded.

The entrances to **Sadat metro station** serve as pedestrian underpasses linking these depots and buildings with the main roads leading off Tahrir. Despite clear labelling in English, it's easy to go astray in the maze of subways and surface at the wrong location. Many Cairenes prefer to take their chances crossing by road – a nerve-wracking experience for newcomers. Though some **landmarks** are obvious, rooftop billboards and neon signs flanking the end of streets like Talaat Harb (between *Leccio* and *Sprite*) or Qasr el-Nil (beside the *Cleopatra Hotel*) also help with orientation. To watch the square over tea, try one of the Arab cafés beneath the *Saudia* sign; the one with a new brick facade was bombed by Islamic radicals in 1993.

Tahrir landmarks

Abutting the grounds of the Antiquities Museum to the south, the blue and white **Nile Hilton** – the first modern "international" hotel built along the Corniche – stretches down to where the Tahrir Bridge runs between guardian lions towards Gezira Island. The tan-coloured edifice just beyond the *Hilton*, built during the 1960s to serve as the secretariat of the Arab League, now stands as a vestige of the time when Egypt was acknowledged leader of the "progressive" Arab cause. After Sadat's treaty with Israel, the headquarters of the **Arab League** moved to Tunis and most of its members severed relations with Egypt. Mubarak's policy of rapprochement was finally rewarded in

1992, when the League returned to Cairo and, with it, posses of limos and gun-toting guards. Further down the Corniche, roughly opposite the new **Helnan Shepheard Hotel**, was the site of the Thomas Cook landing stage, where generations of tourists embarked on Nile cruises and General Gordon's ill-fated expedition set off for Khartoum in 1883.

Across the Tahrir Bridge ramp from the Arab League building, Egypt's Ministry of Foreign Affairs is less conspicuous than the **Omar Makram Mosque**, where funeral receptions for deceased VIPs are held in brightly coloured marquees. But dominating the southern end of Midan Tahrir is a concave office block that inspires shuddering memories: **the Mugamma**. A "fraternal gift" from the Soviet Union in the 1960s, this Kafkaesque warren of gloomy corridors, dejected queues and idle bureaucrats houses the public departments of the Interior, Health and Education ministries, and the Cairo Governorate. How many of the 50,000 people visiting *El-Mugamma* each day suffer nervous breakdowns from sheer frustration is anyone's guess; an African supposedly flung himself through a window several years ago. (For advice on handling the Mugamma, see p.236.) On the corner of Sharia Qasr al-Aini, opposite the Mugamma, a handsome pseudo-Islamic facade masks the old campus of the **American University in Cairo** (entered via Sheikh Rihan Street; the Library is one block northeast). Responsible for publishing some of the best research on Egypt in the English language, the AUC is also a Western-style haven for wealthy Egyptian youths and US students doing a year abroad, its shady gardens and preppy ambience seeming utterly remote from everyday life in Cairo. Visitors might experience a premonitory shiver that Iran's gilded youth probably looked pretty similar before the Islamic Revolution. Egyptian Marxists and Islamic fundamentalists regard the AUC as a tool of US and Zionist imperialism.

Five or so minutes' walk north from the main AUC entrance, near the University Library at **Midan Falaki** (or walk along Sharia Tahrir from the square), you'll find a pedestrian bridge of the kind that circumvented Midan Tahrir before its subways were dug. Off to the right, a broad street awash with fruit and vegetable stalls runs alongside **Bab al-Luq market**. Not a place for the squeamish, and overpriced compared to other markets, it's still an interesting spot to watch haggling and gossiping over trussed poultry or tea and *sheeshas*. It also holds a number of extremely cheap eating places. Across the bridge, a coffee merchant's store fills the square with the fine aroma of cardamom-spiced *'ahwa mahaweka*.

Moving on from Tahrir you can continue south and east to explore the Garden City and the Abdin quarter (see below), or walk back to the square and take either Sharia Talaat Harb or Qasr el-Nil to head for the shops and restaurants of downtown Cairo (see p.106).

Garden City and the Abdin quarter

Spreading south from the square towards Old Cairo and the Islamic districts are two very different, yet historically interlinked, quarters. Deluxe hotels follow the Corniche towards Roda Island, separating the old diplomatic quarter from the Nile just as Sharia Qasr al-Aini divides the leafy winding streets of **Garden City** from the grid of blocks where Egypt's ministries and parliament are located. Like a spider in its web, the ex-royal, now presidential Abdin Palace lends its name to the convoluted **Abdin quarter** that merges into Saiyida Zeinab.

Since Garden City and Abdin meet around Midan Tahrir, both can claim to host Egypt's **National Assembly** (*Maglis al-Shaab*). During the late 1980s, Cairenes were agog over abusive exchanges and fisticuffs in parliament, as the hardline Minister Zaki Badr replied to allegations of torture, wrongful arrest and bugging by the **Interior Ministry**, sited a couple of blocks to the west in Abdin. Badr has long since gone, but the ministry's repressive activities continue: Amnesty International reports cases of torture from Alexandria to Aswan. The road on which both buildings stand is barricaded at either end against suicide car bombers, floodlit at night and perpetually guarded by machine-gunners.

Garden City

When Ibrahim Pasha's al-Dubbarah Palace was demolished in 1906, British planners developed the site for diplomatic and residential use, laying down crescents and cul-de-sacs to create the illusion of lanes meandering through a **Garden City**. Until the Corniche road was ploughed through, embassies and villas boasted gardens running down to the Nile; nowadays, fishermen's shacks and vegetable plots line the river's edge.

Aside from the traffic, it's a pleasant walk along the Corniche towards Roda Island, past a cluster of **feluccas** available for Nile cruises (see p.222). Further inland, Art Deco residences mingle with heavily guarded **embassies** (for addresses, see p.237). Despite being outsized by the US – whose embassy here is the largest in the world – the British enjoy grander buildings with more spacious grounds, a legacy of their pre-eminence in the days of Lord Cromer and Sir Miles Lampson. The main artery, running south from Tahrir towards Old Cairo, is **Sharia Qasr al-Aini**, which goes from riches to rags, banks and villas yielding to cheap backstreet eating places near the Sayala Bridge. A bygone "Palace of the Spring" lends its name to the mixed neigh-bourhood between Garden City and the slaughterhouse district (see "Old Cairo", p.162), and to Cairo's largest public **hospital**, erected in the 1960s, where Yusuf Idris practised as a doctor before devoting himself to writing (see "Books" in Contexts chap-ter). **Roda Island** and the mainland **further south** are described under "Old Cairo" (see pp.163–165).

WAR STORIES

During World War II, much of Garden City was commandeered by military organiza-tions. At GHQ – which rapidly outgrew "Grey Pillars" to fill an entire neighbourhood – **R.A. Bagnold** proposed the formation of the Long Range Desert Group, whose daring raids (with David Stirling's SAS) behind enemy lines were the genesis of a martial leg-end.

On Sharia Rustrum, the Middle Eastern headquarters of the **SOE** (Special Operations Executive) plotted operations from Yugoslavia to Libya, involving Fitzroy McLean, Evelyn Waugh and Patrick Leigh Fermor, among others. At no. 13 Sharia Ibrahim Pasha Naguib, novelist **Olivia Manning** and her husband Reggie (the model for Guy Pringle in *Fortunes of War*) lived beneath Stirling's brother, Peter, who hosted wild parties in a flat crammed with captured ammunition.

British sang-froid only cracked once, when the Afrika Korps seemed poised to seize Alexandria and advance on Cairo. On **"Ash Wednesday"** (July 1, 1942) GHQ and the Embassy burned their files, blanketing Garden City with smoke. Half-charred classified documents were wafted aloft to fall on the streets, where peanut vendors twisted them into little cones.

The Abdin quarter

With hindsight, several rulers must have regretted that Ismail moved the seat of state from the Citadel to what is now the **Abdin quarter**, where tenements surrounded the palace enclave long ago. When Ismail began building the European-style **Abdin Palace**, in the 1860s, a worldwide scarcity of cotton had raised the value of Egypt's export crop to £25 million a year, and his own civil list was double that of Queen Victoria. After prices slumped and creditors gathered, the palace was bequeathed to his successors together with vast debts that reduced them – and Egypt – to near vassal status.

The nadir of humiliation came in February 1942, when British armoured cars burst through the palace gates and Ambassador Lampson demanded that King Farouk sack the prime minister or abdicate himself. It was this that resolved Nasser to assemble the Free Officers, seize power and redeem Egypt. Ten years later, as Farouk displayed his long-awaited son at a magnificent reception, rioters burned downtown Cairo within earshot of the palace; six months afterwards, the Free Officers deposed him and declared a Republic.

Another mass protest – against Sadat's abolition of subsidies on bread and other essentials in January 1977 – actually happened outside the palace on **Midan el-Gumhorriya** (Square of the Republic). Chanting "Thieves of the *Infitah*, the people are famished", crowds overwhelmed Central Security and rampaged against symbols of wealth and authority until the subsidies were restored. Still the state headquarters of Egypt's president, the Abdin Palace is flanked to the north by the Cairo Governorate building. During Ramadan a large tent is pitched in the middle of the square, in which virtuoso performers recite the Koran.

Behind the palace grounds are blocks of crumbling tenements where families lower baskets from the upper windows to passing street vendors. The neighbourhood is chiefly residential, with many Nubians and Sudanese, several street **markets** (around Midan Lazoghli) and a reputation for *ghorzas* (see p.119). **Sharia Bur Said** (Port Said), which divides it from the Saiyida Zeinab quarter, marks the course of the Khalig al-Masri canal that was filled in early last century after the Aswan Dam reduced Cairo's dependency on Nile floodwater. Various stretches of Bur Said carry buses and minibuses to diverse locations around the city, but you need to know the routes well to take advantage of them. Easier to suss is the Saiyida Zeinab to Matariyya tram service, which runs along the street.

Downtown Cairo

The layout of **downtown Cairo** goes back to the 1860s, when Khedive Ismail had it rebuilt in the style of Haussman's new Paris boulevards to impress dignitaries attending the inauguration of the Suez Canal. Cutting an X-shaped swathe through the area are the main throughfares of **Talaat Harb** and **Qasr el-Nil** (each about 1km long), which contain most of the city's budget hotels, airlines and travel agencies. Almost every visitor gravitates here at least once, while many spend a lot of time checking out the restaurants, shops and bars. Inevitably, hustling tourists is a major industry; the guys touting for perfume shops are especially adept at distinguishing gullible newcomers from *khawaga*s who've been around a while. But don't brush off every approach as a sales ploy – passers-by may bid you "Welcome to Egypt" with no motive other than courtesy.

Although overshadowed by Talaat Harb and Qasr el-Nil, four streets running east off the northern end of Talaat Harb are equally integral to downtown Cairo: **Sharia Abdel Khaliq Sarwat**, **Sharia Adly**, **26th July Street** and **Sharia Alfi Bey**.

Talaat Harb

Fifty years ago, Suleyman Pasha Street was lined with trees and sidewalk cafés, a gracious ornament to the Europeanized city centre built in the late nineteenth century. Since being renamed **Sharia Talaat Harb**, the street's once elegant facades have been effaced by grime and neglect, tacky billboards and glitzy facings – yet its vitality and diversity have never been greater. Overflowing the pavements, thousands of Cairenes window-shop, pop into juice bars and surge out of cinemas. Imelda Marcos would drool over the profusion of shoe shops, some devoted to butterfly creations fit only for a boudoir. In the shadows of Western-style affluence, beggars lie with palms outstretched and barefoot urchins hump garbage pails onto donkey carts – an accepted part of Cairo's streetlife.

Almost every tourist seeks a break from the crowds and culture shock at one of three places along the initial stretch of Talaat Harb. **Felfela's Restaurant**, just around the corner of Hoda Shaarawi, is followed shortly by the **Café Riche**, where the Free Officers supposedly plotted their overthrow of Egypt's monarchy; another version maintains that they communicated over the telephone in **Groppi's**, a famous coffee house on **Midan Talaat Harb**, the intersection with Qasr el-Nil. Here stands a statue of Talaat Harb (1876–1941), nationalist lawyer and founder of the National Bank.

Up to this point traffic runs both ways, but thereafter northbound vehicles are restricted to Qasr el-Nil; because the streets cross over, it's easy to take the wrong one by mistake if you're on foot. Between Midan Talaat Harb and 26th July Street, Talaat Harb abounds in takeaways, **cinemas** and cheap **hotels**.

Qasr el-Nil

Although the racecourse that once ran beside **Sharia Qasr el-Nil** disappeared last century, northbound traffic tries to rival bygone derbys, and the shops, though functional enough, play second fiddle to Talaat Harb's. Heading up from Tahrir you'll pass American Express and the l'Orientaliste Bookshop before coming upon a stall devoted to foreign newspapers and magazines, outside *Groppi's*.

Two blocks beyond Midan Talaat Harb, a side street on the right allows a glimpse of the carmine and gold Art Nouveau **Cosmopolitan Hotel**, an elegant leftover from colonial times. Kalashnikov-toting police and Central Security troops are ubiquitous in downtown Cairo, but never threatening. An amiable bunch lounge outside the **National Bank** on the corner of Sharia Sherif.

Harbouring bookshops, bars and health clubs, some of the **backstreets** here also serve as **outdoor mosques**. For midday prayers on Fridays, the one running into Abdel Khaliq Sarwat is carpeted with green mats where the faithful perform a succession of *rekas*, swaying their heads, raising their hands and prostrating themselves while reciting parts of the Koran.

Sharia Abdel Khaliq Sarwat and Sharia Adly

After the Khan el-Khalili bazaar, **Sharia Abdel Khaliq Sarwat** – the first major street you reach after the Midan Talaat intersection – has the city's highest concentration of **jewellers**, particularly around the Midan Opera end, where a street of goldsmiths called Sikket al-Manakh leads off to the south. Because their marked prices are higher, canny shoppers can use them as benchmarks when haggling for lower rates in the Khan (see p.228).

The vast Edwardian neo-Gothic apartment block at the junction of Abdel Khaliq Sarwat and Mohammed Farid frowns its northern face upon **Sharia Adly**. Heading east along this street you'll find a buff, temple-like edifice with Central Security guards posing on a Cecil B. de Mille-like stairway. The arborial reliefs on its columns represent the Tree of Manna whence Heaven's bounty fell upon the Israelites, for the building is Cairo's last working **synagogue**. Discreetly open on Saturday mornings, its opulent marbled interior receives few worshippers these days, the city's Jewish community having dwindled to around fifty, all aged. For Rosh Hashana and Passover a rabbi is flown in from Tel Aviv; otherwise, there's only the melancholy custodian and his Christian friend.

One block along is Cairo's main **tourist office**, with the **tourist police** sited above; for details of both, see p.76. Across the road, **Garden Groppi's** spacious patio and panelled salon are in contrast to the *Groppi's* on Midan Talaat Harb. During World War II, this was one of the few posh establishments open to ordinary British troops – "other ranks", as they were called – who the military top brass had decided should not mix socially with officers. Its high prices nonetheless ensured that officers, Egyptian *pashas* and their fur-draped Levantine mistresses predominated. Nowadays it's frequented by courting couples, journalists and bourgeois matrons.

Another colonial institution that bit the dust still survives in moribund form north of Sharia Adly's termination at Midan Opera. Before World War I, tourists could buy "anything from a boa constrictor to a fully grown leopard" outside the grandiose **Continental-Savoy Hotel** – where one scandalized missionary insisted on providing trousers to cover the genitals of a performing baboon. Orde Wingate, the eccentric military genius who liberated Abyssinia from Italian rule for Emperor Haile Selassie, attempted suicide in his room here.

26th July Street and Sharia Alfi Bey

The busiest, widest thoroughfare of downtown Cairo is **Sharia setta w'ashreen Yulyu** – more easily rendered as **26th July Street** – which runs all the way from Ezbekiya Gardens across the Nile to Zamalek. Formerly called Fouad I, after Ismail's son, its current name commemorates the date of King Farouk's abdication in 1952, following a bloodless coup by the Free Officers three days earlier.

Besides a slew of hotels – most noticeably the *Grand* – this stretch of the street features two sleazy **nightclubs**, a couple of liquor stores, and cages full of pigeons awaiting buyers, plus almost as many shoe shops and pavement hawkers as Talaat Harb. Behind the Cicurel department store, expropriated from its Jewish owner in 1957, is a vintage Cairene restaurant, *El Haty*.

Better still for eating and drinking is **Sharia Alfi Bey**, two blocks north – known by locals as the Cairene Champs-Élysées. At one end is **Midan Orabi**, frequented round-the-clock by Cairenes noshing on falafel and kebabs bought from one of the many takeaways here. Walking down from here you'll find the *Alfi Bey* restaurant, opposite a dirt-cheap 24-hour *taamiya* joint called *Akher Sa'a* (next door to the Nile Christian Bookshop), and further along the street a wonderfully relaxed bar inside the *Windsor Hotel*. Opposite the hotel entrance are two funky Arab cafés. Though perfectly safe late at night, the backstreets that link these thoroughfares retain an aura of illicit goings-on. When Lawrence Durrell and his wife were evacuated from Greece to Cairo in 1941, they discovered that their refugee hotel here doubled as a brothel.

Midan Opera and Midan Ataba

During the 1860s, when the centre was rebuilt (see p.106), an Opera House was also constructed; symbolically, the building faced west, overlooking **Midan Opera** and the modern city rather than Islamic Cairo. Although the opening night saw a lavish production of *Rigoletto*, it was surpassed a year later by the anniversary celebrations, when an opus that had been specially commissioned to have an imperial Egyptian theme was first performed – Verdi's *Aida*. An equestrian statue of Ibrahim Pasha, by Cordier, honours Ismail's father. Though still the sprucest bit of greenery in central Cairo, the square lost its namesake when the Opera House burned down in 1971; a multistorey car park now occupies the site.

Almost a century after Ismail mortgaged Egypt to foreign creditors, anti-colonial resentments exploded here on **"Black Saturday"** (January 26, 1952). The morning after British troops had killed native policemen in Ismailiya, demonstrators were enraged to find an Egyptian police officer drinking on the terrace of *Madame Badia's Opera Casino* (where the Opera Cinema stands today). A scuffle began and the nightclub was wrecked; rioting spread quickly, encouraged by the indifference of Cairo's police force. As ordinary folk looted, activists sped around in jeeps torching foreign premises. Similarly, during the bread riots of 1977, nightclubs and boutiques were specifically targeted by the radical Islamic group *Al-Taqfir w'al-Higrah* (Repentance and Holy Flight).

Midan Ataba

Behind Midan Opera car park, a minibus depot and split-level thoroughfares render **Midan Ataba** just as Yusuf Idris described it in *The Dregs of the City*: "a madhouse of pedestrians and automobiles, screeching wheels, howling klaxons, the whistles of bus conductors and roaring motors". Originally called the Square of Green Steps, Ataba should rightly be renamed the Square of Flyovers.

There is one attraction, however, that you might want to visit, the **Post Office Museum** on the second floor of the Central Post Office (daily except Fri 9am–4pm; £E2; tickets sold in the post office itself, near the commemorative stamps office, then go upstairs through the guarded entrance on the east side of the building). The museum houses exhibits from Egypt's postal service through the ages, with stamps galore (including the rare Suez Canal commemorative issue), Egypt's oldest mailboxes, and a picture of the Sphinx and Pyramids composed entirely of stamps bearing images of the same.

The minibus terminal is around the back of the multistorey car park; for local **transport** details, see p.77.

From Midan Ataba you can also take a number of **walking routes into Islamic Cairo** (see p.114).

Ezbekiya Gardens and north to Ramses

The **Ezbekiya Gardens**, to the north of Opera and Ataba squares, were laid out in the 1870s by the former chief gardener of Paris, forming a twenty-acre park. Subsequent extensions to 26th July Street reduced them to trampled islands amidst a sea of commerce and traffic, but the right-hand one has now been enclosed to preserve its magnificent banyan tree, while the other remains a pitch for hawkers of Islamic arts, gewgaws and incense. Beyond the clothes stalls on the right stands the **Cairo Puppet Theatre** (see p.225).

In medieval times a lake fed by the Nasiri Canal and surrounded by orchards existed here, but in 1470 the Mamluke general Ezbek built a palace, inspiring other beys and wealthy merchants to follow suit. During the French occupation Napoleon commandeered the sumptuous palace of Alfi Bey, and his successor Kléber promoted Western innovations such as windmills, printing presses, and a balloon launch which embarrassingly failed. Another novelty was *Le Tivoli* club, where "ladies and gentlemen met at a certain hour to amuse themselves"; unheard of in a society where men and women socialized separately.

During Mohammed Ali's time, visitors could still witness Cairenes celebrating the Prophet's Birthday here (12 Rabi al-Awwal) with unrestrained fervour. Sufi dervishes entranced by *zikr*s lay prostrate to be trampled by their mounted sheikh in the famous *Doseh* (Treading) ceremony. However, snake-swallowing had already been ruled "disgusting and contrary to their religion" by the sheikh of the Sa'adiya, and under British rule popular festivals were discouraged and dispersed around the city. Nowadays, El-Hussein and other squares are more active during the *Moulid al-Nabi*.

Though nothing remains of them today, two bastions of colonialism once overlooked Ezbekiya from a site bounded by Alfi Bey and El-Gumhorriya, where Scottish pipers once played. Here, *Shepheard's Hotel* (founded in 1841) flourished alongside the

Thomas Cook Agency, which pioneered tourist "expeditions" in the 1870s. Rebuilt more grandly in 1891, *Shepheard's* famous terrace, Moorish Hall, Long Bar and Ballroom (featuring "Eighteenth Dynasty Edwardian" pillars modelled on Karnak) were destroyed by Black Saturday rioters in 1952.

Between Ezbekiya and Ramses

When Mohammed Ali created a military high road to link the Citadel with Cairo's new railway station, and named it after the French physician Antoine Clot – whom he ennobled for introducing Western ideas of public health to Egypt – nobody foresaw that **Sharia Clot Bey** and the fashionable area north of Ezbekiya would degenerate into a vice-ridden "Open Land". By World War I, however, the quarter was full of honky-tonk bars, backstreet porn shows and brothels; shacks and plush establishments alike paying tribute to Ibrahim el-Gharby, the fearsome transvestite "King of the *Wasa'a*". (In the Mahfouz novel and classic Egyptian movie *The Beginning and the End*, the main character's hash-dealing brother set up shop here.) During World War II, activities centred around Wagh el-Birket, known to troops as **"the Berka"**: a long street with curtained alleys leading off beneath balconies where the prostitutes sat fanning themselves. Only after the killing of two Australian soldiers (who were notorious for throwing women and pianos out of windows) was the Berka closed down in 1942.

Nowadays shabbily respectable, with cheap shops and cafés, this past has been further effaced by renaming Clot Bey **Sharia Khulud**. Any bus heading up it from the gardens towards Ramses will take you past the hulking nineteenth-century **Cathedral of St Mark**, now superseded by the new Coptic cathedral in Abbassiya. The derelict Moorish pile at the Ramses end of **Sharia el-Gumhorriya** (which runs up from the west side of the gardens) was the original premises of *Al-Ahram* (The Pyramids), the first – if not still the foremost – newspaper in the Arab world.

Ramses Station and around

The Ramses Station area is the northern ganglion of Cairo's transport system. Splayed flyovers and arterial roads haemorrhage traffic onto darting pedestrians, keeping **Midan Ramses** busy round the clock. Its main focus is **Ramses Station** itself, a quasi-Moorish shoe box to which a major **post office** and the **Egyptian Railways Museum** are appended. The museum (Tues–Thurs, Sat & Sun 8.30am–1.30pm, Fri 8.30am–noon & 2–4pm; £E1.50, £E3 on Fri & public holidays), at the east end of the station, houses a cast of antique steam engines, headed by Ismail's private train.

In ancient times, when the Nile ran further east, Ramses was the site of *Tendunyas*, the port of Heliopolis. Renamed *Al-Maks* (the Customs Point) by the Arabs, it was incorporated within Cairo's fortifications by Salah al-Din, whose Iron Gate was left high and dry as the Nile receded westwards, and was pulled down in 1847 to make way for the station. A nine-metre high red granite **Colossus of Ramses II**, moved here from Memphis in 1955, now stands diminished by the Heliopolis flyover and an overhead walkway; it is becoming so corroded by pollution that experts have long been insisting it be removed. It was due to be transported to the junction of Pyramids Road and the Alexandria Desert Road, out by the Giza Pyramids, despite lobbying from local Egyptologists to have it returned to its original site – pehaps this wrangling is why it's still slowly dissolving *in situ*. A modern replica of this colossus stands beside the airport road.

Near Ramses Station, there are two main **inter-city bus terminals** – Koulali and Ahmed Helmi – and several **service taxi depots** (see "Travel details" at the end of the chapter). Koulali Terminal is off the road beneath the 6th October flyover; to get to Ahmed Helmi Terminal, you have to cross the humpbacked iron bridge. This used to overlook Cairo's army surplus market, which had to be removed to prevent fundamen-

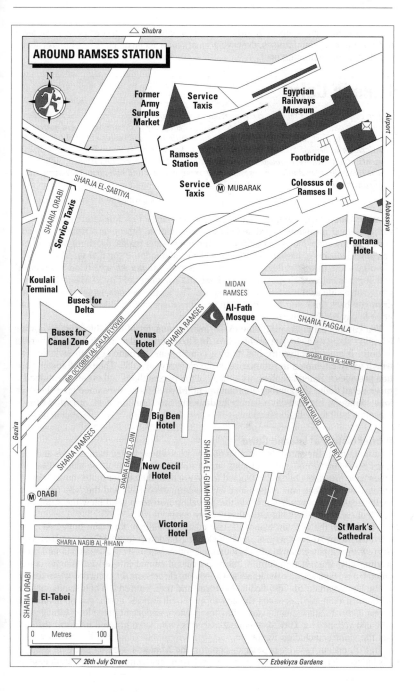

AROUND RAMSES STATION

△ Shubra

N

Former Army Surplus Market

Service Taxis

Egyptian Railways Museum

△ Airport

Ramses Station

Footbridge

Service Taxis

Ⓜ MUBARAK

Colossus of Ramses II

△ Abbassiya

SHARJA EL-SABTIYA

SHARIA ORABI

Service Taxis

Fontana Hotel

Koulali Terminal

Buses for Delta

MIDAN RAMSES

Al-Fath Mosque

SHARIA FAGGALA

6th OCTOBER (AL-GALA) FLYOVER

Buses for Canal Zone

Venus Hotel

SHARIA RAMSES

SHARIA BAYN AL-HARET

△ Gezira

SHARIA RAMSES

SHARIA EMAD EL-DIN

Big Ben Hotel

SHARIA KHULUD (GLOT BEY)

New Cecil Hotel

Ⓜ ORABI

SHARIA EL-GUMHORRIYA

St Mark's Cathedral

Victoria Hotel

SHARIA NAGIB AL-RIHANY

SHARIA ORABI

El-Tabei

0   Metres   100

▽ 26th July Street

▽ Ezbekiyza Gardens

talists from donning uniform in order to impersonate military officers. The *Fontana*, a **hotel** south of Midan Ramses, deserve a mention for its facilities: it lets non-residents use its rooftop swimming pool.

Islamic Cairo

The core of the city itself was circumscribed by the river and hills of refuse, the castle, the aqueduct and the abandoned slums. Most of the bazaars lay in the densely packed quarters of the North-East, nestling in amongst and parasitic upon the rubble of the old Fatimid palaces, and behind the commercial streets one found small courtyards and large tenements, into which were crowded communities of closely knit creeds and tribes . . . The city was like a disordered mind, an expression of archaic wishes and half-submerged memories of vanished dynasties.

Robert Irwin, *The Arabian Nightmare*

Islamic Cairo sustains fantasy and confounds certainty. Few foreigners enter its maw without equal measures of excitement and trepidation. Streets are narrow and congested, slimy underfoot with donkey shit and burst water mains, overhung with latticed balconies. Mosques, bazaars and medieval lanes abound; the smell of *sheeshas* and frying offal wafts through alleys where muezzins wail "*Allahu Akbar!*" (God is Greatest) and beggars entreat "*Ya Mohannin, ya Rabb*" (O Awakener of Pity, O Master) – as integral to streetlife as the artisans and hawkers. The sights, sounds, smells and surprises draw you back time after time, and getting lost or dispensing a little *baksheesh* is a small price to pay for the experience.

You can have a fascinating time exploring this quarter of the city without knowing anything about its history or architecture, but to describe Islamic Cairo one has to refer to both. Islamic architecture has its own conventions, terminology and stylistic eras, which we've attempted to summarize in the glossary on p.686. The potted history section provides a general context, with many of the personalities and events mentioned in more detail under the appropriate monument. Most of these are named after their various founders; modern-day Islamic fundamentalists shun them as *mesjid el-derar* – mosques built for self-glorification.

A brief history of Islamic Cairo

Islamic Cairo is the sum total of half a dozen cities whose varied names, ages and locations make for an unusually complex urban history. One helpful constant is that new cities have invariably been constructed to the north of the old, for quite simple reasons: an east–west spread was constrained by the Muqattam Hills and the Nile (which ran further east than nowadays), while the prevailing northerly wind blew the smoke and smell of earlier settlements away from newer areas.

Thus when the Muslim troops of Amr conquered Egypt for Islam in 641 AD, they sited their city, **Al-Fustat**, just north of Coptic Babylon (see "Old Cairo", p.161). Here it grew into a powerhouse of religious conversion, surpassing Alexandria as Egypt's leading city, though remaining a mere provincial capital in the vast Islamic empire ruled from Damascus by the khalifs, whose only direct contact occurred when the last of the **Umayyads** (661–750) fled to Al-Fustat, and then burned it. Their successors, the **Abbasids** (750–935), ordered the city to be rebuilt further north, and so *Medinet al-Askar* (City of Cantonments) came into being. More important in the long term was the Abbasid reliance on Turkish-speaking warriors, who were granted fiefdoms throughout the empire, including Egypt.

In 870, encouraged by popular discontent, the Abbasids' viceroy in Egypt asserted his independence, and went on to wrest Syria from their control. Like his predecessors,

Ahmed **Ibn Tulun** founded a new city, reaching from Medinet al-Askar towards a spur of the Muqattam. Inspired by the imperial capital of Samarra, it consisted of a gigantic congregational mosque, palace and hippodrome, surrounded by "the Wards" (*Al-Qitai*) or military quarters after which the city was named. However, when the Abbasids invaded Egypt in 905, Al-Qitai was razed and ploughed under, sparing only the great Mosque of Ibn Tulun, which stands to this day.

The city regained a shadow of its former importance under the **Ikhshidids** (935–969), who seceded from the later Abbasid khalifs. But the impetus for its revival, and that of the Islamic empire, came from Tunisia, where adherents of Shia Islam had created their own theocracy, ruled by a descendant of Ali and Fatima – the dynasty of **Fatimids**. Aiming to seize the khalifate, they hit upon Egypt as an ill-defended yet significant power base, and captured it with an army of 100,000 in 969. The Fatimid general, Gohar (Jewel), a converted Greek, immediately began a new city where the dynasty henceforth reigned (969–1171).

By this time distinctions between the earlier cities had blurred, as people lived wherever was feasible amidst the decaying urban entity known as **Masr** (which also means "Egypt"). The Fatimids distanced themselves from Masr by building their city of **Al-Qahira** (The Conqueror) further north than ever, where certain key features remain. It was at the Al-Azhar Mosque that Al-Muizz, Egypt's first Fatimid ruler, delivered a sermon before vanishing into his palaces (which, alas, survive only in name); while the Mosque of Al-Hakim commemorates the khalif who ordered Masr's destruction after residents objected to proclamations of his divinity. You can also see the great Northern Walls and the Bab Zwayla gate, dating from Al-Gyushi's enlargement of Al-Qahira's defences. But as the Fatimid city expanded, Fustat began disappearing as people scavenged building material from its abandoned dwellings; a process that spread to Masr, creating great swathes of *kharab*, or derelict quarters.

The disparate areas only assumed a kind of unity after **Salah al-Din** (Saladin to the Crusaders) built **the Citadel** on a rocky spur between Al-Qahira and Masr, and walls which linked up with the aqueduct between the Nile and the Citadel, so as to surround the whole. Salah al-Din promoted Sunni, not Shia, Islam and built madrassas to propagate orthodoxy; he ruled not as khalif, but as a secular *sultan* (power). His successors, the **Ayyubids**, erected pepperpot-shaped minarets (only one remains, on Sultan Ayyub's Madrassa and Mausoleum, see p.121) and the magnificent tombs of the Abbasid Khalifs and Imam al-Shafi'i (which still exist) in the Southern Cemetery, but they made the same error as the Abbasids: depending on foreign troops and bodyguards. When the sultan died heirless and his widow needed help to stay in power, these troops, the Mamlukes, were poised to take control.

The **Mamlukes** were a self-perpetuating caste of slave-warriors, originally from Central Asia but later drawn from all over the Near East and the Balkans. Their price in the slave markets reflected the "value" of ethnic stock – 130–140 ducats for a Tartar, 110–120 for a Circassian, 50–80 for a Slav or Albanian – plus individual traits: sturdy, handsome youths were favoured. Often born of concubines and raised in barracks, Mamlukes advanced through the ranks under amirs who sodomized and lavished gifts upon their favourites. With the support of the right amirs, the most ruthless Mamluke could aspire to being sultan. Frequent changes of ruler were actually preferred, since contenders had to spread around bribes, not least to arrange assassinations. The Mamluke era is divided into periods named after the garrisons of troops whence the sultans intrigued their way to power: the Qipchak or Tartar **Bahri Mamlukes** (1250–1382), originally stationed by the river (*bahr* in Arabic); and their Circassian successors, the **Burgi Mamlukes** (1382–1517), quartered in a tower (*burg*) of the Citadel.

Paradoxically, the Mamlukes were also renowned as aesthetes, commissioning mosques, mansions and *sabil-kuttabs* that are still the glory of today's Islamic Cairo. They built throughout the city, from the Northern to the Southern Cemetery, and the

APPROACHING AND EXPLORING ISLAMIC CAIRO: PRACTICALITIES

The best (if not only) way **to explore Islamic Cairo** is by walking. Basically, you decide on a starting point that's readily accessible from downtown Cairo, and then follow an itinerary on foot from there. The most obvious **starting points** are Khan el-Khalili, the Bab Zwayla and the Citadel; see the beginning of each of these sections for details on getting there by public transport (also see the bus/minibus information on p.81). If you want to walk from the downtown area, there are four approaches to Islamic Cairo from **Midan Ataba** (see p.109), using the Ataba post office and fire station for orientation:

THE MUSKI is the classic approach to **Khan el-Khalili**: a narrow bazaar, identifiable by the crowds passing between the *El-Mousky* hotel and a clump of luggage stalls. For more details, see "Around Khan el-Khalili and Al-Azhar" (p.116).

SHARIA AL-AZHAR. Overshadowed by a flyover running from Midan Ataba to the heart of Islamic Cairo, Sharia al-Azhar – which runs parallel to the Muski – buzzes with traffic and cottage industries. Buses and minibuses push their way through the crowds and traffic, past **Al-Azhar bus terminal** (for the Western Desert Oases) and across one of Cairo's few remaining tram routes at the Bur Said overpass, taking you on to the **Al-Azhar Mosque**, just south of **Midan el-Hussein**. By walking back from the square along the Muski to the junction with Sharia al-Muizz, you can go south to **Bab Zwayla**.

SHARIA QALAA (formerly Boulevard Mohammed Ali), across from the fire station. This street runs directly to the **Citadel** (2km). When Ismail's Minister of Public Works ordered the thoroughfare ploughed through the old quarter, he asked rhetorically: "Do we need so many monuments? Isn't it enough to preserve a sample?" The stretch down to Midan Ahmed Maher – where the **Islamic Arts Museum** is located – features musical instrument shops, all-night stalls and cafés. In pre-revolutionary times, brothels and hashish dens infested the stepped lanes that rise between its tenements.

SHARIA EL-GEISH. Also topped by a flyover, "Army Street" runs out towards Abbassiya and Heliopolis. The main reason for venturing beyond the Paper Market is to visit the Mosque of Beybars the Crossbowman on Midan Zahir and the Sakakini Palace beyond.

Many of the **itineraries** given on the following pages can be linked up or truncated; the main limitations on how much you can see are time and your own stamina. It makes sense to read up on an area before striking out on foot. The streets of Islamic Cairo are labyrinthine and, while getting lost among them can result in the richest experiences, some visitors prefer to be shown round by a **guide**. The tourist office can put you in touch with authorized guides, and unofficial ones may accost you on the street. If you are in an official or student group you could try the Tourist Friends Association (9th floor, 33 Sharia Qasr el-Nil; ☎392-2036); its tours are free, as the main motive of its members – all students – is to practise their English.

Most of Islamic Cairo's **monuments** are self-evident and often identified by little green plaques with Arabic numbers; these correspond to the numbers on Lehnert & Landrock's map of Cairo and the listings in the exhaustive *Islamic Monuments in Cairo: A Practical Guide*, published by the AUC. Although the area **maps** printed in this book

Citadel to the Nile, and although urban life was interrupted by their bloody conflicts, the city nevertheless maintained civilized institutions: public hospitals, libraries and schools bequeathed by wealthy Mamlukes and merchants. The caravanserais overflowed with exotica from Africa and the spices of the East, and with Baghdad laid waste by the Mongols, Cairo had no peer in the Islamic world, its wonders inspiring many of the tales in the *Thousand and One Nights*.

But in 1517 the **Ottoman Turks** reduced Egypt from an independent state to a vassal province in their empire, and the Mamlukes from masters to mere overseers. When should suffice, the AUC book and three fold-out maps published by SPARE (Society for the Preservation of the Architectural Resources of Egypt) have the advantage of greater detail.

Likewise, we can't hope to match the wealth of detail or evocations of time and place in certain **books**. Edward Lane's *The Manners and Customs of the Modern Egyptians* illuminates life during Mohammed Ali's time. The changes wrought last century underlie Naguib Mahfouz's *Midaq Alley* and *Cairo Trilogy*. Mamluke Cairo is the setting for Robert Irwin's surreal *The Arabian Nightmare*, whereas its fevered demise haunts *Zayni Barakat* by Gamal al-Ghitani. Life in the Cities of the Dead is captured in *Down to the Sea* by Gamil Attiyah Ibrahim. For straight – but never dull – history, try James Aldridge's *Cairo* or, if you can get your hands on a copy, Desmond Stewart's *Great Cairo, Mother of the World*. All of these works are reviewed under "Books" in Contexts chapter and a selection is available at bookstores such as Al-Shourouk on Midan Talaat Harb, the Anglo-Egyptian Bookshop at 169 Sharia Mohammed Farid and the AUC bookstore at the back of the main campus.

The more commonly visited **mosques** and **madrassas** charge an **entry fee**, usually £E6 (students pay half). **Opening hours** are roughly 9am to 7pm daily, though they may well open up later, depending on when the guardian turns up, and will probably close an hour or two earlier in winter. During Ramadan, when everybody wants to be at home by sunset in order to eat, you will not be able to visit after about 4pm. Entry charges and opening hours are only given in the text when they differ significantly from the above. You will also not be welcome during **prayer times** and the Friday noon assembly, which lasts over an hour. A couple of mosques are permanently closed to non-Muslims (as indicated in the text). Apart from an admission charge, and especially when there isn't one, guardians generally expect *baksheesh*: the footwear custodian merits 50pt, while someone who takes you into a tomb or up a minaret rates £E1–2 (which you should pay after your visit). Excessive demands should be politely resisted, and asking for change is awkward, so bring lots of small bills. Old **mansions** charge along similar lines and in theory have set opening hours, but in practice are often closed after 3pm, and all day Friday, whatever the official schedule.

How you **dress** is important. Wearing shorts automatically diminishes prestige in Egyptian eyes, and women wearing halter-necks, skimpy T-shirts, miniskirts, etc, will attract gropers and the disapproval of both sexes. Mosques baulk at admitting the "immodestly" dressed, and for Muslims and unbelievers alike it's obligatory to remove shoes (or don overshoes) to avoid sullying the sacred precincts. Comfortable, easy to slip off footwear is recommended; sandals offer scant protection against manure and leaking drains. Women may feel more comfortable with a male companion, and covering their hair and shoulders with a shawl or headscarf.

It shouldn't need saying that intimate **behaviour** in public is a definite no-no. By remaining courteous and alert, you minimize the risk of hassles on the crowded streets. An effective yet graceful way of brushing off hustlers is to intone *la shukran* (no thank you) while smiling, touching your heart (a gesture of sincerity) and hurrying on. But never begrudge the effort of politeness, nor mistake every approach for a sales ploy. Ordinary Egyptians enjoy welcoming *khawagas* with the right attitude as much as they like watching arrogant tourists get misdirected and cheated.

the French and British extended the Napoleonic War to Egypt they found a city living on bygone glories: introspective and archaic, its population dwindling as civil disorder increased. Eighteenth-century travellers like R.R. Madden were struck by "the squalid wretchedness of the Arabs, and the external splendour of the Turks", not to mention the lack of "one tolerable street" in a city of some 350,000 inhabitants.

The city's renaissance – and the ultimate shift from Islamic to modern Cairo – is owed to **Mohammed Ali** (1805–48) and his less ruthless descendants. An Ottoman servant who turned against his masters, Mohammed Ali effortlessly decapitated the vestiges of Mamluke power, and raised a huge mosque and palaces upon the Citadel. Foreigners were hired to advise on urban development and Sharia Qalaa (Blvd Mohammed Ali) was ploughed through the old city. As Bulaq, Ezbekiya and other hitherto swampy tracts were developed into a modern, quasi-Western city, Islamic Cairo ceased to be the cockpit of power and the magnet for aspirations. But as visitors soon discover, its contrasts, monuments and vitality remain as compelling as ever.

Around Khan el-Khalili and Al-Azhar

Khan el-Khalili bazaar and the Mosque of Al-Azhar form the commercial and religious heart of Islamic Cairo, and the starting point for several walking tours. **To get there**

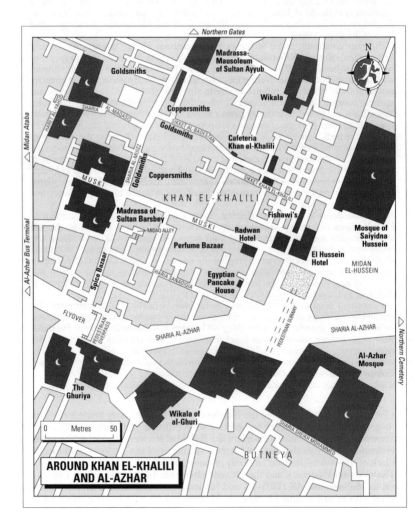

AROUND KHAN EL-KHALILI AND AL-AZHAR

from downtown Cairo you can take a taxi, bus, or walk. Taxis (which usually go via the Al-Azhar flyover) shouldn't cost more than £E3–5, although drivers normally try to overcharge tourists bound for Midan el-Hussein – the main square adjoining Khan el-Khalili that's best given as your destination. For details of the buses from downtown see p.81.

Approaching on foot: the Muski

Walking **from Midan Ataba** there are two basic routes: along Sharia al-Azhar (beneath the flyover), which takes ten to fifteen minutes; or via the Muski, a more interesting, slightly longer approach. It's best to go one way and return by the other.

The **Muski** is a narrow, incredibly congested street running eastwards from Midan Ataba; look for the faded Arabic sign of the *El-Mousky Hotel* on the corner. Worming your way through the crowds – past windows full of wedding gear, tape decks and fabrics, and vendors peddling everything from salted fish to socks – beware of mopeds and other traffic thrusting up behind. Barrow-men still yell traditional warnings – "*Riglak!*" (Your foot!), "*Dahrik!*" (Your back!), "*Shemalak!*" (Your left side!). Itinerant drinks-vendors are much in evidence. Although the *saqi* (water-sellers) have been made redundant by modern plumbing, *susi* dispensing liquorice-water and *sherbutli* with their silver-spouted lemonade bottles remain an essential part of streetlife.

Halfway along the Muski you'll cross Sharia Bur Said; beyond here the Muski turns touristy, with hustlers emerging as it nears Khan el-Khalili.

Midan el-Hussein

Midan el-Hussein, framed by an eclectic mix of architecture, is a central point of reference. To the north stands the tan-coloured **Mosque of Saiyidna Hussein**, where the Egyptian president and other dignitaries pray on special occasions; it's a sacred place, off-limits to non-Muslims. Its cool marble, green and silver interior guards the relic of a momentous event in Islamic history: the **head of Hussein**. The grandson of the Prophet Mohammed, Hussein was killed in Iraq in 680 by the Umayyads, who had earlier been recognized as Mohammed's successors against the claims of his son-in-law, Ali, Hussein's father, whom they had murdered. This generational power struggle over the khalifate caused an enduring schism within Islam. The Muslim world's *Sunni* ("followers of the way") majority not only recognized the khalifate, but forbade the office to anyone of Ali's line. Conversely, the *Shia* ("partisans of Ali") minority refused to accept any khalif but a descendant of Ali, and revered Hussein as a martyr. In predominantly Sunni Muslim Egypt, he's nevertheless regarded as a popular saint, ranked beside Saiyida Zeinab, the Prophet's granddaughter.

Hussein's annual moulid is one of Cairo's greatest **festivals** – a fortnight of religious devotion and popular revelry climaxing on the *leyla kebira* or "big night", the last Wednesday in the Muslim month of *Rabi al-Tani*. Here the Sufi brotherhoods parade with their banners and drums, and music blares all night, with vast crowds of Cairenes and *fellaheen* from the Delta (each of whose villages has its own café and dosshouse in the neighbourhood). El-Hussein is also a focal point during the festivals of *Moulid al-Nabi*, *Eid al-Adha*, *Ramadan* and *Eid al-Fitr*, all well worth seeing. A balcony room at the *El-Hussein Hotel* provides a perfect vantage point, but don't expect to get any sleep. Ablaze with neon lights (including green "Allahs"), the minarets boom sleepers into wakefulness around dawn with their amplified muezzins – and that's on ordinary nights of the year.

The Khan el-Khalili bazaars

Above all, the **Khan el-Khalili** quarter pulses with commerce, as it has since the Middle Ages. Except on Sundays, when most shops are shut, everything from spices to silk is sold in its bazaars. What follows is primarily a guide to the sights; for hard facts about merchandise, dealers and bargaining, see "Shopping", p.225. Generically speaking, all the bazaars around here are subsumed under the name Khan el-Khalili – after Khalil, a Master of Horse who founded a caravanserai here in 1382. However, the Khan itself is quite compact, bounded by Hussein's Mosque, Sharia al-Muizz and the Muski, with two medieval lanes (Sikket al-Badestan and Sikket Khan el-Khalili) penetrating its maze-like interior.

Most of the shop fronts conceal workshops or warehouses, and the system of selling certain goods in particular areas still applies, if not as rigidly as in the past. **Goldsmiths**, jewellers and souvenir-antique shops mostly congregate along the lanes, which retain a few arches and walls from Mamluke times. When you've tired of wandering around, duck into **Fishawi's** via one of the passages off the Muski or the square. Showing its age with tobacco-stained plaster and cracked gilded mirrors, this famous café has been open day and night every day of the year for over two centuries, an evocative place to sip mint tea, eavesdrop, and risk a *sheesha*.

South off the Muski, along Sharia al-Muizz, you'll find the *Souk al-Attarin* or **Spice Bazaar**, selling dried crushed fruit and flowers besides more familiar spices. On the corner of the same street, screened by T-shirt and *galabiyya* stalls, stands the **Madrassa of Sultan al-Ashraf Barsbey**, who made the spice trade a state monopoly, thus financing his capture of Cyprus in 1426.

Sharia Sanadiqiya (off Sharia al-Muizz) will take you into the **Perfume Bazaar**, a dark, aromatic warren sometimes called the *Souk es-Sudan* because much of the incense is from there; in the last century, Baedeker's *Guide for Travellers* also noted "gum, dum-plant nuts" and "ill-tanned tiger-skins" amongst the merchandise. Mamluke sultans appointed a *Muhtasib* to oversee prices, weights and quality. Empowered to inflict summary fines and corporal punishments, he was also responsible for public morals – "enjoining what is right and forbidding what is wrong". The first passage on your left off Sharia Sanadiqiya leads up a flight of steps to a tiny cul-de-sac. This is Zuqaq al-Midaq, or **Midaq Alley**, immortalized by Naguib Mahfouz in his novel of the same name, and made into a film, which was shot here. There is no street sign apparent; it's kept in the tiny (and easy to miss) café, where they'll ask you if you want to photograph it – for *baksheesh*, of course.

Al-Azhar Mosque

To the southwest of Midan el-Hussein, a pedestrian underpass leads towards the **Mosque of Al-Azhar** (pronounced "Al-*Az*har"), whose name can be translated as "the radiant", "blooming" or "resplendent". Founded in 970, as soon as the enclosure walls of Fatimid Al-Qahira were completed, Al-Azhar claims to be the world's oldest university (a title disputed by the Kairaouine Mosque in Fes, Morocco). For more than a millennium, though, Al-Azhar has provided students from all over the Muslim world with free board and with an education that, despite Nasserite reforms, remains largely as it was during the classical Islamic era. *Muqawrin* study every facet of the Koran and Islamic jurisprudence (*fiqh*); logic, grammar and rhetoric; and how to calculate the phases of the lunar Muslim calendar. Much of this involves listening in a circle (*halqa*) at the feet of a sheikh, and rote memorization; but with greater knowledge, students may engage in Socratic dialogue with their teachers, or instruct their juniors.

Given this, and the Sheikh al-Azhar's status as the ultimate theological authority for Egyptian Muslims, it's unsurprising that the mosque has always been politically significant. Salah al-Din changed it from a Shi'ite hotbed into a bastion of Sunni orthodoxy, while Napoleon's troops savagely desecrated it to demonstrate their power. (Omitting any mention of this, Baedeker cautioned visitors to this "fountain-head of Mohammedan fanaticism . . . not to indulge in any gestures of amusement or contempt".) A nationalist stronghold from the nineteenth century onwards, Al-Azhar was chosen by Nasser as the venue for his speech of defiance during the Suez invasion of 1956. When Saudi King Fahd prayed here with Mubarak in 1989 it symbolized Egypt's return to the conservative Arab fold; yet, paradoxically, many of Al-Azhar's 90,000 students revere the blind fundamentalist sheikh Omar Abd al-Rahman, currently serving a life sentence in the US for his part in the 1993 World Trade Center bombing.

THE MOSQUE
The ticket for the mosque (£E12, students £E6) is also valid for admission to the Mosque-Madrassa and Mausoleum of Al-Ghuri (p.126). Women are provided with shawls to cover hair and shoulders, while bare legs rules out entry for either sex.

The **mosque** itself is an accretion of centuries and styles, harmonious if confusing. You come in through the fifteenth-century **Barber's Gate**, where students traditionally had their heads shaved, onto a great **sahn** (courtyard) that's five hundred years older, overlooked by three minarets. The *sahn* facade, with its rosettes and keel-arched panels, is mostly Fatimid, but the latticework-screened *riwaqs* (residential quarters) of the **madrassas** (theological schools) on your right-hand side date from the Mamluke period. Unfortunately, these are rarely opened for visitors, but you can walk into the carpeted, alabaster-pillared **qibla liwan**, where the *mihrab*, or prayer niche facing Mecca, is located.

The **roof** and minarets (the latter currently under restoration) offer great views of Islamic Cairo's timeless vista of crumbling, dust-coloured buildings that could have been erected decades or centuries ago, the skyline bristling with dozens of minarets.

Butneya – and leaving Al-Azhar
The warren of lanes and tenements behind Al-Azhar – an area known as **Butneya** – could be described as Cairo's "Thieves' Quarter", except that racketeering and drugs are more important. Until 1988, the main business was hashish: sold from "windows" and "green doors", it could be smoked with impunity in *ghorzas* (literally "stitches", small and hidden places) throughout the quarter. Local drugs barons like Kut Kut and Wilad Nasare entered Cairene folklore for their ostentatious wealth and devotion to their neighbourhood; Mustafa Marzuaa built a fifteen-room villa, with VCRs in every room, smack in the middle. After the great crackdown in December 1988, when scores of corrupt officials were arrested, the drugs "mafiosi" decamped to the suburbs, leaving Butneya to local racketeers. Some gangs cream the profits from organized garbage collection and begging; others extort money from shops or restaurants, and one gang even specializes in weddings: families pay them to stay away rather than risk disturbances – to hire bouncers would be a shameful admission of family weakness.

None of this should affect foreigners who stay outside the quarter (though you might be offered hashish, or even regaled with stories of the "good old days" when slabs were carved up on tables outdoors). In any case, the well-defined tourist trail leads elsewhere. **Leaving Al-Azhar** by the Barber's Gate, you can turn left down an alley to reach the Wikala of al-Ghuri and other monuments described in the next-but-one walking tour; or return to Midan el-Hussein and check out the following itinerary.

To the Northern Gates and back again

As described below, this itinerary covers an array of monuments from different eras, occupying the one-time heart of Fatimid Cairo. Although one can walk the route – from Midan el-Hussein to the Northern Gates and back again – within an hour, checking out the interiors of all the monuments could take half a day or more, so you might wish to be selective. If your time is limited, it's probably best to concentrate on the three big attractions: the Qalaoun–al-Nasir–Barquq complex, Al-Hakim's Mosque and the Beit al-Sihaymi.

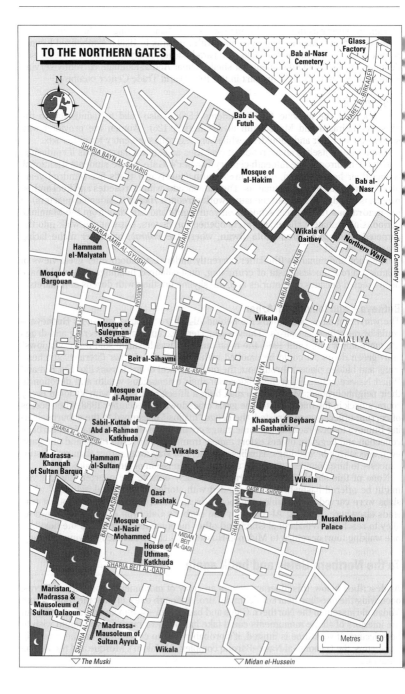

TO THE NORTHERN GATES

N

Glass Factory

Bab al-Nasr Cemetery

Bab al-Futuh

SHARIA BAYN AL-SAYARIG

Mosque of al-Hakim

Bab al-Nasr

HARET EL-BIRKADER

Northern Cemetery

SHARIA AMIR AL-GYUSH

Wikala of Qaitbey

Northern Walls

Hammam el-Malyatah

SHARIA AL-MU'IZZ

SHARIA BAB AL-NASR

HARET

Mosque of Bargouan

BARQUAN

SIKKET BARQOUAN

Wikala

Mosque of Suleyman al-Silahdar

EL-GAMALIYA

Beit al-Sihaymi

DARB AL-ASFUR

Mosque of al-Aqmar

SHARIA GAMALIYA

Sabil-Kuttab of Abd al-Rahman Katkhuda

SHARIA AL-KHRUNFISH

Khanqah of Beybars al-Gashankir

Wikalas

Madrassa-Khanqah of Sultan Barquq

Hammam al-Sultan

Wikala

BAYN AL-QASRAYN

Qasr Bashtak

QASR EL-SHOOK

SHARIA GAMALIYA

Mosque of al-Nasir Mohammed

MIDAN BEIT AL-QADI

Musafirkhana Palace

House of Uthman Katkhuda

SHARIA BEIT AL-QADI

Maristan, Madrassa & Mausoleum of Sultan Qalaoun

SHARIA AL-MU'IZZ

Madrassa-Mausoleum of Sultan Ayyub

Wikala

0   Metres   50

▽ *The Muski*

▽ *Midan el-Hussein*

Midan el-Hussein to Bayn al-Qasrayn

Starting from Midan el-Hussein (see the map opposite), walk 200m west along the Muski to a crossroads with two mosques, and then turn right onto the northern extension of **Sharia al-Muizz**. Here, jewellers' shops overflowing from the Goldsmiths Bazaar soon give way to vendors of pots, basins, and crescent-topped finials, after whom this bit of street is popularly called *Al-Nahaseen*, the **Coppersmiths Bazaar**.

In Fatimid times this bazaar was a broad avenue culminating in a great parade ground between khalifal palaces – hence its name, **Bayn al-Qasrayn** (Between the Two Palaces), which is still used today although the palaces vanished long ago. Robert Irwin writes evocatively of the place as it was during the Mamluke era, when it was customary "for the men and even a few of the women to promenade in the cool twilight. Later, when respectable people had gone back to their homes, the streets were left to the lamplighters, carousing mamlukes, prostitutes and the sleepers."

To the right of the bazaar, a minaret poking above a row of stalls gives away the unobtrusive **Madrassa and Mausoleum of Sultan Ayyub**, more interesting for its historical associations than anything else. Its founder, the last Ayyubid sultan, was responsible for introducing Mamlukes, or foreign slave troops (originally Qipchaks from the lower Volga region), an act pregnant with consequences for Egypt. As related under "Cities of the Dead" (see p.144), the sultan's widow's daring bid for power made the Mamlukes aware that they were kingmakers – whence it was a short step to ruling Egypt themselves, as they did from 1250 onwards. From an architectural standpoint, Ayyub's madrassa (built 1242–50) was the first to incorporate all four *mahhabs* (rites) of Sunni Islam, and be linked to its founder's mausoleum, thus serving as the prototype for the Mamlukes' great mosque-madrassa-mausoleum complexes. Beneath the minaret, whose *mabkhara* (incense burner) or "pepperpot" crown is the sole example of this Ayyubid motif left in Cairo, an alleyway with a gate (on the left) leads into the courtyard of what used to be the madrassa. A sixteenth-century *sabil-kuttab* (Koranic school and fountain) protrudes from the wall between the minaret and Ayyub's domed mausoleum (usually locked), further up the street.

The Qalaoun–Al-Nasir–Barquq complex

Across the road from the madrassa, the medieval complex of buildings endowed by the sultans **Qalaoun**, **Al-Nasir** and **Barquq** forms an unbroken and quite breathtaking 185-metre-long facade. Founded by three of the most significant of the Mamlukes, each of these building groups was designed to serve several functions, yet to form a harmonious whole. Depending on restoration work, parts of the buildings may be off-limits to visitors, but it's worth trying to see as much as you can. There is a £E6 admission charge for each of the three ensembles.

THE QALAOUN COMPLEX

Influenced by the Syrian and Crusader architecture its founder had encountered while fighting abroad, **Sultan Qalaoun's Maristan, Madrassa and Mausoleum** arguably inaugurated the Burgi Mamluke style, which is typified by lavish ornamentation and execution on a grand scale. If modern visitors are impressed by the fact that these structures were completed in thirteen months (1284–85), Qalaoun's contemporaries were amazed.

The **Maristan** provided free treatment for every known illness (including cataract removals), storytellers and musicians to amuse the patients, and money to tide them over following their discharge. A modern eye clinic now occupies the site of Qalaoun's hospital, of which only three *liwans* remain; to see them, walk down the tree-shaded lane that starts opposite the *sabil-kuttab* mentioned above.

Further up the street, a main door clad in bronze with geometric patterns gives access to a corridor running between the madrassa and the mausoleum. The damaged

Madrassa (entered to the left off this corridor) has a sanctuary *liwan* recalling the three-aisled churches of northern Syria, with Syrian-style glass mosaics around its prayer niche.

But the real highlight of the ensemble is Qalaoun's **Mausoleum**, across the corridor. First comes an atrium court with a *mashrabiya* doorway, surmounted by a beautiful stucco arch worked with interlocking stars, floral and Koranic motifs, as intricate as lace. Beyond is the tomb chamber, thirty metres high, with its soaring dome pierced by stained-glass windows in viridian, ultramarine and golden hues. Elaborately coffered, painted ceilings overhang walls panelled in marble, with mother-of-pearl mosaics spelling out "Mohammed" in abstract calligraphy. Until this century the *mihrab* was credited with healing powers, so supplicants could be seen "rubbing lemons on one of its pilasters, and licking up the moisture", while a stick hanging from the tomb's railings was used "to cure fools or idiots by striking them on the head".

Qalaoun himself was a handsome Qipchak, purchased for one thousand dinars during Ayyub's reign. He rose through the ranks due to the patronage of Sultan Beybars al-Bunduqdari, whose seven-year-old son he eventually deposed in 1279. Qalaoun's sonorous titles *Al-Mansour* and *Al-Alfi* ("the Thousand", after his high price) were mocked by his name, which sounds comical in Arabic; it's supposedly derived from the Mongolian word for "duck", or an obscure Turkish noun meaning "great ransom" or "rich present". A tireless foe of the Crusaders – he died en route to Acre fortress in 1290, aged 79 – Qalaoun imported Circassians to offset Qipchak predominance amongst the Mamlukes, and founded a dynasty that ruled for almost a century (barring hiccups).

THE AL-NASIR COMPLEX

Qalaoun's second son, responsible for the **Mosque of Al-Nasir Mohammed** next door, had a rough succession. Only nine years old when elected, he was deposed by his regent, then restored but kept in miserable conditions for a decade by Beybars al-Gashankir. He finally had Beybars executed and subsequently enjoyed a lengthy reign (1293–1340, counting interregnums), which marked the zenith of Mamluke civilization.

The building of thirty mosques, the great aqueduct and a canal north of Cairo attests to Al-Nasir's enthusiasm for public works (matched apparently by his devotion to horses and sheep). If the **madrassa** is still undergoing restoration, you'll have to be content with the **minaret** – a superb ensemble of stuccoed kufic and naskhi inscriptions, ornate medallions and stalactites, probably made by North African craftsmen. Al-Nasir is actually buried in Qalaoun's mausoleum, and his own son occupies the **mausoleum** intended for him.

At the time of writing, the complex was undergoing heavy restoration work and most of it was closed to public access.

THE BARQUQ MADRASSA AND KHANQAH

The adjacent **Madrassa and Khanqah of Sultan Barquq** appears in a much reproduced nineteenth-century drawing by Owen Carter, which also depicts the Sabil-Kuttab of Ismail Pasha, opposite Al-Nasir's mosque. Its broad facade, divided into shallow recesses, echoes Qalaoun's madrassa, although Barquq's complex (1384–86) has the taller dome, and also boasts a minaret.

Barquq was the first Circassian sultan (1382–98), a Burgi Mamluke who seized power by means of intrigue and assassination. His name, meaning "plum" in Arabic, appears on the raised boss in the centre of the bronze-plated doors, behind which a vaulted passageway leads to an open court. The **madrassa**'s sanctuary *liwan* (on the right as you enter) has a beautiful ceiling supported by porphyry columns of pharaonic origin; upstairs are the cells of the Sufi monks who once inhabited the **khanqah** (monastery). To one side of the *qibla liwan*, a splendid domed mausoleum upheld by gilded pendentives contains the tomb of Barquq's daughter.

Mansions and Sabil-Kuttabs

The domestic architecture of the Mamlukes was no less sophisticated: perfectly adapted to Cairene conditions, it offered greater comfort than contemporary European homes – for the well-to-do, at least. An example close at hand is the **House of Uthman Katkhuda**, so called after an eighteenth-century resident, although the mansion itself dates from 1350. You'll find it on the left-hand side of Sharia Beit al-Qadi, which runs eastwards opposite Qalaoun's mausoleum; look for the little green plaque halfway along. Knock, and someone should usher you into the *qa'a*, a narrow, sixteen-metre-high reception hall with a handsome fountain and wainscotting, cooled by a north-facing *malqaf*, or air scoop, on the roof. The curator expects *baksheesh* for showing you around.

Back on Sharia al-Muizz, walk past Barquq's complex (where the street name changes to Bayn al-Qasrayn) and cross the road, turning into a muddy alleyway on the right, where the second door on the left opens onto the fourteenth-century **Qasr Bashtak**. Here the *qa'a* is upstairs, with *mashrabiya*-screened galleries that permitted ladies to witness the amir's parties, and similar devices overlooking the street. Amir Bashtak was married to Al-Nasir's daughter, so he could afford a five-storey palace with running water on every floor; alas, only a section has survived. If the Qasr Bashtak is locked when you arrive, its custodian can usually be found at the *sabil-kuttab* diagonally opposite.

Back on Bayn al-Qasrayn and situated on a fork in the road just beyond the Qalaoun, Al-Nasir and Barquq complex, the **Sabil-Kuttab of Abd al-Rahman Katkhuda** rises in tiers of airy wooden fretwork above solid masonry and grilles at street level. Founded by an eighteenth-century amir who wished to make amends for roistering, this is an Ottoman-influenced example of a type of building once widespread throughout Cairo, intended to provide the "blessings" of water and education, mentioned in the Holy Koran. Thus, local people could draw water from the *sabil* on the ground floor (where the Ka'ba at Mecca is depicted in Syrian tilework), while their sons learned Koranic precepts in the *kuttab* upstairs. (Girls were deemed unworthy of schooling.) An old proverb suggests that teaching methods were simple: "A boy's ear is on his back – he listens when he is beaten."

By taking the left-hand fork at the *sabil-kuttab* and walking 70m north you reach the **Mosque of Al-Aqmar** (on the right). Newly restored, its most salient feature is the facade, whose ribbed shell hood, keel arches and stalactite panels were the first instance of a decorated mosque facade in Cairo. Built between 1121 and 1125 by the Fatimid khalif's grand vizier, the mosque gets its name – "the moonlit" – from the glitter of its masonry under lunar light. Notice the intricate medallion above the door; the way that the street level has risen well above the mosque's entrance; and the "cutaway" corner up the road, designed to facilitate the manoeuvring of loaded camels.

One block further north, turn right into Darb al-Asfur, where the broad wooden door at no. 19 (on the left, halfway along) belongs to the finest mansion yet. The **Beit al-Sihaymi** (currently closed for restoration) surrounds a lovely courtyard filled with bird noises and shrubbery, overlooked by a *maq'ad* or loggia, where males enjoyed the cool northerly breezes; the ground-floor reception hall with its marble fountain was used during winter, or for formal occasions. The *haramlik* section, reserved for women, is equally luxurious, adorned with faïence, stained glass, painted ceilings and delicate latticework. When the mansion eventually reopens, the guided tours should include a visit to the bathhouse (lit by star-shaped apertures) and a small room with whalebones on the floor, over which women are invited to jump to ensure marriage and pregnancy.

Returning to the main street and continuing north brings you to the **Mosque of Suleyman al-Silahdar**, recognizable by its "pencil" minaret, a typically Ottoman feature. Built in 1839, the mosque reflects the Baroque and Rococo influences that reached Cairo via Istanbul during Mohammed Ali's reign – notably the fronds and garlands that also characterize *sabil-kuttabs* from the period. Shortly afterwards the street widens into a triangular square, beyond which it's busy with the colourfully painted carts of garlic and onion sellers who roll in through the mighty gate ahead.

Mosque of Bargouan

The gateway by the southern side of Silahdar's mosque leads onto Haret Bargouan, named after a Mamluke governor of the area. The **Mosque of Bargouan** is shored up with wooden beams and closed to the public at the time of writing, but is due to be opened for viewing after restoration and can be found by following the street round half a dozen bends. It harbours a non-Islamic curiosity, for Bargouan was secretly a Zoroastrian and installed a concealed Zoroastrian temple underneath his mosque. The religion was founded in sixth-century BC Persia by the prophet Zarathustra, whose followers are commonly known as "fire worshippers" because they pray in front of a sacred flame. When such "pagan practices" were discovered, Bargouan was executed and the temple walled up, though you can see one of the entrances in the bottom of the northern wall, behind the piles of firewood.

Al-Hakim's Mosque and the Northern Gates

The **Mosque of Al-Hakim**, abutting the Northern Walls, commemorates one of Egypt's most notorious rulers. **Al-Hakim bi-Amr Allah** (Ruler by God's Command) was only eleven years old when he became the sixth Fatimid khalif, and fifteen when he had his tutor murdered. His reign (996–1021) was capricious and despotic by any standards, characterized by the persecution of Christians, Jews and merchants and by a rabid misogyny: Al-Hakim forbade women to leave their homes (banning the manufacture of women's footwear to reinforce this) and once had a group of noisy females boiled alive in a public bath. His puritanical instincts were also levelled at wine, chess and dancing girls – all of which were prohibited – and all the city's dogs were exterminated as their barking annoyed him. Merchants found guilty of cheating during Al-Hakim's inspections were summarily sodomized by his Nubian slave, Masoud, while the khalif stood upon their heads – comparatively restrained behaviour from a man who once dissected a butcher with his own cleaver.

In 1020, followers proclaimed Al-Hakim's divinity in the Mosque of Amr, provoking riots which he answered by ordering Fustat's destruction, watching it burn from the Muqattam Hills, where he often rode alone at night. However, legend ascribes the conflagration to Al-Hakim's revenge on the quarter where his beloved sister, **Sitt al-Mulk** (Lady of Power), took her lovers. Only after half of Fustat-Masr was in ruins was she examined by midwives and pronounced a virgin, whereupon he surveyed the devastation and asked, "Who ordered this?" Allegedly, it was his desire for an incestuous marriage that impelled her to arrange Al-Hakim's "disappearance" during one of his nocturnal jaunts.

By governing as regent for the child-khalif Zahir and dying peacefully in her bed, Sitt al-Mulk forfeited the eternal fame that later accrued to Shagar al-Durr, renowned as the only female ruler of Egypt since Cleopatra (see p.145). Meanwhile, Al-Hakim's disciple, **Al-Durzi**, persuaded many foreign Muslims that he would be reincarnated as the Messiah – the origin of the tightly knit **Druze** communities that still exist in Syria, Lebanon and Israel, and whose doctrines are secret. Conversely, the Copts maintain that Al-Hakim experienced a vision of Jesus, repented, and became a monk.

At all events, though, his huge **mosque** (£E6 to enter the mosque, £E6 for the roof and interior walls – see below) was thereafter shunned or used for profane purposes until 1980, when it was restored by a sect of Isma'ili Shi'ites from Brunei, which venerates Al-Hakim. The sect's addition of brass lamps, glass chandeliers and a new *mihrab* outraged purists, but the original wooden tie-beams and stucco frieze beneath the ceilings remain. From the roof, you can gaze over Bab al-Nasr Cemetery (see below) and admire the mosque's minarets, which resemble bastions and are its only original features.

THE NORTHERN GATES
In times past, the annual pilgrim caravan returning from Mecca would enter Cairo via the **Bab al-Futuh** (Open Gate), drawing huge crowds to witness the arrival of the *Mahmal*. This decorative camel litter once carried Ayyub's widow on her pilgrimage, but thereafter it symbolized rather than signified the sultan's participation. Islamic pageantry is still manifest during the **Moulid of Sidi Ali al-Bayoumi**, in early October, when the Rifai brotherhood parades behind its mounted sheikh with scarlet banners flying. The procession starts from El-Hussein, passes through the Bab al-Futuh and north along Sharia Husseiniya, where locals bombard the sheikh and his red-turbanned followers with huge sweets called *arwah*.

From Al-Hakim's Mosque, you can gain admission to a **prison** in the dark interior of the **Northern Walls**, whose custodian will point out archers' slits and bombardiers' apertures, shafts for pouring boiling oil onto enemies entering through the Bab al-Futuh below, and bits of pharaonic masonry (featuring Ramses II's cartouche and a hippo) filched from Memphis, striking matches if you haven't brought a torch. The ceiling of the 200-metre tunnel is vaulted, which allowed mounted guards passage through. At its end lies a grim and cavernous judgement room where the condemned, if found guilty, were hanged immediately, their corpses unceremoniously dumped through a hole in the floor, into the waters of the moat.

Erected in 1087 to replace the original mud-brick ramparts of Fatimid Al-Qahira, the walls were intended to rebuff the Seljuk Turks, but never put to the test, although they later provided a barracks for Napoleonic, and then British, grenadiers. The French attempted to rename the bastions of Bab al-Futuh and the next gate along, **Bab al-Nasr** (Gate of Victory), and titles such as "Tour Julien" and "Tour Pascal", are still inscribed on them. Bab al-Nasr can be reached, like Bab al-Futuh, from the roof of Al-Hakim's mosque. The gate's inscription – "No deity but Allah; Mohammed is the Prophet of God" – includes a defiant Shi'ite addition, "And Ali is the Deputy of God". It was after entering this gate in 1517 that the victorious Ottoman sultan Selim the Grim had eight hundred Mamlukes decapitated, and their heads strung on ropes on Gezira Island. Directly opposite the gate lies **Bab al-Nasr Cemetery**, nowadays so overbuilt with houses that you can hardly see the tombs. At the top end of Haret al-Birkhader is a primitive glass factory where they hand-blow Muski glass.

From Bab al-Nasr you could catch a taxi or walk 1500m east, following the Walls and then Sharia Galal, to reach Barquq's complex in the Northern Cemetery (see p.146).

Heading back along Sharia Gamaliya
Re-entering Islamic Cairo along Sharia Bab al-Nasr you pass into **El-Gamaliya**, whose name derives from the old camel road, Sharia Gamaliya, off which the quarter's alleys run; in one of them, Nobel prizewinning author Naguib Mahfouz was born in 1911. Immediately to your right stands the sturdy fifteenth-century caravanserai or **Wikala of Qaitbey**, now occupied by tinsmiths and their families. Such caravanserais naturally clustered near the city gates, and the facades of three more *wikalas* (the last reduced to a mere portal) are visible beyond a small domed mausoleum on the other side of Sharia Gamaliya.

Beyond these *wikalas* stands the **Khanqah of Beybars al-Gashankir**, with its unmistakably bulbous dome and stumpy minaret. Founded in 1310, and thus the oldest Sufi monastery in Cairo, the *khanqah* is entered via a "baffled" corridor that excludes street noises from the inner courtyard. Without tiles or mosaics, the courtyard escapes severity by the variety of its windows: ribbed, S-curved or keel-arched in styles derived from the Fatimid era. Al-Gashankir's tomb (off the corridor) is spectacular by comparison, with sunbeams falling through stained glass onto marbled walls inset with radiating polygons, and his cenotaph within its ebony *mashrabiya* cage. Sultan for one year only, Beybars was dubbed *Al-Gashankir* (the Taster) to distinguish him from Beybars al-Bunduqdari (the Crossbowman), a mightier predecessor.

If you haven't yet seen the Beit al-Sihaymi, it can be reached by heading west along the Darb al-Asfur, which starts opposite the *khanqah*. Otherwise, continue south along Sharia Gamaliya for 100m, past a ruined *wikala*, a fifteenth-century mosque built above shops (whose rent finances the mosque's maintenance), and then another mosque. Immediately after this, turn left into Qasr el-Shook, an alleyway that bends left around a high stone wall to reach the **Musafirkhana Palace** (daily except Fri 9am–4pm; £E6). Though semi-derelict and undergoing slow restoration, this eighteenth-century mansion (where Khedive Ismail was born) retains beautiful *mashrabiyas*, decorative ceilings, a fountain in the reception hall, and a peaceful atmosphere rarely disturbed by visitors.

Returning to the main street, you'll find that it narrows and forks as it runs south. Precise directions are difficult, but by turning right at one fork and passing through a medieval-looking gate, you should emerge onto a square with shops selling scrap metal and weighing machines, behind the El-Hussein Mosque.

Between Al-Azhar and the Bab Zwayla

Some of the most arresting sights in Islamic Cairo cluster between **Al-Azhar Mosque** and the medieval gate known as the **Bab Zwayla** – a fairly brief itinerary (20–60min) that can be followed in either direction. We've described the sequence of places starting from Al-Azhar and finishing at the gate, but you could equally well start at the Bab Zwayla (a short walk from the Islamic Art Museum) and work north from there.

Bab Zwayla is also the starting point for **longer walking tours** of the Qasaba and Darb al-Ahmar, winding up beneath the Citadel, as described in the section following; so you could also take this itinerary in reverse from there.

The Wikala, Mosque-Madrassa and Mausoleum of Al-Ghuri

The **Wikala of Al-Ghuri** is Cairo's best-preserved merchants' hostel (twenty such squatted or derelict structures remain, out of the 200 active in 1835). Its upstairs rooms have been converted into artists' studios (arrive before lunchtime if you want to see them), with a small exhibition on the culture of the Oases on the ground floor (£E3). With its stables and lock-ups beneath tiers of spartan rooms, the *wikala* is uncompromisingly functional, yet the rhythm of *ablaq* (striped) arches muted by the sharp verticals of shutters, and the severe masonry lightened by *mashrabiya*s and a graceful fountain, achieves elegance.

Although it was built (in 1505) just as the new Cape route to the East Indies was diminishing Cairo's role as a spice entrepôt, the *wikala* doubtless witnessed the kind of scenes described in *The Arabian Nightmare*:

> *The Muhtasib stood immovable, flanked by two huge Turks who carried lanterns on great staves. Black slaves staggered under trunks of merchandise that were being fought over. A party of men were unsuccessfully trying to persuade a camel to leave by the same gate that it had come in by. A sheep was being roasted in the centre of the compound.*

Located on a side street off Sharia al-Azhar, the *wikala* can be reached by turning left on leaving the Mosque of Al-Azhar, then following the alley round past a market; or you can visit it after seeing the **Ghuriya** – the mausoleum and mosque-madrassa of Al-Ghuri. Boldly striped in buff and white, this pair of buildings forms a set piece at the junction of Sharia al-Muizz and the Al-Azhar high road, plainly visible from the foot-

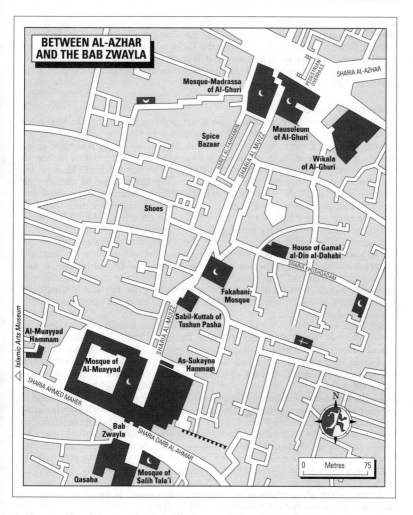

BETWEEN AL-AZHAR AND THE BAB ZWAYLA

Mosque-Madrassa of Al-Ghuri

Spice Bazaar

Mausoleum of Al-Ghuri

Wikala of Al-Ghuri

SHARIA AL-AZHAR

PEDESTRIAN OVERPASS

HARET AL-TAHHAMIN

SHARIA AL MUIZ

Shoes

House of Gamal al-Din al-Dahabi

SHARIA KHUSHQADAM

Fakahani Mosque

Sabil-Kuttab of Tushun Pasha

SHARIA AL-MUIZ

Al-Muayyad Hammam

As-Sukayna Hammam

Mosque of Al-Muayyad

SHARIA AHMED MAHER

Islamic Arts Museum

Bab Zwayla

SHARIA DARB AL-AHMAR

N

Qasaba

Mosque of Salih Tala'i

0   Metres   75

bridge. To the right (west) of the bridge stands the **Mosque-Madrassa**, offering glimpses of the Spice Bazaar from its rear windows, and a grand view of the neighbourhood from its rooftop, though it's currently closed for repairs following the earthquake. Across the way is Al-Ghuri's domed **Mausoleum** (also closed for restoration) and the Al-Ghuri Palace, which now serves as an adult educational centre, with temporary exhibitions on North African cultures, and a theatre with a splendid ceiling where performances by **Whirling Dervishes** are regularly held (see p.222).

Sixty years old when he became the penultimate Mamluke sultan in 1500, **Qansuh al-Ghuri** remained vigorous into his seventies, playing polo, writing poetry and discoursing with Sufis – not forgetting traditional pursuits like building, intrigue and arbitrary justice. Though not averse to filching marble for his mosque-madrassa, Al-Ghuri wished to be remembered for his strict enforcement of Koranic precepts: sentencing a dervish accused of "atheism, sorcery, and the use of milk for his ablutions and intimate toilet" to be paraded naked on a camel, and then hanged; and berating his judges for laxity. Al-Ghuri was killed in 1516 fighting the Turks outside Aleppo; his body was never found and his intended tomb was occupied by his luckless successor, Tumanbey (see below). Gamal al-Ghitani's novel *Zayni Barakat* is a fictionalized account of this Mamluke twilight.

Towards the Bab Zwayla

In olden times the **Sharia al-Muizz**, the street between the Ghuriya buildings, was roofed over, forming the Silk Bazaar where carpets were sold, the subject of a famous drawing by David Roberts. Nowadays, shops along here sell mostly household goods, making fewer concessions to tourism than Khan el-Khalili. At the time of writing, the last fez* workshop in Cairo was situated on the right, 75m past Al-Ghuri's Mosque, kept just alive by sales to five-star hotels and tourists. The street is named after the conquering Fatimid khalif and it was the chief thoroughfare of Islamic Cairo, running from the Northern Gates down towards the Citadel, and meeting another main road – the Darb al-Ahmar – at the Bab Zwayla. Traditionally, each stretch of Al-Muizz had its own name, usually derived from the merchandise sold there.

Roughly 200m down the street you'll find the "Fruit Seller" or **Fakahani Mosque**, whose arabesque-panelled doors are all that remain of the twelfth-century original after its reconstruction in 1735. The nearby **House of Gamal al-Din al-Dahabi**, at no. 6 Sharia Khushqadan (aka "Haret Hoche Kadam"), was the home of seventeenth-century Cairo's foremost gold merchant, and today houses the Egyptian Archeological Organization's (EAO) Islamic Section Documentation Centre. Its magnificent interior is alas closed to sightseers.

South of the Fakahani Mosque, Sharia al-Muizz curves around a row of shops that almost conceals the **Sabil-Kuttab of Tusun Pasha**, adorned with wrought-iron sunbursts, garlands and fronds. Shortly afterwards the street passes between two buildings structurally adjacent to the Bab Zwayla, whose formidable outline dominates the view ahead. To your left, the wall of a *mashrabiya*-fronted *wikala* is preceded by an unobtrusive door (next to a jewellers' shop) that leads into the eighteenth-century **as-Sukanya Hammam**. The fires that heat the water for this grubby men's bathhouse are also used to cook *fuul mudammas* (broad beans) for the neighbourhood's breakfast. The traditional extra allure of such baths was described by Flaubert in 1839: "You reserve the bath for yourself (five francs including masseurs, pipe, coffee, sheet and towel) and you skewer your lad in one of the rooms." Today, such practices continue more furtively, with none of Flaubert's "naked *kellaas* . . . turning you over like embalmers preparing you for the tomb", although many bathhouses still double as gay brothels (see "Hammams", p.223).

Across the way, the **Mosque of Al-Muayyad** – also known as the "Red Mosque" for the colour of its exterior – occupies the site of a prison where its founder was once incarcerated for plotting against Sultan Barquq. Plagued by lice and fleas, he vowed to transform it into a "saintly place for the education of scholars" once he came to power. When he did, 40,000 dinars were dutifully lavished on the mosque's construction (1415–22).

The building is entered via a nine-tiered stalactite portal with a red and turquoise geometric frame around its bronze door. Off the vestibule lies a mausoleum where Al-

---

*The **fez**, called a *tarboush* in Egypt, was originally a mark of Ottoman allegiance, which came to represent the secular, Westernized *effendi*, as opposed to the turbaned traditionalist. Still later, the *tarboush* was stigmatized as a badge of the *ancien regime* that the Nasserite revolution aimed to dispossess. Waiters and entertainers are the main wearers nowadays, but demand is so small that the craft of fez-making seems likely to perish.

Muayyad and his son are buried in befittingly sized cenotaphs. The kufic inscription on Al-Muayyad's reads: "But the god-fearing shall be amidst gardens and fountains: Enter you them, in peace and security" – which seems appropriate for the mosque's courtyard, half filled with palms and open to the sky. Beneath the roofed section a thickly carpeted sanctuary precedes the *qibla* wall, niched and patterned with polychrome marble and mosaic. But best of all is the **view** from one of the minarets, sited atop the Bab Zwayla (*baksheesh* expected, though you may be asked to pay this as an extra £E4 charge on entry).

The Bab Zwayla

The Al-Muayyad's minarets make **Bab Zwayla** look far mightier than the Northern Gates. All of the Fatimid city's defences (which included sixty gates) were in fact reinforced during the 1090s, using Anatolian or Mesopotamian Christian architects and Egyptian labour. Originally the main south gate, Bab Zwayla later became a central point in the Mamluke city, which had outgrown the Fatimid walls and pushed up against Salah al-Din's extensions. Nevertheless, the practice of barring the gates each night continued well into the nineteenth century, maintaining a city within a city. There's a strikingly medieval passage just on the north side of the gate, but the full awesomeness of the Bab itself is best seen from the south side. Note the barbells high up on the western gatetower: a relic of medieval keep-fit enthusiasts.

The gate was named after Fatimid mercenaries of the Berber al-Zwayla tribe, quartered nearby, whom the Mamlukes displaced. Through the centuries it was the point of departure for caravans to Mecca and the source of the drum rolls that greeted the arrival of senior "Amirs of One Hundred". Dancers and snake charmers also performed here, and from the fifteenth century onwards punishments provided another spectacle. Dishonest merchants might be hung from hooks or ropes; garrotting, beheading or impalement were favoured for common criminals; while losers in the Mamluke power struggles were often nailed to the doors. It was here that Tumanbey, the last Mamluke sultan, was hanged in 1517, after a vast crowd had recited the *Fatah* and the rope had broken twice before his neck did. However, Bab Zwayla's reputation was subsequently redeemed by its association with Mitwalli al-Qutb, a miracle-working local saint said to manifest himself to the faithful as a gleam of light within the gatehouse.

A whole slew of places to the south of the Bab are covered by the next itinerary (see p.132), but it's worth mentioning an alternative: namely, heading westwards along Sharia Ahmed Maher **towards the Islamic Art Museum** (see below). En route you'll pass stalls selling waterpipes and braziers, piles of logs destined for the **Al-Muayyad Hammam** (another dubious men's bathhouse, see p.224), a nineteenth-century *sabil-kuttab* and a fifteenth-century mosque. It's a ten-minute walk or a short minibus ride (#68) to the museum. The neighbourhood between Bab Zwayla and the Abdin district is known as the **Bab el-Khalq quarter**, after a long-since vanished medieval gate. On your right off Sharia Ahmed Maher, just before Sharia Bur Said (the entrance to the museum is off this street), is Derb es-Saada, a street of carpenters' workshops, which backs onto a local remand prison. Relatives of the inmates can often be seen on unofficial visits, lining the street and calling up to the windows of the cells.

The Museum of Islamic Art

Try to visit the **Museum of Islamic Art** (daily except Fri 9am–3pm; £E4, students £E2, photography permit £E10) midway through exploring Islamic Cairo, since the historic architecture lends meaning to the museum's artefacts, which, in turn, enhance your appreciation of the old city. It was the ruinous state of many of its mosques and mansions that impelled Khedive Tewfiq and the historians Herz and Cresswell to establish an Islamic collection in 1880. Pieces were stored in Al-Hakim's Mosque until 1902, when a museum was created on the ground floor of the imposing neo-Mamluke *Dar al-Kutub* (National Library) at the junction of Bur Said and Qalaa streets, 600m west of the Bab Zwayla (see map on p.92).

The museum is currently entered from Sharia Bur Said via its garden door, which messes up the already confusing arrangement of **exhibits** by period and medium. To view them in order, walk straight through Rooms 7, 10, 4B and 2 (which contain some of the finest work) and begin with Room 1. However, the cool, deserted halls tempt one to wander through the collection, which can be seen in around ninety minutes.

Because Sunni Muslims extended the Koranic strictures against idolatry to any images of humans or animals, these are largely absent. Instead of paintings and statues, there are exquisite designs based on geometry, Islamic symbolism, plant motifs and Arabic calligraphy – a totally different aesthetic. You'll also notice that dates are given as *AH* – After the Hegira (Mohammed's flight from Mecca) – the starting point of Islamic chronology (622 AD by Western reckoning).

Touring the museum

Assuming you proceed through the central halls without getting sidetracked by the marvellous woodwork and fountains, the exhibition starts with a display of **recent acquisitions** in **Room 1**. If time is short, take the opportunity to visit the **masterpieces** in **Room 13**, next door, which include mosque lamps, carpets, glassware, ceramics, and a lavish door from the Mosque of Saiyida Zeinab.

During the **Umayyad period** (661–750), art was representational and influenced by Hellenistic and Sassanian traditions. Amongst an assembly of objects in **Room 2** are a bronze ewer with a spout in the form of a crowing cockerel, which probably belonged to the last Umayyad khalif (who was slain near Abu Sir), and an **early Muslim tombstone**, dated AH 31.

In **Abbasid and Tulunid times** (750–905), **stucco** was developed into a high art form, principally in Iraq. From being deeply cut and crisply textured with relatively naturalistic vines and acanthus scrolls, stucco panels became increasingly abstract and flowing, no longer carved but moulded. The three different styles from Samarra were

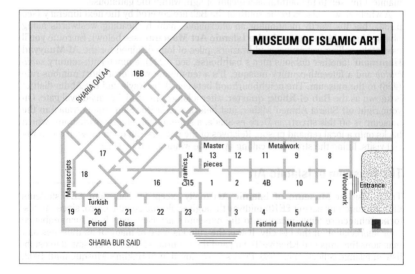

MUSEUM OF ISLAMIC ART

SHARIA QALAA

16B

17

18

Manuscripts

Turkish
19 Period 20 Glass 21   22   23

16

Ceramics
14 C15

Master
13 pieces 12

1   2

3

Metalwork
11   9   8

4B 10 7

Fatimid Mamluke
4   5   6

Woodwork

Entrance

SHARIA BUR SAID

also imitated by the Tulunids in wood; compare the stucco panels with the woodwork from Al-Qitai in **Room 3**.

Passing through a huge door from Sultan Qalaoun's *Maristan* into **Room 4**, you enter the **Fatimid era** (969–1171). As Shi'ites, the Fatimids had no doctrinal objection to depicting animals and birds (a theme popular amongst their co-religionists in Persia), as attested by **panels from the Western Palace**. Also exhibited are inlaid ivory and jewellery, rock crystal, and early **lustre ware from Fustat**. **Room 4B** (part of the main hall) is a lovely composite of Mamluke columns, an Ottoman fountain and floor, and intricate *mashrabiya* work.

Walking from Room 4 into Room 5, you pass through the original doors of the Mosque of Beybars, surmounted by stained-glass "moon windows" set in open plasterwork, from Ottoman times. **Room 5** covers the **Mamluke period** (1250–1517) and centres upon a lovely sunken mosaic fountain, which the curator sometimes turns on. Round about are displayed **mosque lamps** and stucco *mihrabs*; enamelled glass, woven and printed textiles; inlaid metalwork, polychrome pottery, and a wooden **cenotaph from the El-Hussein Mosque**. At the far end of the room is a wooden door from the Mosque of Sultan Ayyub, bearing square kufic and cursive naskhi inscriptions.

A pair of doors from the Al-Azhar Mosque lead into **Room 6**, the first of three devoted to **woodwork**, whose evolution paralleled that of stucco. The deeply incised, naturalistic forms of Umayyad woodcarving gave way to interlocking arches and concentric circles under the Abbasids, followed by bevelled, stylized birds and animals in Tulunid times. Gradually confined to small areas during the Fatimid era, figures were then progressively simplified into arabesques by Ayyubid craftsmen. However, representational art could still be found under the early Mamlukes, as evinced by a **frieze from Qalaoun's Maristan**, which shows hunting, music and dancing. Also featured in **Room 6** are carved panels from the Western Palace, the original *mihrab* from Saiyida Ruqayya's Mashrad, and a portable prayer niche for use on military campaigns. **Room 7** contains a series of *mashrabiyas*, while in **Room 8** there is a *minbar*, a panelled ceiling and a wooden frieze in Hebrew script.

Wooden caskets overspill into **Room 9**, where bronze mirrors and brass lamps inaugurate the metalwork section. Room 10, next door, reflects Ottoman tastes in **interior design**. Beneath an exquisitely coffered ceiling, guests could socialize around a graceful fountain, secretly overlooked by the women of the household. The furnishings in here date from the seventeenth and eighteenth centuries.

From Mosul in Iraq came the technique of inlaying copper or silver into bronze, which was to characterize Egyptian **metalwork**. A brass-plated door from the Mosque of Salih Tala'i stands at the entrance to **Room 11**. Inside you'll find candlesticks and vases; incense burners inlaid with gold and silver (some with Christian symbols); a fourteenth-century hand-warmer; and a case of astrolabes, used by Muslim navigators. **Room 12** contains a fraction of the Mamluke **Armoury** (most of which was taken to Istanbul by Selim the Grim). Case 7, on the left of the door to Room 11, holds the swords of Mehmet II and Suleyman the Magnificent (the respective conquerors of Constantinople and the Balkans).

Rooms 14–16 shift the focus to **ceramics**, ranging from native bowls and ewers to tiles from Tunisia and Turkey; potshards from Italy, Holland and Spain show the extent of Fustat's commercial reach. Notice in **Room 16** the *ahlaq* (chokes) that were inserted in the necks of Fatimid water jars to regulate their flow, fretted with bird, animal and calligraphic motifs. The room also contains stucco *mihrabs*, a tiled **Turkish fireplace**, and a section of an old **kuttab** (Koranic school) with a niche for the teacher to sit beneath its *murqana'd* ceiling.

With Rooms 17 and 18 closed, you proceed to **Room 21**, devoted to Egyptian **glass**. Various techniques perfected in ancient times continued to be used; lustre ware (a Fatimid speciality) and enamelled glass were the chief innovations in the Islamic period. Amongst the **Persian objects** of the ninth to seventeenth centuries in **Room 22**, notice the ceramic camel with a litter on its back. **Room 20** is stuffed with **Ottoman material**, some of it influenced by European Baroque – the bejewelled, gold-encrusted perfume sprayer and incense burner most of all.

Room 19 showcases **calligraphy and bookbinding**, including Persian and Indian illustrated manuscripts, but primacy is accorded to the word of God, with numerous medieval Korans from the collection of King Farouk. The first mass-produced, totally standardized Korans were made in Egypt following Napoleon's introduction of the printing press; Cairo is still the main publishing centre of the Arab world. The north-west wing of the museum has coins, weights, medals and glass seals in **Room 16B**, and a few wood friezes in the adjacent room.

One hall of the **upper floor** (signposted from the stairs) wraps up the exhibition with a display of **textiles**. Early native weavings have a Coptic flavour, despite the decorative use of Arabic script (known as *tiraz*, Persian for embroidery). There's also a superb range of carpets from Turkey, Yemen, Iran and Central Asia.

Between the Bab Zwayla and the Citadel

There are two basic walking **routes between Bab Zwayla and the Citadel**: via the Qasaba, Sharia al-Muizz and Sharia Qalaa; or following the old **Darb al-Ahmar** (after which this quarter of Islamic Cairo is named). It's possible to get the best of both worlds by combining the Darb al-Ahmar with a detour into the **Qasaba** and **Saddlemakers Bazaar**, located on the other route: a total distance of about 1500m. Assuming you're **starting from the Bab Zwayla** as in the itinerary below, it's logical to visit the Qasaba before embarking on the Darb al-Ahmar; whereas the reverse holds true if you're **coming from the Citadel**. Starting with the "Blue Mosque" of Aqsunqur on Sharia Bab al-Wazir (the Citadel end of Darb al-Ahmar), you can backtrack through the text from there.

From the Bab Zwayla into the Qasaba

Emerging from the Bab Zwayla, you'll see a cluster of Islamic monuments across the street, which is often flooded by burst water mains. On the right-hand corner stands a Sufi establishment, the **Zawiya of Farag ibn Barquq** (currently closed for restoration), whose inlaid marble lintels and *ablaq* panels may be hidden by stalls. Opposite the *zawiya*, the **Mosque of Salih Tala'i** withdraws behind an elegant portico with five keel arches – a unique architectural feature. The shops around its base (whose rents again contribute to the mosque's upkeep) were once at street level, but this has risen well over a metre since the mosque was built in 1408. The last of Cairo's Fatimid mosques, the building shows an assured use of the motifs that were first employed on the Mosque of Al-Aqmar: ribbed and cusped arches and panels, carved tie beams and rosettes. Notice the capitals, plundered from pre-Islamic buildings, and the "floriated kufic" script around the arches.

Straight ahead lies the **Qasaba**, where colourful fabrics, appliqué and leatherwork are piled in dens ranked either side of a gloomy, lofty passageway. Erected by Ridwan Bey in 1650, this is one of the best-preserved examples of a covered market left in Cairo. It is popularly known as the *Khiyamiyya*, or **Tentmakers Bazaar**, as colourful printed fabrics are used here to make tents for moulids and weddings, and to screen unsightly building work – a big improvement on tarpaulins. Printed fabric is sold by the metre, quite cheaply; labour-intensive appliqué work is much pricier (see "Shopping", p.225).

Beyond the Qasaba

Emerging from the southern end of the Qasaba, **Sharia al-Muizz** extends its path between two mosques and the facade of Ridwan Bey's former palace, beyond which the

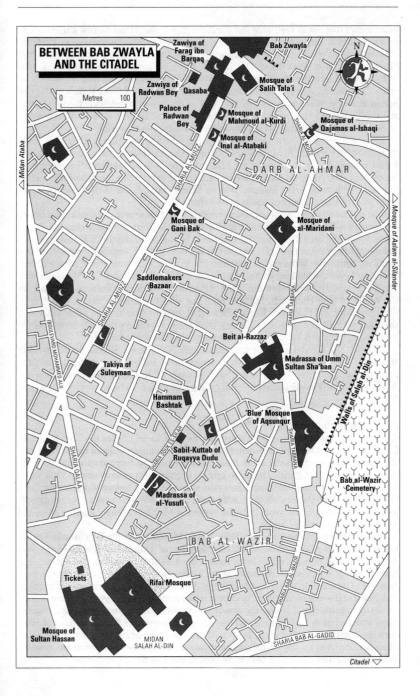

BETWEEN BAB ZWAYLA AND THE CITADEL

0   Metres   100

Zawiya of Farag ibn Barqaq

Bab Zwayla

Zawiya of Radwan Bey

Qasaba

Mosque of Salih Tala'i

Palace of Radwan Bey

Mosque of Mahmoud al-Kurdi

Mosque of Qajamas al-Ishaqi

Mosque of Inal al-Atabaki

DARB AL-AHMAR

Mosque of Gani Bak

Mosque of al-Maridani

Saddlemakers' Bazaar

Beit al-Razzaz

Madrassa of Umm Sultan Sha'ban

Takiya of Suleyman

Hammam Bashtak

'Blue' Mosque of Aqsunqur

Sabil-Kuttab of Ruqayya Dudu

Madrassa of al-Yusufi

Bab al-Wazir Cemetery

BAB AL-WAZIR

Tickets

Rifai Mosque

Mosque of Sultan Hassan

MIDAN SALAH AL-DIN

SHARIA BAB AL-GADID

△ Midan Ataba

△ Mosque of Aslam al-Silander

SHARIA AL-MUIZZ

[BOULEVARD MOHAMMED ALI]

SHARIA QALAA

SHARIA SOUL ES SUKA

SHARIA TABBANA

Walls of Salah al-Din

SHARIA BAB AL-WAZIR

Citadel ▽

monuments thin out as vegetable stalls and butchers congest the narrow street – some of which is still supported by scaffolding, following earthquake damage in 1991. By Mamluke times most of the older quarters here were semi-derelict, merging into the "Tartar Ruins" near the Citadel. The Tartars, recruited by Sultan Kitbugha (1296–96), were despised by other Mamlukes as horse-eaters, and billeted in a quarter that's long since disappeared. About 150m on you'll pass the **Mosque of Gani Bak**, a protégé of Sultan Barsbey, who was poisoned by rivals at the age of twenty-five. Beyond, a few stalls selling donkey and camel wear constitute what remains of the *Souk es-Surugiyyah*, or **Saddlemakers Bazaar**, which produces all kinds of leatherware.

Assuming you don't turn back here to pursue the Darb al-Ahmar, it's a fairly mundane 350-metre walk to Al-Muizz's junction with **Sharia Qalaa**. The Sultan Hassan and Rifai mosques below the Citadel are plainly visible at the boulevard's southern end, 300m away. You could do the last leg by bus, or use services in the opposite direction to reach the Islamic Arts Museum, 1km up Sharia Qalaa. Some of the buses continue on to Midan Ataba, others to Abdin or Al-Azhar.

Adventurous types might consider visiting the **Hammam Bashtak** bathhouse (women 9am–3pm, men before and after), deep in the Darb al-Ahmar quarter. To get there, follow the backstreet running eastwards behind the Takiya of Suleyman, a block before Al-Muizz's junction with Sharia Qalaa. After 250m it reaches a square, where you'll recognize the baths on the western side by their elaborate portal, whose ribbed keel arch bears the napkin symbol of a *jamdar* or "Master of Robes". In Mamluke society, this position ranked below the "Men of the Sword" (cabinet ministers, chosen from the Amirs of One Hundred), but was on a par with the sultan's Taster, Cup-Bearer, Slipper-Holder and Polo-Stick Keeper. Several Mamlukes who became sultans included their former rank (or slave price) among their titles. Nowadays the bath serves people from the neighbourhood whose own tenements lack washing facilities.

To reach the Citadel from the hammam, walk 300m down **Sharia Souk es-Silah** (formerly the Weapons Bazaar, now a secondhand ballbearings market), past the neglected gingerbread facade of the **Sabil-Kuttab of Ruqayya Dudu** and then the **Madrassa of al-Yusufi** (currently undergoing restoration), whose founder was a Cup-Bearer.

Along the Darb al-Ahmar

An alternative, more picturesque route towards the Citadel follows the "Red Road", or **Darb al-Ahmar**. Originally a cemetery beyond the southern walls of the Fatimid city, this quarter became a fashionable residential area in the fourteenth century, as Al-Nasir developed the Citadel. The thoroughfare acquired its present name in 1805, when Mohammed Ali tricked the Mamlukes into staging a coup before slaughtering them "Between the Two Palaces". Stuffed with straw, their heads were sent to Constantinople as a sign of his power; six years later the surviving Mamlukes fell for another ruse, and were massacred on the Citadel.

Start by walking 150m east from Salih Tila'i's Mosque near the Bab Zwayla. On the corner where the Darb turns south, the **Mosque of Qajmas al-Ishaqi** looms over workshops sunk beneath street level. Its founder's blazon – a napkin, penbox, cup and horn of plenty – appears on the knots of the window grilles, indicating the various positions that Qajmas held under Sultan Qaitbey. A marble panel with swirling leaf forms in red, black and white surmounts the entrance to a vestibule with a gilded ceiling; left off this is the mosque itself. Notice the sinuous decorations on the *mihrab* (incised grooves filled with red paste or bitumen) and the fine panelling on the floor near the *qibla* wall (ask the custodian to lift a mat). Best of all are the stained-glass windows in the tomb chamber occupied by one Abu Hurayba. A raised passage connects the mosque with a *sabil-kuttab* across the street; both were built in the 1480s.

A SHORT DETOUR: AL-SILAHDAR'S MOSQUE

If you're not pushed for time, consider detouring off the Darb to visit the **Mosque of Aslam al-Silahdar**. From Qajmas's Mosque, walk through the tunnel around the side and on past a shrine where the street forks (either one will do); Al-Silahdar's Mosque lies 250m ahead. The marble panel outside is typical of exterior decoration during the Bahri Mamluke period; inside, the layout is that of a cruciform **madrassa**. Students used to live in rooms above the north and south *liwans*, behind an ornate facade of stucco mouldings and screened windows. The mosque's founder was a Qipchak Mamluke who lost his position as Swordbearer after Sultan al-Nasir believed rumours spread by his enemies, and imprisoned him, only to reinstate Aslam as *silahdar* (swordbearer) six years later. To return to the Darb, either retrace your steps or take the street running southwest off the square, which joins the Darb further south, beyond Al-Maridani's Mosque.

SOUTH ALONG THE DARB AL-AHMAR

South from the Qajmas Mosque, the Darb al-Ahmar passes the **Mosque of Al-Maridani**, built in 1340 and still a peaceful retreat from the streets. The mosque is usually entered via its northern portal, offset by a stalactite frieze with complex patterns of joggled voussoirs and *ablaq* panels. Inside, a splendid *mashrabiya* screen separates the open courtyard from the *qibla riwaq*, whose stained-glass windows and variegated columns (Mamluke, pre-Islamic and pharaonic) can be glimpsed through the lattice. Because it was economical with wood, and minimized the effect of warping in a hot, dry climate, *mashrabiya*-work was an ideal technique for Egyptian craftsmen. Architecturally speaking, the minaret marks the replacement of the Ayyubid "pepper-pot" finial by a small dome on pillars, which became the hallmark of Mamluke minarets. Below the dome and above the *minbar*, arboreal forms in stucco may allude to the Koranic verse, "A good word is as a good tree – its roots firm, its branches in heaven".

Leaving via the southern entrance, you'll need to turn left to rejoin the Darb – or **Sharia Tabbana** as it's called at this point. Roughly 200m on, past a small Turkish mosque, stands the hulking **Madrassa of Umm Sultan Sha'ban**. *Umm* (Mother of) Sha'ban was the concubine of a son of Al-Nasir, whose own son erected the madrassa (1368–69) as a gesture of gratitude after he became sultan at the age of ten; murdered in 1376, he preceded her to the grave and was buried here since his own madrassa was unfinished. A wealth of *murqanas* and *ablaq* rims the entrance, which is flanked by a *sabil* and a drinking trough. Watering animals was meritorious in the eyes of Islam; the Prophet himself had seen a prostitute give water to a thirsty dog, and promised her, "For this action you shall enter paradise"; but if you want to enter the mosque, you'll have to find the guardian, which is easier said than done. Behind it, and entered by the neighbouring doorway (no. 56), lurks the **Beit al-Razzaz**, a rambling, derelict palace which the American Research Centre hopes to restore.

THE BLUE MOSQUE

Further along the street, now called **Sharia Bab al-Wazir** after the Gate of the Vizier that once stood here, lies the **"Blue Mosque"** or **Mosque of Aqsunqur** (£E6, students £E3), which is directly accessible via #68 minibus from Midan Ramses and the Bab Zwayla, or #75 from Midan Tahir. Blue-grey marble outside and a *qibla* wall covered in indigo and turquoise tiling – with cypresses, tulips and other floral motifs either side of the magnificently inlaid *mihrab* – explain the mosque's name and popularity with tourists. Originally the mosque was plainer, its *ablaq* arches framing a *sahn*, now battered and dusty, with a palm tree and chirping birds. The Iznik-style tiles (imported from Turkey or Syria) were added in the 1650s by Ibrahim Agha, who usurped and redecorated the fourteenth-century mosque. However, the *minbar* inlaid with salmon, plum, green and grey stone is from the original building. The recently restored minaret affords a superb **view** of the Citadel, and on a clear day you can even make out the Pyramids on the far side of the city.

The mosque's founder, Shams al-Din Aqsunqur, intrigued against the successors of Sultan al-Nasir, his father-in-law – whose son Al-Ashraf Kuchuk (Little One) was enthroned at the age of six, "reigned" five months, and was strangled by his brother three years later. The reign of Al-Kamil Sha'ban (not to be confused with Sha'ban II, who erected the madrassa) lasted a year, ending in a palace coup and the crowning of his brother-in-law, Muzaffar Hadji. Recalling how Aqsunqur had manipulated Kuchuk (who's buried just inside the mosque's entrance) and deftly organized the coup against Sha'ban, Muzaffar promptly had him garrotted.

From this mosque, Bab al-Wazir gradually slopes up to meet the approach road **to the Citadel**. If that's your destination, turn left and keep climbing.

The Citadel and around

The Citadel is the natural focus of a visit to Islamic Cairo; while the area just below it, around Midan Salah al-Din, features two of the city's greatest monuments – the **Sultan Hassan** and **Rifai mosques**. To do justice to these, and to the Citadel itself, you need a good half a day.

To reach the Citadel area, you can either catch a taxi from downtown (£E5–7), or a bus (see p.81 for bus routes) – if you've got the energy, it's also an interesting walk. Any of these approaches will leave you beneath the Citadel, either on Midan Salah al-Din or lower down behind the Sultan Hassan and Rifai mosques. Depending on how much time you have, you may only want to visit the Citadel, but it is well worth stopping in Midan Salah al-Din to take in the arresting mix of sounds and the views (see below). For information on moving on from the Citadel and connecting up with other walking itineraries, see p.140.

Midan Salah al-Din

Prosaic traffic islands and monumental grandeur meet beneath the Citadel on **Midan Salah al-Din**, where makeshift swings and colourful tents are pitched for local moulids. With an audience of lesser mosques on the sidelines, the scene is set for a confrontation of behemoths, given voice when the **muezzins** call. Both the Rifai and Sultan Hassan mosques have powerfully voiced muezzins whose duet echoes off the surrounding tenements. This amazing aural experience is best enjoyed seated in the **outdoor café** beside Sultan Hassan's Mosque; never mind that its tea is vastly overpriced.

From this café vantage point you can survey the Rifai and Sultan Hassan mosques, built so close as to create a knife-sharp, almost perpetually shadowed canyon between them. The dramatic angles and chiaroscuro, coupled with the great stalactite portal on this side of the Rifai, make this facade truly spectacular, although the view from Midan Salah al-Din and the Citadel takes some beating. A few centuries ago, all this area would have been swarming with mounted Mamlukes, escorting the sultan to polo matches or prayers.

The Citadel

The Citadel (*Al-Qalaa* – usually pronounced "Al-'Alaa"; daily: winter 8am–5pm; summer 8am–6pm; mosques closed Fri; museums refuse entry 30min before closing; £E20, students £E10) presents the most dramatic feature of Cairo's skyline: a centuries-old bastion crowned by the needle-like minarets of the great Mosque of Mohammed Ali. This fortified complex was begun by **Salah al-Din**, the founder of the Ayyubid dynasty – known throughout Christendom as Saladin, the Crusaders' chivalrous foe. Salah al-Din's reign (1171–93) saw much fortification of the city, though it was his nephew, Al-

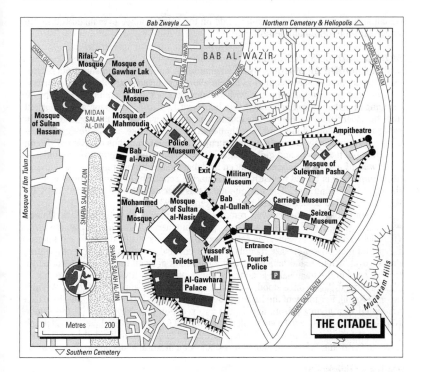

Kamil, who developed the citadel as a royal residence, later to be replaced by the palaces of Sultan al-Nasir.

The main features of the Citadel as it is today, however, are associated with **Mohammed Ali**, a worthy successor to the Mamlukes and Turks. In 1811 he feasted 470 leading Mamlukes in the Citadel palace, bade them farewell with honours, then had them ambushed in the sloping lane behind the **Bab al-Azab**, the locked gate opposite the Akhur Mosque. An oil painting in the Manial Palace on Roda Island depicts the apocryphal tale of a Mamluke who escaped by leaping the walls on his horse; in reality he survived by not attending the feast.

Nowadays the **main entrance** to the Citadel is at a higher level, closer to the centre of the complex; the road there curves up from Midan Salah al-Din in a clockwise direction, past the start of Sharia Bab al-Wazir. Having passed through the gate-tunnel and the inner Bab al-Wustani, you emerge into a courtyard with the **Police National Museum** on one side. This quirky exhibition includes sanitized "cells throughout the ages"; rooms devoted to Egypt's most sensational murders and assassinations (Sadat's is conspicuously absent); and a risible US "how to recognize drugs" kit. Apropos of Sadat and drugs, the late president is reputed to have been a keen hash smoker, and his brother Esmat to have received a percentage on every kilo sold in Cairo. Note that the café here not only has a pleasant terrace with good views over Cairo, but is also a lot cheaper than the indoor café or the drinks-sellers scattered around the Citadel – they'll charge you £E5 for a bottle of water.

There is a superb **view** of the entire city from the Citadel's terrace, to the right of which, in a pit, are the **excavated remains of the Qasr al-Ablaq** or Striped Palace of

Sultan al-Nasir, whose mosque still stands on the Citadel, albeit overshadowed by the loftier Mosque of Mohammed Ali.

MOHAMMED ALI'S MONUMENTS

The **Mohammed Ali Mosque**, which so ennobles Cairo's skyline, disappoints at close quarters: its domes are sheathed in tin, its alabaster surfaces grubby. Nonetheless, it exudes *folie de grandeur*, starting with the ornate clock given by Louis Philippe (in exchange for the obelisk in the Place de la Concorde, Paris), which has never worked; and the Turkish Baroque ablutions fountain, resembling a giant Easter egg. Inside the mosque, whose lofty dome and semi-domes are decorated like a Fabergé egg, the use of space is classically Ottoman, reminiscent of the great mosques of Istanbul. A constellation of chandeliers and globe lamps illuminates Thuluth inscriptions, a gold-scalloped *mihrab* and two *minbars*, one faced in alabaster, the other strangely Art Nouveau. Mohammed Ali is buried beneath a white marble cenotaph, behind a bronze grille on the right of the entrance. The mosque itself was erected between 1824 and 1848, but the domes had to be demolished and rebuilt in the 1930s.

Due south of here stands what remains of Mohammed Ali's **Al-Gawhara Palace**, where he waited while the Mamlukes were butchered. Also known as the *Bijou* (Jewelled) Palace, its French-style salons exhibit portraits of the khedives and kings of Egypt and their wives; life-size models of monarchs and courtiers in nineteenth-century dress; royal furniture and tableware; and a collection of awful Impressionist works; the trompe l'oeil in the main salon is none too successful either. It was around here that Al-Nasir's Striped Palace once stood, and that St Francis of Assisi preached to the Ayyubid ruler Al-Kamil. For many of the hapless boy-sultans chosen by the Mamlukes, the palace amounted to a luxury prison, and finally an execution cell. Nevertheless, the Citadel remained the residence of Egypt's rulers for nearly 700 years, and Mohammed Ali prophesied that his descendants would rule supreme as long as they resided here. Ismail's move to the Abdin Palace did indeed foreshadow an inexorable decline in their power.

MEDIEVAL REMAINS

For an idea of the Citadel's appearance before Mohammed Ali's grandiose reconstruction programme, visit the **Mosque of Sultan al-Nasir** (also called the Mosque of Ibn Qalaoun, after Al-Nasir's father). The Mamlukes and the Mongols of Persia enjoyed good relations when the mosque was constructed (1318–35), and a Tabriz master mason probably designed the corkscrew minarets with their bulbous finials and faïence decorations, if not the dome, which also smacks of Central Asia. Since Selim the Grim carted its marble panelling back to Turkey, the mosque's courtyard has looked ruggedly austere, with rough-hewn pillars supporting *ablaq* arches linked by Fatimid-style tie-beams – although the *mihrab* itself is a feast of gold and marble. Notice the stepped merlons around the parapet, and the blue, white and silver decorations beneath the sanctuary *liwan*.

If you leave the mosque, turn right and walk clockwise around it, you'll find a wasteland with barbicans at the far end. There, a locked gate prevents admission to **Yussef's Well**, which spirals down 97m to the level of the Nile, whence water percolates through fissures in the bedrock. Dug by prisoners between 1176 and 1182, this so-called "Well of the Snail" had its steps strewn with soil to provide a footing for the donkeys that carried up water jars. The Citadel's infamous Jubb dungeon, "a noisome pit where foul and deadly exhalations, unclean vermin and bats rendered the pitchy darkness more horrible", was blocked up by Al-Nasir in 1329, but reactivated under the latterday Mamluke sultans.

THE NORTHERN ENCLOSURE

Passing through the Bab al-Qullah, you'll enter the Citadel's northern enclosure, open to visitors despite a military presence. Straight ahead, beyond a parade of Soviet and

US-made tanks from four Arab–Israeli Wars, Mohammed Ali's old Harim Palace is occupied by the **Military Museum**. This vast exhibition devotes more space to ceremonial accoutrements than the savage realities of war, and even pacifists should enjoy the main salon, with its spectacular trompe l'oeil. While in a military vein, it's worth recalling that the Citadel fell to Mohammed Ali after he stationed cannons on the Muqattam heights. The military electronics that festoon them now are a reminder that strategic ground seldom loses its utility.

By turning right at the barracks near the enclosure entrance and following the lane around, you'll come out into a compound with a formal garden. At the northern end stands the **Carriage Museum**, with its row of horseheads. Inside are six royal carriages and two picnic buggies, one of them an infant prince's; the largest state carriage – heavy with gold – was presented as a gift to Khedive Ismail by Emperor Napoleon and Empress Eugénie. Just beyond is the small **Seized Museum**, displaying various pharaonic, Roman, Coptic and Islamic antiquities recovered from smugglers before they left Egypt.

Behind here are two of the many bastions along the Citadel's ramparts, each with evocative names. Although the derivation of **Burg Kirkyilan** (Tower of the Forty Serpents) is unknown, the **Burg al-Matar** (Tower of the Flight Platform) probably housed the royal carrier pigeons. Neither can be entered, but it's worth visiting a neglected treasure at the other end of the compound. A cluster of verdigris domes and a pencil-sharp minaret identify the **Mosque of Suleyman Pasha** as an early sixteenth-century Ottoman creation, borne out by the lavish arabesques and rosettes adorning the interior of the cupola and semi-domes. Inside, cross the courtyard to find a **mausoleum** where the tombs of amirs and their families have *tabuts* indicating their rank: turbans or hats for the men, floral-patterned *lingums* for the women. Adjacent to the courtyard is a **madrassa** where students took examinations beneath a *riwaq* upheld by painted beams.

The Mosque of Sultan Hassan

Raised at the command of a son of Al-Nasir, the scale of the **Mosque of Sultan Hassan** (daily: winter 8am–5pm; summer 8am–6pm; £E6, students £E3; the ticket office is behind the mosque) was unprecedentedly huge when it was begun in 1356, and some design flaws soon became apparent. The plan to have a minaret at each corner was abandoned after the one directly above the entrance collapsed, killing 300 people; then Hassan himself was assassinated in 1391, two years before the mosque's completion. After another minaret toppled in 1659, the weakened dome collapsed; and if this wasn't enough, the roof was also used as an artillery platform during coups against sultans Barquq (1391) and Tumanbey (1517). But the mosque is big enough to withstand a lot of battering: 150m long, covering an area of 7906 square metres, its walls rise to 36m and its tallest minaret to 68m.

The mosque is best seen when the morning sun illuminates its deep courtyard and cavernous mausoleum, revealing subtle colours and textures disguised by shadows later in the day. Entering beneath a towering stalactite hood, you're drawn by instinct through a gloomy domed vestibule with *liwans*, out into the central **sahn** – a stupendous balancing of mass and void. Vaulted **liwans** soar on four sides, their height emphasized by hanging lamp chains, their maws by red and black rims, all set off by a bulbous-domed ablutions fountain (probably an Ottoman addition). Each *liwan* was devoted to teaching a rite of Sunni Islam, providing theological justification for the cruciform plan the Mamlukes strove to achieve regardless of the site. At Sultan Hassan, four **madrassas** have been skilfully fitted into an irregular area behind the *liwans* to maintain the internal cruciform.

Soft-hued marble inlay and a band of monumental kufic script distinguish the sanctuary *liwan* from its roughly plastered neighbours. To the right of the *mihrab* is a bronze door, exquisitely worked with radiating stars and satellites in gold and silver; on the other side is **Hassan's mausoleum**. Cleverly sited to derive *baraka* from prayers to Mecca, while overlooking his old stamping grounds, the mausoleum is sombre beneath its restored dome, upheld by stalactite pendentives. Around the chamber runs a carved and painted *Thuluth* inscription, from the Throne verse of the Koran. Note also the ivory-inlaid *kursi*, or Koranic lectern.

The Rifai and Amir Akhur Mosques

The **Rifai Mosque** (same opening hours, entrance price and ticket office as Sultan Hussan's Mosque) is pseudo-Mamluke, built between 1869 and 1912 for Princess Khushyar, the mother of Khedive Ismail. With the royal entrance now closed, you enter on the side facing Sultan Hassan. Straight ahead in a sandalwood enclosure lies the **tomb of Sheikh Ali al-Rifai**, founder of the Rifai *tariqa* of dervishes, whose moulid occurs during the sixth month of the Muslim calendar, *Gumad el-Tani*. Off to your left are the *mashrabiya*-screened **tombs of King Fouad** (who reigned 1917–36), his mother, the last **Shah of Iran** and **King Farouk** of Egypt (who likewise died in exile). The monumental sanctuary (on the left) is impressive, but after Ismail's chief eunuch had overseen its forty-four columns, nineteen types of marble, eighteen window grilles costing £E1000 apiece, and £E25,000 dispersed on gold leaf, dowdiness was scarcely possible: what it lacks is the power of simplicity embodied by the mosques of Ibn Tulun and Sultan Hassan.

Finally, facing the Citadel, you can't miss the **Mosque of Amir Akhur** (on the left), with its bold red and white *ablaq*, breast-like dome and double minaret finial, incorporating a *sabil-kuttab* at the lower end of its sloping site.

On from the Citadel

Of the various itineraries emanating from the Citadel, the shortest takes you to the awesome Mosque of Ibn Tulun, whilst the longest ones (requiring transport) involve the Cities of the Dead; both are covered in sections following. The section before this one details the route along the Darb al-Ahmar/Sharia Bab al-Wazir from the Bab Zwayla; you could pick up the trail at the Blue Mosque (see p.135) and follow the directions in the text in reverse.

The Mosque of Ibn Tulun and the Saiyida Zeinab quarter

Two aspects of Islam are strikingly apparent in the great **Mosque of Ibn Tulun** and the quarter of the city named after Egypt's beloved saint, **Saiyida Zeinab**. The mosque evokes the simplicity of Islam's central tenet, submission to Allah, whereas the surrounding neighbourhoods are urban stews seething with popular cults. **Zeinab's moulid** is the wildest festival in Cairo, sucking 500,000 people into a pulsing vortex around her mosque, 1km west of Ibn Tulun's. Its high-octane blend of intense devotion and sheer enjoyment is also characteristic of **other moulids** honouring Saiyida Nafisa, Ruqayya and Aisha, whose shrines lie between Ibn Tulun and El-Khalifa (the Southern Cemetery).

The following section covers only Ibn Tulun, Saiyida Zeinab and sites along Sharia Saliba, which are shown in relation to the Citadel and Southern Cemetery on the **map** opposite. Conceivably, you could visit all of them in a single day – though a more leisurely approach seems advisable.

APPROACHES TO THE QUARTER

Bus #174 and minibus #54 provide the easiest access to Saiyida Zeinab **from Midan Tahrir**, running through the quarter past its namesake shrine and within sight of Ibn

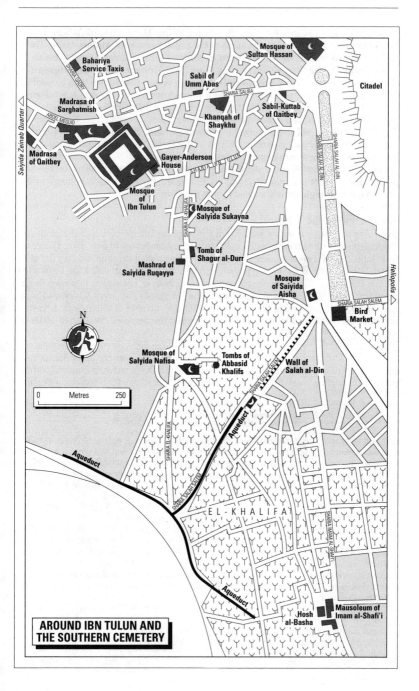

AROUND IBN TULUN AND
THE SOUTHERN CEMETERY

Tulun's Mosque, towards the Citadel, and on to the Mausoleum of Al-Shafi in the Southern Cemetery. Alternatively, minibus #56 and #81 run **from Midan Ataba**. There is also a **metro station** within five to ten minutes walk from Midan Saiyada Zeinab.

Alternatively, the fifteen-minute walk **from the Mosque of Sultan Hassan** to Ibn Tulun takes you along **Sharia Saliba**, past a prison that serves as a barometer of law and order: whenever there's been a crackdown you can see several arms thrust from each cell window. Next comes the lofty **Sabil-Kuttab of Qaitbey**, with its bold red, white and black facade. Further along, beyond the **Khanqah of Shaykhu**, Sharia al-Khalifa turns off **towards the Southern Cemetery**, as described in the following section, "Cities of the Dead". By ignoring this and carrying on past the nineteenth-century *sabil* **of Umm Abbas**, with its blue and red panels and gilt calligraphy, you'll see the huge walls of Ibn Tulun's Mosque on the left. Its entrance is that way, too, and not via the nearest portal, which belongs to the **Madrassa of Sarghatmish**, closed to non-Muslims.

The Mosque of Ibn Tulun

Ibn Tulun's Mosque is a rare survivor of the classical Islamic period of the ninth and tenth centuries, when the Abbasid khalifs ruled the Muslim world from Iraq. Their purpose-built capital, Samarra, centred upon a congregational mosque where the entire population assembled for Friday prayer, and this most likely provided the inspiration for the Ibn Tulun. You enter the mosque via a **ziyada**, or enclosure, designed to distance the mosque from its surroundings; to the left stands the Gayer-Anderson House (see below). It's only within the inner walls that the vastness of the mosque becomes apparent: the courtyard is 92 metres square, while the complex, measuring 140m by 122m, covers six and a half acres.

Besides sheer size, the **mosque** impresses by its simplicity. Strewn with pebbles and open to the sky, its vast court has the grandeur of a desert where all of Allah's worshippers are prostrated equally beneath the sun. Ibn Tulun's architects understood the power of repetition – see how the merlons echo the rhythm of the arcades – but also

---

IBN TULUN AND AL-QITAI

It was from Iraq that the Abbasids made **Ahmed Ibn Tulun** governor of Fustat in 868, and smarted as he declared his independence. Ibn Tulun (the "Son of Tulun", a Turkish slave) founded the Tulunid dynasty that ruled Egypt until 905, and established a new city to the northeast of Fustat. According to legends, Noah's Ark had come to rest on this site when the Flood receded; Moses confronted the pharaoh's magicians here; and Abraham had been ready to sacrifice his son on a nearby hillock. Unperturbed by this, nor by the existence of Christian and Jewish cemeteries on the site, he dictated the construction of **Al-Qitai**, called "the Wards" after its division into military cantonments.

Ibn Tulun's performance on the polo field filled his doctors with foreboding, for in sickness he "refused to follow their orders, flouted their prescribed diet, and when he found himself still sinking, he had their heads chopped off, or flogged them till they died". But under his soft-living successor the Al-Qitai *midan* was converted into a garden with a quicksilver lake, where the insomniac Khomaruya lolled on an airbed guarded by a blue-eyed lion. The Tulunids could afford such luxury, for their annual revenue amounted to 4,300,000 dinars.

When the Abbasids subsequently reconquered Egypt in 905, they destroyed everything here but the mosque, which became derelict. Exploited as a makeshift caravanserai, and a hideout for bodysnatchers during the terrible famine of 1200, it was belatedly restored in 1296 by Sultan Laghin, who had hidden there as an amir suspected of murdering the sultan.

restraint: small floral capitals and stucco rosettes seem the only decorative motifs, although that isn't so. Beneath the arcades you'll find a sycamore-wood frieze over two kilometres long, relating roughly one fifth of the Koran in kufic script. The severely geometric *mida'a*, an inspired focal point, was added in the thirteenth century, when the *mihrab* was also jazzed up with marble and glass mosaics – the only unsuccessful note in the complex.

The **minaret** (entered from outside the mosque) is unique for its exterior spiral stair-case, which gives the structure a helical shape. Supposedly, Ibn Tulun twisted a scrap of paper into a spiral, and then justified his absent-minded deed by presenting it as the design for a minaret. But the great minaret at Samarra (itself influenced by ancient Babylonian ziggurats) seems a likelier source of inspiration.

The Gayer-Anderson House

From the *ziyada* of the Ibn Tulun mosque a sign directs you to the **Gayer-Anderson House** (Mon–Thurs, Sat & Sun 9am–4pm, Fri 9–11am & 1.30–3.30pm; £E12, students £E6, camera £E10), otherwise known as the *Beit al-Kritiliya* (House of the Cretan Woman), which abuts the southeast corner of the mosque.

Gayer-Anderson was a retired British major who during the 1930s and 1940s refur-bished two mansions dating from the sixteenth and eighteenth centuries, filling them with his Orientalist bric-a-brac. Amongst the many paintings is a self-portrait of Gayer-Anderson wearing a pharaonic headdress. **Tours** of the house (the buildings are linked by a passage on the third floor) are conducted by charming curators. There are Persian, Chinese and Queen Anne rooms, and an amazing guest bedroom named after Damascus, whence its opulent wooden panelling originated. Women can sneak through a camouflaged *dulap* (wall cupboard) into the screened gallery overlooking the *salam-lik*, as in olden days. With its polychrome fountain, decorated ceiling and kilim-covered pillows, this is the finest reception hall left in Islamic Cairo. It was the set for a tryst and murder in the James Bond film *The Spy Who Loved Me*.

Saiyida Zeinab

The backstreets west of Ibn Tulun harbour another gem of Islamic architecture in the **Madrassa of Qaitbey**. Ignore the dust and grime and tip the curator to unlock the building, whose mosaic floors and *minbar* are superb examples of fifteenth-century craftsmanship.

Real aficionados can also track down other monuments in the area, detailed in the AUC guide. Otherwise, ride further west into the densely populated **Saiyida Zeinab quarter**, where Islamic and modern Cairo merge in a confusion of tenement blocks and **markets**. Midan Lazoghli, on the edge of the Abdin quarter, hosts a daily car spares and repairs souk, while a **bird market** is held beneath an overpass in the direc-tion of Qasr al-Aini Hospital on Mondays and Thursdays – hence its name, the *Souk Itnayn w Khamis*.

Like Saiyida Zeinab metro station, the market is on the quarter's periphery, where it merges with Garden City and Old Cairo (see the map on p.150). To the northeast of the slaughterhouse district and the Al-Abdin Mosque lies the **Brooke Hospital for Animals**. Founded by Dorothy Brooke in 1934, the hospital treats infirm donkeys and other beasts of burden free of charge, purchases the incurables and puts them out to grass. Egyptians find the whole idea bizarre, but appreciate the service; a stream of patients wends its way up Sikket el-Masbah, off Sharia Bayram el-Tonsi. Phone if you want to visit (☎364-9312).

The quarter's highlight is the annual **Moulid of Saiyida Zeinab**, which features parades of Sufi orders by day, and nocturnal festivities that attract half a million people. Ecstatic devotion and pleasure rub shoulders (and other parts of the anatomy, if you're a woman) in this seething, mostly male crowd, transfixed by the music and spectacles. To see the *zikrs*, snake charmers, conjurers, nail-swallowers and dancing horses performing, you'll have to force your way through a scrum of people and tents – don't bring any valuables. The fifteen-day event takes place during *Ragab*, the seventh month of the Muslim calendar.

The focal point for these celebrations is the **Mosque of Saiyida Zeinab** (closed to non-Muslims), off Sharia Bur Said. Born in 628 AD, Zeinab, the Prophet's granddaughter, emigrated to Fustat after the Umayyads slew her brother, Hussein, and died there shortly afterwards. For Egyptian Muslims – especially women – Zeinab is a protectress whose *baraka* (blessing) is sought in matters of fortune and health; in other words, a popular saint. Although the Koran forbids the deification of mortals, the human urge to anthropomorphize religious faith seems irresistible. Every Muslim nation has its own "saints" (chosen by popular acclaim rather than a supreme authority), and respects bloodlines descended from the Prophet or his immediate kin. For the Shia, the martyrdom of Ali and Hussein is a parable of their own oppression, while Zeinab (whose moulid attracts foreign Shia) is honoured as their closest kinswoman.

Before heading back into town, you might want to try one of Saiyida Zeinab's many cheap but renowned **eating places**, for more on which see p.211. To return to downtown Cairo from here, catch a bus or minibus from near Zeinab's mosque (see above for bus numbers), or ask for directions to the nearest metro entrance (ten minutes' walk). From Saiyida Zeinab station you can ride two stops north to Tahrir, or two stops south to reach Old Cairo (Mari Girgis station).

Cities of the Dead

It's thought that at least 300,000 Cairenes live amid the **Cities of the Dead**: two vast cemeteries that stretch away from the Citadel to merge with newer shantytowns below the Muqattam. The Southern Cemetery, sprawling to the southeast of Ibn Tulun's mosque, is only visible from the Muqattam, or at close quarters. The Northern Cemetery, by contrast, is an unforgettably eerie sight, with dozens of mausolea rising from a sea of dwellings along the road from Cairo Airport.

Although tourists generally – and understandably – feel uneasy about viewing the cemeteries' splendid **funerary architecture** with squatters living all around or in the tombs, few natives regard the Cities of the Dead as forbidding places. Egyptians have a long tradition of building "houses" near their ancestral graves and picnicking or even staying there overnight; other families have simply occupied them. By Cairene standards these are poor but decent neighbourhoods, with shops, schools and electricity, maybe even piped water and sewers. The saints buried here provide a moral touchstone and *baraka* for their communities, who honour them with **moulids**.

Though generally not a dangerous quarter, it's best to exercise some caution when **visiting**. Don't flaunt money or costly possessions, and be sure to dress modestly; women should have a male escort, and will seem more respectable if wearing a headscarf. By responding to local kids (who may request *baksheesh*) with the right blend of authority and affection, you can win the sympathy of their elders and seem less of an intruder; react wrongly, and you might be stoned out of the neighbourhood. You'll be marginally less conspicuous on Fridays, when many Cairenes visit their family plots; but remember that mosques can't be entered during midday prayers. At all events, leave the cemeteries well before dark, if only to avoid getting lost in their labyrinthine alleys – and don't stray to the east into the inchoate (and far riskier) slums built around the foothills of the Muqattam.

The Southern Cemetery (Al-Qarafrah al-Kubra)

The older and larger **Southern Cemetery** is broadly synonymous with the residential quarter of **El-Khalifa**, named after the Abbasid khalifs buried amidst its mud-brick tenements. The area is noted for drug dealing and quite unsafe after dark. Although the Abbasid tombs aren't half as imposing as those of the Mamlukes in the Northern Cemetery, one of the approach routes passes several shrines famous for their moulids, while another moulid is held at the beautiful **Mausoleum of Imam al-Shafi'i**, best reached by bus as a separate excursion. For this reason, we've described two different routes into what Egyptians call "the Great Cemetery" (*Al-Qarafah al-Kubra*).

SHARIA SALIBA TO THE TOMB OF THE ABBASID KHALIFS

This walking route passes through one of the oldest poor neighbourhoods in Cairo, where it's thought that people started settling around their saints' graves as early as the tenth century. None of the tombs are remarkable visually, but the stories and moulids attached to them are interesting. The trail begins where **Sharia al-Khalifa** turns south off Sharia Saliba, just after the Khanqah of Shayku (see map on p.141).

Heading south along this narrow street, full of commerce and capering children, you'll be pestered past a succession of tombs. The second on the left, within a green and white mosque, is that of **Saiyida Sukayna**, a daughter of Hussein, whose moulid (held during *Rabi el-Tani*) is attended by several thousand locals and features traditional entertainments like dancing horses and stick-twisters.

Such saintly graves invariably acquired an oratory (*mashrad*) or mosque, unlike the **Tomb of Shagar al-Durr**, 100m further on: a derelict edifice sunk below street level. Shagar al-Durr (Tree of Pearls) was the widow of Sultan Ayyub, who ruled as *sultana* of Egypt for eighty days (1249–50) until the Abbasid khalif pronounced "Woe unto nations ruled by a woman", compelling her to marry Aybak, the first Mamluke sultan, and govern "from behind the *mashrabiya*". In 1257 she ordered Aybak's murder after learning that he sought another wife, but then tried to save him; the assassins cried, "If we stop halfway through, he will kill both you and us!" Rejecting her offer to marry Qutuz, their new leader, the Mamlukes handed Shagar al-Durr over to Aybak's former wife, whose servants beat her to death with bath clogs and threw her body to the jackals. Now totally gutted, her locked tomb once contained a *tabut* inscribed: "Oh you who stand beside my grave, show not surprise at my condition. Yesterday I was as you, tomorrow, you will be like me".

Slightly further down and across the street, three shrines are grouped within a compound entered via a green and white doorway. The **Mashrad of Saiyida Ruqayya**, on the left, commemorates the stepsister of Saiyida Zeinab, with whom she came to Egypt; the name of her father, Ali, adorns its rare Fatimid *mihrab*, and the devotion she inspires is particularly evident during Ruqayya's moulid.

Ruqayya's devotion doesn't, however, compare with that accorded to the **Mosque of Saiyida Nafisa**, 100m to the south, past the market square. This, Egypt's third-holiest shrine, is closed to non-Muslims, though visitors can still appreciate the good-natured crowd that hangs around after Friday noon prayers, or Nafisa's moulid, usually held in the middle of the month of *Gumad al-Tani* (see p.220). Honoured during her lifetime as a descendant of the Prophet, a *hafizat al-Qur'an* (one who knows the Koran by heart) and a friend of Imam al-Shafi'i, Nafisa was famed for working miracles and conferring *baraka*. Her shrine has been repeatedly enlarged since Fatimid times – the Southern Cemetery possibly began with devotees settling or being buried near her grave – and the present mosque was built in 1897.

If you walk through the passage to its left, turn right at the end and then right again, you should find yourself outside the compound enclosing the **Tombs of the Abbasid Khalifs** (open 24hr). Having been driven from Baghdad by the Mongols, the khalifs' surviving relatives gratefully accepted Beybars's offer to re-establish them in Egypt, only to discover that they were "No longer Commander of the Faithful, but Commander of the Wind". Beybars appropriated the domed mausoleum (usually kept locked) for his own sons; the khalifs were buried outdoors in less than grandiose tombs. Notice the beautiful foliate kufic inscription on the cenotaph of Khadiga, under the wooden shed. In 1517 the last Abbasid khalif was formally divested of his office, which the Ottomans assumed in 1538, and Ataturk abolished in the 1920s.

An alternative route back towards the Citadel passes the **Mosque of Saiyida Aisha**, whose **moulid** occurs during *Sha'ban*. To get there, retrace your steps to the market square south of Ruqayya's shrine and take the road leading off to the right. It's roughly 500 metres' walk to Aisha's Mosque on Sharia Salah Salem, which runs southwest alongside the medieval **Wall of Salah al-Din**. From here you can simply follow the tramlines **towards the Citadel** (1km). If you happen to be here on Friday, consider making a detour to the **bird market** (*Souk al-Asafeer* or *Souk al-Gom'a*), held on a side street to the south of the Salah Salem overpass.

THE MAUSOLEUM OF IMAM AL-SHAFI'I

Imam al-Shafi'i, revered as the founder of one of the four rites of Sunni Islam, occupies a great mausoleum 2km from the Citadel. Aside from catching a taxi from there (for about £E3–5), the mausoleum is accessible by bus #81 or #89 from Midan Ataba, or bus #160 from Midan Ramses, or more comfortable #54 minibuses from Tahrir, which turn off Sharia Imam al-Shafi'i, 100m beforehand. If you miss the turn-off, ride on to the terminal, have a glass of tea with the driver, and get dropped at the corner on the way back.

Recognizable by its graceful dome, crowned by a metal boat like a weather vane, the **Mausoleum of Imam al-Shafi'i** lurks beside a mosque at the end of the street (free but *baksheesh* appropriate). The largest Islamic mortuary complex in Egypt, it was raised in 1211 by Al-Kamil, Salah al-Din's nephew, a propagator of Sunni orthodoxy like the Imam himself, who died in 820. Al-Shafi'i's teak cenotaph – into which the faithful slip petitions – lies beneath a magnificent dome perched on stalactite squinches, painted red and blue, with gilt designs. The walls are clad in variegated marble, dating from Qaitbey's restoration of the building in the 1480s. In times past, the boat on the roof was filled with birdseed and water; boats are vehicles of spiritual enlightenment in Islamic symbolism, while birds are associated with souls.

Al-Shafi'i's **Moulid** attracts many sick and infirm people, seeking his *baraka*. The festival occurs in *Sha'ban*, the eighth month of the Muslim calendar, but the starting date varies. Normally it's the first Wednesday of the month; however, if this falls on the first or second day of *Sha'ban*, the moulid is delayed until the following Wednesday. Either way, it ends on Wednesday evening the following week. More prosaically, the street leading northwards to the mausoleum from the Al-Basatin quarter is used for scrap, clothing and livestock **markets** every Friday morning.

By walking clockwise around the block in which the Imam's mausoleum is located, you'll find a five-domed complex directly behind it. Inside the courtyard are clumps of cenotaphs decorated with garlands and fronds, topped by a turban, fez or other headdress to indicate the deceased's rank. These constitute the **Hosh al-Basha**, where Mohammed Ali's sons, their wives, children and retainers are buried. The conspicuously plain cenotaph belongs to a princess with radical sympathies, who abhorred ostentation. The body of King Farouk himself, who died in exile, now reposes in the Rifai Mosque. In a separate room, forty statues commemorate the five hundred Mamlukes butchered by Mohammed Ali in the Citadel (see p.137).

The Northern Cemetery (Al-Qarafat al-Sharqiyyah)

The finest of Cairo's funerary monuments – erected by the Burgi Mamlukes from the fourteenth to sixteenth centuries – are spread around the **Northern Cemetery**. The majority of tourists who venture in from Sharia Salah Salem are content to see three main sites, plus whatever crops up in between, over an hour or so.

Aside from catching a taxi (ask for the *Qarafat al-Sharqiyyah* – Eastern Cemetery – in Arabic), the surest way of **getting there** is to walk **from Al-Azhar**. This will take

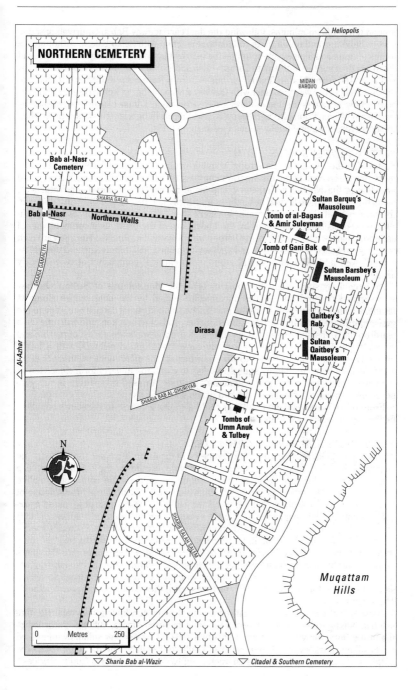

NORTHERN CEMETERY

△ Heliopolis

MIDAN BARQUO

Bab al-Nasr Cemetery

SHARIA GALAL

Bab al-Nasr

Northern Walls

SHARIA GAMALIYA

◁ Al-Azhar

Sultan Barquq's Mausoleum

Tomb of al-Bagasi & Amir Suleyman

Tomb of Gani Bak

Sultan Barsbey's Mausoleum

Qaitbey's Rab

Sultan Qaitbey's Mausoleum

Dirasa

SHARIA BAB AL-GHURIYAB

Tombs of Umm Anuk & Tulbey

N

SHARIA SALAH SALEM

Muqattam Hills

0   Metres   250

▽ Sharia Bab al-Wazir   ▽ Citadel & Southern Cemetery around ten to fifteen minutes, following the dual carriageway Bab al-Ghuriyab past university buildings and uphill to its roundabout junction with Salah Salem. Although the tombs of Anuk and Tulbey are amongst the nearby mausolea, you might prefer to head 250m north along the highway to Dirasa – also accessible by minibus #77, #102 or #103 and bus #186 **from Midan Tahrir** or bus #65 from **Ramses** – and then cut east into the cemetery. That way you start with Qaitbey's Mausoleum (a known point on the circuit), whose ornate dome and minaret are clearly visible. Dirasa can also be reached by tram from Midan Triomphe in Heliopolis, and there will be a metro station here when the new cross-town line finally opens (see map on p.79).

SULTAN QAITBEY'S MAUSOLEUM

Sultan Qaitbey was the last strong Mamluke ruler, and a prolific builder of monuments from Mecca to Syria; his funerary complex (depicted on £E1 notes) is among the grandest in the Northern Cemetery. His name means "the restored" or "returned", indicating that he nearly died at birth; as a scrawny lad, he fetched only fifty dinars in the slave market. The rapid turnover in rulers after 1437 accelerated his ascent, and in 1468 he was acclaimed as sultan by the bodyguard of the previous incumbent, an old comrade-in-arms who parted from Qaitbey with tears and embraces. His 28-year reign was only exceeded by Al-Nasir's, and Qaitbey remained "tall, handsome and upright as a reed" well into his eighties, still attentive to citizens' complaints at twice-weekly *diwaniyyas*.

An irregularly shaped complex built in 1474, the **Mausoleum of Sultan Qaitbey** (9am–8pm; £E6, students £E3) is dynamically unified by the bold stripes along its facade, which is best viewed from the north. The trilobed portal carries one's eye to the graceful **minaret**, soaring through fluted niches, stalactite brackets and balconies to a teardrop finial. Inside, the **madrassa** *liwans*, floors and walls are a feast of marble and geometric patterns, topped by elaborately carved and gilded ceilings, with a lovely octagonal roof lantern. Qaitbey's **tomb chamber** off the *qibla liwan* is similarly decorated, its lofty dome upheld by squinches. Ask to climb the minaret for a close view of the marvellous stone carving on the dome's exterior. A raised star-pattern is superimposed over an incised floral one, the two designs shifting as the shadows change.

From this minaret vantage point you could also plot a course to Barsbey's complex, further up the narrow, winding street.

THE BARSBEY AND BARQUQ COMPLEXES

As the street jinks northwards from Qaitbey's Mausoleum it passes (on the left) the apartment building, that Qaitbey deeded to provide income for the building's upkeep and employment for poor relations. Such bequests could not be confiscated, unlike merchants' and Mamlukes' personal wealth, which partly financed the **Mausoleum of Sultan al-Ashraf Barsbey**, 200m beyond the building. Based on a now-ruined *khanqah*, the complex was expanded to include a mausoleum and mosque-madrassa (1432) after Barsbey's funerary pile near Khan el-Khalili was found lacking. If there's a curator around, ask him to lift a mat hiding the marble mosaic floor inside the long mosque, which also features a superb *minbar*. At the northern end, a great dome caps Barsbey's tomb, its marble cenotaph and mother-of-pearl-inlaid *mihrab* softly lit by stained-glass windows, added at a later date. The stone carving on the dome's exterior marks a transition between the early chevron patterns and the fluid designs on Qaitbey's Mausoleum.

Barsbey was the sultan who acquired young Qaitbey at a knockdown rate. He himself had been purchased in Damascus for eight hundred dinars, but was "returned to the broker for a filmy defect in one of his blue eyes". Unlike other sultans who milked the economy, Barsbey troubled to pay his Mamlukes regularly and the reign (1422–38) of this well-spoken teetotaller was characterized by "extreme security and low prices".

Fifty metres up the street, another finely carved dome surmounts the **Tomb of Gani Bak**, a favourite of Barsbey's, whose mosque stands near the Saddlemakers Bazaar.

The third – and oldest – of the great funerary complexes can be found 50m further north, on the far side of a square with a direct through road onto Sharia Salah Salem. Recognizable by its twin domes and minarets, the **Mausoleum of Sultan Barquq** (daily 8am–8pm; £E6, students £E3) was the first royal tomb in a cemetery that was previously noted for the graves of Sufi sheikhs. Its courtyard is plain, with sere, stunted tamarisks, but the proud chevron-patterned domes above the sanctuary *liwan* uplift the whole ensemble. Barquq and his son Farag are buried in the northern tomb chamber; his daughters Shiriz and Shakra in the southern one, with their faithful nurse in the corner. Both are soaring structures preceded by *mashrabiyas* with designs similar to the window screens in Barquq's madrassa, "Between the Two Palaces". The sinuously carved *minbar* was donated by Qaitbey to what was then a Sufi *khanqah*; stairs in the northwest corner of the courtyard lead to a warren of dervish cells on the upper floors, long since deserted.

The complex was actually erected by Farag, who transferred his father's body here from the madrassa on Sharia al-Muizz. Farag was crowned at the age of ten and deposed and killed in Syria after thirteen years of civil strife: it's amazing that the mausoleum was ever completed in 1411.

Depending on your route out, you might pass the minor **Tombs of Barsbey al-Bagasi and Amir Suleyman**, or those of **Princess Tulbey and Umm Anuk**, nearer Bab al-Ghuriyab and visible from the highway.

Old Cairo, Roda Island and the southern suburbs

The southern sector of the city is divisible into three main areas, the most interesting of which is **Old Cairo** (*Masr al-Qadima*), the historic link between Egypt's pharaonic and Islamic civilizations. Here, the fortress-town of **Babylon**, where the Holy Family is thought to have taken refuge, developed into a powerhouse of native Christianity which today remains the heart of Cairo's **Coptic community**. Featuring several medieval churches, the superb **Coptic Museum** and an atmospheric synagogue, it totally eclipses the site of **Fustat** – Egypt's first Islamic settlement, of which little remains but the much-altered **Mosque of Amr** – or the largely uninteresting **southern suburbs** of Ma'adi and Helwan.

Connected by bridge to Old Cairo – and so covered in this section, too – is **Roda Island**, which boasts a venerable Nilometer and the wonderfully kitsch Manial Palace. The Nilometer is best visited in combination with Coptic Cairo, but the palace is more easily accessible from central Cairo.

Approaching Old Cairo: transport links

Depending on whether it's broadly or narrowly defined, **Old Cairo** covers everything south of Garden City and Saiyida Zeinab – from the slaughterhouse district beside the Mamluke Aqueduct out to the ancient Jewish cemetery of Al-Basatin – or a relatively small area near the Mari Girgis metro station, known to foreigners as **"Coptic Cairo"**. Cairenes themselves distinguish between the general area of *Masr al-Qadima* and specific localities such as *Fumm al-Khalig* (Mouth of the Aqueduct) or *Qasr el-Sham'ah* (the erstwhile fortress of Babylon). Most tourists concentrate on Coptic Cairo, followed by a brief look at the Mosque of Amr.

The Coptic quarter is rapidly accessible by taking the **metro** from downtown Cairo to the **Mari Girgis** station (four stops from Midan Tahrir in the Helwan direction;

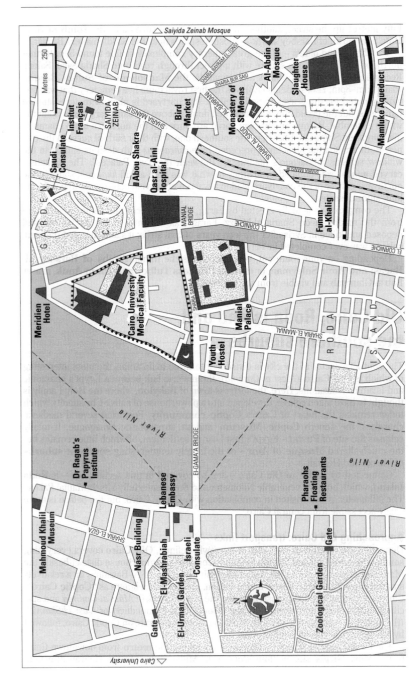

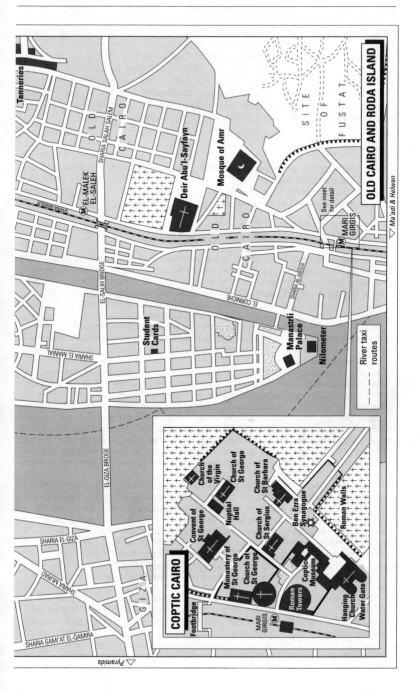

OLD CAIRO AND RODA ISLAND

Tanneries

OLD CAIRO

SHARIA SALAH-SALEM

EL-MALEK EL-SALEH Ⓜ

Deir Abu'l-Sayfayn

Mosque of Amr

SITE OF FUSTAT

OLD CAIRO

MARI GIRGIS Ⓜ

See inset for detail

SHARIA AL-ADUA

EL CORNICHE

EL-SALIH BRIDGE

Student Cards

SHARIA EL-MANIAL

Manastrli Palace

Nilometer

River taxi routes

▽ Ma'adi & Helwan

EL-GIZA BRIDGE

SHARIA EL-GIZA

SHARIA MURAD

SHARIA GAMI'AT EL-QAMIRA

GIZA

▽ Pyramids

COPTIC CAIRO

Church of the Virgin

Church of St George

Convent of St George

Nuptial Hall

Church of St Barbara

Monastery of St George

Church of St Sergius

Ben Ezra Synagogue

Footbridge

MARI GIRGIS Ⓜ

Church of St George

Roman Towers

Coptic Museum

Roman Walls

Hanging Church

Water Gate

50pt). Another possibility is the **river-taxis** (aka water buses; 25pt) that leave from the Maspero Dock (see p.82), zigzagging southwards upriver. On Fridays and during Ramadan, however, some may sail no further than Roda. The Mari Girgis stop is the fifth one; to reach the Coptic quarter from there, head inland, turn left and then cross the tracks at the end of the road. **Taxis** from downtown Cairo are reluctant to accept less than £E10, while **buses** from Tahrir and **minibuses** from Midan Ataba to Amr's Mosque (see p.81 for bus numbers) are usually packed on the outward journey but fine for getting back. To reach other points, see the directions below.

Coptic Cairo

Coptic Cairo recalls the millennial interlude between pharaonic and Islamic civilization, and the enduring faith of Egypt's Copts (see below). Though not a ghetto, the quarter's huddle of dark churches suggests a mistrust of outsiders – an attitude of mind that has its roots in the Persian conquest and centuries of Greek or Roman rule.

THE COPTS

While most Egyptians are Muslims, about ten percent of the population are Coptic Orthodox Christians. **The Copts** share a common national culture with their Muslim compatriots, but remain acutely conscious of their separate identity. Because intercommunal marriages are extremely rare, it's often said that the Copts are "purer" descendants of the ancient Egyptians than the Muslims – overlooking the infusions of Nubian, Greek, Jewish and Roman blood that occurred centuries before the Arab conquest. Though some maintain that they have higher cheekbones or almond-shaped eyes, Copts are rarely recognizable other than by tokens of their faith (wearing a cross around their neck, or tattooed on their wrist) or by forenames such as Maria, Antunius (Antony), Girgis (George) and Ramses.

Coptic Christianity differs from the Eastern Orthodox and Roman churches over doctrine and ritual. The Coptic Orthodox Church and its pope (chosen from the monks of Wadi Natrun) are totally independent from the Vatican, which only recently agreed to disagree for the sake of ecumenical harmony. The Coptic Bible (first translated from Greek c.300AD) antedates the Latin version by a century. While Coptic services are conducted in Arabic, portions of the liturgy are sung in the old Coptic language descended from ancient Egyptian, audibly prefiguring the Gregorian chants of Eastern Orthodoxy. However, the Coptic influence goes well beyond music, for it was in Egypt that the monastic tradition, the cult of the Virgin and – arguably – the symbol of the cross originated.

Christianity reached Egypt early: tradition holds that **St Mark** made his first convert (a Jewish shoemaker of Alexandria) in 45 AD. From Jews and Greeks the religion spread to the Egyptians of the Delta – which teemed with Christian communities by the third century – and thence southwards up the Nile. The persecution of believers began under Emperor Decius (249–51) and reached its apogee under Diocletian, whom the Copts accuse of killing 144,000 Christians; the Coptic Church dates its chronology from his accession (284). During this **Era of Martyrs** many believers sought refuge in the desert. Paul of Thebes, Antony and Pacome – the sainted **"Desert Fathers"** – inspired a multitude of hermits and camp followers whose rude communities became the first **monasteries**.

The Christian faith appealed to Egyptians on many levels. Its message of resurrection offered ordinary folk the eternal life that was previously available only to those who could afford elaborate funerary rituals. And much of the new religion's **symbolism** fitted old myths and images. God created man from clay, as did Khnum on his potter's wheel, and weighed the penitent's heart, like Anubis; Confession echoed the Declaration of Innocence; the conflict of two brothers and the struggle against Satan the myth of

Perhaps as early as the sixth century BC, a town grew up in this area, built around a fortress intended to guard the canal linking the Nile and the Red Sea. Some ascribe the name of this settlement – **Babylon-in-Egypt** – to Chaldean workmen pining after their home town beside the Euphrates; another likely derivation is *Bab il-On*, the "Gate of Heliopolis". Either way, it was Egyptian or Jewish in spirit long before Emperor Trajan raised the existing fortress in 130 AD. Resentful of Greek domination and Hellenistic Alexandria, many of Babylon's inhabitants later embraced Christianity, despite bitter persecution by the pagan Romans. Subsequently, after the emperor Constantine's conversion, the community was further oppressed by Byzantine clerics in the name of Melkite orthodoxy. Thus when the Muslim army besieged Babylon in 641, promising to respect Copts and Jews as "People of the Book", only its garrison resisted.

The Roman fortress

Almost opposite the **Mari Girgis** (St George) metro station you'll see the twin circular **towers** of Babylon's western gate. In Trajan's day, the Nile lapped the base of this gate

Osiris, Seth and Horus. Scholars have traced the **cult of the Virgin** back to that of the Great Mother, Isis, who suckled Horus. The resemblance between early **Coptic crosses** and pharaonic *ankhs* has also led some to argue that Christianity's principal symbol owes more to Egypt than Golgotha.

Although Emperor Constantine converted to Christianity and legalized his adopted faith throughout the empire (313–30), Byzantine converts known as **Melkites** continued to oppress the Copts. Political tensions were expressed in bitter theological disputes between **Arius** and **Athanasius** of Alexandria, which the Nicene Council (325) failed to resolve. When the Copts rejected the compromise verdict of the Council of Chalcedon (451) that Christ's human and divine natures were both unmixed and inseparable, and insisted that his divinity was paramount, they were expelled from the fold for this **Monophysite heresy** (monophysite meaning "single nature", a misrepresentation of their stance on Christ's divinity).

The association between Coptic Christianity and proto-nationalism was plain to Egypt's foreign rulers. "Copt" derives from the Greek word for Egypt, *Aigyptos*, truncated to *gibt* in Egyptian Arabic. Most Egyptians remained Christian long after the Arab conquest (640–41) and were treated justly by the early Islamic dynasties. Mass **conversions to Islam** followed harsher taxation, abortive revolts, punitive massacres and indignities engendered by the Crusades, until the Muslims attained a nationwide majority (probably during the thirteenth century, though earlier in Cairo). Thereafter Copts still participated in Egyptian life at every level, but the community retreated inwards and its monasteries and clergy stagnated until the nineteenth century, when Coptic reformists collaborated with Islamic and secular nationalists bent on overhauling Egypt's institutions.

In recent decades the Coptic community has undergone a **revival** under the dynamic leadership of its current pope, **Shenouda III**. The monasteries have been revitalized by a new generation of highly educated monks; community work and church attendances flourish as never before. Undoubtedly, this Coptic solidarity also reflects alarm at rising Islamic fundamentalism: what frightens the Copts is the state's strategy of wooing Islamist opinion by discriminating against non-Muslims. Merely to open a new church requires presidential permission; one in Ma'adi was closed by security forces backed up by armoured cars. Over 200 converts to Christianity have been arrested under the National Security Act, and in 1999, a local bishop accused the security forces of atrocities against the Copts of El-Qusiya, in Middle Egypt.

Fortunately, it's relatively few Muslims that actively support this kind of sectarian repression – which is at least a source of comfort for Egypt's six million Copts and 200,000 **Christians of other denominations** (Greek Orthodox, Maronite, Armenian, Catholic, Anglican and Baptist).

and was spanned by a pontoon bridge leading to the southern tip of Roda. Today, Babylon's foundations are buried under ten metres of accumulated silt and rubble, so the churches within the compound and the streets outside are nearly at the level of the fortress's ramparts. The right-hand tower is ruined, exposing a central shaft buttressed by masonry rings and radial ribs, which enabled it to withstand catapults and battering rams. Atop the other tower stands the Orthodox Church of St George (see below). Both towers are encased in alternating courses of dressed stone (much of it taken from pharaonic temples) and brick, a Roman technique known as *opus mixtum* or "mixed work".

By purchasing a ticket for the Coptic Museum, you can walk through the fortress's inner courtyard and down into the old **Water Gate** beneath the Hanging Church. The gate is now partly flooded and, though its arches and walls are visible from precarious walkways, the interior is only accessible by a stairway behind the three stone piers supporting the back of the church (bring a torch). It was through this gate that the last Byzantine viceroy, Melkite bishop Cyrus, escaped by boat under cover of darkness before Babylon surrendered to the Muslims.

While exploring the Coptic quarter, you'll also notice various sections of Babylon's Roman **walls**, rebuilt during the fourth and fifth centuries.

The Coptic Museum
Nestled between the Hanging Church and the Roman towers of Babylon, the **Coptic Museum** is one of the highlights of Old Cairo (daily 9am–5pm; Ramadan 9am–3pm; £E16, students £E8, camera permit £E10, video permit £E100; tickets are sold even after the museum stops admitting visitors one hour before closing). Its peerless collection of Coptic artefacts is enhanced by the beautiful carved ceilings, beams and stained-glass domes inside its *mashrabiya*'d wings, which enclose peaceful gardens. Founded in 1908 under the patronage of Patriarch Cyril V and Khedive Kamil, the museum was intended to save Christian antiques from the ravages of neglect and foreign collectors, but soon widened its mandate to embrace secular material. With artefacts from Old Cairo, Upper Egypt and the desert monasteries, the museum traces the evolution of Coptic art from Greco-Roman times into the Islamic era (300–1000 AD). Notwithstanding debts to pharaonic and Greco-Roman culture, its spirit was refreshingly unmonumental: "realistic, at times humorous", Coptic art reflected "plebian or agricultural concerns" (Stewart) and often seems homespun compared to pharaonic and Islamic craftsmanship; appropriately enough, its finest expression was in textiles.

Though spread over three floors, the collection isn't so large that visitors become jaded. You can do it justice within a couple of hours, or cover it at a trot in half that time. A **café** in the grounds sells tea and biscuits; the gateway beyond gives access to the courtyard of the Hanging Church (see p.157).

NEW WING
Entering the museum grounds from Mari Girgis street, you'll find the **New Wing**, built in 1937, straight ahead. The **ground floor** is arranged in chronological order in an anticlockwise direction, starting with **Room 1**. The other exit from this room leads into a garden containing tombstones and funerary steles, with stairs down to the Water Gate beneath the Hanging Church and up into the old wing.

Centred upon a fountain from one of the old houses of the quarter, **Room 1** displays **pagan reliefs and statues** of figures from Classical mythology. Their squat proportions and oversized heads make Aphrodite, Daphnae, Pan, Leda and the Swan look more African than Greco-Roman. The tendency to superimpose two flat layers, and the motif of a broken pediment with a shell, were both characteristic of proto-Coptic art. Artefacts in **Room 2** evince a **shift towards Christian symbolism** from the third century onwards. Pharaonic *ankhs* (see p.255) are transmuted into looped crosses, while

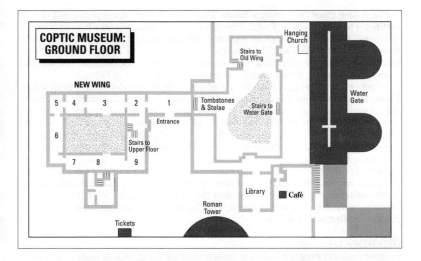

COPTIC MUSEUM: GROUND FLOOR

true crosses appear on the shell pediments and coexist with Horus hawks on a basket-weave capital.

Coptic artistry reached its zenith between the sixth and ninth centuries, as exemplified by the **stone-carvings and frescoes from Bawit Monastery**, near Assyut. Along the north wall of **Room 3** is a splendid apse niche depicting Christ enthroned between the creatures of the Apocalypse and the moon and sun; below, the Virgin and Child consort with Apostles whose homely faces can still be seen in any Egyptian city today. In **Room 4**, notice the eagle, an early Christian symbol of resurrection (as was the peacock). **Room 5** is also filled with miscellaneous objects, notably a painted capital carved with sinuous acanthus leaves, a motif borrowed from the Greeks and Romans but apparently devoid of symbolic meaning for the Copts.

Capitals with acanthus leaves and grapevines mingle with pharaonic palm fronds and lotus motifs in **Room 6**. Among other **objects from the Monastery of St Jeremiah** at Saqqara is the earliest known example of a stone pulpit, possibly influenced by the *heb-sed* thrones of Zoser's funerary complex. The fresco to its right, like the Bawit apse, subtly identifies the Virgin Mary with Isis. Other instances of recycled iconography can be seen around the corner in **Room 7**: a frieze of the grape harvest (a theme favoured by pharaonic nobles) and a small sphinx-like lion figure between two stylized versions of itself.

Room 8 moves on to **Biblical scenes** (Abraham and Isaac, Christ with angels) and **friezes** of animals offset in plant rondels – a motif that was later adopted by Fatimid woodcarvers. Entering **Room 9** you'll encounter a tenth-century panel from Umm al-Birgat (in the Fayoum), depicting Adam and Eve before and after the Fall, for which he blames her in the latter scene while a serpent relishes the denouement. In the centre of the hall is an elaborate papyrus and lotus basket-weave capital, hollowed out to form a **baptismal font**.

Climbing the staircase to the **upper floor**, you come to casefuls of *ostraca* and manuscripts produced by monastic scriptoriums, including several papyrus sheets from the **Gnostic Gospels of Nag Hammadi**, whose 1200 pages shed light on the development of early Christianity and its mystic tradition. The Gospels (translated from Greek into Coptic) were probably buried during the purges against Gnostics in the fourth and fifth centuries; farmers unearthed the sealed jar in 1945.

Proceeding clockwise through **Room 10**, a 1600-year-old towel presages a host of **textiles**. From the third or fourth century onwards, Coptic weavers (chiefly women) developed various techniques to a pitch of sophistication. Tapestry and pile weave designs blended human and bird forms with plant motifs; tunics were appliquéd with bands and rondels. In **Room 12** there's a magnificent silk robe embroidered with pictures of the Apostles, dating from the eighteenth century.

Room 13 displays Alexandrian-style **ivory-work** and cruder efforts from Upper Egypt, alongside a selection of **icons** from Old Cairo, Aswan and Kharga Oasis. Some believe that the change from murals to icons resulted from the need to hide sacred treasures from hostile interlopers. The next three rooms showcase **metalwork**, ranging from crosses and censers to musical instruments and tools. In **Room 15** are patriarchal crowns, a lamp emblazoned with both a Christian cross and an Islamic crescent, and an eagle from the Fortress of Babylon.

The upper floor concludes with an exhibition of **Nubian paintings** salvaged during the 1950s and 60s from villages about to be drowned by Lake Nasser. Like Isis-worship in ancient times, Christianity persisted as the dominant religion in Nubia for several centuries after it had waned in Egypt. The figures are darker, with larger eyes and rounder heads than the Copts.

OLD WING

Entered via stairs from the sculpture garden, the **Old Wing**, with its even finer ceilings and *mashrabiyas*, is currently closed for renovation. If it has reopened by the time of your visit, the items on show and their layout may be slightly different from this description.

On the left as you enter **Room 22** are the original **fourth-century altar** and a Fatimid-era dome from the Church of St Sergius. In the other direction lie two halls full of Nubian wall paintings, plus a pair of lunettes (semicircular paintings) from Bawit Monastery (**Room 23**). Rounding the corner, an original screen from the Church of St

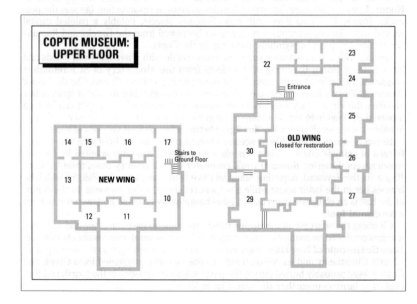

Barbara inaugurates the **woodwork** section. Fragments in the following alcove show a similar mixture of Hellenistic mythology, pharaonic symbolism and Coptic naturalism to the stone-carving in the other wing, while later pieces feature human activities. A **panel depicting Christ's entry into Jerusalem**, taken from the Hanging Church, is the high point of **Room 25**.

Sharing **Room 26** with Coptic toys and domestic utensils are several **mummy portrait panels**, latter-day versions of the Roman "Fayoum Portraits" displayed in the Egyptian Antiquities Museum. In the far right-hand corner is a remarkable **Early Coptic crucifix** (one of the few in existence), which combines a beardless Christ with a Horus hawk and sun disc. Byzantine and Sassanid (Persian) influences underlie the **friezes** of hunting scenes and fabulous creatures – motifs which continued into Islamic times until the Sunni restoration. The episcopal chairs in the annexe to **Room 27** are similar to the reception thrones used by wealthy amirs.

The last quarter of the wing displays **pottery**, arranged by type or form rather than antiquity. Ancient motifs such as fish, ducks and plants are widely employed. At the end of **Room 29** are **Pilgrims' flasks** showing St Menas between two camels (see p.509). Amongst the later work in **Room 30** are lustre ware pieces like those made by Muslim potters at Fustat, but here emblazoned with a Coptic fish or cross. The annexe beyond contains a small collection of **glassware**.

The Hanging Church

Built directly above the water gate, the **Hanging Church** (*Al-Mu'allaqah*, "The Suspended" in Arabic) can be reached via an ornate portal on Mari Girgis street. Ascending a steep stairway, you enter a nineteenth-century vestibule displaying cassettes and videos of Coptic liturgies and papal sermons. Above this are the monks' quarters; beneath it lies a secret repository for valuables, only discovered last century.

The main **nave** – whose ceiling is ribbed like an upturned boat or Ark – is separated from its side aisles by sixteen pillars, formerly painted with images of saints. Behind the marble pulpit, beautifully carved screens hide three **haikals** (altar areas) from the congregation. Accentuated by inlaid bone and ivory, their star patterns are similar to those found in mosques. Both pulpit and screens date from the thirteenth century, but the church was founded at least six hundred years earlier and may even have originated in the fourth century as a chapel for the soldiers of the bastion. Amongst its relics, the church once claimed to own an olive stone chewed by the Virgin Mary, to whom *Al-Mu'allaqah* is dedicated.

Coptic Masses are held on Fridays (8–11am) and Sundays (7–10am).

The Monastery of St George and into the Old Quarter

Returning to the Coptic Museum and heading north, go through the first gateway beyond the Coptic Museum entrance (ignoring demands for cash from "doormen") to reach the precincts of the **Monastery of St George**, now the seat of the Greek Orthodox Patriarchate of Alexandria. The monastery itself rarely admits tourists, but it's worth looking into the neighbouring **Church of St George** (daily 8am–12.45pm & 2.30–3.15pm). The only round church in Egypt, its dark interior is perfumed with incense and pierced by sunbeams filtered through stained glass. A (barred) flight of steps descends into the bowels of the Roman tower, once believed to be "peopled by devils". The present church was built in 1904 after a fire destroyed the original tenth-century structure. Notwithstanding the church's Orthodox allegiance, its **Moulid of Mari Girgis** (April 23) is one of the largest Coptic festivals in Cairo.

Further up the main road, a **subterranean gateway** leads into the oldest part of Old Cairo, whose cobbled lanes flanked by high-walled houses wend between **medieval churches and cemeteries**. In 1929, Evelyn Waugh wrote disparagingly of a "constricted slum" whose Coptic residents hardly differed from their Muslim neighbours: "the only marked sign of their emancipation from heathen superstition was that the swarm of male and juvenile beggars were here reinforced by their womenfolk, who in the Mohammedan quarters maintain a modest seclusion." Since the late 1970s, the quarter has been gradually sanitized and tarted up for tourists, and now seems quite spruce compared to Islamic Cairo.

The most interesting of the churches is reached through the first gate on the left, after you pass through the subterranean gateway. This is the Coptic **Convent of St George** (*Deir Mari Girgis*), whose main building, still a nunnery, is closed to visitors. However, you can walk down into a lofty hall that once belonged to a Fatimid mansion and into the chapel beyond, with its tall, narrow wooden doors, which boasts a cedar-wood casket containing relics of St George. To the left of this building is a small room used for the "**chain-wrapping ritual**", symbolizing the saint's persecution by the Romans. Several of the nuns speak English and welcome questions about their faith; they might even wrap you in chains for a souvenir photo.

Upon leaving the convent, walk on to the end of the lane, where it meets another thoroughfare. At this intersection, turn right around the corner to stumble upon the Church of St Sergius, or head left to explore the quarter's northern reaches.

North to the churches of St George and the Virgin

The north part of the Coptic quarter contains nothing special, but its solitude is refreshing and you might enjoy wandering around the overgrown **cemeteries** – so far unsquatted Cities of the Dead.

Fifty metres up the road from the intersection, an alley to the right leads to yet another **Church of St George**, founded in 681 by Athanasius the Scribe. From the original foundation only the Hall of Nuptials survived a conflagration in the mid-nineteenth century, after which the current structure was erected.

Beyond it, at the end of the road, stands the smaller **Church of the Virgin**, also known as *Qasriyyat al-Rihan* (Pot of Basil) after the favourite herb of the Orthodox Church. Because Al-Hakim's mother was of that faith, the church was given to the Greek community for the duration of his reign, but later returned to the Copts. Largely rebuilt in the eighteenth century, it's chiefly notable for several icons painted by John the Armenian in 1778.

The churches of St Sergius and St Barbara

Heading right from the intersection beyond the convent, you pass a tourist bazaar before reaching the **Church of St Sergius** (daily 8am–4pm), whose site below street level attests to its great age. Probably founded in the fifth century and continuously rebuilt since medieval times, *Abu Serga* retains the basilical form typical of early Coptic churches. The low ceiling and the antique columns topped with Corinthian capitals support the women's gallery, where you can inspect its thirteenth-century *haikal* screen and bits of frescoes and mosaics in the central apse. Steps to the right of the altar descend into a **crypt** where the Holy Family are believed to have stayed. A Coptic **festival** (June 1) commemorates their sojourn.

From St Sergius, you can wander along to the end of the lane where another thoroughfare leads to the Church of St Barbara (to the left) and Ben Ezra Synagogue (on the right).

The eleventh-century **Church of St Barbara** replaced an earlier Church of SS. Cyrus and John, which was razed during Al-Hakim's assault on Fustat. Unlike others in the quarter, its wooden-vaulted roof is lofty, with skylights and windows illuminating a nave flanked by Arabic arches with Fatimid tie beams. Nor would its *minbar*-esque pulpit and inlaid *haikal* screen look amiss in a mosque. As if to refute such comparisons, the right-hand wall relates the life of Jesus in colourful tableaux, while the western sanctuary contains the relics of *Sitt Barbara*. Tradition holds that she was the daughter of a pagan merchant who was murdered for preaching Christianity in the third century, but sceptics might note that her belated recognition followed another questionable case (see "The Monastery of St Catherine" on p.600).

The Ben Ezra Synagogue

Down the road, behind a wrought-iron fence, the **Ben Ezra Synagogue** is a unique relic of Cairo's ancient Jewish community. Bereft of its former host of worshippers (see the box below), the synagogue would have crumbled away were it not for the efforts of one "Rabbi" Cohen, who shamelessly overcharged for souvenir postcards to fund repairs for twenty years, until the American Jewish Congress and the Egyptian government stepped in to restore it. Today it is as good as new again.

THE JEWS OF EGYPT

Egypt's Jewish community is dying out: fewer than two hundred *Yahud* remain in Alexandria, Old Cairo and the Jewish Old People's Home in Heliopolis. The three synagogues that still exist will become empty memorials within a decade or so – a melancholy end to a story that begins in the **Old Testament**. The book of Genesis relates how the descendants of Abraham escaped famine in Canaan (Palestine) by migrating to Egypt at the behest of Joseph, the pharaoh's favourite. Settling in the "Land of Goshen", they "multiplied and waxed mighty" until a new pharaoh enslaved them to build "the treasure-cities, Pithom and Raamses". Their flight from Egypt to the Promised Land is described in Exodus.

Squaring this with ancient Egyptian **history** presents difficulties. Whereas numerous sites are suggestive of Pithom and Raamses, there's no mention of the Exodus in pharaonic records. Assuming the Old Testament is based on genuine history, the Jews probably arrived sometime in the Ramessid era (c.1320–1237 BC), while the Exodus is generally ascribed to the reign of Merneptah (1236–1223 BC). There's some evidence for the Prophet Jeremiah's foundation of a new community at Babylon-in-Egypt after the destruction of Jerusalem (585 BC), but there is no firm historical ground until the second century BC, when it is known that the Ptolemies encouraged an influx of Jews into Alexandria.

In contrast to the Alexandrian fusion of Greek and Jewish culture, the Jews of Babylon were more akin to native Egyptians. Mutual sympathies were strengthened by the **Jewish revolt** against Roman rule (115–17 AD) and the Coptic belief in the **Egyptian exile of the Holy Family**. Babylon's Jewish community would have been a natural haven for Mary, Joseph and the baby Jesus when Herod's wrath made Palestine too dangerous (it's harder to see why they should have hidden out near Assyut, as is also claimed).

As "People of the Book", Egypt's Jews were treated about as well (or badly) as the Copts **during the Islamic period**, acting as small traders, gold and silversmiths, moneychangers or moneylenders. In Mohammed Ali's day, Lane estimated that they numbered about five thousand. The British, however, introduced a new element: Jews who came as Europeans and shared the Brit-colonial disdain for the natives. Most of these new arrivals were merchants or professionals and settled in Alexandria or Cairo. A few families of *haute Juiverie* – the Menasces, Rolos, Hararis and Cattauis – were financiers who moved in royal circles. These **foreign Jews** lamented post-revolutionary restrictions on business and left en masse before and after the Suez Crisis (1956).

Meanwhile, native Jews were torn between Egypt and **Israel** as each war eroded their security. By the time of the 1967 war their numbers had declined from 75,000 to 2600 (mostly living in Cairo), though the capital still had 26 working synagogues, until mobs attacked them for the first time during the conflict. Thereafter, all but a few hundred Jews emigrated, leaving the poor, now aged community that remains today.

In form, the synagogue resembles a basilical church of the kind that existed here between the fourth and ninth centuries. Sold to the Jews in order to pay taxes raised from the Copts to finance Ibn Tulun's Mosque, this church was either demolished or incorporated within the synagogue, which Abraham Ben Ezra, the Rabbi of Jerusalem, restored in the twelfth century. The inlaid marble and gilded stalactite niche date from around then, but most of the graceful mouldings and floral swirls are the result of nine-teenth-century repairs, which unearthed a huge cache of medieval manuscripts, includ-ing a sixth-century Torah written on gazelle hide (now dispersed around Western libraries).

However, Jewish and Coptic traditions invest the site with ancient significance. Here, the pharaoh's daughter found Moses in the bulrushes; Jeremiah gathered survivors after Nebuchadnezzar destroyed Jerusalem; and the temple named after him provided a haven for the Holy Family, who lived amongst the Jews of Babylon for three months. Moreover, the Copts believe that Peter and Mark pursued their apostolic mission in Egypt, whence Peter issued the First Epistle General. The rest of Christendom dis-agrees, however, arguing that the Biblical reference to Babylon (I Peter 5:13) is only a metaphor for Rome.

Around the back of the synagogue are a newly restored chunk of the Roman walls and a derelict Jewish Refuge founded by one Ralph Green.

The Mosque of Amr, Deir Abu'l-Sayfayn and Fustat

To get a feel for what happened after Babylon and Egypt surrendered to Islam, return to Mari Girgis Street and follow it northwards, past the turning for Fustat and a small bus depot, to the **Mosque of Amr**. Though continuously altered, not to mention dou-bled in size in 827, this boasts direct descent from Egypt's first ever mosque, built in 641. A simple mud-brick, thatch-roofed enclosure without a *mihrab*, courtyard or minaret, it was large enough to contain the Muslim army at prayer. At its inauguration, **Amr Ibn al-As** told his 3500 Arab warriors:

> *The Nile floods have risen. The grazing will be good. There is milk for the lambs and kids.*
> *Go out with God's blessing and enjoy the land, its milk, its flocks and its herds, and take good*
> *care of your neighbours, the Copts, for the Prophet of God himself gave orders for us to do so.*

Until the fratricidal struggle between Sunni and Shia, this injunction was honoured: aside from paying a poll tax, non-Muslims enjoyed equal rights. It was Ibn Tulun and Al-Hakim who introduced the discrimination (or worse), that later rulers either foreswore on principle or practised for motives of bigotry, fear or greed. But on an everyday level, citizens of each faith amicably coexisted within the city of Fustat-Masr, as they do in modern Cairo.

The site of the mosque was indicated by Allah, who sent a dove to nest in Amr's tent while he was away at war; on returning he declared it sacrosanct, waited until the dove's brood was raised, then built a mosque. The existing building follows the classic congregational pattern, arched *liwans* surrounding a pebbled *sahn* centred on an ablu-tions well. Believers pray or snooze on fine carpets in the sanctuary *liwan*, whose orig-inal *mihrab* is misaligned towards Mecca. When Amr introduced a pulpit, he was rebuked by Khalif Omar for raising himself above his Muslim brethren. The *mashra-biya'd* **mausoleum** of his son, Abdullah, marks the site of Amr's house in Fustat. A nearby column bears a gash caused by people licking it until their tongues bled, to obtain miraculous cures. None of the mosque's two hundred **columns** is identical, inci-dentally; the pair on the left as you come in are said to part to allow the truly righteous to squeeze through, and another was whipped from Mecca by Omar. From the mosque's **well**, it is said, a pilgrim retrieved a goblet dropped into the Well of Zemzem in the Holy City.

Non-Muslims are charged £E6 **admission** to the mosque (or more if they don't know any better), and its curators are the most *baksheesh*-hungry in Cairo.

Deir Abu'l-Sayfayn

If the Coptic quarter hasn't satisfied your curiosity about medieval churches, pay a visit to **Deir Abu'l-Sayfayn**, northwest of Amr's Mosque. This high-walled enclosure (daily 9am–5pm; £E6, students £E3) is entered via a humble wooden door; the original iron-bound door is now in the Coptic Museum. Within the compound are several churches of indeterminate age. First mentioned in the tenth century (when it served as a sugar-cane warehouse) and totally rebuilt after the burning of Fustat, the **Church of St Mercurius** claims older antecedents. Beneath its northern aisle lies a tiny crypt where St Barsum the Naked lived with a snake until his death in 317; a special Mass is held here on his name-day (September 10).

A doorway beside the crypt stairway leads through into the rest of the complex. The Upper Church, reached by steps, contains five disused chapels. Of more interest are the Small Church with its *haikal* dedicated to St James the Sawn-asunder, and the early seventh-century **Church of St Shenute**, featuring beautiful cedarwood and ebony iconostases. From the same period comes the diminutive, icon-packed **Church of the Holy Virgin**, beyond which stands the **Convent of St Mercurius**, still inhabited by nuns. The liturgy is celebrated in all the churches (Wed 8am–noon, Fri 7–11am & Sun 6–10am). Adjacent to Deir Abu'l-Sayfayn are extensive Protestant and Maronite **cemeteries**.

The remains of Fustat and Cairo's zebaleen

En route to Amr's Mosque you'll pass a turn-off to the right, lined with piles of earthenware pots, jars and waterpipes. Behind them, smouldering rubbish tips and hovels sprawl beneath a pall of smoke, seemingly as far as the Citadel. The hundred-year-old shantytown on the site of ancient Fustat looks – and smells – daunting, but is actually a success story in Third World terms. Its US-sponsored health centre is the most conspicuous example of many recent improvements in a community that used to be at the bottom of the Cairene heap. Should you care to explore, a twenty-minute walk alongside the shantytown will bring you to the **remains of Fustat** (daily: winter 9am–6pm; summer 9am–9pm; £E3). Bring water, a few stones to deter dogs, and above all tread carefully – much of the site consists of centuries-old rubbish tips and kilns, prone to caving in. The foundation walls and water system (still being excavated by the American University) hardly do justice to Fustat's past, though the pottery shards that blanket the site are evocative; some fine early medieval and imported Chinese ware can be seen in the Islamic Arts Museum.

Originally a cluster of tribal encampments around Amr's Mosque, Fustat (City of the Tent) evolved into a mud-brick beehive of multistorey dwellings with rooftop gardens, fountains, and a piped water and sewage system unequalled in Europe until the eighteenth century. As the Abbasids, Tulunids and Ikhshidids also built their own cities ever further to the northeast, a great conurbation known as **Fustat-Masr** was formed. Its decline began in Fatimid times, as the noxious potteries encouraged migration towards Al-Qahira; thieves moved in and dereliction spread like cancer. In 1020, the mad khalif Al-Hakim ordered his troops to sack Fustat-Masr for reasons worthy of Caligula (see p.124). Yet even in 1168, what remained was so vast that Vizier Shawar decided to evacuate and burn it rather than let the Crusaders occupy the old city beyond Al-Qahira's walls. Set ablaze with 10,000 torches and 20,000 barrels of naphtha, Fustat smouldered for 55 days.

Today the Fustat shantytown is inhabited by seventeen thousand people whose filthy work keeps Cairo tolerably clean. Whole families of **potters** slave over beehive kilns, churning out domestic ware for *baladi* households and piping for sewers and water mains. Even more important are the *zebaleen* or **rubbish-gatherers**. These families collect and sift Cairo's rubbish for anything edible or recyclable. All the glass, cardboard, metal, rags and leather are sold as raw materials to over five hundred factories. Though previously regarded as an embarrassment by the authorities, the *zebaleen* have made an indispensable contribution to Cairo's ecology, recognized by the award of a prize at the World Earth Summit and an official government contract in 1991. Community amenities are being improved through self-help projects with foreign backing, in a development programme that could be a model for others in the Third World.

To return to central Cairo, walk to El-Malek el-Saleh metro station, or head back to the Amr's Mosque and catch a bus (#814 and #945/ to Midan Tahrir; #134/ and #135 to Tahrir and Ramses) or minibus (#53 to Midan Ataba; #58 to Midan Ramses and Midan Tahrir).

North to the Aqueduct

Travelling between Coptic and central Cairo by bus or taxi, you'll catch sight of the great **Aqueduct** that carried water to the Citadel. Originally a mere conduit supported by wooden pillars, it was solidly rebuilt in stone by Sultan al-Nasir in 1311 and subsequently extended in 1505 by Al-Ghuri to accommodate the Nile's westward shift, to a total length of 3405m. River water was lifted by the **Burg al-Saqiyya**, a massive hexagonal water-wheel tower near the Corniche. On its western wall can be seen Al-Ghuri's heraldic emblem and slots for engaging the six oxen-powered water wheels, which remained in use until 1872.

The site of this tower is known as **Fumm al-Khalig** (Mouth of the Canal), after the waterway that once ran inland to meet the walls of Fatimid al-Qahira. This *Khalig Masri* (Egyptian Canal) supplied most of Cairo's water during Mamluke and Ottoman times, and was also linked to the ancient Nile Delta–Red Sea waterway, re-dug by Amr and Al-Nasir. In an annual ceremony to mark the *Wafa el-Nil*, or Nile flood, the dike that separated it from the river was breached, sending fresh water coursing through the city. Pleasure boats were launched onto the lakes near Bab al-Luq and Ezbekiya, while fireworks heralded nocturnal revelries. But the taming of the Nile spelt the end of this practice, and after piped water was introduced early last century the canal was filled in to create Bur Said and Ramses streets.

Further inland

From the Fumm al-Khalig roundabout, Sharia al-Sadd al-Barrani runs up to Saiyida Zeinab (2km) past a swathe of **Christian cemeteries**. Within the northernmost cemetery, high walls enclose the **Monastery of St Menas** (*Deir Abu Mina*), whose sunken basilical church has been endlessly rebuilt since 724. Having returned the holy remnants of St Menas to his desert monastery (see p.509), the church now gives pride of place to the relics of saints Behnam and Sarah, who were martyred by their own father. The monastery receives very few visitors and has no set opening hours.

Further south, the Aqueduct bestrides a medieval slum centred around a huge **slaughterhouse** and reeking **tanneries**. To outsiders, stark poverty seems all-pervasive; yet among those who live here, social distinctions are keenly felt. A slaughterhouse worker and his boss will both wear bloodstained *galabiyyas* during working hours, and possibly live on the same street – but the former can only speculate on what riches the latter keeps indoors. Conversely, people will salvage designer-label bags and boxes to flaunt on the streets as if they were returning with a purchase.

Unlike the tanneries of Morocco, this is hardly on the tourist trail. Gustave Flaubert spent an afternoon here in 1850, shooting birds of prey and "wolf-like dogs", but the only recent case I've come across was that of two young Russian women who somehow wandered into the area, and were treated like princesses. However, the odd tourist has been known to attend Saturday evening *zikrs* outside the **Mosque of Sidi Ali Zein al-Abdin**, on the periphery of the quarter of Saiyida Zeinab (see p.143).

Roda Island

The narrow channel between **Roda Island** and the mainland is bridged in such a way that the island engages more with Garden City than with Old Cairo – a reversal of historic ties. As its much-rebuilt **Nilometer** suggests, it was the southern end of Roda that was visited by ferries en route between Memphis and Heliopolis, and Roman ships bound for Babylon-in-Egypt. However, nothing remains of the Byzantine fortress that defied the Muslim invasion, nor the vaster Ayyubid *qasr* where the Bahri Mamlukes were garrisoned, since Roda reverted to agricultural use as Cairo's focus shifted northeastwards. The island's main sight, the **Manial Palace**, re-established a fashion for palatial residences early this century, though it wasn't until the 1950s that Roda experienced a building explosion similar to Zamalek's.

APPROACHING THE SIGHTS
With Roda's tourist attractions sited 3km apart, choice of **transport** is a major consideration. The Nilometer is best reached on foot from Old Cairo via the footbridge from the Corniche. You can take a minibus – see p.81 for numbers – or *service* taxi from the centre to Old Cairo; alternatively Mari Girgis metro station is just two blocks southeast of the footbridge. Should you decide to settle for only one site, make it the palace, which is easily accessible from central Cairo. Aside from a taxi (£E4–5), a #8 or #900 bus is the fastest way of getting there from Midan Tahrir: alight on Sharia Sayala, near the palace gates (this is also the last stop for minibus #90 from Midan Ataba). Walking takes about half an hour from downtown Cairo, and on hot days can leave you totally bushed. Should you decide to anyway, don't cross the first bridge unless you visit the **Meridien Hotel**, which commands superb river views and offers a pool-and-buffet deal but is almost isolated from other parts of Roda (if you do need to get from the hotel forecourt to the rest of the island, a set of stairs leads down to the tradesmen's entrance).

The Qasr al-Aini Bridge leads down to **Cairo University Medical Faculty**. By walking 150m south from here you can reach the palace gates without crossing the Manial Bridge, used by traffic heading for Giza. Cairo's **youth hostel** overlooks the El-Gama'a Bridge, 500m further west.

The Manial Palace

The **Manial Palace** (daily 9am–5pm; £E20, students £E10) is a Cairo must. Built in 1903, its fabulously eclectic architecture reflects the taste of King Farouk's uncle, Prince Mohammed Ali, author of *The Breeding of Arabian Horses* and the owner of a flawless emerald that magically alleviated his ill health (so legend has it). Each of the main buildings manifests a different style – Persian, Syrian, Moorish, Ottoman and Rococo – or mixes them together with gay abandon.

Having bought your ticket, make a beeline for the **Reception Palace** just inside the gateway. Its magnificent *salamlik*, adorned with stained glass, polychrome tiles and ornate woodcarving, prepares you for the opulent guest rooms upstairs; the finest is the Syrian Room, which was quite literally transplanted from Damascus. On the stairs you'll notice a scale model of Qaitbey's Mausoleum, made entirely of mother-of-pearl.

Leaving the Reception Palace and turning right, you come upon a pseudo-Moroccan tower harbouring the prince's **mosque**, whose lavish decor is reminiscent of the great mosque of his namesake in the Citadel. Further along, the grotesque **Hunting Museum** features scores of mounted ibex heads, gorgeous butterflies and ineptly stuffed fowl, a hermaphrodite goat, a table made from elephants' ears and a vulture's claw candlestick.

The **Prince's Residence**, deeper into the banyan-shaded garden, is richly decorated in a mixture of Turkish and Occidental styles. The drab-looking building out back contains a long **Throne Hall** whose red carpet passes life-size royal portraits hung beneath a sunburst ceiling. Around the outside of this hall are the skeletons of the prince's horse and camel, and a stairway to the upper level (often closed). If accessible, visitors can admire its Obsidian Salon and the private apartments of the prince's mother, enriched by a silver four-poster bed from the Abdin Palace. Lastly, follow the signs to the **Private Museum**, a family hoard of manuscripts, carpets, glassware and silver plate – notice the huge banqueting trays.

The Nilometer

From ancient times into the present century, Egyptian agriculture depended on the annual **flooding of the Nile**. Crop yields were predicted and taxes were set according to the river's level in August, as measured by Nilometers. A reading of 16 *ells* (8.6m) foretold the valley's complete irrigation; significantly more or less meant widespread flooding or drought. Public rejoicing followed the announcement of the *Wafa el-Nil* (Abundance of the Nile), while any other verdict caused gloom and foreboding.

Although the southern tip of Roda has probably featured a **Nilometer** (daily 9am–6pm; £E6) since pharaonic times, the existing one dates from 861 and its Turkish kiosk is actually a modern replica, built in 1947 and recently restored. Descending well below the level of the Nile, its stone-lined shaft was connected to the river by three tunnels (now sealed) at different heights – the uppermost is still accessible. Around the shaft's interior are Koranic verses in kufic script, extolling rain as God's blessing; its central column is graduated into 16 *ells* of roughly 54cm each. The Nilometer is often locked, but its caretaker will turn out for rare visitors. The ticket for the Nilometer also admits you to the neighbouring **Monastirli Palace**, a Rococo confection dating from 1850. Built as a conference centre, the palace is now undergoing transformation into an arts centre with a theatre, exhibition hall and library.

The southern suburbs

South of Old Cairo, a ribbon of development follows the east bank of the Nile down to Helwan. Though easily reached by metro, these **southern suburbs** hold little attraction for tourists, notwithstanding Ma'adi's popularity as an expatriate residential area. However, even the least-favoured quarters cast some light on various facets of Egyptian life.

Al-Basatin: the Jewish cemetery

A case in point is the **Jewish cemetery of Al-Basatin**, 3km beyond El-Khalifa (minibus #54 or bus #160/ from Midan Tahrir; bus #72 from Midan Ramses; or minibus #57 from Midan Ataba). Tens of thousands of graves, up to nine hundred years old, have been stripped of their marble slabs, while squatters have occupied any mausolea going (Al-Basatin has few of these compared to the Muslim and Coptic cemeteries). During the late 1980s, the elders of Cairo's depleted Jewish community agreed to accept US$80,000 in return for allowing a highway to be ploughed through Al-Basatin. When foreign rabbis intervened, the whole affair acquired diplomatic overtones and turned into a massive legal wrangle.

Ma'adi and the quarries of Tura

With its Corniche boutiques and take-aways, and acres of villas set amidst luxuriant grounds, **Ma'adi** is unmistakably wealthy. Besides native millionaires and Gulf Arabs, most of Egypt's American community lives here. US citizens can enjoy a free **Fourth of July Party** at the American School, courtesy of taxpayers back home (bring your passport). Trendy **restaurants** include the Thai *Bua Khao*, at 9 Road 151 (daily 11.30am–11.30pm; ☎350-0126) and the *Seahorse* on Ma'adi's Corniche (☎363-8830), near the **As-Salam International Hospital**. Ma'adi also has a handful of Chinese restaurants, including a branch of the city-wide *Peking* chain; an Indian, the *Bukhara*, 43 Sharia Misr Helwan (☎375-5999); and an outpost of *Felfela*'s on the Corniche.

The **Military Hospital**, further north, is the largest of its kind in the Middle East. It was here that the ex-Shah of Iran died of cancer, and President Sadat was rushed by helicopter from the blood-soaked reviewing stand in Medinet Nasr. As a young officer during World War II, Sadat was actually stationed in Ma'adi when he became embroiled in a Nazi spy ring (see p.172). Ma'adi is directly accessible from Midan Tahrir by minibus (#52 & #58; or #56 from Midan Ataba), microbus *service* taxi or metro (25min).

Further south amidst the Muqattam foothills, the **quarries of Tura** have yielded fine limestone since pharaonic times (it was here that pyramid casing blocks were quarried), and now also produce cement.

Helwan

The once-fashionable spa of **Helwan** is now grossly polluted by a gigantic **iron- and steelworks** that exploits power from the Aswan Dam and iron ore from the Western Desert. The steelworks wreak eco-death on a nineteenth-century **Japanese Garden** (daily except Tues 9am–6pm; £E5) – complete with Buddhas and a pagoda – five blocks east from Helwan metro station (turn left as you exit); ask for *Ganenit el-Arbaine Harami*. One hundred metres south of Ain Helwan metro station, one block back, a tacky **Waxworks Museum** (daily 9am–4pm; £E5) portrays such moments in Egyptian history as the death of Cleopatra, and Salah al-Din's meeting with Richard the Lionheart. The sulphurous **Ain Helwan Baths** (daily 24 hours; free) are less than 100m northwest of the same station; being outdoors, they are not used in winter, but the main building doubles up as a nightclub and restaurant.

Gezira and the west bank

Flowing northwards through Cairo, the Nile divides into channels around the two major islands of Roda and Gezira. **Gezira**, the larger island, is further from the centre than Roda and notably more spacious and verdant than the rest of Cairo.

Across the island, elevated highways bear cross-town traffic to diverse **districts on the west bank** of the Nile, collectively known as **Giza** and administered as a separate governorate from Cairo. Moving south through its neighbourhoods, **Imbaba** is a working-class district and former site of Cairo's main camel market – a world apart from the adjoining **Aguza**, with its Corniche nightlife, and even more from the Dallas-style pretensions of **Mohandiseen**. Further south and east is **Dokki**, whose wealthy enclaves give way to *baladi* market quarters, the green lungs of Cairo's zoo and scattered university faculties, before the dusty expanse of Giza city extends to the Pyramids. Giza's **transport** and utilities are functionally integrated with Cairo's.

Gezira and Zamalek

Gezira (literally "island") dominates the waterfront from Garden City to Bulaq, its three sets of bridges spanning the Nile. Nearly 4km long and 1km wide, the island is big enough to encompass two distinct zones. The southern half, featuring the Opera House complex, parks, a viewing tower and famous sporting clubs, is Gezira proper. **Zamalek** (pronounced "Zah-*mah*-lek"), further north, is pure real estate – apartments,

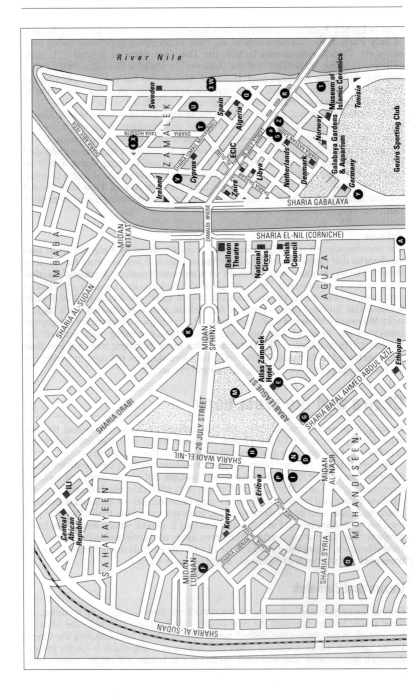

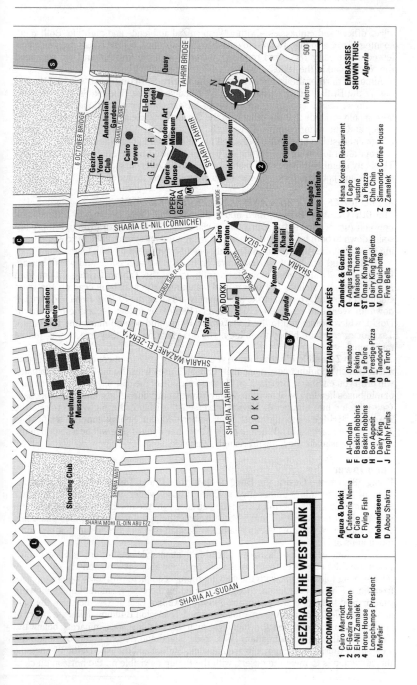

GEZIRA & THE WEST BANK

ACCOMMODATION

1 Cairo Marriott
2 El-Gezira Sheraton
3 El-Nil Zamalek
4 Horus House
   Longchamps President
5 Mayfair

Aguza & Dokki
A Cafeteria Nema
B Ciao
C Flying Fish

Mohandiseen
D Abou Shakra

E Al-Omdah
F Baskin Robbins
G Baskin Robbins
H Bon Appetit
I Dairy King
J Fraghly Fruits

RESTAURANTS AND CAFÉS

K Okamoto
L Peking
M La Poire
N Prestige Pizza
O Tandoori
P Le Tirol

Zamalek & Gezira
Q Angus Brasserie
R Maison Thomas
ST Omar Khayyam
U Dairy King Rigoletto
V Don Quichotte
   Five Bells

W Hana Korean Restaurant
X Il Capo
Y Justine
   La Piazza
   Chin Chin
Z Simmonds Coffee House
a Zamalek

EMBASSIES SHOWN THUS:
Algeria

villas, offices and embassies – with a Westernized ambience and nightlife. Both seem so integral to Cairo that it's hard to envisage their absence, yet the island itself only coalesced in the early 1800s and remained unstable until the first Aswan Dam regulated the Nile's flood in the 1900s.

Almost a third of the island belongs to the **Gezira Sporting Club** (see p.224), laid out by the British Army on land given by Khedive Tewfiq. The club's main pursuits were horse racing and polo, imbued with an extraordinary mystique. "It is on the Gezira polo grounds that the officers of the Cavalry Brigade are tested for military efficiency and fitness for command", wrote C.S. Jarvis in the 1920s. Diplomats and selected upper-crust Egyptians also belonged to the club, and after Nasser decided against expropriation following the revolution it soon acquired members from the new elite. The hefty membership fees still restrict access to its golf course, tennis courts, stables, gardens and pet cemetery; non-members are resolutely excluded.

APPROACHES TO GEZIRA AND ZAMALEK: THE BRIDGES

The **6th October Bridge**, high above the Sporting Club, is more of a direct link between Aguza and central Cairo than a viable approach to Gezira (though there are stairs down to both banks of the island). However, it does overlook the offices and training ground of the **Ahly (National) Club**, one of Egypt's top football teams.

It's the southern bit of **Gezira**, however, that's most accessible and worth seeing. Despite heavy traffic, it's enjoyable to walk across the **Tahrir Bridge** (200m from Midan Tahrir), catching the breeze and watching barges and feluccas on the river. Gaining the island, you can strike 200m northwards past the *El-Borg Hotel* and turn left down an avenue to reach the Cairo Tower (10min), or follow the traffic heading for Dokki, which brings you to the Cairo Opera House and several museums (5–10min). Taxis or *caleches* are happy to oblige if you'd rather ride, but they expect the "tourist minimum".

To get to **Zamalek**, it's best to save yourself a long walk from central Cairo and grab a taxi (which shouldn't cost more than £E3–5). Buses from Midan Tahrir to Zamalek will drop you on Sharia Gabalaya on the western side of the district, and there's no lack of minibuses heading west along 26th July Street from Midan Ataba and Midan Ramses (see p.81 for bus numbers). Having traversed the island, the highway crosses the **Zamalek Bridge** onto the west bank, where Midan Sphinx funnels traffic into Mohandiseen (see p.171). When the new Metro line opens there will be a station in the north of the island called, unsurprisingly, Zamalek.

Cairo Tower

Rising 187m above Gezira, the **Borg al-Qahira** or **Cairo Tower** offers a stupendous view of the seething immensity of Cairo (daily: winter 9am–midnight; summer 9am–1am; £E25, video permit £E15); the entrance is to the north of the tower in Sharia el-Borg. Built between 1957 and 1962 with Soviet help, the tower combines pharaonic and socialist realist motifs within a latticework shaft of poured concrete that blossoms into a lotus finial.

On the fourteenth floor is an overpriced "Egyptian-style" restaurant (set meal £E60; ticket from the entrance) that occasionally revolves; above it is a similarly styled cafeteria serving tolerable tea, with the viewing room – complete with telescopes – upstairs from here. The real attraction, though, provided by the café, restaurant and a **viewing platform** at the top, is the **panoramic vista of Cairo**. East across the river, the blue and white *Nile Hilton* and the antenna-festooned Television Building delineate an arc of central Cairo. Beyond lies the medieval quarter, bristling with minarets below the Citadel and the serene Muqattam Hills. Roda Island and deluxe hotels dominate the view south (upriver); to the north are Zamalek, Shubra and the Nile Delta. Westwards, the city extends to meet the desert, with the Pyramids visible on the horizon on clear days. Come a while before sunset to witness Cairo transformed by nightfall, as a thousand muezzins call across the water. Below the tower is the *Legends* nightclub which has belly dancing every night and a minimum charge of £E30.

The Opera House complex

Fans of postmodernist architecture should check out the **Cairo Opera House**, which is near Tahrir Bridge and directly connected to the metro (the station is called "Opera", but is confusingly marked as "Gezira" on the metro-map). Outwardly Islamic in style, its interior melds pharaonic motifs with elements of the Baroque opera houses of the nineteenth century: an audacious blend of Oriental and Occidental by Japanese architect Koichiro Shikida. A US$30 million gift from Japan, it was built in 1988, belatedly replacing the old building on Midan Opera, which burned down in 1971. Off to the right as you walk towards the Opera House is the **Modern Art Museum** (Tues–Sun 10am–1pm & 5–9pm, Fri 10am–noon; £E10), which displays paintings, sculptures and graphics by Egyptian artists since 1908; there is always something new on show.

Following Sharia Tahrir towards the west bank, you'll pass the old Gezira Exhibition Grounds with their dilapidated pavilions housing the **Gezira Museum** (objets d'art collected by the royal family), the **Museum of Egyptian Civilization** (illustrating national history from pharaonic to modern times) and a **Planetarium**; all are closed for long-term renovation. Across the road to the south, just before the Galaa Bridge, the **Mukhtar Museum** (also currently closed for restorations; ☎340-2519) honours the sculptor Mahmoud Mukhtar (1891–1934), who is buried in the basement. Working in bronze and marble, he created several patriotic sculptures, including the "Renaissance of Egypt" monument that welcomes drivers into Dokki.

The 27-storey **El-Gezirah Sheraton** at the southern tip of the island can be reached by slip roads from the Tahrir and Galaa bridgeheads. On public holidays, a **fountain** in the middle of the Nile between Gezira and Roda shoots an immense jet of water into the sky.

Zamalek

Originally a very British neighbourhood, despite its Continental grid of tree-lined boulevards, **Zamalek** still has bags of social cachet: renting a flat here is the Cairene equivalent of moving into Manhattan. Unlike most parts of Cairo, the quarter feels very private; residents withdraw into air-conditioned high-rises or 1930s apartment buildings, and with so many foreign companies and **embassies** in the area (see p.237), most of the streets are lifeless after dark.

Somewhat paradoxically, Zamalek also features some of the trendiest **nightspots** in Cairo. Near the Aguza side of the Gezira Sporting Club on Sharia Hassan Sabry, the *Four Corners* complex contains, among others, a deluxe French restaurant, *Justine* (see p.212); there are more bars and restaurants to be found in the *Marriott Hotel*. Other places congregate north of the 26th July flyover. Gay men and British expats favour *Pub 28,* at the junction of Shagar al-Durr and Hassan Assim streets. The *Longchamp* disco is just around the corner on Sharia Ismail Mohammed. For eating with live music, there's *El-Patio* on Sharia Sayed al-Bakry, *Il Capo* on Sharia Taha Hussein next to *President Hotel*, and *Five Bells* on Sharia Ismail Mohammed. For Arab music and belly dancing, the top venue in Zamalek is the *Empress Show Lounge* at the *Marriott Hotel*.

Zamalek by day has less to offer, though children may enjoy the **aquarium grotto** in **Galabaya Park** (daily 8.30am–3pm; 50pt), entered from Sharia Galabaya. For more cultural pursuits, head for the other end of Sharia el-Gezira as it curves around the northeastern edge of the Sporting Club. Here, a graceful nineteenth-century villa now houses the Museum of Islamic Ceramics (see below); the **Mahmoud Khalil Museum** that was formerly housed here is now in Dokki (see p.173). The modern annexes of the adjacent **Cairo Marriott Hotel** screen what was originally a "madly sumptuous palace" built for Empress Eugénie, later sold to wealthy Copts in lieu of Ismail's debts and turned into a hotel. Non-residents can wander in and loll amidst khedival splendour for the price of a drink.

MUSEUM OF ISLAMIC CERAMICS
Housed in a white-domed villa close to the *Cairo Marriott*, the newly-opened **Museum of Islamic Ceramics** (Tues–Thur, Sat & Sun 10am–1pm & 6–9pm, Fri 10am–1pm; free) is one of Cairo's most agreeable museums. Built by Prince Amru Abrahim in the late nineteenth century, the structure itself is worth a look for its elaborate marble inlays and floors, while the collection inside contains pieces from Egypt, Persia, Syria, Turkey, Morocco, Iraq and even Andalucia, ranging from the seventh century to the present. The illustrated guidebook (£E25) explains each piece in English and also gives a thorough account of the history of Islamic ceramics. Downstairs there's a museum of fine art (same hours; free) that exhibits original paintings and sculptures as well as prints by modern Egytian artists such as Asraf and Alzamzami. All the works exhibited are for sale.

Imbaba and the new Bil'esh Camel Market

From Midan Kit-Kat, 300m north of Zamalek Bridge, Sharia al-Sudan arcs through the **Imbaba** district, whose overspill covers the site of the "**Battle of the Pyramids**" where Napoleon's army routed the Mamlukes on July 21, 1798, prior to taking Cairo. Unfortunately for Napoleon – who dreamed of "founding a religion, marching into Asia riding an elephant", bearing "the new Koran that I would have composed to suit my needs" – his strategic ambition to disrupt British power in India was literally scuppered when Nelson sank his fleet at Abu Qir Bay. Within eighty years, the Suez Canal had cemented the link between naval power, control of Egypt and Britain's empire "East of Suez"; a bond later reinforced by aviation. Although flying boats on the famous Cape-to-Cairo run used the Nile, most Imperial Airways flights used **Imbaba Airport**, now a flying school.

Formerly in Imbaba, but now held way out to the north at **Bil'esh**, is Cairo's Friday **Camel Market**, a weekly feast of drama and cruelty. Beaten into defecating ranks, the hobbled camels are assessed by traders who disregard their emaciation – caused by a month-long trek from northwestern Sudan to Aswan, followed by an overnight truck ride to Cairo – and concentrate on other features.

Strength and speed are discernible in the legs, chest, eyes, ears and position of the hump, while teeth reflect age; the clearly knackered are evaluated for their meat and hide. During rutting season, signs of irritation (an inflated mouth sac, ferocious slobbering and gurgling) often herald a kick or bite from an enraged bull camel. Docile females are generally preferred as mounts. They're also exchanged for goats and other livestock, while Bishari herdsmen and Egyptian merchants gossip over tea, unperturbed by throat-slittings and disembowelments near the piles of saddlery and tack. In an adjacent compound is a furniture and bric-a-brac market, not unlike a car boot sale.

Lasting from dawn till early afternoon every Friday, the *Souk el-Gamal* (pronounced "Gah*mell*") is busiest between 6 and 8.30am. To get there by taxi will cost around £E20, but the market is also accessible by *service* taxi microbus from the old site at Imbaba, or from Warraq (a village halfway between Imbaba and Bil'esh). Both are served by microbus from Sharia Sabtiya, off Midan Ramses; you then have to take another microbus for the final leg. Alternatively, you can catch the #214 bus from the *Nile Hilton* terminal in Midan Tahrir to Manashi by the Nile Barrage at Qaratir (45min) and take a *service* taxi microbus from there. Going back into town, you should be able to find direct *service* taxis to Midan Ramses.

Mohandiseen

Laid out during the 1960s to house Egypt's new technocrats, "Engineers' City" (as the suburb was initially called) responded to an influx of business and media folk during the Sadat era by shortening its name to **Mohandiseen** and emulating America. Nowhere else in Cairo can you cruise down a boulevard glittering with boutiques and junk food outlets, squint and imagine that you're in LA. Even the palm trees seem to hail from Hollywood, rather than the Nile. But around midday on Fridays, the illusion is ruptured as herds of camels are driven through Mohandiseen en route to the slaughterhouse, bringing traffic to a standstill.

Sharia Orabi runs northwest for 1.5km (strictly speaking, this area is called Sahafeyeen), but except for the **International Language Institute** (ILI), two blocks from the Al-Sudan ring road, it has no more to offer than the continuation of 26th July Street. Most of the action occurs along Mohandiseen's main axis, **Arab League Street** (Sharia Gameat al-Dowal al-Arabiya), also known as "The Mall", which is bisected by palms and shrubbery for its three-kilometre length. Due to its orientation, you can look down it on a clear day (admittedly rare in Cairo) and see the Pyramids of Giza in the distance. During summer Cairene families picnic here – an indication of how few green spaces are available. The avenue's main landmark is the **Atlas Zamalek Hotel**, 500m past Midan Sphinx. Starting with a pharaonic-style *McDonald's* opposite the *Atlas*, fast food proliferates along the way to Midan al-Nasr, the centre of a radial grid of streets harbouring a dozen **embassies** (among them Kenya, the CAR and Eritrea).

To **reach the quarter** from central Cairo, you can catch buses from Midan Falaki, Midan Tahrir, Midan Ataba or Midan Ramses that end up on Sharia al-Sudan near Midan Lubnan. Alternatively, to get to Midan al-Nasr on Arab League Street, you can take buses from Falaki or Tahrir (Arab League Building), Ramses or Ataba (see p.81 for all the bus numbers). A faster way is to jump on a *service* taxi microbus at Ataba or along 26th July Street and get whisked across Zamalek to Midan Sphinx or Arab League Street (but make sure of the destination of the microbus).

Beyond the ring road

Beyond the Al-Sudan ring road lies **Bulaq al-Dakhrour**, an unplanned sprawl of ramshackle dwellings built by migrant *fellaheen* from Upper Egypt and the Delta. Devoid of any proper sewage network (like parts of Imbaba and Giza), the neighbourhood is a sanitary inspector's nightmare. While some houses have cesspits, many households empty their waste into the drainage canals whose water is used by others for washing or drinking. Installing sewers here is merely one of the challenges facing the Cairo Wastewater Organization (see box on p.172).

Bulaq al-Dakhrour ends at the **Maryotteya Canal**, beyond which the village of **Kerdassa** (see p.190) precedes another canal before the strip of luxury hotels (*Môvenpick Jol lie-Ville, Ramada Renaissance, Oasis*) along the Desert Road to Alexandria.

Aguza and Dokki

A 100-metre-wide channel separates Zamalek and Gezira from the west bank districts of **Aguza and Dokki**. Being mainly residential and devoid of major "sights", they're only worth considering as a quieter place to stay than central Cairo, or for their nightlife – although you might just have business with certain local institutions. Yet it's typical of Cairo that these prim-looking neighbourhoods have generated as much scandal as the Clot Bey and Abdin quarters once did.

THE CAIRO WASTEWATER PROJECT

Designed by British engineers in 1910 to serve a population of one million, **Cairo's sewage system** reached breaking point in the late 1970s. Fractured pipes regularly flooded at 120 locations (in one incident, exposed power cables electrocuted a donkey cart driving through a puddle). Worse still, a quarter of Cairo's by then twelve million population lived in areas beyond the sewage network. Cases of what was termed "summer sickness" (in fact, cholera) occurred annually. Besides the risk of epidemics, the practice of flushing raw sewage into the Nile also threatened the ecology of Lake Manzala, the richest fishing grounds in the Delta. Action was urgently needed.

With US and British backing, the **Cairo Wastewater Project** (CWC) aims to remedy these problems over the first few years of this century. On the west bank, where many areas have no sewers at all, an entirely new system is being created. The densely populated east bank poses a greater challenge, requiring extensive "blind" tunnelling. Plans of the old system were lost long ago; urban myth has it that a group of sewer repairmen have passed down their secret underground geography from father to son. Existing sewers are being fed into a huge new tunnel running from Fustat to Cairo's northern outskirts, where a gigantic pumping station is under construction; eventually, the sewage will also be treated at another plant. Given additional investments, the wastewater and nutrient-rich sludge could be used to irrigate and fertilize barren land.

Aguza

Wedged between Mohandiseen and the Nile, **Aguza** ("Old Woman") stretches its legs **along the Corniche**. At the northern end of Sharia el-Nil, near the Zamalek Bridge, are the **Balloon Theatre** – a regular venue for the National and Reda dance troupes – and Egypt's **National Circus** (see p.225). Further south at no. 192 is the **British Council**, a fulcrum of expat life and a sought-after place of employment (see p.61 and p.239). Beyond the *Scherezade Hotel* and Aguza Hospital, couples seek privacy in nooks along the embankment, oblivious to cruising cars. A popular stopover for taxi drivers and nightclubbers is the 24-hour *Cafeteria Nema*, opposite the Police Hospital near the 6th October Bridge.

From here down to Dokki the riverside is colonized by **casinos**. These are family-oriented places for eating and listening to music (gambling isn't involved) that really come alive on Thursday nights. Some are taken over by wedding parties with traditional musicians and a bellydancer. Should you be invited to join a bash, accept without hesitation – they're always fun (see p.216). Street urchins and passers-by peer through the gates, shouting blessings or ribald comments. The downside to the casinos is that some have poor food, and all of them are swarming with mosquitoes.

Fifty years ago the Corniche was also a mooring place for houseboats – then a fashionable alternative to rented flats. It was here that the Nazi spy Eppler used a famous belly dancer, Hekmet Fathy, to inveigle secrets from Allied staff officers aboard her *dahabiya*. Also involved was a young Egyptian officer, Anwar Sadat, who attempted to convey messages to Rommel and was subsequently jailed by the British for treason. Post-revolutionary Egypt was austere by comparison, but hardly innocent. In 1988 the government tried to suppress the memoirs of Eitimad Khorshid, a *femme fatale* who cut a swathe through the Nasserite establishment of the 1950s, and promised to reveal all in what became an underground bestseller.

To reach any of the above locations, catch a taxi via 26th July Street or the 6th October Bridge. An elevated extension of the latter pushes 500m inland towards the **Agricultural Museum** (daily 9am–3pm; 20pt) in the grounds of the Ministry of Agriculture; the entrance is on the south side of the estate. A group of six pavilions – some closed for renovation, others that could themselves almost be museum pieces – these solemnly dingy museums of yesteryear contain exhibits on ancient farming techniques, with stuffed animals and models of native village life. There are also quirky items such as prettily arranged displays of insects and a rather horrific demonstration of various animal diseases. The **Cotton Museum** (daily 9am–4pm; £E6, students E£3), gives the rundown on Egypt's main cash crop. The Ministry of Agriculture marks the point where Aguza merges into Dokki.

Dokki

The social geography of **Dokki** (usually pronounced "Do'i", with a glottal stop in the middle) is more complex than Aguza's. Broadly speaking, the rich occupy the land nearest the river and the Dokki Sporting Club, with a phalanx of private hospitals, VD clinics and covert bordellos separating their villas and apartments from the poorer market quarter to the southwest.

Coming over the Galaa Bridge from Gezira Island, you'll see Mahmoud Mukhtar's **Renaissance of Egypt statue** and the twin towers of the **Cairo Sheraton**. The hotel forecourt is the departure terminal for **buses to Tel Aviv and Jerusalem** (see p.246). From here, Sharia al-Sad al-Ali itself continues on to meet Suleyman Gohar, Dokki's vibrant **market quarter**. For **cinemas** and **restaurants**, look along Sharia Tahrir and Sharia al-Misaha, radiating west and southwest from the Galaa Bridge.

Two main roads head south from the *Sheraton*. Running one block inland, **Sharia el-Giza** passes the **Russian Embassy** and the former residence of President Sadat, where his widow, Jihan, still lives in guarded seclusion (photography is prohibited in this area). Another once-famous resident of Dokki was Field Marshal Amr, a long-time friend and ally of Nasser's who committed suicide after being accused of plotting a coup against him, and was posthumously scapegoated for Egypt's defeat in the 1967 war.

The main feature of interest on Sharia el-Giza, however, is the **Mahmoud Khalil Museum** (daily 10am–6pm; ☎336-2376; £E25; wheelchair access), two blocks south of the *Sheraton*, housed in the refurbished mansion where Khalil, a pre-war politician and Agriculture Minister, lived with his French-born wife, Emeline Hector. Together they built up this magnificent collection of art and sculpture, mostly French Impressionist and Post-impressionist works by the likes of Monet, Renoir, Gauguin and Pissarro, but also featuring artists such as Van Gogh, Delacroix and Rodin. There are information sheets on the artists in various languages, but the computer screens that tell you about the Khalils and their home are, unfortunately, in Arabic only.

Running parallel to Sharia el-Giza is the Corniche, **Sharia el-Nil** (now officially Sharia Gamal Abdel Nasser). Three boats moored 200m south of the *Giza Sheraton* house **Dr Ragab's Papyrus Institute** (daily 9am–9pm; free), where the ancient craft of papyrus making (which died out in the tenth century AD and was revived in modern times by Dr Ragab) is demonstrated. Although more of a papyrus emporium than a museum (and pricey to boot), you are not harassed to buy.

Beyond the Papyrus Institute are Cairo's **Rowing Club** and **Yacht Club**, both citadels of privilege. A few blocks nearer Giza, the Nasr Building contains two excellent **restaurants** owned by SwissAir: *Le Chalet* and *Le Château*.

Dokki is well served by buses (#19, #166, #182, #186, #194, #203 and #815) and minibuses (#77 & #102) from the Arab League Building on Midan Tahrir, but you'll have to check which route suits your objective. "Dokki" metro stop is on Sharia Tahrir, which is close to both the Mahmoud Khalil Museum and Dr Ragab's Papyrus Institute.

Giza

In pharaonic times **Giza** lay en route between Heliopolis and Memphis and probably also housed the skilled corps of pyramid-builders. As Memphis declined during the Christian era, so Giza flourished, thanks to its proximity to the Fortress of Babylon, across the river; Amr's reopening of the ancient Delta–Red Sea canal subsequently boosted its prosperity under Muslim rule. Giza's apogee coincided with the reign of Salah al-Din – the Moorish traveller Ibn Jubayr described it as a "large and important burgh with fine buildings" – when its Sunday market attracted vast crowds. But the area's vulnerability to floods caused stagnation, and it wasn't until Ismail laid the Pyramids Road, drained swamps and built a palace in the 1860s that Giza became fashionable again. By Nasser's time, however, expansion was proceeding virtually unchecked. As Giza's population topped a million, a tide of high-rise hovels, tacky nightclubs and roaring flyovers devoured crumbling villas, erstwhile farmland and desert, right to the Giza Plateau beneath the Pyramids.

Transport from Midan Tahrir approaches Giza via Gezira and Dokki (bus #30, #108, #200, #356, #357 or #997), or crosses over from Roda Island (bus #803); either route serves to reach the zoo or Midan Giza.

Around Cairo Zoo and University

The extensive grounds which Deschamps laid out for Ismail's palace are now divided into Cairo's **Zoological Garden** – which is packed on Fridays and public holidays, but fun to visit at other times (see p.224) – and the smaller **El-Urman Garden**. Like the **Israeli Consulate** and the **floating restaurants** near the **El-Gama'a Bridge**, they're marked on the "Old Cairo and Roda Island" map (see p.150). The bridge is named after **Cairo University**, which was founded in 1908 as a counterweight to traditionalist Al-Azhar but has never been any the less political. Access to its scattered faculties is controlled by Central Security, so foreigners may need a letter of introduction (or at least their passport) to pass beyond the gates. Aside from making student friends, morbid curiosity might inspire a visit to the Agricultural Faculty, near the bottom of Sharia Gameat al-Qahira. Occupying a former palace of Mohammed Ali, its basement holds remnants of his torture chamber.

Midan Giza and Pyramids Road

West of the **El-Giza Bridge** and south of the university belt, Cairo's second largest **bus and taxi terminal** agitates **Midan Giza**. Even more chaotic than Tahrir, its seething ranks include buses to the Pyramids; minibuses to Tahrir, Ramses and Heliopolis; and *service* taxis to Fayoum city, Beni Suef and the Red Sea Coast. A few minutes' walk south is **Giza Station**. More flyovers funnel traffic onto the **Pyramids Road** (Sharia al-Ahram), which runs the gauntlet of **nightclubs** and tourist bazaars for 8km. It was outside a hotel on this avenue that seventeen Greek tourists were shot dead by Islamic radicals, who mistook them for a group of Israelis, in spring 1996. A couple of kilometres before the Pyramids of Giza, Sharia al-Ahram crosses two canals in quick succession; the second one marks the turning (left) for Saqqara. See pp.181–205 for details of both sites.

The northern suburbs

During last century, Cairo's **northern suburbs** swallowed up villages and farmland and expanded far into the desert to form a great arc of residential neighbourhoods stretching from the Nile to the Muqattam. **Heliopolis**, with its handsome boulevards and Art Deco villas, is still favoured above the satellite suburbs that have mushroomed in recent decades, and retains a sizeable foreign community. Otherwise, tourists usually only venture into **Abbassiya** for the Sinai Bus Terminal, or to visit the Coptic Patriarchate and Sakakini Palace, and you have to be fanatically keen to bother hunting down the Virgin's Tree in **Matariyya**, Sadat's tomb in **Medinet Nasr**, or Mamluke edifices in **Bulaq**. See the "Greater Cairo" map on p.74 for a guide to the location of these areas.

Bulaq, Shubra and Rod el-Farag

Bulaq and its neighbours **Shubra** and **Rod el-Farag** (northwest of central Cairo) are run-down and overcrowded, averaging 170,000 residents per square kilometre – ten times the density of Garden City – and have a predominantly *baladi* ambience. But though more or less bereft of "sights", these quarters might appeal to visitors fascinated by ordinary Cairene life. **Getting there**, bus #134 serves Shubra from Midan Falaki, Tahrir and Ramses. However, it's probably easiest to reach these districts using shared taxis. Look for vehicles heading in the right direction on Midan Tahrir, 26th July, or off Midan Ramses.

Bulaq

Immediately east of the 6th October flyover (see the "Central Cairo" map on p.92) lies the oldest of the northern suburbs, **Bulaq**, whose name derives from the Coptic word for "marsh". During medieval times, the westward shift of the Nile turned a sandbank into an island, which merged with the east bank as the intervening channel silted up. As the Fatimid port of Al-Maks was left high and dry, Bulaq became the new anchorage in the 1350s, rapidly developing into an entrepôt after Sultan Barsbey re-routed the spice trade and encouraged manufacturing. When Mohammed Ali set about establishing a foundry, textiles factory and modern shipyards here in the 1820s, Bulaq was the obvious site. Unfortunately, the Ottomans permitted free trade, enabling British manufacturers to undersell local industries and force Egypt back into its dependency on cotton exports to the Lancashire mills.

Since then, small workshops and apartment buildings have taken over Bulaq, while world affairs are handled in two towering landmarks along the Corniche: the **Television Building** and the **Cairo Plaza**. Inland of the latter is a one-time hostel for members of the Rifai order, next to the **Mosque of Sinan Pasha**, a sixteenth-century hybrid of Mamluke and Ottoman styles, attached to a still-working **hammam**. More revered by locals for its namesake's *baraka* is the fifteenth-century **Mosque of Abu'l'Ila**, on 26th July Street just west of the Corniche. Nearby stand the former royal stables of Mohammed Ali, due to open soon as the **Royal Carriage Museum**. An annexe to the Carriage Museum at the Citadel, equestrian follies from the royal collection will be displayed here.

Shubra

Two million Cairenes live in the sprawling beehive known as **Shubra,** the older part of which is called Shubra al-Balad to distinguish it from the newer outgrowth beyond the Ismailiya Canal, dubbed Shubra el-Kheima. Originally an island (its name, "Elephant", supposedly comes from a ship that ran aground), Shubra became attached to the mainland about the same time as Bulaq, but was given over to orchards and villages until the nineteenth century. In 1808, Mohammed Ali built a summer palace here that caused Europeans to snigger ("The taste, alas! of an English upholsterer"), where he later died insane. Other palaces were erected by Ismail, who also laid a carriage road to the original residence, planted with sycamore-fig and acacia trees, where Cairenes promenaded.

The 1891 edition of *Murray's Handbook* deemed **Sharia Shubra** "the most republican promenade in the world. No description of vehicle, nor manner of animal, biped or quadruped, is excluded, and the Khedive and his outriders are jostled and crossed in a most unseemly fashion by files of bare-boned and sore-covered mules and donkeys, whipped in by ragged urchins." Nowadays the avenue seems thoroughly proletarian, for Shubra has long since evolved from a garden suburb into densely packed quarters where educated Copts and Muslims rub shoulders with poor rural migrants.

Though self-help projects have improved some of the bleak low-rise estates in Shubra el-Kheima, dire poverty inclines a minority towards radical Islam, and reinforces the traditional superstitions that most Cairenes at least half-believe. *Baladi* folk turn instinctively to **magic**, whereas educated people will exhaust rational solutions before resorting to a *sheikh* or *sheikha*. What psychologists might regard as mental illnesses are treated as cases of demonic possession, possibly caused by deliberate cursing. (One method of hexing is to recite the 33rd *sura* of the Koran backwards.) While certain moulids feature public **exorcisms**, most are private, especially those with pagan elements. Joseph McPherson, Cairo's secret police chief in the 1920s, witnessed a *zaar* where celebrants whirled to ancient and Muslim incantations, cymbals clashed, and a ram, ganders, doves and rabbits were sacrificed, their blood being daubed on the participants, whose frenzy increased:

> *Sometimes they bent their bodies back, till they formed a writhing and vibrating bow, resting on the ground by the heels and back of the head, whilst the muscles of their bodies carried on the dance with unbelievable contortions.*

When all concerned believe in the ritual's spiritual efficacy, the desired result is frequently achieved.

Rod el-Farag

During the 1950s, a slice of Shubra al-Balad was developed as a separate residential and commercial district, named "Farag's Orchard" after its previous role. The name remains appropriate, since **Rod el-Farag** hosts Cairo's largest **fruit and vegetable market**, Abu el-Farag. Like the others, it's the exclusive preserve of one of two cabals of wholesalers. In Rod el-Farag's case, they hail from the villages around the capital, whereas elsewhere *Saiyidis* from Upper Egypt may control trade. The modern **Port of Cairo** is another local source of wealth with a shady underside.

Abbassiya, Hada'iq al-Qubba and Medinet Nasr

In practice, the demarcation lines between these northeastern districts (which subdivide into other quarters) and Heliopolis are blurred by sheer density, overcrowding and interlocking transport networks.

Abbassiya

The sprawling **Abbassiya** district gets its name from a palace built by Mohammed Ali's grandson, Pasha Abbas I, who dreaded assassination during his brief reign (1848–54) and kept camels saddled there for rapid flight into the desert – to no avail, for he was murdered by his servants. Previously, the area was called Ridaniya and was the site of the last battle between the Mamlukes and the invading Ottoman Turks, who went on to take Cairo. Nearer the centre, the British established the Abbassiya Barracks (where the nationalist leader Orabi surrendered after his defeat at Tell el-Kebir), which vastly expanded during wartime. Like the Army GHQ (still located in Abbassiya), it was later seized by the Free Officers in a bloodless coup against Egypt's monarchy on the night of 22 July, 1952. Cairenes awoke next day to learn of a "revolution" led by General Naguib – a nominal figurehead, since it was Nasser who had engineered it and secretly controlled affairs until his public emergence as leader.

Abbassiya's Janus profile juxtaposes spacious institutions and crowded slums, marshalling yards and hospitals. Its main thoroughfare, Sharia Ramses, divides the oil-depot zone of Al-Sharabiyya from Gamra and El-Sakakini, two residential market quarters. On Sharia Sakakini, near Ghamra metro station, the ornate Rococo **Sakakini Palace**, built in 1898 for an Italian nobleman, will again house a **Museum of Hygiene and Medicine** once restoration work is complete. At the end of Sharia Sakakini, on

Sultan Hassan and Rifai mosques, viewed from the Citadel, Cairo

Khan el-Khalili, Cairo

Mosque of Mohammed Ali, Cairo

Panel from Tutankhamun's throne

Great Pyramid of Cheops, Giza

The Muski, Cairo

The "Collapsed Pyramid", Maidum

Christian icons for sale in Coptic Cairo

Film poster, central Cairo

Abu Simbel - the Sun Temple of Ramses II

Coffee house, Cairo

Stone relief, Kom Ombo Temple

Midan al-Zahir, the thirteenth-century **Mosque of Beybars the Crossbowman** is also undergoing extensive restoration, but can be visited in the meantime. Its sturdy walls enclose a vast open courtyard, surrounded by a rather heavy arcade. A more conspicuous edifice is the curvaceous **Coptic Cathedral of St Mark**, the seat of the Coptic Patriarchate since it was raised in the 1970s. Visitors interested in joining pilgrim excursions to the Red Sea Monasteries should contact officials in the adjacent Church of SS. Peter and Paul (*Al-Batrussiya*), at 222 Sharia Ramses (☎821-274).

Other landmarks include the **Misr Travel Tower**, housing the Ministry of Tourism, 500m from the **Sinai Bus Terminal** near the junction of Salah Salem and Al-'Urubah, and a similar distance from the Engineering Faculty of **Ain Shams University**. Roundabout are sited numerous clubs (*nady*) and training schools belonging to professional unions, the police and military.

To get to Abbassiya, buses (#400 from Tahrir, #500 from Ataba) and minibuses (#30 & #32 from Tahrir) run to the Sinai Terminal.

Hada'iq al-Qubba: Nasser's Tomb

Northeast of Abbassiya along 23rd July Street (a continuation of Sharia el-Geish), a modern mosque stands beside a dusty shrine containing the **Tomb of Gamal Abdel Nasser**. When Nasser died in September 1969, a million Egyptians followed his bier through the streets of Cairo and the whole Arab world mourned. His cult was subsequently downplayed by Sadat (who feared comparisons) and in recent years most of the visitors to Nasser's shrine have been foreign admirers or gloating Israelis. Whatever Egyptians may think about Nasser's son, Khalid – who was finally acquitted of involvement in *Thawraat Masri* (Egypt's Revolution), a Libyan-backed group that attacked US and Israeli targets in the 1980s – his father's legend remains a potent one. Saddam Hussein's claim to be Nasser's "spiritual heir" was only the latest attempt by an Arab leader to metaphorically wrest the sword from the stone.

The tomb lies on the edge of **Hada'iq al-Qubba**, a district named after Ismail's **Qubba Palace**. Its four hundred rooms were inherited by Khedive Tewfik and later contained King Farouk's vast collection of rare stamps, coins and other treasures, ranging from medieval Korans to a Fabergé thermometer. Now a presidential residence used for state conferences, it was here that the Shah of Iran spent the last days of his exile, mortally stricken by cancer. The palace's walled grounds can be seen along the #420 bus route from Abbassiya; bus #300 and #803 also run through Hada'iq al-Qubba along Sharia el-Gash, en route between Tahrir and the Ain Shams quarter (see below).

Medinet Nasr – and Sadat's Tomb

During the 1960s and 70s a whole new satellite-suburb was created on the site of the Abbassiya Rifle Ranges, and many government departments were relocated in this "Victory City". But unless you've got business with the Inland Revenue or Transport Ministry, there's little in **Medinet Nasr** worth noting. Travellers coming in from Suez will pass the Olympic-sized **Cairo Stadium** at one end of Sharia al-Nasr, where the country's football cup finals are held (see p.224).

Alongside the boulevard is a landscaped parade ground centred on a pyramid-shaped **Victory Memorial** to the 1973 war. In 1981, Islamic radicals infiltrated the 6th October anniversary parade and blasted the reviewing stand with machine guns and grenades, fatally wounding President Sadat (Mubarak, who stood beside him, was unharmed). **Sadat's Tomb** is beneath the Victory Memorial, by the huge **October War Panorama**, opened in 1989, where 360° "sensaround" war films are screened (daily except Tues 9.30am, 11am and 6pm; Ramadan closed; £E8). Mubarak apparently got the idea for the Panorama from a similar pavilion in the North Korean capital, Pyongyang.

Medinet Nasr is connected to Midan Roxi in Heliopolis by bus #67 (starting from Tahrir). From Midan Ataba minibus #34 runs through Abbassiya to the quarter and past the tomb. Minibuses #32 and #35 from Midan Tahrir also runs past the tomb, as do trams from Heliopolis.

Heliopolis (Masr el-Gadida)

By the end of the nineteenth century, the doubling of Cairo's population and the exponential growth of its foreign community had created a huge demand for new accommodation, which fired the imagination of a Belgian entrepreneur. Baron Empain proposed creating a garden city in the desert, linked to the downtown area by an overground metro; a commercial venture attractive to investors, since Empain's company would collect both rents and fares from commuting residents of **Heliopolis**. Laid out by Sir Reginald Oakes in radial grid patterns, the suburb's wide avenues were lined with apartment blocks ennobled by pale yellow Moorish facades and bisected by shrubbery. Named after the ancient City of the Sun near Matariyya (see p.179), Heliopolis soon acquired every facility from schools and churches to a racecourse and branch of *Groppi's*.

Wealthy Egyptians settled here from the beginning; merely prosperous ones moved in as foreigners left in droves throughout the 1950s. Meanwhile, poorer quarters started growing up around Heliopolis, ending its privileged isolation from Greater Cairo. During the 1970s, air-conditioned towers began to replace spacious villas, the racecourse was turned into a fun park, and burger joints proliferated. Today, visitors come for the restaurants and nightlife, or to admire the stylish architecture along its central boulevards; many foreigners also rent apartments or work in Heliopolis, which is nowadays called "New Cairo" (*Masr el-Gadida*).

Transport: the Heliopolis metro

Depending on your starting point, choice of transport, and whether it's rush hour, Heliopolis is between fifteen and thirty minutes' ride from downtown Cairo. The fastest way is to hail **service taxis** heading there from Bab al-Luq, Midan Opera and Midan Tahrir, via Salah Salem, which charge fixed rates. To reach Midan Roxi in Heliopolis, it's almost as quick to use **buses** or **minibuses** (see p.81).

During the rush hour, **buses** from Tahrir and Ramses are slower than the suburb's **original tram system**, known as the **Heliopolis metro**, which begins at Abdel Mouneen Riyad (between the Antiquities Museum and the *Ramses Hilton*), running under the elevated roadway from there up Sharia Gala'a to Midan Ramses. From there, its three tram lines follow the same track through Abbassiya, diverging shortly before Midan Roxi. Each has its own colour-coded direction boards.

• The **Abd al-Aziz Fahmi line** (green) runs past Merryland and Heliopolis Hospital on Sharia al-Higaz, before heading off towards the Shams Club.

• More centrally, the **Nouzha line** (red) veers off Sharia Merghani near the Heliopolis Sporting Club, and follows Al-Ahram and Osman Ibn Affan up to Midan Triomphe.

• Initially running alongside the red line, the **Merghani line** (yellow) then follows the street of that name past the International Language Institute (ILI) to Midan Triomphe, and out towards the Armed Forces Hospital.

Sights and activities

Nouzha-line, red-coded trams run through the heart of Heliopolis, whose finest **architecture** lines the boulevards between Sharia Merghani and Abu Bakr al-Saddiq. Stay on board to review Sharia al-Ahram's parade of handsome arcades topped with Andalusian balconies and pantiles, or alight near the **Heliopolis Sporting Club** and walk around the corner of the **Urubah Palace** onto Sharia Ibrahim. Other side streets have more of a 1920s feel, with crisply graceful Art Deco apartments. But the most famous landmark lies off Sharia al-'Urubah, further southeast. Resembling a Hindu

ANCIENT HELIOPOLIS, THE ENNEAD AND THE CULT OF RE

Although Anthony Trollope scoffed "Humbug!" when he saw what little remained in 1858, the site of **ancient Heliopolis**, near modern Matariyya, originally covered perhaps five square kilometres. The City of the Sun (called *On* by its founders, but better known by its Greek appellation) evolved in tandem with Memphis, the first capital of Dynastic Egypt (see p.201). As Memphis embodied the political unification of Upper and Lower Egypt, so Heliopolis incarnated its theological aspect, syncretizing diverse local cults into a hierarchical cosmogony that proved more influential than other creation myths of the Old Kingdom.

COSMOGONY

Shu, Nut and Geb

In the **Heliopolitan cosmogony**, the world began as watery chaos (Nun) from which Atum the sun-god emerged onto a primal mound, spitting forth the twin deities Shu (air) and Tefnut (moisture). They engendered Geb (earth) and Nut (sky), whose own union produced Isis, Osiris, Seth and Nephthys. Later texts often regarded this divine **Ennead** (Nine) as a single entity, while the universe was conventionally represented by the figures of Shu, Nut and Geb. Meanwhile (for reasons unknown), the primal deity Atum was subsumed by Re or Ra, a yet mightier aspect of the sun-god.

Re manifested himself in multiple forms: as hawk-headed Re-herakhte (Horus of the Horizon); the beetle Khepri (the rising sun); the disc Aten (the midday sun); and as Atum (the setting sun). The Egyptians believed that Re rose each morning in the east, traversed the sky in his solar barque and sank into the western land of the dead every evening, to voyage through the Duat (netherworld) during the night, emerging at sunrise. This journey inevitably linked Re to the Osirian myth, and from the V Dynasty onwards it became *de rigueur* for pharaohs to claim descent from Re by identifying themselves with Horus and Osiris. The **cult of Re** was exclusive, for only the pharaoh and priesthood had access to Re's sanctuary, whose daily rituals were adopted by other divine cults and soon became inextricably entangled with Osiris-worship (see "Karnak" and "Abydos", Chapter Two). Ordinary folk – whose participation was limited to public festivals – worshipped lesser, more approachable deities.

Re

REMAINS

Having been eclipsed by Karnak and Amun-worship during the New Kingdom, Heliopolis was devastated by the Persians in 525 BC. Once rebuilt, however, its intellectual reputation attracted visitors such as Plato, Eudoxus (who probably invented the sundial after studying Egyptian astronomy) and Herodotus. But as Alexandria became the new focus for science and religion, Heliopolis inexorably declined; Strabo found it nearly desolate and the Romans totally ignored it. Today, the only tangible reminders of its existence are **Senusert's obelisk** and the **Spring of the Sun**, where Atum supposedly washed himself at the dawn of creation.

temple, **Baron Empain's Palace** originally boasted a revolving tower that enabled its owner to follow the sun throughout the day. The now derelict structure (dubbed "Le Baron" by locals) can be glimpsed from some of the airport-bound buses.

Not far away – and directly accessible by Merghani tram – the **International Language Institute** (ILI) offers Arabic classes and also employs many foreigners as teachers (see p.61 and p.239). Along the Merghani tram route, too, are the Heliopolis and Heliolido **sporting clubs**, with tennis and squash courts, swimming pools and gymnasiums. The Heliopolis Sporting Club only admits foreigners in the summer and seems snootier than the Heliolido. Northeast of the latter, **Merryland** contains a boating lake and funfair, a small zoo and an overpriced café – nothing to get excited about, but it's nice to be surrounded by greenery – and it's a safe place for children to play. Green-coded trams continue on past Merryland, up Al-Higaz towards Midan Heliopolis.

Matariyya and beyond

Northwest of Heliopolis, several former villages have evolved into ramshackle *baladi* suburbs. **El-Zeitun** (the Olives) merits a footnote in history as the site of Sultan Selim's defeat of the Mamlukes in 1517 and of conspiratorial gatherings of Free Officers during the early 1950s. The adjacent **Helmiya** quarter gets its name from yet another khedival palace built last century. But for actual sights you have to venture even further out, into Matariyya.

The modern suburb of **Matariyya** traces its antecedents way back to the Old Kingdom and claims later acquaintance with the infant Christ. As evidence of the former, the neighbourhood's Midan al-Misallah displays a 22-metre-high, pink granite **Obelisk of Senusert I**. One of a pair raised to celebrate the pharaoh's Jubilee Festival (c.1900 BC), it originally stood outside the Temple of Re, erected by Amenemhat I, Senusert's father, who founded the XII Dynasty. Another pair, belonging to the XVIII Dynasty ruler Tuthmosis III, were moved by the Romans to Alexandria, whence they ended up in New York's Central Park and on London's Embankment. However, the significance of this site and its cult of the sun-god are far older, dating back to the earliest dynasties.

Cairo's metro makes this sector of the northern suburbs readily accessible from the centre. Matariyya metro station is eleven stops from Tahrir, in the direction of El-Marg; the neighbourhood can also be reached by tram from Heliopolis and along Sharia Bur Said from Saiyida Zeinab.

The Spring of the Sun, Virgin's Tree and Ain Shams
Nowadays, the **Spring of the Sun** waters a famous Christian relic, the **Virgin's Tree**. Located 500m south of the obelisk, this gnarled sycamore-fig is supposedly descended from a tree whose branches shaded the Holy Family during their Egyptian exile. Tradition has it that they rested here between Bilbeis and Babylon-in-Egypt (see p.159), and Mary washed the clothes of the baby Jesus in the stone trough that still lies beside the tree. Early this century, "Christian souvenir-hunting was so bad that the owner of the sycamore tied a knife to the tree and put up a notice begging people not to hack at it any more with axes, and to leave some of it for others" (Aldridge). Now enclosed within a compound, it grows near the **Church of the Virgin**, a modern building on the site of far older churches.

The spring's Arabic name has attached itself to the **Ain Shams** quarter, one metro stop beyond Matariyya. Densely populated and solidly working-class, the neighbourhood is regarded by the police as a hotbed of Islamic fundamentalism.

The Lake of the Pilgrims
Still further out, beyond El-Marg, caravans once prayed beside the **Lake of the Pilgrims** (*Birket el-Hagg*) before embarking on their journey to Mecca. Today, alas, the "covered litters of the female pilgrims and the picturesque corps of mounted *Bashi-*

Bazouks" no longer "moves slowly forward on its desert route". Instead, the barren wastes outside Cairo have for several decades harboured rocket ranges, chemical weapons factories and other **military installations**, rendering vast tracts off-limits. Ironically, much of this research was undertaken in collaboration with Iraq, Egypt's main Arab ally before the Gulf War, during which they fought on opposite sides.

THE PYRAMIDS

All things dread Time, but Time dreads the Pyramids

Anonymous proverb

For millions of people **the Pyramids** epitomize ancient Egypt: no other monument is so instantly recognized the world over. Yet comparatively few foreigners realize that at least 97 pyramids are spread across seventy kilometres of desert, from the outskirts of Cairo to the edge of the Fayoum. The mass of **theories, claims and counter-claims** about how and why the Pyramids were built contributes to the sense of mystery that surrounds them. Some of the recent contributions to this debate include *The Orion Mystery* (1994*)*, in which Robert Bauval asserts that the orientation of the Giza Pyramids corresponds to the three stars in Orion's Belt, and the "ventilation" shafts in the Geat Pyramid were aligned with Orion's Belt and Alpha Draconis. Graham Hancock took this a stage further in *Fingerprints of the Gods* (1995), arguing that the entire pyramid field corresponded to an astronomical map. In later books he says that the Sphinx and Pyramids are far older than reckoned, and recall a vanished ur-civilization that was destroyed in 12,000 BC, having left its stamp on Angkor Wat, the Maya and Easter Island. Egyptologists have since been lining up to refute these theories; meanwhile you can read up on the latest crop – including some that figure Martians into the equation – at *www.nauticom.net/users.ata/egypt.html*.

Most visitors are content to see the great **Pyramids of Giza** and part of the sprawling necropolis of **Saqqara**, both easily accessible from Cairo (tours to Saqqara often include a visit to the ruins of the ancient city of **Memphis**). Only a minority ride across the sands to **Abu Sir**, or visit the **Dahshur** pyramid field (see the map on p.69 for the location of all these sites). Still further south, the dramatic "Collapsed Pyramid" of **Maidum** and the lesser Middle Kingdom pyramids of **Hawara**, **El-Lisht** and **Lahun** are easier to reach from the Fayoum, so for the sake of convenience we've covered them in Chapter Three (see p.428). The pyramid at Abu Ruash, to the west of Cairo, inaccessible and little more than a pile of sand, is only of interest to specialists (if you do want to find it, *service* taxis from Midan Giza serve the nearby village of Abu Ruash).

The Pyramids in history

The derivation of the word "pyramid" is obscure. *Per-em-us*, an ancient Egyptian term meaning "straight up", seems likelier than the Greek *pyramis* – "wheaten cake", a facetious descriptive term for these novel monuments. Then again, "obelisk" comes from *obeliskos*, the ancient Greek for "skewer" or "little spit".

Whatever, the Pyramids' sheer **antiquity** is staggering. When the Greek chronicler Herodotus visited them in 450 BC, as many centuries separated his lifetime from their creation as divide our own time from that of Herodotus, who regarded them as ancient even then. For the Pyramid Age was only an episode in three millennia of pharaonic civilization, reaching its zenith within two hundred years and followed by an inexorable decline, so that later dynasties regarded the works of their ancestors with awe. Fourteen centuries after the royal tombs of the Old Kingdom were first violated by robbers, the Saïte (XXVI) Dynasty collected what remained, replaced missing bodies with surrogates, and reburied their forebears with archaic rituals they no longer comprehended.

The Pyramid Age began at Saqqara in the 27th century BC, when the III Dynasty royal architect Imhotep enlarged a *mastaba* tomb to create the first **step pyramid**. As techniques evolved, an attempt was made to convert another step pyramid at Maidum into a true pyramid by encasing its sides in a smooth shell, but the design was faulty and the pyramid collapsed under its own weight, necessitating hasty alterations to its counterpart at Dahshur. Not until the IV Dynasty were all the problems solved and a sheer-sided **true pyramid** arose at Giza. After two more perfect pyramids, less resources and care were devoted to the pyramid fields of Abu Sir and South Saqqara, and the latterday pyramids near Fayoum Oasis never matched the standards of the Old Kingdom.

Their enigma has puzzled people ever since. Whereas the ancient Greeks vaguely understood their function, the Romans were less certain; medieval Arabs believed them to be treasure houses with magical guardians, and early European observers reckoned them to be the Biblical granaries of Joseph. The nineteenth century was a golden era of discoveries by Belzoni, Vyse, Petrie, Mariette, Maspero and Lepsius, which all suggested that the pyramids were essentially containers for royal tombs and nothing else. It was also the heyday of Pyramidologists like Piazzi Smyth and David Davidson, who averred that their dimensions in "pyramid inches" proved the supremacy of Christianity and the Jewish origin of the pyramid-builders.

Archeologists now agree that the pyramids' **function** was to preserve the pharaoh's **ka**, or double: a vital force which emanated from the sun-god to his son, the king, who distributed it amongst his subjects and the land of Egypt itself. Mummification, funerary rituals, false doors for his **ba** (soul) to escape, model servants (*shabti* figures) and anniversary offerings – all were designed to ensure that his *ka* enjoyed an afterlife similar to its former existence. Thus was the social order perpetuated throughout eternity and the forces of primeval chaos held at bay, a theme emphasized in tomb reliefs at Saqqara. On another level of **symbolism**, the pyramid form evoked the primal mound at the dawn of creation, a recurrent theme in ancient Egyptian cosmogony, echoed in megalithic *benben* and obelisks whose pyramidal tips are sheathed in glittering electrum.

Although the limestone scarp at the edge of the Western Desert provided an inexhaustible source of building material, finer stone for casing the pyramids was quarried at Tura across the river, or came from Aswan in Upper Egypt. Blocks were quarried using wooden wedges (which swelled when soaked, enlarging fissures) and copper chisels, then transported on rafts to the pyramid site, where the final shaping and polishing occurred. Shipments coincided with the inundation of the Nile (July–November), when its waters lapped the feet of the plateau and Egypt's workforce was released from agricultural tasks.

Herodotus relates that a hundred thousand slaves took a decade to build the causeway and earthen ramps, and a further twenty years to raise the Great Pyramid of Cheops. Archeologists now believe that, far from being slaves, most of the workforce were actually peasants who were paid in food for their three-month stint (papyri enumerate the quantities of lentils, onions and leeks), while a few thousand skilled craftsmen were employed full time on its **construction**. One theory holds that a single ramp wound around the pyramid core, and was raised as it grew; when the capstone was in place, the casing was added from the top down and the ramp was reduced. Other ramps (recently found) led from the base of the pyramid to the quarry. Apparently, pulleys were only used to lift the plug blocks that sealed the corridors and entrance; all the other stones were moved with levers and rollers. It is estimated that during the most productive century of pyramid building, some 25 million tons of material were quarried. To put this in perspective, this is equivalent to one month's quarrying in Britain – or the material for 125 miles of motorway.

Whether or not the ancient Egyptians deemed this work a religious obligation, the massive levies certainly demanded an effective bureaucracy. Pyramid-building therefore helped consolidate the state. Its decline paralleled the Old Kingdom's, its cessation and resumption two anarchic eras (the First and Second Intermediate Periods) and the short-lived Middle Kingdom (XII Dynasty). By the time of the New Kingdom, other monumental symbols seemed appropriate. Remembering the plundered pyramids, the rulers of the New Kingdom opted for hidden tombs in the Valley of the Kings.

The Pyramids of Giza

Of the Seven Wonders of the ancient world, only the **Pyramids of Giza** have withstood the ravages of time. "From the summit of these monuments, forty centuries look upon you", cried Napoleon; "A practical joke played on History", retorted another visitor. The Great Pyramid of Cheops has inspired more learned and crackpot speculation than any

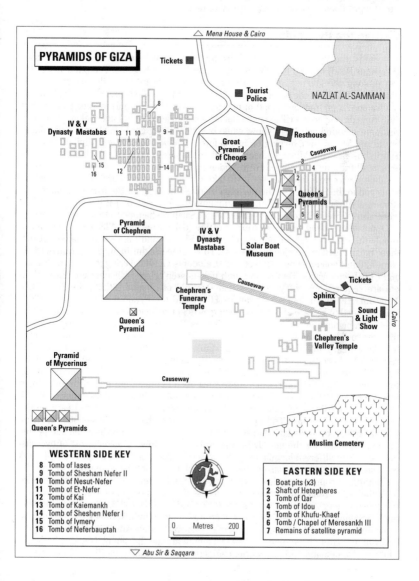

△ Mena House & Cairo

PYRAMIDS OF GIZA

Tickets ■

Tourist Police ■

NAZLAT AL-SAMMAN

IV & V Dynasty Mastabas

8

13 11 10   9

Great Pyramid of Cheops

Resthouse

Causeway

3   4

15
16   12   14

1 2

Queen's Pyramids

5   6

Pyramid of Chephren

IV & V Dynasty Mastabas

Solar Boat Museum

Causeway

Tickets ■

Sphinx

Chephren's Funerary Temple

Sound & Light Show

▷ Cairo

Queen's Pyramid

Chephren's Valley Temple

Pyramid of Mycerinus

Causeway

Queen's Pyramids

Muslim Cemetery

WESTERN SIDE KEY
 8 Tomb of Iases
 9 Tomb of Shesham Nefer II
10 Tomb of Nesut-Nefer
11 Tomb of Et-Nefer
12 Tomb of Kai
13 Tomb of Kaiemankh
14 Tomb of Sheshen Nefer I
15 Tomb of Iymery
16 Tomb of Neferbauptah

N

EASTERN SIDE KEY
1 Boat pits (x3)
2 Shaft of Hetepheres
3 Tomb of Qar
4 Tomb of Idou
5 Tomb of Khufu-Khaef
6 Tomb / Chapel of Meresankh III
7 Remains of satellite pyramid

0   Metres   200

▽ Abu Sir & Saqqara

monument on earth. For millions of people, the Giza Pyramids embody antiquity and mystery. Burdened with expectations, you may find the reality disappointing. Resembling small triangles from afar and corrugated mountains as you approach, their gigantic mass can seem oddly two-dimensional when viewed from below. Far from being isolated in the desert as carefully angled photos suggest, they rise just beyond the outskirts of Giza City. During daytime, hordes of touts and tourists dispel any lingering mystique, as do the Sound and Light Shows after dark. Only at sunset, dawn and late at night does their brooding majesty return.

Visiting the Pyramids

The site is directly accessible from Cairo by the eleven-kilometre long Sharia al-Ahram (Pyramids Road) built by Khedive Ismail for the Empress Eugénie. Though heavy traffic can prolong the journey, **getting there** is straightforward. Taxi drivers often quote upwards of £E20, but the proper fare is £E10–15 for a one-way trip. A cheaper option is to catch a bus (25pt), minibus (35pt) or microbus *service* taxi (50pt) from Midan Tahrir. Bus #913 runs directly to the village of Nazlat al-Samman, near the Sphinx, making it ideal for visiting the Sound and Light show, while bus #900 (£E2) goes via Qasr al-Aini, Manial Island and Midan Giza, turning off just before the *Mena House* hotel. Minibus #83 from Tahrir, bus #30 from Midan Ramses and microbus *service* taxis from both also run more or less all the way to the site. From Midan Ataba, there are less frequent (but larger) minibus *service* taxis, and bus #924 will take you to the top of Sharia Abu el-Hol, which leads you to the Sphinx. (All the downtown drivers heading for the pyramids shout, "Al-Ahram, al-Ahram".) An easier one-day, minimum-effort way to visit the Giza Pyramids, while also taking in Saqqara, is to go on one of Salah Mohammed's tours (see p.194).

Opposite the *Mena House* is a **tourist office** (daily 8am–5pm; ☎383-8823), which can supply the official rates for horse and camel rides around the Giza plateau – not that these mean much in practice (see below). To visit the site during **opening hours** (daily 7am–7.30pm) you must buy a ticket (£E20, students £E10) covering the site, the Sphinx and Chephren's Valley Temple – though tickets aren't rigorously checked. Extra **tickets** are required for entry to the Great Pyramid of Cheops (£E20), the Solar Boat Museum (£E10), Chephren's Pyramid (£E10) and the Pyramid of Mycerinus (£E5). You still need to beware of con men posing as ticket collectors or "special guides", who offer commentary along the lines of "Cheops Pyramid very old" – ignore them, or threaten to call the tourist police if necessary. Also ignore horse and camel touts on the way in who try to tell you that their stables are at the site entrance ("no ticket required"). However, all this is set to change under the "Giza Plateau Conservation Project" (due to open in 2000, but don't hold your breath). The project will include an Imax cinema, cultural centres and more sites open to the public, and, with the plateau effectively cut off from Nazlat al-Samman village, will exclude cars and touts.

Plan on spending half a day at the Pyramids, which are best entered early in the morning before the heat and crowds become unbearable (tour buses start arriving from 10.30am), or in the late afternoon – by 5pm most tour groups have left and people have yet to arrive for the nightly **Sound and Light Show**. These consist of two one-hour shows in different languages (call ☎385-7320/2880, or check *Egypt Today, Cairo's* or *www.sound-light.egypt.com/pyr.htm* for schedules, which vary seasonally). As the melodramatic commentary is rather crass, you might prefer one of the performances in Arabic. Hundreds of Egyptians enjoy a free show from vantage points such as past the Muslim cemetery, eschewing seats (£E33, video camera £E33) on the terrace facing the Sphinx. Bring a sweater, since nights are cold even in summer.

Behind the grandstand is a row of stables **renting horses and camels** that are generally in no better shape than the animals touted around the site by Nagama Bedouin. They tend to demand £E50 for a brief camel ride (never mind the official hourly rate of

£E10 for either a camel or horse) and resort to tricks like setting your horse charging into the desert, only curbing its flight in return for *baksheesh*. As the site is small enough to cover on foot, riding is more of an experience than a timesaver, and haggling with these guys just might ruin your visit.

In Baedeker's day, it was *de rigueur* for visitors to climb the Great Pyramid: while two Bedouin seized an arm apiece and hauled from above, a third would push from below. **Climbing the pyramids** is now forbidden and it is undoubtedly very dangerous, although attempts are still made. Though **going inside** is quite safe, anyone suffering from claustrophobia or asthma should forget it. Clambering through all three shafts in the Great Pyramid will make your leg muscles ache the following day.

As site plans suggest, the pyramids' **orientation** is no accident. Their entrances are aligned with the Polar Star (or rather, its position 4500 years ago); the internal tomb chambers face west, the direction of the Land of the Dead; and the external funerary temples point eastwards towards the rising sun. It is also claimed that the trio of pyramids represents the three stars in Orion's belt. Less well preserved are the causeways leading to the so-called valley temples, and various subsidiary pyramids and *mastaba* tombs. The entire site is being renovated by the EAO, and continues to yield surprises: notably the recent discovery of a possible secret chamber within the Great Pyramid, which some think will contain treasures as stunning as those from Tutankhamun's tomb; a previously unknown small pyramid by the southeastern corner of Cheops', with the oldest pyramidion (capstone) yet discovered; and tunnels under the seats in front of the Sphinx, whose age and purpose are so far unknown.

The Great Pyramid of Cheops (Khufu)

The oldest and largest of the Giza Pyramids is that of the IV Dynasty pharaoh **Khufu** – better known as **Cheops** – who probably reigned between 2589 and 2566 BC. Called the "Glorious Place of Khufu" by the ancient Egyptians, it originally stood 140m (roughly 480ft) high and measured 230m along its base, but the removal of its casing stones has reduced these dimensions by three metres. The pyramid is estimated to weigh six million tons and contain over 2,300,000 blocks whose average weight is 2.5 tons (though some weigh almost 15 tons). This gigantic mass actually ensures its stability, since most of the stress is transmitted inwards towards its central core, or downwards into the underlying bedrock. Until recently, the pyramid was thought to contain only three chambers: one in the bedrock and two in the superstructure. Experts believe that its design was changed twice, the subterranean chamber being abandoned in favour of the middle one, which was itself superseded by the uppermost chamber. By the time archeologists got here, their contents had been looted long ago, and the only object left *in situ* was Khufu's sarcophagus. However, in April 1993, a German team of scientists using a robot probe accidentally discovered a door with handles supposedly enclosing a fourth chamber, apparently never plundered by thieves, which might contain the mummy and treasures of Cheops himself. The head of the Giza Antiquities Inspectorate, Dr Hawas, argues that there is no chamber, and that the "door" was a device for smoothing the inside of the shaft – but until investigations resume, the truth will not be known.

Cheops

Inside the Great Pyramid

You enter the pyramid (daily 8.30am–4.30pm; £E20, camera £E15, video camera £E150) via an opening created by the treasure-hunting Khalif Ma'mun in 820, some distance below the original entrance on the north face (now blocked). After following this downwards at a crouch, you'll reach the junction of the ascending and descending corridors. The latter – leading to an unfinished chamber below the pyramid – is best

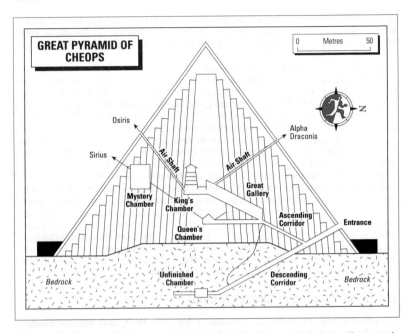

GREAT PYRAMID OF CHEOPS

0   Metres   50

Osiris

Alpha Draconis

Sirius

Air Shaft

Air Shaft

Great Gallery

Mystery Chamber

King's Chamber

Ascending Corridor

Entrance

Queen's Chamber

Bedrock

Unfinished Chamber

Descending Corridor

Bedrock

ignored or left until last, and everyone heads up the 1.6-metre-high **ascending corridor**. According to medieval Arab chroniclers, intruders soon encountered an "idol of speckled granite" wreathed by a serpent which "seized upon and strangled whoever approached", but latterday visitors are merely impeded by the 1:2 gradient of the passage, which runs for 36m until it meets another junction.

To the right of this is a **shaft** that ancient writers believed to be a well connected to the Nile; it's now recognized as leading into the subterranean chamber and thought to have been an escape passage for the workmen. Straight ahead is a horizontal passage 35m long and 1.75m high, leading to a semi-finished limestone chamber with a pointed roof, which Arabs dubbed the "**Queen's Chamber**". Petrie reckoned this was the *serdab*, or repository for the pharaoh's statue, while the eccentric Davidson saw it as symbolizing the ultimate futility of Judaism. Either way, there's no evidence that a queen was ever buried here. In the northern and southern walls are two holes made in 1872 for the purpose of discovering the chamber's ventilation shafts; it was through one of these that the robot probe discovered the "secret chamber", at the end of a 65m passageway only twenty centimetres high and the same distance wide, which is aligned with the Dog Star, Sirius (representing the goddess Isis).

However, most people step up into the **Great Gallery**, the finest section of the pyramid. Built of Muqattam limestone, so perfectly cut that a knife blade can't be inserted between its joints, the 47-metre-long shaft narrows to a corbelled roof 8.5m high. (Davidson believed that its length in "pyramid inches" corresponded to the number of years between the Crucifixion and the outbreak of World War I.) The incisions in its walls probably held beams that were used to raise the sarcophagus or granite plug blocks up the steep incline (nowadays overlaid with wooden steps). Though no longer infested by giant bats, as nineteenth-century travellers reported, the Great Gallery is sufficiently hot and airless to constitute something of an ordeal, and you'll be glad to reach the horizontal antechamber at the top, which is slotted for the insertion of plug blocks designed to thwart entry to the putative burial chamber.

The **King's Chamber** lies 95m beneath the apex of the pyramid and half that distance from its outer walls. Built of red granite blocks, the rectangular chamber is large enough to accommodate a double-decker bus. Its dimensions (5.2 by 10.8 by 5.8 metres) have inspired many abstruse calculations and whacky prophecies: Hitler ordered a replica built beneath the Nuremberg Stadium, where he communed with himself before Nazi rallies. To one side of the chamber lies a huge, lidless **sarcophagus** of Aswan granite, bearing the marks of diamond-tipped saws and drills. On the northern and southern walls, at knee height, you'll notice two air shafts leading to the outer world, aligned with the stars of Orion's Belt and Alpha Draconis (representing Osiris and the hippo goddess Rer respectively).

Unseen above the ceiling, five **relieving chambers** distribute the weight of the pyramid away from the burial chamber; each consists of 43 granite monoliths weighing 40 to 70 tons apiece. These chambers can only be reached by a ladder from the Great Gallery, and then a passage where Colonel Vyse found Khufu's name inscribed in red (the only inscription within the Giza Pyramids), but the flow of people normally rules this out.

On your way back down, consider investigating the 100-metre-long **descending corridor**, which leads to a crudely hewn **unfinished chamber** beneath the pyramid. There's nothing to see, but the nerve-wracking descent is worthy of Indiana Jones.

Subsidiary tombs

East of the Great Pyramid, it's just possible to discern the foundations of Khufu's funerary temple and a few blocks of the causeway that once connected it to his valley temple (now buried beneath the village of Nazlat al-Samman). Nearby stand three ruined **Queens' Pyramids**, each with a small chapel attached. The northern and southern pyramids belonged to Merites and Hensutsen, Khufu's principal wife (and sister), and the putative mother of Chephren, respectively; the middle one may have belonged to the mother of Redjedef, the third ruler of the dynasty. Between that and the Great Pyramid, the remains of a fourth satellite pyramid have recently been discovered, including its capstone, the oldest yet found, but the pyramid's purpose is so far unknown.

Just northeast of Queen Merites's pyramid is a **shaft** where III Dynasty pharaoh Snofru's wife Queen Hetepheres's sarcophagus was found, having been stashed here following lootings at its original home in Dahshur. To the east of it are the tombs of Qar and his son Idou, which contain life-size statues of the deceased and various reliefs. To the east of Queen Hensutsen's pyramid are the tombs of Cheops' son Khufu-Khaef, and Chephren's wife (also Hetepheres's daughter) Meres-ankh, the best preserved of all the tombs on the Giza plateau, complete with statues in the niches and reliefs showing scenes of daily life, with much of the paintwork intact. To get into these tombs, ask at the custodian's hut beside Hetepheres's shaft; naturally, the custodian will appreciate a tip for opening up.

To the west of the Great Pyramid lie dozens of **IV and V Dynasty mastabas**, where archeologists have uncovered a 4600-year-old mummified princess, whose body had been hollowed out and encased in a thin layer of plaster – a hitherto unknown method of mummification. Here are more **tombs** that until 1995 had been closed to the public since their discovery in the nineteenth century. In general, these are less interesting than those on the eastern side of the Great Pyramid, but that of Neferbauptah – almost parallel with the west side of Chephren's pyramid – has a dinosaur fossil preserved in the fifth block from the right of the second row up on its north side. Should you want to enter any of these tombs, ask at the Inspectorate office to the north. Beware of deep shafts with no fences around them.

The Solar Boat Museum

Perched to the south of the Great Pyramid, across the road from another cluster of *mastabas*, is a humidity-controlled pavilion (daily: winter 9am–4pm; summer 9am–5pm; £E20, students £E10; cameras £E10, video camera £E100) containing a 43-metre-long **boat** from one of the five boat pits sunk around Khufu's Pyramid. (Another boat has been located by X-rays and video cameras, but for the present remains unexcavated.)

When the pit's limestone roofing blocks were removed in 1954, a faint odour of cedarwood arose. Restorer Hagg Ahmed Yussef subsequently spent fourteen years rebuilding a graceful craft from 1200 pieces of wood, originally held together by sycamore pegs and halfa-grass ropes. Archeologists term these vessels "solar boats" (or barques), but their purpose remains uncertain – carrying the pharaoh through the underworld (as shown in XVII–IX Dynasty tombs at Thebes) or accompanying the sun-god on his daily journey across the heavens are two of the many hypotheses.

The Pyramid of Chephren (Khafre)

Sited on higher ground, with an intact summit and steeper sides, the middle or **Second Pyramid** seems taller than Khufu's. Built by his son **Khafre** (known to posterity as Chephren), its base originally covered 214.8 square metres and its weight is estimated at 4,883,000 tons. As with Khufu's Pyramid, the original rock-hewn burial chamber was never finished and an upper chamber was subsequently constructed. Classical writers such as Pliny believed that the pyramid had no entrance, but when Belzoni located and blasted open the sealed portal on its north face in 1818, he found that Arab tomb robbers had somehow gained access nearly a thousand years earlier, undeterred by legends of an idol "with fierce and sparkling eyes", bent on slaying intruders. In March 1993, several tourists were injured by an explosion inside Chephren's Pyramid, probably caused by a bomb.

If the pyramid is open, you can follow one of the two entry corridors downwards, and then upwards, into a long horizontal passage leading to Chephren's **burial chamber**, where Belzoni celebrated his discovery by writing his name in black letters. This ebullient circus strongman-turned-explorer went on to find Seti I's tomb in the Valley of the Kings, and died searching for the source of the River Niger. Set into the chamber's granite floor is the sarcophagus of Khafre, who reigned c.2558–2533 BC. The square cavity near the southern wall may have marked the position of a canopic chest containing the pharaoh's viscera.

Chephren's Funerary Complex and the Sphinx

The funerary complex of Chephren's Pyramid is the best-preserved example of this typically Old Kingdom arrangement. When a pharaoh died, his body was ferried across the Nile to a riverside valley temple where it was embalmed by priests. After the process was complete, mourners gathered here to purify themselves before escorting 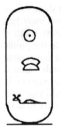 his mummy up the causeway to a funerary (or mortuary) temple, where further rites preceded its interment within the pyramid. Thereafter, the priests ensured his *ka*'s afterlife by making offerings of food and incense in the funerary temple on specific anniversaries.

Chephren's **funerary temple** consists of a pillared hall, central court, niched storerooms and a sanctuary, but most of the outer granite casing has been plundered over centuries and the interior may not be accessible. Amongst the remaining blocks is a 13.4-metre-long monster weighing 163,000 kilos. Flanking the temple are what appear to be boat pits, although excavations have yielded nothing but pottery fragments. From here you can trace the foundations of a **causeway** that runs 400m downhill to his valley temple, near the Sphinx.

Chephren

The **valley temple** (daily 9am–4pm) lay buried under sand until its discovery by Mariette in 1852, which accounts for its reasonable state of preservation. Built of limestone and faced with polished Aswan granite, the temple faces east and used to open onto a quay. Beyond a narrow antechamber you'll find a T-shaped hall whose gigantic architraves are supported by square pillars, in front of which stood diorite statues of Chephren. Contrary to the widely accepted theory, a few scholars believe that mummification occurred at Memphis or Chephren's mortuary temple, this edifice being reserved for the "Opening of Mouth" ceremony, whereby the *ka* entered the deceased's body.

The Sphinx

This legendary monument is carved from an outcrop of soft limestone that was supposedly left standing after the harder surrounding stone was quarried for the Great Pyramid; however, since the base stone was too soft to work on directly, it was clad in harder stone before finishing. Conventional archeology credits Chephren with the idea of shaping it into a figure with a lion's body and a human head, which is often identified as his own (complete with royal beard and *uraeus*, see p.255), though it may represent a guardian deity. Some thousand years later, the future Tuthmosis IV is said to have dreamt that if he cleared the sand that engulfed the **Sphinx** it would make him ruler; a prophecy fulfilled, as recorded on a stele that he placed between its paws. All these notions went unchallenged until 1991, when two American geologists argued that the Sphinx was at least 2600 years older than had been imagined: its bedrock was heavily weathered and eroded by water, probably during the Nabtian Pluvial era (3000–1200 BC). This argument is dismissed by Dr Hawas, who cites an analysis of the Sphinx's bedrock by the Getty Institute, which concludes that the erosion was caused by the action of mineral salts within the plateau and/or the wind. The controversy delighted the maverick Egyptologist John West, who has long claimed that Egyptian civilization was the inheritor of a more ancient, lost culture – the mythical Atlantis. The name "Sphinx" was actually bestowed by the ancient Greeks, after the legendary creature that put riddles to passers-by and slew those who answered wrongly; the Arabs called it *Abu el-Hol* (the awesome or terrible one).

Used for target practice by Mamluke and Napoleonic troops, the Sphinx lost much of its beard to the British Museum and was sandbagged for protection during World War II. Early modern repairs did more harm than good, since its porous limestone "breathes", unlike the cement that was used to fill its cracks. There is also the problem of chemical pollutants from sewage and fires in the neighbouring settlement of Nazlat al-Samman. A more recent long-term **restoration project** (1989–1998) involved handcutting ten thousand limestone blocks, to refit the paws, legs and haunches of the beast; the missing nose and beard have not been replaced, deliberately.

Three **tunnels** exist inside the Sphinx, one behind its head, one in its tail and one in its north side. Their function is unknown, but none of them go anywhere. Other tunnels have been unearthed in the vicinity of the Sphinx; again, we don't know who built them or what they were for, but one suggestion is that they were created by later ancient Egyptians looking for buried treasure.

During Sound and Light shows, the Sphinx is given the role of narrator.

The Pyramid of Mycerinus (Menkaure)

Sited on a gradual slope into undulating desert, the smallest of the Giza Pyramids speaks of waning power and commitment. Though started by Chephren's successor, **Menkaure** (called Mycerinus by the Greeks), it was finished with unseemly haste by his son Shepseskaf, who seemingly enjoyed less power than his predecessors and depended on the priesthood. Herodotus records the legend that an oracle gave Mycerinus only six years to live, so to cheat fate he made merry round the clock, doubling his annual quantum of experience. Another story has it that the pyramid was

KERDASSA AND HARRANIYYA

These two villages have no connection with the pyramids, but tour groups often pay one or both of them a visit. **KERDASSA**, roughly due west of Imbaba (but accessible by minibus from Midan Giza), is where most of the scarves, *galabiyyas* and shirts in Cairo are made, plus carpets, which are sold by the metre. Although no longer a place for bargains, it's still frequented by collectors of ethnic textiles, particularly Bedouin robes and veils (the best-quality ones retail for hundreds of dollars). In times past, Kerdassa was also the starting point of the camel trail across the Western Desert to Libya.

Folks on Salah's tours (see p.194) are inevitably taken to **HARRANIYYA**, the site of the famous **Wissa Wassef Art Centre** (daily 10am–5pm; ☎385-0403). Founded fifty years ago by Ramses Wissa Wassef, an architect who wanted to preserve village crafts and alleviate rural unemployment, the centre teaches children to design and weave carpets, and has branched out into batik work and pottery. Superintended by his widow and the original generation of students, pupils produce beautiful tapestries, which now sell for thousands of dollars and are imitated throughout Egypt. You can see them at work between 10am and 5pm (except at lunchtime and on Fridays), and admire a superb collection in the museum designed by Hassan Fathy, a masterpiece of mud-brick architecture. To reach the Art Centre under your own steam, catch a taxi or minibus 4km south along the Saqqara road (Maryotteya Canal, west bank) from Pyramids Road, and follow the signs to *Salma* (or *Salome*) campsite, next door.

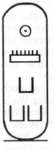

Mycerinus

actually built by Rhodophis, a Thracian courtesan who charged each client the price of a building block (the structure is estimated to contain 200,000 blocks). In any event, no subsequent pyramid ever matched the standards of the Giza trio.

Because its lower half was sheathed in Aswan granite, this is sometimes called the **Red Pyramid** (a name also applied to one of Snofru's pyramids at Dahshur). Its relative lack of casing stones is due to a twelfth-century sultan whose courtiers persuaded him to attempt the pyramid's demolition, a project he wisely gave up after eight months. Medieval Arab chroniclers frequently ascribed the Giza Pyramids to a single ruler, who supposedly boasted: "I, Surid the king, have built these pyramids in sixty-one years. Let him who comes after me attempt to destroy them in six hundred. To destroy is easier than to build. I have clothed them in silk; let him try to cover them in mats." The **interior** (daily 8.30am–4.30pm; £E20, students £E10) is unusual for having its unfinished chamber in the superstructure and the final burial chamber underground. Here Vyse discovered a basalt sarcophagus later lost at sea en route to Britain, plus human remains that he assumed were Menkaure's, but which are now reckoned to be a XXVI Dynasty replacement and rest in the British Museum.

The complex also features three subsidiary pyramids, a relatively intact funerary temple, and a causeway to the now-buried valley temple. Northwest of the latter lies the sarcophagus-shaped **Tomb of Queen Khentkawes**, an intriguing figure who appears to have bridged the transition between the IV and V dynasties. Apparently married to Shepseskaf, the last IV Dynasty ruler, she may have wed a priest of the sun-god after his demise and gone on to bear several kings who were buried at Saqqara or Abu Sir (where she also built a pyramid).

The Pyramids of Zawiyat al-Aryan

The **Zawiyat al-Aryan pyramid field** lies roughly midway between Giza and North Saqqara and about 3.5km from the Sun Temples of Abu Ghurab at Abu Sir (see below), and can be seen if you ride across the desert. Both its pyramids are sanded over and scarcely worth a detour, but Egyptologists still ponder their place in the evolution of pyramid-building.

The northerly **Unfinished Pyramid** makes extensive use of granite, suggesting that it might hail from the IV Dynasty, but never got beyond its foundations and enclosure wall – unfinished blocks and stone chippings are scattered all around. To the southeast lies a **Layer Pyramid** built of small stone blocks, which seems to have been intended as a step pyramid and thus presumably belongs to the III Dynasty.

The Pyramids of Abu Sir

This necropolis of V Dynasty (c.2494–2345 BC) pharaohs covers an arc of desert beyond the village of **ABU SIR**. The mortuary complexes here are smaller than the Giza Pyramids of the previous dynasty, suggesting a decline in royal power; their ruinous state and the effort required to reach them also mean that few tourists come here. Those who do often feel that Abu Sir's splendid isolation compensates for its monumental shortcomings. However, the site is bound to lose some of its enchantment, having opened as an official tourist site in 1999, complete with visitors' centre (daily: winter 8am–5pm; summer 8am–4pm), entry charge (£E10, students £E5) and a steadily increasing stream of tour buses along the new asphalt road.

Getting there

The Pyramids of Abu Sir can now be reached by taxi from Saqqara (£E5–8), or by minibus #333 from Giza. The boldest option, however, is to visit them **en route between Giza and Saqqara** by horse or camel, spending three hours in the saddle. Making a round trip **from North Saqqara** (see below) is less demanding, but still requires commitment. With the Pyramids clearly visible 6km away, you can either walk (1hr 30min–2hr) or conserve energy by renting a horse or camel from near the refreshments tent (£E15–20 one-way). Getting to Abu Sir **from Cairo** is more time-consuming: you need to catch a bus to Maryotteya Canal on Pyramids Road (any of the buses to the Pyramids or the Sphinx will do, see p.81), then a *service* taxi microbus from the west bank to Shabramant, and from there another to Abu Sir.

The pyramid complexes

The four pyramid complexes are ranged in an arc that ignores chronological order. At the southern end of the pyramid field a low mound marks the core of the unfinished **Pyramid of Neferefre**, whose brief reign preceded Nyuserre's. As the core is composed of locally quarried limestone and was never encased in finer Tura masonry, no causeway was ever built. However, the desert may yet disgorge other structures: during the 1980s, Czechoslovak archeologists uncovered another pyramid complex, thought to belong to Queen Khentkawes, the mother of Sahure.

Dominating the view north is the much larger **Pyramid of Neferirkare**, the third ruler of the V Dynasty, who strove to outdo his predecessor, Sahure. If finished, it would have been 70m high – taller than the third pyramid at Giza – but Neferirkare's premature demise forced his successor to hastily complete a modified version using perishable mud-brick. Although too dangerous to climb, its summit commands a view of the entire pyramid field, from the three at Giza and the four at Saqqara to the Red and Bent Pyramids at Dahshur, and even the Collapsed Pyramid of Maidum on the distant horizon. The valley temple and grand causeway of Neferirkare's Pyramid were later usurped to serve the **Pyramid of Nyuserre**, further north. A battered mortuary temple with papyriform columns mocks the original name of this dilapidated pyramid,

"The Places of Nyuserre are Enduring"; the pharaohs who followed him preferred burial at Saqqara. A cluster of *mastabas* to the northwest includes the **Tomb of Ptahshepses**. Currently entered via a rickety ladder, the tomb's most curious feature is the double room off the courtyard, which may have held solar boats. If so, the only other known example of this in a private tomb is that of Kagemni in North Saqqara. Ptahshepses was Chief of Works to Sahure, the first of the V Dynasty kings to be buried at Abu Sir.

The **Pyramid of Sahure** is badly damaged, but its associated temples have fared better than others in this group. A 235-metre-long causeway links the ruined valley temple to Sahure's mortuary temple on the eastern side of the pyramid. Though most of its reliefs (which were the first to show the king smiting his enemies, later a standard motif) have gone to various museums, enough remains to make the temple worth exploring. It's also possible to crawl through a dusty, cobwebbed passage to reach the burial chamber within the pyramid (whose original name was "The Soul of Sahure Gleams"). Just to the north of the causeway, a series of fascinating reliefs show scenes from the building of a pyramid, notably of workers dragging a pyramidion (capstone) covered with white gold, while dancers celebrate the pyramid's completion.

The Sun Temples of Abu Ghurab

Just northeast of Abu Sir is the site known as **Abu Ghurab** (if you are riding between Giza and Saqqara, you could ask the guide to stop here). Its twin temples were designed for worship of Re, the sun-god of Heliopolis, but their Jubilee reliefs and proximity to a pyramid field suggest a similar function to Zoser's Heb-Sed court at Saqqara.

Unlike the ruinous **Sun Temple of Userkaf**, 400m from Sahure's Pyramid, the more distant **Sun Temple of Nyuserre** repays a visit. At its western end stood a colossal *benben* or megalith as tall as a pyramid, symbolizing the primordial mound – of which only the base remains. Approached from its valley temple by a causeway, the great courtyard is centred on an alabaster altar where cattle were sacrificed. From the courtyard's vestibule, corridors run north to storerooms and south to the king's chapel. The "Chamber of Seasons" beyond the chapel once contained beautiful reliefs; to the south you can find the remnants of a brick model of a solar boat.

North Saqqara

While Memphis (see p.201) was the capital of the Old Kingdom, Egypt's royalty and nobility were buried at **Saqqara**, the limestone scarp that flanks the Nile Valley to the west – the traditional direction of the Land of the Dead. Although superseded by the Theban necropolis during the New Kingdom, Saqqara remained in use for burying sacred animals and birds, especially in Ptolemaic times, when these cults enjoyed a revival. Over three thousand years it grew to cover seven kilometres of desert – not including the associated necropolises of Abu Sir and Dahshur, or the Giza Pyramids. As such, it is today the largest archeological site in Egypt. Its name – pronounced "sa' *'ah*-rah" – probably derives from Sokar, the Memphite god of the dead, though Egyptians may tell you that it comes from *saq*, the Arabic word for a hawk or falcon, the sacred bird of Horus.

Besides the pyramids and *mastabas* seen by visitors, Saqqara has an incalculable wealth of monuments and artefacts still hidden beneath the windblown sands. In 1986, the **tomb of Maya**, Tutankhamun's treasurer, was discovered, stuffed with precious objects (it won't be open to the public for some time). Yet aside from Zoser's Pyramid, the site was virtually ignored by archeologists until Auguste Mariette found the Serapeum in 1851.

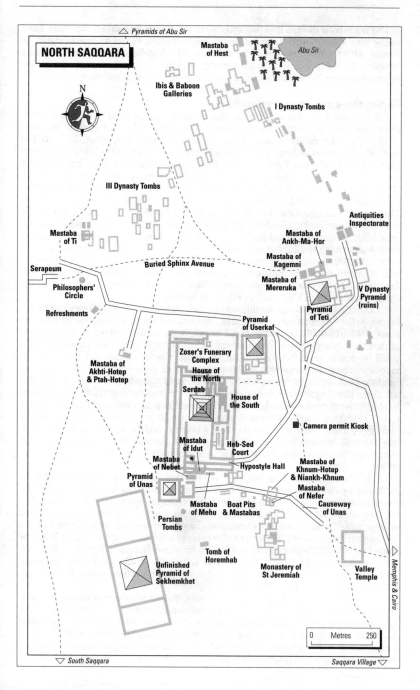

NORTH SAQQARA

△ Pyramids of Abu Sir

Mastaba of Hest

Abu Sir

Ibis & Baboon Galleries

I Dynasty Tombs

N

III Dynasty Tombs

Antiquities Inspectorate

Mastaba of Ti

Mastaba of Ankh-Ma-Hor

Mastaba of Kagemni

Serapeum

Buried Sphinx Avenue

Mastaba of Mereruka

V Dynasty Pyramid (ruins)

Philosophers' Circle

Pyramid of Teti

Refreshments

Pyramid of Userkaf

Mastaba of Akhti-Hotep & Ptah-Hotep

Zoser's Funerary Complex

House of the North

Serdab

House of the South

Camera permit Kiosk

Mastaba of Idut

Heb-Sed Court

Mastaba of Nebet

Hypostyle Hall

Mastaba of Khnum-Hotep & Niankh-Khnum

Pyramid of Unas

Mastaba of Nefer

Mastaba of Mehu

Boat Pits & Mastabas

Causeway of Unas

Persian Tombs

Memphis & Cairo ▷

Unfinished Pyramid of Sekhemkhet

Tomb of Horemhab

Monastery of St Jeremiah

Valley Temple

0   Metres   250

▽ South Saqqara

Saqqara Village ▽

The necropolis divides into two main sections: **North Saqqara** – the more interesting area – and **South Saqqara**. North Saqqara alone boasts a score of sights, so anyone with limited time should be selective. The **highlights** are Zoser's funerary complex, the Serapeum, and two outstanding *mastabas*; if time allows, add other tombs to your itinerary. To take in the whole site you would need several days.

Getting there and other practicalities

North Saqqara lies 21km south of the Giza Pyramids as the camel trundles, or 32km from Cairo by road, being roughly opposite Helwan on the east bank of the Nile. Getting there **by public transport** is awkward and time-consuming. The quickest method takes about an hour: go by bus to Pyramids Road, get off at Maryotteya Canal (about 1km before the Pyramids) and take a *service* taxi microbus from there to Saqqara – be sure not to take one going to Abu Sir village, as you'll then have to walk all the way accross the site to get to the ticket-office. You can also take bus #987 from Midan Ramses to El-Badrasheen, and then a minibus to Saqqara, by way of Memphis. Alternatively, take the metro to Helwan station (30min; 80pt), then a minibus to Tibiin, near the Mazniq bridge (20min; 50pt); another *service* across to El-Badrasheen on the west bank (15min; 50pt); and finally a minibus to Saqqara, again via Memphis (25pt). One disadvantage of all these methods is that they leave you in Saqqara village, still over a kilometre from the site entrance. Getting back to Cairo, it is wise not to leave too late, or you may not find transport in Saqqara village, and will have to either pay well over the odds for a taxi, or walk another 5km to El-Badrasheen (or at least to the Pyramids Road) to pick up a bus or microbus back to Cairo.

To save time and energy for the site, it's best to avail yourself of **tours** run by the affable Salah Mohammed Abdel Hafiez. You can contact him by phone (☎298-0650, mobile 012/313-8446), or send an email (*samo@intouch.com*); you'll also find his flyers posted up in budget hotels – he may call in from time to time. Leaving around 8am, you'll be driven in an A/C minibus to Memphis, North Saqqara, the Wissa Wassef tapestry school at Harraniyya and the Pyramids of Giza – all accompanied by an English-speaking Egyptologist – before returning to Cairo at about 5pm. Be sure to ask to see the Mastaba of Ti during your trip. The price of the tour (£E40, £E5 discount to *Rough Guide* readers who book direct) doesn't include admission tickets. Thomas Cook, Misr Travel and American Express also run tours to Saqqara for upwards of £E50 per person. Another option is to rent a **private taxi** for the day (£E60–80), splitting the cost between however many people you can assemble. Be sure to specify which sites are included and how long you expect to stay when you negotiate with the driver.

Lastly, you could plump for riding **across the desert from the Pyramids of Giza by horse or camel** (3hr). Although touts swear that the route takes you through the desert, past Zawiyet al-Aryan, the Sun Temples of Abu Ghurab and the Pyramids of Abu Sir, they often guide you along a more direct village track on the edge of the cultivated area, supposedly due to military restrictions. Either way, the journey will leave you stiff for days afterwards (see p.44 for the rudiments of camel-handling). Most people opt for a one-way ride (£E40–50 for a horse, £E35–45 for a camel); return trips cost twice that, plus a negotiable sum for waiting time (say £E100–120 in all). Be warned that some guides threaten to abandon travellers in the middle of nowhere unless they receive hefty *baksheesh*; it's usually safe to call their bluff.

Even if you don't emulate Lawrence of Arabia, bear in mind **conditions** at Saqqara. Over winter, the site can be swept by chill winds and clouds of grit; during the hottest months walking around is exhausting. Beware of deep pits, which aren't always fenced off. Bring at least one litre of water apiece, as vendors at Memphis and the refreshments tent at North Saqqara are grossly overpriced, like every restaurant along the Saqqara road; a packed lunch is also a good idea.

Though **opening hours** are 8am–5pm daily, guards start locking up the tombs at least half an hour early. A kiosk on the approach road sells **tickets** (£E20, students £E10), while another just up from the car park has camera (£E5) and video camera (£E25) permits. A separate ticket (£E10; no student reduction) from the car-park kiosk is needed to visit four nobles' tombs, those of Neferhenenptah, Irukaptah, Niankh-Khnoum and Khnum-hotep. It's a good idea to check at the kiosk which tombs are open – especially those further afield – as they often close due to restoration work. Some guards encourage unauthorized snapping in the expectation of *baksheesh*, but aside from this you're not obliged to give anything unless they help with lighting or provide a guided tour. If you don't want a running commentary, make this clear at the outset.

To reduce foot-slogging around the site, consider **renting a camel, horse or donkey** (roughly £E3–5 per hour after bargaining) from outside the refreshments tent near the Serapeum.

Zoser's funerary complex

The funerary complex of King Zoser (or Djoser) is the largest in Saqqara, and its **Step Pyramid** heralded the start of the Pyramid Age. When Imhotep, Zoser's chief architect, raised the pyramid in the 27th century BC, it was the largest structure ever built in stone – the "beginning of architecture", according to one historian. Imhotep's achievement was to break from the tradition of earthbound *mastabas*, raising level upon level of stones to create a four-step, and then a six-step pyramid, which was clad in dazzling white limestone. None of the blocks was very large, for Zoser's builders still thought in terms of mud-brick rather than megaliths, but the concept, techniques and logistics all pointed towards the true pyramid, finally attained at Giza.

Before it was stripped of its casing stones and rounded off by the elements, Zoser's Pyramid stood 62m high and measured 140m by 118m along its base. The original entrance on the northern side is blocked, but with permission and keys from the site's Antiquities Inspectorate you can enter via a gallery on the opposite side, dug in the XXVI Dynasty. Dark passageways and vertical ladders descend 28m into the bedrock, where a granite plug failed to prevent robbers from plundering the burial chamber of this III Dynasty monarch (c.2667–2648 BC).

Surrounding the pyramid is an extensive **funerary complex**, originally enclosed by a finely cut limestone wall, 544m long and 277m wide, now largely ruined or buried by sand. False doors occur at intervals for the convenience of the pharaoh's *ka*, but visitors can only enter at the southeastern corner, which has largely been rebuilt. Beyond a vestibule with simulated double doors (detailed down to their hinge pins and sockets) lies a narrow colonnaded corridor, whose forty "bundle" columns are ribbed in imitation of palm stems, which culminates in a broader **Hypostyle Hall**.

From here you emerge onto the **Great South Court**, where a rebuilt section of wall (marked * on our site plan) bears a **frieze of cobras**. Worshipped in the Delta as a fire-spitting goddess of destruction called Wadjet or Edjo, the cobra was adopted as the emblem of royalty and always appeared on pharaonic headdresses – a figure known as the *uraeus*. Nearby, a deep shaft plummets into Zoser's **Southern Tomb**, decorated with blue faïence tiles and a relief of the king running the *Heb-Sed* race. During the Jubilee festival marking the thirtieth year of a pharaoh's reign, he had to sprint between two altars representing Upper and Lower Egypt and re-enact his coronation, seated first on one throne, then upon another, symbolically reuniting the Two Lands. Besides demonstrating his vitality, the five-day festival confirmed the renewal of his *ka* and the obedience of provincial dignitaries.

Although the festival was held at Memphis, a pair of altars, thrones and shrines were incorporated in Zoser's funerary complex to perpetuate its efficacy on a cosmic timescale. The B-shaped structures near the centre of the Great Court are the bases of these altars;

the twin thrones probably stood on the platform at the southern end of the adjacent **Heb-Sed Court**. Both shrines were essentially facades, since the actual buildings were filled with rubble. This phoney quality is apparent if you view them from the east: the curvaceous roof line and delicate false columns wouldn't look amiss on a yuppie waterfront development. Notice the four **stone feet** beneath a shelter near the northern end of the court.

Beyond this lies the partially ruined **House of the South**, whose chapel is fronted by proto-Doric columns with lotus capitals, and a spearhead motif above the lintel. Inside you'll find several examples of XVIII–IXX Dynasty tourist graffiti, expressing admiration for Zoser or the equivalent of "Ramses was here" – banalities which one scornful ancient graffitist likens to "the work of a woman who has no mind". Continuing northwards, you'll pass a relatively intact row of casing stones along the eastern side of Zoser's Pyramid. The **House of the North** has fluted columns with papyrus capitals; the lotus and papyrus were the heraldic emblems of Upper and Lower Egypt.

On the northern side of the pyramid, a tilted masonry box or **Serdab** ("cellar" in Arabic) contains a life-size statue of Zoser gazing blindly towards the North and circumpolar stars, which the ancients associated with immortality; seated thus, his *ka* was assured of eternal life. Zoser's statue is a replica, however, the original having been removed to Cairo's Antiquities Museum. The ruined mortuary temple to the right of the *Serdab* is unusual for being sited to the north rather than the east of its pyramid, and for the underground tunnel which originally led to Zoser's burial chamber.

South of the complex

South of Zoser's funerary complex are several tombs and other ruins, dating from various dynasties. During the Old Kingdom, nobles were buried in subterranean tombs covered by large mud-brick superstructures; the name *mastaba* (Arabic for "bench") was bestowed upon them by native workmen during excavations last century. Three such edifices stand outside the southern wall of Zoser's complex, although two of them are currently closed. The open one, the **Mastaba of Idut**, has interesting reliefs in five of its ten rooms. Among the fishing and farming scenes, notice the crocodile eyeing a newborn hippo, and a calf being dragged through the water so that cows will ford a river. The chapel contains a false door painted in imitation of granite, scenes of bulls and buffaloes being sacrificed, and Idut herself. Idut was the daughter of Pharaoh Unas, whose pyramid stands just beyond the **Mastaba of Nebet**, his queen. If accessible, its reliefs are also worth seeing: in one scene, Nebet smells a lotus blossom.

The Pyramid of Unas

Although its frontal aspect resembles a mound of rubble, the **Pyramid of Unas** retains many casing stones around the back, some carved with hieroglyphs. A low passageway on the northern side leads into its **burial chamber**, whose alabaster walls are covered with inscriptions listing the rituals and prayers for liberating the pharaoh's *ba*, and the articles for his *ka* to use in the afterlife. These **Pyramid Texts** are the earliest known example of decorative writing within a pharaonic tomb chamber, and formed the basis of the New Kingdom *Book of the Dead*. They speak of the pharaoh becoming a star and travelling to Sirius and other constellations. Painted stars adorn the ceiling, while the sarcophagus area is surrounded by striped, checked and zigzag patterns. Thomas Cook & Sons sponsored the excavation of the tomb by Gaston Maspero in 1881.

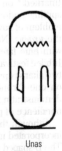

Unas

Unas was the last pharaoh of the V Dynasty, so his pyramid follows those of Abu Sir, which evince a marked decline from the great pyramids of Giza. Given the duration of pharaonic civilization, it's sobering to realize that only 350 years separated the creation of the Step Pyramid from this sad reminder of past glories. Originally, it was approached by a 1km-long **causeway** enclosed by a roof and walls. Reliefs inside the short reconstructed section depict the transport of granite from Aswan, archers, prisoners of war, and a famine caused by the Nile failing to rise. The ruins of a valley temple face the ticket office below the plateau.

To the south of the causeway are two gaping, brick-lined **boat pits** that may have contained solar barques like the one at Giza, or merely symbolized them, since nothing was found when the pits were excavated.

Other tombs and ruins

A stone hut to the south of the Unas Pyramid gives access to a spiral staircase that descends 25m underground, to where three low corridors lead into the vaulted **Persian Tombs**. Chief physician Psamtik, Admiral Djenhebu and Psamtik's son Pediese were all officials of the XXVII Dynasty of Persian kings founded in 525 BC, yet the hieroglyphs in their tombs invoke the same spells as those written two thousand years earlier. The dizzying descent and claustrophobic atmosphere make this an exciting tomb to explore. Though often locked, it's not "forbidden" as guards sometimes pretend, hoping to wangle excessive *baksheesh*.

Further to the southeast lies the recently rediscovered **Tomb of Horemheb**. Built when he was a general, it became redundant after Horemheb seized power from Pharaoh Ay in 1348 BC and ordered a new tomb to be dug in the Valley of the Kings, the royal necropolis of the New Kingdom. Many of the finely carved blocks from his original tomb are now in museums around the world. Another set of paving stones and truncated columns marks the nearby **Tomb of Tia**, sister of Ramses II. The **Tomb of Maya**, Tutankhamun's treasurer, was found nearby in 1986 and is still under excavation. Due east lie the sanded-over mudbrick ruins of the **Monastery of St Jeremiah**, which the Arabs destroyed in 960, four hundred years after its foundation. Practically all of the monastery's carvings and paintings have been removed to the Coptic Museum in Old Cairo. Just to its north, on the causeway of Unas, are the four *mastabas* that you need an extra ticket to visit (see p.198).

It's indicative of how much might still be hidden beneath the sands at Saqqara that the **unfinished Pyramid of Sekhemkhet** was only discovered in 1950. Beyond his monuments, nothing is known of Sekhemkhet, whose step pyramid and funerary complex were presumably intended to mimic those of his predecessor, Zoser, and may also have been built by Imhotep. The alabaster sarcophagus inside the pyramid (which is unsafe to enter) was apparently never used, but the body of a child was found inside an auxiliary tomb.

From Sekhemkhet's pyramid and the monastery it's roughly 700m to the nearest part of South Saqqara (see p.202).

Around the Pyramids of Userkaf and Teti

While neither of these pyramids amounts to much, the *mastabas* near Teti's edifice contain some fantastic reliefs. If you're starting from Zoser's complex, it's only a short walk to the pulverized **Pyramid of Userkaf**, the founder of the V Dynasty, whose successors were buried at Abu Sir (see p.191). From here, a track runs northwards to the **Pyramid of Teti**, which overlooks the valley from the edge of the plateau. Excavated by Mariette in the 1850s, it has since been engulfed by sand and may be closed; in one of the funeral chambers (accessible by a sloping shaft and low passageway), the star-patterned blocks of its vaulted roof have slipped inwards.

Although most of the VI Dynasty kings who followed Teti chose to be buried at South Saqqara, several of their courtiers were interred in a **"street of tombs"** beside his pyramid, which was linked to the Serapeum by an Avenue of Sphinxes (now sanded over). To do justice to their superbly detailed reliefs takes well over an hour, but it's rare to find all of them open.

Teti

The Mastaba of Mereruka

The largest tomb in the street belongs to **Mereruka**, Teti's vizier and son-in-law, whose 32-room complex includes separate funerary suites for his wife Watet-khet-hor, priestess of Hathor, and their son Meri-Teti. In the entry passage, Mereruka is shown playing a board game and painting at an easel; the chamber beyond depicts him hunting in the marshes with Watet-khet-hor (the frogs, birds, hippos and grasshoppers are beautifully rendered), along with the usual farming scenes. Goldsmiths, jewellers and other artisans are inspected by the couple in a room beyond the rear door, which leads into another chamber showing taxation and the punishment of defaulters. A pillared hall to the right portrays them watching sinuous dancers; a room to the left depicts offerings, sacrifices and birds being fed, with a *serdab* at the far end.

Beyond the transverse hall, with its tomb shaft, false door and reliefs of grape-treading and harvesting, lies the main offerings hall, dominated by a statue of Mereruka emerging from a false door. The opposite wall shows his funeral procession; around the corner are boats under full sail, with monkeys playing in their rigging. To the left of the statue, Mereruka is supported by his sons and litter bearers, accompanied by dwarves and dogs; on the other side, children frolic while dancers sway above the doorway into Meri-Teti's undecorated funerary suite.

To reach **Watet-khet-hor's suite**, return to the first room in the *mastaba* and take the other door. After similar scenes to those in her husband's tomb, Watet-khet-hor is carried to her false door in a lion chair.

The Mastabas of Kagemni and Ankh-ma-hor

East of Mereruka's tomb and left around the corner, the smaller **Mastaba of Kagemni** features delicate reliefs in worse shape. The pillared hall beyond the entrance corridor shows dancers and acrobats, the judgement of prisoners, a hippo hunt and agricultural work, all rich in naturalistic detail. Notice the boys feeding a puppy and trussed cows being milked. The door in this wall leads to another chamber where Kagemni inspects his fowl pens while servants trap marsh birds with clap-nets; on the pylon beyond this he relaxes on a palanquin as they tend to his pet dogs and monkeys. As usual in the offerings hall, scenes of butchery appear opposite the false door. On the roof of the *mastaba* (reached by stairs from the entrance corridor) are two boat pits. As vizier, Kagemni was responsible for overseeing prophets and the estate of Teti's pyramid complex.

The **Mastaba of Ankh-ma-hor** is also known as the "Doctor's Tomb" after its reliefs showing circumcision, toe surgery and suchlike, as practised during the VI Dynasty. If the tomb is open it's definitely worth a look, unlike the sand-choked **I Dynasty tombs** that straggle along the edge of the scarp beyond the **Antiquities Inspectorate**.

Two outstanding mastabas

If your time is limited, these are the tombs to visit: the **Double Mastaba of Akhti- and Ptah-Hotep** lies 200m off the road to the refreshments tent, while the **Mastaba of Ti** is 500m in the other direction and easiest to get to from the Serapeum (see below). Outside the **refreshments tent** (£E4 minimum charge) you'll be importuned to rent a horse or camel.

The Mastaba of Akhti-Hotep and Ptah-Hotep

This *mastaba* belonged to **Ptah-Hotep**, a priest of Maat during the reign of Unas's predecessor, Djedkare, and his son **Akhti-Hotep**, who served as vizier, judge and overseer of the granaries and treasury. Though smaller than Ti's *mastaba*, its reliefs are interesting for being at various stages of completion, showing how a finished product was achieved. After the preliminary drawings had been corrected in red by a master artist, the background was chiselled away to leave a silhouette, before details were marked in and cut. The agri-

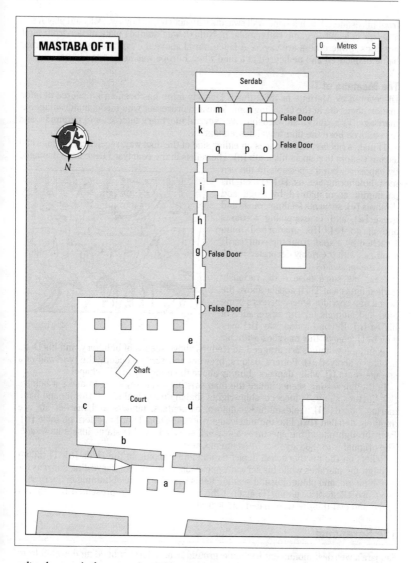

MASTABA OF TI

0   Metres   5

Serdab

l   m   n   False Door

k

q   p   o   False Door

i   j

h

g   False Door

f   False Door

e

Shaft

Court

c   d

b

a

N

cultural scenes in the entrance corridor show this process clearly, although with the exception of Ptah-Hotep's chapel, none of these reliefs was ever painted.

Off the pillared hall of Akhti-Hotep is a T-shaped chapel whose inside wall shows workers making papyrus boats and jousting with poles. More impressive is the chapel of his father, covered with exquisitely detailed reliefs. Between the two door-shaped steles representing the entrance to the tomb, Ptah-Hotep enjoys a banquet of offerings, garbed in the panther-skin of a high priest. Similar scenes occur on the facing wall, whose upper registers show animals being slaughtered and women bringing offerings from his estates. The left-hand wall swarms with activity, as boys wrestle and play *Khaki la wizza* (a leapfrog game still popular in Nubia); wild animals mate or flee from hunting dogs, while others are caged. A faded mural above the entrance shows the priest being manicured and pedicured at a time when Europe was in the Stone Age.

The Mastaba of Ti

Discovered by Mariette in 1865, this V Dynasty tomb has been a rich source of information about life in the Old Kingdom. A royal hairdresser who made an advantageous marriage, **Ti** acquired stewardship over several mortuary temples and pyramids, and his children bore the title "royal descendant".

Ti makes his first appearances on either side of the doorway, receiving offerings and asking visitors to respect his tomb **[a]**. The reliefs in the courtyard have been damaged by exposure, but it's possible to discern men butchering an ox **[b]**, Ti on his palanquin accompanied by dogs and dwarves **[c]**, servants feeding cranes and geese **[d]**, and Ti examining accounts and cargo **[e]**. His unadorned tomb (reached by a shaft from the courtyard) contrasts with the richly decorated interior of the *mastaba*.

Feeding cranes

Near his son's false door, variously garbed figures of Ti **[f]** appear above the portal of a corridor where bearers bring food and animals for the sustenance of his *ka* **[g]**. Beyond a doorway **[h]** over which Ti enjoys the marshes with his wife, funerary statues are dragged on sledges above scenes of butchery, and his Delta fleets are arrayed **[i]**. Potters, bakers, brewers and scribes occupy the rear wall of a storage room **[j]**, while dancers shimmy above the doorway to Ti's chapel.

In the harvesting scene, notice the man twisting a donkey's ear to make it behave **[k]**. Further along, Ti inspects shipwrights shaping tree trunks, and sawing and hammering boards **[l]**. Goldsmiths, sculptors, carpenters, tanners and market life are minutely detailed **[m]**, like the musicians who entertain Ti at his offerings table **[n]**. Peer through one of the apertures and you'll see a cast of his statue inside its *serdab*. The original is in the Egyptian Museum in Cairo.

Reliefs on the northern wall depict fishing and trapping in the Delta **[o]**; Ti sailing through the marshes while his servants spear hippopotami **[p]**; harvesting papyrus for boat-building, and ploughing and seeding fields **[q]**. The scene of hunting in the marshes is also allegorical, pitting Ti against the forces of chaos (represented by fish and birds) and evil (hippos were hated and feared).

The Serapeum

Saqqara's weirdest monument lies underground near a derelict building downhill from the refreshments tent. Discovered by Mariette in 1851, the rock-cut galleries of the **Serapeum** held the mummified corpses of the Apis bulls, which the Memphites regarded as manifestations of Ptah's "blessed soul" and identified with Osiris after death.

Having been embalmed on alabaster slabs at Memphis, the bulls were interred in sarcophagi weighing up to seventy tons apiece. Meanwhile, the priests began searching for Ptah's reincarnation amongst the sacred herd. Once a new bull had been chosen, it spent forty days at Nilopolis (across the river from Memphis), where women were allowed to approach it *only* to expose their vulvas (a practice believed to ensure fertility). After the full moon the bull was taken to its future residence in Memphis, where it had its own priestly attendants and a harem of cows.

The **cult of the Apis bulls** was assailed by Egypt's Persian conqueror, Cambyses, who stabbed one to disprove its divinity, whilst Artaxerxes I avenged his nickname "the donkey" by having a namesake beast buried here with full honours. But the Ptolemies encouraged native cults and even synthesized their own. "Serapeum" derives from the fusion of the Egyptian Osarapis (Osiris in his Apis form) and the Greeks' Dionysos into the cult of *Serapis*, whose temple stood in Alexandria.

Now that the lighting has been improved, the Serapeum galleries are much less spooky than when Mariette broke in. Although tomb robbers had plundered them centuries before, he found a single tomb miraculously undisturbed for four thousand years. The finger mark and footprints of the ancient workman who sealed the tomb were still visible, and Mariette also found a mummified bull and the coffin of Khamenwaset, son of Ramses II and high priest of Ptah. Sadly, none of the mummified bulls remains *in situ*.

The oldest of the galleries dates from that era, and is now inaccessible, the second is from the Saite period, and the main one from Ptolemaic times. Enormous granite or basalt **sarcophagi** are ranged either side of the Ptolemaic gallery, at the end of which is a narrow shaft whereby robbers penetrated the Serapeum. The finest sarcophagus squats on the right, while another one lies abandoned near the entrance to the Ramessid gallery.

Other curiosities

En route to the Serapeum you'll notice a concrete slab sheltering broken statues of Plato, Heraclitus, Thales, Protagoras, Homer, Hesiod, Demetrius of Phalerum and Pindar – the **Philosopher's Circle**. The statues formerly stood near a temple that overlaid the Serapeum, proof that the Ptolemies juxtaposed Hellenistic philosophy and ancient Egyptian religion with no sense of incongruity.

A cluster of **III Dynasty tombs** to the east of Ti's *mastaba* is now reckoned a likely site for the tomb of Imhotep, as yet undiscovered. The architect of Zoser's Step Pyramid was revered throughout pharaonic history and eventually became a demigod, credited with powers of healing; the Ptolemies associated him with Asclepius, the Greek god of medicine. Further northeast lie the **Ibis and Baboon Galleries** sacred to Thoth, which Flaubert visited in the 1840s: "We go down into a hole and then crawl along a passageway almost on our stomachs, inching over fine sand and fragments of pottery; at the far end the jars containing ibises are stacked like blocks of sugar at a grocer's, head to foot".

Memphis

Most tour excursions to Saqqara include a flying visit to the scant **remains of Memphis** in the village of **MIT RAHINA**. Sadly, these hardly stir one's imagination to resurrect the ancient city effaced over centuries by Nilotic silt, which now lies metres below rustling palm groves and oxen-ploughed fields. Although something of its glory is evident in the great necropolises ranged across the desert, and the countless objects in Cairo's Antiquities Museum, to appreciate the significance of Memphis you have to recall its history.

The city's foundation is attributed to Menes, the quasi-mythical ruler (known also as Narmer – and possibly a conflation of several rulers) who was said to have unified Upper and Lower Egypt and launched the I Dynasty around 3100 BC. At that time, Memphis was sited at the apex of the Delta and thus controlled overland and river communications. If not the earliest city on earth, it was certainly the first imperial one. Memphis was Egypt's capital throughout the Old Kingdom, regained its role after the anarchic Intermediate Period, and was never overshadowed by the parvenu seat of the XII Dynasty. Even after Thebes became capital of the New Kingdom, Memphis still held sway over Lower Egypt

THE CULTS OF PTAH AND SOKAR

In pre-Dynastic times, **Ptah** was the Great Craftsman or Divine Artificer, who invented metallurgy and engineering. However, the people of Memphis esteemed him as the Great Creator who, with a word, brought the universe into being – a concept that never really appealed to other Egyptians. Like most creator gods, he was subsequently linked with death cults and is shown dressed in the shroud of a mummy. The Greeks equated him with *Hephaestus*, their god of fire and the arts.

Another deity closely associated with Memphis is **Sokar**, originally the god of darkness but subsequently of death, with special responsibility for necropolises. He is often shown, with a falcon's head, seated in the company of Isis and Osiris. Although his major festival occurred at Memphis towards the end of the inundation season, Sokar also rated a shrine at Abydos, where all the Egyptian death gods were represented.

Ptah

and remained the nation's second city until well into the Ptolemaic era, only being deserted in early Muslim times after four thousand years of continuous occupation.

Alas for posterity, most of this garden city was built of mud-brick, which returned to the Nile silt whence it came, and everyone from the Romans onwards plundered its stone temples for fine masonry.

Nowadays, leftover statues and steles share a garden (daily: winter 7.30am–4pm; summer 7.30am–5pm; £E7, camera £E10, video camera £E25) with souvenir kiosks. The star attraction, found in 1820, is a limestone **Colossus of Ramses II**, similar to the one on Midan Ramses, but laid supine within a concrete shelter. A giant **alabaster sphinx** weighing eighty tons is also mightily impressive. Both these figures probably stood outside the vast Temple of Ptah, the city's patron deity.

By leaving the garden and walking back along the road, you'll notice (on the right) several alabaster **embalming slabs**, where the holy Apis bulls were mummified before burial in the Serapeum at Saqqara. In a pit across the road are excavated chambers from Ptah's temple complex; climb the ridge beyond them and you can gaze across the cultivated valley floor to the Step Pyramid of Saqqara.

South Saqqara

Like their predecessors at Abu Sir, the pharaohs of the VI Dynasty (c.2345–2181 BC) established another necropolis – nowadays called **South Saqqara** – which started 700m beyond Sekhemkhet's unfinished pyramid and extended for over three kilometres. Unfortunately for sightseers, the most interesting monuments are those furthest away across the site; renting a donkey, horse or camel (£E10–15 for the round trip) will minimize slogging over soft sand. It is also possible to walk from Saqqara village: just keep heading west until you emerge from the palm trees. If you stop to ask directions, bear in mind that, whatever you say (even if you say it in Arabic), the villagers will almost certainly assume you are looking for the Step Pyramid, and direct you accordingly.

Once you reach the site, two tracks run either side of several pyramids before meeting at the Mastabat al-Faraun. The western one is more direct than the route that goes via Saqqara village, set amidst lush palm groves 2km from North Saqqara's ticket office. There is no official entrance fee to the site, and you probably won't see another tourist. Apart from the tranquillity, however, what you get here, with the pyramids of North Saqqara clearly visible to your north, and those of Dahshur to your south, is the feeling of being in the midst of a massive pyramid field, somewhere very ancient and vast.

The site

Heading south along either track, you'll pass a low mound of rubble identified as the **Pyramid of Pepi I**. The name "Memphis", which Classical authors bestowed upon Egypt's ancient capital and its environs, was actually derived from one of this pyramid's titles. To the southwest, another insignificant heap indicates the **Pyramid of Merenre**, who succeeded Pepi. French archeologists are excavating the latter's pyramid, but neither site is really worth a detour.

Due west of Saqqara village, sand drifts over the outlying temples of the **Pyramid of Djedkare-Isesi**. Known in Arabic as the "Pyramid of the Sentinel", it stands 25m high and can be entered via a tunnel on the north side. Although a shattered basalt sarcophagus and mummified remains were found here during the 1800s, it wasn't until 1946 that Abdel Hussein identified them as those of Djedkare, the penultimate king of the V Dynasty. Far from being the first ruler to be entombed in South Saqqara, Djedkare was merely emulating the last pharaoh of the previous dynasty, whose own mortuary complex is uniquely different, and the oldest in this necropolis.

Built of limestone blocks, Shepseskaf's mortuary complex resembles a gigantic sarcophagus with a rounded lid; another simile gave rise to its local name, **Mastabat al-Faraun** – the Pharaoh's Bench. If you can find a guard, it's possible to venture through descending and horizontal corridors to reach the burial chamber and various storerooms. The monument was almost certainly commissioned by Shepseskaf, who evidently felt the need to distance himself from the pyramid of his father, Mycerinus. However, the archeologist Jequier doubted that the complex was ever used for any actual burial and Shepseskaf's final resting place remains uncertain.

Northwest of here lies the most complete example of a VI Dynasty mortuary complex, albeit missing casing stones and other masonry that was plundered in medieval times. The usual valley temple and causeway culminate in a mortuary temple whose vestibule and sanctuary retain fragments of their original reliefs. Beyond this rises the **Pyramid of Pepi II**, whose reign supposedly lasted 94 years, after which the VI Dynasty expired. A descending passage leads to his rock-cut burial chamber, whose ceiling and walls are inscribed with stars and Pyramid Texts. These also appear within the subsidiary pyramids of Pepi's queens, Apuit and Neith, which imitate his mortuary complex on a smaller scale. Various nobles and officials are buried roundabouts.

Dahshur

The **Dahshur pyramid field** (daily 8am–5pm; £E10, students £E5) contains some of the most impressive of all the pyramids, and some of the most significant in the history of pyramid-building. **Getting to Dahshur** may prove problematic. The easiest way to reach the site is by taxi, though you can get there on foot from El-Badrasheen if you don't mind a very long walk. Otherwise, you should be able to get *service* taxi microbuses from El-Badrasheen or Giza train station (a short walk from Midan Giza) going to Dahshur village, which will drop you at the site entrance. Gettting back to Cairo, however, should not be left too late or you may find yourself stranded with the nearest public transport 10km away in El-Badrasheen.

The pyramids are in two groups. To the east are three **Middle Kingdom complexes**, dating from the revival of pyramid building (c.1991–1790 BC) that culminated near the Fayoum. Though the pyramids proved unrewarding to nineteenth-century excavators, their subsidiary tombs yielded some magnificent jewellery (now in the Antiquities Museum). To the north, the pyramids of XII Dynasty pharaohs Seostris III and Amenenkhet II are little more than piles of rubble, but the southernmost of the three, the **Black Pyramid** of Amenemhet III (Joseph's pharoah in the Old Testament, according to some), is at least an interesting shape: though its limestone casing has long gone, a black mud-brick core is still standing (its black basalt capstone is in the Antiquities Museum). More intriguing, however, are the two **Old Kingdom pyramids** further into the desert, which have long tantalized archeologists with a riddle.

Both of these pyramids are credited to **Snofru** (c.2613–2588 BC), father of Cheops and founder of the IV Dynasty, whose monuments constitute an evolutionary link between the stepped creations of the previous dynasty at North Saqqara and the true pyramids of Giza. Despite its lower angle (43.5°) and height (101m), Snofru's northern **Red Pyramid** (named after the colour of the limestone it was built from) clearly prefigures his son's edifice, which is also the only pyramid that exceeds it in size, Snofru's Red Pyramid being larger than Chephren's Pyramid at Giza. It was probably Snofru's third attempt (see below) at pyramid building, but he was not laid to rest in any of the three burial chambers here – all were unused. Snofru was in fact buried in the pyramid to the south, a monument that is not only the most intriguing of all the pyramids, but, because of its state of preservation, also the most breathtaking.

The Bent Pyramid

What makes Snofru's final resting place different from all the other pyramids is its change of angle towards the top: it rises more steeply (54.3°) than the Red Pyramid or Giza pyramids for three-quarters of its height, before abruptly tapering at a gentler slope – hence its sobriquet, the **Bent Pyramid**. The explanation for its shape, and why Snofru should have built two pyramids only a kilometre apart, is a longstanding conundrum of Egyptology.

Mindful of the truism that a pharaoh required but one sanctuary for his *ka*, many reasoned that the Bent Pyramid resulted from a change of plan prompted by fears for its stability, and when these persisted, a second, safer pyramid was built to guarantee Snofru's afterlife. But for this theory to hold water, it's necessary to dismiss Snofru's claim to have built a *third* pyramid at Maidum as mere usurpation of an earlier structure; and the possibility that its sudden collapse might have caused the modification of the Bent Pyramid must likewise be rejected on the grounds that he needed only one secure monument.

In 1977, a professor of physics at Oxford University reopened the whole debate. Arguing that Snofru did, indeed, build the "Collapsed Pyramid" at Maidum, whose fall resulted in changes to Dahshur's Bent Pyramid, Kurt Mendelssohn overcame the "one pharaoh–one *ka*–one pyramid" objection by postulating a pyramid production line. As one pyramid neared completion, surplus resources were deployed to start another, despite the satisfaction of the reigning king's requirements. The reason for continuous production was that building a single pyramid required gigantic efforts over ten to thirty years; inevitably, some pharaohs lacked the time and resources. A stockpile of half-constructed, perhaps even finished, pyramids was an insurance policy on the afterlife.

Egyptologists greeted Mendelssohn's theory with delight or derision, but unlike the Great Pyramids, or the lives of Hatshepsut, Nefertiti and Akhenaten, the enigma of Snofru's pyramids has never excited much public interest. Nevertheless, of all the pyramids, the Bent Pyramid probably scores the most highly on the "ooohs" and "aaahs". The reason it seems so impressive lies in the fact that, although its corners have fallen away at the base, the pyramid's limestone casing is still largely intact, giving a clear impression of what it once looked like – smooth and white, it was visually stunning. All the Old Kingdom pyramids were originally clad in limestone, their surfaces smooth like this one, but they have almost all been stripped, the stone burned for lime. The Bent Pyramid escaped that fate because its narrower angle made it harder to remove the facing, though this has disappeared from much of the base.

In fact, the removal of the lowest courses of limestone cladding enables you to see not only how closely the blocks were slotted togeth-

Snofru

er, but something else too. On the ground at the northwest corner of the pyramid, pits and grooves have been carved into the bedrock. These were used to dress the pyramid, and presumably were carved before the pyramid was begun, indicating that construction began with the marking out of a base on the cleared bedrock.

The Bent Pyramid is unusual in one final respect: it has two entrances, one on its west side as well as the more conventional one in its north face. The reason for this is unknown. To its south is a subsidiary queen's pyramid, possibly belonging to Snofru's wife Hetepheres (though some say Snofru himself was buried here). If it did belong to her, she didn't stay there too long: after robbers had entered both of Snofru's pyramids at Dahshur, Hetepheres's sarcophagus was moved to Giza for safekeeping, and hidden down a shaft next to the Great Pyramid of her son Cheops.

CONSUMERS' CAIRO

As befits its size, Cairo has the most varied culinary scene, shopping and nightlife in North Africa. Much of it is new, having developed in the Sadat era after decades of Nasserite austerity, and for those that can afford it conspicuous consumption is very much the order of the day. As a visitor, you're well catered for, whether you're into sailing on the Nile, watching a belly dancer, or absorbing a whole world of popular culture at Cairo's religious festivals. All of this is fun to discover but more mundane practicalities can involve hassles and bureaucracy, mysteries and intricacies which we've tried to unravel beginning with "Money" on p.234.

Eating and drinking

The culinary scene in Cairo has diversified enormously since the 1970s, making it possible to eat anything from *sukiyaki* to Kentucky Fried Chicken. Don't fall into the trap of eating only in tourist restaurants or thinking that Egyptian food doesn't rise beyond *koftas* and kebabs. You can satisfy most tastes if you know where to look. The options range from Arab cafés offering a few simple dishes to extravagant "food weeks" at deluxe hotels (advertised in *Egypt Today*). Though few natives would agree with them, foreigners are generally pleasantly surprised by the cost of eating out in Cairo. Nearly all the downtown coffee houses, restaurants, cafés and bars are keyed to the map on p.206; for places in Zamalek and on the west bank, see the map on p.166. Drinking, though somewhat limited, is also quite affordable – see p.214.

Coffee houses, patisseries and juice bars

Cairene males have socialized in **coffee houses** or **tearooms** (*ahwa*) ever since the beverage was introduced from Yemen in the early Middle Ages (for a rundown on coffee and tea drinking and preparation, see p.52). Although professional *qasas* (storytellers) have largely been supplanted by broadcast or taped music, other traditional diversions such as backgammon and dominoes are still popular, and smokers remain loyal to their waterpipes. Most *ahwas* are shabby hole-in-the-wall places, with chairs overlooking the street, while a few – such as *Fishawi's* and *Al-Shataranji* – are large and more sophisticated, often with high ceilings and tall mirrors (these often also sell pastries, see below). Certain *ahwas* are the haunt of hobbyists – chess players at *Al-Shataranj* in Saiyida Zeinab, literati at the *Ali Baba* on Midan Tahrir (where Mahfouz takes coffee) or rural migrants (oasis folk frequent *Al-Wahia* on Sharia Qadry, off Sharia Bur Said), but most have an eclectic clientele. **All-night** *awhas* can be found around Bab al-Luq, Midan Ramses and Sharia Qalaa; those around the Saiyida Zeinab end of Sharia Mohammed Farid and Sharia el-

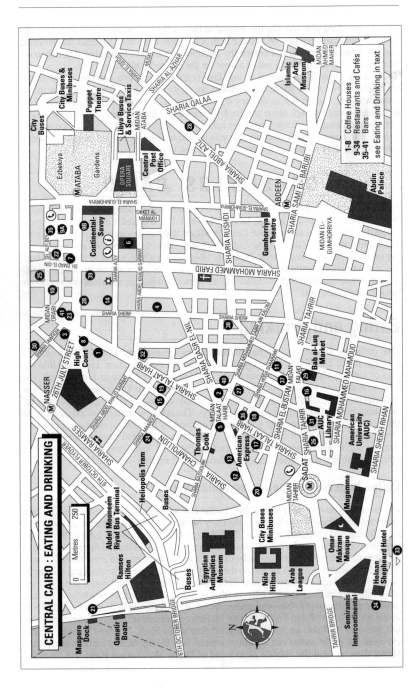

CENTRAL CAIRO: EATING AND DRINKING

1–8 Coffee Houses
9–34 Restaurants and Cafés
35–41 Bars
see Eating and Drinking in text

Nasireya show videos (sometimes in English) throughout the night. There are also modern all-night coffee shops in the *Intercontinental, Meridien* and other deluxe hotels.

For daytime snacks, the upmarket coffee houses and tearooms (more akin to Western cafés than traditional *ahwas*) serve selections of pastries, rice pudding, creme caramel and suchlike – the most famous are the branches of *Groppi's* (see below). As well as being great places to stop off during the day, they also provide a welcome alternative to the monotony of standard hotel **breakfasts** (rolls and jam and/or cheese spread). Another option is to try one of the breakfast **buffets** offered by a range of deluxe hotels and open to non-residents (see listings overleaf).

To take away or consume on the spot, however, it's cheaper to buy at **patisseries** like *Haroun al-Rashid* (no. 25) on Talaat Harb, *El-Sarkia* on Sharia Alfy Bey, or branches of the city-wide chain **La Poire**, where pastries are normally sold by weight with the price per kilo posted. The original and most central branch, at 1 Sharia Amerika Latina (near the British Embassy in Garden City), offers home-made *baklava* (£E25 per kilo) and éclairs (£E2.40); other branches are in Mohandiseen (opposite the *Atlas Hotel*), Giza (Sharia el-Nil, 100m south of the Gama'a Bridge), Heliopolis (92 Sharia al-Higaz, near Midan Heliopolis), the *Ramses Hilton* and elsewhere.

Every main street has a couple of tiled stand-up **juice bars** (usually open 8am–10pm), recognizable by their displays of fruit, where you can pick up a glass of freshly squeezed juice – a great way to get the appetite going before breakfast. The ones near the *Café Riche* and *Felfela* charge more than most, but they're never expensive. The best one in Cairo is *Fraghly Fruits*, 71 Arab League Street, in Mohandiseen. Normally, you order and pay at the cash desk before exchanging a plastic token for your drink at the counter (where customers leave a 5–15pt tip). You'll also see a number of **nut shops** (*ma'la*) on the main thoroughfares, offering all kinds of peanuts (*fuul sudani*), edible seeds, and often candies and mineral water, too. See Basics for more on the various types of juices and nuts.

Ice cream in Cairo is usually not very good, though you may find interesting flavours like guava and mango. A cut above the rest are the *Dairy King* outlets (in Zamalek, Mohandiseen and Heliopolis), but traditionally *Rigoletto*, in Zamalek's Yamaha Centre (3 Sharia Taha Hussein), is considered the best, serving delicious ice cream (£E1.75 a scoop) and cheesecake (daily 9am–11.30pm; £E3 minimum charge to eat in). If you're desperate for the real thing, *Baskin & Robbins* (branches in Modandiseen, Heliopolis and Pyramids Road) has ice cream for the connoisseur, but at a comparatively high price (£E3.50 a scoop).

Coffee houses and buffet breakfasts

As *ahwas* are numerous, pretty standard, and do not sell food, the listings below concentrate on more Western-style coffee houses and tearooms.

GROPPI'S COFFEE HOUSE

Synonymous with Cairo's erstwhile European "café society", the classic **Groppi** chain now has five locations. The once-palatial branch on Midan Talaat Harb **(5)** has lost much of its charm since renovation, but the pastries are just as tasty, and its A/C salon restful (daily 7am–11pm). The panelled interior of *Garden Groppi's* **(6)** on Sharia Adly (daily 7am–10pm; minimum charge £E3) hasn't changed much since World War II – when soldiers in the lower ranks weren't allowed in – but its patio is a letdown. There's a far nicer terrace attached to *Groppi's in Heliopolis*, at 21 Sharia al-Ahram (daily 7am–midnight). Lacking the style of the others are two with the same name, *Groppi's Al'Americaine* (open daily 7am–11pm) at 44 Sharia Emad el-Din **(7)** and Sharia Talaat Harb **(8)**, both on the corner of 26th July Street. Most branches double as delicatessens and all serve terrible coffee.

DOWNTOWN

Brazilian Coffee Shop (1), 36 Talaat Harb. Café au lait, espresso and cappuccino, plus greasy burgers and grills; seats upstairs. Daily 6am–midnight.

La Chesa (14), 21 Sharia Adly. The coffee shop attached to the restaurant (see below) is a must for coffee-addicts; it serves the best espresso downtown, rivalled only by the five-star hotels.

Ibis Café, on the ground floor of the *Nile Hilton*. Breakfast buffet is open daily 5–11am (£E45); there's also an unlimited all-day salad bar (£E30). Daily 24hr.

Lappas (2), 17 Sharia Qasr el-Nil. A shiny delicatessen-cum-supermarket with an upstairs cafeteria offering Egyptian breakfasts (£E7) and light meals. Daily 8am–11pm.

New Sun Café (3), in the passage by 4 Sharia Tawfiqia. A *shai* and *sheesha* bar only really notable for its incredibly kitsch decor, but film-extra recruiting agents come here looking for Westerners most mornings around 10am. Daily 6am–10pm.

Simonds Coffee Shop (4), 29 Sharia Sherif. A branch of the French-style café in Zamalek (see below) with a vintage *Gaggia* espresso machine and delicious pastries. Daily 9am–7pm.

RODA ISLAND

Le Brasserie, in the *Meridien Hotel* on Roda Island. Continental (£E25) or buffet (£E37) breakfast daily 7.30–10.30am; also sumptuous buffet lunches and suppers. Daily 24hr.

ISLAMIC CAIRO AND SAIYIDA ZEINAB

Al-Shataranj, 26 Midan Saiyida Zeinab. A meeting place for chess players; the top ones move on to *El-Horea* on Midan Falaki (see "Drinking").

Naguib Mahfouz Coffee Shop, 5 Sikket al-Badestan. Upmarket A/C tourist café in the heart of the bazaar, serving snacks, coffee, mint tea and orange juice. Attached to the *Cafeteria Khan el-Khalili* (see p.211). Daily 11.30am–1.30am.

Fishawi's, behind the *El-Hussein Hotel* in Khan el-Khalili. Cairo's oldest tea house has been managed by the same family – and remained perpetually open – since 1773. Cracked mirrors, battered furniture, haughty staff and wandering vendors; imbibe the atmosphere with a pot of mint tea and a *sheesha*.

ZAMALEK

Simonds Coffee Shop, 112 26th July St, near the Hassan Sabry intersection. Excellent cappuccino, hot chocolate, lemonade, fresh croissants and *ramequins* (cheese puffs). Daily 7.30am–9.30pm.

HELIOPOLIS

Al-Sokkareya, 61 Sharia Abdul Hamid Bedawi, near the *Al-Salam Hyatt* (bus #50, #128 or #330 from downtown). An upmarket garden café featuring singers, musicians and sideshows only open during Ramadan (10pm–3am); the admission charge (around £E15) includes one soft drink and a *sheesha*. Call the *Hyatt* (☎245-5155) to confirm shows.

PYRAMIDS OF GIZA

Khan el-Khalili Coffee Shop, in the *Mena House*. Luxurious A/C cafeteria near the Pyramids. Skip the paltry Continental breakfast and have a £E29 "special". The "Oberoi" version includes fruit juice, pancakes and croissants; the "Egyptian" one yoghurt with honey and *fuul* with eggs. Also snacks and main meals. Daily 24hr. Breakfast served 3–11am.

Restaurants, cafés and street food

Restaurants, cafés and street food comprise a culinary spectrum rather than distinctly separate categories. **Restaurants** run the gamut from *nouvelle cuisine* salons to back-street kebab houses, while **cafés** range from air-conditioned bourgeois havens to open-fronted tiled diners. The ones devoted to *kushari* (£E1–2 a bowl) or *fuul* and *taamiya* (£E1.50 with salad and pickles) provide the cheapest nutritious meals going. A third type of outlet purveys *fatir* or Egyptian pizzas, which are tastier and cheaper (£E6–10 depending on size and ingredients) than most Western-style pizzas in Cairo.

Despite the blurred line between hole-in-the-wall eateries and outright **street food**, running water remains a crucial factor – anywhere without it is risky. Markets and terminals offer the best outlets; a number of places off Ramses, Orabi, Ataba, Falaki, Lazoghli and Giza squares, and midway down Sharia Qalaa function **all night**.

At the other end of the gastro-cultural spectrum, every hotel rated three stars or above has at least one restaurant and coffee shop (maybe 24hr) that's accessible to non-residents (see above). If familiar food and no hassle are top priority, **hotel dining** is usually a safe bet. For those who need them, *McDonald's, Pizza Hut* and *KFC* have also arrived (with branches on Sharia Mohammed Mahmoud, opposite the north entrance to the American University). *Wimpy* have been here longer (their main downtown branch is at 8 Sharia Talaat Harb). All of them have several outlets around the centre as well as in Mohandiseen and Heliopolis. Perhaps surprisingly to Westerners, these fast-food chains are considered posh eating places by Cairenes, who may even dress up to go to them.

Between these extremes there's a huge variation in **standards** of cleanliness and presentation, and whether somewhere seems okay or grotty depends partly on your own values. We've tried to present a cross section of what's available in various parts of the city. The majority of places listed have **menus** in English or French and staff who understand both, but others deal only in Arabic; fortunately, many of them display what's on offer, so you only have to point (for information on tipping, see p.48).

In the following listings, we've given the following guide to cost: **inexpensive** means that you can get a full meal (starter, main course and soft drink) for £E20 or less, **moderate** means that a full meal costs £E20–40, and **expensive** will set you back over £E40 for a full meal. Many restaurants sell seafood and *kofta* and kebab by weight: a quarter of a kilo is one portion; a full kilo is usually enough for three to four people. Note that telephone numbers have been included for all restaurants where **reservations** are a good idea. At others, there's no need to bother – assuming you could get through and make yourself understood.

Downtown Cairo

Aside from Egyptian restaurants, which range from very upmarket establishments to cheaper *kushari* diners (see "Really Cheap Downtown Options" below), downtown Cairo has a fair number of different international cuisines to choose from, with several French, Levantine, Chinese and Korean eating places, and others offering a variety of Western dishes – however, you'll have to go further afield, mostly to the west bank, to find specifically Italian, Indian and Japanese restaurants.

Al-Haty (9A), 3 Sharia Halim, off 26th July St, behind the *Windsor Hotel*. Vintage decor, with mirrors and fans. The fare is inexpensive and traditional: kebab, fish, stuffed vine leaves, *mezzas*, roast lamb. No alcohol. Daily 11am–11pm (Ramadan 7–11pm). There is another, older branch (**9B**) in the passage off no. 8, on the other side of 26th July St, open daily noon–midnight (Ramadan 1pm–10pm).

Alfi Bey (10), 3 Sharia Alfi Bey. Another vintage restaurant run by strict Muslims. Some of the staff claim to have been here since the 1940s; the panelling and chandeliers certainly have. Best for lamb dishes, chicken, macaroni, or pigeon stuffed with liver; good value and moderate prices. Daily noon–midnight.

American Fried Chicken (11), 8 Sharia Hoda Shaarawi. This places also serves inexpensive spaghetti, burgers and milkshakes. Daily 11am–11pm.

Arabesque (12), 6 Sharia Qasr el-Nil (☎574-8677). French and Levantine cuisine, strong on soups and meat dishes, but chiefly remarkable for its oriental decor and contemporary art gallery rather than the quality of the food. Wine and beer are served. Moderate. Daily noon–4pm & 7.30pm–midnight (Ramadan 5pm–midnight).

La Bistro (11), 8 Sharia Hoda Shaarawi, next door to *American Fried Chicken* (☎392-7694). A bright, clean little place serving delicious French food, though the blue and white decor is a little jarring and the muzak excruciating. Moderate. Daily 11am–11pm.

Caroll (13), 12 Sharia Qasr el-Nil (☎574-6434). Getting a bit tatty nowadays and usually full of package tourists, this restaurant serves reasonable Franco-Levantine food at expensive prices; wine and beer are also available. Daily noon–3.30pm & 7.30–11.30pm.

La Chesa (14), 21 Sharia Adly (π393-9360). Salubrious, SwissAir-managed café serving good Western food, scrumptious pastries and great coffee. Expensive but worth it. Daily 7am–midnight.

Coin de Kebab (15), aka *Kebab Corner*, one block west off Talaat Harb, towards the *Odeon Palace Hotel*. Cosy and inexpensive kebab house. Daily 1pm–2am, closed Ramadan.

El-Guesh (16), 32 Midan Falaki, on the corner of Tahrir and Falaki streets. A family place serving spicy kebab; inexpensive. Daily 11am–midnight.

Estoril (17), 12 Sharia Talaat Harb – in the passage (π574-3102). Similar menu and better food than *Caroll*, at cheaper prices and in quieter surroundings. Its vintage bar deserves a Bogart. Moderate. Daily noon–midnight; closed Aug.

Felfela (18), 15 Sharia Hoda Shaarawi. A tourist favourite, offering inexpensive, diverse veggie and meaty Egyptian dishes in a long, funkily decorated hall. Sells beer. Service can be a little snooty if you're scruffily dressed. Daily 6am–midnight. *Felfela's* **takeaway**, around the corner on Talaat Harb, does inexpensive *shwarmas* and *taamiya* sandwiches.

Fu-Shing (19), 28 Talaat Harb – in the passage. Founded by ethnic Muslim refugees from China, this moderately priced restaurant serves filling quasi-Chinese meals in a relaxed ambience. The spring rolls make a great snack. Sells beer. Daily noon–10.30pm.

Greek Club (5), above *Groppi's* on Midan Talaat Harb – entrance on Sharia Bassiouni. The cuisine is not particularly Greek, but the food is good and inexpensive, and the summer terrace pleasant. Serves alcohol, including *Oúzo*. Evenings only, 6pm–1.30am.

Kowloon Restaurant (20), entered via the *Hotel Cleopatra* on the corner of Midan Tahrir and Sharia el-Bustan. Expensive, but superb Korean and Chinese food cooked by Korean chefs. Menu includes several pork dishes and the place is popular with Japanese diners. Daily 11am–11pm, closed Sun.

Paprika (21), 1129 Corniche el-Nil, just south of the TV Building (π578-9447). Based on a mix of Hungarian and Egyptian food, this place does tasty paprika-based dishes and *mezzas*. Frequented by media folk (including Omar Sharif) and footballers, it's especially busy at weekends. Expensive. Daily 11am–1am.

Peking Restaurant (22), 14 Sharia Saray el-Azbakiya (π591-2381), off 26th July, near the *Windsor Hotel*. More upmarket than the *Fu-Shing*, but still not prohibitively expensive. They have branches in Mohandiseen and Heliopolis and do takeouts and delivery. Moderate. Daily noon–midnight.

Valley of the Kings (23), on the 1st floor of the *Grand Hotel*. Complete with elegant fountain and stained-glass windows overlooking 26th July St. Moderate prices with good Franco-Levantine cuisine and special meal-deals for £E20. Seldom crowded. Daily 11am–6pm & 7pm–midnight.

REALLY CHEAP DOWNTOWN OPTIONS

There are hundreds of *kushari* diners in downtown Cairo, and opinion is divided as to which is the best, but basically it boils down to one of three: *Abou Tarek*, *Lux* or *El-Tahrir*. Most other really cheap eats are concentrated around Midan Orabi (especially on Sharia al-Tawfiqia and along the first block of the small street between the two patisseries) and Midan Falaki (especially on Sharia Mansur, outside Bab al-Luq market). All the following fall into the lower end of the inexpensive price band; you can fill up for under £E10.

Abou Tarek (24), 40 Sharia Champollion, at the corner of Sharia Maarouf. New, clean and A/C diner serving excellent *kushari* on two floors, with rice pudding for afters. You can't miss it as it's lit up like a Christmas tree. Daily 9am–9pm.

Akher Sa'a (25), 8 Sharia Alfi Bey, next to the Nile Christian Bookshop (Arabic sign only). A very popular 24hr *fuul* and take-away with a sit-down restaurant attached. Not a bad place for breakfast either – *fuul*, omelette, bread and *tahina* for £E4.25.

Fatatri Pizza el-Tahrir (26), Sharia Tahrir, one block east of Midan Tahrir (look for the marble facade on the right-hand side). *Fatirs* (with meat and egg) and crustier versions topped with hot sauce, cheese and olives make a delicious meal for around £E6–10. Also pancake-*fatirs* filled with apple jam and icing sugar. Daily 24hr.

Al-Gazaz (27), 38 Sharia Abo Alaam. Clean, inexpensive 24hr diner, just off Midan Talaat Harb. Tasty kebabs, *taamiya*, and other fried food, served in a tiny A/C dining room upstairs. You'd be hard-pressed to spend more than £E10.

Lux, 26th July St, near the corner of Sharia Qasr al-Aini **(28)**. Traditional in style and the original holder of the Cairo *kushari* title, with two offshoots at 68 Sharia Qasr al-Aini in the Garden City and on the south side of Midan Falaki **(29)**. All open daily 7am–2am.

Samak Bur Said (30), 15 Sharia al-Tawfiqia. Fish (£E6 a quarter-kilo) and prawns (£E12). The sign is in Arabic only, but helpfully has a picture of a fish on it. For starters, the *kushari* joint four doors to the east serves very good lentil soup. Daily 9am–midnight.

El-Tabei, 31 Sharia Orabi, north of Midan Orabi. Delicious pick'n'mix *mezze* and a very passable moussaka head the list of Middle Eastern dishes served in this souped-up *fuul* and *taamiya* diner. The take-away sandwiches, though, are less good. Daily 9am–1am.

El-Tahrir (31), Sharia Tahrir between Midan Tahrir and Midan Falaki. An old-fashioned place, always good, but not as good as the new, A/C branch at 19 Sharia Abdel Khaliq Sarwat, just off Sharia Talaat Harb **(32)**, which connoisseurs say knocks spots off even *Abou Tarek* – although the service is sometimes slow. Daily 5am–2am.

Garden City

Besides its hotels, a floating restaurant (see p.214) and *fuul, fatir* and *kushari* joints (east off Qasr al-Aini before the hospital), Garden City can also offer the following.

Abou Shakra, 69 Sharia Qasr al-Aini, opposite the hospital (☎364-8811). Decorated in marble and alabaster, this famous, strictly Muslim establishment specializes in *kofta* and kebab sold by weight (around £E60 per kilo). Take-away service (around £E40 per kilo, meat only). Daily 1pm–1am (Ramadan 7pm–1am).

Sit-In Restaurant (33), 1 Sharia Amerika Latina. Look for the Donald Duck sign, opposite the UK Embassy. Inexpensive sandwiches, hamburgers, grilled chicken and other dishes. Daily 9am–11pm.

Islamic Cairo and Saiyida Zeinab

Although every main street and square in **Islamic Cairo** features poky eating places serving cheap grub, most tourists stick to the four places in Khan el-Khalili detailed below. But for those inured to flies and roaches, there are discoveries to be made, like the hole-in-the-wall near the market on Sharia Qalaa, which does freshly grilled shrimp sandwiches. If you are prepared to wander into **Saiyida Zeinab**, you can find some excellent, and low-priced, traditional Egyptian food, especially at night; a couple of places are listed here.

Cafeteria Khan el-Khalili, 5 Sikket al-Badestan. Expensive, A/C "oriental" café/restaurant managed by the *Mena House Oberoi*, near the old gate 40m west of El-Hussein's Mosque. Western and Egyptian snacks and meals (£E28–50) are served in the dining room (all-day minimum charge £E10, plus £E1.20 "entertainment tax"; also see p.208) as well as a range of fancy ice creams (£E3.50–20). Daily 10am–2am.

El-Dahan, on the Muski, beneath the *El-Hussein Hotel*. An excellent kebab house, where a quarter kilo of mixed kebab with salad and *tahina* costs £E15. No alcohol. Daily noon–2am.

Egyptian Pancake House, between Midan el-Hussein and al-Azhar. Made-to-order *fatirs* filled with meat, egg, cheese, coconut, raisins, jam or honey (or any combination thereof). Soft drinks only. Inexpensive. Daily 24hr.

El-Gahsh, a block along Sharia Abdel Meguid from Midan Saiyida Zeinab, on the way to Ibn Tulun Mosque (look for the mule's-head sign). It may not look much, but it is generally held to do the best *fuul* in Cairo (*fuul* sandwich 50pt). Daily 24hr.

Haram Zeinab, on the corner of Sharia Abdel Meguid and Midan Saiyida Zeinab (next to *Al-Shataranj*, the chess players' coffee house). Serves excellent *fatirs* at half the price you'd pay downtown. Daily 24hr.

El-Hussein, on the roof of the *El-Hussein Hotel*. Fantastic views over Islamic Cairo; food inexpensive but grotty. Used for wedding parties at least two nights a week. *Loud* music. Daily 7am–1am.

Rifai, 37 Midan Zeinab, opposite Saiyida Zeinab Mosque (hidden up an alley by the Sabil Kuttab of Sultan Mustapha). A renowned night-time *kofta* and kebab joint – people are known to drive from Heliopolis for a take-away. Inexpensive at about £E55 a kilo for either. Open 9.30pm–5am.

Zamalek

As befits a high-rent, cosmopolitan neighbourhood, Zamalek boasts several upmarket restaurants devoted to foreign cuisine, plus **trendy nightspots** like *Matchpoint, Longchamp* and *Pub 28* (see "Drinking" below, and the "Discos" section, p.218). Most of them are within ten minutes' walk of 26th July Street.

Angus Brasserie, 34 Sharia Yehia Ibrahim, inside the *New Star Hotel* (☎340-1865). Charcoal-grilled steaks and other Argentine specialities; a T-bone steak costs £E32. Daily 8am–1am.

Don Quichotte, 9a Sharia Ahmed Heshmat (☎340-6415). Tiny, elegant restaurant sampling great cuisines of the world. The speciality of the house is *coquille bonne femme* (seafood in white wine sauce). Very expensive. Reservations advisable. Daily 12.30–4pm & 7.30pm–midnight.

Five Bells, corner of Adil Abu Bakr and Ismail Mohammed, north of the Zamalek Bridge (☎340-8635). It's worth dressing up for this swish Italianate joint, complete with garden and fountain. Expensive and there's a £E2.50 cover charge. Daily 12.30pm–1am.

Hana Korean Restaurant, Sharia Mohammed Mazar, next to the *El-Nil Zamalek Hotel* (☎341-9734). Small, friendly place offering various Asian dishes. A huge portion of *sukiyaki* (do-it-yourself stir-fry soup) costs £E25. Also does deliveries. Daily noon–11pm.

Il Capo, 22 Sharia Taha Hussein, next to the *President Hotel* (☎341-3870). Tasty *antipasti*, pizzas and spaghetti dishes in slick, A/C surroundings. Moderate to expensive. Daily noon–1am.

Justine, 4 Hassan Sabry, in the Four Corners complex 2 blocks south of Galabaya Park (☎341-2961). Probably the finest and one of the most expensive restaurants in Cairo. *Nouvelle cuisine*, soft lighting, music and formal dress. Daily 1pm–3pm & 8–11pm. On the same floor (same phone number also) are: **La Piazza**, a stylish, much cheaper Italian restaurant (pasta dishes £E14–19), which is open daily 12.30pm–12.30am; the moderate–expensive **Chin Chin** Chinese restaurant (daily 7pm–midnight); and the **Matchpoint** video snack bar.

Maison Thomas, 157 26th July St opposite the *Marriott Hotel* (☎340-7057). Deli-diner-take-away-delivery place serving freshly made baguettes and pizzas (both around £E10–12) as well as light meals (£E20–25). They make their own pork sausages and *mozzarella* and also do bacon and eggs (£E17). They will deliver to anywhere in central Cairo – even beer at £E4.45 a bottle.

Zamalek Restaurant, 118 26th July St, near the intersection with Sharia al-Aziz Osman. Sit-down joint for *taamiya*, *fuul* and *tahina* (meals £E3–4). Soft drinks only. Daily 7am–1am.

Mohandiseen

The 1980s saw a proliferation of fast-food outlets and chic restaurants, mostly situated along or just off Arab League Street (*Sharia Gameat al-Dowal al-Arabiya*, also nicknamed "The Mall") and Sharia Batal Ahmed Abdel Aziz. Among more recent additions are a pharaonic-style *McDonald's* opposite the *Atlas Zamalek Hotel*, and the local branch of an Indian-ish city-wide chain called *Chicken Tikka* at 47 Sharia Batal Ahmed Abdel Aziz (☎346-0393). There are also two branches of *Peking*, the popular downtown Chinese restaurant (26 Sharia al-Atebba, ☎349-9086; 9 Sharia al-Kawthar, ☎349-9860); and another outlet of the famous Garden City kebab and *kofta* restaurant *Abou Shakra* (17 Arab League Street, ☎344-2299). All of these restaurants will deliver within Mohandiseen/Dokki/Zamalek.

Bon Appetit, 21 Sharia Wadi el-Nil (☎346-4937). Elegant decor and *haute cuisine* variations on native light meals such as fish kebab and shrimp *kofta*. Better known for appetizers, pastries (try the mousse), take-away club sandwiches and fantastic *espresso* coffee. Moderate. Daily 9am–3am.

Al-Omdah, 6 Sharia al-Gaza'ir, around the corner from the *Atlas*. An island – albeit A/C and priced over the odds for pukka Egyptian food (*kushari* £E3–6; *kofta* and kebab £E40 and £E65 per kilo respectively) – in a sea of plastic fast food. Daily 10am–3am, with takeaway downstairs.

Okamoto, 7 Sharia Ahmed Orabi, off Midan Sphinx (☎346-5264). Excellent Japanese food, well worth the expensive prices; serves *sake*. Daily noon–3pm & 6–10.30pm, closed Wed. Last orders 30min before closing.

Prestige Pizza, 43 Gazirit al-Arab, just east of Sharia Wadi el-Nil (☎347-0383). A smart Italian restaurant with a more casual pizzeria attached for a choice of ambience – and price. Moderate–expensive. Daily 10am–1am.

Tandoori, 11 Sharia Shehab, 2 blocks west of Arab League St (☎348-6301). Run by an ex-employee of the *Mogul Room* this place has fine service and Indian cuisine. Try the tandoori chicken, curried lamb (*kema*) or prawns (*jhinga*). Moderately-priced though take-aways and deliveries cost less. Also has some European and Egyptian dishes. No alcohol. Daily noon–midnight.

Le Tirol, 38 Sharia Gazirit al-Arab, just west off Sharia Wadi el-Nil (☎344-9725). Swiss-chalet decor and tasty Central European cuisine at European prices. An Italian menu (*La Toscana*) is also available. Serves alcohol. Daily noon–1am.

Aguza, Dokki and Giza

The rest of the west bank is less tempting than Mohandiseen, but hardly bereft of options. Cheap eating places abound in market quarters like Suleyman Gohar (Dokki) and Midan Giza, while overpriced kebab restaurants and hotel dining loom large along the Pyramids Road. Visitors with children should enjoy the **outdoor family restaurants** – such as *La Rose* or *Felfela Village* – beside the Maryotteya Canal (bring mosquito repellent), or the floating restaurants near the El-Gama'a Bridge (see the next section).

AGUZA AND DOKKI

Cafeteria Nema, 172 Corniche el-Nil, Aguza, opposite the Police Hospital near the 6th October Bridge. The best takeaway *fuul* and *taamiya* sandwiches in Cairo – so taxi drivers swear. Hamburgers and *shwaarma* rolls £E1.60. Daily 24hr.

Ciao, 10 Midan al-Misaha, Dokki (☎352-2482). Genuine wood-oven pizzas, albeit with beef instead of ham and pepperoni, are the main attraction at Dokki's leading Italian restaurant. Moderate, with pizzas £E9–24 and the service charge at your discretion. Daily noon–midnight.

Flying Fish, 166 Corniche el-Nil (☎349-3234). Seafood specialities such as squid or octopus (£E10–13 a kilo), stuffed fish and lobster (£E99 a kilo!). Another Omar Sharif hang-out. Daily noon–1.30am.

GIZA

Le Chalet, in the Nasr Building (see map on p.150). Run by SwissAir, clean and pleasant, with fine views of the Nile. Offers salads and pasta, hot meat or fish platters and delectable pastries and ice creams; also a children's menu. Moderate. Daily 8.30am–11.30pm. The plush **Le Chateau** restaurant upstairs offers rich – and expensive – main courses and scrumptious desserts; expect a lot of corporate diners. Daily noon–12.30am. Reservations advisable for both (☎361-0165 or 348-6270).

El-Mashrabiah, 4 Sharia Ahmed Nessim, opposite the El-Urman Garden (☎348-2801). Elegant Moorish decor and excellent Middle Eastern and Egyptian food. Fairly expensive salads, lamb, *kofta* and turkey dishes. No alcohol. Daily 12.30pm–1.30am (Ramadan till 3.30am).

PYRAMIDS AREA

China Restaurant, 7 Sharia Abu el-Hol (☎385-2023). A highly rated Chinese-run restaurant in the street leading to the Sphinx. Inexpensive–moderate. Daily 10am–9pm.

Felfela Café, 200m up the Alexandria Desert Road, turn right off Pyramids Road between the turn-off for the Sphinx and the Pyramids site entrance (☎383-0234). An offshoot of *Felfela's*, whackily adorned with fake birds and trees, with a similar menu and prices to the downtown branch. Has an A/C dining room upstairs. Daily 9am–1am (nightly entertainment during Ramadan).

Felfela Village, Maryotteya Canal (☎383-4209). On a canal that crosses Pyramids Road, 1km north on the east bank. This rambling outdoor complex features a zoo and playground and a show with camel rides, acrobats, puppets and belly dancers – even dancing horses. The show (1–7.30pm) is presented during summer, Fri and Sun only. Restaurant open daily 10am–7pm.

The Moghul Room, in the *Mena House*. Cairo's top Indian restaurant with a choice of set menu or à la carte. All curries are normally served in mild versions, including the vindaloo, so remember to tell them if you want full strength. Expensive. Daily 12.30–2.45pm & 7.30–11.45pm.

Pyramids Restaurant, 9 Sharia Abu el-Hol, two doors down from the *China*. A plain honest-to-goodness chicken and kebab house with normal *baladi* prices (quarter-kilo *kofta*, chicken or kebab £E10, salad and *tahina* cost extra), in spite of the plethora of tourists. Daily 10am–3am.

Heliopolis

The deluxe hotels in Heliopolis offer a variety of restaurants, coffee shops, nightclubs and snack bars. In the way of offshoots from popular downtown places, *Peking* have a branch at 115 Sharia Osman Ibn Affan (☎418-5612), and *Abou Shakra* have one at 82 Sharia Merghani (☎418-8891).

Amphitrion, Sharia al-Ahram, on the corner of Sharia Ibrahim al-Laqqani (☎258-1379). A restaurant with bar and snack bar/take-away attached, serving Middle Eastern and Western dishes, tea and coffee. Pleasant terrace. Moderate. Daily 8am–1.30am.

Mashawina, 3 Sharia Abdel Moneim Hafez (☎290-9816). Tasty, authentic Lebanese cooking in a relaxed environment. Moderate. Daily 8.30am–2am.

Petit Palmyra, 27 Sharia al-Ahram (☎415-6836). Looks quite posh but prices are very low: kebab, *kofta* and grilled pigeon cost around £E11, though European dishes are significantly more expensive. Daily 1pm–1am.

El-Tekia, 105 Sharia al-Higaz (☎248-4343). Jazzed-up Arab food, including couscous with duck, fried rabbit with rice and mixed grills. Inexpensive. No alcohol. Daily 1pm–2am.

Floating restaurants

Floating restaurants can be an agreeable way to enjoy the Nile, but business has been badly hit by the slump in tourism. As cruise schedules change, it is wise to phone and check, and, with trade now recovering somewhat, make a booking, too. The price quoted is per person.

Nile Maxim (☎340-8888 ext 8383). Docked in front of and managed by the *Marriott*, runs lunch (2.30–4.30pm; £E45) and dinner (8–10pm & 11pm–1am; £E95–135) cruises with live Egyptian music; dinner show features belly dancing.

The Nile Pharaoh & Golden Pharaoh (☎570-1000). Pair of mock-pharaonic barges complete with scarab friezes, picture windows, and golden lotus flower or figures of Horus mounted on the stern and prow. Moored 1km south of the El-Gama'a Bridge (see map on p.150) and operated by *Oberoi Hotels*, they cruise for lunch (2.30–4.30pm; £E72), sunset (Fri only 5–6.30pm; £E45) and dinner (8–10pm, 8.45–10.45pm, 10.30pm–12.30am & 11.30pm–1.30am; £E95). You should check in half an hour before sailing. The dinner cruises feature music and a belly dancer, the lunch cruises have live "oriental" music.

Scarabee (34) (☎355-4481). Docked on the Corniche near *Helnan Shepheard's Hotel*. Sails four times daily: 2.30–4pm (£E50 including lunch); 6–7.30pm ("sunset cruise"; minimum charge £E21); 8–10pm & 10.30pm–12.30am (both £E85 including dinner). The last features an "oriental" floor show, belly dancer and a dance band.

Drinking

As throughout Egypt, the sale of alcohol is banned during Ramadan and other major Muslim festivals, and drinking is limited to indoor locations at all times. Besides restaurants and hotels, there are various **bars**. The cheapest of these are rather rough male-only hard-drinking dens. Others are chiefly meeting places for men and prostitutes (the only Egyptian women found there). The more upmarket bars often have a minimum charge, often unadvertised (usually around £E10–20).

Inevitably, there's also some overlap between bars and nightclubs (covered under "Nightlife and entertainment" on p.215).

Downtown

Spit-and-sawdust dens, usually open until around midnight – definitely not recommended for women on their own – include the *Stella Cafeteria* on the corner of Sharia Talaat Harb and Sharia Hoda Shaarawi, by *Felfela's* takeaway; the *Cap d'Or Cafeteria* at 31 Sharia Abdel Khaliq Sarwat; the *Cafeteria Port Tawfik* in Midan Orabi on the corner of Sharia Orabi; the *Mourias* at 4 Sharia Adly; a couple by the Forex bureaux on Sharia Alfi Bey; and a slew of bars in the block on the western edge of Midan Ataba. Beer (Stella is £E5–6 in most of these) is usually served with free nibbles and lots of drunken bonhomie. Of the following bars, probably only the *Barrel Lounge*, *Café Riche*, *El-Horea* and *Taverne du Champs de Mars* offer hassle-free drinking for women.

Barrel Lounge (35), on the first floor of the *Windsor Hotel*, Sharia Alfi Bey. Faded Anglo-Egyptian decor and charming ambience; popular with Cairene intellectuals. Foreigners can buy alcohol during Ramadan. Native rum or brandy with Coke is the cheapest drink, followed by Stella and *zibib*. Daily 9am–2am.

Café Riche (36), 17 Sharia Talaat Harb. Once a hang-out for artists and intellectuals, practically every Arab revolutionary of the last century has visited at least once – including Saddam Hussein – and although now strictly for tourists, it still oozes history. Have a chat with the owner, who can give you the full story; he was a pilot during the wars with Israel..

El-Horea (37), Midan Falaki. A mirrored, very 1930s café that's hardly changed since then. Chess players meet here in the evening and people gather to watch them play – though drinking isn't allowed round the boards. Daily 8am–11pm.

Gamaika (38), Sharia Sherif, a small street off Sheria Sharif. Apparently named after Jamaica (the owner's sister went there once), this cosy little dive has £E5 Stella, *sheesha* and no bar girls.

Honololo (39), opposite the *Pensione Roma* on Sharia Mohammed Farid. A "cafeteria restaurant" where only *sheesha*, Stella, Heineken (£E18) and bar girls are in evidence – belly dancers after midnight. Daily 11am–4am.

King's Restaurant (40), Sharia Ibrahim el-Kabari (off Sharia Qasr el-Nil, 20m east of Midan Talaat Harb). This pick-up joint serves kebab as well as beer and whisky. Daily 11am–1am.

Al-Shemi (41), opposite the *Grand Hotel*, in a passage off Sharia Talaat Harb and 26th July St. Bar girls, beer and *sheeshas* – a little bit quieter upstairs. Daily 10am–2am.

Taverne du Champs de Mars, in the *Nile Hilton*. Come evening this spendidly ornate reconstructed *fin-de-siècle* Brussels tavern becomes a predominantly gay pick-up joint. Draught Stella beer is £E11, but they also serve Guinness, Kilkenny, Fosters and Carlsberg which, along with spirits, are all more expensive. Daily 3pm–1am; till 3am Thurs.

Zamalek & Mohandiseen

Harry's Bar and **Eugene's Bar**, in the *Marriott Hotel*. Both are extremely popular with expats; the latter is exquisitely decorated in the khedival Arabesque style.

Matchpoint, in the Four Corners complex, 4 Sharia Hassan Sabry. A pseudo-American video snack bar, frequented by rich young Cairenes attending the AUC. It's easy to exceed the minimum charge. Daily 4pm–1am; minimum charge £E20 (£E25 on Thurs). Couples only – though if you're smartly dressed and behave respectably there shouldn't be a problem.

Pub 28, 28 Shagar al-Durr. The bar section – modelled on a British pub – is popular with expats and gay men but noted for its peremptory evictions. There's also an inexpensive restaurant serving *mezzes*. Daily noon–2am.

Nightlife and entertainment

For current information about **what's on** at cinemas, concert halls and nightclubs, get hold of the daily *Egyptian Gazette* (on Saturday, the *Egyptian Mail*); the monthly *Cairo's* (£E4) or *Egypt Today* (£E9); the weekly *Middle East Times* (£E3); or the Thursday (English) edition of *Al-Ahram* newspaper (75pt). Also useful is the free listings magazine *Croc*, which caters to the young expat/affluent-Cairene and AUC student crowd – it's available from five-star hotels and Western-style bars and clubs.

Music

Aside from discos and the Opera House, you're unlikely to hear much Western music outside of tourist restaurants – Egyptians prefer music from the Arab world. For contemporary music, by far the liveliest time of year is after the school and university exams, from late June to November; you'll need an Arabic-speaking friend to tell you what's happening as none of it is advertised in the foreign press. Note that Egyptians make a clear distinction between a disco, where you dance to records, and a nightclub, where you have dinner and watch a floorshow; should you wish to go "clubbing", it's a disco, not a nightclub, that you want.

Contemporary and dance music

Contemporary Egyptian music can be categorized as either *Shaabi*, the urban folk music of *baladi* Cairo, blending traditional *mawals* (laments) with raunchy, satirical lyrics; or *Al-Jeel,* a fusion of Nubian, Libyan and Bedouin rhythms with a disco beat, reflecting the tastes of upwardly mobile Cairene youth.

Though both sounds are played everywhere, live acts are more elusive. *Shaabi* stars now perform at nightclubs along Pyramids Road, at rich weddings and private parties. Hotel nightclubs, open-air concerts at the Gezira and Heliopolis clubs or Cairo University (usually during summer vacation) are likelier venues for *Al-Jeel* stars. Up-and-coming performers might appear at downtown nightclubs.

Cairo's nightclubs harbour **oriental dance music**, whose golden age was the 1940s and 1950s. Purists distinguish between classical *raqs sharqi* and music influenced by Umm Kalthoum or Western jazz – the torrid sounds associated with belly dancing and pre-revolutionary Cairo. Meanwhile, those who can afford it lap it up regardless at weddings (see p.221) and nightclubs (see below).

Folk, classical Arab and religious music

During the Nasser era, numerous troupes were established to preserve Egyptian folk music and dance in the face of urbanization. Traditional rural numbers like *The Gypsy Dance* or *The Mamluke* are performed at the **Balloon Theatre** (☎347-1718) on Aguza's Corniche by the **National Troupe** and the **Reda Troupe**, while the **Folklore Orchestra of Egypt** (aka the Nile Music Orchestra) plays reproduction ancient instruments at various venues (☎574-3373 for information). However, none of this music commands a wide following today. There's also a nightly show (dinner 8–10pm, show 10–11.30pm) at the *Felafel Restaurant* in the *Ramses Hilton* (☎575-8000), which centres around the Hassan folkloric troupe and costs £E105.

Another tradition on the wane is **classical Arab music**, with its oriental scales and passionate rhetoric, bravura soloists, massed orchestras and male choirs. Real enthusiasts should attend the **Saiyid Darwish Concert Hall** on Sharia Gamal al-Din al-Afghani, behind the City of Art, south of Pyramids Road (☎560-2473), where the **Umm Kalthoum Classical Arabic Music Troupe** fronts a choral ensemble backed by violinists and cellists twice a month on Thursday or Sunday evenings from October to April. The concert hall, named after the blind musician who revived and adapted this form of music early this century, is around £E7 by taxi from downtown Cairo.

All the moulids listed on p.220 feature **religious music** (the reading or chanting of the Koran), while few everyday sounds are more evocative than the call to prayer. Outstanding muezzins inspire local pride and professional jealousy. (In a celebrated court case it was ruled that no copyright existed on any expression of the Koran, since Allah created it.) The duets between the Rifai and Sultan Hassan mosques, and the muezzin near the *Pension Roma*, are superb.

Bellydancing and nightclubs

A Marxist critique of **bellydancing** would point the finger at imperialism, and with good reason. The European appetite for exotica did much to create the art form as it is known today: a sequinned fusion of classical *raqs sharqi* (oriental dance), stylized harem eroticism and the frank sexuality of the *ghawazee* (public dancers, many of whom moonlighted as prostitutes during the nineteenth century). The association with prostitution has stuck ever since, notwithstanding the fact that most dancers today are dedicated professionals, and the top stars wealthy businesswomen. When Fifi Abdou bought an apartment in the deluxe Giza Towers, other tenants, such as the Saudi royal family, protested that she lowered the tone of the place.

The homegrown tradition is now under threat from competition by Russian dancers and the increasing social stigma that deters Egyptian women from entering the profession. The Sheikh of Al-Azhar has decreed that pilgrimages to Mecca undertaken by dancers and actresses are invalid unless they renounce their jobs. "They should give up their sins and return to God," he said.

Despite all the scandalous perceptions, customers are not allowed to touch the dancers, no matter how much they pay in tips.

Five-star venues

If you want to see top acts, the place to go is the nightclub of one of the **five-star hotels**. All of these provide a delicious four-course meal to tide you through the warm-up acts until the star comes on sometime between midnight and 3am. There's usually a minimum rate or flat charge (£E100–200) for the whole deal. Reservations and smart dress are required. The main five-star venues are *Cairo Sheraton* in Dokki (☎348-8600), *Semiramis Intercontinental* (☎355-7171), *Meridian Heliopolis* (☎290-5055), *Helnan Shepheard* (☎355-3800), *Cairo Meridian* (☎362-1717) and *Nile Maxim* (☎340-8888 ext 8383). The number one dancer for the last decade or so has been **Fifi Abdou,** who exemplifies the *bint balad,* or streetwise village girl in the big city. Her act includes circus tricks, vulgar posturing and rapping. Now in her sixties – and despite trips to the US for plastic surgery – Fifi's dancing days look to be well and truly numbered.

The big three dancers at present are **Dina, Lucy** and **Montaha**, while two foreign up-and-coming names to look out for are **Yasmina** (British, known to perform with a chandelier on her head) and the Argentine **Asahan**.

Cheaper venues

A step down from this are the somewhat sleazy, rip-off nightclubs **along Pyramids Road,** where the entertainments are varied and sometimes good, but the food is usually poor. Two places that are halfway recommendable are *El-Leil* and the smaller *Pariziana* (both known to taxi drivers), where the music and dancing start around midnight. Dinner is served as early as 9pm (minimum charge £E120). A better-value alternative to these is *Back of the Moon* (minimum charge £E40) on Sharia Faisal (north of and parallel with Pyramids Road) at the corner of Maryotteya Canal (west bank), with a variety programme starting at 10.30pm (get there early for a good seat).

Even cheaper places lurk **downtown**. *Scheherzade*, at the western end of Sharia Alfi Bey (10pm–5am; £E2.50), presents an enjoyable mixture of variety acts in a lovely vaudeville-style hall. Another venue that's reasonably decent is the *Fontana*, in the hotel of the same name on Midan Ramses (Thurs & Sun; £E22 minimum charge). Other nightclubs are definitely seedy (prostitution is rife) but can be good fun for mixed groups or self-confident males. The *Arizona*, opposite the *Scheherzade*, is open from 10.30pm, charges £E3–10 admission (depending on your haggling skills), and £E15 for a beer (which costs much less in the bar below the nightclub). This offers the experience of seeing drunken Egyptians dancing on stage with the dancers, and flinging money in the air from wads carried specifically for the purpose, while an employee scurries around on the floor collecting it all. The *Miami* (in a passage opposite the Chemla store on 26th July Street; minimum charge £E15) and the more popular *New Miami* next door charges a little less. All these cheaper places will try and rip you off with overpriced nibbles put at your table (if you don't eat them, don't pay for them), service charges, taxes, or may simply refuse to give change – even for a £E50 note. The dancers who perform any time before the small hours of the morning are uniformly awful; if it's late enough and you're lucky, you might catch one who has a little rhythm.

Discos

Cairo has a fair number of **discos** (the term "nightclub" is only used in its old-fashioned sense of a sit-down venue with a meal and floorshow) but nowhere to rave about. The music is usually last year's hits back home or current Egyptian stuff; light shows are unsophisticated. But dance floor manners are good, boozy boors are at a minimum and casual dress is acceptable at all but the ritziest places. More problematical is the trend towards a **couples-only policy**. Though you might imagine this is to prevent women from being swamped, locals say that it's to stop discos from becoming **gay haunts** or pick-up joints for prostitutes (see "Drinking", p.214). In practice, women can usually get into discos without escorts, but men without women have little chance. Call first to avoid disappointment.

Unless otherwise specified, all of the venues below are open nightly.

Hotel venues

Most of the hotel discos cater to rich foreigners and Westernized Egyptians. *Jackie's* in the *Nile Hilton* (9pm–4am) admits hotel guests and members only. Other places maintain their cachet by high prices and standards of dress: *Le Disco* in the *El-Gezirah Sheraton* (11.30pm–6am; minimum charge £E150); *Windows on the World*, on the 36th floor of the *Ramses Hilton* (6pm–2am; minimum charge £E45); and *The Saddle* in the *Mena House* (10pm–3am; £E30). More aggravatingly, the *Tamango* atop the *Atlas Zamalek Hotel* in Mohandiseen (10.30pm–3am; minimum charge £E30) restricts admission to couples. However, singles are admitted to *The Castle* in the *Helnan Shepheard* (daily 11pm–5am, also Thurs & Fri 4.30–9pm "matinee"session; minimum charge £E50), which has a couples-only policy from Thursday to Sunday, with singles allowed in on other days. The disco in the *Pharoah's Hotel*, 12 Sharia Lotfi Hassouna in Dokki, is one of the few places in Egypt which regularly plays hip-hop and rap.

Cheaper venues

Less fastidious, **cheaper venues** include *Longchamp* at 21 Sharia Ismail Mohammed, Zamalek (7pm–1am), and the *Fontana Hotel* disco (daily except Sun & Thurs when there is belly dancing instead; £E18 minimum charge).

One of the city's most popular discos is the new, Western-style *Crazy House Disco* (daily midnight–6am; £E25, Thurs £E50), in the enormous Cairo Land entertainment complex at 1 Sharia Salah Salem, near the Southern Cemetery. Entry price includes two drinks, and there's a strict over-21's policy. Another popular place is the *Casanova*, on the 7th floor of the *Hotel el-Borg* on Gezira Island, just north of Tahrir Bridge (11pm–4am; couples only). The *Gowhara*, on the 9th floor of 35 Sharia Qasr el-Nil, is a disco (5–10pm) which becomes a nightclub (11pm–7am; £E50 including dinner). For something a little more interesting, seek out *Borsalino's* (minimum charge £E20), near the Sudanese consulate in the Garden City, or *Africana* on the Pyramids Road in Giza, both of which have a largely African crowd and play mostly African and reggae music. They can be a little seedy, however, and may be frequented by prostitutes. *Pub 36* in Ma'adi (take a taxi and ask the driver to get directions from locals) is good for **jazz and African music**. *After Eight*, in the passage at 6 Sharia Qasr el-Nil (8pm–2am; closed Sun, Ramadan & Aug) also has DJs and a small dance floor with Arabic singers after 2am; it also serves good food. Thursday night at *El Gato Negro* is known as the "Big Lizard", and has a minimum charge of £E30 (including two beers), the small dance floor packed with a young and trendy Cairene/AUC crowd till 2am; Wednesday is '70s and '80s night.

Cinemas

Most of the older **cinemas** in downtown Cairo are Art Deco relics of the 1930s and '40s, purpose-built for foreigners and trashed by rioters on "Black Saturday" in 1952. Never properly refurbished and now distinctly seedy, they still attract huge, virtually all-male audiences, who cat-call at anything remotely risqué. Lurid hoardings portray grotesquer versions of Hollywood mega-heroes, or the stock characters beloved of *baladi* films (indomitable matriarch, broken patriarch, star-crossed lovers, the hussy and the villain).

Though **foreign movies** are shown throughout the year, there's most choice during winter and Ramadan; see listings in the *Egyptian Gazette* or *Middle East Times*. Because they're subtitled in Arabic, audiences chatter and vendors hawk snacks, drowning out the soundtrack – you have to sit near the front to hear anything. However, the last few years have seen an explosion of expensive new cinemas, most in shopping centres: Al-Tahrir Cinema on Sharia Tahrir, in Dokki (☎335-4726; £E10–15); MGM on the top floor of the Maadi Grand Mall (☎352-6095; £E15); and Ramses Hilton Centre, next to the hotel (☎574-7435; £E25). All have plush seats, stereo sound, A/C (turned to arctic setting), and prohibit chattering and smoking. Elsewhere, it's usually okay to buy tickets (£E2.50–5) an hour or so beforehand, except during Ramadan, when extra evening showings draw full houses and the Metro Cinema on Talaat Harb screens a different movie every night (no reserved seats), as does the Al-Tahrir.

To a greater or lesser extent, all films suffer from **censorship**, which sometimes leaves the plot in shreds. The only chance to view uncensored foreign movies comes during the **Cairo International Film Festival**, usually held during autumn or in December. Check the *Egyptian Gazette* or the tourist office for details.

Opera, ballet and theatre

The **Cairo Opera House** on Gezira (☎339-8132 or 339-8144, *opera@link.eg*) is the chief centre for performing arts. Its main hall hosts performances by prestigious foreign acts (anything from Kabuki theatre to Broadway musicals) and the **Cairo Ballet Company** (Sept–June); the Cairo Opera season begins in March. The smaller hall is used by the **Cairo Symphony Orchestra**, which gives concerts there every Saturday from September to mid-June. During July and August all events move to the marble-clad open-air theatre where you can catch anything from Nubian folk-dancing to Egyptian pop to jazz. Programme listings appear in *Egypt Today* and the *Al-Ahram* weekly, and are available in more detail from the ticket office. Tickets (£E5–25) should be booked several days beforehand (daily 10am–3pm & 4–9pm). A jacket and tie are compulsory for men attending events in the main hall.

Another venue for Western-style performing arts is the AUC's **Wallace Theatre** (☎357-5436), which produces two English-language **plays** or **musicals** and sponsors diverse concerts from October to May, advertised on campus and in local newspapers. You might also hear about productions run by two theatre groups run by Cairo's expat community, the **Cairo Players** (☎340-0137) and the **Ma'adi Community Players** (☎353-1026), both open to anyone who's interested; while for those who understand Arabic, the range encompasses everything from **comedy** at the **Thalia Theatre** (☎593-7948) on Midan Ataba to **political satire** at the **Miami Theatre** on Talaat Harb (☎574-5651; closed Mon).

Religious festivals and weddings

Though few foreign visitors frequent them, Cairo's **religious festivals** are quite accessible to outsiders – and a lot of fun. Many begin with a *zaffa* (parade) of Sufis carrying banners, drums and tambourines, who later perform marathon *zikrs*, chanting and swaying themselves into the trance-like state known as *jazb*. Meanwhile, the crowd is entertained by acrobats, stick dancers, dancing horses, fortune-tellers and other side shows – Cairenes see nothing incongruous in combining piety with revelry.

MUSLIM FESTIVALS

MOHARRAM. New Year begins on **Ras el-Sana el-Hegira**, the first day of *Moharram*. The initial ten days of this first month are blessed, especially the eve of the tenth day (*Leylat Ashura*), which commemorates the martyrdom of Hussein at Karbala. Until this century, it witnessed passionate displays by Cairo's Shia minority – the men would lash themselves with chains. Nowadays, Sunni Muslims observe the next day (*Yom Ashura*) with prayers and charity; the wealthy often feed poor families, serving them personally to demonstrate humility. But aside from *zikrs* outside Hussein's Mosque, there's little to see.

SAFAR AND RABI AL-AWWAL. In olden days the **return of the pilgrims** from Mecca (*Nezlet el-Hagg*) occasioned great festivities at the Bab al-Futuh towards the end of *Safar*, the second month. Nowadays, celebrations are localized, as pilgrims are feasted on the evening of their return, their homes festooned with red and white bunting and painted with *Hadj* scenes. However, it's still customary to congregate below the Citadel a week later and render thanksgiving *zikrs* in the evening. Previously, these gatherings blended into the **Prophet's birthday** (*Moulid al-Nabi*) celebrations during the next month, *Rabi al-Awwal*, which run from the third day to the night of the twelfth, the last being its great day. The eve of the twelfth – known as the Blessed Night (*Leylat Mubarak*) – witnesses spectacular processions and fireworks, with *munshids* (singers of poetry) invoking spiritual aid while crowds chant *"Allahu Hei! Ya Daim!"* (God is Living! O Everlasting!). Midan el-Hussein, the Rifai Mosque and Ezbekiya Gardens are the best vantage points.

RABI EL-TANI. During the fourth month, *Rabi el-Tani*, the **Moulid of El-Hussein** gathers pace over a fortnight, its big day usually a Tuesday, its *leyla kebira* on Wednesday night. Hussein's Mosque in Khan el-Khalili is surrounded by crowds chanting *"Allah Mowlana!"* (God is our Lord!), dozens of *zikrs* and amplified *munshids*, plus all the usual side shows. Also in this month is the smaller **Moulid of Saiyida Sukayna** – at her mosque on Sharia el-Khalifa (see map on p.141).

GUMAD EL-TANI. On a Thursday or Friday in the middle of the sixth month, *Gumad el-Tani*, Sufis of the Rifai order attend the **Moulid of Al-Rifai** at his mosque below the Citadel. Those carrying black flags belong to the mainstream Rifaiyah; subsects include the Awlad Ilwan (once famous for thrusting nails into their eyes and swallowing hot coals) and the Sa'adiya (snake charmers, who used to allow their sheikh to ride over them on horseback). Dervishes are less evident at the **Moulid of Saiyida Nafisa** (on a Wed or Thurs mid-month, or a Tues towards the end of the month), but the event is equally colourful.

Whereas most festivals are specifically Muslim (see the box above) or Christian (see below), people of both faiths attend the birthday or name-day celebrations of holy persons with *baraka* (the power of blessing) – known as **moulids**. Aside from the crowds (don't bring valuables, or come alone if you're a woman), the only problem is ascertaining festival **dates**. Different events are related to the Islamic, Coptic or secular calendar, and sometimes to a particular day rather than a certain date, so details below should be double-checked with Egyptian friends or the tourist office. As a rule, all the longer moulids climax in a *leyla kebira* (literally "big night") on the last evening or the eve of the last day – the most spectacular and crowded phase.

Coptic festivals

It should be emphasized that **Coptic festivals** are primarily religious, with fewer diversions than Muslim ones. Unless you're into church services, the "moveable" feasts centred around Easter (which follows the Coptic calendar rather than the Western one), Christmas (January 7), Epiphany (January 19) and the Feast of Annunciation (March 21) have little to offer.

RAGAB. The seventh month is dominated by the great **Moulid of Saiyida Zeinab**, Cairo's "patron saint", which lasts for fifteen days and attracts up to a million people on its big day and *leyla kebira* (a Tues & Wed in the middle of the month). A much smaller, "local" event is the **Moulid of Sheikh al-Dashuti** on the 26th day of *Ragab*, at his mosque near the junction of Faggala and Bur Said streets, 1km northwest of the Bab al-Futuh. The eve of the 27th is observed by all Muslims as the *Leylat el-Mirag* or **Night of Ascension**, with *zikrs* outside the Abdin Palace and principal mosques.

SHA'BAN. During the eighth month, *Sha'ban*, the week-long **Moulid of Imam al-Shafi'i** enlivens his mausoleum in the Southern Cemetery (see p.145) from one Wednesday to the next. The eve of the 15th is believed to be the time when Allah determines the fate of every human over the ensuing year, so the faithful hope to gain *baraka*.

RAMADAN AND THE EID AL-FITR The sighting of the new moon on the *Leylat er-Ruyeh* (Night of Observation) marks the onset of **Ramadan**, a month of fasting from sunrise to sunset, with festivities every night (see p.57). *Zikrs* and Koranic recitations draw crowds to El-Gumhorriya and El-Hussein squares, while secular delights are concentrated around Ezbekiya and other areas. The *Leylat el-Qadr* (Night of Power) on the eve of the 27th of the month was traditionally marked by Whirling and Howling Dervishes at Mohammed Ali's Mosque at the Citadel. The end of Ramadan heralds the three-day **Eid al-Fitr** or "Little Feast", when people buy new clothes, visit friends, mosques, shrines and family graves. In the past, this was followed by the procession of the *kisweh* (the brocaded cloth which covers the sacred Ka'ba at Mecca), a prelude to the departure of the pilgrims around the 23rd day of *Shawwal*. Given modern transport, however, most pilgrims now depart in the following month, *Zoul Qiddah*, with local send-offs that counterpoint the *Nezlet al-Hagg*.

ZOUL HAGGA. The twelfth month, *Zoul Hagga*, is notable for the "Feast of Sacrifice" or **Eid al-Adha** (the "Great Feast", **Corban Bairam**), which involves the mass slaughter of sheep and other livestock on the 10th, commemorating Ibrahim's willingness to sacrifice Ismail to Allah (the Muslim version of the story of Abraham and Isaac).

MOULID OF SIDI ALI AL-BAYOUMI. Last but not least, there's another colourful parade of Dervishes at the **Moulid of Sidi Ali al-Bayoumi**, the Rifai sects proceeding from El-Hussein's Mosque to the Bab al-Futuh and thence into the Husseiniya quarter. Unlike most Muslim festivals, this is unrelated to the Islamic calendar, happening in early **October**.

However, there's more to enjoy at two festivals in Old Cairo: the **Moulid of Mari Girgis** at the round Church of St George (April 23) and the **Moulid of the Holy Family** at the Church of St Sergius (June 1). Moreover, all Egyptians observe the ancient pharaonic-Coptic spring festival known as **Sham el-Nessim** (literally "Sniffing the Breeze"), when families picnic on salted fish, onions and coloured eggs in gardens and cemeteries.

Weddings

There's nothing bashful about Cairo **weddings** or the curiosity of spectators. On Thursday nights the city resounds with convoys of honking cars conveying guests to Nile-side hotels and casinos; and with ululations, drums and tambourines welcoming the newlyweds (often preceded by a belly dancer), whom relatives shower with rose petals. In poorer quarters all the bridal furniture and wedding guests are first displayed to admiring neighbours.

At the reception itself, the couple sit receiving congratulations ("*Alf mabrouk*" is the formal salutation) while relatives and friends perform impromptu dances. Guests may

WHIRLING DERVISHES

The *Mowlawiyya* are Egyptian adherents of a Sufi sect founded in Konya, Turkey, during the mid-thirteenth century, and known to Westerners as the **Whirling Dervishes**. Their Turkish name, *Mevlevi*, refers to their original Master, who extolled music and dancing as a way of shedding earthly ties and abandoning oneself to God's love. The Sufi ideal of attaining union with God has often been regarded by orthodox Muslims as blasphemous, and only during Mamluke and Ottoman times did the Whirling Dervishes flourish without persecution.

In modern Egypt the sect is minuscule compared to other Sufi orders, and rarely appears at moulids, but a tourist version of the famous whirling ceremony is staged at the Ghuriya cultural centre in Al-Ghuri's Mausoleum (see map on p.127). If the *Mowlawiyya* are in Cairo, **performances** are held on Wednesdays and Saturdays starting at 9pm; arrive early to get a good seat, although this may entail getting cooked by the heat. The performances are free, sponsored by the government, and last for about an hour. Photos are permitted but not videos – if you bring a video camera along you'll have to leave the battery at the desk.

Each element of the **whirling ceremony** (*samaa*) has symbolic significance. The music symbolizes that of the spheres, and the turning of the dervishes that of the heavenly bodies. The gesture of extending the right arm towards heaven and the left towards the floor denotes that grace is being received from God and distributed to humanity without anything being retained by the dervishes. Their camelhair hats represent tombstones; their black cloaks the tomb itself; their white skirts shrouds. During the *samaa* the cloaks are discarded.

be segregated, allowing both sexes to let their hair down: women can dance and smoke, men indulge in spirits (or hashish, in private homes). Although it's not uncommon for foreign onlookers to be invited into middle-class or *baladi* wedding parties, rich ones are predictably exclusive, but good for a brief show.

Activities and kids' stuff

The two classic tourist activities are riding in the desert near the Pyramids and sailing on the Nile in a felucca. Other more or less adventurous trips are covered at the end of this chapter under "Excursions from Cairo" (see p.242).

Riding in the desert

Despite the pitfalls mentioned under "The Pyramids of Giza", **riding in the desert** is a fantastic experience. Unless you relish haggling, authorized stables are a safer bet than footloose Bedouin operators; in either case, check to see that your horse is in good condition. Stables behind the Sound and Light grandstand near the Sphinx include AA (☎385-0531), which is good for children, Eurostables (☎385-5849) and MG Stables (☎385-1241). For Omar Stables (☎385-0301), ask for Mohammed or Adel Omar in the Pyramids Bazaar opposite the *Mena House*. All of the above charge £E20 an hour. Children and adults can take riding lessons (£E10 for 30min) at Heliopolis Racing Club (9am–5pm; ☎245-4090).

Felucca sailing

Something as restful as **sailing on the Nile in a felucca** can hardly be termed an activity. Since the boatman does all the work, the only effort involved is negotiating rental rates. Most of the feluccas moored along the river bank opposite the *Helnan Shepheard* and the northern tip of Roda can seat eight people and charge £E20–30 per hour. Bring a picnic and lots of mosquito repellent. For rather less cost, you can join one of the boats just south of Maspero Dock, which do round trips to the Nile Barrages at Qanatir (£E5). Shorter jaunts are available on boats from the quay just north of Tahrir Bridge on Gezira Island (£E2 for 30min). For an even cheaper no-frills ride on the Nile, catch a river-taxi (25pt) from the Maspero Dock to Giza or Old Cairo or, on Fridays and Sundays, up to Qanatir (£E1.50).

Parks

Cairo is incredibly densely populated, with green spaces few and far between. Even in prosperous Mohandiseen, local residents are forced to make use of the central reservations of the main boulevards for sitting out or picnicking. Downtown, the nearest thing to a park you will find is the **Andalusian Garden** (50pt), complete with Cleopatra's Needle-style obelisk, on the east side of Gezira Island just south of 6th October Bridge. By 6th October Bridge on the other side of the island, Gezira Youth Club is used by locals and residents as a park. The adjoining Gezira Sporting Club has a massive green space – the largest in Cairo – but keeps its fees high and its doors resolutely closed to non-members. However, **Saiyida Park**, in Saiyida Zeinab (on Sharia Qadry, one block off Sharia Bur Said; daily 8am–10pm), is a public landscaped garden in traditional Arabic style not far from the Ibn Tulun Mosque, a very welcome green lung in one of the most crowded parts of town, and an excellent place for a breather after a day's sightseeing in Islamic Cairo.

Further afield, the grounds of the **Agriculture Museum** in Aguza (Tues–Sun 9.30am; 20pt; see p.172) are rather more enticing than the museum itself, and there is also the **Japanese Garden** in Helwan (daily except Tues 9am–6pm; £E1; see p.165). Other options are Galabaya Park in Zamalek, El-Urmen Gardens and the zoo in Giza, and Merryland in Heliopolis, all dealt with under "Chiefly for children", below.

Swimming pools

Swimming pools take on an extra allure in Cairo, whose only "public" pool is the spa at Ain Helwan (daily 8am–3pm; £E2; see p.165). The Heliolido (☎258-0070) off Midan Roxi is open to members only, but offers monthly memberships for £E250 (open July–Sept). The nearby Heliopolis Sporting Club (☎417-0010) on Sharia Merghani has a larger pool and admits foreigners over the summer (bring your passport), but the entrance fee (£E20) doesn't include use of the other facilities. The Olympic-size pool at the Ahli Club by the Opera House on Sharia Om Kalthoum is for more serious swimmers and also has women-only sessions – monthly membership costs US$50.

Hotel pools are more accessible, the best being the *Semiramis InterContinental* (£E84), *Cairo Marriott* (£E63) and *Atlas Zamalek* (£E28.50). The rooftop pool of the *Fontana Hotel*, off Midan Ramses, is cheaper for dipping (£E10) but hardly big enough for a swim.

Hammams

A totally different experience is available at traditional **hammams** (bathhouses), whose nondescript facades conceal gloomy warrens of sweatrooms and tubs. Some baths serve men in the morning and women in the afternoon; others assign them separate days, or only admit one sex. With no mixed bathing, Egyptian women can ignore taboos and talk frankly; foreigners may be adopted into their circle, which usually includes children being scrubbed. For men, baths are something of a centre for gay prostitution, and have been since Ottoman times, so many avoid them for that reason, although you can generally go there just for a bathe without being hassled. Egyptians pay £E3–5, but foreigners are likely to be charged £E10. Ask **around Islamic Cairo** – most of the baths are located on maps in that section. The oldest, dating from 1261, is the Hammam al-Sultan, four doors north of Barquq's complex on Sharia al-Muizz (daily 10am–6pm).

Nearer to the Northern Walls are the eighteenth-century Hammam al-Malatyah (on Sharia Amir al-Gyushi) and the harder-to-find Hammam al-Tanbali (near the El-Geish end of Bayn al-Haret, 1km east of Ramses). Around the Bab Zwayla are the As-Sukayna and Al-Muayyad baths – both Mamluke (see map on p.127) - and the rather grubby Ottoman Hammam al-Sukkariyya. A medieval facade halfway down Sharia es-Silah screens the modernized Hammam Bashtak (daily: women noon–5pm; men 7–10pm; Ramadan men only). For a cleaner, more expensive and less traditional venue, around £E25 buys a **sauna** at the *El-Gezirah Sheraton*, a sau*na and* Turkish bath at the *Nile Hilton*, or both plus Jacuzzi at the *Ramses Hilton*.

Sports: participatory and spectator

Keeping fit in Cairo is difficult but not impossible. The expat Hash House Harriers (☎350-5577) is one of several clubs organizing **street running**, best done on Gezira, Roda or the west bank Corniche, before 8am or after 10pm to avoid heavy traffic and air pollution. Alternatively, by paying £E1.50 to enter the Youth Club under the Giza side of the 6th October Bridge, you can "stray" into the Gezira Sporting Club – just keep away from the built-up area near the running track, where guards check for tickets.

Although the Gezira Sporting Club's extensive facilities are only available to members and guests (see above), anyone can use the **gymnasiums** in the *Ramses Hilton* (£E25), *Nile Hilton* (£E54) and *Atlas Zamalek* (£E10 per day) hotels; or call the Community Services Association, 4 Road #21, Ma'adi (☎350-5284), which runs a fitness centre with a weight room.

Of the city's spectator sports, **football** is the most exciting. During the season (Sept–May), premier league teams Ahly and Zamalek take on challengers like Mahalla and Masri at the Cairo Stadium or the Maoulin el-Arab ground, both in Medinet Nasr (Fri, Sat & Sun; £E3–15; kickoff is at 3 or 4pm). Riot policemen with machine guns are regularly in attendance at matches since football riots, though infrequent, can be extremely bloody.

The Saturday *Egyptian Mail* gives details of **horse racing** at both the Heliopolis Hippodrome Course and the Gezira race track, from mid-October to mid-May. Races start at 1.30pm every other Saturday and Sunday; the international ones and the local derby are both enjoyable. From November to April, Cairo's bridges provide a fine view of **rowing** races every Friday.

Chiefly for children

Besides the following places, children (and adults) should enjoy felucca and camel rides, the Sound and Light show, and theme restaurants like *Felfela Village* on Maryotteya Canal at Giza (see "Eating"). Because of Cairo's density, most of the parks and pleasure grounds are on the islands or the west bank (see above).

The Aquarium and zoo

The **Aquarium Grotto** in Galabaya Park in Zamalek (daily 8.30am–3pm; 50pt) displays 195 kinds of tropical fish amidst a labyrinth of passageways and stairs that children will love to explore. The entrance is on Sharia Galabaya, on the western side of the park.

For a larger park and more to see, check out **Cairo Zoo** in Giza (daily 8.30am–4.30pm; last entry 3.30pm; 10pt, camera 20pt, £E5 to hold an animal); and the **El-Urman Gardens** (daily: winter 8.30am–4pm; summer 8.30am–5pm; 50pt, camera 50pt) across Sharia el-Gamia, a stately remnant of the Khedival Gardens laid out by the French (see the map on p.150). Both can be reached from Midan Tahrir by buses

(#900, #115, #913 and many others) that run past the Manial Palace (see p.163) – another place that children should enjoy. Try to avoid Fridays, weekends or public holidays, when the zoo is packed with picnicking families.

Dr Ragab's Pharaonic Village

Reached by half-hourly boats from the corniche 2km south of the Giza Bridge, **Dr Ragab's Pharaonic Village** (daily: winter 9am–5pm; summer 9am–9pm; £E40, children under six £E20; ☎571-8675) is a kitsch simulation of ancient Egypt on Jacob Island, upriver from Roda in Dokki. During the two-hour tour, visitors survey the Canal of Mythology (flanked by statues of gods) and scores of costumed Egyptians performing tasks from their floating "time machines", before being shown around a replica temple and nobleman's villa.

The circus and the puppet theatre

Those who enjoy animals performing tricks, acrobats, clowns and trapeze artists should visit the **National Circus** (☎347-0612) in Aguza, next to the Balloon Theatre near the Zamalek Bridge. The box office is open from 10am to 10pm (tickets £E20–75); performances run from 9pm to midnight daily. Another traditional diversion is the **Cairo Puppet Theatre** (Thurs–Sun 11.30am; ☎591-0954) in Ezbekiya Gardens, which stages *Sinbad the Sailor*, *Ali Baba* and other favourites, or campy musicals during season (Oct–May).

Rides and games

Fun rides and games are on offer at the **Cookie Amusement Park** near the Giza Pyramids (3pm till late; opens at noon on Fri) and the larger **Sinbad Amusement Park** near Cairo Airport, which has bumper cars, a small roller coaster and lots of rides for tots (daily: winter 9–11pm, opens 10am on Fri; summer 9pm–2am; £E5 entry plus £E3–5 per ride). A much smaller mini-fairground can be found on 26th July Street in Mohandiseen, just before Midan Sphinx if you're coming from Zamalek (daily 8am–4pm; entry 75pt, rides 25pt–£E1). **Merryland** on Sharia al-Higaz, off Midan Roxi in Heliopolis, is a safe environment to play, with a merry-go-round, pedalo lake and small zoo (daily: winter 8am–4.30pm; summer 8am–7pm; 50pt at weekends, £E1 Fri & public holidays).

Shopping: bazaars and markets

Shopping in Cairo is a time-consuming process, which suits most locals fine. Cairenes regard it as a social event involving salutations and dickering, affirmations of status and servility; smoothly impersonal transactions are not an ideal. Excluding government stores, there are basically three types of retail outlet. **Department stores** (generally open Mon–Sat 9am–1pm & 5–8pm) have fixed prices and the tedious system where you select the goods and get a chit, pay the cashier and then claim your purchases from a third counter. **Smaller shops**, usually run by the owner, stay open till 9 or 10pm and tend to specialize in certain wares. Although most of them have fixed prices, tourists who don't understand Arabic price tags or Egyptian currency are liable to be overcharged (around the Khan el-Khalili bazaar and Talaat Harb, especially). If you know the correct price, attempts can be thwarted by handing over the exact sum (or as near as possible).

In **bazaars** and **markets** haggling prevails, so it's worth window-shopping around fixed-price stores before **bargaining** for lower rates in bazaar stalls. When asked for a quote, merchants often riposte: "What do you think?" Suggest an absurdly low sum to

---

RAMADAN HOURS

During Ramadan (see p.57), shopping hours go haywire, as some places close all day and operate through the night, while others open later and close earlier. Given that people splurge after sundown, Cairo's boutiques and bazaars are as busy then as Western stores before Christmas.

---

make them respond and don't be fazed by mockery – it's all part of the game. Buyers' tactics include stressing any flaws that might reduce the object's value; talking of lower quotes received elsewhere; feigning indifference or having a friend urge you to leave. Avoid being tricked into raising your bid twice in a row, or admitting your estimation of the object's worth (just reply that you've made an offer). Providing you don't make an offer they're willing to accept, it's okay to terminate a lengthy session without buying anything.

Souvenirs, antiques and film

Scores of shops in the Khan and central Cairo purvey **souvenirs**, mostly kitsch reproductions of pharaonic art – scarabs, statuettes of deities, busts of Nefertiti, eyes of Horus – which are cheaper to buy at source in Luxor or Aswan.

Sheets of **papyrus** painted with scenes from temples or tombs are equally ubiquitous, though much of it is actually made from banana leaves – genuine papyrus

---

MARKETS

Although the bazaars deal in more exotic goods, Cairo's **markets** provide an arresting spectacle, free of the touristy slickness that prevails around the Khan el-Khalili bazaar in Islamic Cairo. Watch how people bargain over the humblest items (often recycled from other products), a paradigm of free enterprise in the gutter. What isn't apparent are the customs, guilds and rackets that govern business, as exemplified by the vast wholesale market at Rod el-Farag (see p.176), whence **fruit and vegetables** are distributed throughout the city. Street markets in central Cairo can be found at Bab al-Luq, halfway up Sharia Orabi, at the eastern end of Sheikh al-Rihan, and along Sharia Qalaa – all of which do business through the night, accompanied by local coffee houses. With the kilo price displayed on stalls in Arabic numerals, you shouldn't have to bargain unless they try to overcharge.

Elsewhere haggling is *de rigueur*. Promising locations are listed below.

• Secondhand clothing can be found in the *canto* section of the **Imam al-Shafi'i Market**, which straggles for 1km along the road leading from Al-Basatin to the Imam's mausoleum in the El-Khalifa district. Other parts of this Friday morning market sell scrap, grain, poultry, sheep and cattle.

• The **Camel Market** at Bil'esh is described on p.170.

• Cairo's **Bird Markets** (10am–2.30pm) are named after the days on which they're held: *Souk al-Hadd* (Sun; Giza Station), *Souk al-Gom'a* (Fri; by the Salah Salem overpass, south of the Citadel) and *Souk Itnayn w Khamis* (Mon & Thurs; in the Abu Rish area of Saiyida Zeinab). The locations of the last two are shown on p.141 and p.150.

• On Sharia el-Geish near Midan Ataba there's a daily **Paper Market**, selling all types of paper, dyed leather and art materials.

• For **fabrics** (from hand-loomed silk to cheap offcuts), **tools** and much else, you can't beat the daily **Wikalat al-Bulah**, on Sharia Abu'l'Ila in the Bulaq district.

should be able to withstand crumpling without cracking (though paint won't!). But the important thing is whether you like the painting. Prices range from around £E2 to £E80, depending on size, intricacy, the quantity of gold paint used and where you're buying: places around the Pyramids, in big hotels and the Khan tend to be overpriced; if you've got the stomach to bargain them down, itinerant street vendors give better deals. You can see papyrus-making demonstrated at Dr Ragab's Papyrus Institute (p.173).

Copies of **prints** by David Roberts and other nineteenth-century illustrators also make nice souvenirs. For cheap poster-sized or postcard editions, check out Reader's Corner and Lehnert and Landrock; costlier original engravings are sold at L'Orientalist (addresses under "Books and newspapers" on p.233). Old Egyptian **stamps**, **coins** and **postcards** can also be found at 33 Sharia Abdel Khaliq Sarwat, among other places.

Selling fake *antikas* (with spurious certificates) is an old tradition. Genuine pharaonic, Coptic or Islamic **antiques** cannot be exported without a licence from the Department of Antiquities. Old reproductions and foreign-made antiques are a safer bet. Dealers in the Khan include Lotus Palace (7 Sharia Khan el-Khalili), and Oriental Souvenirs and Ahmed Dahba (both at 5 Sikket al-Badestan).

Film and processing

Outside of big hotels, you can buy **film** fairly cheaply. Actina (4 Sharia Talaat Harb; Mon–Fri 9am–8pm; ☎757-5236) and Photo Greenwich (16 Sharia Adly; ☎360-6990) both sell Kodachrome and Agfa film for £E12 and also offer **photo-processing** and **printing**. Other outlets where you can get film developed include: Kodak Shop, 20 Sharia Adly (Mon–Sat 9am–9pm; ☎394-2263); and Best Foto/Misr 2000, 6 Sharia Alfi Bey (daily except Fri 9am–9pm; ☎574-3975). Developing is £E4 at the Kodak Shop, £E2.50 at Best Foto/Misr 2000; both charge 60pt per print (9x13), and £E2 extra to get them done in an hour. Don't risk your film at the Kodak kiosk on 26th July Street. For where to get passport photos, see p.237.

Brass and copper ware

Egyptian craftsmen have been turning out **brass and copper ware** for over a thousand years, and aside from the tourist trade there's still a big domestic market for everything from banqueting trays to minaret finials. Amongst the items favoured as souvenirs are candlesticks, waterpipes, gongs, coffee sets, embossed plates and inlaid or repoussé trays (the larger ones are often mounted on stands to serve as tables). All of these are manufactured and sold within the Khan, particularly along the stretch of Sharia al-Muizz just before Qalaoun's complex, known as the **Coppersmiths Bazaar** (*Souk al-Nahhasin*).

Although the Khan offers the best range of decorative pieces, it's cheaper to buy **Turkish coffeepots** and hookah pipes between the Ghuriya and the Bab Zwayla, along Ahmed Maher, or from workshops on Sharia Khulud and other streets around Ramses. Be sure that anything you intend to drink out of is lined with tin or silver, since brass and copper react with certain substances to form toxic compounds. Test **waterpipes** for leaky joints and remember to call them *sheeshas* or *narghiles* rather than *hubbly bubblies* (which signifies hashish-smoking). Two shops facing the Barquq complex specialize in waterpipes, backgammon boards and other coffee house sundries; proceeding north from there up Sharia al-Muizz, there's a passage on the left just before the Sabil-Kuttab of Abd al-Rahman that is full of shops selling pipes. Expect to pay £E30–70, depending on the size; the ones with stainless steel rather than brass fittings are better made and more durable.

Gold and silver jewellery

Most Egyptians still regard **jewellery** as safer than money in the bank; for women, in particular, it constitutes a safety net in case of divorce or bereavement. Pharaonic, Coptic and Islamic motifs, Bedouin, Nubian and oasis designs, work from Syria, Jordan, Yemen and Arabia – Cairo's jewellers stock them all, and can also make pieces to order.

Gold and silver are sold by the gramme, with a percentage added on for workmanship. Bullion prices fluctuate but Egyptian wages remain low. The current ounce price of gold is printed in the daily *Egyptian Gazette*; one ounce equals about 28 grammes. Barring antiques, all **gold** work is stamped with Arabic numerals indicating its purity: usually 21 carat for Bedouin, Nubian or *fellaheen* jewellery; 18 carat for Middle Eastern and European-style charms and chains. Sterling **silver** (80 or 92.5 percent) is likewise stamped, while a gold camel in the shop window indicates that the items are **gold-plated brass**.

The Goldsmiths Bazaar

Downtown jewellers are concentrated along Sharia Abdel Khaliq Sarawt and Sikket al-Manakh, near Midan Opera. In Islamic Cairo, the **Goldsmiths Bazaar** (*Souk es-Sagha*) covers Sharia al-Muizz between the Muski and Sultan Qalaoun's complex, and infiltrates the heart of the Khan via Sikkets al-Badestan and Khan el-Khalili, two medieval lanes whose gateways now denote addresses (for example, Bab al-Awwal, "First Gate"). For gold-plated *fellaheen* designs, check out Sigal and Al-Gamal Jewellery on Sharia al-Muizz. Oasian gold can be found at Adel Rizk, off to the right near Bab al-Awwal, and at Gundi Shenouda, Bab al-Talat; the latter also sells original *faraoni* necklaces from Upper Egypt. Adly Fam (72 Muski) specializes in 21-carat *fellaheen* jewellery. There are several good **silversmiths** in the Wikala al-Gawarhergia (ask for directions).

The most popular souvenirs are gold or silver **cartouches** with given names in hieroglyphics. The price depends on the quantity of metal used, and whether the characters are engraved or glued on. Thin gold cartouches with glued letters cost about £E60; thicker ones with soldered letters £E90–170; silver cartouches cost much less (£E10 upwards). The cheapest way to get these is to go directly to a workshop where they are made. There are several above the passage of waterpipe suppliers off Sharia al-Muizz (left just before the Sabil-Kuttab of Abd al-Rahman Katkhuda, if coming from the Muski – the stairs are towards the end of the passage on the left). As well as getting a better price, you'll be able to see your piece being made; the disadvantages are that you won't see a selection of items on display here, and you'll be lucky to find anyone who speaks English.

Carpets, tent-making, appliqué and basketwork

Pure wool kilims and knotted carpets are an expensive (and bulky) purchase in any country, so serious buyers are advised to read up on the subject before spending hundreds of pounds on one. As most Egyptian **kilims** (pile-less rugs) and **knotted carpets** have half as many knots (16 per centimetre) as their Turkish counterparts, they should be significantly cheaper – especially the ones made from native wool rather than the high-grade imported stuff used in finer kilims. Prices posted in downtown stores like Omar Effendi (42 Sharia Sherif) and Abdou Moustafa (23 Sharia Sherif) can give you an idea of what to aim for in the bazaar.

Tapestries and rugs

More affordable – and ubiquitous – are the **tapestries and rugs** woven from coarse wool and/or camel hair. These come in two basic styles. Bedouin rugs carry geometric patterns in shades of brown and beige and are usually loosely woven (often purely from camel hair). The other style, deriving from the famous Wissa Wassef School at Harraniyya (see p.190), features colourful images of birds, trees and village life. Beware of stitched-together seams and gaps in the weave (hold pieces up against the light), and unfast colours – if any colour wipes off on a damp cloth, the dyes will run when the rug is washed.

While the suburban village of Kerdassa (p.190) replicates every style imaginable, the only authorized outlet for genuine Wissa Wassef Harraniyya tapestries and batiks is Senouhi, on the fifth floor of 54 Sharia Abdel Khaliq Sarwat (Mon–Fri 10am–5pm, Sat 10am–1pm; ☎391-0955). Crammed with carpets, jewellery, Bedouin embroidery and modern paintings, this small store is a fascinating place to browse. The best site in the bazaar is Haret al-Fahhamin (see "Spices and perfume", p.231), where you can compare Rashidi and Shahatta Talba Manna (both at no. 11) with Hamid Ibrahim Abdel Aal (no. 5). Unfortunately, none of them is recognizably signposted (or even numbered), so you'll have to ask for directions to the right shop.

Tent-making and appliqué

The traditional Cairene crafts of tent-making and appliqué work are still practised in half a dozen tiny workshops inside the Qasaba, near the Bab Zwayla – hence its sobriquet, the **Tentmakers Bazaar** (*Souk al-Khiyamiyya*). Colourful **appliqué work** comes in various forms. Some designs are pictorial, based on pharaonic motifs or romantic Arab imagery; others are abstract, delicate arabesques (which tend to be dearer). Prices vary according to size and intricacy. A zippered pillowcase or cushion cover costs £E15–25; larger pieces, to be used as hangings, go for upwards of £E100, with bedspread-sized ones starting at roughly £E300. A much cheaper alternative is the riotously patterned **printed tent fabric** used for marquees at moulids, or to screen unsightly building work. This costs about £E5 per metre, cut from a bolt of cloth roughly 1.5m wide; offcuts are cheaper still.

Another cheap souvenir is palm-frond **basketwork**, mostly from the Fayoum and Upper Egypt. Fayoumi baskets (for sewing, shopping or laundry) are more practical, but it's hard to resist the woven platters from Luxor and Aswan, as vibrantly colourful as parrots. You may also find baskets from Siwa Oasis, trimmed with tassels.

Clothing, bellydancing costumes and leatherwork

As a cotton-growing country with a major textiles industry, Egypt is big on retail **clothing**. Smartly dressed Cairenes are forever window-shopping along Talaat Harb and 26th July Street (downtown), Sharia al-Ahram (Heliopolis) and Arab League Street (Mohandiseen), to name only the main clusters of **boutiques** (open till 9–10pm). For those who want familiar labels, there are branches of Benetton at 41 Sharia Qasr el-Nil and at 11 Sharia Hassan Saby in Zamalek, plus several more at other locations around the city. Staider threads can be had in **department stores** like Chemla and Cicurel on the downtown section of 26th July Street, or Omar Effendi at 2 Talaat Harb and 25 Sharia Adly (Mon–Fri 9.30am–2pm & 5–8.30pm, Sat 9.30am–2.30pm). The cheapest outlets for clothes are **street vendors** along the Muski.

Egyptian clothes

Although few tourists can wear them outdoors without looking silly, many take home a caftan or *galabiyya* for lounging attire. Women's **caftans** are made of cotton, silk or wool, generally A-line, with long, wide sleeves and a round or mandarin collar (often braided). Men's **galabiyyas** come in three basic styles. *Ifrangi* (foreign) resembles a floor-length tailored shirt with collar and cuffs; the *Saudi* style is more form-fitting, with a high-buttoned neck and no collar; *baladi galabiyyas* have very wide sleeves and a low, rounded neckline. The fixed prices in downtown shops should be beatable by hard bargaining **in the Khan**, where there are also two fixed-price stores. Ouf (pronounced "oaf"), at the end of an alley leading west off the Spice Bazaar, stocks a wide assortment of ready-mades at reasonable prices, including black dresses with Bedouin-style embroidery. Atlas, on Sikket al-Badestan, does made-to-order garments in handwoven fabrics with intricate braidwork (allow several weeks; keep all receipts). Their cheapest caftans and *galabiyyas* are dearer than most garments in other shops.

Another fetching item is the heavy, woven, fringed or tassled black **shawls** worn by *baladi* women, which are sold along the Muski for upwards of £E10, depending on their size and composition (nylon or silk); check for any snags or tears in the weave. If you want to go the whole hog, invest in a *melaya*, the flowing black ankle-length wraps that *baladi* women wear over their house dresses when they go outdoors.

Bellydancing costumes

Cairo is the cheapest place in the world to buy bellydancing costumes, and many foreign dancers come here just to buy all the gear. Forget the rubbish sold to tourists, and look for one of the tiny specialist emporiums in Khan el-Khalili. The best one is upstairs immediately to the right of the passage leading from the Muski to *Fishawi's* café. There's a woman to help fit the costumes; anything they don't have in stock they can make in a few days. Lavishly beaded and sequinned bras and hipbands, with a skirt and veil, cost £E150–300; the more you buy, the lower the price. If you're really serious, go to Amira el-Khattan, 27 Sharia Basra, Mohandiseen (☎349-0322), where a full tailor-made costume will set you back about £E1800. For belly dancing tapes and videos of the great artistes, pay a visit to Es-Sawy, on the left of the passage just before you reach *Fishawi's*. If you're interested in lessons, Miss Raqia Hassan (☎348-2338) in Dokki comes recommended by several dancers who are now professional.

Leatherwork

Egyptian **leatherwork** is nice and colourful, if not up to the standards of its Turkish rival. You can get an idea of the range of products from several shops along Sikket Khan el-Khalili. Leather jackets cost upwards of £E100. Cheaper wallets, handbags and pouffes (tuffets) are sold throughout the Khan and central Cairo, whilst camel saddles in a variety of colours and sizes (£E100) are still produced in the **Saddlemakers Bazaar** (*Souk es-Surugiyyah*), south of the Qasaba (see the map on p.127).

Glass, ceramics and precious stones

Primitive factories on Haret al-Birkedar just outside the Northern Gates still produce **Muski glass**, a form of hand-blown glassware popular in medieval times, which is nowadays made from recycled bottles. Recognizable by its air bubbles and extreme fragility, Muski glass comes in five main colours (navy blue, turquoise, aquamarine, green and purple) and is fashioned into inexpensive glasses, plates, vases, candle holders and ashtrays – sometimes painted with arabesque designs in imitation of enamelled Mamluke glassware. In the bazaar, the main stockist is Saiyid Abd al-Raouf (8 Sikket Khan el-Khalili), but it's better to go to the factory, where you can see the glass being blown, and also get a better price. The main one is called Al-Daour, and can be found by leaving the walled city through Bab al-Futuh, crossing the main road (Sharia Galal) and finding Haret al-Birkedar about 50m to your right behind the first row of shops; the factory is more or less at the end of it.

A very different kind of glassware is the elegant handmade **perfume bottles** sold in the bazaars. The cheaper ones are made of glass and are as delicate as they look

(£E2–10). Pricier versions (costing about four times more) are made of Pyrex and are a little sturdier (they should also be noticeably heavier).

Pottery and alabaster

Robust **household pottery** is sold outdoors near the Mosque of Amr in Old Cairo, along Sharia al-Ahram in Giza and the Corniche between Cairo and Ma'adi. For more refined **ceramics**, check out Senouhi (see p.229), Sornaga, on Sharia Ibrahim el-Kabani, just behind Midan Talaat Harb between Sharia Qasr el-Nil and Sharia Mohammed Sabri, and Ma'adi galleries such as Al-Patio (6 Road # 77c) and Haddouta (Sharia Amira, New Ma'adi). Vases and sculptures made from **alabaster** are ubiquitous in Cairo's tourist marts, but you can get better deals at source, in Luxor.

Precious stones

Although nothing can substitute for experience, it's worth relating a few tips about **precious stones**, which Egypt imports from all over, having exhausted its own supply through centuries of mining. Most emeralds in Egypt are of poor quality (good ones are clear, dark green); very large or transparent rubies (from India and Burma) are almost certainly fake; and real sapphires should be opaque. True amber will float when put in salt water. Pearls (from the Gulf Emirates and Japan) should feel like glass if tapped against your teeth; German onyx should be opaque and make a sharp sound if dropped onto glass; and genuine turquoise (from Sinai, Iran or the USA) should contain streaks and impurities. To test the authenticity of Brazilian topaz, amethyst or aquamarine, place them on a sheet of white paper – genuine ones should have only two shades within the stone.

Mashrabiya and inlay work

With little demand for the huge latticed screens that once covered nearly every window in Cairo, modern **mashrabiya work** is usually confined to decorative screens and table stands (see "Brass and copper ware", above). Generally made of imported red birch or oak, they consist of scores or hundreds of turned wooden beads, joined by dowels and glue, without nails. The technique is also applied to Koran stands (which make splendid magazine racks), the fancier ones being embellished with mother-of-pearl, bone and other inlays.

Inlaid **boxes** come in all sizes, from cigar holders to multi-drawer jewellery caskets. Small boxes cost upwards of £E7; prices increase with size and quality of workmanship. **Backgammon boards** (*thowla* – pronounced "dow-la") come in two broad varieties: very simple, with minimal (often poor-quality or plastic) inlay, for around £E35; and larger sets made of hard woods, intricately inlaid with mother-of-pearl, bone or ivory. A multiple box set can cost £E140 or more.

Many backgammon sets have chessboards on the back; **chesspieces** in every style and material are widely available, but good backgammon counters are hard to find. Now that Egypt has stopped legal imports, fresh supplies of **ivory** (whose sale is not illegal) are smuggled in from Sudan and Kenya, where poachers are decimating elephant herds. If that's not sufficient reason to boycott ivory products, numerous countries (including Australia, Britain, Germany and the USA) prohibit their importation. Inlaid or carved **bone** makes an acceptable, cheaper substitute.

Spices and perfume

As the world's main spice entrepôt from Fatimid times until the eighteenth century, Cairo remains the largest market for perfumes and spices in the Arab world, with some of its business still conducted in bazaars.

Spices and herbs

The Muski end of the **Spice Bazaar** is generally disappointing, with tourist tat imping-ing on old shops like Donia al-Henaur (incense, spices, candles) and Khedar al-Attar (herbal cures), between the Madrassa of Barsbey and Sharia al-Azhar. However, at the other end of the *Souk al-Attarin*, a narrow lane behind the Mosque-Madrassa of Al-Ghuri – the **Haret al-Fahhamin** – is a welter of vivid colours and aromas, mingling with the dirt and stench of ages. Here, piled high and named in Arabic, *'irfa* (cinnamon) and *simsim* (sesame) are still evocative of distant lands. Saffron (*za'faraan*) costs a hun-dred times less than you'd pay back home, but the quality is very poor.

Some shop owners are also **herbalists** (*etara*), whose traditional remedies for every ailment from impotence to constipation are widely used. There are several *etara* on Al-Fahhamin and outside Barsbey's madrassa, but the most famous establishment is Abdul Latif Mahmoud Harraz (39 Sharia Ahmed Maher), in the Bab el-Khalq quarter, which has been run by the same family since 1885.

Incense and perfume

Just as herbal medicine blends into folk magic (many stalls purvey amulets), both make use of **incense**. The Spice and Perfume bazaars offer the widest range of musks and resins, but you can also find Sudanese vendors squatting beside aromatic cones and medicinal roots in the Ezbekiya Gardens.

Alongside the northern half of the *Souk al-Attarin* lies a warren of covered alleys that forms the **Perfume Bazaar**. Egypt produces many of the **essences** used by French perfumiers, which are sold by the ounce to be diluted 1:9 in alcohol for perfume, 1:20 for eau de toilette and 1:30 for eau de cologne. Local shops will duplicate famous per-fumes for you, or you can buy brand imitations (sometimes unwittingly – always scru-tinize labels).

Reputable shops like Princess Perfumes at 4 Sharia Bud al-Gadid (by the corner of Sharia Bab al-Wazir, near the Citadel) charge £E1 a gramme, depending on the type of essence, and will only dilute to order, but many places overcharge and cheat – around Talaat Harb especially. Boasting that their "pure" essence is undiluted by alcohol, crooked salesmen will omit to mention that oil has been used instead, which is why they rub it into your wrist to remove the sheen.

Musical instruments and recordings

Cairo is a good place to buy **traditional musical instruments** such as the *kanoon* (dulcimer), *oud* (lute), *nai* (flute), *rabab* (viol), *mismare baladi* (oboe), *tabla* (drum), *riq* and *duf* (both tambourines; the latter is played by Sufis). All of them are made and sold by half a dozen shops on the right-hand side of **Sharia Qalaa** (walking from Midan Ataba towards the Islamic Art Museum), which also deal in Western instruments and cheaper imitations from China.

Traditional instruments are also sold by itinerant vendors, especially during moulids, when a favourite buy is a hand-held dummy that claps its cymbals together when squeezed (known as a *Shoukoukou* after the famous comic monologist).

As the centre of the Arab music world and a melting pot for every tradition (see "Music" in Contexts chapter), Cairo is a superb place to buy **recordings**. Authorized cassettes (there are very few CD recordings of Arab music and no one uses vinyl LPs) and pirated versions are sold from kiosks where it's quite acceptable (indeed, advis-able) to listen before buying. Given that non-Arabic labelling is minimal, it helps to rec-ognize labels like *Sout el-Beiruit* (a green cedar-pine logo; Gulf and Levantine music), *SLAM!* (mostly *Al-Jeel* music) and the *Shaabi* imprint *Fel Fel Phone* (which has a retail outlet on Sharia Khulud, near Midan Ramses).

The kiosk beside the *Café Riche* is good for all kinds of music, whereas those on Ezbekiya chiefly stock religious and folk cassettes (often cheap, inferior copies). For quality recordings of Umm Kalthoum, Abdel Wahaab and orchestral music, visit Sono Cairo on Sikket Ali Labib Gabr, between Qasr el-Nil and Talaat Harb (opposite the Radio Cinema). Cairo's main distributor, Abdullah, has a shop in the alley behind the *Café al'Americaine* at the top of Sharia Talaat Harb, with vast stocks and an even bigger mail-order catalogue of new wave Arab music. Western music is also available in many kiosks on tape, but for CDs try the shopping malls in places like Heliopolis or Dokki.

Books and newspapers

Egypt is the world's largest publisher of Arabic books and newspapers, so those who know the language can find almost any type of **Arab literature** in Cairo. Aside from magazine and paperback stalls along the downtown thoroughfares, good sources include Dar al-Kitab al-Masri wal-Loubnani (on the first floor of 33 Sharia Qasr el-Nil) and Dar al-Maaref (27 Sharia Abdel Khaliq Sarwat); for Islamic heritage books, try Dar el-Tarath (22 Sharia Gumhorriya) and around Ezbekiya Gardens.

Unlike most other places in Egypt, Cairo also has plenty of **books in foreign languages** (chiefly English, French and German). Generally, bookshops charge the original cover price for imported editions – usually at an unfavourable rate. For a huge range of material on all things Egyptian, plus novels, travel guides and dictionaries, visit the American University in Cairo Bookshop (closed Aug) at the back of the main campus (use the entrance on Sharia Mohammed Mahmoud). Also good for fiction, Egyptology and local literature are Shorouk (on Midan Talaat Harb), who seem to have the best prices for AUC publications, and keep a stash of out-of-print literature published by the Egyptian Book Organization (ask if you want to see it). Other good downtown bookshops are Lehnert & Landrock (44 Sharia Sherif) and Reader's Corner (33 Abdel Khaliq Sarwat). The Anglo-Egyptian Bookshop (169 Sharia Mohammed Farid) specializes in Arab politics, history and culture, but has an excellent all-round collection; Al-Ahram (165 Sharia Mohammed Farid) and Madbouli (Midan Talaat Harb) also sell books in English. L'Orientalist (15 Sharia Qasr el-Nil) specializes in rare and antique editions, all of which are pricey. Most of these **downtown bookshops** are closed on Sunday.

Since the wonderful old booksellers on Ezbekiya have been forced to disperse, few outlets for **secondhand books** remain. But you can find downtown secondhand bookstalls outside *Groppi's* on Sharia Qasr el-Nil (fair selection), outside 26 Sharia Talaat Harb (a bit pricey), and on Midan Tahrir between Sharia Champollion and Sharia Qasr el-Nil (mostly pulp novels).

Newspapers and magazines

Foreign newspapers and magazines can be found in the bookshops of the five-star hotels or downtown at the stall on Qasr el-Nil, outside *Groppi's*, and another on Sharia Mohammed Mahmoud by *McDonald's*, which sometimes even carries the *New York Times* and also a few foreign-language novels. Purchasers of weekend editions of British papers should note that colour supplements are sold separately. You'll be hard-pressed to find a newspaper less than a few days old, so if you need the latest news you'd be better off paying £E10–15 at an Internet café and accessing the Web site of your favourite read.

Booze and cigarettes

For those who enjoy tippling in their room or want a cache for consumption in "dry" parts of Egypt, there are several places which sell alcohol.

Downtown **liquor stores**, run by Greek or Maronite Christians, maintain a low profile; furtive Muslim customers are served at once, with hardly a word exchanged. You'll find Orphanides, opposite the High Court on 26th July Street, and a small shop on the same block, 20m west of Sharia Talaat Harb; Nicolakis, on the corner of Sharia Talaat Harb and Sharia Suq al-Tawfiqia; Gianacus, below the *Hotel Claridge* at 41 Sharia Talaat Harb; Cava Kasr el-Nil at 24 Sharia Bassiouni. All stock Egyptian beer, wine, *zibib*, *raki*, brandy and dubious lookalike brands such as *Johnny Wadie Whisky* (Red and Black labels) and *Gardan's Gin*: checking out the windows can be fun. Most are open from mid-afternoon till 8pm, Monday to Friday, and close down entirely during Ramadan and other major Muslim festivals.

Liquor regulations entitle foreigners to buy up to four litres of **imported alcohol at duty-free prices** within 24 hours of arrival in Egypt, and a further three litres within the next month. To take advantage of this, bring your passport – you'll get a stamp in it saying what you've bought – along to the well-stocked Diplomatic Section of the Egypt Free Store, 500m beyond the *Atlas-Zamalek Hotel* on Arab League Street in Mohandiseen (daily 10am–3pm), or to the *Sheraton* in Dokki, or you can save about US$1 on a bottle by going to the shop at the airport.

Beware of Egyptians who accost you in the street asking if you'll buy them some duty-free booze "for my sister's wedding". Buying alcohol for someone else is fine, but under no circumstances should you allow a stranger to be involved in the actual transaction inside the store. The paperwork for any duty-free purchase is filled out in Arabic, and some travellers have discovered on leaving Egypt that a TV or video has been bought duty-free with their passport. Being unable to produce the item for customs officials, they've had to pay duty on it, just as if they'd purchased and then sold it while in Egypt.

With **cigarettes** available on every corner, only smokers addicted to certain foreign brands need hunt down specialist outlets. Try Carvellis Frères (32 Sharia Talaat Harb), which also sells pipe tobacco, rolling tobacco (100g Drum £E25, 50g Samson £E15) and cigarette papers, and never overcharges. Refilling stalls all over the city can recharge your lighter (even if it's "non-refillable") for 35–50pt, or change flints for 25pt.

Money

Though rates of exchange vary slightly, **banks** are chiefly distinguished by their opening hours and relative (in)efficiency. The main high street banks are the National Bank of Egypt (Mon–Thurs & Sun 8.30am–2pm), Banque Misr (Mon–Thurs & Sun 8.30am–2pm) and the Bank of Alexandria (Mon–Thurs & Sun 8.30am–2pm). Most downtown banks are also open between 3 and 5pm.

Aside from Thomas Cook or American Express (see below), it's usually quickest to **exchange money** or **travellers' cheques** at the **24hr** Banque Misr exchange bureaux in the *Nile Hilton* and the *Ramses Hilton*, and outside the *Helnan Shepheard*; or at branches in other major hotels and off Midan Ramses, which are open daily till 8pm. However, none of the banks will change NZ dollars, Irish pounds, or Scottish and Northern Irish sterling banknotes. **Visa** or **MasterCard** holders can obtain cash advances in £E from the Bank of America at 106 Sharia Qasr al-Aini (☎354-7788, fax 355-5023; Mon–Thurs & Sun 8.30am–2pm), a couple of blocks south of Midan Tahrir; it takes about an hour to get confirmation by telex. **Payouts** for Visa and MasterCard are usually in Egyptian currency only.

Two sets of **ATMs** now accept cashcards and credit cards (but are frequently out of order). The Egyptian British Bank (Visa, Cirrus, Electron, Plus, MasterCard, Express Net, Global Access, Electro Bank and Marine Machine) has them at their hotel branches (*Nile Hilton, Ramses Hilton, Marriott, Cairo Sheraton* and *Semiramis*

Intercontinental), as well as at the Abu el-Feda Tower in Zamalek; behind the Grand Mall in New Maadi; at 1 Midan Roxy in Heliopolis; and the World Trade Centre on the Corniche at Bulaq. They can also be found at Alfa Market in Dalla Towers, Ma'adi and ABC Supermarkets in Zamalek, Heliopolis and El-Manial. Other ATM machines which accept Visa, Plus, MasterCard and Cirrus are outside Banque Misr branches in Sharia el-Bustan (at the corner of Sharia Talaat Harb); Midan Orabi; at 151 Sharia Mohammed Farid; in Midan Roxi in Heliopolis; and in Dokki, Ma'adi, Helwan and Pyramids Road. The National Bank of Egypt has also begun to install ATMs, the first being at the Sharia Talaat Harb branch.

Forex

Private exchange bureaux – known as **Forex** – are usually open daily. They are faster and give a better rate for cash than banks and, unlike banks, will usually change Israeli shekels, and Jordanian and Libyan dinars – though again not NZ, Irish, Scottish or Northern Irish notes. In general, they will not accept travellers' cheques either. Downtown Forex bureaux include the Horus and the Al-Fakahany (better rates), two doors from each other in Sharia Alfi Bey (they will change travellers' cheques, but at a low rate, and may demand to see receipts); others are at 6 Sharia el-Bustan, 14 Sharia el-Bustan, 29 Sharia Emad el-Din by the *New Cecil Hotel*, and on the corner of Sharia Qasr el-Nil and Sharia Sherif. There are also two in Midan Ataba, one in Midan Orabi and one on Midan Hussein, up a flight of stairs opposite *Fishawi's*.

American Express

Aside from its overpriced tours and travel services, **American Express** (Amex for short) can be useful to travellers. Their main office at 15 Sharia Qasr el-Nil (Sat–Thurs 8.30am–5pm; Fri 8.30am–3pm; during Ramadan daily 8.30am–3.30pm; ☎574-7991, fax 574-7997) is the best place to send money or letters, although this mail service (closed Fri) is only available to holders of Amex travellers' cheques or cards. As a rule, it's quicker to change foreign currency or Amex cheques here than in commercial banks. Refunds for lost or stolen cards or travellers' cheques can take weeks, though they claim it's the next day. Amex is acutely suspicious of fraud, which is widespread in Cairo.

Other Amex branches can be found in the *Nile Hilton* (☎578-5001), at 21 Sharia Giza in Giza (☎570-3411), and 72 Sharia Omar Ibn el-Khattub in Heliopolis (☎418-2144). Most of them will pay out US$ for Amex travellers' cheques, and allow cardholders to draw out emergency cash on a personal cheque.

Transferring money from abroad via MoneyGram is explained below.

Thomas Cook

The modern-day descendant of the world's first tourist company, **Thomas Cook** can change foreign currency and most brands of travellers' cheques into Egyptian money. Their central branch at 17 Sharia Bassiouni (daily 8am–5pm; ☎574-3955, fax 576-2750) also sells travellers' cheques in return for dollars or sterling, with no nonsense about cardholders. It will also exchange one hard currency for another in the form of travellers' cheques. However, they have a bad reputation when it comes to lost or stolen travellers' cheques; you may have to kick up a fuss – or even demonstrate outside – to get a full refund.

There are **other branches** of Thomas Cook in the *Semiramis Intercontinental* (☎355-7171 ext 1918); *Mena Palace Hotel* (☎382-2688) near the pyramids; in Heliopolis (7 Sharia Baghda, ☎417-3511); Mohandiseen (10 26th July St, ☎346-7187); and Ma'adi (88 Street 9, Station Square, ☎351-1419).

Money transfers

There are several ways of **transferring money from abroad**. Amex in Sharia Qasr el-Nil will accept instant Moneygram transfers, or you can transfer money through Thomas Cook from any of their offices abroad (see Basics chapter, p.24, for details of both of these). Most banks will transfer money by telex in two working days and charge US$3 for US$1000, regardless of charges paid at the sender's end. They will also usually only deal with their own branches or corresponding banks abroad.

Banks include: Cairo Barclays International Bank (☎354-2195, fax 355-2746, telex 92343 CABAR UN), opposite the AUC on Sharia Qasr al-Aini; The Bank of America at 106 Sharia Qasr al-Aini (☎354-7788, fax 355-5023), with a good reputation for transfers from the US; Citibank, 4 Sharia Ahmed Pasha, Garden City (☎355-1877, fax 355-7743, telex 92162 CITAR UN); Credit Suisse, 32 Sharia Haroun, Dokki (☎348-4777, fax 348-5237, telex 94128 CSCA UN); Banque du Caire, 38 Sharia Abdel Khaliq Sarwat (☎323-2439, fax 391-9080, telex 22898 BDCSR UN).

If you wish to use money received at banks to **buy travellers' cheques** at Thomas Cook or Amex, you must produce a Certificate of Transaction (which you have to request at the issuing bank) rather than an ordinary exchange receipt, proving that your Egyptian currency was legally acquired.

Bureaucracy

Foreigners are no longer required to register with the authorities when entering Egypt; however, any **bureaucratic matters** involving visa extensions, travel permits and the like are almost certain to induce frustration. There's little choice but to relax and go with the flow – we've included some guidelines here to help ease your way through the ordeal.

Visa extensions at the Mugamma

Extending your visa entails visiting the **Mugamma**, that bureaucratic behemoth on Midan Tahrir (Mon–Wed, Sat & Sun 8am–1.30pm, Thurs 8am–12pm & 2–8pm; closed Fri; variable hours during Ramadan). Display patience and good humour when dealing with the Mugamma; only stage a tantrum or nervous breakdown as a last resort. To avoid the crush, arrive first thing in the morning or during the evening shift. Unless you're certain which numbered "window" is currently appropriate (details below may become outmoded), check with the **information** desk on the second floor, before going through the door on your left.

For a six-month **tourist visa extension**, go to desk #50 – accessed via entrance 3 or 4 on the same floor – and pick up a form. You need to provide a photocopy of the page in your passport with your photo on and also the page which carries your original visa – there are copying facilities on the ground floor. Pay the fee (£E8.20) and go to window #28 where your new visa will be issued; you have to pay another £E3.10 for the stamp. Windows #27–29 issue **tourist residence visas**; **re-entry visas** are handled by #16 and #17. In case of lost or stolen passports (see below), replacement entry stamps are obtainable from room #1 & #2; however, these may not pass muster with the Libyan, Syrian or Sudanese consulates.

Travel permits: the Ministry of the Interior

Other matters are dealt with by the **Ministry of the Interior** on Sharia Sheikh Rihan in the Abdin quarter (daily except Fri 9am–2pm; ☎355-6301 or 354-8661), whose Travel Permits Department can grant **permission to travel in restricted areas** (off *piste* in the deep desert; on minor Delta and Sinai roads; between Mersa Matrouh and Libya, or Mersa Allam and the Sudanese border). Applications require two photos and photocopies of the identifying pages of your passport and your Egyptian entry visa; plus a justification for your journey. Processing takes anywhere between four and fourteen days.

Student cards

ISIC student cards are obtainable at Egyptian Student Travel Services, 23 Sharia el-Manial (☎531-0330), on Roda Island. You can get there by walking from El-Malek el-Suleh metro. The card costs £E18, and you'll need one passport photo as well as proof of student status – a letter or ID card from your own university is best. ISIC cards can also be obtained unofficially – at more than double the price – through some of Cairo's budget hotels. You can find out which ones by asking around, but remember there's no guarantee that you won't be sold a fake card.

Passport photos, photocopying and translations

Passport photos can be obtained from the studio in room #99 on the ground floor of the Mugamma (colour £E10, b/w £E5), or from photo booths in places like the *Nile Hilton* and even some metro stations. The best deal is offered by Mitry Colour, 3rd floor, 127 Sharia Ramses (Mon–Sat 9am–9pm), which charges only £E10 for a dozen photos delivered later the same day, or £E4 if you are prepared to wait until the next day to collect them. Another good deal is at the Kodak Shop, 20 Sharia Adly (see "Film and processing"); they have a digital camera system and charge £E15 for twenty photos ready in five minutes – and you can have as many poses as you want.

Several shops along 26th July Street and Sharia Mahmoud (near the AUC Library) advertise **photocopying** services. For cheap **translations**, contact Fouad Nemab downtown (2nd floor, 37 Sharia Qasr el-Nil; Mon–Thurs & Sun, 8.30am–3pm; ☎392-2124) or in Heliopolis (14a Sharia Sherif; ☎256-7808). Hany Eskander, 11 Midan Tahrir (☎575-7331) also does translations and has a PC and laser printer which you can make use of for specific jobs.

Embassies, foreign visas and missing passports

Cairo is a major centre for acquiring visas, and travellers embarking on trans-African or Middle Eastern journeys, or long-distance flights, would do well to sort things out here. Most embassies and consulates are in Garden City, Zamalek, Dokki or Mohandiseen. Since everyday business is handled by consulates rather than embassies, we've listed the former only if there are two separate addresses.

For those applying for **foreign visas**, some countries require you to provide a **letter of recommendation** – which basically approves your visa application – from your own embassy. For some nationalities they're free, while others have to pay through the nose for them.

Lost or stolen passports should be reported to the police as soon as possible. You'll receive a slip of paper indicating the police file number; take this and two photos plus any personal ID to your consulate to apply for a new passport. Then bring this and the police report to the Mugamma for verification of entry (see above). You'll also need to obtain a new Egyptian visa.

Algeria, 14 Sharia Brazil, Zamalek (☎341-8527, fax 341-4158). You need 4 photos, a letter of recommendation and hard cash to get a visa – £E150 for one month and £E180 for three months. Mon, Wed & Sat 9am–2.30pm, Thurs 9am–1pm.

Australia, 11th floor, World Trade Centre, 1191 Corniche el-Nil, Bulaq; 200m north of the 26th July Bridge (☎575-0444, fax 341-4158). Letters of recommendation A$15. Mon–Wed & Sun 9am–12.30pm & 1–4pm, Thurs 8am–1.30pm.

Canada, 3rd floor, 5 Sharia Saraya al-Kubra, Garden City (☎ & fax 354-3110). Letters of recommendation £E24. Daily except Fri 8.30am–4.30pm.

C.A.R., 41 Sharia Mahmoud Aziza, off Sharia Ahmed Orabi (☎349-0865). Two photos but no letter of recommendation required; 24–48hr to issue (roughly FF300). Mon–Fri 9am–2pm.

Cyprus, 23a Sharia Ismail Mohammed, Zamalek (☎341-1288, fax 341-7299). Visas dealt with Mon & Fri only, but most nationalities don't need them. Mon–Fri 8am–3.30pm.

Denmark, 12 Sharia Hassan Sabri, Zamalek (☎340-2502 or 340-7411, fax 341-1780). Letters of recommendation £E75. Mon–Thurs & Sun 9am–2pm.

Eritrea, 13 Sharia Mohammed Shafi, Mohandiseen (☎303-0517, fax 303-0516). Two photos and letter of recommendation required, and usually an onward ticket. Visas £E135. Daily except Fri 8am–2pm.

Ethiopia, 6 Sharia Rahman Hussein, Dokki (☎335-3696, fax 335-3699). One photo, a letter of recommendation and an onward ticket (or at least a booking, which you can cancel) are required. Visas (US$63, though US citizens pay US$70) are issued in 24–48hr, or same day if you get there before 10am. Mon–Thurs & Sat 8am–2pm.

Germany, 8b Sharia Aziz Abaza, Zamalek (☎341-0015, fax 341-0530, visa section ☎340-1076). Letters of recommendation DM20. Mon–Fri 8am–2pm.

India, 2nd floor, 37 Talaat Harb (☎393-9152, fax 393-6702). Two photos and letter of recommendation required; visas (£E102 for 6 months) issued within 2–3 days. Special permits for places like Sikkim not issued. Mon–Thurs & Sun 9.30am–12.30pm.

Ireland, 7th floor, Abu el-Feda Tower, just north of the Zamalek Bridge, Zamalek (☎340-8264, fax 341-2863). Free letters of recommendation. Mon–Thurs & Sun 9am–noon.

Israel, 6 Sharia Ibn Malek, Giza; near the El-Gama'a Bridge (☎361-0380, fax 361-0414). Look for the security guards at the entrance or the Israeli flag flying aloft. Most foreigners can, in fact, obtain tourist visas at the border. Mon–Thurs & Sun 10.30am–12.30pm.

Jordan, 6 Sharia Gohini, Dokki, 2 blocks west of the *Sheraton* (☎349-9912, fax 360-1027). No letter of recommendation needed; visas issued same day if you apply before noon – bring along one photo. Free for Australians, but not Brits and other EU citizens (£E63), US citizens (£E231) or Canadians (£E91). Mon–Thurs & Sun 9am–noon.

Kenya, 7 Sharia Muhandes Galal, off Sharia Libnan, Mohandiseen (☎345-3628, fax 344-3400). One-month single-entry visas (usually free) issued in 24hr (use in 3 months); two photos and correct change required – for a two-month visa they'll ask for £E178. Winter Mon–Fri 8.30am–2.30pm, summer 8am–2pm; closed Egyptian and Kenyan public holidays.

Lebanon, 5 Sharia Ahmed Nassim, Giza (entrance on Corniche; ☎361-0623, fax 361-0463). Letter of recommendation, a photo and 3 passport photocopies required; takes 3 days. Mon–Fri 9.30am–12.30pm.

Libya, 7 Sharia Saleh el-Ayoub, Zamalek (☎340-1865, fax 340-0072). Visas generally only issued to Egyptian residents, but they may be open to persuasion if you have an invitation from someone in Libya. Americans are forbidden to visit Libya by the US State Department. Two photos, a letter of recommendation and a stamp in your passport giving its details in Arabic are required; most embassies supply one free, except Britain (£E25; see p.237 for cheaper translations). Daily except Fri 9am–2pm.

Netherlands, 18 Sharia Hassan Sabry, Zamalek (☎340-1936, fax 341-5249). Letters of recommendation £E12.

New Zealand, "represented' in Cairo by the UK (see below). Mon–Thurs & Sun 8am–3.30pm.

Norway, 8 Sharia al-Gezira, Zamalek (☎341-3955, fax 342-0709). Letters of recommendation free. Mon–Thurs & Sun 8.30am–3.30pm.

Saudi Arabia, 2 Sharia Ahmed Nessim, Giza (☎349-0775, fax 349-4590). Transit visas issued the same day provided you already have a visa for your next destination (for example, Yemen) plus a letter of recommendation from your embassy. Mon–Wed, Sat & Sun 8.30–11.30am.

South Africa, 18th floor, 21–23 Giza (☎571-7238 or 571-7239, fax 571-7241). Mon–Thurs & Sun 9am–noon. Letter of recommendation free.

Spain, 41 Sharia Ismail Mohamed, Zamalek (☎340-6397, fax 340-3685). Mon–Fri 9am–3pm.

Sudan, 1 Sharia Mohammed Fahmi el-Sayed, Garden City – see central Cairo map on p.92 (☎354-9661, fax 354-2693). Five photos and a letter of recommendation needed; visas (US$50 cash only) take between 14 days and a month to process: it *may* be possible to get 2-week transit visas faster, but you have to ask specially. Daily except Fri 9am–1pm.

Sweden, 13 Sharia Mohammed Mazhar, Zamalek (☎341-4132, fax 340-4357). Charges £E55 for a letter of recommendation. Mon, Wed, Thurs & Sun 9–11am.

Syria, 3 Sharia el-Ibrahimi (☎337-7020, fax 335-8232). Prices and requirements for visitors vary: high for Brits (£E198) and Americans (£E136), but no letter of recommendation needed; cheaper for Australians (£E20) and free for Canadians, but letters of recommendation required. Two photos needed for all. Visas take 1–3 days to issue. Daily except Fri 9am–2pm (Ramadan 9am–1pm).

Tunisia, 26 Sharia Gezira, Zamalek (☎341-8962, fax 341-2479). Passport photocopy, 2 photos and a letter of recommendation required: visas (£E23) take 15 days, but can be obtained routinely at the border by those Western nationals who need them. Daily except Fri 10am–1pm.

Turkey, 25 Sharia Falaki, Bab al-Luq (☎356-3318, fax 355-8110). Most Western nationals apart from Australians don't require visas; British and Irish citizens can obtain them routinely on arrival. Mon–Fri 9–11am.

Uganda, 9 Midan al-Misaha, Dokki (☎348-5544, fax 348-5980). Mon–Fri 8.30am–2.30pm (Ramadan 8.30am–1.30pm). Ask for latest requirements; visa currently £E100.

UK, 7 Sharia Ahmed Ragheb, Garden City (☎354-0852, fax 354-0859). Really only interested in helping business people. Charges £25 sterling for each letter of recommendation. Also grudgingly "looks after" New Zealand nationals. Mon–Wed & Sun 8.30am–1.30pm.

United States, 5 Sharia Amerika Latina, Garden City (☎355-7371, fax 357-2300) – see map of central Cairo (p.92). Lost or stolen passports replaced overnight for £E216; limited passports issued for travel to Israel on request. Letters of recommendation free. Mon–Thurs & Sun 8am–noon.

Yemen, 28 Sharia Amin Bey al-Rafi'i, off Midan al-Misaha, Dokki (☎361-4224, fax 360-4815). Letter of recommendation and 2 photos required; visas (£E130) issued in 24hr if applied for early. Mon–Thurs & Sun 9am–1pm (Ramadan 10am–1.30pm).

Zaire, 5 Sharisa Mansur Mohammed, Zamalek (☎340-3662 or 341-1069, fax 340-4342). Visas cost £E300 for a 1-month single entry – enquire at consulate for longer stays. Two photos and a letter of recommendation required. Mon–Fri 10am–1pm.

Cultural centres, clubs and language courses

Cultural centres are good for catching up on home news and making contacts; longer-staying visitors can join their libraries and sign up for **language courses**. Other courses are on offer at AUC Public Service Division, 28 Sharia Falaki (☎357-6873 or 357-6872, *hamgiagi@aucegypt.edu*), and the International Language Institute (ILI), 2 Sharia Mohammed Bayoumi, off Sharia Merghani, Heliopolis (☎418-9212 or 291-9295, *ili@ritsec3.com.eg*). **Private tutors** advertise in all these places. To find out about public lectures at the AUC, contact Mona Zaki (Oct–May; ☎357-5021, *monazaki@aucegypt.edu*).

Institutes

American Research Center in Egypt, 1st floor, 2 Midan Simon Bolivar, Garden City (☎354-8239). Organizes lectures and day-trips.

British Council, 192 Corniche el-Nil, Aguza; near the Circus (☎344-8445, *www.britcoun.org.eg/*). Large library (annual membership £E40), including videos and cassettes. Also sponsors visiting cultural acts. Mon–Thurs & Sat 9am–2pm & 3–7.30pm, Fri 9am–2pm.

Canadian Research Center, 32 Road 103, Ma'adi (☎350-7214). Monthly lectures. Oct–April Mon–Thurs & Sun 8.30am–4pm.

Egyptian Centre for International Cultural Cooperation (ECIC), 11 Sharia Shagar al-Durr, Zamalek (☎341-5419). Organizes Arabic classes, exhibitions, recitals and occasionally tours. Daily except Fri 10am–1pm & 5–7pm.

Goethe Institute, 2nd floor, 2 Sharia el-Bustan (just off Tahrir) (☎575-9877). Public reading room; library membership and borrowing rights with ID. Mon–Thurs 1–7pm, Fri 8am–noon.

Israeli Academic Centre in Cairo, 92 Sharia el-Nil, Dokki (☎348-8995). Lectures. Mon–Thurs & Sun 9am–3pm.

Netherlands Flemish-Institute, 1 Sharia Mahmoud Azmi, Zamalek (☎340-0076, *nvic@rite.com*). English lectures about Egypt on Thurs at 5.30pm (Sept–June). Mon–Fri 9am–2pm.

Health care

For minor complaints, simply consult the nearest **pharmacy**; pharmacists can prescribe a wide range of drugs, including antibiotics. There are a number of 24-hour pharmacies, including: Al-Ezabi, 1 Sharia Ahmed Taysir, Heliopolis (☎415-3409); As-Salam International Hospital, Ma'adi (see below); Seif, 76 Sharia Qasr el-Aini, Garden City (☎354-2678).

There are English- or French-speaking **private doctors** all over Cairo. A consultation normally costs £E40–50, excluding drugs. Some practices that are used to foreign patients include: Dr Naguib Badir at the Anglo-American Hospital, next to the Cairo Tower on Gezira Island (general practice; ☎340-6162); Dr Doss or Dr Emad Rushdi, *Nile Hilton Hotel* clinic (☎578-0444); Dr Zoheir Farid, 16 Abdel Khaliq Sarwat (tropical medicine; ☎392-5023).

Hospitals require a cash deposit of at least £E150 (it can go as high as £E1000) to cover the cost of treatment; medical insurance is *not* accepted (though you can reclaim expenses later). The following are well equipped and used to foreigners: Anglo-American Hospital (see above for address; ☎341-8630); As-Salam International Hospital, on the Corniche to Ma'adi (☎363-8050 or 363-4196 or 363-8424); Cairo Medical Centre, on Sharia Higaz, by the *Andalus* restaurant, just off Midan Roxi, Heliopolis (☎258-1206 or 258-0566). For any of these hospitals, take a taxi if you can; otherwise use the private **As-Salam ambulance service** (same phone numbers as the hospital). **Public ambulances** offer free transport to whichever hospital is the nearest: call ☎123.

There are two places that provide **vaccinations** against cholera, yellow fever and other diseases. The Egyptian Organization for Biological Products and Vaccines, at 51 Sharia Wazart el-Zaraa (☎348-3205; daily 24hr), 100m north of the 6th October Bridge/Agricultural Museum intersection – take the first right inside the gate, then go round the side of the building on the left and up the stairs. It has English-speaking doctors and vaccines against cholera (£E6.65 for 10 doses), yellow fever (£E30.75) and meningitis (£E15.50), with a £E5 charge for the certificate. The Public Health Vaccination Centre (daily except Fri 10am–1pm & 6–7.30pm), at the rear of the lobby of the *Hotel Continental-Savoy* on Midan Opera, is highly efficient, with no red tape or fuss. They do cholera (£E1.50) and yellow fever, but not meningitis. If you need a **dentist**, try Dr Amr Waguih (☎310-8574) whose clinic is in Mohandiseen.

Post and phones

The **central post office** on Midan Ataba (daily except Fri 8am–6pm; during Ramadan daily 9am–4pm) and other main branches (daily except Fri 8.30am–3pm; during Ramadan daily 9am–3pm) are often extremely crowded. Mail can be sent to Ataba's **poste restante** (daily except Fri 8am–6pm, Fri 8am–noon; Ramadan 9am–4pm; Poste Restante, Post Office Ataba, 11511 Cairo). Go to counter #10 (signposted "Private boxes"), where they hold mail for a month, with no charge to collect – just be sure to bring your passport. They are prone to file letters under the wrong name, but it helps if your surname is underlined and highlighted on anything sent to you. Problems are less likely to occur if you have mail sent **c/o American Express** on Sharia Qasr el-Nil (see p.235); however, this service is only for holders of Amex cards or Amex travellers' cheques.

Although letters posted in the lobby of the *Nile Hilton* are said to arrive faster than those dropped in ordinary mailboxes (painted blue for overseas mail), **airmail letters** can still take two weeks to reach Europe, and three weeks to the US. However, Ataba's **express mail service** – opposite the Poste Restante – (daily except Fri 8am–7pm) promises delivery to Europe and the US in two days; items under 100 grammes cost £E38–50, plus a dubious £E5 charge for "customs-clearing". Any post office can send **registered letters**. It's quicker to buy **stamps** from hotel shops or cigarette kiosks, which charge about 5pt above normal rates (£E1.25 for a postcard/letter to anywhere in the world).

Parcels can only be sent abroad from the Ramses Square post office, where unsealed packages must be inspected by customs before weighing and sealing. The overseas rate is about £E4 a kilo. Anyone **receiving parcels** in Egypt should beware of **import duty** (for example, £E40 on a pair of contact lenses). If you really want to be sure of receiving a pakage, DHL couriers have an office in Garden City at 21 Gamal el-Abu el-Maasen (☎355-7301).

Phones

Cairo's telephone system has undergone major restructuring in recent years, with new exchange numbers and/or extra digits being introduced. A few older places may still have six-digit numbers, but most are now seven digits.

International calls can now be made using phonecards (see Basics p.54) at Menatel and Nile kiosks, or the orange direct-dial phones installed at Cairo's main **telephone and telegraph offices** (open 24hr) and other locations. There are four main offices: at 8 Sharia Adly; alongside the *Windsor Hotel* on Alfi Bey; on Sharia Ramses, opposite Sharia Tawfiqia; and 13 Midan Tahrir (the smallest). There are others further afield, sometimes worth trying if you want to avoid queuing; for example, the one on Sharia Maglis al-Shad, by the National Assembly (ten minutes south of Midan Tahrir). However, it remains slightly cheaper to make calls at a telephone office in the old way rather than the phonecard kiosks or hotel. Calls are booked and paid for in advance, and can either be taken in a booth or directed to an outside number such as a hotel.

Select locations in Cairo also boast special phones for **direct dialling** to a specific country: **USA Direct** phones at American Express on Sharia Qasr el-Nil, and in the *Marriott, Ramses Hilton, Nile Hilton* and *Semiramis* hotels; and **BT Direct** phones in the British Airways office on Midan Tahrir. These are the only phones in Egypt that allow **credit card and collect calls**. You can also make calls over the **Internet** using the net2phone and MediaRing systems – so far only available at the *Berlin Hotel*, which charges £E3 a minute to anywhere in the world.

Telegrams, telexes and faxes

Telephone offices can also send **telegrams**, which you pay for by the word (including the address) – 60pt a word to the US, for example. Like the 24-hour **telegraph and telex office** on Midan Ataba (opposite the post office), they also handle **telexes**.

Faxes can be sent and received at the four downtown telephone offices (open 24hr); the EMS office by Ataba post office (daily except Fri 8am–7pm); the *Grand Hotel* (daily except Thurs 8am–4pm) on 26th July; or the *Berlin Hotel* (daily 8pm–11pm) on Sharia Qasr el-Nil. The EMS office offers the lowest sending rates per page (UK & US £E13.20; Australasia £E19.80), but it is cheaper to receive one-page faxes at the *Grand Hotel* (£E3 per page) or American Express (free for Amex clients). Phone offices charge £E8.25 a minute to send or receive a fax and, along with EMS, will inform you of its arrival if your name and phone number are at the top of the page. Fax numbers: Amex (☎574-7997); EMS (☎393-4807); *Grand Hotel* (☎575-7593); *Berlin Hotel* (☎395-7502); downtown telephone offices at Sharia Adly (☎393-3909), Sharia Ramses (☎578-0977), Alfi Bey (☎589-7662) and Midan Tahrir (☎578-0979).

EXCURSIONS FROM CAIRO

The Nile Valley – most people's target after Cairo – is too distant for **day excursions** from the city. Elsewhere, however, you can choose between a jaunt to the seaside or remoter pyramids, a river trip or desert monasteries – and still be back in Cairo the same night. The notes below are an outline of possibilities and are intended (with the exception of the entries on the Nile Barrages and Muqattam Hills) to be used in conjunction with the full accounts in other chapters.

THE NILE BARRAGES AT QANATIR

Roughly 20km downriver from Cairo, the Nile divides into two great branches which define the Delta, whose flow is controlled by the **Nile Barrages** at **Qanatir**. Decoratively arched and turreted, this splendid piece of Victorian civil engineering is surrounded by shady parks and lush islets – an ideal spot for a picnic.

Originally conceived by Mohammed Ali's French hydro-engineer, Mougel Bey, the Barrages were later realized as part of the nationwide hydrological system designed by Sir Colin Scott-Moncrieff. At the eastern end of the 438-metre-long Rosetta Barrage lies the *Istarahah al-Qanatir* or **Presidential Villa** that Islamic Jihad once considered attacking with an anti-aircraft cannon from the garden of one of their member's homes, across the river. Egypt's **State Yacht** (originally King Farouk's, on which he sailed into exile) is often moored at the quay.

Providing you don't come on Friday, when the area is ridiculously crowded, the Barrages make a pleasant excursion. Qanatir is accessible by bus #210 from the *Nile Hilton* terminal on Midan Tahrir, or by ferry from the Maspero Dock in front of the Television Building. Ferries leave hourly (6am–6pm; £E1.50) on Friday and Sunday and take two hours; or you can take a pleasure boat (daily round trips; £E5) to the south of Maspero Dock; the bus journey is less appealing. Travelling by felucca is very slow, since the mast has to be lowered at every bridge.

THE MUQATTAM HILLS AND WADI DIGLA

The **Muqattam Hills**, rising beyond Cairo, are seldom visited by tourists but readily accessible by #401 buses from Midan Ataba and Tahrir. Zigzagging up the hillside past caves and quarries, ruined shrines and guarded outposts, they terminate at **Medinet Muqattam**, an upmarket suburb whose avenues are flanked by villas and casinos. The Muqattam Corniche, circling the edge of the plateau, offers spectacular views across the Citadel and most of Cairo – an unforgettable vista at sunset.

People planning desert expeditions might consider a few training runs below the Muqattam. Victorian travellers used to engage a dragoman to lead them to the **Petrified Forests** – two expanses littered with broken, fossilized trunks, thought to date from the Miocene Period. The larger one (marked on our map of Greater Cairo) is really only accessible with a guide, but would-be explorers can easily find the "Little Forest" on the Jebel el-Khasab plateau, north of the Digla–Ain Sukhna road.

The **Digla–Ain Sukhna road** turns east off the Nile Valley expressway near a *zebaleen* village beyond Ma'adi. Roughly 25km from the turn-off, you'll pass the Jebel el-Khasab on the left; if you keep on, you'll notice various tracks leading off to the right, which eventually converge on a main desert track running east–west. By following it west, back towards Digla, you'll pass through several meandering wadis before the way is blocked by **Wadi Digla**. This miniature canyon is good for **rock-climbing** and **bird-watching**; bring water, food and shade.

THE FAYOUM

Fayoum Oasis, 100km southwest of Cairo, is another place to escape. Though Fayoum City holds little appeal, you can walk from its centre into lush countryside within half an hour. Irrigated by water wheels and canals, the Fayoum was a major centre during the Middle Kingdom, Ptolemaic and Roman times, as evinced by various ruins around its periphery. While some involve bumpy rides into the desert, others are reasonably accessible from Fayoum City by local bus or *service* taxi, with a pleasant walk to the site itself. The **ruins of Karanis** lie just off the Fayoum–Cairo road; the dramatic **"Collapsed Pyramid" of Maidum** a short ride from El-Wasta. Both sites are usually deserted, in blissful contrast to Giza and Saqqara. Either makes a good day excursion, but you should bring food and drink and be on your way by mid-morning. *Service* taxis from Midan Giza are the fastest way of reaching Fayoum City (2hr). See p.419 in Chapter Three for details.

ALEXANDRIA AND THE MONASTERIES OF WADI NATRUN

A three-hour journey from Cairo, Egypt's second city and summer capital embraces the Mediterranean with its sweeping Corniche. **Alexandria** has little to show for its ancient glory (personified by Cleopatra) or former decadence (celebrated by Lawrence Durrell), but its fresh seafood and cool breezes are delightful. However, with the discovery of Cleopatra's Palace on the ocean floor in Alex's Eastern Harbour (see p.496 for details), there may soon be more to occupy visitors to Alex than a quick spin through the Greco-Roman museum and a literary pilgrimage around the haunts of Durrell, E.M. Forster and the poet Constantine Cavafy. The world's first underwater museum is planned for the remains of the royal enclosure, although it may be a few years before this comes to fruition. Alex can be reached by bus, train or *service* taxi. For details, see p.482 in Chapter Four.

The Desert Road to Alex passes the turn-off for the fortified **Monasteries of Wadi Natrun**, which have long provided the Coptic Church's spiritual leadership. When not undergoing periodic fasts, the monks welcome pilgrims and other visitors. The most accessible of the monasteries are **Deir Anba Bishoi** and **Deir al-Suryani**, 10km from the rest stop on the highway (which can be reached by bus or *service* taxi from Cairo). To visit all four, it's best to rent a taxi or car for the day, either in Cairo or at the rest stop, which is roughly midway between Alexandria and Cairo. For more on Wadi Natrun and how to get there, see p.415 in Chapter Three.

Unless you start very early or have a car, it's not really feasible to visit both Alexandria and the monasteries in one day.

ISMAILIYA, AIN SUKHNA AND THE RED SEA MONASTERIES

The canal city of **Ismailiya** is verdantly peaceful, with handsome promenades and colonial-era villas – a nice place to stroll or bicycle, also favoured by Egyptians as a honeymoon destination. Its museum and Garden of Stelae attest to ancient canals that once linked the Delta with the Red Sea; the House of Ferdinand de Lesseps commemorates the founder of the Suez Canal, one of the world's crucial waterways. Outside town you can watch boats slip between the desert on either side. Along the eastern embankment runs the Bar-Lev Line, a fortified Israeli barrier that was stormed on the first day of the 1973 war. Ismailiya itself can be reached by bus or *service* taxi from Cairo's Koulali Terminal (2–3hr). For details, see Chapter Six (p.542).

Cairenes with transport visit **Ain Sukhna** on the Gulf of Suez for its **beaches** and offshore coral reefs. If you fancy swimming and **snorkelling**, it's worth renting a car for the day rather than switching buses at Suez and having to hitch back. Bring food and drink (plus snorkel if required), since they're not obtainable there. Don't wander into areas ringed by barbed wire, which are still mined. Ain Sukhna is approachable via Suez (3hr) or by the Digla–Ain Sukhna desert road (see opposite). Further south and high inland are the **Red Sea Monasteries** of St Paul and St Anthony. With a car, you could combine a visit to St Anthony's with a swim at Ain Sukhna, but unless you leave at the crack of dawn it's impossible to get to both monasteries and return the same night. All three places are described in Chapter Eight.

travel details

Cairo is the linchpin of Egypt's transport network and its main link to the outside world. Many parts of the country are accessible from the capital by several forms of transport, while numerous airlines compete over flights to Europe, Africa and Asia.

TRAINS

Virtually all trains depart from **Ramses Station** (*Mahatat Ramses*), a cavernous beehive seemingly designed to bemuse. Almost all trains to points south halt at **Giza Station** 15min after leaving Ramses.

Ramses Station

Entering **Ramses Station** from Ramses Square, you'll find the tourist information office, tourist police, *wagons-lits* and sleeper booking offices on the left; through to your right are the platforms serving Alexandria, the Delta and Canal Zone. Tickets for these destinations are sold at the rear, left-hand side of the main hall, where a round **information** kiosk should be able to advise on muddles, rescheduling and other problems (although you may need to fall back on the tourist office if no one in the information booth can speak English). Card-carrying members of the Tourist Friends Association may also approach you, offering to help; they're quite sincere and don't expect *baksheesh*.

Through the back of the hall are platforms 8–11, for southbound trains to Upper Egypt, linked by an underpass to the ticket offices beyond platform 11.

Tickets

Buying tickets is rarely easy. Both sets of ticket offices have separate windows for 1st class/2nd class superior seating (which is reservable and has A/C) and ordinary 2nd class/3rd class (which isn't and doesn't); the placement of these windows varies from day to day. You have to find the right queue and get your requirements (it helps to have them written down in Arabic) across to clerks who may not give a damn. Tickets can be booked up to a week in advance and should be booked at least a day in advance; 1st and 2nd class superior seats sell out first. The peak seasons for travel are winter (for Upper Egypt) and summer (for Alexandria).

Card-carrying **students** are eligible for 30 percent **reductions** on all trains except sleepers and *wagons-lits*, which must be booked at their own counters in the main hall. Prices given below are full adult fares.

Regular services and sleepers

As **timetables in English** are not on sale at present, you'll have to hope that schedules are posted in the station, or worm the information out of someone. All **services** are individually numbered, and the number should be written on your ticket when you reserve a seat. Foreigners are not encouraged to buy ordinary 2nd or 3rd class tickets, and strongly discouraged from using anything but the official tourist trains (see below).

There are four kinds of trains **to Alexandria**. The fastest are the Turbini services (leaving around 8am & 7pm; 2hr 20min) and trains belonging to the French line (3 daily between 9am and 6pm; 2hr 20min), followed by the slightly cheaper tourist trains (noon & 10.30pm; 2hr 30min); all are fully air-conditioned and require reservations. Lastly, there are regular trains, composed only of 2nd and 3rd class, which leave every ninety minutes or so and don't need reservations. Prices on all trains except the Turbini and French line are: 1st class £E20, A/C 2nd class £E12, non-A/C 2nd class £E5.50, 3rd class £E2.50.

Although there are nine daily departures for **Aswan** (14–17hr) and five more for **Luxor** (11–12hr), at present tourists are only authorized to use two of these trains (departing at 7.30am & 10pm) and are placed in special coaches guarded by armed plainclothes policemen. Tourists may not be allowed to buy tickets for any other train. In principle this is for protection from "terrorists", but it does tend to make the tourist trains potential targets for snipers, who have been known to take pot-shots at them on their way through Middle Egypt (see box on p.258). Fares for ordinary seats (not sleeping berths) are £E51 in 1st class and £E31 in 2nd for Luxor, £E63 and £E37 for Aswan.

With no direct A/C services **to Mersa Matrouh**, it is better to spend extra on a *wagons-lit* or travel by bus instead (see below) rather than endure the interminable journey (up to 24hr!) in non-A/C 2nd (£E4.50) or 3rd class (£E2.50).

Wagons-lits services

In addition to regular services, there are daily **wagons-lits** services (8pm) to **Upper Egypt**, which include a bar and disco on the train. The cost per person for a double cabin is £E314.50 to Luxor or Aswan (£E579 return). Solo travellers can reserve the entire cabin for £E435, or consent to share it with a stranger of the same sex and pay the normal fare. Although these services are much more comfortable than the other "tourist" trains, they are also regular targets for gunmen and are probably best avoided. During summer, there are also thrice-weekly *wagons-lits* to **Mersa Matrouh** (Mon, Fri & Sat; £E270 per person).

The Ramses *wagons-lits* **bookings office** is notoriously bloody-minded: they'll happily announce that everything's booked solid for the next fortnight, while denying that one can reserve more than seven days ahead. You can, in fact, do this at their branch in the *Helnan Shepheard* hotel (daily 8.30am–4.30pm), or at their main offices: 2 Sharia Ibrahim el-Lakani, Heliopolis (☎257-4297), and 48 Sharia el-Giza, Giza (☎348-7354 or 349-2536). Bring the passports of everyone travelling with you.

INTER-CITY BUSES

Inter-city buses reach most parts of Egypt, making equal or better time than trains. Vehicles range from sleek A/C Superjet buses serving overpriced snacks to battered rattletraps missing panes of glass; a lot of nominally A/C services are actually ventilated by ill-fitting rear doors. Services depart from several terminals, none of which will take **bookings** over the phone; tickets must be purchased in person. Unless stated otherwise, all services below run daily; however, **schedules** change, so you shouldn't rely on our timings. Since Cairo's bus terminals are undergoing major restructuring, don't rely on them staying in the same place either – ask as many people as possible, and take the majority decision. If in doubt, the **Turgoman Garage** should be the first place to enquire, although the least expensive (and least comfortable) buses start from the **Ahmed Helmi Terminal**. You can usually only get information on the spot, but wherever possible we've listed telephone numbers; whether you can get hold of someone who speaks English is of course another matter. As with most things in Egypt, persevere and you'll get there in the end.

Turgoman Garage

In theory, the new **Turgoman Garage** in Bulaq – 600m west of Ramses Station – will handle the majority of A/C (and many non-A/C) buses to destinations within Egypt. At present, Turgoman is basically a small tract of desert with six huts for ticket offices. Hopefully, as it's developed further, this new terminal will make getting a bus out of Cairo relatively hassle-free.

Two companies operate services **to Alexandria**; the smart A/C Superjet (☎579-8181) buses leave every 30min (6am–10pm; 2hr 30min–3hr; £E20), while West Delta Bus Co (☎576-5582) services leave hourly (5.30am–midnight; 3hrs; £E16–20). The West Delta Bus Co also has four daily departures **to Mersa Matrouh** (3hr; £E25–35).

Superjet and the Upper Egypt Bus Co (☎576-0261) both have services to **Hurghada** (4 daily each; 5–6hr; £E45), the latter also serving **Luxor** (2 daily; 9hr; £E50) and **Aswan** (2 daily; 12hr; £E55). However, the train is similarly priced and much more comfortable.

Other buses from here include East Delta Bus Co (☎576-2293) services to **Dahab** (4 daily; 9hr; £E55; £E75 for overnight bus), **St Catherine's** (1 daily; 7hr 30min; £E35) and **Sharm el-Sheikh** (6 daily; 7hr 30min; £E50 or £E65 for overnight bus). Superjet have a fast daily bus to Sharm el-Sheikh (5hr; £E55), as well as ten buses daily to **Port Said** (3hr; £E15).

East Delta buses depart every 30–40min (between 6.30am and 9.30pm) to: **Port Said** (3hr; £E12), **Suez** (1hr 30min–2hr; £E6), **Ismailiya** (2hr; £E6.50) and **El-Mansura** (2hr 30min; £E8.50); hourly services go to **Damietta** (3hr 30min; £E15) and **Ras el-Bahr** (3hr; £E18). **Nuweiba** (3 daily; 9hr; £E50), **Taba** (3 daily; 10hr; £E70) and **El-Arish** (4 daily; 5hr; £E35) are also covered by East Delta. The other company operating from here is the Middle Delta Bus Co, which runs services to smaller Delta destinations such as **El-Mahalla** (7 daily; 2hr; £E7) and **Tanta** (hourly, 7am–9pm; 1hr 30min; £E6) among others – though many more go from the **Aboud Bus Station** (see below).

Also from here, dusty government-run buses embark on lengthy journeys to the **Western Desert Oases** (excluding Siwa, which is reached from Mersa Matrouh or Alexandria). Except on Friday, when there is only one, there are four daily departures to the **Bahariya Oasis** (6hr; £E12–18), two of which (on Mon, Thurs & Sat only) continue to **Farafra Oasis** (8hr; £E25). A/C buses for **Kharga Oasis** (10hr; £E21–35) via Assyut also depart four times daily, with two continuing on to **Dakhla Oasis** (14–16hr; £E42). It's best to buy tickets for government-run bus services two days beforehand, and be sure to bring food and drink for the journey as refreshment stops may be infrequent or non-existent.

There are currently no city buses that go to Turgoman Garage; your best option is to take a taxi (£E1.50 from Ramses Station or £E3–5 from downtown).

Aboud Bus Station

The **Aboud Bus Station**, 500m north of Ramses station by the Sharia Shubra and Sharia Ahmed Helmi intersection, has many services to **Middle Egypt**. The West Delta Co (☎431-6742) covers **Minya** (hourly 7.30am–midnight; 4hrs; £E11), **Assyut** (hourly 6.30am–1am; 6–7hrs; £E18–20), **Sohag** (hourly 6.30am–1am; 8–9hrs; £E18–21) and **Qena** (hourly 6.30am–1am; 9–10hrs; £E19–21). There are also East Delta (☎431-6723) services to **Zagazig** (every 30min 6am–10pm; 1hr 30min; £E5.50), **Faqus** (hourly 6.30am–7pm; 2hr) and **Benha** (every 30min 6am–8pm; 1hr; £E2.50). To get here, take bus #24 or #176 from Ataba, bus #34 from Tahrir; otherwise a taxi will cost around £E2 from Ramses Station, £E5–6 from downtown.

Sinai (Abbassiya) Bus Terminal

While the **Sinai Bus Terminal** (☎482-4753) will doubtless continue serving **all parts of the Sinai Peninsula**, schedules and prices change so rapidly that it's impossible to predict either with any accuracy. When last heard, East Delta buses ran from here to **Sharm el-Sheikh** (10 daily; 7hr; £E35–65); **Dahab** (4 daily; 9hr; £E55, £E75 for the overnight bus); **Nuweiba** (2 daily; 9hr; £E50–55), continuing to **Taba** (10hr; £E50–70); the morning bus bus goes via **St Catherine's Monastery** (7hr 30min; £E35). For those on tight budgets, the cheapest way to reach Sinai is to take a *service* taxi to Suez, and then a bus on from there (see p.538), or a direct service minibus from Ahmed Helmi Terminal.

All seats should be booked the day before. You can reach the terminal by bus (for details of bus numbers see p.81) – look for the yellow billboard 500m beyond the Misr Travel Tower in Cairo's Abbassiya district.

Ahmed Helmi Terminal

The **Ahmed Helmi Terminal** behind Ramses Station (see map on p.111) is more noticeable for its *service* taxis than for the muddy yard screened by fruit stalls that is used by the bus companies. **Non-A/C buses** depart from here to **most destinations within Egypt** except the oases, with prices considerably lower than the equivalent A/C services. This is also where the eleven-seater *service* minibuses fill up for destinations in the **Sinai** and **Red Sea Coast**. As with *service* taxis, check to see what other passengers are paying before handing over your cash.

Koulali terminal:
Canal Zone and the Delta

From beside Ramses Station (see map p.111) the **Koulali Terminal** (also notable for its *service* taxis) is a second Cairo stop for the East Delta buses that cover the **Canal Cities** and much of the **Delta**, picking up extra passengers after setting out from Turgoman. It's unclear what the future holds for this terminal, but at present the buses still stop here.

INTERNATIONAL BUSES

International buses are highly vulnerable to political upheavals, so none of the schedules and fares mentioned below can be taken for granted – double-check everything, including the availability of foreign visas (see p.237).

Of most interest to tourists are the services **to Tel Aviv and Jerusalem** – an 11–12hr journey via El-Arish and Rafah, skirting most of the Gaza Strip. Travco (13 Sharia Mahmoud Azmi, near the *Marriott Hotel*, Zamalek; daily 9am–4pm; Ramadan 9am–3.30pm; ☎340-4493) runs a service to both cities, departing from the *Cairo Sheraton* in Dokki at 5.30am (daily except Sat; £E120 one-way, £E160 return). Tickets are also available from Spring Tours (11 Sharia Talaat Harb; ☎393-2573) and Misr Travel (7 Sharia Talaat Harb; ☎393-0201). Note that at the border you'll be stung for £E17 departure tax as well as £E10 for the shuttle bus from the Egyptian immigration hall to the Israeli one.

Less well known are the Superjet services **to Jordan, Syria, Saudi Arabia and Libya** from Midan Almaza in Heliopolis (take minibus #39 to the end of the line). Tickets can be bought from their office here (☎290-9017). There are departures for **Amman** (3 weekly; 20hr;US$67 including ferry crossing), **Damascus** (1 weekly service; 20hr; US$80), and **Tripoli** (daily; 30hr; US$86) via **Benghazi** (18hr; US$68). Note that these services may run from Turgoman Garage in the future.

Various destinations in **the Gulf** and Libya can be reached from Sinai Bus Terminal via Nuweiba-Aqaba: for **Kuwait**, **Jeddah** and **Riyadh**, contact the East Delta Bus Co (☎419-8503), who also run daily services to Benghazi and Tripoli (£E100 & £E180). There are also plusher A/C buses to Benghazi (daily; 16hr; £E120), leaving from Midan Ataba. Buy tickets from Hebton Misr Travel (☎590-0963), which also runs cheaper *service* taxis to the same destinations (see below).

INTER-CITY SERVICE TAXIS

If you don't mind a slightly cramped and definitely hair-raising journey, **service taxis** (and their slightly cheaper relatives the *service* minibuses) are usually the fastest way to reach a host of destinations. Their biggest advantage is that they leave as soon as they're full; just turn up, and you'll probably be away in 15min (morning and late afternoon are prime times).

Drivers drum up custom by shouting out their destinations; anybody can point you towards the right taxi(s) for your destination. Prices are posted in Arabic on the windscreen; **fares** to specific destinations are detailed in subsequent chapters, but generally work out 20–30 percent above the bus fare. Watch what Egyptians pay and you can hardly go wrong. If you're alighting halfway (for example, at Wadi Natrun, along the Desert Road to Alex), it's normal to pay the full fare.

The map on p.111 gives an idea of *service* depots around the **Koulali and Ahmed Helmi terminals**, which serve the **Delta** and **Canal Zone**, **Alexandria** and the **Mediterranean coast** (including El-Arish), the **Red Sea Coast** down to Hurghada and the **Nile Valley** as far south as Minya (5hr) or Assyut (6hr), from where there are connections further south. If in doubt about which depot to go to, try Ahmed Helmi first. A third terminal on **Midan Giza** serves the Fayoum (£E6); *service* taxis to El-Badrashein (for Saqqara) and Dahshur depart from **Giza Station** nearby; while at least one vehicle a day departs from the **Wahia Café**, 28 Sharia Qadry, in Saiyida Zeinab, bound for the desert oasis of Bahariya (£E15).

INTERNATIONAL SERVICE TAXIS

Amazingly, there are also **international** *service* taxis to neighbouring countries. Hebton Misr Travel (between Midan Ataba and Midan Opera, in the block behind the multistorey car park; ☎591-9124) arranges seats on cars bound for Benghazi (18hr; £E80) and Tripoli (36hr; £E120). The taxis leave from in front of the booking office. The same firm also runs Superjet buses to Benghazi (see above). It is also possible to get to Palestine and Israel by *service* taxi in stages, by taking one from Midan Ramses to the border at Rafah, then to Khan Yunis, Gaza and finally Jaffa (a suburb of Tel Aviv). If you do this, you will need to set out early to avoid being stranded at Khan Yunis.

DOMESTIC FLIGHTS

EgyptAir (for information ☎245-0260) flies 2–5 times a day to Aswan, Luxor, Hurghada, Sharm el-Sheikh and Alexandria (the maximum number of flights a day in the winter), and daily to Abu Simbel (return flight compulsory). Over the summer there are also three flights a week to El-Arish. Its Cairo offices (generally open daily except Fri 8am–5pm) include: 6 Sharia Adly (☎390-0999); 9 Sharia Talaat Harb (☎393-2836); *Nile Hilton* (daily till 8pm; ☎579-3049); *Cairo Sheraton*, Dokki (☎348-8630); Zamalek Club Fence, 26th July Street (☎305-1431); and 22 Sharia Ibrahim al-Lakani, Heliopolis (☎290-8453).

Tickets and terminals

During winter, EgyptAir flights to the Nile Valley or Hurghada are often fully booked by groups – reserve as far in advance as possible, or hope to get a cancellation on stand-by. Although **tickets** must be purchased in Egyptian currency backed by an exchange receipt, fares are generally reckoned in $US. The following one-way **fares** are only estimates: Luxor £E419, Aswan £E576, Abu Simbel £E816 (you can only buy a return ticket), Sharm el-Sheikh £E477, Hurghada £E453, Alexandria £E248. Return fares cost double. **Students** may qualify for a reduction, but since EgyptAir enjoys a monopoly it rarely offers big discounts.

All these flights leave **from Terminal 1**, the "old airport" (*Al-mattar qadima*), which can be reached by bus or minibus or by taxi (drivers usually demand £E30). During rush hour the journey takes over an hour. Always allow plenty of time.

INTERNATIONAL FLIGHTS

Many airlines make Cairo a stopover between the Near and Far East, or between Europe and sub-Saharan Africa, ensuring a competitive market in fares, student and youth discounts – but also heavy demand for flights. Don't leave **buying tickets** until the last moment. Especially during August, you should book weeks in advance on Eastern European airlines (which often have the cheapest flights to Turkey, Greece and Western Europe) or for popular long-haul destinations like Nairobi, Bangkok and Delhi.

All **reservations** should be **reconfirmed** 72 hours before departure. Also check which terminal you are flying from – most Western airlines use **Terminal 2**, the "new airport" (*Al-mattar gadid*). Rather than rely on buses or minibuses, it's safer to take a taxi.

Agents and tickets

It's worth shopping around **agents**, who can often find seats when the airline itself swears that none exist, and may offer discounts. Places to try include Spring Tours (11 Sharia Talaat Harb; ☎392-2627), Norma Tours (10 Sharia Talaat Harb; ☎576-0007), and Bon Voyage Egypt (16 Sharia Adly; ☎390-8099 or 391-2345, *bonvoyag@intouch.com*). Expect queuing and shoving in agencies and offices.

Although some agents and airlines may accept credit card payments for **tickets**, most don't – it's certainly not something to count on.

Student and youth discounts

To qualify for student discounts (20–50 percent) you must have a valid ISIC card and be under an age limit (24–31 years, depending on the airline or agency). Another age limit (24–26) determines eligibility for youth discounts, which don't require an ISIC card. There are rarely any **student/youth discounts** on flights to sub-Saharan Africa, India and the Far East.

Airline offices

Most of the **airline offices** are in central Cairo; some are represented by local travel agents.

Air Canada, 26 Sharia Bassiouni (☎575-8939 or 761-769). Daily 9am–4pm (Ramadan 9.30am–4.30pm).

Air France, 2 Midan Talaat Harb (☎575-8899, fax 577-1744, *www.airfrance-me.com*). Daily except Fri 8.30am–4.30pm.

Air India, 1 Sharia Talaat Harb (☎393-4875). Mon–Thurs & Sat 8am–3pm.

Air Sinai, *Nile Hilton* arcade (☎ & fax 576-0948). Flies daily except Tues and Sat to Tel Aviv. Daily 8.30am–6pm.

Alitalia, *Nile Hilton* arcade, Tahrir entrance (☎578-5823, fax 578-6924, *caiupaz @alitalia-egypt.com*). Daily except Sat 9am–4pm.

American Airlines, 2 Talaat Harb (☎574-9360 or 390-7045). Daily 9am–5pm. Also handles **TAP**, **Korean Air** & **Air Malta**.

British Airways, corner of Sharia Bustan and Midan Tahrir (☎578-0743/4/6, fax 574-7674). Daily 8am–4pm.

Bulgarian/Balkan Airlines, Sharia Mohammed Sabry al-Alam, 20m east of Midan Talaat Harb (☎393-1211, fax 393-9199). Daily except Fri 9am–5pm.

CSA, 9 Talaat Harb (☎393-0395, fax 392-0463). Daily 8am–4pm.

EgyptAir (see "Domestic flights" on previous page).

El Al, 1st floor, 5 Sharia el-Makrizi, just south of the Zamalek Bridge, Zamalek (☎ & fax 341-1620). Daily 8.30am–5pm.

Delta, 17 Sharia Ismail Mohammed, Zamalek (☎340-1948). Daily 8.30am–5pm.

Ethiopian Airlines, *Nile Hilton* arcade (☎574-0603, fax 574-0189, *ethiocai@giganet*). Daily 8.30am–4.30pm.

Iberia, 15 Midan Tahrir (☎579-5800, fax 576-1988). Daily except Fri 8am–4pm.

Kenya Airways, *Nile Hilton* arcade (☎762-494). Mon–Thurs & Sun 9am–4pm.

KLM, 11 Sharia Qasr el-Nil (☎574-7004, fax 574-7330, *www.klm.com.eg*). Daily except Fri 8.30am–4.30pm.

LOT, 1 Qasr el-Nil (☎578-7312). Mon–Thurs & Sun 9am–2pm, Sat 9am–noon.

Lufthansa, 9 Talaat Harb (☎393-0366). Daily except Fri & Sat 8am–4.30pm. Also handles United Airways.

Malév, upper floor, 10 Talaat Harb (☎576-4251, fax 575-3111). Daily 9.30am–3.30pm.

Olympic Airways, 23 Qasr el-Nil (☎393-1318). Daily 8.30am–4pm.

Singapore Airlines, *Nile Hilton* arcade (☎575-0276, fax 574-7084). Daily 8.30am–4.30pm.

Sudan Airways, 1 Sharia el-Bustan (☎374-7145). Daily 8am–7pm.

Thai Air, 16 Sharia Adly (☎390-5090 or 390-8099). Daily 9am–4pm.

THY Turkish Airways, 3 Midan Mustafa Kemal (☎390-8960). Daily 9am–4.30pm.

TWA, 1 Qasr el-Nil (☎574-9904). Daily 8am–4.30pm.

BOATS – NILE CRUISES AND INTERNATIONAL LINES

Although luxury cruises operated by the *Hilton*, *Sheraton* and *Mena House Oberoi* remain prohib-itively expensive, budget travellers may consider less ritzy boats run by agencies such as Eastmar Tours (in the passage of 13 Sharia Qasr el-Nil; ☎574-5024), which charges – depending on sea-son – US$40–65 a night per person for a 4- to 7-night cruise. Be aware, however, that better deals could well be available from local agents in either Luxor or Aswan. For information on Nile cruises, see Basics, p.43, and for more on cruises and sail-ing on a felucca – a funkier and much cheaper experience – see Chapter Two, p.392.

International lines

Several agencies can supply information and tick-ets for **international lines**, though, to be honest, the incentives for leaving Egypt by sea are mini-mal.

For details of the ferry service from Aswan to Wadi Halfa in **Sudan**, see p.406; for information on ferries from Suez to the Saudi port of **Jeddah**, see p.539.

THE NILE VALLEY

Egypt has been called the gift of the Nile, for without the river it could not exist as a fertile, populous country, let alone have sustained a great civilization five thousand years ago. Its character and history have been shaped by the stark contrast between the fecund **Nile Valley** and its Delta (covered in Chapter Five), and the arid wastes that surround them. To the ancient Egyptians, this was the homeland or *Kemet* – the Black Land of dark alluvium, where life and civilization flourished as the benign gods intended – as opposed to the desert that represented death and chaos, ruled by Seth, the bringer of storms and catastrophes.

Kemet's existence depended on an annual miracle of rebirth from aridity, as the Nile rose to spread its life-giving waters and fertilizing silt over the exhausted land during the season of inundation. Once the flood had subsided, the *fellaheen* (peasants) simply planted crops in the mud, waited for an abundant harvest, and then relaxed over summer. While empires rose and fell, this way of life persisted essentially unchanged for over 240 generations, until the Aswan Dam put an end to the inundation in 1967 – a breathtaking period of continuity considering that Jesus lived only about eighty generations ago.

This continuity and ancient history is literally underfoot. Almost every Nile town and village is built upon layers of previous **settlements** – pharaonic, Ptolemaic, Roman and Coptic – whose ancient names, modified and Arabized, have often survived. When treasure-hunting "archeologists" first turned their attention to the ancient temples and tombs in the 1830s, they had to sift through metres of sand and debris before reaching their goal. Yet the centuries of burial preserved a panoply of ancient reliefs and carvings that would otherwise have been defaced by Coptic or Muslim iconoclasts, who hacked away at the pagan gods on the accessible friezes, pillars and ceilings, and plundered masonry for their own churches and mosques.

After a century and a half of excavation by just about every Western nation – and by the Egyptians since independence – the Nile's **monuments** constitute the greatest open-air museum in the world. Revealed along its banks are several thousand **tombs** (Thebes alone has over 900) and scores of **temples**: so many, in fact, that most visitors feel satiated by just a fraction of this legacy.

To enjoy the Valley, it's best to be selective and mix sightseeing with felucca rides on the river, roaming around bazaars and camel markets, or attending the odd moulid.

ACCOMMODATION PRICE CODES

Throughout the guide, hotels and pensions are graded on a scale of ① to ⑨, indicating the price (including tax) of the **cheapest double room** in each establishment in high season (for places that offer **dorm beds**, rates per person are given in £E). Please note that most hotels in categories ⑧ and ⑨ quote rates in US$, but will accept payment in £E. For a full explanation of the following categories, see p.46. The price bands to which these codes refer are as follows:

① under £E20/US$7
② £E20–30/US$7–10
③ £E30–45/US$10–15
④ £E45–65/US$15–20
⑤ £E65–100/US$20–35
⑥ £E100–150/US$35–50
⑦ £E150–300/US$50–100
⑧ US$100–200/£E300–600
⑨ US$200/£E600 upwards

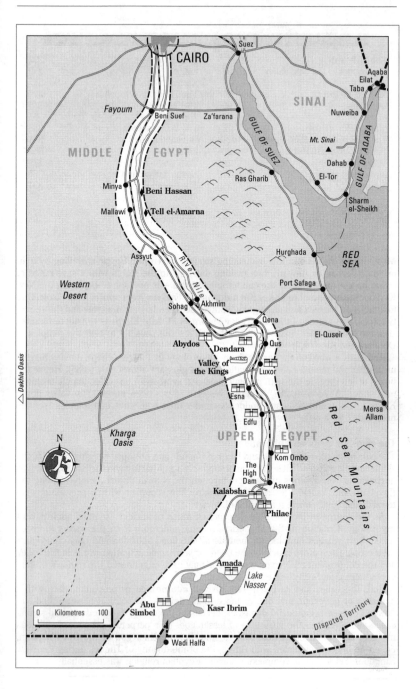

Most visitors succeed in this by heading straight for **Upper Egypt**, travelling by train or air to **Luxor** or **Aswan**, then making day-trips to the sights within easy range of either base – most notably the cult temple at **Edfu** – in addition to exploring the New Kingdom temples and tombs of **Karnak** and the **Theban Necropolis** from Luxor. Due to attacks on tourists and an ongoing conflict between Islamic militants and the security forces, the stretch of the Nile Valley known as **Middle Egypt** is considered a risky area for tourists (see box on p.258), though it's still possible to visit the temples of Dendara and Abydos, beyond Qena.

And lastly a word on the **terms from Egyptology** that fill this chapter: many may be unfamiliar and need a fuller explanation than a glossary allows (see p.685). Hence the boxes at intervals in the text: on statehood and symbolism on p.255; temple architecture under "Abydos" (p.288); funerary beliefs and practices, under "The Valley of the Kings" (p.336); and gods and goddesses under their respective cult temples (see the main index for a list).

The river, its gods and pharaohs

The Nile originates in the highland lakes of Uganda and Ethiopia, which give rise to the White and Blue Niles. These join into a single river at Khartoum in the Sudan, then flow northwards over a series of cataracts through the Nubian desert, before forming the Egyptian Nile Valley. The river's northward flow, coupled with a prevailing wind towards the south, made it a natural highway.

As the source of life, the Nile determined much of ancient Egyptian **society and mythology**. Creation myths of a primal mound emerging from the waters of chaos reflect how villages huddled on mounds till the flood subsided and they could plant their crops. Even more crucially, the need for large-scale irrigation works in the Valley and the consequent mobilization of labour may have engendered the region's system of centralized authority – in effect, the state.

Both the Valley and its Delta were divided into **nomes** or provinces, each with a monarch or governor, and one or more **local deities**. As political power ebbed and flowed between regions and dynasties, certain of the deities assumed national significance and absorbed the attributes of lesser gods in a perpetual process of religious mergers and takeovers. Thus, for example, Re, the chief god of the Old Kingdom, ended up being assimilated with Amun, the prime divinity of Thebes during the New Kingdom. Yet for all its complexity, ancient Egyptian religion was essentially practical and intended to get results. Its pre-eminent concerns were to perpetuate the beneficent sun and river, maintain the righteous order personified by the goddess Maat, and achieve resurrection in the afterlife.

Abundant crops could normally be taken for granted, as prayers to Hapy the Nile-god were followed by a green wave of humus-rich water around June. However, if the Nile failed to rise for a succession of years there ensued the "years of the hyena when men went hungry". Archeologists reckon that it was **famine** – caused by overworking of the land, as well as lack of the flood waters – that caused the collapse of the Old and Middle Kingdoms, and subsequent political anarchy. But each time some new **dynasty** arose to reunite the land and re-establish the old order. This remarkable conservatism persisted even under foreign rule: the Nubians, Persians, Ptolemies and Romans all continued building temples dedicated to the old gods, and styled themselves as pharaohs.

The people of the Nile Valley

Although the Nile Valley and its Delta represents a mere four percent of Egypt's surface area, it is home to 95 percent of the country's population. While Cairo and Alexandria account for about a quarter of this, the bulk of the people still live in small towns and villages and, as in pharaonic times, the **fellaheen** or peasant farmers remain the bedrock of Egyptian society.

Most **villages** consist of flat-roofed mud-brick houses, with chickens, goats, cows and water buffalo roaming the unpaved streets, and elaborate multistorey pigeon coops (the birds are eaten and their droppings used as fertilizer). The plastered outside walls of the houses are often painted light blue (a colour believed to ward off the Evil Eye), and if the householder has made the pilgrimage to Mecca, they will be decorated with characteristic *Hadj* scenes (recalling the journey with images of ships and charter jets, lions and the sacred Ka'ba). Children begin work at an early age: girls feed the animals, fetch water and make the dung patties which are used for fuel (though primus stoves are increasingly popular), while by the age of nine or ten, boys are learning how to farm the land that will one day be theirs.

Rural life might appear the same throughout the Nile Valley, but its character changes as you go further south. The northern part of the Valley is wider and greener, unconstrained by the desert hills; its people have a reputation for being quietly spoken and phlegmatic, notwithstanding a recent turn towards Islamic radicalism. By contrast, Egyptians characterize the **Saiyidis** of Upper Egypt as mercurial in character, alternating between hot-blooded passion and a state known as *kismet* – a kind of fatalistic stasis. To non-Saiyidis, they are also the butt of jokes mocking their stubbornness and stupidity. A further ethnic contingent of the southern reaches of the Valley are the black-skinned **Nubians**, whose traditional homeland extended into Sudan, but has now been submerged beneath the waters of Lake Nasser.

Nile wildlife

The exotic Nile wildlife depicted on ancient tomb reliefs – hippos, crocodiles, elephants and gazelles – is largely a thing of the past, though you might just see a croc near Aswan. However, the Valley has a rich diversity of **birds**. Amid the groves of palms (dates all along the Valley and dom palms south of Assyut), fruit and flame trees, sycamores and eucalyptus, and fields of *besoom* (Egyptian clover) and sugar cane, you can spot hoopoes, turtle- and laughing-doves, bulbuls, bluethroats, redstarts, wheatears and dark-backed stonechats; purple gallinules, egrets and all kinds of waders are to be seen in the river; while common birds of prey include a range of kestrels, hawks and falcons.

Approaches to the Nile Valley

Setting out from Cairo, you are faced with a variety of approaches to the Valley (for details of ticket buying, prices, departure and journey times, see "Travel Details" at the end of the Cairo chapter).

TRANSPORT SECURITY IN THE NILE VALLEY

Since the first attacks on tourists in the early 1990s, transport in the Nile Valley has been subject to various **controls**, which were tightened dramatically after the Hatshepsut Massacre in November 1997. The exact nature of these controls fluctuates, but generally involves the following:

Buses: All tourist traffic in the Nile Valley travels in police-escorted convoys, which run between the main tourist centres (Luxor and Aswan). However, in practice it is often possible to catch any bus from Luxor, and sometimes from Aswan. Between Luxor and Aswan, the towns of Esna, Edfu and Kom Ombo enforce the rules less strictly.

Sevice taxis: Foreign tourists are currently banned from *service* taxi depots in Luxor and Aswan. It may at times be possible to travel by *service* taxi between other towns in the region, so details of routes and fares have been included in most town accounts.

Trains: Tourists are only allowed to travel on two regular (guarded) A/C trains a day between Cairo, Luxor and Aswan, as well as the deluxe *wagons-lits* service (see p.244).

Note: For further information on terrorism in Middle Egypt, see box on p.258.

• **Trains** from **Ramses Station** run as far south as Aswan. Following terrorist ambushes in Middle Egypt (see box p.258), tourists are only allowed to travel on two trains a day (guarded by plainclothes cops with Uzis) between Cairo, Luxor and Aswan. The journey is quite comfortable if you travel in 1st or A/C 2nd class, which have padded swivel seating and carpets. Besides the two "tourist" trains, there is a deluxe *wagons-lits* service with a restaurant and bar, which was subjected to sniper attacks, but has not been targeted recently.

• **Buses** leave from the **Aboud** and **Turgoman Terminals**. There are several daily services to Luxor and Aswan that are A/C. The journey time is the same as by train, and the risk of attack much less; but the buses are a lot less comfortable than 1st or 2nd class train travel. Additionally, there are non-A/C buses to the main towns of Middle Egypt: Beni Suef, Minya, Assyut and Sohag. In theory all tourists in the Nile Valley must travel in police-escorted convoys, which run between the main tourist centres (Luxor and Aswan). However, in practice it is often possible to catch any bus from Luxor, and sometimes from Aswan. Between Luxor and Aswan, the towns of Esna, Edfu and Kom Ombo enforce the rules less strictly.

• **Service taxis** also leave from **Aboud**, bound for Minya or Assyut, whence there are connections further south – but this is a dangerous route, due to the hazards associated with Middle Egypt and also reckless driving. Foreign tourists will not be admitted to the *service* taxi depots in Luxor or Aswan, but in the towns between the two it is usually possible to escape the attention of the police. Details of *service* taxi routes have been included in this chapter in case the security situation eases.

• A quicker, safer but considerably more expensive way to travel is by plane. There are up to a dozen **flights** a day to Luxor, Aswan and Abu Simbel, affording amazing views over the Valley's green belt of cultivated land.

• With the slump in tourism, prices for **Nile cruises** have never been lower, whether arranged before you leave (see the "Getting There" sections in Basics chapter) or on the spot. Most boats start off in Luxor, and sail down to Aswan, with stops at Esna, Edfu and Kom Ombo, over three to five days. For more on cruises and information on **felucca** rides from Aswan, see p.392.

THE TWO LANDS, PHARAONIC SYMBOLS AND CARTOUCHES

Much of the symbolism of ancient Egypt referred to the union of the **Two Lands**, the **Nile Valley** (Upper Egypt) and its **Delta** (Lower Egypt), whose establishment marked the onset of the Old Kingdom (c.3100 BC).

Each Land had its own deity – the Delta had **Wadjet**, the cobra goddess, while the Valley had **Nekhbet**, the vulture goddess. With union, however, their images were combined with the

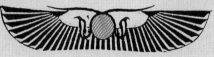

winged sun-disc

sun-disc of the god Re to form the **winged sun-disc**, which often appeared on the lintels of temple doors. Another common image was that of the Nile-god, **Hapy**, binding together the **heraldic plants** of the Two Lands, the papyrus of the Delta and the lotus of the Valley.

Much the same process can be observed in the evolution of **pharaonic crowns**. At state rituals, the pharaoh customarily wore first the **White Crown** of Upper Egypt and then the **Red Crown** of Lower Egypt, although by the time of the New Kingdom (c.1570 BC) these were often subsumed into the **Combined Crown**. Pharaonic crowns also featured the **uraeus** or fire-spitting cobra, an incarnation of Wadjet believed to be a guardian of the kings.

Another image that referred to the act of union (an act which had to be repeated at the onset of the Middle and New Kingdoms) was the **Djed column**, a symbol of steadfastness. Additional symbols of royal authority included the **crook** (or staff) and the **flail** (or scourge), which are often shown crossed over the chest – in the so-called Osiride position – on pharaonic statues. A ubiquitous motif was the **ankh**, symbolizing breath or life, which pharaohs are often depicted receiving from gods in tombs or funerary texts.

Hapy binding the Two Lands

However, the archetypal symbol of kingship was the **cartouche**, an oval formed by a loop of rope, enclosing the hieroglyphs of the pharaoh's nomen and **prenomen**. Traditionally a pharaoh's title consisted of five names: four adopted on accession to the throne (Horus name, Nebty name, Golden Horus name and prenomen) and a birth name (nomen), roughly corresponding to a family name. The prenomen was introduced by a group of hieroglyphs meaning "He who belongs to the sedge and the bee" and was nearly always compounded with the name of Re, the sun-god. The nomen – the name by which pharaohs are known to posterity – was likewise introduced by an epithet, "Son of Re".

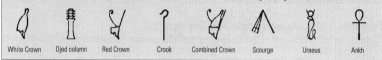

| White Crown | Djed column | Red Crown | Crook | Combined Crown | Scourge | Uraeus | Ankh |

At the time of writing, Dendara and Abydos could be visited by taxi or cruise boat on day-trips from Luxor; cruise boats carrying foreign tourists are restricted from travelling any further north than Qena.

MIDDLE EGYPT

It was nineteenth-century archeologists who coined the term **Middle Egypt** for the stretch of river between Cairo and the Qena Bend; in native usage and current administration there's no such area, unlike Upper and Lower Egypt, which are ancient divisions. Nevertheless, it's a handy label for a region that's subtly distinct from Upper Egypt, further south (in this guide, the Middle Egypt account ends at Sohag; the sites to the south – at Abydos and Dendara – are dealt with in the Upper Egypt account as the best access to them is from Luxor). Owing little to tourism, the towns are solidly provincial, with social conservatism providing common ground for those wanting to preserve peaceful relations between the Muslim majority and Middle Egypt's Coptic community (about 20 percent of the local population, roughly double the national average). In recent years, a spate of **terrorism** has heightened tensions and made much of the region a **no-go zone** for tourists (see below).

Even before this, most foreigners rated Middle Egypt a low priority, as towns like **Minya** and **Sohag** lack the romance of Aswan or the stupendous monuments of Luxor, for all that the local antiquities have fascinated scholars. The rock tombs of **Beni Hassan** and the necropolis of **Tuna al-Gabel** are well-preserved relics of Middle Kingdom artistry and Ptolemaic cult-worship, while the desolate remains at **Tell el-Amarna** stand as an evocative reminder of the "heretic" Pharaoh Akhenaten. Unfortunately, all these sites lie in the heart of the danger zone and are unlikely to be open even if you're bold enough to risk a visit.

As the situation is fluid and might improve, we haven't deleted Middle Egypt from this edition, even though it was unsafe to visit at the time of writing. The following accounts are *not* a recommendation to go, merely an acknowledgement that places still exist and life goes on there.

Beni Suef

The ramshackle provincial capital of **BENI SUEF** is only 130km from Cairo, but there's no reason to come here except to switch transport for the Red Sea Coast, Fayoum Oasis or the Pyramid of Maidum. Should this mean staying overnight, your best option is the hotel *Semiramis* (☎082/322-092; ③), up the road to the left.

The **bus and taxi stations** are 75m further down Bur Said. There are buses to Fayoum City every half-hour, and frequent *service* taxis. Morning is the best time to find taxis to Za'farana on the Red Sea Coast, a route that passes the turn-off for St Anthony's Monastery (see p.614), 150km east of Beni Suef. Alternatively, you can aim for the Pyramid of Maidum (p.429), 30km north of Beni Suef, which involves taking a minibus to the Nile Valley town of El-Wasta, and then a *service* to Maidum. **Minibuses** for El-Wasta leave from a separate depot, 500m north along Sharia Salah Salem, which forks off Bur Said near the bus station.

Forgotten cities: Heracleopolis and Oxyrhynchus

Though nothing remains of them, two ancient cities once flourished along this stretch of the Nile Valley.

Heracleopolis is marked by a huge mound of rubble near the village of Ihnasya el-Medina, 15km west of Beni Suef. Founded early in the Old Kingdom and long the capital of the twentieth nome, its rise coincided with the decline of the VIII Dynasty, which barely controlled the region around Memphis by 2160 BC. While anarchy reigned throughout the Two Lands, **Achthoes**, the nomarch of Heracleopolis, forged a new dynasty. Although his successors never achieved control of southern Egypt, their

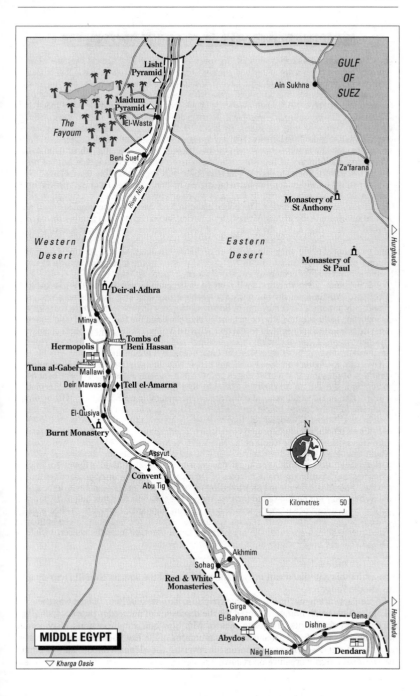

TERRORIST ATTACKS IN MIDDLE EGYPT

In 1992, a spate of **terrorist attacks on tourists** in Middle Egypt made headline news abroad. Tourist buses were ambushed outside Qena, Assyut and Dairut, and a Nile cruiser was machine-gunned near El-Qusiya. Each year since, there have been a few attacks on passing trains, and on buses or taxis around Qena, with sporadic outbursts in Cairo. The situation peaked in November 1997, when over sixty people, mostly foreign tourists, were killed at Hatshepsut Temple on Luxor's west bank. Tourism dried up completely and the government introduced severe security measures. By late 1999, the situation had stabilized, but police remain vigilant and still assign escorts to any foreigners they see. Independent travellers continued to visit Minya and Sohag – until their embassies issued **warnings** about them too. Perversely, the Ministry of Tourism continues to assert that the region is safe, but has privately told travel agencies to drop it, while the police have their own policy (see below).

The reality is a **wider conflict** between Islamic militants (called "Islamists" or "terrorists" in the media) and the security forces, in which arrests and shoot-outs occurred weekly but seldom made headlines. The police claim to have narrowed the Islamists' field of operations down to the Minya–Mallawi area, having "neutralized" them in other towns or forced them to hide out in the desert. Cane fields alongside the train tracks have been burned to deny cover to snipers; traffic is filtered through checkpoints on trunk routes and roads out of town; and some places are under dusk-to-dawn curfew. Torture is routine during police interrogations and in two special prisons in the mountains outside Qena; rumour has it that policemen are rewarded for each "terrorist" shot dead.

Ask Egyptians about this, and their reply often depends on whether they're Muslim or Christian. **Muslims** usually downplay the problem, insisting that there is no sectarian angle, only terrorists backed by Iran or Sudan. **Christians** (in private) tell a different story, of extortion and assaults, petty restrictions on churches, and the fear that local officials are unsympathetic to their plight. In recent times there have been disturbing accounts of police brutality against Copts, including rapes, beatings and even simulated crucifixions. Whilst the lurid details may be exaggerated, the basic scenario is not unlikely.

Officially, **foreigners** are free to visit any part of Middle Egypt; **police** on the spot interpret this as meaning that a brief visit is permissable, but staying is not. If you're bent on reaching a site and no transport is available, they'll even drive you there under armed escort. The aim is to get you out of the area (and preferably back in Luxor) well before nightfall. In many towns, hotels have been told not to take foreign guests, so that if one has to stay, it must be somewhere that supposedly affords protection. One is also shadowed by plainclothes or uniformed cops, which precludes much contact with other people. This applies along the whole of the Nile Valley between Cairo and Qena. When asked about trouble, local cops invariably dismiss the notion – whatever the situation is.

Bearing all this in mind, you must choose whether to skip Middle Egypt entirely; chance a trip from Luxor to the temples of Dendara (near Qena) or Abydos; or venture further. Should you decide to risk **travelling on**, *service* taxis may be an option, although foreigners may not be allowed to travel in them in some areas (see box on p.254). Most of the time, things seem pretty normal by Egyptian standards, though the police presence is larger. Their hardware reflects the level of tension: one ammunition clip in their rifles means things are relatively relaxed; two taped together indicates concern; while flak-jackets and machine-gun nests signify a heavy situation.

reassertion of centralized authority in the north paved the way for the XII Dynasty and the Middle Kingdom.

Of similarly academic interest, **Oxyrhynchus**, 9km west of Beni Mazar, was the capital of the nineteenth nome. It's noted for the discovery of numerous papyri – including third-century fragments of the gospels of Matthew and John; portions of plays by Sophocles, Euripides and Meander; and summaries of the lost books of Livy. More frivolously, it deserves to be remembered for revering the elephant-snout fish – perhaps the weirdest totemic creature on record.

Minya, Mallawi and surrounding sites

Unfortunately, the best archeological sites in Middle Egypt are in what is now the most dangerous zone, around **Minya**, 109km south of Beni Suef, and **Mallawi**, 47km further south. Even before the area became dangerous, the relative isolation of the sites around the towns made it hard to reach more than one or two places in a single day without private transport. The usual strategy was to rent a private taxi and visit two or three sites in succession, which wasn't too costly if there was a group of you. Now, however, the police insist on accompanying foreigners, so finding a driver willing to take you is far from easy, and much more expensive. Moreover, since few tourists visit, finding someone to open the sites can be a problem.

The main attractions are the rock tombs of **Beni Hassan**, roughly midway between the towns, which contain the finest surviving murals from the Middle Kingdom. Nearer to Mallawi are the ruins of **Hermopolis** and its partially subterranean necropolis, **Tuna al-Gabel**, while the Coptic **Monastery of the Virgin** lies across the river north of Minya. The major site of Tell el-Amarna, 12km south of Mallawi on the east bank, is covered separately on p.267; although the Burnt Monastery is closer to Mallawi, it is safer to travel there from Assyut (see p.280).

Most **trains** between Cairo and Luxor stop at Minya which takes about four hours. There are **buses** from Cairo's Aboud and Turgoman Terminals (5hr) and **service taxis** (4hr) from the adjacent depot or Midan Giza. If you're **driving**, use the expressway that runs down the east bank of the Nile; despite rough patches, you'll make better time than on the congested west bank "highway". Coming up **from Luxor** by bus or *service* taxi usually entails a change of vehicles at Assyut.

Minya

Though **MINYA** is further from most of the sites, it used to be infinitely preferable to Mallawi as a base for excursions. The provincial capital, it derives considerable charm from the old villas built by Italian architects for Greek and Egyptian cotton magnates – now picturesquely decaying amidst their overgrown gardens – and from its people, known in Egypt for their warmth and honesty. Beneath the palm trees that shadow its squares, couples canoodle and vendors hawk sweet potatoes, and during Ramadan half the population seems to sleep outdoors. In happier times, Minya was called the "Bride of Upper Egypt".

Outside the train station is a square redolent of some ex-colonial *ville* in North Africa. **Sharia Gumhorriya** leads past a row of cafés to reach **Midan Tahrir** (aka Midan Qasr), the hub of small-town life by day. Come evening, locals promenade between Tahrir and **Midan Sa'a** (Clock Square), past shops and eating places replicated further up Gumhorriya, which terminates at the **Corniche** (aka Sharia el-Nil).

Across the river rise the striated hills of the Eastern Desert. Thus constrained, Minya spreads alongside the riverbank and westwards across the **Ibrahimiya Canal**, encroaching on the agricultural plain beyond.

Practicalities

Minya's **tourist office** (daily except Fri 8.30am–8.30pm; ☎086/343-500) is anxious to please but short on hard facts. It can even be wrong about whether sites like Beni Hassan and Hermopolis are open, so it's best to double-check vital information with the **tourist police** (☎086/364-527). Visitors are bound to come to the attention of the **security department**, which shares a building on the Corniche with the regular **police** (☎123).

There's a 24-hour **telephone office** opposite the station, while the main **post office** (daily 8.30am–3pm) is at the rear of a white building near the tourist office, with a **pass-**

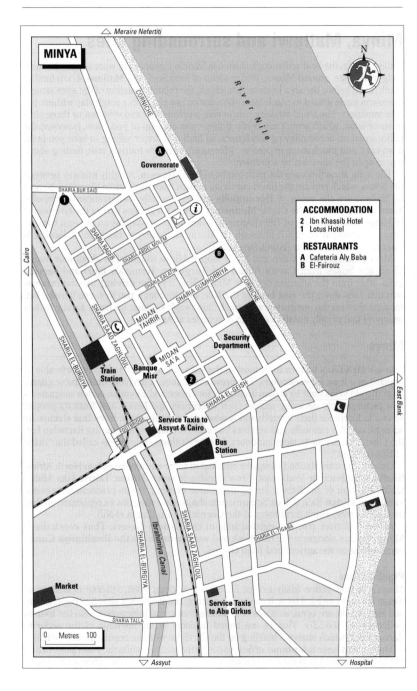

△ Meraire Nefertiti

MINYA

N

River Nile

CORNICHE

Ⓐ
Governorate

SHARIA BUR SAID
❶

SHARIA RAGEB

ⓘ

SHARIA ABDEL MOLEM

SHARIA SALATIN

Ⓑ

SHARIA GUMHORRIYA

CORNICHE

◁ Cairo

ACCOMMODATION
2 Ibn Khassib Hotel
1 Lotus Hotel

RESTAURANTS
A Cafeteria Aly Baba
B El-Fairouz

MIDAN
TAHRIR
Ⓒ

SHARIA SAAD ZAGHLOUL

**Security
Department**

SHARIA EL-BURGIYA

MIDAN
SA'A

**Train
Station**

**Banque
Misr**

❷

SHARIA EL-GEISH

▷ East Bank

FOOTBRIDGE

**Service Taxis to
Assyut & Cairo**

**Bus
Station**

Ibrahimya Canal

SHARIA SAAD ZAGHLOUL

SHARIA EL-TIGARA

SHARIA EL-BURGIYA

Market

0 Metres 100

SHARIA TALLA

**Service Taxis
to Abu Qirkus**

▽ Assyut   ▽ Hospital

port office (daily except Fri 8.30am–2pm) on the floor above. Banque Misr on Midan Sa'a (daily except Fri 8.30am–2pm) does cash advances on Visa cards; another branch on Sharia Gumhorriya, and the National Bank of Egypt (daily except Fri 8.30am–2pm & 6–9pm) at the Corniche end of Sharia Gumhorriya, only **change money** and travellers' cheques. There is a **hospital** just south of town along the Corniche (☎086/634-098). The Monday **market**, to the southwest of town, has been a fixture since Ottoman times.

TRANSPORT

Though *hantours* (horse-drawn buggies) are widely used for getting around, Minya is compact enough for walking, with its local and long-distance transport depots fairly close together.

Service taxis are the fastest way to reach anywhere between Cairo and Assyut (the point to change for destinations further south). The "local" and inter-city *service* depots between the station and the bus terminal cover all destinations except for Abu Qirkus (the jumping-off point for Beni Hassan), which is handled by a depot 300m further south. Many routes are also plied by **pick-ups** (mini-vans or covered trucks), which charge similar rates to *service* taxis.

Trains are generally slower than other transport to most points in the Nile Valley. **Buses** for Assyut leave every hour on the hour; services to Cairo (5hr) every two hours on the half-hour.

ACCOMMODATION

Even if you wish to stay, finding a hotel willing to accept foreigners can be problematic; it all depends on the local police. Visiting businessmen are secluded in the *Mercure Nefertiti*, outside town; otherwise, the likeliest places are the hotels on the Corniche, near police headquarters. It's wise to phone ahead to enquire.

Ibn Khassib, 5 Sharia Ragab (☎086/324-535). Nice garden and vintage rooms, available with or without private baths, and dinner. Bar and restaurant. ③.

Lotus, 1 Sharia Bur Said (☎086/324-500). Decent A/C rooms with showers, and a top-floor restaurant with fine views, serving beer and wine. ③.

Mercure Nefertiti, 1km north of Minya by the Nile (☎086/331-515, fax 326-467). Guarded four-star retreat with A/C rooms or bungalows with TV, private bathroom and phone, with its own pool and restaurants. ⑦.

EATING

Discounting the restaurants in the *Mercure Nefertiti*, there are few **places to eat** worth considering. Avoid the garishly painted *El-Fairouz* on the corner of Sharia Salatin and the Corniche, and the restaurant in the *Akhnaton Hotel*. The *Lotus Hotel* offers better meals, but the best chicken, kebabs and desserts are sold at the *Cafeteria Aly Baba*, north of the Governorate building. The *Savoy Restaurant*, next to the *Savoy Hotel*, is also good for kebab and *kofta*, while the *Sabah al-Kheer*, across the road, does cheap *fuul* and eggs. Both Minya's main squares feature the usual array of cafés, *kushari* and grilled-chicken take-aways.

Mallawi

MALLAWI has gone to the dogs ever since Minya supplanted it as the regional capital. Its streets are littered and stink of open drains; hovels are more prevalent than villas. To Egyptians, it is best known as the birthplace of Sadat's assassin, Khalid al-Islambouli, and his brother Shawky, who fought with the Afghan *mujahadin* and later formed his own terrorist group in Egypt. Its economy has been crippled by the conflict; with 25,000 jobless, the town is sullen with repressed anger and frustration. At the time of writing, it was under **curfew**, with armoured cars on the streets, and was obviously the last place anyone would want to visit. However, the details below might prove useful if the situation ever improves – in which case, don't miss the derelict Hindu-Gothic-style **feudal palace**, 150m in from the main road.

Practicalities

Mallawi straggles along both sides of the Ibrahimiya Canal, and unfortunately for those seeking **transport** on to Beni Hassan, Tuna al-Gabel or Tell el-Amarna, the various terminals are dispersed. On the **east bank** are the train station and, further south, the depot for *service* taxis to all points south of Mallawi. Northbound taxis leave from a depot 200m north of the canal bridge. On the other side of this is **Sharia Essim**, the main drag, along which buses and *service* taxis shuttle between Minya and Assyut. Also on Sharia Essim is a **restaurant which** serves meat and rice with salad and bread, soft drinks and tea, while on Sharia Bank al-Misr, across the bridge from the station, the *El-Horriya Restaurant* does hearty *kofta* meals. There are no tourist hotels in town, and this is not a place where you would want to be stuck overnight.

Mallawi's Banque Misr (Sun–Thurs 8am–2pm & 6–9pm) can **exchange** currency and travellers' cheques. To reach the **post office** (daily except Fri 8.30am–3pm), follow the dirt road to the left of the bank and turn left after 100m.

Across the river from Minya

Before describing the pharaonic sites south of Minya, it's worth mentioning two places across the river and north of town: Minya's **City of the Dead**, and the **Monastery of the Virgin**. Thanks to the Minya Bridge and *service* taxis from the "local" depot, both are reasonably easy to reach. Formerly, you could also visit the ruined Greco-Roman temple of **Tehna al-Gabel**, but this has been closed for years and is unlikely to reopen soon.

Minya's City of the Dead and the Church of Aba Hur

Beyond the east bank village of Al-Sawadah, 4km south of Minya, stretches an immense cemetery resembling Cairo's City of the Dead. Dubbed **Zawiyet el-Mayyiteen**, the "Corner of the Dead", it consists of thousands of mausolea: confessional enclaves interspersed with the homes of the living. A rash of mud-brick domes marks the Muslim quarters; a forest of crosses marks the Coptic burial grounds. Somewhere amongst them lies the **Mausoleum of Hoda Shaarawi**, an early twentieth-century feminist who campaigned for women's liberation.

Traditionally, locals visit their ancestral tombs during the Muslim months of *Shawwal*, *Ragab* and *Zoul-Hagga*, at the time of the full moon. On July 6, the cemetery also serves as a camping ground for Coptic pilgrims attending the **Mouild of Aba Hur** at the subterranean rock church of **Deir Aba Hur**, a kilometre from Al-Sawadah. The church – entered via a narrow, stepped tunnel – contains finely inlaid *haikal* screens and a nineteenth-century icon of Aba Hur, a blacksmith's son whose faith under torture converted the Roman governor of Pelusium to Christianity.

Deir al-Adhra: the Monastery of the Virgin

About 20km downriver from Minya, the east bank extrudes a cliff-like hill known as **Gabel et-Teir** (Bird Mountain), after the flocks said to haunt it on the birthday of a local saint – a name that's also applied to the Coptic monastery on its summit. The **Monastery of the Virgin**, properly called **Deir al-Adhra**, was inhabited until late last century, when Baedeker dismissed it as a "group of miserable huts, occupied not only by the monks but by laymen with their wives and children", whose reaction to passing

tourist steamers had previously amused Gustave Flaubert: "You see these fellows, totally naked, rushing down their perpendicular cliffs and swimming towards you as fast as
they can, shouting '*Baksheesh, baksheesh*'."

Nowadays a place of pilgrimage, the monastery's rude outbuildings screen a **rock-
hewn church**, reputedly founded in 328 AD by Empress Helena, inside a cave where
the Holy Family sheltered. One of its six columns has been hollowed out and serves for
baptisms; the tales attached to it are only surpassed by the miraculous cures attributed
to a picture of the Virgin that weeps holy oil. Forty days after the Coptic Easter, thousands of pilgrims come here for the week-long **Feast of the Assumption**; at other
times the church is locked, but a caretaker can admit visitors.

Getting there from Minya involves catching a *service* taxi 30km north to Samalut;
alighting at the canal bridge, taking a pick-up to the Nile, a boat to the east bank, and
walking through a field to the rock-hewn stairway that ascends the cliff to a hamlet
beside the monastery – also accessible by a bumpy track and the odd pick-up truck.
During the festival, minibuses run there directly from Minya.

The rock tombs of Beni Hassan

Roughly midway between Minya and Mallawi, a range of barren cliffs east of the Nile
shelters the **rock tombs of Beni Hassan** (daily 9am–4pm; £E12, camera permit £E5),
named after an Arab tribe that once settled hereabouts. The vivid murals in this necropolis shed light on the Middle Kingdom (2050–1800 BC), a period when provincial dignitaries showed their greater independence by having grand burials locally, rather than
at Saqqara. A path links the tombs to the isolated temple of **Speos Artemidos**, 3km
away. Neither site offers food or water.

The traditional way of **getting there** is to catch a pick-up or *service* taxi (30–40min)
from Minya or Mallawi to the large village of **ABU QIRKUS**, although this will depend
on the security situation (see box on p.254). Cross the main canal bridge and grab
another pick-up at the end of the street for the 3km ride to the river bank. An office by
the Nile sells tickets valid for the ferry crossing and minibus ride to and from the
tombs, 500m inland on the east bank of the Nile.

The tombs

Although most of Beni Hassan's 39 tombs are unfinished, the four shown to visitors
evince a **stylistic evolution** during the XI–XII Dynasties. Their variously shaped chambers represent a transitional stage between the lateral *mastaba* tombs of the Old
Kingdom and the deep shafts in the Valley of the Kings, gradually acquiring porched
vestibules and sunken corridors to heighten the impact of the funerary effigies at the
back. The actual mummies were secreted at the bottom of shafts, accompanied by
funerary texts derived from the royal burials of the Old Kingdom. Pharaonic iconography and contemporary reportage are blended in the **murals**, whose innovative
wrestling scenes presaged the battle vistas of the New Kingdom. Though battered or
effaced in parts, their details reward careful study; the following descriptions are keyed
to the tomb plans.

TOMB OF BAQET III (#15)

Taking the chambers in chronological order, you should begin with the **Tomb of
Baqet III**. Like other tombs, its images are arranged in "registers" (rows), whose
height above floor level reflects their spatial relationship. Thus, Nile scenes go below
those involving the Valley, above which come desert vistas, the highest ones most distant. Mural **[a]** shows papyrus gathering in the marshes; **[b]** a desert hunt (notice the
copulating gazelles) above pictures of ball players, women spinning and fullers beating

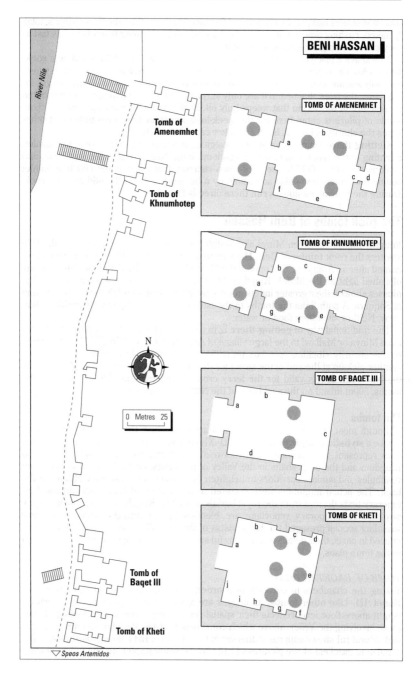

BENI HASSAN

TOMB OF AMENEMHET

TOMB OF KHNUMHOTEP

TOMB OF BAQET III

TOMB OF KHETI

Tomb of Amenemhet

Tomb of Khnumhotep

River Nile

N

0 Metres 25

Tomb of Baqet III

Tomb of Kheti

▽ Speos Artemidos

cloth. The rear wall [c] depicts nearly 200 wrestling positions, while the south wall [d] is covered with episodes from the life of this XI Dynasty nomarch; in one scene, his underlings count cattle and punish tax defaulters.

TOMB OF KHETI (#17)

Baqet bequeathed the governorship of the Oryx nome to his son, who was buried in the nearby **Tomb of Kheti**, which retains two of its structurally inessential papyrus-bud columns. In the murals, hippopotami ignore the papyrus harvest [a], as desert creatures are hunted [b] above registers of weavers, dancers, artists and *senet*-players (*senet* is a game a bit like draughts); metalsmiths labour, musicians entertain Kheti and his wife [c], and minions bring offerings of gazelles and birds [d].

On the rear wall, warriors storm a fortress below a compendium of wrestling positions [e]. Grape harvesting and wine-making [f], herding cattle [h] and ploughing [i] are only some of the tasks overseen by Kheti, who appears beneath a sunshade attended by his dwarf and fan-bearers [g], and elsewhere receives offerings. Notice Kheti's boats, and bulls locking horns, near the entrance [j].

TOMB OF AMENEMHET (#2)

Columned porticos and a niche for statues (which replaced the Old Kingdom *serdab* or secret chamber) are hallmarks of the XII Dynasty tombs, 150m north. Proto-Doric columns uphold a vaulted ceiling painted with checkered reed-mat patterns in the **Tomb of Amenemhet**. This nomarch's campaign honours are listed beside the door near a text relating the death of Senusert I. Leather-workers, armourers, masons and weavers [a] precede the customary hunting scene [b], beneath which Amenemhet collects tribute from his estates – a scene with scribes brow-beating defaulters at the bottom. Below the wrestling and siege tableaux, boats escort him towards Abydos [c], while a niche [d] holds broken effigies of Amenemhet, his mother and his wife Heptet, who sits at her own table to receive offerings [e]. Fish are netted and spit-roasted above a false door flanked by scenes of music making, cattle fording and baking [f].

TOMB OF KHNUMHOTEP (#3)

Amenemhet's successor was also governor of the Eastern Desert, hence the imposing portal framed by proto-Doric columns outside the **Tomb of Khnumhotep**. Left of the *muwu* dancers accompanying his cortege [a], servants weigh grain and scribes record its storage in granaries; while agricultural scenes surmount Khnumhotep's voyage to Abydos [b]. Beneath the desert hunt [c], Semitic Amus from Syria pay their respects to him, their alien costumes, flocks and tribute all minutely detailed – the governor is shown accepting eye paint.

Remnants of his statue in the niche are eclipsed by vivid scenes of him netting birds, hunting with a throwing stick [d], and spearing fish from a punt in the marshes [e], above a hippo, crocodiles and fishermen. After the usual offerings [f], he inspects boat-building timber from a litter and then sails to Abydos [g]. Higher and lower registers portray laundrymen, weavers and various other artisans.

Speos Artemidos

The cliffside path at Beni Hassan affords a fine view of the Nile and the abrupt transition from cultivation to desert. From the Tomb of Kheti, it continues 2.5km south and then heads 500m up a wadi whose south face is pimpled by the small rock-hewn **temple of Speos Artemidos**. Begun by Queen Hatshepsut, whose claims to have restored order after Hyksos misrule are inscribed above its door (but typically usurped by Seti I), the temple has only roughed-out Hathor-headed columns, and its sanctuary – dominated by a statue of the lion-goddess Pakht – is largely unfinished. However, scenes of Hatshepsut making offerings to the gods have been executed in the hall.

Just before the site there's a small **grotto** (*speos*), whence comes the temple's Greek name. Further into the desert are early Christian **hermit cells**, after whom the wadi was called the Valley of the Anchorites.

Antinopolis

The ancient city of **Antinopolis**, 10km south of Beni Hassan, deserves a mention for its origins alone. Touring Egypt with his lover Antinous in 130 AD, the Roman emperor Hadrian was warned by an oracle to expect a grievous loss, whereupon Antinous drowned himself in the Nile to prevent a greater calamity befalling his master. In grief, Hadrian deified the youth and founded a city in his honour before continuing south to Thebes with his unloved wife Plotina.

Today, little remains but some fine red granite columns; most of the **ruins** were used to build the neighbouring village of Sheikh Abadah, or turned into cement in the last century.

Tuna al-Gabel and Hermopolis

Northwest of Mallawi are two sites whose vestigial remains are less dramatic than their mythical associations. According to one tradition, the Creation began on a primordial mound near **Hermopolis**, where two stone baboons recall the long-vanished Temple of Thoth. Rather more remains of the city's necropolis, **Tuna al-Gabel**, where thousands of sacred baboons and ibises were buried in underground galleries.

To get here, rent a **taxi** from Mallawi and visit either both sites in a half-day excursion, or Tuna al-Gabel alone in a couple of hours – neither place being worth the trouble of getting to by public transport. Although both sites are now open daily (9am–4pm; £E12 each site), hardly any tourists have come here since two guards were shot at Hermopolis in 1995.

THOTH AND THE HERMOPOLITAN OGDOAD

In Egyptian mythology, **Thoth** was the divine scribe and reckoner of time, the inventor of writing and the patron god of scribes. His cult probably originated in the Delta, but achieved the greatest following in Middle Egypt; later, by association with Khonsu, he acquired the attributes of the moon-god and mastery over science and knowledge. Though usually depicted with a man's body and the head of an ibis (his sacred bird), Thoth also assumed the form of a great white baboon, invariably endowed with an outsize penis. Baboons habitually shriek just before dawn, and the Egyptians believed that a pair of them uttered the first greetings to the sun from the sand dunes at the edge of the world.

Thoth's role is rather more complex in relation to the Hermopolitan cosmogony, which ordained that the chaos preceding the world's creation had four characteristics, each identified with a pair of gods and goddesses: primordial water (*Nun/Nanuet*), infinite space (*Heh/Hehet*), darkness (*Kek/Keket*) and invisibility (*Amun/Amunet*). From this chaos arose the primeval mound and the cosmic egg whence the sun-god was hatched and proceeded to organize the world. While stressing the role of this **Hermopolitan Ogdoad** (company of eight), Thoth's devotees credited him with laying the cosmic egg in the guise of the "Great Cackler", so it's difficult to know who got star billing in

Thoth

this Creation myth. By the New Kingdom it had generally succumbed to the version espoused at Heliopolis (see p.179), but Thoth's cult continued into Ptolemaic times.

Tuna al-Gabel

The **necropolis** gets its name from the small town of **TUNA AL-GABEL**, 6km from the site. Halfway along the road from town, a boundary stele on a distant cliff marks the edge of the agricultural land claimed by Tell el-Amarna, across the river (see section following). The necropolis itself is awash with sand, wind-rippled drifts casting its angular mausolea into high relief, but obscuring other features.

A path to the right of the entrance leads to the **catacombs** (*As-Saradeb*), which some believe stretch as far as Hermopolis. The accessible portion consists of several main corridors with blocked-off side passages, where the mummified baboons and ibises were stacked (a few bandages remain). A shrine near the ladder contains a baboon fetish and a pathetic-looking mummy; baboons were sacred to Thoth (see above). Beneath the main gallery lies the tomb of a temple priest.

Further along the main track is a miniature **City of the Dead**, with "streets" of mausolea that mostly reflect Hellenistic influences. The finest structure is the **Tomb of Petosiris**, High Priest of Thoth (whose coffin is in the Cairo Antiquities Museum), dating from around 300 BC. Its vestibule walls depict traditional activities such as brick-making, sewing and reaping (left), milking, husbandry and wine-making (right) – with all the figures wearing Greek costume. Inside the tomb are colourful scenes from the *Book of Gates* and the *Book of the Dead*. The most vivid scene shows nine baboons, twelve women and a dozen cobras, each set representing a temporal cycle. Notice the Nubians at the bottom of the opposite wall.

Behind this is another "house" whose upper room displays the **Mummy of Isadora**, a young woman from Antinopolis who drowned in the Nile around 120 BC. Victims of the life-giving river acquired posthumous sanctity, but the leathery state of Isadora's corpse owes to 2000 years of desert air rather than embalming techniques, which had by then degenerated. Beyond Isadora's tomb, and some **columns** from the Temple of Thoth that once dominated the site, lies the brick superstructure of *As-Saqiyya*, a **well** that once supplied the necropolis and its sacred aviary with fresh water, drawn up from 70m below the desert by a huge **water wheel**. The well is infested with bats.

The ruins of Hermopolis

The pulverized ruins of Hermopolis spread beyond the village of **ASHMUNEIN**, off the secondary road linking Mallawi with Tuna al-Gabel. An access road curving off to the west of Ashmunein brings you to a pair of **giant sandstone baboons** that once sported erect phalluses (hacked off by early Christians) and upheld the ceiling of the Temple of Thoth. Built by Ramses II using masonry from Tell el-Amarna, the temple stood within an enclosure covering 640 square metres, the spiritual heart of the city of the moon-god.

Hermopolis was a cult centre from early Dynastic times, venerated as the site of the primeval mound where the sun-god emerged from a cosmic egg. Like Heliopolis (which made similar claims) its priesthood evolved an elaborate cosmogony, known as the Hermopolitan Ogdoad (see previous page). Though ancient Egyptians called the city *Khmunu*, history remembers it as **Hermopolis Magna**; its Ptolemaic title reflects the Greek association of Thoth with their own god Hermes. However, none of the mounds of earth and rubble that remain seems credible as the site of Creation, and there's little to see except 24 slender rose granite **columns**, further south. Re-erected by archeologists who mistook the ruins for a Greek *agora*, they previously supported a Coptic basilica, but originally belonged to a Ptolemaic temple.

Tell el-Amarna

TELL EL-AMARNA is the familiar name for the site where **Pharaoh Akhenaten** and **Queen Nefertiti** founded a city dedicated to a revolutionary idea of God, which later rulers assailed as heretical. During their brief reign, Egyptian art cast off its preoccupation with death and the afterlife to revel in human concerns; bellicose imperialism gave way to pacifistic retrenchment; and the old gods were toppled from their pedestals. The interplay between personalities, beliefs and art anticipates the Renaissance – and their story beats Shakespeare for sheer drama.

The interest of the **site** (see p.271 for access details) is chiefly romantic, for what remains is hardly comparable to the great temples further up the Nile. Only the faintest outline of the city is discernible, while the reliefs in its rock-cut tombs have been badly mutilated (initially by reactionaries, who defaced the images of Akhenaten and his deity). Nonetheless, it strikes some visitors as intensely evocative: a place of mystery whose enchantment grows the more one knows about it.

The story of Akhenaten and Nefertiti

Few figures from ancient history have inspired as much conjecture as Akhenaten and Nefertiti, as scholars dispute even fundamental aspects of their story – let alone the interpretation of the events.

The tale begins with Pharaoh **Amenophis III**, who flouted convention by making Tiy, his Nubian concubine, Great Wife, despite her lack of royal blood. **Queen Tiy** remained formidable long after Amenophis entered his dotage and their eldest son ascended the throne as **Amenophis IV**. Some believe this event followed his father's death, others that mother and son ruled jointly for twelve years. To square the former theory with the period of his reign (c.1379–1362 BC) and his demise around the age of thirty means accepting that Amenophis Jr embarked on his religious reformation between the ages of nine and thirteen. It seems an unusually early age, though a marriage at thirteen is quite likely.

The origins of Amenophis's wife, **Nefertiti**, are obscure. Her name – meaning "A Beautiful Woman Has Come" – suits the romantic legend that she was a Mesopotamian princess originally betrothed to Amenophis III. However, others identify her as Amenophis III's child by a secondary wife, or as the daughter of his vizier **Ay**, whose wife, **Tey**, was almost certainly Nefertiti's wet nurse. The pharaonic custom of sister–brother and father–daughter marriages allows plenty of scope for speculation, but the fair-skinned bust of Nefertiti in the Berlin Museum suggests that she wasn't Tiy's child, at any rate. (Amid all the fuss about Cleopatra being black, nobody seems to have noticed that Queen Tiy – and therefore her son, Amenophis IV – were indubitably so.)

Early in his reign, Amenophis IV began to espouse the **worship of Aten** (see above), whose ascendancy threatened the priesthoods of other cults. The bureaucracy was equally alarmed by his decree that the spoken language should be used in official documents, contrary to all tradition. To escape their influence and realize his vision of a city dedicated to Aten, the pharaoh founded a **new capital** upon an empty plain beside the Nile, halfway between Memphis and Thebes, which he named **Akhetaten**, the "Horizon of the Aten".

It was here that the royal couple settled in the fifth year of their reign and took Aten's name in honour of their faith. He discarded Amenophis IV for **Akhenaten** (Servant of the Aten) and vowed never to leave the city, while she took a forename meaning "Beautiful are the Beauties of the Aten", styling herself **Nefernefruaten-Nefertiti**. Her status surpassed that of any previous Great Wife, approaching that of Akhenaten himself. Bas-reliefs and steles show her participating in state festivals and her own cartouche was coupled with Aten's – an unprecedented association. Tableaux from this period depict an idyllic royal family life, with the couple embracing their daughters and banqueting with Queen Tiy.

There's no sign that their happiness was marred by his decision to take a second wife, **Kiya**, for dynastic ends; nor of the degenerative condition that supposedly afflicted Akhenaten in later life. However, the great ceremony held at Akhetaten in their

ATEN-WORSHIP AND AMARNA ART

Many scholars herald **Aten-worship** as a breakthrough in human spirituality and cultural evolution: the world's first monotheistic religion, and thus representing "a peak of clarity which rose above the lowlands of superstition".

Aten was originally just an aspect of the sun-god (the "Globe" or "Disc" of the midday sun), ranking low in the Theban pantheon until Amenophis III privately adopted it as a personal deity. Then Akhenaten publicly exalted Aten above other gods, subsuming all their attributes into this newly omnipotent being. Invocations to Maat (truth) were retained, but otherwise the whole cast of underworld and celestial deities was jettisoned. Morbid Osirian rites were also replaced by paeans to life in the joyous warmth of Aten's rays (which are usually shown ending in a hand clasping an *ankh*), as in this extract from the *Hymn to Aten*:

> *When you rise from the horizon the earth grows bright; you shine as the Aten in the sky and drive away the darkness; when your rays gleam forth, the whole of Egypt is festive. People wake and stand on their feet, for you have lifted them up . . . Then the whole of the land does its work; all the cattle enjoy their pastures, trees and plants grow green, birds fly up from their nests and raise their wings in praise of your spirit. Goats frisk on their feet and all the fluttering and flying things come alive.*

Similarities between the *Hymn* and *The Song of Solomon* (supposedly written 500 years later) have encouraged speculation about the influence of Atenism on early Jewish monotheism. In *Moses and Monotheism*, Freud argued that Moses was an Egyptian nobleman and the Biblical Exodus a "pious fiction which a remote tradition has reworked in the service of its own biases". Conversely, a book by Ahmed Osman advances the theory that Akhenaten's deity derived from tales of the Jewish God related to him by his maternal grandfather Yuya, the Joseph of the Old Testament (see p.347).

Equally intriguing is the artwork of the Amarna period and the questions it raises about Akhenaten. **Amarna art** focused on nature and human life rather than the netherworld and resurrection. Royal portraiture, previously impersonally formalized, was suffused by naturalism (a process which began late in the reign of Amenophis III, as evinced by the stele depicting the obese king listlessly slumped beside Tiy). While marshes and wildlife remained a popular subject, they no longer implicitly associated birds and fish with the forces of chaos. The roofless Aten temples made new demands on sculptors and painters, who mixed sunk- and bas-relief carving to highlight features with shifting shadows and illumination.

Most striking is the rendering of **human figures**, especially Akhenaten's, whose attenuated cranium, curvaceous spine and belly, and matronly pelvis and buttocks (evident on the colossi in the Cairo Museum) have prompted speculation that the pharaoh may have suffered from Marfan's syndrome – a rare genetic disorder that leads to feelings of alienation and a slight oddness in physical appearance – or was possibly a hermaphrodite. Some argue that the Amarna style was essentially an

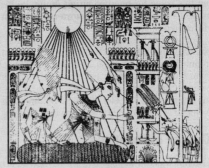

Nerfertiti and Akhenaten

acquiescence to Akhenaten's physiognomy, others that such distortions were simply a device that could be eschewed, as in the exquisite bust of Nefertiti. Advocates of the "Akhenaten was sick" theory point out that this was the only time when vomiting was ever represented in Egyptian art; however, Amarna art also uniquely depicted royalty eating, yet nobody asserts that other pharaohs never ate.

twelfth regnal year marked a turning point. Whether or not this was Akhenaten's true coronation (following his father's death), he subsequently launched a **purge against the old cults**. From Kom Ombo to Bubastis, the old temples were closed and their statues disfigured, causing widespread internal unrest. Although this was quelled by Akhenaten's chief of police, **Mahu**, his foreign minister apparently ignored pleas from foreign vassals menaced by the Hittites and Habiru, and the army was less than zealous in defending Egypt's frontiers. Akhenaten was consequently blamed for squandering the territorial gains of his forefathers.

What happened in the last years of Akhenaten and Nefertiti's reign is subject to various interpretations. The consensus is that Nefertiti and Akhenaten became estranged, and he took as co-regent **Smenkhkare**, a mysterious youth married to their eldest daughter, **Meritaten**. While Nefertiti withdrew to her Northern Palace, Akhenaten and his regent lived together at the other end of the city; the poses struck by them in mural scenes of the period have prompted suggestions of a homosexual relationship. Whatever the truth of this, it's known that Smenkhkare ruled alone for some time after the **death of Akhenaten** (c.1362 BC), before dying himself. Nefertiti's fate is less certain, but it's generally believed that she also died around the same time. To date, none of their mummies have been found (or, rather, definitely identified).

In the late 1970s, a novel solution to the puzzle of Smenkhkare's identity and the **fate of Nefertiti** was advanced by Julia Samson of the Petrie Museum in London. Samson argued that Smenkhkare *was* Nefertiti, who, far from being spurned by Akhenaten, finally achieved pharaonic status, adopting Smenkhkare as her "throne name". Since the faces on the steles depicting Akhenaten and his co-regent have been obliterated, only their cartouches identify them; and previous hypotheses have never satisfactorily explained why Smenkhkare's should be coupled with "Nefernefruaten", Nefertiti's Aten-name. Conversely, the youth shown with a princess isn't identified as her husband, nor by name, but he does wear the royal *uraeus* (see p.255 for information on pharaonic symbols). Unfortunately, this figure looks too old to be the famous boy-king who succeeded Smenkhkare at the age of nine – known to posterity as **Tutankhamun**. Tut's own genealogy is obscure (some hold that his parents were Amenophis III and his half-sister Sitamun; others favour Ay and Tey, or Akhenaten and Kiya), but it's certain that he was originally raised to worship Aten, and named Tutankh*aten*. By renouncing this name for one honouring Amun, he heralded a return to Thebes and the old gods, fronting a **Theban counter-revolution** executed by Vizier Ay and General Horemheb.

Some think this was relatively benign while Tut and his successor Ay ruled Egypt, blaming **Horemheb** and Seti I for a later and ruthless extirpation of Atenism. Certainly, in time-honoured tradition, Seti plundered the abandoned city of Akhetaten for masonry to build new temples, ordered its site cursed by priests to deter reoccupation, and excised the cartouches of every ruler tainted with the "Amarna heresy" from their monuments and the List of Kings. So thorough was this cover-up that Akhenaten and Nefertiti remained unknown to history until the nineteenth century.

The site of Akhetaten

The remains of Akhenaten's city are spread across a desert plain girdled by an arc of cliffs. Except for a few palm groves beside the Nile, the site is utterly desolate, a tawny expanse of low mounds and narrow trenches littered with potshards. These fragments of pale terracotta, cream and duck-egg blue-glazed pottery seem more tangible links to the city's past than its vestigial remains. Because the city was created from scratch and deserted soon after Tut moved the court back to Thebes, its era of glory lasted only twelve years, and much of the building was never completed, so don't expect to find imposing ruins or statues, as everything of value has been removed to museums.

However, a century of archeological research has identified the city's salient features, assisted by pictures found in contemporary tombs.

Visiting Tell el-Amarna

Tell el-Amarna (daily 9am–4pm; £E12) lies on the east bank of the Nile, 12km south of Mallawi and roughly halfway between Minya and Assyut. Starting from either of the latter, an excursion will take the best part of a day, as the widely dispersed attractions are time-consuming and tiring, unless you have a car.

Wherever you start out from, **Mallawi** is the jumping-off point. From here, drivers should turn east at Kafr Khuzm, the second village south of town, to reach the ferry crossing. By public transport, any southbound bus or local pick-up truck from the depot south of Mallawi's train station can take you out to the ferry crossing on the west bank. From here, you can either cross by felucca, car ferry (last one at 6pm) or canopied motorboat to the village of El-Till. There are also smaller ferries from Deir el-Mawas to the southern village of El-Hagg Qandil, but this isn't such a good approach.

Landing at **EL-TILL**, you'll be greeted by hordes of children touting colourful basketwork. Left of the landing stage is a small office selling **tickets** which cover the entrance to the ruins of the city, and transport to and from the Northern Tombs by a spine-jolting **tractor-driven trailer** or occasional minibus; the former returns to El-Till via the palace district of the ruined city. To see more than that, you'll have to find a car-owner willing to risk his car's suspension **driving around** the site. To enter the Northern or Southern Tombs requires another ticket, sold on the spot, plus a photo permit if you want to take any pictures. Though most people head directly for the Northern Tombs, we've described the city first; an idea of how it was and who lived there adds to an appreciation of the tombs.

The City

The dirt track running south from El-Till follows the old **Royal Road** that formed ancient Akhetaten's main axis, and is known locally as the *Sikket es-Sultan*, the Road of the Sultan. A twenty-minute walk brings you to a Muslim cemetery, which overlies part of a vast rectangle stretching eastwards towards the ridge.

This was once the **Great Temple of Aten**, whose northern wall incorporated the Hall of Foreign Tribute where emissaries proffered treasure (as depicted in tombs). Unlike traditional temples, which got darker as one approached the sanctuary, Aten's was roofless, admitting the rays of its namesake. It's thought that Horemheb ordered the temple's destruction after Akhenaten's death, and Ramses II quarried its foundations for his temples at Hermopolis, across the Nile.

Further south (and hard to distinguish beneath shifting sands) are the remnants of the Foreign Office **Archives**, where the *Amarna Letters* were discovered. Written in the Akkadian script used for diplomatic correspondence with Asiatic states, these clay tablets have revealed much about the period. Over 360 letters have been found, but more were undoubtedly lost, leaving an incomplete puzzle for archeologists to piece together and argue over. David Rohl believes that some refer to the Israelite monarchs Saul and David.

Next come three excavated rectangles that were once the **Royal Residence**. Their private apartments were separated from the stately reception halls that ran through the centre of the huge palace compound. When Flinders Petrie excavated Nefertiti's suite, he found wall tiles decorated with fruit and flowers, and a painted floor depicting fish, birds and insects (later smashed by a farmer who resented tourists walking across his fields). Across the Royal Road stood an even larger **State Palace**, with a dock for the royal barge. Both palaces were connected by a covered "flyover" spanning the road (part of one pylon remains), into which was set the **Window of Appearances**, whence

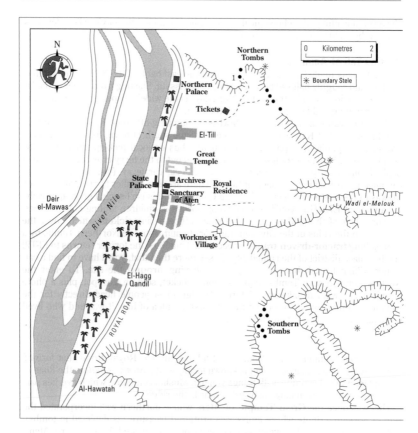

Nefertiti and Akhenaten showered favoured courtiers with gold collars and other rewards.

To the south of their residence lay the **Sanctuary of Aten**, probably used for private worship by the royal family, and the home of the High Priest, Panehsi. Beyond spread the city's **residential quarters**; the richest homes beside the road, the poorest hovels backing onto desert. Also in this quarter was the workshop of the sculptor Tuthmosis, where the famous bust of Nefertiti was uncovered in 1912, before being smuggled to Berlin's Ägyptisches Museum.

Outlying palaces and steles

The best-preserved outline of an Amarna building is Nefertiti's **Northern Palace** or summer residence, 1500m from El-Till. Low walls and hollows delineate rooms and courtyards grouped around a garden which once contained a pool that cooled the palace by evaporation. Like all Amarna residences, it was divided into public and private quarters, with north-facing doors to catch the prevailing wind. Rooms were plastered and painted, lit by oil lamps hung from pegs or set in niches, and warmed by braziers over winter. Fitted toilets and bathrooms also featured in the homes of the well-to-do. Although you can walk on bits of mosaic floor once trodden by Nefertiti, the finest sec-

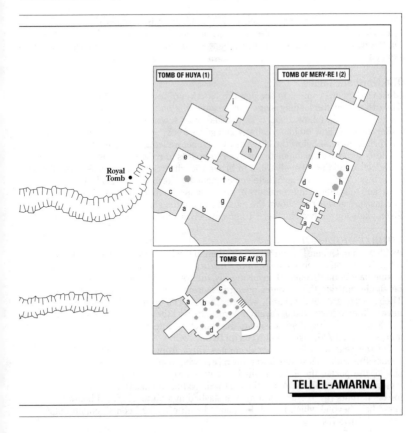

tion of painted flooring – depicting wildfowl and fish in the marshes – now lies in the Cairo Antiquities Museum. Unlike traditional marsh scenes, Amarna tableaux rarely feature hunting, suggesting that Akhenaten abjured the sport of kings.

In summer, Akhenaten and Nefertiti would ride in their electrum-plated chariot to the other end of the Royal Road, where another palace called Maru-Aten stood near the modern-day hamlet of Al-Hawatah. Alongside this **Southern Palace** lay a pleasure lake surrounded by trees and shrubs, which fed smaller pools within the palace. The walls of its columned hall were painted with flowers and inlaid with figures and Aten symbols. It was here that Petrie found hundreds of glazed pieces and flakes of paint adhering to blocks that bore Meritaten's cartouche superimposed over another, assumed to be that of Nefertiti – the rather shaky basis upon which archeologists devised the theory of Nefertiti's rejection in favour of Smenkhkare. In 1974, however, Professor John Harris re-examined the fragments and concluded that the hidden cartouches really belonged to Kiya, whose existence had been unknown to earlier scholars. From this point on, Samson developed her theory that Nefertiti and Smenkhkare were one and the same.

Akhetaten's periphery was defined by **boundary steles** carved high up on the cliffs (marked * on our map); erected over successive years, their inscriptions and family portraits have enabled archeologists to deduce many events during Akhenaten's reign.

Fine alabaster for the temples and public buildings was dragged from the **Hatnub Quarries**, 10km southeast of the city (only accessible by donkey or four-wheel drive). On the way up the wadi are the remains of workmen's huts and pottery from diverse periods.

The Northern Tombs

Most visitors are content to see just the **Northern Tombs**, 4km from El-Till village. The office near the landing stage can arrange lifts on the tractor-pulled trailer, while motorists should follow a poorly signposted track towards the cliffs. Tickets are sold either at the yellow building halfway along the track, or at the **café** (with toilets and overpriced drinks) below the cliffs; ask which before leaving El-Till.

Although guards manipulate foil-covered boards to reflect sunlight into tombs without electric lighting, it's advisable to bring a torch to study the reliefs and paintings (now less clear than the exquisite copies made by Norman de Garis Davies, a century ago), and to spotlight uneven floors or deep shafts with flimsy railings. Note that, unless you insist, you won't be shown the most distant of the six **tombs** (#1 and #2). We have given plans for the two Northern Tombs, which are the most rewarding to visit.

TOMB OF HUYA (#1)

As Steward to Queen Tiy and Superintendent of the Royal Harem, **Huya** is shown praying at the entrance, beside a *Hymn to Aten* [a] – see plan no. 1 on the map. In the following banqueting scene [b], involving Tiy, the royal couple and two princesses, it may be significant that the dowager queen is merely drinking (which was acceptable by Theban standards of decorum), whereas the Amarna brood tuck in with gusto (an act never hitherto portrayed of royalty). Across the way they imbibe wine, *sans* princesses [c], followed by a royal procession to the Hall of Tribute, where emissaries from Kush and Syria await Akhenaten and Nefertiti [d].

On the rear wall, Akhenaten decorates Huya from the Window of Appearances (notice the sculptor's studio, lower down [e]), who displays his awards [f] on the other side of the portal, the lintel of which portrays three generations of the royal family, including Amenophis III. Along the east wall, Akhenaten leads Tiy to the temple built for his parents [g]. Huya's mummy was stashed in a burial shaft [h] below the transverse hall, beyond which is a shrine painted with offerings, containing an unfinished statue of Huya [i].

TOMB OF MERY-RE II (#2)

The last resting place of **Mery-Re II**, Overseer of the Two Treasuries, is similar in shape to Huya's tomb, but was constructed late in Akhenaten's reign, since his cartouches have been replaced by Smenkhkare's, and Nefertiti's by Meritaten's. Beyond the entrance (whose adoration scene and *Hymn to Aten* are largely destroyed), the inner walls portray Nefertiti straining a drink for the king, who is seated beneath a sunshade (to your left); and Mery-Re receiving a golden crown, followed by a warm welcome from his household (right). The rear wall bears an unfinished scene of Mery-Re being rewarded by Smenkhkare and Meritaten, drawn in black ink.

TOMB OF AHMOSE (#3)

This battered tomb is one of the four that visitors usually see. The entrance walls show **Ahmose**, Akhenaten's fan-bearer, praying to Aten, with a now-illegible inscription enjoining the deity to ensure "that there is sand on the shore, that fishes in the stream have scales, and cattle have hair. Let him sojourn here until the swan turns black and the raven white". Inside, you can just discern Ahmose carrying an axe and a fan, his official regalia. On the left-hand wall are reliefs of archers, shield-bearers and pikemen, crouched and moving, followed by an outsized horse and chariot outlined in red pigment (presumably intended to represent Akhenaten leading his army into battle, which never happened).

TOMB OF MERY-RE I (#4)
High Priest **Mery-Re I** (father of Mery-Re II) rated a superior tomb (see plan no. 2 on the map), with a coloured cornice around its entrance **[a]** and columns of painted flowers at the rear of the vestibule **[b]**. Reliefs of Mery-Re and his wife, Tenro, at prayer flank the portal **[c]** into the main chamber, which retains two of its original papyrus-bud columns. Proceeding clockwise round the room, one sees Mery-Re's investiture with a golden collar **[d]** and the royal family leaving the palace **[e]**, and Akhenaten in a chariot (his face and the Aten symbol have been chiselled out, as usual). Scenes of offerings **[f]** and Aten-worship **[g]** flank the doorway into the unfinished rear chamber, which lacks any decoration. More interesting is the eastern wall **[h]**, depicting Akhenaten and the Great Temple (which has helped archeologists visualize the city's appearance). Notice the sensitive relief of blind beggars awaiting alms, low down in the corner **[i]**.

TOMBS OF PENTU (#5) AND PANEHSI (#6)
The third tomb in this cluster belongs to **Pentu**, the royal physician, whose statue in the endmost chamber has been disfigured. Its reliefs are in even worse shape, so there's no point wasting time here when you could be checking out the isolated tomb of High Priest **Panehsi**, 500m south along the cliff path. Unlike most of the others, its decorative facade has remained intact, but the interior has been modified by Copts who used it as a chapel. On the left of the entrance the royal family pray above their servants. The painted, apse-like recess in the main chamber is probably a Coptic addition. In one corner, steps spiral down into an underground sarcophagus chamber containing broken urns. Lower down the cliff are strata of rubble and potshards – vestiges of a medieval Coptic village.

Unas

The Royal Tomb
Secreted in a wild valley 5.5km from the plain, the **Royal Tomb** is kept locked to prevent further damage, but the office in El-Till can arrange for it to be opened. Assuming there's a taxi willing to make the journey (which involves negotiating the vehicle through patches of soft sand), the round trip takes three to four hours.

The tomb is the first from the XVIII Dynasty to run directly from a corridor to a burial chamber. The burial scene and text were virtually obliterated by Amun's priests, and no mummies were ever found here. However, one of the side chambers off the main corridor contained fragments of a granite sarcophagus bearing Tiy's cartouche, suggesting this might have been a family vault. Almost certainly, it served for the burial of Meketaten, the royal couple's second-eldest daughter, for the walls bear scenes of her funeral and their grief. No one knows whether Akhenaten and Nefertiti were interred here (and perhaps dragged out to rot a few years later) or somewhere else. Some believe that the mysterious mummy found in Tomb #55 in the Valley of the Kings is Akhenaten's (see p.347).

The Southern Tombs
Visiting the **Southern Tombs** entails a separate 14km excursion, and tracking down the custodian with the keys. The tombs are scattered over seven low hills in two clusters: #7–15 and #16–25. Amarna notables buried here include Tutu, the foreign minister, and Ramose, Steward of Amenophis III; but the ones to look out for are Mahu and Ay.

TOMB OF MAHU (#9)

Set amongst the northernmost group is the **Tomb of Mahu**, Akhenaten's chief of police and frontier security. The structure has a long, rough-cut corridor without decoration. On the right-hand entrance wall of the first chamber, Mahu appears before the vizier with two intruders whom he accuses of being "agitated by some foreign power". Further back are two more chambers at different levels, linked by a winding stairway and decorated with scenes of Mahu mixing with royalty.

TOMB OF AY (#25)

Ay's Tomb, the finest at Tell el-Amarna (see plan no. 3 on the map), lies some distance beyond the southern group and was never finished, since Ay built himself a new vault at Thebes after the court returned there under Tutankhamun. However, such paintings as were executed show the Amarna style at its apogee.

Both sides of the tomb's vestibule **[a]** are decorated. On the left, the king and queen, three princesses, Nefertiti's sister Mutnedjmet and her dwarves lead the court in the worship of Aten. Across the way is a superb relief of Ay and his wife Tey rendering homage and the most complete text of the famous *Hymn to Aten*. The really intriguing scenes, however, are in the main chamber. On the left side of the entrance wall, Ay and Tey are showered with decorations from the Window of Appearances, acclaimed by fan-bearers, scribes and guards **[b]**. Palace life is intimately observed: a concubine has her hair done, while girls play the harp and dance, cook and sweep; further along, Ay is congratulated by his friends, as servants carry the gifts away **[c]**. The top register shows doormen and peasants gossiping, whores and soldiers, and other streetlife. Along the rear wall are a ruined door-shaped stele **[d]** and a stairway leading to an unfinished burial shaft.

Ay and Tey are mysterious figures, honoured as "Divine Father and Mother", but never directly identified as being royal. Some reckon **Ay** was a son of Yuya and Thuya, Akhenaten's maternal grandparents; others that Tey bore Nefertiti, or that both conceived Tutankhamun. Certainly, Ay was vizier to Amenophis III, Akhenaten and Tutankhamun, and reigned briefly himself (1352–1348 BC). He was ultimately buried in the Valley of the Kings (see p.348).

Assyut and around

Every country has at least one city which is universally loathed by all but those who live there. In Egypt, Assyut holds this honour.

Douglas Kennedy, *Beyond The Pyramids*

Assyut was the first part of Middle Egypt to become a virtual **no-go zone** for tourists, as locally based Islamic radicals targeted foreigners as well as the security forces in their war against the state. Since a tour bus was ambushed outside town and a Nile cruiser was shot up near El-Qusiya, tourist buses have avoided this stretch of the Valley entirely; ordinary traffic is filtered through multiple checkpoints along the main roads, and the whole area crawls with troops and police spies. Giving the city a wide berth is obviously a prudent move, and no great loss either. Aside from the monasteries outside town, Assyut never had very much going for it. The introduction of a new road (albeit with no public transport, at least for now) and a weekly train service from Luxor to Kharga has somewhat alleviated the "Assyut dilemma" when wishing to commence the Great Desert Circuit from Kharga.

Previously it was necessary to backtrack through some of the oases, or otherwise risk a **fleeting contact** with Assyut. It is now possible to start the circuit in Bahariya or Kharga, continuing around and back to Cairo or Luxor and missing Assyut altogether.

TROUBLE IN ASSYUT

In the late 1970s, **Assyut University** became a stronghold of **Islamic Societies** (*Gamaat Islamiya*) bent on turning Egypt into an Islamic republic. They managed to get music and co-ed drama banned, and cafeterias segregated by sex; violations of their standards were liable to be punished by club-wielding militants. Today's terrorist violence is rooted in a vicious cycle of reprisals going back to 1981, when Sadat cracked down on religious extremism after years of tolerating it as a counterweight to the Left.

In response, members of the secret group **Al-Jihad** (Holy Struggle) assassinated Sadat in Cairo and stormed Assyut police headquarters the following day, hoping to launch a revolution. Two days of rioting ensued, causing 55 deaths. Among those later indicted at the "Trial of the Jihad 302" was the blind university theologian **Sheikh Omar Abd el-Rahman**, their "spiritual leader". Acquitted but exiled to the Fayoum, he later moved to America, where in 1995 he was sentenced to life imprisonment for conspiring to blow up the World Trade Center in New York.

Meanwhile, offshoots of Al-Jihad led by self-styled "Amirs" spread the conflict across Middle Egypt. Nowadays, Assyut is less of a trouble-spot than Minya or Mallawi, but the police and army presence remains formidable.

Bear in mind, however, that some buses between Kharga and Cairo go via Assyut while others don't; breezing in and out of Assyut by local transport in this manner involves very little risk of being targeted; unpremeditated assault is unlikely, as foreigners quickly acquire a police escort (unasked for).

Information and accommodation

The low-key **tourist office** (☎088/310-010) on the second floor of the Governorate building has little to offer except a brochure, but may be worth contacting if you're intending to stay more than a few hours, or make any excursions – they'll alert the police to keep tabs on you. Assyut's 24-hour **telephone exchange** is beside the train station; the **post office** is on a side street which leads on to Midan Talaat Harb, where three **banks** are located. Though none do cash advances, you can change Eurocheques at the Bank of Alexandria (Mon–Thurs & Sun 8.30am–2pm, also Sun 6–9pm & Wed 5–8pm). In case of emergencies, the **police** (☎122) are on the Corniche, and there's a **hospital** (☎088/322-016) attached to Assyut University; dial ☎123 for an ambulance.

Accommodation

Should you get stuck here by some mischance, it's best to hole up in a hotel near the station. The police prefer that foreigners stay in upmarket hotels, and have told the managers of low-budget places not to accept foreign guests. Depending on how many comply, your options may be limited. The *Venus*, *Semiramis* and *Lotus* hotels are not recommended.

Akhnaton, Sharia Mohammed Tewfik Khashaba (☎088/337-723, fax 331-600). Cramped but comfortable A/C rooms, with private baths and TV. ③.

Assiutel, 146 Sharia el-Nil (☎088/312-121, fax 312-122). Agreeable but overpriced three-star place, near the Governorate building on the Corniche. ⑥.

Badr, Sharia el-Thallaga (☎088/329-811, fax 322-820). Aspiringly palatial, the *Badr* cocoons VIPs within its padded, mirrored chambers, which come equipped with a video channel, mini-bar and A/C. ⑨.

Casablanca, Sharia Mohammed Tewfik Khashaba (☎088/337-662, fax 336-662). Slightly less plush than the *Badr*, though more pricey. ⑥.

Hotel El-Haramein, Sharia el-Hellaly (☎088/320-426). Clean, simple rooms with fans, and shared hot-water bathrooms, in a quiet location. ②.

Reem, Sharia el-Nahda (☎088/311-421, fax 311-424). Carpeted rooms with private baths and A/C; those overlooking the street are noisy. ⑥.

YMCA, Sharia Salah al-Din al-Ayubi (☎088/323-218). The old section contains simple, clean doubles with fridges; the newer wing has large carpeted rooms with A/C, TV and private bath for just over double the price. ①–②.

Youth Hostel, Lux Houses, 503 Sharia al-Walidiya (☎088/324-846). Shabby dorm beds, out near the Assyut Barrage. Doesn't require HI membership. £E6.

The City

Hopefully, nothing worse than seething traffic awaits visitors to downtown **ASSYUT**, whose street names (mostly in Arabic or outdated) are even less help than usual,

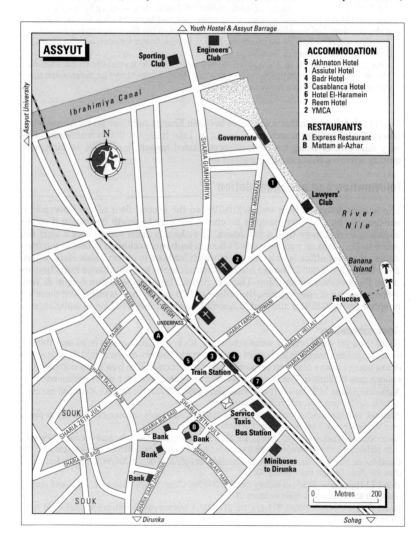

ASSYUT

△ Youth Hostel & Assyut Barrage

Sporting Club
Engineers' Club

Assyut University

Ibrahimiya Canal

N

Governorate

SHARIA GUMHORRIYA

SHARIA MOHAFAZA

ACCOMMODATION
5 Akhnaton Hotel
1 Assiutel Hotel
4 Badr Hotel
3 Casablanca Hotel
6 Hotel El-Haramein
7 Reem Hotel
2 YMCA

RESTAURANTS
A Express Restaurant
B Mattam al-Azhar

Lawyers' Club

River Nile

SHARIA YAGER
SHARIA EL-GEISH

Banana Island

Feluccas

SHARIA FAROUK KISWANI
SHARIA EL-HELLALY
SHARIA MOHAMMED FARID

UNDERPASS

SHARIA TAHRIR

5 3 4 6

Train Station

7

SOUK

SHARIA TALAT HARB
SHARIA 26TH JULY
SHARIA BUR SAID

Service Taxis
Bus Station

Bank
B
Bank

Bank

SHARIA BUR SAID
SHARIA SAAD ZAGHLOUL
SHARIA TALAAT HARB

Minibuses to Dirunka

Bank

SOUK

0 Metres 200

▽ Dirunka

Sohag ▽

though hotel billboards facilitate orientation. Happily for those hoping to escape as soon as possible, the bus, train and *service* taxi stations are right next to each other. Our account makes transport top priority, followed by places to stay and eat. The inclusion of sights and excursions that once attracted tourists is *not* a recommendation to visit, but it seems shameful to excise places that still exist, so we haven't.

Assyut has largely erased its own history. Scores of rock tombs west of town are the only sign of pharaonic Sawty, a nome capital which the Greeks renamed Lycopolis (Wolftown) after the local god, **Wepwawet**, "Opener of the Ways". Represented as a wolf or jackal of the desert, he was an apt symbol for a city which later prospered from slavery, for it was here that survivors of the Forty Days Road (see p.460) emerged from the desert to be traded wholesale. Trafficking may have continued until 1883, although Amelia Edwards saw nothing amiss a decade earlier, when she enthused over the "quaint red vases" and "bird-shaped bottles" in Assyut's souks.

Nowadays the souks purvey nothing worse than flyblown meat at the seedy end of the sprawling commercial district that opens with jewellers on Talaat Harb and peters out beside a fetid canal. A shopper's mecca it's not, but **carpets** are a local speciality, and there used to be pleasure in wandering the backstreets of decaying colonial mansions smothered in creepers, trying to locate a derelict **khan** that once stabled camels or the **Hammam al-Qadim** bathhouse, with its fine marble fountain.

On the other side of the tracks, Assyut's **riverside quarter** is freshened by breezes and greenery. Sharia el-Hellaly leads directly to the Nile, where a felucca can be rented to reach **Banana Island** (*Gezira el-Mohz*), a lush picnic spot. Assyut's elite can be found in the Governorate building and private clubs en route to the British-built (1898–1903) **Assyut Barrage**, 2km downriver, which acts as a bridge across the Nile. The Lawyers', Engineers' and Sporting clubs are on the "mainland", the Officers' Club on the east bank.

Eating and drinking

Most of the upmarket hotels incorporate **restaurants**, but the only one worth the cost is the *Badr*'s, which is also the sole outlet for alcohol in the centre. Other middle-class establishments include the Officers', Lawyers', Engineers' and Sporting **clubs,** housed in former consulates beside the Nile, which generally admit *pukka*-looking foreigners.

Assyut's commercial district, west of the station, features **cheaper eating options**. The *Express Restaurant*, 100m along 26th July Street, sells hamburgers and *shawarma* or kebab sandwiches, while you can buy a whole grilled chicken at the *Mattam al-Azhar*, 100m down Sa'ad Zaghloul (on the left, with a fancy screen above the door), whose second floor overlooks the quarter. There are juice bars, patisseries and *kushari* joints along 26th July and Talaat Harb streets; coffee houses and *taamiya* stands cluster opposite the station.

Moving on from Assyut

A dozen or so **trains** per day make the 375km run to Cairo (5–7hr), stopping at Mallawi (2hr), Minya (3hr) and Beni Suef (5hr) along the way. Heading south, half a dozen trains call at Sohag (2hr), Qena (4hr) and Luxor (6hr) en route to Aswan (12hr). Alternatively, there are several daily **buses** to Cairo (4–7hr), Qena (4hr) and Luxor, plus half-hourly services to Sohag or Minya (2hr) between 6am and 6pm. You'll have to check exactly when the four daily buses to Kharga Oasis (4hr) leave, and which one continues on to Dakhla (7–8hr).

In the morning, it's easier to reach Kharga by shared **service taxi** (4hr) from the depot south of the station. *Service* taxis also run to every town along the Valley between Minya and Qena, and a few points further afield.

Around Assyut

In the vicinity are two monasteries that testify to the roots Christianity put down in this region in the fourth century. Both are much visited by Copts and attract hordes of pilgrims on holy days.

Dirunka: the Convent of the Virgin

The Copts believe that when the Holy Family fled from Herod into Egypt, they sought refuge in caves at **DIRUNKA**, 12km outside Assyut – as did later Christians. From such troglodyte origins, however, the present **Convent of the Virgin** (aka *Deir el-Adhra,* or Santa Maria) on the site has grown into what resembles a fortified campus – cynics might say a refuge for Assyut's Coptic population, should the worst ever occur.

The expansion is justified by the monastery having to accommodate 50,000 pilgrims for the **Moulid of the Virgin** (August 7–22). This occasions the parading of icons around the spacious cave church where they stand for most of the year. Coptic altars face east because it's from there that Jesus will return, but also because He is "the sun" of their religion. Pilgrims are photographed against a huge portrait of the Virgin, or the verdant plain overlooked by the convent's terrace, below which is a Coptic village where nuns operate a dispensary. In 1994, many homes were destroyed when a liquid-gas tank exploded.

Getting to the monastery by private taxi (£E6–10 round-trip) saves a fifteen-minute uphill slog from the roadside, where minibuses from Assyut (25pt) drop visitors. If you can't beg a lift back at the convent, returning minibuses can be flagged down on the main road. The ridge between Dirunka and Assyut is honeycombed with long vandalized rock tombs from pharaonic times.

The Burnt Monastery

By taking a *service* taxi 42km north to **EL-QUSIYA** (1hr; £E2) and asking directions for this small town's other taxi depot, you can catch a covered pick-up 5km out to the **Burnt Monastery** (*Deir el-Muharaaq*), near the desert's edge. Its tinderbox surroundings explain the name and protective walls; the crenellated inner rampart is still blackened from a conflagration that occurred during the **Moulid of the Virgin** (June 21–28) some years ago.

Except on fast days, visitors are shown around the thriving, modernized establishment. Many of the hundred students at its Theological College will become monks when they turn twenty-five. Within the compound are grouped the Abbot's residence, a fourth-century keep and two churches. Believers maintain that the **cave sanctuary** of the **Church of the Anointed** (*El-Azraq*) once hid the Holy Family for a month, and what is now the altar stone was used to block its entrance. When an abbot ordered its replacement, the mason's hand was paralysed and a vision of Jesus appeared, intoning "Leave it alone." The *Virgin and Child* icon is said to be painted by St Luke; those in the **Church of St George** come from Ethiopia.

Foreigners with passports might be allowed to stay at the monastery's **guesthouse**, where simple meals are provided. Even for brief visits, a donation seems appropriate.

Sohag

Set on a rich agricultural plain bounded by the hills of the Eastern and Western deserts, **SOHAG** (pronounced "Sohaj") is an industrious town of 75,000 with a large Christian community and a small university. Before the conflict in Middle Egypt, Sohag made a nice, relaxed stopover and a base for visits to the nearby **Red and White monasteries**, or Abydos Temple, further away (see p.286). Nowadays tourists are afraid to come

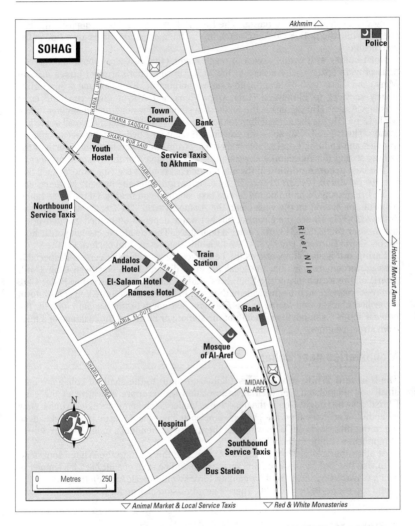

Akhmim △

Police

SOHAG

SHARIA EL JIHAD

SHARIA SAQQAFA

Town Council

Bank

SHARIA BUR SAID

Youth Hostel

Service Taxis to Akhmim

SHARIA ABU AL-MUNIM

Northbound Service Taxis

R i v e r   N i l e

△ *Hotels Meryut Amun*

Andalos Hotel

SHARIA EL

Train Station

El-Salaam Hotel
Ramses Hotel

SHARIA EL-QUTE

SHARIA EL MAHATTA

Bank

Mosque of Al-Aref

MIDAN AL-AREF

SHARIA EL GIRGA

N

Hospital

Southbound Service Taxis

0   Metres   250

Bus Station

▽ *Animal Market & Local Service Taxis*   ▽ *Red & White Monasteries*

here, despite valiant efforts by the council to woo visitors by creating an archeological museum, and a tourist village in the mountains 12km east of town (both near completion). Aside from these, Sohag hosts a huge **animal market** just off the Girga road, known as the *Souk el-Itnayn* because it's held on Monday (6am–noon), and the **Moulid of Al-Aref** – Sohag's patron saint – a few weeks before the nationwide feast of Eid al-Adha. Last but not least, there's a colossal statue of an ancient Egyptian princess in the town of **Akhmim**, just across the Nile from Sohag.

Practicalities

International calls can be made from the **post and telephone office** on the Corniche; the 24-hour branch inside the train station is only for domestic calls. Further north along the Corniche are two **banks**. The **hospital** (☎093/332-007) is opposite the bus station, while the **police** (☎093/654-800) are by the mosque on the eastern side of the Nile bridge.

Don't bother with **trains** except to reach Luxor (4hr) or Cairo – buses and *service* taxis provide faster, easier access to the Valley towns. There are five **buses** daily to Minya and Cairo (6.30–10.30am), and a similar number to Luxor (last one at 3pm). Half-hourly services to El-Balyana (1hr), Qena (3hr) and Assyut (2hr) run until early evening. Assyut (1hr 30min) is the furthest destination for northbound **service taxis**, while Qena (1hr) is the normal limit for southbound vehicles, which also call at the bus station. The trip to El-Balyana – the jumping-off point for Abydos – takes between thirty minutes and an hour. Local *service* taxis depart from two separate depots: north of the railway station (for Akhmim) and west of the bus terminal (for the White Monastery).

The best **accommodation** in town is on the east bank of the Nile, where you'll find the *Meryut Amun* (☎093/601-985; ⑤) by turning right after the mosque at the far end of the bridge; any Akhmim-bound *service* taxi can drop you nearby. Of the three hotels opposite the station on the west bank, the *Andalos* (☎093/334-328; ③) and *El-Salaam* (☎093/333-317; ④) are the cleanest, but hot water depends on bottled gas deliveries; the *Ramses* (☎093/332-313; ①) comes a poor third. There's also a spartan **youth hostel** on Sharia Bur Said (☎093/324-395; lock-out 10am–2pm; 1am curfew; £E10).

Eating out is similar, insofar as the best places are outside the centre. Respectably dressed foreigners may join the local worthies dining at the Northern Club (*Nady Bahri*) on the west bank, or the Engineers' Club (*Nady el-Mohandiseen*) or Police Club (*Nady esh-Shorta*) on the other side of the Nile. In the centre of town, you can sit down for grilled chicken and *tahina* at the *El-Eman*, just north of the *Andalos*; look for the *kushari* shops 100m north and south of the station; or rustle up the makings of a meal from street vendors.

Monasteries near Sohag

The **Red and White monasteries** (daily 9am–5pm) to the south of Sohag are both small and dilapidated, yet their near-desolation seems more evocative of the early Christians who sought God in the desert than busier establishments like Dirunka. Only a handful of acolytes tend the chapels, timeworn stones and plastic medallions attesting to the thousands of Copts who visit them during Shenoudi's *moulid*, when dozens of minibuses shuttle in the pilgrims.

At other times local *service* taxis (50pt) only run the 10km to the White Monastery, so to visit the Red Monastery (4km further on) and be sure of a lift back it's simpler to rent a **private taxi**. After hard bargaining (drivers only speak Arabic), the price for the round trip seems to be £E15–20. There's no admission charge for the monasteries, but *baksheesh* is appreciated.

The White Monastery

Across the plain from Sohag, near an arabesqued mosque, high limestone walls enclose the **White Monastery** (*Deir al-Abyad*). Named for the colour of its masonry (mostly taken from pharaonic or Roman buildings), the monastery had some two thousand monks during its heyday. Today it has only three residents, and its courtyard is flanked by ruined cloisters and cells, while discarded millstones and soot-blackened vaults show where the kitchen once stood. Remove your shoes before entering the **Church of St Shenoudi**, a lofty basilica admitting breezes and birdsong, observed by a stern-faced Christ Pantokrator. Note the monolithic granite pulpit halfway along the northern wall, Roman columns in the apses, and pharaonic hieroglyphics on the outer rear wall.

The monastery is also known as *Deir Anba Shenouda* after its fifth-century founder, who enforced the monastic rule with legendary beatings – on one occasion, fatally. Shenoudi condemned bathing as an upper-class luxury maintained by the sweat of the poor; early monks cleansed themselves by rolling naked in the sand. During **Shenoudi's moulid** (July 14), childless women roll down nearby hills in sacks, hoping to obtain divine intervention.

The Red Monastery

Down the road past walled Coptic and Muslim cemeteries, a straggling village conceals the **Red Monastery** (*Deir al-Ahmar*) in an unobtrusive cul-de-sac. Built of dark red brick, the monastery is attributed to St Bishoi, a penitent armed robber who became Shenoudi's disciple (retaining his club as a reminder); hence its other sobriquet, *Deir Anba Bishoi*.

The monastery's principal **church** is darker than Shenoudi's, its blackened tenth-century murals less remarkable than the finely carved tiers of niches. Whereas purloined Roman columns and the White Monastery's pharaonic-style corvetto cornice betray artistic debts, the intricate floral capitals inside the outer gate show that Coptic architecture soon transcended mere imitation. In the courtyard's far corner squats the smaller **Red Church**, whose inner sanctum is barred to women.

Akhmim

Only a century ago, guidebooks ranked Sohag as less important than **AKHMIM**, across the Nile – a place reckoned "the oldest city in Egypt" by the sixteenth-century Moorish geographer-historian Leo Africanus. Akhmimis have built on the rubble of their ancestors since pre-Dynastic times, so the whole town rests on a mound of remains, with a maze-like street plan essentially unchanged since the Middle Ages. The town's name derives from the Coptic *Khmim*, itself derived from the name of an ancient local fertility god, Khente-Min, who was often represented by a giant phallus.

Its **weaving** tradition is equally old: legend has it that the pharaohs were buried in shrouds of Akhmim silk. Early last century, imported textiles closed hundreds of local workshops and concentrated production into four factories, which used power looms from Rochdale in England. The hand-weaving tradition was only preserved by a missionary-inspired **Women's Cooperative** (*Rahabaat*), founded in the 1920s, whose tapestries are now sold as highly priced works of art. The weavers forgo celebrity and high earnings in order not to irritate their menfolk, so visitors are unwelcome.

Akhmim's main sight is an eleven-metre-high limestone **statue of Meryut Amun**, accidentally uncovered in 1981 along the main road running east from the market. Little is known about Princess Meryut Amun, who may have been a daughter (or wife) of Ramses II, but her statue is memorably vivid, with curled hair and rouged lips. En route is a waste ground used for the weekly **Animal Market** (Wed morning), which is even bigger and livelier than the one in Sohag. Down by the river on the other side of town are communities of **boat builders** and **potters**, and a noxious tannery.

Another reason for making the trip is that many of the *service* taxis that shuttle between Sohag and Akhmim (25pt) are lovely **vintage cars** from the 1930s and 1940s. These drop you at an intersection in Akhmim's centre known as "Setta Aziza"; from here, follow a road jinking north towards the market and the **Al-Amri Mosque**, founded not long after the Mosque of Amr in Cairo. In the grounds of the mosque are Roman pillars and a grave of similar antiquity.

UPPER EGYPT

In antiquity, **Upper Egypt** started at Memphis and ran as far south as Aswan on the border with Nubia. Nowadays, with the designation of Middle Egypt, borders are a little more hazy, though the **Qena Bend** is generally taken as the region's beginning and **Aswan** is still effectively the end of the line.

Within this stretch of the Nile is the world's most intensive concentration of ancient monuments – temples, tombs and palaces constructed from the onset of the Middle Kingdom (c.1990 BC) up until Roman and Byzantine times. The greatest of the buildings are the **cult temples** of **Abydos**, **Dendara**, **Karnak**, **Esna**, **Edfu**, **Kom Ombo**, **Philae** and **Abu Simbel**, each conceived as "homes" for their respective deities and an accretion of centuries of building. Scarcely less impressive are the multitude of tombs in the **Theban Necropolis**, most famously in the **Valley of the Kings**, across the river from **Luxor**, where Tutankhamun's resting place is merely a hole in the ground by comparison with those of such great pharaohs as Seti I and Ramses II.

Monuments aside, Upper Egypt marks a subtle shift of character, with the desert closing in on the river, and dom palms growing alongside barrel-roofed houses, designed to reflect the intense heat. One of the greatest pleasures to be had here – indeed one of the highlights of any Egyptian trip – is to absorb the riverscape slowly from the vantage point of a **felucca**. This is easily arranged on the spot at Luxor or Aswan – the latter being the preferred starting point, so that you can sail downriver with no fear of being becalmed.

Abydos

As Muslims endeavour to visit Mecca once in their lifetimes and Hindus aspire to die at Benares, the ancient Egyptians devoutly wished to make a pilgrimage to **ABYDOS**, cult centre of the god Osiris. Those who failed to make it hoped to do so posthumously; relatives brought bodies for burial, or embellished distant tombs with scenes of the journey to Abydos (represented by a boat under sail, travelling upriver). Egyptians averred that the dead "went west", for the entrance to the underworld was believed to lie amidst the desert hills beyond Abydos. By bringing other deities into the Osirian fold, Abydos acquired a near monopoly on death cults, which persisted into Ptolemaic times, while its superbly carved **Temple of Seti I** has been a tourist attraction since the 1830s. Although it's seldom visited since the campaign of terrorism began in 1992, the temple is open to tourists, with transport to and from Luxor under armed guard.

Getting there from Luxor and El-Balyana

Abydos lies 10km outside the small town of **EL-BALYANA**, midway between the provincial capitals of Qena and Sohag. Before the unrest in Middle Egypt, it made an easy half-day's excursion from either town, but now the few tourists who come invariably make a long **day trip from Luxor**, perhaps visiting Dendara Temple on the way (see p.294). A **taxi** should cost £E95–140, depending on the number of passengers and your bargaining skills.

Travel restrictions for foreigners may apply in this area (see box p.254 for details); we've included the following public transport information in case the security situation changes. As **trains** and **buses** from Luxor to Qena and El-Balyana are excruciatingly slow, it's best to catch a **service taxi** directly to El-Balyana (£E5) or, failing that, to Nag Hammadi (£E4), and then another *service*. At El-Balyana itself, ask to be dropped at the checkpoint by the bridge, where your arrival will fluster the police. They want you gone by nightfall, so staying in El-Balyana is not an option.

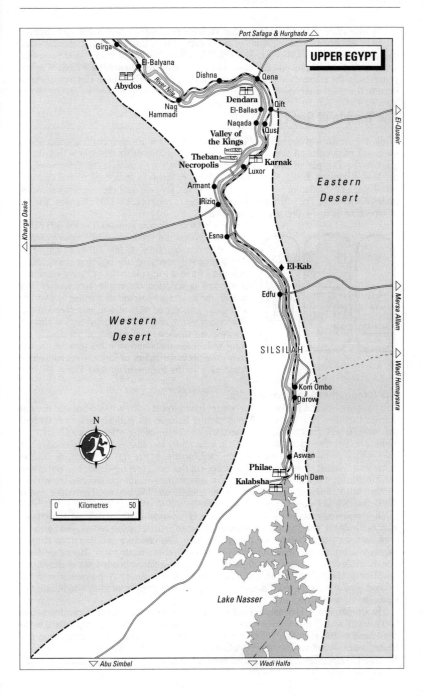

The **site of Abydos** (daily 9am–4pm; £E12) is reached by a well-surfaced road used by carts and camels bearing loads of sugar cane, which terminates on the spruced-up main square of **AL-ARABA EL-MADFUNA** village, beside the ruins, where souvenir and soft-drink stalls precede the ticket kiosk. Bring a **torch** to see the darkened reliefs properly. In the interests of "security", visitors are constantly followed by a custodian – even to the toilet washroom!

The Temple of Seti I

While the temples of Karnak and Deir el-Bahri at Luxor are breathtaking conceptions executed on a colossal scale, it is the exquisite quality of its bas-reliefs that distinguishes the **Temple of Seti I** at Abydos. The reliefs are amongst the finest works of the New Kingdom, harking back to Old Kingdom forms in an artistic revival that mirrored Seti's political efforts to consolidate the XIX Dynasty and recover territories lost under Akhenaten. The official designation of Seti's reign (1318–1304 BC) was "the era of repeating births" – literally a renaissance.

Seti I

It was in fact Seti's son, Ramses II (1304–1237 BC), who completed the reconquest of former colonies and the construction of his father's temple at Abydos. Strictly speaking, the building was neither a cult nor a funerary temple in the ordinary sense (for a general description of temple architecture, see p.288), for its chapels contained shrines to a variety of deities concerned with death, resurrection and the netherworld, and one dedicated to Seti himself. Its purpose was essentially political: to identify the king with these cults and with his putative "ancestors", the previous rulers of Egypt, thus conferring legitimacy on the Ramessid dynasty.

The forecourt and Hypostyle Halls

The temple's original **pylon** and **forecourt** have almost been levelled but you can still discern the lower portion of a scene depicting Ramses II's dubious victory at Qadesh **[a]**, women with finely plaited tresses **[b]**, and Seti making offerings to Osiris (in a niche, nearby). From the damaged statues currently stored in the upper, second court, your eyes are drawn to the square-columned **facade**, where tiny birds inhabit fissures in the wall behind pillars covered with scenes of Ramses greeting Osiris, Isis and Horus **[c]**. Originally, the temple was entered by seven doors (corresponding to the shrines within), but Ramses ordered all except the middle one blocked up. The upper part of the facade has been crudely rebuilt in concrete.

The ponderous sunk-reliefs in the **outer Hypostyle Hall**, completed by Ramses after Seti's death, suggest that he used second-rate artists, having redeployed Seti's top craftsmen on his own (now destroyed) temple. The entrance wall portrays Ramses measuring the temple with the goddess Selket and presenting it to Horus on Seti's behalf, while on the wall to your right Ramses offers a falcon-headed box of papyrus to Isis, Horus and Osiris, and is led to the temple by Horus and Wepwawet (the jackal-headed god of Assyut) to be doused with holy water (represented by the interlinked signs for life and purity) **[d]**.

The deeper **inner Hypostyle Hall** was the last part of the temple decorated before Seti's death, and some sections were never finished, but others are exceptional. On the right-hand wall Seti stands before Osiris and Horus – who pour holy water from garlanded vases – and makes offerings before the shrine of Osiris, who is attended by Maat and Ronpet (the goddess of the year) in front, with Isis, Amentet (goddess of the

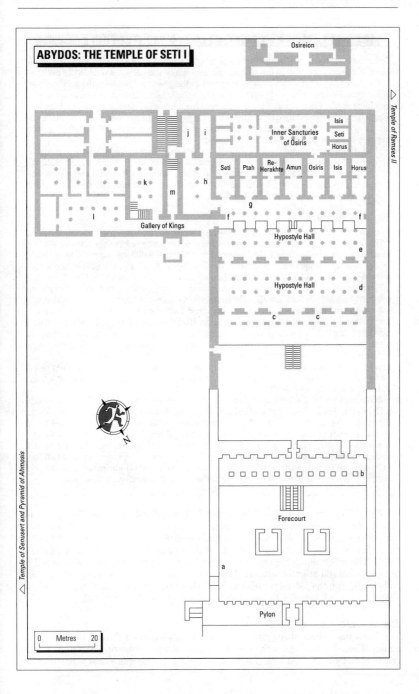

ABYDOS: THE TEMPLE OF SETI I

Osireion

Temple of Ramses II ▷

Isis
Seti
Horus

Inner Sancturies
of Osiris

j i

Seti Ptah Re-
Herakhte Amun Osiris Isis Horus

k

h

m

g

f   f

l

Gallery of Kings

Hypostyle Hall

e

Hypostyle Hall

d

c   c

◁ Temple of Senusert and Pyramid of Ahmosis

N

b

Forecourt

a

Pylon

0   Metres   20

ANCIENT EGYPTIAN TEMPLE ARCHITECTURE

From earliest times, two distinct types of temple evolved in Egypt: **cult temples**, dedicated to the principal god of the region, and **mortuary temples**, devoted to the worship of the dead king. Cult temples were regarded as the *pr-ntr* or "house of the god", whose effigy was cosseted with daily rituals and periodically taken to visit its divine spouse in another temple. Such centres were elaborate from the start, unlike mortuary temples, which began as two-roomed structures attached to the king's pyramid and joined to a valley temple by a causeway, only being divorced from their tombs and burgeoning into massive complexes during the New Kingdom.

Most of the great temples of the Nile Valley embody centuries of work by successive kings and dynasties, some of whom added major sections while others merely decorated a wall or carved their name on another pharaoh's statue. Built from stone, to last forever, their general form and layout hardly changed over millennia, and were still being imitated during Ptolemaic and Roman times.

TEMPLE LAYOUT

Because each temple was envisaged as a progression from this world into the realm of divine mysteries, halls got darker and lower and doors narrowed as they approached the sanctuary. In accordance with this convention, additional halls or pylons had to increase in size as they grew more distant from the sanctuary. As a corollary of this, the architecture is generally older the further in you venture.

Temples were seldom accessible to commoners, being set within enclosures surrounded by lofty mud-brick walls. These **precincts** often contained priestly residences, workshops and storehouses, along with a **Sacred Lake** for ritual ablutions. In Ptolemaic and Roman times, they also usually featured a **Birth House** or *Mamissi*, which emphasized the king's divine antecedents. Entering the temple proper meant passing through a series of gated **pylons** whose towers bore giant reliefs of the pharaoh making offerings to the gods and smiting Egypt's enemies. A few also boasted graceful **obelisks** whose tips were sheathed in gold or electrum (an alloy of gold and silver). Between the pylons were open **courts**, often flanked with **colonnades** of Osiride pillars and guarded by **colossi** of a pharaoh or deity.

Another pylon (or a screen wall surmounted by open columns) divided the court from a **Hypostyle Hall**, whose forest of columns was intended to resemble a papyrus thicket, dimly illuminated by shafts of sunlight penetrating apertures in the roof. Beyond lay a series of **vestibules** or antechambers (often preceded by a smaller Hypostyle Hall), climaxing in the **sanctuary** where the deity's effigy and sacred boat reposed. Smaller rooms and **chapels** for storing valuables or worshipping subsidiary deities were grouped off the halls and behind the sanctuary. Some temples also had a **rooftop shrine** or kiosk for celebrating the resurrection of Osiris and revitalizing the divine effigy at New Year.

---

west) and Nephthys behind [**e**]. Seti's profile is a stylized but close likeness to his mummy (in the Cairo Antiquities Museum). The east and west walls are of sandstone, the north and south of limestone. Two projecting piers [**f**] near the back of the hall depict Seti worshipping the *Djed* column while wearing the crown of Upper or Lower Egypt. The reliefs along the rear wall – showing him being anointed and crowned by the gods – are still brightly coloured. Best of all is a scene of Seti kneeling before Osiris and Horus, with the sacred persea tree in the background, which appears above head height on the wall between the sanctuaries of Ptah and Re-Herakhte [**g**].

The sanctuaries

The finest **bas-reliefs** at Abydos are inside the sanctuaries dedicated to Seti and six deities. Though retaining much of their original colouring (showing how most temple reliefs once looked), their graceful lines and subtle moulding are best appreciated on

DECORATION

Virtually every temple wall is covered in **reliefs**, either carved proud (bas-reliefs, the most delicate and time-consuming method), recessed into the surface (sunk-reliefs) or simply incised (the quickest form to execute). They are arranged in rows called "registers", counted from the bottom of the wall upwards. Doorway lintels are always adorned with a winged sun-disc, symbolizing the Two Lands whose heraldic plants are a common motif. Some Ptolemaic temples also feature astronomical ceilings depicting heavenly bodies and creatures of the zodiac. Since reliefs were generally painted in bright colours, temples must once have looked far gaudier than their present state suggests.

Also striking are the variegated **columns**, which evolved from two basic types. Square-sectioned pillars were sometimes faced with a statue of the pharaoh as a god (usually Osiris – hence the term Osiride pillars) or crowned with the head of the goddess Hathor (perhaps surmounted by a sistrum, her sacred instrument). A wider variety derived from plant forms, with different permutations of shafts and capitals. The palm column had a plain shaft and leafy capital; the papyrus column chevron markings and a flowering or closed bud capital; while a cluster of rounded stems gave the lotus column its distinctive "bundle" appearance. By Ptolemaic times, capitals resembled Baroque bouquets and the established forms were mixed to create composite columns.

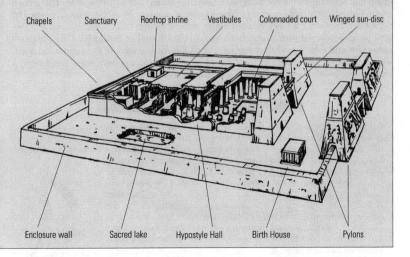

| Chapels | Sanctuary | Rooftop shrine | Vestibules | Colonnaded court | Winged sun-disc |

| Enclosure wall | Sacred lake | Hypostyle Hall | Birth House | Pylons |

the unpainted reliefs. Seti's classical revival eschewed both Amarna expressionism and the bombastic XVIII Dynasty imperial style, which his son embraced and raised to new heights of megalomania. The seven sanctuaries are roofed with false vaults carved from rectangular slabs, and culminate in false doors (except for Osiris's chamber, which leads into his inner sanctuaries).

To ancient Egyptians, these chambers constituted the abode of the gods, whom the king (or his priests) propitiated with daily rituals, shown on the walls. Having opened the shrine, the pharaoh offers the god sacrifices and washes and dresses its statue, which is then purified and presented with gifts. After further offerings before the god's barque, he scatters sand on the floor, sweeps away his footprints and withdraws, leaving the deity alone till next morning.

An exception to this rule is the **Sanctuary of Seti**, which emphasizes his recognition by the gods, who lead him into the temple and ceremonially unite the Two Lands along the northern wall. Below the barque near the back of the left-hand wall, Seti receives a list of offerings from Thoth and the High Priest Iunmutef, wearing the leopardskin and braided side lock of his office. Finally, Seti leaves the temple, his palanquin borne by the souls of jackal-headed deities from the Upper Egyptian town of Nekhen and hawk-headed gods from the Delta capital of Pi-Ramses.

The fine unpainted reliefs of Seti and seated deities in Re-Herakhte's chamber make interesting comparison with similar painted scenes in the sanctuaries of Ptah, Amun, Osiris and Isis. On the side wall just outside the Sanctuary of Horus, the pharaoh presents Maat to Osiris, Isis and Horus, a XIX Dynasty motif symbolizing righteous order and the restoration of royal legitimacy.

The **inner sanctuaries of Osiris** boast three side chapels whose colours were still fresh and shiny in the 1980s, but are now blackened by mould – a rapid rate of deterioration affecting many of the temples and tombs in the Nile Valley.

The southern wing

From the inner Hypostyle Hall you can enter the southern wing of Seti's temple. The portal nearest his sanctuary leads into the columned **Hall of Sokar and Nefertum**, two deities of the north representing the life-giving forces of the earth and the cycle of death and rebirth, who were integrated into the Osirian cult by Seti's time. The niches along the left-hand wall once contained Osiride statues. Reliefs across the way **[h]** depict Seti receiving a hawk-headed Sokar, and Nefertum in both his human and leonine forms (crowned with a lotus blossom). In the **Chapel of Sokar [i]**, Osiris appears in his bier and returns to life grasping his penis (near the back of the right-hand wall), while Isis hovers over him in the form of a hawk on the opposite wall. You'll need a torch to see inside the **Chapel of Nefertum**, next door **[j]**.

THE CULT OF OSIRIS

Originally the corn god of Busiris in the Delta, **Osiris** attained national significance early in the Old Kingdom, when he was co-opted into the Heliopolitan Ennead. According to legend, Re (or Geb) divided the world between Osiris and his brother Seth, who resented being given all the deserts and murdered Osiris to usurp his domain. Although the god's body was recovered by **Isis**, the sister-wife of Osiris, Seth recaptured and dismembered it, burying the pieces (and feeding the penis to a crocodile, in one version). Aided by her sister Nephthys, Isis collected the bits and bandaged them together to create the first mummy, which they briefly resurrected with the help of Thoth and Anubis. By transforming herself into a hawk, Isis managed to conceive a child with Osiris before he returned to the netherworld to rule as lord and judge of the dead. Secretly raised to manhood in the Delta, their child **Horus** later avenged his father and cast Seth back into the wilderness (see p.369).

Osiris

As the reputed burial place of the torso (or head) of Osiris, **Abydos** was the setting for two annual **festivals**. The "Great Going Forth" celebrated the search for and discovery of his remains, while the Osiris Festival re-enacted his myth in a series of Mystery Plays. In one scene, the god's barque was "attacked" by minions of Seth and "protected" by **Wepwawet**, the jackal-headed god of Assyut. This marked the final stage in a process of religious mergers, for it was Wepwawet who supplanted **Khentamenty**, the original death god of Abydos, as the "Foremost of the Westerners", before his own assimilation into the cult of Osiris. The total identification of Abydos with **death cults** was completed by its association with **Anubis**, the jackal-headed god of embalming, always present in funerary scenes.

The other portal leads through into the **Gallery of Kings**, so called after the list of Seti's predecessors carved on the right-hand wall. For political reasons, the Hyksos pharaohs, Hatshepsut, Akhenaten and his heirs have all been omitted, and Seti has recorded his own name as *Menmare Osiris-Merneptah* (rather than *Menmare Seti-Merneptah*) to distance himself from his namesake Seth, the killer of Osiris. Nonetheless, the list has proved immensely useful to archeologists, naming 34 kings (chiefly from the VI, VII, XII, XVIII and XIX Dynasties) in roughly chronological order. Seti and his son Ramses stand facing the list of their "ancestors", which begins with Menes (Zoser).

With the **Sanctuary of the Boats [k]** and the **Hall of Sacrifices [l]** off-limits, the best course beyond here is to follow the side corridor **[m]** past a vivid relief of Seti and Ramses harnessing a bull and running to greet Wepwawet, then go out through a rear door to the Osireion, behind the temple.

The Osireion and other remains

Recent discoveries at Abydos have reopened the debate over its role as a pharaonic cemetery, antedating the great Old Kingdom necropolis of Saqqara, outside Cairo. When Flinders Petrie excavated Abydos at the beginning of the 20th century, he uncovered numerous *mastabas* which he believed to be royal tombs from the Old Kingdom, but which later Egyptologists held to be cenotaphs or Osirian burial places – dummy tombs, built to promote a closer association between the pharaoh's *ka* and Osiris, while his mummy reposed elsewhere, with Re. In 1991, however, a team from Pennsylvania University found a dozen royal **Solar Boats** buried at Abydos, estimated to be five thousand years old, or four hundred years older than the Solar Boat at Giza. This raises the possibility that the early Dynastic burials attributed to Saqqara may have occurred at Abydos instead, and thus some of its presumed Osirian burial places were really once royal tombs. Don't get too excited, though – the Solar Boats aren't likely to be open to the public for years to come, and no one has found an intact royal tomb yet.

The only Osirian burial place visible nowadays is the Cenotaph of Seti I – more commonly known as the **Osireion** – and even this is half-buried and rendered partly inaccessible by stagnant water. Built of massive blocks, it once enclosed a room containing a mound surrounded by a moat (symbolizing the first land arising from the waters of Chaos at the dawn of Creation), where a pseudo-sarcophagus awaited resurrection.

Abydos once covered a huge area, with various temple complexes, necropolises and sacred lakes, and a town centred upon the great Temple of Osiris. Nowadays, almost

---

THE GNOSTIC GOSPELS

The **Nag Hammadi Codices** – better known as the **Gnostic Gospels** – were found near the town, below the caves of Jebel et-Tur, in 1945. The gospels are fourth-century Coptic translations of second-century Greek originals, although the Gospel of Thomas might date from 50–100 AD, and therefore be as early as – or even older than – the gospels of Matthew, Mark, Luke and John.

The Gnostics (from *Gnosis*, Greek for "knowledge") were early mystics who believed that God could only be known through self-understanding and that the world was illusory. Regarding self and the divine as one, they saw Jesus as a spiritual guide rather than the crucified son of God, pointing to his words in the Gospel of Thomas: *"If you bring forth what is within you, what you bring forth will save you. If you do not bring forth what is within you, what is within you will destroy you."* But the official church thought otherwise and condemned Gnosticism as a heresy; hence the burial of these codices (some of which can be seen today in Cairo's Coptic Museum).

everything has been demolished or sanded over, and not many visitors bother with what remains. If you feel like stretching your legs, however, the **Temple of Ramses II** is 300m from the Osireion. Though now much ruined and reduced in height, the temple was surely once magnificent, incorporating fine limestone, red and black granite and alabaster masonry. Fragments of scenes of the Battle of Qadesh and offerings can be discerned on the remnants of its enclosure walls and pillared courtyard.

Although there are other ruins further afield, they are really only of interest to specialists, and usually kept locked.

Nag Hammadi and Dishna

At **NAG HAMMADI** (pronounced "Naja Ham*maadi*"), 40km south of El-Balyana, the Nile sweeps into the **"Qena Bend"**, and the main road and train tracks transfer from the west bank to the other side of the river. Nag Hammadi itself is an important agricultural centre with a large cement factory, otherwise only known for its past association with the Gnostic Gospels (see previous page). Travellers should beware that, after dark, road traffic to the east bank may be suspended for security reasons; it's hard to know whether this is due to the conflict in Middle Egypt as a whole, or the traditional state of lawlessness in Dishna, across the river.

DISHNA looks much like any other small town in the Valley, but is something of a bad joke amongst Egyptians. In the surrounding countryside, almost every male above the age of puberty carries a gun, owing to a century-old vendetta between two neighbouring villages. The local police seldom leave their fortified post, and never get involved in fights. The gunmen come into their own at night, when it's not unknown for cars to be held up; in daytime, the road is perfectly safe and you'd never notice anything amiss. Dishna folk are actually renowned for their hospitality to guests; their hostility is reserved for their neighbours.

Qena and Dendara

Until recently, tourists went to **Qena** for two reasons: its **connections** between the Nile Valley and the Red Sea Coast, and local transport to the fantastic **temples** of **Dendara** (8km west of town) and **Abydos** (see preceding section). Nowadays, however, Nile cruisers only dock there under guard, and few independent travellers make the day-trip from Luxor and use the town as a springboard for reaching Dendara Temple. The method of getting there outlined below is meant to minimize contact with Qena and get you to Dendara (and back) as fast as possible.

Qena

QENA (pronounced "*Ge*na") has the dubious distinction of being the place where the first attack on tourists occurred, in the summer of 1992. (The killers were traced to a nearby village, whose entire population was evicted, and their homes demolished, for "harbouring terrorists".) Given Qena's reputation for being an Islamist stronghold, one can hardly believe that it was a hotbed of vice during the mid-nineteenth century, when many of the professional singers whom Mohammed Ali exiled from Cairo for their "indecent" dances and prostitution settled here – nor that Qena's air base was a staging post during the abortive mission to rescue the US hostages from Iran, in 1980. Such ironies aside, Qena feels a world apart from Luxor, with no obvious disparities between rich and poor, nor even any noticeable differences in lifestyles.

Due to the Qena Bend, the banks of the Nile lie north and south, rather than east and west of the river. The town is on the north bank, with a bridge to the other side,

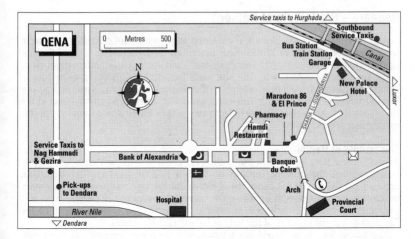

where Dendara is located. All the government buildings in Qena are sited near the Nile in a kind of security zone. Further inland, once-graceful colonial villas give way to low-rise flats that resemble rejects from Eastern Europe, or maze-like tenements that defy cartographers to produce an accurate map of town. Fortunately, everything one needs to know about is easily found, using the two mosques on the main drag as landmarks. The older mosque (with one minaret) contains the tomb of a twelfth-century sheikh, who is honoured by the **Moulid of Abdel Rahim al-Qenawi**, on the 14th day of *Sha'ban*.

Transport from Luxor and other practicalities

Tour groups are only taken to Dendara on **day cruises from Luxor** aboard the *Lotus* (departs from near the *Novotel*) or *Tiba Star* (beside the *Winter Palace Hotel*) which dock in Qena's security zone while passengers are whisked off to the temple under armed guard. The once or twice weekly excursion costs £E150 per person and anyone can sign up. **Travel restrictions** for foreigners may apply in this area (for further details, see box on p.254); the following information will therefore only be relevant if the situation alters. Reaching Dendara by public transport involves crossing the Nile to Gezira by 9am and catching a *service* taxi to Qena (£E2; 1hr), which drops you at a taxi depot near the Nile bridge, on the edge of town, close to where pick-ups (50pt) depart for Dendara village, not far from the temple. Failing that, you can take a *service* taxi bound for Nag Hammadi, but get off soon after passing beneath a massive bridge that will eventually carry the new train line between Hurghada and the Nile Valley. The signposted side road to Dendara (1km) is 200m along, on the left.

The only **accommodation** in Qena (where hotels have been told to remove signs in English to discourage foreigners) worth considering is the seedy *New Palace Hotel* (☎096/322-509; ③), in the turquoise building behind the garage outside the station. Standard Egyptian **meals** are available at *El-Prince* (which sells beer) and *Maradona 86*, by the intersection, and at the *Hamdi Restaurant* on the main drag, where the souk begins.

There are two **banks** (daily except Fri 8am–2pm & 6–9pm) for changing cash and travellers' cheques. The **post office** (daily except Fri 8.30am–2pm) and the 24-hour **telephone exchange** are a short walk from the main intersection, while the **police** (☎096/325-284) can be found in the train station.

Dendara – the Temple of Hathor

Across the Nile, fields of onions and clover recede towards the cliffs of the Western Desert and the Temple of Hathor near the village of **DENDARA**. One of the few Egyptian temples whose rooftop remains intact – and accessible – it offers great views of the surrounding countryside. The **site** (daily 9am–4pm; £E12) deserves at least an hour and a half, and you'll need a torch to illuminate its darker recesses. The nearby *Hotel Dendara* (③) has recently reopened, providing the only accommodation at the site – book through the *New Palace* in Qena (see p.293). There is also a **café** at the site, serving soft drinks.

The Temple of Hathor

Although there have been shrines to Hathor, the goddess of joy, at Dendara since pre-Dynastic times, the existing **Temple of Hathor** is a Greco-Roman creation, built between 125 BC and 60 AD. Since the object of the exercise was to confer legitimacy on Egypt's foreign rulers, it emulates the pharaonic pattern of Hypostyle Halls and vestibules preceding a darkened sanctuary, "a progression from the light of the Egyptian sun to the mystery of the holy of holies" (T.G.H. James).

The temple **facade** is shaped like a pylon, with six Hathor-headed columns rising from a screen. Here and inside, Hathor appears in human form rather than her bovine aspect (see overpage). Because this section was built during the reign of Tiberius, its reliefs depict Roman emperors making offerings to the gods, namely Tiberius and Claudius before Horus, Hathor and their son Ihy **[a]**, and Tiberius as a sphinx before Hathor and Horus **[b]**. Nineteenth-century engravings show the temple buried in sand almost to the lintel of its portal, which explains why its upper sections bore the brunt of Coptic iconoclasm.

THE HYPOSTYLE HALL

Entering the **Hypostyle Hall** with its eighteen Hathor-headed columns, let your eyes grow accustomed to the gloom before examining its famous **astronomical ceiling**, which retains much of its original colouring. This is not a sky chart in the modern sense, but a symbolic representation of the heavenly bodies, the hours of the day and night, and the realms of the sun and moon. Although the Qena Bend dictates a north–south orientation rather than the customary east–west axis (since temples always faced the Nile), the ceiling maintains the traditional dichotomy between the northern and southern halves of the sky.

Above the central aisle, a row of flying vultures and winged discs separates the left-hand bays representing the southern heavens from those to the right, dedicated to the northern sky. Here, the first row **[c]** begins with the Eye of Re in its barque, above which appear the fourteen days of the waning moon. Beyond the full moon in the centre come the fourteen stages of the waxing moon (each with its own deity), culminating in the full disc worshipped by Thoth, and lastly the moon as Osiris, protected by Isis and Nephthys. Souls in the form of jackals and birds adore Re's barque as it journeys across the sun's register **[d]**.

Following these are two bands **[e]** showing the planets, the stars of the twelve hours of the night, and the signs of the zodiac. The end rows **[f]** are dominated by Nut, who gives birth to the sun at dawn and swallows it at dusk. On one side, the rising sun Khepri (the scarab beetle) is born **[g]**; on the other, the sun shines down on Hathor **[h]**.

THE HALL OF APPEARANCES

The Ptolemaic section of the temple begins with the columned **Hall of Appearances**, where Hathor consorted with fellow deities before her voyage to Edfu (see below). With a torch, you can examine reliefs on the entrance wall depicting offerings **[i]**, and

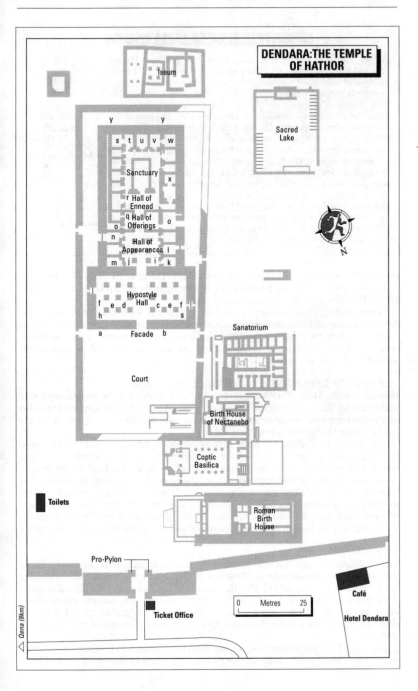

DENDARA: THE TEMPLE OF HATHOR

Iseum

Sacred Lake

N

y   y

s   t   u   v   w

Sanctuary   x

r Hall of
   Ennead
o q Hall of
      Offerings   o
n
   Hall of
   Appearances   l
m j   i k

Hypostyle
f e d Hall c e f
h   s

a   Facade   b

Court

Sanatorium

Birth House
of Nectanebo

Coptic
Basilica

Roman
Birth
House

Toilets

Pro-Pylon

Qena (8km)

0   Metres   25

Café

Ticket Office

Hotel Dendara

THE CULT OF HATHOR

Worshipped from the earliest times as a cow goddess, **Hathor** acquired manifold attributes – body of the sky, living soul of trees, goddess of gold and turquoise, music and revelry – but remained essentially nurturing. Her greatest role was that of wet nurse and bed mate for **Horus**, and giver of milk to the living pharaoh. In her human aspect (with bovine ears and horns), the goddess paid an annual visit to Horus at his temple in Edfu. Escorted by priests and cheered by commoners, her barque proceeded upriver, where Horus sailed out to meet her on his own boat. After much pomp and ritual, the idols were left alone to reconsummate their union while the populace enjoyed a **Festival of Drunkenness**, which led the Greeks to identify Hathor with their own goddess of love and joy, Aphrodite. However, drunkenness at other times drew condemnation, as in this timeless rebuke to a lager lout: "You trail from street to street smelling of beer, you have been found performing acrobatics on a wall, people run from your blows. Look at you beating on your stomach, reeling and rolling about on the ground covered in your own filth!"

Hathor

the foundation of the temple and its presentation to the gods **[j]**. Holy objects of precious metal were kept in the Treasury **[k]**, to your right. Next door is the so-called Nile Room **[l]**, which provided access to a well outside.

Corresponding chambers across the hall include the laboratory **[m]**, where perfumes, incense and unguents were mixed and stored (notice the reliefs showing recipes, and bearers bringing exotic materials from afar); and another room for storing valuables. A liturgical calendar listing festivals celebrated at the temple appears on the inner side of its doorway **[n]**.

THE HALL OF OFFERINGS AND THE HALL OF ENNEAD
Beyond lies the **Hall of Offerings**, the entrance to the temple proper, with twin **stairways** to the roof (see opposite) up which sacrificial animals were led **[o]**. A list of offerings appears on the rear wall **[p]**, across the way from a relief showing the king offering Hathor her favourite tipple **[q]**.

Next comes the **Hall of the Ennead**, where statues of the gods and kings involved in ceremonies dedicated to Hathor once stood. Her wardrobe was stored in a room to your left, where reliefs show the priests carrying the chests that held the sacred garments. Just outside the sanctuary you can see the text of the Hymns of Awakening. The **Sanctuary** housed Hathor's statue and ceremonial barque, which priests carried to the riverside and placed upon a boat that worshippers towed upriver to Edfu for a conjugal reunion with Horus. Reliefs depict the daily rituals (described in the Abydos account – see p.284), and the king presenting Maat to Hathor, Horus and Harsomtus (rear wall).

SIDE CHAPELS
Two corridors with side chapels run alongside (and meet behind) the sanctuary. Above the doorway into the Corridor of Mysteries, Hathor appears as a cow within a wooden kiosk mounted on a barque **[r]**. Past the chapels of Isis, Sokar and the Sacred Serpent, you'll find the "Castle of the Sistrum" (Hathor's musical instrument), where niches depict her standing on the sky, and the coronation of Ihy as god of music **[s]**. This is entered via the darkened *Per-Nu* chapel **[t]**, whence Hathor embarked on her conjugal voyage to Edfu.

The New Year procession began from the *Per-Ur* chapel **[u]**, where nowadays a shaky ladder ascends to a small chamber containing reliefs of Hathor, Maat and Isis. In the *Per-Neser* chapel **[v]**, one of the custodians will lift a hatch and guide you down into a low-ceilinged **crypt** carved with cobras and lotuses (*baksheesh* expected). The chapel itself shows Hathor in her terrible aspect as a lioness, for by Ptolemaic times she had assimilated the leonine goddess Sekhmet and the feline goddess Bastet. The temple's most valuable treasures were stored underneath the Chapel of Re **[w]**.

If you haven't already stumbled upon it, return to the Hall of the Ennead, bear left through an antechamber and then right, to find the "Pure Place" **[x]** or **New Year Chapel**, whose ceiling is covered by a relief of Nut giving birth to the sun, which shines on Hathor's head. It is here that rituals were performed prior to Hathor's communion with the sun on the temple's roof. Check out the rooftop shrines (see below) before leaving the temple and walking round to the rear wall, where two defaced reliefs **[y]** of Cleopatra and her son Caesarion feature in a procession of deities. The chubby face below the Hathor crown is so unlike the beautiful queen of legend that most people prefer to regard this as a stylized image rather than a lifelike **portrait of Cleopatra**.

ROOFTOP SANCTUARIES
From either side of the Hall of Offerings, a stairway ascends to the roof of the temple; the scenes on the walls depict the New Year procession, when Hathor's statue was carried up to an open kiosk on the rooftop to await the dawn. Touched by the rays of the sun, her father, Hathor's *ba* (soul) was revitalized for the coming year. Besides the sun kiosk there are two suites of rooms dedicated to the death and resurrection of Osiris, behind the facade of the Hypostyle Hall. Although such **rooftop sanctuaries** were a feature of most temples, those at Dendara are uniquely intact.

The one on the left (as you face south) is notable for the reliefs in its inner chamber, which show Osiris being mourned by Isis and Nephthys, passing through the gates of the netherworld, and finally bringing himself to erection to impregnate Isis, who appears as a hovering kite.

The other suite contains a plaster cast of the famous **Dendara Zodiac** ceiling filched by Lelorrain in 1820 and now in the Louvre. Upheld by four goddesses, the circular carving features a zodiac which only differs from our own by the substitution of a scarab for the scorpion, and the inclusion of the hippo goddess Tweri. The zodiac was introduced to Egypt (and other lands) by the Romans. Mind your head on the low doorway.

Outlying buildings
Surrounding the temple are various other structures, now largely ruined. Ptolemaic temples were distinguished by the addition of *mamissi* or Birth Houses, which associated the pharaoh with Horus, the deified king. When the Romans surrounded the temple with an enclosure wall, it split in two the **Birth House of Nectanebo** (XXX Dynasty), compelling them to build a replacement. The **Roman Birth House** has some fine carvings on its south wall, and tiny figures of Bes and Tweri on the column capitals and architraves. Between the two *mamissi* lies a ruined, fifth-century **Coptic Basilica**, built with masonry from the adjacent structures; notice the incised Coptic crosses.

As a compassionate goddess, Hathor had a reputation for healing and her temple attracted pilgrimages from the sick. In the **Sanatorium** here patients were prescribed cures during dreams, probably induced by narcotics. Water for ritual ablutions was drawn from a **Sacred Lake** now drained of liquid and full of palm trees and birds.

Nearby stands a ruined **Iseum** erected by Augustus and used for the worship of Isis and Osiris, whose cults were ubiquitous by then.

Between Qena and Luxor

As things stand at present, tourists are disinclined to visit any of the other sites **between Qena and Luxor**, which previously attracted people as "undiscovered" loca-

---

THE PRIMAL ALPHABET

During ancient times there was a road between Abydos and Luxor through the Western Desert, which followed the **Wadi el-Hol**. In 1999 a team under John Darnell of Yale University identified two **rock inscriptions** there as the earliest known examples of a **phonetic alphabet**. The alphabet was previously thought to have been developed by Semitic-speaking people in ancient Palestine around 1600 BC, but the Wadi el-Hol inscriptions date from two or three centuries earlier. Darnell believes that Semitic merchants living in Egypt developed a "shorthand" based on Egyptian hieroglyphics. For example, "A" was the pictogram for a bull's head, turned upside down; the semitic for bull is *Aleph*, the first letter of the Hebrew alphabet, pronounced with the same "aah" sound as the Latin letter. It is possible that other symbols may be the precursors of the letters "L", "M", "T" and "R".

---

tions. As most of them lie along the east or west bank roads, they're accessible by *service* taxi from Luxor or Qena (£E2); buses only run along the east bank. By day, ferries cross the Nile between El-Ballas and Qift, and Naqada and Qus. There are no bridges until south of Luxor.

Along the west bank

EL-BALLAS, 23km from Qena, has manufactured white earthenware jars since antiquity; they are sold at Qena's **pottery** market alongside the town's own traditional wares – the porous water jars that women carry on their heads from childhood. South of here lay ancient Ombos, whose crocodile-worshipping residents never forgave the people of Dendara for eating one: a grudge reaffirmed at every Festival of Drunkenness (see box on p.296).

Further south, the predominantly Coptic village of **NAQADA** lends its name to two **pre-Dynastic cultures** that are reckoned to have existed between around 4000 and 3000 BC: Naqada I (early) and Naqada II (late). However, the reason to come here is to see the huge **Pigeon Palace**, built by a monk just over a century ago. Located in a field 200m west of the main road, the mud-brick *Qasr el-Hamam* enables ten thousand birds to recuperate from their flight over the Western Desert; food is provided – and in turn the keepers eat their resident charges. There are frequent *service* **taxis** (50pt) between Naqada and Gezira, across the Nile from Luxor.

Along the east bank

Crowded with traffic for Luxor, the east bank marks the start of hairpin desert roads to El-Quseir and Port Safaga on the Red Sea Coast. The Valley comes closest to the coast near **QIFT**, ancient *Kebt* or *Koptos*: a mining depot which became a commercial entrepôt once a route to the coast was found. Nowadays well paved but lacking petrol stations, the 216-kilometre-long **road to El-Quseir** is covered in Chapter Eight.

South towards Luxor, a new factory for converting *bagasse* (the waste product of sugar refining) into paper presages the large town of **QUS**, which was second only to Cairo during Fatimid and Mamluke times, when it served as a place of exile for deposed sultans. A relic of its former status is the eleventh-century **Al-Amri Mosque**, containing a fine arabesque *mihrab* and teak *minbar*.

Further south, near Khuzam, a side road leads to the Coptic community of **GARAGOS**, which produces artistic **ceramics** and **textiles**. Garagos is hard to reach by public transport, but Luxor's tourist office can arrange a private taxi there and back. Nearing Luxor, you pass by **EL-MADAMUD**, which harbours a **ruined Temple of Mont** whose Ptolemaic-Roman avenue of sphinxes and monumental gateway belie its Old Kingdom origins.

Luxor

LUXOR has been a tourist mecca ever since Nile steamers began calling in the nineteenth century to view the remains of Thebes, ancient Egypt's New Kingdom capital, and its associated sites – the concentration of relics in this area is overwhelming. The town itself boasts **Luxor Temple**, a graceful ornament to its waterfront and "downtown" quarter, while just to the north is **Karnak Temple**, a stupendous complex built over 1300 years. Across the river are the amazing tombs and mortuary temples of the **Theban Necropolis**, and as if this wasn't enough, Luxor also serves as a base for trips to Esna, Edfu, Dendara and Abydos temples, up and down the Nile Valley.

In a town where **tourism** accounts for 85 percent of the economy, it's hardly surprising that you can't move without being importuned to step inside a shop, rent a *caleche*, or

THE TOURISM SCENE

Since many visitors fly directly to Luxor, it's worth outlining a few features of the local tourism scene. In recent years its tone has been set by independent travellers rather than package tourists, especially by young backpackers travelling through the Middle East, whose Egyptian itinerary is confined to Aswan, Luxor, Hurghada and Dahab. However, if the recovery in package tourism continues, the balance may tip in the other direction. Meanwhile, though, Luxor remains a kind of Goa on the Nile.

Some travellers expect to get the cheapest price as a matter of right, never considering things **from the locals' standpoint**. Hoteliers, felucca captains and salesmen earn good money one day, then little or nothing for ages – even in high season. The children who try to sell you *The Egyptian Gazette* for ten times its cover price are family breadwinners who tramp the streets till late at night. The hotel touts who swear that your place of choice is closed or dirty know that most hotels in Luxor are half empty – so every guest counts. At **no-star hotels**, the price depends on how full they are, how many there are of you, and at what time you arrive – the cost per person is negotiable. Be fair and realistic, even if you're on a tight budget. To get a room with a private bath for £E7–10 per person is a good deal by any standards; trying to force them to go any lower is really taking advantage.

Where such hotels make their money is by charging exorbitant sums for **taxi, caleche or donkey tours**. Although it's wise not to take the first deal offered, also bear in mind that the lowest price may not necessarily be a good deal: you could end up with someone who's so bad that they have to undercut better guides in order to get any work. The easiest way to spoil your day is to ask what someone else paid; if you're happy with what you've done and can afford it, why worry about what amounts to the price of a cup of tea or coffee back home?

That said, it's best to be forewarned about a few scams. Shopkeepers often ask tourists to **read a letter** from abroad, which is invariably a pretext to lure you into their shop. Another trick is to ask you to **buy duty-free alcohol** for their "brother's wedding" – a way of acquiring cheap booze for resale to hotels. If you want to go ahead, fine, but you're entitled to a commission on the deal. Taking **commissions** is universal practice; tour guides get a percentage of every transaction they facilitate. Finally, foreign women should be wary about holiday romances: **gigolos** abound in Luxor – for more on this, see p.33 in Basics chapter.

Hissed invitations and whiffs of smoke by the Nile attest to a smoking sub-culture that's stronger in Luxor than anywhere else in Egypt except Dahab. **Bango** (marijuana) is easy to obtain if you know where to ask, and smoking shouldn't cause any problems if it's done discreetly; several low-budget hotels have a liberal atmosphere in this respect. A packet (*talga*) costs £E15–20, or less if one buys several. **Hashish** is costlier and usually adulterated with henna. *Bango*, too, may be cut with *molukhiyya* (a vegetable), so it's better to buy whole buds, not broken stuff. *Caleche* drivers are likeliest to sell you rubbish.

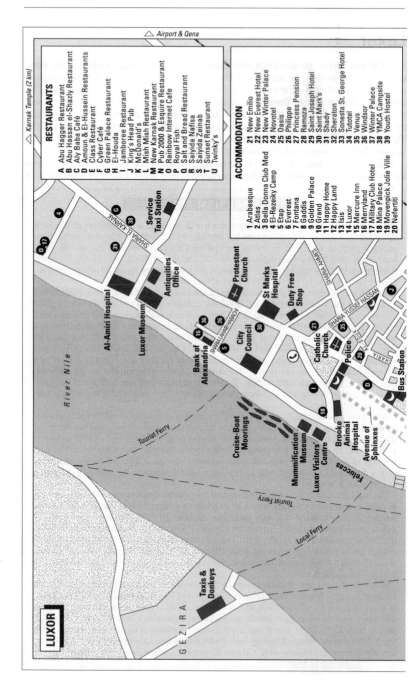

LUXOR

△ Airport & Qena

△ Karnak Temple (2 km)

RESTAURANTS

A Abu Hagger Restaurant
B Abu Hassan el-Shazly Restaurant
C Aly Baba Café
D Amoun & El-Hussein Restaurants
E Class Restaurant
F Cyber Café
G Green Palace Restaurant
H El-Houda
I Jamboree Restaurant
J King's Head Pub
K McDonald's
L Mish Mish Restaurant
M New Karnak Restaurant
N Pub 2000 & Esquire Restaurant
O Rainbow Internet Cafe
P Royal Fish
Q Salt and Bread Restaurant
R Saiyida Nafisa
S Saiyida Zeinab
T Sunset Restaurant
U Twinky's

ACCOMMODATION

1 Arabesque
2 Atlas
3 Bella Donna Club Med
4 El-Rezeiky Camp
5 Etap
6 Everest
7 Fontana
8 Gaddis
9 Golden Palace
10 Grand
11 Happy Home
12 Happy Land
13 Isis
14 Luxor
15 Mercure Inn
16 Merryland
17 Military Club Hotel
18 Mina Palace
19 Movenpick Jolie Ville
20 Nefertiti
21 New Emilio
22 New Everest Hotel
23 New Winter Palace
24 Novotel
25 Oasis
26 Philippe
27 Princess Pension
28 Ramoza
29 Saint Joseph Hotel
30 Saint Mark's
31 Shady
32 Sheraton
33 Sonesta St. George Hotel
34 Tutotel
35 Venus
36 Windsor
37 Winter Palace
38 YMCA Campsite
39 Youth Hostel

River Nile

GEZIRA

Tourist Ferry

Tourist Ferry

Local Ferry

Feluccas

Taxis & Donkeys

Service Taxi Station

Antiquities Office

Al-Amiri Hospital

Luxor Museum

Bank of Alexandria

City Council

SHARIA LABIB HABACHI

SHARIA EL-KARNAK

Protestant Church

St Marks Hospital

Duty Free Shop

Catholic Church

Police

SHARIA AHMED

SHARIA YUSSEF HASSAN

Bus Station

Avenue of Sphinxes

Brooke Animal Hospital

Luxor Visitors' Centre

Mummification Museum

Cruise-Boat Moorings

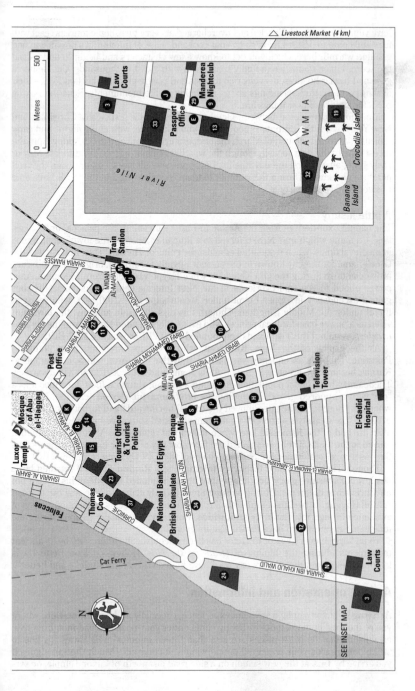

Livestock Market (4 km)

Law Courts

Manderea Nightclub

Passport Office

Metres
0 500

River Nile

AWMIA

Crocodile Island

Banana Island

Train Station

SHARIA RAMSES

SHARIA CLEOPATRA

SHARIA AL-KORTA

MIDAN AL-MAHATTA

SHARIA AL-MAHATTA

SHARIA EL-ADASI

SHARIA MOHAMMED FARID

SHARIA AHMED ORABI

Post Office

Mosque of Abu el-Haggag

Luxor Temple

(SHARIA AL-BAHRI)

SHARIA EL-KARNAK

Tourist Office & Tourist Police

Television Tower

MIDAN SALAH AL-DIN

El-Gadid Hospital

SHARIA EL-MADINA EL-MINAWRA

National Bank of Egypt

Banque Misr

British Consulate

SHARIA SALAH AL-DIN

Thomas Cook

Feluccas

CORNICHE

Car Ferry

SHARIA IBN KHALID WALID

Law Courts

SEE INSET MAP

N

have your shoes shined. Hassled and overcharged at every turn, some tourists react with fury and come to detest Luxor. Keep your cool and sense of humour; it's possible to find genuine warmth here. Once you get to know a few characters and begin to understand the score, Luxor seems like a funky soap opera with a cast of thousands. Cool feluccca guys and bazaar hustlers, nervous rich tourists and piastre-pinching backpackers – their dealings and misunderstandings are as intriguing as the monuments. Read the box on p.299 for an idea of how things are.

Most foreigners come between October and February (especially Christmas and New Year), when the **climate** is cooler than you'd imagine, with chilly nights and early mornings. Around the end of March the temperature shoots up 10°C, making April the nicest time of the year to visit, though the weather remains agreeable until late May or early June, after which the daytime heat is oppressive till late October, when the temperature plummets. During the summer tourism is well down, and the locals have time to sleep by day and party at night.

A little history

The name Luxor derives from the Arabic *El-Uqsur* – meaning "the palaces" or "the castles" – a name which may have referred to a Roman *castrum* or the town's appearance in medieval times, when it squatted admidst the ruins of **Thebes**. This, in turn, was the Greek name for the city known to the ancient Egyptians as *Weset*, originally an obscure provincial town during the Old Kingdom, when Egypt was ruled from Memphis. After power ebbed to regional overlords in the First Intermediate Period, Weset/Thebes gained ascendancy in Upper Egypt under Mentuhotpe II (c.2100 BC), who reunited Egypt under the Middle Kingdom. Though this dissolved into anarchy, the town survived as a power base for local princes who eventually liberated Egypt from the Hyksos invaders, reunited the Two Lands and founded the XVIII Dynasty (c.1567 BC).

As the capital of the **New Kingdom**, whose empire stretched from Nubia to Palestine, Thebes's ascendancy was paralleled by that of **Amun**, whose cult temple at Karnak became the greatest in Egypt. At its zenith under the XVIII and XIX dynasties, Thebes may have had a population of around a million; Homer's *Iliad* describes it as a "city with a hundred gates". Excluding the brief **Amarna Period** (c.1379–1362 BC), when the "heretic" Akhenaten moved the capital northwards and forbade the worship of Amun, the dynasty's – and city's – supremacy lasted some five hundred years. Even after the end of the Ramessid line, when the capital returned to Memphis and thence moved to the Delta, Thebes remained the foremost city of Upper Egypt, enjoying a final fling as a royal seat under the **Nubian** rulers of the XXV Dynasty (c.747–645 BC).

Though Thebes persisted through **Ptolemaic** into **Roman** times, it retained but a shadow of its former glory, and might have been abandoned like Memphis were it not for Christian settlements. During Muslim times its only claim to fame was the tomb of Abu el-Haggag, a twelfth-century sheikh. However, Napoleon's expedition to Egypt awakened foreign interest in its **antiquities**, which were gradually cleared during the nineteenth century, and have drawn visitors ever since.

To be fair, not every visitor to Luxor has been unequivocally impressed by its ancient monuments: during the filming of *Death on the Nile*, Hollywood icon Bette Davis famously remarked that "In my day we'd have built all this at the studio – and better".

Arrival, orientation and information

Arriving in Luxor can be a stressful experience, especially at the **train station**, where you're mobbed by hotel-touts thrusting cards under your nose and bad-mouthing rival establishments. As most places are less than fifteen minutes' walk away, it's fine to strike out towards your preferred option without further ado. Much the same goes if you arrive **by bus** at the new station on a side road just north of Luxor Temple, or **ser-**

vice taxi at the depot off Sharia el-Karnak, just to the north of the centre. You can walk from the latter to the centre in under twenty minutes, but may prefer to catch a minibus, *caleche* or taxi if you are heading for the southern part of town around Television Street. Travellers who've come up **from Aswan by felucca** are dependent on private taxis from Esna or Edfu, whose drivers will rendezvous with hustlers at the checkpoint south of Luxor and steer you to their hotels. If you're not being met at **Luxor Airport**, a taxi into town should cost £E10–12, depending on the size of the car.

Orientation

Luxor spreads along the east bank of the Nile, its outskirts encroaching on villages and fields. For a general layout of the town along with Karnak and the Theban Necropolis, see the map on p.328; a more detailed map appears on pp.300–301. **Orientation** in central Luxor is simplified by a relatively compact tourist zone defined by three main roads. **Sharia al-Mahatta** runs 500m from the train station towards Luxor Temple, where it meets **Sharia el-Karnak**, the main drag heading north to Karnak Temple (2.5km). Karnak is also accessible via the riverside **Corniche**, though tourists generally stick to the 1.5km stretch between Luxor Museum and the *Winter Palace Hotel*. The "circuit" is completed by a fourth street, **Sharia el-Birka** – also known as **Sharia al-Souk** after its bazaar. In the last decade or so Luxor has expanded south towards the village of Awmia, with dozens of new hotels and other facilities along **Sharia Ibn Khalid Walid** (running 3km from the *Novotel* to the *Sheraton*) and **Television Street** (named after its TV tower), which now constitute extensions of the tourist zone.

Information

Once you've found somewhere to stay, it's a good idea to visit the **tourist office** (daily 8am–8pm; ☎095/372-215 or 373-294) south of Luxor Temple to discover the latest official rates for taxis, *caleches*, feluccas or any other service you might be interested in. Confusingly, there are two offices next door to each other; you want to go into the one signposted "Egyptian Tourist Authority", not "Luxor City Information". There's also a branch at the airport (☎095/372-306), open 24 hours during winter and another at the train station (generally open daily 8am–6pm). Finally, there's the **Luxor Visitors' Centre** (daily 9am–1pm & 7–10pm), in the riverside mall near the temple, which shows films, sells books and sponsors seminars about Luxor.

The **tourist police**'s "front" office lies across the way from the tourist office, while their headquarters is upstairs, around the back of the building (☎095/373-845; 24hr). They also have a branch in the station (daily 8am–11pm; ☎095/372-120). The regular **police** (☎095/382-006) are based off Sharia el-Karnak, north of Luxor Temple, and supplemented on the streets by a host of plainclothes agents known as the "*galabiyya* police". Whatever your problem, it's always best to go to the tourist police first.

Transport

Although you can easily explore central Luxor **on foot**, it takes some time to get used to the traffic (a balletic melee of bikes, cars, carts and minibuses) and being importuned at every step. **Caleches** are fun to ride and useful if you're burdened with luggage, but a bit pricey for regular use. Fares are set by the authorities but drivers charge whatever they can get. Expect an argument if you pay the official rate (£E4 for a ride within Luxor; £E12 for 1hr tour); rides to Karnak are a special case (see p.317). The Brooke Animal Hospital asks tourists to dissuade drivers from galloping their horses or taking more than four passengers. **Taxis** serve for trips to outlying hotels (£E5–9) or the airport, but are fairly superfluous around the centre (£E3–5). As with *caleches*, you'll have to haggle over the price, which is bound to exceed the cost of public transport.

Surprisingly few visitors take advantage of the fleet of blue-and-white **minibuses** that shuttle between outlying points, constantly passing through the centre along Sharia el-Karnak. Northbound minibuses either turn off towards the taxi depot (*mogaf*), or run straight on to Karnak and sometimes to the *Nile Hilton*. Heading in the opposite direction, they terminate at the public hospital (*moustashfa*) far down Television Street, or at Awmia, beside the *Sheraton*. The *moustafsha*-bound ones detour inland via the train station, while Awmia buses stick to Sharia Ibn Khalid Walid. The tactic is to wave down any minibus heading in the right direction, shout "*mogaf*", "*Hilton*", "*moustafsha*" (or whatever), and hop in if they're going there. There's a flat fare of 25pt on all routes.

Many tourists rent **bicycles** from shops on Sharia al-Mahatta, Television Street and other localities, where prices vary from £E3–7 a day in the winter to £E4–5 over summer. Most of these bikes are one-speed only, if not defective in some respect, so you may prefer to rent a better model from the *Etap*, *Windsor*, *Sheraton* or *Hilton* (£E5 per hour/£E15 per day). In any case, it's always wise to check the machine and do a short test ride. A passport or other ID is generally required as security. You can also rent 150cc **motorbikes** from a host of places, including *Sinbad*, opposite the *Ramoza Hotel* on Sharia al-Mahatta, for about £E30 a day. The owner doesn't care whether you've got a licence or not, but the police will. Bikes can be carried on local ferries to the west bank, for getting around the Theban Necropolis.

Accommodation

The cost and availability of **accommodation** varies with the time of year and fluctuations in tourism. Officially, there are just "high" (Nov–May) and "low" (June–Oct) **seasons**, the first more expensive than the second. In practice, however, prices also rise or fall depending on **demand**, which used to be so great that hotels jacked their rates up during the peak period (coinciding with the Egyptian school vacation, Dec 10–Jan 10), but then fell so low that many offered discounts during high season. **Hotel-touts** refer to netting tourists as "fishing", and happily poach them from rivals. So long as you end up somewhere okay, it shouldn't matter too much if you get taken to a different hotel from the one you expected. If not, look elsewhere. With over eighty hotels in town, there's no shortage of alternatives.

As some places calculate prices on a per-person basis, and others by the room, the scope for **bargaining** varies. Three-star hotels may waive taxes, particularly newly opened places that haven't yet got many customers, or older ones threatened by better competitors. No-star hotels and pensions rarely charge tax anyway, and will often shave a few pounds off the price, or let you sleep on the roof for as little as £E2, plus breakfast. As this is the same everywhere except for top hotels, you needn't pay attention to lavish descriptions of **breakfast** – though a **restaurant** with a good cook and a licence to sell **alcohol** are definite advantages. One last factor is the **staff**: places that were good can become bad (or vice versa), merely because the manager or receptionist changes.

The following are all in Luxor; hotels on the west bank are detailed on p.333.

Low-budget hotels and pensions
Low-budget hotels and pensions range from cosy home-from-homes to utter fleapits, all varieties being represented on and off **Yussef Hassan**, **Al-Mahatta** and **Television** streets. The biggest selection lies around Television Street, no more than fifteen minutes' walk from Luxor Temple or the station. Despite its unpaved backstreets, this is an up-and-coming area that's safe to stay in and quieter than the centre of town, which offers few low-budget options. Unless stated otherwise, you should be sure of getting hot water and breakfast.

Atlas, off Sharia Ahmed Orabi (☎095/373-514). Clean, simple rooms with fans and private baths; no singles. Friendly atmosphere. ②.

Everest, Sharia el-Salam, off Television St (☎095/373-260). Clean, simple rooms with fans or A/C, many with baths. Washing machine and shaded rooftop terrace. ②.

Fontana, Sharia Radwan, off Television St (☎095/380-663). Decent rooms with fans or A/C, some with private baths. Small library, kitchen and washing machine. Mr Magdy will let you sleep on the roof for the price of breakfast. ③.

Grand, off Sharia Mohammed Farid (☎095/382-905). Quiet, clean semi-carpeted doubles with fans and shared bathrooms. Also has a nice rooftop terrace. ①.

Happy Home, off Sharia al-Mahatta (☎095/378-511). Tiny pension with a liberal atmosphere. Three rooms share a bath on each floor and guests can use the kitchen. ①.

Happy Land, Sharia el-Kamrr, off Television St (☎095/371-828). Small, quiet and hyper-clean. All rooms with fans, some A/C, most with private baths. Towels, toilet paper and mosquito-zappers provided. Good, cheap food served on the rooftop terrace. ②.

Nefertiti, Karnak Temple St (☎095/372-386). Exceptional value for its central location, clean, renovated rooms and honest, friendly staff, the *Nefertiti* is Luxor's best choice in this price range. The management offer the usual tours of the major sites, but without being pushy. Breakfast here is well above average too, served on the hotel's roof-terrace which overlooks the *souk* and Luxor Temple. ③.

New Everest, off Sharia al-Mahatta (☎095/370-017). Clean, simple rooms with fans, some with A/C and bathroom (£E15). Tranquil and comfortable roof terrace. ①.

Oasis, Sharia Mohammed Farid (☎095/381-699). Spacious, semi-carpeted doubles with fans or A/C (plus bath), and clean shared facilities. Shaded rooftop with washing machine, and a video in the lobby. ①.

Princess Pension, off Sharia Ahmed Orabi (☎095/373-997). Clean-ish and friendly; popular with Japanese travellers. Dorm beds £E4 including breakfast. ①.

Venus, Sharia Yussef Hassan (☎095/372-625). Perhaps the best low-budget choice in the centre (offers discounts for *Rough Guide* users). Simple rooms with fans or A/C, most with baths and some with double beds. Washing machine. Free pool table and satellite TV in the *Mars Bar* (see p.311), which serves cheap food and Stella with a view of streetlife near the bazaar. Friendly staff and liberal atmosphere. You can sleep on the roof for £E5. ①.

Mid-range hotels

Mostly modern or modernized, the following mid-range hotels feature private bathrooms, A/C, TV and include breakfast unless otherwise stated. Being geared to tour groups, some of them treat independent travellers rather shabbily.

Arabesque, Sharia Mohammed Farid (☎095/371-299, fax 372-193). Clean, simple rooms, some overlooking the palmy garden of the *Luxor*. Nice rooftop terrace with a tiny pool and splendid views of the Nile and Luxor Temple. No alcohol. ⑤.

Golden Palace, 600m down Television St (☎095/382-972, fax 382-974). Attractive new three-star place with nice rooftop, garden, bar, restaurant and swimming pool. ④.

Mercure Inn, beside the *Luxor* (☎095/373-321, fax 373-051). Has totally separate facilities, but still seems a poor relation of its neighbour. Run by the company that manages the *Etap* (see below). ⑥.

Merryland, Sharia Nefertiti, near the Corniche (☎095/381-746 or 376-903). Tastefully decorated, with a rooftop bar and sundeck. Some rooms have Nile views and all have balconies. ⑥.

Military Club, on the Corniche, 500m north of the hospital (☎095/370-500). Large rooms with fridges and Nile views. No English is spoken. ⑤.

Mina Palace, on the Corniche near Luxor Temple (☎095/372-074, fax 382-194). Old-fashioned, but most rooms overlook the Nile; the "06" ones have an extra temple-facing balcony. Restaurant, bar and terrace. ⑤.

Philippe, Sharia Labaib Habachi (☎095/373-604, fax 380-060). Nice rooms with fridges. Rooftop pool and terrace with a view of town. Bar and restaurant. ⑥.

Ramoza, Sharia al-Mahatta (☎095/372-270, fax 381-670). Very clean bathrooms but otherwise a bit shabby. Caters to low-budget tour groups. Bar. ⑤.

Saint Joseph, Sharia Ibn Khalid Walid, near the *Sonesta St.George* (☎095/381-707, fax 381-727). Clean rooms, some with balconies. Rooftop pool and bar with good views. Popular with British tour companies. ⑥.

Saint Mark's, Sharia el-Karnak (☎095/373-532, fax 371-032). Chiefly remarkable for its oddly shaped bathrooms and a rooftop terrace overlooking the *Etap* pool. ④.

Shady, Television St (☎095/381-262, fax 374-859). Salubrious good-value rooms. Large pool in the garden; rooftop sundeck. Disco, bar and restaurant. Laundry service. ⑤.

Windsor, Sharia Nefertiti, near the Corniche (☎095/375-547, fax 373-447). Rooftop pool and bar, restaurant, private disco, gym and sauna. ⑥.

Upmarket hotels

The slump in tourism has hit **upmarket hotels** especially hard, since tour groups are their mainstay. Though quoted prices for walk-in guests remain high, you shouldn't be shy about angling for reductions if business looks slack. Many places charge premium rates for Nile-facing rooms; the prices below are for the least expensive (garden- or street-facing) rooms.

Bella-Donna Club Med, Sharia Ibn Khalid Walid, 700m beyond the *Novotel* (☎095/380-850, fax 380-879). Stylish, self-contained resort by the banks of the Nile, with a pool and disco. Children under five stay free, older children get discounts. ⑦.

Etap, on the Corniche between Luxor Temple and the museum (☎095/380-944, fax 374-912). Modern complex run by the *Mercure* chain, featuring several restaurants, a nightclub/disco and pool. ⑦.

Gaddis, Sharia Ibn Khalid Walid, 1km south of the *Novotel* (☎095/382-838, fax 382-837). Very clean and stylish rooms; some suites have double beds. Smallish pool, plus there's a bar, disco and laundry service. Fifty percent discount for *Rough Guide* readers. ⑦.

Isis, 500m beyond the *Bella-Donna* (☎095/373-366, fax 372-923). Five-star complex set in lush grounds with wonderful views of the river. Owned by a relative of President Mubarak, who has a penthouse suite and a helipad on the roof. Italian and Chinese restaurants. Two pools, one heated. ⑦.

Karnak, 1km north of Karnak Temple, opposite the *Nile Hilton* (☎095/376-155, fax 374-155). Large, clean rooms with satellite TV, no balconies. Swimming pool and pleasant atmosphere. ⑦.

Luxor Sheraton Hotel & Resort, Sharia Ibn Khalid Walid, 4km south of Luxor Temple (☎095/374-544, fax 374-941). Good facilities and service, but it's not worth paying premium rates for "Nile view" rooms. Courtesy bus from outside the Luxor Museum five times daily. ⑦.

Luxor, Sharia el-Karnak, near Luxor Temple (☎095/380-018, fax 379-849). This renovated 1920s pile retains a Moorish-style verandah and some Art Deco features; the bar and billiards table are great. Set in a garden with a pool. ⑦.

Môvenpick Jollie Ville, on Crocodile Island, 5km south of Luxor (☎095/374-855, fax 374-936). Comfy bungalows in extensive grounds, with tennis courts, a pool and a children's playground. Hourly courtesy bus to the *New Winter Palace*, and a motorboat three times daily. ⑧.

New Emilio, Sharia Yussef Hassan (☎095/376-666, fax 370-000). Centrally located and popular with tour groups. Comfortable rooms with video channel; restaurant, disco and rooftop pool. ⑦.

Nile Hilton, 4km north of downtown Luxor, and 1km from Karnak Temple (☎095/374-933, fax 376-571). Club class, Nile-view and garden-facing rooms in an enclave beside the river, with tennis courts, a giant chessboard and other diversions. Hourly courtesy bus from outside the *Mercure Inn* (see above). ⑧.

Novotel, near the Nile 1km south of Luxor Temple (☎095/380-925, fax 380-972). Small as *Novotels* go, but with the usual atrium and facilities, and a popular disco aboard the *Lotus* cruise boat. ⑦.

Sonesta St. George, in between the *Club Med* and *Isis* (☎095/382-575, fax 382-571, *sonesta@iec.egnet.net*). The latest addition to Luxor's luxury hotel collection has Italian and Japanese restaurants, *Nobles Bar*, 24hr business centre and a Nile-side pool. ⑧.

Tutotel, Sharia Salah Al-Din, inland from the *Novotel* (☎095/377-990, fax 372-671). A would-be luxury hotel. Most rooms have balconies, pool is unfinished. Bar and disco. Way overpriced. ⑦.

Winter Palace, on the Corniche south of Luxor Temple (☎095/380-422, fax 374-087). The doyen of Luxor's hotels, founded in 1887, has played host to heads of state, Noël Coward and Agatha Christie (parts of *Death on the Nile* were written and filmed here). Combines old-fashioned elegance with modern facilities; rooms overlook the Nile, or a huge garden with a pool. Snazzy *Royal Bar* and *Victoria Lounge*. Beside the "Old" Winter Palace stands a **New Winter Palace**, which lacks its splendour, but shares the same facilities. ⑧.

Hostels, camping and apartments

All things considered, **hostels** and **campsites** have less to offer than hotels, even if saving money is your main concern. However, the *El-Rezeiky Camp* does have a pool, which is more than you can say for the cheapo hotels in town.

If you want to stay a long time in Luxor, it's easy to negotiate big discounts at hostels, especially over summer. For more privacy and independence, **renting an apartment** is appealing. A decent one-bedroom place in the centre costs about £E350 a month, plus bills. Ask around and landlords will make themselves known. For total immersion in Egyptian life you could **stay with a family** in Luxor or on the west bank. There's no formal way of arranging this, so you'll need to forge your own contacts and be committed to the idea.

El-Rezeiky Camp, halfway between Luxor and Karnak temples, 15 minutes' walk from the town centre (☎095/381-400). Partly shaded campsite where you can pitch your own tent (£E10 per person) or stay in rooms with A/C and bathrooms. Swimming pool, bar and restaurant. Laid-back atmosphere. ④.

YMCA campsite, Sharia el-Karnak, a little nearer the centre (☎095/372-425). Tent space (£E3 per person) and hot showers, chiefly used by Egyptian families and tour groups, who party till midnight or later; the site is guarded 24 hours. Charge for motorbikes (£E2.80), cars (£E5) or caravans (£E25).

Youth Hostel, on a side street across the road from the *YMCA* (☎095/372-139, fax 370-539). Dorms with bunks or "lux" rooms with three beds. Crowded with Egyptian students in winter; closed over summer. 10am–2pm lockout and 11pm curfew. HI membership obligatory, available here for £E20. Breakfast included; £E13.

Luxor Temple

Luxor Temple (daily: winter 6am–9pm; summer 6am–10pm; Ramadan 6am–6.30pm & 8–11pm; £E20) stands aloof in the heart of town, ennobling the view from the waterfront and tourist bazaar with its grand colonnades and pylons, which are spotlit at night. Though best explored by day – when its details can be thoroughly examined in a couple of hours – you should come back after dark to imbibe its atmosphere and drama with fewer people around. For a general guide to temple architecture see p.288.

The temple's dedication and construction

Dedicated to the Theban Triad of Amun-Min, Mut and Khonsu (see p.318), Luxor Temple was the "Harem of the South" where Amun's consort Mut and their son Khonsu resided. Every spring a flotilla of barques escorted Amun's effigy from Karnak Temple to this site for a conjugal reunion with Mut in an *Optet* or fertility festival noted for its public debauchery.

Whereas Karnak is the work of many dynasties, most of Luxor Temple was built by two rulers during a period when New Kingdom art reached its apogee. The temple's founder was **Amenophis III** (1417–1379 BC) of the XVIII Dynasty, whose other monuments include the Third Pylon at Karnak and the Colossi of Memnon across the river. Work halted under his son Akhenaten (who erased his father's cartouches and built a sanctuary to Aten alongside the temple), but resumed under Tutankhamun and Horemheb, who decorated its court and colonnade with their own reliefs. To this, **Ramses II** (1304–1237 BC) of the XIX Dynasty added a double colonnaded court and a great pylon flanked by obelisks and colossi. Despite additions by later pharaohs and the rebuilding of its sanctuary under Alexander the Great, the temple has a coherence that reproaches Karnak's inchoate giganticism.

The clarity of its **reliefs** owes to the temple having been half-buried by sand and silt, and overlaid by Luxor itself. Nineteenth-century visitors found a "labyrinthine maze of mud structures" nesting within its court; colonnades turned into granaries where dishonest merchants were hung by their ears. "So stirs a mini-life amid the debris of a life that was far grander", wrote Flaubert. When the French desired to remove an obelisk, and archeologists to excavate the temple, they had to pay compensation for the demolition of scores of homes.

Approaching the temple

The ticket office is on the Corniche side, where the gradual slope inside the entrance obscures the fact that the site lies several metres below street level – a measure of the debris that accumulated here over centuries. At the end of the ramp, to your left, is a neglected mud-brick **Roman chapel** containing a headless statue of Isis wearing a toga. Beyond this, the courtyard opens into an **Avenue of Sphinxes** with human faces that once led to Karnak Temple – a XXX Dynasty addition by Nectanebo I.

The temple gateway proper is flanked by massive pylons and enthroned colossi, with a single **Obelisk** soaring 25m high. Carved with reliefs and originally tipped with electrum, this was one of a pair until its mate was removed in 1835, taken to France and re-erected on the Place de la Concorde. The four dog-faced baboons at the base of each obelisk also sported erect phalluses until prudish Frenchmen hacked them off. Behind loom three of the six **colossi of Ramses II** that originally fronted the pylon (four seated, two standing). The enthroned pair have Schwarzenegger physiques and double crowns; reliefs of the Nile-god binding the Two Lands adorn their thrones.

Notched for flagpoles and carved with scenes of Ramses' victory at Qadesh (the battle uppermost, the Egyptian camp below), the **Pylon** was later embellished by Nubian and Ethiopian kings, as shown by the relief of Pharaoh Shabaka running the *heb* race before Amun-Min, high up on the left as you walk through.

Courts and colonnades

Beyond the pylon lies the **Court of Ramses II**, surrounded by a double row of papyrus-bud columns, once roofed over to form arcades. The courtyard is set askew to the temple's main axis, doubtless to incorporate the earlier **barque shrine** of Tuthmosis III, whose triple chapels were dedicated to Khonsu (to the right as you enter), Amun (centre) and Mut (nearest the river).

Incongruously perched atop the opposite colonnade (which is still bricked up to its capitals), the **Mosque of Abu el-Haggag** is a much-rebuilt edifice bearing the name of Luxor's patron saint, whose demolition the townsfolk refused to countenance when the temple was excavated. To the right of the portal at the back of the court, you'll see the lower half of a frieze depicting Amun's procession approaching the temple during the Optet festival, when the god was presented with lettuces, symbolizing his fertility. Here, Ramses makes offerings to Mut and Mont (the Theban war god), observed by his queen and seventeen of the hundred or so sons that he sired over ninety years. Notice the bullocks in the corner of the wall.

The portal itself is flanked by black granite statues of Ramses, their bases decorated with bound prisoners from Nubia and Asia. Beyond lies the older section of the temple, inaugurated by the lofty **Colonnade of Amenophis III**, with its processional avenue of giant papyrus columns whose calyx capitals still support massive architraves. On the walls are more damaged scenes from the Optet festival, intended to be "read" in an anti-clockwise direction. After sacrifices to the boats at Karnak (northwest corner), Amun's procession (west wall) arrives at Luxor Temple (southeast corner), returning to Karnak 24 days later (east wall). The pharaoh shown here is Tutankhamun, who had the colonnade decorated, but the cartouches honour his successor, Horemheb.

Since piped water was installed in Luxor, the rising water table has undermined the foundations of the great **Court of Amenophis III**, at the end of the avenue. Previously the temple's crowning glory, it is currently bereft of one of its colonnades, whose massive columns have been dismantled while new foundations are laid. The two remaining colonnades consist of papyrus-bundle columns with bud capitals – the most elegant form devised by the ancient Egyptians. Its decorations include artwork from the time of Alexander and Philip of Macedon, with some traces of colour still visible on the eastern colonnade. The southern one merges into a **Hypostyle Hall** with 32 papyrus columns, serving as a vestibule to the temple proper. Between the last two columns on the left of its central aisle is a Roman altar dedicated to Emperor Constantine (before his conversion to Christianity). On either side of the hall's rear wall, Amenophis makes offerings to the gods.

The inner sanctums

Beyond the hall lies a columned **portico** or antechamber, whose central aisle was flanked by the barque shrines of Mut and Khonsu. Roman legionaries later plastered over the pharaonic reliefs and turned it into a chapel where local Christians were offered a choice between martyrdom or obeisance to the imperial cults. Paintings of Roman emperors are visible near the top of the walls; elsewhere the stucco has fallen away to reveal Amenophis offering sacrifices to Amun. In the smaller, four-columned **Hall of Offerings**, beyond, reliefs show the pharaoh leading sacrificial cows and presenting incense and sceptres.

By erecting a granite chapel within the next columned hall, Alexander the Great converted it into the **Sanctuary of Amun's Barque**, adorned with "doors of acacia inlaid with gold". The remaining chambers to the south constituted the private apartments of the gods, reached by a **transverse hall**. However, this section of the temple is badly damaged and really only notable for the name *Rimbaud*, carved high up on the wall near the river. Rimbaud spent the last sixteen years of his life roaming the Near and Far East; while living in Ethiopia he was feared dead, so Verlaine published his poems (all written by the age of 21), which took Paris by storm and inspired the Decadent movement.

More battered reliefs survive in two rooms situated alongside the Sanctuary and Hall of Offerings. The first, opening eastwards (left) off the Sanctuary, contains hacked-about scenes of Amenophis III being crowned, and hunting in the marshes. From here, you can walk north into the **Birth Room**, whose left-hand wall emphasizes his divine paternity. The ravaged lower register shows Amun, Hathor and Queen Mutemuia embracing; and Thoth leading Amun (disguised as Tuthmosis IV) into the queen's bedchamber. Examined from left to right, the middle register depicts Thoth foretelling Amenophis's birth; Mutemuia's pregnancy and confinement; Isis presenting the child to Amun; and the god cradling his son. Along the top register, Amenophis and his *ka* are nurtured by deities and presented to Amun; in the far right corner, Amenophis becomes pharaoh.

It was near this room in 1989 that workers uncovered a cache of 26 New Kingdom statues which are now on show in the Luxor Museum.

Luxor Museum

Luxor Museum (daily: winter 9am–1pm & 4–9pm; summer 9am–1pm & 5–10pm; Ramadan 10am–4pm; £E30, camera permit £E10, no flashes or tripods, camcorder £E100) complements the town's monumental assets, containing a small but choice collection of statues and funerary goods from local temples and the Theban Necropolis. The museum is well laid out with clear labelling in English, but some names may be rendered differently from those in this book (eg Amenhotep for Amenophis). An illustrated guidebook can be purchased at the information desk.

Works in stone include a large pink granite head of Amenophis III; a fine statue of Tuthmosis III in green-black schist; a jug-eared Senusert III (XII Dynasty); a human-bodied, crocodile-headed Sobek in alabaster; and two haunting busts of Amenophis IV

(Akhenaten) from his temple at Karnak. Figures on a lovely mural from this temple demonstrate the strange physiognomy associated with Akhenaten's reign.

From **Tutankhamun's tomb** in the Valley of the Kings come a funerary bed, two model boats and a stunning gold-inlaid cow's head representing Merit Weri (an aspect of Hathor); the rest of the Tut finds are housed in Cairo. **Other highlights** include a dazzling mummy casing from the tomb of Lady Shepenkhonsu; canopic jars with animal- or human-headed lids; and a scowling statue of Amenhotep, Steward of Amenophis III, the probable architect of Luxor Temple.

The **New Hall** displays the cache of statues found in the temple. The most impressive ones are larger than life, amongst them Amenophis III, Tutankhamun, Ramses II, Queen Nefertari, Hathor and Horus. Archeologists disagree over whether the statues were cached at the start of the Roman occupation or nine hundred years earlier, when Egypt was invaded by the Assyrians, whose armies sacked Thebes in 664 BC.

Mummification Museum

The **Mummification Museum** (daily: winter 9am–1pm & 4–9pm; summer 9am–1pm & 5–10pm; £E20, students £E10, camera permit £E10, camcorder £E100) is a recent addition to Luxor's sights, detailing the history and beliefs about mummification with its exhibits of human, reptile and bird mummies as well as the instruments used in the process. The museum provides a valuable insight into the painstaking process of mummification and its importance in the life-cycle of the people of ancient Egypt.

Eating and drinking

The culinary scene is less diverse than in Cairo or Alexandria, but there's no shortage of places to eat. Upmarket **hotel restaurants** offer A/C, good service and cuisines such as Chinese (at the *Isis*), Japanese (at the *Sonesta St. George*), Italian or French (most places). Prices are usually steep, but there are some good deals, like the all-you-can-eat **salad bars** in the *New Winter Palace* and the *Etap* coffee shop, or the rich spaghetti bolognese served at the *Gaddis*. Elsewhere you'll mainly find pizzas, kebabs, omelettes and other dishes palatable to tourists. Menus are written up outside and all the waiters know English, so it's easy to order. Providing you're ready for service charges and tax (up to 21 percent), the total cost shouldn't come as a shock.

All the usual **street food** can be found along El-Karnak, Ramses and Yussef Hassan streets, but it's hard for foreigners to avoid being overcharged, even if they know the proper price. The same is also true for tea, coffee and *sheeshas* at cafés, cigarettes, pastries and other items. One 24-hour **bakery** near the corner of Sharia al-Mahatta and the souk turns out pretzels and rolls, while *Twinky's*, at the station end of Sharia al-Adasi, abounds in sticky confectionery. The poolside *gelateria* in the *Mövenpick Jolie Ville* serves the best **ice cream** in Luxor.

Most of the following **restaurants** are inexpensive by Western standards, and largely cater to low-budget tourists. All are open from mid-morning (or earlier) till 9–10pm (or later), but the range of meals diminishes as the evening wears on. Unless stated otherwise, they don't sell alcohol. We've only listed **cafés** that sell food, but there are scores of local coffee houses where you can sample exotic beverages – try *helba*, a bright yellow tea made from fenugreek.

Abu Hagger Restaurant, Sharia al-Adasi. Fronted by bloodstained haunches in display cabinets, it is said by locals to do the best kebab and *kofta* in town. A bit overrated but not bad for the price, which is reasonable.

Abu Hassan el-Shazly Restaurant, Sharia al-Adasi. Just along from *Abu Hagger*, its murals and stained glass make it look a more enticing prospect, and the menu also runs to pizzas and fish. Prices, though, are slightly higher.

Aly Baba Café, on the corner near the *Luxor*. Usual dishes but overpriced. The main attraction is the view of Luxor Temple and the hotel gardens. Waiters call "Hey you" to solicit custom.

Amoun Restaurant, in the tourist bazaar on Sharia el-Karnak. Chicken, fish, omelettes, soup and other staples. The shaded tables outside are plagued by hustlers; inside is A/C. Average prices.

Champollion Snack Bar, in the *Etap*. Pizza, burgers, cakes and beer. £E17 minimum charge.

Class Restaurant, Sharia Khalid Ibn Walid, near the *Isis*. An upmarket A/C joint popular with hotel guests and good for splurging out. Sells beer and wine.

El-Houda, Television St. Shorter on quality than its long menu of grills, kebabs and pizzas suggests. Average prices.

El-Hussein, in the tourist bazaar on Sharia el-Karnak. Like the *Amoun*, next door, it has become smarter but less welcoming since it moved into the bazaar. Their menus are almost identical.

Green Palace Restaurant, Sharia el-Karnak, next to the *YMCA*. Smart place with good Italian and Egyptian food and a swimming pool. Expensive (main courses £E25 upwards).

Jamboree, 29 Sharia el-Montazah, between the fire station and the telephone exchange. Spotlessly clean place with roof terrace, serving a range of mid-priced Egyptian and international dishes including Cajun chicken (£E22.50) and tasty jacket potatoes (£E9–13). Owned and run by a friendly Scottish couple. Daily 10.30am–2.30pm & 6.30–10.30pm.

King's Head Pub, Sharia Ibn Khalid Walid, near the passport office. Club sandwiches (£E17), soups and main dishes, with a real British Sunday lunch of roast beef and Yorkshire pud (£E20).

Maharba, above the tourist office, with a rooftop terrace overlooking the Theban Hills and a darkened indoor restaurant. Serves the usual food (plus beer) at fairly upmarket rates. No hustlers.

Mish Mish, Television St. A friendly A/C pizza outlet that's popular with tourists. Its name means "apricot". Reasonably priced.

New Karnak Restaurant, below the hotel of the same name, opposite the station. Omelettes, soups, salads, curries and spaghetti with a smidgin of sauce. Inexpensive.

Peace Abouzeid Restaurant, north of town on the Corniche. Range of tasty Arabic dishes in a pleasant setting. Expensive (mains £E27 upwards).

Pub 2000 and Esquire Restaurant, just off Sharia Ibn Khalid Walid near the Law Courts. Mock pub serving passable food at reasonable prices (main courses £E10–40). Special "backpacker deal" chicken and chips for £E9. Imported beer and Stella (£E9). Happy hour 7.30–8.30pm.

Royal Fish, off Television St beside the bus garage. Tasty meals of Red Sea fish with rice, chips, salad and *tahina* (£E10). Basic decor. Daily 8am–midnight.

Saiyida Nafisa, Sharia Mustafa Kamel, just past the mosque at the end of Sharia Yussef Hassan. Rather shabby, but does a great *kushari*. Open till midnight.

Saiyida Zeinab, at the start of Television St. Sparklingly clean place, serving excellent *kushari*. Open till late.

Venus Garden, opposite the *Venus Hotel* on Sharia Yussef Hassan. Tasty, inexpensive light meals and beer.

Victoria Lounge in the *Winter Palace*. Does a spiffing afternoon tea (£E25) from 3 to 6pm.

Drinking and duty-free shops

If you don't mind paying over the odds, the nicest place to sink a cold Stella beer is the garden terrace of the *Winter Palace*. The next best is the *Mina Palace*'s terrace, on the Corniche, where the ambience is less grand but the view is good and the prices reasonable. For a livelier atmosphere, visit the *King's Head Pub* on Sharia Ibn Khalid Walid (daily 9am–3am) – which offers meals, cocktails (£E12), Stella (£E8), darts and billiards – or the *Venus Hotel*, where the excellent *Mars Bar* sells local (£E6) and imported draught beer, and has satellite TV, a pool table and Western music. There are ritzier **bars** in all the big hotels – in particular, the elegant *Royal Bar* in the *Winter Palace*.

Imported beer and spirits cost a fortune in hotels, but a modest sum at **duty-free shops**, where you pay in hard currency. There's a flourishing black market in which tourists buy booze for middlemen, who sell it to hotels (whose official quota doesn't cover their needs). Visitors can buy duty-frees twice: in the arrivals section of the airport, and then at the duty-free shop in town (daily 10am–3pm & 7pm–midnight). You'll need your passport, in which the transaction(s) will be noted. The cheapest buy is Borzon vodka (US$4). Egyptian beer and spirits can be purchased at an inconspicuous liquor shop near the cinema on Sharia al-Mahatta.

Nightlife

Aside from the **Sound and Light show at Karnak Temple** – which is the best in Egypt (see p.317) – Luxor's nightlife is similar to Cairo's. The liveliest **hotel discos** are aboard the *Lotus* boat by the *Novotel* (nightly 10pm–2am) – which often waives its £E10 minimum charge – and in the *Etap* (£E20 minimum charge), which has a belly dancer from 11.30pm to 12.30am. Less active spots include the *Shady* (free), *Luxor Sheraton* (11pm–2am; £E20 admission), *New Emilio* (£E10) and *Gaddis* (8.30pm–3am; free). The *Isis* disco (9pm–2am; free) has a slightly risqué Russian dance show. Smart-casual dress is okay at all of them.

During winter, several also lay on a programme of **music and belly dancing**, with a buffet meal included in the price (drinks cost extra). The most elaborate shows – including stick-fights and other folkloric routines – are in *Fellah's Tent* in the *Môvenpick Jolie Ville* (£E110 per person), and the *Luxor Sheraton*'s "Nubian Night" (Sat; £E100). There are less extravagant bashes in the *Nile Hilton* (Fri & Sat; £E85), the *El-Darweesh* in the *New Winter Palace* (Tues; £E76), the *Dawar el-Omda* in the *Mercure Inn* (Thurs; free with dinner), and on board the *Tiba Star* docked by the *Winter Palace*. Sanitized and tweely "ethnic", they are hardly a wild night out. **Karaoke nights**, usually in English, are held in the bar of the *Gaddis Hotel*.

The alternative is to visit a **real Egyptian nightclub**, where the decor is seedy and the clientele raucous (women are best off going with male companions); the music is brilliant and the dancers get sexier as the night wears on. You have to stay through till dawn to savour the build-up, as they tease gold-bedecked businessmen into throwing £E100 notes around, to shimmy alongside or toast themselves over the echo machine. The cash is collected in a box, which is dragged off at the end of each act and split equally among the dancer, the bandleader and the club. If the woman fails to arouse enthusiasm, the manager shoos her off and orders another on. Rich clients may demand a "White" (pale-skinnned, blond) dancer, or come to blows over a woman, while poorer spectators sit in the shadows, quaffing booze and smoking *bango*. The only drinks sold are Johnny Walker (£E80–100 a bottle) and Stella beer (£E7); forget about food. Luxor now has only one such club, the *Manderea*, up a side street beside the passport office on Sharia Ibn Khalid Walid, which is open from 11pm to 5am, depending on how many patrons are still spending. They'll try to add an entry charge to your bill, but there isn't one.

For locals who can't afford such pleasures, the main diversions are playing backgammon (*thowla*) or dominoes in **cafés** like the one bearing a huge portrait of the singer Oum Kalsoum, near the Abu el-Haggag Mosque. Though café life is exclusively masculine, foreign women can usually feel comfortable there, even alone. Most places stay open as long as there are customers; Sharia Ramses has several all-nighters. Trashy movies are regularly screened at the **cinema** on Sharia al-Mahatta.

Festivals

Aside from an **International Rowing Festival** around December 18–22, it's hard to predict what kind of tourist events will occur during high season. *Aida* was staged at Hatshepsut Temple in 1996 and 1997, but has not been re-scheduled since. In any event, the tourist office can supply details of whatever entertainments are scheduled.

Depending on the Islamic calendar, your visit might coincide with a **moulid**, which could be a local affair attended by a few thousand people, or a huge carnival attracting half a million *fellaheen* from Upper Egypt. Most of them happen during the two months of the Muslim calendar preceding Ramadan; locals can rarely tell you the exact date, but always know when one is due. Foreigners are welcome to attend; just beware of pickpockets.

The largest and most famous is the **Moulid of Abu el-Haggag** (pronounced "Hajjaj"), honouring Luxor's patron sheikh, whose mosque overlooks the temple. **Yussef Abu el-Haggag** (Father of the Pilgrimage) was born in Damascus (c.1150), moved to Mecca in his forties and finally settled in Egypt, where he founded a *zawiyah* in Luxor and met with other Sufi sheikhs such as Al-Mursi and Al-Shazli. Many of his descendants still live in the area, and the tradition of venerating local sheikhs is strong in villages around Luxor. During the festival, giant floats move through the densely packed streets, some dedicated to trades (the *caleche* drivers' bears a carriage), others to the sheikh himself. The parading of a large **boat** (or even three boats) is often compared to the solar barque processions of pharaonic times, though in Islamic symbolism boats represent the quest for spiritual enlightenment. Vast crowds attend the *zikrs* outside Abu el-Haggag's Mosque, and revel in traditional entertainments. There are **stick fights** (*tahtib*) to the music of drums and *mizmars* (a kind of oboe), and **horse races** (*mirmah*) where the riders gallop hell for leather, halting in a flurry of dust just before they plough into the crowd. Booze and *bango* are consumed quite openly. The festival occurs two weeks before the start of Ramadan, and lasts for two days. During **Ramadan** itself, townsfolk compensate for its daytime rigours by gathering to hear *zikrs* and dance outside Abu el-Haggag's Mosque in the evenings.

Sheikh Ali Musa of Karnak was actually born in another village, and when he died the villagers demanded that his body be buried there instead. The Karnakis said, "Let the Sheikh decide", so his coffin was borne to the crossroads, whereupon it turned to face Karnak and was taken back in triumph. His moulid lasts a week, its *leyla kebir* (Big Night) falling on the 6th of *Rageb*. You can't miss the music, swings and lights around his tomb, near the entrance to Karnak village.

About the same time, on the other side of town, Awmia village honours its own **Sheikh Ahmed al-Adasi** with a week-long festival, whose curtain raiser is a day of stick fights, horse and **camel races** on a nearby wasteground. For the moulid itself, Awmia's main street is enclosed by a tent, where *munshids* sing at ear-splitting volume; further in are fairground rides and a tent of Sufis in a *zikr*. Following the *leyla kebir* on the 14th of *Rageb,* there's a final day of celebrations called *Ed-Dara*, when camels and horses are paraded through the streets and villagers throw candies at each other. Al-Adasi is known for appearing in the dreams of Egyptians working in Italy and Morocco.

Yet another moulid occurs in Old Qurna, across the Nile (see p.334).

Shopping: bazaars and markets

The streets around Luxor Temple are infested with **tourist bazaars** whose salesmen use every trick in the book to lure you into their shops. Despite fierce competition, you must bargain hard for a good price, since merchants can rely upon fresh-off-the-plane tourists to pay way over the odds. Fixed-price shops are rare, but can provide a rough benchmark for bargaining at other places. Gold and silver are usually sold by weight and so prices should be roughly fixed; El Safa Bazar on Sharia Labaib Habachi is friendly and honest. As a rule, it should be cheaper to buy alabaster or papyrus on the west bank. The Nefertari Papyrus Institute is one of the few fixed-price shops on that side of the Nile. In Luxor, curio and carpet shops have long been driving hardware, spices and clothing stalls northwards up Sharia el-Birka, the traditional **souk**. On Tuesdays, there's a **fruit and veg market** there, and on Sharia el-Madina el-Minawra, near Television Street. Most non-tourist shops close for a **siesta** (2–5pm).

Luxor's weekly **livestock market** is smaller and less camel-oriented than the *Souk el-Gamal* at Darow, near Aswan, or Cairo's market at Bil'esh, but just as rough on the nerves of animal lovers. The name of the route to the site – Sharia es-Salakhana, "Slaughterhouse Street" – says it all. The market is held every Tuesday (7–11am) in the village of El-Hebel, 4km outside Luxor (£E6–7 by taxi). To reach El-Hebel by bicycle, follow Sharia Mustafa Kamel across the train tracks, turn right down Es-Salakhana and simply follow the stream of traffic.

Activities

Sailing on the river in a **felucca** is a relaxing way to spend an afternoon, while a sunset cruise is the perfect way to end the day. Expect to pay about £E20 an hour for a boat carrying two people, £E30 upwards for a craft seating six or seven. The favoured destination is **Banana Island** (*Gezira el-Mozh*), a lush peninsula 4km upriver, where visitors are charged £E5 apiece to land. There are souvenir and drinks stalls, and lads who hijack the clothes of tourists stripping to swim and hold them to ransom. The round trip takes between two and three hours depending on the wind, and costs £E50 per boatload. To the felucca men's dismay, **motorboat cruises** are an increasingly popular alternative. Though package tourists are gulled into paying £10/US$20 a head for cruises on the *Lotus* boat, you should be able to rent a smaller *zobak* for £E40 an hour by negotiating directly with boatmen (for more on cruises between Luxor and Aswan, see p.392). The best felucca and *zobak* captains are allocated berths below Luxor Temple and the *Winter Palace*; less skilled ones tie up nearer the *Etap* and *Novotel*. Smara of the *African Queen* is a good felucca captain.

Most hotels with **swimming pools** let non-residents use them. The *Windsor*, *Philippe*, *New Emilio* and *Shady* charge £E7 admission; the *Luxor Sheraton* £E20; the *Gaddis* and *Sonesta St. George* £E25; and the *Winter Palace* charges £E50. The *Luxor* (£E10), *Mercure Inn* and *Novotel* (£E15), *Bella-Donna Club Med* (£E18) and *Isis* (£E25) levy a minimum charge for snacks and drinks, while the entry price at the *Etap* (£E25) includes a drink or snacks. There are **tennis** courts at the *Winter Palace*, *Luxor Sheraton* and *Nile Hilton*, while **horse-riding** on the west bank can be arranged through the *Etap* (£E55; 2hr), or by visiting one of the stables in Gezira, where you should be able to negotiate the price to £E10 an hour. The *Pharaonic* and *Arabian* stables both have Arabian thoroughbreds. You can play **billiards** in the *King's Head Pub* (£E10), the *Nile Hilton* (£E20) or the *Luxor* (£E15). The *Luxor* has the nicest billiards room after the *Winter Palace*'s, which is not for use by non-residents but worth a look for its Edwardian splendour.

Finally, if money is no object, there's the luxury of drifting over the Necropolis in a **hot-air balloon**, which affords an awesome view of the temples, villages and mountains; to get the best photographic results use 200 or 250 ASA film. Cruising at 300 metres, you can smell the cooking fires and donkeys and overhear conversations below, in an eerie silence punctuated by the roar of the balloon's gas-burners. The course is determined by meteorological conditions and the skill of the pilot, so each flight is different – but you'll probably spend about an hour aloft. The two balloon companies operating in Luxor are fully insured and CAA-approved. Hod-Hod Soliman (☎ & fax 095/370-116) is a locally based firm with a British pilot, while Balloons Over Egypt (BOE; ☎095/376-515) holds a franchise from Virgin. Both offer two or three flights daily in season (Oct–May), subject to cancellation at short notice. BOE charges US$250 per person, including a champagne breakfast or buffet in the desert; Hod-Hod trips cost US$200, with a slap-up breakfast at the *Môvenpick*. Bookings can be made through travel agents, or by phone; BOE is also represented at the *Isis* and *Hilton* hotels.

Listings

American Express In the arcade outside the *Winter Palace*. Changes money and travellers' cheques, makes cash advances and transfers, sells cheques to Amex cardholders, and holds mail. Daily 8am–8pm (☎095/378-333, fax 372-862).

Banks and exchange Banque Misr, Sharia Labaib Habachi (daily 8.30am–9pm, Fri closed between 11.30am & 3pm), has a cash dispenser (Visa, MasterCard, Cirrus) outside. Other banks include National Bank of Egypt, 50m south of the *Winter Palace* (daily except Fri 8.30am–2pm & 5–9pm, Fri 8.30–11am & 5–9pm); Banque du Caire, Midan Salah al-Din, near Television St (winter daily except Fri 8.30am–2pm & 5–8pm, summer same days till 9pm). The Bank of Alexandria on the Corniche between the City Council and Luxor Museum exchanges cash, travellers' cheques and does Visa cash advances (Mon–Thurs & Sun 8.30am–2pm; Ramadan 10am–1.30pm). Many of the luxury hotels also do currency exchange.

Bookshops Aboudi and Gaddis in the bazaar near the tourist office, and Hachette, in the arcade of the *Etap*, stock loads of novels and books on Egyptology in foreign languages. A kiosk on the Corniche near the tourist office sells foreign newspapers. The best place for postcards is on the corner of Sharia al-Souk and Sharia Yussef Hassan.

British Consul (Honorary) Mr Ehab A.A. Gaddis can help British citizens in the event of trouble. Contact him at the "consulate" at the *Gaddis* Hotel (Mon–Thurs & Sat 10am–2pm & 7–10pm; ☎095/382-838).

Dentist Dr Moneer el-Shaoly, on Sharia al-Mahatta (☎095/373-710).

Doctors Dr Makrus Faoze, Sharia al-Adasi (☎095/382-614, mobile 01234/00729); dermatologist Dr Selim Fakhri (☎095/372-028); urologist Dr Samy Fakhri (☎095/374-964).

EgyptAir In the arcade outside the *Winter Palace* (daily 8am–8pm; ☎095/380-580).

Hospital The El-Gadid is at the far end of Television St (☎095/382-698); the new St Mark is on Sharia el-Karnak opposite the hotel of the same name (☎095/370-465), while the older Al-Amiri is on the Corniche near the Luxor Museum (☎095/372-025); all open 24hr. English is spoken but they're all pretty grim – seek treatment in Cairo if you can. Ambulance ☎123.

Internet cafés *Cyber*, Sharia al-Adasi (daily except Fri 7am–11pm; Internet £E45/hr, £E5 to send or receive an email); *Aboudi*, in bookshop of the same name (see above; daily 8am–10pm; Internet £E25/hr); *Rainbow Internet Café*, on the Corniche at the entrance to the Military Club (daily 9am–midnight; Internet £E30/hr, £E5 to send or receive an email).

Passport office On Sharia Ibn Khalid Walid (Mon–Thurs & Sat 8am–2pm; ☎095/380-885). Visa extensions cost £E12 and require one photo. Some English spoken.

Pharmacies Exist all over town and have a rota for working nights, posted in Arabic. Hotels are generally aware of likely locations.

Post office At the temple end of Sharia al-Mahatta (Mon–Thurs & Sun 8am–2pm), with a branch in the station (daily 8am–8pm) and another next to the telephone exchange on Sharia el-Karnak (daily 8am–8pm). *Don't* use the poste restante; have letters sent c/o American Express or the *Winter Palace*. It's less hassle to send packages with DHL, on the Corniche next to the *Mina Palace Hotel* (daily 8am–6pm).

Telephone calls The cheapest way to call abroad is with a phonecard (£E15–30), sold at the 24-hour telephone office off Sharia el-Karnak, which can also be used in phones in the station. However, not enough lines exist to meet demand in off-peak hours (8pm–8am), so you may have to try several different phones before getting a connection. This enables hotels with a private line to get away with charging £E35 (minimum 3min) for international calls.

Thomas Cook Outside the *Winter Palace*. Changes currency and sells travellers' cheques. Also does tours and makes reservations (daily 8am–8pm; ☎095/372-402, fax 376-502).

Excursions from Luxor – and moving on

With Karnak Temple and the Theban Necropolis (see following sections) in the immediate vicinity, it'll be a while before you start considering **excursions** to other sites up and down the Nile Valley. However, the **temples of Esna, Edfu and Kom Ombo** are spaced along the way to Aswan, and bolder tourists may also hanker after **Abydos** and **Dendara**, around Qena, despite these areas being affected by the troubles in Middle Egypt (see p.258). Any of these sites makes a feasible day excursion from Luxor.

Travel restrictions for foreigners may apply in this area (for further details see box on p.254), and timings of police-escorted convoys may be less than convenient, so it's easier and more pleasant to visit the temples of Esna, Edfu and Kom Ombo from a cruise boat or felucca. The initial stretch is frustratingly slow in a felucca as the Theban

Hills block the wind from the north, so most visitors prefer to sail downriver from Aswan. (The ins and outs of felucca trips are covered on p.392.) Nevertheless, for those who are committed to visiting these temples from Luxor, it is feasible to visit Esna and Edfu by private taxi in a day (around £E80 for a five-seater). Heading north, day-trips by private taxi to **Dendara or Abydos** can be arranged through many of the hotels (£E120 return for a five-seater to both sites). Cruise boats now also make day-trips to Dendara, docking at Qena (*Lotus* and *Tiba Star* both charge £E150 per person including lunch, tea and entrance fees). For details, see the accounts of Qena, Dendara and Abydos, earlier in this chapter.

Moving on to these and other points in Egypt may be affected by seasonal factors. Flights and trains are quite heavily booked over winter, as are direct buses to Hurghada on the Red Sea.

Buses

Luxor's inter-city **bus station** has recently moved to a side road off Sharia el-Karnak, just north of Luxor Temple. It's fairly easy to obtain information on buses here, and you can sometimes buy tickets the day before (if not, get them on the bus). There is one express bus to **Cairo** (7pm; 10hr; £E51) every day, plus the chance of seats on the A/C through-service from Aswan. Seedier southbound buses run every hour or so in the morning, and less frequently in the afternoon to **Aswan** (£E6.50–8). The morning services make longer stops at **Esna** (£E2.50), **Edfu** (£E3.75) and **Kom Ombo** (£E5). There are five direct services a day to **Hurghada** (4hr; £E13–21), from where you can catch a boat to **Sharm el-Sheikh** (Mon, Tues & Sat). Alternatively, you can get one of the four daily buses to Suez (9hr; £E31–41) and pick up a *service* taxi or through bus from Cairo to the Sinai resorts. The *Happyland Hotel* arranges direct buses to **Dahab** (13hr; cost depends on the number of passengers), though it could take a few days to get enough people together to make it viable. There are six buses a day to **Qena** (1hr; £E3). All of these services are subject to convoys.

Trains

For reasons of security, foreigners are only allowed to buy tickets for two trains to **Cairo** (12–14hr), as well as the exorbitant *wagons-lits* (£E313). It might be possible to travel on other trains, but there's bound to be hassle. The overnight service (leaving at 11.30pm) is more popular than the daytime one (departing at 7.50am), since both 1st (£E51) and A/C 2nd (£E31) class are comfortable to sleep in. There is a similar restriction on trains to **Aswan** (4hr), where the afternoon service (5pm) is preferred to the morning one (7am). First class costs £E20; A/C 2nd £E14. Tickets should be purchased the day before for morning departures, and as early as possible on the day for later services. There is also a weekly train to **Kharga** (Thurs 7am; 6–8hr; £E10).

Service taxis

Luxor's **service taxi depot** is just off Sharia el-Karnak. At the time of writing, foreigners were forbidden to travel in *service* taxis outside of Luxor (see box on p.254); we have included some routes and fares in the event that restrictions are lifted. With a sign in English for each destination, you can't go wrong in identifying which twelve-seater minivan you want. Just turn up and you should be off within fifteen minutes. Journey times and per-person prices are: **Esna** (1hr; £E2), **Edfu** (1hr 30min; £E4), **Kom Ombo** (2–3hr; £E7), **Aswan** (3–4hr; £E8).

Flights

Flight schedules vary seasonally, so get the latest details from **EgyptAir** (daily 8am–8pm; ☎095/380-580). Current one-way ticket prices are: **Cairo** (US$123), **Aswan**

(US$56) and **Sharm el-Sheikh** (US$122); return tickets cost double, and student rates are about 25 percent lower. Book as far in advance as you can, or try for last-minute cancellations. There may also be a chance of **standby charter flights to Europe**, which can be extremely cheap. Ask at the airport, or approach tour reps at the big hotels.

Luxor **Airport** (☎095/384-655) is 6km east of town (£E10–12 by taxi).

Karnak

The temple complex of **Karnak** beats every other pharaonic monument but the Pyramids of Giza. Built on a leviathan scale to house the gods, it comprises three separate temple enclosures, the grandest being the **Precinct of Amun**, dedicated to the supreme god of the New Kingdom – a structure large enough to accommodate ten great cathedrals.

Karnak's magnitude and complexity owes to 1300 years of aggrandizement. From its XII Dynasty core, Amun's temple expanded along two axes – towards the river and the **Temple of Mut** – while its enclosure wall approached the **Precinct of Mont**. Though Pharaoh Akhenaten abjured Amun, defaced his images and erected an Aten Temple at Karnak, the status quo ante was soon restored at the behest of Amun's priesthood.

At the zenith of its supremacy Karnak's wealth was staggering. A list of its assets during the reign of Ramses III includes 65 villages, 433 gardens, 421,662 head of cattle, 2395 square kilometres of fields, 46 building sites, 83 ships, and 81,322 workers and slaves. The Egyptologist T.G.H. James likened it to an industrial giant "which generated a mass of business subsidiary to the practice of the cults and a huge army of officials and working people". Yet ordinary folk were barred from its precincts and none but the pharaoh or his representative could enter Amun's sanctuary. The whole area was known to the ancient Egyptians as *Iput-Isut*, "the most esteemed of places".

Visiting Karnak

The **site** of Karnak covers over 100 acres, 2.5km north of central Luxor. The only part that's readily accessible is the Precinct of Amun (daily: winter 6am–5.30pm; summer 6am–6.30pm; £E20, students £E10), which hosts nightly Sound and Light shows. This alone covers almost 62 acres, requiring at least two hours for a lookover, three or four hours for a closer examination. As there's little shade, it's best to wear a hat and bring water. Usually the temple is busy with tour groups in the morning, but almost deserted from mid-afternoon onwards, so if you can stand the heat, that's the best time to come. A café by the Sacred Lake sells tea and soft drinks, and toilets can be found near the grandstand and the open-air museum. A separate ticket (£E10) is required for the museum.

There are two **approaches** from town: via the Corniche, which turns inland further north, or along Sharia el-Karnak, roughly following the **Avenue of Sphinxes** that once connected Luxor and Karnak temples, past the towering **Gateway of Euergetes II** and the precinct's **enclosure wall**. You could cycle or walk, but it's best to conserve your energy for the site. The cheapest way to get there (and back) is by minibus (25pt per person). The official rates for a one-way taxi (£E5–9) or *caleche* (£E5) ride provide a benchmark for haggling with drivers; if you rent them for the return journey, be sure to agree on the time to be spent at Karnak and remember your *caleche* number.

Expect to pay a bit more for rides to the **Sound and Light show** (£E33 tickets sold on the spot; no reductions). The first half consists of a four-stop tour through the temple, ineffably grander when gloomy and spotlit. Although the second half – when you view the ruins from a grandstand beyond the lake – drags on too long, the whole experience is unforgettable. *Caleches* cram in extra passengers for the homeward journey, and race back for a second load. There are three or four shows each night, at least one of them in English. Schedules are posted in the tourist office.

The Temple of Amun

The great **Temple of Amun** seemingly recedes towards infinity in an overwhelming succession of pylons, courts and columned halls, obelisks and colossi. Compared by T.G.H. James to "an archeological department store containing something for everyone", it bears the stamp of dozens of rulers, spanning some thirteen centuries of ancient history. Half-buried in silt for as long again, the ruins were subsequently squatted by *fellaheen*, before being cleared by archeologists in the mid-nineteenth century. The Karnak thus exposed was far more ruinous than today, with columns and colossi lying amidst piles of rubble and frogs croaking from the swampy enclosure. Since major repairs early last century, the temple has been undergoing slow but systematic restoration.

AMUN AND THE THEBAN TRIAD

Originally merely one of the deities in the Hermopolitan Ogdoad (see p.266), **Amun** gained ascendancy at Thebes shortly before the Middle Kingdom, presumably because his cult was adopted by powerful local rulers during the First Intermediate Period. After the expulsion of the Hyksos (c.1567 BC), the rulers of the XVIII Dynasty elevated Amun to a victorious national god, and set about making Karnak his principal cult centre in Egypt.

As the "Unseen One" (whose name in hieroglyphic script was accompanied by a blank space instead of the usual explicatory sign), Amun assimilated other deities into such incarnations as **Amun-Re** (the supreme Creator), **Amun-Min** (the "bull which serves the cows" with a perpetual erection) or ram-headed **Auf-Re** ("Re made Flesh"), who sailed through the underworld revitalizing the souls of the dead, emerging reborn as Khepri. However, Amun most commonly appears as a human wearing ram's horns and the twin-feathered *atef* crown.

His consort, **Mut**, was a local goddess in pre-Dynastic times, who became linked with Nekhbet, the vulture protectress of Upper Egypt. Early in the XVIII Dynasty she was "married" to Amun, assimilated his previous consort Amunet and became Mistress of Heaven. She is customarily depicted wearing a vulture headdress and *uraeus* and the Combined Crown of the Two Lands.

Amun and Mut's son **Khonsu**, "the Traveller", crossed the night sky as the moon-god, issued prophecies and assisted Thoth, the divine scribe. He was portrayed either with a hawk's head, or as a young boy with the side lock of youth.

Karnak was the largest of several temples consecrated to this **Theban Triad** of deities.

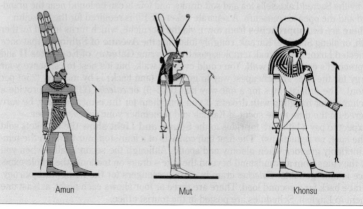

Amun   Mut   Khonsu

Making sense of its convoluted layout is not easy, with the ruins themselves getting denser and more jumbled the further in you go. To simplify **orientation**, we've assumed that the temple's alignment towards the Nile corresponds with the cardinal points, so that its main axis runs east–west, and the subsidiary axis north–south.

It's worth following the main axis all the way back to the **Festival Hall**, and at least seeing the **Cachette Court** of the other wing. A break for refreshments by the lake is advisable if your itinerary includes the **open-air museum** or the **Temple of Khonsu**, off the main circuit.

Entering the temple

Walking towards the Precinct of Amun from the ticket office, and crossing over a dry moat, you'll pass the remains of an **ancient dock**, whence Amun sailed for Luxor Temple during the Optet festival. Before boarding a full-sized boat, his sacred barque rested in the small **chapel** to the right, which was erected (and graffitied by mercenaries) during the brief XXIX Dynasty. Beyond lies a short **Processional Way** flanked by ram-headed sphinxes (after Amun's sacred animal) enfolding statues of Ramses II, which once joined the main avenue linking the two temples.

Ahead of this rises the gigantic **First Pylon**, whose yawning gateway exposes a vista of receding portals, dwarfing all who walk between them. Composed of regular courses of sandstone masonry, the 43-metre-high towers are often attributed to the Nubian and Ethiopian kings of the XXV Dynasty, but may have been erected as late as the XXX Dynasty (when Nectanebo I added the enclosure wall). Although the northern tower is unfinished and neither is decorated, their 130-metre width makes this the largest pylon in Egypt. High up on the right as you walk through the pylon, Napoleonic surveyors have inscribed Karnak's vital statistics and the distances to other temples in Upper Egypt.

The **Forecourt** is another late addition, enclosing three earlier structures. In the centre stands a single papyriform pillar from the **Kiosk of Taharqa** (an Ethiopian king of the XXV Dynasty), thought to have been a roofless pavilion where Amun's effigy was placed for its revivifying union with the sun at New Year. Off to the left stands the so-called **Shrine of Seti II**, actually a way station for the sacred barques of Amun, Mut and Khonsu, built of grey sandstone and rose granite.

The Temple of Ramses III to the Second Pylon

The first really impressive structure in the precinct is the columned **Temple of Ramses III**, which also held the Theban Triad barques during processions. Beyond its pylon, flanked by two colossi, is a festival hall with mummiform pillar statues, behind which are carvings of the annual festival of Amun-Min. A Hypostyle Hall precedes the darkened barque shrines of the temple, whose dedication reads in part: *"I built it, sheathed it with sandstone, bringing great doors of fine gold; and I filled its treasuries with offerings that my hands had brought."*

Though the pink granite **Colossus of Ramses II** beside the vestibule to the Second Pylon **[a]** is an immediate attention-grabber, it's worth detouring round the side of his temple to pass through the **Bubastite Portal**, named after the XXII Dynasty that hailed from Bubastis in the Delta. En route you'll pass some holes in the Second Pylon, where in 1820 Henri Crevier uncovered a host of statues and blocks from the demolished Aten Temple (including the colossi of Akhenaten in the Luxor and Cairo museums), which Horemheb used as in-fill for his pylon.

Pass through the Portal and turn left to find the **Shoshenk relief**, commemorating the triumphs of the XXII Dynasty Pharaoh Shoshenk. Traditionally, scholars have identified him as the Biblical Shishak (I Kings 14: 25–26) who plundered Jerusalem in 925 BC, thus establishing a crucial link between the chronologies of ancient Egypt and the

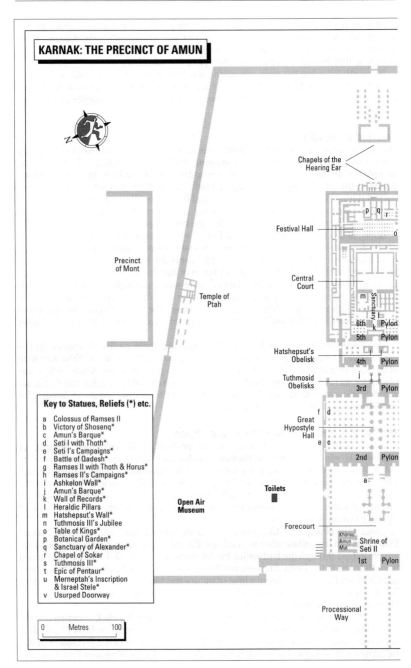

KARNAK: THE PRECINCT OF AMUN

Chapels of the
Hearing Ear

Festival Hall

Precinct
of Mont

Precinct
of Mont

Central
Court

Temple of
Ptah

Sanctuary

6th Pylon
5th Pylon

Hatshepsut's
Obelisk

4th Pylon

Tuthmosid
Obelisks

3rd Pylon

Great
Hypostyle
Hall

2nd Pylon

Key to Statues, Reliefs (*) etc.

a   Colossus of Ramses II
b   Victory of Shosenq*
c   Amun's Barque*
d   Seti I with Thoth*
e   Seti I's Campaigns*
f   Battle of Qadesh*
g   Ramses II with Thoth & Horus*
h   Ramses II's Campaigns*
i   Ashkelon Wall*
j   Amun's Barque*
k   Wall of Records*
l   Heraldic Pillars
m   Hatshepsut's Wall*
n   Tuthmosis III's Jubilee
o   Table of Kings*
p   Botanical Garden*
q   Sanctuary of Alexander*
r   Chapel of Sokar
s   Tuthmosis III*
t   Epic of Pentaur*
u   Merneptah's Inscription
    & Israel Stele*
v   Usurped Doorway

Toilets

**Open Air
Museum**

Forecourt

Khonsu
Amun
Mut
Shrine of
Seti II

1st Pylon

Processional
Way

0   Metres   100

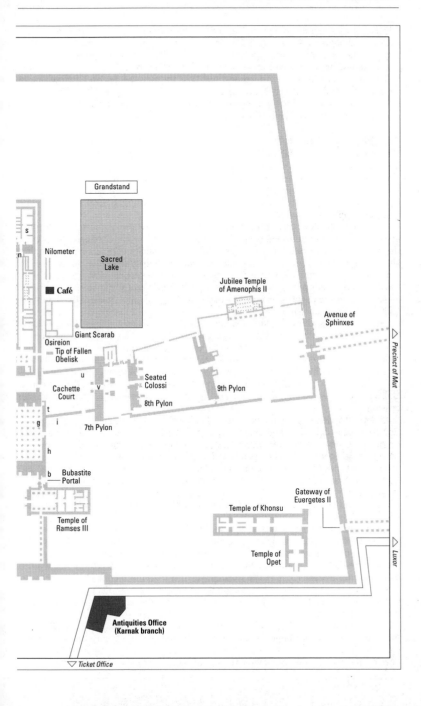

Grandstand

s

Nilometer

n

Café

Sacred
Lake

Jubilee Temple
of Amenophis II

Avenue of
Sphinxes

Osireion

Giant Scarab

Tip of Fallen
Obelisk

Seated
Colossi

9th Pylon

Precinct of Mut

u

v

Cachette
Court

8th Pylon

t

g

i

7th Pylon

h

b

Bubastite
Portal

Gateway of
Euergetes II

Temple of Khonsu

Temple of
Ramses III

Temple of
Opet

Luxor

Antiquities Office
(Karnak branch)

▽ Ticket Office

Old Testament – an orthodoxy challenged by David Rohl's book, *A Test of Time* (see below). Although Shoshenk's figure is almost invisible, you can still see Amun, presiding over the slaughter of Rheoboamite prisoners in Palestine **[b]**. The scenes further along the wall are best seen after visiting the Great Hypostyle Hall.

To reach this, return to the forecourt and pass through the **Second Pylon**, one of several jerry-built structures begun by Horemheb, the last king of the XVIII Dynasty. The cartouches of Seti I (who completed the pylon) and Ramses I and II (Seti's father and son) appear just inside the doorway.

The Great Hypostyle Hall

The **Great Hypostyle Hall** is Karnak's glory, a forest of gigantic columns covering an area of 6000 square metres – large enough to contain both St Peter's Cathedral in Rome and St Paul's Cathedral in London. Its grandeur is best appreciated early in the morning or late in the afternoon, when diagonal shadows enhance the effect of the columns. In pharaonic times the hall was roofed with sandstone slabs, its gloom interspersed by sunbeams falling through windows above the central aisle.

The hall probably began as a processional avenue of twelve or fourteen **columns**, each 23m high and 15m round (requiring six people with outstretched arms to encircle their girth). To this, Seti I and Ramses II added 122 smaller columns in two flanking wings, plus walls and a roof. All the columns consist of semi-drums, fitted together without mortar. The central ones have calyx capitals that once supported a raised section of the roof incorporating clerestory windows (the stone grilles of several remain in place), elevated above the papyrus-bud capitals of the flanking columns. Some of the lintels are still painted, as in ancient times.

Their **carvings** show the king making offerings to Theban deities, most notably Amun, who frequently appears in a sexually aroused state. Some Egyptologists believe that the temple priestesses kept Amun happy by masturbating his idol. Similar cult scenes decorate the side and end walls of the hall, which manifest two styles of carving. While Seti adorned the northern wing with bas-reliefs, Ramses II favoured cheaper sunk-reliefs for the southern wing. You can compare the two styles on the Hypostyle Hall's entrance wall, which features nearly symmetrical scenes of Amun's barque procession.

In Seti's **northern wing**, the procession begins on the north wall with a depiction of Amun's barque, initially veiled, then revealed **[c]**. Thoth inscribes the duration of Seti's reign on the leaves of a sacred persea tree **[d]** just beyond the doorway. By walking out through this door you'll come upon **Seti I's battle scenes**, whose weathered details are best observed in the early morning or late afternoon. One section **[e]** relates the capture of Qadesh from the Hittites in Syria (lower rows), and Seti's triumphs over the Libyans (above). Depicted elsewhere **[f]** are his campaigns against the Shasu of southern Palestine and the storming of Pa-Canaan, which the Egyptians "plundered with every evil".

Returning to the Hypostyle Hall, you can find similar reliefs commissioned by Ramses II in the **southern wing**, retaining traces of their original colours. Beyond the barque procession on the inner wall, Ramses is presented to Amun and enthroned between Wadjet and Nekhbet, while Thoth and Horus adjust his crowns **[g]**. On the outer wall are **Ramses II's battle scenes**, starting with the second Battle of Qadesh (c.1300 BC) **[h]**. Though scholars reckon it was probably a draw, Ramses claimed total victory over the Hittites. The text of their **peace treaty** (the earliest such document known) appears on the outer wall of the Cachette Court **[i]**.

This is known as the **"Ashkelon Wall"** after one of the four battle scenes flanking the treaty; another may depict a fight with the Israelites. Rohl argues that the enemy chariots in this scene contradict established chronology, since the Israelites didn't develop them until King Solomon's reign, but Ramses is conventionally supposed to have been the Pharaoh of the Oppression in the time of Moses, centuries earlier. Other clues from the Ashkelon Wall, Shoshenk's reliefs (see above) and the Israel Stele (see p.325) led Rohl to surmise that the Biblical Shishak was not Shoshenk, but Ramses II, and that the established synchronicity between Biblical and Egyptian history is three centuries out, due to an overestimation of the duration of the Third Intermediate Period (Dynasties XXI–XXV). See p.647 in Contexts chapter for more about Rohl's New Chronology hypothesis.

Pylons and obelisks

Beyond the XIX Dynasty Hypostyle Hall lies an extensive section of the precinct dating from the XVIII Dynasty. The **Third Pylon** that forms its back wall was originally intended by Amenophis III to be a monumental gateway to the temple. Like Horemheb forty years later, he demolished earlier structures to serve as core filler for his pylon. Removed by archeologists, these blocks are now displayed – partly reassembled – in the open-air museum. Two huge reliefs of Amun's barque appear on the far wall of the pylon **[j]**.

The narrow court between the Third and Fourth pylons once boasted four **Tuthmosid Obelisks**. The stone bases near the Third Pylon held a pair erected by Tuthmosis III, chunks of which lie scattered around. Of the pink granite pair erected by Tuthmosis II, one still stands 23m high, with an estimated weight of 143 tons. Once tipped with glittering electrum, the finely carved obelisk was later appropriated by Ramses IV and VI, who added their own cartouches.

At this stage it's best to carry on through the **Fourth Pylon** rather than get side-tracked into the Cachette Court on the temple's secondary axis (see p.325). Beyond the pylon are numerous columns which probably formed another hypostyle hall, dominated by the rose granite **Obelisk of Hatshepsut**, the only woman to rule as pharaoh. To mark her sixteenth regnal year, Hatshepsut had two obelisks quarried in Aswan and erected at Karnak, a task completed in seven months. The standing obelisk is over 27m high and weighs 320 tons, with a dedicatory inscription running its full height. Its fallen mate has broken into sections, now dispersed around the temple. After Hatshepsut's death, the long-frustrated Tuthmosis III took revenge, defacing her cartouches wherever they occurred and hiding the lower part of her obelisks behind walls – which inadvertently protected them from further vandalism during the Amarna Period.

The carved **tip** of Hatshepsut's fallen obelisk can be examined near the Osireion and Sacred Lake. On the way there, you'll pass a granite bas-relief of Amenophis II target-shooting from a moving chariot, protruding from the **Fifth Pylon**. Built of limestone, this pylon is attributed to Hatshepsut's father, Tuthmosis I. Beyond it lies a colonnaded courtyard with Osiride statues, built by one of the Tuthmosid pharaohs and possibly part of a large inner court surrounding the original Middle Kingdom temple of Amun.

Though the **Sixth Pylon** has largely disappeared, a portion either side of the granite doorway remains. Its outer face is known as the *Wall of Records* **[k]** after its list of peoples conquered by Tuthmosis III: Nubians to the right, Asiatics to the left. Beyond the latter is a text extolling the king's victory at Megiddo (Armageddon) in 1479 BC. By organizing tribute from his vanquished foes rather than simply destroying them, Tuthmosis III was arguably the world's first imperialist.

Around the Sanctuary

The section beyond the Sixth Pylon gets increasingly confusing, but a few features are unmistakable. Ahead stand a pair of square-sectioned **heraldic pillars**, their fronts carved with the lotus and papyrus of the Two Lands, their sides showing Amun embracing Tuthmosis III **[l]**. On the left are two **Colossi of Amun and Amunet**, dedicated by Tutankhamun (whose likeness appears with them) when orthodoxy was re-established after the Amarna Period. There's also a seated **statue of Amenophis II**.

Next comes a granite **Sanctuary** built by Philip Arrhidaeus, the cretinous half-brother of Alexander the Great, on the site of a Tuthmosid-era shrine which similarly held Amun's barque (whose pedestal is still *in situ*). The interior bas-reliefs show Philip making offerings to Amun in his various aspects, topped by a star-spangled ceiling. On the outside walls are sunk-reliefs depicting his coronation, Thoth's declaration of welcome, and Amunet suckling the young pharaoh, some still brightly coloured.

Around to the left of the sanctuary and further back is a wall inscribed with Tuthmosis III's victories, which he built to hide a wall of reliefs by Queen Hatshepsut, now removed to another room **[m]**. **Hatshepsut's Wall** has reopened after lengthy restoration, as has the facing portion, where Tuthmosis replaced her image by offerings tables or bouquets, and substituted his father's and grandfather's names for her cartouches.

Beyond here lies an open space or **Central Court**, thought to mark the site of the original temple of Amun built in the XII Dynasty, whose weathered alabaster foundations poke from the pebbly ground.

The Jubilee Temple of Tuthmosis III

At the rear of this court rises the **Jubilee Temple of Tuthmosis III**, a personal cult shrine in Amun's back yard. As at Saqqara during the Old Kingdom, the Theban kings periodically renewed their temporal and spiritual authority with jubilee festivals. The original entrance **[n]** is flanked by reliefs and broken statues of Tuthmosis in *hed-seb* regalia. A left turn brings you into the **Festival Hall**, with its unusual tentpole-style columns, their capitals adorned with blue and white chevrons. The lintels – carved with falcons, owls, *ankhs* and other symbols – are likewise brightly coloured. During Christian times the hall was used as a church, hence the haloed saints on some of the pillars.

A chamber off the southwest corner **[o]** contains an eroded replica of the *Table of Kings* (the original is in the Louvre), depicting Tuthmosis making offerings to previous rulers – Hatshepsut is naturally omitted from the roll call. Behind the hall are further chambers, mostly ruinous. The so-called **Botanical Garden** is a roofless enclosure containing painted reliefs of plants and animals which Tuthmosis encountered on his campaigns in Syria **[p]**. Across the way is a roofed chamber decorated by Alexander the Great, who appears before Amun and other deities **[q]**. The **Chapel of Sokar** constitutes a miniature temple to the Memphite god of darkness **[r]**, juxtaposed against a (now inaccessible) shrine to the sun. A further suite of rooms is dedicated to Tuthmosis **[s]**.

Chapels of the Hearing Ear

Excluded from Amun's Precinct and lacking a direct line to the Theban Triad, the inhabitants of Thebes used intermediary deities to transmit their petitions. These lesser deities rated their own shrines, known as **Chapels of the Hearing Ear** (sometimes actually decorated with carved ears), which straddled the temple's enclosure wall, presenting one face to the outside world. At Karnak, however, they became steadily less approachable and were finally surrounded by the present enclosure wall.

Directly behind the Jubilee Temple is a series of chapels built by Tuthmosis III, centred upon a large alabaster statue of the king and Amun. On either side are the bases of another pair of obelisks erected by Hatshepsut, of which nothing else remains. Still further east lie the ruined halls and colonnades of a Temple of the Hearing Ear built by Ramses II. Behind this stands the pedestal of the tallest obelisk known (31m), which Emperor Constantine had shipped to Rome and erected in the Circus Maximus; it was

SEKHMET

Sekhmet – "the Powerful" – was the violent counterpart of the Delta goddess Bastet (see p.527). As the daughter of Re, she personified the sun's destructive force, making her a worthy consort for Ptah, the Memphite creator-god. In one myth, Re feared that humanity was plotting against him and unleashed his avenging Eye in the form of Sekhmet, who would have massacred all life had not Re relented and slaked her thirst with red beer, which the drunken goddess mistook for blood.

With the rise of Thebes and Amun's association with Ptah, a corresponding relationship was made between their consorts, Mut and Sekhmet. The New Kingdom pharaohs adopted Sekhmet as a symbol of their indomitable prowess in battle: the statues of the goddess at Karnak bear inscriptions such as "smiter of the Nubians". As "Lady of the Messengers of Death", Sekhmet could send – or prevent – plagues, so her priestesses also served as healers and veterinarians.

Sekhmet

later moved to Lateran Square, hence its name, the **Lateran Obelisk**. As the ancient Egyptians rarely erected single obelisks, it was probably intended to be accompanied by the Unfinished Obelisk that lies in a quarry outside Aswan, abandoned after the discovery of flaws in the rock.

Around the Sacred Lake

A short walk from Hatshepsut's Obelisk or the Cachette Court brings you to Karnak's **Sacred Lake**, which looks about as holy as a municipal boating pond, with the grandstand for the Sound and Light show at the far end. The main attraction is a shady (and pricey) **café** where you can take a break from touring the complex and imagine the scene in ancient times. At sunrise, Amun's priests would take a sacred goose from the fowl-yards which now lie beneath the mound to the south of the lake, and set it free on the waters. As at Hermopolis, the goose or Great Cackler was credited with laying a cosmic egg at the dawn of Creation; but at Karnak the Great Cackler was identified with Amun rather than Thoth. During the Late Period, Pharaoh Taharqa added a subterranean **Osireion**, linking the resurrection of Osiris with that of the sun. The **giant scarab beetle** nearby represents Khepri, the reborn sun at dawn.

The north–south axis

The temple's **north–south axis** is sparser and less variegated than the main section, so if time is limited there's little reason to go beyond the Eighth Pylon. The Gate of Ramses IX, at the southern end of the court between the Third and Fourth pylons, gives access to this wing of the temple, which starts with the Cachette Court.

The **Cachette Court** gets its title from the discovery of a buried hoard of statues early last century. Nearly 17,000 bronze statues and votive tablets, and 800 figures in stone, seem to have been cached in a "clearance" of sacred knick-knacks during Ptolemaic times. The finest statues (dating from the Old Kingdom to the Late Period) are now in the Cairo Museum. The court's northwest corner incorporates a mass of hieroglyphics known as the *Epic of Pentaur* [t], which recaps the battles of Ramses II depicted on the outside of the Great Hypostyle Hall. Diagonally across the court are an eighty-line inscription by Merneptah and a copy of the **Israel Stele [u]** that's in Cairo, which contains among a list of conquests the only known pharaonic reference to Israel: "Israel is crushed, it has no more seed". Rohl argues that the stele has been misread, and really relates the achievements of Merneptah's father and grandfather, Ramses II and Seti I.

More proof of the complexities of Egyptology is provided by the **Seventh Pylon**, which was built by Tuthmosis III, but decorated – and usurped – during the XIX Dynasty, a century or so later, when the cartouches on its door jambs **[v]** were altered to proclaim false ownership. It is fronted by seven statues of Middle Kingdom pharaohs, salvaged from pylon cores. On the far side are the lower portions of two **Colossi of Tuthmosis III**.

Although repair work has closed the **Eighth Pylon**, you might be able to walk around the edge for a distant view of its **four seated colossi**, or pay some *baksheesh* to be sneaked in for a closer look. The most complete figure is that of Amenophis I. Beyond a featureless court rises the **Ninth Pylon**, one of three erected by Horemheb and stuffed with masonry from the demolished Aten Temple, which is currently being rebuilt. Flanking the east wall of the final court is the ruinous **Jubilee Temple of Amenophis II**, which fulfilled a similar function to Tuthmosis III's temple in the main wing. The mud-brick houses of Karnak village are visible beyond the **Tenth Pylon**, whence an **Avenue of Sphinxes** once led to the Precinct of Mut.

The Temples of Khonsu and Opet

Located in the southwest corner of Amun's Precinct are two smaller temples related to his cult. The **Temple of Khonsu** is dedicated to the son of Amun and Mut. Mostly built by Ramses III and IV, with additions by later kings, it is well preserved but crudely carved and dark inside. Many of the reliefs depict Herihor, first of Thebes' priest kings, who ruled Upper Egypt after the Ramessid pharaohs moved their capital to the Delta. This shift in power is also evident on the pylons, which show Pinundjem, another high priest, worshipping the gods as a king.

Alongside stands a smaller **Temple of Opet**, the hippopotamus goddess traditionally believed to be the mother of Osiris. Its reliefs – dating from Ptolemaic and Roman times – are finer than Khonsu's, but it may not be possible to enter. The towering **Gateway of Euergetes I**, with its winged sun-disc cornice, was raised in Ptolemaic times and is now barred shut.

The open-air museum

The northern sector of Amun's Precinct contains an **open-air museum**, for which a separate ticket (£E10) must be bought before entering Karnak. Its prime attractions are two early barque shrines, reassembled from blocks found inside the Third Pylon. From the XII Dynasty comes a lovely **White Chapel**, carved all over with bas-reliefs. While most depict *Djed* columns, *ankhs* and other symbols, it's the scenes of Senusert I embracing a priapic Amun-Min that one remembers. The plainer **Alabaster Chapel** of Amenophis I contains more innocuous scenes of the pharaoh making offerings to Amun and his barque. Along the way you'll pass rows of blocks from Hatshepsut's **Red Chapel**, which archeologists have been unable to reconstruct since each block features a self-contained design rather than a segment of a large relief. This hasn't deterred Egyptologists from trying the same feat with the **Shrine of Tuthmosis III**, with more success. You'll also notice granite **statues of Sekhmet**, taken from a small **Temple of Ptah** alongside Karnak's enclosure wall, whose ruins aren't much reward for a 300-metre trek across broken ground.

Other temples at Karnak

Beyond the Precinct of Amun is a host of other ruins, intermingled with canals and villages. None of them is readily accessible or officially open to tourists, and sites under excavation are supposedly off-limits without permission from the **Antiquities Office** in Luxor (behind the museum) or Karnak (outside the precinct), whose Head and Deputy flit between offices, making it hard to catch them.

The Precinct of Mont

Dedicated to the falcon-headed Theban war-god of the Old Kingdom, who continued to be venerated after Amun gained primacy, the overgrown and ruinous **Precinct of Mont** is unusual for being oriented northwards rather than towards the river. Its main **Temple of Mont** (or Montu) dates from the XVIII–XIX Dynasty, while the **Temple of Amun** was added in the XXX Dynasty. Both are currently being excavated by the French Institute of Archeology in Cairo.

Also worth noting are the **chapels of Amenirdis**, daughter of the Nubian king Kashta (honoured by another chapel at Medinet Habu in the Theban Necropolis), and **Nitocris**, daughter of Psammetichus I, who is said to have avenged her brother's murder by constructing a sunken festival hall near the Nile, inviting the suspects to party, then opening hidden sluices and drowning them all – the basis of a short story by Henry James.

The Aten Temple

Likewise undergoing excavation, the **Aten Temple** 100m east of Amun's Precinct was demolished by Horemheb during the Theban counter-revolution that followed the brief Amarna Period. The temple was constructed early in Akhenaten's reign, before he quit Thebes for Tell el-Amarna, and, like the Aten shrine at Luxor Temple, constituted his opening move towards a revolutionary monotheism. Its reconstruction from the thousands of blocks scattered around the site or used as pylon-filling is based on a computer programme devised by a retired US diplomat in 1965. The Canadian Egyptologist John Redford, who spent over a decade excavating here, reckons that Akhenaten was an indolent paranoiac with an Oedipal complex, who compelled his acolytes to worship beneath the burning sun, rather than in shadowy temples.

The Precinct of Mut

As Amun's consort, the goddess Mut rated her own temple complex, linked to her husband's by an Avenue of Sphinxes. The **Precinct of Mut** covers roughly twice the area of Mont's enclosure, and centres around a kidney-shaped **lake**. Locals informed Flaubert that Karnak's priests submerged all the gold and silver ornaments here when the Persian emperor Cambyses sacked Thebes, but so far the site has merely yielded masonry. Near the enclosure entrance lies a headless granite colossus, which has been matched with a serene head and mighty forearm held by the British Museum (attributed to Amenophis III, Tuthmosis II or Ramses II). It was Amenophis III who commissioned the scores of grey diorite **statues of Sekhmet** that rise from the long grass.

The Theban Necropolis

Across the Nile from Luxor, the **Theban Necropolis** testifies to the same obsession with death and resurrection that produced the pyramids. Mindful of how these had failed to protect the mummies of the Old Kingdom pharaohs, later rulers opted for concealment, sinking their tombs in the arid Theban Hills while perpetuating their memory with gigantic mortuary temples on the plain below. The Necropolis straddled the border between the lands of the living and the dead: verdant flood plain giving way to boundless desert, echoing the path of the dead "going west" to meet Osiris as the sun set over the mountains and descended into the underworld.

Though stripped of its treasures over millennia, the Necropolis retains a peerless array of funerary monuments. The grandest of its tombs are in the **Valley of the Kings** and the **Valley of the Queens**, but there's also a wealth of vivid detail in the smaller **Tombs of the Nobles**. Equally amazing are the mortuary temples which enshrined the deceased pharaoh's cult: among these, **Deir el-Bahri** is timelessly magnificent and

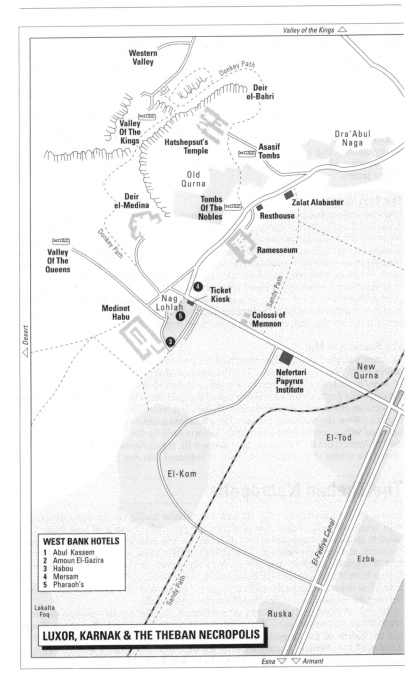

Valley of the Kings △

Western
Valley

Donkey Path

Deir
el-Bahri

Valley
Of The
Kings

Hatshepsut's
Temple

Asasif
Tombs

Dra'Abul
Naga

Old
Qurna

Deir
el-Medina

Tombs
Of The
Nobles

Zalat Alabaster

Resthouse

Donkey Path

Ramesseum

Valley
Of The
Queens

Sandy Path

⁴ Ticket
Kiosk

Nag
Lohlah

⁵

Medinet
Habu

△ Desert

³

Colossi of
Memnon

New
Qurna

Nefertari
Papyrus
Institute

El-Tod

El-Kom

El-Fadiya Canal

Ezba

WEST BANK HOTELS
1 Abul Kassem
2 Amoun El-Gazira
3 Habou
4 Mersam
5 Pharaoh's

Lakalta
Foq

Ruska

LUXOR, KARNAK & THE THEBAN NECROPOLIS

Esna ▽   ▽ Armant

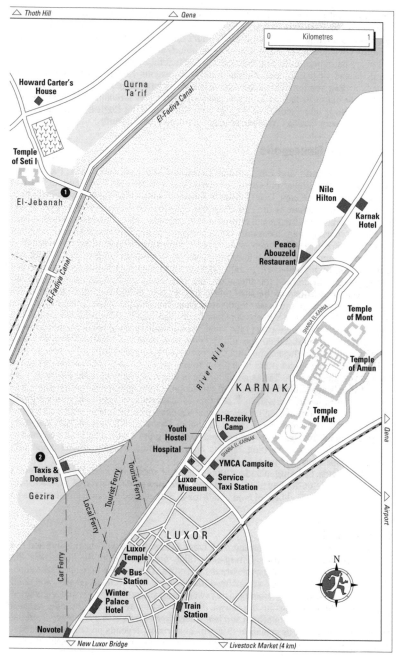

△ Thoth Hill △ Qena

0 Kilometres 1

Howard Carter's House

Qurna Ta'rif

El-Fadiya Canal

Temple of Seti I

❶

El-Jebanah

El-Fadiya Canal

Nile Hilton

Karnak Hotel

Peace Abouzeld Restaurant

SHARIA EL KARNAK

Temple of Mont

River Nile

Temple of Amun

KARNAK

Temple of Mut

El-Rezeiky Camp

Youth Hostel

SHARIA EL-KARNAK

Hospital

YMCA Campsite

❷

Taxis & Donkeys

Service Taxi Station

Gezira

Luxor Museum

Tourist Ferry

Tourist Ferry

△ Qena

△ Airport

Local Ferry

LUXOR

Car Ferry

Luxor Temple

Bus Station

N

Winter Palace Hotel

Train Station

Novotel

▽ New Luxor Bridge ▽ Livestock Market (4 km)

Medinet Habu rivals Karnak for grandeur, while the shattered **Ramesseum** and **Colossi of Memnon** mock the pretensions of their founders. On a humbler level, but still executed with great artistry, are the funerary monuments of the craftsmen who built the royal tombs, and the ruins of their homes at **Deir el-Medina**.

Beside its monuments, the west bank is interesting by way of contrast with Luxor: rural instead of urban, and making fewer concessions to foreigners. Many of the Egyptians that you'll meet in Luxor actually come from villages on the west bank, and a lot of the money made in Luxor is invested there. The symbiosis between the two communities is underscored by the fact that, when speaking English, locals invariably refer to the west bank as "**the other side**" (in Arabic, *min Gharb*).

Visiting the Necropolis

Spread across wadis and hills beyond the edge of the cultivated plain, the Theban Necropolis is too diffuse and complex to take in on a single visit. Even limiting yourself to the Valley of the Kings, Deir el-Bahri and one or other of the major sites, you're likely to feel all tombed out by the end of the day. Most people favour a series of visits, taking into account the climate and crowds – both major factors in the enjoyment of a visit. In **winter**, mornings are pleasantly hot, afternoons baking but bearable, and most bus tours are scheduled accordingly, making the Valley of the Kings crowded between 9am and 2pm (other sites are less overrun). As lots of people come early "to beat the crowds", the royal tombs are actually emptiest in the late afternoon. In **summer**, it's simply too hot throughout the afternoon, and you should get here as early as possible.

The **opening hours** of the sites reflect this: almost all are open daily from 6am to 5pm, though some of the lesser tombs may close two or three hours earlier over summer, and Nefertari's tomb keeps separate hours (see p.358). Making a full tour of the Necropolis is expensive – except for those with a **student card**, which entitles you to a 50 percent discount. When you add the **cost** of getting around the Necropolis, *baksheesh* and a few purchases, the total expense may be considerable.

Hotels and tours reps strive to sell you **tours**, which come in all shapes and sizes. Even if you like the idea, don't sign up for the first one offered – at least, not without an idea of what's available elsewhere, and the scope for **independent travel** (see opposite). All tours include a visit to a papyrus or alabaster "factory" where your guide stands to earn a commission on **sales**; some agencies own the shops where they send their clients (for example, Seti I Travel and Sobek Papyrus). There's no point in getting indignant about this, but bear in mind that the asking price will initially be determined by the company you're keeping, since a bus-load of middle-aged tourists is patently wealthier than a few backpackers on donkeys.

Useful **things to bring** include a torch, plenty of water and small change. If you're planning to cycle or donkey it, a hat and double rations of water are vital. A snack, too, is a good idea, as the choice of food and drink is limited, and prices are higher than in Luxor.

Crossing the Nile

There are several ways of crossing over **from Luxor** to the west bank. Blue-and-red Misr Travel **tourist ferries** sail frequently (daily 6am–5pm) from the docks near the *Etap* and *Winter Palace* hotels; the fare is £E2 return. You can also take one of the shabby **local ferries** (24hr) that depart from the riverside below Luxor Temple, and dock near **Gezira village** on the west bank. Crowded with villagers, bicycles and baggage, it puts you in the mood for the day ahead. Though locals pay 10pt for the ride, tourists are charged £E1. Between March and late November, there's also a **car ferry** from the *Novotel* to Gezira, but its schedule (5.30am–9pm) really depends on business, and services may be suspended if the river drops too low. During winter, when the Nile is at its lowest, ferries sometimes get stranded on **sandbanks** for hours, and irate passengers have been known to rip up the seats in a Nilotic version of road rage.

This is less of a problem for the private **feluccas and motorboats** that inveigle for custom by the water's edge. In recent years, the motorboat operators have poached customers from the feluccas by charging passengers as little as £E1 a head (£E5 minimum per boatload), and providing a quicker crossing to Gezira. Nonetheless, you'll still have to haggle over the price.

You should be able to take **bicycles** for free on all these vessels, but **motorbikes** can only be carried aboard the local and car ferries.

The opening of **Luxor Bridge**, 7km south of Luxor at Bogdadi, now makes road travel to the west bank sites substantially easier, meaning less business for the ferries, feluccas and west bank taxi men. Crossing by boat remains the more pleasant option however, and costs only a little more than going by bus or taxi.

Getting around

Once across the Nile, how you choose to get around will depend on the time of year and what you plan to see, your budget and your sense of adventure. If you intend to visit the Necropolis more than once, try using various modes of transport. As most entail negotiating a price, it helps to know the ins and outs beforehand. None of the prices given below include the cost of admission tickets.

• Assuming that you're reasonably fit, the cheapest way – aside from walking – to cover the Necropolis is by **cycling**. During winter, you'll feel cool when riding but start sweating once you stop. Guard against heatstroke and keep swigging water. A day's touring might involve cycling 30km: for example, 3km from the river bank to the ticket kiosk, 8km from there to the Valley of the Kings (mostly uphill – beware of traffic), and 3km from Deir el-Bahri to Medinet Habu. The main drawback is that you can't walk over the hills from the Valley of the Kings to Deir el-Bahri. Cycling during summer is a lot more demanding, so it's imperative to take the long uphill stretch to the Valley of the Kings early in the morning, allowing you to coast back downhill in the afternoon heat. Roads vary from smooth tarmac to stony *pistes*. Bicycles are best rented in Luxor (see p.304), where they cost £E3–7 a day, or £E15 for a superior model from a top hotel. Alternatively, you could get around by **motorbike**. Several bike shops rent them by the day; after much haggling, you can probably get one for £E30-40. Be especially careful of children and livestock when riding on the west bank.

• Getting around by **private taxi** is economical for groups, and the least tiring way of visiting a lot of sites. Taxis are usually engaged for four to six hours; the tourist office advises paying £E40 for six hours, but you'll have to haggle over the time and price. You can also hire slightly cheaper, non-private taxis, which scoot off for other business while you're exploring, and catch up with you when needed later on. Taxis wait by both landing stages on the west bank, but it's best to strike a deal at Gezira, where the competition is fiercer. Arranging a taxi through a hotel in Luxor will almost certainly mean paying more.

• Travelling by **donkey** is an unforgettable experience, offering the thrill of riding up the Theban Hills as mist cloaks the plain, skirting precipices and abandoned tombs before you descend into the Valley of the Kings; and returning via Deir el-Bahri and the Tombs of the Nobles. Light relief is provided by the donkeys, who disobey commands of *Hoosh!* (stop) or *Hatla!* (faster) whenever they encounter another beast on heat, or anything edible. As "mountain" donkeys know the trail, mishaps are more comical than serious. The problem with trying to rent your own donkey is that you risk getting a "field" animal, or an unlicensed guide who's neither helpful nor informative. The best guide is an English-speaking German, Enric Franken, whose donkeys bear apt names like Roadrunner and Ferrari – if you're feeling macho, ask to ride the impetuous

Saddam. You can find Enric at the *Venus Hotel*; his rates are what you'd pay at most other low-budget hotels (£E20–30 per person; discounts given to *Rough Guide* users) – though at some places, tourists who don't know better are charged £E60–80. Women should never travel alone with a guide, particularly a guy called Shahat, who is missing one finger.

• One option that's often overlooked is exploring parts of the Necropolis **on foot**, having got there by public transport. From the far end of the taxi rank above the ferry landing stage in Gezira, covered pick-up trucks shuttle passengers to Old Qurna (known to drivers as *Qurna Foq*), bringing you within fifteen minutes' walk of Medinet Habu, the Valley of the Queens or the Ramesseum, for a mere 25pt. Some pick-ups run on to Dra' Abu Naga, leaving you closer to the Tombs of the Nobles or Hatshepsut's temple. The drawback with this strategy is that the Valley of the Kings remains out of reach unless you're up to hiking over the hills and back again. In summertime, it's only feasible to cover shorter distances, and then only in the morning.

• If you'd prefer to travel in comfort with everything organized, **guided tours** can be booked through any hotel or travel agency in Luxor. Some will tag you onto existing groups, travelling in A/C buses; others may lay on a minibus and tailor the trip to your specifications. Two veteran guides with a good knowledge of Egyptology are Mahmoud Abdullah (Sunshine) and Abu Nagga (Moonshine), whose **minibus trips** cost about £E50 per person if booked through a small hotel, or £E100 at a large one. Bus tours from agencies like Misr Travel can easily cost £E150. If you're not fussy about your guide, trips can cost as little as £E15 per person – ask at the *Happy Land Hotel*. Most tours feature the tombs of the Kings and Queens, Deir el-Bahri and the Colossi of Memnon. Tour groups get priority access to the royal tombs and a higher standard of commentary than is offered by unofficial guides, but lack atmosphere and spontaneity.

• An alternative way of viewing the Theban Necropolis is to take a **hot-air balloon flight** – an amazing experience. Full details are given on p.314.

Buying tickets for the Necropolis

Currently, **tickets** for the various sites must be bought at the main **ticket kiosk** which is just past the Colossi of Memnon. The only exception is the ticket for Tutankhamun's tomb, which you buy from a kiosk at the Valley of the Kings itself. Of the various tomb tickets available, most people start with a "Valley of the Kings" ticket, which is valid for three tombs in the Valley of the Kings, excluding Tut's tomb. This is generally enough for most people, but should you decide that you want to view some of the other tombs, it is usually possible to have a guard go back to the main kiosk to get tickets for you – a little *baksheesh* will of course be in order. Bear in mind that you can't buy tickets at the individual sites, nor gain admission without them.

It's unlikely that you'll use more than six or seven tickets in a day's outing, and they are only valid for the day of purchase (with no refunds for unused ones). Students pay half the full-rate **prices** given below. Tickets are numbered as follows.

#1	Valley of the Kings (three tombs)	£E20
#2	Tomb of Tutankhamun	£E40
#3	Deir el-Bahri (Hatshepsut's temple)	£E12
#4	Medinet Habu (Temple of Ramses III)	£E12
#5	Ramesseum	£E12
#6	Asasif Tombs (Kheru-ef, Ankh-hor)	£E12
#7	Tombs of Nakht and Menna	£E12
#8	Tombs of Rekhmire and Sennofer	£E12
#9	Tombs of Ramose, Userhat and Khaemhat	£E12

#10	Deir el-Medina (two tombs)	£E12
#11	Valley of the Queens	£E12
#12	Tomb of Nefertari	£E100
#13	Temple of Seti I	£E12
#14	Tomb of Pabhasa	£E12
#15	Tomb of Peshedu (Deir el-Medina)	£E12
#16	Tomb of Ay (Western Valley)	£E12
#17	Khokha Tombs	£E20
#18	Tombs of Khonsu, Userhet and Benia	£E12

Dusk and early morning are the best times to capture the landscape and temples of the west bank. To photograph inside the tombs you'll need **photo permits** (£E5 per tomb), sold at both ticket kiosks. There's a £E50 surcharge for using a tripod. Flashes are forbidden as they harm the paintings, so sensitive film is required. Illegal flash-photography may result in the film being confiscated. Video cameras are not allowed into the Valley of the Kings, but can be stashed at the entrance. Like tickets, photo permits are non-refundable and valid only on the day of issue. There are no student discounts.

Some suggested itineraries

If you're forced to cram the highlights into half a day, a **minimalist schedule** might run: **Valley of the Kings** (2hr); **Deir el-Bahri** (20min); the **Tombs of the Nobles** (30min–1hr); **Medinet Habu** (30min) and/or the **Ramesseum** (30min).

If you're limited to a couple of days, two **itineraries** make sense:

Day one: catch a taxi to the **Valley of the Kings** before 9am, spend a couple of hours there and then walk over the hills to **Deir el-Bahri**, arranging to be met there for another ride to **Medinet Habu** or **Deir el-Medina** and the **Valley of the Queens**. Alternatively, you could spend time at the **Tombs of the Nobles** and the **Ramesseum** before returning to the landing stage.

Day two: this is basically devoted to whatever you missed the first time around.

For those who like to linger over every carving, the tombs and temples on the west bank easily require three or four days.

Staying on the west bank

Staying on the west bank might seem a good way to avoid the hassles of Luxor and to get closer to the sights, but it won't save you any money. Tourists staying there are deemed to be "living in Kuwait": charged more for rooms and meals than they'd pay in Luxor – and a captive market for local hustlers. Still, the pleasure of living beside an ancient temple or fields alive with birds may outweigh the disadvantages. The **hotels** (located on the map on p.328) vary greatly in quality, but most are pretty small. Though they're rarely (if ever) full, it's advisable to phone ahead before crossing the Nile with your luggage. Some of the hotels are accessible by *service* taxi (25pt); a private taxi from the landing stage costs £E3–4. All rates quoted below include breakfast.

Abul Kassem, east of Seti I's temple, so distant from the other sites; take El-Jebanah- or Qurna Ta'rif-bound *service* taxis (☎095/310-319). Carpeted, airy rooms with fans and (mostly) hot showers. Quiet and friendly; tasty meals. Bikes and donkeys available. ③.

Amoun el-Gazira, in Gezira village, 300m from the landing stage (☎095/310-912). Clean rooms, some with private baths, near the Pharaonic Stables; turn off the main road at the El-Tayeb Pharmacy. Well managed and agreeably situated. ④.

Habou, directly opposite Medinet Habu temple (☎095/372-477). Simple rooms with fans; dirty shared bathrooms with hot water. Nice rooftop, garden and terrace, if you can take the mosquitoes. ④.

Marsam, off the main road to the Tombs of the Nobles (☎095/372-403). Simple rooms with fans; clean, shared hot-water bathrooms. Pleasant courtyard overlooks fields and palms. Doubles and triples (④) only; run by an Australian woman. ③.

Pharaoh's, in Nag Lohlah village, 100m from the ticket kiosk along an unpaved road (☎095/310-702). Clean, carpeted, cosy rooms with A/C or fans, and shared hot-water bathrooms. Set in a lovely garden with table tennis. Serves beer and meals. ⑤.

The west bank villages

The **west bank villages** are incidental to most tourists visiting the Theban Necropolis, but integral to the landscape and atmosphere. Their fields stretch from the river banks to the temples on the desert's edge; their goats root amidst the Tombs of the Nobles. Though land remains paramount, almost every family is involved in tourism, either renting out donkeys or making souvenirs on the west bank, commuting to hotel jobs in Luxor, or sailing feluccas on the Nile. Family and village ties bind them together and help them exploit the stream of rich visitors that flows across their land. Crafty, warm-hearted and proud, they are worth getting to know. Richard Critchfield's *Shahhat* (sold in most Luxor bookshops) gives a fascinating glimpse into their lives a generation ago.

Your first encounter is likely to be with **GEZIRA**, where local ferries disgorge crowds of villagers returning from Luxor, and tourists clutching bicycles. Up the slope are private and *service* **taxis** to most villages on the west bank, plus **donkeys** and their guides, awaiting clients. The village straggles almost to the El-Fadiya Canal, where **EL-TOD** begins. Its inhabitants call the canal "the Nile", and those residing on one side of it regard themselves as superior to folks on the other, whom they scornfully describe as *mi'afin* (despicable).

Across the main road lies **NEW QURNA** (*Qurnat el-Jedid*), whose spacious mud-brick homes were designed by Hassan Fathy, a lifelong advocate of architecture suited to local conditions. Alas, this model village has not lured many people away from insalubrious **OLD QURNA** (*Sheikh Abd el-Qurna*, or *Qurna Foq*), which hugs the barren slopes of the Theban Hills, a mile down the road. Besides a sentimental attachment to their ancestral homes (many of them painted with splendid *Hadj* scenes), the villagers are loath to lose a traditional source of income – **tomb-robbing**. Over nine hundred tombs are dug into the hills, and rumours of undisclosed finds persist. Formerly, the villagers were also skilled at **faking antiquities** (passing a scarab through the intestines of a turkey will apparently give it an aged finish) – but standards have sunk so low that only the most gullible are deceived.

Qurna's **Moulid of Abu Qusman** (March 29) still features the practice of *doseh* (treading), where the sheikh walks over his followers. Many tales are told about Abu Qusman, who died in 1984. On one occasion he supposedly crossed the Nile on his handkerchief after the ferry refused to take him because he lambasted the tourists on board for immorality.

Skirting the Tombs of the Nobles, the road runs on to **DRA' ABUL NAGA**, whose blue-and-yellow houses contrast with the arid moonscape all around, which glitters with light reflected off mica and alabaster dust. The village manufactures the statues and ashtrays sold in tourist shops throughout Egypt. Its **alabaster workshops** vie for attention with garish murals and craftsmen shaping vases and bowls with hand-grinders, outside the showroom. Zalat Alabaster offers the widest choice.

At Dra' Abul Naga, a side road turns off towards Hatshepsut's temple, while the main road carries on to a crossroads beside a cemetery, where the road to the Valley of the Kings begins. The mud-brick complex on the hilltop was **Howard Carter's residence** during his search for Tutankhamun's tomb.

The Colossi of Memnon

A kilometre or so beyond New Qurna the main road passes the **Colossi of Memnon**, rearing nearly 18 metres above the fields to the right. This gigantic pair of enthroned statues originally fronted the mortuary temple of Amenophis III, which later pharaohs plundered for masonry until nothing remained but the king's colossi. Both have lost their faces and crowns, and the northern one was cleaved to the waist by an earthquake in 27 BC. Subsequently, this colossus was heard to "sing" at dawn – a sound probably caused by particles breaking off as the stone expanded, or wind reverberating through the cracks. The phenomenon attracted many visitors during antiquity, including the Roman emperors Hadrian (130 AD) and Septimus Severus, who gave orders for the statue to be repaired (199 AD), after which it never sang again.

Previously, the sound had been attributed to the legendary Memnon, whom Achilles killed outside the walls of Troy, greeting his mother, Eos, the Dawn, with a sigh. The Greeks identified the colossi with Memnon in the belief that his father, Tithonus, had been an Egyptian king. Before this, the colossi had been identified with Amenhotep, Steward of Amenophis III, whom posterity honoured as a demigod long after his master was forgotten. This association had some grounds in truth, since it was Amenhotep who supervised the quarrying of the monoliths at Silsilah, and their erection on the west bank. He was also probably responsible for Amenophis III's section of Luxor Temple.

At close quarters you can appreciate what **details** remain, mostly on the thrones and legs of the sandstone colossi. On the sides of the nearer one, the Nile-gods of Upper and Lower Egypt bind the heraldic plants of the Two Lands together. The legs of each colossus are flanked by smaller statues of Queen Tiy (right) and the king's mother, Mutemuia (left). As high as one can reach, both are covered in graffiti, including Roman epigrams.

The Valley of the Kings

Secluded amidst the bone-dry Theban Hills, removed from other parts of the Necropolis, the **Valley of the Kings** was intended as the ultimate insurance policy on life eternal. These secretive tombs of New Kingdom pharaohs were planned to preserve their mummies and funerary impedimenta for eternity. While most failed the test, their dramatic shafts and phantasmagorical murals are truly amazing. The descent into the underworld and the fear of robbers who braved the traps is still imaginable in the less crowded, darker tombs.

Seal of the Valley of the Kings

Royal burials in the "Place of Truth" date from the early XVIII to the late XX Dynasty. The first to be buried here was probably Tuthmosis I (1525–1512 BC). Until the time of Ramses I, queens and royal children were entombed here. **The tombs** were hewn and decorated by skilled craftsmen (known as "Servants at the Place of Truth") who dwelt at nearby Deir el-Medina. Work began early in a pharaoh's reign and never exceeded six years duration; even so, some tombs were hastily pressed into service, or usurped by later kings. Broadly speaking, there are two types: the convoluted, split-level ones of early XVIII rulers such as Tuthmosis I and Amenophis II, and the straighter, longer tombs of the XIX–XX dynasties.

The weaker rulers of the XX Dynasty were unable to prevent **tomb-robbing** on a massive scale. Both the vizier and police chief of Thebes were implicated in the disposal of treasure, while many of the robbers were the workmen who had built the

MUMMIFICATION AND THE UNDERWORLD

The **funerary beliefs** manifest in the Valley of the Kings derive from two myths, concerning Re and Osiris. In that of **Re**, the sun-god descended into the underworld and voyaged through the hours of night, emerging at dawn to sail his barque across the heavens until sunset, when the cycle began anew. **Osiris**, king of the underworld, offered hope of survival in the afterlife through his death and resurrection.

MUMMIFICATION AND BURIAL

To attain the afterlife, it was necessary that the deceased's name (*ren*) and body continued to exist, sustaining the **ka** or cosmic double that was born with every person and inhabited their mummy after death. **Mummification** techniques evolved over millennia, reaching their zenith by the New Kingdom, when embalmers offered three levels of mummification. The deluxe version entailed removing the brain (which was discarded) and the viscera (which were preserved in canopic jars); dehydrating the cadaver in natron salts for about forty days; packing it to reproduce lifelike contours, inserting artificial eyes and painting the face or entire body red (for men) or yellow (for women); then wrapping it in gum-coated linen bandages, and finally cocooning it in mummiform coffins. On the chest of the mummy and its coffin were placed heart scarabs, designed to prevent the deceased's heart from bearing witness against him during the judgement of Osiris.

    Royal burials were elaborate affairs. Escorted by priests, mourners and musicians, the coffin was dragged on a sledge to the Valley of the Kings, where the sarcophagus was already occupied by a *sem* (death) priest, who performed the **Opening of the Mouth** ceremony, touching the lips of the mummy with an adze and reciting spells. As the mummy was lowered into its sarcophagus, priests slashed the forelegs of sacrificial animals, whose limbs were burned as the tomb was sealed. The tomb's contents (intended to satisfy the needs of the pharaoh's *ka* in the afterlife) included food, drink, clothing, furniture, weapons, and dozens of *shabti* figures to perform any task that the gods might require. Then the doors were walled up, plastered over and stamped with the royal seal and that of the Necropolis. To thwart robbers, royal tombs featured deadfalls and false burial chambers; however, none of these devices seem to have succeeded in protecting them.

The Journey of Re
From right to left: Sunset; Year; Eternity; Everlasting; Maat (justice); Re; Heka; Sunrise

tombs, embittered over arrears in pay. In desperation, the priests reburied many sarcophagi and objects in two **secret caches** that were only discovered in the late nineteenth century.

    The exploration of the Valley began in earnest with a series of **excavations** sponsored by Theodore Davis in 1902–14, when over thirty tombs and pits were cleared. In 1922, the discovery of Tutankhamun's tomb made headlines around the world, while as **recently** as 1995 a mass tomb for the sons of Ramses II was uncovered beneath tomb KV5, long regarded as empty. Using clues from a papyrus codex in Turin, Professor Kent Weeks found a complex of over one hundred rooms, some as large as four hundred square metres. Though inscriptions suggest that fifty of Ramses's one hundred or

THE JOURNEY THROUGH THE UNDERWORLD AND JUDGEMENT OF OSIRIS

Funerary artwork dwelt on the journey through the underworld, whose pictorial representation inverted the normal order, so that each register was topped by sand instead of sky. The **descent** into the underworld, or *Duat*, echoed that of a sarcophagus into its tomb, involving ramps, ropes and gateways. Each of the twelve **gates** was personified as a goddess and guarded by ferocious deities (for example, the "Lady of Duration" and the "Flame-eyed" serpent at the fifth gate). In the darkness between them lay twelve **caverns** inhabited by beings such as the jackal-headed gods who fed on rottenness at the first cavern, or the wailing goddesses with bloody axes who waited at the tenth. Voyaging through the twelve **hours** of the night in his solar barque, Re had to overcome the serpent Apopis and other lesser denizens of **primeval chaos**, which threatened the **righteous order** personified by the goddess Maat.

It was Maat's Feather of Truth that was weighed against the deceased's heart (believed to be the seat of intelligence) during the **Judgement of Osiris**. With Anubis on the scales and Thoth waiting to record the verdict, the deceased had to recite the **negative confession** before a tribunal of 42 **assessor gods**, each attuned to a sin. While the hearts of the guilty were devoured by crocodile-headed Ammut, the righteous were pronounced "true of voice" and led into the presence of Osiris to begin their **resurrection**, which paralleled Re's passage through the underworld. Helped by Anubis, Isis and Nephthys (often shown as serpents), Aker the earth-god (whose back bore Re's barque) and Khepri the scarab beetle, Re achieves rebirth in the fifth hour, and is fully restored to life by the tenth. Here the two myths part company, for whereas Re emerges from the body of the sky-goddess Nut to travel the heavens again, the Osirian journey concludes in an afterlife that is sometimes identified as the **Fields of Yaru**.

Since many of the scenes were supplemented by papyri buried with the mummy, funerary **artwork** is categorized in literary terms. The *Book of the Dead* is the name now given to the compendium of Old and Middle Kingdom Pyramid Texts and spells, known in the New Kingdom as the *Book of Coming Forth*. Other **texts** associated with the New Kingdom include the *Book of Gates*, *The Book of Caverns*, *Book of Hours*, *Book of Day and Night* and *Book of Amduat* (That which is in the Underworld).

The Judgement of Osiris
From left to right: Anubis escorts the deceased and weighs his heart before Ammut and Thoth; then Horus leads him to Osiris, Isis and Nephthys

so sons were meant to be interred here, only the remains of four adults in their twenties have thus far been found – DNA samples from these have been taken to compare with those from Ramses's mummy in the Cairo Museum. There are almost certainly more tombs awaiting discovery in the Valley of the Kings.

Alas, the Valley is endangered by mass **tourism** and changes in the local **geology**. During the 1990s, cracks appeared in three tombs and the ceiling of a fourth collapsed. To prevent further damage to the **reliefs** and pigments, caused by friction, carbon dioxide and moisture (the average visitor leaves behind 2.8 grammes of sweat), the Antiquities Council has installed glass screens or dehumidifers. A graver threat is posed by a sub-stratum of grey shale, which has expanded upwards beneath the lime-

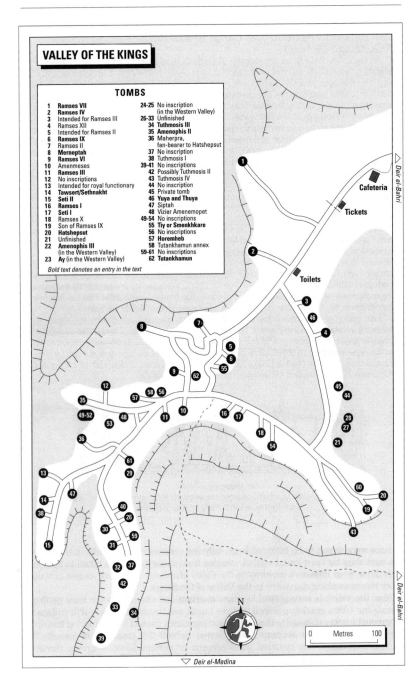

VALLEY OF THE KINGS

TOMBS

1	**Ramses VII**
2	**Ramses IV**
3	Intended for Ramses III
4	Ramses XII
5	Intended for Ramses II
6	**Ramses IX**
7	Ramses II
8	**Merneptah**
9	**Ramses VI**
10	Amenmeses
11	**Ramses III**
12	No inscriptions
13	Intended for royal functionary
14	**Tawsert/Sethnakht**
15	**Seti II**
16	**Ramses I**
17	**Seti I**
18	Ramses X
19	Son of Ramses IX
20	**Hatshepsut**
21	Unfinished
22	**Amenophis III** (in the Western Valley)
23	**Ay** (in the Western Valley)

24-25	No inscription (in the Western Valley)
26-33	Unfinished
34	**Tuthmosis III**
35	**Amenophis II**
36	Maherpra, fan-bearer to Hatshepsut
37	No inscription
38	Tuthmosis I
39-41	No inscriptions
42	Possibly Tuthmosis II
43	Tuthmosis IV
44	No inscription
45	Private tomb
46	**Yuya and Thuya**
47	Siptah
48	Vizier Amenemopet
49-54	No inscriptions
55	**Tiy or Smenkhkare**
56	No inscriptions
57	**Horemheb**
58	Tutankhamun annex
59-61	No inscriptions
62	**Tutankhamun**

Bold text denotes an entry in the text

Cafeteria

Tickets

Toilets

Deir el-Bahri

Deir el-Bahri

Deir el-Medina

0   Metres   100

stone, rupturing several tombs from below. Some blame this on 25 years of leaks from a (now demolished) tourist resthouse, while others contend that the water table has risen due to the High Dam.

The upshot is that tombs may be closed for years at short notice or reopened after ages under wraps. Remember that the artwork is **fragile**, so help preserve it by not touching the walls.

Visiting the tombs

The main **approach** to the valley (known as *Biban el-Melouk*, "Gates of the Kings" in Arabic) is via a serpentine road that follows the route of ancient funeral processions. Before the road, when donkeys were the only means of travel, its silence and emptiness were striking ("White earth; sun; one's rump sweats in the saddle", noted Flaubert). Nowadays, though, you'll only get this feeling on the trail across the hills from the Workers' Village, which is still travelled by donkeys (see p.348).

The valley is surrounded by limestone crags, the loftiest of which was the abode of Meretseger, snake goddess of the Necropolis. This natural suntrap is hot even in winter, the heat permeating the deepest tombs, whose air is musty and humid (drink plenty of water). The **site** resembles a Nevada missile base on open day, sightseers wandering from one bunker-like entrance to another. It's hard to predict exactly which tombs will be open in the future, so we have left unchanged entries for tombs which may be closed during your visit.

Most people find three to five **tombs** enough for one visit; of the 64 tombs (numbered in order of discovery, not chronologically), less than a score merit attention. A "Valley of the Kings" ticket is valid for three tombs only, and you can only buy **tickets** for Tutankhamun's tomb once you reach the site itself. Video cameras must be deposited at the kiosk just inside the barrier. A **cafeteria** in the car park sells costly snacks and drinks.

Tomb of Tutankhamun (#62)

One of the world's most famous tombs, this is neither large nor imposing by the standards of the Valley of the Kings, reflecting Tutankhamun's short reign (c.1361–1352 BC; see p.270) as an XVIII Dynasty boy-pharaoh. Its renown stems from its belated discovery and its amazing hoard of treasures (now mostly in the Cairo Museum). After archeologist **Howard Carter** had dug in vain for five seasons, his financial backer, **Lord Carnarvon**, was on the point of giving up when the tomb was found on November 4, 1922. Fears that it had been plundered were dispelled when they broke through the second sealed door – officially on November 26, though in fact Carter and Carnarvon secretly entered the previous night, stole several items and resealed the door. Otherwise, the tomb was cleared meticulously. Each of its 1700 objects was documented, drawn and photographed *in situ* before being removed to an impro-

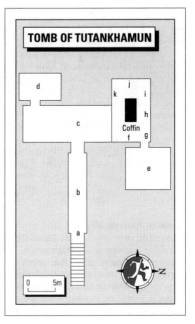

vised laboratory in the tomb of Seti II, for stabilizing and cleaning by Arthur Mace. Unpacking everything took nearly ten years, the whole process being recorded in over 1800 superb photographs by Harry Burton, who converted an empty tomb into a dark-room.

Lord Carnarvon's death in Cairo from an infected mosquito bite in April 1923 focused world attention on a warning by the novelist Marie Corelli, that "dire punishment follows any intruder into the tomb". (At the moment of Carnarvon's death, all the lights in Cairo went out.) The **Curse of Tutankhamun** gained popular credence with this and each successive "mysterious" death. The US magnate Jay Gould died of pneumonia resulting from a cold contracted at the tomb; a famous Bey was shot by his wife in London after viewing the discovery; a French Egyptologist suffered a fatal fall; Carter's secretary died in unusual circumstances at the Bath Club in London; and his right-hand man Arthur Mace sickened and died before the tomb had been fully cleared. However, of the 22 who had witnessed the opening of Tut's sarcophagus, only two were dead ten years later. Howard Carter died in 1939 at the age of 64, while others closely involved lived into their eighties (not least Dr Derry, who performed the autopsy which suggested that Tut died from a blow to the head, aged about nineteen). Notwithstanding this, a new explanation for the "curse" was advanced by a scientist at Cairo University in 1991. Professor Thebat believes that Carnarvon and Mace were fatally weakened by radioactivity emanating from an unknown substance used as part of the mummification process, which had accumulated in the tomb over 3000 years; he also claims to have detected radioactivity in seventeen of the mummies in the Egyptian Museum.

As for the tomb itself, it is now glassed over to protect its paintings, and the number of visitors has been reduced by a steep admission charge. **Tickets** (£E40) for Tut's tomb are only available at the entrance to the Valley of the Kings. You might well decide that the tomb isn't worth it.

In 1922, Carter found the door at the bottom of the stairway **[a]** walled up and sealed with Tut's cartouche and the seal of the Necropolis, but signs of repairs, the detritus in the corridor **[b]** and another resealed door at the end indicated that robbers had penetrated the antechamber **[c]** during the XX Dynasty.

Most of the funerary objects now in the Cairo Museum were crammed into the undecorated chambers **[c, d** (now walled up) and **e]**. Another wall (now replaced by a barrier) enclosed the burial chamber, which was almost filled by four golden shrines packed one inside another, containing Tut's stone sarcophagus and triple-layer mummiform coffin, of which the innermost, solid **gold coffin** – and **Tut's mummy** – remain.

The colourful murals run in an anticlockwise direction, starting with the funeral procession where nine friends and three officials drag Tut's coffin on a sledge **[f]**. Next, his successor Ay performs the Opening of the Mouth ceremony **[g]** and makes sacrifices to the sky-goddess Nut **[h]**. The deceased king embraces Osiris, followed by his *ka* (in the black wig) **[i]**. His solar boat and sun-worshipping baboons appear on the left wall **[j]**. On the hard-to-see entrance wall, Anubis and Isis escort Tutankhamun to receive life from Hathor **[k]**.

Tomb of Ramses VI (#9)

One reason why Tut's tomb stayed hidden for so long was that it lay beneath mounds of rubble from the tomb of Ramses VI (1156–1148 BC), which has been a tourist attraction since antiquity, when the Greeks called it the "Tomb of Memnon". The first two corridors have suffered from centuries of graffiti, but far worse occurred in 1992, when the ceiling fell down and had to be glued back on.

It was begun by Ramses V but usurped and enlarged by his successor, whose offering of a lamp to Horus of the Horizon opens the *Book of Gates* **[a]**, which faces other

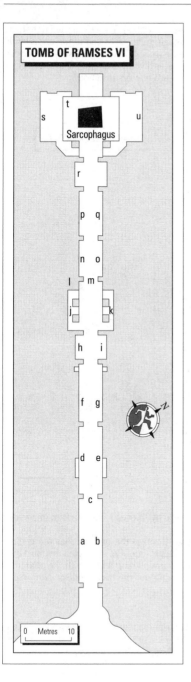

TOMB OF RAMSES VI

t
s   u
Sarcophagus

r

p   q

n   o

l ⊐ ⊏ m ⊏
j ⊏   ⊐ k
h   i

f   g

d   e

c

a   b

0   Metres   10

sunk-reliefs from the *Book of Caverns* **[b]**. Like the astronomical ceiling, this continues through a series of corridors (note the winged sun-disc over the lintel and Ramses' cartouches on the door jambs **[c]**). Where the *Book of Gates* reaches the Hall of Osiris **[d]**, a flame-breathing snake and catfish-headed gods infest the *Book of Caverns* **[e]**. As Re's barque approaches the Seventh Gate, beyond which twelve gods hold a rope festooned with whips and heads **[f]**, the *Book of Caverns* depicts a procession of *ka* figures **[g]**. From here on, the astronomical ceiling features an attenuated sky-goddess and the *Book of Day and Night*.

The eighth and ninth divisions of the *Book of Gates* **[h]** and fifth division of the *Book of Caverns* **[i]** decorate the next chamber, originally a vestibule to the hall beyond, which marked the limits of Ramses V's tomb. This contains the concluding sections of the *Book of Gates* **[j]**, the seventh division of the *Book of Caverns* **[k]** and a summary of the world's creation **[l]**. The rear wall also features a scene of Ramses VI making offerings and libations to Osiris. On the pillars, he makes offerings to Khonsu, Amun-Re, Meretseger, Ptah-Sokar, Ptah and Re-Herakhte **[m]**.

The descent to the next corridor is guarded by winged serpents representing the goddesses Nekhbet and Neith (left), Meretseger and Selket (right). On the corridor walls appear the introductory **[n]** and middle sections **[o]** of the *Book of Amduat*; on the ceiling, extracts from the *Books of Re* and the *Book of Day and Night*. Scenes in the next corridor relate the fourth and fifth **[p]** and eighth to eleventh **[q]** chapters of the *Book of Amduat*. The small vestibule beyond contains texts from the *Book of Coming Forth by Day*, including the "negative confession" **[r]**. On the ceiling, Ramses sails the barques of Day and Night across the first register, while Osiris rises from his bier in the second.

Lovely back-to-back versions of the *Book of Day* and *Book of Night* adorn the ceiling of Ramses VI's burial chamber, where his image makes offerings at either end of one wall [s]. The rear [t] and right-hand walls carry portions of the *Book of Aker*, named after the earth-god of the underworld who fettered the coils of Apopis, safeguarding Re's passage. Incarnated as a ram-headed beetle, the sun-god is drawn across the heavens in his divine barque [u]. The king's black granite **sarcophagus** was smashed open by treasure hunters in antiquity.

Tomb of Merneptah (#8)

Merneptah (1236–1223 BC), the fourteenth son of Ramses II, didn't become pharaoh until his fifties, having outlived thirteen brothers with prior claims on the throne. On the evidence of his mummy, he was afflicted by arthritis and hardening of the arteries, and underwent dental surgery in old age. On the strength of his "Israel Stele" at Karnak and the identification of his father as the Pharaoh of the Oppression, many scholars hold that Merneptah was the Pharaoh of the Exodus (although this is disputed by David Rohl, see p.647).

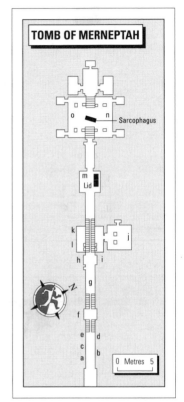

Like other tombs of the XIX Dynasty, his descends in corridors, with a total length of about 80m. Merneptah is welcomed by Re-Herakhte and Khepri [a], the *Litany of Re* [b] unfolds opposite the sixteen avatars of Osiris [c], Re's barque is pulled through the underworld [d], and Nekhebkau leads his soul towards Anubis [e]. Beyond a pit watched by Thoth and Anubis [f], another corridor decorated with the *Book of Amduat* [g] leads to an antechamber with images of Osiris and Nepthys [h], and Merneptah as Imutef [i].

The next hall is a false burial chamber (a trick that seldom fooled robbers) decorated with hymns to Osiris [j] and scenes from the *Book of Gates*. Notice the binding of the Serpents of Chaos [k], a tug-o-war over a "rope" of human souls [l], and the Osirian avatars above the lintel. The final corridors are largely bare, but you'll stumble upon the outer **lid** of Merneptah's sarcophagus – left there by thieves – and the faint image of a monkey [m].

In the real burial chamber, the gods voyage through the night across the ceiling, while murals show the metamorphosis of Khepri into Re, encircled by bird-men requesting the deceased's *ba* (soul) [n], and Khnum piloting a boat with the pharaoh's mummy floating above [o]. There is a carving of the sky-goddess Nut inside Merneptah's massive granite **sarcophagus**.

Tomb of Ramses IX (#6)

This monument belonged to one of the last rulers (1140–1123 BC) of the XX Dynasty, towards the end of the New Kingdom. It's indicative of waning majesty that the initial scenes in sunk-relief soon give way to flat paintings, akin to drawings. The walls of its stepped corridor (originally bisected by ramps, for moving the sarcophagus) depict Ramses before the gods, and symbolic extracts from the *Book of Caverns*. Notice the solar barques bearing crocodiles, heads and other oddities, on the left-hand wall. The burial chamber is memorable for its *Book of Night* in yellow upon a dark blue background. Two sky-goddesses stretch back-to-back across the ceiling, encompassing voids swirling with creatures, stars and heavenly barques. While the king's sarcophagus pit gapes empty, his resurrection is still heralded on the walls by Khepri, the scarab incarnation of the reborn sun at dawn.

Tomb of Seti I (#17)

It was Seti I (1318–1304 BC) who consolidated the XIX Dynasty, regained the colonies lost under Akhenaten, and paved the way for Ramses II to reach new heights of imperialism. Found in 1817, Seti's tomb is the longest (100m) and finest in the valley, boasting carvings and gilded paintings comparable to those in his temple at Abydos. Unfortunately, the tomb suffered badly from the rising water table and the exhalations of tourists, necessitating its closure. Following years of restoration and the installation of dehumidifiers, it remains to be seen whether the tomb will ever reopen.

The tomb descends through several corridors, their ceilings painted with flying vultures. In the first, Seti appears before falcon-headed Re-Herakhte **[a]**, Aten, Khepri and other solar incarnations, in a *Litany of Re* that continues along the facing wall **[b]** and both sides of the stairway beyond, flanked by Isis and Nephthys. On the upper part of the left-hand recess **[c]** are depicted the 37 forms of the sun-god, whose journey through the underworld features in the next corridor **[d]**. In the fifth hour of the night (left), Re overcomes the Serpent of Chaos. His own ram-headed form is that of Re-made-Flesh, whose mortal avatar – the king – consorts with deities **[e]**. Beyond a pit lies a pillared hall depicting the fifth division of the *Book of Gates* **[f]**;

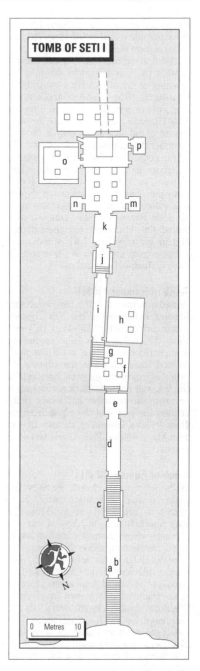

TOMB OF SETI I

Horus presenting Seti to Osiris **[g]** near the stairs into a Hall of Offerings **[h]**; and extracts from the *Book of Amduat*.

The descent continues via steps across another pit, into a corridor showing the Opening of the Mouth **[i]**; a winged disc surmounting the portal to another passage, where Seti sits before an offerings table **[j]**; and a *Litany of the Eye of Horus* to the left of the door at the end. In the next chamber **[k]** he is embraced and given life by the gods. The pillared hall **[l]** forms an anteroom to the burial chamber, which features an astronomical ceiling, scenes from the *Book of Amduat*, and a depression where Seti's sarcophagus (now in the Sir John Soane Museum, London) once rested. One of the side chambers depicts Nut in her cow form **[m]**; others carry extracts from the *Book of Gates* and the *Book of Amduat* **[n, o and p]**.

Tomb of Ramses I (#16)

Buried next door to Seti is his predecessor Ramses I, founder of the XIX Dynasty, whose brief reign (1320–1318 BC) only allowed a modest tomb. Its steep, featureless corridor leads to a small but finely painted burial chamber, the colours still bright against a blue-grey background. On the left wall are nine black sarcophagi in caverns, above twelve goddesses representing the hours of the night, from the *Book of Gates*. Elsewhere, Ramses appears with Maat, Anubis, Ptah, Osiris and other deities.

Tomb of Ramses III (#11)

With Seti's tomb closed, Ramses III's makes a fair consolation prize, being almost as grand. His reign (1198–1166 BC) marked the heyday of the XX Dynasty, whose power declined under the later Ramessids. Like his temple at Medinet Habu, the tomb harks back to the earlier glories of the New Kingdom. Uniquely for royal tombs, its colourful sunk-reliefs include scenes of everyday life. From another vignette derives its popular name, the Tomb of the Harpers.

Off the entrance corridors lie ten side chambers, originally used to store funerary objects. Within the first pair are frag-

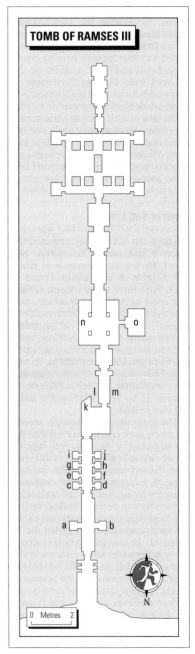

TOMB OF RAMSES III

mentary scenes of butchery, cooking and baking **[a]**, and ships setting sail, those with furled sails bound downriver **[b]**. Next, Hapy blesses grain-gods and propitiates snake-headed Napret, with her escort of aproned *uraei* **[c]**. The bull of Meri (right) and the cow of Hesi (left) coexist with armoury scenes **[d]**, while hermaphrodite deities bring offerings **[e]** to a treasury **[f]**. Ramses owns cattle and minerals **[g]**, and from his boat inspects peasants working in the Fields of Yaru **[h]**. In a famous scene, two harpists sing to Shu and Atum, while Harsomtus and Anhor greet the king; the lyrics of the song cover the entrance wall **[i]**. The twelve forms of Osiris **[j]** are possibly linked to the twelve *decans* (divisions or hours) of the night.

The dead-end tunnel **[k]** shows where diggers accidentally broke into a neighbouring tomb, at which point the original builder, Pharaoh Sethnakht, abandoned it and appropriated Tawsert's (see below). When construction resumed under Ramses, the tomb's axis was shifted west. The corridor has scenes from the fourth **[l]** and fifth **[m]** hours of the *Book of Amduat*. Part of the *Book of Gates* specifies four races of men: Egyptians, Asiatics, Negroes and Libyans (along the bottom) **[n]**. On the facing wall, the pinioned serpent Apopis is forced to disgorge the heads of his victims, in the fifth chapter of the *Book of Gates*. In the side room **[o]** are scenes from the *Book of Amduat*. The rest of the tomb has been barred since its ceiling fell down.

Tomb of Horemheb (#57)

General **Horemheb** was the power behind the throne of Tutankhamun and his aged successor Ay, and finally became pharaoh himself. His reign (1348–1320 BC) marked the height of the Theban counter-revolution against the Amarna heresy and the last gasp of the XVIII Dynasty, and was spent shoring up the crumbling empire bequeathed by his predecessors. According to Rohl's *A Test of Time*, Horemheb gave his daughter as a bride to King Solomon, to seal an alliance with the Israelites.

Due to reopen early in the new millennium, the tomb's layout prefigures Seti's (see p.343), with a long, steep descent through undecorated corridors to a well room which depicts Horemheb with deities, highly detailed and coloured. Hathor, Isis, Osiris, Horus and Anubis reappear in the anteroom before the burial chamber, whose entrance is guarded by Maat. Its unfinished scenes range from stick-figure drawings to fully worked carvings; the *Book of the Dead* begins to your left and runs clockwise round the chamber, whose huge sarcophagus is carved with a relief of Nut. In the second room to the left, you can see Osiris before a *Djed* pillar.

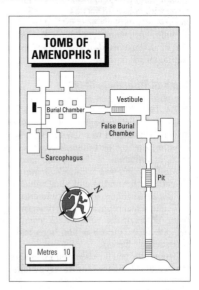

Tomb of Amenophis II (#35)

One of the deepest tombs in the valley lies at the head of the wadi beyond Horemheb's tomb. Built for Amenophis II (1450–1425 BC) midway through the XVIII Dynasty, it gets hotter and stuffier with each lower level, having over ninety steps. When the tomb was discovered in 1898, the body of the king was still in its sarcophagus and nine other royal mummies were found stashed in another chamber. The tomb's defences included a deep pit (now bridged) and a false burial chamber to distract robbers from the lower levels (which would have been sealed up and disguised).

From a pillared vestibule, steps descend into the huge chamber. On its six square pillars, Amenophis is embraced and offered *ankhs* by various gods. Beneath a star-spangled ceiling, the walls are painted yellow and inscribed with the entire *Book of Amduat*, like a continuous scroll of papyrus. When found in his quartzite sarcophagus (still *in situ*), the king's mummy had a floral garland around its neck. The second chamber on the right served as a cache for the mummies of Tuthmosis IV, Merneptah, Seti II, Ramses V and VI (hacked to pieces) and Queen Tiy, after their original tombs proved insecure.

Tomb of Tawsert/Sethnakht (#14)

Located en route to Seti II's tomb, this originally held the mummy of his wife, Queen Tawsert, but was usurped by Pharaoh Sethnakht (c.1200–1085 BC) after his own tomb (now Ramses III's) ran into difficulties. In the first corridor one finds Sethnakht making offerings to Horus and Isis, and Osiris enshrined. Further on, a ram-headed god with a knife is followed by Anubis and Wepwawet. Texts from the *Book of the Dead* cover what was meant to be Tawsert's tomb chamber beyond which steps lead down towards Sethnakht's vault.

At the bottom of the stairs, the pharaoh's soul attains harmony with Maat, cherishing the Papyrus and Lotus of the Two Lands; while Anubis embalms his mummy in a side chamber further on. A hall of texts from the *Book of Caverns* and the Opening of the Mouth ceremony precede the burial chamber, whose pillars show the gods greeting Sethnakht, while the walls depict the resurrection of Osiris and Re's journey through the night.

Tomb of Seti II (#15)

At the end of the wadi lies the seldom-visited tomb of Seti II (1216–1210 BC), which Arthur Mace used as a storage and restoration area during the excavation of Tutankhamun's tomb. Its long, straight corridors are typical of the XIX Dynasty, decorated with colourful scenes. Due to Seti's abrupt demise, however, there was only time to carve sunk-reliefs near the entrance, and the rest was hastily filled in with paintings or outline drawings. The king's mummy was later hidden in tomb #35 and replaced by that of an anonymous dignitary, which was plundered by thieves, who left only the sarcophagus lid.

Tomb of Tuthmosis III (#34)

Likewise secreted in a separate wadi, high up in a cleft, the tomb of Tuthmosis III (1504–1450 BC) is one of the oldest in the valley. Its concealment and (futile) defences make this tomb especially interesting, though some are disappointed by its artwork. Having ascended a wooden stairway to the cleft, you descend through several levels, crossing a pit by footbridge to reach a vestibule. Its walls depict 741 deities as stick figures, in imitation of the format used on papyrus texts from the Middle Kingdom onwards, which was favoured for murals early in the New Kingdom. Reduced to their essentials, the ramps and shafts that led into the underworld, and Khepri's role in pulling Re's barque, are clearly visible.

The unusual rounded burial chamber is also decorated with outline figures and symbols. Although the yellow background simulates aged papyrus, the texts were only painted after Tuthmosis had been laid to rest; there's a crossed-out mistake on the "instruction" fresco.

Elsewhere you'll notice double images, used to suggest motion (as at Abu Simbel). On one of the pillars, Tuthmosis's mother stands behind him in a barque; the register

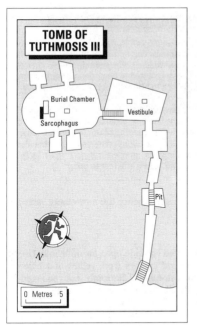

TOMB OF
TUTHMOSIS III

Burial Chamber
Sarcophagus
Vestibule
Pit
N
0 Metres 5

below shows three wives and a daughter, to the right of which a tree-goddess suckles the young king. By shining a torch inside the quartzite sarcophagus, you can admire a lovely carving of Nut, whose arms would have embraced his mummy before priests removed it to a safer hiding place near Deir el-Bahri (see below).

Tomb of Queen Tiy/Smenkhkare (#55)

This undecorated tomb has been a conundrum ever since its discoverer, Theodore Davis, failed to record its contents before removing the mummy in 1907, thus destroying crucial evidence. The decrepit mummy was initially attributed to Queen Tiy – the wife of Amenophis III – due to its pelvic shape and "feminine" position (left arm bound across the chest, right arm alongside the body), and a gilded panel that depicted her with Akhenaten. Later, however, the bones were identified as those of a man under 26 with signs of hydrocephalus, which seemed to fit Pharaoh Akhenaten instead. Yet another examination in 1933 found no signs of water on the brain (hydrocephalus), but diagnosed a platycephalic (abnormally flat) skull similar to Tutankhamun's – suggesting that this was the mummy of his mysterious predecessor, Smenkhkare.

Although new evidence has since been advanced for this being the mummy of Akhenaten, the Egyptian Museum remains unconvinced, and still attributes it to Smenkhkare.

Tomb of Yuya and Thuya (#46)

Another tomb with nothing to see (its contents are in the Cairo Museum) but a story attached is that of Yuya and Thuya, the parents of Queen Tiy. Though seemingly not of noble birth, Yuya was the highest official under Tuthmosis IV and Amenophis III. The latter's marriage to their daughter led to Thuya and Yuya becoming the grandparents of Pharaoh Akhenaten. In *Stranger in the Valley of the Kings*, Ahmed Osman argues that Yuya – whose mummy has a non-Egyptian appearance – was the Biblical Joseph (Genesis 41:39–40), whose talk of Yahweh subsequently inspired the monotheistic religion of Akhenaten (see "Tell el-Amarna", p.269). However, others believe that Yuya and Thuya were of Nubian origin, as evinced by a famous bust of Tiy, whose face is indubitably African.

Tomb of Ramses IV (#2)

This tomb has much of the appeal of Ramses VI's (which it resembles), but is less crowded with visitors. Its cheerful colours make amends for the inferior carving and abundant Greek and Coptic graffiti (notice the haloed saints on the right near the entrance). The ceiling of the burial chamber is adorned with twin figures of Nut. On the enormous pink granite sarcophagus are magical texts and carvings of Isis and Nephthys, to protect the mummy from harm. When these seemed insufficient, the

---

HIKING ACROSS THE HILLS TO DEIR EL-BAHRI

This wonderfully scenic hike is easiest over winter, but feasible at other times so long as you guard against heatstroke. Though **the hike** can be done in thirty minutes, it's worth taking it slowly once you've shaken off the souvenir vendors who wait above the start of the trail, where the donkey guides rest up. If you're tempted to be rude, remember that the vendors only come here because they can't afford to bribe the police to let them work in the Valley of the Kings.

When the path forks, take the left-hand track running flat along the top of a rock "loaf", before crossing the ridge to behold the Nile Valley. Directly beneath the sheer cliff lies Hatshepsut's temple; to see it, walk right for a bit before peering *carefully* over the edge. To descend, follow the path alongside the trampled fence till you reach a crag where the trail divides. Ignore anyone who tries to lure you down the steepest trail, to render "help" for *baksheesh* – the slightly less precipitous left-hand path is the one to take.

---

priests stashed Ramses in the tomb of Amenophis II, whence the now empty sarcophagus has been returned.

Tomb of Ramses VII (#1)

Set apart near the entrance to the valley, this tomb lay wide open for millennia. Greek and Roman graffiti mars its sunk-reliefs and vivid colours (red, yellow and blue on white), whose freshness is obviously due to restoration (the tomb was reopened in 1995). Amid the standard imagery are odd details like the figures entombed in cartouches on the right-hand wall of the first corridor, while the hippo goddess Tweri is prominent in the nocturnal pantheon on the ceiling of the burial chamber. The tomb isn't visited much, so you can wander round in peace.

The Western Valley and Thoth Hill

A neglected offshoot of the Valley of the Kings, the **Western Valley** contains only four tombs (two of them royal), of which just one is open. The **Tomb of Ay** (#23) was built for Tutankhamun's successor, who had earlier been Akhenaten's vizier and prepared himself a tomb at Tell el-Amarna. His crypt in the Western Valley is notable for the blend of royal and noble imagery in the burial chamber, where the *Book of Amduat* is juxtaposed with a typical nobles' vignette of the deceased spearing fishes and birds. Unfortunately, given the distance by road off the main route to the Valley of the Kings (the Western Valley is clearly signposted), you can only get there by car or bike.

Locals call the valley "Wadi Monkey", after the caches of mummified baboons found there, probably connected with a remote **sun temple** of Thoth (to whom baboons were sacred), which is now being excavated by Hungarian Egyptologists. Uniquely for an Egyptian temple, it is sited 400m above the Nile, atop a spur of the Theban range that the Magyars call **Thoth Hill**. The temple is distantly visible at the start of the serpentine route to the Valley of the Kings, but can only be reached on foot or by donkey (1hr 30min–2hr starting from near Howard Carter's house). If you're seriously interested, the two-man Hungarian team can be contacted at the *Abul Kassem Hotel*. It won't be open to tourists for a few years, and at present you can't enter it.

Deir el-Bahri

Of all the sites on the west bank, none can match the breathtaking panache of **Deir el-Bahri**. Set amidst a vast natural amphitheatre in the Theban Hills, the temple rises in imposing terraces, the shadowed verticals of its colonnades drawing power from the massive crags overhead. Its great ramps and courts look modern in their stark simplicity, but in ancient times would have been softened and perfumed by gardens of fragrant trees. Although its uppermost level may still be off-limits, the lower colonnades and chapels attest to a woman's will and a man's spite. *Deir el-Bahri* (Northern Monastery) is the Arabic name for the **Mortuary Temple of Hatshepsut**, the only woman ever to reign over Egypt as pharaoh (1503–1482 BC). A daughter of Tuthmosis I, married to his successor Tuthmosis II, Hatshepsut was widowed before she could bear a son. Rather than accept relegation in favour of a secondary wife who had produced an heir, Hatshepsut made herself co-regent to the young Tuthmosis III and soon assumed absolute power.

To legitimize her position, she was depicted in masculine form, wearing a pharaoh's kilt and beard; yet her authority ultimately depended on personal will-power and the devotion of her favourite courtier, Senenmut, who rose from humble birth to the stewardship of Amun's estates, before falling from grace for reasons unknown. When Tuthmosis came into his inheritance after her death, he defaced Hatshepsut's cartouches and images, consigning her memory to oblivion until her deeds were rediscovered by archeologists.

In 1995, the temple was used to stage Verdi's *Aïda*, which was a financial flop due to poor promotion and colossal expenditure, not least on building a road to the Nile so that VIPs could arrive by boat from Karnak, which has hardly been used since. However, dozens of bus parties arrive along the road from Dra' Abul Naga, making this one of the busiest sites in the Necropolis.

In November 1997 Hatshepsut's temple made international headlines when 58 tourists and several locals were shot and stabbed to death by Muslim extremists (see box p.258).

Hatshepsut's temple

Hatshepsut called her temple *Djeser Djeseru*, the "Splendour of Splendours". In ancient times an avenue of sphinxes probably ran from the Nile to its **Lower Terrace**, which was planted with myrrh trees and cooled by fountains (the stumps of a few 3500-year-old trees remain). At the top and bottom of the ramp to the next level stood pairs of stone lions (one of each pair is still *in situ*). Before ascending the ramp, check out its flanking **colonnades**, whose reliefs were defaced by Tuthmosis III, and later by Akhenaten. While Hatshepsut's image remains obliterated, those of Amun were restored after the Theban counter-revolution. Behind the northern colonnade (right of the ramp) are idealized scenes of rural life;

Hatshepsut

reliefs in the southern (left) colonnade show the transport by river of two obelisks from Aswan – doubtless the pair that she erected at Karnak.

The **Middle Terrace** once also boasted myrrh trees, which Hatshepsut personally acquired from the Land of Punt in a famous expedition that's depicted along one of the square-pillared colonnades flanking the ramp to the uppermost level. Together with the Birth reliefs behind the other colonnade, and scenes in the chapels at either end, these are the highlights of her temple.

THE BIRTH AND PUNT COLONNADES

To the right of the ramp is the so-called **Birth Colonnade**, whose reliefs assert Hatshepsut's divine parentage. Starting from the left, its rear walls show Amun (in the guise of Tuthmosis I) and her mother Queen Ahmosis (seated on a couch), their knees touching. Next, bizarre deities lead the queen into the birth chamber, where the god Khnum fashions Hatshepsut and her *ka* (both represented as boys) on his potter's wheel. Her birth is attended by Bes and the frog deity Heqet; goddesses nurse her, while Thoth records details of her reign. The sensitive expressions and delicate modelling convey a sincerity that transcends mere political expediency.

At the far end of the colonnade, steps lead back into a **Chapel of Anubis** with fluted columns and colourful murals. Tuthmosis III and a falcon-headed sun-god appear over the niche to the right; Hathor on the facing wall; offerings by Hatshepsut and Tuthmosis to Anubis on the other walls. As elsewhere, the images of Hatshepsut were defaced after her death by order of Tuthmosis.

On the other side of the ramp is the famous **Punt Colonnade**, relating Hatshepsut's journey to that land (thought to be modern-day Somalia). Though others had visited Punt to obtain precious myrrh for temple incense, Hatshepsut sought living trees to plant outside her temple. Despite the faintness of the reliefs, you can follow the story as it unfolds (left to right). Commissioned by Amun "to establish a Punt in his house", the Egyptian flotilla sails from the Red Sea Coast, to be welcomed by the king of Punt and his grotesquely fat wife (perhaps afflicted by elephantitis). In exchange for metal axes and other goods, the Egyptians depart with myrrh trees and resin, ebony, ivory, cinnamon wood and panther skins; baboons playing in the ships' rigging. Back home, the spoils are dedicated to Amun and the precious myrrh trees bedded in the temple gardens.

The Punt Colonnade leads into a larger **Chapel of Hathor**, whose face and sistrum (sacred rattle) form the capitals of the square pillars. In the first pillared chamber, the goddess appears in her bovine and human forms, and suckles Hatshepsut (whose image has not been defaced here) on the left-hand wall. The next chamber features delicate reliefs of festival processions (still quite freshly coloured) in a similar location. Peering into the gated sanctuary, you'll see another intact Hatshepsut worshipping the divine cow (left), and an alcove (right) containing a **portrait of Senenmut**, which would have been hidden when the doors were open. Apocryphally, it was this claim on the pharaoh's temple that caused his downfall. After fifteen years of closeness to Hatshepsut and her daughter Neferure (evinced by a statue in the Cairo Museum, which some regard as proof of paternity), Senenmut abruptly vanished from the records late in her reign.

THE UPPER TERRACE AND SANCTUARIES

Reached by a ramp terminating in vultures' heads, the **Upper Terrace** is now emerging from decades of research and restoration work by Polish and Egyptian teams, but is still off-limits to visitors. Beyond its Osiride portico lies a courtyard flanked by colonnades and sanctuaries. In the **Sanctuary of Hatshepsut** (left) are stylish reliefs of priests and offerings bearers. On the other side is the **Sanctuary of the Sun**, an open court with a central altar.

The central **Sanctuary of Amun** is dug into the cliff, aligned so that it points towards Hatshepsut's tomb in the Valley of the Kings on the other side of the mountain. In Ptolemaic times the sanctuary was extended and dedicated to Imhotep and Amenhotep, the quasi-divine counsellors of Zoser and Amenophis III. Beneath it lies another burial chamber for Hatshepsut, presumably favoured over her pro forma tomb in the Valley of the Kings, since it was dug at a later date.

Other temples

From the heights of Hatshepsut's temple you can gaze southwards over the ruins of two similar edifices. The **Mortuary Temple of Tuthmosis III** was long ago destroyed by a landslide, but a painted relief excavated here can be seen in the Luxor Museum; more remains of the far older **Temple of Nebhetepre Mentuhotpe**, the first pharaoh to choose burial in Thebes (XI Dynasty). Unlike his XVIII Dynasty imitators, Nebhetepre was actually buried in his mortuary temple; his funerary statue is now exhibited in the Cairo Museum.

Secret tombs and lavatory humour

Whereas Nebhetepre's remains weren't discovered till modern times, many of the New Kingdom royal tombs were despoiled soon after their final burial in the Valley of the Kings. Towards the end of the XXI Dynasty, the priests hid forty mummies in a **secret cache** in the next hollow to the south above Nebhetepre's temple, which the villagers of Qurna found in 1875 and quietly sold off for years until rumbled by the authorities, who forced them to reveal the cache's location. Amongst the mummies recovered were Amenophis I, Tuthmosis II and III, Seti I and Ramses II and III. Archeologists were baffled to find a XXII Dynasty coffin, beyond a passage blocked by royal mummies from an earlier period. As the steamer bore them downriver to Cairo, villagers lined the banks, wailing in sorrow or firing rifles in homage.

Worth a look if you can persuade a guard at Deir el-Bahri to unlock it is the **Tomb of Senenmut**, just beyond the temple precincts. Its steep shaft descends past a bust of Senenmut into a chamber with a lovely astronomical ceiling; on its walls are extracts from the *Book of the Dead*. Why Senenmut should have built this tomb when he already had one at Qurna is uncertain; in any event, its unfinished burial chamber was never used.

Finally, there's a rare example of ancient Egyptian **lavatory humour** in a cave to the north of Hatshepsut's temple (in line with its lower colonnade). Amongst the doodles and inscriptions is a drawing of a man buggering a figure wearing pharaonic headgear and women's underwear. Could this be Senenmut and Hatshepsut – or a fantasy of revenge by the juvenile Tuthmosis?

The Asasif Tombs

Midway between Deir el-Bahri and the Tombs of the Nobles lies a burial ground known as the **Asasif Tombs**, currently being studied by several archeological teams. While some of its 35 tomb chapels date from the XVIII Dynasty, the majority are from the Late Period (XXV–XXVI Dynasty), when Thebes was ruled by Nubian kings, and then from the Delta. Several of the tombs may be open to visitors (ask at the ticket office).

The most likely to be open is the **Tomb of Pabasa (#279)**, the steward to a Divine Votaress of Amun during the XXVI Dynasty. His tomb reflects the Saïte Dynasty obsession with the Old Kingdom, having a similar design to tombs at Saqqara. Its massive gateway leads into a pillared court with scenes of hunting, fishing and viticulture (note the bee-keeping scene on the central column). A funeral procession and the voyage to Abydos appear in the vestibule.

Also worth noting is the **Tomb of Kheru-ef (#192)**, a steward of Queen Tiy during the Amarna period. His scenes depict a Jubilee Festival, Tiy and Amenophis III, musicians, dancers and playful animals – as lyrical as those in Ramose's tomb (see p.353). Roughly 10m north of here lies the **Tomb of Kiki (#409)**, whose soul is weighed by Anubis and Thoth at the entrance. In the unfinished burial shrine are faceless figures outlined in red.

The Tombs of the Nobles

The **Tombs of the Nobles** are a study in contrasts to their royal counterparts. Whereas royalty favoured concealed tombs in secluded valleys, Theban nobles and high officials were ostentatiously interred in the limestone foothills overlooking the great funerary temples of their masters and the city across the river. The pharaohs' tombs were sealed and guarded; the nobles' were left often, for their descendants to make funerary offerings. Wheras royal tombs are filled with scenes of judgement and resurrection, the nobles' chosen artwork dwells on earthly life and its continuation in the hereafter. Given more freedom of expression, the artists excelled themselves with vivid **paintings** on stucco (the inferior limestone on this side of the hills militates against carved reliefs).

The **tombs' layout** marks a further evolution in funerary architecture since the Middle Kingdom tombs of Beni Hassan. Most are entered via a courtyard, with a transverse hall preceding the burial shrine with its niche containing an effigy of the deceased (or statues of his entire family). Strictly speaking, they are tomb chapels rather than tombs, since the graves themselves lie at the bottom of a shaft (usually inaccessible).

Excluding the Asasif Tombs nearer Deir el-Bahri (see above), all the tombs open to visitors cluster around the village of Old Qurna, where they're divided into four groups (each requiring a separate ticket), namely: **Rekhmire and Sennofer; Ramose, Userhat and Khaemhat; Nakht and Menna; and Khonsu, Userhet and Benia**. The first two lie furthest west and back from the road; the next trio downhill towards the Ramesseum; and the last two sets of tombs to the northeast, closer to Deir el-Bahri. Until signposting improves, you'll have to ask children for directions or try to locate them by their modern brick enclosure walls.

As visiting all seven tombs takes an hour or so, most people limit themselves to a single group or the highlights from each (marked * in the accounts following). Unlike at the Valley of the Kings, the guards often hassle visitors for *baksheesh*. If you don't want a guided tour, politely refuse at the start.

Tomb of Rekhmire (#100)*

This richly decorated tomb casts light on statecraft and foreign policy under Tuthmosis III and Amenophis II, whom Rekhmire served as vizier. The badly damaged murals in its transverse hall show him collecting taxes from Upper **[a]** and Lower **[b]** Egypt, and inspecting temple workshops, charioteers and agricultural work **[c]**. Around the corner from his ancestors **[d]**, grapes are trod in large tubs and the juice is strained and stored in jars **[e]**.

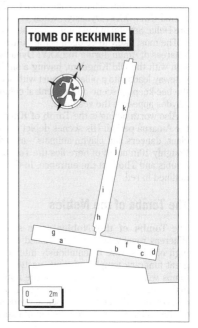

TOMB OF REKHMIRE

Along the rear wall are depicted a desert hunt **[f]** and a famous scene of Rekhmire receiving tributes from foreign lands **[g]**. Amongst the gifts shown are vases from Crete and the Aegean Islands (fourth row); a giraffe, monkeys and elephant tusks from Punt and Nubia (third row); and chariots and horses from Syria (second row).

Growing in height as it recedes towards the false door at the back, the long corridor is decorated with scenes of work and daily life. Slaves store grain in silos **[h]**, whence it was later disbursed as wages to armourers, carpenters, sculptors and other state-employed craftsmen **[i]**. An idealized banqueting scene with female musicians **[j]** merges into an afterworld with a lake and trees **[k]**. Also note Rekhmire's funeral procession and offerings to sustain him in the afterlife **[l]**.

Tomb of Sennofer (#96)

From Rekhmire's tomb slog 50m uphill to the left to find another colourful tomb, in better condition. Entered by a low, twisting stairway, it is known as the "Tomb of Vines" after the grapes and vines painted on the textured ceiling of the antechamber. As mayor of Thebes and overseer of Amun's estates under Amenophis II, Sennofer's responsibilities included local viticulture. The walls of the burial shrine depict his funeral procession (left), voyage to Abydos (back, right) and mummified sojourn with Anubis (right). Its square pillars bear images of Hathor, whose eyes follow you around the room; a small tree-goddess appears on the inner side of the rear left-hand pillar.

Tomb of Ramose (#55)*

Down a dirt road to the southeast lies the tomb of Ramose, who was vizier and governor of Thebes immediately before and after the Amarna revolution. His spacious tomb captures the moment of transition from Amun- to Aten-worship, featuring both classical and Amarna-style reliefs, the latter unfinished since Ramose followed Akhenaten to his new capital. Besides its superb reliefs, the tomb is notable for retaining its courtyard – originally a feature of all these tombs.

Along the entrance wall of its pillared hall are lovely carvings that reflect the mellowing of classicism during the reign of Amenophis III, Akhenaten's father. Predictable scenes of Ramose and his wife [a], Amenophis III and Queen Tiy [b] making offerings come alive thanks to the exquisite rendering of the major figures, carried over to their feasting friends and relatives [c]. The sinuous swaying of mourners likewise imparts lyricism to the conventional, painted funerary scene [d], where Ramose, wife and priests worship Osiris.

The onset of Aten-worship and the Amarna style is evident in the reliefs at the back, despite their battered condition. Those on the left [e] were carved before Amenophis IV changed his name to Akhenaten and espoused Aten-worship, so the pharaoh sits beneath a canopy with Maat, the goddess of truth, receiving flowers from Ramose. (At the far end, note the red grid and black outlined figures by which the artist transferred his design to the wall before relief-cutting took place.) However, the corresponding scene [f] depicts the pharaoh as Akhenaten, standing with Nefertiti at their palace window, bathed in the Aten's rays. Ramose is sketched in below, accepting their gift of a golden chain; his physiognomy is distinctly Amarnan, but rather less exaggerated than the royal couple's (see p.269).

By a quirk of Egyptian security, a low wall bars access to Ramose's inner shrine, but there is nothing at all to prevent one from venturing into a dark tunnel leading off the hall, which suddenly plummets into his grave, 15m below – beware.

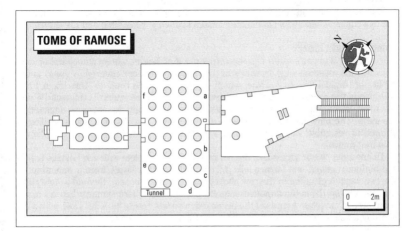

Tomb of Userhat (#56)

Immediately south of Ramose's tomb lies that of Userhat, a royal scribe and tutor in the reign of Amenophis II. Although some of the figures were destroyed by early Christian hermits who occupied the shrine, what remains is freshly coloured, with unusual pink tones. The tomb is also interesting in that it's still illuminated by means of a mirror reflecting sunlight inside, just as it was when the artists decorated the tomb.

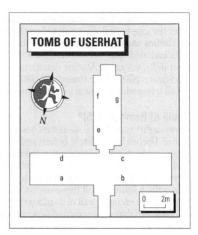

Along the entrance wall of the antechamber are scenes of wine-making, harvesting, herding and branding cattle, collecting grain for the royal storehouse [a], and the customary offerings scenes [b]. On the rear wall are reliefs of baking, assaying gold dust, and – lower down – a barber trimming customers beneath a tree [c]. The funerary feast scene [d] was extensively damaged by hermits, particularly the female figures. The inner hall contains paintings of Userhat hunting gazelles, hares and jackals from a chariot in the desert [e]; fowling and fishing amidst the reeds [f]; and funerary scenes [g]. In a niche at the end is a headless statue of the deceased's wife.

Tomb of Khaemhat (#57)

Next door is the tomb of Khaemhat, royal scribe and inspector of granaries under Amenophis III, which is reached via a forecourt off which two other tombs, now locked, once led. Flanking its doorway outside are battered reliefs of Khaemhat worshipping Re, and the complete set of instruments for the Opening of the Mouth ceremony (right). In the transverse antechamber with its red and black patterned ceiling, the best reliefs are on the left as you enter. Although Renenet the snake-headed harvest-goddess has almost vanished, a scene of grain boats docking at Thebes harbour is still visible nearer the niche containing statues of Khaemhat and Imhotep. In the bottom row to the left of the door into the corridor, Hathor breastfeeds a boy-king, surrounded by sacred cows.

Fishing, fowling and family scenes decorate the right-hand wall of the corridor, leading to a triple-niched chapel containing seated statues of Khaemhat and his family.

Tomb of Nakht (#52)*

Northeast of Ramose's tomb lies the burial place of Nakht, whose antechamber contains a small museum with drawings of the reliefs (which are covered in glass) and a replica of Nakht's funerary statue, which was lost at sea en route to America in 1917. Nakht was the overseer of Amun's vineyards and granaries under Tuthmosis IV, and the royal astronomer, but stargazing does not feature among the activities depicted in his tomb. The only decorated section is the transverse antechamber, whose ceiling is painted to resemble woven mats, with a *kherker* frieze running above the brilliantly coloured murals.

To one side, Nakht supervises the harvest in a scene replete with vivid details [a]. In the bottom register, one farmer fells a tree, while another swigs from a waterskin; of the two women gleaning in the row above, one is missing an arm. Beyond a stele relating Nakht's life [b] is the famous banqueting scene [c], where sinuous dancers and a blind harpist entertain friends of the deceased, who sits beside his wife, Tawi, with a cat scoffing a fish beneath his chair; sadly, their figures have been erased.

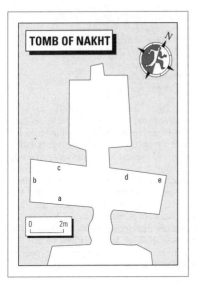

The defacement of Nakht's image and Amun's name is usually ascribed to Amarna iconoclasm, but the gouging out of his eyes and throwing sticks in the hunting scene **[d]** suggests a personal animus. Happily, this has not extended to the images in the corner **[e]**, where peasants tread grapes in vats, and birds are caught in clap-nets and hung for curing (below). The plain inner chamber has a false door painted to resemble Aswan granite; and a deep shaft leading to the (inaccessible) burial chamber.

Tomb of Menna (#69)

More scenes of rural life decorate the nearby tomb of Menna, an XVIII Dynasty inspector of estates. Accompanied by his wife and daughter, Menna worships the sun in the entrance passage. In the left wing of the first chamber, he supervises field labour (notice the two girls pulling each other's hair, near the far end of the third row), feasts and makes offerings with his wife. Across the way they participate in ceremonies with Anubis, Osiris, Re and Hathor. Though chiefly decorated with mourning and burial scenes, the inner chamber also features a spot of hunting and fishing, vividly depicted on the right-hand wall. The niche at the end contains the legs of Menna's votive statue.

Notice the finely painted **Hadj scene** on the outside of the house near the tomb.

Tombs of Khonsu, Userhet and Benia

This trio of small tombs near those of Nakht and Menna was opened to the public in 1992, after restoration. The themes are standard, with scenes of offerings, hunting, fishing and funerary rites. In the tomb of Userhet (not to be confused with the Userhat in tomb #56), the guard will produce a mummified head for *baksheesh*.

The Ramesseum

The **Ramesseum** or mortuary temple of Ramses II was built to awe the pharaoh's subjects, perpetuate his existence in the afterlife and forever link him to Amun-United-with-Eternity. Had it remained intact, the Ramesseum would doubtless match his great sun temple of Abu Simbel for monumental grandeur and unabashed self-glorification. But by siting it beside an earlier temple on land that was annually inundated, Ramses unwittingly ensured the ruination of his monument, whose toppled colossi would later mock his presumption, inspiring Shelley's sonnet *Ozymandias*:

I met a traveller from an antique land
Who said: Two vast and trunkless legs of stone
Stand in the desert . . . Near them on the sand,
Half sunk, a shattered visage lies, whose frown,
And wrinkled lip, and sneer of cold command
Tell that its sculptor well those passions read
Which yet survive, stamped on these lifeless things,

Ramses II

The hand which mocked them, and the heart that fed.
On the pedestal these words appear:
'My name is Ozymandias, King of Kings:
Look upon my works ye Mighty, and despair!'
Nothing beside remains. Round the decay
Of that colossal wreck, boundless and bare
The lone and level sands stretch far away.

Nineteenth-century writers knew the ruins as the *Memnonium*. Their present name only caught on late last century, by which time the Ramesseum had been plundered for statuary – not least the seven-ton head of one of its fallen colossi, now in the British Museum. Yet its devastation lends romance to the conventional architecture, infusing it with the pathos that moved Harriet Martineau to muse how "violence inconceivable to us has been used to destroy what art inconceivable to us had erected". As bus parties seldom intrude, the Ramesseum seems peaceful, its tranquillity enhanced by some trees near the First Pylon, which offer a pleasant contrast to the desolation of other sites in the Necropolis. Sadly, the trees may be felled soon, as their roots are damaging the foundations of the pylon, which has been shored up with buttresses. Half an hour suffices to see the famous colossi and the best reliefs, but you may care to linger. The nearby **Ramesseum Resthouse** sells overpriced drinks and snacks, and has toilets.

Exploring the Ramesseum

Like other mortuary temples in the Theban Necropolis, the Ramesseum faces southeast towards the Nile, and was originally entered via its **First Pylon**. Wrecked by the earthquake that felled the colossi, the pylon stands marooned in the scrub beyond a rubble-strewn depression that used to be the **First Court**. In 1983, Rohl found evidence for his "New Chronology" in an inscription on a block balanced atop the pylon, asserting that during the eighth year of his reign, Ramses plundered a city named "Shalem", which Rohl thinks was Jerusalem in the time of King Solomon (see p.647).

Visitors enter the temple via the northern flank of its **Second Court**, to be confronted by the awesome **fallen colossus of Ramses II**. This seated megalith once towered over the stairs from the first into the second court; over 18m tall and weighing about 1000 tons, it was only surpassed by the Colossi of Memnon thanks to their pedestals. When it toppled some time after the first century AD, its upper half smashed through the Second Pylon into the court, where its head and torso lie today, measuring 7m across the shoulders; the cartouche on its bicep reads: "Ruler of Rulers". In the lower court are other fragments, notably feet and hands. As Dean Stanley wrote in 1852, "You sit on his breast and look at the Osiride statues which support the porticos of the temple, and they seem pygmies before him".

Behind the chunky Osirian pillars rises what's left of the **Second Pylon**, whose inner face bears scenes from the second Battle of Qadesh, surmounted by a register depicting the festival of the harvest-god Min. At the far end of the second courtyard, where three stairways rise to meet a colonnaded portico, is a **smaller fallen colossus** of Ramses, more fragmented, though its face has suffered merely nasal damage. Originally there were two colossi, but the other – dubbed the "Young Memnon" – was acquired for Britain in 1816 by Belzoni. The name "Ozymandias" arose from the ancient Greeks' misreading of one of the king's many titles, *User-Maat-Re*.

Beyond here, the core of the Ramesseum is substantially intact. The first set of reliefs worth noting occurs on the front wall of the **portico**, between the central and left-hand doorways. Above a bottom row depicting eleven of his sons, Ramses appears with Atum and Mont (who holds the hieroglyph for "life" to his nose), and kneels before the

Theban Triad (right) while Thoth inscribes his name on a palm frond (centre). The top register shows him sacrificing to Ptah and making offerings to an ithyphallic Min.

The **Great Hypostyle Hall** had 48 columns, of which 29 are still standing. The taller ones flanking the central aisle have papyrus shafts and lotus capitals that support a raised section of roof; the lower side columns have papyrus-bud capitals. On the wall to the left as you come in, reliefs depict Egyptian troops storming the Hittite city of Dapur, using shields to protect themselves from arrows and stones. At the back of the hall, incised reliefs show lion-headed Sekhmet (far right) presenting Ramses to an enthroned Amun, who gives him an *ankh*; along the bottom are depicted some of the king's hundred sons.

Beyond this lie two **smaller Hypostyle Halls**. The first retains its astronomical ceiling, featuring the oldest known twelve-month calendar (whether lunar or solar months is debatable). Notice also the barques of Amun, Mut and Khonsu on the entrance wall, and the scene of Ramses beneath the persea tree with Sheshat and Thoth, on the wall at the far end (right). "Pukler Muskan" is the oddest of the many names scrawled on the columns over millennia. The ruined **sanctuaries** were presumably dedicated to Amun, Ramses the god and his glorious ancestors, for the edifice stood alongside an earlier temple of Seti I, which itself contained shrines to Seti and his father, Ramses I, both of whom were linked to Amun. Its scant remains lie to the northeast of the portico and Hypostyle Hall.

The whole complex is surrounded by mud-brick **magazines** that once covered about three times the area of the temple and included workshops, storerooms and servants' quarters, all originally enclosed by high walls.

Other mortuary temples

In ancient times, the Ramesseum was one of half a dozen mortuary temples ranged along the edge of the flood plain with no regard for chronological order. To the southwest were arrayed the mortuary temples of Tuthmosis IV, Merneptah and Amenophis III (of which only the last's colossi remain), followed by those of Tuthmosis II, Ay and Horemheb. The furthest temple at Medinet Habu was closely modelled on the Ramesseum (see above).

Since most are virtually nonexistent, the only one worth consideration is the **Temple of Seti I**, near the village of Qurna Ta'rif (accessible by pick-ups from Old Qurna or Gezira). The site is still being excavated by German Egyptologists, but you can enter its temple, a hulking affair with crude reliefs dedicated to Amun, Seti and Ramses I.

Deir el-Medina: the Workers' Village

Deir el-Medina, the **Workers' Village**, housed the masons, painters and sculptors who created the royal tombs in the Valley of the Kings. Because many were literate and left records on papyrus or *ostracae*, we know such details as who feuded with whom, and about labour disputes. As state employees, they were supposed to receive fortnightly supplies of wheat, dried meat and fish, onions, pulses and beer, corresponding in value to the price of a bull. When these failed to arrive (as often happened during the ramshackle XX Dynasty), the workers downed tools, staged sit-ins at Medinet Habu, or demonstrated in Luxor.

Normally they worked an eight-hour day, sleeping in huts near the tombs during their ten-day shift before returning to their families at Deir el-Medina – a pattern followed over generations, as most occupations were hereditary. In their spare time craftsmen worked for private clients or collaborated on their own tombs, built beneath man-sized pyramids. Their own murals appropriated imagery from royal and noble tombs, which was parodied in the famous *Satirical Papyrus*, showing animals judging souls, collecting taxes and playing *senet*.

Anyone taking the donkey trail to the Valley of the Kings can get a fine **overview** of the village from the hillside – but the real attraction is its tombs. Visitors should know that the "Deir el-Medina" **ticket** (#10) doesn't cover the tomb of Peshedu, which needs a separate ticket (both only sold at faraway kiosks). You can easily walk to Deir el-Medina from the main road; it's also feasible to do so from the Valley of the Queens or Medinet Habu.

The nearest pyramid to the entrance marks the **Tomb of Sennedjem** (or Sennutem), whose vaulted burial chamber is reached by steep flights of steps and two antechambers. Its colourful murals feature ithyphallic baboons (right end wall), Osiris and the Fields of Yaru, and Anubis ministering to Sennedjem's mummy (facing wall, far left). The **Tomb of Ankherha** (#359) has a similar design, with an antechamber whose ceiling is decorated with intricate abstract patterns. On the left wall of the burial chamber, Ankherha appears with Wepwawet and Khepri; Anubis breathes life into his mummy; his wife adores Horus as a falcon; and his naked daughters make libations. In the **Tomb of Peshedu** (#3), one can see the deceased praying beneath the tree of regeneration, below which flow the waters of the *Amuntit*, the "Hidden Region" where souls were judged. Unusually for Deir el-Medina, the **Tomb of Iphy** (#217) eschews ceremonial scenes and deities for tableaux from everyday life.

Just north of the village stands a **Ptolemaic temple** dedicated to Maat and Hathor, whose head adorns the pillars between the outer court and naos. Each of its three shrines is decorated with scenes from the *Book of the Dead*; near the back of the left-hand shrine, a hyena-like "Devourer of Souls" awaits those who fail the Judgement of Osiris. Ancient Greek graffiti is scrawled around the temple's entrance. Early in the Christian era, the temple and the workers' village were occupied by monks – hence the site's Arabic name of *Deir el-Medina* (Monastery of the Town).

The Valley of the Queens

The **Valley of the Queens** is something of a misnomer, for it also contains the tombs of high officials (who were interred here long before the first queen was buried in this valley during the XIX Dynasty) and royal children. Polygamy and concubinage produced huge broods whose blood lines were further entangled by incestuous marriages between crown princes and their sisters, in emulation of Osiris and Isis. Princes were educated by priests and scribes, taught swimming, riding and shooting by officers, and finally apprenticed to military commands around the age of twelve. Less is known about the schooling of princesses, but several queens were evidently well versed in statecraft and architecture.

Originally named the "Place of Beauty", but now known in Arabic as *Biban el-Harem* (Gates of the Harem), the valley contains nearly eighty tombs, most of which are uninscribed and simple in plan. Although the finest murals rival those in the Valley of the Kings for artistry, many have been corroded by salt deposits, or badly vandalized.

Tomb of Queen Nefertari (#66)

After years of work cleansing its reliefs of salt deposits and stabilizing the plasterwork, Queen Nefertari's tomb looks fabulous – but is so fragile that only 150 visitors a day are allowed in for exactly ten minutes only, for £E100 a head. Assuming you're willing to spend that much, **tickets** go on sale at 6am, at the ticket kiosk on the Qurna road. Buying a ticket is less chaotic than it used to be – when touts fought to buy all the tickets and re-sold them to travel agencies, or sometimes in the Valley of the Queens – as the tourist police are keeping tighter controls, but individual travellers still need to come early. The tomb is **open** from 7.30am in summer and 8.30am in winter until noon.

Descending a stairway and passing beneath a lintel bearing Nefertari's titles and a winged sun-disc flanked by Isis and Nephthys, you enter a hall ablaze with murals. On either side are extracts from the *Book of Gates*, and Nefertari before Osiris. To the right of the hall, two projecting sections feature Anubis and Neith, Osiris and Selket, while the sons of Horus appear over the portal of a corridor slanting off towards the burial chamber. At the entrance to the latter, Nefertari makes burnt offerings to Amun and Isis; inside she venerates the *Book of Gates* to ensure her safe passage through the underworld, by formulae depicted on the far wall. The colours in Nefertiti's tomb are rich and soothing, with an unusual preference for hues of green.

Nefertari was the principal wife of Ramses II, with whom she had achieved almost equal status by the end of his reign. Her ascendancy was signified by the appearance of her image beside the king's on the pylon of Luxor Temple; the dedication of a shrine within the Ramesseum to Nefertari and the Queen Mother, Tuya; and finally by a massive temple at Abu Simbel, which identifies her with the goddess Hathor. After Ramses' death, Nefertari may have retired to a palace near the Fayoum or died herself; for no more is heard of her.

Tomb of Prince Khaemweset (#44)

Relatively few tourists visit this colourfully painted tomb, which lies uphill behind the souvenir stalls. Prince Khaemweset was one of several sons of Ramses III who died in a smallpox epidemic, and the murals in his tomb give precedence to images of Ramses, making offerings in the entrance corridor and worshipping funerary deities in the side chambers. In the second corridor, decorated with the *Book of Gates*, Ramses leads Khaemweset past the fearsome guardians of the Netherworld to the Fields of Yaru; bearing witness for him before Osiris and Horus in the burial chamber. Notice the four sons of Horus on the lotus blossom.

Tomb of Queen Titi (#52)

Sited along the well-trodden route to Amun-Hir-Khopshef's tomb, this cruciform structure was commissioned by Queen Titi, wife of one of the Ramessid pharaohs of the XX Dynasty. A winged Maat kneels in the corridor (where Titi appears before Thoth, Ptah and the sons of Horus) and guards the entrance to the burial chamber with Neith (left) and Selket (right).

The burial chamber itself boasts jackal, lion and baboon guardians, plus three side chambers, the finest being the one to your right. Here, Hathor emerges from between the mountains of east and west in her bovine form, while the tree-goddess pours Nile water to rejuvenate Titi, who reposes on a cushion across the room. Unfortunately, most of these murals are faded or damaged.

Tomb of Amun-Hir-Khopshef (#55)

Further along lies the tomb of Khaemweset's brother, Amun-Hir-Khopshef, who was given a royal burial and portrayed as a boy with the braided side lock of a prince, even though he died in infancy. Descending the steps, you'll find a hall and corridor with lustrous murals of Ramses conducting him through funerary rituals, and beyond, past the Keepers of the Gates, an unfinished burial chamber containing a granite sarcophagus. A glass case displays a shrivelled foetus which his mother supposedly aborted through grief – a grisly curio which makes this the most visited tomb in the Valley of the Queens.

Medinet Habu

Medinet Habu (Habu's Town) is the Arabic name for the gigantic **Mortuary Temple of Ramses III**, a structure second only to Karnak in size and complexity, and better preserved in its entirety. Modelled on the Ramesseum of his illustrious ancestor,

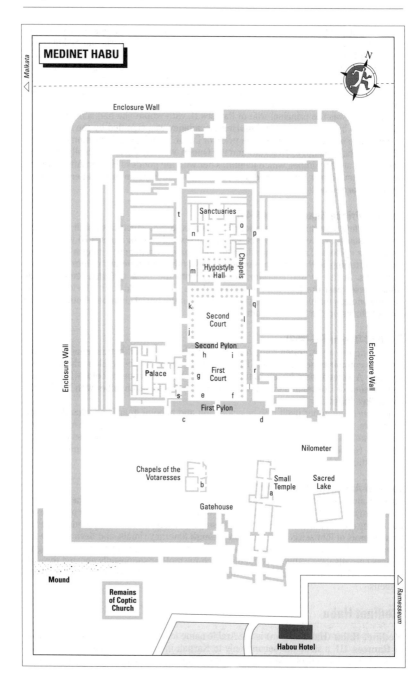

MEDINET HABU

N

Malkata

Enclosure Wall

t   Sanctuaries
          o
n   p

          Chapels

m   Hypostyle
     Hall

k
     Second
     Court   l

j
     Second Pylon

          h   i

Palace   First
          g   Court   r

s   e   f

First Pylon

c   d

Enclosure Wall   Enclosure Wall

Nilometer

Chapels of the
Votaresses
          b   Small
                    Temple   Sacred
                    a   Lake

Gatehouse

Mound

Remains
of Coptic
Church

Habou Hotel

Ramesseum

Ramses II, this XX Dynasty extravaganza deserves more attention than it usually gets, being the last stop on most tourists'
itinerary. The site itself was hallowed long before Ramses
erected his "House of Millions of Years" and is still imbued
with magical significance by the local *fellaheen*. Its massive
brick enclosure walls sheltered the entire population of
Thebes during the Libyan invasions of the late XX Dynasty and
for centuries afterwards protected the Coptic town of *Djeme*,
built within the great temple. You can get a fine **overview** of
Medinet Habu from the top of the mound of earth near the
southeast corner, or by drifting low over the temple in a hot-air
balloon (see p.314).

Ramses III

The temple precincts

The entire complex was originally surrounded by **enclosure walls**, sections of which
rise at intervals from the plain. You enter the temple precincts through a lofty towered
Gatehouse resembling an Assyrian fortress. The two statues of Sekhmet by the
entrance may have served to transmit the prayers of pilgrims to Amun, who "dwelt"
within the temple. Ramses himself would relax with his harem in a suite above the gate,
decorated with reliefs of dancers in slinky lingerie. Ravaged by vandals over the centuries, these are slowly being restored, so the upper chambers are off-limits.

North of here stands a **Small Temple**, reputedly sited where the primeval mound
arose from the waters of Chaos, preceding the creator-god Re-Atum of the
Hermopolitan Ogdoad. The existing structure was built and partly decorated by
Hatshepsut, whose cartouches and images were erased by Tuthmosis III. Akhenaten
did likewise to those of Amun, but Horemheb and Seti replaced them. Some defaced
reliefs **[a]** show Tuthmosis presiding over the foundation ceremonies, "stretching the
cord" before the goddess Seshat, "scattering the gypsum" and then "hacking the earth"
before a priapic Min.

Wheras the Small Temple antedates Ramses' work by three centuries, the **Chapels
of the Votaresses** are Late Period additions. Several date from the XXV Dynasty of
Nubian kings, who appointed these high priestesses of Amun and de facto governors
of Thebes. The best reliefs are in the forecourt **[b]** and shrine of Amenirdis, sister of
King Shabaka, whose alabaster funerary statue is now in the Cairo Museum. Ironically,
these chapels remained objects of veneration long after Ramses' temple had been abandoned.

In the right-hand corner of the enclosure are the remains of a **Sacred Lake** where
childless local women came to bathe at night and pray to Isis for conception. Behind
this lies a ruined **Nilometer**, once fed by a canal from the river. Originally, this whole
area was a garden.

Entering the Mortuary Temple of Ramses III

Like Deir el-Bahri and the Ramesseum, this mortuary temple was a focus for the
pharaoh's cult, linking him to Amun-United-with-Eternity. The effigies of Amun, Mut
and Khonsu paid an annual visit during the Festival of the Valley, while other deities
permanently resided in its shrines. Ramses himself often dwelt in the adjacent palace,
his Libyan and Sardinian bodyguard billeted nearby. Aside from its lack of freestanding
colossi, the sandstone temple gives a good idea of how the Ramesseum must have
looked before it collapsed.

Had it not lost its cornice and one corner, the **First Pylon** would match Luxor
Temple's in size. For *baksheesh*, a guard may unlock a stairway to the top, which offers
a panoramic view of the temple, Theban Hills and Nile Valley. Reliefs on the outer walls

(copied from the Ramesseum) show Ramses smiting Nubians **[c]** and Syrians **[d]**, though he never warred with either. Those on the inner wall relate genuine campaigns with Ramessid hyperbole. An outsized Ramses scatters hordes of Libyans in his chariot **[e]**. Afterwards, scribes tally the severed hands and genitals of dead foes (third row from the bottom) **[f]**.

Until the nineteenth century, the ruined houses of Coptic Djeme filled the **First Court**, now cleared to reveal its flanking columns. Those on the right bear chunky Osiride statues of the king, attended by knee-high queens. The other side of the court abuts the royal palace (now ruined and entered from outside). In the middle of this wall was a Window of Appearances **[g]** flanked by reliefs of prisoners' heads, whence the king rewarded loyal commanders with golden collars. Yet more scenes of triumph cover the outside of the **Second Pylon**, where Ramses leads six rows of prisoners to Amun and Mut **[h]** (those in the third row are Philistines) and a long inscription lauds his victories in Asia Minor **[i]**. The winged cobras and sun-discs on the ceiling of the pylon's gateway are still coloured.

Halls and sanctuaries

During Coptic times most of the Osiride pillars were removed to make room for a church, and a thick layer of mud was plastered over the reliefs in the **Second Court**. Now uncovered, these depict the annual festivals of Min **[j]** and Sokar **[k]**, with processions of priests and dancers accompanying the royal palanquin, the original colouring still intact. Elsewhere, the events of Ramses' fifth regnal year are related in a long text lower down the wall **[l]**.

The now-roofless **Hypostyle Hall**, beyond, once had a raised central aisle like the great hall at Karnak, and still has some brightly coloured pillars at the back. To the right lie five **chapels** dedicated to Ramses, his XIX Dynasty namesake, Ptah, Osiris and Sokar. On the opposite side are several (locked) treasure chambers whose reliefs show the weighing of myrrh, gold, lapis lazuli and other valuables bestowed upon the temple **[m]** – also visible on the outer walls.

Beyond this lie two **smaller halls** with rooms leading off. To the left of the first hall is the funerary chamber of Ramses III **[n]**, where Thoth inscribes his name on the sacred tree of Heliopolis. The other side – open to the sky – featured an altar to Re. On the lintels that once supported the roof **[o]**, Ramses and several baboons worship Re's barque. The central aisle of the next hall is flanked by statues of Ramses with Maat or Thoth. At the back are three **sanctuaries** dedicated to the Theban Triad of Mut (left), Amun (centre) and Khonsu (right). The false door behind the central one was for the use of Ramses' *ka*.

Along the outer walls

Some of the best reliefs at Medinet Habu are on the **outer walls** of the temple, involving a fair slog over broken ground. As most are quite faint, they're best viewed early or late in the day, when shadows reveal details obscured at midday. The famous **battle reliefs of Ramses II** run along the temple's northern wall, starting from the back. Although you'll encounter the last or middle scenes first, we've listed them in chronological order, as Ramses intended them to be seen. The first section **[p]** depicts the invasion of land-hungry Libyans, early in his reign. In the vanguard of the battle are Ramses, a lion and the standard of Amun. Afterwards, scribes count limbs and genitals to assess each soldier's reward in gold or land. Yet despite this victory, Ramses was soon beleaguered on two fronts, as the Libyans joined with the Sea Peoples (Sardinians, Philistines and Cretans) in a concerted invasion of the Nile Delta. A giant Ramses fires arrows into a melee of grappling ships, in the only Egyptian relief of a sea battle **[q]**. A third invasion by the Libyans **[r]** was also thwarted, but their descendants would eventually triumph and rule Egypt as the XXIII and XXIV dynasties.

On the other side of the temple behind the First Pylon is a dramatic relief of Ramses hunting antelopes in the desert and impaling wild bulls in a marsh **[s]**, near a ruined **Palace** where he resided during visits. A calendar of festivals appears at the far end of the temple **[t]**, which is surrounded on three sides by mud-brick **storehouses**, eroded into worm-like shapes.

Nag Lohlah, Armant and Riziq

Having seen Medinet Habu temple, consider dropping in for a chat with Hagg Ali, the aged proprietor of the *Habou Hotel*, who appears in Richard Critchfield's superb book *Shahhat*. Its eponymous hero was also born in **NAG LOHLAH** village, and most of the characters described by Critchfield still live here, or in other villages such as El-Tod. Though collectively known as "Berat", Gezira, Ezba, Ruska and El-Kom jealously guard their separate identities. Every family has someone working in tourism in Luxor or Hurghada, and others farming on the west bank, so that one finances the other as fortune allows.

Their fields have almost effaced the **remains of Malkata**, a pleasure palace erected by Amenophis III, where Akhenaten spent his youth. However, you can still discern a huge depression and rows of parallel mounds, where the king created a lake connected to the Nile, for Queen Tiy to sail in the royal barge, *Aten Gleams*. But unless you fancy a walk through the countryside, there's no reason to make the kilometre trek from Medinet Habu.

In December and in the spring, the villagers harvest their crops of sugar cane, which are transported by train to the refinery at **ARMANT**. As the cane's value declines the longer it sits in the sun, farmers are anxious to load it quickly. But wagons are in short supply, leading to accusations of favouritism and bribery, and even fights. Armant itself was anciently known as *Pathyris* and used to have a temple built by Cleopatra and Ptolemy Caesarion (her son by Julius Caesar). The modern town is on both banks of the Nile, with ferries shuttling between *Armant min Gharb* (west) and *Armant min Sharq* (east).

Further south, the small town of **RIZIQ** (or *er-Rizeiqat*) deserves a mention for its annual **Moulid of St George**, on November 11, which draws Copts and Muslims alike. Though worth attending, the festival is not for the squeamish, involving mass circumcisions and the slaughter of animals. *Service* taxis run there from the west bank. Riziq is also the start of a **new road to Kharga Oasis**, so far used only by the army. There's no water or petrol en route and safety dictates that cars travel in pairs, so taxis are averse to the journey, despite the road being in fine condition.

Esna and around

Small-town life and ancient stone are boldly juxtaposed at **ESNA**, where a huge pit in the centre of town exposes part of the **Temple of Khnum**. Some visitors are disappointed by what they find: the only part to have been excavated is the Hypostyle Hall, whose somewhat inferior reliefs detract from the forest of columns and lofty astronomical ceiling. That said, Esna is worth a stopover en route to the fabulous temple at Edfu, 50km upriver, and is often the last port of call for feluccas from Aswan. Unless you care to visit the early Saturday morning **camel market**, there's no reason to linger after seeing the temple, which takes under an hour.

Visible just north of Esna are two **barrages** that act as bridges over the Nile. The nearest was built by the British in 1906 as part of a grand scheme to tame the Nile, with barrages at four points along its length. In the 1990s, the river was further exploited by an Italian-built hydroelectric barrage, known to locals as the "Electricity Bridge". Both

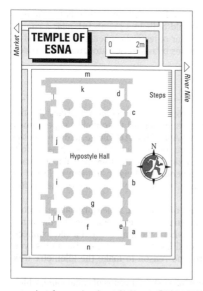

TEMPLE OF
ESNA

0   2m

Market

River Nile

m

k   d   Steps

c

l

j

Hypostyle Hall

N

i   b

g

h

f   e   a

n

barrages have locks to allow vessels to pass through, while trucks and carts trundle across the top. Also worth a passing mention is **Deir Manayus w al-Shuhada**, 6km southwest of town, a relic of the time when Esna was a centre of early Christianity. Founded in the fourth century AD, the high-walled "Monastery of Three Thousand Six Hundred Martyrs" now contains two churches, one of them decorated with a wonderful series of tenth-century murals.

Practicalities

Esna lies on the west bank of the Nile 54km south of Luxor and 155km north of Aswan. Although **service taxis** are the fastest way of getting there from Luxor (1hr; £E2), Aswan (2–3hr; £E6) or Edfu (1hr; £E2), foreigners may be subject to **travel restrictions** (for further details, see box on p.254), forcing you to rely on trains; buses and private taxis in convoy; or going by cruise boat/felucca. Though **buses** are frequent in the morning, anyone boarding at Esna could find all the seats taken, while only 2nd and 3rd class **trains** stop at the train station, which is further from the temple (take a *caleche*; £E2).

It's easy to get lost amidst Esna's muddle of unpaved streets. The best way to reach the temple is to follow the Corniche south past the Nile cruiser berths, or surrender yourself to the flow of the crowd through the souk, until you reach the sandbagged **police** station. Backtrack one block and turn right down a narrow side street, which should bring you out by the temple. Another advantage of the riverside route is that it takes you past some old *mashrabiya'* houses, a **bank** (daily except Fri 8.30am–2pm, also Sun 6–9pm & Wed 5–8pm; during Ramadan daily except Fri 10am–1.30pm) and a **post office** (daily except Fri 7am–2pm). The **tourist police** (☎095/400-686) are located

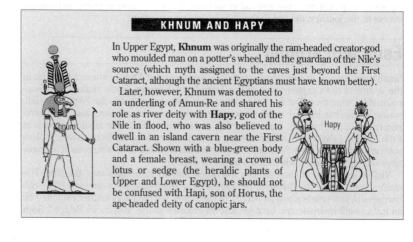

KHNUM AND HAPY

In Upper Egypt, **Khnum** was originally the ram-headed creator-god who moulded man on a potter's wheel, and the guardian of the Nile's source (which myth assigned to the caves just beyond the First Cataract, although the ancient Egyptians must have known better).

Later, however, Khnum was demoted to an underling of Amun-Re and shared his role as river deity with **Hapy**, god of the Nile in flood, who was also believed to dwell in an island cavern near the First Cataract. Shown with a blue-green body and a female breast, wearing a crown of lotus or sedge (the heraldic plants of Upper and Lower Egypt), he should not be confused with Hapi, son of Horus, the ape-headed deity of canopic jars.

Khnum

Hapy

near the temple ticket booth, further down the Corniche. By walking a kilometre past the kiosk, then heading 100m inland beside a concrete building and turning left, masochists can find the grimy, fanless *El-Haramin* (☎095/400-340; double £E12), Esna's only **hotel**. A terraced café near the cruiser berths and a humbler place on the corner by the temple serve **meals**; street food is sold in the souk.

The Temple of Khnum

When Amelia Edwards visited Esna, the **Temple of Khnum** (daily: winter 6am–5.30pm; summer 6am–6.30pm; £E12) was "buried to the chin in the accumulated rubbish of a score of centuries" and built over with houses. To minimize their destruction, only a portion was excavated in the 1860s. Now 10m below ground level, the temple resembles a pharaonic Fort Knox: its boxy mass fronted by six columns rising from a screen, the open space above them covered with wire mesh to discourage nesting birds. **Tickets** are sold at the riverside kiosk beyond the covered tourist bazaar, which runs between the temple and the river, five minutes' walk from the souk.

A Ptolemaic-Roman replacement for a much older structure dedicated to the ram-headed creator-god of ancient myth, the temple faced eastwards and probably rivalled Edfu's for size. Since what you see is merely the Roman section (dating from the first century AD), the **facade** bears the cartouches of Claudius **[a]**, Titus **[b]** and Vespasian **[c]**, and the battered sun-disc above the entrance is flanked by votive inscriptions to these emperors.

Entering the lofty **Hypostyle Hall**, your eyes are drawn upwards by a forest of columns that bud and flower in variegated capitals. Their shafts are covered with festival texts (now defaced) or hieroglyphs in the form of crocodiles **[d]** or rams **[e]**. The hall's **astronomical ceiling** rivals Dendara's for finesse and complexity, but gloom, soot and distemper render much indiscernible. However, the zodiac register **[f]** visibly crawls with two-headed snakes, winged dogs and other creatures. Notice the pregnant hippo goddess Tweri (whom the Greeks called Thoeris), and the scorpion in the next aisle **[g]**. Registers on the walls below show Septimus Severus, Caracalla and Geta before the gods.

The last Roman emperor mentioned is Decius **[h]**, whose persecution of Christians (249–51) anticipated the "Era of Martyrs" under Diocletian. Further along **[i]** is the cartouche of Ptolemy VI Philometor (Mother Lover), whose father began the construction of Esna temple. To the right of the portal, Decius makes offerings to Khnum, including a potter's wheel **[j]**. The liveliest reliefs are near the foot of the northern wall **[k]**, where Khnum, Horus and Emperor Commodus net fish and malignant spirits. To the left of this tableau stands an ibis-headed Thoth; to the right, Sheshat, goddess of writing. Around the outer walls of the temple are texts dedicated to Marcus Aurelius **[l]** and stiffly executed scenes of Titus, Domitian and Trajan smiting Egypt's foes before the gods **m** and **n**. Several blocks from an early Christian church lie in front of the temple.

Edfu

The provincial town of **EDFU** boasts the best-preserved **cult temple** in Egypt, dedicated to the falcon-headed god Horus (see p.367). Though actually built in the Ptolemaic era, this mammoth edifice respects all the canons of pharaonic architecture, giving an excellent idea of how most temples once looked. In terms of sheer monumental grandeur, it ranks alongside Karnak and Deir el-Bahri as one of the finest sites in the Nile Valley.

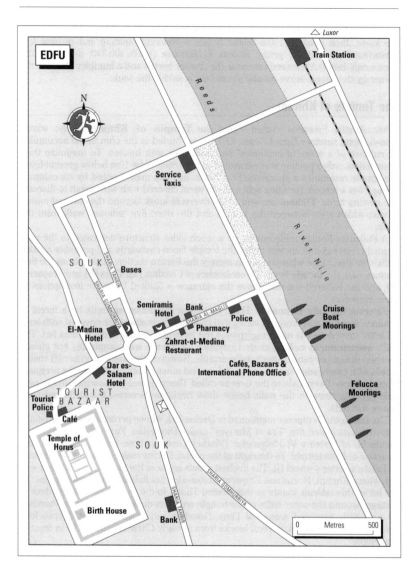

△ Luxor

EDFU

Train Station

Reeds

River Nile

N

Service
Taxis

S O U K

Buses

SHARIA TAHRIR

SHARIA GOMHOURIYA

Semiramis
Hotel

Bank

SHARIA AL-MAGLIS

Police

El-Madina
Hotel

Pharmacy

Zahrat-el-Medina
Restaurant

Dar es-
Salaam
Hotel

Cafés, Bazaars &
International Phone Office

Cruise
Boat
Moorings

TOURIST
BAZAAR

Tourist
Police

Café

Felucca
Moorings

Temple of
Horus

S O U K

SHARIA GOMHOURIYA

SHARIA TAHRIR

Birth House

Bank

0   Metres   500

Practicalities

Situated on the west bank of the Nile, roughly equidistant from Luxor (115km) and
Aswan (105km) and 65km north of Kom Ombo, Edfu is readily accessible by public
transport – though at the time of writing, *service* taxis were not an option for foreigners.
Buses terminate along Sharia Tahrir, or you can jump off a Luxor-bound bus which
leaves you at the junction with the bridge on the east bank; arriving by 2nd or 3rd class
train also leaves you on this side of the river. From here you can catch a pick-up (25pt)

or taxi (£E5) to the west bank and the temple. *Caleches* shuttle furiously between the cruise boat moorings and the temple; the ride costs around £E5, depending on your bargaining skills.

Sharia al-Maglis, Edfu's main street, leads past a **police** station (☎097/700-866) and a **bank** (winter Mon–Thurs & Sun 8.30am–2pm & 5–8pm; summer 8.30am–2pm & 6–9pm) to a circular junction named Temple Square. Further along, the temple lies off the tourist bazaar; the **tourist police** are based at the site entrance. Edfu's fruit and vegetable souk occupies an unpaved area of Tahrir and Gumhorriya streets, with the latter continuing south into a textiles souk, while Tahrir carries on past the **post office** (daily except Fri 8am–2.30pm).

Should you feel like staying in Edfu, the *Dar es-Salaam* **hotel** (☎097/701-727; ①) has sporadic hot showers, but there's a much friendlier ambience at the *El-Madina* (☎097/701-326; ③), which offers a delicious, filling breakfast that compensates for the lack of hot water. Across the road is the *Zahrat el-Medina* **restaurant**, which is reasonably clean but nothing special; you can also buy *fuul* and grilled fish in the fruit and vegetable market.

Returning to Luxor, buses depart from the vicinity of Sharia Tahrir.

The Temple of Horus

The **site** (daily: winter 7am–4pm; summer 7am–5pm; £E20) is a large excavated compound overlooked by mud-brick houses and catcalling children. Ahead stretch the sandstone enclosure walls and towering pylon of the **Temple of Horus**, which lay buried to its lintels until the 1860s, when Auguste Mariette cleared the main building; a splendid drawing by David Roberts shows the courtyard full of sand and peasant houses built atop the Hypostyle Hall. Yet the mammoth task of excavation was nothing compared to the temple's construction, which outlasted six Ptolemies, the final touches being added by the twelfth ruler of that dynasty.

Modern-day visitors approach the temple from the rear and have to walk its full length in order to enter through a gate in the pylon, fronted by two black granite **falcons**. The **Pylon** was erected by Ptolemy IX before he was ousted from power by his brother Alexander, who was later usurped by another ruler, for its exterior reliefs show Neos Dionysos smiting foes before Horus the Elder [a].

Entering the immense **Court of Offerings**, you can study the festival reliefs on the inner walls of the pylon, which continue around the court along the bottom of the wall. In the *Feast of the Beautiful Meeting*, Horus's barque tows Hathor's to the temple, where the deities retire to the sanctuary after suitable rituals [b]. Later they emerge from the temple, embark and drift downstream to the edge of the Edfu nome, where Horus takes his leave [c]. Beneath the western colonnade, Ptolemy IX makes offerings to Horus, Hathor and Ihy [d]; his successor appears before the Edfu Triad across the way [e]. However, most visitors are content to photograph the pair of **Horus statues** outside the Hypostyle Hall [f]. One hawk stands higher than a man, the other lies legless in the dust.

The great **Hypostyle Hall** dates from the reign of Ptolemy VII (145–116 BC), known to his contemporaries as "Fatty". With a torch, you can examine two small rooms in the entrance wall: the Chamber of Consecrations, where the king or his priestly stand-in dressed for rituals [f]; and a Library of sacred texts adorned with a relief of Sheshat, the goddess of writing [g]. The reliefs showing the foundation of the temple and the deification of Horus [h] have been mutilated by iconoclasts. From here on you encounter the oldest section of the temple, begun by Ptolemy III in 237 BC and completed 25 years later by his son, who styled himself Philopator (Father Lover).

Try to imagine the shadowy halls during the annual festivals rhapsodized in temple texts, when the **Festival Hall** was decorated with faïence, strewn with flowers and

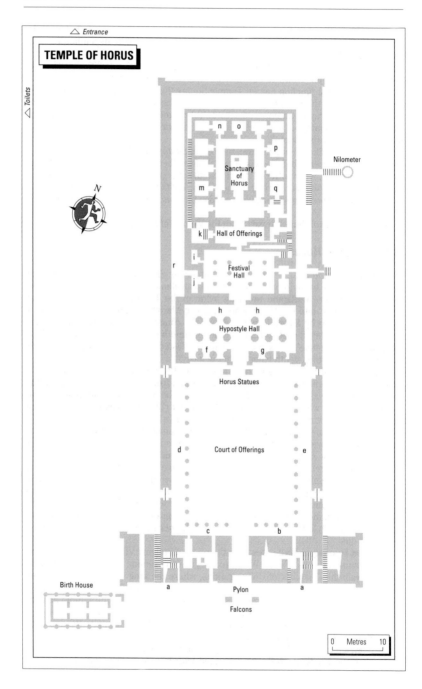

△ Entrance

TEMPLE OF HORUS

△ Toilets

N

Nilometer

n o

p

Sanctuary
of
Horus

m

q

k Hall of Offerings

i

r

Festival
Hall

j

h   h

Hypostyle Hall

f   g

Horus Statues

d   Court of Offerings   e

c   b

Birth House

a   a

Pylon

Falcons

0   Metres   10

THE CULT OF HORUS

Originally the sky-god of the Nile Valley, whose eyes were the sun and moon, the falcon deity **Horus** was soon assimilated into the Osirian myth as the child of Isis and Osiris (see p.290 and p.399). Raised in the swamps of the Delta by Isis and Hathor, Horus set out to avenge his father's murder by his uncle Seth. During their titanic struggle at Edfu, Horus lost an eye and Seth his testicles. Despite this, Seth almost prevailed until Isis intervened on her son's behalf and Osiris pronounced judgement upon them from the netherworld, exiling Seth back to the wilderness and awarding the throne to Horus. Thus good triumphed over evil and Osiris "lived" through his son.

Horus

All pharaohs claimed to be the incarnation of Horus the "living king" and reaffirmed their divine oneness in an annual **Festival of Coronation**. A live falcon was taken from the sacred aviary, crowned in the central court and then placed in an inner chamber where it "reigned" in the dark for a year as the symbol of the living king. Another event, sometimes called the **Festival of Triumph**, commemorated the Contendings of Seth and Horus in a series of Mystery Plays. At the equally lavish **Feast of the Beautiful Meeting**, his wet nurse and wife Hathor sailed from Dendara aboard the *Lady of the Lake* to be met near Edfu by his own barque, *The First Horus*. Public ceremonies preceded their conjugal encounters in the privacy of the temple's sanctuary. Besides these festivals, Horus also underwent a reunion with the sun-disc at New Year, similar to Hathor's at Dendara.

To complicate the cult of Horus still further, he was also associated with the Divine Ennead of Heliopolis and another variant of the Creation myth. Having distinguished the Osirian Horus from the Heliopolitan deity by terming the latter **Horus the Elder**, the Egyptians split him into archetypes such as **Herakhte** (often conjoined with Re), **Hariesis** (stressing his kinship to Isis) and **Haroeris** (see p.371). His priesthood asserted a place for Horus in the Creation myth by crediting him with building the first house amidst swamps at the dawn of the world, or even laying the Cosmic Egg whence the sun-god hatched. In rituals associated with the **Myth of the Great Cackler**, they launched a goose onto the sacred lake near Edfu temple, whose egg contained air and the potential for life – crucial elements in the world's creation.

herbs and perfumed by myrrh. Incense and unguents were blended according to recipes inscribed on the walls of the Laboratory **[i]**. Nonperishable offerings were stored in the room next door **[j]**, while liquids, fruit and sacrificial animals were brought in through a passageway connected to the outside world.

The sacred barques of Horus and Hathor appear in glorious detail on either side of the doorway into the **Hall of Offerings**. During the New Year Festival, Horus was carried up the ascending stairway **[k]** to the rooftop; after being revitalized by the sun-disc, his statue was returned to the sanctuary via the descending stairway **[l]**. The ritual is depicted on the walls of both stairways, but you'll need a torch, and locked gates may prevent you from going far. Otherwise, carry on to the **Sanctuary of Horus**, containing a shrine of polished black granite and an offerings table. Reliefs on the lower half of the right-hand wall show Philopator entering the sanctuary and worshipping Horus, Hathor and his deified parents.

There are several chambers worth noting off the corridor surrounding the sanctuary. The Linen Room **[m]** is flanked by chapels to Min and the Throne of the Gods, while a suite nominally dedicated to Osiris contains colourful scenes of Horus receiving offerings [n], a life-size model of Horus's barque [o] and reliefs of his avatars [p]. Equally arresting is the **New Year Chapel**, with a blue-coloured relief of the sky-goddess Nut stretched across its ceiling [q].

Returning to the Festival Hall, you can gain access to an external corridor running between the inner and outer walls, where the priesthood tallied tithes assessed on the basis of readings from the temple's own **Nilometer**. On the other side are tableaux from the Triumph of Horus over Seth, depicting Mystery Plays in which Seth was cast as a hippopotamus, lurking beneath his brother's boat [r].

Don't miss the colonnaded **Birth House**, a focus for the annual Coronation Festival re-enacting the divine birth of Horus and the reigning pharaoh. Around the back of the building are reliefs of Horus being suckled by Isis, both as a baby (low down on the rear wall) and as a young man (on the inside of the columns).

Around Edfu: El-Kab and Silsilah

Fifteen kilometres downriver from Edfu, the east bank road between Luxor and Kom Ombo passes the site known as **EL-KAB**, once the ancient city of *Nekheb*, dedicated to the vulture goddess of Upper Egypt. Only opened to tourists in the late 1980s, the **scattered ruins** are meagre compared to other sites and you have to be pretty keen to bother. Tickets are sold from a kiosk by the highway, which bisects the site.

The most conspicuous part of **the site** (daily 8am–6pm; £E10) lies towards the Nile, where the vast mud-brick **walls** that once enclosed the city stand, along with the conjoined **temples** of Nekhbet and Thoth, now reduced to stumps of painted columns and a series of **crypts** (notable for a scene of baboons dancing to the rituals of Mut). Across the road and up the slope from the ticket office, other ruins are scattered eastwards across the desert. You may not fancy hiking 3.5km to a small Chapel of Thoth and a Ptolemaic Temple of Nekhbet, but there are four **tombs** dug into the nearest ridge of hills. The best preserved is that of **Daheri**, royal scribe and tutor, and son of Tuthmosis I, which features ranks of lotus-sniffers and field workers. Next door are the lacklustre tombs of **Setau**, high priest of Nekhbet, and the commander **Aahmes**; superintendent **Renini** has a sprucer tomb, to the left.

Travelling between Edfu and Kom Ombo by felucca, you'll pass a succession of ancient quarries, most notably at **Silsilah**, where the river is constricted by sheer cliffs and the bedrock changes from Egyptian limestone to Nubian sandstone. The site's ancient name, *Khenu* (Place of Rowing), suggests that rapids once existed here during the season of inundation. If your boatman is willing to stop, the most imposing **quarries** lie on the east bank, approached by a narrow defile down which cut stones were dragged to waiting barges. Workmen's graffiti covers the rocks, while two formal inscriptions record the cutting of stone for Aten's temple at Karnak, and the reopening of the quarry early last century to provide stone for the Esna Barrage.

Lastly, real devotees of off-the-beaten-track experiences should bear in mind the **desert road** linking Edfu to the Red Sea Coast. Once a year, trucks decked with banners and loudspeakers convey thousands of Sufis along this route to Wadi Humaysara, high in the Red Sea Hills, for the **Moulid of Abul Hassan al-Shazli** (see p.642).

Kom Ombo

Thirty kilometres downriver from Aswan, the arid hills of the Eastern Desert recede from the river banks and bumper crops of sugar cane are harvested on reclaimed land. Here, too, around the town of **KOM OMBO**, many of the **Nubians** displaced by Lake Nasser have settled. In ancient times this town stood at the crossroads of the caravan route from Nubia and trails from the gold mines of the Eastern Desert, becoming the capital of the Ombos nome and a training depot for war elephants during the Ptolemaic era.

While modern-day Kom Ombo is known to the *fellaheen* for its sugar refinery and felucca-building yards, tourists associate it with the Ptolemaic **Temple of Haroeris and Sobek**, 4km from the town centre. Unlike other temples in the valley, this still stands beside the Nile, making the approach by river one of the highlights of a felucca journey. (Another way to see it is to join a day cruise from Aswan.)

Practicalities

Kom Ombo lies along the east bank "highway" between Luxor (170km) and Aswan (45km), roughly 60km south of Edfu. Although buses and slow trains call at Kom Ombo, the quickest way of **getting there** is by *service* taxi, but given the possible security restrictions (see box on p.254), a visit by cruise **boat** or **felucca** is probably easier, and is in any case a more pleasant way to get there, either from Aswan or Luxor. The temple can, however, be reached by *service* taxi from Edfu (1hr; £E2) or Aswan (45min; £E1.50). Approaching from Aswan or Darow, you can ask to be dropped at the signposted "tembel" turn-off, 2km south of town, whence it's a 1500m walk past cane fields to the temple site, by the Nile. Should you start from town instead, the cheapest method is to catch a pick-up to the ferry landing stage a few hundred metres north of the temple. Pick-ups leave from behind a mosque with a minaret on Sharia Gumhorriya, one block off the highway, and charge 25pt per head, but don't always run all the way to the river. Alternatively, you can engage a private taxi for the trip (£E3–5 one-way).

Kom Ombo's **service taxi depot** is on 26th July Street, just south of the intersection with Sharia Gumhorriya (which crosses the highway to meet the train station); continue south on 26th July Street for another 400m to find the **bus station**.

Should you wish **to stay**, try the *Cleopatra Hotel*, by the taxi depot (☎097/500-325; £E24), which has clean rooms with fans and balconies and rather basic bathrooms. In town, the *Restaurant El-Noba*, south of the mosque, provides an alternative to **eating** at *fuul* and *taamiya* stands; out near the temple, the *Venus Cafeteria* sells *kofta* sandwiches, ice cream and beer.

A small alley next to the mosque harbours a **bank** (daily: winter 8.30am–2pm & 5–8pm; summer 8.30am–2pm & 6–9pm; Ramadan 10am–1.30pm). The **police** (☎097/500-023) are located 50m north of Sharia Gumhorriya.

The Temple of Haroeris and Sobek

The **Temple of Haroeris and Sobek** stands on a low promontory near a bend in the river whose sandbanks were a basking place for crocodiles in ancient times. This proximity to the Nile has both preserved and damaged the **site** (daily 7am–5.45pm; £E8), covering the temple with sand which protected it from Coptic iconoclasts, but also washing away its pylon and forecourt, and undermining columns within the temple. What remains was aptly described by Amelia Edwards as a "magnificent torso"; truncated and roofless, it is still imposing, with traces of its original paint. It was further damaged in the 1992 earthquake, and sections are still propped up by scaffolding.

However, its main characteristic is its bisymmetry, with twin entrances and sanctuaries, and halls that are nominally divided down the middle. The left side is dedicated to the falcon-headed Haroeris the "Good Doctor" (a form of Horus the Elder) and his consort Ta-Sent-Nefer the "Good Sister" (an aspect of Hathor). The crocodile-god Sobek (here identified with the sun as Sobek-Re), his wife (another form of Hathor) and their son Khonsu-Hor are honoured on the right side of the temple.

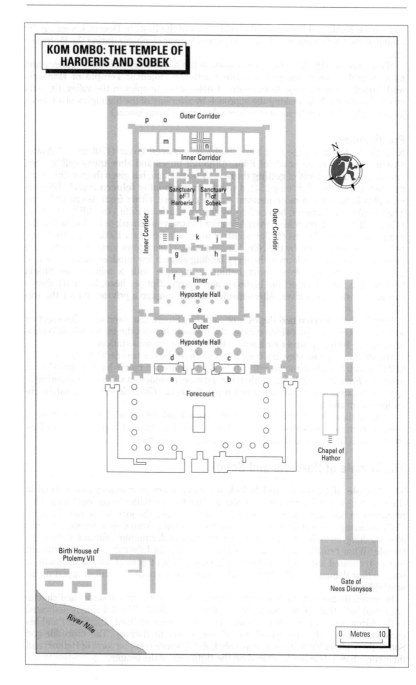

KOM OMBO: THE TEMPLE OF
HAROERIS AND SOBEK

Outer Corridor

p   o

m

n

Inner Corridor

Sanctuary
of
Haroeris

Sanctuary
of
Sobek

l

Inner Corridor   Outer Corridor

i   k   j

g   h

f   Inner
       Hypostyle Hall

e

Outer
Hypostyle Hall

d   c

a   b

Forecourt

Chapel of
Hathor

Birth House of
Ptolemy VII

Gate of
Neos Dionysos

River Nile

0   Metres   10

The facade and Hypostyle Halls

With the forecourt (added by Trajan in 14 AD) reduced to low walls and stumps of pillars, your eyes are drawn to the **facade** of the Hypostyle Hall. Rising from a screen wall, its surviving columns burst in floral capitals beneath a chunk of cavetto cornice bearing a winged sun-disc and twin *uraei* above each portal. Bas-reliefs on the outer wall show Neos Dionysos being purified by Thoth and Horus **[a]**, and yet again in the presence of Sobek **[b]**. Around the lintels and jambs of the easternmost portal, the Nile-gods bind the Two Lands together.

Wandering amidst the thicket of columns inside the **outer Hypostyle Hall**, notice the heraldic lily of Upper Egypt or the papyrus symbol of the Delta carved on their bases. On the inner wall of the facade are splendid paintings of Neos Dionysos's coronation before Haroeris, Sobek, Wadjet and Nekhbet (the goddesses of the north and south) **[c]**, and his appearance before Isis, Horus the Elder and a lion-headed deity **[d]**. Having propitiated four weird creatures by the easternmost door, he mingles with Nile-gods and field-goddesses along the side walls and appears with hymnal texts at the back of the hall, whose left side retains much of its roof, decorated with flying vultures.

Entering the older, **inner Hypostyle Hall**, you'll find a relief of Sobek in his reptilian form between the two portals **[e]**. Ptolemy VII makes sacrifices to diverse gods on the shafts of the columns, while his elder brother does likewise to Haroeris at the back of the hall. However, the finest reliefs occur on the left at the back, where Ptolemy VII receives the *hps* (sword of victory) from Haroeris, accompanied by his sister Cleopatra and his wife of the same name **[f]**. Between the two doors at the back of the hall are lists of temple deities and festivals.

Vestibules and sanctuaries

Beyond lies the first of three **vestibules** (each of which sits a little higher than the preceding one) decorated by Ptolemy VI. Scenes at the back depict the foundation of the temple, with Sheshat, goddess of writing, measuring its dimensions **[g]**; and offerings and libations to Sobek **[h]**. To maintain the temple in a state of purity, these foundation rituals were periodically repeated. Only priests were admitted to the next vestibule, which served as the Hall of Offerings. The ruined chambers either side once held vestments and sacred texts, as at Edfu and Dendara. Offerings to Haroeris **[i]**, a description of the temple and an address to Sobek **[j]** appear on the southern wall. Notice the tiny relief of a woman giving birth between the doors to the inner vestibule, at roughly waist height **[k]**.

A fine relief between the doors of the sanctuaries **[l]** shows Ptolemy and his sister-wife being presented with a palm stalk from which hangs a *heb-sed* sign representing the years of his reign. Khonsu does the honours, wearing a blue crescent and red disc, followed by Haroeris in blue and Sobek in green (representing air and water, respectively); Ptolemy himself sports a Macedonian cloak. Because so little remains of the **sanctuaries**, you can espy a secret corridor between them, whence the priests would "speak" for the gods. This was accessible from one of the chapels off the inner corridor **[m]** via an underground crypt, now exposed. Stairs in the central chapel **[n]** allow an overview of the temple.

The outer corridor and Birth House

In the **outer corridor** between the Ptolemaic temple and its Roman enclosure wall, pilgrims scratched graffiti on the pavements to while away the time before their appointment with the Good Doctor, who was represented by a statue in the niche behind the central chapel. The carved ears heard their pleas and the eyes symbolized the health they sought. Though these carvings have been gouged away by supplicant fingers, other reliefs are in better shape. One shows Marcus Aurelius offering a pectoral to Ta-Sent-Nefer, the Good Sister (aka Sennuphis) **[o]**. The other testifies to sophisticated

---

THE LAST FORTY DAYS ROAD

The camel trail from northern Sudan to Upper Egypt is one of the last great desert drov-
ing routes still active. The camels are reared in Sudan's Darfur and Kordofan provinces
and herded 300–400km eastwards across the Libyan Desert to Dongola on the Nile,
whence they follow the river into Egypt. Herdsmen call this month-long route the **Forty
Days Road** (*Darb al-Arba'in*), perhaps from folk memory of the old slave trail from
Kobbe to Assyut (see p.460), which was even longer and harder.

Now, as then, the drovers are usually Bishari or Rizayqat nomads, who sometimes
appear at Egyptian markets in their traditional garb of flowing trousers, woollen cloak,
dagger and sword (serious weapons like AK-47s are stashed before crossing the border).
For what amounts to three months' work in atrocious conditions, each drover receives
the equivalent of £100 sterling, the guide about £150. The camel owners are town-
dwelling Sudanese merchants who fly up to supervise the sale, on which they can expect
to make a profit of 500 percent.

---

surgery nearly 2000 years ago, depicting instruments such as scalpels, suction cups,
dental tools and bone saws **[p]**.

Time has been crueller to the temple's *mammisi*, half of which fell into the Nile in the
nineteenth century. The only scene of note in what's left of the **Birth House of Ptolemy
VII** actually shows Ptolemy IX. Accompanied by two gods, he navigates through a
papyrus thicket alive with birds, observed by an ithyphallic Min-Amun-Re clutching lettuces – Freud would have loved to get the Ptolemies on his couch. The **Gate of Neos
Dionysos** is another teaser, since scholars disagree over the number, order and dates
of the various Ptolemies, each of whom adopted a title such as Soter (Saviour),
Euergetes (Benefactor) or Philometor (Mother Lover). Some identify Neos Dionysos as
Ptolemy XII, others as Ptolemy XIII; however, there's general agreement that he
fathered the great Cleopatra, had an interrupted reign (80–58 and 55–51 BC) and was
nicknamed "The Bastard". Before leaving, peer through the bars of the small **Chapel of
Hathor** to see three **mummified crocodiles**, found nearby during roadworks.

Darow Camel Market

Traditionally, **DAROW** (pronounced "De-*rau*") marks the point where Egypt begins to
shade into Nubia: a distinction underlined by its camel market, which is attended by
tribesmen from the northern deserts of the Sudan. The village is a ramshackle sprawl
of mud-brick compounds either side of the highway and railway line, where *service* taxis
from Kom Ombo (10min; 50pt) or Aswan (40min; £E1) will drop you near a bridge that
functions as a taxi depot, level crossing, bus stop and general meeting point. Private
taxis in Darow might agree to take you to Kom Ombo Temple and back for about £E10.

The **Camel Market** (*Souk el-Gamal*) happens every **Tuesday** throughout the year,
and maybe also on Sundays or Mondays over winter. Although hours (7am–2pm)
remain constant, with activities winding down after 11am, the location of the market
changes seasonally. Over winter, it's often held in two dusty compounds on the eastern
outskirts of Darow (15 minutes' walk from the main intersection; cross the bridge, walk
on past the cane fields and turn right down a lane flanked by mud-brick walls). During
summer, it may take place on the other side of town beyond the fruit, vegetable and
poultry souk – just follow the crowds. The giveaway is truckloads of camels bumping
hither and thither along a dusty lane.

At the end you'll find several hundred camels with their forelegs hobbled in the traditional manner, and scores of drovers and buyers drinking tea and smoking *sheeshas*
beneath awnings. As the principal camel market between Dongola and Cairo, Darow is

a good place to do business. A prime *hageen* (riding camel) costs 25 to 50 percent less than at Cairo's Imbaba market. The buyers are Egyptian peasants who need a beast of burden, or merchants who plan to sell the camels for a profit in Cairo or abroad. More notable – but negligibly rewarded – are the herdsmen who drive the camels up the Forty Days Road (see box opposite).

The Tuesday *Souk el-Gamal* coincides with a **livestock market** where donkeys, sheep and cows jostle for space with people and trucks amidst trampled mud and dung. Over summer, the two markets are often held side by side. It's also worth catching Darow's annual **Moulid of Sidi Amr**, should you happen to be around between the 13th and 15th of *Sha'ban*.

Aswan and around

Egypt's southernmost city (population 150,000) and ancient frontier town has the loveliest setting on the Nile. At **ASWAN** the deserts close in on the river, confining its sparkling blue between smooth amber sand and rugged extrusions of granite bedrock. Lateen-sailed feluccas glide past the ancient ruins and gargantuan rocks of Elephantine Island, palms and tropical shrubs softening the islands and embankments till intense blue skies fade into soft-focus dusks. The city's **ambience** is palpably African; its Nubian inhabitants are lither and darker than the *Saiyidis*, with different tastes and customs. Although its own monuments are insignificant compared to Luxor's, Aswan is the base for **excursions** to the **temples of Philae and Kabasha**, near the great dams beyond the First Cataract, and the Sun Temple of Ramses II at **Abu Simbel**, far to the south. It can also serve for day-trips to Darow Camel Market, Kom Ombo, Edfu and Esna – the main temples between here and Luxor. But the classic approach is to travel upriver by felucca, experiencing the Nile's moods and scenery as travellers have for millennia. The delights and pitfalls of **felucca journeys** are described on p.392. However, Aswan itself is so laid-back that one could easily spend a week here simply hanging out, never mind going anywhere. The **tourism** scene is much the same as in Luxor (see box on p.299).

Climate

The time of year is a major influence on people's level of activity. Situated near the Tropic of Cancer, Aswan is hot and dry nearly all the time, with average daily **temperatures** ranging from a delicious 23–30°C in the winter to a searing 38–54°C over summer. Late autumn and spring are perfect times to visit, being less crowded than the peak winter period, yet not so enervating as summer, when long siestas, cold showers and air-conditioning commend themselves, and the number of tourists dwindles.

Aswan in history

Elephantine Island – opposite modern Aswan in the Nile – has been settled since time immemorial, and its fortress-town of *Yebu* (or *Abu*) became the border post between Egypt and Nubia early in the Old Kingdom. Local governors, known as the "Guardians of the Southern Gates", were responsible for border security and trade with Nubia, for huge quarries for fine red granite, and mining in the desert hinterland of amethysts, quartzite, copper, tin and malachite. Military outposts further south could summon help from the Yebu garrison by signal fires and an Egyptian fleet patrolled the river between the First and Second Cataracts.

Besides this, Yebu was an important cult centre, for the Egyptians believed that the Nile welled up from subterranean caverns at the **First Cataract**, just upriver (see p.391). Its local **deities** were Hapy and Satet, god of the Nile flood and goddess of its fertility, though the region's largest temple honoured Khnum, the provincial deity (see preceding Esna section).

THE NUBIANS

The **Nubians** – the primary people of the Nile between Aswan and Khartoum – are seemingly unrelated to other Nilotic or desert tribes of the same region, where they have lived as long as anyone can establish. In ancient times, when the region was known as **Kush** (covering parts of modern-day Egypt and Sudan), the pharaohs used the Nubians as mercenaries and traders – roles in which they are often depicted in tomb and temple art. Almost all of the XXV Dynasty ("Ethiopian" or "Kushite") pharaohs were of Nubian birth, and some claim that Cleopatra (or *Kilu baba tarati* – "Beautiful Woman") was a Nubian born near Wadi Halfa.

Traditional Nubian life centred around **villages** of extended families, each with its own compound of domed houses. The people made a livelihood farming the verges of the river, planting date palms, corn and *durra* melons, as well as fishing and transporting trade goods. Socially and spiritually, the Nile formed the basis of their existence. The whole village celebrated births, weddings and circumcision ceremonies with Nile rituals, and, despite converting first to Christianity and then to Islam, they retained a belief in water spirits, petitioning them for favours. They also brewed beer and date wine.

This way of life – which had existed pretty much unchanged for five millennia – was shattered by the **Aswan Dams**. The first dam, built in 1902 and successively raised, forced the Nubians to move onto higher, unfertile ground: unable to subsist on agriculture, many of the menfolk left for Cairo and the cities, sending back remittances to keep the villages going. With construction of the High Dam, the Nubians' traditional homeland was entirely submerged, displacing the entire 800,000-strong community. Around half of them moved north, settling around Aswan and Kom Ombo, where the government provided homes and assistance with agriculture and irrigation. The rest were repatriated to Sudan, where many ended up in the Kassala/New Halfa area, a thousand miles to the south.

In Egypt, the **Nubian community** has done well. Many have taken advantage of higher education and business opportunities, making their mark in government, commerce and tourism (85 percent of Nubian males in Aswan earn their living from tourism). Others from the first wave of emigration continue to provide the backbone of Cairo's janitors and servants; Nubians as a whole have always been noted for their honesty and reliability. Remarkably, the community has maintained its cultural identity, with the resettled villages (which took their old names) acting as guardians of tradition.

A few Nubian phrases (accents indicate stress)

Er raigráy? or *er-minnabóu?*	How are you? (to a man or woman)
Ai raigérry	I'm fine
Ekináira?	What's your name?
Aigi	My name is . . . (followed by *-era*)
Er fárdiray?	Are you busy?
Tégus	Sit down
Er wenáyseso	I am honoured
Asálgi	Tomorrow
Kattaháiruk	Thank you
Ena fiadr	Goodbye

During settled periods, the vast trade in ivory, slaves, gold, silver, incense, exotic animal skins and feathers spawned a **market town** on the east bank (slightly south of modern Aswan, its linear descendant), but the island remained paramount throughout classical times, when it was known by its Greek appellation, *Seyene*. In the Ptolemaic era, the Alexandrian geographer **Eratosthenes** (276–196 BC) heard of a local well into which the sun's rays fell perpendicularly at midday on the summer solstice, leaving no shadow; from this he deduced that Seyene lay on the Tropic of Cancer, concluded that the world was round and calculated its diameter with nearly modern accuracy – being only 80km out. (Since that time, the Tropic of Cancer has moved further south.)

The potency of the **cult of Isis** at nearby **Philae** (see p.399) made this one of the last parts of Egypt to be affected by **Christianity**, but once converted it became a stronghold of the faith. From their desert Monastery of St Simeon, monks made forays into Nubia, eventually converting the local Nobatae, who returned the favour by helping them to resist Islamic rule through Fatimid times, until finally subjugated by Salah al-Din. However, Bedouin raiders persisted through to 1517, when Sultan Selim garrisoned an entire army here, by which time the town's name had changed from Coptic *Sawan* to its present form, and the population had embraced **Islam**.

From the early nineteenth century onwards, Aswan was the base for the conquest of the Sudan and the defeat of the Mahadist Uprising (1881–98) by Anglo-Egyptian forces. As British influence grew, it also became the favourite **winter resort** of rich, ailing Europeans, who flocked to Aswan for its dry heat and therapeutic hot sands, luxurious hotels and stunning scenery, spiced with the thrill of being "at the edge of civilization". Its final transformation into the Aswan of today owes to the building of the **High Dam**, 15km upriver, which flooded Nubia, compelling its inhabitants to settle in new villages built around Kom Ombo and Aswan itself, which is now predominantly Nubian.

To assert its identity, the city has undertaken two projects: an **Africa University** for the study of African science and culture, and a **Nubia Museum** tracing the Nubians' history. The relationship between the Egyptian and Sudanese governments has been somewhat fragile, however, and the weekly ferry between Aswan and Wadi Halfa was suspended for a time during the mid-1990s because of political tensions. At the time of writing, the ferry is running and relations between the two governments seem relatively stable (see box "Visiting Sudan" on p.406).

Arrival, information and transport

Most tourists travel directly to Aswan from Cairo (889km) or Luxor (215km), as detailed in the introduction to this chapter; a few arrive by *service* taxi from Esna, Edfu or Kom Ombo (see the respective entries for details), or by felucca from Luxor.

Aside from **Aswan airport**, 23km south of town (£E20 by four-seater taxi), points of arrival are fairly central. The **train station** lies in the northern part of town, five minutes' walk from the Corniche or the bazaar quarter. The inter-city **bus station** is smack in the centre on Sharia Abtal el-Tahrir, while **feluccas** tie up alongside the Corniche. The inter-city **service taxi** depot is more awkwardly located, across the tracks and south of the train station; at the time of writing it was off-limits to foreign tourists.

Information and assistance

The **tourist office** (daily: winter 9am–3pm & 6–8pm; summer 9am–3pm & 7–9pm; Ramadan 10am–2pm; ☎097/312-811) is housed in a domed Nubian-style building outside the station. The erudite and charming Shukri Sa'ad and Hakeem Hussein can answer just about any question, and will recommend good felucca captains, if asked beforehand – they won't pass judgement if you've already made a deal. They also provide current private taxi rates. Shukri is worth talking to about anything, having read and travelled widely, whilst remaining a real Nubian.

The **tourist police** (☎097/316-436) are based near the Corniche, with a branch in the train station; both are open round the clock. The Aswan Governorate's **Police Department** occupies a grand modern tower on the Corniche, fronted by machine-gunners and a notice welcoming tourists to the building, which also contains the passport office. There is another, colonial-style police station on Sharia Abtal el-Tahrir.

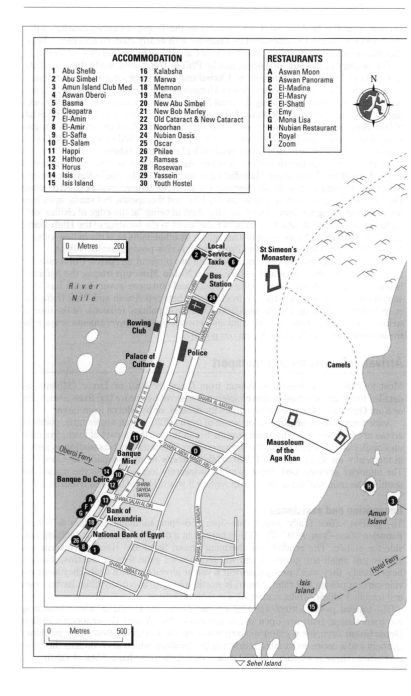

ACCOMMODATION

1 Abu Shelib
2 Abu Simbel
3 Amun Island Club Med
4 Aswan Oberoi
5 Basma
6 Cleopatra
7 El-Amin
8 El-Amir
9 El-Saffa
10 El-Salam
11 Happi
12 Hathor
13 Horus
14 Isis
15 Isis Island
16 Kalabsha
17 Marwa
18 Memnon
19 Mena
20 New Abu Simbel
21 New Bob Marley
22 Old Cataract & New Cataract
23 Noorhan
24 Nubian Oasis
25 Oscar
26 Philae
27 Ramses
28 Rosewan
29 Yassein
30 Youth Hostel

RESTAURANTS

A Aswan Moon
B Aswan Panorama
C El-Madina
D El-Masry
E El-Shatti
F Emy
G Mona Lisa
H Nubian Restaurant
I Royal
J Zoom

Sehel Island

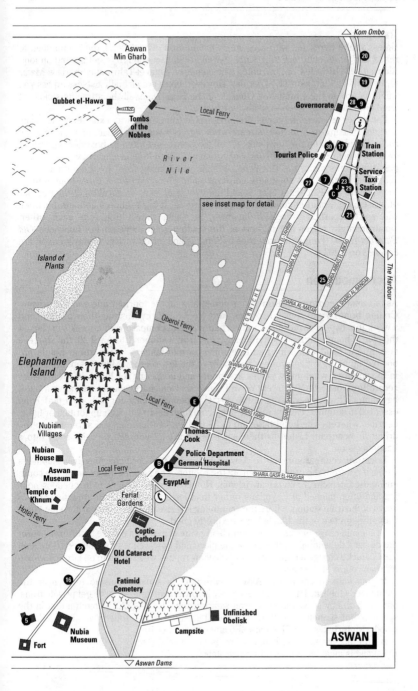

△ Kom Ombo

20
19
28 9

Qubbet el-Hawa ■   Governorate ■   i

Aswan
Min Gharb

Tombs
of the
Nobles   Local Ferry

River
Nile   Tourist Police   30 17   Train
                                                            Station

                                                            Service
                                                            Taxi
                                            27   7   23   Station
                                                         J
                                                         C 29

                    see inset map for detail   21

Island of
Plants   ▷ The Harbour

                                        SHARIA EL TAHRIR
                                                                25
                         4   Oberoi Ferry

Elephantine   CORNICHE
Island   SHARIA AL MATAR
                                                      SHARIA ABDEL MAGID ABU ZID
                                        Local Ferry

Nubian   SHARIA SALAH AL-DIN
Villages   SHARIA SHARD AL-BANDAR
                                            E
Nubian   Thomas
House   Cook
        Local Ferry
Aswan   Police Department
Museum   B 1   German Hospital   SHARIA QASR EL-HAGGAR

Temple of   EgyptAir
Khnum
                        Ferial   ☎
        Hotel Ferry   Gardens
                                        ✚
                        Coptic
              22   Cathedral

                        Old Cataract
                        Hotel
        16
                        Fatimid
                        Cemetery   Unfinished
                                                         Obelisk
5
                Nubia   Campsite
        Fort   Museum   **ASWAN**

▽ Aswan Dams

Transport

Unless you're burdened with luggage or bound for a distant hotel, there's no need to rent a **taxi** or **caleche** (£E4–5), since Aswan is compact enough to get around on foot. Alternatively, **bicycles** can be rented from shops on Abtal el-Tahrir and Sharia al-Matar for roughly £E1 an hour, £E10 per day. However, bikes are virtually useless unless you want to cycle to the Unfinished Obelisk or the High Dam; all the attractions close at hand are reached by river – mostly by felucca.

For better or worse, **feluccas** are inseparable from the Aswan experience. It's wonderfully relaxing to drift downstream while egrets swoop overhead, or tack between rocky islands, but on the downside, it's all too easy to get irked by boatmen who fritter away time before demanding *baksheesh* for an unfulfilled itinerary; or get wearied of the persistent touts along the Corniche. Despite **rates** being fixed by the authorities at £E18 per boatload for an hour's constant sailing, or £E40 for a three-hour tour of Elephantine and Kitchener islands and the west bank sites (regardless of the number of passengers), market rules and haggling prevail. If big spenders abound, boatmen will sniff at official rates; if business is slack, they'll undercut each other. Unsurprisingly, prices are highest at the landing stage beneath the luxurious *Old Cataract Hotel.* (Longer felucca trips to Sehel Island, or downriver towards Luxor, are covered on p.392.)

Accommodation

As in Luxor, **accommodation** varies depending on the tourist trade and the season. **Cruise boats** try to steal customers away from hotels by slashing their prices – and a week in a two- or three-star hotel certainly cannot compare with a week's cruise on the Nile. Though high season officially runs from October 1 to April 30, the squeeze is only felt (if at all) from mid-December to mid-January, when some hotels are booked up by Egyptian groups. The nadir of the low season (May 1–Sept 30) comes in the summer, when most places are empty and desperate for business. Many offer **reductions** of 15 to 50 percent or will waive service charges and taxes after a bit of haggling. With temperatures in the 50s°C, air-conditioning (or at least a fan) is an essential in summer. Guests may be subjected to **pressure** to sign up for taxi or felucca trips, whereby the hotel takes up to 50 percent of whatever you agree to pay the driver or boatman. Listen to their spiel, but don't let yourself be railroaded into a hasty decision.

Location counts for much in Aswan: hotels on the Corniche may have fabulous views, if not from the rooms, then from the rooftop. The poshest places are at the south end of the Corniche, or on private islands. Hotels in the bazaar tend to be cheaper, noisier, and often pitched at Egyptians rather than foreigners. The least attractive area is north of the train station, where the crumbling low-rise buildings are hardly what you'd want, though two of the hotels here are pretty good.

Of the mid-range places – aside from being sure of getting a private bathroom – **standards** vary depending on the age of the place and how well it's maintained. Hotels on the Corniche charge a higher rate for Nile-view rooms, which tend to be larger and better than rooms at the back.

If you want to camp, the **Aswan campsite** is situated outside town near the Unfinished Obelisk. This site is hopelessly inconvenient unless you've got private transport, and chiefly serves trans-African safari groups. It costs £E3 to pitch a tent in the spacious but shadeless compound, which has showers and toilets (vendors sell firewood). Motorbikes cost £E2, cars £E5 and caravans £E10.

All the accommodation listed below is keyed to the map on the previous pages. Breakfast is included unless otherwise stated.

Low-budget hotels

Abu Shelib, Sharia Abbas Farid, off the lower end of the bazaar (☎097/303-051). Tatty but clean rooms with fans or A/C, washbasins or baths – unfortunately within earshot of a mosque. Restaurant with good food (no alcohol); breakfast not included. Friendly. ③.

Abu Simbel, on the Corniche (☎097/302-888). The rooms here are somewhat shabby but they're spacious and clean, with small Nile-facing balconies. Garden out front; sells beer. Mostly used by Egyptians, the place is rather noisy. ③.

El-Amin, just off the bazaar (☎097/301-213). Basic cleanish singles, doubles and triples with fans (some with showers). Mostly used by Egyptians. Noisy; breakfast not included. ②.

Hathor, midway along the Corniche (☎097/314-580, fax 303-462). Plain A/C rooms: only the Nile-view ones are carpeted. Also cheaper, spartan rooms on the tatty 2nd floor. Restaurant, bar and rooftop with a small pool and view of Elephantine. ③.

Marwa, in an alley near the youth hostel (☎097/308-532). Clean, plain rooms with fans (a few have A/C), and two hot showers on each floor. Hard beds. ①.

Mena, north of the station (☎097/304-388). Clean, pastel-painted and carpeted rooms, some with double beds, most with A/C and all with private baths. Nice restaurant. ③.

New Abu Simbel, behind the football club at the northern end of the Corniche (☎097/306-090). A/C rooms with bedside lamps, some facing the Nile or a pleasant garden; those with fridge and TV cost extra. Spacious and carpeted throughout. Friendly ambience. Sells beer. ③.

New Bob Marley, off Sharia al-Souk (☎097/301-839). Simple, clean rooms with fans or A/C, some with private showers. Liberal atmosphere. ①.

Noorhan, off Sharia al-Souk near the station (☎097/316-069). Reasonable rooms with fans, some have bathrooms and/or A/C. Rooftop with washing machine. Beer and simple meals are available; breakfast not included. Liberal atmosphere. ①–②.

Nubian Oasis, corner of Sharia al-Souk (☎097/312-123, fax 312-124). Though a bit gloomy, rooms have A/C, soft beds and decent bathrooms. Liberal atmosphere, but bad for hustling. Sells beer, and there's a dry-cleaners downstairs. Breakfast not included. ②.

Oscar, Sharia Abbas el-Abkad (☎ & fax 097/306-066). Nice, clean, comfortable place, with traces of former elegance. All rooms with bath and A/C; some have bedside lamps and balconies. Sells beer. Honest management. ③.

Rosewan, north of the station (☎097/304-497). Welcoming and reasonably clean, with fans in all rooms, and large beds and bathrooms in some doubles. Erratic hot water, but Internet access may be some compensation. The owner makes things from papier mâché and will invite you to visit his studio. ②.

Yassein, next to the *Noorhan,* off Sharia al-Souk (☎097/317-109). Recently renovated place with clean doubles with bathrooms and a choice of fan or A/C. Friendly staff. ②.

Youth Hostel, Sharia Abtal el-Tahrir, near the station (☎097/302-313). Beds in musty, crowded dorms for £E7.60 (£E1 extra for non-members); some A/C doubles also available (②). Vague curfew around midnight.

Mid-range hotels

El-Amir, one block inland from the lower end of the Corniche (☎097/314-732). Clean, smart place aimed at Gulf Arabs. Some rooms with double beds; all A/C. Restaurant (no alcohol). Large rooftop sundeck. ⑥.

El-Salam, midway along the Corniche (☎097/302-651, fax 303-649). Simple, carpeted rooms, mostly with fans rather than A/C. All Nile-facing ones rent as doubles; there are also triples with corner balconies. Restaurant overlooking Elephantine. ④.

Happi, just off the Corniche (☎097/314-115, fax 307-572). Cosy, clean, attractive A/C rooms overlooking the bazaar or the Nile; the restaurant faces Elephantine and sells beer. Reduced rate for use of the *Cleopatra*'s pool (£E5). Internet access. ⑤.

Horus, on the Corniche (☎097/303-323, fax 313-313). Clean A/C rooms with tiled floors; the ones upstairs and at the back are shabbier. Pleasant roof garden with fine view (sells beer). Not as good value as the *Hathor*. ④.

Memnon, further down the Corniche from the *Horus*; the entrance is round the back. (☎097/300-483). Tiled or carpeted A/C rooms with bedside lamps. The hotel is crassly decorated and has a tiny lift. ④.

Philae, on the Corniche (no phone). Nile-view or airless back rooms, all clean and modern with baths. ⑤.

Ramses, Sharia Abtal el-Tahrir (☎097/304-000, fax 315-701). Modern, centrally located and covered in mock-pharaonic carvings. Carpeted A/C rooms with fridges, phones and satellite TV. Restaurant and bar. ⑤.

Upmarket hotels

Amun Island Club Med, on its own island, across from the *Old Cataract* (☎097/313-800, fax 317-190). Small resort set amid a lush garden and exotic birdlife; pool, bars and restaurant. A/C bungalows with private bathrooms. Reservations advisable in high season. Reached by private ferry. ⑧.

Aswan Oberoi, on Elephantine Island (☎097/314-667, fax 313-538). Resembling an airport control tower, this five-star blight is reached by a ferry done up like a pharaonic barge. Rooms, or villas with private gardens. Restaurants, nightclub and disco. ⑧.

Basma, on the hillside above the *Old Cataract* (☎097/310-901, fax 310-907). Cool, stylish rooms with satellite TV. Large, kidney-shaped pool. Splendid Nile view. Hourly free bus from the *Isis*, in town. ⑦.

Cleopatra, Sharia al-Souk, near the bazaar (☎097/314-001, fax 314-002). Clean, carpeted A/C rooms, some with fridges and TV. Restaurant, bar and pool. ⑦.

Isis, on the Corniche (☎097/315-100, fax 315-500). Single and double bungalows with A/C and TV, in a small garden with a pool. Italian and Egyptian restaurants. ⑦.

Isis Island, on its own island upriver from Aswan (☎097/317-400, fax 317-405). Opulent five-star colossus, owned by a relative of Mubarak. All mod cons and flourishes. Reached by private ferry. ⑧.

Kalabsha, inland of the *New Cataract* (☎097/302-666, fax 305-974). Doesn't merit its four stars. Plain rooms with TV, fridge and erratic hot water. Bar and restaurant. Use of the *New Cataract*'s pool. ⑦.

New Cataract, by the Ferial Gardens (☎097/316-000, fax 316-011). Less classy modern annexe to the *Old Cataract*, next door. Disco, bar, 24-hour café and several restaurants. Its best feature is an Olympic-sized pool. ⑦.

Old Cataract, by the Ferial Gardens (☎097/316-000, fax 316-011). A splendid Edwardian-Moorish relic, tastefully refurbished. River-facing rooms with glorious views, and others overlooking a fine garden. For US$700 a night you can stay in the Agatha Christie or King Farouk suite. Shares all facilities with the *New Cataract*. ⑧.

The Town

Ignoring the residential and industrial suburbs (as every tourist does) greatly simplifies **orientation**. Although Aswan's sinuous **Corniche** follows the river bank for over 4km, most things worth noting lie along the 1500-metre stretch between the Palace of Culture and **Ferial Gardens** (where the road swings inland), culminating in the *Old Cataract Hotel* facing the southern end of **Elephantine Island**. Otherwise, the main focus of interest is **Sharia al-Souk** (aka Sharia Sa'ad Zaghloul), which runs two to three blocks inland as it snakes down from the train station to Sharia Abbas Farid. For about half this distance it is paralleled by another busy thoroughfare, **Sharia Abtal el-Tahrir**, which runs ever closer to the Corniche but never quite touches it, and finishes up as a narrow backstreet (not all the streets off the bazaar appear on our **map** of town).

The bazaar and Corniche

Aswan's **bazaar** is renowned as the best in Egypt outside Cairo, and is not yet entirely corrupted by tourism. Traditional wares such as spices, ebony, basketwork and rugs are still in evidence, but souvenir shops are gradually forcing humdrum vendors into the alleys off Sharia al-Souk. Nonetheless, it's a pleasure to wander around, with its smells and colours evoking the Sudan and camel caravans across the Sahara. Fresh produce is chiefly sold around the junction of Sharia Saiyida Nafisa (running inland from the *Isis Hotel*) and Sharia al-Souk, and at the station end of the latter, where pickled fish is displayed in jars. Shop in the morning, since quality drops as the temperature rises. Conversely, the spice, textiles and jewellery souks are barely active before 3pm, but thronged after sundown. The most attractive part is the stretch of tall wooden shopfronts to the north of Sharia Abdel Magid Abu Zid, mostly given over to souvenirs.

The city's **Corniche** is the finest in the country, less for its architecture (which is mostly modern and undistinguished) than for the superb vista of Elephantine Island, and feluccas gliding over the water like quill pens across papyrus, with the tawny wastes of the Western Desert on the far bank. Unfortunately, you can't walk along the esplanade without being pestered by boatmen or their juvenile sidekicks; stay on the other side of the street and they'll leave you alone. Sunset is best enjoyed from the rockbound **Ferial Gardens** or the grand terrace of the **Old Cataract Hotel** (featured in the movie *Death on the Nile*), which afford a sublime view of Elephantine's headland and the smaller islands beyond.

Two reasons for going further are visible on the hillside beyond the *Old Cataract*. Halfway up is a gleaming structure resembling a modernistic *qasr*, housing the Nubia Museum, which contains 5000 exhibits and serves as a cultural centre. Higher uphill above the *Basma Hotel* stands a derelict mud-brick **fort** with a watchtower, built in Mohammed Ali's time, which offers a great view of the First Cataract and the Eastern Desert, and the Fatimid Cemetery in the other direction.

The Nubia Museum

The Nubia Museum (daily: winter 9am–1pm & 5–9pm; summer 9am–1pm & 6–10pm; £E20, camera permit £E10, camcorder £E20), partly funded by UNESCO, opened in 1998 and has proven a big success. It houses an excellent collection of artefacts from the realm of Nubia (roughly Aswan to south of Khartoum), and the combination of well-organized exhibits and clear labelling in English make this a "must see" introduction to the history and culture of the Nubians.

On entering you will see a scale model of the Nile Valley sites, which helps put the magnitude of ancient Egypt's architectural achievements into perspective. The museum traces the formation of the Nile Valley and the peoples of the region from pre-history through to the present, including sections on the cult of Isis, the spread of Christianity and Islam, and finally the massive **UNESCO project** to move some of Nubia's monuments – currently endangered by the rising waters of Lake Nasser – onto higher ground. The *piece de resistance* is the central exhibition hall which contains tombstones, frescoes and statues, the most imposing of which is an eight-metre high Ramses II, built by Setau, the Viceroy of Kush, and which still holds traces of its original colour.

There follows an impressive exhibition of Nubian culture and crafts – some of the human models looking scarily alive. The garden houses further monuments and exhibits, including the mausoleum of 77 *wali* (venerated Muslim sheikhs), a traditional Nubian house, and a cave containing rock art removed from now inundated areas.

The Museum is situated south-east of *The Old Cataract* about thirty minutes' walk from the town centre, though most people take taxis (£E10 return).

Elephantine Island

Elephantine Island takes its name from the huge black rocks clustered around its southern end, which resemble a herd of pachyderms bathing in the river. Its spectacular beauty is marred only by the towering *Aswan Oberoi Hotel*, reached by its own private ferry and cut off from the rest of the island by a lofty fence. (An even larger hotel lies semi-constructed beyond the *Oberoi* and seems likely to remain unfinished as investors have backed out.).

South of this, three **Nubian villages** nestle amidst lush palm groves, their houses painted sky-blue, pink or yellow and often decorated with *Hadj* scenes. Alongside the houses run mud-brick alleys where chickens peck around in the dust and tethered goats chew garbage. The villagers prefer foreigners to keep out unless invited in, as they don't want to become a tourist sideshow. However, this doesn't cause any problems since all the tourist attractions are at the southern end of the island, accessible by public **ferries** from the landing stage near EgyptAir; ferries also run from a second landing stage a little further north, opposite Thomas Cook (every 15min 6am–10pm; 25pt). Alternatively you could get there by felucca (negotiable rates), which dock just below the Aswan Museum.

The Aswan Musuem

The small **Aswan Museum** (daily: winter 8.30am–5pm; summer 8.30am–6pm; £E10 ticket also valid for the Nilometer and ruins further south) casts light on the island's past, when its southern end was occupied by the town of *Yebu* (meaning both "elephant" and "ivory" in the ancient Egyptian language). Most of the museum's best exhibits have been moved to the Nubia Museum, but a mummified gazelle and jewellery found at the island's Temple of Satet are worth a look. The museum was originally the villa of Sir William Willcocks, who designed the first Aswan Dam, and is set amidst fragrant subtropical **gardens**. Come back and enjoy them once you've visited the Nilometer and the ruins of Yebu.

The Nilometer

In ancient times the **Nilometer** at Aswan was the first to measure the river's rise, enabling priests to calculate the height of the inundation, crop yields over the next year and the rate of taxation (which peasants paid in kind). Ninety enclosed rock-hewn steps lead down to a square shaft by the riverside; the stair walls are graduated in Arabic, Roman and (extremely faint) pharaonic numerals, reflecting its usage in ancient times and during the late nineteenth century. To get there from the museum, follow the path southwards for 300m to find a sycamore tree (the pharaonic symbol of the tree-goddess, associated with Nut and Hathor), which shades the structure. Its custodian keeps the barbed-wire gate shut in the hope of exacting *baksheesh*.

Should you approach the Nilometer by river, notice the rock embankments to the south, which bear **inscriptions** from the reigns of Tuthmosis III, Amenophis III and the XXVII Dynasty ruler Psammetichus II.

The ruins of Yebu

The southern end of the island is littered with the **ruins** of the ancient town, which covered nearly two square kilometres by Ptolemaic times. To the southwest of the Nilometer, a massive platform and foundation blocks mark the site of the **Temple of Khnum**, god of the Aswan nome, founded in the Old Kingdom (when it accounted for two-thirds of the town's area) but entirely rebuilt during the XXX Dynasty. On its north side are the remains of pillars painted by the Romans, and Greek inscriptions; to the west stands the imposing gateway added by Alexander II, shown here worshipping Khnum.

Depending on the state of excavations, parts of the area to the north may be off-limits. Immediately to the north lies a Greco-Roman **Necropolis of Sacred Rams**, unearthed in 1906. Further to the northwest stands the small **Temple of Hekayib**, a VI Dynasty nomarch buried in the Tombs of the Nobles (see p.386) who was later deified; the steles and inscriptions found here by Labib Habachi in 1946 revealed much about Aswan during the Middle Kingdom.

Due east lies a **Temple of Satet** where excavations continue to produce discoveries (closed to visitors). Built by Queen Hatshepsut around 1490 BC, it was the last of more than thirty such temples on this site, dating back four millennia, dedicated to the goddess who incarnated the fertile aspect of the inundation. Beneath the temples, German archeologists have found a shaft leading 19m into the granite bedrock, where a natural **whirl hole** is thought to have amplified the sounds of the rising water table (the first indication of the life-giving annual flood) and was revered as the "Voice of the Nile". Although the High Dam has since silenced its voice, a half-buried statue near the temple still draws new brides and barren women longing for the gift of fertility.

To the southwest of Khnum's temple, the layered **remains of ancient houses** have yielded Aramaic papyri attesting to a sizeable **Jewish colony** on Elephantine in the sixth century BC. A military order by Darius II permitting the Yebu garrison to observe Passover in 419 BC suggests that they defended the southernmost border of the Persian empire. Although nothing remains of their temple to Yahweh, the German team have used leftover blocks from Kalabsha (see p.402) to reconstruct a **Ptolemaic sanctuary** with decorations added by the Nubian Pharaoh Arkamani in the third century BC, at the southern tip of the island.

The rocky passage between Elephantine and Amun Island looks its best from a felucca. If you're not already waterborne, the surrounding coves are frequented by lads who'll happily sail you across to the Island of Plants or the west bank, but drive a hard bargain. **Amun Island** itself features a reclusive *Club Med*, reached by private ferry from a landing stage near the telephone office. Further south you'll see a new and grander hotel complex on **Isis Island**, likewise accessible by private ferry.

The Island of Plants

Almost hidden from town by the bulk of Elephantine, the smaller, lusher **Island of Plants** (*Geziret an-Nabatat*) is still commonly referred to by tourists as "Kitchener's Island". Presented with the island in gratitude for his military exploits in the Sudan, Consul-General Kitchener here indulged his passion for exotic flora, importing shrubs and seeds from as far afield as India and Malaysia. This beautiful island-wide **botanical garden** (daily 7am–sunset; until 5/6pm in summer; £E5) is an ideal place to spend the afternoon, having seen the other sites, with colourful **birdlife** flitting through the trees.

The island is accessible by local ferry (50pt from the west side of Elephantine Island), rowing boat or felucca (£E3–5 from the west bank or Elephantine Island).

The west bank

The main attractions on the **west bank** of the river are the **Mausoleum of the Aga Khan** and the desert **Monastery of St Simeon**. Unless you're prepared to hike for over 2km across the hills, the more northerly **Tombs of the Nobles** are best visited as a separate excursion. When negotiating a price for a felucca, be sure to establish how long you plan to spend at both sites.

The Aga Khan's Mausoleum

Just uphill from the embankment is a walled estate comprising a private villa and riverside garden, and a stairway ascending the barren hillside to the **Mausoleum of the Aga Khan** (Tues–Sun 9am–1pm; free). Outwardly modelled on the Fatimid tombs of Cairo, its open court culminates in a Carrara marble *mihrab* and sarcophagus, enshrining Aga Khan III, the 48th Imam of the Isma'ili sect of Shi'ite Muslims, who was weighed in jewels for his diamond jubilee in 1945. After his death in 1957, his tomb attracted hordes of pilgrims, whose camps posed a health hazard until the government forbade mass pilgrimages.

The Aga Khan was initially drawn to Aswan by its climate and hot sands, which relieved his rheumatism; subsequently he fell in love with its beauty, built a villa and spent every winter here. His widow, the Begum, still does likewise, and ensures that a fresh red rose is placed on his sarcophagus every day; legend has it that when none were available in Egypt, a rose was flown in by private plane from Paris on six successive days. Currently you can walk around the outside, but not enter the mausoleum.

The Monastery of St Simeon

Unless you walk across the desert from the Tombs of the Nobles (see below), the ruined **Monastery of St Simeon** (daily 7am–5pm; £E12) must be approached from the valley below. You can either slog uphill through soft sand (30min) or rent a camel from the pack near the landing stage (£E35 round trip with half an hour's waiting; a camel seats two); the latter is more fun and less effort, but whichever way you approach, it's a good idea to bring water.

Founded in the seventh century and rebuilt in the tenth, *Deir Anba Samaan* crowns the head of a desert valley, which used to be cultivated down to the river's edge. Built like a fortress, it was originally dedicated to Anba Hadra, a local saint of the fourth century who encountered a funeral procession the day after his wedding and decided to renounce the world for a hermit's cave before the marriage was consummated. From here, monks made evangelical forays into Nubia, where they converted the Kingdom of the Nobatae to Christianity. After the Muslim conquest, the Nobatae used the monastery as a base during their own incursions into Egypt, until Salah al-Din had it wrecked in 1173.

One of the custodians will show you around the split-level complex, whose lower storeys are made of stone, the upper ones of mud-brick. The now-roofless **Basilica** bears traces of frescoes of the Apostles, their faces scratched out by Muslim iconoclasts. In a nearby chamber with a font, you're shown the place where St Simeon (about whom little is known) used to stand sleeplessly reading the Bible, with his beard tied to the ceiling so as to deliver a painful tug if he nodded off. The central **Keep** has room for three hundred monks sleeping five to a cell, a tunnel-like refectory, bathhouse, ovens and bakeries (notice the millstones). Beware of sheer drops when exploring. At sunset the surrounding desert turns madder-red and violet; foxes emerge to hunt and hawks soar aloft.

The Tombs of the Nobles

Relatively few tourists bother with the **Tombs of the Nobles** (daily 7am–5pm; £E12, camera permits £E10 per tomb), which are hewn into the hillside further up the west bank and whose artwork has an immediacy and concern for everyday life that makes a refreshing change from royal art. If you're curious, **local ferries** ply between the station end of the Corniche and the landing stage of the west bank village of **ASWAN MIN GHARB** (every 30min 6am–10pm). The fare is 25pt, but they'll try to charge £E1 (preferably each way). At the site kiosk, beware of being palmed off with used **tickets**. As there are no slides of these tombs available commercially, consider buying a couple of photo permits; the custodian might let you photograph additional tombs without extra permits, for *baksheesh*. In order to combine a visit with the monastery and mausoleum, start early with the tombs, then ascend to the domed hilltop Muslim shrine known as **Qubbet el-Hawa** (Tomb of the Wind), and walk across the desert to St Simeon's (45min; bring plenty of water). Alternatively you could do the route in reverse, being dropped off below the monastery from which point you can hire a camel to do the legwork between the sites for you (£E45 for two people on one camel).

The Tombs of the Nobles lie at different heights (**Old and Middle Kingdom** ones uppermost, **Roman** tombs nearest the waterline), and are numbered in ascending order from south to north. Taking the path up from the ticket kiosk you reach the high-numbered ones first.

TOMB OF SIRENPUT I (#36)

Turn right at the top of the steps and follow the path downhill around the cliffside to find the tomb of **Sirenput I**, overseer of the priests of Khnum and Satet and Guardian of the South during the XII Dynasty. The six pillars of its vestibule bear portraits and biographical texts. On the left-hand wall he watches bulls fighting, and spears fish from a papyrus raft, accompanied by his sandal-bearer, sons and dog. On the opposite wall he's portrayed with his mutt and bow-carrier, and also sitting above them in a garden with his mother, wife and daughters, being entertained by singers; the lower register shows three men gambling. Amongst the badly damaged murals in the hall beyond, you can just discern fowlers with a net (on the lower right wall), a hieroglyphic biography (left), and a marsh-hunting scene (centre). Beyond lies a chapel with a false door set into the rear niche; the corridor to the left leads to the burial chamber.

TOMBS OF PEPI-NAKHT (#35) AND HARKHUF (UNNUMBERED)

To reach the other tombs from Sirenput I's, return to the top of the steps and follow the path southwards. Amongst a cluster of tombs to the left of the steps are two rooms ascribed to Hekayib (whose cult temple stands on Elephantine), called here by his other name, **Pepi-Nakht**. As overseer of foreign troops during the long reign of Pepi II (VI Dynasty), he led colonial campaigns in Asia and Nubia, which are related on either side of the door of the left-hand room.

A bit further south lies the (unnumbered) tomb of **Harkhuf**, who held the same position under Pepi I, Merenre and Pepi II. A badly eroded hieroglyphic biography just inside the entrance mentions his gifts to the young Pepi II, which included incense, leopard skins and ebony, and a "dancing dwarf from the land of spirits" (thought to be a pygmy from Equatorial Africa).

TOMBS OF SIRENPUT II (#31)

The largest and best-preserved tomb belongs to **Sirenput II**, who held the same offices as his father under Amenemhat II, during the apogee of the Middle Kingdom. Beyond its vestibule (with an offerings slab between the second and third pillars on the right) lies a corridor with six niches containing Osiride statues of Sirenput, still brightly coloured like his portraits on the four pillars of the chapel, where the artist's grid lines are visible in places. Best of all is the recess at the back, where Sirenput appears with his wife and son (left), attends his seated mother in a garden (right), and receives flowers from his son (centre). Notice the elephant in the upper left corner of this tableau.

TOMB OF MEKHU (#25) AND SABNI (#26)

At the top of the double ramps ascending the hillside (up which sarcophagi were dragged) are the adjacent tombs of a father and son, which are interesting for their monumentality – a large vestibule with three rows of rough-hewn pillars, flanked by niches and burial chambers – and for their story. After his father **Mekhu** was killed in Nubia, **Sabni** mounted a punitive expedition which recovered the body. As a sign of respect, Pepi II sent his own embalmers to mummify the corpse; Sabni travelled to Memphis to personally express his thanks with gifts, as related by an inscription at the entrance to his tomb. Both tombs are crudely constructed and decorated, with small obelisks at their entrances, and twin vestibules which form a single rectangular room. Sabni's chapel has columns painted with fishing and fowling scenes.

Eating and drinking

Eating out in Aswan offers the pleasures of fresh fish and Nubian dishes such as okra in spicy tomato sauce, in riverside **restaurants** which are great on balmy nights but empty when it's cold. You won't find any Chinese food, and Italian or French cuisine is limited to a few big hotels. The bazaar is good for **street food**, with *fuul* and liver sandwiches sold near the station end of the street, and fruit and nuts on every corner. There are simple **cafés** for chicken and fish meals or *kushari*, and the usual array of juice bars and coffee houses. All the Corniche places are **open** till around midnight (or later if there is custom); the cafés in the bazaar may close earlier at around 10–11pm. The cheapest place for **drinking** is the bar in the *Oscar Hotel* (Stella £E6).

Aswan Moon, on the Corniche near the *Horus*. Distinguished by its castle gate and a floating extension. Cool by day, loud and lively at night; a place to meet felucca captains and hear Nubian music. Fish, chicken, vegetable dishes and meaty *kab hala* stew. Beer and wine. Fun, but service is sometimes poor. Main dishes £E5–15, plus tax.

Aswan Panorama, on the Corniche opposite Duty Free. Serves a wide range of entrées, so-called vegetarian dishes, iced drinks and herbal teas. Try the rice pudding with nuts and rosewater. Similar prices to the *Aswan Moon*.

El-Madina, Sharia al-Souk, near the *Cleopatra*. Clean, share-a-table diner with set meals (£E6–16) of liver, chicken or fish with salad, *tahina*, vegetable stew, rice, bread and Coke. No alcohol.

El-Masry, Sharia Abdel Magid Abu Zid. Nice, authentic place decorated in arabesque tiles, serving tasty meals based around fish or kebab. Moderate prices. No alcohol.

El-Shatti, on the riverside, opposite *Thomas Cook*. Has several pleasant terraces, okay for drinking beer (£E6), but the food is often poorly cooked. Inexpensive.

Emy, on a boat on the Corniche, just south of the *Aswan Moon*. Slightly shabbier and less popular than the *Moon*, but with better views and a good breeze. Tasty food at reasonable prices (mains £E9–10) in a tranquil setting.

Mona Lisa, on the Corniche, near the *Aswan Moon*. A sweatbox during the summer, with painfully slow service at lunchtime, but the food is okay and the fruit-juice cocktails delicious. Prices are lower than at the *Aswan*. Sells beer (£E6).

Nubian Restaurant, on a tiny island just south of Elephantine. Tasty Nubian set meals (£E55) and a show after dinner. Serves beer and wine. Free transport from the dock opposite EgyptAir. Expensive.

Old Cataract Buffet, on the hotel terrace from 4pm to sunset. Earl Grey tea, cakes and sandwiches (£E35); after sunset the terrace is free for non-residents.

Royal Restaurant, Pub and Coffee Shop, on the Corniche, above Duty Free. Clean, spacious place with good views, Internet access, TV, beers (£E6) and reasonable food, but not much in the way of character. Inexpensive.

Zoom, Sharia al-Souk, just north of the *El-Madina*. No-frills sit-down patisserie with ice cream and sticky cakes; cheap – mostly under £E1.50.

Activities and entertainments

Traditional Aswani diversions are promenading along the Corniche and bazaar, meeting friends in riverside restaurants, and listening to Nubian music. For tourists, during the day you can go swimming – or you could go in search of alligators, by boat; at night there's the Philae Sound and Light show and nightclubs to consider.

Swimming – and alligators in the Nile

Sooner or later, you'll find the idea of **swimming** irresistible. Non-residents may use the pools at the *Cleopatra* (£E8) and *Isis* (£20), but foreigners aren't admitted to the municipal baths on the Corniche. Although local boys happily bathe in the Nile, tourists seldom do for fear of bilharzia, and would be even less inclined if they knew that some **alligators** have slipped through the High Dam and established a breeding colony just upriver from Aswan. However, the tourist office asserts that they are too nervous of humans to pose a threat, and can arrange a **boat trip** to view them if anybody is interested. There are also some crocodile farms on Lake Nasser, which are harder to reach.

Music and nightclubs

Although Nubian stars like Hassan Jazuli and Khitr al-Atar only visit town occasionally, taped music plays everywhere and impromptu sounds can be heard in cafés and backstreets, or sometimes at Ferial Gardens. Live bands are chiefly found at weddings, during the summer months. Over winter, locals flock to see the **Nubian Folk Troupe** perform stories of village life, wedding and harvest numbers and the famous Nubian stick dance, which pantomimes a sword fight. Performances at Aswan's Soviet-inspired **Palace of Culture** (☎097/313-390) usually take place every night (9.30–11pm) except Friday from October to May and throughout Ramadan; tickets (roughly £E10) are sold on a first-come, first-served basis. The *Nubian Restaurant* (see above) also has nightly shows with dinner, but is expensive (£E55 not including drinks); cheaper options are to visit the *Nubian House* on Elephantine Island (£E35 for dinner and music) or the house of Omar Abdel Aziz on Sehel Island (☎097/301-514; £E25 including transport, music and dancing, and a tasty dinner in beautiful adobe surroundings). Omar can usually be found at the felucca dock opposite EgyptAir.

When not attending the **Sound and Light Show at Philae** (see p.397), package tourists usually opt for **nightclubs** in the *Oberoi* and *New Cataract* hotels, which offer a floor show of Nubian and Western music, with a minimum charge (£E30–55 per person), which is easy to exceed given the high price of drinks (ask at reception for details). The *Isis Hotel* runs a nightly **disco** (except Monday, 11pm–3am) year-round, which is usually free for non-residents.

Festivals and weddings

On **Aswan Dam Day** (January 15), the Corniche witnesses a good-natured parade of civic and military hardware; fire engines and ambulances following jeep-loads of perspiring frogmen and rubber-suited decontamination troops. To appreciate the joke, catch the farcical orgy of drilling and polishing that transpires outside the Police Department and the Governorate Building the day before.

Although Aswan itself isn't noted for religious festivals, **Nubian weddings** are celebrated on a lavish scale, with guest musicians who charge as much as £E5000. The bridegroom recoups the expense by inviting hundreds of his friends and charging them £E10 apiece, which makes summer – the wedding season – an expensive time for locals. The wedding ceremony is followed by a week of celebrations, culminating in "pigeon nights" when guests devour quantities of pigeon to increase their sexual potency. (King Farouk was said to consume the juice of six birds a day.) As guests from foreign lands are held to be auspicious, tourists are often invited (but should never presume) to attend weddings in the villages around Aswan. However, beware of crooks inveigling you to their village with a phoney invitation in the hope of getting you drunk or stoned, to rob or molest you later.

Listings

Airline EgyptAir on the Corniche (daily 8am–8pm; ☎097/315-000) and at the airport (☎097/480-568) near the High Dam, 23km south of town (£E20 by taxi). Airport police ☎097/480-509.

American Express In the *New Cataract* (Sun–Thurs 8am–5pm, Fri & Sat 9am–4pm; ☎097/306-983, fax 302-909). No longer does currency exchange, but will hold client mail and organize travel.

Banks Banque Misr (Sun–Thurs 8.30am–9pm) has a cash dispenser (Visa/MasterCard) outside; Banque du Caire (Sun–Thurs 8.30am–2pm & 3–10pm), Bank of Alexandria (Sun–Thurs 8am–2pm) and the National Bank of Egypt (Sun–Thurs 8.30am–2pm) are all on the Corniche, and change currency and travellers' cheques.

Dry-cleaners On the ground floor of the *Nubian Oasis Hotel* (50pt–£E6 per item).

Duty Free at the southern end of the Corniche (daily 10am-3pm & 7-12pm). Often poorly stocked and involves the usual shuffling from counter to counter. Alcohol and cigarettes are upstairs.

Foreign newspapers and books Sold on the Corniche near the *Horus*, *Hathor* and *Philae* hotels.

Internet Currently there are three places in Aswan, but all have to wait and connect to a provider in Cairo. *Happi Hotel* charges £E50/hr or £E5 to send or receive an email. *Royal Restaurant* (above Duty Free) is cheaper at £E30/hr or £E2.50 per email, whilst the *Rosewan Hotel* is £E60/hr and £E2 per email.

Medical emergencies The German Evangelical Hospital (☎097/302-176) near the Police Department will provide treatment and accept insurance payments later, and does check-ups (Mon–Sat 7am–noon & 4–6pm). There is also a public hospital (☎097/302-855; ambulance ☎123). Both are open 24 hours for emergencies. The tourist office can recommend doctors.

Passport office On the 2nd floor of the Police Department (Sun–Thurs 8am–2pm; ☎097/312-238). Registration all day; visa extensions mornings only.

Pharmacies El-Nile, next to the Banque du Caire on the Corniche (daily 8am–1am, closed 1–5pm on Fridays; ☎097/302-674); Galal, next to the *Happi Hotel* (daily 7am–3pm & 6–12pm; ☎097/303-011). Others are dotted all over town – ask at your hotel for the nearest.

Photo developing Photo Sabry on the Corniche near EgyptAir (Sat–Thurs 9am–2pm & 6.30–11.30pm, Fri 7–11pm; ☎097/306-452). Sells film.

Post office Main GPO (daily except Fri 8am–2pm) near the Rowing Club; the section for poste restante (Sat–Thurs 9am–2pm) is one block inland behind the Bank of Alexandria. Outward-bound mail arrives quicker if posted from a major hotel.

Telephones International calls can be made from the 24-hour telephone office near EgyptAir, or by using a phonecard in the branch in the station (daily 8am–10pm). It costs less to send a fax at the telephone office than at the Business Centre one block south of the Police Department, or in major hotels. Off-peak rates 8pm–8am.

Thomas Cook On the Corniche near the Police Department (daily 8am–8pm; ☎097/304-011, fax 306-209). Changes money, sells cheques and arranges tours to Abu Simbel.

Excursions from Aswan

Aswan is a base for **excursions** to numerous sites, some of which can only be reached from here, while others are also accessible from Luxor. Providing you start early enough, it's possible to fit two or more sites into a **full day's itinerary**, albeit one that doesn't allow you to linger at each place for long. Much depends on whether you engage a private taxi or rely on public transport, which is more time-consuming. Some tourists try to cram the highlights into two long day-trips: south to Abu Simbel and Philae; and north to Kom Ombo, Edfu and Esna.

The classic half-day excursion is to **Philae Island** with its lovely Temple of Isis, situated in the lake between the **Aswan Dams**. Typically, groups of tourists rent a private taxi to take them to the Philae launch dock, then the dams and back to Aswan, briefly visiting the **Unfinished Obelisk** and the **Fatimid Cemetery** on the outskirts of town (another short trip from town is to **Sehel Island**). For a four-hour tour (which suffices), four-seater taxis should accept about £E50; larger Peugeot 504s, seating seven or eight, roughly £E65. For £E60–80, you can probably persuade them to extend the tour to include **Kalabsha Temple**, which otherwise entails a separate trip.

As far as **Abu Simbel** goes (and it *is* far), at the time of writing the only way for foreigners to get there was by plane, or on a Lake Nasser Cruise – both expensive options. The road closed shortly after the Hatshepsut Massacre in November 1997, and although it has reopened for Egyptians, foreigners are still forbidden to travel on it.

The other main circuit takes in one or more of the **temples between Aswan and Luxor**. Relying on public transport, you could feasibly combine **Kom Ombo** with **Edfu**, but to see **Esna** as well really calls for a private taxi. Expect to pay £E150 for a four-seater taxi, or nearer £E200 for a larger vehicle to take you to each site for an hour and then on to Luxor. Currently you have to travel in one of three daily convoys. By starting early, it's also possible to combine Kom Ombo and/or Edfu with the **Camel**

Market at Darow (see under respective towns for details). Alternatively, you can visit these temples while sailing between Aswan and Luxor in a felucca (see p.392).

The sites nearer town are described below; for accounts of the Aswan Dams, Philae, Kalabsha Temple and Abu Simbel, see the subsequent sections; for information on moving on from Aswan and felucca trips see below.

The Unfinished Obelisk and the Fatimid Cemetery

Past the Aswan campsite, off the highway south, is one of the **granite quarries** that supplied fine red stone for temples and colossi in ancient times (daily 7am–5pm; £E12). In one section lies a gigantic **Unfinished Obelisk**, roughly dressed and nearly cut free from the bedrock, but abandoned after a flaw in the stone was discovered. Had it been finished, the obelisk would have weighed 1168 tons and stood nearly 42 metres high. It's reckoned that this was the intended mate for the so-called Lateran Obelisk in Rome, which originally stood before the temple of Tuthmosis III at Karnak and is still credited as being the largest obelisk in the world. From chisel marks and abandoned tools, archeologists have been able to deduce pharaonic quarrying techniques, such as soaking wooden wedges to split fissures, and using quartz sand slurry as an abrasive.

Beside the turn-off and sprawling back towards town are hundreds of mud-brick tombs ranging from simple enclosures to complex domed cubes. This veritable lexicon of Islamic funerary architecture is known as the **Fatimid Cemetery**, though the majority of tombs actually date from Tulunid times. Unfortunately, most of their marble inscriptions were removed to Cairo in 1887 without any record of their original locations, leaving the tombs starkly unadorned.

Though neither of these sites is worth the effort of getting there by yourself, which involves a two-kilometre walk or bike ride, taxi tours to Philae often stop here on the way back for a brief look.

Sehel Island and the First Cataract

Travellers enamoured of felucca journeys (see overleaf) should consider visiting **Sehel Island**, 4km upriver. With a strong wind behind you, it can be reached in an hour or so; on calmer days, allow longer. The official rate for a three-hour felucca trip is about £E45. Bring water and a hat, and come well shod: although the river is cool, the rocks and sand are scorchingly hot. Landing on the east side of the island, you may be lured into the **Nubian village** (to the west) by promises of tea, or mobbed by children eager to lead you to the "ruins" (south); the expected *baksheesh* supplements family incomes.

Sehel is dominated by two hills of jumbled boulders bearing over 250 inscriptions from the Middle Kingdom until Ptolemaic times, "bruised" rather than carved into the weathered granite. The majority record Egyptian expeditions beyond the First Cataract or prayers of gratitude for their safe return, but atop the eastern hill you'll find a Ptolemaic **Famine Stele** (#81). Backdated to the reign of Zoser, it relates how he ended a seven-year famine during the III Dynasty by placating Khnum, god of the cataract, with a new temple on Sehel and the return of lands confiscated from his cult centre at Esna, which had provoked Khnum to withhold the inundation.

The summit provides a superb view of the **First Cataract**, a cliff-bound stretch of river divided into channels by outcrops of granite. Before the Aswan Dams, the waters foamed and boiled, making the cataract a fearsome obstacle to upriver travel. Until early last century, it was necessary to offload cargo and transport it overland while the lightened boats risked rowing against the rapids. Amelia Edwards described "the leap – the dead fall – the staggering rush forward", waves and spray flooding the boat and the oars audibly scraping the rocks on either side.

In ancient times the cataract was credited as being the source of the Nile (which was believed to flow south into Nubia as well as north through Egypt) and the abode of the

FELUCCA JOURNEYS AND CRUISES BETWEEN ASWAN AND LUXOR

The Nile's timeless scenery is best appreciated on longer felucca journeys between Aswan and Luxor, or aboard a Nile cruiser. While cruisers are more comfortable and predictable, feluccas offer an unforgettable, uniquely Egyptian experience, which many travellers rate as the highlight of their trip – though tales of misery aren't uncommon either. Whether your felucca trip is blissful or boring, tragicomic or simply unpleasant, largely depends on a host of factors and your own expectations.

Firstly, bear in mind the time of year and **conditions on the river**. Feluccas are dependent on the wind, which nearly always blows south. Travelling downstream (towards Luxor) therefore involves constant tacking, unless you simply drift with the sluggish current. Travelling upstream towards Aswan you'll make better **time** with the wind behind you, but face being becalmed if it drops – as happens between Edfu and Kom Ombo, especially in summer, which is why most tourists start from Aswan. During winter, when daylight hours are short, anyone sailing from there is unlikely to reach **Edfu** in less than three nights. As feluccas are prohibited from sailing after 8pm, most stop at sunset for an evening round a campfire, enlivened by Nubian singing and drumming. Each day will be different from the last: stow your watch and take things as they come.

Another crucial factor is the **water level**. Between October and May, so little is allowed through the Aswan Dam that feluccas must be careful near shore; the object is to conserve water for the summer, but in drought years the Nile may become so shallow that cruise boats cannot use the river at all. Lastly, from June 1–16 every year, the Esna lock is closed for maintenance, and boats may only pass through in the early morning. Year-round most felucca trips end at **Edfu**.

ARRANGING A FELUCCA TRIP

Assembling a group of five to eight people is easily done by asking around in Corniche restaurants or responding to messages posted in the tourist office. Since you'll be spending many hours in close proximity, the character and habits of your fellow travellers are a prime consideration (vid. Sartre, "Hell is other people"). Women will benefit from teaming up with a couple of men for the duration: an all-female group is likely to have problems.

The **tourist office** can recommend good captains and where to find them, but won't deliver a verdict on guys with whom you've already started negotiations. Organizing things through a hotel will probably work out costlier than finding your own captain, and in the event of a dispute it will be harder to recover any cash, since the hotel will have taken a hefty commission. On the other hand, hotels usually vet their captains, minimizing the risk of you ending up with a baddie. Try socializing with a few before **choosing a captain** and opening negotiations. Would-be voyagers are entitled to a free cruise around Aswan "bay" to check out the boat and its crew in action. Typically, a large vessel has an English-speaking Nubian captain and carries up to eight passengers who sleep either ashore after the boat has tied up, or on mattresses aboard. Nights are chilly (and maybe damp) for much of the year, so a sleeping bag or plenty of blankets are essential. Ensure that the **boat** has a canvas awning to protect you from the sun (which doubles as a tent at night), adequate mattresses, a jerry can for water, a kerosene stove and lamp, proper cutlery and a padlocked luggage hold. It is unwise to travel on a felucca lacking any of these items. Some captains have been guilty of taking tourists for a jaunt on a

deity who controlled the inundation (either Hapy or Khnum, or perhaps both working in tandem). The foaming waters were thought to well up from a subterranean cavern where the Nile-god dwelt. Offerings continued to be made at Sehel even after its putative location shifted to Biga Island during the Late Period or Ptolemaic times (see "Philae", p.397).

smart boat, and then substituting an inferior vessel (or crew) on the day of departure. If this happens, simply refuse to set sail.

RATES AND REGISTRATION

Rates vary according to the length and duration of the journey, but also (unofficially) with fluctuating demand. The tourist office quotes £E55 per person (including food) for a group of six to eight to sail between Aswan and Edfu over two nights, stopping at Kom Ombo en route. Many travellers prefer to sail only as far as Edfu (£E45), or even just to Kom Ombo (£E25), travelling on to Luxor or returning to Aswan by *service* taxi. Though most captains will accept less in the summer, travellers who push the price too low risk being robbed by a crew bent on getting proper remuneration. Don't pay the whole amount until you reach your destination, lest the boat "break down" and curtail the trip prematurely, and be sure that all members of the group know what has been negotiated, to ensure solidarity in the event of a dispute with the crew.

Travellers are required to register with the River Police before leaving Aswan or Luxor. Felucca captains will organize this if passengers surrender their passports (or two photocopies of the relevant pages), or it can be done by local travel agencies – all of which charge £E5 per person for the effort, though there is no official fee.

HYGIENE

There's a real risk of getting sick on a felucca journey if hygiene precautions aren't observed. Bring extra strong sterilizing tablets to purify the jerry can of Nile water used for washing up (one tab per 25 litres); also purchase carbolic soap and be sure that everyone uses it (food is mostly eaten with fingers); burn rubbish and bury excrement (the Nile's banks are badly littered) – few captains will bother with any health precautions unless pressed. Also strongly recommended are a hat and sunscreen (the river feels cool but reflects sunlight with great intensity) and bug repellent (the shallows swarm with mosquitoes).

RECOMMENDED FELUCCAS

Good boats include *Wien Magic Express*, owned by Omar Abdel Aziz, who can usually be found at the felucca dock opposite EgyptAir, or on ☎097/301-504 in the evenings; also *Jamaica* and six other boats owned by a family who live on Elephantine Island near the more northerly local ferry landing stage – "Captain Jamaica" (aka Ahmed Gendor) runs the show.

CRUISE BOATS

Nile cruise boats offer a more comfortable ride and better meals, at the cost of distancing you from the river and lumping you in with a large group and a rigid schedule. All of them have bars and restaurants, and pools are *de rigueur* on the ritzier vessels. You should be able to find a berth at short notice in Luxor or Aswan without much trouble, though getting the best deal will require some hunting. If you've got the patience, try negotiating directly with the reception staff on boats moored along the Corniche. Travel agents can offer good deals, too, but the price will inevitably include a commission. It's possible to pay as little as US$50 per day for a double cabin and meals for two. Ask around.

Moving on

The most important considerations with onward travel are likely to be **restrictions for foreigners**; security measures in force at time of writing remain subject to change (see box on p.254).

Private and service taxis

The convoy rule definitely applies to **private taxis** to Kom Ombo and other points north of Aswan, so if you're renting a *special* taxi for an excursion, be prepared to start with the police convoy even if you quit it later. The main *service* taxi depot beyond the train tracks serves **Darow** and **Kom Ombo** (£E1.50), **Edfu** (£E3.50), **Esna** (£E6), **Luxor** (£E8) and other points north. **Aswan environs**, **Hazan/the Old Dam** (50pt) and **points south** are served by a smaller depot on a side street around the corner from the *Abu Simbel Hotel*.

Buses

Slower public **buses** feel safer than taxis, but have their own drawbacks. The police have decreed that tourists may only ride in buses in the convoy, so you may not be allowed to buy tickets for many of the buses **between Aswan and Luxor** (4hr; £E8), which stop at each town en route, or are "expresses" that only call at **Kom Ombo**, **Edfu** and **Esna**. There are two direct A/C buses from Aswan to **Cairo** (13hr), leaving at 3.30pm (£E55) and 6.30pm (£E50). Travellers bound for the Red Sea Coast or Sinai can use one of the five daily buses which go to **Hurghada** (7hr; £E25–40) and then on to **Suez** (12hr; £E45).

Trains

It's only worth using trains for long hauls. There are six daily services to **Luxor** (4hr; 1st class £E22, A/C 2nd class £E15), which continue on to **Cairo** (14hr; 1st class £E63, A/C 2nd class £E37), but tourists are only allowed to buy tickets for two of these trains (departing at 5am and 8.45pm), while the only sleeper service open to them is the deluxe *wagons-lits* (£E313), leaving at 5.15pm. Most tourists economize by travelling on a regular train, as both 1st and A/C 2nd class have comfortable seating that makes an overnight journey quite tolerable.

Flights

For those with sufficient money, EgyptAir does flights to Luxor (45min; US$56), Cairo (90min; US$169) and Abu Simbel (30min; US$85). The prices quoted are one-way fares – except for Abu Simbel, which is usually visited on a day-return ticket that includes transfers between the temple and the airport. Several charter companies such as Luxor Air, Orca, Pharaoh and Scarabee now run flights to Abu Simbel for around $5–10 less than EgyptAir, but flights are subject to demand and, as such, are less reliable than EgyptAir.

The Aswan Dams

Under a good administration the Nile gains on the desert;
under a bad one the desert gains on the Nile.

Napoleon

The **Aswan Dams** attest that Egypt's fundamental dilemma is more intractable than suggested by John Gunther's pithy diagnosis: "Make more land. Make fewer people. Either solution would alleviate the problem, but neither is easy." Although each dam has brought large areas under cultivation, boosted agricultural productivity and provided hydroelectricity for industry, the gains have been eroded by a population explosion that again threatens to outstrip resources.

Ever conscious of the dams' significance, Egyptians are inclined to view them as a tourist attraction, whereas most foreigners simply regard the edifices as a route to the temples of Abu Simbel, Philae and Kalabsha, which were reassembled on higher ground following construction of the High Dam. Views from the top of the dams are spectacular, though, so don't begrudge tours' obligatory stopovers.

The Old Dam

Just upriver from the First Cataract stands the old **Aswan Dam**, built by the British (1898–1902) and subsequently twice raised to increase its capacity. Once the largest dam in the world, it stands 50m tall, 2000m long, 30m thick at the base and 11m at the top. Driving across, you'll notice the 180 sluice gates that used to be opened during the inundation and then gradually closed as the river level dropped, preserving a semi-natural flood cycle. Now that its storage and irrigation functions have been taken over by the High Dam, it chiefly serves to generate hydroelectricity for the nearby Kima factory, producing chemical fertilizers. Philae is visible amongst the islands to the south of the dam.

Near the eastern end of the dam lies a former Reservoir Colony, now called **HAZAN**, where colonial villas nestle amidst peaceful gardens.

The High Dam (Al-Sadd al-Ali)

By 1952 it was apparent that the Aswan Dam could no longer satisfy Egypt's needs nor guarantee security from famine. Nasser pledged to build a new **High Dam**, 6km upstream, that would secure Egypt's future, power new industries and bring electricity to every village. When the World Bank reneged on its promised loan under pressure from the US, Nasser nationalized the Suez Canal to generate revenue for the project and turned to the USSR for assistance. The dam's construction (1960–71) outlasted his lifetime, however, as well as the era of Soviet–Egyptian collaboration. When Egypt decided to install more powerful turbine generators in the late 1980s, they were bought from America.

Lake Nasser and environmental consequences

The most visible consequence of the High Dam is **Lake Nasser**, which backs up for nearly 500km, well into Sudan. Over 180m deep in places, with a surface area of 6000 square kilometres, the lake is the world's largest reservoir. During the decade of drought that saw the Nile fall to its lowest level in 350 years, it saved Egypt from the famine that wracked Ethiopia and Sudan. When heavy rainfall caused the Nile to flood in August 1988, the High Dam prevented Aswan from being inundated like Khartoum. Since a dam burst would wash most of Egypt's population into the Mediterranean, its security is paramount. The surrounding hills bristle with radar installations and anti-aircraft missiles; threats to bomb the dam made by Israel during the 1967 and 1973 wars, and by Gadaffi in 1984, have not been forgotten.

Although its human, cultural and environmental costs are still being evaluated, the dam has delivered most of its promised **benefits**. Egypt has been able to convert 700,000 *feddans* (a measurement of land roughly equal to one acre) of cultivated land from the ancient basin system of irrigation to perennial irrigation – doubling or tripling the number of harvests – and to reclaim over one million *feddans* of desert. The dam's turbines have powered a 30 percent expansion of industrial capacity, too; humming pylons carry megavolts to Aswan's chemical and cement factories, the Helwan Iron and Steel Mill, and the refineries of Suez. A fledgling fishing industry on Lake Nasser provides an additional source of protein and a livelihood for the locals. Evaporation from the lake has caused haze, clouds and even rainfall over previously arid regions, and the water table beneath the Sahara has risen as far away as Algeria. The main losers have been the **Nubians**, whose homeland was submerged by Lake Nasser (see p.376).

Other **environmental consequences** are still being assessed. Because the dam traps the silt that once renewed Egypt's fields, farmers now rely on *Nitrokima* fertilizers, which have entered the food chain. The soil salinity caused by perennial irrigation can only be prevented by extensive drainage projects, which create breeding grounds for mosquitoes and bilharzia-carrying snails. Ancient monuments have been affected by damp and salt-encrustation, blamed on the rising water table and greater humidity. Some even think that this has made Egypt more vulnerable to earthquakes. And with no silty deposits to replenish it, the Delta coastline is rapidly being eroded by the Mediterranean.

It's estimated that the lake itself will be filled by silt within five hundred years. But whereas some reckon that the Nubian desert may have reverted to its prehistoric lushness by then, others fear international conflicts over water resources within the first century of the new millennium. Civil wars have hitherto prevented Ethiopia and Sudan from harnessing the White Nile and the watery Sudd for their own needs, but Egypt has already expressed its objections, citing a vested interest in the Nile's headwaters. Former UN Secretary-General Boutros-Boutros Ghali prophesied that Egypt may go to war over the Nile during this century.

Visiting the High Dam

The High Dam can be crossed anytime between 7am and 5pm; all vehicle passengers are charged a £E5 **toll**, and may also have to show their passports. Along the western approach, a giant lotus-blossom **tower** built to commemorate Soviet–Egyptian friendship now symbolizes goodwill and the dam's benefits, as depicted in heroic, Socialist Realist bas-reliefs; its observation deck, reached by elevator, is sometimes open. Off the road at the east end of the dam is a **visitor's pavilion** (daily 7am–5pm), which the curator will unlock for *baksheesh*. Exhibits include a fifteen-metre-high model of the dam, plans for its construction (in Russian and Arabic), and a photo narrative of the relocation of Abu Simbel.

However, unless you ask to visit the tower (*burg*) or "model" (*mekat*), taxis will only **stop midway across the dam** for a brief look. From this vantage point the dam's height (111m) is masked by the cantilever, but its length (3830m) and width at the top (40m) and base (980m) are impressive. From the southern side of the dam you can gaze across Lake Nasser to Kalabsha Temple. The **view** northwards includes the huge 2100-megawatt power station on the east bank and the channels through which water

---

CRUISES ON LAKE NASSER

Since 1993, the *M/S Eugénie* has been making three-, four- and seven-day cruises to Abu Simbel, offering a unique opportunity to see other temples that were also salvaged and reassembled on higher ground, but can't be reached by road yet (this may change in a few years). Passengers visit Abu Simbel twice (at dawn, and after everyone has left), and make landings at Kalabsha Temple near the High Dam and at the isolated temples of Kasr Ibrim, Amada, Derr, Wadi el-Seboua, Mehrarakka and Dakka – not to mention the Tomb of Penout. Except for Kalabsha, all these sites are so remote that the only people there are the guards, who work three-week shifts.

There are now similar cruises available aboard the *M/S Nubian Lake, Prince Abbas* and *Qasr Ibrahim*. These are all luxurious vessels with pools and A/C. Cruises cost US$75 to $120 a day per person, which includes delicious meals, and entrance fees to the sites. The main agent for the *Eugénie* and *Ibrahim* is Belle Epoque in Cairo (17 Sharia Tunis, New Ma'adi; ☎02/353-7935, fax 353-6114), but any travel agent can secure reservations. In Aswan, try Travco on the 3rd floor next to the National Bank of Egypt on the Corniche (☎097/316-393, fax 315-960).

is routed into the Nile, rushing out amidst clouds of mist, sometimes crowned by a rainbow. Philae lies amongst the cluster of islands further downriver.

Trains south from Aswan (9 daily 6am–10.30pm; 25pt) terminate at **Sadd al-Ali Station**, 5km south of the High Dam. Nearby is the **dock** from which ferries to Wadi Halfa depart (see box on p.406).

Philae

The island of **PHILAE** and its **Temple of Isis** have bewitched visitors since Ptolemaic times, when most of the complex was constructed. The devout and curious were drawn here by a cult that flourished throughout the Roman empire well into the Christian era. Although the first Europeans to "rediscover" Philae in the eighteenth century could only marvel at it from a distance after their attempts to land were "met with howls, threats and eventually the spears of the natives living in the ruins", subsequent visitors revelled in this mirage from antiquity. "If a procession of white-robed priests bearing aloft the veiled ark of the God were to come sweeping round between the palms," mused Amelia Edwards, "we would not think it strange."

After the building of the first Aswan Dam, rising waters lapped and surged about the temple, submerging it for half the year, when tourists would admire its shadowy presence beneath the translucent water. However, once it became apparent that the new High Dam would submerge Philae forever, UNESCO and the EAO organized a massive operation (1972–80) to **relocate its temples** on nearby **Aglika Island**, which was landscaped to match the original site. The new Philae is magnificently set amidst volcanic outcrops, like a jewel in the royal blue lake, but no longer faces Biga Island, sacred to Osiris, whence its holiness derived.

Getting there

Most people visit Philae on **taxi tours from Aswan** (see p.390), which is the best way of getting there and back. The alternative entails catching a *service* taxi (if allowed; see box on p.254) from Aswan to the checkpoint at the eastern end of the Old Dam, and then walking 2km to the Shallal motorboat dock, where taxis drop visitors and you buy site **tickets** (daily 7am–5pm; Ramadan 7am–4pm; £E20). Having agreed on a price for a motorboat to the island (officially £E20 return per boat-load or £E2.50 each for more than eight people), you shouldn't pay anything until you're back on shore, obliging the boatman to wait while you explore; if you linger more than an hour, however, *baksheesh* is in order. There's nowhere to buy food or drink on the island, and the toilets are grisly.

Sound and Light show

Some reckon that Philae's **Sound and Light show** is even better than the one at Karnak, due to its island setting. There are two or three performances nightly; check the schedules at the tourist office. As at Karnak, the show consists of an hour-long tour through the ruins, whose floodlit forms are more impressive than the melodramatic soundtrack. By manoeuvring yourself into the front row, you can enjoy a panoramic view of the entire complex without having to swivel your head during the second act. **Tickets** (£E33; no student reductions) are sold at the dockside just before the first show begins. You'll need to rent a **taxi** to take you there and back; expect to pay £E20 for a four-seater cab (including waiting time).

The Temple of Isis

Philae's cult status dates back to the New Kingdom, when Biga Island was identified as one of the burial places of Osiris – and the first piece of land to emerge from the pri-

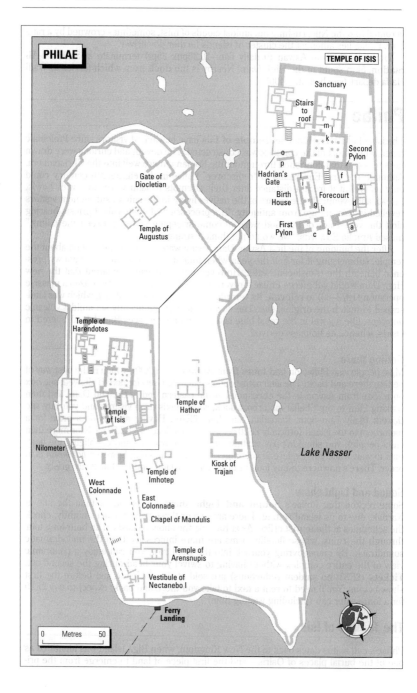

PHILAE

Gate of
Diocletian

Temple of
Augustus

Temple of
Harendotes

Temple
of Isis

Nilometer

Temple of
Hathor

West
Colonnade

Temple of
Imhotep

East
Colonnade

Chapel of Mandulis

Temple of
Arensnupis

Vestibule of
Nectanebo I

Ferry
Landing

Kiosk of
Trajan

Lake Nasser

0   Metres   50

N

TEMPLE OF ISIS

Sanctuary

Stairs
to roof

n

m

k

Second
Pylon

o

p

Hadrian's
Gate

f

i

Birth
House

g   h

Forecourt

e

d

First
Pylon

c   b

a

THE CULT OF ISIS

Of all the cults of ancient Egypt, none endured longer or spread further than the worship of the goddess **Isis**. As the consort of Osiris, she civilized the world by instituting marriage and teaching women the domestic arts. As an enchantress, she collected the dismembered fragments of his body and briefly revived him to conceive a son, Horus, using her magic to help him defeat the evil Seth and restore the divine order. As pharaohs identified themselves with Horus, the living king, so Isis was their divine mother; a role which inevitably associated her with Hathor, the two goddesses being conflated in the Late Period. By this time Isis was the Great Mother of All Gods and Nature, Goddess of Ten Thousand Names, of women, purity and sexuality.

By a process of identification with other goddesses around the Mediterranean, **Isis-worship** eventually spread throughout the Roman empire (the westernmost *Iseum* or cult temple extant is in Hungary). The nurturing, forgiving, loving Isis was Christianity's chief rival between the third and fifth centuries. Many scholars believe that the cult of the Virgin Mary was Christianity's attempt to

Isis

wean converts away from Isis; early Coptic art identifies one with the other, Horus with Jesus, and the Christian cross with the pharaonic *ankh*.

mordial waters of Chaos. Since Biga was forbidden to all but the priesthood, however, public festivities centred upon neighbouring **Philae**, which was known originally as the "Island from the Time of Re".

Excluding a few remains from the Late Period, the existing **Temple of Isis** was constructed over some eight hundred years by Ptolemaic and Roman rulers who sought to identify themselves with the Osirian myth and the cult of Isis (see above). An exquisite fusion of ancient Egyptian and Greco-Roman architecture, the temple complex harmonizes perfectly with its setting, sculpted pillars and pylons gleaming white or mellow gold against Mediterranean-blue water and black Nilotic rock.

Approaching the temple

Motorboats land near an ancient quay at the southern end of the island. In ancient times, on the original Philae, visitors ascended a double stairway to the **Vestibule of Nectanebo** at the entrance to the temple precincts. Erected by a XXX Dynasty pharaoh in honour of his "Mother Isis", this was the prototype for the graceful kiosks of the Ptolemaic and Roman era. Notice the double capitals on the remaining columns: traditional flower shapes topped with sistrum-Hathor squares that supported the architrave. The screens that once formed the walls are crowned with cavetto cornices and rows of *uraeus* serpents, a motif dating back to Zoser's complex at Saqqara, nearly three thousand years earlier.

Beyond the vestibule stretches an elongated trapezial courtyard flanked by colonnades. The **West Colonnade** is the better preserved, with fine carved capitals, each slightly different. The windows in the wall behind once faced Biga, the island of Osiris; the one opposite the first two columns is topped by a relief of Nero offering two eyes to Horus and Isis. The plainer, unfinished **East Colonnade** abuts a succession of ruined structures. Past the foundations of the **Temple of Arensnupis** (worshipped as the "Goodly Companion of Isis" in the Late Period) lies a ruined **Chapel of Mandulis**, the Nubian god of Kalabsha. Near the First Pylon, an unfinished **Temple of Imhotep** honours the philosopher-physician who designed Zoser's Step Pyramid and was later deified as a god of healing. Its forecourt walls show Khnum, Satis, Anukis, Isis and Osiris, and Ptolemy IV before Imhotep.

The Pylons and Forecourt

The lofty **First Pylon** was built by Neos Dionysos, who smites enemies in the approved fashion at either corner, watched by Isis, Horus and Hathor. Set at right angles to the pylon, the Gate of Ptolemy II **[a]** is probably a remnant of an earlier temple. The pylon's main portal **[b]** is still older (dating from the reign of Nectanebo II) and was formerly flanked by two granite obelisks; now only two **stone lions** remain. Inside the portal are inscriptions by Napoleon's troops, commemorating their victory over the Mamlukes in 1799. The smaller door in the western section of the pylon leads through to the Birth House and was used for *mamissi* rituals; the entrance depicts the personified deities of Nubia and the usual Egyptian pantheon **[c]**. On the back of the pylon are scenes of priests carrying Isis's barque.

Emerging into the **Forecourt**, most visitors make a beeline for the Birth House (see below) or the Second Pylon, overlooking the colonnade to the east. Here, reliefs behind the stylish plant columns show the king performing rituals such as dragging the barque of Sokar **[d]**. A series of doors lead into six rooms which probably had a service function; one of them, dubbed the Library **[e]**, features Thoth in his ibis and baboon forms, Maat, lion-headed Tefnut and Sheshat, the goddess of writing. At the northern end stands a ruined chapel **[f]**, which the Romans erected in front of a granite outcrop that was smoothed into a stele under Ptolemy IV and related his gift of lands to the temple.

Set at an angle to its forerunner, the **Second Pylon** changes the axis of the temple. A large relief on the right tower shows Neos Dionysos placing sacrifices before Horus and Hathor; in a smaller scene above he presents a wreath to Horus and Nephthys, offers incense and anoints an altar before Osiris, Isis and Horus. Similar scenes on the other tower have been defaced by early Christians, who executed the paintings in the upper right-hand corner of the pylon passageway, leading into the temple proper.

The Birth House

The western side of the forecourt is dominated by the colonnaded **Birth House** of Ptolemy IV, which linked his ancestry to Horus and Osiris. Most of the exterior reliefs were added in Roman times, which explains why the Emperor Augustus shadows Buto, goddess of the north, as she plays a harp before the young, naked Horus and his mother at one end of the central register, behind the Hathor-headed colonnade **[g]**. Further south and higher up, the Roman reliefs overlie inscriptions in hieroglyphs and demotic characters that partly duplicate those on the Rosetta Stone **[h]**. Inside the *mamissi*, a columned forecourt and two vestibules precede the sanctuary, which contains the finest scenes **[i]**. Although iconoclasts have defaced the goddess suckling the child pharaoh on the left-hand wall, you can see Isis giving birth to Horus in the marshes at the bottom of the rear wall. Around the back of the sanctuary behind the northern colonnade is a corresponding scene of Isis nursing Horus in the swamp **[j]**.

Inside the Temple of Isis

Immediately behind the Second Pylon lies a small open court that was originally separated from the **Hypostyle Hall** by a screen wall, now destroyed. A lovely drawing by David Roberts shows this "Grand Portico" in its rich original colours: the flowering capitals in shades of green with yellow flowers and blue buds; crimson and golden winged sun-discs flying down the central aisle of the ceiling, which elsewhere bears astronomical reliefs. The unpainted walls and column shafts show the hall's builder, Ptolemy VII Euergetes II, sacrificing to various deities. After the emperor Justinian forbade the celebration of Isis rituals at Philae in 550 AD, Copts used the hall for services and chiselled crosses into the walls. On the left-hand jamb of the portal **[k]** into the vestibule beyond, a piece of Roman graffiti asserts *B Mure stultus est* ("B Mure is stupid").

As at other temples, the **vestibules** get lower and darker as you approach the sanctuary. By a doorway **[l]** to the right of the first vestibule, a Greek inscription records the "cleansing" of this pagan structure under Bishop Theodorus, during the reign of Justinian. On the other side of the vestibule is a room giving access to the **stairs** to the roof (see below). The next vestibule has an interesting scene flanking the portal at the back **[m]**, where the king offers a sistrum (left) and wine (right) to Isis and Harpocrates. On the left-hand door jamb, he leaves offerings to Min, a basket to Sekhmet and wine to Osiris, with the sacred bull and seven cows in the background. In the partially ruined transverse vestibule, the king offers necklaces, wine and eye paint to Osiris, Isis, Hathor and Nephthys, outside the sanctuary **[n]**.

Dimly lit by two apertures in the roof, the **sanctuary** contains a stone pedestal dedicated by Ptolemy III and his wife Berenice, which once supported the goddess's barque. On the left wall, the pharaoh faces Isis, whose wings protectively enfold Osiris. Across the room, an enthroned Isis suckles the infant Horus (above) and stands to suckle a young pharaoh (below, and now defaced). The other rooms, used for rites or storage, contain reliefs of goddesses with Nubian features.

The Osirian Shrine

Try to persuade a guard to unlock the stairway to the roof, where a series of sunken rooms dwells on the resurrection of Osiris. After scenes of lamentation in the vestibule of this **Osirian Shrine**, you can see Isis gathering up his limbs, and the slain god lying naked and tumescent upon a bier (as always, the phallus has been vandalized). Mourned by Isis and Nephthys, Osiris revives to impregnate his sister-wife, while Selket and Douait reconstruct his body for its solar rebirth. Cast as the hawk-headed Sokar, Osiris is borne away to a papyrus swamp by the four sons of Horus, to be anointed with holy water with Anubis in attendance.

Hadrian's Gate

By leaving the temple through the western door of the first vestibule you'll emerge near **Hadrian's Gate**, set into the girdle wall that once encircled the island. Flanking your approach are two walls from a bygone vestibule, decorated with notable reliefs. The right-hand wall **[o]** depicts the origin of the Nile, whose twin streams are poured forth by Hapy the Nile-god from his cave beneath Biga Island, atop which perches a falcon. To the right of this, Isis, Nephthys and others adore the young falcon as he rises from a marsh.

Above the door in the opposite wall **[p]**, Isis and Nephthys present the dual crowns to Horus, whose name is inscribed on a palm stalk by Sheshat (right) and Thoth (left). Below, Isis watches a crocodile drag the corpse of Osiris to a rocky promontory (presumably Biga). Around the gate itself, Hadrian appears before the gods (above the lintel) and the door-jambs bear the fetishes of Abydos (left) and Osiris (right). At the top of the wall, Marcus Aurelius stands before Isis and Osiris; below he offers Isis grapes and flowers.

North of the gateway lie the foundations of the **Temple of Harendotes** (an aspect of Horus), built by the emperor Claudius.

The Temple of Hathor and Trajan's Kiosk

To complete the cast of deities involved in the Osirian myth, a small **Temple of Hathor** was erected to the east of the main complex. Aside from two Hathor-headed columns *in situ* and fragmented capitals out back, the ruined temple is only notable for a relief of musicians, amongst whom the god Bes plays a harp. More eye-catching and virtually the symbol of Philae is the graceful open-topped **Kiosk of Trajan**, nicknamed the "Pharaoh's Bedstead". Removed from its watery grave by a team of British navy divers, the reconstructed kiosk juxtaposes variegated floral columns with a severely classical superstructure; only two of the screen wall panels bear reliefs.

Last in order of priority come the ruined **Temple of Augustus** and the **Gate of Diocletian**, which shared the northern end of old Philae with a mud-brick Roman village that was so eroded by repeated soakings that it was left to be submerged by the lake. The **toilets** lie in this direction.

Kalabsha Temple

The hulking **Temple of Kalabsha** broods beside Lake Nasser near the western end of the High Dam, marooned on an island or strung out on a promontory, depending on the water level. Between the site and the dam lies a graveyard of boats and fishy remains, enhancing its mood of desolation. The main temple originally came from Talmis (later known as Kalabsha), 50km to the south of Aswan; in a German-financed operation, it was cut into 13,000 blocks and reassembled here in 1970, together with other monuments from Nubia. Although military restrictions were lifted in 1987, the site only became readily accessible in the early 1990s, and is still pleasantly under-visited in comparison to other temples. Strictly speaking, "Kalabsha" refers to the site rather than the temple, which is named after the god Mandulis, and has no historic connection with two smaller monuments in the vicinity, relocated here from other sites in Nubia.

Getting there

Taxis are the best way of getting to Kalabsha and back. Official rates for a round trip from Aswan are about £E25 for a four-seater taxi, £E45 for a seven-seater Peugeot. Better still, include Kalabsha in a half-day taxi tour taking in Philae, the dams and the Unfinished Obelisk (see p.391). Either is preferable to the penny-pinching alternative of taking a **train** to Sadd al-Ali Station (see p.397), then walking or hitching up to the dam and across to the other side of the lake (almost 10km in all).

In recent years it has been necessary to reach Kalabsha **by boat**. Motorboats will take you there and back for £E20 (for the whole boat; 6–8 people) with an hour at the site (daily 7am–5pm; £E12) which is sufficient; tickets are sold at the temple itself.

The Temple of Mandulis

The **Temple of Mandulis** is a Ptolemaic-Roman version of an earlier XVIII Dynasty edifice dedicated to the Nubian fertility god Marul, whom the Greeks called Mandulis.

By Ptolemaic times, Egypt's Nubian empire was a token one, dependent on the goodwill of the powerful Nabatean empire ruled from Merowe near the Fourth Cataract, about 400km south of Abu Simbel. Having briefly restored old-style imperialism, the Romans abandoned most of Nubia during the reign of Diocletian, falling back on deals with local rulers to safeguard Egypt's southern border. As the linchpin of the last imperial town south of Aswan, the temple bears witness to this patronage and the kingdoms that succeeded the Nabatean empire, which disintegrated under the onslaught of marauding Blemmyes (c.550 AD), a group of nomadic tribes who were perhaps the ancestors of the modern Beja.

The causeway, court and facade

Approaching the sandstone temple from behind, you miss the dramatic effect of the great **causeway** from the water's edge, used by pilgrims in the days when Kalabsha was a healing temple, like those at Edfu and Dendara. For reasons unknown, its chunky **pylon** is skewed at a slight angle to the temple, a blemish rectified by having a trapezial **courtyard** whose pillars are set closer together along the shorter, southern side.

The first batch of reliefs worth a mention occurs on the **facade** of the Hypostyle Hall at the back of the court. While Horus and Thoth anoint the king with holy water in a conventional scene to the left of the portal, the right-hand wall bears a decree excluding swineherds and their pigs from the temple (issued in 249 AD); a large relief of a horseman in Roman dress receiving a wreath from the winged Victory; and a text in poor Greek lauding Siklo, the Christian king of the Nabatae, for repulsing the Blemmye.

The Hypostyle Hall and Sanctuary

The now roofless **Hypostyle Hall** is distinguished by columns with ornate flowered capitals, and some interesting reliefs along the rear wall. Left of the portal, a Ptolemaic king offers crowns to Horus and Mandulis, while Amenhotep II (founder of the XVIII Dynasty temple) presents a libation to Mandulis and Min. Across the way, a nameless king slays a foe before Horus, Shu and Tefnet.

Within the **vestibules** beyond, look for figures personifying the Egyptian nomes, below a scene of the king offering wine to Osiris and a field to Isis and Mandulis (near the stairs off the pronaos or outer vestibule); and a rare appearance by the deified Imhotep (low down on the left-hand wall of the naos or inner vestibule).

The **Sanctuary** is similar in size to the vestibules and, like them, once had two columns. Along its back wall you can identify (from left to right) the emperor offering lotuses to Isis and the young Horus, and milk to Mandulis and Wadjet; then incense to the former deity and lotuses to the latter. Although the god's cult statue has vanished, Mandulis still appears at either end of the scene covering the temple's **rear wall**: in his royal form, with a pharaonic crown, sceptre and *ankh* sign (right); and as a god whose ram's horn crown is surmounted by a solar disc, *uraeus* and ostrich plumes (left).

From the temple's pronaos, you may be able to ascend a stairway to the **roof**, which features an abbreviated version of the Osirian shrines found at other complexes.

The Kiosk of Qertassi and Beit al-Wali

Re-erected near the lakeside at the same time as Kalabsha Temple, the **Kiosk of Qertassi** resembles a knocked-about copy of the "Pharaoh's Bedstead" at Philae, but actually came from another ancient settlement, 40km south of Aswan. Aside from its fine views of Lake Nasser, this Ptolemaic-Roman edifice is chiefly notable for two surviving Hathor-headed columns, which make the goddess look more feline than bovine.

The oldest monumental relic from Nile-inundated Nubia is a temple dug into the hillside behind Kalabsha Temple. Originally hewn under Ramses II, who left his mark throughout Nubia, this cruciform rock-cut structure is known by its Arabic name, **Beit al-Wali** (House of the Governor). The weathered reliefs flanking its narrow court depict the pharaoh's victories over Nubians and Ethiopians (left), Libyans and Asiatics (right). By contrast, scenes in the transverse hall are well preserved and brightly coloured. Here, Ramses makes offerings before Isis, Horus and the Aswan Triad (Hapy, Satet and Khnum), and is suckled by goddesses inside the sanctuary, whose niche contains a mutilated cult statue of three deities.

Abu Simbel

The great **Sun Temple** of **Abu Simbel** epitomizes the monumentalism of the New Kingdom during its imperial heyday, when Ramses II (1304–1237 BC) waged colonial wars from the Beka'a Valley in the Lebanon to the Fourth Cataract. To impress his power and majesty on the Nubians, Ramses had four gigantic statues of himself hewn from the mountainside, whence his unblinking stare confronted travellers as they entered Egypt from Africa. The temple he built here was precisely oriented so that the sun's rays reached deep into the mountain to illuminate its sanctuary on his birthday and the anniversary of his coronation. The deified pharaoh physically overshadows the sun-god **Re-Herakhte**, to whom the temple is nominally dedicated, just as his queen, **Nefertari**, sidelines **Hathor** in a neighbouring edifice, also hewn into the mountain.

The first European to see Abu Simbel since antiquity was the Swiss explorer Burckhardt, who found the temples almost completely buried by sand drifts in 1813. Although Belzoni later managed to clear an entrance, lack of treasure discouraged further efforts and the site was soon reburied in sand so fine "that every particle would go through an hourglass"; a process repeated throughout the nineteenth century. After Robert Hay took a cast of the face of the northern colossus, leaving it disfigured by lumps of plaster, Amelia Edwards ordered her sailors to remove the residue and tint the white stains with coffee, dismaying the vessel's cook, who had never "been called upon to provide for a guest whose mouth measured three feet and a half in width". Finally cleared, the temple became the scenic highlight of Thomas Cook's Nile cruises.

It was the prospect of losing Abu Simbel to Lake Nasser that impelled UNESCO to organize the salvage of Nubian monuments in the 1960s. Behind the temporary protection of a coffer dam, Abu Simbel's brittle sandstone was stabilized by injections of synthetic resin and then hand-sawn into 1050 blocks weighing up to thirty tons apiece. Two years after the first block was cut, Abu Simbel was reassembled 210m behind (and 61m above) its original site, a false mountain being constructed to match the former setting. The whole operation (from 1964 to 1968) cost US$40 million and is still being paid for; the cost of Egyptian tourist visas supposedly goes towards repayments.

Visiting Abu Simbel

Abu Simbel lies on the west bank of Lake Nasser, 280km south of Aswan and 40km north of the Sudanese border. A road runs there from Aswan, but this is out of bounds for tourists, so it can only be reached by water or by air. Roads are currently being built to other temple sites around Lake Nasser, which at present are only accessible via **luxury cruises to Abu Simbel** (see p.396).

Getting there

Since November 1997 the road to Abu Simbel has been closed to tourists for reasons of security and to carry out repairs. Local sources suggest that the road may reopen to foreigners during 2000, when it is likely that minibus and taxi tours from Aswan will resume. Those organized by budget hotels such as the *Noorhan* or *Nubian Oasis* were good value at around £E25 (3hr 30min each way with 1hr 30min at the site).

Therefore, the choice remains to fork out for the EgyptAir return flight or take a luxury cruise (see p.396). EgyptAir usually has four flights a day from Aswan (US$85 return, including transfers to the site – it's wise to book a few days in advance (at any EgyptAir office). Several charter airlines have started flying to Abu Simbel, most easily arranged if you have a large group. Luxor Air (☎012/317-0464), Orca (☎012/218-5257), Pharaoh (☎012/316-9947) and Scarabee (☎012/322-0104) flights are usually US$5–10 cheaper than EgyptAir, but are less relible or frequent (inqure at travel agents to find out if flights are operating). That said, EgyptAir flights are often cancelled or delayed, especiallly during summer. Planes often circle the temple – sit on the left to enjoy the best view.

Abu Simbel town: practicalities

Roughly 2km before the temple site you'll pass the new **town** of **ABU SIMBEL**, a huddle of breeze-block dwellings in a dusty wilderness that belies its Arabic name, "Father

---

PHOTOGRAPHING ABU SIMBEL

Abu Simbel is an awkward subject for photography. The immense facade should be snapped in the morning before it's cast into shadow, and needs a wide-angle lens to do it justice; whereas details are best captured with a telephoto lens (it also helps to underexpose the shot by 1–1.5 stops). To photograph Abu Simbel from the air, sit on the left side of the plane and use a telephoto (at least 200mm) lens with a haze filter. Unless you get there very early or just before the temple closes, its interior is so crowded that photography is hopeless; if you do want to attempt to capture the interior on film, there is no photo permit charge but for camcorders you have to pay £E400.

---

of the Ear of Corn". It has a **post office** and a **hospital**; the police station is 400m up the dead-end road from the temple; the **tourist police** are across the street from the *Nobaleh Ramses Hotel*. Although you can call Abu Simbel from outside, there are no phone numbers as such in town; simply pick up the phone, dial zero, and the operator will connect you.

Should you decide **to stay** overnight to enjoy the temples at their deserted best, there are two hotels and the possibility of camping at one of them. It's forbidden to sleep out, and the rule is strictly enforced. The *Nefertari Abu Simbel*, 400m from the temple (☎097/400-509, fax 400-510; ⑨), has A/C rooms, a pool and tennis courts, and the price includes breakfast; room rates are 30 percent lower in the summer. They may also allow visitors to pitch their own tents and use the pool for £E15 per person. The other option is the fairly spartan state-owned place, the *Nobaleh Ramses Hotel*, 1.5km from the temple (☎097/400-380, fax 400-381; ⑥), where package tourists are fed and watered. Singles cost almost the same as doubles; breakfast is included.

The Sun Temple of Ramses II

Rounding a shoulder of the hill from the ticket office, visitors are confronted by the great **Sun Temple** (daily 6am–5pm, later if planes land in the evening; £E36 including local guide), seemingly hewn from the cliffs overlooking Lake Nasser. Having been depicted on everything from T-shirts to £E1 notes, its impact is perhaps a little diminished by familiarity: the technicolour contrast between red rockscape and aquamarine water is more startling than the clean-swept facade, which looks less dramatic than the sand-choked Abu Simbel of nineteenth-century engravings. For all the meticulous reconstruction and landscaping, too, it's hard not to sense its artificiality . . . then the temple's presence asserts itself and your mind boggles at its audacious conception, the logistics of constructing and moving it, and the unabashed megalomania of its founder.

Although Re-Herakhte, Amun-Re and Ptah are also billed as patron deities, they're clearly secondary to Ramses, the pharaoh-god whom courtiers feared as "a powerful lion with claws extended and a terrible roar".

The colossi and facade

The temple facade is dominated by four enthroned **Colossi of Ramses II**, whose twenty-metre height surpasses the Colossi of Memnon at Thebes (though one lost its upper half following an earthquake in 27 BC). Their feet and legs are crudely executed but the torsos and heads are finely carved, and the face of the left-hand figure is quite beautiful. Between them stand figures of the royal family, dwarfed by Ramses' knees. To the left of the headless colossus is the pharaoh's mother, Muttuy; Queen Nefertari stands on the right of the colossus; Prince Amunherkhepshef between its legs. On the left leg of this same figure, an inscription records that Greek mercenaries participated in the Nubian campaign of the Saïte king Psammetichus II (c.590 BC).

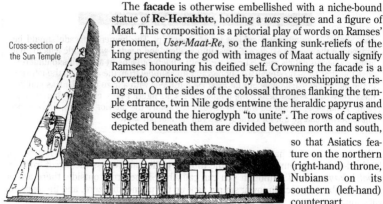

Cross-section of
the Sun Temple

The **facade** is otherwise embellished with a niche-bound statue of **Re-Herakhte**, holding a *was* sceptre and a figure of Maat. This composition is a pictorial play of words on Ramses' prenomen, *User-Maat-Re*, so the flanking sunk-reliefs of the king presenting the god with images of Maat actually signify Ramses honouring his deified self. Crowning the facade is a corvetto cornice surmounted by baboons worshipping the rising sun. On the sides of the colossal thrones flanking the temple entrance, twin Nile gods entwine the heraldic papyrus and sedge around the hieroglyph "to unite". The rows of captives depicted beneath them are divided between north and south, so that Asiatics feature on the northern (right-hand) throne, Nubians on its southern (left-hand) counterpart.

The Hypostyle Hall and Sanctuary

This schematic division reappears in the lofty rock-cut **Hypostyle Hall**, flanked on either side by four pillars fronted by ten-metre-high statues of Ramses in the Osiris position, carrying the crook and flail (the best is the end figure on the right). Beneath a ceiling adorned by flying vultures, the walls crawl with scenes from his campaigns, from Syria to Nubia. On the entrance walls, Ramses slaughters Hittite and Nubian captives before Amun-Re (left) and Re-Herakhte (right), accompanied by his eight sons or nine daughters, and his *ka*. But the most dramatic **reliefs** are found on the side walls (all directions as if you're facing the back of the temple).

The right-hand wall depicts the **Battle of Qadesh** on the River Orontes (1300 BC), starting from the back of the hall. Here you see Ramses' army marching on Qadesh, followed by their encampment, ringed by shields. Acting on disinformation tortured out of enemy spies, Ramses prepares to attack the city and summons his reserve divisions down from the heights. The waiting Hittites ford the river, charge one division and scatter another to surround the king, who single-handedly cuts his way out of the trap. The final scene claims an unqualified Egyptian triumph, even though Ramses failed to take the city. Notwithstanding this, the opposite wall portrays him storming a

Syrian fortress in his chariot (note the double arm, which some regard as an attempt at animation), lancing a Libyan and returning with fettered Nubians. Along the rear wall, he presents them to Amun, Mut and himself (left), and the captured Hittites to Re-Herakhte, lion-headed Wert-Hekew and his own deified personage (right).

The eight **lateral chambers** off the back of the hall were probably used to store cult objects and tribute from Nubia. Reliefs in the smaller **pillared hall** show Ramses and Nefertari offering incense before the shrine and barque of Amun (left) and Re-Herakhte (right). Walk through one of the doors at the back, cross the transverse vestibule and head for the central **Sanctuary**. Originally encased in gold, its four (now mutilated) cult statues wait to be touched by the sun's rays at dawn on February 22 and October 22. February 21 was Ramses' birthday and October 21 his coronation date, but the relocation of Abu Simbel has changed the timing of these **solar events** by one day. Perhaps significantly, the figure of Ptah is situated so that it alone remains in darkness when the sun illuminates Amun-Re, Re-Herakhte and Ramses the god. Before them is a stone block where the sacred barque once rested.

The false mountain

To see behind the scenes at Abu Simbel, look for a grey door in the mountainside beyond the northern colossus. Inside you'll find air-conditioning, a guy selling soft drinks, and stairs which lead up into a vast dome ringed by a walkway. Here, displays show how the temple was removed from its original site and reassembled beneath the dome, which was covered with landfill to create a **false mountain**. The revelation is just as startling as Abu Simbel itself.

The Hathor Temple of Queen Nefertari

A little further north of the Sun Temple stands the smaller rock-hewn **Temple of Queen Nefertari**, identified here with the goddess Hathor, who was wife to the sun-god during his day's passage and mother to his rebirth at dawn. As with Ramses' temple, the rock-hewn facade imitates a receding pylon (whose corvetto cornice has fallen), its plane accentuated by a series of rising buttresses separating six **colossal statues of Ramses and Nefertari** (each over 9m tall), which seem to emerge from the rock. Each is accompanied by two smaller figures of their children, who stand

---

THE TOSHKA AND EAST OWEINAT IRRIGATION PROJECTS

The **Toshka Irrigation Scheme**, inaugurated by President Mubarak in January 1997, is a huge-scale project whose long-term goal is to settle 25 percent of Egypt's landmass (at present only five percent of Egypt is actually populated). To this end, the **world's largest pumping station** is being built to take 177 billion cubic feet of water from Lake Nasser annually, to irrigate 500,000 acres of desert northwest of Abu Simbel, much of which is potentially fertile alluvial land. Already some thirty kilometres of canal have been built (the projected length when finished is 550km) with help from French, Norwegian and British construction firms. The government plans to deliver water to the edge of each property, leaving the owner with the responsibility for its distribution across their land. One such investor is Saudi Prince Alwaleed Bin Talal, who has bought 100,000 acres. The government has set up an experimental farm and reports that cotton, cucumbers, tomatoes, watermelon, bananas, grapes and wheat grow well. A separate project underway to the west of Abu Simbel, known as **East Oweinat**, will irrigate land using aquifer water. Some fear that these projects are too ambitious and may turn out to be white elephants; however, the same was said of the High Aswan Dam, without which – even given the huge problems it has caused – Egypt simply could not sustain herself.

knee-high in the shadows. A frieze of cobras protects the door into the temple, which is simpler in plan than Ramses', having but one columned hall and vestibule, and only two lateral chambers.

The best **reliefs** are in the hall with square, Hathor-headed pillars whose sides show the royal couple mingling with deities. On the entrance wall Nefertari watches Ramses slay Egypt's enemies; on the side walls she participates in rituals as his equal, appearing before Anuket (left) and Hathor (right). In the transverse vestibule beyond, the portal of the sanctuary is flanked by scenes of the royal couple offering wine and flowers to Amun-Re and Horus (left), Re-Herakhte, Khnum, Satet and Anuket (right). The **Sanctuary** niche contains a ruined cow statue of Hathor, above which vultures guard Nefertari's cartouches. On the side walls, she offers incense to Mut and Hathor (left), while Ramses worships his own image and that of Nefertari (right). The predominance of yellow in the paintings may allude to Hathor's title, "The Golden One".

CHAPTER THREE

THE WESTERN DESERT OASES

For the ancient Egyptians civilization began and ended with the Nile Valley and the Delta, known as the "Black Land" for the colour of its rich alluvial deposits. Beyond lay the "Red Land" or desert, whose significance was either practical or mystical. East of the Nile it held mineral wealth and routes to the Red Sea Coast; west of the river lay the Kingdom of Osiris, Lord of the Dead – the deceased were said to "go west" to meet him. But once it was realized that human settlements existed out there, Egypt's rulers had to reckon with the **Western Desert Oases** as sources of exotic commodities and potential staging posts for invaders. Though linked to the civilization of the Nile Valley since antiquity, they have always been different – and remain so.

Siwa Oasis, far out near the Libyan border (and covered last in this chapter as it is furthest away), is the most striking example: its people speak another language and have customs unknown in the rest of Egypt. Its ruined citadels, lush palm groves, limpid pools and golden sand dunes epitomize the allure of the oases.

The four "inner" oases of **Bahariya**, **Farafra**, **Dakhla** and **Kharga** lie on the "**Great Desert Circuit**" that begins in Cairo or Assyut – a Long March through the New Valley Governorate, where modernization has affected each oasis to a greater or lesser extent. While Bahariya and Farafra remain basically desert villages, living off their traditional crops of dates and olives, Dakhla and Kharga have full-blown modern towns. The appeal of the latter two is stronger in the journeying – across hundreds of miles of awesome barrenness, most of it gravel pans rather than pure "sand desert".

Much nearer to Cairo (and suitable for day excursions) are two quasi-oases: the Fayoum and Wadi Natrun. The **Fayoum** is more akin to the Nile Valley than the Western Desert, with many ancient ruins to prove its importance since the Middle Kingdom. Though a popular holiday spot for Cairenes, it doesn't attract many foreign

ACCOMMODATION PRICE CODES

Throughout the guide, hotels and pensions are graded on a scale of ① to ⑨, indicating the price (including tax) of the **cheapest double room** in each establishment in high season (for places that offer **dorm beds**, rates per person are given in £E). Please note that most hotels in categories ⑧ and ⑨ quote rates in US$, but will accept payment in £E. For a full explanation of the following categories, see p.46. The price bands to which these codes refer are as follows:

① under £E20/US$7	④ £E45–65/US$15–20	⑦ £E150–300/US$50–100
② £E20–30/US$7–10	⑤ £E65–100/US$20–35	⑧ US$100–200/£E300–600
③ £E30–45/US$10–15	⑥ £E100–150/US$35–50	⑨ US$200/£E600 upwards

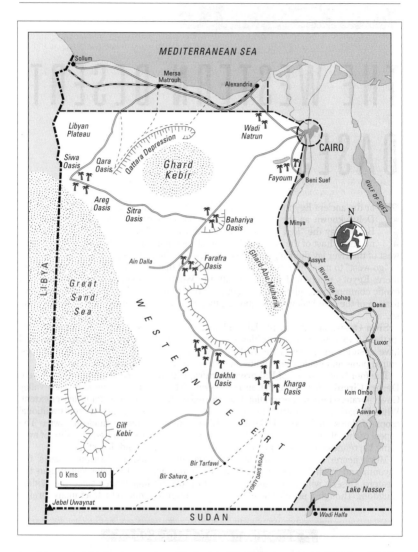

tourists except for hunters and ornithologists. **Wadi Natrun** is significant mainly for its Coptic monasteries, which draw hordes of Egyptian pilgrims but comparatively few foreigners.

The desert

Much of the fascination of this region lies in the desert itself. It's no accident that Islam, Judaism and Christianity were forged in deserts whose vast scarps and depressions displayed the hand of God writ large, with life-giving springs and oases as manifestations of divine mercy in a pitiless landscape. Although much of this landscape was once savannah, it was reduced to its current state millennia ago by geological processes and overgrazing by Stone Age pastoralists.

The **Western Desert**, which covers 681,000 square kilometres (over two-thirds of Egypt's total area), is merely one part of the Sahara belt across northern Africa. Its anomalous name was bestowed by British cartographers who viewed it from the perspective of the Nile – and, to complicate matters further, designated its southern reaches and parts of northwestern Sudan as the "Libyan Desert". Aside from the oases, its most striking features are the **Qattara Depression**, whence dunes extend 700km southwards, and the **Great Sand Sea** along the Libyan border. Both are discussed under "Siwa Oasis", while the old slave trail from the Sudan is covered after "Kharga Oasis", the penultimate stop on the **Forty Days Road**.

All the **practicalities** of visiting the oases (including the best times to go) are detailed under the respective entries in this chapter. The most comprehensive source of historical and geographical **information** is Cassandra Vivian's *Islands of the Blest: A Guide to the Oases and Western Desert of Egypt* (1990; new edition due out in 2000), sold in Cairo, which includes a useful set of pull-out maps.

WADI NATRUN

The quasi-oasis of **Wadi Natrun**, just off the Desert Road between Cairo and Alexandria, takes its name – and oasis stature – from deposits of natron salts, the main ingredient in ancient mummifications. Wadi Natrun's most enduring legacy, however, is its **monasteries**, which date back to the dawn of Christian monasticism, and have provided spiritual leadership for Egypt's Copts for the last 1500 years. Their fortified exteriors, necessary in centuries past to resist Bedouin raiders, cloak what are today very forward-looking, purposeful monastic establishments. Coptic monasticism experienced a revival during the 1980s, twenty years after an English writer dismissed the monasteries as "of little interest except to the specialist".

The area surrounding Wadi Natrun is known as **Liberation Province** (*Mudiriyat el-Tahrir*). In the 1950s, model villages, olive groves and vineyards were planted here to reclaim 25,000 hectares of land from the desert, a project initially financed by the sale of King Farouk's stamp collection and other valuables. The soil is potentially fertile, but lacks water; hitherto, the main springs and lakes in Wadi Natrun have been saline.

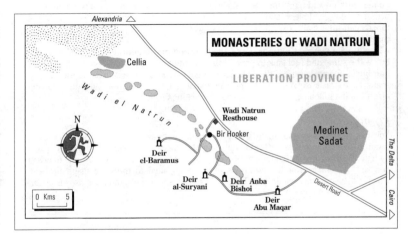

DESERT DRIVING

Although most of the places in this chapter can be reached by public transport or locally arranged excursions, a few of them entail real **desert expeditions**. The following advice should be borne in mind even if you're going to stick to main roads; for motorists considering more ambitious trips, it's only the bare outline of what you need to know. (For detailed handbooks, see "Books" in Contexts chapter.)

An easier option is to take an **organized desert safari**, though you should enquire well in advance, since they're often booked from abroad. Cairo-based firms include Albarai Desert Travel (16 Sharia Sherif Pasha; ☎393-5094), El Badawiya Safari (☎345-8524), El-Tahawy Tops (15 Sharia Haroun, Dokki; ☎348-6782) and *Siag Pyramids Hotel* (59 Saqqara Road; ☎385-6022). El-Tahawy Tops also **rents 4WD vehicles**.

PERMITS

When visiting sites within the limits of the oases, the main considerations are your vehicle, supplies and driving skills. Things get more complicated, however, if you're aiming for a remote location or planning to cross the desert by an unusual route. For their own safety, motorists are required to stick to the main roads between the oases, and any major detours need official **permission**. The main issuing authority is Military Intelligence in Cairo (Army Group 26, Sharia Manshia el-Bakry, Heliopolis), whose remit covers the whole Western Desert. Permission to travel to Qara Oasis or the Qattara Depression may also be obtained from Military Intelligence in Mersa Matrouh (see p.518). No permit is required to drive from Siwa to Bahariya.

VEHICLES

The desert is a potentially lethal environment, so it's crucial to get the right vehicle. If you're not planning anything ambitious, a **camper** (mobile home) might be worth considering. The high price may be affordable when shared among four or five people; ask at Starco (1 Midan Talaat Harb, downtown Cairo; ☎574-6963). However, campers are too ponderous for crossing soft sand, salt flats or boulder-strewn pans, and their fuel consumption is prodigious (carry a full extra tank in reserve), ruling them out for serious ventures off-road.

Providing they're up to scratch, **cars** are better. Mechanical reliability, high ground clearance and four-wheel drive are absolutely vital; non-automatic gears, a water-cooled engine and an electrical fuel pump are strongly advised. Tyres should be in good condition and have inner tubes; always carry two spare wheels, a tyre pump and pressure gauge, levers and a jack. A fire extinguisher, vital spares and a full tool/repair kit are also essential. El-Tahawy Tops (see above) can usually provide cars that fit the bill.

Ideally, your vehicle should also have the following **modifications**: steel plates welded below the sump and fuel tank to prevent them being holed, fireproof lagging around the fuel lines where they pass the exhaust manifold, crossover seat belts, fabric-covered seats, an extra, false roof above the cab (painted gloss white for maximum cooling effect), and a mileometer for navigational calculations.

EQUIPMENT

You can never carry too much **water** (in metal or heavy-duty polythene jerry cans, securely fixed to brackets) or **fuel** – travelling off *piste* can reduce a car's normal mileage by half. Even staying within the limits of an oasis depression, it's vital to be able to orient yourself. A vehicle-mounted **compass** must be adjusted to the car's magnetic field, which will also distort readings on hand-held compasses if you stand too close (as do ferrous rocks in Bahariya Oasis).

DESERT DRIVING

Decide from the start whether you plan to travel on paved roads, unpaved tracks (*pistes*), or through trackless open desert. It's safe to travel alone by road, as the police checkpoints at either end (and at intervals along major routes) will raise the alarm if you fail to arrive. Always **travel in pairs** of vehicles if you're going off-road (though locals often drive alone on familiar territory). Never set off – or keep going – during **sandstorms**; should you get caught in one, turn the car's rear end towards the wind, lest it sand-blast the front windscreen and headlights into opacity.

Driving at **night** is likewise taboo: potholes are vicious and it's easy to crash or get lost. The **best times for driving** are early morning and late afternoon, when there's less risk of overheating or misjudging the terrain. During the middle of the day, the details of the landscape are lost in the glare, making it harder to judge **distances and scale**. Both are distorted by the desert, where drivers often perceive near-vertical slopes as level ground, or discarded jerry cans as villages. These kind of optical illusions are commoner than **mirages** of shimmering "lakes".

If you are driving cross-country, stay alert for **changes in the desert's surface**, often indicated by a shift in colour or texture. Wheel ruts left by other vehicles can also yield clues: a sudden deepening and widening usually means softer sand (another sign of which is vegetation around the edges of dunes). Generally speaking, gravel plains provide a firm surface, while salt flats and dunes are the most unstable. Deflating one's **tyres** increases their traction on soft sand, but also their surface temperature and the car's fuel consumption, so keep a conservative speed.

DUNES

There's no substitute for experience of **dunes**, but a few points need making. Never crest a dune at high speed, in case the far side has collapsed, leaving a slipface. If you do go over, accelerate hard (which tends to lower the rear of the vehicle), charge down the slope and hope to butch it out. Braking or slewing sideways seems the natural reaction, but it's likely to somersault or roll the car over the edge.

When deflating tyres for better traction, do this just before you drive onto sand, and pump them up again before gaining firm ground. Shifting into a lower gear should likewise be done in advance. If stuck in soft sand, revving the engine will only dig you in deeper. Stop at once, change into low gear and try driving out slowly. If this fails, deflate the tyres as far as possible (or put traction mats, brushwood etc, beneath the rear wheels) and try again.

EMERGENCIES

Getting stuck, breaking down or crashing in the desert can be fatal if you compound the misfortune by acting wrongly. Assuming you're driving solo, *never leave your own vehicle* unless you're within 5km of a plainly visible settlement or major highway. Otherwise, stay put, keep cool (literally) and try to attract attention. By day you can burn oil-soaked sand or bits of rubber to produce thick black smoke; at night, make a fire. A vehicle, smoke or fire are hard enough for search parties to locate; a person on their own is virtually impossible.

Other **emergencies** arise simply through drivers getting lost. The moment you suspect this, stop and try to get oriented using a compass, the sun, or the watch or stick method; take your time calculating how much water and fuel remain, then deciding on a course of action. The worst thing to do is simply drive on by instinct – it's a sure way of wandering even further in the wrong direction.

Although proper spares are obviously preferable, **improvised materials** can serve for vital **repairs**: nylon tights make a substitute fan belt and chewing gum can plug holes in fuel tanks or radiators.

MAPS

For details of the best relevant maps for exploring the oases, see p.32.

Land reclamation has turned the desert green for much of the way along the road to Alex, with ranks of saplings receding up to the horizon. To the east of the highway, a whole new conurbation, **MEDINET SADAT** (Sadat City), represents Egypt's aspirations for the 21st century: a dormitory suburb, science park and film studio rolled into one. On the other side of the highway, motels have sprung up around the turn-off for Wadi Natrun, which runs via the ramshackle township of **BIR HOOKER** (named after Mr Hooker, an early manager of the Egyptian Salt & Soda Co.) into the Natrun Valley.

Visiting the monasteries

Wadi Natrun makes a memorable **day excursion** from Alex or Cairo, but a few caveats are in order. Getting within striking distance requires little effort, time or cash, but reaching more than one or two of the monasteries can be difficult without using rented vehicles – see below for transport details.

Visiting hours vary from monastery to monastery, as does the extent to which each closes during the five seasons of **fasting**: 43 days before the Nativity, 3 days in commemoration of Jonah in the Whale, 55 days preceding Lent, the fast of the Holy Apostles (from Pentecost to July 12), and 15 days marking the Assumption of the Virgin Mary (Aug 7–22). Deir Anba Bishoi alone is open every day of the year; Deir al-Suryani and Deir el-Baramus have regular opening times but close during most of the feasts; while Deir Abu Maqar will only admit those with a letter of introduction from the **Coptic Patriarchate** in Cairo (next to the Cathedral of St Mark, 222 Sharia Ramses, Abbassiya; ☎02/282-5374 or 284-3159) or Alexandria (in the Cathedral of St Mark on Rue d'Iglise du Copte; ☎03/483-5522). The Patriarchate can verify the opening dates of specific monasteries. Fridays, Sundays and public holidays are best avoided when visiting any of the monasteries as they are often swarmed by Coptic pilgrims from all over Egypt.

Male tourists interested in **staying the night** in a monastery must get written permission from the appropriate "residence" in Cairo: Deir Anba Bishoi (☎591-4448); Deir al-Suryani (☎590-5161); Deir el-Baramus (☎592-2775); Deir Abu Maqar (☎770-614). As other guests are devout pilgrims, you should make at least a token effort to attend prayers, and leave a donation in return for the tea and bread that's provided. Women are not allowed to sleep in any of the monasteries. Otherwise, there are several swanky motels (⑤–⑥) along the Desert Road, near the turn-off for Wadi Natrun.

GETTING THERE

Unless you rent a car, or take a taxi (£E100–150 depending on how many monasteries you visit), reaching the monasteries is a two-stage process. The best way of **getting there** from Cairo is by the West Delta buses that leave from the Aboud terminal (hourly 6.30am–6.30pm; £E3). Tickets are bought on the bus, which terminates at Bir Hooker, where you should be able to catch a pick-up (50pt) to Deir Anba Bishoi. Otherwise, you can get a *service* taxi from Cairo (Aboud terminal) or Alex (Midan el-Gumhorriya) to the **Wadi Natrun Resthouse** on the Desert Road – a bunch of motels, gas stations and cafés where non-express inter-city buses also stop. From here, you can negotiate a private taxi ride to the nearest monastery (£E5 one-way), or hope to be offered a lift by one of the busloads of Coptic pilgrims that come this way.

Returning to Cairo or Alex by bus or *service* taxi from the Resthouse, you'll probably have to pay the full inter-city rate. There are hourly buses to Cairo until 7pm; departures for Alex are fewer and further between, with perhaps only two buses in the afternoon, when people are most likely to be leaving having visited the monasteries.

The monasteries of Wadi Natrun

Christian monasticism was born in Egypt's Eastern Desert, where the first Christian hermits sought to emulate St Anthony, forming rude communities; however, it was at Wadi Natrun that their rules and power were forged. Peter Levi's study of monasticism, *The Frontiers of Paradise*, notes how this coincided with the persecution of Christians in urban areas, especially under Diocletian. Certainly, several thousand **monks** and hermits were living here by the middle of the fourth century, harbouring bitter grudges against paganism, scores which they settled after Christianity was made the state religion in 330 by sacking the temples and library and murdering scholars in Alexandria. E.M. Forster judged them "averse to culture and incapable of thought. Their heroes were St Ammon, who deserted his wife on their wedding eve, and St Anthony, who thought bathing was sinful and was consequently carried across the canals of the Delta by an angel". The Muslim conquest and Bedouin raids encouraged a siege mentality amongst the monks, who often lapsed into idle dependence on monastic serfs. Nineteenth-century foreign visitors unanimously described them as slothful, dirty, bigoted and ignorant – the antithesis of the monks here today.

The **four Wadi Natrun monasteries** have all been totally ruined and rebuilt at least once since their foundation during the fourth century; most of what you see dates from the eighth century onwards. Each has a high wall surrounding one or more churches, a central keep entered via a drawbridge, containing a bakery, storerooms and wells, enabling the monks to withstand siege, and diverse associated chapels. Their low doorways compel visitors to humbly stoop upon entry (don't forget to remove your shoes outside).

Their **churches** – like all Coptic chapels – are divided into three sections. The *haikal* (sanctuary) containing the altar lies behind the iconostasis, an inlaid or curtained screen, which you can peer through with your escort's consent. In front of this is the choir, reserved for Coptic Christians, and then the nave, consisting of two parts. *Catechumens* (those preparing to convert) stand nearest the choir, while sinners (known as "weepers") were formerly relegated to the back.

Deir Anba Bishoi

The most accessible monastery is **Deir Anba Bishoi**, 10km from the highway, with a signpost of sorts on the mostly paved road. Over one hundred and fifty monks and

---

THE MONASTIC RULE AND WORKING DAY

All Egyptian monasteries are cenobitic, meaning that the monks share food and possessions and unconditional submission to the rule of their abbot (a word that derives from the Arabic *abd*, "father").

The **monastic day** begins at 3am with an hour of silent prayer in individual *laura* (cells), before two hours of collective worship in the chapel, followed by unrelenting labour until the main meal of the day at noon. Afterwards, the monks work until 5pm, assemble for prayers and then return to their tasks until sheer exhaustion forces them to bed.

Work and prayer are seen as equal holy obligations, and many of the younger monks and novices are qualified engineers or scientists. High-tech coexists with spiritualism, which is clearly apparent during liturgies. Black garments symbolize their death to the world of bodily desires; their hoods (possibly representing the "helmet of salvation" in Ephesians 6) are embroidered with twelve crosses, after Christ's disciples.

novices live here, and the monastery of St Bishoi receives a stream of Coptic pilgrims (daily: winter 7am–6pm; summer 7am–8pm). Foreigners are usually shown around by the English-speaking Father Shedrak.

The legend of **Bishoi** suggests he was one of the earliest monks at Wadi Natrun. An angel told the saint's mother that he was chosen to do God's work even before his birth in 320; two decades later he moved here to study under St Bemoi alongside John "the Short". Adopting a rather imaginative chronology, the legend also recalls that Bishoi later met Christ as an old man, carried him to church, washed his feet and was allowed to drink the water as a reward. Whatever the truth, since Bishoi's death in 417 his body has reportedly remained uncorrupted, and occasionally reaches out from beneath its red shroud to shake the hands of devout believers. Next to him lies Paul of Tammuh, who was revered for committing suicide seven times.

St Bishoi's is the oldest of the five **churches** in the monastery, and features three *haikals* dating from the fourth, ninth and tenth centuries. The **keep**, built three to four hundred years later, has chapels at ground level (around the back) and on the second storey, one floor above its drawbridge. There's also a fifth-century **well** where Berber tribesmen washed their swords after massacring the 49 Martyrs of the Monastery of St Makarius.

The multi-domed building furthest away from the entrance is the **residence of Pope Shenouda III**, the current Coptic Pope. He uses it normally as an occasional retreat, though he was exiled here for some years by Sadat. Most of the Coptic popes have been chosen from the monks of Wadi Natrun, and Deir Anba Bishoi in particular.

Deir al-Suryani

A sixth-century dispute over the theological importance of the Virgin led dissenting monks to found another monastery, 500m from St Bishoi's. After they returned to the fold it was purchased for a group of Syrian monks, hence its name, **Deir al-Suryani** (winter Mon–Fri & Sun 9am–6pm, Sat 9am–3pm; summer Mon–Fri & Sun 9am–7pm, Sat 9am–5pm). It was here that Robert Curzon came searching for ancient manuscripts (the ostensible reason for his tour of Balkan and Levantine monasteries in the 1830s), and found them lying on the floor or serving as covers for jars, all "well begrimed with dirt". The keep's oil cellar held a "mass of loose vellum pages", while the consistory of Abyssinian monks contained a library of Aramaic texts, hanging from pegs in individual leather satchels. Nowadays, the monastery's antique volumes are lovingly maintained in a modern **library**. The monastery also boasts the remains of some twelve saints and a lock of hair from Mary Magdalene.

Deir al-Suryani's principal **Church of the Virgin** (*al-Adhra*), built around 980, contains a *haikal* with stucco ornamentation, and a superb ebony "**Door of Prophecies**", inlaid with ivory panels depicting the disciples and the seven epochs of the Christian era, culminating in the split with the Orthodox Church and the Coming of Islam. A dark passageway at the back of the church leads to the **cave** where Bishoi tied his hair to a chain hanging from the ceiling to prevent himself sleeping for four days, until a vision of Christ appeared. The marble basin (*lakan*) in the nave is used by the abbot to wash the feet of twelve monks on Maundy Thursday, emulating Christ's act during Passion week.

The large **tamarind tree** in the grounds is said to have grown from the staff of St Emphram, who, as a monk, thrust it into the earth after his fellows criticized it as a worldly affectation. As Coptic pope, he established cordial relations with the Fatimid khalif in 997.

Deir el-Baramus

If you're keen on seeing one of the remoter monasteries, **Deir el-Baramus** fits the bill (daily: winter 9am–5pm; summer 9am–6pm). A road running 4km north from the vicinity

Obelisk and head of Ramses II, Luxor Temple   Camel market at Darow, near Aswan

Feluccas near Elephantine Island, Aswan

Kom Ombo Temple of Haroeris and Sobek   Tomb of Amenophis II, Valley of the Kings

Nile ferry, Luxor

Avenue of the Sphinxes, Luxor Temple

Al-Qasr, Dakhla Oasis

The Great Sand Sea, Siwa Oasis

Toilet at military checkpoint, Siwa to Bahariya road

The White Desert, Farafra Oasis

of St Bishoi's Monastery has reduced its isolation amidst barren sands, but it still feels far from the madding crowd. Visitors are greeted outside by a picture of St Moses the Black, a Nubian robber who became a monk under the influence of St Isidore. The monastery itself was founded by St Makarius (see below) in 340, making it the oldest of the four that remain in Wadi Natrun. Its name, "Monastery of the Romans", honours Maximus and Domidus, two sons of the Roman Emperor Valentinus who died from excessive fasting; the younger one was only nineteen years old.

Their bodies are reputedly buried in a crypt below the **Church of the Virgin**, whose principal altar is only used once a day, since Mary's womb begot but one child. An adjacent altar, normally curtained off, serves the "Immaterial Fathers", the spirits of bygone saints and abbots who occasionally leave droplets of water sprinkled there. The relics of Moses and Isidore are encased in glass; pilgrims drop petitions into the bier. Notice the photo of a T-shirt bearing a bloody cross, resulting from an exorcism.

Restoration work has revealed layers of medieval **frescoes** in the nave, the western end of which incorporates a fourth-century **pillar** with Syriac inscriptions. It was behind here that St Arsanious prayed with a pebble in his mouth, regretful only of the few words that he'd spoken (including a statement to that effect).

The ninth-century church (whose belfries of unequal height symbolize the respective ages of Maximus and Domidus) shares a vine-laden courtyard with a **keep** and four other churches. Deir el-Baramus has eighty monks and novices, one of whom will show you around.

Cellia and birdlife

The monks may also tell you about **Cellia** (or El-Muna), the name given to the **ruins** of some five hundred hermitages, spread over a wide area 30km north of Deir el-Baramus. Cellia was founded by St Anthony, who is said to have told monks at Wadi Natrun who wished to live as hermits, "Let us take food at the ninth hour and then go forth and pass through the desert and consider the place." It's thought that Cellia maintained links with the pilgrim city of Abu Mina (see p.509) until their freshwater springs dried up. In 1995 American archeologists unearthed the Monastery of St John, plus traces of five subterranean monasteries that had been "lost" since their discovery by Prince Tousoum in 1930.

This remote part of Wadi Natrun has a melancholy beauty, its numerous **saline lakes** rimmed by crusts of **natron**, a mixture of sodium carbonate and sodium bicarbonate, which the ancient Egyptians used for dehydrating bodies and making glass. Ducks, waterhens, jacksnipes and sandpipers are typical of the **birdlife** around these lakes, which also harbour Egypt's last surviving wild **papyrus**. Due to the salinity, it is a dwarf subspecies of the plant that once flourished throughout the Nile Valley, but gradually became extinct; the last large papyrus (which could reach 6m) was found by a Prussian soldier in the Delta in the mid-nineteenth century. Today it exists only on small plantations, thanks to Dr Rageb, who rediscovered the lost technique of making papyrus paper and began to manufacture souvenirs from the stuff.

You'll need a **car** to explore the area.

Deir Abu Maqar

The oldest and furthest of the monasteries, **Deir Abu Maqar** lies 18km southwest of St Bishoi and can also be reached by an eight-kilometre spur off the Desert Road, midway between the main turn-off and Sadat City. It is not open to casual visitors, but will admit those with a letter of authorization from the Patriarchate.

Enclosed by a circular wall ten metres high, the monastery requires visitors to pull a bell rope; in times past, two giant millstones stood ready to be rolled across to buttress the door against Bedouin raiders. Its founder, **St Makarius**, died in 390 "after sixty years of austerities in various deserts", the last twenty of which were spent in a hermit's cell at Wadi Natrun. He's said to have been so remorseful over killing a gnat that he withdrew for six months to the marshes, getting stung all over until "his body was so much disfigured that his brethren on his return only knew him from the sound of his voice". A rigorous faster, his only indulgence was a raw cabbage leaf for Sunday lunch.

Despite repeated sackings, Abu Maqar has hung onto the bodies of the numerous Coptic popes that have been buried here, plus the 49 Martyrs whom the Berbers killed in 444. In 1978, monks discovered what they believed to be the head of John the Baptist; however, this is also claimed to be held in Venice, Aleppo and Damascus. Since its nadir in 1969, when only six monks lived here, the monastery has acquired a hundred brethren, a modern printing press and a farm employing six hundred workers. The monks have mastered pinpoint irrigation systems and bovine embryo transplant technology in an effort to meet their abbot's goal of feeding a thousand laypersons per monk, revitalizing a landscape which "might be supposed to boast of nothing but the salt and natron for which it is indebted to its barrenness and its name" (*Murray's Handbook*, 1891).

THE FAYOUM

Likened in Egyptian tradition to a bud on the stem of the Nile and an "earthly paradise" in the desert, the **Fayoum** depends on river water – not springs or wells, like a true oasis. The water is distributed around the depression by a system of canals going back to ancient times, creating a lush rural enclave of palm trees dividing cotton and clover fields, orchards, and carefully tended crops of tomatoes and medicinal plants in the sandier outlying regions. Pigeons nest in mud-brick coops shaped like giant Victorian trifles, blindfolded cattle turn threshing machines and water buffalo plod home for milking. Along one shore of Lake Qaroun are fishing communities, while on the periphery are encampments of semi-nomadic Bedouin. About two million people live here, in half a dozen towns and 158 villages.

Visiting the Fayoum

Given easy access from Cairo, there have to be good reasons why foreign tourists are so thin on the ground. Number one is the Governorate capital, **Fayoum City**, which has all of Cairo's **drawbacks** and few of its advantages. Avaricious drivers bedevil day excursions to the distant **antiquities**, whilst *baksheesh*-hungry locals pester visitors to **Lake Qaroun**, where wealthy tourists are bussed in for shooting holidays. It is possible to get into the diverse **birdlife**, local **moulids** or **desert expeditions**, but you have to be committed. If you're only lukewarm, a brief day-trip will probably discourage further contact.

As for the **best time to go**, the Fayoum's winters are warmer and drier than Cairo's, its summers milder than in Upper Egypt; however, cold winds in spring – known as the *khamseen*, coat everything with dust. At other times, the clarity of the air causes the sun's rays to burn more strongly than you'd expect.

GETTING THERE

The **road from Cairo** to the Fayoum starts near the Pyramids of Giza, whose silhouette sinks below the horizon as the road gains a barren plateau dotted with army bases, then (76km later) reaches the edge of the Fayoum depression. Once here, the Ptolemaic-Roman site of Kom Oshim is passed (on the left) before you sight Lake Qaroun and cruise down through Sinnuris into Fayoum City, driving past the Obelisk of Senusert I. **Buses** (£E3.50) from Cairo's Ramses and Giza terminals (every 15–30min between 6.15am and 6.45pm) do the 100km journey in two hours; advance bookings are usually only necessary from midday Thursday till late on Saturday, or during Ramadan, Fayoumi moulids and public holidays. An alternative is to go to Midan Giza and grab a **service taxi**. These seven-seater Peugeots or pack-'em-in minibuses run practically non-stop from early morning to late at night, charging £E5 for a stomach-churning high-speed ride past the wrecks of previous crashes, reaching Fayoum City in just over an hour – *inshallah*. For those with more time on their hands, the daily **train** from Cairo's Ramses and Giza stations (3rd class; £E3) takes a leisurely two or three hours to reach Fayoum City's central train station.

Coming from the **Nile Valley**, catch one of the half-hourly buses or *service* taxis **from Beni Suef**, which reach Fayoum City in an hour. The road runs through a cultivated strip beside the Bahr Yussef, so there's little sense of entering an oasis; en route it passes the start of tracks to the Lahun and Hawara pyramids. Buses and *service* taxis coming from this direction terminate at the Hawatim depot in the southwest of town.

Fayoum City

A kind of pocket-sized version of Cairo, with the Bahr Yussef canal in the role of the Nile, **FAYOUM CITY*** makes a grab at the wallets of middle-class Egyptians who come to bask beside Lake Qaroun during summertime, and any foreigners that come to hand. Most of the latter are whisked through in buses and remain immured in luxury hotels, so independent travellers bear the brunt of local hustlers – and obnoxious teenagers, if you're a woman. Another major drawback is that mosquitoes swarm from every nook and waterway, making evenings a misery. Add makeshift buildings, weaving traffic and malodorous canals and you've got half a dozen reasons not to linger.

On the plus side, the city has the cheapest accommodation in the area and serves as the jumping-off point for almost everywhere you might consider visiting in the oasis. It also musters a pleasant **souk**, a couple of venerable **mosques** and some colourful **moulids** – the biggest of which (see p.422) is that of *Ali er-Rubi* in the middle of the month of *Sha'ban*.

Arrival, orientation and accommodation

Trains terminate at the station in the centre of town, while buses and *service* taxis stop slightly further out beyond the Gamal Abdel Nasser Mosque. Coming from Beni Suef you arrive at the Hawatim depot behind the old town, which is too far from town to walk – the local minibus routes (25pt) are hard to figure out without local knowledge, so it's best to get a taxi or horse-drawn cab (*hantour*), which shouldn't cost over £E5.

Once downtown, most things worth seeing can be reached on foot, with the Bahr Yussef canal facilitating **orientation**. The **tourist office** is in a prefab hut near the four water wheels (daily except Fri 9am–2pm; ☎084/342-586, ext. 177). Their colourful map of town isn't much use, but determined enquiries might yield some details of buses or taxi fares to places of interest in the oasis.

Accommodation
Outside of *Er-Rubi*'s festival, there shouldn't be any difficulty **finding a room** in town, where there are four hotels, plus a hostel. Other options exist at Ain es-Siliyin, Lake Qaroun and Kom Oshim (see sections following).

---

*The city is officially **Medinet el-Fayoum**, but known as **El-Fayoum** or **Fayoum** in colloquial usage (not *El-Medina*, as some guidebooks say). The word "Fayoum" probably derives from *Phiom*, the Coptic word for "sea", although folklore attributes it to the pharaoh's praise of the Bahr Yussef: "This is the work of a thousand days" (*alf youm*).

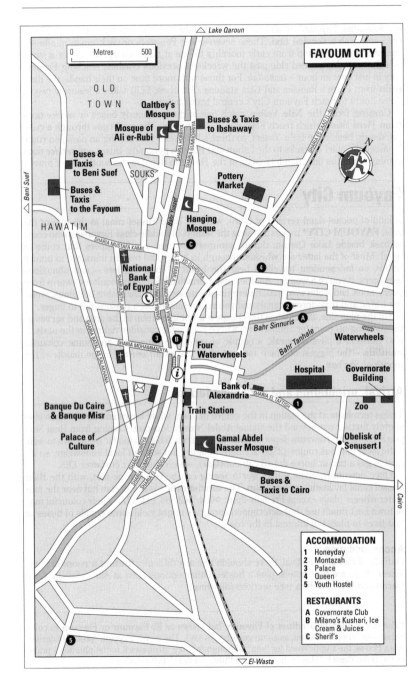

△ Lake Qaroun

FAYOUM CITY

Metres 0 — 500

OLD TOWN

Qaltbey's Mosque

Mosque of Ali er-Rubi

Buses & Taxis to Ibshaway

Buses & Taxis to Beni Suef

SOUKS

Pottery Market

Buses & Taxis to the Fayoum

HAWATIM

Hanging Mosque

C

SHARIA MUSTAFA KAMIL

National Bank of Egypt

4

Bahr Sinnuris

A

2

Bahr Tanhale

Waterwheels

Four Waterwheels

3 B

SHARIA MOHAMMADIYA

i

Hospital

Governorate Building

Bank of Alexandria

SHARIA EL TAFTISH

1

Zoo

Banque Du Caire & Banque Misr

Train Station

Palace of Culture

Gamal Abdel Nasser Mosque

Obelisk of Senusert I

Buses & Taxis to Cairo

▷ Cairo

5

▽ El-Wasta

ACCOMMODATION
1 Honeyday
2 Montazah
3 Palace
4 Queen
5 Youth Hostel

RESTAURANTS
A Governorate Club
B Milano's Kushari, Ice Cream & Juices
C Sherif's

Honeyday, Sharia Gamal Abdel Nasser (☎084/340-105, fax 341-205). Ten minutes walk from town, this new hotel has clean A/C rooms with TV and fridge. Breakfast included. ⑤.

Montazah, Sharia Ismail al-Medany (☎084/348-662). North of the centre in the quiet residential area of Munsha'at Lotfallah. Tatty rooms with TV and phone; some are A/C. Bearable bathrooms. Run by Copts. ②–③.

Queen, Sharia Ata-Allah Hassan (☎084/346-819, fax 346-233). Also in Munsha'at Lotfallah, this is the best place in town. Spotless rooms with private bathrooms. Good restaurant. ⑥.

Palace, by the Bahr Yussef (☎084/351-222). Dead central, with a wide range of rooms, mostly quite decent. Meals may be available, but it's better to eat out. ③–④.

Youth Hostel, Block #7 Flat 7–8 (☎084/323-682). Located on a nameless street 2km from the centre, the *Beit es-Shabab* is a last resort, with 44 beds. £E7 including breakfast.

The City

Groaning away behind the tourist office are four large wooden **water wheels**, symbolic of Fayoumi agriculture. Because Nile water is introduced into the sloping depression at its highest point, gravity does half the work of distribution. Sluices at El-Lahun regulate the current, which is strong enough to power water wheels for lifting irrigation water where needed – except during January, when the whole system is allowed to dry out for cleaning and maintenance.

Coptic and Muslim folklore ascribes the **Bahr Yussef** (River of Joseph) to its Biblical namesake, who's believed to have been the pharaoh's vizier and minister for public works. Originally a natural waterway branching off the Nile near Beni Suef, it was regulated from the XII Dynasty onwards, and since the building of the Ibrahimiya Canal in the nineteenth century, has drawn water from the Nile at Dairut, nearly 300km further south.

Walking west alongside the canal and crossing the fourth bridge from the tourist office, you'll notice a side street with a wooden roof. This is the city's **souk**: a compact labyrinth of alleys with stalls selling copperware and spices, grain and pulses, clothing and other goods – all without a hint of tourism. Behind the souk, keeping slightly aloof, the street of **goldsmiths** (*Es-Sagha*) is crammed with jewellery shops, mostly owned by Christians. (There's a church nearby, and three larger ones on 26th July Street.)

More persistent hawkers flog ornamental baskets (*sabat*) near the four water wheels. For ceramics, there's more choice at the **pottery market** off Sharia el-Mudaris (Tues only). Most of the red, pink or unglazed pots are made at the village of Nazla, south of Ibshaway.

The **Mosque of Khawand Asal-Bey**, west of the souk, is the oldest in the Fayoum. Traditionally attributed to Sultan Qaitbey, who's said to have ordered it built for his favourite concubine in 1499, the mosque could actually be older. Ancient columns from Kiman Faris (see box on p.424) uphold its dome, while the stone carving around the doorway, and the ebony *minbar* inlaid with Somalian ivory, are distinctly Mamluke.

The twin-arched bridge nearby, once also named after Khawand, is now called the "Bridge of Farewells" because it leads to a cemetery. By walking east and turning right before the next bridge, and then right again further up the street, you should come upon the **Mosque** and **Mausoleum of Ali er-Rubi**. The *darih* or carved box frame around the tomb is often surrounded by Fayoumis muttering or shouting supplications to this revered sheikh. On the other bank opposite the souk, the **Hanging Mosque** – built above five arches – is undergoing slow restoration.

In the other direction from the tourist office, the Bahr Yussef is dominated by two public buildings. The **Gamal Abdel Nasser Mosque** is one of many that Nasser had built in provincial towns in the 1960s, and which bear his name. Just before this you'll see the city's newest landmark: the upside-down pyramid-shaped **Palace of Culture** housing a cinema, theatre and library, which should open in 2000.

The Seven Water Wheels and the Obelisk of Senusert I

For a pleasant half-hour's walk in the morning or evening, follow the Bahr Sinnuris northwards out of town to reach the **Seven Water Wheels** (not to be confused with the four by the tourist office). First comes a single wheel near a farm; slightly further on, a quartet revolves against a backdrop of mango trees and palms; the final pair is a little way on, near a crude bridge. The Fayoum has about two hundred such water wheels (introduced by Ptolemaic engineers in the third century BC), which have a working life of ten years if properly tarred and maintained. They act as pumps rather than powering machinery, using the flow of the stream to lift the water to a higher level, for irrigation.

Entering or leaving town by the Cairo road, you'll see the thirteen-metre-high red granite **Obelisk of Senusert I**, which doesn't merit a closer look. Senusert was the second king of the XII Dynasty, who displayed a special fondness for the Fayoum and was the first to regard it as more than just a hunting ground, building the Lahun and Hawara pyramids, Medinet Madi and Qasr es-Sagha. Following the XII Dynasty (1991–1786 BC), interest in the Fayoum declined, and didn't properly revive until the advent of the Ptolemies, fourteen centuries later.

Eating, drinking and other practicalities

You can **change money** or travellers' cheques and get a Visa cash advance at the Bank of Alexandria on Sharia El-Taftish (Sun–Thurs 8.30am–2pm; during Ramadan 10am–1.30pm). There are a further four banks along the Bahr Yussef – the new Banque du Caire (same times as Bank of Alexandria) is the most efficient and offers an **ATM** as well as foreign exchange facility. The **post office** (daily except Fri 8am–3pm) has EMS and *poste restante*, and you can make international calls from the **telephone exchange** which is next to the post office. A Xerox office and a photo shop can be found nearby.

You can fill your stomach with *kushari* or *felafel* at **stalls and cafés** along both sides of the Bahr Yussef, or go in search of a chicken- or *kofta*- based meal. The places listed below are the best the town can offer. For those with money, a splurge at the *Auberge du Lac-Fayoum* is recommended (see p.425).

Cafeteria el-Medina, by the four water wheels. A bit of a rip-off, but you might succumb to breakfast. The service is good and the food tasty. A full meal costs about £E25.

Governorate Club (*Nady al-Muhafza*), north along Bahr Sinnuris. Does excellent kebab and some Western-style dishes, with a nice garden out back. Open till 1am.

Milano's, a green and yellow place 100m northwest of the tourist office on the Bahr Yussef, where you can get tasty *kushari* and great juices and ice cream.

Queen Hotel, Sharia Ata-Allah Hassan. Nicely decorated, with a longish menu. Try the *shish tawouq* or *escalope panée* (£E13).

Sherif's, Mustapha Kamil, between Bahr Yussef and Sharia Ramleh. Unexceptional *kofta*, chicken and kebab at average prices.

Festivals

It's worth visiting the city purely for its festivals, as lots of *fellaheen* do. Hotels overflow during **Ali er-Rubi's moulid** in *Sha'ban*, when the alleys around his mosque are crammed with stalls purveying sugar dolls and horsemen, and all kinds of amusements, while the devout perform *zikrs* in the courtyard.

The other big occasion is the "viewing" (*Er-Ruyeh*) of the new moon that heralds **Ramadan**. This calls for a huge procession from the Gamal Abdel Nasser Mosque. Headed by the security forces, followed by imams and sheikhs, a parade of carnival floats "mimes" the work of different professions and bombards spectators with "lucky" prayer leaflets.

During the month of Ramadan, there's a small moulid at the domed white tomb of **Sheikha Mariam** (between the sluice of the Bahr Sinnuris and the *Cafeteria el-Medina*). The **Great Feast** (starting on the tenth of *Zoul Hagga*) is a more private occasion, with most eateries closed, so avoid coming then.

On the Monday after the movable **Coptic Easter**, locals and day-trippers from Cairo picnic along the canalsides and the shore of Lake Qaroun, in the popular festival of "Smelling the Breeze" (*Sham el-Nessim*).

Around Fayoum Oasis

The oasis's other populous centres – Sinnuris, Ibshaway, Itsa and Tamiya – hold little interest. However, there are enjoyable scenic spots easily accessible from Fayoum City in the form of the springs of **Ain es-Siliyin** and **Lake Qaroun**. Reaching the waterfalls of **Wadi Raiyan** or the seldom-visited **ancient sites** on the periphery of the oasis is more tricky, so don't undertake a jaunt lightly nor set off without adequate water and food for the day – you can't rely on finding either in the remoter places.

Perhaps the best way of **getting around** is to rent a bicycle (£E15), motorbike (£E40) or car (£E70) for the day from the *Montazah Hotel*. Otherwise, you can rent a private taxi, or rely on *service* taxis, covered pick-ups (with fixed fares and routes) or local buses. Pick-ups and taxi drivers frequently overcharge, so it's wise to check fares

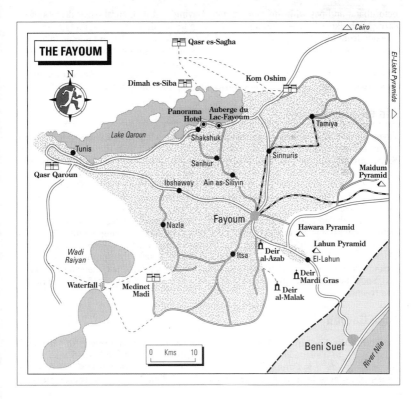

SOBEK AND CROCODILOPOLIS

Kiman Faris (Horseman's Mounds) is the local name for a site on the northern outskirts of Fayoum City, rapidly disappearing beneath new colleges. Although nothing exists to justify a visit, it deserves a mention as the **site of Crocodilopolis** (later renamed *Arsinoë* after Ptolemy II's sister-wife), the Fayoum's ancient capital and centre of the **crocodile cult**. This supposedly began with Pharaoh Menes, the legendary unifier of Upper and Lower Egypt, whose life was saved by a croc while he was hunting in the Fayoum marshes. Crocodiles infested the lake beyond Kiman Faris (which was much larger in ancient times), so an urge to propitiate the creatures is understandable.

The crocodile deity, **Sobek,** was particularly favoured by Middle Kingdom rulers but assumed national prominence after he became identified with Re (as Sobek-Re) and Horus. He was variously depicted as a hawk-headed crocodile or in reptilian form with Amun's crown of feathers and ram's horns. At the Sacred Lake of Crocodilopolis, reptiles were fed and worshipped, and even adorned with jewellery, by the priests of Sobek.

Sobek

beforehand and pay with the exact money. Having said that, rural truck drivers often carry hitchhikers for free, and it's worth trying to flag down anything that moves.

Aside from being alert for tractors, children and livestock, **drivers** should take care in visiting the remoter sites. You'll need a car with high ground clearance, if not 4WD; adequate water (for humans and radiators); and shovels and traction mats or boards (for digging cars out of soft sand). Always travel with at least one other car and heed local advice about the weather; never travel during the *khamseen*.

Ain es-Siliyin

Fayoumis rate **Ain es-Siliyin** as a major beauty spot – and perhaps it was so in the days before cafeterias, a football pitch, pool and chalets were built in the hollow where the Siliyin **springs** bubbled forth. Nowadays they spurt from pipes, and hordes of picnickers (Fridays are busiest) have trampled the surrounding vegetation. The pool itself (25pt admission) is perennially packed with children and, whatever Egyptians say, it's *not* a good idea to drink the spring water, which is rich in titanium and supposedly good for hypotension.

To reach the springs, which are sited 9km north of town just before the village of the same name, ask for directions to the taxi and pick-up depot serving Sanhur, Shakshuk and other points north. This is currently located just off the railway tracks several blocks west of Bahr Sinnuris. Public **transport** is cheap: to the springs or Sanhur by pick-up costs about 50pt; don't be fooled into renting a private taxi instead of a *service* taxi. Should you want **to stay**, the *Ain as-Siliyin Hotel* (☎084/500-062; ②) has seedy, fanless rooms.

Lake Qaroun

To reach **Lake Qaroun**, ride on to Sanhur and catch a pick-up heading for "*El-Birka*" (The Pond), as it's familiarly known. Some pick-ups join the lakeside road 3km east of the *Auberge du Lac-Fayoum* hotel and then run west along the shore towards Shakshuk; others head directly for Shakshuk and then continue eastwards past the hotels. West of Shakshuk, the holiday villas of wealthy Cairenes spread out along a new road, that will soon run all the way to Wadi Raiyan (see below). If you've got a car, keep going, since local women and children pester you remorselessly for *baksheesh*.

The lake

Birket Qaroun (Lake of Horns) takes its name from the serrated hills on its far shore, where the Western Desert begins; looking especially incongruous when the fishing boats are out. Described by nineteenth-century guidebooks as "glassy and brooding, surrounded by beaches encrusted with salts, the recipient of all the drainage canals in the region", it makes an unlikely resort. Egyptians seem undeterred by the beach of broken shells and a lack of showers for removing saline gunk, but you may feel rather less like **swimming**. (The enthusiastic may be glad to note that, though foul-tasting, the lake's water is at least free of bilharzia.)

The view can be enjoyed from the jutting *La Promenade Café* of the **Auberge du Lac-Fayoum**, a luxury hotel that was once King Farouk's hunting lodge, where Allied leaders met after World War II to carve up the Middle East. Besides renting parasols and rowing **boats** (£E15 per hour) there, it's possible to negotiate trips to Dimeh es-Siba (see below) or the barren **Horn Island** (*Geziret el-Qorn*), where *Murray's Handbook* advised its travellers to camp in order "to avoid the hyenas and Arabs".

Covering 214 square kilometres at 45m below sea level, the **lake** is indeed a mere *birka* (pond) compared to when the Nile first broke into the wind-eroded Fayoum depression seventy thousand years ago, forming a lake 40m above the current level. Egyptian mythology identified this with *Nun*, the waters of chaos and primeval life; from the Stone Age onwards people lived around the lake, which had shrunk considerably by Dynastic times.

Although the Middle Kingdom emerged at nearby Heracleopolis, it wasn't until Pharaoh Amenemhat I moved his capital from Upper Egypt to Lisht that the Fayoum became important. He had canals dug and the channel to the Nile deepened, draining parts for agriculture and submerging a greater area with what the ancients called **Lake Moeris**. It was this that the Ptolemies lowered to reclaim land for their settlements, whose decline by the end of the Roman period matched the lake's drop to 36m below sea level. Increasing salinity was a problem by medieval times, and after the lake came into equilibrium with the water sheet 40m beneath the Libyan Desert in 1890, it became too salty for its freshwater fish; since then, new marine species have been introduced.

Eating and accommodation

The four-star *Auberge du Lac-Fayoum* (☎084/700-002, fax 700-730; ⑨) is the swankiest of the lakeside **hotels**. Its restaurant is renowned for wild duck and other game dishes, pandering to the rich hunters that patronize the *Auberge*. Expect a full meal to set you back £E80–100; a beer on the terrace costs £E6. A few kilometres west is the *Oasis Tourist Village* (☎084/701-565; ④) of A/C rooms with rather erratic power and water; followed by the *Panorama Shaksouk Hotel* (☎084/701-314, fax 701-757; ⑦), a good three-star place where a meal costs £E20–25. If you're driving on to Wadi Raiyan, you'll also pass by the *Geziret el-Bat Hotel* (☎084/749-288; ③) in the village of Manshiet El-Sadat.

Qasr Qaroun

Qasr Qaroun, the best preserved and most accessible of the Fayoum's Ptolemaic temples (daily 8am–4pm; £E16), lies on the northwestern edge of the oasis, roughly 45km from Fayoum City. **To get there**, take a *service* taxi from the rank on the canal near Khawand's Mosque to Ibshaway, and then another one from there towards the village of Qaroun; the temple is close to the road, just before its namesake.

Not a palace as its Arabic name suggests, Qasr Qaroun is an outwardly plain but inwardly labyrinthine temple. You'll need a torch to explore its warren of chambers, stairs and passageways at different levels; beware of scorpions, bats, snakes and lizards – the last resemble miniature crocodiles, as befits a temple dedicated to Sobek. Round about are the **ruins of Dionysias**, a Ptolemaic-Roman town believed to have been abandoned in the fourth century AD when the lake shrank (it's now 45 minutes' walk away), leaving dessicated stalks of vegetation. Early European travellers undertook nine-hour horse rides to this site, believing that it was the famous Labyrinth described by Herodotus and Strabo (see below).

Wadi Raiyan

Wadi Raiyan is a separate depression outside the Fayoum, which has become a wildlife haven and beauty spot thanks to human ingenuity. The idea of piping excess water from the Fayoum into the wadi was first mooted by the British, but only put into practice after the completion of the Aswan High Dam. In the thirty years since, three lakes and a waterfall have formed, vegetation has flourished and the area has become a major nesting ground for birds. The lakes have been stocked with fish and a small fishing industry established, while the tourist board is now promoting Wadi Raiyan as a major attraction.

Now that the new access road is finished you can drive here easily. After about half an hour a sign will point you to the left; the village of Tunis is to the right. Its domed houses were designed by Hassan Fathy, the advocate of traditional architecture for the poor. The wadi's azure freshwater **lakes** are visible well before you reach a toll station, where you pay £E5 per person and £E5 per car. There's a blue sign 13km later on; turn left down a short sandy road to find the **waterfalls**. This is a great spot for swimming, sunbathing and watching **birds**. Besides the ubiquitous cattle egrets and grey herons, there are hard-to-spot wagtails, skylarks, kestrels, kites and coucals from Senegal. The reed beds developing here are being colonized by wetland species such as the little bittern, adding to the diversity of the habitat. If you want to stay in this idyllic spot, the *Paradise Safari Camp* has basic tents right on the lakeshore for £E20 per person, including breakfast.

Drivers with 4WD can return to Fayoum City by a different scenic route starting on the far side of the falls, which you must drive across. Otherwise, retrace your way to Lake Qaroun.

Medinet Madi

Medinet Madi (City of the Past) is another temple site in the desert, roughly 35km southwest of Fayoum City. **Getting there** entails catching the El-Qasmiya bus from the Hawatim depot and riding on through Itsa, El-Minia and Abu Gandir. Ask to be dropped off at Menshat Sef, roughly one hour later. From this bridge it's about an hour's walk to the temple. Turn right, follow the canal to the next bridge, cross over and take a narrower canal path past a small village on your left, aiming for a stone hut on the rise ahead, beyond which lies the site.

Squatting in a sandy hollow where excavations are revealing an avenue of sphinxes and lions (one of them ruffed and bearded like a Renaissance grandee), the **Temple of Medinet Madi** was built for the XII Dynasty pharaohs Amenemhat III and IV, and dedicated to twin deities. Sobek appears in relief on the outside of the rear wall, while Renenutet the serpent-goddess (also associated with harvests) can be seen in the left-hand room of the limestone edifice. Ptolemaic additions include two female winged sphinxes, and the **ruined town** of mud- and fired bricks to the southeast. Although legend attributes its destruction to a tribe of eleventh-century Nejd warriors enraged by the town's refusal of hospitality, the real cause of its blight was probably the shrinking of the lake. What looks like an embankment north of the temple was actually the storm beach of the lake in ancient times, 68m above its present level.

To return to Fayoum City, catch the bus from Menshat Sef (going in the same direction, as the route is circular).

Kom Oshim: ancient Karanis

The most accessible of the ancient sites in the Fayoum is **Kom Oshim** (daily 8am–4pm; £E18), 30km north of Fayoum City, where the Cairo road descends into the depression. Ask a bus or taxi driver to drop you at *Mat'haf Kom Oshim*, the small **museum** by the road, where **site tickets** are sold. Its curator speaks good English and is keen to explain details. Pottery and glassware, terracotta figures used for modelling hairstyles and a lifelike "Fayoum portrait" (see p.428) convey the wealth and sophistication of the ancient frontier town whose ruins lie behind the museum.

The **ruins of Karanis** clearly show the layout of this Ptolemaic-Roman town, founded by Greek colonists during the third century BC, which had a population of three thousand or so until the 5th century AD. Although the mud-brick houses have been reduced to low walls, two stone temples are better preserved – no thanks to the nineteenth-century Antiquities Department, which allowed contractors to destroy Roman buildings for their bricks.

Professor Scott Woodward of Bringham University believes that the population of Fayoum Oasis was the most genetically diverse in ancient times, and is reflected in the genetic make-up of Egyptians today. He reckons that over one million corpses are buried around the edges of the oasis, and at Karanis in particular, where eighty-five percent of the upper strata are blond-haired (northern Mediterraneans), and couples are genetically dissimilar; by contrast, the lower layers contain evidence of many brother-sister marriages. Scott attributes the change to the advent of Christianity (with its taboo on incest) in the Fayoum, which seems to have happened in the first century AD, two hundred years earlier than was previously thought.

There's a **campsite** (☎084/501-825) which also has chalets (②) and some food stalls nearby. To return to Fayoum or Cairo, flag down any passing bus or *service* taxi. During opening hours the museum can usually provide a guide for excursions to Qasr es-Sagha and Dimeh es-Siba (see below).

Qasr es-Sagha and Dimeh es-Siba

Adventurous types might go for visiting the ancient sites of **Qasr es-Sagha** and **Dimeh es-Siba** in the desert north of Lake Qaroun. Because of looting, you need to obtain permission from the Karanis museum (see above), which strongly recommends that you take a guide. Even with the right sort of vehicle it's important to stick to the vaguely marked track (starting by the police station opposite the museum), for soft sand lurks off *piste*. The forty-kilometre journey to Qasr es-Sagha takes about ninety minutes; Dimeh, 9km further south, can also be reached by paying a boatman to row you across the lake (1–2hr) and return some hours later; either way, the excursion will take the best part of an afternoon.

Qasr es-Sagha (Palace of the Jewellers), a small Middle Kingdom temple, nestles inconspicuously halfway up a scarp. Although lacking any friezes or inscriptions, it's still remarkable for its masonry, which is unlike that of any other Egyptian temple. The blocks are irregularly shaped, with odd angles and corners fitting together like a jigsaw; the overall effect is of a transplanted Inca edifice. Lake Qaroun, which once lapped its feet, now lies 11km away, beyond the ruins of a Ptolemaic settlement that pegged out as the lake shrank.

Starkly visible against the desert, the ruins of **Dimeh es-Siba** (Dimeh of the Wolves) are ringed by a wall up to 10m high and 5m thick. In the centre is a rough-hewn, ruined temple that was dedicated to Soknopaios, a form of Sobek (see p.424); the hill on which it stands was originally an island in the crocodile-infested lake. Approaching from that direction – a 2.5km walk – you'll come first to a 400-metre-long road (flanked by stone lions as late as the nineteenth century), running past ruined houses into the temple enclosure.

Pyramids around the Fayoum

The Fayoum is associated with four separate **pyramid sites**, two of them beyond its limits, the other pair more conveniently sited off the Beni Suef road. The latter, at **Lahun** and **Hawara**, both date from the XII Dynasty, which governed Egypt – and ordered the waterworks that transformed the Fayoum – from its capital *Itj-tway* (Seizer of the Two Lands). This lay 30km to the northeast, near **El-Lisht**, where the dynasty's founder Amenemhat I built his own pyramid.

The fourth site, **Maidum**, is unconnected with the others (which it predates by seven centuries), but its dramatic-looking "Collapsed Pyramid" marks an evolutionary step between the pyramids at Saqqara and Giza.

Hawara Pyramid

Stripped of its limestone casing, the mud-brick **Pyramid of Amenemhat III** (daily 8am–4pm; £E8) has degenerated into a humpy mound offering great views of the surrounding area. Unlike most pyramids, its entrance (now blocked) was on the south side: one of many ruses devised to foil tomb-robbers – to no avail. The body of the pharaoh (1842–1797 BC) had been looted and burned centuries before Petrie redis-covered his sarcophagus alongside that of his daughter, Nefru-Ptah, which was stored here while her own tomb was being constructed. It was found intact with her treasures in 1956. East of the pyramid (the direction from which visitors approach) lies a bone-and bandage-littered necropolis, with deep shafts to ensnare the unwary.

To the south, towards and beyond the canal, a few column stumps and masses of lime-stone chippings mark the **site of the Labyrinth**. All that's known about this building in antiquity comes from Strabo and Herodotus (who was prone to exaggeration). Reportedly, it contained over three thousand chambers hewn from a single rock, half of them underground (where the kings and mummified crocs are buried), surpassing all the "great works of the Greeks . . . put together". Most archeologists think that it was Amenemhat III's mortuary temple, although Rohl argues that it may have been an eter-nal representation of the bureaucracy and waterworks that Joseph devised to prepare Egypt for the seven years of famine foretold by the pharaoh's dream (Genesis 41:1–4).

Amenemhat III

During the early excavations at Hawara in the nine-teenth century, Petrie unearthed 146 brilliantly natural-istic **"Fayoum Portraits"** (100–250 AD) in the Roman cemetery to the north of the pyramid. Executed in beeswax-based paint while their sitters were alive, they were cut to size and stuck on to the bandaged cadavers, whose mummification was perfunctory compared to the embalming of Dynastic times. One such portrait graces the Karanis museum (see p.427); others can be admired in Cairo's Egyptian Museum.

Getting to the pyramid involves a ten-kilometre *ser-vice* taxi ride from the Hawatim depot to just beyond the village of Hawara, whence you take the left-hand turning, cross the Bahr Yussef by a shaky bridge and walk on for about 3km until the pyramid appears. From its summit (easily reached by climbing the southwest corner) you should be able to see the Lahun Pyramid on the south-eastern horizon.

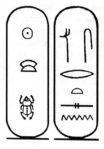

Senusert II

Lahun Pyramid

Nine kilometres beyond Hawara, the incoming Nile waters pass through El-Lahun, where modern sluices stand just north of the **Qantara of Sultan Qaitbey**, the thirteenth-century equivalent of the regulators installed by Amenemhat III. (Photographing these installations is forbidden.) Lahun gets its name from the ancient Egyptian *Le-hone* (Mouth of the Lake), and gives it to the Pyramid of Senusert II sited 5km away. Most of the *service* taxis from the Hawatim depot to El-Lahun stop where the track leaves the main road; it's well over an hour's walk to the pyramids from there.

Built seven or eight centuries after the pyramids at Giza, the **Pyramid of Senusert II** (daily 8am–4pm; £E8) employed a new and different technique. The core consists of a rock knoll on which limestone pillars were based, providing the framework for the mud-brick overlay, which was finally encased in stone. Mindful of flooding, the pharaoh's architect, Anupy, surrounded the base with a trench full of sand and rolled flints, to act as a "sponge".

The subsequent removal of its casing stones left the mud-brick pyramid exposed to the elements, which eroded it into its present mess. When Petrie entered the pyramid and found Senusert's sarcophagus it had been looted long ago; however, Brunton discovered the jewellery of Princess Sat-hathor, which is now divided between Cairo's museum and the Metropolitan Museum of Art in New York.

Senusert II (1897–1878 BC), Amenemhat III's grandfather, ordered eight rock-cut *mastabas* for his family to the north of his pyramid; east of them is the shapeless so-called Queen's Pyramid, apparently lacking any tomb.

Maidum Pyramid

Although technically outside the limits of the Fayoum, the **"Collapsed Pyramid" of Maidum** (daily 8am–4pm; £E18) is best reached from there. Take an early morning train from Fayoum to El-Wasta (1hr), and then a *service* taxi to the village of Maidum (10–15min). From the far end of the village it's a short walk across the fields and two canals into the desert; beware of potholes and skulls underfoot. The pyramid is visible from the Nile Valley road, and during the last stage of the train journey. Tickets include admission to two *mastabas* and a ruined mortuary temple. Ask to see them or you won't get into either.

Standing isolated and truncated amidst the sands "with much of its outer layers collapsed into piles of rubble, it looks more like the keep of a medieval castle than a proper pyramid", as T.G.H. James observed. It rises in sheer-walled tiers above mounds of debris: a vision almost as dramatic as the act of getting inside used to be, when "visitors had to hang by their hands from the ledge above and drop into the entry guided by a guard". Nowadays you climb a 30m stairway on the north side, descend to the bedrock via a passageway, and then ascend to the airless, corbelled burial chamber (bring a torch). Round about the pyramid are subsidiary, unfinished buildings, reduced to "ruinous lumps", where the exquisite "Maidum Geese" frieze and the famous statue of Prince Ra-Hotpe and his wife Nofret were found (both can now be seen in Room 32 of the Cairo Egyptian Museum).

Archeologists ascribe the pyramid to **Snofru** (see p.204), the first king of the IV Dynasty (c.2613–2494 BC), or to **Huni**, the last ruler of the preceding dynasty.

Partisans of Huni argue that Snofru is recognized as having built the Red and Bent pyramids at Dahshur, and would therefore not have needed a third repository for his *ka*. Mendelssohn's *The Riddle of the Pyramids* advances the contrary theory that Maidum was started by Snofru as a step pyramid (like Zoser's at Saqqara), and then later given an outer shell to make it a "true" pyramid. But the design was faulty, distributing stresses outwards rather than inwards, so that its own mass blew the pyramid apart. Mendelssohn argues that Snofru had already embarked on another pyramid at Dahshur, whose angle was hastily reduced (hence the Bent Pyramid), and that the Red Pyramid was a final attempt to get things right. Crucial to his argument is the idea that pyramids were built in production-line fashion, whether there were pharaohs to be buried in them or not; thus, kings who died before the completion of their own pyramid could be allotted one from the "stockpile".

El-Lisht Pyramids

The **Pyramids of El-Lisht** are the most inaccessible and ruined of the Fayoum collection, with little claim to anyone's attention. The larger of them, the **Pyramid of Amenemhat I** (1991–1962 BC), commemorates the founder of the XII Dynasty, whose capital, *Itj-tway*, was somewhere in the vicinity. Slightly to the south and harder to reach is the **Pyramid of Senusert I**, Amenemhat's son.

Fayoumi monasteries

Tradition has it that St Anthony personally inspired the first hermits in the Fayoum during the fourth century, and within two hundred years the depression held 35 monastic communities. As elsewhere in Egypt, Coptic monasticism gradually declined after the Muslim conquest, and only started to revive during last century. But the habit of pilgrimage never faded, and still ensures visitors to monasteries that are virtually deserted except on holy days.

Deir al-Azab, the nearest monastery to Fayoum City, is reached by heading 5km out along the Beni Suef road, and turning left at a fork; the monastery is on the right after just over a kilometre. Founded during the twelfth century and recently rebuilt *sans* style, the "Bachelor's Monastery" no longer houses monks, but draws many Coptic visitors on Fridays and Sundays, and also holds the **Moulid of the Virgin** (Aug 15–22). It's the burial place of St Abram, the revered Bishop of Fayoum and Giza between 1882 and 1914, whose portrait is said to reach out and shake hands with blessed visitors.

The remoter, more picturesque **Deir el-Malak** (Angel Monastery) squats on a desert hillside overlooking the cultivated lowlands, a single monk in attendance. Pilgrim buses may turn up for the **Moulid of Archangel Gabriel** (Dec 18), but otherwise it's very quiet. Wolves have been known to make their dens in the hillside caves; from the ridge you can see the Lahun gap, and sometimes the Lahun and Hawara pyramids. *Service* taxis for Qalamsha run past a yellow stone barn in the village of Qalhana, whence a dirt track leads to the monastery (1hr walk).

Two yet remoter sites are the monasteries of St George and St Samuel. **Deir Mari Girgis** was restarted early this century by two monks whose relics are in the refectory, and hosts the **Moulid of St George** a week before the Feast of Ascension. **Deir Anba Samwil** is totally isolated in the desert, 30km south of the oasis rim, and can only be reached (with a guide) by donkey or four-wheel drive. Two neighbouring springs sustain it in the Valley of Salts (*Wadi al-Mawalih*); St Samuel and other early hermits lived in caves on Jebel al-Qalamun, 4–5km east of the present monastery, which has been rebuilt by monkish engineers.

THE GREAT DESERT CIRCUIT

Only feasible for tourists since the 1980s, the **Great Desert Circuit** is one of the finest journeys Egypt has to offer. Starting from Cairo, Luxor or Assyut, it runs for over 1000km through a desert landscape pockmarked by dunes and lofty escarpments. En route, amid wind-eroded depressions, **four oases** are sustained: Bahariya, Farafra, Dakhla and Kharga. Unlike Siwa, these "inner oases" have been almost continuously under the control of the Nile Valley since the Middle Kingdom, ruled by the pharaohs, Persians, Romans, Mamlukes, Turks and British, who have left their mark in the form of temples, tombs, forts, mosques or roads.

Although each oasis has a central focus, the differences between them are as marked as their similarities. **Bahariya** and **Farafra** both score highly on their hot springs and palm groves, but Bahariya seems corrupted by Cairene ways and tourism, whereas Farafra is more rural and traditional. In **Dakhla** and **Kharga** the modern centres are less appealing than the ancient ruins and villages on their periphery, redolent of historic links with the Nile Valley or caravan routes from Sudan. Staying overnight in the haunting **White Desert** between Bahariya and Farafra is a must, while for those with transport and a lust for adventure there are remoter destinations like **Ain Dalla** (requiring military permission), or the desolate road **to Siwa Oasis**, which allows die-hard travellers to visit all of the main Western Desert oases in a mega-circuit of over 1400km. If you haven't got a car, this journey is only really possible in the other direction, starting from Siwa.

For those limited to **public transport**, travelling the whole circuit from Bahariya to Kharga will take at least a week. As the nearest oasis to Cairo, Bahariya attracts many who fancy a few days in the desert but aren't committed to doing more. If you're short on **time**, it may seem enough; carrying on to Farafra via the White Desert will add two or three days to your schedule, while once past Farafra there's little point in turning back. Motorists can now use a **new direct road** from Luxor to Kharga, which alleviates somewhat the "Assyut dilemma" (see p.277), although as yet – despite much speculation – there is no public transport on this route. Previously there was no means of travelling between Luxor and Kharga, but with the new road and the **weekly train service** (departs Luxor Thurs 7am; 6–8hr; £E10), it is now feasible to tackle the circuit in either direction. Hiring a **taxi** for the journey will cost around £E300.

Visiting the oases

Though **conditions** are getting easier, you shouldn't expect comforts in the oases. Accommodation (in government resthouses or private hotels) is generally basic; there's little choice of things to eat, rarely any alcohol, and no bright lights. Passengers might have to stand during long bus journeys, while motorists must reckon on pot-holed roads and very few petrol pumps, hundreds of kilometres apart. Keep your passport handy to show at checkpoints. There are **banks** in the "capitals" of Bahariya, Dakhla and Kharga oases, and all the oases now have **telephone** links with the outer world.

Broadly speaking, the oases share the **climate** of Nile Valley towns on the same latitude – Bahariya is like Minya, and Kharga like Luxor – but the air is fresher (although the dust sometimes causes swollen sinuses). Winter is mild by day and near freezing at night (bring a sleeping bag); during summertime temperatures can soar to 50°C at midday and hover in the 20°s after dark. From October to April, each oasis can usually muster half a dozen visitors, making it easy to assemble a group for excursions to hot springs and other sites – unlike over summer, when tourism evaporates. Spring and

---

THE NEW VALLEY

The four "Great Desert Circuit" oases are situated along a dead, prehistoric branch of the Nile, and depend on springs and wells tapping the great aquifer beneath the Libyan Desert. In 1958 the government unveiled plans to exploit this, irrigate the desert, and relocate landless peasants from the overcrowded Nile Valley and Delta to the "**New Valley**" (*El-Wadi el-Jedid*). A special New Valley Governorate was set up to run Kharga, Dakhla and Farafra oases, in collaboration with the Giza Governorate, which administers Bahariya Oasis.

Work on the New Valley began in the 1970s, but the project has since been scaled down: investments proved costlier than expected, and doubts surfaced about the subterranean water table. Previously it was thought to be replenished by underground seepage from Lake Chad and Equatorial Africa, whereas nowadays it's believed to be a finite geological legacy, sufficient for between one and seven hundred years. As a result, the oases have been caught in mid-stride, partly modernized but unsure of their long-term viability. Hopes of prosperity and fears of decline still turn on the caprices of hydrology and the wits of the oasis people, as they have since ancient times.

---

autumn are the **best times** to visit the oases, with the orchards in bloom or being harvested, and enough fellow travellers around to make sharing costs easy.

Tourism is in the hands of local officials and entrepreneurs whose competence and honesty varies. Hustling is big in Bahariya but nonexistent in Kharga; Farafra and Dakhla fall somewhere in between. Tourist officials claim to be able to arrange trips at lower prices than private operators charge. In some places this may be true, in others not. The only way to be sure is to sound out different sources and compare what they're offering. But don't let over-suspicion sour things, since you really need local help to get the best from the oases and will have to strike a deal with somebody in the end – preferably one that both sides feel happy with, as disgruntled guides or tourists can spoil the most magical spot.

Visitors should respect local values by dressing modestly and observing the conventions on bathing in **outdoor springs** (mostly concrete tanks, fed by a pipe or water percolating up from below). The ones nearest town are always used by local men; if women bathe there, it is only after dark, never when males are present, and only fully covered by a *galabiyya*. Tourists can avoid these restrictions by bathing in more isolated spots (or in the enclosed pools attached to resthouses), but most **women** cover up anyway to discourage lechery from guides and hangers-on. Women on their own should beware of entering palm groves or gardens – regarded here as an invitation to sex – or accepting rides from drivers who haven't been cleared with the tourist office.

Transport from Cairo or the Nile Valley

Starting from Cairo, book seats a day beforehand at the new Turgoman bus terminal. **Buses** to Bahariya (6hr; £E12) leave every day at 7am, 8am, 3pm and 6pm. The 7am and 6pm services continue on to Farafra (8hr; £E22) and Dakhla (12hr; £E32). Direct buses from Cairo to Dakhla or Kharga oasis are routed via the Nile Valley and Assyut–Kharga road; some enter Assyut, while others bypass the city. There are daily services to Kharga (8hr; £E28–35) at 9am, 7pm, 8pm and 9pm; the 7pm service continues to Dakhla (11hr; £E37.50). The journey times given here are only estimates; it can take longer if the bus has a wheezy engine or bursts a tyre. All Upper Egypt and Superjet buses running these routes are A/C – whether it works is another matter.

As many people from the oases moved to Cairo in the 1940s and 50s, Bahariya is also accessible by **service taxi** from the Al-Wahia café on the corner of Sharia Qadry (a few blocks south of Sharia Bur Said) in Cairo's Saiyida Zeinab quarter, where the immigrants congregated. Taxis leave in the early morning or mid-afternoon; seats are first-come, first-served, the fare £E15 apiece if the vehicle is full.

EgyptAir has two **flights** a week to the oases. A Wednesday morning flight leaves Cairo for Kharga (1hr; US$132) and continues to Dakhla (US$160) before returning to Cairo. The Sunday morning flight is routed via Assyut to Kharga and then back to Cairo. The view of the desert from the air is awesome.

Kharga – and, to a lesser extent, Dakhla – is also accessible by daily **buses** and **service taxis from Assyut** (see p.279 for details); the bus to Kharga takes four to five hours (£E6–10), and a few continue on to Dakhla (8hr; £E10–12). *Service* taxis run between Assyut and Kharga (£E8–9), from where you can pick up another *service* to Dakhla.

For details of the journeys to (and between) each oasis, see the relevant section.

Bahariya Oasis

Bahariya Oasis is the smallest of the four depressions, only 94km long and 42km wide; its desert floor and lower escarpments formed of Cretaceous sandstone, overlaid by limestone and basalt from the Eocene period, rich in fossils. Yet despite having the high-

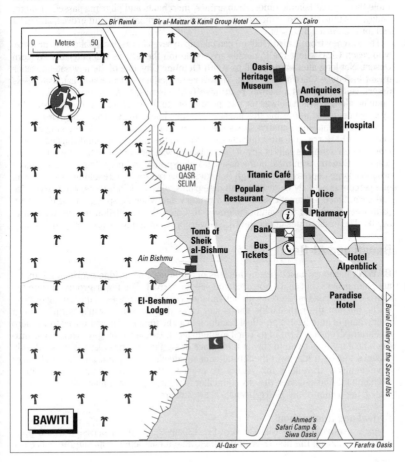

VALLEY OF THE MUMMIES

In 1996 a donkey stumbled and broke through the desert's surface near the ruined Temple of Alexander, to reveal the first of hundreds, possibly thousands, of Greco-Roman tombs. The area has been named "the Valley of the Mummies" and constitutes the **largest concentration of mummies ever found**. Excavations will continue for years to come, and at present no tourist visits are allowed. Already the cache is yielding evidence that for the Greco-Romans, mummification was a traditional rather than religious practice, as much of the typical pharaonic detail (mummies facing east, the presence of coffins and canopic jars) is missing.

est elevation above sea level of the four oases, its water table is nearer the surface, making agriculture easier here. It is known to have been under pharaonic control by the Middle Kingdom, when *Zezes* (as the oasis was known) exported wine to the Nile Valley.

During the Late Period Bahariya thrived as an artery between Egypt and Libya, while throughout Islamic times, Arab armies, merchants and pilgrims passed through. Today, it is tourists who come here to enjoy the hot springs and palm groves, and get a feel for the Western Desert.

The **journey from Cairo** (360km) can take up to seven hours; it can take an hour merely to reach Giza, where the Pyramids are visible (on the left) as you enter the Western Desert. Not long afterwards you'll pass **6th October City**, one of the new satellite cities meant to reduce Cairo's congestion. To relieve the tedium of traversing flat, featureless desert, vehicles stop at a halfway **resthouse** (with biscuits, *fuul*, soft drinks and toilets). Running alongside is a railway for transporting ore to the steel mills at Helwan, supplied by a vast open-cast iron **mine** that imparts a ferrous hue to the surrounding desert.

Soon after entering Bahariya Oasis the road passes a gravel track to the outlying settlement of El-Harra, and subsequently side roads to the villages of Mandisha and Agouz. Don't get off if the bus calls at any of these places – wait for the end of the line at the oasis "capital", **Bawiti**. As in most of the oases, people, springs and palm groves are scattered around a large depression. Although Bahariya's covers 1200 square kilometres, less than one percent is actually cultivated, with date palms, olive and fruit trees, vegetables, rice and corn. Since a dramatic slump half a century ago when 32 springs dried up, 63,900 palm trees died, and thousands emigrated to Cairo, the population has risen again to 30,000. The oasis comes under the Giza Governorate, owing to its proximity to Cairo.

Bawiti and Al-Qasr

BAWITI harbours a picturesque nucleus of old houses on a ridge overlooking luxuriant palm groves, but that's not what you see on **arrival**. The lower ground beside the Cairo–Farafra road is littered with half-finished New Valley projects, disrupting donkey traffic but not the ramshackle shops and cafés that enliven Bawiti's "strip". Almost everything of note from a practical standpoint can be found here, and buses from Cairo or Farafra drop you right in it. You'll immediately be accosted by guys from **rival outfits** who'll try to get you to stay at their place or sign up for trips. Animosity seethes in Bawiti's tourist trade; over-the-top tales of misdeeds, corruption and hotel closures have amused travellers for years. At present, things are under the thumb of Mohammed Abd el-Qader, the city councillor for tourism, but familiar figures like Salah Sherif, the owner of the *Hotel Alpenblick*, are still around.

Arrival and information

There's a **tourist office** (daily except Fri 8.30am–2pm and on occasion also 5–8pm; ☎018/802-222) on the first floor of the government compound opposite the police station; out of hours, look for Mohammed Abd el-Qader in the *Paradise Hotel*. He claims to be able to arrange taxi trips for less than the price asked by operators like Salah, Yehi, or Badry at the *Popular Restaurant*. All of them are useful **contacts** to some extent, and with a bit of luck you may be able to play one off against another when negotiating the price of an excursion

Accommodation

Currently, tourists can choose between three **hotels** in Bawiti, a fourth about 5km north of town, and two **campsites** miles into the desert. The choice comes down to whether you want desert seclusion, or prefer to have the "facilities" of Bawiti closer at hand.

El Beshmo Lodge, near the Tomb of Sheikh al-Bishmu (☎018/802-177). Situated above palm groves with the desert lying beyond, the location reminds you that you are actually in an oasis. Its clean singles, doubles and triples have fans and are available with or without private bathroom. Breakfast is included, other meals are served and there is a laundry service. ④–⑤.

Hotel Alpenblick (☎018/802-184). This perennial survivor remains the choice of most tourists for its clean, spacious rooms, pleasant garden and patio area. Range of overpriced double and triple rooms with and without bath; hot water at times if you're lucky. Breakfast is included and other meals and beer can be provided. ③–④.

Kamil Group International Health Centre, on the very edge of Bawiti below the Black Mountain (☎018/802-322). Rooms are clean and pleasant with en-suite facilities, but overpriced even though rates include half-board and use of the hot springs and small gym. There is also a sauna (£E20) and massage room (£E35). ⑦.

Paradise Hotel, on the main street, opposite the post office (☎018/802-600). Offers grimy triples and a single bathroom, slightly redeemed by a garden. £E5 per person including breakfast. ①.

CAMPSITES

Ahmed's Safari Camp, 4km south of Bawiti (☎018/802-770). Features a variety of basic thatched huts, clean and simple rooms with fan and bathroom, plus has two overpriced "luxury" rooms with a few furnishings and breakfast included. There's a hot spring nearby and guests are promised free transport into town, although this may not materialize. Food is allegedly available 24 hours, and there's a washing machine. Bikes are available for £E10 per day. ①–④.

Salah's Campground, out at Bir el-Ghaba (see map p.422; no phone, contact through the *Alpenblick*). Perfect for hermits and nature-lovers, the hot springs and scenery here are utterly relaxing, but you must bring food and drink, plus candles, since the site is far from anywhere and lacks electricity. As jeep-loads of tourists visit the spring most nights during winter, you should be able to get a lift back eventually. The campsite consists of straw huts with mattresses and nothing else. ①.

Eating and other practicalities

Eating out in Bawiti is unexciting, as in most of the oases. Travellers tend to make a beeline for the *Popular Restaurant*, as it sells **beer** (£E8) and is almost the only place to eat; the owner, Mohammed Bayoumi Gahsh, gets irked by people asking the cost of dishes, asserting that if the meal is good, what does the price matter? The nearby *Titanic Café* only serves drinks. You can change **money** (but not travellers' cheques) at the National Bank for Development, by the government building. The **telephone** office (daily 8am–midnight) just off the main road can reach the rest of Egypt, but struggles to place international calls despite improvements to the phone system. The **post office** (daily except Fri 8am–2pm) is also located on the main drag.

Local sights

The only "sight" in new Bawiti is a small **Oasis Heritage Museum** (no set hours) of clay figures in scenes from oasis life, by a young local artist, Mohammed Eed, who is obviously inspired by the example of Badr in Farafra (see p.441). Admission is free but donations are welcome; some figures are for sale. Better to follow the side road past the *Popular Restaurant* and find Bawiti's **old quarter**, a huddle of mud-brick homes and mausolea flanking a main street where elders sit and gossip on *mastabas*. To appreciate its commanding position, enter the alley winding off behind an incinerator on a square, which leads to **Ain Bishmu**. A craggy fissure in the bedrock where a spring was hewn in Roman times, it gushes hot water (30°C) into a natural basin where boys swim and girls wash clothes, before flowing into the **palm groves** below. Mostly owned by the Dawawida family (like the spring itself), the gardens look especially lovely when spangled with apricot blossom in spring. Also nearby lies the dovecote shaped **Tomb of Sheikh al-Bishmu** which local children will happily lead you into.

The street runs on into **AL-QASR**, an older village built directly over the capital of the oasis in pharaonic times and continuously inhabited since then. Its houses incorporate odd walls and stones from a bygone XXVI Dynasty temple, and a Roman triumphal arch that survived until the mid-nineteenth century. The ancient town extended for 3km to **Ain al-Muftillah**, where four **ruined chapels** depict King Amasis and various deities, amongst them Bes, whose leering visage used to be a favoured tattoo on the thighs of dancing girls. By crossing the rise and a dune beyond, you can enjoy a **panoramic view** of Al-Qasr, Bawiti, and the springs and mountains described below. To avoid going astray, it's best to reach Ain al-Muftillah by taking the Siwa road at the main fork, then turning left at the first side road and again at the second. This should take you past the Tomb of Sheikh Mubarak in Al-Qasr; turn right at the next fork and follow the road to the end to reach the ruins.

Ask at the tourist office or the Antiquities Department about the current status of other sites near Bawiti, which have been closed for years but are always said to be about to reopen. Within the village itself, the Egyptologist Ahmed Fakhry discovered two painted tombs on the small hill of **Qarat Qasr Salim**. For obvious reasons, oasis burial grounds are always on barren ridges or flats. The most extensive is the ancient **Burial Gallery of the Sacred Ibis**, whose tunnels run beneath a modern cemetery outside town. Owing to the thousands of mummified birds found there, locals call it **Qarat al-Faragi** (Ridge of the Chicken Merchant). In Bahariya, the burials of old people are accompanied by rituals to prevent younger kinsfolk from following them to the grave.

If you're unsure about finding your way around the ridges and palmeries, **tours** of the locality are offered by *Hotel Alpenblick* and *The Paradise* for about £E10 a head (less for large groups).

Around the oasis

With none of its antiquities open to the public at present, trips around Bahariya Oasis focus on bathing in **hot or cold springs** – various operators with cars or pick-ups will be happy to take groups for a negotiable sum; bargain hard. Closer to town, you can walk out to the palms for a glimpse of the oasis ecology and **wildlife**: Bahariya abounds in insect and birdlife – most noticeably wheatears, which semaphore to each other with their black and white tails, while birds of prey stay aloft, soaring on thermals.

The hottest (45°C) and nearest spring is **Bir Ramla**, a nice 2km walk from Bawiti past palm and fruit orchards, but quite exposed. Males can bathe here in shorts; women only at night, in full-length opaque clothing. Similar rules apply to **Bir al-Mattar**, a concrete tank of tepid (25°C), faintly sulphurous water, 7km northeast of Bawiti by desert track (£E10 return by taxi, group rate). This "Well of the Airport" gets its name from an abandoned wartime airstrip, visible en route. Skirting palm groves and fields where camels graze, the track carries on to **Bir el-Ghaba** (Well of the Forest), a hot and a cold spring in a eucalyptus grove. As both men and women can swim here, it's the most popular spot with tourists (group-rate return £E25). Some find it so idyllic that they **stay** at *Salah's Campground*; bring food if you're tempted.

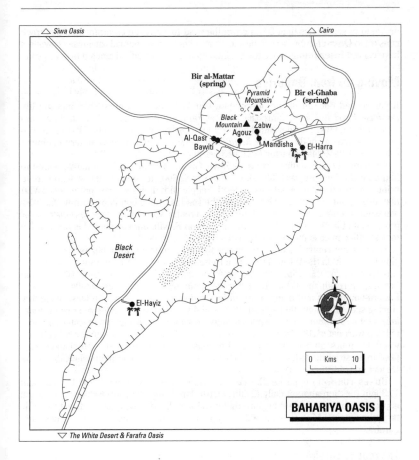

△ Siwa Oasis   △ Cairo

Bir al-Mattar
(spring)

Pyramid
Mountain

Bir el-Ghaba
(spring)

Black
Mountain ▲ Zabw
Agouz
Al-Qasr ● ●
Bawiti Mandisha
El-Harra

Black
Desert

El-Hayiz

N

0   Kms   10

BAHARIYA OASIS

▽ *The White Desert & Farafra Oasis*

Visiting Bir el-Ghaba by day affords a view of mountains and hills that can be excursions in themselves. Jebel Dist (Mountain of the Pot) is more accurately described by locals in the tourist trade as **Pyramid Mountain**. It is a great spot for hunting **fossils**; geologists have found dinosaur remains here. Another trip is to Jebel Mayisra, whose mass is capped by black dolorite and volcanic basalt, plus a ruined look-out post manned in 1916 by Captain Williams, for which it is nicknamed the **Black Mountain** or the "English Mountain". Most of the inhabited parts of the oasis are visible from its summit. To reach either site requires a car, preferably 4WD.

Most tourists pay little heed to the **villages** outside Bawiti, whose people are friendly and hospitable. It's feasible to walk to **AGOUZ** (Old One), only 2km away via the first paved road to the left off the Cairo highway. Agouz is unique for being inhabited by the descendants of families banished from Siwa Oasis for the loose morals of their women. Like many old oasis villages, its maze-like core of mud houses goes back to medieval times and covers an ancient site, while a new settlement lies closer to the road. Seven kilometres out is another turn-off that runs past a field of **dunes** named Ghard Mandisha, after the village of **MANDISHA**. Paltry compared to the dune fields in other oases, they still pose a real threat to neighbouring **ZABW**, where houses and palm groves have been drowned in sand. Less than 500m down the road towards the escarpment, a dirt track runs off to **Qasr el-Zabw**, a rock beside a trail where Libyan nomads and other travellers have carved **inscriptions** since the twelfth century – now badly damaged by quarrying.

Moving on from Bahariya

If you've had enough of the desert, you can get a bus to **Cairo** from opposite the *Paradise Hotel* in Bawiti (6hr; £E12–14) at 7am and 3pm daily; those starting from Farafra on Sunday, Tuesday and Thursday leave Bawiti at around 3pm. There may also be *service* taxis from the *Popular Restaurant* at 8am and mid-afternoon, terminating in Cairo's Saiyida Zeinab quarter (£E10–15 per person).

Although there is a direct **road to Siwa Oasis** (420km) you'd be hard pressed to find a local driver prepared to risk it for under £E600, nor enough fellow travellers to bring the cost down to an affordable level. People with their own car (preferably 4WD) may use it, but should exercise caution; the road is in bad condition with no facilities whatsoever, only checkpoints at intervals. Currently, you simply have to register your passport and licence with Military Intelligence in Bawiti, but you should enquire at the tourist office in case the rules have changed.

Tourists not returning to Cairo invariably carry on to **Farafra Oasis**, maybe stopping for a night in the **White Desert** en route. As Bawiti's tour operators demand £E35 (group rate) for this trip, you may prefer to take a cheaper excursion (£E25) from Farafra, or reach the White Desert under your own steam. This entails catching a Farafra-bound bus and being dropped in the desert 20–40km before Qasr al-Farafra. Having spent the night there, return to the highway and wait for a lift into town (*inshallah*). Out of summer, it's a feasible strategy providing you bring lots of water and gear to keep warm at night. If you want a hot meal, you'll also need to bring (or collect) firewood. On tours, an evening meal and breakfast should be included, and blankets supplied to those without sleeping bags. The route to Farafra is described below; the White Desert on p.442.

Buses run from opposite *The Paradise Hotel* in Bawiti to Farafra at 11.30am and 11.30pm (or thereabouts) daily (2–3hr; £E10). **Hitching** a lift from Bahariya to Farafra is possible, but you should be sure that it's going all the way; quiz drivers at the military checkpoint. Motorists should carry ample **petrol** as there are no pumps until Farafra.

The road to Farafra

The 180-kilometre journey to Farafra takes about three hours, so motorists hoping to reach the White Desert before sunset should allow a bit longer. For part of the way the road crosses a gravelly **Black Desert** with charred outcrops and table-top rocks. Some stretches are quite smooth, but others are like solidified lava flows and compel detours off *piste*. Roughly 30km from Bawiti there's a white **tomb** atop a crag in the desert to the right: a monument to Swiss man René Michel, a pioneer of tourism to Bahariya, who died here from heatstroke in 1986. Another 10km on, the road passes **EL-HAYIZ**, Bahariya's southernmost oasis, with two villages (pop. 4000) and some ruins from early Christian times, when the community was far larger. The Copts believe that one of Christ's apostles, St Bartholomew, visited Bahariya before his martyrdom, and perhaps even died there. Military permission is required to visit the **ruined Roman camp and church**, marked with Coptic graffiti. Fakhry reckons that El-Hayiz was the "fourth oasis" described by texts in the temple at Edfu (see p.367).

Gigantic drifts of sand buttress the escarpment that separates the oasis depressions; a magnificent sight from the **Naqb el-Sillum** (Pass of the Stairs). In the excitement of photographing it, don't point your lens anywhere near the microwave mast. As the road descends into the Farafra depression, you'll see the landmark **Twin Peaks** at the end of the range of hills on the left, while 10km later the first chalk inselbergs appear on the horizon. These rock formations occur all over the northern part of Farafra Oasis, but are most profuse in the **White Desert**, which most guides take to mean somewhere within 20–40km of Qasr al-Farafra, though sometimes as far out as 80km. If you're not going to get out there, sit back and enjoy the view, which peters out into a dusty chalk pan for the last 10km to Qasr al-Farafra.

Farafra Oasis

Farafra Oasis is the least populous, most isolated of the four oases on the circuit. When camels were the only means of travel, the Farafonis had less contact with Bahariya (a journey of four days) than with Dakhla, which was tenuously connected to the Forty Days Road. Fakhry relates how the villagers once lost track of time and could only ascertain the right day for Friday prayers by sending a rider to Dakhla. Before the paved road was built in 1978 it took 4WD and a winch truck a whole day to climb the Bahariya escarpment. Yet the oasis had dealings with the Nile Valley as early as the V Dynasty, when it was called *Ta-ihw*, the "Land of the Cow". Even today, Farafra's cows are of the same breed as those depicted in ancient tombs and temples, though no pharaonic monuments have been found in the oasis.

Qasr al-Farafra was the only village in the oasis before the New Valley scheme seeded five new hamlets across the depression. Four extended families account for

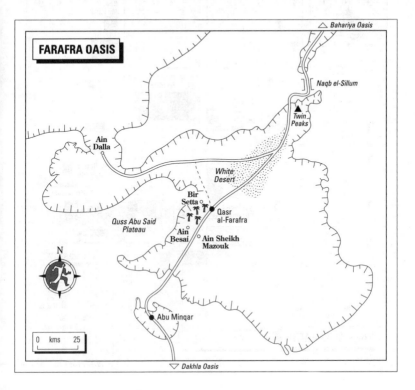

most of its 4000 inhabitants, whose tight-knit community is noted for its piety, apparent during Ramadan, when the mosque overflows with robed imams and sheikhs. Tourists are kept at a distance, except by a genial clique of fixers, who are keen to arrange excursions to the White Desert and other beauty spots in the oasis.

There are now **buses** as well as **service taxis** that run several times daily from Farafra to Bahariya and Dakhla oases.

Qasr al-Farafra

As in Bawiti, the low ground in **QASR AL FARAFRA** has been colonized by New Valley infrastructure, which obscures your view of the hilltop village, backing onto palm groves. Its traditional mud houses have an austere beauty, their low windowless facades topped by flowing pediments or crenellations. Facing the street are broad *mastabas* where mothers chat and elders ruminate. Everyone knows each other and their lineage; many are of Libyan ancestry and bear the surname Senussi. Farafra's pop-

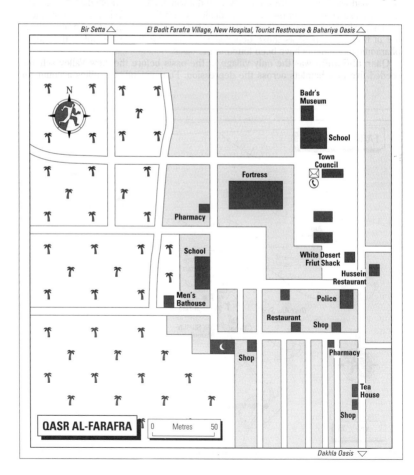

ulation has long been minuscule (only 542 in 1892), and agriculture limited to the near-by palm groves and a few outlying springs, keeping the oasis poor (hence its lack of tra-ditional jewellery). Even now its shops and market are meagre compared with those of other oases, and frugality is the order of the day – yet there's plenty to enjoy if you meet the right people.

Arrival, accommodation and information

Unless you ask to be dropped at one of the two places to stay in Farafra, you will arrive at a tea house on the main road near the centre. Your first choice of **accom-modation** is the *Badit El Farafra Village* (Cairo ☎02/345 8524; ③–⑤), whose rooms are tastefully designed, many with split-levels – a lower seating area and a raised bed with mosquito net. There are double rooms with and without facilities, and the shared bathrooms are immaculate. There are also some quad-share rooms and you can pitch a tent for £E5 per person. Good meals are available (£E5–25) and can be eaten on the rooftop terrace, and Stella is also served. The grim tourist resthouse (①) at the entrance to town is only worth considering if you're seriously broke.

Stay a day here and you're bound to meet a handful of **local characters** with an interest in tourism. Saad, Hamdy and Atif Ali, of the *Badit El Farafra*, organize excur-sions, and nighttime parties with Bedouin music and dancing (you'll be expected to par-ticipate). Though women might feel uneasy with the dancing, the guys are basically trustworthy. You may also encounter "Mr Socks", selling home-made camel-hair wool-lies; the artist Badr (see below) and his jeep-driving brother, Gamel; or even the Mayor of Farafra, Mohammed Ra'afat, who brags endlessly of his plans for the oasis. As these guys constitute the only game in town and the number of tourists is tiny, how good a time you have boils down to personal chemistry.

The village

Behind the school you'll find **Badr's Museum**, the creation of a self-taught artist who has successfully exhibited in Germany, France and Britain, but stayed in the oasis, about which he feels passionately. Badr detests the urban-style buildings of New Valley, believing that Farafra can be developed in harmony with its traditional character. His museum resembles a *qasr*, with reliefs of camels and farmers decorating its walls, and an antique wooden lock on the door. Its dozen-odd rooms exhibit Badr's rustic sculp-tures and surreal paintings; stuffed wildlife, weird fossils and pyrites. The Farafonis find his desert garden incomprehensible, but relish his portraits of local people. The museum opens when Badr wishes; there's no admission charge, but donations are appreciated.

Previously, he painted *Hadj* **murals** of snarling lions and flying eagles on local hous-es. Sadly they have all vanished due to salt corrosion and only two more have been painted since – one for Atif and one for Badr's parents. Badr's "Fourth Dream" (as he puts it) is a studio-house embodying his ideas about architecture and creativity – if you're invited to visit, accept the offer.

Otherwise, you can investigate the mud-brick **fortress** (*qasr*) that gives the village its name (though the full appellation is rarely used in everyday speech). Until early this century, the Farafonis would retreat inside when invaders came; each family had a des-ignated room, where, during normal times, provisions were stored and guarded by a watchman. Damaged by heavy rainfall, it began to crumble in the 1950s; the less dam-aged parts are now home to a few families, and blend into the surrounding houses.

Last but not least, you can wander around the **palm groves** behind the village, which look especially lovely an hour before sunset. They are divided into walled gardens planted with olive and fruit trees as well as date palms (whose branches are used to fence the land). You can walk the paths freely, but shouldn't enter the gardens uninvited; for single women to do so is regarded as provocative. Likewise, avert your eyes from the **men's bathhouse** on the edge of the village, where youths splash around in a concrete tank fed by a pipe gushing warm water. Foreigners are expected to bathe at other springs.

Eating and other practicalities

It doesn't take long to sample the culinary delights of Farafra. Aside from *Badit El Farafra*, the *Hussein Restaurant* does beans and egg-fried *taamiya* for breakfast, and maybe chicken later in the day; a few other small restaurants dotted around the village serve similar fare. For *sheeshas* and tea or Turkish coffee, there's a single tea house.

There's a **post office** (daily except Fri 8am–2pm) and a **telephone exchange** (24hr) which should be able to take international calls by the end of 2000. In the absence of a bank, you may be able to change small amounts of **cash** with locals. There's a new **hospital** between *Badit El Farafra* and the tourist resthouse. Once a year doctors from Cairo come here for a week and treat locals free of charge.

The White Desert and other sites

If they haven't already done the trip from Bahariya, most tourists want to visit the **White Desert**, camping out to experience its magic. A surreal landscape of fungoid shapes that glint pale gold in the midday sun and turn pink and violet around dusk, resembling icebergs at dawn and snowdrifts by moonlight, the chalk outcrops loom over dusty ground littered with fossils, quartz crystals and iron pyrites shaped like sea-urchins or twigs. Herds of **gazelles** may be glimpsed at daybreak, when they forage for a couple of hours. The White Desert extends on both sides of the highway starting only 20km from Farafra, but the *yardangs* (rocks) are finer further away from the road. Tourists are often taken into the area behind **Bir al-Akhbar**, a **hot spring** signposted near the roadside 33km from Farafra.

Getting there (and back) is a toss-up between effort and economy. Coming from Bahariya, the cheapest way is to visit the White Desert before Farafra, by getting off the bus at a promising spot and hitching into town next day. Although it's feasible to hitch out from Farafra, local drivers are likely to charge for rides, and could ask as much as £E50. Forget about using the bus to Bahariya, which either leaves so early that you'd be stranded all day in the desert before sunset came, or too late to see it at all. The alternative is to muster a group to share the cost of an overnight **excursion** (£E250) through Hamdy & Co, using a jeep that can cavort among the *yardangs* over a wider area than you'd cover on foot. They'll provide blankets (vital if you haven't got a sleeping bag), water, firewood and hot food, which independent campers would otherwise have to arrange for themselves.

Another popular excursion is to **Bir Setta** (Well Six), 6km west of town, a concrete tank of sulphurous hot water that's good for wallowing but stains clothes brown. You're taken there at night, to bathe under the stars and have a party. The unfinished construction of a hotel has somewhat diminished the place's appeal, however, and trips may be on offer to other nearby springs. If you do want to stay longer here, bring supplies of everything, including water. It's feasible to walk from town to Bir Setta once you've seen the route; coming back, Farafra's palm groves are unmistakable. The group rate for an evening trip is £E40. A jeep can carry eight people, nine at a pinch.

Hamdy confesses that he's tired of always visiting Bir Setta and the White Desert, when he knows many other beauty spots in the oasis. Twelve kilometres west of town there is a man-made lake, which, although slimy-bottomed, is a great spot for a refreshing swim – Hamdy organizes return trips there for a couple of hours for £E10 per person. At **Ain Besai**, 15km from town, there are small rock tombs and chapels of a settlement abandoned in Christian times and dug up by treasure-hunters, near a cold

---

AIN DALLA AND THE LOST ARMY OF CAMBYSES

Though off-limits without permission from Cairo, **Ain Dalla** (Spring of the Shade) deserves a mention for its epic part in the history of the Westen Desert. As the last water-hole before the Great Sand Sea, used by raiders and smugglers since antiquity, motor-ized explorers during the 1920s and 1930s, and the Long Range Desert Group in World War II, it now has a small Egyptian army garrison that chases smugglers. Both sides use 4WD instead of camels, as in the days of the Frontier Camel Corps, which once pursued a caravan of hashish all the way across the desert to Giza. The 120-kilometre paved road to Ain Dalla begins 75km from Farafra, at a checkpoint between two stretches of White Desert; there are great rock formations for most of the way.

Some believe that Ain Dalla was the last-known location of the **Lost Army of Cambyses**. Despatched by Egypt's Persian conqueror to destroy the famous Oracle of Amun at Siwa Oasis, the entire 50,000-strong army disappeared en route in 524 BC. Herodotus relates how the troops were resting when a sandstorm blew up and complete-ly buried them; Fakhry reckons that they separated, panicked and got lost, eventually dying of thirst. Archeologists still dream of finding Cambyses' army beneath the outlying dunes of the Great Sand Sea (see p.474), but admit that the likelihood of doing so is nil.

---

freshwater spring where you can bathe in summer; the pool is surrounded by vegeta-tion and 4m deep in the middle. Another spot is the small, uninhabited oasis of **Ain el-Tanien**, where you can also bathe. Both are well off the main road, so you can't get there alone; the rate for an overnight trip to either is £E40 per person. **Ain Sheikh Mazouk** is an old palm-garden 23km south of town, sufficiently near the main road that you could hitch there. It has a hot sulphur spring feeding a concrete tank where local men bathe, and an ancient Roman well of fresh water. Alas, women can't swim in either. Altogether there are 26 ancient wells or springs in Farafra.

Moving on from Farafra

If you're doing the circuit in reverse, **buses to Bahariya** (2–3hr; £E10) and **Cairo** (8hr; £E25) leave at around 10am and 10pm daily. You buy tickets on board and there's usually no problem getting a seat, but be sure to arrive in good time, as the bus may leave before its scheduled departure time. Otherwise, there's a faint chance of **service taxis** to Bahariya, or lifts from cars that have just deposited tourists after a night in the White Desert and are heading back. Expect to pay about £E15 per person for a full taxi load.

Buses to Dakhla Oasis (4hr; £E12) are scheduled to leave around 2pm and 2am daily. *Service* taxis also cover the route, maybe once or twice a day. In a fully loaded vehicle passengers pay £E15 each; fewer individuals pay more. If you're planning to do this, spread the word so drivers know that you're interested. Buses both ways can be flagged down from the tourist resthouse or the *Badit El Farafra* and they stop at the tea house in town for a few minutes. **Hitchhiking** from the military checkpoint outside town is also feasible, but be sure your ride is going all the way.

The road to Dakhla

Relatively few vehicles follow the 310-kilometre road **between Farafra and Dakhla Oasis**, where the only fuel en route is reserved for road gangs and military outposts. Once past Ain Sheikh Mazouk, the desert shifts from white stone to gravel and sand until you reach **Abu Minqar** (Father of the Beak). A green smudge in the wilderness, where wells have been sunk and houses built in an effort to attract settlers, it is the westernmost point on the oases route, only 100km from the Libyan border. There's a

tea house 105km from Farafra, after which the road skirts the edge of the vast escarpment that delineates **Dakhla Oasis**, where you'll pass through Al-Qasr and Mut Talatta
before reaching Mut, Dakhla's main centre.

Dakhla Oasis

Verdant cultivated areas and a great wall of rose-hued rock across the northern horizon make a feast for the eyes in **Dakhla Oasis**. Partitioned by dunes into more or less
irrigated, fertile enclaves, the oasis supports 75,000 people living in fourteen settlements strung out along the Farafra and Kharga roads. Although it's the outlying sites
that hold most attraction, the majority of travellers base themselves in **Mut** (pronounced "moot"), Dakhla's "capital", which has better facilities. Buses and pick-ups
between Mut and the villages enable you to see how the Dakhlans have reclaimed land,
planted new crops, and generally made the best of New Valley developments. Water is
relatively abundant in the oasis, which has over 520 wells in its 410 square kilometres.

Most **villages** have spread down from their original hilltop maze of medieval houses
and covered streets, into breeze-block houses with schools and other public buildings
near the roadside. Besides this exotic architecture, Dakhla has pharaonic, Roman and
Coptic antiquities, dunes, palm groves and hot springs to explore. It was in this region
that the *Breitling Orbiter 3*, the first balloon to circumnavigate the globe, touched down
after twenty days above the earth, on March 21, 1999.

Mut

Dakhla's capital, **MUT**, was branded a miserable-looking place by travellers early last
century, but it has come on apace since the 1950s, as the Dakhlans have subverted or
embraced planned "modernity" according to their needs and tastes. The architect of
Mut's already crumbling low-rise flats is unlikely to have foreseen their balconies being
converted into extra rooms or pigeon coops, and the four-lane road that snakes through
town rarely carries anything heavier than cyclists. Yet the locals welcome the hospital
and schools, and big capital investments like the Fish Pond wastewater project.

Information and accommodation
The energetic, conscientious Omar Ahmed flits between the new **tourist office**
(☎092/821-686), 300m west of Midan Tahrir, and the old office in the *Tourist Resthouse* on
New Mosque Square (both daily 8am–2pm, and maybe 6–9pm). He also swears that you
can contact him at home (☎092/820-782) at other times. Besides Omar there are unofficial **fixers** like Nasser (who owns the *Nasser Hotel* in Sheikh Wali and whose brothers
own the *Ahmed Hamdy*, *Hamdy* and *Abu Mohammed* restaurants) or the boss of *Anwar
Paradise Restaurant*, who often approach visitors. All of them are useful sources of information, bearing in mind that they'll badmouth their rivals and try to persuade you to sign
up for an excursion (see below). Mut also has a conspicuously new **State Information
Office**, which offers no help but is often mistaken for the tourist office.

ACCOMMODATION
As oases go, Dakhla offers a fair range of **accommodation**: in Mut; at Mut Talatta
springs (3km north); or out in the villages of Sheikh Wali (5km), El-Douhous (7km)
and Al-Qasr (32km). Foreigners can no longer stay in the *Dar al-Wafden* government
hotel, and the Tourist Village designed by Hassan Fathy remains unfinished. Several
other places are due to open soon, including the renovated tourist resthouse and a hotel
above the *Anwar Paradise Restaurant*, but as always in Egypt it's a game of wait and see.
All the places listed except *Gardens* and *Mebarez* serve Stella.

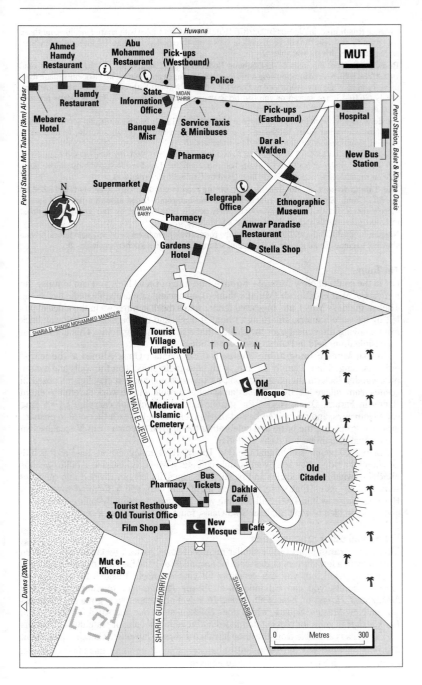

Al-Qasr Resthouse, in Al-Qasr (☎092/876-103). Five spartan triples with shared facilities, for those who want to stay near the village. Excellent view from the rooftop. Satellite TV, international phone and table-tennis. Meals available. ①.

Bedwen Campe, just outside El-Douhous Bedouin village, signposted off the Budkhulu road (☎092/850-605). Scenic location atop a hill overlooking dunes and fields. The basic huts made from palm fronds are slightly overpriced at £E30 for a double without bathroom, but it's a magical spot. Meals (£E10–15) are served or you can bring your own food and cook it. Camel safaris are also arranged from here. ②.

Gardens, an easy walk from everywhere in Mut (☎092/821-577). Simple mosquito-screened rooms with fans and rather dingy bathrooms; there's also a palm garden restaurant, roof terrace and a washing machine. Favoured by low-budget travellers. ②.

Mebarez, out past Midan Tahrir and the tourist office (☎092/821-524). Clean, carpeted rooms with soft beds and choice of fan or A/C; private bathroom optional. Breakfast included, other meals available on request. International phone line. Used by Explore tour groups. ④.

Mut Talatta Resort, at Mut Talatta, 200m off the road (☎092/821-530). Recently refurbished by the MG Group. Six immaculate rooms with fan and bathroom, based around a large hot spring; there's also a villa that can accommodate thirty people (mostly used by tour groups). Breakfast included, other meals and drinks served at a premium. ⑥.

Nasser, in Sheikh Wali (☎092/822-727). Adobe rooms with palm frond beds and sand floors; private showers to come. Small garden in a peaceful setting. Meals and a kitchen available. ②.

TheTown

Off to the south of **New Mosque Square** (the hub of social life), you can glimpse the remains of **Mut el-Khorab** (Mut the Ruined), an ancient city probably dedicated to the Theban goddess Mut. Cute, big-eared fennec foxes dwell in burrows in the sides of pits left by treasure-hunters, emerging to hunt at dusk, and can be seen on the way back from enjoying the sunset over the **dunes** that rise beyond the fields. This is the most accessible dune field in Dakhla, but not the finest.

To visit Mut's **Ethnographic Museum** (£E2), contact Omar Ahmed at the tourist office. Arranged like a family dwelling with household objects on the walls and a complex wooden lock on the palm-log door, its seven rooms contain clay figures posed in scenes from village life, by the Khargan artist Mabrouk, whose work is reminiscent of Badr's in Farafra Oasis. Notice the gazelle-hide receptacle for carrying fat on long camel journeys, and the spiked basket that Dakhlans hid beneath the sand to ensnare gazelles. Preparing the bride and celebrating the pilgrim's return from Mecca are two scenes that remain part of oasis life today.

About 2000 people still inhabit the **Old Town**, which many visitors miss as it is hidden behind a ridge crowned by an Islamic cemetery. Mut originated as a hilltop *qasr* or **citadel** of windowless facades and twisting passages, its interior divided into quarters separated by gates that were locked at night; and was still a fortified town when Harding-King saw it in 1909. Still bustling with life though gradually falling into ruin, it gives you an idea of what Shali, in Siwa Oasis, must have been like a century ago.

Eating and other practicalities

Most **restaurants** in Mut offer similar menus of soup, pasta, vegetable stew, chicken or *kofta*, with a few starters or desserts for around £E6–10 all in. They don't always have everything listed, but you can certainly fill your stomach. Besides the *Gardens* or *Mebarez* hotels, you can eat indoors at *Anwar Paradise*, or outdoors at the *Abu Mohammed*, *Hamdy* or, best of all, *Ahmed Hamdy*. For cheaper eats, go to the nameless café on New Mosque Square, which does chicken, stew, rice and salad for £E3–5. The *Dakhla Café* is good for playing dominoes and meeting people, or watching Arab films on TV. Stella is available from the shop beside the *Anwar Paradise*. There's a small fruit and vegetable **market** on Midan Tahrir.

Mut's Banque Misr (daily except Friday 8.30am–2pm & sometimes 6–8pm) can change **money** or travellers' cheques. International calls can be made from the **telephone exchange** (24hr) or, more expensively, from either the new telephone office 100m west of Midan Tahrir or the *Mebarez Hotel*. The telegraph office is next to the exchange, while the **post office** is on New Mosque Square (daily except Fri 8am–2pm).

Mut's **hospital** (☎092/821-555; ambulance ☎123) is well equipped by the standards of the Western Desert, and most of the villages have a medical post. You'll pass the **police station** (☎092/821-500) en route to the hospital, and tyre-repair shops and a **petrol station** along the road to Mut Talatta. A small shop opposite the New Mosque is one of a few in Mut that sells **film**.

Transport and excursions around the oasis

Transport around Dakhla is hit and miss, depending on your destination. **Taxis** are the priciest option, with hard bargaining required should you wish the driver to wait at sites and then return to Mut. Omar at the tourist office says he can fix one for a decent rate, with no hassle; also a **minibus** or **4WD** vehicle, with driver. Sceptics could try both approaches, before committing themselves. Whatever the cost, it's obviously more economical for groups than for solo travellers.

Most Dakhlans get around by covered **pick-ups**, which speed out towards both ends of the oasis from depots either side of Midan Tahrir. They can be flagged down at any point and charge a flat(ish) fare of 50pt. Some **minibuses** also cover the same routes; those leaving from beside the hospital are for the eastern villages beyond Balat, which is the terminus for pick-ups from the eastbound depot. Both kinds of vehicle are faster

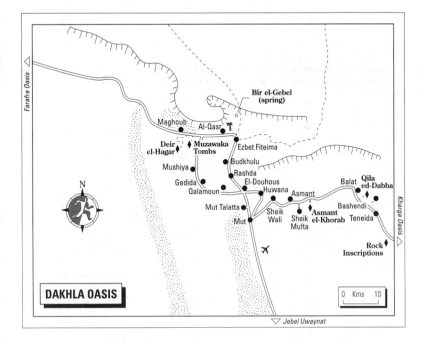

than local buses, and most active in the morning. Beware that drivers may be tempted to charge "special" rates if you request somewhere like Mut Talatta late at night; or if there are no other Egyptians on board.

Cranky **local buses** from New Mosque Square stop at villages en route to Al-Qasr or Teneida (50pt). They run to no specific timetable so it's a case of getting there and waiting. Some may be routed via Gedida instead of Budkhulu, so you should check with the driver. You can also use long-distance buses to reach outlying villages. In both cases, simply buy tickets on board.

Out of town it's always worth **hitching** if you're stuck somewhere. Although payment at pick-up rates is customary, you might get a free lift. If you're into cycling – feasible in wintertime – **bicycles** can be rented from the *Abu Mohammed Restaurant* (£E5) or the *Gardens Hotel* (£E7). You need to be fit, though, since visiting outlying villages will involve a round trip of at least 60km.

As many places are hard to reach, and it takes local knowledge of natural beauty spots to get the best from Dakhla, organized **excursions** kill two birds with one stone. Omar, Nasser and others all offer much the same locations, on day-trips, overnight or two-day safaris. Omar can arrange half-day trips either to the east or the west (£E40 for the car) or a full day-trip to both (£E80). Roughly speaking, half-day camel trips including one meal are £E50 per person and an overnight excursion with three meals is £E120. Nasser arranges overnight 4WD desert tours which cost £E350 for the vehicle including food.

West of Mut

Most visitors are initially drawn to the western part of the oasis by the village of **Al-Qasr**, which is deservedly renowned for its medieval mud-brick architecture, and easily reached by public transport. Should they reopen (as was promised as far back as 1977), the colourful **Muzawaka Tombs** are also within striking distance; if not, consider visiting **Deir al-Hagar**, a Roman temple near a hot spring, further from the main road. To cover more ground than this requires days to spare or private transport. Compare what Nasser and Omar have to say about trips to other villages, or **springs** and **dunes** you can reach by camel at sunset (staying overnight if desired) – then take the better deal.

The routes

There are two **routes** to Al-Qasr via different villages, so, if you can, it's worth following one out and the other one back. Most traffic leaves Mut by the main road (and shorter route; 32km), with buses and pick-ups stopping at Rashda and Budkhulu; while along the secondary loop road they call at Qalamoun, Gedida and Mushiya. On the way you'll pass the **hot springs** and resort at **Mut Talatta** (3km) and the drainage lake for irrigation water known as the **Fish Pond**. With private transport, try a brief initial **detour** along the desert road via **Huwana**, to see the domed and coffin-shaped tombs of an **Islamic cemetery** between Huwana and the Bedouin village of **El-Douhous**, where the desert road joins the highway and the loop road begins.

On the main road beyond El-Douhous, olive groves and orchards presage the clifftop village of **Rashda**, set far back from the highway. The local custom that when he marries, a man must build a new house for his bride, accounts for Rashda's modern appearance. A nicer stopover is **BUDKHULU**, where new buildings flank an **old quarter** of covered streets and houses with carved lintels, like the ones at Al-Qasr. On a hill to the west is a **Turkish cemetery**, visible from the main road. During the Islamic era, Budkhulu was a customs post on the caravan routes between Kharga, Assyut and Farafra. Further out, beyond **Ezbet Fiteima**, the highway curves west as it nears the cliff wall and a track runs 5km off to the sulphurous hot spring of **Bir el-Jebel** (aka the

Tourism Wells). Though a bit remote for those without transport (you might get a lift on a truck bound for the quarry nearby), Bir el-Gebel is fit for camping out if you bring food and water.

The **loop road** to Al-Qasr runs past three villages interspersed by stagnant pools and desert. **QALAMOUN** dates back to pharaonic times, and the old hilltop village is a wonderful maze of lanes and mud-brick houses, centred on an **Ayyubid mosque** – though, as in Budkhulu, you must first pass through a new settlement nearer the road. Many families are descended from Mamluke and Turkish officials once stationed here, whose mausolea are dotted across the cemetery. The next village is only 200 years old – hence its name, **GEDIDA** (New). Mut's tourist office can arrange a visit to the **mashrabiya factory**, a new source of employment in a village whose men have traditionally worked in Cairo, taking it in turns to share the same job with a friend back home. Shortly before reaching **Mushiya**, the road passes **Bir Mushiya**, a keyhole-shaped tank fed by a tepid spring, where tourists are taken to bathe.

The side road joins the highway between Al-Qasr and the turn-off for the Muzawaka Tombs, opposite a golden **dune field**. Originating on the plateau above the escarpment, the dunes cascade down the cliff and reform below, to continue their way southwards. Tourists are brought here by jeep or camel to enjoy rolling down the dunes, and the view at sunset. The dunes have occasionally been heard to "sing" in a slow rhythm that locals have traditionally attributed to spirits, and scientists explain as the friction of one layer of sand slipping over another.

Al-Qasr

Built over Roman foundations, **AL-QASR** may be the longest continually inhabited site in the oasis, and was indubitably Dakhla's capital in medieval times. Its romantic **old town** crowns a ridge above the palm groves, visible beyond sprawling New Qasr, whose main street is called Sharia al-Kuwait after the source of the remittances that financed it. Buses should drop you by the *Al-Qasr Resthouse* and a path leading to Old Qasr. Mud-walled alleys snake through dark passageways upheld by palm trunks, between tall houses with acacia-wood lintels whose cursive or kufic inscriptions name the builders or occupants (the oldest dates from 1518), of which only three are still inhabited. The Nasr el-Din Mosque has a 21-metre-high, twelfth-century **minaret** with a "pepperpot" finial, typical of Ayyubid architecture. You can follow the signs to a tenth-century **madrassa** (school and court) offering great views from its rooftop, or visit a **pottery** and an ancient **water wheel** (*saqqiya*) accompanied by local children, who may want to sell pots or baskets, or simply practise their English. Qasr's schoolteachers also enjoy a chat, and the guys in the resthouse will happily accept a challenge to ping-pong.

The Muzawaka Tombs

Five kilometres west along the highway from Al-Qasr, a signpost indicates the track to the **Muzawaka Tombs**, a twenty-minute walk or a slow drive through the silent desert, past rock buttes gouged with empty tombs. Of the three hundred or so recorded by Fakhry in 1972, two deserve his exclamation "Muza!" (Colour), from which their name derives – and will hopefully reopen soon. The **Tomb of Petosiris** is vividly painted with Roman-nosed blonds in pharaonic poses, curly-haired angels and a zodiac with a bearded Janus figure on the ceiling. In the back right-hand corner is a man standing on a turtle, holding a snake and fish aloft – a curious amalgam of Egyptian and Greco-Roman symbolism. Better-preserved, cruder murals in the **Tomb of Sadosiris** show Anubis (weighing the deceased's heart in one scene), Osiris judging on the rear wall, and another Janus – looking back on life and forward into the hereafter – just inside the entrance.

Heading back, you can try hitching towards Al-Qasr, or cut across the desert towards the village. There's little risk of getting lost, since by climbing a table plateau you can always get oriented – and the views are splendid.

Deir al-Hagar

Unless you've rented a taxi, getting to **Deir al-Hagar** (daily 8am–5pm; £E20) demands commitment. The trail begins 2km further west along the highway, where an unmarked road runs south past some Roman ruins to a small village (1km); beyond here a track crosses a ridge, whereupon the temple becomes visible on the right. Notwithstanding its Arabic name, "Stone Monastery", Deir al-Hagar is actually a Roman temple dedicated to the Theban Triad and the god of the oasis, Seth, the "evil" brother of Osiris, depicted with a blue body and a falcon's head. Its sandstone Hypostyle Hall, sanctuary and brick enclosure wall were built in the first century AD, under emperors Nero, Vespasian and Titus. Besides their cartouches, its walls are inscribed with the names of almost every explorer who visited Dakhla in the nineteenth century, including Edmonstone, Cailliaud, and the entire Rohlfs expedition. Local legend has it that Rohlfs sacrificed a servant to the spirits guarding the temple's treasury, in order to rob it. Having looked around, you can relax in a sulphurous **hot spring**, nearby.

East of Mut

Villages on the east side of the oasis are more or less accessible by pick-ups (which rarely venture far beyond Balat) or Teneida-bound buses. Unfortunately, most places of interest lie some way from the main road, so visiting more than one or two could be hard without transport. Bring food and water.

Heading out from town, you'll see where irrigation canals have enabled wheat, rice and peanuts to be grown on once barren land. Should you feel like stopping only 5km from Mut, **SHEIKH WALI** backs onto desert, with olive groves and goat-pens surrounding a Biblical **water wheel**, while **dunes** swell in the distance. **Asmant**, 6km on, has the usual sprawl of modern buildings by the roadside and a high-walled **old village** on the hill further back.

Asmant el-Khorab

Asmant lends its name to an ancient site 9km further east and 1km off the highway. **Asmant el-Khorab** (Asmant the Ruined) is the local name for the **ruins of Kellis**, a Roman and Coptic town inhabited for seven centuries, whose two cult temples and three churches mark the shift from pagan Rome to Byzantine Christianity. Fragmentary paintings appear in the larger, eastern temple, while the churches are mud-brick with plastered walls. The barely excavated site includes the remains of aqueducts, tombs and farmhouses, where archeologists have found wooden codices, casting light on religion and daily life in the third century AD. If you're curious to explore it, head south down the track running off the highway 4km past the spur-road to Sheikh Mufta. The track is okay for bikes or regular cars.

Balat and Qila ed-Dabba

After the swathe of desert beyond Asmant one welcomes the tree-lined road through **BALAT**, whose tea house with a mud-brick bench outside is a *de facto* bus stop. As usual, the modern village screens an older hilltop one, whose narrow **covered streets** protected the villagers from sun and sandstorms and prevented invaders from entering on horseback. Still inhabited, some of the houses have carved lintels and wooden locks, operated by peg-keys. Although the oldest dates from Mamluke times, Balat was a town and a governors' seat (its name means "Palace of the Lord") way back in the Old Kingdom, when it prospered through trade with Kush (ancient Nubia).

There's proof of this in Balat's ancient necropolis, where five mud-brick *mastabas* akin to step pyramids mark the **tombs of VI Dynasty governors**. One from the reign of Pepi II was discovered intact by French archeologists in 1977, and is now open to the public (daily 8am–5pm; £E20). Though its paintings are battered and the governor's mummy has been removed, the site itself merits a look, being a kind of provincial Saqqara without any sightseers. Known to the locals as **Qila ed-Dabba** (or "Ed-Dabba"), it can be reached by turning off the road 100m past Balat's tea house and following a track into the desert for 1km, whence another track carries on to **Ain Asil** (Spring of the Origin), where excavations have indicated that a large farming community existed in the Old Kingdom. You can walk on to Bashendi from there by back road – about 5km in all.

Bashendi

Alternatively, buses can drop you at the highway turn-off for **BASHENDI**, with its sign promising carpet-weaving and Roman tombs. Having walked 3km across a landscape of acacia trees and red earth, you reach the village, whose sugary pink mosque with three white domes resembles a marquee from afar. The name Bashendi derives from "Pasha Hindi", a medieval sheikh who is buried in the local cemetery, which dates back to Roman times. Tombs form the foundations of many of the houses, which are painted pale blue with floral friezes and *Hadj* scenes, merging into the ground in graceful curves. The village is renowned throughout Egypt for its tidiness and order, though perversely the place is plagued by flies.

The cemetery is at the back, where the desert begins. Some empty sarcophagi separate the domed tomb of Pasha Hindi (where locals pray for the recovery of lost items) from the square **Tomb of Kitnes**. While both structures are of Roman origin, the latter still retains its original funerary reliefs, depicting Kitnes meeting the desert-gods Min, Seth and Shu. Its key is held by a villager who can be fetched, but since admission costs £E16, you might settle for viewing its pharaonic lintels.

There is also a **carpet-weaving** factory, established with the help of Helwan University of Fine Arts, to train youths in making rugs and kelims. Ask at Mut's tourist office to arrange a visit (£E1.50 entrance fee).

Teneida and beyond

TENEIDA, Dakhla's easternmost settlement, is a modern affair centred on a leafy square, whose only "sight" is a **cemetery** on the outskirts with weird tombstones resembling houses, painted blue or white. In desert lore, Teneida is known for the three Zwayah tribesmen who staggered out of the desert in 1931, alerting the authorities to a tragedy that was already weeks old. Bombed from their homes at Kufra Oasis in Libya by the Italians, five hundred Zwayah nomads had trekked 320km south over waterless desert to Jebel Uwaynat, where they found springs but no grazing. Faced with starvation, half the tribe struck out towards Dakhla without knowing the way, while the others remained to await their end. Thanks to the men's 21-day, 670km march (a feat of endurance with few parallels), search parties managed to rescue almost three hundred stragglers from the wilderness.

With a car you can press on to see some curious **rock inscriptions** just off the highway 10km past Teneida. Among the sandstone outcrops on the south side of the road, four in the form of a sphinx or a camel flank a large rock whose base is covered in inscriptions. You can discern prehistoric and Bedouin drawings of giraffes, camels and hunters, plus the name of Jarvis (British governor of Dakhla and Kharga in the 1930s) and many other visitors.

Moving on

Upper Egypt **buses** leave for **Kharga** (3hr; £E8) daily at 6am, 8am, 2pm, 5pm and 10pm; all but the 2pm run on to **Assyut** (8hr; £E15). For **Farafra** (4hr; £E12), **Bahariya**

(6hr; £E22) and **Cairo** (13hr; £E32–35) the bus departs at 6am and 6pm. Superjet run two buses a day to Cairo (13hr; £E37.50–£E42); both run via Kharga (3hr; £E12) and the earlier one calls at Assyut (8hr; £E18). All buses leave from the new bus station which is on a side road just after the hospital on the road to Kharga; they also pick up passengers from the ticketing office in New Mosque Square. **Minibuses and service taxis** also run to the other New Valley oases and charge similar rates to the buses providing they are full; it's best to try and leave early to ensure this is the case – the rank is opposite the police station. One bus a day leaves at 5am for **Luxor** (10hr; £E28) via Kharga and Assyut, though this is a very indirect way of getting there. Before leaving Mut, motorists should fill up at the gas station, as there's no more **petrol** until Kharga or Farafra. There is also now a weekly EgyptAir **flight** to Cairo (Wed 8am; US$160) from Dakhla Airport.

The road to Kharga

Beyond Teneida's last flourish of greenery, wind-sculpted rocks soon give way to dun table-tops and gravelly sand, persisting for most of the way from Dakhla to Kharga (197km). Following the ancient *Darb el-Ghabari* (Dust Road), the modern road skirts the phosphate-rich Abu Tartur Plateau that separates the two depressions. The appearance of a phosphates factory and railroad 45km outside Kharga alerts you for a treat to follow. Golden **dunes** march across the depression, burying lines of telegraph poles and encroaching on the highway. Villagers faced with their advance have been known to add an extra storey to their house, live there while the dune consumes the ground floor, and move back downstairs once it has passed on. These dunes are outstretched fingers of the Ghard Abu Muharik (Dune with an Engine) range, of the type known as "whalebacked". Folk wisdom asserts that the less common *barchan* or crescent-shaped dunes are always separate from whalebacks; you'll see a cluster of baby ones in the desert to the left, nearer town.

Kharga Oasis

If your time or appetite for the desert is limited, **Kharga Oasis** is the one to consider missing. Of the 65,000 people in the oasis, 50,000 live in sprawling, modern **El-Kharga** city, which has adequate facilities and a decent museum, but nothing to get excited about. That said, there are some fine Christian and pharaonic ruins near town, others at remoter points in the oasis (some accessible by 4WD only), and the prospect of dramatic scenery as you ascend the scarp wall en route to Assyut.

Submerged by the sea aeons ago, leaving fossils on the high plateau, the Kharga depression is hemmed in by great cliffs and broken up by massifs, with belts of dunes advancing across the oasis. It's thought that there were no dunes in Kharga during Roman times; myth has it that they erected a brass cow on the escarpment, which swallowed up the sand. Historically, Kharga's importance owes to the desert trade routes that converged on the oasis, notably the **Forty Days Road** (see p.460). Deserted Roman forts and entire villages that claim descent from Mamluke soldiers attest to centuries of firm control by Egypt's rulers, who have used Kharga as a place of exile since the fourth century. In modern times, Mustafa Amin, the founder of the popular daily newspaper *Al-Akhbar*, was banished here by Nasser after the Revolution. Since 1994, Islamists have been incarcerated in **Kharga Prison**, a maximum security jail where at least thirty prisoners have died in custody (visible from the highway as one enters the oasis from the north).

Note that the **name** Kharga may be pronounced "Harga" or "Harjah", depending on who's talking. Both the oasis and its capital are called Kharga; we've used the prefix "El-" to denote the city.

El-Kharga

As the capital of the New Valley Governorate (comprising Kharga, Dakhla and Farafra oases), **EL-KHARGA** has grown into a sprawl of mid-rise buildings and highways that belies romantic stereotypes of an oasis town, unless you go searching around the souk. Hotels, banks and offices line the main drag, Sharia Gamel Abdel Nasser, which is too long and monotonous for pleasant walking. But **getting around** is easy, with covered pick-ups shuttling non-stop between Midan Showla and the Mabrouk Fountain, at either end of town. Midan Mesaha, near the *Hotel Waha*, marks the "fare stage", being a 10pt ride from each terminus; the full journey costs 20pt. Ring the bell on the roof to let the driver know when you want to get off.

Information and accommodation

Almost everywhere you might need to visit can be reached by pick-up, not least the **tourist office** (Sat–Thurs 8am–2pm, Fri 2–10pm; ☎092/921-206, fax 921-205), which can advise on transport to *outré* destinations. The **tourist police** (☎092/921-367; 24hr) are next door and the regular **police** (☎092/920-700; 24hr) across the road.

ACCOMMODATION

Buses entering town can drop you off at a hotel if they pass by en route to Midan Showla; otherwise, catch a pick-up. By oasis standards there's a good choice of **accommodation** spread over the town, but most places are expensive. Book ahead if you're fussy about where you stay.

Aldar Al Bidaa, just off Midan Showla (☎092/921-717). This recent addition has clean doubles, triples and quads, some with fan and bathroom. Unhelpful staff and noisy, but handy for the souk and bus station. ①–③.

Chalet (or *Villa*). Spacious carpeted chalets holding up to nine people with TV, bath, phone, fan or A/C. Behind the tourist office, which handles reservations. Probably the best deal in town at £E20 per person. ③.

Hamadalla (☎092/920-638, fax 925-017). Clean A/C rooms with soft beds; some have bathrooms, fridges and even balconies. Friendly staff. Restaurant. Breakfast included. ④–⑤.

Hotel Waha (☎092/920-393). Simple rooms with grungy shared bathrooms; it's worth paying for a "lux" one with private facilities and a fan. ①–②.

Kharga Oasis (☎092/921-500). Large A/C rooms with soft beds, bathrooms, and balconies overlooking a palm garden – it sounds great, but the hotel is always empty, as if waiting for a convention or tour party that never arrives. The restaurant serves Stella. ⑤.

Pioneer (☎092/927-982, fax 927-983, *mgg@mggroup.com.eg*). Out towards the Temple of Hibis, this garish pink five-star pad has all the facilities you'd expect and a price tag to match. Non-residents can use the pool for £E30 per day. ⑧.

The Town

Opened in 1994 after years of setbacks, the **Museum of Antiquities**, on Sharia Gamal Abdel Nasser (daily 8am–3pm; £E20), contains many items that have never before been exhibited, from sites scattered across three oases. Of the exhibits on the ground floor (mostly labelled in English), the most impressive are Greco-Roman: painted sarcophagi from Maks al-Qibli and Dakhla; death masks from Qasr el-Labeka; and mummified rams, eagles and ibises from the Muzawaka Tombs. The Old Kingdom is represented by an offerings tablet, scarabs and headrests from the tombs of the VI Dynasty governors in Balat. Upstairs you'll find Coptic textiles and pottery, and floral friezes from the Fatimid and Ottoman eras, mostly unlabelled.

While in the vicinity, don't miss the (dry) **Mabrouk Fountain**, just up the road at the main junction, created by a local artist in three days. Its lusty figures symbolize Mother Egypt dragging her unwilling children towards their destiny. Aside from the

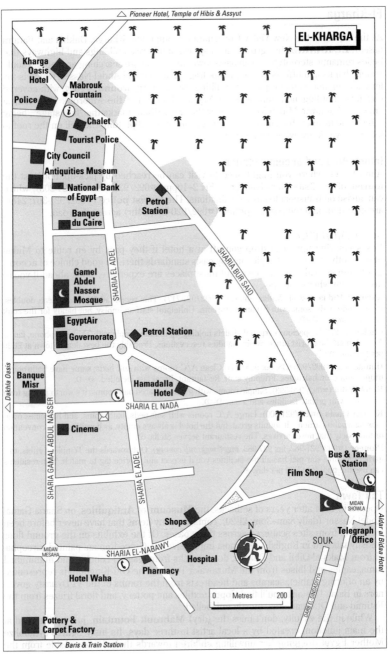

Pioneer Hotel, Temple of Hibis & Assyut

EL-KHARGA

Kharga Oasis Hotel

Mabrouk Fountain

Police

Chalet

Tourist Police

City Council

Antiquities Museum

National Bank of Egypt

Banque du Caire

Petrol Station

SHARIA EL ADEL

SHARIA BUR SAID

Gamel Abdel Nasser Mosque

EgyptAir

Governorate

Petrol Station

Banque Misr

Hamadalla Hotel

SHARIA GAMAL ABDUL NASSER

SHARIA EL NADA

Cinema

SHARIA EL ADEL

Bus & Taxi Station

Film Shop

MIDAN SHOWLA

Aldar al Bidaa Hotel

Telegraph Office

Shops

SOUK

MIDAN MESAHA

SHARIA EL-NABAWY

Hospital

N

DARB EL SINDADIYA

Pharmacy

Hotel Waha

0   Metres   200

Pottery & Carpet Factory

Dakhla Oasis

Baris & Train Station

Gamel Abdel Nasser Mosque (one of dozens that Nasser built in provincial towns in the 1960s), and a **Coptic Church** discreetly located off the highroad, there's nothing else to see until you reach the lower part of town (it's best to take a pick-up, unless you fancy the 2–3km walk).

Here, dusty **Midan Showla** is abuzz with people and traffic, a lively **souk** running off into an old quarter of mud houses painted apricot or azure and daubed with the Hand of Fatima. Turn right at the intersection and then left and you should find yourself in the **Darb el-Sindadiyya**, a dark, twisting street roofed with palm trunks, which once extended over 4km; its oldest part dates from the tenth century. Only the initial stretch is inhabited nowadays and most of the passageways are used as barns. Foreigners aren't discouraged from entering, but it's wise not to venture too far in without a guide.

The tourist office can arrange visits to El-Kharga's **pottery and carpet factory**, or the **date factory** (both daily except Fri 8am–2pm; free) down the road.

Eating and other practicalities

Eating out is mediocre. Simple meals of chicken, beans, rice and salad are all you can hope for in the nameless cafés by the *Hotel Waha* and on Midan Showla, where you can also buy *felafel* sandwiches at the entrance to the souk. The restaurants in the *Hamadalla* and *Kharga Oasis* hotels offer much the same fare (at a higher price), plus mutton stew.

You can change **money** and travellers' cheques at the Banque du Caire (daily except Fri 8.30am–2pm) and Banque Misr (Sun–Thurs 8.30am–2pm & 5.30–8pm). The **hospital** (☎092/920-777) is on Sharia el-Nabawy and the **post office** (daily except Fri 9am–2pm) and 24-hour **telephone** exchange are located on side streets near the Banque Misr. You can also make international calls and send faxes from the *Hamadalla Hotel*.

There are **petrol** stations on Sharia Bur Said and Sharia El Adel, and a tyre-repair place off Sharia el-Nabawy.

Moving on from El-Kharga

If you've got the money, EgyptAir **flights** from El-Kharga's New Valley Airport can get you to Cairo in two hours. Departures are on Wednesday and Sunday mornings, and a one-way ticket costs the equivalent of US$132; book through their office on the main street. The airport turn-off is 3km north along the Assyut road, then 2km southeast; a taxi costs £E5–10.

Otherwise, there are daily **buses** to Cairo (9pm & 11pm departures run direct to Cairo and cost £E37.50 for the 7hr journey; 6am & 10pm services cost £E32 and stop at many towns along the way, including Assyut and Minya), Dakhla (six daily; £E6–10) and Assyut (nine daily; £E6–10), whence you can reach most points along the Nile Valley. The journey to Assyut takes four to five hours – it's worth travelling by day and getting seats on the left to see the magnificent rock escarpment, one of the most dramatic vistas Egypt has to offer. All buses, minibuses and **service taxis** leave from Midan Showla. Minibuses and *service* taxis run to all the previously listed destinations and, providing they are full, cost a little more than the buses, and are usually slightly quicker.

A **train** leaves every Friday at 7am for Luxor, taking between six and eight hours (£E16). The train station is 5km out along the road to Baris.

There is also a **direct road to Luxor** (275km), which quits the oasis between Jaja and Baris. As yet, there are no buses, however, so you really need your own vehicle; a taxi might agree to do the journey for £E300. The road varies from good to poor, with checkpoints every 60km, but no facilities. Ask the tourist office if any formalities such

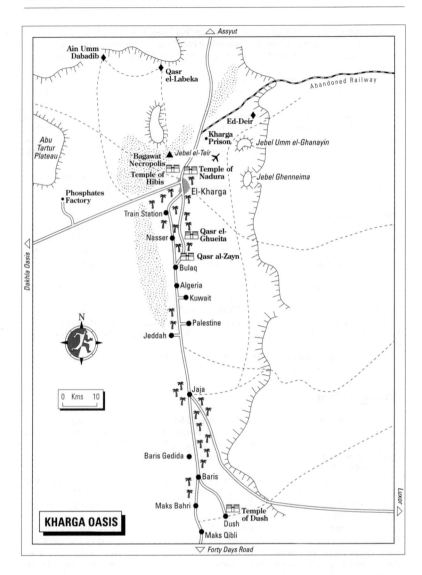

KHARGA OASIS

as registering your vehicle apply. The road meets the Nile Valley at Riziq, 15km south of Luxor.

North of El-Kharga

Compensating for the paucity of sights in El-Kharga, two of the finest ancient monuments in the oasis are just a few miles from the town. The **Temple of Hibis** is the best-preserved temple in the Western Desert, while the **Bagawat Necropolis** is among the oldest Christian cemeteries in Egypt. Further north, the depression is pock-marked with ruins of ancient towns and forts, with tunnels and other feats of Roman engineering waiting to be explored – but only accessible by 4WD with a guide who knows the way. Talk to the tourist office if you're serious about visiting **Ed-Deir**, **Qasr el-Labeka** or **Ain Umm Dabadib**; if not, forget 'em.

To the Temple of Hibis

Although you can get there by taxi (£E5–10), it's fun to walk if you're feeling energetic. Take a pick-up to the Mabrouk Fountain and walk two kilometres out along the Assyut road. You'll catch sight of the ruined Ptolemaic **Temple of Nadura** atop a low hill in the desert to your right – and although its sandstone wall and pronaos aren't worth the trudge, the view is.

The **Temple of Hibis** (accessible any time; free) stands just up the road amidst the palm groves on the left, a short walk away by tarmac path beyond the swamp. Besides reminding sightseers that most pharaonic sites originally looked verdant, the lush vegetation around it covers the site of ancient Hibis, a XVIII Dynasty settlement that prospered under the Saïtes, Persians and Ptolemies.

One of the few Persian monuments left in Egypt, the sixth-century BC temple is dedicated to Amun-Re. Well preserved from the Third Pylon onwards, it has painted vultures (beneath the pylon), squat columns with variegated capitals, and (locked) Hypostyle Halls – which the guard will unlock for *baksheesh*. You can see graffiti by Francis Catherwood, later famous for discovering Mayan temples in Central America. Carrying a stone to deter wild dogs, walk around the outer walls, with their huge reliefs of Darius I greeting Egyptian gods, and noticeably Persian hairstyles. The guard will also unlock an unsafe subterranean tomb containing fine reliefs of dolphins – again *baksheesh* is expected.

The Bagawat Necropolis

A hundred metres beyond the Hibis Temple road turn-off, a dirt track leads off towards crumbling ruins in the desert. Follow this beside a palm grove and then cut across to a **ruined Christian village**, where the sand chokes low walls with flowery friezes, and disgorges shards of Coptic pottery. From here you can see the **Bagawat Necropolis** – 263 mud-brick chapels ascending a ridge (daily: summer 8am–6pm; winter 8am–5pm; £E20).

Used for Christian burials between the third and seventh centuries, these **chapels** display diverse forms of mud-brick vaulting or Roman-influenced portals, but they are best known for their Coptic murals. A guard should appear to unlock the **Chapel of Peace**, whose dome is decorated with images of Adam and Eve, the Ark, Abraham and Isaac, sadly defaced by Greek inscriptions. Flowery motifs and doves of peace can be seen inside **Tomb #25**, one of three adjacent family vaults on the ridge, where the guard usually asks *Shouf bebe?* If you reply affirmatively he'll produce a hideous mummified child, expecting male tourists to react with sang-froid and women tourists with dismay; not to mention *baksheesh* worthy of his efforts. Give him his due, but not until you've seen the frescoes in the **Chapel of the Exodus**. Crudely executed yet vivid, they depict Roman-looking pharaonic troops pursuing the Jews, led by Moses, out of Egypt, and other Biblical scenes.

From behind the chapel you can gaze across the desert to the scarp wall. Notice how the four mighty crescent **dunes** to the north have spawned two infants downwind, either side of the Assyut road, near a crowd of whalebacks. Though disproving the notion that *barchan* and *seif* dunes don't mix, its physical causes are still explicable in terms of formulae devised by the explorer Ralph Bagnold, whose classic book *The*

Physics of Blown Sand and Desert Dunes (1939) later helped NASA to interpret data from its Martian space probes. The book was written after five years' experimentation with a home-made wind tunnel and builder's sand; after his desert journeys of the 1920s, Bagnold felt "it was really just exploring in another form".

Other sights

For those with a **4WD car** (or dirt bikes) and a local guide, there are many other sites to explore. The most rewarding area lies west of the Assyut road, where a track from Bagawat skirts the foothills of the fox- and snake-infested **Jebel el-Teir** (Bird Mountain), whose wadis contain prehistoric, ancient and Arabic **inscriptions**. It then diverges into two trails leading to the finest **Roman fortresses** in the oasis. Invariably built near springs, they once guarded, taxed and sheltered caravans on the road to Assyut. As a single caravan contained thousands of people and animals, they probably settled for the night in several forts; the bustle is unimaginable in the desolate ruins today.

Qasr el-Labeka is secluded in a wadi at the base of the northern escarpment, its twelve-metre walls enclosing sand-filled chambers. On an outcrop further north stands a ruined mud-brick temple, where one of the lintels still bears a painted vulture. Between the two buildings lies the spring that sustained the fort – a subterranean aqueduct (now silted up) of the kind found on a grander scale at **Ain Umm Dabadib**. Though it's only 18km from Qasr el-Labeka, the track to Ain Umm Dabadib is extremely rough; approaching it from the south means locating a corridor through the dune fields. The site covers 60,000 acres, including a ruined fortress, churches and tombs, plus a remarkable **underground aqueduct** that worked by liberating ground-water, like the qanats of ancient Persia (Fakhry suggests that the system originated under Persian rule). The shaft runs for 15km with access holes every few metres, filled with sand and rubble.

Far across the oasis near the eastern scarp wall, **Ed-Deir** once guarded the shortest camel route to the Nile, which climbs out of the depression at the Abu Sighawal (Father of Underwear) Pass. The fort lies 1km beyond the end of a track starting near Munira (the checkpoint on the road as you enter Kharga Oasis from the north), which later turns into decrepit asphalt, so you could risk it in a regular car, walking over the dunes at the end. Its twelve towers are connected by a gallery, and the surviving rooms covered in **graffiti** drawn by generations of soldiers: Turks in fezzes, tanks, airplanes, and obscenities.

South towards Baris

Exploring the southern spur of the oasis means flitting between sites off a highway, which isn't a prospect to relish if you're reliant on buses (hitching is not advised). On the positive side, access roads have been improved to the point that the temples can be reached by regular car. The tourist office reckons that a pick-up will drive you to Qasr el-Ghueita, Qasr al-Zayn and Bulaq and back for £E50. **Taxis** may agree to visit all three, plus the Temple of Dush near Baris, for £E100. Venturing any further south you need to be a committed desert-buff with a 4WD. **Buses** bound for Baris (2hr; £E1.75) leave El-Kharga at 7am, noon and 2pm, making it essential to start early if you want to visit at least one site, and not be stranded. There are basic government **resthouses** in Bulaq and Baris and one operated by the MG Group in Nasser – it has a cold spring pool and basic rooms for £E20. You can pitch your tent here (£E12) or use the pool for £E7, including a drink; contact the *Pioneer Hotel* in Kharga to organize a stay.

Qasr el-Ghueita and Qasr al-Zayn

The fortified temple of **Qasr el-Ghueita** (Fortress of the Beautiful Garden) can be found 18km south of El-Kharga and 2km off the main road, crowning a hilltop (daily

8am–5pm; £E16). The climb lets you appreciate its commanding view of the area, which was intensively farmed in ancient times. Ten-metre-high walls enclose a sandstone temple dedicated to the Theban Triad, built by Darius I on the site of an older shrine, and modified by the Ptolemies. Its Hypostyle Hall contains scenes of Hapy the Nile-god holding symbols of the nomes of the Upper and Lower Egypt. Nearby you can see the adobe remnants of a Ptolemaic settlement.

Five kilometres south by highway there's a paved turn-off to **Qasr al-Zayn** (daily 8am–5pm; £E16), a Ptolemaic-Roman temple that lends its name to a village built over the ancient town of *Tkhonemyris*. This proximity to daily life helps you imagine it as a bustling settlement in antiquity. As at Qasr el-Ghueita, the temple is enclosed within a mud-brick fortress, together with living quarters for the garrison, a cistern and a bakery. Its portal bears the cartouches of Antonius Pius, who restored the temple in 138 AD. The plain hereabouts is 18m below sea level, the lowest point in Kharga Oasis.

The first large settlement you encounter, **BULAQ** ("to watch"), is divided into a picturesque old village to the west, and a larger modern one east of the highway. Its **resthouse** (£E15 per person) and **hot springs** are visible immediately before you enter town, on the right. Leaving Bulaq, you pass the whitewashed tomb of Sheikh Khalid shortly before the microwave tower that presages a string of New Valley settlements founded in the 1980s, named Algeria, Kuwait, Palestine and Jeddah in a gesture of Arab solidarity. Only Jaja is of ancient lineage, but it looks as modern as the others. The **new road to Luxor** (275km) turns off midway between Jaja and Baris.

Baris and beyond

BARIS is the second largest settlement after El-Kharga; a sign at the entrance to town welcomes you to "Paris", but don't expect to find anything grand. Half a dozen kiosks and a place dispensing *fuul* and *felafel* (except on Fridays) ensure that you won't starve here, and there's an unsignposted **resthouse** (£E5 per person) on the northern edge of town, at right angles to the highway. Before this, you'll pass the abandoned village of **Baris Gedida** (New Baris), which the architect Hassan Fathy based on the principles of traditional oasis architecture, including wind shafts to cool the marketplace. Alas for his idealism, work was halted by the Six Day War of 1967 and never resumed, so the initial settlers soon drifted away. Baris itself is just a place to stay and/or hire a pick-up to reach the Roman Temple of Dush (£E20 return, with waiting time).

A paved road runs 23km southeast from Baris, directly to the site. Potsherds, cemeteries and the ruins of ancient *Kysis* are scatttered around a hilltop fortress, whose ruined walls are six metres high. Abutting this is the **Temple of Dush** (8am–5pm; £E16), built by Domitian and enlarged by Hadrian and Trajan. Reputedly once sheathed in gold, it is covered in dedications to the last two emperors, and the gateway in graffiti by Cailliaud and other nineteenth-century travellers. The discovery of an elaborate system of clay pipes and a Christian church suggests that the town was abandoned when its wells dried up, some time after the fourth century AD. "Dush" is believed to derive from *Kush*, the name of the ancient Sudanese kingdom with which the Egyptians traded along the Nile.

It's uncertain when desert routes to Sudan developed, but the introduction of camels to North Africa after the Persian invasion of 525 BC enabled travellers to cover far greater distances between wells, making new routes feasible. However, caravans lacked an incentive to make such a long and dangerous journey until the Mamluke era, when rising tolls and bribes for customs officials along the Nile made a desert route more profitable. Thus arose the infamous *Darb al-Arba'in* or **Forty Days Road** (see below), which entered the oasis and came under scrutiny at **MAKS BAHRI** (Customs North) and **MAKS QIBLI** (Customs South). Today, there's no evidence of their slave-trafficking past in either village, though in Maks Qibli you can still see a small mud-brick watchtower, the **Tabid el-Darawish**, built by the British after the Dervish invasion of 1893.

THE FORTY DAYS ROAD

Of all the trade routes between North Africa and the tropical south, the **Forty Days Road** (*Darb al-Arba'in*) was the one most involved in **slavery** – the only business profitable enough to justify the risks and rigours of the thousand-mile journey. The slaves, purchased at the Dongola slave market or kidnapped by the fierce desert tribes, were assembled at **Kobbé**, a town (no longer existing) 60km northwest of El-Fasher, the capital of Sudan's Darfur Province, once an independent kingdom.

After a few days' march from Kobbé, the slaves were unchained from their yokes, for there was no way to escape. With no permanent water source until Bir Natrun, 530km away, they could only survive on the ox skins of water that burdened the camels. From **Bir Natrun**, caravans trekked 260km northeast across waterless, open sands, vulnerable to attack by bandits from the Arab Kababish and Bedayatt tribes, or the black Gor'an from Nukheila Oasis. The next stop, **Laqiya al-Arba'in**, had water but scant grazing for camels, and with their reserves of fodder exhausted they could easily weaken and stumble along the rocky 280-kilometre journey to **Selima Oasis**. While human losses were erased by the sands, the road gained definition from its Bactrian casualties; a 1946 survey of north-western Sudan noted "a track about one mile wide marked with white camel bones".

W.G. Browne, the first European to complete the route, estimated the slave caravan's value at £115,000 sterling – a huge sum for the time (1762). Egyptian customs posts taxed caravans arriving in **Kharga Oasis**, the last stage before their ultimate destination, Assyut. As the caravans approached, small boys were hidden in empty water skins to evade tax, but officials would beat them to thwart this ploy. The most valuable slaves were young Nubian women – prized as concubines because their skin remained cool whatever the heat. Having sold their chattels at **Assyut**, traders bought "fabrics, jewellery, weaponry and kohl" for the return journey.

The Forty Days Road effectively ended in 1884, after the rise of the Dervish empire closed the Egyptian–Sudanese border. When it reopened slavery had been prohibited, rendering its premier commodity worthless, so the caravans ceased. As the illiterate slave-drivers died off, memories of the *Darb al-Arba'in* faded, as Michael Asher discovered when he tried to retrace the route from Darfur in the 1980s. Since then, however, it seems to have revived as a conduit for drugs and arms, and two American women accomplished the perilous journey just a few years ago.

The Gilf Kebir and Jebel Uwaynat

The final frontier is the wilderness to the southwest of Kharga and Dakhla oases, called the **Darb al-Arba'in Desert** by some geographers. Drier than the rest of the Western Desert, with less than a millimetre of rain a year, this most isolated part of Egypt is still largely *terra incognita*. But in the past decade roads have penetrated the region, and it's not impossible that tourism will be encouraged one day.

On a map of North Africa, the ruler-straight borders of Libya, Egypt and Sudan intersect at **Jebel Uwaynat**, the highest point in the Libyan Desert. A flat-topped block of sandstone 16km wide, it rises from foothills through a "vertical battlement" to heights of 1800m, just enough to attract a little rainfall, which collects in pools at either end of the massif's southern face. The soil is fertile, sustaining small communities since prehistoric times, but the massif's location remained a mystery to the outside world until 1923, when it was reached by Hassanein Bey from Kufra Oasis in Libya.

This spurred attempts by Dr Ball, Prince Kemal al-Din and other motorized explorers to find a route from Egypt, circumventing the Great Sand Sea and the plateau of the **Gilf Kebir**, described by Bagnold as "unscalable":

For a hundred miles the great cliff went on. It seemed like the frontier of some "lost world"
. . . unbroken except where the mouths of deep unlit gorges appeared as black slits, from the

bottom of which an ancient debris of boulders spilled out fanwise for miles into the plain. It was tempting to go and explore one of those gorges. What might there not be far inland up the valleys which they drained? . . . But it was impossible to get close to the foot of the cliff without risking the cars.

In 1932, Count Almassy and Clayton led an expedition to explore the Gilf Kebir by air and discovered several valleys with lush vegetation, grazed by nomads, which some thought to be the "Lost Oasis" of Zerzura (see p.475). More **recently**, satellites have revealed clusters of craters as far afield as Kufra Oasis in Libya and Gilf Kebir; while the Egyptians have embarked on a bold project to create a sustainable farming community at Uwaynat, using subterranean water and modern irrigation methods.

The **route** to Gilf Kebir and Jebel Uwaynat is known as the *Darb el-Tarfawi*, and starts from Mut in Dakhla Oasis. There is a minor road as far as Abu Ballas, about halfway to Gilf Kebir. To attempt this 700-kilometre round trip without proper equipment would be madness, and one definitely needs military permission. Armchair travellers can visit via the pages of Bagnold's *Libyan Sands*.

SIWA OASIS

Isolated by hundreds of kilometres of desert, **Siwa Oasis** remained virtually independent from Egypt until the late nineteenth century, sustaining a unique culture. Yet despite – or because of – its isolation, outsiders have been drawn here since antiquity. The legendary Army of Cambyses was heading this way when it disappeared into a sandstorm; Alexander the Great journeyed here to consult the famous Oracle of Amun; and Arabic tales of *Santariyah* (as the oasis was known) were common currency into the last century. In modern times, Siwa has received visits from kings and presidents, anthropologists and generals. Tourism only really began in the mid-1980s but has gathered steam in recent years as Siwa has become a firm favourite with independent travellers and adventure tour groups. Though welcoming its economic benefits, the Siwans want to keep tourism within bounds, and insist that direct charter flights into Siwa are not on the cards.

The oasis offers all you could ask for in the way of desert **beauty spots**: thick palm groves clustered around freshwater springs and salt lakes; rugged massifs and enormous dunes. Equally impressive are the **ruins** of Shali and Aghurmi, labyrinthine mud-built towns that once protected the Siwans from desert raiders. Scattered around the oasis are ruined temples that attest to Siwa's fame and prosperity during Greco-Roman times; some claim that the tomb of Alexander the Great lies here. Visitors are also fascinated by **Siwan culture**, and how it is reacting to outside influences like TV, schooling and tourism. Nowadays, it is mostly only older women who wear the traditional costume, silver jewellery and complex hair-braids; younger wives and unmarried women dress much the same as their counterparts in the Nile Valley. But the Siwans still observe their own festivals and wedding customs; and among themselves they speak *Siwi*, a Berber tongue. Though things are changing, the Siwans remain sure of their identity and determined to maintain it.

A little history

Beyond the fact that it supported hunter-gatherers in Paleolithic times, little is known about Siwa Oasis before the XXVI Dynasty (525–404 BC), when the reputation of its **Oracle** spread throughout the Mediterranean world.

Siwa's inhabitants – who probably migrated here from the Libyan oases – were always at risk from predatory desert tribes, so their first settlement was a fortified acropolis. Classical accounts of the Oracle reveal little about this beyond its name, **Aghurmi**, and its position as a major caravan stop between Cyrenaica and Sudan. Its later history, however, is detailed in the *Siwan Manuscript* (its whereabouts are a closely guarded secret), a century-old compilation of oral histories that relates how Siwa's rulers considered poisoning the springs with mummies in order to thwart the Muslim conquest (date uncertain), and how Bedouin and Berber raids had reduced Aghurmi's population to a mere two hundred by the twelfth century AD.

HALI AND SIWAN SOCIETY

Roundabout 1203, seven families quit Aghurmi to found a new settlement further west, called **Shali** (the Town). Their menfolk are still honoured as the "forty ancestors", and these pioneering families were probably the most vigorous of the surviving Siwans. Like Aghurmi, Shali was walled and built of *kharsif*: a salt-impregnated mud which dries cement-hard, but melts during downpours – fortunately, it only rains heavily here every fifty years or so. Fearful of raiders, Shali's *agwad* (elders) forbade families to live outside the walls, so as the population increased the town could only expand upwards. Siwan households added an extra floor with each generation, while the *agwad* regulated the width of alleys to one donkey's breadth in an effort to ensure some light and air within the labyrinth.

Siwan bachelors aged between twenty and forty were obliged to sleep in caves outside town, guarding the fields – hence their nickname, the "club-bearers". Noted for their love of palm liquor, song and dance, these *zaggalah* shocked outsiders with their open **homosexuality**. Homosexual marriages were forbidden by King Fouad in 1928, but continued in secret until the late 1940s. Today, Siwans emphatically assert that homosexuality no longer exists in the oasis.

Another feature of Shali was the tradition of violent **feuds** between two neighbourhood clans – the Westerners and Easterners – in which all able-bodied males were expected to participate. Originally ritualized, with parallel lines of combatants exchanging blows between sunrise and sunset while their womenfolk threw stones at cowards and shouted encouragement, feuds became far deadlier with the advent of firearms, occasioning gun battles "on the slightest grounds". (Even now, Siwans know which clan they're descended from, and the town council is sited exactly midway between the two neighbourhoods.) Yet they immediately closed ranks against outsiders – Bedouin raiders, khedival taxmen or European explorers.

EGYPTIAN AND BRITISH CONTROL

Visitors of the eighteenth and nineteenth centuries regularly experienced Siwan **xenophobia**. "Whenever I quitted my apartment, it was to be assailed with stones and a torrent of abusive language," Browne wrote in 1762. Having poked around the antiquities in Muslim guise, Frederick Hornemann was pursued into the desert, where "the braying of three hundred donkeys announced the arrival of the Siwan army", and only escaped thanks to his assistant's recitation of Koranic verses. Frederic Cailliaud was permitted to visit the gardens and ruins in 1819, but the town remained barred to strangers until six hundred troops sent by Mohammed Ali compelled the oasis to recognize **Egyptian authority** in 1820.

Although the Siwans subsequently revolted against their governor and defaulted on taxes (payable in dates) half a dozen times over the next sixty years, the oasis began to change. With the desert tribes suppressed, and Shali rendered unsafe by heavy rains, the *agwad* permitted families to settle outside the walls. From the 1850s onwards the great reformist preacher Mohammed Ibn Ali al-Senussi cast a spell over the desert peoples from Jaghbub Oasis just over the border, and Siwa – the site of his first *zawiya* – supported **Senussi** resistance to the Italian conquest of Libya (1912–30), until it became clear that their Senussi "liberators" would not restore Siwan independence. Thus in 1917, British forces were "welcomed by the cheering Siwans, who declared their loyalty as they always did with every new victorious conqueror" (Fakhry).

SIWI

Siwi is the mother tongue of all native Siwans; children only start to learn Arabic from the age of six, in school. However, as Arabic is used in public life, visitors needn't deal with Siwi unless they want to. A few phrases can get you started.

yes	*mashi*	donkey(s)	*yeizite (zitan)*
no	*oola*	horse	*agmare*
How are you?	*Tanta elhalenik?*	camel(s)	*alghum*
What's your name?	*Bit in insmitinik?*	dates	*tenii*
Where are you going?	*Imani tehab?*	olives	*azumour*
What do you want?	*Tanta ekhsitta'?*	water	*aman*
Give me . . .	*ooshi . . .*		

Anglo-Egyptian control of Siwa was maintained by the Frontier Camel Corps and Light Car Patrols. Agricultural advisors, a school and an orthodox imam were introduced following King Fouad's visit to the oasis in 1928. When the British withdrew as the Italians advanced across North Africa in 1942, the Siwans accepted Axis **occupation** with equal resignation. Unlike Rommel, who made a favourable impression during his flying visit, King Farouk dismayed the Siwans by wearing shorts, and asking if they "still practised a certain vice" when he visited the oasis in 1945.

MORE RECENTLY . . .
Paradoxical as it sounds, Siwa's biggest problem is an excess of fresh water, which gushes from springs and drains into salt lakes, increasing their volume and salinity. As the explorer Bagnold put it: "the air, hot and breathless, has a characteristic oasis smell, slightly sweet, of rank grass faintly charred, decaying through increasing saltiness". Smelly, mosquito-infested ponds all over town attest that the **water table** lies only twenty centimetres underground. **Land reclamation** projects have tried to tackle the problem since 1907, but creating drainage catchment areas in an oasis lying 18m below sea level has always proved hugely expensive.

While Egyptian military bases exist here on sufferance, the Siwans have welcomed developments in healthcare, education and communications. A public hospital treats patients who once had to travel to Mersa Matrouh. Over thirty Siwans have graduated from university, and returned to live in the oasis. The road to Matrouh (completed in 1984) has encouraged exports of dates and olives, and tourism to the oasis. In 1995, the prospect of the "discovery" of Alexander the Great's tomb, which a Greek couple proclaimed to the media (see p.472), increased interest in Siwa. A year later, President Mubarak flew in to inaugurate the Siwa mineral water factory, north of town – although the new olive oil factory, nearby, actually contributes more to the local economy.

Visiting Siwa

Visitors to Siwa Oasis no longer require **military permission**, unless they wish to travel to the remoter oases of Girba, Qara, Areg or Sitra. This can be obtained from Military Intelligence in Mersa Matrouh (see p.518) or Cairo (p.237) and in Siwa itself. You do not require permission to drive from Siwa to Bahariya. Aside from lacking a **bank** (bring enough cash for your stay), Siwa has all the basic facilities – though **petrol** might be unavailable until the delivery truck shows up.

The **best time** to come is during spring or autumn, when the Siwans hold festivals and the days are pleasantly warm. During winter, windless days can also be nice, but nights – and gales – are chilling. From May onwards, rising temperatures keep people indoors between 11am and 7pm, and the nights are sultry and mosquito-ridden. Even when the **climate** is mild you'll probably feel like taking a midday siesta or a swim.

Siwa is well known for its conservatism in matters of **dress** and **behaviour**. Notices request visitors to refrain from public displays of affection or drinking alcohol (which is not sold here), and women to keep their arms and legs covered – especially when bathing in pools. Women should also avoid wandering alone in places with few people around. Local people are generally more reserved than the Egyptians, and invitations home are less common. Siwan households are segregated, with the women's quarters on the ground floor; foreign women who get invited upstairs have reason to be suspicious.

Besides the official ban on **photographing** military installations (including the airport, and sandbagged dugouts in unexpected locations), visitors should respect Siwan feelings on the issue. As a rule, local women are taboo subjects, whereas Siwan males – particularly the younger ones – don't mind being snapped (but always ask them first). Discreet long shots are easier than close-ups. For streetlife and visual clarity, take your pictures before 9am, or during the hour or so before sunset; people stay indoors when the sun is high, and its glare bleaches colours and textures from photographs.

Getting there: the routes
Unless you sign up with a desert safari – which might reach Siwa via the Qattara Depression – there are only two possible **approaches**. One is via the dire road from Bahariya Oasis (see p.438); the other is from Alexandria or Mersa Matrouh – the route favoured by most visitors.

There is one A/C **bus** daily from Sidi el Gaber in Alexandria to Siwa (11am; 9hr; £E27), which calls briefly at Moharrem Bey. It takes on extra passengers at Mersa Matrouh, three to four hours later. Matrouh is also the starting point for a further three buses a day to Siwa (4–5hr; £E12), leaving at 7.30am, 1.30pm and 4pm. You may also be able to catch a *service* taxi or **minivan** from Matrouh to Siwa; the fare is £E10 per person.

The 300km **journey** from Matrouh to Siwa takes four hours by car or bus. If you're driving, the Siwa road turns off the highway 20km west of Matrouh, at a checkpoint. There are minefields to the left for 50km into the desert, marked by triangular signs. About 100km further there are two tiny **resthouses**, 300m apart on opposite sides of the road, one of which is called **Bir Nous** (Halfway Well), selling tea, soup and soft drinks. Its toilets are the nearest one gets to the horrors of this route before the road was built. Until last century there was only a camel trail (eight days from Matrouh) across this flat desert and the few landmarks might be obscured by dust clouds or sandstorms. The sharp limestone ridges and hollows beneath the powdery surface of this *shabak* (net) desert also made the route hazardous for early motorists, who followed the line of telegraph poles. Nowadays the monotonous vistas – interspersed with army camps – keep going until the last 40km, when rock outcrops presage the appearance of the oasis.

Siwa Town

Most visitors rate **SIWA TOWN** and the pools, rocks and ruins around as the oasis's main attractions, and not many bother to visit the outlying villages. Siwa Town has grown as its population has risen to 18,000 (at least 1000 of them from outside the oasis), and people have moved into breeze-block houses or low-rise flats, forsaking their traditional mud-brick dwellings as their ancestors had previously abandoned the fortified hilltop city of Shali, whose ruins overlook the modern town. A triumphal arch and broad roads debouch onto a central market area, but the town slips away into a

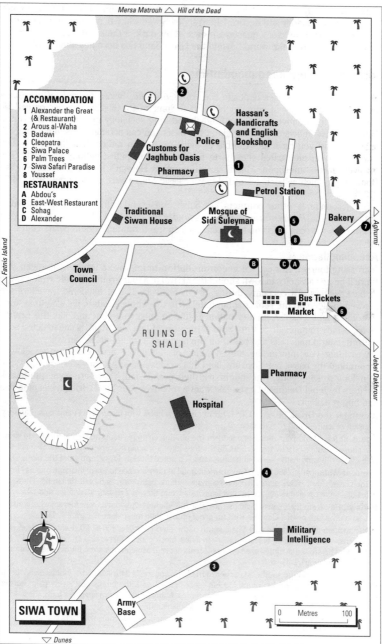

Mersa Matrouh △ Hill of the Dead

ACCOMMODATION
1 Alexander the Great
   (& Restaurant)
2 Arous al-Waha
3 Badawi
4 Cleopatra
5 Siwa Palace
6 Palm Trees
7 Siwa Safari Paradise
8 Youssef

RESTAURANTS
A Abdou's
B East-West Restaurant
C Sohag
D Alexander

Hassan's
Handicrafts
and English
Bookshop

Customs for
Jaghbub Oasis

Police

Pharmacy

Petrol Station

Traditional
Siwan House

Mosque of
Sidi Suleyman

Bakery

Town
Council

RUINS OF
SHALI

Bus Tickets

Market

Pharmacy

Hospital

Military
Intelligence

N

SIWA TOWN

Army
Base

△ Fatnis Island

△ Aghurmi

▷ Jebel Dakhrour

0 Metres 100

▽ Dunes

maze of alleyways, and loses itself amidst the encircling palms. Boys driving donkey carts transport fodder and decorously wrapped Siwan women, and the braying of donkeys resounds from every quarter of town. After dark, a thousand stars emerge and Siwa's isolation from the world beyond the Great Sand Sea becomes almost palpable.

Information and accommodation

Housed in new premises opposite the *Arous al-Waha*, Siwa's **tourist office** (daily except Fri 9am–2pm; in summer also Fri 6–8pm; ☎046/460-2338) is personified by Mahdi Hweity, a native Siwan and English-speaking sociology graduate of Alexandria University. He knows everything about the oasis and can arrange trips to outlying villages. Should you have any trouble in Siwa, go to him rather than the police. The Siwans rely on nine tribal sheikhs to resolve their disputes; nobody wants the law involved. In the afternoon, Mahdi can be found at Hassan's Handcrafts and English Bookshop (which sells copies of Fakhry's classic *Siwa Oasis*) or at home (☎046/460-2130).

You'll soon make **other contacts**, like Salah, Yousef and Ahmed, who run Siwa Safari Tours from the *Restaurant and Hotel Alexander the Great*, or Abu Bakr at *East West Restaurant*, who can help you to organize a jeep trip through Bedouin Safari Tours.

Accommodation

Increasing tourism has caused **accommodation** to improve a lot, but can mean that there'll be no vacancies in town should the arrival of a tour group coincide with a surge of backpackers – a certainty during Siwan festivals. If that happens, travellers are allowed to sleep on the roof at some hotels. On the whole, though, it's safe to assume that you'll find a bed. A further option is due to open sometime in 2000; the *Ecology Hotel*, twenty minutes drive from Siwa at the base of Jafa Mountain, is constructed solely from natural materials and based on the layout of a traditional Siwan village.

Providing you inform the tourist office or the police first, **camping** is allowed throughout the oasis, but since any land that's cultivated or near a water source is sure to belong to somebody, you should ask their permission. There are some mud-brick shelters by Jebel Dakhrour if you just want a roof over your head. Bring a sleeping bag and bug repellent.

Alexander the Great (☎046/460-0512). Friendly new hotel with clean rooms and fans. Laundry, pleasant restaurant and roof terrace. ②.

Amun, at Jebel Dakhrour, 4km outside town (no phone). Grungy rooms and squat toilets; no showers, shops or cafés. Strictly for hermits, but it does have a wonderful view of the oasis. £E5 per person, £E25 with sand bath (burial in baking sand is a noted therapy for arthritis and the like). ①.

Arous al-Waha (☎046/460-2100). Government hotel at the entrance to town; its name means "Bride of the Oasis". Very clean, semi-carpeted rooms with fans, bathrooms and bedside lamps. There are two 4-bed suites available (⑦). Breakfast is included, and there's a restaurant and garden. ⑤.

Badawi, 1km from the centre, near the hospital (no phone). Only opens when everywhere else is full, so truly a last resort. Couples without proof of marriage must sleep separately. ①.

Cleopatra, on the main road past Shali, south of the market (☎046/460-2148). Range of clean double rooms, some with toilet, balcony, fan, or in a new block with all three; also one suite with TV and A/C (⑥). The shared facilities are spotless. Meals served. Mosquitoes are a big problem, due to a stagnant pond nearby. ①–③.

Palm Trees, just off the southeast corner of the main square (☎046/460-2304). Not as clean as the *Cleopatra* and with unreliable plumbing but more central, with the bonus of a lovely palm garden out back where you can enjoy meals and table tennis. Many rooms have a fan and a bath; those without are cheaper. Friendly staff; laundry service available. ①.

Siwa Palace Hotel (☎046/460-2048). Recently refurbished. Clean rooms with fans but shared facilities. The usual plans for a rooftop restaurant. ①.

Siwa Safari Paradise, a few hundred metres along the road to Aghurmi (☎046/460-2289, fax 460-2286). 34 A/C rooms with fridge, bathroom and satellite TV, 20 bungalows with fan, heater, bathroom and TV, and 25 small basic huts. All immaculately clean. Restaurant with traditional Siwan feast once a week. Best of all is a large cold spring pool which non-residents can use for a minimum charge of £E10. Huts ②; rooms and bungalows ⑦.

Youssef Hotel (☎046/460-2162). Has a variety of clean rooms, some with bathrooms and/or balconies. There's no garden, but work is underway on a rooftop café. Laundry service. ①.

City sights: Shali and the Hill of the Dead

The **ruins of Shali**, looming above the centre and floodlit in the evening, are a constant invitation to explore. Until late last century this hermetic labyrinth attained a height of over sixty metres, with many levels of chambers, passages and granaries. Its surreal remains cover the entire saddle of rock below a **mosque**, which is said to have been the last one in Egypt where the muezzin still shouted out the call to prayer without the benefit of a loudspeaker. Down behind the hill around the back of Shali is a donkey-driven **oil-press** that dates back centuries. From vantage points in Shali, you can see the whole modern town, its palm groves, the salt lakes and table-top rocks beyond; and providing you don't peer too obviously into the houses below, it's possible to glimpse the Siwans at home. Downstairs, women busy themselves with cooking (cockerels and goats roam the alleys) and childcare; a few mats and painted chests, used for storing the family valuables, constitute the only furniture.

You can get a closer look at home life at the sanitized **Traditional Siwan House** (daily except Fri 10am–noon; £E1.50). Funded by the Canadian Ambassador, who feared that few such mud-brick dwellings would survive another deluge and the trend towards breeze-block housing, it serves as a museum of traditional dress, jewellery and toys, resembling a handicrafts shop. There are several others in the vicinity of the **market** on the main square, which is busiest on Fridays, when villagers come in to buy and sell. The other focus of life is the **Mosque of Sidi Suleyman**, built by King Fouad next to the tomb of Siwa's patron sheikh, who is honoured by a festival (see below).

By following the Matrouh road out of town and then bearing right, you'll reach the unmistakable Jebel al-Mawta, or **Hill of the Dead**, also known as the Ridge of the Mummified. Amongst scores of XXVI Dynasty and Ptolemaic tombs reused by the Romans, who cut *loculli* for their own burials, four locked ones still retain murals or inscriptions. A custodian who lives nearby will unlock them if you make your presence known (daily 9am–2pm; admission free but *baksheesh* expected).

In the **Tomb of Si-Amun**, murals depict a bearded, Greek-looking merchant and his family worshipping Egyptian deities with great artistry; unfortunately, they were vandalized by Allied soldiers after the tomb's discovery in 1940, when the Siwans dug into the necropolis to escape air raids and also found the **Tomb of Mesu-Isis**. Another third-century BC creation, this was used for two burials although the decorators never got far beyond the entrance.

Whereas Si-Amun's tomb bespeaks of Cyrenaic influence, the **Tomb of the Crocodile** reflects Siwa's longstanding ties to the Fayoum, where the crocodile cult (see p.424) flourished – with a dash of Hellenistic style in the painting of gazelles nibbling at a tree.

Lastly, there's the battered XXVI Dynasty **Tomb of Niperpathot**, with a ruined court, side rooms, and a tiny burial chamber covered with red inscriptions, including praise of Niperpathot as "the straightforward one". It also contains a once-mummified skull, complete with hair, which the custodian will produce with a flourish in the hope of startling visitors.

SIWAN FESTIVALS AND WEDDINGS

Siwan festivals are the most public side of a largely private culture, so it's worth making an effort to attend one. Since many Egyptians enjoy going to them, it is wise to reserve a room well in advance, and get there several days early, as buses to the oasis fill up nearer the time.

The largest and most famous is the **Siayha**, or **Tourism Festival**, which, despite its name, is a genuine event with a long tradition. Some 10,000 Siwans assemble at Jebel Dakhrour for three days of feasting, dancing and relaxation – acting as tourists in their own oasis. A sheikh from Sidi Barrani comes in to bless the feast with an inaugural *Bism'allah!* (in the name of God). Many non-Siwans and foreigners come too, and are made welcome. *Siayha* always occurs during the period of the full moon in October.

Two other festivals are celebrated by Muslims everywhere: the **Lesser Bairam**, at the end of Ramadan, occasioning festivities similar to those elsewhere in Egypt; and the **Corban Bairam** (Great Feast), which starts earlier in Siwa. The gathering of fuel and salt over the preceding nine days is reckoned as much a part of the event as the mass slaughter of sheep after festival prayers on the tenth day of *Zoul Hagga*. The sheep's hide is stewed together with its offal in an earthenware pot; its head and stomach are eaten the next day, when cuts of meat are distributed amongst relatives (new brides especially); and finally, any leftovers are preserved.

The **Moulid of Sidi Suleyman** is a less carnivorous affair, with banners, candles and Dervishes performing *zikrs* outside his tomb beside the mosque. Siwans recall how its doors refused to open after their ancestors spurned some poor Bedouin pilgrims, and how Sidi Suleyman once conjured up a sandstorm to bury an army of Tibbu raiders. Held just after the corn harvest, his moulid subsumes two older, pagan festivals, where vast amounts of palm-liquor were openly consumed. Such excesses no longer occur. The festival is also known as the *Moulid en Tagmigra*. Less noticeably, 21 other sheikhs are honoured by small moulids throughout the year.

Ashura, on the tenth of *Moharram*, was once Siwa's principal feast, and fervently Shi'ite; the Fatimid Shia reached Egypt via the North African oases. Nowadays it's chiefly an event for children, who decorate their homes with palm stalks soaked in olive oil, and fire them at sunset, singing while the town is illuminated by torchlight. Afterwards the children go from house to house exchanging presents.

WEDDINGS

Although you might be invited to join the tea-drinking crowd outside the bridegroom's family house, foreigners rarely witness the intricate ritual of **Siwan weddings**. Preceded by reciprocal visits of kinsfolk, and a ritual bath where the removal of an item of jewellery symbolizes her abandonment of maidenhood, the bride is "kidnapped" by her spouse's family, returned, and then delivered wrapped in a sheet. The wedding dress of embroidered shawls and skirts is as flamboyant as the outdoor garb of married women is drab. Nowadays, unmarried girls wear Egyptian fashions rather than Siwan costume, and the usual age of marriage has risen from fourteen to sixteen years (the national average) since the mid-1980s.

Traditionally, a Siwan widow commanded the same *mahr* (dowry) as a virgin since both were "daughters of the forty ancestors", but could only remarry after one year of bereavement. Cruelly, the Siwans regarded newly bereaved widows as "devourers of the soul" (*ghulah*), and forced them to spend forty days in solitary confinement before they were "cleansed" – a taboo now happily lapsed.

Crafts

Traditional **crafts** still flourish in the oasis, particularly pottery and basket-making. Embroidery had been declining, but has now revived owing to tourists' liking for dresses, shawls and waistcoats. Most of the work is done at home by women and marketed through informal co-operatives in handicrafts shops. The price has already been set so there's no point in bargaining (unless you're in direct negotiation with the owner of something for sale). Many women now earn significant sums for this work, belying the stereotype of passive, dependent Siwan womanhood. Other products made mostly by the women include black **robes** with orange or red piping; intricately embroidered **wedding clothes** spangled with antique coins; and all kinds of woven **baskets**, often brightly tasselled. They also mould **pottery** and fire it at home in bread-ovens: robust cooking and storage pots, delicate oil lamps, and a kind of baptismal crucible called the *shamadan en sebaa*.

Unlike the gold-loving Egyptians, the Siwans have traditionally preferred **silver jewellery**, which likewise served as bullion assets for a people mistrustful of banks and paper money. The designs are uniquely Siwan, influenced by Berber rather than Egyptian jewellery. Local silversmiths once produced most of it, but in modern times it has largely come from Khan el-Khalili; the last Siwan master craftsman died in 1952. Broad silver bracelets and oval rings wrought with geometric designs are the most popular items with visitors, while *Al-Salhat*, with its six pendants hung from silver and coral beads, is the easiest type of necklace to identify. You'll also recognize the *tiyalaqan*, a mass of chains tipped with bells, suspended from huge crescents; and an ornament for the head, consisting of silver hoops and bells suspended from matching chunks of bullion, called a *qasas*. Finally, there's the *aghraw*, a silver collar from which girls hang a decorative disk or *adrim*, which is removed on their wedding day.

Eating and other practicalities

As the oases go, Siwa is good for **eating**; although service is slow, its humble restaurants offer a fairly wide range of dishes, including Indian. You'll soon discover what is best cooked in one place, or cheaper in another; their menus are similar, but prices vary. *East West Restaurant* offers good food and is a great place to watch everyday life in Siwa, while the new and immaculately clean *Restaurant Alexander the Great* is friendly and definitely worth a try. Also good, reasonably priced and relatively free of flies is *Abdou's*, which organizes Siwan music parties at the Cleopatra Spring if there are enough tourists; the neighbouring *Sohag Restaurant* is really only fit for tea. Providing there are customers, all are open till around midnight. Local **shops** are well supplied with canned goods, sweets, juices and bottled water, while fresh bread is available from a hole-in-the-wall **bakery**. If you're serious about self-catering, the market stocks seasonal vegetables, dates and olive oil galore.

Aside from a bank, Siwa has all the basic facilities. There are two **pharmacies** in the centre and a **hospital** on the outskirts. The police (☎046/460-2008) share a building with the **post office** (daily except Fri 8am–2pm), which is quite reliable. Currently there are public (24hr) and private (9am–midnight) **telephone exchanges**, both of which can make local and international calls; a new government telephone exchange is due to open in 2000. Siwa's **petrol station** is the only one in the oasis, and the last until Mersa Matrouh or Bahariya Oasis.

Moving on from Siwa

Buses depart from the market, where you should buy tickets the night before to be sure of getting a seat (although standing passengers are seldom turned away). There are two daily to **Alexandria** (9hr), leaving at 7am and 10am (£E27). Both call at **Mersa Matrouh** (4hr; £E12), while a third bus, leaving Siwa at 1pm, terminates there. Beware that some Alex buses don't stop in the centre of the city, but run on to Sidi Gaber; if so, you'll be warned to get off at Moharrem Bey and take a taxi. There are a few **service taxis** from Siwa to Matrouh (£E10), leaving from *Abdou's*, usually in the early evening.

The **road to Bahariya Oasis** (420km) gives fabulous views of dunes and scarps and allows travellers to reach the four oases on the Great Desert Circuit directly from Siwa, without having to return to Cairo first – but far fewer people use it than you'd imagine. The road is bad all the way, with no facilities, only army checkpoints. If nothing goes amiss, a jeep can make the journey in eight or nine hours. Crossing in a regular car may be possible, but is not advised as the road is very bumpy and frequently covered in sand. Traffic is very rare, so a breakdown can leave you stranded for days. While motorists might still be game, tourists without a car are often deterred by the **price**; around £E700 by jeep. Finding other travellers to split the cost involves a trade-off; more passengers means greater discomfort but less expense.

Getting a group together could take a few days, depending on how many foreigners are in Siwa. Military permission costs £E10.50 per person, from the Military Intelligence office in Siwa Town; drop off your money and passport in the morning and you can usually collect it later the same day. For those with their own 4WD, the **formalities** are simple: just register your passport and licence number with the police in Siwa before you leave. The turn-off for Bahariya is 6km north of town on the right-hand side of the Mersa Matrouh road.

En route to Bahariya, the road passes four uninhabited oases which travellers are forbidden to enter without military permission (see above). The most beautiful is **Areg Oasis**, behind a cliff off the road, where ancient, often-plundered tombs attest to past habitation. **Bahrein Oasis** is named after its two lakes; the one nearest the road can ensnare vehicles in quicksand. **Nuwamisa Oasis** abounds in sheltered camping spots, but has to be the worst place for mosquitoes in the world. Traversing the depression of **Sitra Oasis**, you come within 4WD range of its lake. The last stage of the journey skirts the **Ghard Kebir** (Great Dunes), whose sandy crests were likened by Bagnold to "unclipped horses' manes". The dunes are slowly making their way south from the Qattara Depression, destined to arrive in Bahariya in a few hundred years.

Around Siwa Oasis

Although the **Siwa Oasis** depression is some 82km long and up to 28km wide, cultivated areas amount to less than 2000 acres and the total population is only 18,000; in some areas both population and cultivation have diminished since salination turned ancient gardens into barren *karshif*. Nearer town, dense **palm groves** and wiry olive trees are carefully tended in mud- and palm-leaf-walled gardens: dates and olives are the chief crops. Siwa has as many as 70,000 olive trees and over 300,000 palm trees, of which around 23,000 are male palms, only valued for the white heart at the top of the tree, a local delicacy.

Palms form the backdrop to most places that you're likely to go, especially the **pools** or **baths**, which for many visitors are the highlight of the oasis. The nearer sites can be reached by bicycle, donkey *caretta* or on foot; just time your visit to avoid travelling in the hottest part of day. **Bicycles** can be rented from Hassan's Handcrafts or places near the *Youssef* and *Palm Trees* hotels, for £E5 a day. *East West Restaurant* offers bikes for the same price, or £E25 with a guide for the day. Test bikes out before embarking on a long ride.

Should you be invited to visit **private springs and gardens**, it's wise to consider your would-be host's motives before accepting. Financial designs aren't necessarily a deterrent – it's quite acceptable to pay for a good time – but lecherous intentions are something else: women without male escorts should definitely be wary.

Aghurmi and Jebel Dakhrour

A *caretta* ride (£E10 return) or a half-hour walk through the palm groves will bring you to **AGHURMI**, just over 1km east of town by a country road; keep going straight on

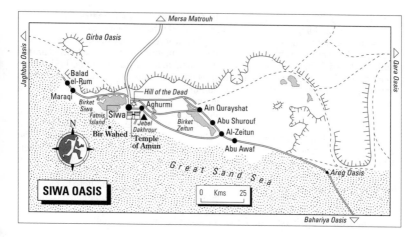

past the crossroads and the modern village appears shortly before the hill where the ancient Siwans built their first fortified settlement. Raised 12m above the plain and entered by a single gateway, Aghurmi had its own deep well (to the left, inside), making it impervious to sieges. The ruins are signposted as the "Alexander Crowning Hall", for it was here that the **Siwan Oracle** reposed in antiquity. Its **temple** is currently being restored, but you are amply compensated by the fabulous **view**, encompassing two salt lakes, Dakhrour and Siwa Town in the distance, and a great mass of palms.

Fakhry dates the existing temple to the reign of Amasis the Drunkard (570–526 BC) but reckons it evolved from a seventh- or eighth-century BC site dedicated to Amun-Re. Though others have attributed the primal shrine to the ram-headed Libyan god Ammon, experts agree that the **Oracle of Amun** was renowned from the XXVI Dynasty onwards.

Its history is subsequently much documented: a Persian army sent to destroy it was obliterated by the desert; emissaries sent by Cimon of Athens were told of his death as it happened; assured of success by the oracle, Eubotas of Cyrenaica took his own victory statue to the 93rd Olympiad; and Lysander tried bribery to win the oracle's endorsement of his claim to the Spartan throne.

But the most famous petitioner was Alexander the Great. Having liberated Egypt from its hated Persian rulers and ordered the creation of a city on the Mediterranean, Alexander hurried to Siwa in the spring of 331 BC. It's thought that he sought confirmation that he was the son of Zeus (whom the Greeks identified with Amun), but the oracle's reply – whispered by a priest through an aperture in the wall of the sanctuary – is unrecorded. Alexander kept it secret unto his death in Asia eight years later. Despite his personal wish to be buried near the oracle, he was probably interred in Alexandria, the capital he never saw – though two Greeks claim to have found his tomb in Siwa (see p.472).

On to Jebel Dakhrour

From the ruins of Aghurmi you can gaze across thickets of palms to a cream-coloured pillar – part of a **ruined Temple of Amun** viewed side-on. To get there, continue along the road and take the signed turn to "Umm Ubayda". A painted bas-reliefed wall and giant blocks of rubble are all that remain of this once-substantial XXX Dynasty creation after it was dynamited by a treasure-hunting governor in 1897. Locals call the ruin *Umm Ubaydah*, but its likely founder was Nectanebo II (360–343 BC), who also rebuilt the Temple of Hibis at Kharga Oasis.

Follow the path on and bear right at the fork to reach the **Cleopatra Bath**, a deep pool of gently bubbling spring water, where local men bathe. Being fully visible to anyone passing along the trail, it is not often a place where women can comfortably swim, although Siwan brides used to do so before ritual ablutions were moved to the **Tamusi Bath**, secluded 150m back along the path. Traditionally, it was here that brides-to-be handed on their *adrims* to their younger sisters, and boys were circumcised. Nowadays, the nuptial couple arrive by car, drive around the pool and away, without bathing at all. There is also a café and toilet near the spring.

Heading on from the Cleopatra Bath, bear left at the fork and take the first path on the right. A ten-minute walk through clover fields and groves of palms will bring you out in the desert near **Jebel Dakhrour**. This rugged massif is the site for the *Siyaha festival* in October, and affords stunning **views** from its summit. In contrast to the verdant oasis and the silvery salt lake, the southern horizon presents a desolate vista of crescent dunes and blackened mesas: the edge of the Great Sand Sea. The **hot sand** at Dakhrour is efficacious for rheumatic conditions, so sufferers come here to be buried up to their necks during the summer months, and there is talk of building a clinic.

To get back from Dakhrour, follow the first dirt road you come to, which enters the centre of town by the *Palm Trees Hotel*. It's about half an hour's walk.

Fatnis Island

The most popular excursion is to "Fantasy" or **Fatnis Island**, on the salt lake of Birket Siwa, 6km west of town. An easy bike ride, it can also be reached by *caretta* (£E8 return) or on foot (1hr). Take the road out past the town council and then the left-hand route every time a fork occurs, except when a sign directs you to the right. En route you'll pass the **Abu Alif Bath**, where farm hands wash; beyond the palm groves, follow a causeway across salt-encrusted pans onto the island, where palms surround a large circular, tiled **pool**, fed by fresh water welling up from clefts in the rock 15m below. It gets busy around sunset, when tourists are joined by off-duty soldiers, so women are advised to bathe earlier.

Before returning, take a look at **Birket Siwa** receding towards the sculpted table-tops on the western horizon. You can see the process of crust-formation at the edges, where evaporation gradually renders fresh water saline, then crystalline, blackening the surrounding vegetation. Like other lakes in the oasis, it spreads or recedes according to the season, so that the desert tracks around its perimeter are underwater in wintertime.

Maraqi and "Alexander's Tomb"

MARAQI is the collective name for several **villages** at the western end of the depression, separated from the main oasis by a rocky desert riddled with caves and tombs. The area was populous and intensively cultivated from Roman times until the fifteenth century, but is now mostly used for grazing by the **Bedouin** Al-Shihaybat tribe, which has settled here. Most buildings are quite new as the old settlements were destroyed by the deluge of 1982, which forced residents to shelter in caves at Balad el-Rum (Town of the Romans).

In early 1995, Maraqi made news when Liana and Manos Souvaltzi announced their discovery of the "**Tomb of Alexander the Great**" beneath a ruined **Doric temple** near the village. The Antiquities Council endorsed their claim, but backed off after the Souvaltzis failed to refute criticism that they had misread vital inscriptions. They now claim that the tomb belonged to a Macedonian VIP and *may* shed light on the whereabouts of Alexander's tomb, which they still believe is in Siwa Oasis. Most scholars agree that he was buried somewhere in Alexandria, though exactly where, and whether his body was destroyed by the Romans, is still debated.

The temple is guarded while excavations continue, and casual visitors are excluded – not that there's much to see above ground anyway. If you're interested in the excavations, talk to Mahdi at the Siwa tourist office, who knows when work is in progress and can arrange a visit to the site. An **excursion** to the tomb and surrounding villages costs £E50 (group rate). You could also reach Maraqi by **bus** (£E1) from Siwa, but since they only run twice a day (7am & 2pm) and remain in Maraqi for just twenty minutes, you'll have to start early and catch the afternoon bus back to avoid being stranded. The temple is also hard to reach, being at the edge of the furthest village, on the left side of the road before the water tower. If you're **driving** from Siwa, turn left off the Matrouh road 1km north of town and keep going until you reach the last village in Maraqi.

Between Maraqi and Siwa a track runs off to **Girba Oasis**, now solely occupied by soldiers. In olden times this was the *Masrab el-Ikhwan* (Road of the Brotherhood) from Jaghbub Oasis in Libya, whereby Senussi preachers reached the Western Desert oases. (*Masrab* is the Siwan word for a camel route, called a *darb* in other oases.) Today the soldiers try to catch **smugglers** of hashish and videos; the punishment for capture is summary execution. Another hazard is the **minefields** along the Libyan border, sown by the British and Italians soon after they defined it in 1938, and by the Egyptians and Libyans since the 1970s. All in all, this is not an area to explore by jeep.

Birket Zeitun and further afield

Other sites **further afield** range the gamut of accessibility. There are no buses, but the tourist office and private operators such as Abu Bakr at *East West Restaurant*, or Siwa Safari Tours offer day-trips to **Birket Zeitun** or **Bir Wahed** for around £E50 per person including lunch and the £E10.50 fee for military permission. *Siwa Safari Paradise* runs more upmarket versions of the same tours in A/C jeeps at £E70 per person for a half day. Travelling beyond Siwa Oasis, the more remote **Qara Oasis** and the **Qattara Depression** can only be reached by 4WD with military permission and a guide.

Birket Zeitun

The largest salt lake in the oasis, **Birket Zeitun** is visible from Aghurmi and Jebel Dakhrour. Only the far shore is inhabited, with villages that flourished in Roman times before centuries of slow decline set in. The lake's increasing salinity is both the cause and result of depopulation: as fewer irrigation works are maintained, more of the fresh water from the **Ain Qurayshat** spring flows unused into the lake, crystallizing mineral salts as it evaporates. The source is enclosed by a pool where you can bathe.

Near the spring are two ancient **ruins**, roughly 100m apart: a heap of rubble, which still constituted a temple during Steindorff's visit in 1900; and the remains of a brick building attributed as "the abode of King Ghashsham" by the *Siwan Manuscript*. Though Siwans still dig round about, in the hope of finding loot, Ain Qurayshat is better for bathing than antiquities.

The best of the lake's **bathing** is around 35km southwest of Siwa Town at **ABU SHUROUF**, whose 500 inhabitants are mostly Siwan. Their houses surround a small stone **temple**, but the village is more remarkable for harbouring all the female **donkeys** in the oasis, which are kept and mated here. In Siwan parlance, "Have you been to Abu Shurouf?" is a euphemism for "Have you had sex?"

Further south along the lake, the village of **AL-ZEITUN** was once a model Senussi community tending the richest gardens in the oasis, until it was abandoned following an Italian bombing raid in 1940. A passage to the left of the mosque leads to a small ancient **temple**, where the locals sheltered from the bombs. Two kilometres further on, the eerie Roman Tombs of **Abu Awaf** are littered with bones, although they bear no inscriptions.

Bir Wahed

Situated 22km from Siwa and several miles into the dunes of the Great Sand Sea (see the following section for more on visiting the Great Sand Sea), **Bir Wahed** is a **hot spring** and a **cold pool** surrounded by vegetation. You can roll and slide down the huge **dunes** or hunt for **fossils** before cooling off or soaking in clean hot water. Accessible only by jeep, it's a magical spot. Overnight excursions are currently on hold as part of a nationwide increase in security, but day-trips are still popular (see start of section for details).

Qara Oasis and the Qattara Depressions

If you have the means and are seriously into desert travel, **Qara Oasis** has a compelling fascination. The smallest and poorest of the inhabited oases, it has been far less touched by the outer world than Siwa. Visitors are so rare that the villagers turn out to welcome them and serve a meal in their honour. Until flooding rendered it unsafe in 1982, the Qarawis occupied a Shali-like labyrinth atop "a solitary white mushroom of rock", edged by a "high smooth wall, impregnable to raiders, with one black tunnel for a street". Now, most families live in new houses on the plain. According to legend, the Qarawis once made a pact (or were cursed) that their population would never exceed 140; whenever a child was born an older person was obliged to leave the oasis.

The shortest **route** from Siwa to Qara is via the Masrab Khidda (125km), but its rough terrain and featureless mud flats make it essential to have someone who knows the way. Alternatively, you can head north towards Matrouh and turn off at the checkpoint just before the Bir Nous resthouse, on to a dirt road to Qara.

Northeast of Qara the land plummets into the **Qattara Depression**, 120–134m below sea level, where a long narrow salt marsh winds "like a petrified river close beneath the cliffs". Ever since Dr Ball first proposed it in the 1920s, Egyptian planners have dreamed of piping water from the Mediterranean to the depression, utilizing the fall in height to generate hydroelectricity, and run desalination plants and irrigation systems. But all attempts have foundered through lack of capital, and nothing seems likely to happen in the foreseeable future. There is, however, exploration for **oil** at many points in the desert between Qattara and Mersa Matrouh, which explains the upgraded tracks that crisscross the wilderness.

The Great Sand Sea and the "Lost Oasis"

The **Great Sand Sea** that laps Siwa and floods the Libyan–Egyptian border still has areas beyond the "limits of reliable relief information" on Tactical Pilotage Charts, but its overall configuration is known. From thick "whalebacks" and a mass of transverse dunes near Siwa, it washes south in parallel ridges (oriented north–south, with a slight northwest–southeast incline) as far as the eye can see.

Although its general existence was known at the time of Herodotus, the extent to which it stretched southwards wasn't realized until the Rohlfs expedition of 1874 headed west from Dakhla into the unknown. With seventeen camels bearing water and supplies, they soon met the *erg*'s outermost ranges: "an ocean" of sand-waves over 100m high, ranked 2–4km apart. Rohlfs estimated that their camels could scale six dunes and advance 20km westwards on the first and second days, but that their endurance would rapidly diminish thereafter, so with no prospect of water or an end to the dunes they were forced to turn north-northwest and follow the dune lanes towards Siwa. Their isolation was intense:

If one stayed behind a moment and let the caravan out of one's sight, a loneliness could be felt in the boundless expanse such as brought fear even in the stoutest heart . . . Nothing but sand and sky! At sea the surface of the water is moved, unless there is a dead calm. Here in the sand ocean there is nothing to remind one of the great common life of the earth but the stiffened ripples of the last storm; all else is dead.

By the eighteenth day the expedition could no longer water every camel and the animals began dying, yet it wasn't until the thirty-sixth day that the party reached Siwa. They had trekked 675km, 480 of them across the waterless dunes.

The feat wasn't repeated until 1921–24, when Colonel de Lancey Forth entered the Sand Sea twice by camel from Dakhla and Siwa. Beneath a layer of sand he found campfires, charred ostrich eggs, flint knives and grinders from Neolithic times, when the desert was lush savannah.

Meanwhile, Ball and Moore had managed to round the Sand Sea's southeastern tip (near latitude 24) by car in 1917. However, it was an Egyptian, Hassanein Bey, who circumvented the Sand Sea's western edge (1923) as part of an extraordinary 3550-kilometre camel journey from Sollum on the Mediterranean to El-Fasher in Sudan's Darfur Province. He also confirmed the existence of the hitherto legendary massif, Jebel Uwaynat, whose water source encouraged motorized explorers of the 1920s to seek new routes to the southwest. For Prince Kemal al-Din in his fleet of caterpillar-tracked Citroens, and Ralph Bagnold and Co. – who found customized Model-T Fords more effective – the next obstacle was the Gilf Kebir: a vast limestone plateau south of the Sand Sea, which barred the way to remoter Libyan oases.

Visiting the Sand Sea

As its outermost dunes are only a few kilometres from Siwa's cultivated edge, it's quite feasible to enter the Sand Sea yourself. You can cycle most of the way there from town by following the road out past the hospital (15min), or walk it in an hour or so. It's safe to leave the bike and trek into the dunes, where you can sleep out. As nights are cold, you may prefer to rent a donkey to carry the water, food and firewood, and a boy to guide the animal. Always keep oriented in relation to the oasis; a compass is essential unless you can take bearings from the sun or stars. The red light on Siwa's radio mast might also be visible at night. Never enter the Sand Sea when a windstorm is rising. See the box on the following page for an account of the formation of sand seas and dunes and more on the consequent dangers.

Zerzura: the "Lost Oasis"

With the "discovery" by motorized explorers of Selima, Merga and the Forty Day Road's water holes, the number of unlocated oases diminished until only the **"Lost Oasis" of Zerzura** remained. First mentioned in 1246 as an abandoned village in the desert southwest of the Fayoum, it reappeared as a fabulous city in the fifteenth-century treasure-hunters' *Book of Hidden Pearls*:

> *This city is white like a pigeon, and on the door of it is carved a bird. Enter, and there you will find great riches, also the king and queen sleeping in their castle. Do not approach them, but take the treasure.*

Citing native sources, the first European reference to Zerzura (1835) placed the oasis "five days west of the road from El-Hayiz to Farafra", or "two or three days due west from Dakhleh". *Murray's Handbook* (1891) reported an "Oasis of the Blacks ... also called Wady Zerzura" to the west of Farafra, and described it quite matter-of-factly. But Zerzura was still unlocated, and the stories placing it west of Dakhla gained credibility after Europeans "discovered" Kufra Oasis in Libya, which the same tales had mentioned. However, both the Rohlfs and Harding-King expeditions heard accounts of black men who periodically raided Dakhla from an oasis seven or eight days' journey to the southwest.

SAND SEAS AND DUNES

The true life of the desert is not made up of the marches of tribes in search of pasture, but of the game that goes endlessly on. What a difference in substance between the sands of submission and the sands of unruliness! The dunes, the salines, change their nature . . . as the code changes by which they are governed.

Antoine de Saint-Exupéry, *Wind, Sand and Stars*

Though gravel plains, limestone pans and scarp account for 90 percent of the Sahara Desert, it's the **sand seas** or **ergs** that captivate the imagination. Covering hundreds of thousands of square kilometres of Algeria, Libya and Egypt, these sand sheets and dune fields are awesomely lifeless, yet shift and reproduce. Formed by wind and particles, vortices and accretion, their shapes, hues and textures are defined by light and shadow, a mutable reality. Venturers into this unearthly world must accept its whims and logic – this is elemental, not mortal terrain. Its sandstorms have buried armies and scoured paint from cars; soft spots and slip faces can trap the unwary, break limbs or axles; getting lost and dying of heat and thirst are real possibilities here.

While prevailing winds are the dominant factor, local geology and whatever precipitation or vegetation exists also determine the shape of **dunes**. Where sand is relatively scarce and small obstructions are common, windblown particles tend to form **crescent-shaped** *barchan* dunes, which advance horns first. Fully-grown specimens (weighing up to 450 million kilos) are capable of spawning infants downwind, but their mass is nothing compared to **ridged** *seif* ("sword") dunes, which can rise over 100m high and run unbroken for 50km – the longest straight lines in nature. Each has a hard-packed windward face, and a softer, gently sloping leeward side. The latter is prone to shallow quicksand spots and sudden slippages (stop and look before cresting dunes!), and even the firm windward surface can become unstable once its "piling" has been disturbed.

It's easy to imagine a sand ridge developing in the lee of soft, eroded rock, but **dune formation** in open desert requires some explanation. The ingredients include coarse sand and gravel whose weight immobilizes them as lag deposit and lighter particles (between 0.1 and 0.5 millimetres in size), which travel by a series of hopping movements, termed saltation. Transverse dunes (producing a "washboard" effect) are generally attributed to multi-directional winds – the prevailing wind moderate, the stronger wind intermittent – but there's disagreement about the cause of parallel ridged dunes. Some think they evolve from transverse dunes buffeted by fierce crosswinds, others that they're whipped up by "longitudinal roll vortices" (horizontal whirlwinds). When the wind direction alters constantly, it can even form star-shaped (*rhord*) or ring dunes.

Having weighed the evidence for various speculative locations in the last chapter of *Libyan Sands*, Bagnold demarcated three zones. The "northern" one – encompassing the whole Sand Sea, but rating the areas west of Dakhla and Farafra as likeliest – was propounded by de Lancey Forth, citing the story of a town with iron gates, seven days' camel journey to the south, in the *Siwan Manuscript*; plus tales of Bedouin chancing upon unknown oases while pursuing missing camels.

Unfortunately, similar yarns also pointed towards the far south – that vast wilderness between Dakhla and the Selima and Merga oases in Sudan. Dr Ball and Newbold favoured this area, largely free of dunes and often low enough to approach the subterranean water table; in addition, Newbold thought he glimpsed an oasis during a flight over the desert (one of several by the Hungarian aviator Count László Almassy).

The third, "central" zone extended southwest from Dakhla as far as Jebel Uwaynat (see p.460). Championed by Harding-King, it rested largely on native accounts of incursions by "strange cows", Tibbu raiders and a "black giantess". When Ball discovered a cache of Tibbu water jars 200km southwest of Dakhla in 1917, it supported the stories but argued against an oasis; if a water source existed, why bother to maintain a depot in the middle of nowhere?

Accepting Ball's theory of a consistent water level beneath the Libyan Desert, Bagnold argued that Zerzura could only exist in low-lying areas or deep, wind-eroded hollows. As the desert was surveyed, the possibility of such sites escaping notice diminished, and Bagnold doubted that an undiscovered oasis existed. Perhaps Zerzura might once have been a water hole or an area favoured with periodic rainfall, but the fabled oasis of palms and ruins must be a figment of wishful thinking: a Bedouin Shangri-la that tantalized foreign explorers.

CHAPTER FOUR

ALEXANDRIA AND THE MEDITERRANEAN COAST

For ancient Egyptians, the **Mediterranean coast** marked the edge of the "Great Green", the measureless sea that formed the limits of the known world. Life and civilization meant the Nile Valley and the Delta – an outlook that still seems to linger in the country's subconscious. For, despite the white beaches, craggy headlands and turquoise sea that stretch for some five hundred kilometres, the Egyptian Med is eerily vacant and underpopulated.

Anywhere on the European side of the sea, mass tourism would have taken hold years ago. Here, though, in part due to a lack of fresh-water sources, towns are few and generally small, and far outnumbered by military bases. Such tourism as exists is largely domestic and overwhelmingly male; there is virtually no alcohol on sale and standards of dress verge on the puritanical. Foreign women, especially, could well find that the hassles far outweigh any pleasure to be gained here – in contrast to the much more relaxed beaches in the Sinai. If you explore nonetheless, the best resorts are **Mersa Matrouh** (a jumping-off point for the Siwa Oasis) and **Sidi Abd el-Rahman**, while historical interest focuses chiefly on the World War II battlefield of **El-Alamein**.

Alexandria, however, at the east end of the coast, is an entirely different animal. Egypt's second city feels as Mediterranean and cosmopolitan as Athens or Marseille, its nineteenth-century architecture redolent of the colonial days immortalized by E.M. Forster, the poet Cavafy and, most famously, Lawrence Durrell. But its sights belong to

---

ACCOMMODATION PRICE CODES

Throughout the guide, hotels and pensions are graded on a scale of ① to ⑨, indicating the price (including tax) of the **cheapest double room** in each establishment in high season (for places that offer **dorm beds**, rates per person are given in £E). Please note that most hotels in categories ⑧ and ⑨ quote rates in US$, but will accept payment in £E. For a full explanation of the following categories, see p.46. The price bands to which these codes refer are as follows:

① under £E20/US$7	④ £E45–65/US$15–20	⑦ £E150–300/US$50–100
② £E20–30/US$7–10	⑤ £E65–100/US$20–35	⑧ US$100–200/£E300–600
③ £E30–45/US$10–15	⑥ £E100–150/US$35–50	⑨ US$200/£E600 upwards

an earlier age, when it was the capital of Greco-Roman Egypt, and the seat of Cleopatra, the last of the Ptolemies.

Finally, a word about the **weather**: Egypt's Med coast gets hotter and drier the further west you travel, but Alexandria can be cold and windy in the winter, with torrential downpours and waves crashing over the Corniche for days on end. Should you happen to be there over New Year, beware of the blizzard of crockery that Alexandrians throw out of their windows at midnight.

> The **telephone code** for Alexandria, Mersa Matrouh and other resorts is ☎03.
> It has to be used even when calling from one place to another within the code area.

ALEXANDRIA (EL-ISKANDARIYA)

Alexandria, princess and whore. The royal city and the anus mundi.
Lawrence Durrell, *The Alexandria Quartet*

ALEXANDRIA turns its back on the rest of Egypt and faces the Mediterranean, as if contemplating its glorious past; a hybrid city characterized by Durrell as the "Capital of Memory". One of the great cities of antiquity, Alex slumbered for 1300 years until it was revived by Mohammed Ali and transformed by Europeans, who gave the city its present shape and made it synonymous with cosmopolitanism and decadence. This era came to an end in the 1950s with the mass flight of non-Egyptians and a dose of revolutionary puritanism, but Alexandria's beaches, restaurants and breezy climate still attract hordes of Cairenes during the summer, while its jaded historical and literary mystique remains appealing to foreigners. And when *El-Iskandariya* (the city's Arabic name) palls, you can easily enough take a bus to Mersa Matrouh and continue on to Siwa Oasis.

Alex in history

When **Alexander the Great** wrested Egypt from the Persian empire in 332 BC at the age of twenty-five, he decided against Memphis, the ancient capital, in favour of building a new city linked by sea to his Macedonian homeland. Choosing a site near the fishing village of **Rhakotis**, where two limestone spurs formed a natural harbour, he gave orders to his architect, Deinocrates, before travelling on to Siwa and thence to Asia, where he died eight years later. His corpse was subsequently returned to Egypt, where the priests refused burial at Memphis; its final resting place remains a mystery, although most archeologists believe it lies somewhere beneath Alexandria.

Thereafter Alexander's empire was divided amongst his Macedonian generals, one of whom took Egypt and adopted the title **Ptolemy I Soter**, founding a dynasty. Avid promoters of Hellenistic culture, the **Ptolemies** made Alexandria an intellectual powerhouse: among its scholars were Euclid, the "father of geometry",and Eratosthenes, who accurately determined the circumference and diameter of the earth. Alexandria's great lighthouse, the **Pharos**, was literally and metaphorically a beacon, rivalled in fame only by the city's **Library**, the foremost centre of learning in the ancient world.

The later, mostly enfeebled Ptolemies, however, increasingly depended on Rome to maintain their position, and even the bold **Cleopatra VII** (51–30 BC) came unstuck after her lover, Julius Caesar, was murdered, and his successor in Rome (and in Cleo's bed), Mark Antony, was defeated by Octavian. The latter proved immune to her charms and in fact so detested Cleopatra's capital at Alexandria that he banned Roman citizens from entering Egypt on the pretext that its religious orgies were morally corrupting.

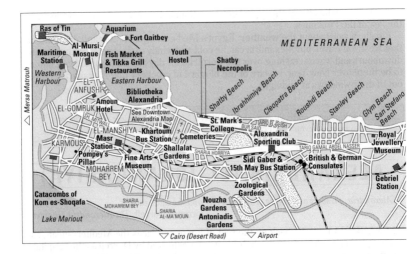

Roman rule and Arab conquest

Whereas Alexandria's Egyptians and Greeks had previously respected one another's deities and even syncretized them into a common cult (the worship of Serapis), religious conflicts developed under **Roman rule** (30 BC–313 AD). The empire regarded Christianity, which was supposedly introduced by St Mark in 45 AD, as subversive, and the persecution of Christians from 250AD onwards reached a bloody apogee under Emperor Diocletian, when the Copts maintain that 144,000 believers were martyred. (The Coptic church dates its chronology from 284 AD, the "Era of Martyrs", rather than Christ's birth.)

After the emperor Constantine made **Christianity** the state religion, a new controversy arose over the nature of Christ, the theological subtleties of which essentially masked a political rebellion by Egyptian **Copts** against Byzantine (ie Greek) authority. In Alexandria, the Coptic patriarch became supreme and his monks waged war against paganism, sacking the Serapis Temple and Library in 391AD, and later murdering the female scholar Hypatia.

Local hatred of Byzantium disposed the Alexandrians to welcome the **Arab conquest** (641 AD), whose commander, Amr, described the city according to what he saw that it contained: "4000 palaces, 4000 baths, 400 theatres, 1200 greengrocers and 40,000 Jews". But while the Arabs incorporated elements of Alexandrian learning into their own civilization, they cared little for a city which "seemed to them idolatrous and foolish", preferring to found a new capital at Fustat (now part of Cairo). Owing to neglect and the silting-up of the waterways that connected it to the Nile, Alexandria inexorably declined over the next millennium, so that when Napoleon's expeditionary force arrived in 1798, they found a mere fishing village with four thousand inhabitants.

Mohammed Ali and colonial rule

Alexandria's **revival** sprang from the sultan Mohammed Ali's desire to make Egypt a commercial and maritime power, which necessitated a seaport. The Mahmudiya Canal, finished in 1820, once again linked Alexandria to the Nile, while a harbour, docks and arsenal were created with French assistance. European merchants erected mansions and warehouses, building outwards from the Place des Consuls (modern-day Midan Tahrir), and the city's population soared to 230,000.

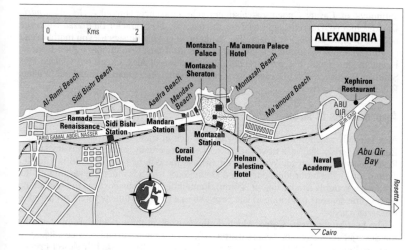

Nationalist resentment of foreign influence fired the **Orabi revolt** of 1882, in retaliation for which British warships shelled the city, whose devastation was completed by arsonists and looters. Yet such was Alexandria's vitality and commercial importance that it quickly recovered.

Having survived bombing during World War II, Alexandria experienced new turmoil in the post-war era, as anti-British riots expressed rising **nationalism**. The **revolution** that forced King Farouk to sail into exile from Alexandria in 1952 didn't seriously affect the "foreign" community (many of whom had lived here for generations) until the Anglo-French-Israeli assault on Egypt during the Suez Crisis of 1956. The following year, however, Nasser expelled all French and British citizens and nationalized foreign businesses, forcing a hundred thousand non-Egyptians to emigrate. Jewish residents also suffered after the discovery of an Israeli-controlled sabotage unit in the city, so that by the year's end only a few thousand Alexandrian Greeks and Jews remained. Foreign institutions, street names and suchlike were Egyptianized, and the custom of moving the seat of government to Alexandria during the hot summer months was ended.

Contemporary Alex

Though "old" Alexandrians undoubtedly regret the **changes** since Suez, Durrell's complaint that they produced "leaden uniformity" and rendered Alexandria "depressing beyond endurance" seems jaundiced and unjustified. Egypt's second city (pop. 5,000,000) has become more Egyptian and less patrician, but it doesn't lack contrasts and vitality (except by comparison with Cairo). The difference is that middle-class Egyptians set the tone, not Greeks, Levantines and European expats. If Cavafy, *arak* and child brothels represented the old days, McDonald's, Coke and Nike symbolize a new and brasher kind of cosmopolitanism. Overcrowding, pollution and traffic have all worsened, but – unlike pressure-cooker Cairo – the Med still keeps Alex cool.

With few monuments to show for its ancient lineage and much of its modern heritage rejected, one seeks Alexandria's past in institutions like *Pastroudis*; minutiae such as old nameplates; the reminiscences of aged Arabs, Greeks and Jews; and in the **literary dimension**. E.M. Forster's *Alexandria: A History and a Guide* (1922) remains the classic source book, but Forster reckoned that the best thing he did was to publicize the work of Alexandrian-born Constantine Cavafy. Nostalgia, excess, loss and futility – the leitmotivs of Cavafy's poems – also pervade Lawrence Durrell's *The Alexandria Quartet*: indeed, Durrell used Cavafy as the basis for his character Balthazar. However, bearing in mind the ancient adage that "a big book is a big nuisance", you might prefer Naguib Mahfouz's *Miramar*, a concise evocation of post-revolutionary Alex from an Egyptian standpoint. For more recent, foreign views of Alex, check out Charlie Pye-Smith's *The Other Nile,* Douglas Kennedy's *Beyond the Pyramids*, and Paul William Roberts' *River in the Desert.*

Approaches to Alex

Alex is easily reached **from Cairo**, with a choice of train, bus, *service* taxi or plane. Buses and *service* taxis offer two routes to Alex, travelling by the flat and dreary Desert Road past the turn-off for Wadi Natrun (whose monasteries are covered in Chapter Three), or by the hazardous, congested Delta Road, which is much slower though the distance is roughly similar (about 225km). Remember that transport can get booked up during "the season" (mid-June to late Sept), so reserve seats unless you're prepared to use *service* taxis.

The best **buses from Cairo**, which do the journey in three hours, are operated by the Superjet company. The fastest **trains**, A/C Spanish and Turbini services, take just over two hours and both leave three times daily. There is also the slightly slower French service that has nine daily departures, takes forty minutes longer and costs thirty percent less. *Service* taxis do the run in about three hours, their advantage being that they leave all through the day, as soon as they're full; in Cairo both car- and minibus-taxis cluster outside Ramses Station, on Koulali Square and around the Ahmed Helmi bus terminal, their drivers bawling "*Iskandariya! Iskandariya!*". For details of bus, train and taxi schedules and terminals, see "Travel Details" at the end of the Chapter One (p.244).

Getting to Alex **from other parts of Egypt**, buses and/or *service* taxis are your best bet. Transport from the Delta and the Canal Zone is fairly regular; from the Nile Valley, daily buses run from Beni Suef. See the relevant chapters for details.

Arrival, orientation and information

A/C West Delta and Superjet **buses** drop passengers at the **15ᵗʰ May Station**, in Sidi Gaber. To get to the centre from here take tram #25, or it's a £E3–5 taxi ride. However, non-A/C Delta buses might terminate instead at **Midan el-Gumhorriya**. This vast square – portioned up into bus parks and taxi ranks – lies about 1km south of Midan Sa'ad Zaghloul, flanked on one side by **Masr Station**. Arriving by **train**, you should get off at Masr Station – don't make the error of getting off at Sidi Gaber Station in the eastern suburbs. From Masr Station/Midan el-Gumhorriya, it's ten or fifteen minutes' walk up Nabi Daniel Street to Midan Sa'ad Zaghloul, or take minibus #700 or #705 to Ramleh. **Service taxis** might drop you at either square, or at **Midan Orabi**, 400m west of Sa'ad Zaghloul. A taxi into the centre should cost £E5. Arriving at the **airport**, 5km south of Alex, catch bus #203 or minibus #703 to Midan Orabi, or a taxi into the centre (£E8–15).

Orientation, maps and street names

Alexandria runs along the Mediterranean for 20km without ever venturing more than 5km inland – a true waterfront city. Its great **Corniche** sweeps around the **Eastern Harbour** and along the coast past a string of city **beaches** to **Montazah** and **Ma'amoura**, burning out before the final beach at **Abu Qir**. (The beaches to the west of Alex are dealt with in the "Mediterranean Coast" account; see p.506.) Away from the beach, visitors hang around the downtown quarter of **El-Manshiya**, where most of the restaurants, hotels and nightclubs are within a few blocks either side, or inland, of **Midan Sa'ad Zaghloul**.

The modern city overlies the ancient one, hence there's a fine collection of Greco-Roman **antiquities**, but few monuments remain *in situ*: a Roman theatre near Masr Station, and Pompey's Pillar and the Catacombs in the **Karmous** quarter. The Islamic era is better represented by **Fort Qaitbey** and the old Turko-Arabic neighbourhoods of **El-Gomruk** and **El-Anfushi**, both of which are notable for their souks and streetlife.

The Corniche (and breezes blowing inland) make basic orientation quite simple, but the finer points can still be awkward. Unlike Cairo, downtown Alex has yet to be properly mapped. The standard Lehnert & Landrock's *Map of Alexandria* omits whole streets and blocks, and our **maps** aren't faultless either. **Street names** are also problematic, for signs don't always square with the latest official designation or popular usage (usually one change behind). Other street names have simply been Arabicized: Rue or Place to Sharia or Midan; "Alexandre le Grand" to "Iskander el-Akbar". In the downtown area, most of the nameplates are in French and Arabic, and people may use either variant when giving directions. For areas away from downtown there's a useful map inside *Alexandria Night and Day*, which also shows the locations of the beaches.

Information

The main **tourist office** on the corner of Midan Sa'ad Zaghloul (daily: 8am–6pm, mid-July to mid-Aug to 8pm; Ramadan 9am–4pm; ☎484-3380), is staffed by very helpful English-speakers, can provide a free information booklet, *Alexandria Night and Day*, and answer most questions. It has branches at the airport (daily 8am–8pm; ☎420-2021) and Masr Station (daily 8am–8pm; ☎492-5985). The university and foreign cultural centres are obvious sources of **contacts** (students and expats); on Thursday nights you'll find half the expat community in bars. If you're considering staying for some time, try getting hold of the *Newcomers' Guide to Alexandria*, written by (and for) resident Americans. There is also a Web site for information on Alex which has photos and a wide selection of links (*ce.eng.usf.edu/pharos/alexandria/*).

City transport

Downtown is compact enough to walk around, and along the Corniche to Pharos makes a healthy constitutional. However, you really need transport to reach other outlying areas. The main downtown terminals are **Ramleh**; the tram, bus and minibus stands on **Midan Orabi**, 400m west of Midan Sa'ad Zaghloul; and **Khartoum** bus station, to the east of the Greco-Roman Museum. Minibuses running along the Corniche can be boarded from the seafront side of both Midan Orabi and Sa'ad Zaghloul.

Trams, buses and minibuses

Trams are integral to Alex life, conveying all classes at a snail's pace and rattling past the houses of rich and poor alike. Services run from 5.30am to midnight (1am in summer), with fares 15–20pt. Destinations and route numbers are in Arabic only, but you can get an idea from the vehicle's livery where it's heading, as all trams running east from Ramleh are painted blue, while those going west are yellow and white. More arcane clues lie in the colour of the background to the numeral(s) on the signboard, which identify routes #1 (green), #2 (red), #3 (blue on yellow), #4 (blue or black on yellow), #5 (black on white) and #14 (blue). On trams with three carriages, the middle one is reserved for women. Some have double-decker carriages, with a fab view from the top floor. Standing downstairs, you may have difficulty seeing the names of the tram stops, which are written in English on certain routes.

Buses (keeping similar schedules and likewise numbered in Arabic; 25–50pt) are dirtier and faster, with passengers boarding on the run between Sa'ad Zaghloul, Orabi,

Tahrir, and El-Gumhorriya squares – the major terminals. They are often very crowded, and made worse by gropers and pickpockets. Whenever possible, it's best to use another form of transport. Fortunately, **minibuses** offer the chance of a reasonably comfortable ride and cover many of the same routes. Those run by the municipality are blue and white, while privately operated minibuses are blue. Both charge the same fares (25–50pt) and run similar hours to trams and buses.

TRAMS

#1 and #2: Ramleh to Victoria, via the Sporting Club and Roushdi.

#8: Ramleh to San Stefano, via the Sporting Club.

#14: Ramleh to Sharia Moharrem Bey (near the Fine Arts Museum), via Midan Orabi and Sharia Abu Dardaa.

#15: Ramleh to Ras el-Tin, via El-Gomruk and El-Anfushi (near Fort Qaitbey).

#25: Ras el-Tin to Sidi Gaber, via Ramleh.

BUSES

#2 and #3: Ramleh to El-Agami (Bitash then Hannoville).

#203: Midan Orabi to the airport, via the zoo.

#260: Ramleh to Abu Qir, via Sharia Iskandar el-Akhbar and the Corniche.

#309 and #709: Ramleh to Pompey's Pillar.

#460: Midan Khartoum to Hanoville, via Corniche.

MINIBUSES

#703: Midan Orabi to the airport, via Ramleh.

#735: Ramleh to Montazah, via the Corniche.

#736: Ras el-Tin to Ma'amoura, via the Corniche.

#728 and #729: Masr Station to Abu Qir.

#736: Midan Orabi to Ma'amoura, via the Corniche.

#750: Khartoum to El-Agami (Bitash), via the Corniche.

#755: Masr Station to El-Agami (Bitash).

#760: Khartoum to El-Agami (Hannoville), via the Corniche.

#765: Masr Station to El-Agami (Hannoville).

Taxis, caleches and car rental

Regular black and orange (or yellow) **taxis** seldom use meters and will charge whatever they can get away with (especially going to Masr Station or some other point of departure). You should pay about £E2 for a ride across downtown (say, to Shatby), £E15–20 for a trip to Hannoville or Montazah. The larger, monochrome Peugeots are a lot pricier than regular taxis, so don't take one by mistake.

Leather-hooded, brass-trimmed **horse-drawn carriages** solicit passengers with cries of "*caleche, caleche*" outside Masr Station and along the Corniche. Providing you don't get stuck in traffic jams or feel self-consciously "colonial", they can be a good way of touring the quieter parts of Alex and enjoying the sea breezes. You'll have to negotiate a price – roughly £E8–10 an hour.

If you want to **rent a car**, try Avis in the Hotel Cecil (daily 8am–8pm; ☎483-1467), which offers Toyota Corollas for US$58 per day. You must be over 25 years old and have an international licence held for at least one year. They can also supply English-speaking drivers at US$15 per (10hr) day. Alternatively, Alex Limousine, 25 Sharia Talaat Harb (☎482-5252), rents luxury cars with drivers.

Accommodation

Alexandria's **hotels** run the gamut from old pensions to glitzy citadels of Sheraton-style internationalism, with something for every visitor's taste and budget. Whereas foreign visitors usually stay downtown, many Egyptian holidaymakers prefer hotels near the Corniche beaches. A sea view is a big plus, and hotels charge accordingly – though in cheap hotels these rooms are freezing in wintertime. Two drawbacks that only later become apparent are **tram noise** and giant orange **cockroaches** – the twin banes of hotels near the waterfront. Basically, you either learn to live with them or move further inland. At some places the staff **hassle** guests to buy duty-free alcohol. Bear in mind that the choice and availability of rooms is limited during high season (June 15–Sept 15), when **reservations** are advisable. **Prices** below are for the high season, and refer to rooms without a sea view. You can count on hot water, and breakfast being included, unless stated otherwise. The downtown hotels are all keyed to the map on p.488.

Downtown hotels

Acropole, 27 Sharia Gamil el-Din Yassin (☎480-5980). Just behind Midan Sa'ad Zaghloul, so central but noisy. Most rooms have sinks, balconies and brass beds. Hot water available in one of the shared bathrooms, which are clean. Only four singles; fills quickly. ③.

Ailema, 21 Sharia Amin Fikhry, 7th floor (☎482-7011, fax 482-2040). Quiet, stylish 1940s place run by Greeks. Very clean, spacious rooms (sea or garden view), some with baths. Restaurant and a private lift. ③.

Cecil, 16 Midan Sa'ad Zaghloul (☎483-7173, fax 483-6401). Dead central, with great views of the Eastern Harbour, the *Cecil* is an Alexandrian institution. Durrell, Churchill, Noel Coward and Somerset Maugham head the list of former guests, but modernization has dispelled the old ambience. Regular rooms are cosy and A/C but nothing special; the corner suites are grander. Restaurants (French and Chinese), coffee shop, nightclub, *Monty's Bar*, Avis desk and a bank. Same rates year-round. ⑧.

Gamil, 28 Sharia Gamil el-Din Yassin, 4th floor (☎481-5458). Old-fashioned pension, one of four in the same building. Cleanish doubles and triples; shared bathrooms. Pushy, crafty manager; door often locked during the day. No breakfast. ③.

Holiday, 14 Midan Orabi (☎ & fax 480-1559). Very noisy location in a busy square. Clean and carpeted but rather dingy. Most rooms with private baths and TV, but no A/C (despite notice outside). ③.

Hyde Park, 21 Sharia Amin Fikhry, 8th floor (☎483-5666). Definitely inferior to the *Ailema*, downstairs, but with the redeeming feature of glassed-in balconies facing the sea. ③.

Leroy, 25 Sharia Talaat Harb, 8th floor (☎483-3439). Huge, shabby, gloomy Art Deco warren with a few nice rooms on the 9th floor, and distant views of the Eastern Harbour. None of the bathrooms – private or communal – appear very clean. No breakfast. ②.

Marhaba, 10 Midan Orabi (☎480-0957, fax 480-2040). Cosy, clean, carpeted rooms with fans and baths. Bar, restaurant and coffee shop, plus a billiards room with kitsch sculptures. A popular choice, despite the noisy square outside. All rooms come with fans and satellite TV. ④.

Metropole, 52 Sharia Sa'ad Zaghloul (☎482-1457). Centrally located period piece with Art Deco features. Rooms are cosy with soft beds and clean baths, and the hotel has been renovated to house an expensive French restaurant, *Versaille*. ⑧.

New Welcome Hotel, 28 Sharia Gamil el-Din Yassin, 5th floor (☎483-6402). Alexandria's cheapest budget hotel. Shabby rooms, reasonably clean bathrooms and a cantankerous owner. Along with the sister hotel **Victoria** (same phone and price) upstairs, it tends to be a bit hot in the summer. Triples also available. ①.

Normandie, 28 Sharia Gamil el-Din Yassin, 4th floor (☎480-6830). Across the landing from the *Gamil*. Cheery lobby and serviceable rooms, some with views of the Corniche. Partly furnished with French antiques, left by the previous owner. Shared bathrooms. No breakfast. ②.

Picadilly, 11 Sharia el-Huria (☎493-2839). An air of crumbling grandeur pervades this hotel, whose lobby is decorated with Art-Deco furniture and oil paintings. However, the rooms are large and airy – if a bit tatty – and it's far better value than most of the other budget options. No breakfast. ①.

Sea Star, 24 Sharia Amin Fikhry (☎480-5343, fax 483-2388). Clean, carpeted rooms with baths; some have double beds. Restaurant and international phone line. Same rates all year. Will send and receive faxes – for a price. ⑤.

Triomphe, 26 Sharia Gamil el-Din Yassin, 5th floor (☎480-7585). A poor relation compared to other places on this street (see above) Not as clean as it could be but the management are friendly and the lounge is pleasant enough. No breakfast. ③.

Union, 164 26th July Street, 5th floor (☎480-7312, fax 480-7350). Three blocks along the Corniche from Midan Sa'ad Zaghloul. Bright, clean Art Deco place with friendly staff and a cool lounge facing the sea. Comfortable carpeted rooms with private baths and TV; the best ones are upstairs. ④.

Near the port and out along the Corniche

There are lots of hotels in the commercial district of El-Manshiya, catering to the Russians who disembark at the Maritime Station, bent on shopping. Affluent tourists are more attracted by the mid-range and upmarket hotels out along the Corniche, towards Montazah. See the map on p.480 for an idea of their location; descriptions of the localities are to be found on pp.499–501.

Amoun, 32 Sharia en-Nasr (☎481-8228, fax 480-7131). Modern, A/C block above a seething shopping district between Midan Orabi and the docks. Fairly plush with a bar, restaurant and satellite TV. ⑦.

Corail, 802 Tariq el-Geish (☎548-0996). Two-star place overlooking Mandara beach, 1km west of Montazah. A bit tatty, but clean and friendly, with a Chinese restaurant. 20 percent more for a seaview. ③.

Helnan Palestine, near Montazah beach and palace (☎547-3500, fax 547-3378). Five-star venue for conferences and bridge tournaments, built to house Arab heads of state attempting to solve the Palestinian problem in 1964, and later refurbished by the Helnan chain. Spacious rooms overlooking the palace or the sea. All mod cons, including a small cinema during the summer. Costs around 30 percent less off-season. ⑨.

Maamura Palace, 100m from Ma'amoura beach (☎547-3450, fax 547-3383). Clean, comfortable rooms with TV, phone, fridge and heater. Park-side rooms are identical to sea-view ones, but over-. look Montazah. Reserve 1–2 weeks ahead in high season, when half-board is obligatory. Prices are 50 percent lower in winter. ⑨.

Montazah Sheraton, Montazah (☎548-0550, fax 540-1331, *smontaza@mail.rite.com*). Five-star tower outside the grounds of the Montazah Palace. Nightclub, disco, heated pool and tennis court. All rooms with twin or double beds, A/C, minibar and satellite TV. Same rates year-round. ⑨

Ramada Renaissance, 544 Tariq el-Geish (☎549-0935, fax 549-7690, *alexandria@renaissance-htl.com.eg*). A similar five-star tower overlooking Sidi Bishr beach, with pool, cocktail-bar, disco and Chinese and Italian restaurants. ⑨.

Salamlek, Montazah gardens (☎ & fax 547-3585, *samalek@inetalex.ie-eg.com*). Further downhill and around the bay from the *Helnan Palestine*, this grandiose pseudo-Alpine chalet was once the residence of the Austrian mistress of Khedive Abbas. By far the plushest hotel in town it features it's own private beach, the only casino in Alex (open to non-residents carrying passport ID; 9pm–5am), French and Italian restaurants and even live chamber music in the lobby – though they do a bit of light jazz as well. ⑨.

Hostelling and camping

Neither is an attractive option. Alexandria's small **youth hostel** (☎597-5459; £E12) is on a main road opposite St Mark's College in Shatby, 1km east of the downtown area. Take tram #1 or #2 from Ramleh to the College and turn towards the Corniche; the hostel is at 32 Sharia Bur Said, next to some Greco-Roman tombs. Non-HI members are allowed to use its shabby dorms (open daily 7am–midnight; strict curfew enforced) for £E1 extra. An even less appealing prospect is to rent a seven-person tent – or pitch your own – at the primitive **campsite** (☎560-1424) in Abu Qir, far to the east of Alexandria (see p.501). The site is on Sharia el-Bahr el-Mayyit, 500m south of the *Zephyrion* restaurant. Moribund out of season and jam-packed over summer, it is the last place to consider staying.

The City

I loved the shabbiness of the streets and cafés, the melancholy which hung over the city late of an evening, the slow decay (not destruction, mind you) of what the Europeans had left behind when they fled.

Charlie Pye-Smith, *The Other Nile*

Alex encourages nostalgia trips and random exploration, if only because "the sights" are limited and chance incidents often more revealing. Don't be afraid of following your nose and deviating from the usual itineraries, which could be completed in a day if done at the trot.

For convenience, these accounts start with the downtown area and work outwards, interweaving the ancient, remembered and existing cities.

Midan Sa'ad Zaghloul to the Roman Theatre – and back to Ramleh

Since E.M. Forster wrote his guide to Alexandria in 1922, the city's centre has shifted eastwards from the former Place Mohammed Ali to the seafront **Midan Sa'ad Zaghloul**, a square named after the nationalist leader (1860–1927) whose **statue** gazes towards the Mediterranean. His deportation by the British to Malta provoked nation-wide rioting (1919) and guaranteed Zaghloul a hero's return, though the national independence he sought was denied for another generation. Zaghloul is referred to as "the Pasha" in Naguib Mahfouz's novel, *Miramar*.

With no trace of the Caesareum that stood here in ancient times (see below), the square today looks post-colonial. Decrepit edifices that could have been lifted from Naples or Athens overshadow the **tourist office**. The dominant building is the pseudo-Moorish **Hotel Cecil**, where British Intelligence hatched the El-Alamein deception plan. No longer the decadent and moribund establishment of *The Alexandria Quartet*, it now belongs to the Sofitel chain.

A similar mystique used to attend Alexandrian **patisseries**, of which there are three nearby. *Délices*, beneath a red awning, has followed the famous old *Trianon*, on the corner, in installing air-conditioning and a doorman. *Athineos*, by Ramleh tram station, used to be the grandest but now has gaping holes in its Art Nouveau decor. All three levy £E3–8 minimum charge per person (plus service tax), so you'll feel that you've been ripped-off if you just order coffee.

Sharia Nabi Daniel and Rue de l'Eglise Copte

Starting as an inconspicuous backstreet beside the tourist office, **Sharia Nabi Daniel** grows wider as it runs south along the route of the ancient **Street of the Soma**. Paved in marble and flanked by marble colonnades, this dazzled the Arabs in 641, even though its finest buildings had already vanished.

Before its destruction by feuding Christians in the fourth century, the north end of the street was crowned by the **Caesareum**, a temple begun by Cleopatra for Antony, which Octavian completed and dedicated to himself. Full of "choice paintings and statues", it was fronted by two obelisks that remained *in situ* until the 1870s, when they were relocated on London's Embankment and in New York's Central Park. Their popular title, "Cleopatra's Needles", is a misnomer: erected in Heliopolis fourteen centuries earlier, the obelisks were moved to Alexandria fifteen years after her death by suicide.

A short way down Nabi Daniel, high wrought-iron gates front Alexandria's principal **Synagogue**, entered via an alley to the north (Mon–Fri 8am–1pm, Sun 10am–1pm; bring your passport). An old woman speaking French, English and a little Hebrew will show you round its pastel-coloured, Italianate interior, turning on giant *menorahs*.

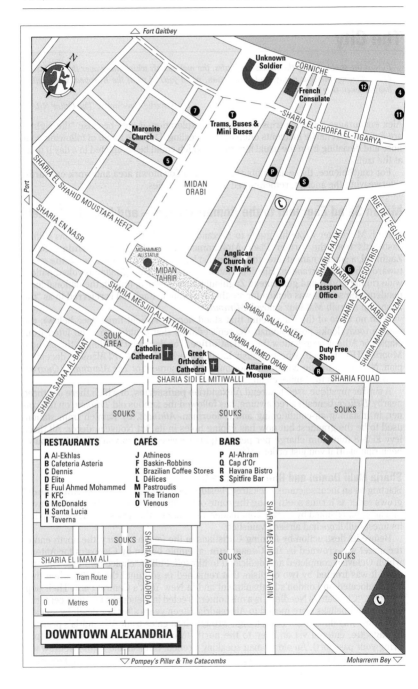

△ Fort Qaitbey

Unknown Soldier

CORNICHE

French Consulate

⑫

④

⑪

⑦

SHARIA EL-GHORFA EL-TIGARYA

T
Trams, Buses & Mini Buses

Maronite Church

⑤

P

S

MIDAN ORABI

C

SHARIA EL SHAHID MOUSTAFA HEFIZ

△ Port

SHARIA EN NASR

RUE DE L'EGLISE

MOHAMMED ALI STATUE

MIDAN TAHRIR

Anglican Church of St Mark

SHARIA FALAKI

SHARIA TALAAT HARB

SHARIA SESOSTRIS

⑥

Q

Passport Office

SHARIA MESJID AL-ATTARIN

SHARIA SALAH SALEM

SHARIA AHMED ORABI

SHARIA MAHMOUD AZMI

SÔUK AREA

Catholic Cathedral

Greek Orthodox Cathedral

Attarine Mosque

Duty Free Shop

R

SHARIA SABAA AL-BANAT

SHARIA SIDI EL MITIWALLI

SHARIA FOUAD

SOUKS

SOUKS

SOUKS

RESTAURANTS	CAFÉS	BARS
A Al-Ekhlas	J Athineos	P Al-Ahram
B Cafeteria Asteria	F Baskin-Robbins	Q Cap d'Or
C Dennis	K Brazilian Coffee Stores	R Havana Bistro
D Elite	L Délices	S Spitfire Bar
E Fuul Ahmed Mohammed	M Pastroudis	
F KFC	N The Trianon	
G McDonalds	O Vienous	
H Santa Lucia		
I Taverna		

SOUKS

SHARIA ABU DADRDA

SHARIA MESJID AL-ATTARIN

SOUKS

SOUKS

SHARIA EL IMAM ALI

SOUKS

– – – Tram Route

0   Metres   100

C

DOWNTOWN ALEXANDRIA

▽ Pompey's Pillar & The Catacombs

Moharrerm Bey ▽

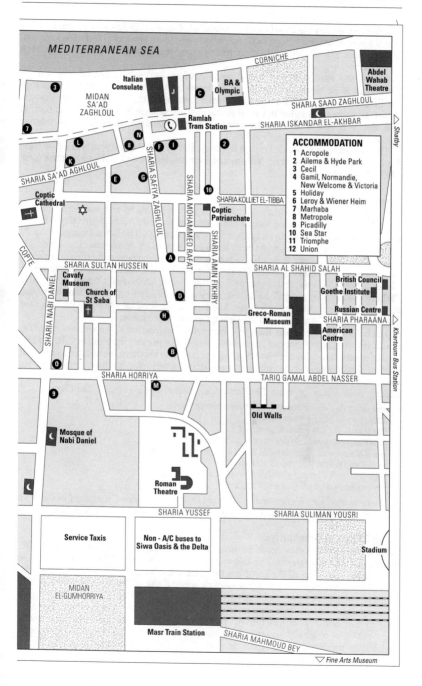

MEDITERRANEAN SEA

CORNICHE

Abdel Wahab Theatre

Italian Consulate

BA & Olympic

MIDAN SA'AD ZAGHLOUL

SHARIA SAAD ZAGHLOUL

Ramlah Tram Station

SHARIA ISKANDAR EL-AKHBAR

▷ Shatby

SHARIA SAFIYA ZAGHLOUL

SHARIA SA'AD AGHLOUL

Coptic Cathedral

SHARIA MOHAMMED RAFAT

SHARIA AMIN FIKHRY

SHARIA KOLLIET EL-TIBBA

Coptic Patriarchate

ACCOMMODATION
1 Acropole
2 Ailema & Hyde Park
3 Cecil
4 Gamil, Normandie,
    New Welcome & Victoria
5 Holiday
6 Leroy & Wiener Heim
7 Marhaba
8 Metropole
9 Picadilly
10 Sea Star
11 Triomphe
12 Union

SHARIA SULTAN HUSSEIN

SHARIA AL SHAHID SALAH

Cavafy Museum

Church of St Saba

SHARIA NABI DANIEL

COPTE

British Council

Goethe Institute

Russian Centre

SHARIA PHARAANA

Greco-Roman Museum

American Centre

▷ Khartoum Bus Station

SHARIA HORRIYA

TARIQ GAMAL ABDEL NASSER

Mosque of Nabi Daniel

Old Walls

Roman Theatre

SHARIA YUSSEF

SHARIA SULIMAN YOUSRI

Service Taxis

Non - A/C buses to Siwa Oasis & the Delta

Stadium

MIDAN EL-GUMHORRIYA

Masr Train Station

SHARIA MAHMOUD BEY

▽ Fine Arts Museum

Tracing its ancestry back to the city's foundation, Alexandria's Jewish community numbered fifteen thousand before 1957; nowadays only about seventy elderly Jews remain, and services are no longer held in the synagogue, although it has recently been restored.

Across the road, another set of gates marked by crosses betrays the **Coptic Cathedral of St Mark**, in a compound enclosed by taller buildings, entered from **Rue de l'Eglise Copte**, which joins Nabi Daniel further south. Named after the Apostle whose body was smuggled out of Muslim-ruled Alexandria in a barrel of salt-pork in 828, the cathedral is an early twentieth-century Byzantine pastiche, whose interior Forster described as "fatuously ugly".

This part of town is classic Durrell territory: Darley and Pombal shared a flat on Nabi Daniel, while Clea, Justine and Nessim had their residences on Rue Fuad Premier (now Sharia Fouad/Sharia Horriya).

Cavafy in the backstreets

A tangible relic of Alexandria's literary heritage can be found in a backstreet just off Nabi Daniel, formerly called Rue Lepsius but now named Sharm el-Sheikh; to find it, turn off onto Sultan Hussein and follow the alley running off beside a luggage shop. At no. 4, near the far end, a sign in Greek identifies the **Cavafy Museum** (Tues, Wed, Fri & Sat 10am–3pm, Thurs & Sun 10am–3pm & 6–8pm; free), re-creating the second-floor flat where **Constantine Cavafy** (1863–1933) lived at the zenith of his poetic talent, above a bordello around the corner from the Greek Orthodox Church of St Saba. "Where could I live better?" he asked, "Below, the brothel caters for the flesh. And there is the church which forgives sin. And there is the hospital where we die." He died there indeed, and was buried in the Greek Cemetery at Shatby.

His belongings were later used to create a small exhibition in the Greek Consulate, which bought Cavafy's former flat and established the present museum in 1992. Its custodian relates how "Cavafis" (as he is known) had nine brothers, loved candlelight, and died of throat cancer from drinking – but draws a veil over his homosexuality ("He never married"). Visitors can see his brass bed, icons, books and death mask, and the modest desk where he wrote *The Barbarians, Ithaca,* and his elegiac *The City*:

> *You won't find a new country, won't find another shore.*
> *This city will always pursue you.*
> *You'll walk the same streets, grow old*
> *in the same neighbourhoods, turn grey in the same houses.*
> *You'll always end up in this city. Don't hope for things elsewhere:*
> *there's no ship for you, there's no road.*
> *Now that you've wasted your life here, in this small corner,*
> *you've destroyed it everywhere in the world.*

There is also a room devoted to the novelist **Stratis Tsikas**, a student of Cavafy's who wrote the trilogy *Drifting Cities*, about wartime Jerusalem, Cairo and Alexandria.

On to Midan el-Gumhorriya

Ancient Alexandria's crossroads lay near the modern-day intersection of Nabi Daniel, Fouad and Horriya streets. The last used to be the **Canopic Way**, lined by marble colonnades extending all the way from the Gate of the Sun, where visitors entered the city. Many scholars believe that this junction was the site of the **Mouseion**, an institution from which our word "museum" derives. Founded by Ptolemy Soter (323–282 BC), it incorporated lecture halls, laboratories, observatories, and the legendary "Mother" Library (see box on p.495). Across the way stood the **Soma**, a temple where Alexander the Great was originally entombed, as were several Ptolemies. Here the victorious Octavian is supposed to have paid his respects to Alexandria's founder but disdained his heirs: "I wished to see a king, I did not wish to see corpses."

Part of the site is occupied by the nineteenth-century **Mosque of Nabi Daniel**, whose modern entrance is set back from the street. The mosque's crypt is popularly believed to hold the remains of the Prophet Daniel (in reality, it contains those of Mohammed Danyal al-Maridi, a Sufi sheikh, and one Lukman the Wise). Legends that Alexander's tomb lay deeper underground impelled the Egyptian Antiquities Organization (EAO) to excavate in the early 1990s, but nothing was found. A Greek journalist has since claimed to have found Alexander's tomb near Siwa Oasis (see p.472), while Professor Fakharani of Alexandria University believes that the Romans reburied him outside the Royal Quarter, where the Christian cemeteries are today.

Sharia Nabi Daniel ends at **Midan el-Gumhorriya**, a seething mass of bus and taxi ranks outside the neo-Baroque **Masr Station**, designed by a Greek and an Italian in 1927. You can beat a retreat westwards into the **souk**, or follow the track behind the station to reach Alexandria's Fine Arts Museum (see below), but the nearest refuge is the Roman Theatre off Sharia Yussef.

The Roman Theatre

Since 1959 Polish archeologists and staff from the Greco-Roman Museum have removed the Turkish fort and slums on *Kom el-Dik* (Mound of Rubble), revealing a substratum of Roman remains beneath a Muslim cemetery (daily 9am–4pm; Ramadan 9am–3pm; £E6, students £E3, cameras free, camcorders £E150). In a hollow to the east lies an elegant **Roman Theatre** with marble seating for seven to eight hundred, cruder galleries for the plebs, and a forecourt with two patches of mosaic flooring. During Ptolemaic times this was the Park of Pan, a hilly pleasure garden with a limestone summit carved into a pine cone, onto which Roman villas and baths later encroached.

Further north they're excavating a **residential quarter** (closed to visitors) whose jumbled arches and walls resolve into streets, shops and houses at close quarters. Many of the buildings are constructed from alternating courses of brick and stone, a technique called *opus mixtum* (mixed work). Five centuries later, the Arabs used the same method to build a wall around the shrunken city, which was reinforced by the Turks. A multi-layered section of the **old walls** remains behind some houses in an alley off Sharia Horriya, which can be seen on the way to the Greco-Roman Museum.

To the Fine Arts Museum

Visiting the **Fine Arts Museum** at 18 Sharia Menasce (daily 9am–1pm & 5–8pm; free) involves walking east from Masr Station along Sharia Mahmoud Bey (parallel to, and south of the tracks) for 150m before turning right; the museum lies ahead. Alternatively, it's two stops on any yellow tram heading east from Masr station. As temporary exhibitions are often held here, it's impossible to predict what you'll find. Modern Egyptian artists have sometimes had to tread warily; Mahmoud Bey Said's Cubist-influenced portraits of urban sophisticates were considered faintly suspect after the Revolution. When "socialist realism" was abandoned in the 1970s, artists leapt at Surrealism and Abstract Expressionism, which is why much of the stuff can seem derivative. Painting in the 1950s, Seif el-Wahly had already captured the essence of the jazz and flamenco era, Alexandria's previous engagement with Mediterranean culture.

Alternatively, you can turn the corner of the archeological site and head northwards up **Sharia Safiya Zaghloul**. In Cavafy's day this was called the Rue Missala and known for its billiard-halls and rent-boys; today the street is noted for its cinemas and restaurants. By turning off just after the Metro Cinema, you'll be on course for the Greco-Roman Museum – its classical facade is visible from the far end of the street.

The Greco-Roman Museum

The **Greco-Roman Museum** contains Egypt's best collection of antiquities from the classical era (Mon–Thurs, Sat & Sun 9am–4pm, Fri 9–11.30am & 1.30–5pm; £E16, students £E6, camera permit £E10, video permit £E150). Turning left off the entrance vestibule into Room 6, you encounter **relics of the Serapis cult** promoted by Ptolemy I. A fusion of Osiris and Dionysos, Serapis was represented as a bearded, avuncular fellow, and by a giant granite bull carved during the reign of Hadrian (who's commemorated by a bust). Besides maintaining the old cults, the Romans added flourishes like the **death masks** they hung indoors as *memento mori*.

The Ptolemies also adopted the Fayoumi cult of Sobek (see p.424), hence the **mummified crocodile**, fragmentary chapel and funerary accoutrements in Room 9. The most remarkable of the human **mummies** bears a superbly lifelike portrait of the deceased, executed in the Fayoum c.100–250 AD, when naturalism was taking hold. Although a life-size Marcus Aurelius dominates the other **statues** in Room 12, it can't distract you from Ptolemy X (who mortgaged Egypt to Rome), whose resemblance to the actor Donald Pleasence is quite remarkable.

Amongst the **busts of Roman emperors** in Room 14 are Julius Caesar, a cold-faced Augustus (Octavian) and a bearded Hadrian, and there's more evidence of sculptural talent in Rooms 16–17, beyond the chunk of wall decorated with a **Ptolemaic mural** of an ox turning a water wheel. The colossal headless red porphyry statue has been identified variously as Christ Pantokrator (Christ in Majesty) or the rabidly anti-Christian Diocletian.

Pharos-shaped lamps can be seen in Room 18, whose annexe showcases delicate **tanagra figures**, buried with young women and children. Notice the hideous effigy of Bes (Room 20) and the finely carved schist head of a young man (Room 23), which precede a huge collection of **antique coins**.

Finally, you can catch a breath of air with **rock-cut tombs** and a giant head of Mark Antony in the garden, before going in search of the mummy with a cross on its neck, amongst the **Christian antiquities** (Rooms 1–5).

While in the neighbourhood, you can investigate the **foreign cultural centres** on Sharia Phara'ana and Sharia Al-Batalssa (aka Rue de Ptolomeés), which are detailed on p.505. This pleasant quarter marks the onset of the Bab Sharq district, covered on p.498.

To return to the downtown area, make your way back to Sharia Safiya Zaghloul and continue north, or take either of the two main streets before it; all will bring you out near **Ramleh tram station**, east of Midan Sa'ad Zaghloul.

Around Midan Orabi and Midan Tahrir

The old heart of "European" Alexandria lies six blocks west of Midan Sa'ad Zaghloul. To get there, you can catch a tram along Sharia el-Ghorfa el-Tigarya, or walk along **Sharia Sa'ad Zaghloul**, which starts as a busy shopping street aglow with neon, and ends as a shadowy alley. Along the way you may meet local **characters** like the stationer whose family escaped the Armenian genocide, arrived here penniless, got rich by founding a piano factory and then lost everything in 1957; a father-and-daughter team of acrobats; or a seedy old guy who pimped for British soldiers in his youth, and will regale you with sordid tales for the price of a drink in one of the backstreet **bars** (see p.503).

Emerging onto **Midan Orabi**, you'll see a Neoclassical **Monument of the Unknown Soldier** towards the seafront, and tram, bus and minibus stops inland. No trace remains of the French Gardens where expatriates once strolled amongst the acacia trees and shrubs, but a derelict synagogue on the corner of Sa'ad Zaghloul and a **Maronite Church** off the square attest to the area's social complexion a century ago.

Midan Tahrir

South of the French Gardens lay "Frank Square", the European city's social hub; "There is nothing in Alexandria but the Frank Square and the huts of the

Alexandrians", wrote Florence Nightingale in 1849. Originally the Places des Consuls, it was renamed in honour of **Mohammed Ali**, whose equestrian **statue** at the far end now barely stands out against the scabrous facades in the background. After the Orabi Revolt of 1882, rebels were tied to the acacias, shot and buried there by British forces. Not surprisingly, its name was changed to Liberation Square – **Midan Tahrir** – following the Revolution.

Midan Tahrir also witnessed two crucial events of the Nasser era. In October 1954, a member of the Muslim Brotherhood fired on Nasser during a public speech; the botched assassination gave Nasser an excuse to ban the Brotherhood and supplant General Naguib (who was falsely implicated in the conspiracy) as Egypt's acknowledged leader. Two years later, on the fourth anniversary of King Farouk's abdication, Nasser delivered a three-hour speech broadcast live from here on national radio, climaxing in the announcement that Egypt had taken possession of the Suez Canal; the repetition of the name "Lesseps" earlier in his peroration was actually the codeword for the operation to begin.

To the Attarine Mosque and beyond

A few streets around Midan Tahrir deserve a mention, if not a ramble. Leading off to the southeast, the erstwhile Bond Street of Alexandria, Rue Chérif Pacha, was Cavafy's birthplace; on the corner stood the Cotton Exchange that once echoed with the cries of European merchants. Renamed **Sharia Salah Salem** after a colleague of Nasser's, the street is less chic but still the place to find **antiques** and **jewellery**. Its main landmark is the Moorish-Gothic **Anglican Church of St Mark**, whose congregation includes many Sudanese. Six blocks further down at no. 30 stands a **copy of the Palazzo Farnese** in Rome, built for an Italian bank and now housing the National Bank of Egypt. In 1942, Durrell worked around the corner in a propaganda bureau at 1 Rue Toussoum Pacha. A plaque at no. 2 marks the first trading company established by the Al-Fayeds – two poor lads born in Alex's Sharbangi Alley, now multimillionaire businessmen and controversial owners of Harrods in London.

Jewellers also crop up in the backstreets north of Salah Salem, and along two thoroughfares further south: Ahmed Orabi and Mesjid al-Attarin. The latter gets its name from the **Attarine Mosque**, which occupies the site of the legendary "Mosque of a Thousand Columns". It was from here that Napoleon's forces removed a seven-ton sarcophagus, thought to be Alexander's, and later surrendered it to the British Museum, which attributed it to Nectanebo I. The Mosque of a Thousand Columns was built over the Church of St Theonas, whose rector Athanasius argued the "dual nature" of Christ against his theological opponent, Arius the Monophysite. The existing mosque has a lacey, multi-tiered minaret, reminiscent of Al-Nasir Mohammed's mosque in Cairo, and likewise dates from the fourteenth century.

Further west are two reminders of the city's multi-sectarian legacy. The **Greek Orthodox Cathedral** underpins a small Hellenistic enclave, while a huge **Catholic Cathedral** stands aloof from the bustling junction of Mesjid al-Attarin and Abu Dardaa streets. Northwest of here, the former European district merges into the erstwhile Turko-Arab Anfushi quarter, via a wide street that was previously notorious for its child bordellos. In *The Alexandria Quartet*, Justine sought her kidnapped daughter here, Mountolive was mauled by child prostitutes, and Scobie killed his neighbours with moonshine whisky. Today, it is a seething **bazaar** of clothes shops, aimed at Russian tourists disembarking at the Maritime Station at the far end of Sharia en-Nasr.

Anfushi and the harbours

In ancient times, the site of Midan Orabi was underwater, and a seven-league dike – the *Heptastadion* – connected Alexandria with Pharos, then an island. Allowed to silt up after the Arab conquest, the Heptastadion gradually turned into a peninsula that the newcomers built over, creating the **Anfushi quarter**. Its Ottoman mosques and some old *mashrabiya*-ed houses are the only "sights" as such, but the variety of streetlife makes this an interesting area to explore. The best strategy is to hop on a #15 tram, running one block inland from the Corniche, which travels past most places of interest.

The **Terbana Mosque**, 700m along, is chiefly remarkable for its antique columns – no one knows where they came from. A huge pair with Corinthian capitals supports the minaret. Lesser columns are ranged eight to an arcade within and painted gloss white; there's also some fine tiling quietly going to pot – the mosque has been subject to slap-dash "improvements" ever since it was built in 1685.

The city's foremost religious building, the **Mosque of Abu al-Abbas al-Mursi** (closed during prayer-time) is located the same distance again further north. It honours the patron saint of Alexandria's fishermen and sailors, a thirteenth-century Andalusian sheikh. Although the present building was erected as recently as 1943 – in gratitude for Al-Mursi's supernatural defence of the quarter against Luftwaffe bombers, so legend has it – it looks as old as the sixteenth-century original. Bold keel-arched panels, elaborately carved domes and cornices make a visually satisfying pastiche. Women are only allowed into a room at the back of the mosque.

After a visit, have a drink in the arcade across the street and watch life go by. If you're feeling adventurous, you can investigate the maze of old houses behind the mosque; otherwise, press on to Qaitbey's Fort.

Fort Qaitbey and the Pharos

One tram stop after Al-Mursi's Mosque and a short walk past the fishing port and boat yard will bring you to the promontory bearing Sultan Qaitbey's Fort. The **Aquarium** and **Institute of Oceanography** en route are not worth the time of day: the first is cramped and miserable, and the second musters a weird collection of lacquered sea creatures.

Fort Qaitbey (daily 9am–4pm; £E12, students £E6, camera permit £E10) is an Alexandrian landmark, a doughty limestone sentinel buffeted by wind-borne spray, its flag forever rippling. Built during the 1480s and later beefed up by Mohammed Ali, it commands great views of the city and the spume-flecked Mediterranean. Within the keep there's a mosque whose minaret was blown away by the British in 1882; upstairs, relics of Roman and Napoleonic sea battles comprise a small **Naval Museum**.

The fort occupies the site of the **Pharos**, Alexandria's great lighthouse, one of the Seven Wonders of the ancient world. A combination of aesthetic beauty and technological ambition, it transcended its practical role as a navigational aid and early-warning system, becoming synonymous with the city itself. Possibly conceived by Alexander himself, it was built during Ptolemy II's reign (c.279 BC) under the direction of an Asiatic Greek, Sostratus, and exceeded 125m – perhaps even 150m – in height, including the statue of Poseidon at its summit.

Its square base contained three hundred rooms* and possibly hydraulic machinery for hauling the fuel up the second, octagonal storey; otherwise, this would have been accomplished by a procession of pack mules climbing a spiral ramp. The cylindrical third storey housed the lantern, whose light is thought to have been visible 56km away. Some chroniclers also mention a "mirror" that enabled the lighthouse keepers to observe ships far out at sea; a form of lens (whose secret was lost) has been postulated.

---

*Legend has it that these rooms once housed the seventy rabbis who translated the Hebrew scriptures into Greek for Ptolemy Philadelphus (c.200 BC), producing identical texts despite having worked alone. In reality, this Septuagint version of the Bible wasn't completed until 130 BC, and the rabbis lived in huts on the island.

Around 700 AD the lantern collapsed, or was demolished by a treasure-hunting Khalif; the base survived unscathed and Ibn Tulun restored the second level, but earthquakes and neglect had reduced the whole structure to rubble by the fourteenth century. Fragments of the Pharos are embedded in the northwest section of the fort's enclosure walls and the facade of its keep. Recently, stone blocks have been found on the seabed that appear to have come from a temple of Isis that stood beside the Pharos.(see box p.496).

The Anfushi Tombs, Ras el-Tin and the Western Harbour

A small park some 2km west of Qaitbey's Fort, near the end of the tram line and Sharia Ras el-Tin, features the seldom-visited **Anfushi Tombs**. Sharing a pair of atriums, these four limestone-cut tombs are painted to simulate costly alabaster or marble. The right-hand set has pictures of Egyptian gods, warships and feluccas, crudely executed around 250 BC; a Greek workman has also immortalized his mate's virtues in graffiti. Hang around and a keeper should appear to unlock the tombs (daily 9am–5pm; £E12, students £E6).

Further west, formal gardens precede **Ras el-Tin Palace**, overlooking the Western Harbour. In the days when Pharos was an island, a Temple of Neptune stood here. Now strictly off limits as Admiralty Headquarters, the "Cape of Figs" palace was built for Mohammed Ali, its audience hall sited so that he could watch his new fleet at anchor while reclining on his divan. Rebuilt and turned into the summer seat of government under Fouad I, it witnessed **King Farouk's abdication** on July 26, 1952. "What you have done to me I was getting ready to do to you," the king informed General Naguib, adding "Your task will be difficult. It is not easy to govern Egypt." Wearing an admiral's uniform, Farouk departed on the royal yacht to a 21-gun salute; with him went the royal family, an English nursemaid, three Albanian bodyguards, a dog trainer and 244 trunks.

Egypt's main port and naval base since the mid-nineteenth century, the **Western Harbour** is not for sightseeing. Inland, blocks of warehouses with their foreign names still faintly visible are given over to the **cotton industry**, "greasy fluff" and rags littering the streets as in Forster's day. Another major industry is smuggling, for which the **port** is notorious. Alexandria handles about 80 percent of Egypt's import and export trade; over 5000 ships dock here every year.

The Eastern Harbour and the Bibliotheka Alexandria

Although the **Eastern Harbour** is no longer the busy port of ancient times, its graceful curve is definitely appealing. At the Qaitbey end, fishermen cast rods and mend nets while the fresh catch is marketed and shipwrights show off their hulls to anyone visiting the boatyard. Nearer to Al-Mursi's Mosque, the Corniche is flanked by stately palms and weathered colonial mansions, calling to mind a set from *Casablanca*, an effect somewhat spoiled by the crass new buildings further east around the bay.

Walking **along the Corniche** from Sa'ad Zaghloul to Al-Mursi takes roughly half an hour, and is highly recommended. If you peg out over longer distances, switch to minibuses or *caleches* – it's a good six-kilometre trek right around the harbour from Qaitbey's Fort to **Silsileh** ("the Chain"). This promontory has shrunk since the days when it enclosed the royal harbour, but recent underwater excavations have uncovered evidence of **Cleopatra's palace** (where she committed suicide) and possibly the **Lighthouse of Pharos** (see box below). Naguib Mahfouz located his fictional *Pension Miramar* near its junction with the mainland, just beyond which rises the **Bibliotheka Alexandria**, the greatest library in the ancient world.

Dedicated to "the writings of all nations", the Bibliotheka Alexandria welcomed scholars and philosophers and supported research and debates. By law, all ships

CLEOPATRA'S PALACE AND OTHER UNDERWATER DISCOVERIES

The location of the **royal court of Cleopatra** has been a mystery since a series of earthquakes and tidal-waves plunged it into the Mediterranean some 1600 years ago. Until 1996 that is, when French marine archeologist Franck Goddio and an international team of underwater experts discovered, less than a kilometre from Alexandria, an extensive area of submerged ruins including red-granite columns, statues, sphinxes (their heads missing as a result of tidal action), pavements, ceramics and a pier. Working with Gaballa Ali Gaballa, head of the Egyptian Supreme Council of Antiquities, Goddio drew up a detailed map of the site, and in October 1998 a sample of the treasures lying below was hauled up to show the world. A 1-metre-tall, black granite figure of the goddess Isis holding a canopic jar and an intact 380kg diorite sphinx – with the face of what is thought to be Ptolemy XII, Cleopatra's father – were the largest and most striking objects raised. Both have since been returned to the seabed. In addition, some huge granite blocks displaying signs of having fallen from a great height could be the **remains of the Lighthouse of Pharos**, one of the Seven Wonders of the Ancient World. Plans are afoot to make the site into the world's first underwater museum – with Plexiglass tunnels allowing visitors to stroll around five metres below the surface – although it is too early even to estimate the time and money required to realize such a project.

docking at Alexandria were obliged to allow any scrolls on board to be copied, if they were of interest to the Library. By the mid-first century BC it held 532,800 manuscripts (all catalogued by the Head Librarian, Callimachus), and later spawned a subsidiary attached to the Temple of Seraphis; the two were known as the "Mother" and "Daughter" libraries. Some of their vast collection was damaged during Julius Caesar's assault on the city, but it was a Christian mob led by Patriarch Theophilius that burned the place to the ground in 391 AD. Medieval Europe mythologized its **destruction** as proof of Arab barbarism; an apocryphal tale had the Muslim leader Amr pronouncing: "If these writings of the Greeks agree with the Koran they are useless, and need not be preserved; if they disagree, they are pernicious, and ought to be destroyed."

In 1987, UNESCO agreed to support the **creation of a new library**, intended to cover all fields of knowledge and attract researchers from the whole Mediterranean region. The competition to build it was won by a Norwegian–Austrian team of architects, whose bold design tilts to face the sea, with an elevated passageway linking it to Alexandria University, further inland. Its cost of US$172 million was met by donations from UNESCO, Saudi Arabia, the Arab Emirates, and Iraq (before the Gulf War) with the Egyptian government donating a further US$182 million for the land and other services. The official inauguration was due to be held sometime in 2000, though the 578 staff will be cataloguing the estimated four- to eight million volumes – covering every language from Polynesian dialects to Mandarin Chinese – for a long time to come. For the latest on the library contact the tourist office or try *www.unesco.org/webworld/ alexandria_new/index.html*.

Pompey's Pillar and the Catacombs of Kom es-Shoqafa

The poor **Karmous quarter** in the southwest of the city contains two of Alex's best-known ancient monuments. **Pompey's Pillar** can be reached by taxi (£E5 from Ramleh). From Pompey's Pillar you can easily walk to the **Catacombs of Kom es-Shoqafa**. If you've just arrived in Egypt, the poverty of the slums in the intervening neighbourhood might seem shocking.

Pompey's Pillar

"An imposing but ungraceful object", **Pompey's Pillar** towers 25m above a limestone ridge and garden, surrounded by the fruits and pits of excavations. Despite its name, the red granite column was actually raised to honour Diocletian, who threatened to massacre the dissenting populace "until their blood reached his horse's knees", but desisted when his mount slipped and bloodied itself prematurely. The column came from the ruined Temple of Serapis, which once rivalled the Soma and Caesareum in magnificence, and contained a "Daughter Library" of religious texts.

Three subterranean galleries where the sacred Apis bulls were interred (see Saqqara, p.201) are all that remain: you'll find them west of the ridge, which also features three sphinxes and some underground cisterns. Overall, however, the **site** (daily 9am–5pm; Ramadan 9am–3pm; £E6, students E£3) is pretty disappointing considering what used to exist here.

The Catacombs of Kom es-Shoqafa

The **Catacombs of Kom es-Shoqafa** combine spookiness and kitsch, never mind their prosaic Arabic name, "Mound of Shards". To reach them, turn right around the corner after leaving Pompey's site and follow the road uphill and straight on for about 500m; the entrance to the catacombs is on the left (daily 9am–5pm; Ramadan 9am–3pm; £E12, students £E6, camera permit £E10).

Visitors descend a spiral stairway, past the shaft down which bodies were lowered. From the vestibule with its well and scalloped niches, you can squeeze through a fissure (right) into a lofty **Caracalla** riddled with tombs, or walk into the **Triclinium** (left), where relatives toasted the dead from stone couches. But the main attraction is the **Central Tomb** downstairs, whose vestibule is guarded by reliefs of bearded serpents with Medusa-headed shields. Inside are comically muscle-bound statues of Sobek and Anubis wearing Roman armour, dating from the second century AD when "the old faiths began to merge and melt" (Forster). Water has flooded the **Goddess Nemesis Hall** (still accessible) and submerged the lowest level, hastening the catacombs' decay.

Moharrem Bey, Nouzha and Bab Sharq

To the east of Karmous lies **Moharrem Bey**, a once-affluent suburb of mansions and villas, now derelict and slummy. The district grew up in the mid-nineteenth century as a result of the **Mahmudiya Canal** (dug at the cost of 20,000 lives), which revitalized commerce and created a mercantile elite who built palatial residences along its banks, described by *Murray's Handbook* as the "fashionable afternoon promenade". Its charm endured for a century, the final decades of which were embellished by the presence of residents like Cavafy (before he moved to the Rue Lepsius) and Durrell. In 1943 **Durrell** rented the top floor and tower of a **villa** on Sharia al-Ma'amoun, where he met his second wife, the Alexandrian Eve Cohen, who became the model for Justine. Subsequently leased to the painter and sculptor Effat Nagui and her husband and fellow artist Sa'ad el-Khadem, the villa now looks likely to be demolished.

Moharrem Bey's **environmental problems** go way beyond the conservation of historic houses. The canal is choked and filthy, a sewer for residents and factories. In 1987, a warehouse explosion produced clouds of gas that killed seven people and hospitalized four hundred; officials described the gas as "non-toxic". Near the Iron and Steel Works in Mex (or Max, an industrialized suburb to the west of the city), madder-rose lakes of industrial effluent are only separated from the reedy fishing grounds of **Lake Mariout** by low dikes. To make matters worse, the sewage that used to be flushed into the sea is now dumped into the lake as well. Fish catches have dropped by 85 percent, and tests have shown them to be contaminated by mercury and cadmium, two to three times above World Health Organization safety levels. Despite dire warnings from local fishermen and academics, the authorities have yet to introduce any pollution controls.

The Zoo and Nouzha Gardens
Half the trams running out along Moharrem Bey carry on to the terminal at Nouzha, a block or so from the entrance to Alexandria's Zoo and two gardens. You can also get there by bus (#203, #310, #234) or minibus (#703, #710, #711, #725) from Midan Orabi. The **Zoological Gardens** (daily 24hr; 50pt) were opened in 1907 and cover 26 acres; the macaws swear like troopers, tutored by long-departed British soldiers.

Next door, a diverse range of trees planted by Khedive Ismail have grown to maturity in the **Nouzha Gardens** (same hours; 25pt), where military bands once played. Here, E.M. Forster had his first date with Mohammed el-Adl, a tram conductor whom he met at Ramleh in the winter of 1916–17. Before Mohammed, Forster's sexual passions had never been reciprocated. The racial, class and sexual barriers it challenged underlie the finale of *A Passage to India*, which Forster was struggling with when he learned of Mohammed's death in Egypt.

Just south of Nouzha are the tranquil **Antoniaidis Gardens** (same hours; 25pt). Embellished with classical statuary, they were once the private grounds of a wealthy Greek family. In ancient times, the Nouzha area was a residential suburb inhabited by the likes of Callimachus (310–240 BC), the Head Librarian of the Bibliotheka Alexandria. It was around here, too, that Amr's Muslim forces camped before entering the city in 641 AD.

Bab Sharq: the Shallalat Gardens and Cemeteries
Separated from Moharrem Bey and Nouzha by the train tracks converging on Masr Station, the **Bab Sharq** district can be as easily approached via the backstreets behind the Greco-Roman Museum (see p.491) or en route to the Corniche beaches (see below). Starting from Moharrem Bey, catch any bus or minibus heading north up the Suez Canal Road, which meets the Corniche near the new Alexandria Library. Halfway, it crosses the main east–west thoroughfare, named Tariq (or Sharia) Gamal Abdel Nasser at this point, and Sharia Horriya further to the west.

The junction is flanked on two sides by the hilly **Shallalat Gardens**, which blaze with scarlet flame trees over summer. Their nineteenth-century French designer utilized remnants of the Arab walls and the Farkha Canal to create rockeries and ornamental ponds; if any trace of it remained, the ancient "Gate of the Sun" would have doubtless been accorded pride of place. There is a boating lake and a restaurant where you can sometimes hear live music.

Across the road lies a sprawling necropolis of high-walled **cemeteries** consecrated to diverse faiths. Though most of the tombs date from the nineteenth or twentieth century, burials have occurred here since ancient times. Professor Fakharani thinks that a marble chamber found beneath the Catholic cemetery near the crossroads may belong to a royal tomb, perhaps even that of Alexander himself. Like the Catholic compound, the Coptic, Greek Orthodox, Armenian, Maronite, Uniate, Protestant and Jewish cemeteries are full of lavish mausolea and sculptures, from the heyday of European supremacy. The necropolis extends nearly as far as St Mark's College in Shatby, in relation to which, the Jewish cemetery is nearest.

During summer, affluent citizens hang out at the **Alexandria Sporting Club**, 1km east along Tariq Gamal Abdel Nasser. Its pool and tennis courts are the best in the city; polo and golf matches, or billiards and movies at night, are just some of the entertainments. Non-members pay £E15 to use the facilities and must be accompanied by a member. All eastbound blue trams stop at Sporting Station.

Corniche beaches

Alexandria's beaches are an overworked asset. Hardly a square metre of sand goes unclaimed during high season, when literally millions of Egyptians descend on the city. Before June the beaches furthest out are relatively uncrowded, with predominantly local users; however, Alexandrians alone can number hundreds on Fridays, Saturdays and public holidays – days to be avoided.

The popularity of the beaches doesn't imply Western-style beach culture. On most of the beaches you will rarely see any woman past the age of puberty wearing a swimsuit – they wander into the sea fully clad. For Western women who want to swim without the hindrance of a *galabiyya*, or a lot of attention, the only place where even a modest one-piece seems OK is the Westernized enclave of **Ma'amoura**. As far as facilities go, most beaches have parasols and chairs for rent, and sometimes public showers, while fish restaurants, soft-drink and snack vendors are ubiquitous. Since 1991, the civic authorities have solved the image problem posed by the 47 sewage outlets that used to pollute the seaside from the centre of town to Montazah, by pumping sewage into Lake Mariout instead, whence it finds its way into the Med more discreetly.

If that deters you, there are still two indisputable attractions: the **Royal Jewellery Museum** in Glym, and the extensive grounds of the **Montazah Palace**, further along the coast. Many visitors go to **Abu Qir** for its seafood – though you can eat just as well in nicer surroundings in central Alexandria.

East to Montazah and Abu Qir

Travelling eastwards past the Corniche beaches looks simple on the map, but isn't so easy in practice, since for much of the day only westbound traffic is allowed along this route. For the initial stretch as far as Cleopatra beach, minibuses (#719, #728, #729, #735 and #736) run a block inland, and tram #2 three to five blocks in, leaving you with only the stops – mostly named after beaches – to go on. As most of the **city beaches** amount to an arc of sand with a few hotels and a casino (for food, drink and light music, not gambling), they're hard to differentiate without a landmark in the vicinity. The following account includes some places a fair way inland.

Shatby to Glym

The district known as **Shatby** (or Chatby) is overshadowed by **Saint Mark's College**, a massive red-brick neo-Baroque edifice whose dome is visible from afar. Founded to educate the city's Christian elite, it now forms part of Alexandria University. On the far side of Sharia Bur Said is the grandly named **Shatby Necropolis** (daily 9am–5pm; Ramadan 9am–3pm; £E6), a small pit exposing some rock-cut ossuaries and sarcophagi from the third century BC, which can be viewed for free by peering over the wall of the nearby youth hostel. Shatby **beach** looks fit to spawn the "Swamp Thing", and subsequently mutates into **Ibrahimiya**.

Shortly before Cleopatra beach, tram #2 turns further inland, visiting **Sidi Gaber Station** and passing through the **Bacos** quarter where Gamal Abdel Nasser was born on January 15, 1918. He was eleven years old when he attended his first nationalist demonstration, got truncheoned and was jailed overnight. Tram #1 runs closer to **Cleopatra** beach, which has no connection with the lady herself, although the nearby **Roushdi** district was the site of *Nikopolis*, which Octavian (or Augustus Caesar, as he then styled himself) founded because he hated living in Alexandria. The British also built barracks and houses there, in the districts they named Stanley, Glym and San Stefano.

The Royal Jewellery Museum

The **Royal Jewellery Museum** (daily 9am–5pm; Ramadan Mon–Thurs, Sat & Sun 9am–3pm, Fri 9–11.30am & 1.30–4pm; £E20, students £E10, camera permit £E10, video permit £E150) is midway between Glym and San Stefano, three blocks in from the Corniche. It's a short walk from the El-Fenoun el-Gamilia and Kasr el-Safa stops on the #2 tram line to the mansion at 27 Sharia Ahmed Yehia, whose decor is as splendidly vulgar as the treasures on display. All the exhibits are labelled, so you'll have no trouble identifying Mohammed Ali's diamond-inlaid snuffbox, King Farouk's gold chess set or the platinum crown with 2159 diamonds. The main gallery downstairs is lined with stained-glass cameos of courtly love in eighteenth-century France, while Provencal farmers, milkmaids and food decorate the service corridors. Upstairs you'll find the wildest his 'n' hers bathrooms; hers with tiled murals of nymphs bathing in a waterfall, his with scenes of Côte d'Azur fishermen. The mansion was built for Mohammed Ali's granddaughter Princess Fatima el-Zaharaa (1903–83) and her husband Ali Heider.

San Stefano and Sidi Bishr

San Stefano – named after a famous resort hotel of the 1930s (now featuring a small private beach) – used to entertain promenaders with an orchestra. As in Forster's day, the tram lines converge here, inland of San Stefano's promontory, terminating at Victoria (now Nasser) College.

Minibuses carry on to **Sidi Bishr**, 14km east of the centre, where Sidi Bishr's Mosque stands between two beaches with the same name. Below the Automobile Club, east of the mosque, are the "**Spouting Rocks**" of Bir Mas'ud, where the ancient Alexandrians placed water-powered horns and mills, delighting in gadgetry. It was here, too, that the geometrician Hero invented the world's first hurdy-gurdy and coin-operated vending machine (dispensing holy water) in the first century AD.

Beyond Sidi Bishr, the **Miami Casino** gives way to two more sandy inlets, **Asafra** and **Mandara**; at the latter, the Chinese restaurant in the *Corail Hotel* makes for a change (see "Eating and drinking").

Montazah

Eighteen kilometres east of downtown Alex you reach **Montazah**, the city's walled pleasure grounds. You can enter the grounds (daily 7am–sunset; £E1) by the gates opposite the *Sheraton*. The 350 acres are well laid-out and tended, with brass lamps, diverse palms and flowers, plus a *Wimpy*, *Pizza Hut* and *Tikka Grill* that might have pleased the gluttonous King Farouk.

Farouk's ancestor Khedive Abbas II ordered the fabulous **Montazah Palace**, a Turko-Florentine hybrid whose central tower mimics the Palazzo Vecchio in Florence; it was from here that Farouk fled to Ras el-Tin before abdicating. Sadat spent £E7 million on restoring the building, which is now a presidential residence and guesthouse, closed to the public. Nearby are two fancy hotels, the *Helnan Palestine* and the *Salamlek*.

Montazah's **beach** is separated from Ma'amoura by a promontory with a picturesque "Turkish" belvedere; gaps in the fence may enable one to reach Ma'amoura directly, rather than via the distant fee-paying entrance. The **Alexandria Diving Centre** offers CMAS courses for £E400; contact Amro Abu el-Soud (☎547-6637) for details.

Ma'amoura and Canopus

East of the palace grounds, **Ma'amoura** has developed into a private enclave of holiday flats and villas, charging visitors £E1 admission before they've even glimpsed the **beach**, access to which costs a further £E5 (deck-chair included). Its sands are cleaner than most, and women can get away with wearing one-piece costumes. The main beach entrance is off a roundabout on the Abu Qir road, about 1km east of the *Sheraton*. A #736 minibus will deliver you to the *Ma'amoura Palace Hotel*, within the enclave.

Past Ma'amoura, the road runs inland of a swathe of military and naval bases, occupying the ancient site of **Canopus**. Not that anything significant remains of this once-great Delta city, which flourished when a branch of the Nile reached the sea by the nearby "Canopic Mouth", but declined as this dried up and Alexandria arose. Classical mythology has it that Canopus was founded by a Greek navigator returning from the Trojan war, whom the locals later worshipped in the form of a jar with a human head. Nineteenth-century archeologists bestowed the title **Canopic jars** on similar receptacles used to preserve mummies' viscera. Each organ had its own protective deity (a minor son of Horus) whose visage adorned the stopper (human heads went out of fashion late in the XVIII Dynasty). Even after XXI Dynasty embalmers began replacing organs in the mummies, the practice of leaving Canopic jars in tombs continued.

Abu Qir

When a straggle of jerry-built houses appears beyond the naval bases, you know you're entering **Abu Qir**. This small fishing town can be reached by *service* taxi, or minibus #728 (from Masr) or #729 (from Orabi); if you're coming from Montazah, the minibus stop is under the bridge and left around the corner of the palace walls from the *Sheraton* – look for knots of people waiting near the butchers. Abu Qir is garbage-strewn and ugly, and the raw sewage flowing down its **beach** should deter anyone but Egyptians from bathing; the only things going for it are itinerant vendors peddling everything from dolls to candelabras, and its **seafood restaurants**. The *Zephyrion* (Greek for "sea breeze") is rated one of the best in Alexandria; it's the blue and white building with green awnings overlooking the beach, next door to the *Bella Vista*.

Formerly, Abu Qir was better known for two **historic battles**. Admiral Nelson's defeat of the French fleet at Abu Qir Bay (1798) effectively scuppered Napoleon's dream of an eastern empire, but Bonaparte had his revenge the following year, when he personally led ten thousand cavalry against fifteen thousand Turks landed by the Royal Navy, pushing them back into the sea. It was the naval battle (remembered as the "Battle of the Nile") that inspired Mrs Hemans to write, "The boy stood on the burning deck . . .". Fittingly, Abu Qir is now the site of Egypt's **Naval Academy**. During summer, it's possible to take a motorboat to **Nelson's Island** (45min; £E40 for three people); ask for El Mu'allim Desouki, on the beach at the end of Sharia el-Bahr el-Mayyit.

Eating and drinking

Alexandria can't match Cairo for culinary variety, but it beats the capital when it comes to **seafood and Greek restaurants** – and when these pall you can always fall back on Egyptian favourites like *shawarmas*, pizzas, *fuul* and felafel, or seek refuge in a few Oriental-ish places. **Coffee houses**, too, are an Alex speciality, and there are some good **bars** if you know where to look.

Alongside all this, Western **fast-food outlets** are springing up all over town. *McDonald's* (daily 10am–11pm) is near the top of Sharia Safiya Zaghloul, around the corner from *Kentucky Fried Chicken* and *Baskin-Robbins* (both daily 10am–2am) on Ramleh. *KFC* has another branch on the Corniche in Roushdi, near *Pizza Hut* (which also has an outlet in Montazah) and *Wimpy* (whose franchise by the Fish Market complex is run by deaf people).

Coffee houses and patisseries

Coffee houses and **patisseries** like *Athineos* and the *Trianon* have accumulated a heavy load of mystique, and even if you couldn't give a toss about Cavafy or Durrell, their opulent interiors and cakes should not be missed. All of them are shown on the map on p.488. For nocturnal types, there are expensive **24-hour coffee shops** in the *Cecil, Montazah Sheraton* and *Ramada Renaissance* hotels.

Traditional **Arab cafés** (*ahwas*) are another world from the European patisseries, and a male preserve not recommended for women on their own. If you're into sipping tea or *karkaday* surrounded by guys slapping down backgammon counters or dominoes between lung-charring tokes on *sheeshas*, there are loads of places around Midan el-Gumhorriya. You can always locate them by the sound of coughing, audible above Koranic recitals or Umm Kalthoum sobbing from the radio.

Athineos, Midan Ramleh. Decorated with classical motifs and mirrors and frequented by eccentrics; beware of the pushy waitress, eager to boost your bill. Check out the gilded friezes and columns in the restaurant upstairs – the entrance is around the corner. Daily 8am–midnight.

Brazilian Coffee Stores, on the corner of Nabi Daniel and Sa'ad Zaghloul streets, near the tourist office. This popular stand-up breakfast spot features antique coffee mills, a glass map of Brazil and other period furnishings. Great coffee – espresso only costs £E1.20 – and greasy pastries. Daily 7am–11pm. There's also a, sit-down branch on Sharia Talaat Harb.

Délices, between Midan and Sharia Sa'ad Zaghloul. Rather uninviting since they smartened it up, junked the teak bar and installed air-conditioning. Sells cakes, soft drinks and beer. Daily 7.30am–midnight.

Pastroudis, 39 Sharia Horriya, 100m from *Vienous*. Established in 1923, this dark-panelled café features in *The Alexandria Quartet*, and was another haunt of Cavafy, but is now a sad parody of itself. Half the place has been converted into a dubious and overpriced French restaurant, with the entrance now round the corner from Sharia Horriya. Daily 9am–midnight.

The Trianon, corner of Sa'ad Zaghloul and Ramleh. Redecorated and air-conditioned, the swankiest of Alexandria's patisseries boasts gilt columns and a splendidly ornate restaurant; Cavafy used to work upstairs. The patisserie serves light meals, pizzas, beer, creamy cakes and beverages (£E8 minimum charge). It also serves a wide range of wines by the bottle; Egyptian at £E32, French £E180 and champagne £E450! If you want to splurge, try the flambé dishes.

Vienous, on the corner of Nabi Daniel and Horriya streets. Faintly chintzy with its cream and gilt Art Deco salon, but very restful. Daily 10am–9pm.

Restaurants and cafés

The following **restaurants and cafés** more or less represent the culinary and budgetary spectrum. Most of them are downtown, in the area delineated by Ramleh, Safiya Zaghloul, Nabi Daniel and Horriya streets (see map on p.488), but there are also some recommendations far along the Corniche (marked on the city plan on p.480). Phone numbers are only given where reservations are advisable.

Al-Ekhlas, 49 Sharia Safiya Zaghloul (☎482-3571). Join the haughty bourgeoisie supping fine Egyptian dishes in the restaurant upstairs, or go for pizzas and a salad bar in the *Papillon Coffee Shop* on the ground floor. Quite expensive. Daily 24hr.

Bella Vista, Abu Qir beach (☎560-0628). Though its decor is less agreeable than that of the *Zephyrion* (see below), its fresh seafood is just as good. Sells alcohol. Daily noon–1am.

Cafeteria Asteria, 40 Sharia Safiya Zaghloul. Sandwiches, macaroni, pizzas, ice cream and hot drinks at reasonable prices. Walk through the outer room to find a nice glass-roofed annexe, popular with lovers. Friendly, English-speaking Greek proprietor. Daily 8am–11pm.

Denis, 1 Sharia Ibn Basaam, off Ramleh. 1930s-style Greek fish bar where you select your *samak* or *calamari* from the freezer. Fish with chips, salad, *tahina* and beer costs around £E35. Sells wine too. Daily 10am–midnight.

Elite, 43 Sharia Safiya Zaghloul. Old-fashioned bohemian place decorated with Chagall and Picasso prints; owner Madame Christina enjoys reminiscing about the artists and writers she has known. Simple Greco-Levantine dishes: choose from the long menu on the wall rather than the short one given to tourists. Serves beer and *ouzo*. Moderate prices. Irregular daytime hours, but usually open till midnight.

Fish Market, on the 2nd floor of a waterfront complex that includes the *Tikka Grill* (see below) and a *Wimpy* (☎480-5119). Spacious and snazzy, with a great view of the harbour. No menus; you choose from a mound of fish (£E45–80 per kilo) and crustaceans (£E105–120). The salad platter is a meal in itself. Wine and beer. Moderately priced, given the quality. Daily 1pm–1am.

Fuul Mohammed Ahmed, 17 Sharia Shakor Pasha, off Sharia Sa'ad Zaghloul. Simple family place serving excellent *fuul*, felafel, and other cheap Egyptian eats. Soft drinks only; takeaways. Daily 6am–1am.

New China Restaurant, in the *Corail Hotel*, Mandara beach (☎548-0996). Established by Chinese Muslims who have since moved on, it still serves authentic meals; the wonton soup is especially good. Sells beer. Does deliveries (£E4). Moderately priced. Daily noon–midnight.

Santa Lucia, 40 Sharia Safiya Zaghloul (☎482-0332). The plushest seafood place in Alex, awarded the Grand Collar in 1980 for being "one of the best in the world" – an accolade it certainly doesn't deserve nowadays. Reckon on paying £E50–60 for a meal; a lot more if you're drinking. Beer and wines; nightclub and pianist. Daily noon–4pm & 7pm–2/3am. Bar closed Wed & Sun.

Taverna, opposite Ramleh tram terminal. Popular chain restaurant with a *shawarma* and kebab takeaway downstairs. Does excellent Egyptian and Western-style pizzas (£E10–18), seafood, soup, and there's a salad bar (£E4). There's also a branch in Montazah Gardens. Both daily 7am–2am.

The Italian Restaurant, in the *Corail Hotel*, Mandara beach (☎548-0996). Really great Italian food, served beside the hotel pool. Moderate prices and suprisingly Italian ambience with pizzas from £E15–25.

Tikka Grill, underneath the Fish Market (☎480-5114). Plush surroundings and great service, though the chicken *tikka* is nothing special. Serves alcohol. Daily 1pm–1am. Has an outlet in the Montazah Gardens.

Zephyrion, Abu Qir beach (☎560-1319). Popular seafood restaurant with a breezy terrace. Select your own fish (£E35–40 per kilo), shrimp (£E80), lobster (£E100) or octopus (£E10 per plate) from the freezer. Beer, wine and spirits. Daily noon–midnight.

Drinking

Although Alex is the centre of Egypt's wine and spirits industry (the vineyards are at Giancolis, near Lake Mariout), **bars** have a fairly low profile. Rather than the pricy *Monty's Bar* (noon–1am) in the *Hotel Cecil*, try some of the places listed below, mostly located on side streets near Midan Orabi. Thursday is the big night out for English teachers and other expats, who start drinking in the *Spitfire Bar* and finish up at the *Havana Bistro*. Imported booze costs less at the **duty-free shop**, 31 Sharia Salah Salem (daily 10am–7pm; Ramadan 10.30am–2.30pm & 8–11pm), which only accepts US dollars or Egyptian currency; there are other shops at the airport and the Maritime Station. The following are all keyed to the map on p.488.

Al-Ahram, off Sharia Sa'ad Zaghloul. Split-level bar and coffee shop refuge for middle-aged sports fans. Upstairs, a beer will cost you £E7 and you can watch satellite TV while you eat – though it's often tuned to German stations. Not a place for women to feel relaxed. Closed Fri.

Cap d'Or, Sharia Adib, off Sharia Sa'ad Zaghloul. Art Nouveau gilded mouldings, carved teak and engraved mirrors. Dubbed "The Trapdoor" by expats, but mostly frequented by Egyptians. Sells shrimps and other snacks (check the price first); a pint of Stella is £E10. Daily noon–3am.

Elite, 43 Sharia Safiya Zaghloul. Simple blue-painted extension to the restaurant of the same name. Frequented by tourists, writers and oddballs. Sells beer, *ouzo* and brandy. Usually open till midnight.

Havana Bistro, Sharia Fouad. Tiny, cosy den known as "Nagy's", after its engaging manager. Popular with expats and locals alike; fine for solo women. Serves tasty food and stocks a wide range of spirits. Knock to be admitted. Open Mon–Sat noon–3.30pm & 7.30pm–1am (or later).

Spitfire Bar, off Sharia Sa'ad Zaghloul. Small, friendly hang-out covered in stickers from engineering companies and warships; all kinds of expats meet here. Owned by five brothers and their "adopted" British sibling. Sells imported as well as domestic liquor. Mon–Sat noon–midnight.

Nightlife and entertainment

Several hotel **nightclubs** offer a programme of dinner with a slightly risqué "Russian Show" and a belly dancer. The best ones are in the *Helnan Palestine* (June–Sept daily

11pm–4am; £E45 minimum charge) and the *Montazah Sheraton* (Thurs 11pm–4am; £E105 minimum charge; June–Sept daily pool-side belly dancing, 11pm–2am; £E35); the show in the *Hotel Cecil* (£E66 minimum charge) is not up to much. Foreigners who turn up at the *Crazy Horse* inside *Athineos* on Midan Ramleh are discouraged from entering the nightclub, which is full of prostitutes (10pm–5am; minimum charge £E75). You're better off heading to the Latin-American Show on the terrace of the *Salamalek* (June–Sept daily 7–11pm; minimum charge £E75), an all-singing, all-dancing affair that also features a DJ.

Young Egyptians prefer the kind of **discos** that exude sweat and Arabic pop from the upper floors of seedy buildings. Unfortunately, they open and close so often that it's hard to be specific about venues – listen out and you might locate one. Punters who aren't in mixed-sex couples may be refused admission to the pricier, Westernized discos in the top hotels, but you could try the *Ramada Renaissance*'s *Black Gold*, which gushes from 6pm to 9pm and 11pm to 4am (minimum charge £E25; closed Tues); *Aquarius* in the *Montazah Sheraton* from 10.30pm to 2am (£E25 minimum charge, £E43 on Thurs; closed Wed).

Arts and festivals

Over summer you can see **belly dancing and folk dances** by the Rida Troupe (*Fir'et Rida*) or the National Troupe (*El-Fir'a el-Qawmiyya*) at the outdoor **Abdel Wahab Theatre** (☎482-3637), on the Corniche east of Midan Ramleh. Nightly shows start at 9.30pm; tickets cost £E3–20, and are best reserved the day before. During summer there is also a **Circus**, which sets up either at Azarita near the *Abdel Wahab Theatre*, or at St Marks College, near the youth hostel. Performances start at 9pm, or 5pm on Fridays and Sundays; tickets cost £E8–31.

September normally witnesses an **International Film Festival**, which gives Egyptians a rare opportunity to see foreign movies in an uncensored state; every cinema in town screens a few. However, film-going is popular throughout the year, with extra showings at the Metro, Amir and Rialto cinemas (all on Safiya Zaghloul) during Ramadan. Come October, Alex holds an **International Yachting Regatta** (details from the tourist office), while every two years the Fine Arts Museum arranges the **Alexandria Biennial**, an exhibition of art from Mediterranean countries. The *Helnan Palestine Hotel* sometimes hosts exclusive **bridge tournaments**, attended by Omar Sharif.

During Ramadan, the Egyptian, Islamic side of Alex revels in five **moulids** over five consecutive weeks, starting with *zikrs* outside the Mosque of Al-Mursi. The day after its "big night", the action shifts to Sidi Gaber's Mosque, then Sidi Bishr's; followed by the moulids of *Sidi Kamal* and *Sidi Mohammed al-Rahhal*.

Listings

Airlines EgyptAir (2–3 daily flights to Cairo; ☎482-5701), BA (☎482-1565) and Olympic (☎482-7295) are on Midan Ramleh; Air France (☎483-8901) at 22 Sharia Salah Salem; Lufthansa (twice weekly flights to Frankfurt; ☎483-5983) at 9 Sharia Talaat Harb. Foreign airlines without an office are represented by local travel agents; most are open Sat–Thurs 9am–4pm.

American Express 34 Sharia el-Moasker el-Romani, Roushdi (☎541-0177 or 543-7343, fax 545-7363), will cash and sell Amex travellers' cheques, and deal with lost cards and cheque refunds.

Arabic language courses Can be arranged through the British Council (see below).

Banks/exchange/ATMs Private exchange bureaux (known as Forex) on the north side of Midan Ramleh offer the best rates for cash; for travellers' cheques try the Bank of Alexandria, 59 Sharia Sa'ad Zaghloul, 23 Sharia Talaat Harb and 26 Sharia Salah Salem (Mon–Thurs & Sun 8.30am–2pm; Ramadan 10.30am–1pm); the National Bank of Egypt in the *Montazah Sheraton* (daily 10am–2pm; ATM accepts MasterCard) or the *Hotel Cecil* (Mon–Thurs & Sun 8.30am–8pm, Fri & Sat 9am–noon & 4–7pm); or Thomas Cook (see below). The Egyptian British Bank has ATMs (accepting Visa,

Cirrus, Electron, Plus and MasterCard) at its branch at 47 Sharia Sultan Hussein (opposite the duty free shop) and the *El Salamlek Palace Hotel*; and there's another ATM accepting Visa, MasterCard, Cirrus and Plus at the Banque Misr on Sharia Talaat Harb.

Bookshops There's some evidence of Alex's old literary cosmopolitanism at Mostakpal Library bookshop at 32 Safiya Zaghloul; the Al-Ahram bookshop at 10 Sharia Al-Haia – stocking a good range of books on Egypt as well as English-language classics – and El-Ma'aref (between Midan and Sharia Sa'ad Zaghloul, next to *Délices*), which offers foreign novels and text books. There's also a secondhand book-stall next to the Amir cinema on Safiya Zaghloul which does trade-ins. Foreign newspapers are sold outside the Ramleh telephone exchange.

Consulates Britain, 3 Sharia Mena, Roushdi (Mon–Thurs & Sun 8am–1pm; ☎546-7001); Germany, 5 Sharia Mena (Mon–Thurs & Sun 10am–noon; ☎545-7050); France, 2 Midan Orabi (Mon–Thurs & Sun 9am–1pm; ☎483-5513); Ireland, 236 Sharia Kafr Abdou, Kafr Abdou (Mon–Thurs & Sun 8am–1pm; ☎546-0081); Israel, 207 Sharia Abd es-Salem Aref, Roushdi (Mon–Thurs & Sun 9.30am–12.30pm; ☎586-0492); Italy, Sa'ad Zaghloul (Mon–Thurs 9am–12.30pm; ☎483-0095); Spain 101 Sharia el-Horreya, el-Shallalat (Mon–Thurs & Sun 9.30am–12.30pm; ☎493-9185). (Australia, New Zealand, the US and Canada have no consular representation; other consulates are listed in *Alexandria Night and Day*.

Cultural centres American Center, 3 Sharia Phara'ana (library Mon–Wed & Sun 10am–6pm, Thurs 10am–4pm; Ramadan Mon–Thurs & Sun 10am–3pm; *Lehrer News Hour* Mon–Thurs noon–1pm; *CBS News* Mon–Thurs & Sun 10.30–11am; ☎482-4117); British Council, 9 Sharia al-Batalssa (Mon–Wed & Sun 10am–7.30pm, Sat & Thurs 9.30am–3.30pm; Ramadan daily except Fri 9.30am–3.30pm; library membership £E25; ☎482-9890); French Centre, 30 Sharia Nabi Daniel (Mon–Thurs & Sun 9am–1pm & 4–8pm; ☎492-0804); Goethe Institute, 10 Sharia al-Batalssa (Mon–Thurs & Sun 10am–1pm & 4–7pm; ☎483-9870); Russian Centre, 7 Sharia al-Batalssa (Mon–Thurs & Sun 10am–1pm & 5–7pm, Fri 10am–1pm; ☎482-5645).

Film processing Kodak film is sold and developed opposite the Rialto Cinema on Safiya Zaghloul; other places can be found on Sharia Sa'ad Zaghloul.

Hospitals The private Al-Madina al-Tibaia, Sharia Ahmed Shawky, Roushdi (☎543-2150 or 543-7402), and Al-Markaz al-Tiby, 14th May Road, Smouha (☎548-6521), are accustomed to dealing with foreigners. For non-emergencies, ask your consulate or hotel to recommend a doctor.

International calls The 24hr exchange on Midan Ramleh has direct-dial phones and sells phonecards; the exchanges on Midan el-Gumhorriya and Sharia Sa'ad Zaghloul (both daily 8am–11pm) work on the pre-booking system. Speedy connections can be obtained at any of the top hotels, which charge 50–70 percent above the normal rate.

Internet cafés Alex has no less than four Internet cafés: *Access Cybercafé* (☎425-5766; *www.cyber-access.com.eg*) in the Zahran Mall, Smouha; *Click-it Internet* (☎311-7520) next door; *Netserv* (☎587-2269; *webmaster@netserv.com.eg*), 678 Tariq al-Horreyya, Loran; and *SatNet*, 603 Tariq al-Horreyya, Zizina (☎312-9985). All charge between £E8–12 for an hour.

Passport office To renew your visa, go to the office at 25 Sharia Talaat Harb (Mon–Thurs, Sat & Sun 8.30am–2pm & 7–9pm, Fri 10am–2pm; ☎482-7873), which is least busy in the evenings.

Pharmacies Khalil, on Sharia el-Ghorfa el-Tigarya, off Midan Sa'ad Zaghloul (Mon–Sat 9am–10pm, Sun 10am–10pm; ☎480-6710). There are others on Safiya Zaghloul and Nabi Daniel streets.

Post offices Midan Ramleh (daily 8am–3pm), Sharia el-Ghorfa el-Tigarya (same hours) and Masr Station (daily 8am–5pm). The poste restante service is unreliable, so ask if you can have mail sent c/o the *Hotel Cecil*. There's an Express Mail Service available at the Masr Station branch.

Swimming pools If you can't gain access to the Alexandria Sporting Club (see p.498), non-residents are sometimes allowed to use the pools at the *Ramada Renaissance* (☎549-0935) or *Montazah Sheraton* (☎540-1331). Phone to check before turning up.

Teaching English Holders of RSA or Trinity TEFL certificates may be able to find work in private schools, for £E1500 a month plus something towards the cost of renting a flat. Make enquiries at the British Council or ask around the expat community.

Thomas Cook 15 Midan Sa'ad Zaghloul (☎484-7830, fax 483-4073). Can change money and travellers' cheques, give cash advances on MasterCard and deal with stolen ones. Daily 8am–5pm.

Tourist police Above the tourist office (☎483-3378); in the Maritime Station (☎480-0100); at the entrance to Montazah gardens (☎547-3814); in the Greco-Roman Museum (☎482-8912). All except the last are open 24 hours.

Moving on from Alexandria

Most of the places covered in the remainder of this chapter can be reached from Alexandria by some form of public transport. Using the quickest available method it's also feasible to make **day excursions** to Rosetta and Tanta in the Delta (see Chapter Five) or the Monasteries of Wadi Natrun (see Chapter Three). Moving on from the city, there are also direct services to the Canal Zone.

Buses

Alexandria's inter-city **bus terminals** are spread around the city.

● **15th May Terminal** Behind Sidi Gaber Station (accessible by tram #2). Hourly A/C services to **Cairo**, operated by the West Delta (5.30am–10.30pm) and Superjet (5.30am–10.30pm) companies; bookings should be made at the appropriate kiosk. West Delta express buses to **Mersa Matrouh** (7am & 3pm) run all year, supplemented by slightly more comfortable – and expensive – Superjet services (daily 7.15am & 8.15am) over the summer. Tickets for West Delta buses can also be bought at their office on Midan Sa'ad Zaghloul.

● **Midan el-Gumhorriya** The bus depot facing the entrance to the Roman Theatre handles non-A/C services to **Siwa Oasis** (10am daily); non-express services calling at **El-Alamein** and **Sidi Abd el-Rahman** en route to Mersa Matrouh (every 1–2hr; 6.30am–1.30am in summer, till 5pm in winter); plus irregular non-A/C buses to **Rashid** and **Damietta**. A kind of sub-depot nearer Masr Station has buses for the **Monastery of Abu Mina** (hourly 8am–6pm). All tickets should be bought on the spot. Daily services also to **Ismailiya** (7am & 2.30pm), **Port Said** (6am, 8am, noon & 4.30pm) and **Suez** (9am & 11pm).

Trains

Train services between Alex and Cairo are detailed on p.244; there are two A/C 2nd class westbound services daily to Mersa Matrouh (6.45am & 1pm; 6–9hr; £E10). Unless you travel in 1st or A/C 2nd class, trains are generally less comfortable than buses or *service* taxis. The staff at the information desk and booking kiosk in **Masr Station** are often slow and unhelpful – you can only hope that you'll get sympathetic treatment. Services to Tanta and Cairo can also be boarded at Sidi Gaber Station.

Service taxis

Midan el-Gumhorriya seethes with Peugeots, Toyota minibuses and minivans going to almost everywhere that's worth mentioning within 200km of Alexandria. Listen for the drivers shouting out destinations, or simply ask for directions to the right clump of *service* taxis. If you don't mind a hair-raising trip with a few strangers, *service* taxis are the quickest way to get anywhere.

THE MEDITERRANEAN COAST

Egypt's 500-kilometre-long **Mediterranean coast** has beautiful beaches and sparkling sea all the way to Libya. However, many stretches are still mined from World War II (see below) or off limits due to military bases, or simply hard to reach – while all the most accessible sites have been colonized by holiday villages. Unlike in Sinai and Hurghada, these cater exclusively to Egyptians, whose beach culture is significantly different from Westerners'.

Most foreign travellers heading this way are aiming for Siwa Oasis (see p.461) rather than the resort town of **Mersa Matrouh**. Aside from the **beaches** near Matrouh, other

MINEFIELDS: A WARNING

Sections of the Mediterranean coast and the desert inland are still littered with **unexploded shells and minefields**. Never stray into wired-off areas or anything that resembles an abandoned camp or airfield. The best indication of safe and dangerous areas is the behaviour of locals. By sticking to well-worn paths and regular beaches, you'll be quite safe.

coastal sites are awkward to reach (or leave) without private transport, though you may consider it worth making the effort to get to the famous World War II battlefield of **El-Alamein**, or the swanky resort at **Sidi Abd el-Rahman**. In general, though, even the sea can seem reclusive here, hidden from sight of the "coastal" highway by **holiday villages** or barren ridges, while the B-road and railway along which many of the region's villages are located run still further inland.

Between Alexandria and El-Alamein

The "sights" **between Alexandria and El-Alamein** are relatively neglected by tourists, in some cases deservedly so. Getting there can involve much toing and froing around unsignposted crossroads miles from anywhere and, without your own transport, none of the places below are easy to reach as stops en route to El-Alamein or Mersa Matrouh. If you're using public transport, it's better to consider them as day excursions from Alex. Conversely, there are many new **holiday villages** along the highway to Matrouh. Some are reserved for elite sections of Egyptian society such as the army, navy and diplomatic corps, while others cater to anyone wealthy enough to afford an apartment there. If you have a car and loads of money, their gorgeous beaches and middling to luxurious facilities could be worth investigating. Otherwise, they're simply blights on the landscape that induce a numbing fatalism, as one succeeds another, for mile after mile.

El-Agami

Some 20km west of downtown Alex is the ever-growing resort of **EL-AGAMI**, whose white sands were first appreciated by rich, villa-building Egyptians in the 1950s. Confusingly, it comprises two resorts: **Bitash** (or "El-Agami"), consisting of villas and upmarket hotels, and **Hannoville**, 1km further west, where flats and cheaper hotels predominate. Each is approached by a separate road turning off the highway to Mersa Matrouh – Sharia Bitash and Sharia Hannoville – which runs towards their respective **beaches**. Both are somewhat less crowded than the Corniche beaches in Alex, but suffer from the same drawbacks, namely litter and sexual harassment. You might encounter foreign expats living here, who commute to work in Alex.

The easiest way of **getting there** from Alex is by minibus from the Sa'ad Zaghloul branch of the Ramleh terminal (#750 to Bitash, #760 to Hannoville) or Masr Station (#755 or #765, respectively). Although #460 buses from Ramleh run to both resorts (first Bitash, then Hannoville), they're incredibly crowded and far slower than minibuses. In Bitash, minibuses drop you across the road from the *Summer Moon Hotel*; in Hannoville, at the *Costa Blanca Hotel*.

Bitash

By Egyptian standards Bitash has a fairly liberal atmosphere, with the odd bikini to be seen on the semi-private **Fardous Beach**, reached by turning left by the telephone

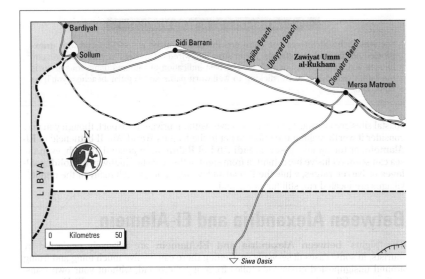

office on Sharia Bitash and carrying on to the end of Sharia Hanafiyya. The best places to stay are the beach-front *Agami Palace* (☎433-0230, fax 430-9364; ⑤) and *Summer Moon* (☎433-0367; ⑥) **hotels**, which have pools, discos and other amenities; their rates include breakfast. There are two other **discos** nearby, at *Felfela* (which also has a swimming pool and billiard room), and the expensive open-air French restaurant, *Michael's*.

Places to eat proli-ferate along Sharia Bitash. *Abu Hussein* and *Mu'min* are cheap and cheerful sandwich bars; *Gino's* does tasty pizzas and pasta; while *Saber* serves up sugary desserts. A right turn at the end of the street will bring you to *La Poire* on Sharia Shahr al-Asal, offering excellent *shawarmas* and chicken sandwiches, next to which are *Pizza Hut*, *Kentucky Fried Chicken* and *Baskin-Robbins*.

There are two private **hospitals** on Sharia Bitash: Al-Wafaa (☎433-8318) at no. 54 and Ibrahim Farouk (☎433-2925) at no. 62. You'll also find a **pharmacy** (daily 9.30am–midnight) at no. 79, a **bank** (Mon–Thurs & Sun 8.30am–2pm) at no. 84, an **Internet café** and a **telephone office** (daily 8am–midnight).

Hannoville

With fewer places to eat and a dirtier beach, **Hannoville**'s main attraction is its cheaper **accommodation**. Two hundred metres before the beach, you pass the clean and friendly *Costa Blanca Hotel* (☎430-3112; ③). Don't bother with the overpriced four-star places on the beach – if you're going to pay that kind of money it's better to stay at Bitash. Inexpensive and outstanding **meals** are available at the *Gad Restaurant*, across the road from the *Costa Blanca*. There's a **bank** (Mon–Thurs & Sun 8.30am–2pm) on the same street.

Abu Sir and Burg al-Arab

A *service* taxi or bus from Midan el-Gumhorriya in Alex can take you 48km west along the H55 to the coastal town of **ABU SIR**. Unremarkable nowadays, it was once **Taposiris**, a contemporary of ancient Alexandria, built upon the same limestone ridge, and likewise devoted to Osiris-worship.

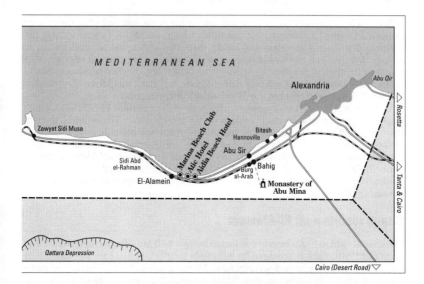

The enclosure walls of a long-vanished temple crown the ridge, with gate towers offering lovely views over the Mariout marshes and the azure sea. A few hundred metres to the east stands the solitary **Burg al-Arab** (Arab's Tower), actually a Ptolemaic lighthouse replicating the Pharos, but one tenth of its size; it was part of a chain that once illuminated the coastline from Alexandria to Cyrenaica.

Just west of Abu Sir, a minor road runs inland across reedy marshes, passing fragments of an ancient causeway (on the left) that connected Taposiris with the desert. There it meets **BURG AL-ARAB**, a "model" village resembling a walled, medieval Italian town, which was designed by the British administrator Wilfred Jennings-Bramly in 1915. Commandeered as the RAF headquarters during the battle for El-Alamein, Burg al-Arab was later graced with a villa (near the carpet factory outside its walls) where President Sadat planned the October War of 1973. The town is on the B-road from Alex to Mersa Matrouh, with a fair chance of *service* taxis to the nearest small town, **Bahig** (also a train stop).

The Monastery of Abu Mina

Seven kilometres along the road from Burg al-Arab to Bahig, a poorly marked track turns off and runs 15km south into the desert, to the Coptic **Monastery of Abu Mina**. The site is directly accessible from Alex by public buses (hourly 8am–6pm) that leave from a small depot in the vicinity of Masr Station.

Deir Mari Mina (as it's known locally) honours **St Menas**, an Egyptian-born Roman legionary who was martyred in Asia Minor in 296 after refusing to renounce Christ. His ashes were buried here when the camel that was taking them home refused to go any further. Miraculous events on the spot persuaded others to exhume Menas in 350 and build a church over his grave, later enclosed within a huge basilica. A pilgrim city grew up as camel trains spread his fame (Menas is depicted between two camels), and "holy" water from local springs was exported throughout Christendom. But when these dried up in the twelfth century, the city and its vineyards were abandoned and soon buried by sand, only a small community of monks remaining.

With its belfry towers visible from way out on the roads east and west, the present **monastery** hides its concrete buildings within a stone enclosure. Erected in 1959, the building is outwardly graceless and luridly decorated within, like all modern Coptic architecture. Not that monks and believers would agree, or even think it relevant; what counts is the spirit of devotion, most evident on November 11, when pilgrims celebrate **St Menas's Day**. (A Coptic encyclical of 1943 asserted that it was Menas the "wonder-worker of Egypt" who ensured the Allies' victory at El-Alamein.)

In addition to Menas, the crypt houses the body of Pope Kyrillos VI (1959–71), whom Copts regard as a saint, writing petitions on his marble grave. Tombs aside, though, there are only paltry **antiquities** to see. Amidst some low mounds several hundred metres beyond the monastery are broken marble paving, granite and basalt columns – the foundations of the original church and the basilica raised around Menas's original tomb. Remnants of the pilgrims' town lie all around (artefacts found here can be seen in Alex's Greco-Roman Museum); to the north is a ruined hospice once equipped with hot and cold baths.

Beach resorts near El-Alamein

The coastal road to El-Alamein is dominated by ugly **holiday villages** that have sprung up in the 1990s. Each is presaged by billboards long before you pass its ostentatious entrance, guarded by armed security men. Mostly moribund over winter, they come alive as BMW-borne families move in for the summer. At some, apartments can be rented on a short-term basis and their beaches and pools are open to non-residents for a charge. Their **beach scene** is more Western than elsewhere on the coast; bikinis and cocktails are taken for granted among the Egyptian smart set.

One top-class place that's open all year is the *Aida Beach Hotel* (☎499-0851, fax 499-0867), 30km from El-Alamein. It has two rates for day-visitors that fluctuate with the season: the lower (£E8–12) rate includes snacks, while the higher one (£E27–35, minimum two people) gets you lunch and the use of a beach cabin. Rent a double room (£E220) or a six-person villa and you'll also get breakfast and dinner. Bookings can be made in Alexandria at 18 Sharia Kolliet el-Tibba (☎ & fax 438-5882).

Barely 16km before El-Alamein, the sprawling low-rise *Atic Hotel* (☎492-1340; ◎) has a beautiful beach. Its day-rate (£E45) includes lunch and the use of two pools and a children's playground; other facilities cost extra. At the vaster condominium spread of the *Marina Beach Club*, 4km on, visitors can use an equally lovely beach (but not the pool) for £E10. Billboards for the resort have barely ceased when the roadside erupts in signs alerting you to the imminence of El-Alamein.

El-Alamein

Before Alamein we never had a victory. After Alamein we never had a defeat.
Winston Churchill, *The Hinge of Fate*

EL-ALAMEIN ("Two Worlds") is an apt name for a place that witnessed the turning point of the North African campaign, determining the fate of Egypt and Britain's empire. When the Afrika Korps came within 100km of Alexandria on July 1, 1942, the city and the capital experienced "The Flap": documents were burned, civilians mobbed railway stations, and Egyptian nationalists prepared to welcome their Nazi "liberators". Control of Egypt, Middle Eastern oil and the Canal route to India seemed about to be wrested from the Allied powers by Germany and Italy. Instead, at El-Alamein, the Allied Eighth Army held, and then drove the Axis forces back, to ultimate defeat in Tunisia. 11,000 soldiers were killed and 70,000 wounded at El-Alamein alone;

total casualties for the North African campaign (September 1940–March 1943) exceeded 100,000.

Travellers who wish to pay their respects to the dead or have an interest in military history should find the **cemeteries** and the **war museum** worth the effort of getting there. Commemorative **services** are held at El-Alamein each October; contact the British, Italian or German embassies in Cairo for details.

Getting there – and leaving

The so-called "City" of El-Alamein squats on a dusty plain 106km west of Alexandria, situated along a spur road that turns inland from the coastal highway. Anyone driving past could blink and see nothing except construction debris until they pass the Italian War Cemetery 9km down the highway. If you can afford it, the easiest way of visiting El-Alamein is by **rented car**. Renting through Avis in Alex (see p.484), you should expect the round trip to cost about £E180. Thomas Cook will do a car with driver for £E200. Depending on your bargaining skills, it should also be possible to rent a **taxi** for the day in Alex, for the same amount or maybe less. Though comparatively expensive, a car enables you to reach the far cemeteries and leave El-Alamein without difficulty – a major advantage over public transport.

Non-express **buses** from Alexandria's Masr Station to Mersa Matrouh (every 1–2hr from 6.30am to 5pm; £E6–7) usually call at El-Alamein's resthouse, which is conveniently close to the War Museum. Leaving can be tricky, however, as buses are packed when they arrive and you can't reserve seats from here. **Service taxis** from Midan el-Gumhorriya could drop you off along their run to Matrouh, but will probably expect the full fare (£E10). If that's the deal, make sure you're dropped at the resthouse and not at some distant intersection. Again, leaving is somewhat dependent on luck; flag down any minibus on the highway heading back to Alex or on to Mersa Matrouh. Staying in town, **accommodation** is fairly limited. The *El-Alamein Resthouse* (☎430-2785; ②) itself is pretty grotty and the *Al-Amana Hotel* (☎492-1340; ②), opposite the museum, is not much better – though it does have a restaurant serving standard Egyptian fare. Otherwise, for something a bit more comfortable, there's the *Hotel Atic* (see above), about 15km east on the Alex road.

The Battle and its legacy

Rather than the dramatic, single clash of forces that people generally imagine, the **Battle of El-Alamein** alternated between vicious fighting and relative lulls over four months (July–November) in 1942. The **Afrika Korps'** initial advance on El-Alamein was stymied by lack of fuel and munitions and stiff Allied resistance organized by Auchinleck. Once resupplied, however, Field Marshal Erwin **Rommel** was able to press the advantage with 88mm cannons that outranged the Allies' guns, as well as faster, better-armoured tanks.

At this time General Bernard **Montgomery** ("Monty") took over the Allied **Eighth Army**, and his first command was that it would retreat no further. He negated his army's weaknesses by digging his tanks into pits with only the gun turrets poking out above ground, protecting them until the German Panzers came within range. Aware that the Allies were being quickly re-supplied, Rommel now launched a huge offensive, attacking Alam Halfa ridge with ten Divisions. Suffering heavy losses (August 31 to September 6) and desperately short of fuel, the Afrika Korps withdrew behind a field of 500,000 landmines; however, Monty patiently re-organized his forces, resisting pressure from his superiors to attack until he had amassed 1000 tanks.

Having cracked the "Enigma" code, the Allies were now able to exploit a huge tactical advantage – it was October 23, Rommel was absent sick in Italy, and the Allies knew it. When they punched a corridor through the minefields of the central front, the

Germans, who had expected the main assault on their southern flank, were taken unawares. Rommel managed to return two days later, but was obliged to concentrate his mobile units further north, thus stranding four Italian divisions in the south. The Allies had established a commanding position at Kidney Hill, from which point Monty launched the decisive strike on November 2, using air power and artillery and leaving Rommel with only 35 operational tanks by the end of the day. The Eighth Army broke out on November 5 and surged west, and the Afrika Korps fought rearguard actions back through Libya until its inevitable surrender six months later.

The War Museum and Cemeteries

Motorists seeking the War Museum and Allied Cemetery should keep driving through El-Alamein City till they sight a Sherman tank (not of World War II vintage, but captured from the Israelis) near a gas station. Follow the road between them to a T-junction and turn left; the museum is on the main square, 200m ahead.

The **War Museum** (daily: summer 8am–6pm; winter & Ramadan 9am–3pm; £E10, students £E5, camera £E5, camcorder £E20) is small but well presented, with guides who can explain each phase of the battle on electronic map boards. Due weight is given to the experience of both sides, and Egypt's role in the Allied struggle is deservedly credited. Outside the museum are two dozen tanks, trucks and cannons, plus all manner of other equipment kept in a good state of preservation by the dry desert air. There's also a restored **Command Bunker** that was used by Monty during the battle, which you'll have to ask a guide to unlock.

The **Allied Cemetery** is 600m down the road, secluded on the reverse slope of a hill. Planted with trees and flowers, it is a tranquil site for the graves of 7367 Allied soldiers (815 of them nameless, only "known unto God"), with memorial cloisters listing the names of 11,945 others whose bodies were never found. Though over half were Britons, the dead include Australians, New Zealanders, Indians, Malays, Melanesians, Africans, Canadians, French, Greeks and Poles. If you want to find a particular headstone, the Commonwealth War Graves Commission in London can tell you exactly where to look. As you walk down towards the cemetery, there is an **Australian Memorial** to the right, and a **South African Memorial** 50m further along the road.

On the highway west of El-Alamein is a **plaque** marking the furthest point of the Axis advance, which asserts: *Manco la Fortuna, Non Il Valore* (Lacking Fortune, Not Valour), *1.7.1942, Alessandria 111km*. Further out you'll glimpse the **German Cemetery**, which overlooks the sea from a peninsula to the north: a squat octagonal building that houses the remains of 4280 German soldiers. An elegant white tower marks the **Italian Cemetery**, 3km further along the highway, which contains a small museum, and a chapel with the dedication: "To 4800 Italian soldiers, sailors and airmen. The desert and sea did not give back 38,000 who are missing".

Another legacy of the conflict, forgotten by the nations that pursued it, are the **minefields** they sowed across the Western Desert, which still kill and maim Bedouin people to this day. Casualties were highest in the 1950s, when a foreign scrap-metal dealer taught the Bedouin to make bombs from unexploded shells, and blow derelict tanks into portable chunks. The hinterland of El-Alamein is *especially dangerous*, as so many strongpoints were located there, but a few Bedouin with 4WDs are prepared to take people to such sites as **Kidney Ridge** and **Tell el-Issa**. The latter was the Afrika Korps' last defensive position, known to the Australian Division that assaulted it as "Hill 33". There are abandoned tanks and minefields as far south as **Naqb Abu Dweis**, the path out of the Qattara Depression (see p.474).

In November 1995, Egypt's Mediterranean coast and Western Desert witnessed the largest **wargames** ever staged in the Middle East, involving Egyptian, US, British, French and United Arab Emirate forces in amphibious and airborne landings, tank battles and missile barrages, repeating the scenario of the liberation of Kuwait, five years earlier.

Sidi Abd el-Rahman

Nine kilometres past the last of the battlefield memorials, a spurt of new housing anounces **SIDI ABD EL-RAHMAN**, which is used as a pit-stop by buses going to Matrouh and Siwa. There's no point in lingering here unless you're going to use the stunning white **beach** at the *El-Alamein Hotel* (☎492-1228, fax 492-1232; ⑧), a fancy resort where the day-charge for a cabin and lunch for two is £E180, and the rooms and villas are reserved up to a year in advance. It lies at the end of a 3km spur road off the highway, a world away from the township established to settle Awlad Ali **Bedouin** who moved in from Libya onto the lands of the weaker Morabiteen tribe a couple of centuries ago. Many have abandoned their traditional goat's-hair tents for stone houses, but they still maintain flocks, which they graze on scrubland or pen behind their now-immobile homes. Ten kilometres into the desert behind them lies a **graveyard of Panzers**, destroyed in the final rout of the Afrika Korps from the battlefield.

Mersa Matrouh

Although **MERSA MATROUH** has grown phenomenally and sees itself as a sophisticated resort, it remains a hick town with donkey carts outnumbering cars on the main street, which in summer is clogged with groups of well-to-do Egyptian and Libyan holidaymakers. All the local **beaches** have been ruined, leaving only the magnificent cove at Agiiba and neighbouring Ubbayad beach, both far from town. Whatever Egyptians might say, by no stretch of the imagination does Matrouh fit the tourist board's promise of a hedonist's playground. The only people likely to think so are the Libyans who've started coming here since the border was reopened; Egyptians go the other way, seeking work in Libya, while Western visitors are generally more interested in reaching Siwa Oasis (see p.518).

A grid of mould-poured low-rise blocks housing forty thousand people, the **town** spreads up from the coast towards a ridge festooned with radar dishes. As Matrouh has gone from being a quiet fishing port to the booming capital of the Mediterranean Governorate, immigrants have poured in from other parts of Egypt, inspiring mixed feelings amongst the locals.

Despite appearances, Mersa Matrouh ("Sheltered Anchorage") has a long **history**. Founded by Alexander the Great on his way to Siwa, it was here that Mark Antony and Cleopatra sought solace after their defeat at Actium, and that her fleet put out to sea for its final battle against Augustus. During the Islamic era, Matrouh was a busy trading port with a sideline in smuggling; its other main industry (dating back to Roman times) was harvesting sponges. Divers came from as far away as the Cyclades – up to two thousand of them per year in the early part of last century. To pluck the sponges from the seabed 60–90m below, they used a stone to make themselves sink faster, which they jettisoned at the bottom. Sponge-harvesting ceased in the early 1980s.

Getting there

The 209km journey **from Alex** is best accomplished **by bus**. There are twelve daily A/C West Delta services (7am & 3pm; £E17) throughout the year, augmented from June to September by more comfortable Superjet buses (7.15am & 8.15am; £E23) that likewise depart from Midan Sa'ad Zaghloul and take about three hours. Don't bother with the West Delta non-A/C buses from the Misr (new) station (every 1–2hr; 6.30am–1.30am in summer, till 5pm in winter; 4–5hr) unless you want to stop over at El-Alamein or Sidi Abd el-Rahman. Quicker but scarier are the **service taxis** that depart from outside Masr Station until around 6pm (£E10; 3hr 30min). **Trains** from Alex can

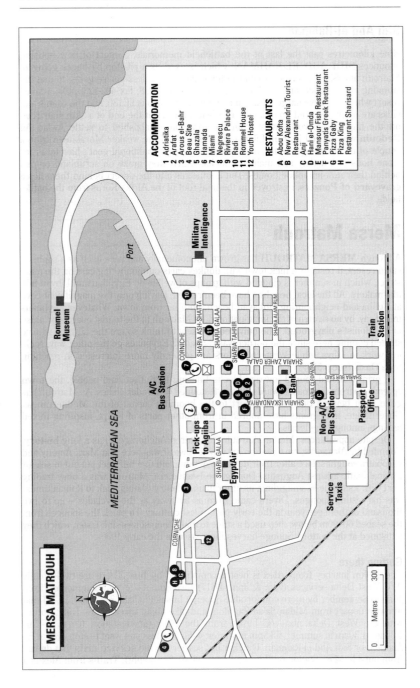

MERSA MATROUH

MEDITERRANEAN SEA

Port

Rommel Museum

Military Intelligence

A/C Bus Station

Pick-ups to Agiiba

EgyptAir

Non-A/C Bus Station

Bank

Passport Office

Service Taxis

Train Station

CORNICHE

SHARIA GALAA

SHARIA ASH-SHATTA

SHARIA TAHRIR

SHARIA GALAA

SHARIA ISKANDARIYA

SHARIA ZAHER GALAL

SHARIA ALAM RUM

SHARIA CLEOPATRA

SHARIA BUR SAID

0   300
Metres

N

ACCOMMODATION
1 Adriatika
2 Arafat
3 Arous el-Bahr
4 Beau Site
5 Ghazala
6 Hamada
7 Miami
8 Negrescu
9 Riviera Palace
10 Radi
11 Rommel House
12 Youth Hostel

RESTAURANTS
A Abou Kofta
B New Alexandria Tourist Restaurant
C Anji
D Hani el-Omda
E Mansour Fish Restaurant
F Panyatis Greek Restaurant
G Pizza Gaby
H Pizza King
I Restaurant Sharisard

take up to nine hours, and consist only of A/C 2nd class (£E10) or 3rd class (£E6.40) carriages.

Matrouh can be reached directly **from Cairo** in about six hours by identically scheduled A/C West Delta and Superjet buses, leaving at 6.15am, 7.15am (both £E35) and 7.45am (£E30) from the Abdel Mouneem Riyad Terminal near the *Ramses Hilton*. Book seats a day or two beforehand. Mornings are the best time to catch sporadic **service taxis** (£E20) from Ahmed Helmi and Koulali squares, near Ramses Station, which take about seven hours; an alternative is to ride to Alex and pick up another *service* taxi there. Over summer there are thrice-weekly **trains** (£E260) from Cairo to Matrouh, but at the price it's hard to imagine a reason for using them – or the EgyptAir **flights** (June–Oct Thurs, Fri & Sun; 1hr; £E344 one-way).

Tourists intent on **travelling to Siwa Oasis without staying in Matrouh** catch either one of the direct services from Alex, or an early morning bus from Cairo to Matrouh, and then the afternoon bus on to Siwa. The former limits your exposure to Matrouh to half an hour; the latter gives you enough time to stroll around and have lunch before returning to fight your way aboard the bus, some time between 3pm and 4pm. Advice on travelling on to Siwa appears at the end of this chapter.

Arrival, information and accommodation

On **arrival**, visitors can easily walk from either bus station to a hotel, though you'll need a taxi from the airport (£E10), if not from the train station (£E3–5). Donkey *carettas* are the mainstay of **transport** around town (£E1–3) and to the nearer beaches, but the animals are so abused that few tourists can bear to use them. The best way to get around is to rent a bike from one of the stands along the Corniche (£E1 per hour, £E5 per day).

The municipal **tourist office** (daily except Fri 8am–2pm; ☎493-1841) on the Corniche can supply a pretty useless map but little other information – especially if you want it in English. The best map of the town is included in *Alexandria Night and Day*, available in Alex or from a few of the more upmarket hotels in Mersa such as the *Miami*.

Accommodation

Many of the pricier **hotels** close down (or slash their prices) over winter, to reopen once the tourist season has got going in May. Visiting during the summer, it's wise to make **reservations** if you're fussy about lodgings.

The **youth hostel** (☎493-2331; £E8, non-members pay £E5 extra), off Sharia Galaa, 800m west of Sharia Iskandariya, has dinky shared rooms (unsuitable for women) and a kitchen. Although you can pitch a tent on Matrouh's beaches for free, you *must* inform the tourist office (who'll notify the tourist police) exactly where you're **camping**. Unauthorized campers risk being taken for smugglers and shot by police patrols.

Where distances are given below, they refer to the distance from Sharia Iskandariya.

Adriatika, 400m west along Sharia Galaa (☎593-5195). Average rooms with baths and balconies. Cafeteria, bar and dry cleaning. Closed out of season. ③.

Arafat, Sharia Tahrir (☎493-3606). Clean rooms with balconies and baths. Next to the *Hani el-Omda Restaurant*; follow the red arrow to the right. ②.

Arous el-Bahr, Corniche (☎493-4420). City-council owned and opposite the Med, which makes up for a lot. Slightly grubby rooms with balconies and bathrooms. Its name means "Bride of the Sea". ⑥.

Beau Site, 1.5km west along the Corniche (☎493-8555, fax 493-3319). Favoured by wealthy Egyptians for its comfortable rooms, fine food and private beach. Open May–Oct only. ⑧.

Ghazala, Sharia Alma Rum (☎493-3519). Clean and simple, this is the budget travellers' favourite. Beds in double, triple or quad-share rooms (without locks). Hot showers may be turned off over summer. Helpful management. ②.

Hamada (aka "Mersa Matrouh"), Sharia Iskandariya (☎493-3300). Cleanish rooms with shared cold-water facilities, above a noisy café. Singles, doubles and triples. ②.

Miami, Corniche (☎493-1400, fax 493-2083). Central three-star hotel with bar and restaurant. ⑦.

Negrescu, 600m west along the Corniche (☎493-4491, fax 493-3960). Spotlessly clean three-star establishment with good facilities. ⑦.

Radi, 500m east along the Corniche (☎ & fax 493-4828). Carpeted rooms with bathrooms and fans; some have TV. Bar and disco. ⑦.

Riviera Palace, Sharia Iskandariya (☎493-3045, fax 493-0004). Nice, spacious, central three-star joint with a good restaurant (no alcohol), and an organist in the lounge most evenings. ⑦.

Rommel House, 300m east along Sharia Galaa (☎493-5466, fax 347-1496). Its name is the main attraction of this overpriced three-star place (half-price in winter). Breakfast included. ⑥.

Beaches

Beaches are Matrouh's saving grace, so it's a real shame that women can't enjoy them. As in Alex, Egyptian women sunbathe and swim fully clothed, accompanied by male relations; a foreigner acting differently can be subject to persistent eyeballing and pestering, and maybe an encounter with an exhibitionist masturbator whom the authorities have tolerated for years. An exception to this rule is the *Beau Site*'s **private beach**, which admits non-residents if they promise to rent a beach umbrella (£E5 per day) or surf kayak (£E5 per hour).

The nearer beaches are accessible by *caretta* (£E5) or rented bicycle; **transport** to the western beaches varies with the season. From June onwards you should be able to catch a shared taxi or microbus from the bus station (£E2–3 each to Agiiba), or a pick-up truck from the stand on the corner of Sharia Galaa (£E1.50 to Agiiba). There is also an open-sided *tuf-tuf* bus (£E1.25 per person) that shuttles back and forth every hour or so from 9.30am to 4pm, between the bus station and Cleopatra and Agiiba beaches.

Beaches close to town

The three beaches around Matrouh's crescent-shaped bay are separated by a litter-strewn swathe and a small port further east. Beyond this, a spit of land curves around to face the town, rimmed on the landward side by **Rommel's Beach**. The Desert Fox supposedly bathed here in between plotting the Alam Halfa offensive from a nearby cave, now turned into a small **Rommel Museum** (daily 10am–5pm; £E1). His maps, desk and greatcoat (donated by his grandson, Manfred) are among the exhibits, which carry amusing captions like: "Rommel was the professor of contemporary military leaders to the extent that he was in every place at the same time".

Having ruined **Lido Beach**, curving west around the bay, litterbugs are doing the same to the **Beach of Lovers** (*Shahata al-Gharam*) on its western horn. Further west (roughly 7km from town) lies the cleaner, windier **Cleopatra Beach**, which drops away sharply a metre offshore. Across the dunes on its far right-hand side is **Cleopatra's Bath**, a hollow rock whirlpool bath where she and Mark Antony reputedly frolicked. Outside of the bath, heavy surf and sharp, slippery rocks make this a bad place to swim. The road to these beaches is a continuation of the Corniche, which turns south at the end of Lido Beach and then winds its way westwards.

Ubayyad and Agiiba beaches

Ubayyad Beach, 14km from town, is a vast expanse of silvery sand where the sea is calm and shallow up to 200m out. As you'd expect, it has not gone uncolonized: besides the Badr Tourist Village (open to the public) there is a private resort for army officers. Five kilometres further on, near the village of Umm Abraham, the sands have disgorged a tiny **ruined temple-fort** dedicated to Ramses II by his general Nebre, which marked ancient Egypt's westernmost port. **Zawiyat Umm al-Rukham** (its local name) isn't signposted from the coastal road, and can really only be reached by private taxi or a long walk from Ubayyad.

From the next headland, 24km from town, a path slopes down to **Agiiba Beach**. Agiiba ("Miraculous") is an apt name for this stunningly beautiful cove, but "beach" is rather a misnomer. To swim in the calm, crystal-clear turquoise water, you can dive off rocky shelves protruding into the sea or wade in off a tiny beach gunked up with algae. From July onwards it's necessary to walk around the headlands and along the shore to find uncrowded sites. Bring food and drink as there's no guarantee of stalls operating on the cliff top, which overhangs some caves.

Eating and nightlife

Matrouh is not exactly a metropolis, but it has a fair spread of restaurants (see below) and most services that you might want to make use of. Sharia Iskandariya overflows with grocery stores, bakeries, fruit and veg stalls and outlets for beach-gear.

Besides the following, there is swanky hotel dining in the *Riviera Palace* and *Beau Site*. Other hotel **restaurants** probably have less to offer than the places listed below, and are bound to charge more. The opening hours given are for summertime; over winter, most places close before midnight, though coffee houses on the main drag and at the bus station square stay open till the small hours.

The *Beau Site* hosts the better of Matrouh's two **discos**; the other, *Disco 54* at the *Radi Hotel*, doesn't get going until well into the tourist season, like the nightclubs in other three-star hotels.

Abdu Kofta, corner of Tahrir and Zaher Galal. Small, clean place to consume grilled chicken (£E14), *kofta* or kebab (£E26–28 per kilo). Try the *molukhiyya* soup. Open daily 10am–2am.

New Alexandria Tourist Restaurant, Sharia Iskandariya. One of the best low-budget options; a full fish meal costs only £E15. May sell beer. Daily 9am–midnight (last orders 10.30pm).

Anji, Sharia Cleopatra. Decent burgers and veggie stew in an environment that's OK for solo women. Also does breakfast and ice cream. Daily 10am–10pm.

Hani el-Omda, Sharia Tahrir. Cool, clean and dimly lit. Good for simple meals: a quarter-kilo of *kofta* with salads and bread costs £E8. Daily 9am–midnight.

Mansour Fish Restaurant, Sharia Tahrir. Attracts trendy young Egyptians who watch videos over their fish or lobster and salad. Pricier than the rest, but worth it. Daily 11am–3am.

Panyatis Greek Restaurant, Sharia Iskandariya. Not especially Greek, but it has been around since 1922. Sells fried fish (£E20), calamari (£E15), salad, *tahina* and beer. Open daily 8am–midnight.

Pizza Gaby, 850m west along the Corniche. Fine, if you can bear its tacky decor and music, intended to lure guests from the *Hotel Negresco*. Daily 11am–midnight.

Pizza King, Beyond the *Gaby*, up an alley to the left past the *New Lido Hotel*. A humbler take-away with tables, but the pizzas (£E7-10) here are better. Daily 6pm–3am.

Restaurant Sharisard, Sharia Iskandariya. Tasty *fuul*, falafel, *shawarmas*, liver and other cheap eats. Claims to be open 24 hours. Highly recommended.

Practicalities

The **tourist police** (☎493-5575) are next to the tourist office on the Corniche, while the regular **police** (☎493-3376) are just inland on Sharia ash-Shatta; both are open 24 hours. On the same street are the **post office** (daily except Fri 8am–3pm) and 24-hour **telephone exchange**, but the latter is so crowded and unreliable for international calls that it's worth paying extra for a direct line at the *Rivera Palace*.

You can **change money** and travellers' cheques at the Banque du Caire (daily 9am–2pm & 6–9pm) on Sharia Bur Said, or the National Bank of Egypt (daily 8.30am–12.30pm & 6–9pm) across the road from EgyptAir (Mon 10am–1pm, Tues–Sun

10am–1pm & 6–9pm; ☎493-4398). Should you need to register or extend your visa, the **passport office** (daily except Fri 9am–2pm & 5–7pm) lies in the vicinity of the train station. Both formalities are handled in the morning, but only registrations in the evening.

Medical emergencies may be referred to the military **hospital** (☎493-5286) on Sharia Galaa, but it's better to go to Cairo for treatment if possible. For less serious ailments, visit the Said Lee Tohaami **pharmacy** (daily: summer 8am–midnight; winter 8am–9pm), eight blocks in from the Corniche on Sharia Iskandariya.

Moving on – Siwa and Libya

As said earlier, you don't have to stay here in order to reach **Siwa Oasis** – actually, there's more call to do so on the way back, if only to break the nine-hour journey from Siwa to Alex. Another possible reason is if you plan to visit remoter oases such as Qara, which still require permission from Military Intelligence (see below).

In any event, there are three **buses** a day from Matrouh to Siwa: a non-A/C rattletrap leaving at 7am (£E7), and two through-buses from Alex, which cram in extra passengers here. The one leaving Matrouh around 1.30pm (£E7) is equally decrepit, while the one going at around 4pm (£E10) is nominally A/C. Try buying tickets the night before, but don't be surprised if they're only sold on the bus, accompanied by a no-holds-barred struggle for seats. There may also be the odd **service taxi** (£E10 per person for a full load), but this should be used only as a last resort, and not in preference to the bus. Bring plenty of food and water for the six-hour journey.

Motorists should avoid travelling in the midday heat and fill up before leaving Matrouh, as there are no petrol stations along the 300km route. The Siwa road is reached by following the Corniche west out of town, turning inland and passing the airport turn-off, and then heading south at the next junction, 20km from Matrouh. There's a police checkpoint, so you can't miss it. Don't stray far from the road if you stop for a leak; there are minefields on either side for miles into the desert.

Permission to visit Qara, Girba, Sitra and Areg oases is obtainable from **Military Intelligence** (daily 8am–2pm & 8–11pm). Knock on the steel gates and you should get taken into the guardhouse to explain yourself. You'll need a photocopy of your passport and Egyptian visa, which can be made on Sharia Iskandariya. The permit should be issued free of charge.

Remember to **change money** before you set out, as Siwa has no bank.

West of Matrouh: the road to Libya

The **road to Libya** reflects relations between the Arab Republic of Egypt and the Libyan *Jamahiriyah* (State of the Masses). During the 1960s, when Gaddafi regarded Nasser's Egypt as the vanguard of revolutionary Arab nationalism, people and goods flowed both ways, encouraging the Libyan leader to propose that the two countries unite in 1973 – an ambition that came to nought as President Sadat cultivated the Western powers and finally signed a peace treaty with Israel. In response, Libya severed relations, closed the border and began agitating for the overthrow of the Egyptian government; a cold war ensued, with sporadic incursions by Libyan war planes and saboteurs during the 1980s.

It wasn't until the end of the decade that relations were restored and the border was reopened. Despite an upturn in civilian traffic, there's still an overwhelming military presence along the 120km to **Sidi Barrani** – a small port named after the Senussi missionary Sidi Mohammed el-Barrani, which was bitterly contested during the Western Desert campaign, but is now just a gas-stop on the road to Sollum (60km). **SOLLUM** is more arresting, overlooking the sea from a 180-metre cliff with a harbour at the bottom. A small **Allied War Cemetery** at the eastern entrance to town recalls the toll exacted at "Hell Fire Pass", where five waves of British tanks were destroyed by German guns dug into the ridge.

Between Sollum and the border (10km) is a **Palestinian refugee camp** whose inmates have languished in limbo since their expulsion from Libya in 1994, lacking visas or funds to move on. The local authorities leave their provisioning to Sollum's merchants, who overcharge for everything. If you happen to be driving this way, even a few crates of bottled water would be welcome; basic medicines, too.

The **border** is officially open 24 hours, but its lethargic customs officials and sweltering queues of vehicles suggest otherwise. While Egyptians and Libyans cross over regularly, foreign tourists are only just beginning to visit Libya, which hardly encourages impulse visits. Libyan **visas** must be obtained beforehand in Cairo (see p.238), and from there a *service* taxi (LD1) can take you to Al-Burdi for buses on to Tobruk and Benghazi. If you're planning to drive your own vehicle along the coast and into Libya, be sure to have your passport and car papers ready to show at the innumerable checkpoints along the way.

CHAPTER FIVE

THE DELTA

While the Nile Valley's place in ancient Egypt remains writ large in extraordinary monuments, the **Nile Delta**'s role has largely been effaced by time and other factors. Although several pharaonic dynasties arose and ruled from this region – Lower Egypt – little of their twenty provincial capitals remains beyond mounds of debris known as *tell* or *kom*. The pharaohs themselves set the precedent of plundering older sites of their sculptures and masonry – hard stone had to be brought to the Delta from distant quarries, so it was easier to recycle existing stocks – and nature performed the rest. With a yearly rainfall of nearly 20cm (the highest in Egypt, most of it during winter) and an annual inundation by the Nile that coated the land in silt, mud-brick structures were soon eroded or swept away. More recently, farmers have furthered the cycle of destruction by digging the mounds for a nitrate-enriched soil called *sebakh*, used for fertilizer; several sites catalogued by nineteenth-century archeologists have all but vanished since then.

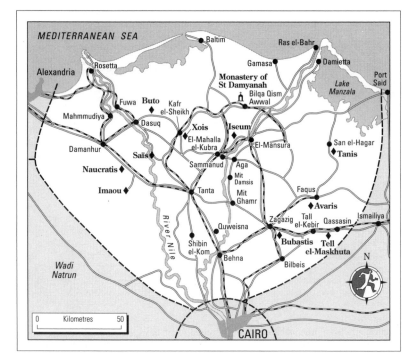

Of the Delta's show of ancient monuments, the ruins of **Tanis**, **Avaris** and **Bubastis** are certainly worth knowing about, if not visiting. As for Islamic architecture, there's a sprinkling of "Delta Style" mansions and medieval mosques in the coastal towns of **Rosetta** and **Damietta**.

Practically everywhere else on the map is an industrialized beehive or a teeming village, only worth visiting for **moulids** or popular festivals, of which the region has dozens. Combining piety, fun and commerce, the largest events draw crowds of over a million, with companies of *mawladiya* (moulid people) running stalls and rides, while the Sufi *tariqas* perform their *zikrs*. People camp outdoors and music blares into the small hours. Smaller, rural moulids tend to be heavier on the practical devotion, with people bringing their children or livestock for blessing, or the sick to be cured.

The great **Moulid of Saiyid el-Bedawi**, held at **Tanta** just after the cotton harvest in October, starts a cycle of **Muslim** festivals lasting well into November. At one- to two-week intervals, pilgrims and revellers congregate for week-long bashes at **Basyouni**, **Dasuq**, **Mahmudiya**, **Fuwa** and **Rosetta**. The Muslim month of *Shawwal* (following Ramadan) also occasions moulids at **Bilbeis** and **Zagazig**. During May, the remote **Monastery of St Damyanah** witnesses one of Egypt's largest **Christian moulids** and, come August, another event transpires at the village of **Mit Damsis**. In January a unique **Jewish moulid** takes place at **Damanhur**.

The Delta's other possible attraction is its flat, intensely green **landscape**, riven by waterways where feluccas glide past mud-brick villages and wallowing buffalo. The northern **lakes** are a wintering ground for herons, storks, great crested grebes and other water birds, while doves and pigeons – reared for human consumption in cotes shaped like Khmer temples – join other **birdlife** pecking around the cotton-, rice- and cornfields. In ancient times, wealthy Egyptians enjoyed going fowling in the reeds, using throwing sticks and hunting cats; their modern-day counterparts employ shotguns. The Delta is also still a habitat for wildcats and pygmy white-toothed shrews, but boars have been driven out and the last hippopotamus was shot in 1815.

More sombrely for the ecology, the Delta is one of the world regions most vulnerable to the effects of **global warming**. Oceanographers predict that a one-metre rise in the sea level would swamp Alexandria and submerge the Delta as far inland as Damanhur, destroying six percent of Egypt's cultivable land and displacing 3.3 million people. The freshwater Delta lagoons, which provide much of the nation's fish catch, would also be ruined. A more immediate threat is **erosion** by the Mediterranean. Now that the Delta is no longer renewed by silt from the Nile, its coastline is being worn away.

Visiting the Delta

As few visitors have time for more than one moulid or site, we've dealt with the region in less detail than other parts of Egypt. Depending on where you're aiming for, it might be better to start from Alex, Cairo or the Canal Zone: Rosetta and Damanhur are easiest to reach from Alex; Tanta from Cairo; and Zagazig from Ismailiya in the Canal Zone. There are direct buses from Cairo to the Delta resorts over summer. In some cases, a shortage of local **accommodation** makes day trips more feasible than overnight stays. Trains are OK for reaching major towns, but *service* taxis and buses are the best way of **getting around**. Renting a car isn't necessarily a good idea: it's easy to have accidents on the Delta roads, and the minor ones are legally off limits to foreign drivers – a hangover from 1960s spy-phobia. Should the police decide to make a fuss, you could conceivably spend a night in jail.

Rosetta, Damanhur and the Western Delta

The broader Rosetta branch of the Nile delineates one edge of the **Western Delta**, whose other flank fades into desert. Its cotton fields and mill towns are visible enough from the Delta Road or the Cairo–Alexandria railway, and few places merit closer inspection. **Rosetta** makes a nice day excursion from Alex (there's no tourist accommodation), and **Damanhur** hosts two remarkable moulids, but you have to be pretty keen on archeology to bother with the *koms* off the Tanta road.

Rosetta (Rashid)

The coastal town of **ROSETTA** has waxed and waned in counterpoint to the fortunes of Alexandria, 65km away. When Alex was moribund, Rosetta burgeoned as a port, entering its heyday after the Ottoman conquest of Egypt in the sixteenth century, only to decline after Alexandria's revival. The modern-day town is still "surrounded by groves of orange and lemon trees", as Eliza Fay wrote home in 1817, but its "appearance of cleanliness . . . so gratifying to the English eye" has dissipated, and these days few tourists come to wander through its run-down, littered streets in search of once-elegant Ottoman mansions. It's certainly a far cry from the early nineteenth century, when E.D. Clarke saw "English ladies from the fleet and the army" wearing "long white dresses", riding "the asses of the country".

This earlier European fascination owed to the discovery of the **Rosetta Stone** by French soldiers in 1799. Their officer realized the significance of this second-century BC basalt slab inscribed with ancient hieroglyphs, demotic Egyptian and Greek script, which was forwarded to Napoleon's savants in Cairo. Although their archeological booty had to be surrendered in 1801 – which is how the Stone, "Alexander's Sarcophagus" and many other objects wound up in the British Museum – it was a French professor, Jean-François Champollion (1790–1832), who finally deciphered the hieroglyphs by comparison with the Greek text, and unlocked the secret of the ancient Egyptian tongue.

Getting there

The quickest way to reach the town is by **service taxi** (1hr; £E4) or hourly **bus** (90min; £E1.50) from Alexandria's Midan el-Gumhorriya; the last bus back to Alex leaves at 5pm. Third-class **trains** are slower, though you might find them useful for reaching Fuwa and Dasuq (on the Tanta line), or Mahmudiya (on the Damanhur branch), in order to attend their moulids. But *service* taxis provide the widest choice of destinations. Most Delta towns are within a couple of hours' ride; to Cairo takes an hour longer. To find a *service* taxi from Cairo to Rosetta, ask around the Aboud terminal.

The Town

Rosetta's main appeal lies in its **"Delta Style"** **architecture**. The Delta hallmarks are pointed brickwork (usually emphasized by white or red paint), inset beams and carved lintels, and a profusion of *mashrabiya*-work. Some of the mansions also incorporate ancient columns. Here, the finest examples lie on, or just off, the main street running parallel to the river, with the railway station at its northern end. Starting from the bus and taxi depot, you can find this by walking past the nearest mosque and taking the second turning on your left. The first house worth investigating stands on the left, 200m ahead, bearing a blue sign in Arabic. It's now a workshop for producing and restoring *mashrabiyas*, but the craftsmen don't mind visitors.

For a better idea of how the Ottomans lived, visit the **Beit al-Amasyali**, 50m further on, straddling a corner. A superb wooden ceiling and mother-of-pearl-inlaid *mashrabiyas* ennoble the reception room upstairs. Downstairs you'll find the Abu Shahim Mill, with its huge wooden grinders and delicately pointed keyhole arches. Both were built around 1808 for the Turkish Agha, Ali al-Topgi, who bequeathed them to his servant Al-Amasyali. From here, you can get directions to the **Beit Kili** off Midan al-Hurriya, an eighteenth-century house containing a small **museum** (daily 9am–4pm; £E20, camera £E10) whose only notable exhibit is a diorama showing British soldiers being trounced by the locals.

To make a day of it, consider an excursion to the **Fort of Qaitbey** (daily 9am–4pm; Ramadan 9am–3pm; also open some evenings; £E20), 5km from town. Built in 1479 to guard the mouth of the Nile, it served as the first line of defence against the Crusaders and was later reinforced by the French, whose use of masonry imported from Upper Egypt led to the discovery of the Rosetta Stone. The fort can be reached from town by green-and-white taxi (£E2–3; £E5 round-trip) or fishing boat (£E5–10 after bargaining). Alternatively, you can visit the tranquil old **Mosque of Abu Mandar**, 5km upriver from Rosetta; taxi boats leave from the docks near Midan al-Horriya – expect to pay £E5–7 after haggling.

Around mid-November, the chain of festivals that started in Tanta the previous month should reach Rosetta. Don't despair if you come a few weeks earlier, since similar **moulids** occur at Fuwa, Mahmudiya and Dasuq, further inland. Salted fish (*fisikh*) and hummus are the traditional snacks at these events.

Damanhur and around

Most of the land between Alex and Tanta is given over to **cotton**, Egypt's major cash crop, whose intensive cultivation began under Mohammed Ali. His French hydro-engineer's scheme to regulate the flood waters by means of barrages across the Rosetta and Damietta branches of the Nile was ultimately realized by Sir Colin Scott-Moncrieff in 1880–90. The shift from flood to perennial irrigation enabled three or four crops a year to be grown in the Delta, as is still the case.

Hardly surprising, then, that local towns are heavily into textiles; particularly the Beheira Governorate capital, **DAMANHUR**, once *Tmn-Hor*, the City of Horus. Although much of it is drably functional, this city of 170,000 people gains a dash of colour from green-shuttered houses and bougainvillea-laden archways, and blossoms during its festival.

Turbaned Sufis perform *zikrs* and *munshids* to enthusiastic crowds during Damanhur's **Moulid of Sheikh Abu Rish**. This occurs in late October or early November, a week after the festival at Dasuq, across the river. With venues so close together, the *mawladiya* (moulid people) can easily move on to the next event; barbers, circumcisers and all.

Egypt's only **Jewish moulid**, held over two days in January, is a very different scene. The shrine of **Abu Khatzeira** (Father of the Mat), a nineteenth-century mystic, is cordoned off by security police who rigorously exclude non-Jewish Egyptians, fearing a terrorist attack. Within the cordon a few thousand mostly French or Israeli visitors bring sick relatives or bottled water to be blessed, and "bid" for the key to Abu Khatzeira's shrine; the money raised supports its upkeep.

Two moulids: Dasuq and Fuwa

A week or so after Tanta's festival (see below), the agricultural town of **DASUQ** holds the **Moulid of Ibrahim al-Dasuqi** (in mid- to late October), drawing almost as many people. Al-Dasuqi (1246–88) was the only native-born Egyptian to found a major Sufi order, the Burhamiya (whose chosen colour is green): the other brotherhoods originated abroad, or were started here by foreigners.

Should you decide to attend the eight-day event, Dasuq is probably easiest to reach from Damanhur by bus or *service* taxi. Coming from Tanta or Rosetta, you could either take a slow, stopping train, or catch a *service* taxi, changing at Kafr el-Sheikh if necessary. Most trains also call at **FUWA**, 13km from Dasuq, where another **festival** occurs in late October or early November.

Between Damanhur and Tanta

A couple of **ancient sites** reduced to *kom* lie off the road **between Damanhur and Tanta** (64km). Roughly 23km out of Damanhur, a track leads three kilometres left off the main road to the village of El-Nibeirah, near two low mounds marking the site of Naucratis. During the XXVI Dynasty, when Egypt was ruled from the Delta, King Amasis (570–26 BC) granted this Greek colony a monopoly of trade between Egypt and Greece. Excavating the site for the British Museum in the nineteenth century, Flinders Petrie found it littered with shards of Greek pottery, and imagined that he was "wandering in the smashings of the Museum's vase-room".

At Itai El-Baroud, the last town before crossing the Rosetta branch of the Nile, another turn-off runs fourteen kilometres south to El-Tud, by the "Mound of the Fort", *Kom el-Hisn*. This used to be **Imaou**, which became the capital of the Third Nome (an administrative district) during the New Kingdom, and was turned into a necropolis by the Hyksos pharaohs. A temple enclosure and numerous tombs are still evident.

Tanta and the Central Delta

Tanta, Egypt's fifth largest city, hosts the country's greatest moulid, which is worth experiencing for at least a day. The city also serves as a jumping-off point for practically everywhere else in the **Central Delta**. Depending on your bent, there are several other moulids and a host of ancient sites scattered around the region. With regular trains and *service* taxis to Alex (a roughly 2hr journey) and Cairo (1hr 30min) running from early morning till nigh on midnight, you don't have to stay in Tanta; indeed, you'd be lucky to find a vacant room while the moulid's on. Elsewhere, tourist accommodation is virtually nonexistent anyway. Because the northwestern corner of this part of the Delta is easier to reach from Damietta or El-Mansura, we've allocated sites there to the "Eastern Delta" section (see p.526).

Tanta

A bustling industrial city with strong rural ties, **TANTA** marks the end of the cotton harvest in October with Egypt's largest festival, the **Moulid of Saiyid Ahmed el-**

Bedawi. Tanta's population jumps from 230,000 to nearly three million as visitors pour in from the Delta villages, other parts of Egypt and the Arab world. Streets and squares fill with tents and stalls; Sufis prepare for *zikrs*, while musicians test their amps ("Allah, two, three"). Thousands camp out amidst heaps of blankets and cooking pots, though sleep seems impossible. With music and chanting, vendors and devotees, a circus with lions and tigers and a levitation act, Tanta becomes a seething cacophony. If you plan to attend the week-long festival, it is best to leave all your valuables somewhere safe. Pickpocketing is rife and injuries may result from crushing or fist-fights in the dense crowd.

The moulid honours the founder of one of Egypt's largest Sufi brotherhoods. Born in Fes in Morocco in 1199, **Saiyid Ahmed el-Bedawi** was sent to Tanta in 1234 by the Iraqi Rifaiyah order, and later established his own *tariqa* (brotherhood), the Ahmediya. His name is invoked to ward off calamity – *"Ya saiyid, ya Bedawi!"* – but his moulid is anything but angst-ridden. "Although a religious festival, pleasure is the chief object of the pilgrims, and a few *fatahs* at the tomb of the saint are sufficient to satisfy every pious requirement", noted *Murray's Handbook* in 1891. The climax to the eight-day festival occurs on a Friday, when the Ahmediya – whose banners and turbans are red – parade with drums behind their mounted sheikh. Events focus on the triple-domed, Ottoman-style **mosque** wherein Bedawi and a lesser sheikh, Abd el-Al, are buried.

Practicalities

Should you wish **to stay** in the vicinity during the moulid (or other festivals – see below), book a room as far in advance as possible. The *Green House Hotel* (☎040/330-760; ⑤) on Sharia el-Borsa has friendly staff who can organize most things for you, while the *Arafa Hotel* (☎040/336-952; ⑤) outside the train station has rooms with A/C, TV and minibars. The only **bank** that cashes travellers' cheques is the Delta Bank, diagonally opposite the *Green House*; there's an ATM for Visa and MasterCard outside the Banque Misr across the road. Tanta's **service taxi** depot is the place to ask about rides to wherever you hope to go.

Sites around Tanta

Some of the places below are directly accessible from Tanta; to reach others you might have to change once or twice. For the committed, renting a private **taxi** gives the greatest scope for excursions.

As a footnote to bygone rulers, it's worth mentioning (but not visiting) the village of **Mit Abu el-Kom**, near the small town of Quweisna to the south of Tanta, as the **birthplace of Anwar Sadat**. Born in 1908, he escaped rural life by joining the army, became a nationalist and conspired with like-minded officers to overthrow King Farouk. As Nasser's heir, President Sadat waged war against, and then signed a peace treaty with Israel, opened Egypt to Western capitalism – generating a consumer boom and massive corruption – and was finally assassinated by Islamic militants in 1981.

Buto and Xois

Only those with private transport and a consuming passion for **ancient sites** will bother trying to reach **Tell al-Faraoun** (Mound of the Pharaoh), on the edge of some marshes north of Ibtu village, itself 5km north off the Dasuq–Kafr el-Sheikh road. The site appears on maps as **Buto**, the Greek name for a dual city known to the ancient Egyptians as *Pr-Wadjet*. **Wadjet**, the cobra-goddess of Lower Egypt (whom the Greeks called Buto) was worshipped in the half of the city known as Dep. The other city, known as Pe, was dedicated to Djbut, the heron-god, who was later supplanted by Horus. Nothwithstanding all this, the 180-acre site had been obliterated down to its paving stones by the time Petrie excavated it.

Should you carry on to **KAFR EL-SHEIKH** and follow the Tanta road south, you'll pass the village of Sakha, occupying the site of **Xois**, ancient capital of the Sixth Nome.

Saïs

Nothing but a few pits filled with stagnant water remains of the once great city of **Saïs**, near the modern village of **SA EL-HAGAR**, beside the Rosetta branch of the Nile. Founded at the dawn of Egyptian history, it was always associated with the goddess of war and hunting, **Neith**, whose cult emblem appeared on pre-Dynastic objects. In Egyptian cosmology, she was also the protectress of embalmed bodies; the Greeks identified her with Athena.

The city became Egypt's capital during the **Saïte Period**, when the XXVI Dynasty (664–525 BC) looked back to the Old Kingdom for inspiration, refurbishing the pyramid tombs and reviving archaic funerary rituals. In 525 BC the Dynasty was overthrown by the Persian emperor Cambyses, who's said to have had the body of the penultimate Saïte king, Amasis "the Drunkard", removed from its tomb, whipped and burnt.

El-Mahalla el-Kubra and Sammanud

EL-MAHALLA EL-KUBRA, 24km northeast of Tanta, is Egypt's fourth largest city (*Omar Khayyam* **hotel** on Midan 23rd July; ☎040/334-299; ⑤), and a taxi staging-post for journeys to the riverside town – almost a suburb, these days – of **SAMMANUD**.

Immediately west of the Sammanud taxi depot, near the hospital, a large mound and a scattering of red and black granite blocks mark the site of the Temple of Onuris-Shu, rebuilt by Nectanebo II to grace **Tjeboutjes**, the capital of the Twelfth Nome. Another city, **Busiris**, occupied a bluff overlooking the river further south, along the road out of Sammanud. However, part of a XXVI Dynasty basalt statue and fragments of a monumental gateway are all that remain of this reputed birthplace of Osiris.

The H8 road, which runs northeast from Sammanud to Talkha, takes you past the site of ancient *Pr-Hebeit*, 10km to the west, better known by its Roman name, **Iseum**. Here, the great **Temple of Isis** which Nectanebo began and Ptolemy II completed has been reduced to an enclosure wall, some carved granite blocks and Hathor-headed capitals. From Talkha, you can easily cross the river to El-Mansura (see p. 530).

The Eastern Delta and the Delta resorts

The **Eastern Delta** scores on several counts. **Tanis**, **Avaris** and **Bubastis** are the best **pharaonic ruins** that Lower Egypt can offer; there are **moulids** aplenty, both Christian and Muslim; and if you include the places on the Central Delta coast, which are easier to reach from here, the region can also claim three low-key **beach resorts** and some fine **bird-watching**.

For some of these destinations it might be simpler to approach the Eastern Delta from Port Said or Ismailiya in the Canal Zone, rather than from Alex.

Zagazig and the ruins of Bubastis

The charmingly named **ZAGAZIG** (pronounced "Za'a'zi") is less appealing in reality, blighted by fumes from a soap factory. Only founded in 1830, it boasts of being the home town of Colonel **Ahmed Orabi** (1839–1911), leader of the 1882 revolt against British rule, whose statue stands outside the station. As a provincial capital with a thriving university, Zagazig is reticent about being the source of most of the **papyri** sold in tourist shops throughout Egypt, which are manufactured in sweatshops and sold to

BASTET

The feline goddess **Bastet** was originally depicted as a lioness, her head surmounted by a solar disc and *uraeus* serpent. As the daughter of Re, she was associated with the destructive force of the sungod's eye. This aggressive side of Bastet can be seen in texts and reliefs describing the pharaoh in battle. Her epithet, "Lady of Asheru", also linked her to the goddess Mut at Karnak, where temple reliefs show the pharaoh running ritual races in front of Bastet.

After about 1000 BC, however, this aspect of Bastet became subsumed by Sekhmet (see p.325), and the goddess herself was portrayed more commonly as a cat, often with a brood of kittens, and carrying a sacred rattle. The *Coffin Texts* of the Middle Kingdom frequently invoke her protection as the first-born daughter of Atum (another aspect of the sun-god). In return, the Egyptians venerated cats and mummified them at several sites, including Bubastis and Memphis.

The Greeks later identified Bastet with Artemis, the Virgin Huntress, who was believed to be able to transform herself into a cat. It's also thought that cats came to Europe from Egypt during or before the fourth century AD.

Bastet

dealers for as little as £E3–4 apiece. From a tourist's standpoint, its attractions are the **Moulid of Abu Khalil**, held outside the main mosque sometime during the month of *Shawwal*, and the paltry ruins of Bubastis, to the southeast of town.

Whatever its shortcomings, Zagazig has the merit of being readily accessible. You can travel the 80km from Cairo by bus (1hr 30min; £E3.25) or *service* taxi (1hr; £E4.25) from the Aboud terminal; *service* taxis from the other major Delta towns and Alexandria also run to Zagazig, and there are hourly bus links with Ismailiya. Should you need to stay, there are two **hotels** (③) opposite the train station.

Bubastis

To reach the site of **Bubastis** (daily 9am–4pm; £E10), ask a taxi driver to take you to Tell Basta. While little remains but scattered blocks and gaping pits, archeologists have found here Old and New Kingdom cemeteries and vaulted catacombs full of feline mummies. The city was known to the ancient Egyptians as *Pr-Bastet* (House of Bastet), after the cat-goddess whom they honoured with licentious festivals. Pilgrims sailed here in high spirits, saluting riverside towns with music, abuse and exposed loins. In the fifth century BC, Herodotus noted that 700,000 revellers consumed more wine than "during the whole of the rest of the year", and described how the city lay on raised ground encircling a canal-girt temple, "the most pleasing to look at" in all of Egypt. Begun by the VI Dynasty pyramid-builders, Bubastis was enlarged and embellished for over 1700 years, attaining its apogee after its rulers established the XXII Dynasty, though the capital in this period was probably still Tanis (see p.528).

Bilbeis and Behna

To the south and southwest of Zagazig a couple of minor towns are worth a passing mention. **BILBEIS**, 10km away by road or rail, hosts a couple of festivals during *Shawwal*: its **moulids** of Abu Isa and Abu Alwan predate Abu Khalil's in Zagazig. Further west, beside the Damietta branch of the Nile, **BEHNA** (on the Cairo–Alex main line; daily half-hourly buses to Cairo 6am–9pm) is near another ancient site. To the northeast of town, 150m off the road, *Kom el-Atrib* is what remains of **Athribis**, once the capital of the Tenth Nome. This was the birthplace of Psammetichus I (664–610 BC), who restored pharaonic authority over Upper and Lower Egypt, replacing the so-called *Dodekarchy* with centralized government by the Saïte dynasty.

Tanis, Avaris and the "Land of Goshen"

Early archeologists were drawn to the eastern marches of the Delta in search of clues to the Israelites' Biblical sojourn, but what they found proved more important to knowledge of ancient Egypt. Fragmented statues and steles, papyrus texts and layers of debris have shed light on dynastic chronologies and religious cults, the movement of Delta waterways and imperial borders, invasions and famines. Fresh discoveries are still being made – particularly at Avaris, a site associated with the Hyksos "Shepherd Kings" who seized control of the Delta after the collapse of the Middle Kingdom, and which may also have been inhabited by the Israelites during their sojourn in Egypt. The following accounts simplify a mass of contradictory evidence and theories thrown up by archeologists.

Tanis

One of the oldest-known sites is a huge *kom* near the village of **San el-Hagar** (San of the Stones), 167km northeast of Zagazig. Barring a stint by Petrie, the excavation has mostly been in French hands since the 1860s. Although best known by its Greek name, **TANIS**, the city was called *Zoan* in the Bible and known to the ancient Egyptians as *Djanet*. It originally stood beside the Tanite branch of the Nile, which has long since dried up. In the film *Raiders of the Lost Ark*, it is here that Indiana Jones uncovers the Ark of the Covenant.

The **age and identity** of Tanis have been much debated, as scholars have frequently conflated it with Avaris, the capital of the Hyksos, or the much later city of Pi-Ramses, supposedly the "City of Bondage" from which the Israelites fled. In recent decades, however, both have been firmly identified with other sites (see below), and Tanis is now thought to have come into existence long afterwards, during the Third Intermediate Period. Some theorize that the XXI Dynasty founded Tanis as their capital at the same time as they abandoned the traditional cult of Seth in favour of the Theban Triad.

The desolate **site** looks as if the huge Ramessid **Temple of Amun** was shattered by a giant's hammer, scattering chunks of masonry and fragments of statues everywhere. Confusingly for scholars, the founders of Tanis plundered masonry from cities all over the Delta (some predating the Hyksos, who had earlier usurped it). In 1939, Pierre Montet discovered the **tombs of Psusennes II and Osorkon II**, containing the "Treasure of Tanis", which is now in the Cairo Museum. Perplexingly, it was soon noted that the tomb of the XXI Dynasty ruler Psusennes seems to have been built *after* that of Osorkon, who is supposed to have lived well over a century later, during the XXII Dynasty. Rohl argues that the two dynasties were actually contemporary, and that by assuming that they were sequential, archeologists have overestimated the duration of the Third Intermediate Period by at least 140 years – thus distorting the whole chronological basis of Egyptology.

While the site can be wandered at will, **getting there** is awkward. The best jumping-off point is **FAQUS**, 37km to the south, which can be reached by *service* taxi from Ismailiya, or by bus from Cairo's Aboud terminal (every 30min 8.30am–6pm). From Faqus, you can catch a local bus or *service* taxi to San el-Hagar, or rent a private taxi for the round trip.

Avaris

Since 1966, excavations by Manfred Bietak at **Tell ed-Daba** (Mound of the Heyena) have yielded many discoveries that have confirmed it as the site of **AVARIS**, the long-vanished **Hyksos** capital. The most sensational find, in 1991, were **Minoan-style frescoes** in a Hyksos-era palace on the western edge of the site, which evinces strong links with the Minoan civilization on Crete, 500 miles away, even if it doesn't disprove the idea that the Hyksos originated in Palestine or Syria. (The term Hyksos derives from *hekaukhasut*, "princes of foreign lands)". Painted as Cretan civilization reached its zenith, the murals feature Cretan mountain landscapes and acrobats vaulting over bulls, as in the Minoan frescoes at Knossos. Both the Minoans and the Hyksos are thought to have associated bulls with the worship of storm gods.

However, the Hyksos finds are only half the story, for Avaris existed long before their invasion, and may hold the key to early Biblical history. Before finding the frescoes, Bietak's team excavated what had been a hilly residential quarter, uncovering grave goods that suggested that the bulk of the population originated from Palestine and Syria. This lay above a stratum of evidence for an older, more sophisticated community of non-Egyptians, where 65 percent of the burials were of children below the age of two. Rohl argues that this represents the **Israelites** during their sojourn in Egypt and the culling of their male newborn by the "pharaoh who did not know Joseph", which places the events of Exodus in the reign of Djudmose of the XIII Dynasty, c. 1447 BC – two or three centuries earlier than is commonly accepted. The plagues that struck Egypt, followed by the Exodus, left the Delta exposed to invasion by the warlike nomads later known as the Hyksos. Having been taken over by these newcomers, Avaris remained the Hyksos capital until its destruction by Ahmosis I, the founder of the New Kingdom.

Tell ed-Dabba is only 7km from Faqus, and although the site is not yet officially open to tourists, you can get permission to visit from the Antiquities Department in Cairo.

The "Land of Goshen"
Many archeologists have striven to uncover the "**Land of Goshen**" where the Israelites toiled for the pharaoh before Moses led them out of Egypt – though some shrewdly plugged the Biblical connection to raise money for digs with other aims (notably Petrie at Tanis). Public opinion was fixated on the Biblical "store cities of Pithom and Raamses", speculatively assigned to many locations between Avaris and the Bitter Lakes (the area through which the Suez Canal runs). "Raamses" has usually been identified as Pi-Ramses, the royal city of the XIX Dynasty pharaoh Ramses II – which is why his successor, Merneptah, regularly gets fingered as the pharaoh of the Exodus. Conversely, Rohl argues that the Bible was really referring to Avaris, but using the name of the Ramessid city that existed at a later date, which would have been familiar due to Ramses II's wars in Palestine.

It is now certain that **Pi-Ramses** was centred on the modern-day village of **QANTIR**, 3km northeast of Tell ed-Daba, but extended far enough to cover most of Avaris, which had been laid to waste centuries earlier. A mud-brick palace dating to the earliest phase of the city was discovered in 1929, and Bietak's excavations have revealed barracks and workshops, also from the Ramessid era. Unfortunately for those who believe that this was the "City of Bondage", no evidence of a foreign population was found in any of the strata associated with the New Kingdom – whereas at Tell ed-Daba, there are extensive traces from the Middle Kingdom, and even mass graves that fit the Biblical account of a calamity. Rather, Pi-Ramses was a parvenu city founded by Seti I and turned into a royal capital by Ramses II, which had dwindled in significance by the end of the New Kingdom. Much of its stonework was later taken to Tanis or Bubastis during the XXI and XXII Dynasties; the most notable bits still *in situ* are the feet and one arm of a colossus of Ramses II, lying 50m apart in a field.

If the Israelites did flee from Avaris, what of the other cities mentioned in the book of Exodus – Pithom and Succoth? Here, the evidence is less conclusive, but they could well have been somewhere around **Tell el-Maskhuta**, an enormous *kom* off the road between Zagazig and Ismailiya. If Tell el-Maskhuta was really Pithom, then another *kom* a few kilometres to the west may have been Succoth.

To reach Sinai, the Israelites presumably went through Wadi Tumaylat, nowadays the route for traffic between Zagazig and Ismailiya (hourly buses). Before Tell el-Maskhuta, it passes **Tell el-Kebir**, where Orabi's rebellion was finally defeated by the British in September 1882. In the 1920s, the government sponsored a reforesting project in what was then virgin desert, and now supports plantations and orchards all the way to Ismailiya.

Mit Damsis and El-Mansura

Trains and inter-city buses take the shortest route **between Zagazig and El-Mansura**, and for most of the year that's a sensible option. In August, however, you might consider the alternative Mit Ghamr–Aga road in order to visit **Mit Damsis** village near the Damietta branch of the Nile, site of the Coptic **Moulid of St George**. Buses and *service* taxis **from Cairo** to El-Mansura, Zagazig and Faqus go from the Aboud terminal.

Mit Damsis

The **Moulid of St George** (August 2–28) is notable primarily for its **exorcisms**. Copts attribute demonic possession to improper baptism or deliberate curses, and specially trained priests bully and coax the *afrit* (demon) to leave through its victim's fingers or toes rather than via the eyes, which is believed to cause blindness.

Egyptian Muslims likewise believe in possession, but don't always regard it as malign; in some cases they try to harmonize the relationship between the spirit and its human host rather than terminate it. Egyptians of both faiths take precautions against the Evil Eye. Christians put store in pictures of St George and the Virgin, while Muslims display the Hand of Fatima – literally hand-printed on the walls of dwellings – and perhaps the legend *"B'ismallah, masha' Allah"* (In the name of God, whatever God wills).

Because the **moulid** is well attended there's a fair chance of lifts along the seven-kilometre track that turns west off the main road, 15km south of Aga. Mit Damsis rarely appears on maps; don't confuse it with Damas, which does.

El-Mansura

EL-MANSURA was founded as the camp of Sultan al-Kamil's army during the 1218–21 siege of Damietta, though its name ("The Victorious") was a premature boast, since the Crusaders reoccupied Damietta in 1247. Weakened by cancer and tuberculosis, Sultan Ayyub was unable to dislodge them, and died here in 1249 – a fact concealed by his widow, Shagar al-Durr, who issued orders in Ayyub's name, buying time until his heir could return from Iraq. Encouraged by the Mamlukes' withdrawal, Louis IX led a sortie against the enemy camp, slaying their general in his bath. But with victory in sight, the Crusaders fell sick after eating corpse-fed fish, just before a devastating counterattack launched by Beybars the Crossbowman. Louis was captured and ransomed for Damietta's return, and later met a similar fate on his Tunisian crusade.

The medieval house where Louis was imprisoned, **Beit Luqman**, still stands near the Mwafi Mosque, but most of today's El-Mansura is modern, with tree-lined avenues, a university, and a central mosque whose twin minarets are visible from far away. For outsiders, the town's most interesting feature is delicious buffalo-milk ice cream.

Buses run between Cairo and El-Mansura every quarter of an hour from 6am to 7pm, as do **service taxis**. These also link El-Mansura with Zagazig and Damietta, plus a number of sites in the Central Delta beyond the west bank suburb of Talkha. El-Mansura proper contains several **hotels**: worth a try are the *Marshal el-Gezirah* on

Sharia Gezirah el-Ward (☎050/368-888; ⑤); the *Cleopatra* at 13 Souk el-Toggar el-Gharby (☎050/341-234; ③); the *Marshal Hotel* on Midan Umm Kathoum (☎050/324-380; ③); or the *Abou Shama Hotel* on Sharia Bank Misr (050/345-227; ②).

The Monastery and Moulid of St Damyanah

Normally difficult to reach without private transport, the **Monastery of St Damyanah** becomes accessible during its namesake's **moulid** (May 15–20), when *service* taxis and private buses convey pilgrims across to the small town of Bilqas Qisim Awwal, whence it's 3km by track to Deir Sitt Damyanah.

The monastery – whose four churches date from the nineteenth and twentieth centuries – is, in fact, rather less interesting than **Damyanah's story** and her **festival**, which is one of the largest Christian moulids in Egypt. The daughter of a Roman governor under Diocletian, she refused to marry and insisted that her father build a palace into which she and forty other virgins could retire. All refused to worship Roman gods, and their example eventually converted her father – enraging Diocletian, who had the lot of them executed.

As with the Church of St George at Mit Damsis, Copts ascribe the building of Damyanah's shrine to St Helena, the mother of the Roman emperor Constantine. Pilgrims bring sick relatives (or livestock) to be blessed, and believe that Damyanah manifests herself at night as a pigeon, which can be distinguished from other birds by the trajectory of its flight. Icons and special pottery (inscribed "Happy returns, Damyanah") are popular buys at the fair, where Muslim tattooists do a brisk trade in St George, Christ on the cross, snakes, birds and other motifs, which punters select from display boards.

Damietta (Dumyat)

Sited near the mouth of the eastern branch of the Nile, the port city of **DAMIETTA** became prosperous in medieval times, through its trade in coffee, linen, dates and oil. However, it was always wide open to seaborne invasions and was seized by the Crusaders in 1167–68 and 1218–21, on the latter occasion accompanied by St Francis of Assisi – who ignorantly imagined that the Sultan al-Kamil knew nothing of Christianity, although he numbered Copts amongst his advisors. The main function of the Crusaders in Egypt, however, was pillage, and Damietta suffered heavily during its occupations. When Louis "the Pious" returned with a further crew in 1247, the inhabitants fled or deliberately sold the Crusaders contaminated fish – one cause of their defeat at El-Mansura (see above). Unfortunately, Damietta suffered a far worse attack under the Mamlukes, who razed the town and rendered its river impassable as a punishment for suspected disloyalty and a precaution against future invasions.

It was the Ottomans who revived the town and built "**Delta Style" mansions** of the kind found in Rosetta; their last pasha surrendered to the Beys here just before the rise of Mohammed Ali. With the opening of the Suez Canal, Damietta had to reorient its trade towards Port Said, some 70km away. Nowadays it's a thriving port city of 120,000 inhabitants, with the status of a provincial capital.

Having said that, there's little call to come here unless you're mad on Delta architecture, or into bird-watching or beachcombing. There are several modest **hotels** on the Nile-side Corniche, plus the *El-Manshy* (☎057/323-308; ③) on Sharia el-Nokrashy. As for **transport**, Damietta is linked by rail to Tanta, Zagazig, Alex and Cairo, and by hourly buses (6am–5pm) or *service* taxis to Cairo. Closer at hand are Port Said (30min drive along the causeway between Lake Manzala and the Med) and the beach resorts of the Central Delta.

Lake Manzala

East of Damietta lies **Lake Manzala**, a great place for **bird-watching** if you can find a boatman to take you through the reeds. Nineteenth-century European visitors tended to be more interested in shooting wildfowl than observing it. "Their compact mass formed living islands upon the water; and when the wind took me to these, a whole island rose up with a loud and thrilling din to become a feathered cloud in the air", wrote one hunter.

Winter is the best time to see herons (*balashon* to locals), spoonbills (*midwas*), pelicans (*begga*) and flamingoes (*basharus*). Along the Nile, these last are called "water camels" (*gamal el-bahr*).

Three Delta resorts

Ranged along the coast of the Central Delta are three beach resorts popular with middle-class Egyptians: **Ras el-Bahr**, **Gamasa** and **Baltim**. During summer, they can be reached by *service* taxis or special A/C buses from Cairo's Koulali terminal, near Midan Ramses. Buses and taxis from Damietta are another option, at least to Ras el-Bahr or Gamasa; Baltim is accessible by *service* taxi from El-Mansura. Out of season many of the resorts' hotels and summerhouses are boarded up.

RAS EL-BAHR, where the eastern branch of the Nile flows into the Med north of Damietta, is a pleasant beach resort with several restaurants and **hotels**. Try *Abu Tabl* (☎057/528-166; ④), *El-Mobasher* (☎057/527-097; ③) or *El-Salam* (☎057/528-156; ④). Across the river lies the busy fishing port of **Ezbet el-Bourg** (unmarked on most maps), named after an abandoned nineteenth-century **coastal fort** that's fun to explore. Hidden beneath a section of the walls is the **command bunker** (code-named Centre #10) containing seven small rooms in which Sadat's generals directed the October War of 1973.

During summer, Ras el-Bahr is readily accessible from Cairo by *service* or private **taxi** from the Koulali terminal, whence there are also **buses** (3hr 30min; £E14). Between 8am and 3pm, there are also hourly buses to **GAMASA**, further along the coast, which has two cabin-type **hotels**, *Beau Rivage* (☎057/760-268; ③) and *Hanoville* (☎057/760-750; ③), plus the slightly fancier *Amun* (☎057/760-660; ③), near the market.

The third resort, **BALTIM**, is actually halfway to Rosetta, but only accessible from there by a long detour inland. It has a couple of simple **hotels**, the *Baltim Beach* (☎047/501-451; ①) and *Cleopatra* (no phone; ①).

CHAPTER SIX

THE CANAL ZONE

N o longer feted as a triumph of nineteenth-century engineering, nor regarded as the linchpin of Britain's empire, the **Suez Canal** seems as Joseph Conrad described it: "a dismal but profitable ditch", connecting the Red Sea and the Mediterranean. Except around the harbour mouths or where ships are glimpsed between sandbanks, it's a pretty dull waterway, too, relieved only by the Canal cities of Port Said and Ismailiya.

With its evocative waterfront, prosaic beaches and duty-free shopping, **Port Said** feels like Alexandria minus its cultural baggage – and a place that's somehow more authentic as a maritime city. By contrast, the canal scarcely impinges on the leafy, villa-lined streets of **Ismailiya**, once the residence of the Suez Canal Company's European staff and now a popular honeymoon destination. Foreigners generally overlook both cities, prejudging them on the basis of **Suez**, a neglected city but a vital transport nexus between Cairo, Sinai and the Red Sea Coast.

Heading to Sinai, bus passengers (or car drivers) cross the Suez Canal at either the **Ahmed Hamdi Tunnel** (12km north of Suez City) or the **car ferry** 7km north of Ismailiya; at **Qantara**, between Ismailiya and Port Said, there's a passenger ferry across to East Qantara, whence *service* taxis run to El-Arish in Sinai, though these days buses and *service* taxis also run direct to El-Arish from Ismailiya. Drivers should be aware that stretches of the canal are **off limits** and should stick to main routes to avoid questioning by the military.

The canal's history

The **first attempts** to link the Red Sea and the Mediterranean by means of a canal are usually attributed to Necho II (610–595 BC) of the XXVI Dynasty. Herodotus claims that 120,000 workers had died before the project was abandoned after an oracle predicted that only Egypt's foes would benefit from it. Sure enough, it was the Persian emperor **Darius**, around 500 BC, who completed the first canal in the region, linking the Red Sea and the Great Bitter Lake, whence an older waterway created by Ramses II connected with Bubastis on the Nile and thence to the Mediterranean.

Refined by the Ptolemies and Trajan (who added an extension leading to Babylon-in-Egypt), this system of waterways was restored by **Amr** following the Muslim conquest

---

ACCOMMODATION PRICE CODES

Throughout the guide, hotels and pensions are graded on a scale of ① to ⑨, indicating the price (including tax) of the **cheapest double room** in each establishment in high season (for places that offer **dorm beds**, rates per person are given in £E). Please note that most hotels in categories ⑧ and ⑨ quote rates in US$, but will accept payment in £E. For a full explanation of the following categories, see p.46. The price bands to which these codes refer are as follows:

① under £E20/US$7	④ £E45–65/US$15–20	⑦ £E150–300/US$50–100
② £E20–30/US$7–10	⑤ £E65–100/US$20–35	⑧ US$100–200/£E300–600
③ £E30–45/US$10–15	⑥ £E100–150/US$35–50	⑨ US$200/£E600 upwards

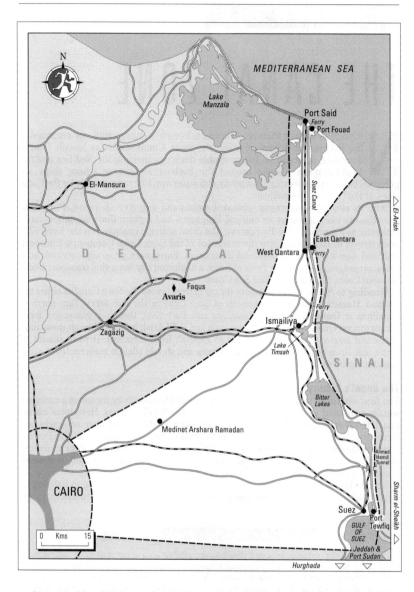

and was used for shipping corn to Arabia until the eighth century, when it was deliberately abandoned to starve out rebels in Medina. Although the Venetians, Crusaders and Ottomans all considered renewing the old system, the idea of a canal running direct between the Red Sea and the Mediterranean was first mooted – and then vetoed – by Napoleon's engineers, who miscalculated a difference of ten metres between the two sea levels.

The discovery of their error, in the 1840s, encouraged a junior French consul, **Ferdinand de Lesseps**, to present his own plan to Said Pasha, who approved it despite British objections. ("It cannot be made, it shall not be made; but if it were made there would be a war between England and France for the possession of Egypt," Palmerston asserted.)

Work began at the Mediterranean end in 1859 and continued throughout the reign of Said's successor, Ismail (hence the names of Port Said and Ismailiya). Of the twenty thousand Egyptians employed in the **construction of the Suez Canal**, a great many died from accidents or cholera, while Ismail himself went bankrupt attempting to finance his one-third share of the £19 million sterling investment, most of which went on bankers' charges.

In 1875, Ismail was forced to sell his shares to Britain for a mere £4 million sterling and the Suez Canal effectively became an imperial concession. By appealing to the Rothschilds for a loan over dinner, Prime Minister Disraeli bought Ismail's shares before France could make an offer, and reported to Queen Victoria: "You have it, Madam." When the canal finally opened in 1888, its vast profits went abroad with the **Suez Canal Company**, which acted as a state within a state, while two world wars saw the **Canal Zone** transformed into the largest military base on earth.

Following the end of World War II nationalist protests against the British presence grew, and guerrilla attacks in the Zone led to the British assault on Ismailiya's police barracks that sparked "Black Saturday" in Cairo (see p.108). After the 1952 Revolution, Egypt's new leaders demanded the withdrawal of British forces and a greater share of the canal's revenue, and when the West refused to make loans to finance the Aswan High Dam, Nasser announced the canal's **nationalization** (July 26, 1956). Britain and France tried to hamper this process, smearing Nasser as an "Arab Hitler". Israel's advance into Sinai that October became the agreed pretext for them to "safeguard" the canal by bombarding and invading its cities. But by standing firm and appealing to outraged world opinion, Nasser emerged victorious from the **Suez Crisis**.

The battered Canal cities had hardly recovered when the **1967 War** with Israel caused further damage and blocked the canal with sunken vessels. The canal was closed and Suez was evacuated during the "War of Attrition" that dragged on until 1969, while Israel fortified the **Bar-Lev Line** along the east bank, which the Egyptians stormed during the **October War** of 1973 (known as the *10th Ramadan* or *Yom Kippur* war, respectively, to Arabs and Israelis). Although the canal was reopened to shipping in 1975, both sides remained dug in on opposite banks until 1982, when Israel withdrew from Sinai. While the canal was closed, supertankers were built to travel around Africa – and were too large to pass through Suez once it reopened.

Despite this, the canal today handles up to ninety ships a day, carrying 14 percent of the world's trade; the direction of traffic is alternated, with an average transit time of fifteen hours. At 167km long, it's the third longest canal in the world and the longest without locks; current plans to deepen the canal and double its width render further statistics pointless.

Suez (El-Suweis) and Port Tewfiq (Bur Tewfiq)

Since its devastation by Israeli bombardments, and the evacuation of almost the entire population between 1967 and 1973, **SUEZ** has risen from the rubble to reclaim its inheritance. Unlike Port Said and Ismailiya, the city's history long predates the canal, going back to Ptolemaic *Klysma*. As Arabic *Qulzum*, the port prospered from the spice trade

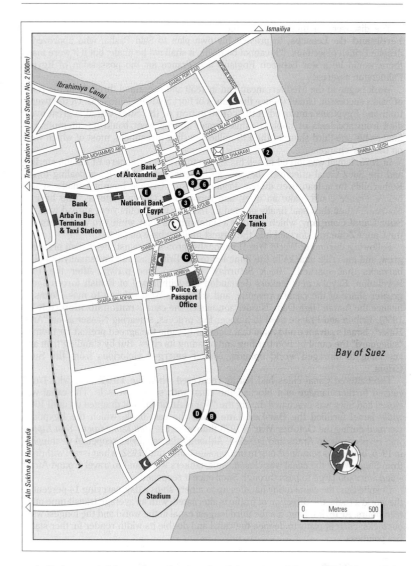

and pilgrimages to Mecca throughout medieval times, remaining a walled city until the eighteenth century, when Eliza Fay described it as "the Paradise of Thieves". The canal brought modernization and assured revenues, later augmented by the discovery of oil in the Gulf of Suez. All this was lost during the wars with Israel, requiring a massive reconstruction programme financed by the Gulf states. While noxious petrochemical refineries, cement and fertilizer plants ring the outskirts, most of the city's 300,000 inhabitants have been rehoused in prefabricated estates or the patched-up remnants of older quarters.

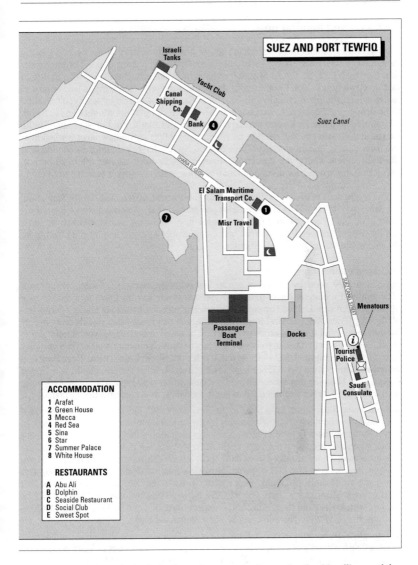

What Suez lacks in looks is made up for to some degree by the friendliness of the local people. For the foreign visitor however, it's best to dress for the city wherever you are, saving your shorts and skimpy tops for the beaches of Sinai. The lack of things to do in Suez is perhaps most keenly felt by the city's young people, most of whom spend their evenings hanging out and smoking joints – the monotony broken only by their home team playing football in the city's stadium. Despite its important contribution to the Egyptian economy, Suez has yet to see significant investment in its infrastructure. Its residents seem to feel they have been largely forgotten by their government.

Arrival – and moving on

Like the other Canal cities, Suez has regular connections with **Cairo** by bus (hourly 6am–6.30pm; £E7) and *service* taxi (more frequently; £E5), from either Turgoman station (see map p.74) or the Al Mazah Terminal in Heliopolis. Both cover the 134km in just over two hours. Don't bother with the hot and uncomfortable trains from Cairo (6 daily), which run on to Ismailiya (6–7hr). Arriving by bus or *service* taxi, you're bound to be dropped at Suez's Arba'in Terminal, where you can get bus connections to **Sinai, Alexandria** and **the Delta** and also *service* taxis to Hurghada. For buses to **Hurghada, Luxor** and **Aswan** you will need to take a minibus (50pt) to the new bus terminal near the train station, known simply as "Bus Station No. 2". There's an information kiosk at the train station where you can check times, but schedules change often, so be prepared to hang around for a connection. The train station – which you are unlikely to need – is 1.5km west of the Arba'in Terminal (50pt by minibus).

For the benefit of people arriving by ship, the **tourist office** (Sat–Thurs 8am–3pm, Fri 9am–2pm; ☎069/331-141) and **tourist police** (24hr) are way out on the edge of Port Tewfiq, on Suez Canal St; you can catch a minibus out along Sharia el-Geish as far as the Passenger Terminal. The tourist office can supply a decent map of the city, but little else in the way of useful information.

Overland connections

Suez is mainly seen by travellers as an **interchange between Cairo, Sinai and Hurghada**. If money is really tight, and you are heading from Cairo to Sinai (or vice versa), you can save £E10–30 by switching transport in Suez, instead of taking a direct bus all the way. Travelling overland from Hurghada, you can reach Suez rapidly and cheaply by *service* taxi, and then get other transport on to Sinai. In both cases you should aim to reach Suez by noon, to be sure of getting a bus to your destination – otherwise you may have to stay overnight. Arba'in bus terminal is for the **Sinai, Cairo, Alex, Port Said** and **Ismailiya**; Bus Station No. 2 (25pt by microbus from Arba'in) for **Hurghada** and **Upper Egypt**. Note however that *service* taxis for all destinations still leave from outside Arba'in terminal. For **El Arish** you will need to get to Ismailiya, then pick up a bus or taxi.

● **Sinai** Most of the buses from Suez to the Sinai start their journey in Cairo. In the past this meant you couldn't always find a seat by the time the bus arrived in Suez. However, direct Superjet buses between Cairo and Sharm el-Sheikh – that don't stop in Suez – are proving popular, lessening demand on the East Delta buses that do, so seat availability has improved. There are five buses daily from Suez to **Sharm el-Sheikh** (8am, 11am, 1.30pm, 3pm & 6pm; 6hr; £E25), two to **Nuweiba** (noon & 3pm; 5hr 30min; £E30), and one each to **Dahab** (12.30pm; 9hr; £E30), **Taba** (3pm; 6hr 30min; £E30) and **St Catherine's Monastery** (2pm; 6hr; £E£25). *Service* taxis are often quicker but will be packed with bodies and there's no A/C – expect to pay around £E35 to Dahab, £E20 to St Catherine's, £E25 to Nuweiba and £E25 to Sharm el-Sheikh.

● **Ismailiya** Buses run every half-hour (6am–4.30pm; 45min–1hr; £E4), and *service* taxis just as frequently (45min; £E5). There are also five buses daily to **Port Said** (7am, 9am, 11.15am, 12.15pm & 3.30pm; 2hr; £E9), a *service* taxi will cost £E10. There are frequent *service* taxis to **Qantara** (see p.546).

● **Alexandria** Two buses daily (7am & 2.30pm; 6hr; £E25), which need to be booked the day before. *Service* taxis charge £E20.

● **Cairo** Buses leave every 30min (£E7) throughout the day.

● **Hurghada** Nine buses daily (6am–10pm; 6–8hr; £E21–26), leave from Bus Staion No. 2; most of these also stop at the nearer Red Sea resort of **Ain Sukhna** (1hr; £E5). *Service* taxis (4–5hr; £E25 per person) leave from Arba'in terminal.

• **Upper Egypt** Buses to Luxor (8am, 2pm & 8pm; £E29–38) and Aswan (5am, 12pm & 5pm; £E36–48) also leave from Bus Station No 2. You can also get buses from here to Assyut (7am & 7pm; £E20–22) and Qena (6am; £E26–33).

International ferries

Suez is the point of departure for passenger **boats to Saudi Arabia and Sudan**; the former are used by migrant workers or pilgrims, the latter by a few determined travellers. Ferries to the Saudi port of **Jeddah** sail every day, and there are additional sailings during the *Hadj* season (six weeks either side of the Muslim month of *Zoul Hagga*). Boats leave around 2pm and arrive in Jeddah around 10am three days later. Prices start at £E125 for deck space and £E220 per person in a four-berth 2nd class cabin (1st class £E250–270). Providing there's not a storm, sleeping on deck represents no real hardship. Whether boats carry on to **Port Sudan** is hard to predict as schedules change from month to month. Optimists should enquire at Misr Travel (☎069/223-949), El Salam Maritime Transport Co. (☎069/326-251 or 326-252) or Menatours (☎069/228-821), all in Port Tewfiq.

Be warned that they won't sell you a **ticket** unless you already have the right visa(s). The Saudi consulate in Port Tewfiq has sections for work and *Hadj* **visas** but tourist visas can be harder to obtain, so it might be a better idea to get a transit visa in Cairo, where you can also obtain a Sudanese visa – *inshallah*. Should you succeed, the ferry takes a week to get to Port Sudan so take enough food and drink for the journey.

Accommodation

Outside of the *Hadj* season, **finding a room** in Suez should be easy. Except where indicated, breakfast is not included in the rates given below.

Arafat Hotel, off Sharia el-Geish in Port Tewfiq (☎069/338-355). Clean, small rooms with balconies and fans, some with bathrooms. The only budget option if you need to stay in the Port area. Manager has information about passenger ships for Saudi Arabia etc. ②–③.

Green House Hotel, corner Sharia el-Geish and El Nabi Mousa St (☎069/331-553, fax 331-554). Smarter sister of the *White House* (see below) though still a little run down. Clean A/C rooms with Gulf views. Swimming pool. No bar, but serves Stella (£E8). Popular with foreign engineers based in the area. ⑦.

Red Sea, Port Tewfiq (☎069/334-302, fax 334-301). Clean and comfortable A/C rooms with bath, phone, balcony and satellite TV – the smartest hotel in Suez. Sixth floor *Mermaid Restaurant* has great views of the canal. Breakfast included. ⑦.

Sina, 21 Sharia Banque Misr (☎069/334-181). Small rooms with fans, TV and clean shared bathrooms, with a fridge on each floor. A good, central, low-budget option. ②.

Star, 17 Sharia Banque Misr (☎069/228-737). A mixture of large and small rooms with fans and balconies; some have baths. Another good budget option, a little cheaper than the *Sina*. ②.

Summer Palace, Port Tewfiq (☎069/224-475, fax 321-944). Run-to-seed three-star hotel, chiefly notable for its Gulf views and freshwater pool. Overpriced, but worth a visit to its alfresco café to enjoy the views. ⑦.

White House, 322 Sharia el-Geish (☎069/331-550). Recently chose to drop its rating by one star (now down to only two) to reduce the price of rooms. Clean, slightly shabby rooms with A/C, TV and bathroom. The bar is gone, but they still serve beer. Restaurant and international phone; breakfast included. ④.

The City

Should you decide to stay (or simply pass a few hours between buses), Suez City is readily accessible from the Arba'in terminal – just follow the alley past some motor dealers to reach **Sharia el-Geish** (Army Street), a two-kilometre-long swathe where cruising minibuses drop and collect passengers along the way to Port Tewfiq. Dusty palms and decrepit colonial-era buildings (including several churches) are followed by a strip of hotels, restaurants and currency exchanges. The stadium on Tariq el-Horriya in the south of the city, is home to Suez FC, enthusiastically supported by the local residents.

The backstreets to the south of El-Geish harbour cheap cafés, while **Sharia Sa'ad Zaghloul** runs past consulates and a fun park towards the Governorate. North of El-Geish, a tawdry souk overflows **Sharia Haleem**, presaging a quarter of workshops and chandlers, crumbling century-old apartments with wooden balconies interspersed by modern low-rises. There's a better **bazaar** to the northwest of the Arba'in bus station.

Along the Bay of Suez promenade and the main **corniche** around **PORT TEWFIQ**'s northeastern corner stand four US-made **tanks** captured from Israel in the 1973 War.

Should you happen to be here in spring, migratory **birds of prey** provide a more arresting sight. Griffon vultures and Imperial and Steppe eagles overfly Suez to avoid crossing the Red Sea, which lacks the rising thermals on which they depend for flight. A more permanent resident is the Indian House crow – recognizable by its ear-splitting *caaarrrr* – which is thought to have arrived from India on ships during the course of last century.

Eating, drinking and other practicalities

Eating out in Suez is limited but adequate. Your best bet for seafood is the *Dolphin* restaurant on Tariq El-Horiya, opposite the Social Club (which also does seafood), or *Abu Ali's* on Sharia el-Geish, near the *White House*. For good value *shawarma*, sandwiches or baked macaroni, check out the *Sweet Spot*, also on Sharia el-Geish, west of the *White House*. For *kushari* there's *Al Tabareh Restaurant* on Sharia Banque Misr near the *Star Hotel*.

Drinking is even more limited, with only one bar, the *Sant George* (next to *Sweet Spot*), where you can be sure of finding Suez's expat community gathered in the evening.

You can **change money** at the Bank of Alexandria on Sharia el-Geish (daily: summer 9am–2pm & 5–8pm; winter 8am–2pm & 6–9pm), the National Bank of Egypt on Sharia Sa'ad Zaghloul (Sun–Thurs 8.30am–2pm & 5–8pm), private exchanges in the souk, or the Banque du Caire in Port Tewfiq (Sun–Thurs 8.30am–2pm & 5–8pm). Also in Port Tewfiq is Menatours (☎069/228-821), the agents for **American Express** (beside the tourist police) and a branch of the **post office** – the main one is on Sharia Hoda Sharawi, in the centre of town (both daily except Fri 8am–3pm). You can make international calls from the **telephone exchange** (daily 8am–midnight) on the corner of Sa'ad Zaghloul and el-Shahada, or extend your visa at the **passport office** (Sat–Thurs 8am–2pm) inside **police** headquarters on Sharia Horriya; as always, arrive early with your passport and photo, a pen, something to read and a sense of humour.

Ismailiya

ISMAILIYA's schizoid character is defined by the rail line that cuts across the city. South of the tracks lies the European-style **garden city** built for foreign employees of the Suez Canal Company, extending to the verdant banks of the Sweetwater Canal. Following careful restoration, its leafy boulevards and placid streets of colonial villas look almost as they must have done in the 1930s, with bilingual street signs nourishing the illusion that the British empire has just popped indoors for cocktails.

North of the train tracks you move into another world of hastily constructed flats grafted onto long-standing **slums**, and a quarter financed by the Gulf Emirates that provides a *cordon sanitaire* for the wealthy suburb of **Nemrah Setta** (Number Six). This

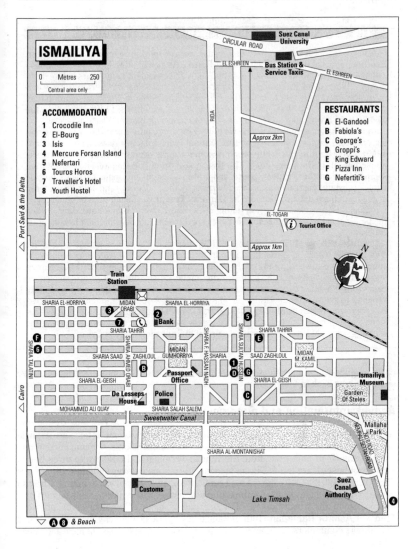

ISMAILIYA

0 | Metres | 250
Central area only

ACCOMMODATION
1 Crocodile Inn
2 El-Bourg
3 Isis
4 Mercure Forsan Island
5 Nefertari
6 Touros Horos
7 Traveller's Hotel
8 Youth Hostel

RESTAURANTS
A El-Gandool
B Fabiola's
C George's
D Groppi's
E King Edward
F Pizza Inn
G Nefertiti's

Janus-profile reflects the city's twentieth-century **history**, when two disparate sons of Ismailiya had a lasting effect on Egyptian society. **Hassan el-Banna** created the Muslim Brotherhood that was the bane of the British, and has vexed Egypt's rulers since independence (see box below). Two generations later, Ismailiya became synonymous with **Osman Ahmed Osman**, a self-made millionaire contractor whom Sadat appointed as Minister of Housing and Reconstruction in 1975. As Gulf investments poured into the Canal Zone, billboard-sized pictures of Osman began to outnumber those of his patron, who finally agreed to opposition demands for an audit. By the time it was discovered that millions had been stashed in Swiss banks, Osman had fled the

THE MUSLIM BROTHERHOOD AND THE BATTLE OF ISMAILIYA

Ismailiya – the most Europeanized of Egyptian towns – was the birthplace of the **Muslim Brotherhood** and its founder, **Hassan el-Banna**. As a child, El-Banna nailed up leaflets calling upon Muslims to renounce gold and silks, and awoke his neighbours before dawn prayers. When older he campaigned against female emancipation, delivering fiery sermons in rented cafés. He founded the *Ikhwan el-Muslimeen* in 1928 and within fifteen years the Brotherhood had spread throughout Egypt and spawned offshoots across the Middle East, articulating an Islamic response to modernization on Western terms.

From campaigning for moral renewal it went on to organize paramilitary training and terrorist cells, and was outlawed by King Farouk (whose agents assassinated El-Banna) in 1949. Despite this, the Brotherhood mounted attacks against the British and an economic boycott in the Canal Zone. The British suspected that they received arms from sympathizers in the Egyptian police and tried to disarm the main barracks outside Ismailiya, whose garrison was ordered to resist by their superiors and only surrendered after fifty of them had been killed. The **Battle of Ismailiya** (January 25, 1952) outraged Egyptians and provoked an orgy of rioting in Cairo next day – **"Black Saturday"** – when the police stood by as Brotherhood activists sped around in jeeps, torching foreign properties.

Legalized after the 1952 Revolution, the Brotherhood was soon suppressed again for trying to kill Nasser in Alexandria. Hundreds of Brothers spent years in concentration camps, until amnestied by President Sadat, who sought to co-opt them as a counterweight to the left. Eventually, their growing influence and criticism of his policies led Sadat to jail them *en masse*, whereupon his assassination by *Al-Jihad* proved that other groups had grown up in the Brotherhood's shadow and surpassed it in radicalism. To isolate these new militants, Mubarak, too, wooed the Brotherhood with all kinds of concessions short of legalization, but in **recent years** has turned against them, ordering the arrest of scores of Brothers and the closure of their headquarters in Cairo.

country. Subsequent investigations into his political connections proved inconclusive and he is now back in business.

Arrival, information and accommodation

Although Ismailiya can be reached by train (6 daily; 3–5hr), buses or taxis are a quicker way of **getting there from Cairo**. Buses (every 30min 6.30am–6.30pm; £E6.50) and *service* taxis (£E6) both leave from the Koulali Terminal and take two to three hours. East Delta buses leave the Al Mazah terminal in Heliopolis (every 40min 7am–7.30pm; £E6.50). The 120-kilometre desert road runs through two places worth noting. **Khanka** contains Egypt's main asylum for the criminally insane, which has made its name a popular synonym for "totally crazy". Further out, a spate of country clubs presages **Medinet Ashara Ramadan** (10th of Ramadan City), a satellite city for the new breed of Cairene commuters, complete with quasi-American suburban homes and steak houses.

All buses and *service* taxis wind up at the new **bus station** on the ring road outside Ismailiya, opposite the massive Suez Canal University building. From here take a taxi (£E2) or microbus (50pt) into the town centre.

The old town's grid-plan and clearly named streets make **orientation** a doddle. The **tourist office** is inside the new Governorate Building on El-Togari Street, in the north of the city 2km from downtown (daily except Fri 9am–2pm; ☎064/321-072 or 321-076); it's an inconvenient location and does little other than supply a booklet with some information and a map. Hotel staff are likely to prove more informative and helpful.

Accommodation

Apart from a couple of smart hotels, most of Ismailiya's accommodation has seen better days. However, the majority of the hotels are safe, reasonably clean and cheap, and Ismailiya only really gets busy during festivals and the summer season – May to September – when it's a popular honeymoon destination for Egyptian couples. Finding accommodation at other times should be easy, with some hotels likely to be empty – a fact reflected by a general lack of atmosphere in town. Breakfast is included in rates given below unless indicated otherwise.

Crocodile Inn, 172 Sharia Sa'ad Zaghloul (☎064/331-555, fax 331-666). The only reasonably smart hotel in the town centre, with a restaurant and 24-hour coffee shop. Nice A/C rooms with balconies, but overpriced. ⑦.

El-Bourg (or *New Palace*), Midan Orabi (☎064/326-327, fax 327-761). A wonderfully pretentious nineteenth-century pile with A/C rooms, satellite TV and private baths. Popular with honeymooners, so often full. A good value option, especially for those travelling on their own, with single rooms just £E35 including breakfast. ④.

Isis, Midan Orabi (☎064/357-821). A range of rooms with fans. Friendly, helpful staff. Reductions for long-staying guests. A low-budget option. Breakfast extra £E4. ②–③.

Mercure Forsan Island, 2km from town (☎064/338-040, fax 338-043). Leafy four-star resort set in 50 acres of grounds. A/C rooms and villas with satellite TV, minibar and international phone. Swimming pool and watersports. ⑨.

Nefetari, 41 Sharia Sultan Hussein (☎064/322-822, fax 321-108). A good choice with agreeable rooms, some with A/C and private baths. ④.

Touros Horos, on Sharia Talatini, next to *Pizza Inn* (☎064/333-990). Basic rooms with fans on a lively and somewhat noisy street. Not recommended for single female travellers as you might have to share bathrooms with Egyptian men, but worth considering for a largish group on a tight budget. Friendly staff. No lift and a lot of stairs. Breakfast £E3 extra. ②.

Traveller's Hotel, Sharia Ahmed Orabi (☎064/358-304). Also called *Hotel des Voyageurs*. Colonial-style hotel that's stronger on atmosphere than creature comforts. Nice rooms with balconies, but no restaurant or anything much else. Fans on request. No breakfast. ②.

Youth hostel, at Sharia Imhara Siyahi, 1km from the centre and £E2 by taxi (☎ & fax 064/322-850). Overlooks Lake Timsah and has its own beach. It has 26 double, triple or six-person rooms with private baths. Double £E44 with breakfast; dorm bed £E18.50. Non-members pay £E1 extra.

The Town and around

Ismailiya's carefully restored old town is a pleasure to walk or bike around, shaded by pollarded trees. Most of the sights can be reached on foot within ten minutes, although a couple of places outside town warrant renting a bicycle in the backstreets off Mohammed Ali Quay, or catching a *service* taxi from the turn-off near Mallaha Park.

Starting on Mohammed Ali Quay, first on the trail is the large, vaguely Swiss-looking **House of Ferdinand de Lesseps**, who lived here during the canal's construction. Disappointingly, you can only visit the interior if you're some kind of VIP, since the house now serves as a private hotel for guests of the Suez Canal Authority. In De Lesseps's study, books and photographs are scattered around his desk and bed as if the Frenchman had been reviewing his life's work, while his carriage stands outdoors, encased in glass. Lone visitors might chance a peek inside if the rear gate is open; otherwise, you could try presenting yourself at the Suez Canal Authority and bluffing the press officer into fixing a visit – though this could well prove a waste of time.

A pleasant fifteen minutes' walk down the street from the De Lesseps House, the **Ismailiya Museum** (Sat–Thurs 9.30am–4pm, Fri and during Ramadan 9.30am–2pm; £E6) leans towards ancient history, devoting a section to the waterways of Ramses and Darius. The highlights of its collection of four thousand Greco-Roman and pharaonic artefacts is a lovely mosaic from the fourth century AD, depicting Phaedra, Dionysos,

Eros and Hercules. Other sections cover the canal in modern history, the Battle of Ismailiya and the "Crossing" of October 1973.

With permission from the museum, one can also visit some plaques and obelisks from Ramses II's time, in the **Garden of Steles** down the road, past the guarded residence of the head of the Canal Authority. It's nicer to wander amid the 500 acres of exotic shrubs and trees of **Mallaha Park**, or stroll alongside the shady **Sweetwater Canal** that was dug to provide fresh water for labourers building the Suez Canal. Previously, supplies had to be brought across the desert by camels, or shipped across Lake Manzala to Port Said.

Lake Timsah

Notwithstanding its name, "Crocodile Lake", there are several nice **beaches** around **Lake Timsah**, which you can reach by taking a taxi or walking 1km out along Sharia Talatini. You can dine outside near picturesque fishing boats, or pay £E5–10 to use the manicured lawns and beaches of the smart resort clubs (which may include snacks and drinks in the deal), but you might find many of these places are closed outside of high season. Wealthier citizens patronize the *Mercure Forsan Island* with its **waterskiing, windsurfing** and **tennis** facilities; you can use the beach and swimming pool for £E20, or £E50 on Fridays and holidays, when the price includes a buffet lunch or barbeque.

The Bar-Lev Line and other excursions

Service taxis turning off near Mallaha Park are usually bound for "Ferri Setta" (50pt), outside town, where locals use a **ferry crossing** to the east bank of the canal. Here, a vast sand rampart breached by deep cuts marks the former **Bar-Lev Line**, named after the Israeli general who designed it. Intended to stall any attack on Sinai for 48 hours, this 25-metre-high embankment was defended by forty mined strongpoints. In the event, they were totally surprised by Egypt's assault on **October 6, 1973**. As hidden artillery opened up at 2pm, eight thousand commandos dragged launches to the water's edge, roared across the 180-metre-wide canal and scaled the ramparts with ladders. Within hours, high-pressure hoses ordered from Bavaria "for the Cairo Fire Department" were blasting gaps for the Egyptian armour massing behind pontoon bridge layers.

However, although "The Crossing" was an Egyptian triumph (still remembered with pride), the war subsequently turned against them. An Israeli force under Ariel Sharon counterattacked across the canal between Lake Timsah and the Great Bitter Lake, wheeled inland to cut the Cairo–Suez road, and had virtually encircled the Egyptian army in Sinai by the time the superpowers imposed a ceasefire. Disengagement on the ground began with UN-sponsored talks at **Kilometre 101** – the nearest Israeli tanks came to Cairo.

A more scenic but distant view of the canal can be had from **Nemrah Setta**, an exclusive suburb of French colonial-style villas on a hilltop outside town, where, in 1969, an Israeli shell killed the Egyptian Chief of Staff, General Abdul-Monaim Riad. To get there costs £E2–3 by private taxi, or take a *service* taxi from Midan Orabi to "Ferri Setta" (50pt) and walk up the hill.

The surrounding countryside also has its charms. By taking a *service* taxi (£E2) from the bus station, out to **El-Mahsama**, and alighting at Dr Hassan's Hospital, you can walk along the Nile tributary past fields irrigated by archaic water-pumps and old men on donkeys – a scene redolent of the Biblical land of Goshen.

Eating, nightlife and other practicalities

Ismailiya is good for **eating out**. When the weather's fine, citizens dine alfresco near the fishing port on Lake Timsah; it's worth the cost of a taxi (£E2–3) out along Sharia

Talatini to eat fish straight from the lake. You might even risk the local speciality, *Umm el-Khaloul* – a kind of shellfish that's best avoided during hot weather. Otherwise, there are several decent restaurants in the centre. The most popular **drinking** spots are *King Edward* (see listings below) and the bar at the *Mercure Forsan Island*, both of which attract an interesting crowd as the night wears on. Alternatively, most of the evening streetlife can be found around Sharia Talatini, Sharia Sa'ad Zaghloul and Sharia el-Geish, where shops, cafés and juice bars are open late into the night.

You can't miss the **post office** (daily except Fri 9am–4pm) and 24-hour **telephone exchange** on Midan Orabi, nor the **passport office** (Sat–Thurs 8am–2pm). You can **change money** at the Bank of Alexandria or National Bank of Egypt (both Sat–Thurs 8.30am–2pm, 5–8pm, Fri 8.30am–12pm; the latter takes Visa and MasterCard) just off Midan Orabi, but you'll get a slightly better rate for cash at the exchange at 22 Ahmed Orabi, near the *Traveller's Hotel*. There are several **pharmacies**, including one near the *Isis* on Sharia el-Horriya and another on Sharia Sa'ad Zaghoul. To buy or develop **film**, try either Kodak or Fuji, both near *Groppi's*. Fuji sells slide and Advantix film.

Restaurants

El-Gandool, the best fish restaurant on Lake Timsah, is past Fayrouz Beach; a £E2–3 taxi ride from town. £E10–20 for their tasty fish dishes.

Fabiola's, off Sharia Sa'ad Zaghloul. Inexpensive pizza joint, but don't bother if empty as this could mean a long wait for mediocre food. Daily 11am–11pm.

George's, Sharia Sultan Hussein. Quiet, A/C Greek restaurant specializing in seafood and kebab. Has a well-stocked bar, the only one in town. £E14–38 for a full meal. Daily 11am–1am.

Groppi's, Sharia Sultan Hussein. Branch of the Cairo patisserie chain. Open 9.30am–9.30pm; closed Sun and during the first half of Ramadan.

King Edward, 171 Sharia Tahrir (☎064/325-451). A/C haunt of expats and affluent natives, offering tasty Continental and Egyptian food (main dishes £E10–30), wine and beer. DJ plays Western and Middle Eastern music, but don't expect it to get going till after 11pm.

Pizza Inn, 41 Sharia Talatini. Busy take-out and sit-down eatery for burgers (from £E4) and pizzas (from £E6). Free delivery. Daily 10am–2am.

Nefertiti's, Sharia Sultan Hussein (☎064/220-494). Specializes in fish (£E15–20) and shrimps (£E36), but does meat dishes, too. Sells beer and wine. Daily noon–midnight.

Festivals

Should you happen to be here around Easter, Ismailiya is a good place to witness the spring festival of **Shams el-Nessim**, when families picnic in the park between the Sweetwater Canal and Lake Timsah, and a **Flower Festival** adds colour to the occasion.

Even better is the "**Doll-Burning**" or **Limbo Festival**, held a week later. Its curious title refers to a hated nineteenth-century local governor – Limbo Bey – effigies of whom were torched by the citizenry. Ever since then, it has been customary to burn dolls resembling one's pet hate: footballers are popular targets whenever Ismailiya's soccer club does poorly. The dolls are burned on the streets after dark.

Moving on

To get anywhere from Ismailiya, it's back to the bus station on the ring road opposite the new Suez Canal University building. Private taxis (£E2–3) or *service* taxis (50pt) to the bus station leave from the rank outside the train station in the city centre.

● **North Sinai** Buses leave six times a day for **El-Arish** (8.30am, 9am, 10am, 12pm, 3.30pm & 5pm; 3hr; £E10); *service* taxis cost £E6. There are also *service* taxis to **Rafah** (£E8).

● **South Sinai** Buses leave throughout the day and night to **Sharm el-Sheikh** (6.30am–midnight; 6hr; £E31), two of which carry on to **Dahab** (2.30pm & midnight; 7–8hr; £E36). A *service* taxi to Sharm el-Sheikh costs £E25. There's also a nightly bus to **Nuweiba** (9pm; 7–8hr; £E48).

● **Canal cities** Buses travel regularly via Ismailiya between **Port Said** (at least hourly 6.45am–6.45pm; 1hr; £E5) and **Suez** (hourly 6.30am–6pm; 1hr; £E4) while *service* taxis are a bit cheaper (Port Said £E4.50; Suez £E3.50). A *service* taxi to **Qantara** is £E1.25.

● **Lower Egypt** There are two buses daily to **Alexandria** (7am & 2.30pm; 4hr; £E17) and frequent departures for **Cairo** (every 45min 6.30am–7pm; 2hr; £E6.50). Outside of these hours you can still get to Cairo by *service* taxi (£E5) or to the Delta town of **El-Mansura** (£E6).

North of Ismailiya – canal crossings

Seven kilometres north of Ismailiya, a **car ferry** crosses the canal more or less non-stop during daylight hours. Together with the Ahmed Hamdi Tunnel outside Suez, it carries almost all the traffic between mainland Egypt and Sinai. By dint of being the most direct route from Cairo to Israel, the car ferry also takes **international and tour buses**.

The only other crossing point is at **QANTARA**, 44km from Ismailiya and 80km from Port Said. As its name ("Bridge") suggests, this was the route used by pilgrims and armies to cross the marshy Isthmus of Suez before the canal was built. Since then, it has been spanned by pontoon bridges in wartime, but is now negotiated by a small passenger ferry, carrying locals, bikes and donkeys from one side of Qantara to the other. Most of the town is on the **west bank**, whose unpaved main drag has a busy souk and lines of **service taxis** going to Cairo and the Canal cities; the battered, poorly rebuilt houses are a reminder that armies clashed here as recently as 1973. On the **east bank** of the canal there's a cafeteria and **service taxis for El-Arish** (2hr 30min; £E5), but it's easier to take one direct from Ismailiya.

Port Said (Bur Said)

Founded at the start of the canal excavations, **PORT SAID** was long synonymous with smuggling and vice, boasting an "even larger stock of improper photos than Brussels or Buenos Aires". The adventurer De Monfreid was amused by the Arab cafés where "native policemen as well as coolies" smoked hashish in back rooms, supplied by primly respectable Greeks. "If anyone had even had the bad taste to pronounce the forbidden word, I believe that they would have all turned into pillars of salt. All the same, every single one of them got his living from trafficking in hashish, either as a retail seller, or as a small-scale smuggler who haunted the liners."

Nowadays, this bustling city of 400,000 people earns its living as a free port and beach resort, yet a faintly raffish atmosphere lingers around its old streets of timber-porched houses, vaguely resembling the French Quarter of New Orleans. *Bur Said* is currently luring native tourists away from Alexandria by promising better shops and less crowded beaches, cheap hotels and good restaurants, only failing to deliver much in the way of nightlife. Aside from day-trippers off cruise liners, foreign tourists seldom visit the city and hustlers are rare, making it an agreeable place to relax for a day or two if you don't mind the lack of "sights" and diversions.

Arrival, information and accommodation

Trains **from Cairo** (six daily) take at least four and a half hours to reach Port Said via Ismailiya, and are grimy to boot, making it more appealing to do the 220km journey by

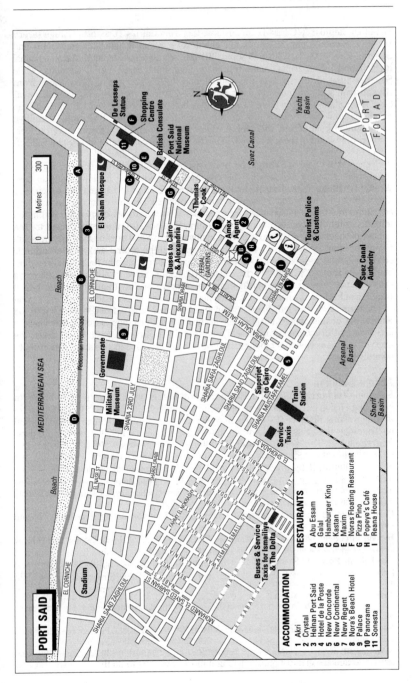

PORT SAID

MEDITERRANEAN SEA

Beach

Beach

EL CORNICHE

Stadium

EL CORNICHE

Pedestrian Promenade

El Salam Mosque

Governorate

Military Museum

SHARIA 23RD JULY

SHARIA ORABI

EL CORNICHE

De Lesseps Statue

Shopping Centre

British Consulate

Port Said National Museum

N

Metres
0   300

Yacht Basin

PORT FOUAD

Suez Canal

Thomas Cook

Amex Agent

FERIAL GARDENS

SHARIA SAAD ZAGHLOUL

SHARIA SAFIA ZAGHLOUL

SHARIA SALAH SALEM

Buses to Cairo & Alexandria

SHARIA ORABI

SHARIA SAAD ZAGHLOUL

Superjet to Cairo

SHARIA MUSTAFA KAMEL

Train Station

Service Taxis

Tourist Police & Customs

Suez Canal Authority

Arsenal Basin

Sherif Basin

EL SHOHADA ST

ABU BAKR EL SIDDIQ ST

SHARIA AL NAHDA

Buses & Service Taxis for Ismailiya & The Delta

ACCOMMODATION
1 Akri
2 Crystal
3 Helnan Port Said
4 Hotel de la Poste
5 New Concorde
6 New Continental
7 New Regent
8 Nora's Beach Hotel
9 Palace
10 Panorama
11 Sonesta

RESTAURANTS
A Abu Essam
B Galal
C Hamburger King
D Kastan
E Maxim
F Noras Floating Restaurant
G Pizza Pino
H Popeye's Café
I Reana House

MOHAMED EL SAFED SARWAN ST

SHARIA SAAD ZAGHLOUL

E NASR ST

EL SABAH ST

AHMED ISMAIL ST

EL SALAM ST

NABIL ST

FANNY EL NURASHI ST

bus (3hr). Regular A/C East Delta buses depart from Cairo's Turgoman Garage (every 30min 6.30am–6.30pm; £E15). East Delta (every 40min 6.30am–7.30pm; £E15) and Superjet (every 30min, 6.30am–5.30pm; £E15) buses also leave from Al-Mazah terminal in Heliopolis; East Delta buses terminate near Port Said's Ferial Gardens, while Superjet buses drop you near the train station. In the absence of direct trains **from Alexandria**, seats on buses (4 daily; 6hr; £E17–22) from the 15th May Terminal near Sidi Gaber Station should be reserved the day before, at the East Delta kiosk on Midan Sa'ad Zaghloul. *Service* taxis provide the fastest transport **from Suez and Ismailiya** and augment buses **from the Delta**, where Damietta and El-Mansura have the best connections. Coming **from El-Arish** in north Sinai, you can catch a *service* taxi (£E8–9) direct to the city.

Because Port Said is a **duty-free port**, visitors are supposed to pass through **customs** upon entering and leaving the city. You may not have to, but if you do pass through customs, it is advisable to declare any cameras or other gadgets, which they might think you bought at a discount here, or you may be subject to a 12 percent levy as you go out (ships' passengers are exempt). Most **points of arrival** are within ten minutes' walk of downtown (along and around Sharia el-Gumhorriya), except for the depot for buses and *service* taxis from Ismailiya, north Sinai or the Delta, which is sufficiently distant to make it worth catching a taxi into the centre (£E2). **Orientation** is straightforward, as most things of interest or use to tourists can be found on three thoroughfares: the waterfront Sharia Filastin (Palestine Street); Sharia el-Gumhorriya (Street of the Republic), two blocks inland; or Sharia 23rd July (named after the date of King Farouk's overthrow).

The **tourist office** (daily 9am–1.30pm & occasionally also 4–8pm; ☎066/235-289) on Sharia Filastin can supply a useful map of the town with listings of hotels and services and some historical background, while the **tourist police** (☎066/228-570) are at the back of the main customs building, and have another office in the train station (both open 24 hours).

Accommodation

Sharia el-Gumhorriya offers the widest range of **hotels**, from modern tower blocks to old-style pensions. If one is full up or seems uncongenial, there's always another within in easy walking distance. Be aware, however, that accommodation can be hard to find on Thursday and Friday nights, when many Egyptians come here to do weekend duty-free shopping. The **youth hostel** on Sharia al-Amin (☎066/228-702, fax 226-433; £E18.50), near the stadium, has clean but gloomy dormitory rooms; it admits non-members (£E1 extra). Rates given below include breakfast unless stated otherwise.

Akri, 24 Sharia el-Gumhorriya (☎066/221-013). Run-down, atmospheric Greek pension near the harbour. Basic, clean rooms and sporadic hot water in shared bathrooms; ask for a balcony. Rooftop restaurant, breakfast not included. ②.

Crystal Hotel, 12 Sharia el-Gumhorriya (☎066/222-747). A big complex which resembles a youth hostel, with large en suite A/C rooms. ⑤.

Helnan Port Said, El Corniche St (☎066/320-8908, fax 323-762). Retains its five-star rating chiefly because of its location on the beach. Has a pool, gym and sauna. ⑦.

Hotel de la Poste, 46 Sharia el-Gumhorriya (☎066/229-655, fax 228-898). Rambling 1940s-style place offering high-ceilinged rooms with fans and baths; TVs and fridges cost extra. Prices vary according to room; breakfast not included. ③.

New Concorde, Sharia Mustafa Kamel (☎066/235-342, fax 235-930). Carpeted rooms with baths, fans and TV, near the train station. Some of the rooms on the upper floors have views of the canal. ⑥.

New Continental, 30 Sharia el-Gumhorriya (☎066/225-024, fax 333-088). Pleasant enough, though a bit shabby; A/C rooms with satellite TV, international phone and balconies. ⑤.

New Regent, off Sharia el-Gumhorriya (☎066/223-802, fax 224-891). Small but comfortable hotel offering A/C rooms all with TV and fridge. ⑥.

Noras Beach Hotel, El Corniche St (☎066/329-834, fax 329-841). Huge beachside complex with 200 apartments and suites – a bit frayed at the edges but still comfortable – with A/C, private bathroom, satellite TV, minibar, balcony or terrace. With its three swimming pools and a health club, it's popular with Egyptian families. ⑤.

Palace, 19 Sharia Ghandi, opposite the Governorate building, near the beach (☎066/239-450, fax 239-464). Pleasantly furnished rooms with A/C and private bathrooms. ⑥.

Panorama Hotel, Shari el-Gumhorriya (☎066/325-101, fax 325-103). A/C rooms with satellite TV, private bathrooms and big balconies. Great views especially from the billiard-room on the 11th floor. A bit worn, but clean and comfortable. ⑥.

Sonesta, Sharia Sultan Hussein (☎066/325-511, fax 324-835). A/C rooms have private bathrooms, satellite TV and a minibar, and overlook the canal entrance and fishing harbour. There's also a nice pool, but no beach. Breakfast costs extra. ⑧.

The City

Sharia el-Gumhorriya reflects Port Said's metamorphosis from a salty entrepôt to a slick commercial centre, plate-glass facades superseding early twentieth century balconies as the street progresses from the Arsenal Basin to Sharia 23rd July.

The adjacent **bazaar** quarter is a microcosm of Egyptian consumer aspirations, ranging from humble stalls on Sharia el-Togary to the smart boutiques on Sharia en-Nahda. These have been joined by designer shops such as Hugo Boss and sports stores like Nike and Reebok at the junction of Sharia el-Gumhorriya with Sharia 23rd July. There is even a Clark's shoe shop downtown and a Marks & Spencer in the shopping centre opposite the Sonesta.

The **Military Museum** (Sat–Thurs 9am–2pm, also Fri in summer 6–10pm; £E2) gives a strong sense of the canal's embattled history. The 1956 Anglo-French-Israeli invasion is commemorated by lurid paintings and dioramas, while another room is dedicated to the October War of 1973. This gives pride of place to the storming of the Bar-Lev Line (see p.544), a heroic feat of arms ultimately wasted by the high command's failure to exploit Egypt's breakthrough in Sinai. Curiously absent from the large display of weaponry are the Soviet-made *Strella* and *Molutka* rockets that enabled Egyptian infantrymen to destroy Israeli jets and armour, rated by strategists as a minor revolution in modern warfare. It's about 15–20 minutes' walk from here to the National Museum.

Opened in 1987, the **Port Said National Museum** (Sat–Thurs 9am–5pm, Fri 9am–noon & 2–5pm; £E12, students £E6, camera £E10) runs the gamut of Egyptian history. Highlights of the well-displayed collection include two mummies, an exquisitely worked faïence shroud and painted coffin, Ptolemaic funerary masks, Islamic tiles and *mashrabiyas*, Coptic textiles (especially a tunic adorned with images of the Apostles) and the coach of Khedive Ismail, used during the canal's inauguration ceremonies. Cool and uncrowded, the museum makes a pleasant retreat from the heat and hubbub around this part of the waterfront.

Come evening, townsfolk and holidaymakers **promenade** along the Corniche, or near the National Museum, watching dozens of vessels at anchor, their bulky hulls dwindling to lights bobbing far offshore. At the far end of the quay is a massive sandstone plinth that used to bear a huge **statue of De Lesseps**, before it was torn down following the 1952 Revolution. For an idea of the canal's workings, take a cruise on the *Noras* floating restaurant or catch the free **ferry** (every 15min) across to Port Fouad (see below).

You can rent chairs and parasols for £E5 on Port Said's shell-strewn **beach**, which has public showers at 100m intervals. For calmer water and more relaxed sunbathing, consider paying £E15 to use the **pool** at the *Sonesta* hotel. The pool at the *Helnan* costs a hefty £E40 but this includes use of the gym and sauna.

Port Fouad

Founded as a suburb for canal bureaucrats in 1927, **PORT FOUAD** is quieter than its
sister city. Residents boast of commuting between Asia and Africa – an enjoyable ride
in a battered ferry reeking of everything but inter-Continental status. The suburb's
decrepit but stylish **1930s architecture** can be appreciated by making a tour of Port
Fouad's Art Deco flats, colonial villas and well-tended gardens. Travellers hoping to
work their passage to the Med or the Indian Ocean could ask around at the **yacht
basin**, although success is far from assured.

Eating and drinking

Eating out in Port Said is enjoyable, as fresh seafood abounds and most places have
tables outdoors, allowing you to savour the bustling streetlife. If you fancy cruising the
Suez Canal while you eat, make a reservation at the *Noras* **floating restaurant** on the
waterfront near the National Museum. The *Noras* sails at least twice daily (2.30pm and
8.30pm) but schedules change so check times at the *Noras Beach Hotel* where you can
also reserve tickets. The 90-minute cruise costs £E10 if you settle for a soft drink, or
£E36–60 including lunch or dinner. Besides the places listed below, there are lots of
patisseries and coffee houses on Sharia el-Gumhorriya. The spit-and-sawdust *Cecil Bar*
beneath the *Reama* restaurant is where to go **drinking** if you want to imbibe an atmosphere redolent of the olden days, in the company of aged Greeks. The bar is open till
midnight or later. There is also the standard duo of *KFC* and *Pizza Hut* on 23rd July if
you're feeling homesick.

Abu Essam, El-Corniche St, diagonally opposite the *Helnan*. Excellent fish restaurant with moderate prices. A full meal costs £E20–30.

Galal, on the corner of Gaberti and El-Gumhorriya. A nice place to sit outside, drink beer and eat
kofta sandwiches or seafood (£E15–20). They also do *shawarma* takeaways. Daily 7am–1am; closed
during Ramadan.

Hamburger King, corner of Sharia el-Gomhorriya and Sharia Tarh el-Bahr (☎066/224-877).
Burger bar popular with young Egyptians. Hamburgers, (£E2) sandwiches, *shawarma* (£E2–6) and
pizza (£E10–20). Also serves fresh fruit juice (£E3) and does home delivery.

Kastan, El-Corniche St, towards the stadium. Large and very busy 24-hr seafood and fish restaurant on the beach. Around £E30 for a full meal. Recommended.

Maxim, in the shopping centre on the corner of El-Gumhorriya and El-Corniche. Port Said's most
expensive fish restaurant, with splendid views of ships entering the canal. A full meal costs £E40–60.

Pizza Pino, on the corner of El-Gumhorriya and 23rd July streets. Popular joint with slick decor
and a seductive range of Italian dishes and ice cream.

Popeye's Café, Sharia el-Gumhorriya, opposite the *Hotel de la Poste*. A burger bar with trimmings
and piped music; serves huge banana splits. Daily 8am–midnight.

Reana House, 5 Sharia el-Gumhorriya, diagonally across from the *Akri Hotel*. Tasty Korean and
Chinese food including vegetarian dishes, at reasonable prices. Serves alcohol. Open till midnight
or later.

Listings

Consulates British (☎066/231-155), French (☎066/322-875) and Belgian (☎066/223-314) con-
sulates are located in the commercial centre just beyond the National Museum, while Denmark and
Norway are represented at the Norwegian Seaman's Service (☎066/336-730) on the 4th floor of 30
Sharia Sultan Hussein, one block north along the waterfront from the tourist office.

Currency exchange Numerous private exchanges around Sharia en-Nahda and the shopping malls
at the northern end of Sharia el-Gumhorriya can change money with less hassle than banks and
sometimes at a slightly better rate. Travellers' cheques can be cashed at the Banque Misr near the
(which will accept Visa or MasterCard), Thomas Cook, at 43 Sharia el-Gumhorriya (daily 8am–5pm;
☎066/227-559, fax 236-111). Menatours, at no. 18 (☎066/225-742), still claim to be the local agents

for American Express, but its role has been usurped to some degree by the arrival of American Express Bank (Sat–Thurs 8am–3pm) on Sharia el-Gomhorriya near the British Consulate.

Hospitals The best equipped and newest hospital is Al-Soliman near the sports stadium (☎066/331-533). Emergencies can also be treated at the Al-Mabarrah (☎066/220-560) or El-Tadaman (☎066/231-790) hospitals.

Passport office In the Governorate building on Sharia 23rd July (Thurs & Sat 8am–2pm).

Pharmacy The 24-hour Hussein pharmacy on Sharia el-Gumhorriya (☎066/339-888) is diagonally opposite the *Hotel de la Poste*.

Post office The main branch (daily except Fri 9am–2pm) is near the southeast corner of Ferial Gardens.

Telephone exchange Just along from the tourist office on Sharia Filastin (24hr).

Moving on

East Delta **buses to Cairo or Alexandria** (most are A/C) leave from the northern side of Ferial Gardens (☎066/226-883), while Superjet A/C services to Cairo depart from a depot near the train station (☎066/328-793). To board either, you must first go through customs, so come half an hour early. The same goes for **buses to Ismailiya or the Delta** leaving from the depot on Sharia al-Amin, though passengers departing in **service taxis** often seem to avoid customs entirely.

To get to **Limassol by ferry**, the *Princess Marissa* departs around 7.30pm every Tuesday and Saturday in the summer (Tues & Fri in the winter), arriving in Limassol the next morning around 10am. The Saturday boat which arrives in Limassol at 10am on Sunday then departs for Haifa at 4pm, arriving in Haifa on Monday at around 8am. The fare to Limassol is US$120 per person one-way for a cabin (4 persons max). Tickets are available from Nasco Tours on Sharia Filastin, north of the tourist office (☎066/329-500, fax 238-850).

CHAPTER SEVEN

SINAI

The **Sinai** peninsula has been the gateway between Africa and Asia since time immemorial and a battleground for millennia. Prized for its strategic position and mineral wealth, Sinai is also revered by disparate cultures as the site of God's revelation to Moses, the wanderings of Exodus and the flight of the Holy Family. As Burton Bernstein wrote, "it has been touched, in one way or another by most of Western and Near Eastern history, both actual and mythic", being the supposed route (there's no archeological proof) by which the Israelites reached the Promised Land and Islam entered North Africa, then a theatre for Crusader-Muslim and Arab-Israeli conflicts, and finally transformed into an internationally monitored demilitarized zone.

Though mostly wilderness, Sinai looks far too dramatic – and too beautiful – to be dismissed as "24,000 square miles of nothing". The interior of southern Sinai is an arid moonscape of jagged ranges harbouring **Mount Sinai** and **St Catherine's Monastery**, where pilgrims climb the Steps of Repentance from the site of the Burning Bush to the summit where God delivered the Ten Commandments. Further north, the vast **Wilderness of the Wanderings** resembles a Jackson Pollock canvas streaked with colour and imprinted with tank tracks. The Sinai is also home to a remarkably high number of plants and wildlife; over sixty percent of Egypt's plant life thrives in this area, and thirty-three species are unique to the Sinai. Among a number of mammals that inhabit the region are the hyena, ibex and the rabbit-like hyrax. Venture into this "desert" on a **camel trek** or **jeep safari** and you will also find remote springs and lush oases, providing some insights into **Bedouin culture**.

Above all, however, the south has the lure of exquisite coral reefs and tropical fish in the **Gulf of Aqaba**, one of the finest **diving** and **snorkelling** grounds in the world. The beach resorts at **Sharm el-Sheikh**, **Na'ama Bay**, **Dahab** and **Nuweiba** cater to every taste and budget. From Sharm or Na'ama Bay you can also make expeditions to Egypt's deepest reefs and most diverse aquatic life at **Ras Mohammed**, a mini-peninsula at the southern tip of Sinai. Northwest of here, the **Gulf of Suez** pales by comparison with its eastern counterpart – there are no reefs and only a few sites to interest the visitor.

Northern Sinai is visited by almost no Western tourists, although in summer it fills up with Egyptian holidaymakers. A barren coastline, which you scarcely glimpse from the road, it has a single town and focus in **El-Arish**, a laid-back if conservative place with a palm-fringed beach and a Bedouin market.

Some history

Fifty million years ago the Arabian Plate began shearing away from the African landmass, tearing the Sinai peninsula from the mainland while the Red Sea inundated the gap. Hot springs on the sea bed indicate that the tectonic forces which created Sinai are still active – the Gulf of Suez is widening by three inches each year. In **prehistoric times** the climate was less arid and Sinai supported herds of gazelles which Stone Age people trapped and slaughtered in stone enclosures.

Bronze Age Semites from Mesopotamia were the first to exploit Sinai's lodes of copper ore and turquoise, foreshadowing the peninsula's colonization by the III Dynasty

ACCOMMODATION PRICE CODES

Throughout the guide, hotels and pensions are graded on a scale of ① to ⑨, indicating the price (including tax) of the **cheapest double room** in each establishment in high season (for places that offer **dorm beds**, rates per person are given in £E). Please note that most hotels in categories ⑧ and ⑨ quote rates in US$, but will accept payment in £E. For a full explanation of the following categories, see p.46. The price bands to which these codes refer are as follows:

① under £E20/US$7	④ £E45–65/US$15–20	⑦ £E150–300/US$50–100
② £E20–30/US$7–10	⑤ £E65–100/US$20–35	⑧ US$100–200/£E300–600
③ £E30–45/US$10–15	⑥ £E100–150/US$35–50	⑨ US$200/£E600 upwards

pharaohs, who enslaved its Semitic population to work the mines, and build roads and fortresses. According to Egyptian mythology, it was in Sinai that Isis sought the dismembered body of Osiris; and Hathor, also associated with the region, was called "Our Lady of Sinai". **Pharaonic rule** continued until the invasion of the Hyksos "Shepherd Kings", whose occupation of northern Egypt lasted well over a century, till Ahmosis I drove them out and finally destroyed their last bastion in Gaza. This was subsequently the route by which Tuthmosis III and Ramses II invaded Palestine and Syria.

The Exodus

Enshrined in the Old Testament and by centuries of tradition, the **Exodus of the Israelites** is a historical conundrum, as no archeological evidence of their journey through Sinai has ever been found – though excavations at Avaris in the Delta (see p.528) suggest that this was the "City of Bondage" from which they fled. This is generally thought to have happened during the reign of the XIX Dynasty pharaoh, Merneptah (1236–1223 BC), although Egyptologist David Rohl argues that it occurred two centuries earlier (c.1447 BC), under Dudimose of the XIII Dynasty (see p.529).

To identify their route and various crucial sites, scholars have compared Biblical descriptions with physical features and tried to reconcile myths with realities. The "**Red Sea**" found in the King James Bible is a mistranslation of the Hebrew *Yam-suf*, or **Sea of Reeds**, which fits the salt lakes and marshes to the north of Suez, known today as the Bitter Lakes. From there, the Israelites proceeded down the coast to **Ain Musa** and followed **Wadi Feiran** inland towards **Mount Sinai**; although a contrary theory has them trekking across northern Sinai and receiving the Ten Commandments at **Jebel Halal**. Either way, the subsequent forty years in the wilderness are only explicable in terms of a lengthy stay at "Kadesh Barnea", identified as the oasis of **Ain Kedirat**, where there are extensive ruins.

Christianity and Islam

Over the next millennium or so, Sinai was invaded by Assyrians, Hittites and Babylonians, recaptured by Egypt, and conquered in turn by the Persians and Greeks. While the Ptolemies built ports along the Mediterranean coast, Semitic tribes from Petra established themselves between Aqaba and Gaza, both ultimately succumbing to the **Romans**. Whether or not the **Holy Family** had previously crossed Sinai to escape Herod's massacre, the region had begun to attract hermits even before Emperor Constantine legalized **Christianity**, which rooted itself in cathedrals and **monasteries** under Justinian's patronage.

In 639–40 the **Arabs** swept into Sinai, fired with the zeal of **Islam**. The new faith suited local tribes, which turned to plundering the desert monasteries while the Arabs

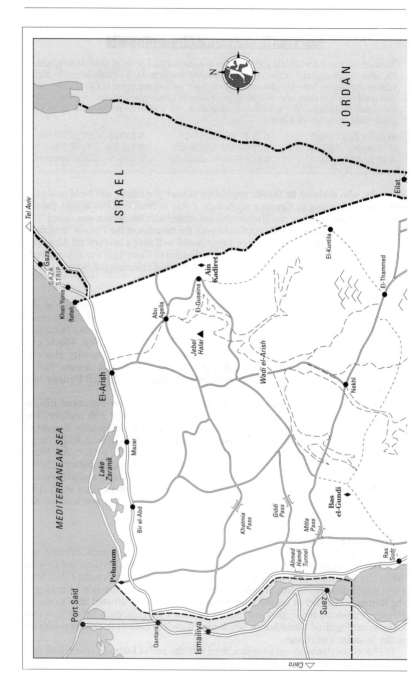

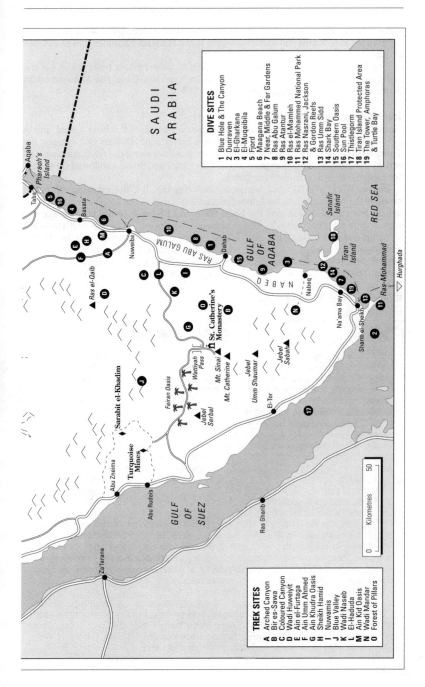

DIVE SITES

1 Blue Hole & The Canyon
2 Dunraven
3 El-Gharkana
4 El-Muqeibila
5 Fjord
6 Maagana Beach
7 Near, Middle & Far Gardens
8 Ras Abu Galum
9 Ras Atantur
10 Ras el-Mamleh
11 Ras Mohammed National Park
12 Ras Nasrani, Jackson
& Gordon Reefs
13 Ras Umm Sidd
14 Shark Bay
15 Southern Oasis
16 Sun Pool
17 Thistegorm
18 Tiran Island Protected Area
19 The Tower, Amphoras
& Turtle Bay

TREK SITES

A Arched Canyon
B Bir es-Sawa
C Coloured Canyon
D Wadi Huweiyit
E Ain el-Furtaga
F Ain Umm Ahmad
G Ain Khudra Oasis
H Sheikh Hamid
I Nuwamis
J Blue Valley
K Wadi Naseb
L El-Haduda
M Ain Kid Oasis
N Wadi Mandar
O Forest of Pillars

sacked the cathedral cities. Northern Sinai eventually became a pawn in the **Crusades**, the area between Aqaba and Rafah belonging to the Frankish Kingdom until its collapse at Acre.

After the Crusades, the victorious Mamlukes reopened Sinai's trade routes but the peninsula remained Egypt's Achilles heel, as the Ottoman Turks and Mohammed Ali demonstrated with their conquests of 1517 and 1831.

Twentieth-century Sinai

Sinai's strategic importance increased with the completion of the **Suez Canal**, and in 1892 Britain compelled Turkey to cede it as a buffer zone. Backed by Germany, the Turks retook it in 1914, laying roads and water pipelines along the northern coast and across the interior. Anglo-Egyptian forces only dislodged them – and went on to take Jerusalem – after a prolonged campaign.

During World War II Sinai witnessed little fighting, but the **creation of Israel** brought the territory right back into the frontline. In 1948 the Israelis repulsed Arab attacks from all sides and took the **Gaza Strip** and **El-Arish** before an armistice was signed, only withdrawing under British pressure. By closing the Gulf of Aqaba to Israeli shipping and nationalizing the Suez Canal, however, Nasser brought together British and Israeli interests. It was Israel's advance into Sinai in October 1956 that was the agreed pretext for Anglo-French intervention in the **Suez Crisis**; though militarily successful, the three states were compelled to quit by international opposition, UN peacekeeping forces establishing a buffer zone in Gaza and guaranteeing free passage through the Gulf of Aqaba.

THE BEDOUIN

Most of Sinai's population are **Bedouin** who claim descent from the tribes of the Hejaz on the Arabian Peninsula, and thus rate themselves amongst the purest Arab genealogies. Only the Jebeliya tribe is anomalous, tracing its origins to the Caucasus.

Traditionally, each tribe roamed its own territory in search of grazing and settled around local oases. The Mizayna claimed the land between El-Tor and Nuweiba; the Tarabeen a swathe from Nuweiba to El-Arish; the Jebeliya the St Catherine's region, and so on*. Tribal and family honour were paramount, raids and camel-rustling a perpetual cause for blood feuds that might persist for generations. Agriculture or fishing was a hand-to-mouth activity, secondary to herding goats and camels – the latter being the measure of a tribe's wealth, with racing camels esteemed above all. Though devout Muslims, the Bedouin retained pagan superstitions and practices from the "time of darkness", with their own common law (*'urf*) instead of regular Islamic jurisprudence.

Unsurprisingly, the Bedouin took advantage of discarded weaponry to resist outside authority, attempts to settle the nomads having little success until the 1970s, when Israel constructed water tanks, schools and clinics at various sites. By providing employment and exposing the Bedouin to Western comforts, the coastal resorts had an equally profound effect on traditional lifestyles. Nowadays, many earn their living through tourism, taxi driving or construction work, and stone huts with corrugated iron roofs and TV antennae are more common than black tents. Where grievances are discernible by outsiders, they usually focus on administrators and entrepreneurs from mainland Egypt, whom many Bedouin regard as here on sufferance.

For more on traditional Bedouin culture see p.606.

---

*The number of **tribes** in Sinai is uncertain, ranging from 14 to 27 depending on which of their subdivisions are counted. Other tribes include the Sawalha, Alekat, Walad Shaheen and Tiyahah. Collectively, they are known as the *Tawarah* ("Arabs of Tor"), after the ancient name of the peninsula, or simply as *Al-Arab*.

But further **Arab-Israeli wars** were inevitable. When Egypt ordered the UN to leave and resumed its blockade in **1967**, Israel launched a pre-emptive strike and captured the entire peninsula, which it retained after the **Six Day War** and fortified with the Bar-Lev Line along the east bank of the Suez Canal. In the **October War of 1973**, Egypt broke through into Sinai but then suffered a devastating counterattack across the canal.

US-sponsored peace negotiations culminated in President Sadat's historic visit to Jerusalem, the **Camp David Accords** and a peace treaty signed in 1979, which led to Egypt's decade-long expulsion from the Arab League. Under its terms Israel evacuated all settlements founded during the occupation of Sinai and the territory reverted to Egypt; a phased transition completed in 1982, except for the disputed enclave of Taba, finally resolved in 1989. The Multinational Force and Observers (**MFO**) based at Na'ama Bay monitors Sinai's "banded" demilitarized zones from orange-flagged outposts around the peninsula.

Introduced to Sinai by the Israelis, **tourism** initially suffered from the handover, as the Camp David Accords forbade any development for five years. Since 1988, however, its recovery has shifted into overdrive: where the Aqaba coast once had five hotels it now has 150, with plans for plenty more. While Ras Mohammed and Nabeq are protected by their status as Nature Reserves, the entire coastline north of Nuweiba is under intense development; the area bounded by Taba Heights, Eilat and Aqaba has become known as the "Red Sea Riviera". With new links between Israel and Jordan, and ever more charter flights from Europe, tourism can only increase further. Sinai's days as a wilderness seem to be numbered.

Visiting Sinai

The differences between Sinai and mainland Egypt can induce culture shock in travellers who arrive from Israel or Jordan, spend some days on a Sinai beach and then go on to Cairo. For those accustomed to Egyptian towns and beaches, Sinai will seem amazingly uncrowded, laid-back and hassle-free – especially so for women. Pressing on into mainland Egypt, of course, you experience the reverse. Native Bedouin and recent settlers from the mainland both assert Sinai's distinctive character and disparage Egyptian government, often comparing it unfavourably with the period of Israeli rule. Even the customary salutation is different: "*Kif halak*" (How is your health/situation?) instead of "*Izzayak*".

For the purposes of this guide, the peninsula divides into three zones – the **gulf coasts of Suez and Aqaba**, the **interior** and **northern Sinai**. Communications between the resorts along the coastal strip of the Gulf of Aqaba and the interior around St Catherine's are well-established (these two areas make up the administrative region of **South Sinai**), but northern Sinai is effectively sundered from both, despite the upgrading of a route between El-Arish and Nekhl. Transport to the zones from mainland Egypt is described at the start of each section, while the **approaches from Israel and Jordan** are covered in Basics – see p.16.

Unlike elsewhere in Egypt, you can visit part of the peninsula on a special **Sinai-only visa** valid for two weeks, which can be obtained at Taba on the border with Israel, the port of Nuweiba where boats arrive from Jordan, or the airports of Sharm el-Sheikh and Taba, where charter flights from Europe land. This is *only* valid for the Aqaba coast down to Sharm el-Sheikh and the immediate vicinity of St Catherine's Monastery (effectively it's a visa for South Sinai); if you wish to visit Ras Mohammed, other parts of Sinai's interior or mainland Egypt, you'll need a **regular Egyptian visa**, which *cannot* be issued at Nuweiba or the Taba border crossing, but can be obtained at Sharm el-Sheikh and Taba airports.

Climate, activities and maps

Sinai's **climate** is extreme. On the coast, daytime temperatures can reach 50°C (120°F) during summer, while nights are sultry or temperate depending on the prevailing wind. In the mountains, which receive occasional snowfall over winter and the odd rainstorm during spring, nights are cooler – if not chilly or freezing. Outside of winter, you should wear a hat, use high-factor sunscreen and drink four to six litres of water a day (more if you're trekking) to avoid sunburn and heatstroke.

The climate is obviously a factor affecting tourist **activities** in Sinai. During summer, the heat is likely to make you spend less time on the beach and more time in the water, and to forgo trekking or camel riding entirely. Happily, **diving** or **snorkelling** can comfortably be done at any time of the year, and constitute Sinai's greatest attraction. If you're new to either or simply unfamiliar with how and where it's done here, the account on pp.560–563 should give an idea of what's on offer. Details of diving centres, courses and trips are given under each resort as appropriate. We've done the same with **camel** and **jeep safaris**, giving a general rundown on p.596 and specifics under the localities where trips are arranged or occur. As a rule, sites near the coast can be visited at any time of the year by jeep, and between October and April by camel, while **trekking** in the High Mountain Region (see p.602) is unfeasible in winter owing to snow, and only possible in summer if you're fit enough to stand the heat.

While the **map** at the start of this chapter indicates the main diving and safari sites, serious divers or trekkers should acquire the 1:250,000 *Sinai Map of Attractions*, an English-language tourist map based on Israeli army surveys, which is sold at the Taba border and most resorts. At a pinch, divers could make do with one of the maps produced by diving centres or travel agents, which outline the chief dive sites and Ras Mohammed National Park. You can pick up a copy of the quarterly **listings magazine** *Sinai Today* at most resorts, for £E5.

Transport, accommodation and costs

All the main tourist spots are accessible by well-paved roads and some form of public transport. Most travellers find it easy to get around, as **buses** are frequent and cheap, and **service taxis** run to and from every resort. The sole exception is the **border at Taba**, which has only a couple of buses a day waiting to take people further south – as well as a few *service* taxis, whose drivers are notorious for taking financial advantage of the shortage of buses. Foreign **motorists** are restricted to main roads; given the baking heat and huge distances, **hitchhiking** is a dubious proposition unless your destination is nearby or you're certain of a ride all the way (or at least to somewhere with shade and buses). Women should *never* hitch alone. MFO personnel are forbidden to give lifts.

The type of **accommodation** varies from resort to resort, with costly holiday villages the norm at Na'ama Bay and cheap campgrounds at Dahab, while other places offer more of a range. Although tourism is a year-round business, there are definite **peak periods** when hotels charge higher prices and are liable to be full. To some extent this depends on the resort: Sharm el-Sheikh and Na'ama Bay receive a surge of European package tourists over spring, autumn and Christmas, while everywhere from Taba to Dahab is flooded with Israelis during Jewish holidays. Also bear in mind Egyptian vacations: December 22–February 2; March 1–May 3 and July 19–October 31. However, don't be discouraged from visiting whatever the time; you're bound to find somewhere to stay eventually.

Aside from accommodation, the **cost** of everyday items, meals and transport is higher in Sinai than anywhere else in Egypt, but still cheaper than in Israel or Europe. In the backpacking resorts like Dahab, essentials like bottled water, toilet paper and tampons can be pricey. There are **banks** in all the main resorts, while US dollars can be exchanged in many shops. Israeli shekels (NIS) are common currency in Dahab and Nuweiba, with an unofficial exchange rate of 1:1 on the £E.

THE GULF COASTS

Sinai rises and tapers as the peninsula runs towards its southern apex, red rock meeting golden sand and deep blue water along two gulf coasts. Even the **Gulf of Suez**, as E.M. Forster noted, looks enticing from offshore – "an exquisite corridor of tinted mountains and radiant water" – though it's nowadays transformed after dark into a vision of Hades by the flaming plumes of oil rigs.

For most travellers, however, Suez is merely an interlude before the **Gulf of Aqaba**, whose amazing coral reefs and tropical fish attract visitors to Na'ama Bay and other resorts. Their beach scene is the best Egypt can offer and should aquatic pursuits pall – if such a thing is possible – there are opportunities for making trips into the wild **interior** by jeep or camel. Even from the beach, the view of the mountains of Sinai and Saudi Arabia is magnificent. All things considered, it's not surprising that some people choose to spend their entire holiday here.

Approaches to the gulf coasts

Aside from those arriving from Israel or Jordan, most travellers approach the gulf coasts from **Cairo**, **Suez** or **Hurghada**, which generally entails following a zigzag route. Note, however, that most services to Taba and Nuweiba travel across the interior of the peninsula, avoiding both gulf coastlines for much of the way.

● Most people come **from Cairo** by **bus** from the **Sinai Terminal** (*Mahattat Seena*) in the Abbassiya district, or from **Turgoman Garage** behind the *Ramses Hilton* in downtown Cairo – from where you can also catch the overnight (11pm) Superjet bus to Sharm. Check schedules and reserve seats the day before (earlier during Ramadan). Eight East Delta buses run daily to **Sharm el-Sheikh** (7–8hr; £E50–65); four to **Dahab** (9hr; £E55–70); four to **Nuweiba** (8–10hr; £E55–70), three of which carry on to Taba (9hr; £E65) and one to **St Catherine's Monastery** (8hr; £E55). All services are A/C, offer on-board snacks and halt at one or two resthouses en route; refreshments are expensive. To save on fares, consider travelling via Suez instead (which most direct buses bypass). At the time of writing, some buses were leaving from the Sinai terminal and some from Turgoman, but the latter seems likely to have frequent departures on all these routes in future.

Rapid access to Sharm and great views of the peninsula might entice those with plenty of cash onto EgyptAir **flights.** There are at least three flights daily (except Fri, one flight only at 6.30pm) from Cairo to **Sharm** (US$138 one-way). There is currently only one flight weekly to **Taba** from Cairo (Mon 8am), but this looks set to increase as the new Taba Heights resort becomes fully operational.

● **Suez City** is the interchange for numerous buses coming from Hurghada, Cairo or northern Sinai. **Buses** leave from the Arba'in terminal going to **Sharm el-Sheikh** (5 daily; 5–6hr; £E25), **Dahab** (daily at noon; 7–8hr; £E30), **Nuweiba** (daily at noon & 3pm; 6–7 hr; £E30), **Taba** (daily at 3pm; 7–8 hr; £E30) and **St Catherine's** (daily at 2pm; 6hr; £E25). **Service taxis** leave from just outside the bus station for Dahab (£E35), St Catherine's (£E20), Nuweiba (£E25) and Sharm el-Sheikh (£E25).

● The third option is to travel directly **from Hurghada** to **Sharm** by **air** (Mon 3.30am, Sat 6am, Sun 11.30pm; one-way US$95) or **sea** (see p.633 for details), or charter a seven-seater **taxi** for the 750km drive (£E700 shared among passengers).

● There are also thrice-weekly EgyptAir **flights** to **Sharm from Luxor** (Tues 9.30pm, Thurs & Sat 9.15pm; one-way US$123) and two a week **from Alexandria** (Mon & Fri 8.45am; one-way US$185).

Diving and snorkelling

The Red Sea offers some of the finest diving and snorkelling in the world, accessible to most travellers at a fraction of the cost of reaching the Seychelles or the Great Barrier Reef. It's also a cheap place to learn open-water diving and gain a PADI or CMAS certificate, entitling you to dive anywhere in the world (NAUII, SSI or MDEA are less widely accepted). You must have an internationally recognized **certificate** in order to rent (or fill) **scuba diving** tanks, though other gear can be rented without one.

Many people visit Sinai simply to acquire this on diving **courses**. The initial step is a five-day **open-water** (OW) course, costing US$280–330 (plus US$30 for the certificate). Most centres offer a supervised introductory dive (US$40–50) for those uncertain about shelling out for a full course. If you're certified but haven't logged a dive in the past three months, they may insist on a trial dive before taking you on sea trips. Qualified divers can progress through **advanced open-water** (AWOD), **dive master** and **instructor** certification, and take **specialized courses** in underwater rescue, night or wreck diving (to name but a few that are available).

When **choosing a diving centre**, the main considerations should be the quality of the instructors and the state of the equipment. Linguistic misunderstandings can be dangerous, so you need an instructor who speaks your **language** well. Ask to see a card proving that he or she is qualified to teach the course (PADI, NAUI or whatever), and not merely a dive master. Amazingly, diving centres in Egypt were virtually unregulated until 1996, and there is still some question over how well the new laws are being enforced. Though centres associated with big hotels are safer bets than outfits on their own, smart premises are less important than the **equipment**. If left lying about, chances are it'll also be poorly maintained. Also notice the location of the compressor, used to fill the tanks; if it's near a road or other source of pollution, you'll be breathing it in underwater. Ask around and then stick to the dive centres that have been there the longest and have proper links with organizations like PADI. Remember that with diving, there is no substitute for a good training and safety record.

Broadly speaking, most dive centres in Sharm el-Sheikh and Nuweiba are fine. In Dahab, however, regulations are less likely to be adhered to and competition between dive centres is cutthroat, encouraging some divers to simply go for the cheapest option. One famous Dahab dive site, the **Blue Hole**, is entirely unsuitable for inexperienced divers – having claimed the lives of several people in recent years.

Diving centres are detailed under each resort, while **dive sites** are summarized below. The type of diving and the degree of experience required are mainly determined by underwater topography and currents. Around Sharm el-Sheikh and Na'ama Bay, the chief activity is **boat diving** (you enter the water offshore) at sites ranging from novice-friendly to demanding. Up the coast past Dahab and Nuweiba this gives way to **shore diving**, where you wade or swim out to the reefs. Some slope gently out to sea while others drop off sharply; the deeper the drop-off the richer the variety of corals and fish. **Liveaboards** are vessels that allow you to spend days or weeks at sea, cruising the dive spots in the Tiran Strait or the Gulf of Suez. During quiet periods, bookings can be arranged at short notice in Sharm, Na'ama or Shark Bay, but to be sure of what you're getting it's best to book in advance through an agent (see Basics chapter for details).

Snorkelling is also great fun and costs much less to get into. If you're planning to do a lot, it's cheaper to buy your own gear in Cairo or Israel than to rent it from dive shops in Sinai (you might be able to sell it when you leave). Coral reefs and spiny urchins can rip unprotected feet to shreds; in all events you should only walk in designated "corridors" to protect the corals – if the water is too shallow to allow you to float above them. However cool the water may feel, the sun's rays can still burn exposed flesh (water

Alexandria

Moulid of el-Bedawi, Tanta

Egyptian fairground, Tanta

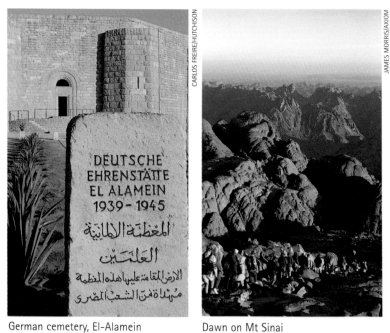

German cemetery, El-Alamein

Dawn on Mt Sinai

Bedouin, Western Desert

St Paul's Monastery, Red Sea Mountains

Fishing boat and cargo ship, Suez Canal

St Catherine's Monastery, Sinai

Fishing boat on beach, Hurghada

Coloured Canyon, Sinai

Moray eel, Red Sea

Clownfish in anemone, Red Sea

magnifies the effects of ultraviolet), so always wear a T-shirt and use waterproof sunscreen.

Always **remember** that reefs are very fragile, so the fundamental rule is: **look but don't touch**. In areas protected by law, you are forbidden to feed the fish, or remove anything from the sea. Don't buy **aquatic souvenirs**, the export of which is illegal. Tourists can help by boycotting stores selling them, and telling the shopkeepers why.

Sinai dive sites

The following sites are all marked on the map on p.554.

Amphoras Between Ras Umm Sidd and Na'ama Bay. Named after a Turkish galleon laden with amphoras of mercury, that lies on the reef – the site is also known as "Mercury".

Blue Hole 8km north of Dahab. The challenge of this 80-metre-deep hole in the reef is to swim through a passage 60m down and come up the other side – which is highly risky even for expert divers. You can safely snorkel around the rim of the hole, however.

Canyon Near the Blue Hole. A narrow reef crack, 50m deep, which is only for experienced divers.

El-Gharkana A luxuriant reef, offshore from mangroves and lagoons with rare waterfowl and flora. Part of the Nabeq protected area.

El-Muqeibila 25km south of Taba. A lovely diving beach stretching 15km from Mersa el-Muqeibila to Ras el-Burqa, often within walking distance of the main road.

Fjord 10km south of Taba. A picturesque cleft with underwater reefs, overlooked by the *Salima* motel and restaurant.

Gordon Reef Off the coast of Ras Nasrani, in the shipwreck-littered Tiran Strait. Sharks and strong currents. Popular with experienced divers; not for beginners.

Jackson Reef A much larger reef between Tiran Island and the mainland, with a 70-metre drop-off, sharks and pelagic fish, and the shipwreck *Lara*. Strong currents; dangerous for beginners.

Maagana Beach 5–10km north of Tarabeen. The reef falls sheer around the "Devil's Head" to the north, getting shallower and less impressive further south.

Near, Middle and Far Gardens 1–5km north of Na'ama Bay. A series of lovely coral reefs, for easy diving and snorkelling. The Near Gardens are within walking distance of Na'ama.

Pharaoh's Island Near Taba. Superb underwater scenery and strong currents; a diving guide is recommended. Israelis call it "Coral Island". Easy access by boat.

Ras Abu Galum 50km south of Nuweiba. A protected area with a deep virgin reef wall and great fish. Access by 4WD or boat.

Ras Atantur Between Dahab and Sharm el-Sheikh. Colourful, abundant reef, with a shipwreck – the *Maria Schroeder* – 10km further south. Access by 4WD.

Ras el-Mamleh 20km south of Nuweiba. Another slab of virgin reef wall on the northern edge of the Ras Abu Galum Protected Area. Access by 4WD or boat.

Ras Mohammed National Park 25km southwest of Sharm el-Sheikh. Wonderful corals, mangrove lagoons, anemone gardens and crevice pools, with shark reefs offshore. The wrecks of the *Dunraven* and the *Thistlegorm* lie further out towards El-Tor.

Ras Nasrani Sheer reef wall riddled with shark caves; the Light and the Point are notable spots. Beware of sharks and strong currents. Not for inexperienced divers.

Ras Umm Sidd Within walking distance of Sharm el-Sheikh. Exquisite fan corals and fish. Up the coast towards Na'ama are other popular sites like Turtle Bay, Amphoras, and The Tower.

Shark Bay Colourful reef just off the beach of a small resort, 10km north of Na'ama Bay. Good for novices and experienced divers alike; snorkellers too.

Southern Oasis Gently sloping reef to the south of Dahab City. Easy diving and snorkelling.

Sun Pool 10–15km from Taba. A gorgeous diving beach extending as far north as the Fjord.

The Tower South of Na'ama Bay. Sheer reef pillar dropping 60m. Easy access from the beach and mild currents; good for novice divers.

Tiran Island Protected Area An archipelago with over 20 dive sites, all amazing. Sharks and strong currents; only for experienced divers unless explicitly stated otherwise.

Turtle Bay Between Ras Umm Sidd and Amphoras. Shallow bay with turtles, easy to enjoy. Access by boat.

Coral reefs and tropical fish

Created by the same tectonic stresses that formed the Dead Sea and East African Rift Valley, the **Red Sea basin** is over three kilometres deep in places, yet effectively separated from the Indian Ocean by an underwater "sill" at Bab el-Mandab, roughly 100m below the surface. Circulation between the Red Sea and the Gulf of Aqaba is similarly limited by the 200-metre-deep Tiran Strait, although the gulf itself attains depths of 1830m. As neither is fed by rivers and their rate of evaporation far exceeds any rainfall, both are exceptionally warm and salty – providing an ideal environment for tropical fish and coral reefs.

It's the warmth of the Red Sea water that is responsible for the Sinai's particular brilliance of coral – a revelation if you have previously snorkelled in such places as Hawaii or the Caribbean, whose reefs will ever after seem dull by comparison.

CORAL REEFS

The **coral reefs** that fringe the Sinai coastline from El-Tor to Taba have been created by generations of minuscule polyps extracting calcium from the sea water and depositing limestone exoskeletons on the remains of their ancestors. Fossilized reefs form the bedrock for living ones, which can grow 4–5cm a year, but are easily bruised or killed; if snapped off, coral loses its colour within hours of being removed from the sea. The lack of rain and rivers allows well-developed fringing reefs to thrive on both coasts of the Red Sea.

Reefs come in all shapes and sizes, some more encrusted with coral growths than others, but the idealized representation given below should give you an idea of where different species might be found. Some corals live 300 metres down, but you'll find most corals within 20–30 metres of the surface. The presence of sharks is usually a sign of a reef's good health.

Just below the shoreline, the warm water and eroded, sand- and rubble-covered bottom of the **lagoon** attract starfish, sea slugs and stinging anemones. Clams and sea urchins hide in crevices, while small yellow anemone fish and schools of viridian and carmine damselfish flit about. Other species include azure and opal blennies, tentacled clown fish and multitudes of butterfly fish.

Beyond lies the **reef flat**, a barren, fossilized shelf curving up towards the **reef crest**, overgrown with organ pipe corals and anemones. Damselfish, angelfish, snappers and parrotfish are ubiquitous, while sea worms and eels emerge from deep **caves** below the crest. Mountain and stag-horn corals encrust the upper **slope**, whose lower section merges into bare terraces or sandy shelves overgrown with **sea grass**, the habitat of sea horses and pipefish.

Close to the surface further out are **pillars**; their own richly developed coral formations attract damselfish, basslets, wrasses and grunts, to name but a few. The **forereef**

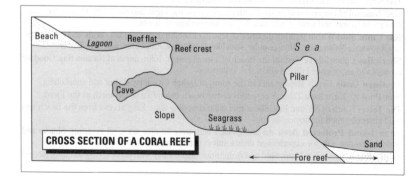

CROSS SECTION OF A CORAL REEF

tends to draw larger fish, octopuses and squids, with stingrays and mantas (whose wingspans can reach nearly 5m) gliding along the sea bed.

TROPICAL FISH AND OTHER CREATURES

The Red Sea's flora and fauna are related to tropical Indo-Pacific species, with no observable migration from the Mediterranean, although blue-speckled parrotfish have travelled the other way. The following are the most basic notes for identification – and avoiding the odd dangerous species.

Wherever soft, stinging anemones cling to the reef you're likely to see yellow **anemone fish**, recognizable by their twin vertical stripes. Equally commonplace are **angelfish**, with their long dorsal fins diminishing to filaments. Crescent angelfish are blue at the front, with a yellow vertical stripe and black hindquarters, while Emperor angelfish are horizontally pinstriped in blue and yellow, and the larger Arabian angelfish (up to 50cm long) is blue all over but for a yellow splotch. The same colour scheme in reverse appears on **butterfly fish**, which favour sunny slopes and forereefs; around lagoons, pillars and crests you'll also see racoon butterfly fish, striped in yellow and black, with a black and white eye patch.

Slopes and forereefs are the habitat of small **goatfish** (red mullet) with horizontal stripes of blue and yellow (or yellow and black in the case of Forsskal's goatfish). Diverse types of **parrotfish** and **snappers** frequent deeper water alongside crests and pillars. Parrotfish are easily recognizable by their beaky mouths and vibrant colours; snappers are similarly sized, with silvery scales striped and spotted in red, green or electric blue. Likewise bulky and diversely hued are **wrasses**, related to the bigger **Napoleon fish**, which can dwarf a person. Dugongs or **sea cows** are equally large and harmless, unlike small, sharp-toothed and armoured **triggerfish**, **filefish** and **porcupine fish**, more commonly found in deeper water.

DANGERS OF THE DEEP

Considering all the **dangerous creatures**, it's remarkable that most visitors get nothing worse than the odd cut from sharp coral. Poisonous species include spiny **scorpion fish**, wildly coloured **turkeyfish** and **dragonfish**, and the oddly finned **lionfish**. By not touching anything remotely fitting their description you should avoid danger from these sources.

The lethal **stonefish**, camouflaged as a gnarled rock, is harder to spot but fortunately rare. You're more likely to be at risk from stinging **purple anemones** and burning **fire coral**, or **black sea urchins** with needle-like spines, which nestle in crevices. Dark caves sometimes harbour razor-toothed **moray eels**, which may bite if they feel threatened. **Stingrays** can deliver a painful dose of venom, and at certain times of the year **jellyfish** arrive in hordes, contact with which can cause mild irritation.

Although makos, hammerheads and other **sharks** frequent the deep waters around Ras Mohammed and the Tiran Strait, they're seldom found near the coast. However, blood in the water can attract them from afar, so never enter the sea with an open wound. Hammerheads and white-tip reef sharks have been known to attack with little provocation, though some divers consider **barracuda** more aggressive. Sighting either predator near shore, climb out quickly but calmly and spread the word; if you're diving in deeper water, keep still and you'll almost certainly be ignored.

Between Suez and Sharm el-Sheikh

The 338km between Suez and Sharm el-Sheikh takes only a few hours by bus or *service taxi*, and there's little point in stopping unless you've got private transport. Such attractions as exist along (or off) the route are otherwise awkward to reach (or leave), so most travellers pass them by. Beyond **El-Tor**, the area's administrative capital, there's little of interest until you reach the diving grounds of **Ras Mohammed**, which draw hordes of people on day-trips from Sharm el-Sheikh. The resort of **Ras Sudr** is becoming increasingly popular for its windsurfing, while, further south, the pharaonic ruins at **Sarabit el-Khadim** are also starting to attract large numbers of visitors. For simplicity's sake, we've covered them here rather than later.

If you're not already booked on a through-service to Sinai, Suez is the place to catch a bus or *service* taxi – an easier, surer way than hoping to cadge a ride at the **Ahmed Hamdi Tunnel**, 17km north of Suez. The tunnel – named after an Egyptian general killed in the October War – is the only road crossing between Sinai and Egypt proper, so most traffic uses it.

South along the Gulf of Suez

Heading south by road, the **Gulf of Suez** is sensed before it appears as a glint on the horizon, beyond the sands that rim the west for much of the way. Roughly 50km past the Ahmed Hamdi Tunnel, a dirt road turns off towards the coast to **AIN MUSA**, the **"Springs of Moses"**. According to scholastic conjecture and local legend, it was here that the Israelites halted after crossing the Red Sea, and Moses threw a tree into the bitter spring of Marah, which miraculously became drinkable (Exodus 15). Ain Musa is recognizable from the highway by the deposits of calcium and magnesium salts that surround the oasis, where only one of the twelve springs mentioned in Exodus remains, yielding water that has a strong chemical odour and acts as a powerful laxative. Many of the palm trees in the oasis were decapitated during various Sinai conflicts; an Israeli battery stationed here shelled Suez and Port Tewfiq during the War of Attrition, until Egypt recaptured Ain Musa in 1973. Camping is possible, although limited by the lack of food and water and transport out. Ask at the village if you're interested, and you may find a willing Bedouin guide. Alternatively, overnight trips (£E20 per person including dinner and guide, minimum of five people) can be arranged at *Marah Beach* hotel in Ras Sudr (see below).

Ras Sudr and Hammam Faraoun

Famed for the variety of seashells washed up on its beach and its perfect windsurfing conditions, **RAS SUDR** is marred by a reeking oil refinery that doesn't seem to bother the middle-class Cairenes who patronize its holiday villages and **hotels**. One of the oldest, *Sudr Beach Inn* (☎069/400-402, fax 400-885; ⑤) is a bit worn, but has clean A/C rooms with baths, TVs and terraces looking onto a pretty beach. Next door, *Marah Beach* (☎069/400-166; ⑤) looks in serious need of refurbishment, but they also have tents on the beach (②) or you can pitch your own. There is little to choose between the holiday villages which pepper the coast road to the north of Ras Sudr; but if you're stuck for somewhere to stay, try *Banana Beach Village* (☎02/247-5258) *Daghash Land Village* (☎069/777-049; ⑧), *Helnan Royal Beach* (☎069/400-101, fax 400-108; ⑧) or *Mesalla Beach* (☎069/678-411; ⑦).

The coast improves 55km further south, where a turn-off leads to **HAMMAM FARAOUN** (Pharaoh's Bath), several near-boiling **hot springs**, which Arab folklore attributes to the pharaoh's struggles to extricate himself from the waves, and local Bedouin use for curing rheumatism. A cave in the hill beside the shore leads into "the sauna", a warren of chambers awash with hot water – but it's more comfortable to bathe where the springs flow into the sea. Plans to build a health resort here were abandoned after the springs mysteriously dried up and only resumed flowing once work had ceased. Though **camping** is allowed, you must tell the soldiers posted nearby, who enforce a ban on visiting the beach after 6pm. Only soft drinks and biscuits are sold, and what little traffic there is rarely goes beyond El-Tor (see below).

A detour to the Turquoise Mines

Down the coast from Hammam Faraoun, the petroleum township of **Abu Zneima** serves as a reminder of Sinai's mineral wealth and of the ancient turquoise mines far inland near Sarabit el-Khadim. The site of the only pharaonic temple and some of the grandest scenery in Sinai, it is becoming a popular destination for **jeep safaris** from Sharm el-Sheikh. Several travel agents offer a day-trip there, while Bedouin guides at the Pigeon House can arrange two- to five-day excursions, including more distant sites. Alternatively, you could **get there** in a rented car (preferably 4WD) by a washed-out road that turns inland just past Abu Zneima, or another bumpy wadi route off the road to St Catherine's from Wadi Feiran – both take about ninety minutes. As the final approach to Sarabit must be made on foot, it's best to rent a **guide** from the Bedouin village 3km away, where you can **camp** out (it's also a good place to buy Bedouin carpets). Ask to speak to the son of Sheikh Barakat.

Sarabit el-Khadim and beyond

Built upon a 755-metre-high summit reached by a tortuous path, the **rock-hewn temple** known as **Sarabit el-Khadim** ("Heights of the Slave" in Arabic) is an enduring symbol of pharaonic power over the nameless thousands that once toiled in the mines of Sinai. Erected during the XII Dynasty, when mining reached its apogee, the temple consists of open courts and sanctuaries dedicated to the goddess Hathor in her aspect "Mistress of Turquoise", and the god Soped, "Guardian of the Desert Ways". Both deities are invoked on rock-cut and freestanding steles relating to mining expeditions, which were only possible for half of the year due to the heat and scarcity of water, which made a permanent colony impossible. The temple (whose precincts were segregated from the mining area by a crude stone wall) was abandoned during the reign of Ramses VII. Known to the Bedouin for centuries, it was first "discovered" by Reinhold Niebuhr in 1792, but not excavated until early last century.

Jeep safaris from Na'ama approach Sarabit from the south, via a track leading off the road from St Catherine's into **Wadi Mukattab** – the Valley of Inscriptions. Here you can find dozens of hieroglyphic texts carved into the rocks, alongside Proto-Sinaitic **inscriptions** that continue into Wadi Maraghah, where ancient mine workings and steles were damaged when the **turquoise mines** were revived by the British and then went bust in 1901. Though Bedouin still glean some by low-tech methods, the amount of turquoise that remains isn't worth the cost of industrial extraction. The ancient Egyptians preferred the greener variety to the more porous blue type, which tends to fade when exposed to the air.

Another picturesque spot near Sarabit is **Jebel Fuga**, whose wadis contain sand and dunes of various colours. If you're smitten by this rugged wilderness and want to go further, ask to visit the **Forest of Pillars**, a unique geological formation on the cliffs of Jebel el-Tih. Though only 40km from Sarabit as the hawk flies, the trail is rather longer and quite arduous. Ample water and an expert guide are imperative. You'll need a rope, too.

El-Tor

Assuming you can stick to the coastal highway – which often veers inland, giving a wide berth to airstrips and oil terminals – there's little to see besides a scattering of holiday resorts all the way to **EL-TOR**, the administrative capital of South Sinai. Originally, the Egyptian government based its administrators at Abu Rudeis, near the fledgling oilfields that were their prime concern – not realizing that this lay outside the territory of the main Bedouin tribal confederation and thus limited their influence over the tribes.

After capturing South Sinai in 1967, the Israelis used ethnographic data to devise a system that exploited tribal allegiances, under a military governor in Sharm el-Sheikh. The Egyptians took note and, once they had recovered the region, established their own South Sinai Governorate at El-Tor, just within the territory of the powerful Mizayna tribe.

The town (or "City") consists of a few government buildings and a mass of housing, offering no inducement to visit – though it is possible to get a **visa extension** from the governorate office here (Sun–Thurs 8am–2pm; ☎069/661-622), rather than having to travel to Cairo. Visitors without a car risk being stranded (there are surprisingly few local buses or *service* taxis to Sharm el-Sheikh, 108km away) with an unenviable choice of **hotels**. The *Delmoun*, at the edge of town by the ocean (☎069/771-060; ⑤), with A/C rooms with baths is your best bet; the *Tur Sinai* (☎069/770-059; ⑤) opposite the bus station is downright grungy.

It's better to settle back in your seat and dream of the reefs that fringe the Gulf coast from El-Tor onwards; the account on pp.560–563 should provide some food for thought.

Ras Mohammed

RAS MOHAMMED is a small peninsula, fringed with lagoons and reefs, that was declared a nature reserve in 1983 and became Egypt's first marine **National Park** in 1989. All of the thousand-odd species of fish that occur in the Red Sea and 150 types of corals are represented here. The age of this amazing ecosystem is evinced by marine fossils in the bedrock dating back twenty million years; on the shoreline are newcomers only 75,000 years old. Since the section entitled "Coral reefs and tropical fish" on pp.562–563 covers in general what you'll see, suffice it to say that Ras Mohammed should not be missed. Though chiefly for **divers**, there are enough calmer reefs for **snorkellers** to have a great time as well. But as the two activities don't really mix, it's important to choose the right kind of excursion.

You can **visit** the National Park any day from sunrise to sunset, providing you have a full Egyptian **visa** and not just a Sinai-only one (they check). The US$5 entry charge is usually included in the cost of excursions from Sharm el-Sheikh or Na'ama Bay (see under both resorts for details). As the number of dive boats allowed each day is limited, you can't be certain of a place at short notice. Alternatively, you could rent a taxi (about £E100) or car for the day. You really need wheels to reach the park and get around – unless, of course, you're taken to the reefs by boat. There are two perimeter gates on the road between El-Tor and Sharm el-Sheikh, leading to a main entrance whence it's 24km to the nearest reefs.

Various trails – accessible by regular car – are marked by colour-coded arrows. The blue one leads to Aqaba Beach, the **Eel Garden**, the Main Beach and a **Shark Observatory** 50m up the cliffside, which affords distant views of the odd fin. Purple and then red shows the route to the Hidden Bay, **Anemone City** and Yolanda Bay, while green signifies the way to the **Crevice Pools** and the **Mangrove Channel**, where children can safely bathe in warm, sandy shallows. Divers prefer the deeper sites that can only be reached by boat, such as the **Shark Reefs** off Yolanda Bay (the place to see sharks, barracuda, giant Napoleon fish and manta rays); and **The Mushroom** or the **wreck** of the *Dunraven*, out towards **Beacon Rock**.

A **visitors centre** (10am–sunset) off the road between the Sharm gate and the main entrance shows videos in English and Arabic on alternate hours, and contains a library, shop and restaurant. Free **telescopes** are located there, at the Shark Observatory, and at Suez Beach. You can't rent diving equipment at Ras Mohammed.

You can pick up a form for a **camping** permit (US$5 per person per night; children under 12 free) at the entrance to the park. There is no shop to buy supplies, the nearest one is in Sharm el-Sheikh, about 30 minutes away by car.

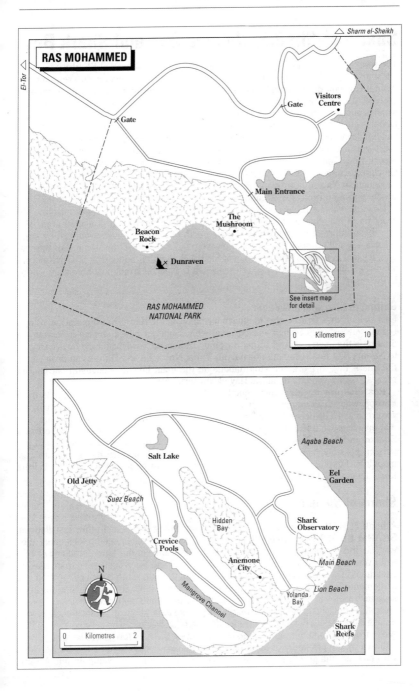

RAS MOHAMMED

Sharm el-Sheikh

El-Tor

Gate

Gate

Visitors Centre

Main Entrance

The Mushroom

Beacon Rock

Dunraven

RAS MOHAMMED NATIONAL PARK

See insert map for detail

0   Kilometres   10

Salt Lake

Aqaba Beach

Eel Garden

Old Jetty

Suez Beach

Hidden Bay

Shark Observatory

Crevice Pools

Anemone City

Main Beach

Mangrove Channel

Yolanda Bay

Lion Beach

N

Shark Reefs

0   Kilometres   2

Sharm el-Sheikh, Na'ama Bay and Shark Bay

The three resorts on the Aqaba coast are a mixed bunch. **Sharm el-Sheikh** ("Sharm" for short) is the largest and most southerly, and comprises several different areas – though constant development means they are slowly merging into one. Its downtown precinct has all the charm of a container port, but the nearby diving grounds are superb, and it makes a cheaper base than **Na'ama Bay**, 7km up the coast. Here, the facilities are top class, in a town almost solely devoted to tourists with its smart hotels and holiday villages, and gorgeous reefs which are within walking distance. Socially the two towns are poles apart: Na'ama Bay is much like any other Mediterranean coastal resort, while Sharm retains a *baladi* ambience like Suez or Cairo, which can come as a shock to package tourists leaving their hotels for the first time. Whereas beachwear is de rigueur at Na'ama, tourists staying in Sharm would do well to **dress** modestly off the beach to avoid unwelcome attention.

Hotel development has not stopped at Na'ama Bay and tourist villages now line the coast up to Ras Nasrani airport and even beyond to the Nabeq protected area. The once-beautiful retreat of **Shark Bay**, 8km north of Na'ama, is now swamped by large resorts – it still boasts a fine beach, however, and a view of Tiran Island. For orientation, try and get hold of the free map of Sharm el-Sheikh produced by Sharm Xplorers which contains listings with map references. It is available from most hotels and shops in the resort.

Getting to Sharm and Na'ama

East Delta **buses from Cairo** to Sharm terminate at the Hay el-Nur bus station, roughly half way between Sharm and Na'ama, while Superjet buses end up in downtown Sharm on the main road to Na'ama Bay; only Dahab- or Nuweiba-bound ones carry on to Na'ama Bay. Buses coming down **from Taba, Nuweiba** and **Dahab** can drop you at the Shark Bay turn-off, and stop outside all the main holiday villages in Na'ama on request, before winding up at the Hay el-Nur terminal.

Ras Nasrani airport, 15km north of Na'ama, is busy with charter flights from Europe, whose passengers are driven off to their holiday villages by bus; arriving on your own you'll be dependent on costly taxis to get anywhere. The **port** where the catamaran arrives from Hurghada is 600m south of downtown Sharm. **Transport between Sharm and Na'ama** is frequently available from the **minibuses** for workers (£E1 per person, possibly more if you have luggage); you won't be sharing space with cosmopolitan Egyptian holidaymakers, so it's advisable to be modestly dressed. Private **taxis** demand £E15–20 per car load.

Sharm el-Sheikh

A hunk of sterile buildings on a plateau commanding docks and other installations, **SHARM EL-SHEIKH** was developed by the Israelis after their capture of it in the 1967 war. Their main purpose was to thwart Egypt's blockade of the Tiran Strait and to control overland communications between the Aqaba and Suez coasts. Tourism was an afterthought – though an important one, helping to finance the Israeli occupation and settlements, which Egypt inherited between 1979 and 1982. Since then, Sharm's infrastructure seems to have expanded in fits and starts, without enhancing its appeal much. Despite some plush hotels and reams of propaganda about it being a slick resort, Sharm is basically a dormitory town for the Egyptian workers who service Na'ama Bay. Aside from package tourists conned by brochures, the only foreigners here are divers – drawn by the proximity of Ras Umm Sidd and other **reefs** – and a few backpackers who take advantage of its lowish-budget accommodation, and commute into Na'ama

Bay. Sharm has no beach to speak of and its small bay is slicked with oil from the near-by marina. The (illegal) daily burning of garbage also detracts from the hotels' "luxu-ry" pretensions. But in its defence the downtown area does have some excellent restau-rants, a good bakery and other shops.

The wealthier residents occupy the cliff above the bay of Sharm el-Maya, in an area called **Hadaba**. Towards the end of this cliff is a lighthouse and restaurant, marking the dive site of **Ras Umm Sidd**, whose name now also applies to the string of hotels and villas that have sprouted along the coast as far north as the **Tower**. While the swanki-est resorts are perched close to the edge of the cliff, cheaper hotels favoured by British tour operators fill up the land behind. This is a rather bleak area, where guests have to rely on shuttle buses to take them to the beach or Na'ama Bay.

The only "sight" is **Ras Kennedy**, a rock formation that resembles the face of the slain US president, visible on the left as you head out towards Na'ama.

Accommodation

Most **accommodation** is either deluxe and costly or simple and inexpensive. The for-mer enables package tourists to ignore Sharm's ugliness, while the latter serves as a fallback if the *Pigeon House* in Na'ama or *Shark's Bay Camp* at Shark Bay are full. Otherwise the windswept clifftop area away from the beach is full of hotels offering mid-priced deals. If you're rich and into diving, you're best choice is a hotel right **next to a dive site** like Ras Umm Sidd, or just up the coast at the Tower (see p.572).

Amar Sina, Sharm's clifftop area (☎069/662-221, fax 662-233). Eclectic but impressively designed hotel, full of domes and arches, designed by its owner in residence. 88 A/C rooms with satellite TV. Nice pool, jacuzzi and gym. ⑦.

Beach Albatros, on the cliff overlooking Sharm el-Maya, with access to the beach below by a very long staircase, or lift (☎069/663-922, fax 663-925). Construction of the beach involved in-filling a stretch at the back of the reef, causing the latter's death; it now has the best beach in this part of town, as well as a great view of the mountains and Ras Mohammed. ⑧.

Clifftop, (☎069/600-251, fax 600-253). A/C boxes in a palmy garden on the hilltop behind the youth hostel. Both were built by the Israelis and are showing their age now. ⑥.

Dive Inn Swiss Resort, Ras Umm Sidd (☎069/660-835, fax 660-834, *swissres@intouch.com*). New four-star place, designed for divers. 135 rooms with balconies, satellite TV etc. ⑧.

Dreams Beach, on the beach at Ras Umm Sidd (☎069/660-170, fax 660-199, *dreamsbeach@sinainet.com.eg*). Large five-star complex with 500 rooms, satellite TV, numerous bars and restaurants. Some rooms have disabled access. ⑧.

El-Kheima, Sharm el-Maya (☎069/600-167, fax 600-166). Its recently upgraded A/C rooms can be booked for any duration, but the four-person bungalows have a one-week minimum stay. Clean and quiet but with little atmosphere. Bungalows ④; rooms ⑥.

Hilton Sharm Waterfall Resort, on the beach at Ras Umm Sidd (☎069/601-071, fax 601-076). *Hilton*'s latest addition to Sharm has 117 A/C rooms with all the trimmings. ⑧.

Horus, on the clifftop at Sharm (☎069/663-103, fax 663-101). Small hotel with 24 A/C rooms with terrace and bath. Shuttle-bus to beach. ⑤.

Iberotel Grand Sharm, on the beach at Ras Umm Sidd (☎069/663-800, fax 663-819). Even larger than the other *Iberotel* with small pockets of beach over coral reef coastline. A/C rooms with satel-lite TV and terrace, pools and the latest in resort facilities. ⑧.

Iberotel Palace, Sharm el-Maya (☎069/661-111, fax 661-293). Over 240 rooms and luxury facilities, but a dirty beach. Lots of restaurants and sports facilities, bicycle rental, bank. ⑧.

Marine Club, Sharm el-Maya (☎069/600-450, fax 600-672). Quite a nice three-star place, offering A/C bungalows with satellite TV; popular with middle-class Egyptian families. ⑤.

Ritz-Carlton, by the beach at Ras Umm Sidd (☎069/661-919, fax 661-920, *ritzcarltonssh@ sinainet.com.eg*). The last word in luxury, this is trumpeted as the first Ritz in Africa and it's full of the latest trends in luxury hotels, including Internet access via the TV in each of the huge A/C rooms. There are 8 restaurants and bars (even a cigar lounge), plus sauna, spa and fitness centre, whirlpool and beauty salon. The hotel's beach has direct access to a reef and 2 pools with a river and waterfall. ⑧–⑨.

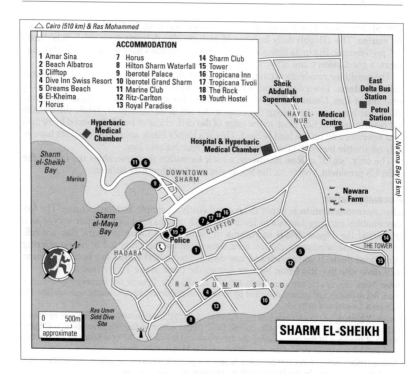

△ *Cairo (510 km) & Ras Mohammed*

ACCOMMODATION

1 Amar Sina	**7** Horus	**14** Sharm Club
2 Beach Albatros	**8** Hilton Sharm Waterfall	**15** Tower
3 Clifftop	**9** Iberotel Palace	**16** Tropicana Inn
4 Dive Inn Swiss Resort	**10** Iberotel Grand Sharm	**17** Tropicana Tivoli
5 Dreams Beach	**11** Marine Club	**18** The Rock
6 El-Kheima	**12** Ritz-Carlton	**19** Youth Hostel
7 Horus	**13** Royal Paradise	

Hyperbaric Medical Chamber

Sharm el-Sheikh Bay

Marina

DOWNTOWN SHARM

Sharm el-Maya Bay

HADABA

Police

CLIFFTOP

RAS UMM SIDD

Ras Umm Sidd Dive Site

0 — 500m approximate

Sheik Abdullah Supermarket

HAY EL-NUR — Medical Centre

Hospital & Hyperbaric Medical Chamber

Nawara Farm

THE TOWER

East Delta Bus Station

Petrol Station

△ *Na'ama Bay (5 km)*

SHARM EL-SHEIKH

The Rock, Sharm clifftop (☎069/661-765, fax 660-203, *therock@sinainet.com.eg*). A/C rooms with TV and bath. Pool and shuttle-bus. Also rents apartments for four or six people. ⑥.

Royal Paradise Hotel, just back from the beach at Ras Umm Sidd (☎069/663-613, fax 661-503). A new and not very attractive hotel, but it's home to the well-reputed Waterland dive centre. ⑦.

Tropicana Inn, at the end of the strip of hotels leading away from the clifftop at Sharm (☎069/663-376, fax 663-375). A/C rooms with satellite TV, plus there's a pool and a shuttle-bus to the beach. Used by Explorers Tours. ⑥.

Tropicana Tivoli, Sharm clifftop (☎069/661-381, fax 661-380). Rooms with A/C and kitchenette, sited around a large pool. Also runs a shuttle-bus to its sister hotel in Na'ama Bay and the beach at Ras Umm Sidd. ⑦.

Youth hostel (☎ & fax 069/600-317). On the left on the top of the cliff; look out for its basketball court. Cramped A/C dorms with bunks, and cleanish bathrooms, but a new building is under construction so things might improve. May be full of young Egyptians or otherwise virtually empty. Non-members admitted (£E1 extra). Breakfast included; £E18.50.

Diving courses and excursions

Most **diving centres** are now firmly attached to hotels, but most are happy to take non-guests for courses and daily boat diving. Before signing up for anything, ask where you'll be doing your training; the water in Sharm's bay is a lot dirtier than in Na'ama Bay. You're better off looking there or at the dive centres around Ras Umm Sidd where you will find the long-established African Divers (see below), Rasta Divers and more recent arrivals Waterland at *Royal Paradise Hotel*. Dive Africa, a five-star PADI centre, recently moved to *Beach Albatros* and claims to be very eco-friendly. Prices for most dive trips and courses mirror those offered by dive centres in Na'ama (see p.575 for details).

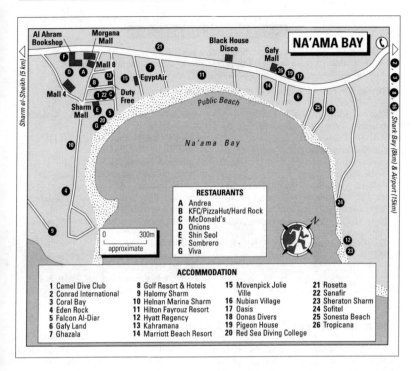

NA'AMA BAY

Al Ahram Bookshop
Morgana Mall
Black House Disco
Gafy Mall

F
D A
Mall 8
B
13 15
EgyptAir
Mall 4
1 22 C
Duty Free
Sharm Mall
E 5
20
G
10

26 19 17
14
6
25 18

Sharm el-Sheikh (5 km)

Public Beach

Na'ama Bay

Shark Bay (8km) & Airport (15km)

RESTAURANTS
A Andrea
B KFC/PizzaHut/Hard Rock
C McDonald's
D Onions
E Shin Seol
F Sombrero
G Viva

0   300m
approximate

24

12
23

ACCOMMODATION

1 Camel Dive Club	8 Golf Resort & Hotels	15 Movenpick Jolie Ville	21 Rosetta
2 Conrad International	9 Halomy Sharm	16 Nubian Village	22 Sanafir
3 Coral Bay	10 Helnan Marina Sharm	17 Oasis	23 Sheraton Sharm
4 Eden Rock	11 Hilton Fayrouz Resort	18 Oonas Divers	24 Sofitel
5 Falcon Al-Diar	12 Hyatt Regency	19 Pigeon House	25 Sonesta Beach
6 Gafy Land	13 Kahramana	20 Red Sea Diving College	26 Tropicana
7 Ghazala	14 Marriott Beach Resort		

In case of **diving emergencies**, contact the Hyperbaric Medical Centre near the Sharm el-Sheikh marina (☎069/660-992, mobile 012/212-4292); there is also a new decompression facility at the International Hospital in Hay el-Nur (☎069/600-893).

Eating, drinking and other practicalities

Aside from **eating and drinking** in hotels, there is a wide range of restaurants, coffeshops and *fuul* and *taamiya* stalls to choose from. One of the best value seafood restaurants is the *Sinai Star* (☎069/600-623) in the main shopping arcade, where a meal will cost you £E15–20. Another, more expensive choice for seafood is *Safsafa* (☎069/660-474) in Asia Mall. The cheapest snacks going are egg or *taamiya* sandwiches, sold in local restaurants and street stalls, and there are also a couple of pizza joints. The best-stocked **supermarket** in downtown Sharm is Sharm Express, located near the 24-hour **laundry**, Bergo's. However, the area's cheapest supermarket, which also offers the most choice, is Sheikh Abdullah's in Hal el-Nur. To the left of *Safety Land*, there is a street leading to a **bakery**. Beer is available from a shop beside the *Sinai Star* in the main arcade (24 cans of Stella costs £E85). Other facilities are concentrated on the hilltop, where an arcade contains three **banks** (daily 8am–2pm & 6–8pm) that change travellers' cheques; a **post office** (daily except Fri 8am–3pm; you can also buy stamps in shops and post letters in hotels) and a **pharmacy** (daily 9am–3pm & 6–11pm). Further on and off to the left is a 24-hour **telephone** exchange that sells international phonecards for £E20 (3min). The **police** and **tourist police** (both open 24hr) share a building in the municipal showpiece zone beyond the mosque.

DIVING CENTRES

Sharm and Na'ama Bay's major diving centres have recently formed the **Sharm Diving Union** (☎ & fax 069/660-418, *sharm_diving_union@sinainet.com.eg*). Among other things they organize regular clean-ups of the sea.

African Divers, Ras Umm Sidd (☎ & fax 069/600-307, *african @sinainet.com.eg*). PADI, CMAS, NAUI, SSI.

Atlantis, *Safety Land* (☎069/601-182, fax 660-334). PADI, CMAS, SSI.

Cali International Dive Centre, *Marine Club* (☎069/661-030, fax 601-031). PADI, NAUI, MDEA.

Colona, *Amar Sina* (☎069/662-222, fax 662-233, *colona@sinainet.com.eg*) PADI. Also offers liveaboard trips (see p.576).

Dive Africa, *Pick Albatros* (☎069/663-122, fax 663-398, *diveafrica@sinainet.com.eg*). PADI and SSI.

Divers Den, *Seti Sharm Hotel* (☎069/600-870, *den@sinainet.com.eg*) Also in Na'ama Bay. PADI, BSAC, CMAS, SSI, NASDS.

Diver's Lodge, *Aida Beach Hotel* (☎ & fax 069/601-255). PADI, SSI.

Leonessa Diving, *Tower Club* (☎069/600-230, fax 600-237). Mainly Italian clientele. PADI.

Rasta Divers, (no dive shop) (☎069/663-086, mobile 012/213-3881, *rasta@sinainet.com.eg*). Somewhat exclusive, caters mostly to private groups. PADI, CMAS, SSI.

Waterland, *Royal Paradise* (☎069/663-613, fax 661-503, *waterland@sinainet.com.eg*). PADI, SSI.

The reefs between Sharm and Na'ama

The fabulous array of **dive spots** between Sharm and Na'ama is the chief attraction of both resorts, offering endless scope for boat or beach diving. Although tourism in these parts was formerly geared to diving-buffs from Northern Europe, the newer developments pander to Italian couples worshipping the body beautiful.The most accessible site is **RAS UMM SIDD**, just around Sharm el-Sheikh's headland, a fifteen-minute walk from the top of the hill. The area is basically all coral reef without any natural sandy beaches – what sand there is has been imported by the hotels to create their own beaches. And the endless construction has inevitably increased the debris many divers now encounter underwater in this area.

From Ras Umm Sidd, a paved road lined with holiday villages and hotels runs to **THE TOWER**, a fine diving beach colonized by the *Tower* (☎069/600-231, fax 600-230; ⑧) and *Sharm Club* (☎069/600-260, fax 600-733; ⑧) **hotels**. The *Tower*'s beach café is a good place for watching oiled and aerobicized Italians – but the real lure is a huge **coral pillar** just offshore, which drops 60m into the depths. As the road rejoins the highway at the gas station midway between Sharm and Na'ama, it's easy to get there by taxi from either resort.

It is no longer possible to access most of the reefs between Ras Umm Sidd and the Tower from land, as hotels along this stretch of coast now effectively block public access to the sea. Diving these reefs by boat, in order of appearance after Ras Umm Sidd, you come to Fiasco, Paradise, Turtle Bay, Pinky's Wall and Amphoras. **Turtle Bay** has warm sun-dappled water that's lovely to swim in, even if there are fewer **green turtles** (*Chelonia myades*) than you'd wish for. **Amphoras** gets its name from the cargo of clay jars aboard an Ottoman ship that sunk on the reef; as the jars contain mercury, it's lucky that they remain sealed. Diving down to the **wreck** is safe enough for novices.

Na'ama Bay

With its fine beach and upmarket facilities, **NA'AMA BAY** has transformed itself so rapidly even the residents have trouble keeping up. In a few short years the bay has grown from a few huts on the beach, to what looks like a mini-city. The amazing diving and snorkelling are still the main draws, with dive centres, hotels and malls being the only points of reference along the beachfront "strip", while a new row of hotels has grown up behind the main highway. The **beach** is divided into hotel-owned plots that are supposedly open to anyone providing they don't use the parasols or chairs – but hippy-looking types may be hassled and topless bathing is not only technically illegal, it is highly unadvisable. One public beach remains, although it's very hard to find, squeezed in next to the *Novotel*.

Accommodation

As pricey **holiday villages** are the norm here, travellers on a tight budget either stay in Sharm and commute by microbus, or roost at the *Pigeon House*, the best cheapish hotel in Na'ama. The *Oasis* next door has similar accommodation but is definitely lacking in atmosphere. Alternatively there are a couple of **diving colleges** that rent out rooms to divers on their courses. The *Red Sea Diving College* (☎069/600-145, fax 600-144, *college@sinainet.com.eg*; ⑤) is central and on the beach with clean, en-suite A/C rooms. They also have dorm beds with A/C and breakfast included for US$10 per person; *Oonas Divers* (☎069/600-581, fax 600-582, *oonas@sinainet.com.eg*; ⑦), at the northern end of the bay, also has A/C rooms. Those with children in tow should note that the *Hilton* and the *Sonesta* both offer decent "Kids Club" facilities. The nearest place to **camp** is at Shark Bay, although this campground may soon be subject to redevelopment; if you have your own transport, you might consider camping at Ras Mohammed (see p.566).

Camel Dive Club Hotel (☎069/600-700, fax 600-601, *reservations@cameldive.com*). A small, but well-designed hotel right in the heart of Na'ama and attached to one of the best dive centres. A/C rooms with satellite TV, some with disabled access. ⑦–⑧.

Coral Bay (aka "Sheikh Coast"), 5km north of Na'ama Bay (☎069/600-610, fax 600-483). A five-star many-domed village with a large private beach and casino, The *Coral Bay* is one of the ritziest places in the area (Omar Sharif has a villa here). Also home to Sinai Wildlife Projects (see p.579). ⑧–⑨.

Conrad International, 14km north of Na'ama, just before Ras Nasrani (☎069/600-175, fax 600-177, *conrad@sinainet.com.eg*). Newly-built mega-complex with its own beach, ten bars and restaurants, shops, watersports etc. ⑧.

Eden Rock, on the southern hill overlooking Na'ama Bay (☎069/602-250, fax 602-257, *edenrock@sinainet.com.eg*). A/C rooms with balcony or terrace and satellite TV; also offers good views and a pool. ⑦.

Falcon Al-Diar, opposite *McDonald's* (☎069/600-827, fax 600-826). Oriental-style hotel with a pool and private beach. A/C rooms with satellite TV, video channel. ⑧.

Gafy Land, on the beach (☎069/600-210, fax 600-216, *gafyland@access.com.eg*). Rooms with A/C, satellite TV and seaviews. Pool. Gafy Mall behind it. ⑧.

Ghazala Hotel, on the beach (☎069/600-150, fax 600-155, *ghazala@sinainet.com.eg*). Medium-sized four-star holiday village with pool and tennis courts. Mainly German and Swiss guests. ⑧.

Golf Resort and Hotels, 7km north of Na'ama, this is the next big resort after *Coral Bay* (☎069/603-200, fax 603-225, *gmgolfsharm@hotmail.com*). Has 270 A/C rooms with views of the resort's own golf course, garden or the sea. Also offers several luxury villas; President Mubarak has his own villa by the sea. ⑧–⑨.

Halomy Sharm, on the cliff at the southern end of the bay (☎069/600-681, fax 600-134). Its 70 A/C chalets have views of the Gulf and nearby reefs; facilities include tennis courts. ⑧.

Helnan Marina Sharm, at the southern end of the bay (☎069/600-751, fax 600-712, *saleshms@helnan.com*). Na'ama's first (Israeli-built) hotel. Some disabled-friendly rooms. Two pools and a good beach. ⑦.

Hilton Fayrouz Resort, on the beach (☎069/600-140, fax 660-040, *Fayrouz@sinainet.com.eg*). Similar facilities and prices to the *Ghazala*, but larger and more comfortable. There's a sports centre, and children up to twelve stay free. Home to one of the locals' favourite pubs, *Pirates Bar*. ⑨.

Hyatt Regency, just north of Na'ama Bay (☎069/601-234, fax 603-600). Another mega-hotel, overlooking the coral gardens which means a poor beach. Rooms for disabled guests, and even non-allergenic sheets and towels. Extensive sports facilities. ⑧.

Kahramana Hotel, in the third row back from the beach (☎069/601-071, fax 601-176). Four-star complex which has a nice bar with a pool table; some notably good value flight/hotel packages available in conjunction with this property. ⑧.

Marriott Beach Resort, (☎069/600-190, fax 600-188) One of the most expensive hotels in Na'ama, with an appropriately pricey Japanese restaurant, the *Kona Kai*, plus a beach and pools. ⑨.

Môvenpick Jolie Ville, smack in the middle of Na'ama (☎069/600-100, fax 600-111). This hotel is so large that it has a shuttle-bus from one end to the other. Its five-star amenities are guarded against interlopers. Popular beach bar. ⑧.

Nubian Village, 25km north of Na'ama, towards Nabeq (☎012/217-6962, fax 215-6364). Very beautiful hotel designed to resemble a Nubian village. Part of the Franco Rosso Group so mainly Italian guests, but it's not overly expensive. Full board only. ⑦.

Oasis (☎ & fax 069/601-602). Next to the better *Pigeon House* (see below) and only worth considering if the latter is full. Similar prices and accommodation, but no atmosphere. ④–⑥.

Pigeon House, on the edge of the desert, 750m from the beach (☎069/600-996, fax 600-995, *pigeon@access.com.eg*). The most popular budget option, with thatched huts and rooms with fans or A/C. Good for solo travellers and meeting people. Arranges safari trips, and guests get a ten percent discount at Anemone Dive Centre. Breakfast included. ④–⑥.

Rosetta, opposite the *Hilton*, on the other side of the highway (☎069/601-888, fax 601-999). A/C rooms with satellite TV; there's a pool and the *Black House* disco, and the hotel is home to Emperor Divers. ⑧.

Sanafir, in central Na'ama, one block back from the beach (☎069/600-197, fax 600-196, *sanafir@access.com.eg*). One of the first hotels in Na'ama, its huts have long gone, replaced by a striking white domed compound of A/C rooms, much imitated in Sharm. There's a pool and several restaurants and bars; popular evening venue and home to the *Bus Stop*, Na'ama's liveliest nightclub. Good buffet breakfast included. ⑦.

Sheraton Sharm Hotel, Resort and Villas, 1km north of Na'ama Bay (☎069/602-070, fax 602-099). Offers 300 rooms, suites and villas overlooking Tiran Strait. An attraction for some will be the Turkish bath, while the resort's *Al Pasha Casino* claims to be the biggest in Egypt. ⑧.

Sofitel Coralia, on the north hill overlooking Na'ama Bay (☎069/600-081, fax 600-085, *h1970@accor-hotels.com*). Impressive-looking resort with 300 A/C rooms with terraces. Pool and beach normally not too unfriendly to (female) interlopers from the *Pigeon House*. ⑧.

Sonesta Beach Resort, at the northern end of Na'ama on the beach (☎069/600-725, fax 600-733, *sonesta.europe@wxs.nl*). Five-star facilities, recently expanded, including water-gym and Kids' Club. ⑨.

Tropicana Hotel, beside the *Pigeon House* (☎069/600-652, fax 600-649). Small complex of A/C rooms, plus there's a pool. Shuttle bus to Ras Umm Sidd beach, or guests can use *Marriott* beach for £E15 a day. Welcoming to disabled guests; used by British tour operators. ⑦.

Diving courses and excursions

Much of Na'ama's appeal lies in its plethora of **diving centres** (see box opposite), which offer an extensive range of courses, trips and equipment rental. Though generally good, their prices and operating styles vary, so it's worth shopping around. Recommended outfits include the Anemone Dive Centre (laid-back, good value), Camel Dive Club (good facilities and lots of daily dive trips), Oonas (a five-star PADI dive centre), Red Sea Diving College (fine facilities and tuition) Shark Bay Dive Centre (quiet and has its own jetty) and Sinai Divers (efficient, experienced). All the centres are open daily (mostly 8.30am–6pm); dive boats leave the marina around 9am.

Total novices can make a supervised **introductory dive**; most places charge US$45–50 including equipment. Five-day Open Water **diving courses** progress from classroom theory to your first dives from the shore at Shark Bay or Ras Umm Sidd, and

DIVE CENTRES

Anemone Dive Centre *Pigeon House* (☎ & fax 069/600-999, *anemone@sinainet.com.eg*). PADI, NAUI, SSI.

Aquamarine Diving Centre *Novotel* (☎069/600-276, fax 600-176, *aquamarine@sinainet.com.eg*). PADI.

Camel Dive Club next to the *Sanafir Village* (☎069/600-700, fax 600-601, *reservations@cameldive.com*). All affiliations.

Colona Dive Club *Oasis* (☎ & fax 069/602-624, *colona@sinainet.com.eg*). PADI, SSI.

Diver's Network *Golf Resort,* Mall 4 & *Ritz-Carlton* (☎ & fax 069/602-033, *hseldin@sinainet.com.eg*). PADI, NAUI, SSI.

Emperor Divers & Red Sea Scuba Schools *Rosetta* (☎069/601-734, fax 601-735, *emperor.divers@sinainet.com.eg*). PADI.

Ocean College *Ocean Sands* (☎069/600-802, *ocean@sinainet.com.eg*). BSAC.

Oonas Divers near the *Sonesta Resort* (☎ & fax 069/600-581 or 600-582, *oonas@sinainet.com.eg*). PADI.

Red Sea Diving College Na'ama beach (☎069/600-145, fax 600-144, *college@sinainet.com.eg*). PADI.

Shark Bay Dive Centre *Shark's Bay Camp* (☎069/600-942, fax 600-944, *umbi@sinainet.com.eg*).

Sinai Dive Club *Hilton Fayrouz Resort* (☎069/600-140, fax 601-040, *dive.club@sinainet.com.eg*). PADI, CMAS, SSI.

Sinai Divers *Ghazala Hotel* (☎ & fax 069/600-158, *sinai_divers@sinainet.com.eg*). PADI, CMAS, SSI.

Subex Diving Centre *Mövenpick Jolie Ville* and *Holiday Sharm* (☎069/600-100, fax 600-111). CMAS.

The Crab *Kahramana* (☎069/600-660, *ssh1@the crab.com*). PADI, SSI.

LIVEABOARDS

Colona, Dive Africa, Diver's Network, Emperor Divers, Rasta Divers, Sinai Dive Club and Sinai Divers are just some of the dive centres that offer liveaboard trips; contact them direct for enquiries/bookings. Alternatively, the following private boats run dive safaris from Sharm el-Sheikh; all are contactable via email for information on prices, boat specifications etc.

Morgaan *morgaan@sinainet.com.eg*
President *president@sinainet.com.eg*
Royal Boats *tdrf@sinainet.com.eg*
Sabeel *sabeel@sinainet.com.eg*
Sea Queen *seaqueen@sinainet.com.eg*

Sinai Sensation *sensation@sinainet.com.eg*
Snefro Boats *snefro@sinainet.com.eg*
Sundance *sundance@sinainet.com.eg*
Tornado Marine *tornado@sinainet.com.eg*
Vip One *vipone@sinainet.com.eg*

finishing with a few boat-dives at the end. Anemone offers one of the cheapest **openwater PADI** courses in Na'ama (US$280, plus US$30 for the certificate) while Emperor and Colona both charge US$290 (plus US$30 for certificate). At the other end of the skill spectrum, you can be trained as an instructor or pursue **specialized courses** like night diving or underwater navigation (US$200–400). Divers are no longer allowed to explore the reefs near Na'ama and Sharm el-Sheikh **independently**; all diving must now be done with a guide, which in practical terms means sticking with trips run by the dive operators.

All centres organize daily **boat trips** to the dive sites. One day's diving at "local" sites like **Ras Nasrani** costs US$45–50 which includes two dives, tanks and weights, while trips further afield to the **Gordon and Jackson reefs** in the Tiran Strait (see p.581) or **Ras Mohammed** will set you back US$50–55. Entry to Ras Mohammed costs US$5 extra and requires a full Egyptian visa, so visitors with Sinai-only visas are not permitted to dive here. Snorkellers can generally join most boats, if there's room, for US$25. If you want to do lots of boat-diving, **dive packages** can be a good deal: Oonas charges

US$210 for a five-day package (10 dives). These rates do not include lunch on the boat (£E25) or **equipment rental**, which costs US$20–25 per day at most centres. Except for *Shark's Bay Camp*, which has its own jetty, all the boats start from the new marina in Sharm el-Maya, entailing a minibus journey there and back – although most dive centres will collect you and drop you off again if you're marooned at one of the hotels on the cliff.

One popular excursion is to the wreck of the **Thistlegorm** (found by Jacques Cousteau), whose wartime cargo of jeeps is eerily visible underwater. A one-day *Thistlegorm* trip with two dives costs US$80 with Camel, US$100 with Colona. Emperor offers a two-day trip with full board and five dives for US$185 (including equipment).

Increasingly popular with those who want intensive diving and longer at sea, is a few days or weeks on a **liveaboard**. The daily cost per person (US$80–200) largely depends on the vessel; some are quite spartan, others luxurious. As many of the boats are leased rather than owned by diving centres, you may be able to strike a deal directly with the captain; in any case, it's wise to inspect vessels at the marina before deciding. One of the most important things to look for, apart from the obvious comforts, is a good diving platform with space for your equipment. Meals (and maybe beverages) are usually included in the price; equipment, apart from tanks and weights, is not.

At time of writing, all dive centres were asking divers for US$1 for each day's diving, towards the cost of maintaining the Hyperbaric Chamber (see p.571).

Snorkelling and watersports

While diving is the main pursuit, Na'ama is also great for **snorkelling** – a less demanding but equally pleasurable activity. If you've never snorkelled before and find breathing through a tube unsettling, start with the baby reefs just off the beach, where the sea is only waist deep. By the time you've circled a reef and seen its profusion of rainbow-hued fish, snorkelling should feel like fun and you'll be ready to move on to bigger things. Unfortunately, visiting the other reefs involves some walking: drinking water, a hat and proper footwear are essential. It's wise to start early as the sea is usually calmest in the morning, an important factor when you've got to swim over serrated reefs.

The best **reefs** – aptly known as coral gardens – run for several miles **north of Na'ama Bay**. They don't get many divers (being deemed inferior to The Tower or Shark Bay) but are ideal for snorkelling. Just look for a safe descent from the rocks and the shortest, smoothest reef flat, with dark water beyond its edge. Bear in mind that these reefs are regularly visited by glass-bottom boats, so you will need to take care while you're in the water. The **Near Gardens** can be reached on foot by following the coast beyond Oonas Dive Centre. Plummeting to unseen depths beyond its crest, the reef has spawned offshore pillars and fantastic encrustations, swarming with angelfish, parrotfish and blue snappers. From here you can swim to the equally amazing **Middle and Far Gardens**, further up the coast.

If you're willing to pay to reach **other sites**, several agencies run overland snorkelling trips to the mangrove forests of **Nabeq** for around US$35 (see below), or boat trips to the less demanding reefs at **Ras Mohammed**, **Ras Nasrani** or **Shark Bay**. The Wave, at *Iberotel Grand Sharm* in Ras Umm Sidd (☎069/663-800), offers a full-day boat trip to Ras Mohammed or Tiran for US$40 (plus US$5 entry fee) as well as sunset (US$20) and night cruises (US$35), while Fanous Moto Safari (☎069/603-059) runs snorkelling trips to the Near and Far Gardens and White Knights. A full-day overland trip to Nabeq, including Shark Bay and Dahab, costs US$70.

Apart from snorkelling, there's a wide variety of watersports on offer at most beachfront hotels, including sailing, windsurfing (instructors for both are available), water skiing, parasailing and pedalos. Thankfully, swimmers are spared having to dodge jetskiers, banned in Na'ama Bay since 1998, when two Italian tourists crashed into each other and were killed. There are, of course, glass-bottom boats if you don't want to get wet at all. The Wave and Sun'n'Fun have boats leaving every two hours throughout the day (1hr 30min; £E55, children £E30).

Overland trips and safaris

Should the wonders of the deep pall, safari and travel agencies (see box below) can arrange jeep, camel, or motorbike trips. "Quads" or **quadrunners**, also known as ATVs (All-Terrain Vehicles) are another popular way of charging into the desert.

Some of the most popular **day excursions** by jeep are a mangrove-and-snorkelling visit to **Nabeq** (The Wave does a half-day trip for US$35); a 4WD trip to the **Coloured Canyon** followed by a swim with the **dolphin** in Nuweiba (most places charge around US$60); or **St Catherine's Monastery** (overnight trip including climbing Mount Sinai for US$50). Nearer to Na'ama lies Wadi Mandar, visited on sunset trips by jeep (US$30) or camel (US$20 with tea, US$35 with dinner). If you see trips advertised for less, they probably involve travelling by bus rather than jeep. A bit further up the road is **Wadi Ain Kid**, a long fertile canyon culminating in an oasis of palm trees, a well and Bedouin farm; overnight excursions with Hussein from the *Pigeon House* cost US$50. Several companies also offer excursions to Sarabit el-Khadem and Hammam Faraoun. If a **longer** time in the wild appeals, Khaled Liston can organize 4WD or diving safaris for around US$100 per person per day, for up to a fortnight; Madian Adventure offers jeep safaris and mountain trekking from US$80 per person per day (for details of both see box below). Most of the sites mentioned above are covered later in this chapter, and are cheaper to reach from Nuweiba.

Horse-riding in the desert can be arranged through Stefano at *Camp Kanasir* at Wadi Khansour (☎012/322-3313); overnight trips start from US$50. Most recreation centres in Na'ama charge US$20 per hour or US$30 for two hours. The norm for **camel rides** is US$20 with a stop for Bedouin tea, or US$35 with dinner.

EXCURSIONS AND SAFARI TRIPS

Excursions to the desert, St Catherine's and the Coloured Canyon, as well as activities like swimming with the dolphin in Nuweiba, can be booked through travel agents, safari operators, or direct with the Bedouin guides hanging out at *Shark's Bay Camp* and the *Pigeon House*.

TRAVEL AGENTS

Abu Noub Morgana Mall (☎069/600-066, fax 600-855). Established, reliable agent.

Nass Tours Plaza Mall (☎ & fax 601-258, *nasstours@sinainet.com.eg*). Can help with booking trips to Petra.

Thomas Cook *Gafy Mall* (☎069/601-808). Friendly service, can help with most general travel arrangements for the rest of Egypt.

Travco Iberotel Palace (☎069/661-111). Sells tickets for the catamaran to Hurghada.

SAFARI OPERATORS

Desert Blues Safaris (☎ & fax 069/660-141, mobile 010/143-6121, *barbara@sinainet.com.eg*). Very experienced Bedouin guide; charges US$80–100 per person per day.

Hussein (☎012/224-6193) Bedouin guide based at *Pigeon House*. US$50 per person per day.

Khaled Liston (☎069/662-068, *khaledliston@hotmail.com*). Desert and diving safaris and boat safaris for US$100–120 per person per day.

Madian Adventure (☎069/662-421, *madian@tecmina.com*). One of the first guides in the area, and very experienced; charges US$80 per person per day.

If you fancy venturing out on your own **by car**, a Jeep Cherokee can be rented for US$90 a day from Avis in Morgana Mall (☎069/602-400) and at the *Sonesta* (☎069/600-979). Prices for a smaller car such as a Ford Fiesta start from US$35 a day; try Shark Limousine (☎069/603-200) at the *Golf*, or Hertz at the *Sanafir* (☎069/600-459). CRC (in Sharm Mall; ☎069/600-407) offers the larger Peugeot 106 with a 100km daily limit for US$45 per day. Of the other major companies, you'll find Budget in the *Marriott* and Thrifty at the *Mövenpick*.

Canyon Safari at the *Pigeon House* (☎069/600-997, mobile 012/315-8121) rents **quads** (double US$28 per hour, single US$18), and also runs a popular guided sunset trip (US$35 double, US$25 single) which takes two hours with a stop for Bedouin tea. Other quad excursions include a six-hour trip to Nabeq with lunch (US$110 double, US$90 single) and a Bedouin dinner trip (US$50 double, US$35 single). Sinai Riders at the *Kahramana* (☎069/601-701, mobile 012/337-6499) has quads at similar rates, and also rents racing **motorbikes** (US$50 per hour); their guided motorbike trips take in Ras Mohammed (US$100, half-day), Dahab, Nuweiba or St Catherine's (US$150, full day).

Keep in mind that is illegal for unaccompanied foreigners to go off-road; there are still many unexploded landmines in Sinai and you won't know where they are.

Eating, drinking and nightlife

There are no really cheap places to eat or drink, so what passes for inexpensive is relative. On the plus side, the quality of the **food** is high and there is wide choice ranging from Egyptian, Italian and seafood to Japanese and Thai; prices tend to be higher along the "strip" outside the *Sanafir* and *Camel Dive Club* hotels. If you want fish, but don't want to travel to *Sinai Star* in Sharm (see p.571), try *Viva Seafood* next to Red Sea Diving College. There's an expensive Japanese restaurant, *Kona Kai*, at the *Marriott*, and if you long for the familiar, you can find *KFC*, *Pizza Hut* and *McDonald's* (☎069/602-110 for *McDonald's* home delivery) within a stone's throw of each other. If you fancy eating by the sea, try the *Hilton's* restaurant, or venture up to the fish restaurant at *Shark's Bay Camp*.

Al-Fanar, at Ras Umm Sidd lighthouse (☎012/215-6583). Excellent Italian food and an unbeatable location on the beach; popular with Italian families. A bit expensive though. Daily 11am–midnight.

Andrea, in the mall opposite *Hard Rock Café* (☎069/600-972). Mostly chicken-based dishes, but also good value Egyptian food; from £E9–12 for a meal.

Bua Khao, at *Sharm Holiday Resort* (☎069/601-391). Thai cuisine is one of the latest arrivals in Sharm, but it's not cheap. Open daily for lunch and dinner.

Da Franco, at the *Ghazala*. Excellent pizza and pasta restaurant; reasonably priced main dishes (£E15–20).

Hard Rock Café (☎069/602-665). Serves hamburgers with all the trimmings; one of the most popular nightspots in Sharm. Daily 12.30pm–2am (till 3am Sat).

Jurgen at the Sombrero, on the highway just before Na'ama Bay (☎012/214-6143). Safe European-style food with a dash of Orientalism.

Kokai, at the *Ghazala*. Japanese restaurant, slightly cheaper than *Kona Kai* at the *Marriott*.

Mashy Café du Liban, also at the *Sanafir*. Alfresco Lebanese cuisine. Good value, especially if you're a meat lover. Open daily for lunch and dinner; dishes £E20–45.

Onions, in the Royal Mall opposite the *Cataract Hotel* (☎069/600-050). Popular place, offering good value, basic food – pasta, salads, kebabs etc. Very good *sheeshas*. Also does take-away and home delivery. Most dishes £E8–25.

Peking, at the *Sanafir*. Chinese and Korean restaurant on the roof of this hotel.

Shin Seol, in the Sharm Mall. Reasonable Chinese restaurant with roof garden. About £E25 for a three-course meal.

Tam Tam, at the *Ghazala* (☎069/600-150). Tasty Egyptian food near the beach with roof-top seating. Excellent *karkade* (hibiscus drink hot or cold), lentil soup and Egyptian sweets. Does take-away. Daily until 1am.

La Trattoria, at the *Sanafir*. Good, basic Italian restaurant, run by Italians. Pasta from £E15.

Viva, next to Red Sea Diving College (☎069/600-964). Reasonably-priced seafood restaurant near the beach. Good pasta too.

NIGHTLIFE

Alcoholic drinks are widely available at European prices; the **duty-free shop** in front of the *Kahramana* (daily 11am–2pm & 6–11pm) sells cheap booze, though at the time of writing you can only buy duty-free within the first 48 hours of arrival in Egypt. The bar at the *Pigeon House* is a good place to start your evening as it often has special promotions, as does Sinai Divers. Currently a favourite with divers is *Chris's Place*, at *Camel Dive Club*, but you will find more locals at the nautically themed *Pirates Bar* in the *Hilton* (happy hour 5.30–7.30pm), which also serves good food. Another popular spot is *Sombrero*, a friendly Mexican-style roof bar on the main highway just south of Na'ama Bay.

Na'ama's premier nightspot is the *Sanafir*, where you'll find a stylish rooftop bar and the *Bus Stop* disco (£E20, includes one drink), which opens at 10pm but doesn't get going until past midnight. Its main competition, notably popular with Italians, is the *Hard Rock Café*, on the main road leading to Na'ama Bay (daily 8pm–2am; until 3am Sat; ☎069/602-665).

Other discos include the *Black House Disco* at the *Rosetta*, *Cactus* at the *Mövenpick*, *Casablanca* at the *Sonesta*, and the Latin-themed *La Luna* at the *Golf*; none is likely to be very lively before midnight. Though most specify "couples only", the rule is seldom enforced. There are **pool tables** in the *Kahramana* bar, in the *Hilton Fayrouz* and in the Lobby Bar of the *Ghazala*. For a more Egyptian-style evening, several coffee shops offer *sheeshas*, backgammon and chess – try *Coffeeshop Mohamed* near the *Sanafir* or *El Fishawys* in Sharm Mall – while *El-Mastaba*, at the *Ghazala Gardens*, offers live entertainment including belly dancing. The *Mövenpick* has a poolside cinema, where you can watch new release Hollywood films for £E50 (including a simple buffet meal).

Listings

Banks and exchange Most banks are open daily (8.30am–2pm & 6–9pm). The National Bank of Egypt has branches in the *Ghazala*, *Mövenpick*, *Hilton* and *Marina Sharm*. You can get cash advances on Visa and MasterCard at the Banque Misr (9am–1.30pm & 5–8pm) in the Sharm Mall. Several banks now have ATMs; one that usually works is at the Egyptian British Bank next to *McDonald's*. For changing money, Swiss Exchange in Morgana Mall (daily 9am–midnight) may offer slightly better rates than the banks (cash only).

Books and newspapers Al Ahram, on the highway just south of Na'ama (9am–1pm & 6–10pm) sells books and international newspapers. You can also get English-language newspapers at the *Hilton* bookshop.

SINAI WILDLIFE PROJECTS

Sinai Wildlife Projects (☎069/601610 ext 241, *swp@sinainet.com.eg*) is a non-profit conservation organization, active in Sharm el-Sheikh since 1992. Some of its most important work takes place during autumn, when 32 different species of raptors and cranes and 82 percent of the world's population of white storks pass through the area on their journey south. Each week over 500 sick and injured birds are treated in SWP's animal hospital at *Coral Bay Hotel*.

One of the organizations most recent acquisitions is **Nawara Farm** (see map on p.570), a striking enclosure of trees on the road from the Tower dive site to the main highway. The farm, open from sunrise to sunset, is a haven of birdlife and there are plans to set up hides for twitchers to be more comfortable.

Periodically volunteers are taken on to work on SWP's various projects; contact the centre for more information.

Dentist Dr Mohammed el-Hadidy, at the Morgana Mall (☎069/601-111, mobile 010/153-5372).

Doctor Dr Wael Habib, at the Mount Sinai Clinic in the *Môvenpick* (☎069/600-100; 24hr mobile 012/218-9889).

Internet Cafés *Cyber Disco* at the *Hilton Fayrouz* (☎069/600-136, *fayrouz@sinainet.com.eg*; £E15 per hour); *Camel Cyber* at *Camel Dive Club* (☎069/600-700, *info@cameldive.com*, £E20 per hour); *GlobalLink* in Mall 8 (daily 10am–midnight; ☎069/601-819, *team@globallink.8m.com*; £E10 for 30min).

Supermarkets Cherry, in Sharm Mall (daily 9am–midnight); Shamandoura, next to the *Sanafir* (daily 9am–midnight); Sheikh Abdullah's in Hay el-Nur is the cheapest and offers the most variety.

Pharmacy Towa, in the Sharm Mall (daily 10am–1am; ☎069/600-779) offers free home delivery if you're too sick to go there in person.

Telephone exchanges Sharm No. 1 on the clifftop in Sharm, and Sharm No.2 opposite the entrance to the Sheraton about 1km north of Na'ama Bay (both daily 10am–10pm).

Thomas Cook In the Gafy Mall (9am–2pm & 5–10pm). Usual range of travel services as well as Visa cash advances.

Western Union At the DHL office in the *Rosetta* (Sun–Thurs 9am–9pm; ☎069/602-222, fax 602-223).

Moving on

Sharm is the transport hub of South Sinai, with overland services to Cairo, the Canal Zone and most points in the peninsula, boats to Hurghada, and flights to domestic and international airports.

The direct A/C Superjet nightbus leaves for **Cairo** at 11pm (£E55) from the Superjet terminal (☎069/601-622) next to EgyptAir on the main highway at the junction leading to downtown Sharm. You will need to buy your ticket in advance to be sure of getting a seat, but this bus is more direct and tends to be quieter than the East Delta buses to Cairo that leave from the bus station in Hay el-Nur (6 daily; £E50; also evening buses at 10pm, 11pm & midnight; £E65). You have to reserve seats in person at the bus station, or the office next to the Superjet terminal in person. It's worth turning up early for the 7.30am bus to **St Catherine's Monastery** (£E25). The 9am service to **Taba** (£E25) also stops at **Dahab** which can also be reached by direct buses at 7.30am, 2.30pm and 5pm (£E10). Both services to **Nuweiba** (9am & 5pm; £E20) can be crowded. Buses also run to the Canal cities of **Suez** (7am, 9am & 10pm; £E30) and **Ismailiya** (7 daily; £E35). It's cheaper to catch a bus to Suez and then a *service* taxi to Cairo than to travel by A/C bus all the way.

In the absence of a bus you'll be thrown back on **service taxis**, whose rates are negotiable. The usual destinations on offer are Suez, Taba and St Catherine's, though others can be agreed if the price is right. The larger the group, the less each person pays.

Voyaging across the Red Sea or the Gulf of Aqaba has been transformed by the **catamaran**, a high-speed service between Sharm and **Hurghada**. The ninety-minute journey across the Gulf of Suez (6pm Mon, Tues, Thurs & Sat; US$33/£E115, cars £E250); can be booked in Sharm el-Sheikh through Travco (☎069/661-111 or 660-764). You can save US$6 by travelling on the much slower **ferry**, but it's prone to breakdowns and delays so it really isn't worth it.

The EgyptAir office in Sharm (daily 9am–2pm & 6–9pm; ☎069/661-056, fax 661-057) can sell tickets for **flights** to other cities in Egypt and Tel Aviv. There are regular flights from Ras Nasrani airport, 10km north of Na'ama to **Alexandria** (Mon & Fri 11.45am; US$185), **Cairo** (Sun 8am, 7.15pm & 9.15pm; Mon, Wed & Fri 8am; Tues 8am & 10.25pm; Thurs 10.30am & 9.15pm; Sat 10.30am & 7pm; US$140), **Hurghada** (Sun 11.30pm, Mon 3.30am, Sat 6am; US$98), **Luxor** (Thurs & Sat 8am; US$123), **Taba** (Mon 9.30pm; US$57) and **Tel Aviv** (Mon & Fri or Thurs & Sun 11.05am; US$139). For flights to Europe, check with the representatives of UK tour operators who might be able to sell you a seat on their charter flights (see p.6).

Shark Bay

Ten kilometres up the coast from Na'ama is the quieter resort of **SHARK BAY**, reached by a well-signposted road that leaves the main road before the turn-off for Ras Nasrani airport (£E15 by taxi). Despite the bay's forbidding name (*Beit el-Irsh*, "House of the Shark" in Arabic), all the sharks have been scared away by divers, leaving a benign array of tropical fish and coral gardens just offshore, with deeper reefs and bigger fish further out. Sheikh Embarak's **Shark's Bay Camp** (☎069/600-942, fax 600-941) is a pleasant mix of bungalows (⑤) and beach huts (⑤) with its own dive centre and jetty – although the nearby *Pyramisa Hotel* now has half the beach. But Shark Bay still attracts many young Israelis, overlanders on stopovers and day-visitors from Na'ama; there's a £E10 charge to use the beach which includes the use of showers and a soft drink. The *Camp*'s **diving centre** runs boat trips to the Tiran Strait (day-dive US$40; liveaboard US$95 a day) while Bedouins who hang out there can arrange jeep safaris into the interior. Its restaurant and Bedouin café are quiet nightspots which close around midnight; guests wanting more action generally club together for a taxi into Na'ama.

Just a kilometre or so north of Shark Bay, **White Knights** is a good place to go beach **diving**; its name derives from coral formations that resemble ghostly warriors.

The Tiran Strait and Nabeq

The headland of Ras Nasrani beyond Shark Bay marks the onset of the **Tiran Strait**, where the waters of the Gulf of Suez flow into the deeper Gulf of Aqaba, swirling around islands and reefs. In 1992, the Tiran archipelago was declared a protected area, which may become a fully fledged national park. Meanwhile, there's no admission charge or facilities and the only access is by boat from Na'ama, Sharm or Shark Bay. This is *not* an excursion for novice divers, as the sea can be extremely rough and chilling (bring high-calorie drinks and snacks to boost your energy).

Sharks, manta rays, barracuda and Napoleon fish are typical of the deepwater sites around the **islands of Tiran and Sanafir**, though there are also shallow reefs like the Small Lagoon and Hushasha. The **Jackson Reef** has a spectacular 70m drop-off and the wreck of the *Lara* to investigate, while the **Gordon Reef** boasts the hulk of the *Lucila*. The multitude of **shipwrecks** in the Gulf is due to treacherous reefs and currents, insurance fraud, and Egypt's blockade of the Strait in the 1960s. Two notable sites at **Ras Nasrani** are the **Light**, with a 40m drop-off and pelagic fish; and the **Point**, with a dazzling array of reef fish.

Beyond the mouth of the Gulf of Aqaba, a swathe of the coast as far north as Dahab City has been designated another protected area, named after the small oasis and **Bedouin village** of NABEQ. As few dive boats come here from Na'ama, the **reefs** are quieter than at Tiran or Ras Mohammed. Most visitors are on half-day trips to see Nabeq's mangrove forests – the most northerly in the world. **Mangroves** can filter salt from sea water and thus survive in tropical coastal areas. As sediment traps, they reduce erosion and provide a habitat for mating fish and migratory birds (in summer and autumn), acting as the ecological interface between the coast and the interior, whose flood-prone wadis sustain ibex, hyrax, foxes and other **wildlife**.

Nabeq can be reached by two main routes. You can either take the road that leads to Ras Nasrani airport, which continues to the entrance (US$5) gates. From here the road changes to a track, best navigated with a 4WD vehicle, which contines as far as Ras Atantur (20km). There are also two signposted tracks off the main road to Dahab, one before and one after the copper mine. They both meet the coast near the stretch of reef bearing the wreck of the *Maria Shroeder*. All approaches are best made by someone who knows the way, wander off the track and you might inadvertently encounter **mines** left over from Israeli-Egyptian wars, which killed a jeep-load of tourists in 1995. The only facilities here are a **cafeteria** and visitors' centre.

Dahab and Asilah

Jagged mountains ranged inland of Na'ama Bay accompany the road 95km northwards, providing a magnificent backdrop for **DAHAB**'s tawny beaches, from which its Arabic name – "gold" – derives. The resort divides into two localities: a cluster of holiday villages catering for affluent visitors, and the Bedouin settlement of **ASILAH** 2.5km up the coast, where younger travellers hang out in a kind of Goa by the Red Sea – though as Asilah moves upmarket, the distinction between them is blurring. A third area is developing to the north of Asilah, near the dive sites of the Canyon and Blue Hole, but most construction was unfinished at time of writing.

Don't be discouraged by **DAHAB CITY**, a colony of municipal housing and offices 1km inland of the holiday villages. The only reason to go there is to use its facilities: a **post office** (daily except Fri 8.30am–3pm) and 24-hour **telephone exchange** (international calls with phonecards); a **bank** which accepts travellers' cheques and Visa (winter Sat–Thurs 8.30am–2pm & 5–8pm, Fri 8.30–11am & 5–8pm; summer Sat–Thurs 9am–12.30pm & 6.30–8.30pm, Fri 10–11.30am & 6.30–8.30pm), and a **supermarket** (daily 8am–10pm). The **tourist police** is conveniently located opposite the *Novotel*, while the nearest **hospital** is in Sharm el-Sheikh.

Most tourists head straight for Asilah; every bus is met by **taxis** and **pickups** that charge £E1 per person for the journey, £E5 for solo travellers. Most places aren't more than ten minutes' walk from the taxi drop-off point.

The **holiday villages** around Dahab Bay are self-contained, with private beaches and access to a coral reef on the headland. Their guests have little in common with the crowd drawn to Asilah, although everyone mingles at the two main discos, *El-Zar* in Asilah and the state-of-the-art *Zanzibar* at the *Helnan* (June–Oct; £E10). The hotels north of the lagoon are covered under Asilah, but some of them are actually closer to the following. The **Ganet Sinai Hotel** (☎069/640-440, fax 640-441; ⑧) has A/C rooms with TVs and seaviews, a private beach without coral (£E15 for outside guests to use the beach which includes a soft drink) and a windsurfing centre. Buffet breakfast is included in the price. Next door is the **Swiss Inn Golden Palace Resort** (☎069/640-471, fax 640-470; ⑦). The newest of the Dahab resorts, the opulent **Hilton Dahab** (☎069/640-310, fax 640-424; ⑧) is about as far away as you can get from hippy huts and if you transgress its boundaries, they'll want a wopping US$20 to use the beach. The **Novotel Coralia Dahab** (☎069/640-301, fax 640-305, *rsrv.novotel.dhb@sinainet.com.eg*; ⑦) is a four-star complex with some charm that monopolizes a windswept bay enclosed by a sandbar, providing an ideal spot for learning how to windsurf (see p.587). Further round the bay the **Helnan Dahab Hotel** (☎069/640-425, fax 640-428; ⑦), offers five-star facilities along with a good beach.

Asilah

If lazing on the beach, stoned, is your idea of heaven, Asilah is the place to be. The music and **ambience** reek of the 1960s, when Israeli troops started coming here for R & R, introducing the Bedouin to another way of life. Nowadays, the *real* Bedouin village of tin shacks and scrawny goats hides behind scores of restaurants and campgrounds, while local children wander beneath the palm trees selling culottes and camel rides. Visitors either stay longer than they'd expected (sometimes until their money or brain cells are gone) or find the whole scene so repellent that they leave immediately.

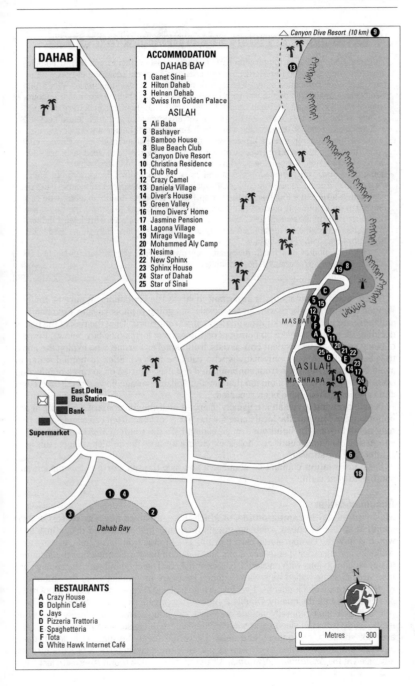

DAHAB

ACCOMMODATION
DAHAB BAY
1 Ganet Sinai
2 Hilton Dahab
3 Helnan Dehab
4 Swiss Inn Golden Palace

ASILAH
5 Ali Baba
6 Bashayer
7 Bamboo House
8 Blue Beach Club
9 Canyon Dive Resort
10 Christina Residence
11 Club Red
12 Crazy Camel
13 Daniela Village
14 Diver's House
15 Green Valley
16 Inmo Divers' Home
17 Jasmine Pension
18 Lagona Village
19 Mirage Village
20 Mohammed Aly Camp
21 Nesima
22 New Sphinx
23 Sphinx House
24 Star of Dahab
25 Star of Sinai

Canyon Dive Resort (10 km) 9

MASBAT

ASILAH

MASHRABA

East Delta
Bus Station

Bank

Supermarket

Dahab Bay

RESTAURANTS
A Crazy House
B Dolphin Café
C Jays
D Pizzeria Trattoria
E Spaghetteria
F Tota
G White Hawk Internet Café

0   Metres   300

N

DRUG SMUGGLING AND CULTIVATION IN SINAI

The Sinai Bedouin have a long tradition of **smuggling** hashish into Egypt. During colonial times the route followed the Mediterranean coast, until the militarization of El-Arish and the Canal Zone compelled smugglers to seek new routes across the interior. When this also became militarized due to war with Israel, they switched their attention to the mountains of South Sinai and the Aqaba coast. Under Israeli rule their activities were tolerated so long as the dope was bound for Egypt, but the emergence of an Israeli market caused a clampdown in the 1970s, at a time when hash supplies from Lebanon were drying up.

Meanwhile, however, foreign hippies were flocking to Sinai and asking the Bedouin for grass (using the Indian term *ganja*, from which *bango*, the Egyptian word for marijuana, derives). Thus was planted the seed of a local **cultivation** industry, which really got going once Sinai was returned to Egypt and its police chief took a hand in the business for a decade. Today, Sinai is one of Egypt's main sources of *bango*, as cultivators can't be prosecuted owing to a loophole in the Camp David Accords – unlike dealers, who risk long-term imprisonment or even hanging, and rely on bribery to get off the hook. But the police must make *some* arrests, so it's rather like an auction where the lowest bidders are cast as scapegoats. This applies equally to **foreigners** – especially those who bring heroin or ecstasy to sell in Dahab.

As an indication of how much marijuana is grown in Sinai, the authorities burned 28 million kilos in 1997 – imagine how much escaped seizure!

Given Asilah's reputation, it's important to stress the limitations on pure hedonism. Women can sunbathe here without any hassle, but **going topless** violates Egyptian law, and there are periodic crackdowns on **dope**: if you consume, it's at the risk of the police deciding they need to make up numbers on their arrest forms (see box below). Beware of being ripped off by resident **con-artists** from Israel or Europe, who exploit the naive travellers' belief that it's only natives who can't be trusted. Stick to bottled water to avoid the risk of **hepatitis** from contaminated cisterns; a dozen or so cases of infection occur every year. Bear in mind too that most of Asilah's sewage flows directly out to sea and cases of typhoid have been reported.

People **arriving** in Asilah are usually dropped near the *Mohammed Aly Camp* at the bottom end of **Masbat**, the local name for the "strip" of beachfront cafés and shops running north beyond the lighthouse on a headland. To the south of *Mohammed Aly* lies a succession of campgrounds and hotels extending towards the holiday villages: this area is known as **Mashraba**.

Basic **orientation** couldn't be simpler: if you face the sea, north is to your left and south is to your right.

Accommodation

Most visitors stay in **campgrounds**, of which there are about fifty. The reason is quite simply that they're cheap, enabling guests to spend their money on drugs instead – which is how the campgrounds earn a profit. They range from basic huts, usually with padlocks and electricity; showers, sinks and toilets in the yard completing the facilities, to upgraded versions with en-suite facilities and A/C. Thatched huts are the coolest, but insecure, so stone-walled huts with thatched roofs are preferable; avoid the stifling tin-roofed or breeze-block shacks. Everywhere charges the same **rates**: £E10–20 per person depending on the quality. Double rooms with a private shower cost £E30–60. These prices, which don't generally include breakfast, can jump dramatically during Israeli holidays. Aside from the sleeping arrangements, factors to consider when choosing a site are: hot showers, mosquitoes and noise (anywhere near the main strip at Masbat). Several camps have added extra storeys and become quasi-hotels – a process furthest advanced at the *Mohammed Aly Camp*. Although it offers 115 rooms, there are just a few appealing ones that overlook the seas and have showers and fans (②–③). *Green Valley* is another camp-hotel, pleasant enough with a pool table and rooms set back from the main strip (②–③). Other camps worth mentioning are *Crazy Camel Camp* (with its famous owner and safari guide, Lobster Man), *Bashayer* and *Ali Baba*.

You can find more "proper" **hotels** in Mashraba but they are also beginning to fill up the vacant land between Asilah and the holiday villages and between Asilah and the dive sites to the north.

Bamboo House Hotel, in Masbat (☎069/640-263). A proper hotel with A/C rooms and a Western Union money transfer service. ⑤.

Blue Beach Club, 300m north of the lighthouse (☎069//640-413). Relatively new Swiss-managed place, has 18 rooms with fans, fridges, balconies with sea views, but it's a very windy spot. ⑦.

Canyon Dive Resort, 11km north of Masbat (☎069/640-413). Attractive two-star place next to Canyon dive site. Worth considering if all you want to do is dive, but otherwise a bit far from town. ⑤.

Christina Residence, Mashraba (☎069/640-390, fax 640-406, *christina_residence@yahoo.com*). Smart, clean Greek-inspired hotel one block back from the beach; currently adding a beachfront extension. Only 10 rooms with A/C or fans but no breakfast. Has a small Internet café. ⑤.

Club Red, at the north end of Mashraba (☎ & fax 069/640-380, *clubred@intouch.com*). This dive centre also offers dorm beds (③) and rooms with fans or A/C and sea views. Discounts with dive packages. ⑤.

Daniela Village, 3km north of Dahab on the way to Canyon dive site (☎02/348-2671, fax 360-7750). Comfortable place with 40 large A/C rooms with sea views, a laundry, shop and bar. ⑦.

Diver's House, tucked away in the south of Mashraba (☎ & fax 069/640-451). Small English-run hotel, nicely designed and very clean. Preference given to divers. ⑤.

Inmo Divers' Home, Mashraba (☎069/640-370, fax 640-372, *inmo@inmodivers.com*). Stylish lodgings around a dive centre. All rooms have double beds and bathrooms; discount for longer stays, divers and advance bookings. ⑥–⑦.

Jasmine Pension, on the beach next to *Divers' House* (☎069/640-370, fax 640-372). Good food and some nice rooms with balconies. ④.

Lagona Village, south of Mashraba, on the way to Dahab Bay (☎069/640-350, fax 640-351). Comfortable rooms facing a private beach. Neat and clean, but a bit isolated. ⑦.

Mirage Village, near the lighthouse (☎069/640-352). Tucked away behind a walled compound; reasonable rooms and the added bonus of being mosquito-free. ③.

Nesima, Mashraba (☎069/640-320, fax 640-321, *nesima@intouch.com*). Possibly the most beautiful hotel in Asilah, with a great pool setting, but marred by some of its staff. Used by Regal and Crusader Travel. Discounts on rooms with fans in quiet periods. ⑦.

New Sphinx, Mashraba (☎ & fax 069/640-032, *sphinx_d@intouch.com*). 40 rooms with bath, A/C and satellite TV, plus there's a pool. ⑦.

Sphinx House, Mashraba (☎ & fax 069/640-032, *sphinx_d@intouch.com*). Older than its sister hotel, *Sphinx House* has 54 rooms with A/C or fans, private or shared baths. Free pool. ③–⑤.

Star of Dahab, Mashraba (☎ & fax 069/640-130). Basic rooms with fans and showers, breakfast not included or even more basic huts without electricity. ②.

Star of Sinai Hotel, at the southern end of Masbat (☎ & fax 069/640-259). Very cheap A/C rooms with bath; the place is a bit bleak, but it does boast an enthusiastic Bedouin owner. Worth considering if beachfront rooms elsewhere are full. Cheaper rooms have fans and shared baths. ②–③.

Eating, drinking and nightlife

A score of **restaurants** by the beach vie for custom by playing 1960s classics, Bob Marley or rave music; floor cushions and posters reflect their amalgam of Bedouin and hippie influences. Everywhere serves soft drinks, and you can sit around for hours without being hassled to eat (dishes take a long time to prepare, in any case). With menus displayed outside, it's easy to compare prices. Ask other travellers where they've eaten (and not got sick) – everyone has their favourite place.

Pancakes with bananas, apples, ice cream or honey are popular for breakfast or late-night munchies, while main **meals** consist of pizzas, pasta or fish. *Jays*, run by an English woman, is popular with resident divers for its safe food. *Crazy House* is one of the few places with tables and chairs, and very clean; their food is good but pricey by local standards and they serve beer. *Tota* (recognizable by its ship facade) is also clean and serves delicious lasagne and a range of pizzas, as does *Pizzeria Trattoria* (from £E8). *Dolphin Café*, just up from the police station, offers reasonable Indian vegetarian baltis and noodles, while the Italian restaurant *Spaghetteria* nearby serves good coffee. Many places display a tempting heap of fresh fish and crustaceans outside; just check the price before ordering. Unless you splash out on lobster, you can eat quite well for £E20–35 a meal, including drinks and dessert. Most places are open until midnight (or later), though the choice of food diminishes after 9pm. There are also numerous **supermarkets** (daily 7.30am–midnight), **fruit stalls** and *taamiya* stands.

With the closure of the infamous *Black Prince Disco*, **nightlife** is now based in the bars and restaurants of Asilah that have licences to sell alcohol. There are two main drinking hangouts: the bars at *Nesima* (happy hour 7–9pm), which stay open until 3am or later and are popular with the diving set; the bar at the *Sphinx House* (happy hour 7–9pm) is more low-life. *El-Zar,* next to *Dolphin Café*, has a bar on the beach, happy hour runs 7–9pm (beer £E5), and a disco from 11pm until 2am. Those who prefer quieter entertainment can take up yoga and meditation at *Club Red, Blue Beach, Nesima* and elsewhere, get a henna tattoo or hair braid, play **pool** at *Napoleon's* (£E10 a game) or borrow a book from the Arabesque Bazaar.

There are several **Internet cafés** dotted along Mashraba, including the *Lagoon* at *Christina Residence* (£E20 per hour, £E3 to send one email) and *White Hawk* (£E1 for 3min). Most have **telephone**, fax and photocopying facilities too; *Lagoon* charges £E7 per minute to call abroad. If you have a phonecard there is a callbox at Baraka supermarket near *Friends* restaurant.

Diving, snorkelling and inland safaris

Despite being smaller than Na'ama Bay, aquatic pursuits are taken just as seriously in Dahab, but beach- rather than boat-diving is the norm. In Dahab Bay the **reefs** are between *Lagona Village* and the *Novotel*, while at Asilah the reefs are meagre and the seabed is covered in rubbish, so most divers head 7–8km up the coast where you can find the Eel Garden, Canyon and Blue Hole dive sites. Trips are arranged by most dive centres every morning, or you can get there by taxi (£E10 per car-load).

The **Canyon** is a dark, narrow fissure that you reach from the shore by swimming along the reef and then diving to the edge of a coral wall. It can be frightening for inexperienced divers, as it sinks to a depth of 50m, but there's plenty to see at the top of the reef. Further north lies the notorious **Blue Hole**, which claims several lives every year. This spectacular shaft in the reef plunges to 80m; the challenge involves descending 60m and swimming through a transverse passage to come up the other side. Divers who ascend too fast risk getting "bent"; inexperienced divers should not attempt this dive under any circumstances. Fortunately, the Hole can be enjoyed in safety by staying closer to the surface and working your way round to a dip in the reef known as the Bridge, which swarms with colourful fish and can even be viewed using snorkelling gear.

Masks and fins can be rented at most campgrounds and shops on Asilah's beach, but to be sure of getting a mask that doesn't leak you should go to a diving centre (see box below). While **renting equipment** (US$35–40) is actually costlier here than in Na'ama, **diving courses** are generally cheaper. Competition means cut-price deals, especially when business is quiet, but saving a few dollars can be dangerous. Stick to the long-established centres like Club Red (OW course US$250 plus US$30 certification),

Adventure Dive Club, at the Lighthouse (☎ & fax 069/640-161). PADI.

Canyon Dive Club, Masbat & at the Canyon (☎069/640-043). PADI.

Dive Zone, in the centre of Masbat. (*divezonedahab@yahoo.com*). PADI.

Fantasea Dive Club, at the Lighthouse (☎ & fax 069/640-043). PADI, SSI.

INMO, Mashraba (☎069/640-370, fax 640-372). PADI.

Lagona Dive Centre *Lagona Village* (☎069/640-356, fax 640-355). CMAS, SSI, PDIC.

Nesima Diving Centre *Nesima* (☎ & fax 069/640-321). PADI. BSAC.

Sinai Dive Club *Novotel Holiday Village* (☎069/640-302, fax 640-303). PADI.

Nesima (OW US$254 plus US$30 for certification), Inmo, or Lagona (which has good facilities for disabled divers), but as ever, ask around and don't be swayed simply by promises of the best price.

The main destination for day-long **dive safaris** is the Ras Abu Galum protected area, a 30km stretch of coast with three diving beaches, accessible by jeep or camel. **Naqb Shahin** – closest to Dahab – has fantastic coral and gold fish but the sea is very turbulent, so many divers prefer **Ras Abu Galum** or **Ras el-Mamleh**, further north. All three sites have deep virgin reefs with a rich variety of corals and fish. Club Red does a one-day, two-dive trip by camel to Ras Abu Galum for US$68 including tanks and weights (US$88 with all diving equipment), while Fantasea does a two-dive trip for US$65, including tanks, weights and lunch. Trips to the *Thistlegorm* (see p.628) are also available from Club Red; US$110 including transport, food and three dives. A quirkier aquatic option is to go **lobster-hunting** at night, when the creatures are at their liveliest; excursions culminate in a lobster feast on the beach. For details, contact Hammad the "Lobster Man" at the *Crazy Camel Camp*.

The wind blows at least two hundred days each year at Dahab, making this area a haven for windsurfers. Fantasea and the **windsurfing** centre at the *Novotel* both rent boards for US$20 an hour; an introductory lesson costs US$35, and a three-day beginner's course is US$180.

Jeep and camel safaris

If you fancy **riding on the beach** at Asilah, there are lots of boys renting out horses (£E50 for one hour) or camels (£E10–15 per hour). A more exciting option is to sign up for trips into the rugged interior, which can be organized by most campgrounds, through the safari agencies below, or by negotiating directly with guides. The most popular **day excursions** are by jeep to the **Coloured Canyon** (see p.591), which costs £E55 per person for a group of six; by camel to **Wadi Gnay**, a Bedouin hamlet with palms and a brackish spring (£E25 per person); or by camel to the mangrove forest of **Nabeq** (£E40–55). Dahab Safari Club (☎069/640-285, *am.ghabour@hotmail.com*) above the *Pizzeria Trattoria* can arrange a three-day camel trip into the desert for £E190 per person, while Embah Safari (☎ & fax 069/640-447, *embah@intouch.com*) offers diving, camel or jeep safaris from US$60 per person per day; dive trips include tanks, weights, food and two dives a day.

Moving on from Asilah and Dahab

Buses leave from Dahab City outside the East Delta ticket office (☎069/640-250). It's wise to arrange an early-morning lift the night before, as tourists in a hurry are ripe for overcharging. Of the buses to **Sharm** (9 daily; 1hr 30min; £E10), seven continue on to

El-Tor (3hr; £E40); there are four buses daily to **Cairo** (7–8hr; £E55; £E70 for 10pm bus), and the 8.15am Cairo bus also stops at **Suez** (4–5hr; £E30). Two buses daily go to **Zagazig** (6–7hr; £E40) and Ismailiya (6–7hr; £E40). There are two daily buses to **Nuweiba** (10.30am and 6.30pm; 1hr; £E10), with the earlier one continuing on to **Taba** (3hr; £E20). The bus to **St Catherine's** (1hr; £E15) leaves around 9.30am.

If you would rather take a shared taxi to your destination, you can book a place in advance at any of the safari agencies and at most camps; it's worth asking around, as prices can vary for the same trip. *Star of Dahab* advertises £E20 to go to Nuweiba, £E30 to Taba, and £E30 for a return trip to St Catherine's, which leaves at 11pm. There is also a microbus service to Cairo (8am £E45; 11pm £E55).

Nuweiba and Tarabeen

NUWEIBA is another resort on the Gulf of Aqaba, consisting of a **port** with nearby tourist complexes, followed 4km up the coast by Nuweiba **"City"**, an administrative and commercial centre grafted on to a former Israeli *moshav* (co-operative village). During the late 1970s, thousands of Israeli and Western backpackers flocked here to party and sleep on the beach; nowadays, the resort attracts a staider crowd of moderately affluent Egyptians and package tourists, for whom it constitutes a kind of cut-price Na'ama Bay. For others, however, Nuweiba is simply a stepping stone to Taba on the border with Israel, or the place to catch ferries to Aqaba in Jordan.

Like Dahab, Nuweiba has also spawned a neighbouring Bedouin settlement, which draws younger, low-budget travellers. Named after the local Bedouin tribe, **TARABEEN** is much like Asilah used to be, but is catching up fast: there are now over twenty campgrounds and a few hotels or semi-hotels on its wide and sandy beach, lined with restaurants and tourist bazaars. As yet though, there are no bars as such. If you want a beer, you'll have to venture to the *Helnan* in Nuweiba City. But if you yearn for the "old days" when you could still see the stars and hear the waves, undisturbed by bright lights or loud music you will need to head to the **DUNAS**, just south of Nuweiba city, or further north to the campgrounds appearing in **BIR SWAIR**. Like Dahab the place is very popular with Israelis due to its proximity to the border. Tarabeen is also a good place to arrange camel or jeep safaris.

Buses from points south call at the port before running on to the *Helnan* in Nuweiba City – or vice versa coming from Taba. Taxis charge £E10 for the journey between Tarabeen and Nuweiba City, £E15–20 to or from the port. You can walk from the *Helnan* to Tarabeen in twenty minutes, via the beach; it takes slightly longer by road. Package tourists fly into **Taba International airport**, near Taba, whence shuttle-buses convey them to the new hotels in Taba Heights (see p.595), the *Coral Hilton* or *Helnan* hotels.

Accommodation

Accommodation is found in three main locations: near the port, Nuweiba City and the Bedouin village of Tarabeen, though there is also some basic accommodation available at *Café & Camp Sinai* (☎069/520-188, *eid-sinai@sinainet.com.eg*; ②) in the Bedouin village of Sayadeen, where the dolphin "Olin" hangs out. Tarabeen is the place to find cheap **campgrounds** (②) à la Dahab, which tend to come and go or evolve into hotels. Bearing that in mind, it's best to sniff around and ask other travellers, but you could start by looking for *Bish Bish, Soft Beach* or *Sunrise Camp* (②). Another popular site is *Swelm* (②), entirely run by Sudanese, as is *Carmina* (☎069/500-477; ②) a relaxed camp, set back from the beach behind *Blue Bus*. The smarter *Prince* has huts (②) and apartments (⑤), while the positively luxurious Nakhil Inn (⑤–⑦) can be found at the northern end of the bay. Some sites still lack electricity, so a torch is useful, but the

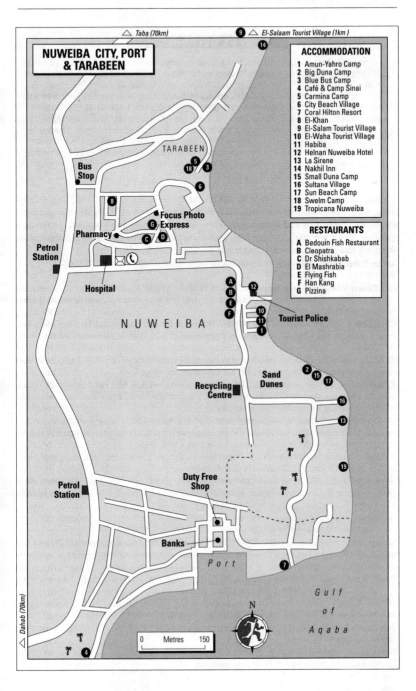

NUWEIBA CITY, PORT & TARABEEN

△ Taba (70km)

⑨ △ El-Salaam Tourist Village (1km)

⑭

TARABEEN

⑤ ⑱ ③

Bus Stop

⑥

⑧

Focus Photo Express

Ⓖ

Pharmacy

Ⓒ Ⓓ

Petrol Station

✉ ☏

Hospital

Ⓐ
Ⓑ ⑫
Ⓔ
Ⓕ
⑩
⑪ Tourist Police
①

N U W E I B A

② ⑮ ⑰
Sand Dunes
⑯
⑬

Recycling Centre

⑲

Petrol Station

Duty Free Shop

Banks

⑦

Port

Gulf of Aqaba

N

0 Metres 150

△ Dahab (70km)

④

ACCOMMODATION

1 Amun-Yahro Camp
2 Big Duna Camp
3 Blue Bus Camp
4 Café & Camp Sinai
5 Carmina Camp
6 City Beach Village
7 Coral Hilton Resort
8 El-Khan
9 El-Salam Tourist Village
10 El-Waha Tourist Village
11 Habiba
12 Helnan Nuweiba Hotel
13 La Sirene
14 Nakhil Inn
15 Small Duna Camp
16 Sultana Village
17 Sun Beach Camp
18 Swelm Camp
19 Tropicana Nuweiba

RESTAURANTS

A Bedouin Fish Restaurant
B Cleopatra
C Dr Shishkabab
D El Mashrabia
E Flying Fish
F Han Kang
G Pizzina

THE DOLPHIN

One of Nuweiba's main attractions is a female **dolphin** named Olin, who lives offshore from the Bedouin fishing village of Sayadeen, in Maagana bay. The story goes that having lost her mate in 1992, the dolphin made friends with **Abdullah**, a deaf fisherman, and has hung around ever since. Abdullah claims that swimming with her has improved his hearing. Scientists have suggested that Olin stays in the bay because she is disturbed and her communication problems prevent her from living normally with other dolphins. In any case she is now a major attraction in Sinai and village entrepreneurs, headed by Abdullah, charge visitors £E10 to "swim" with her. On busy days you'll find over a dozen tourists with a boat or two in attendance and plenty more waiting on the shore; at other times you might get to frolic with her alone.

---

introduction of jet skis to the area means it's rarely quiet. If you really want to get away from it all, head south of Nuweiba City to the sand dunes of **DUNAS**, where *Small Duna*, *Big Duna* (②) and a couple of other camps can give you complete peace and quiet, as they have no electricity. Like Dahab, most camps do not include breakfast in the price and prices can rise dramatically during Israeli holidays.

Amun-Yahro Camp, last camp in Nuweiba City before *Dunas* (☎069/500-555, fax 500-244). Clean with raised huts with electricity. ②.

City Beach Village, between Nuweiba City and Tarabeen (☎069/500-307, fax 500-146). Basic huts (②) or attractive stone-built rooms with baths and A/C or fans. Restaurant, pool table and there's beer available. Safe for valuables. ⑤–⑥.

Coral Hilton Resort, east of the port (☎069/520-320, fax 520-327). Luxury holiday village with two heated pools and lots of sports facilities. Sells catamaran tickets. Outside guests can use the beach for £E20. ⑧.

El-Khan, east of the road between Nuweiba City and Tarabeen (☎069/500-319). Bungalows and rooms. Good restaurant; Bedouin handicrafts exhibition and shop. ④–⑤.

El-Salam Tourist Village, by the beach north of Tarabeen, reached by a signposted track (1km) from the main road (☎ & fax 069/500-440). Nice A/C rooms with baths. Bar, restaurants, two swimming pools and a private beach with a reef. ⑥.

El-Waha Tourist Village, Nuweiba City (☎069/500-421, fax 500-420, *elwaharesort@hotmail.com*). Smart A/C bungalows with bathrooms, TV and telephone, or simple versions with fans and shared showers. You can also camp on their beach if you have a tent. ④–⑥.

Habiba, Nuweiba City (☎069/500-770, *habiba@nuweiba.net*). Comfortable A/C bungalows and huts. Very good restaurant. Breakfast included. ③–⑥.

Helnan Nuweiba Hotel, Nuweiba City (☎069/500-402, fax 500-407). A/C bungalows with TV, a disco, diving centre and private beach. An adjacent compound has beach huts sleeping three (⑤), with electric lighting but no other facilities. Rents bicycles. ⑦.

La Sirene, between Nuweiba City and the port (☎069/500-701, fax 500-702). Attractive A/C bungalows dotted along a beautiful stretch of beach, and there's a dive centre. ⑥–⑦.

Nakhil Inn, north end of Tarabeen (☎069/500-879, fax 500-878, *surf@sinainet.com.eg*). Newly built rooms, all with A/C, satellite TV, bath and international telephone. Children under 12 are free. ⑤–⑦.

Small Duna, south of Nuweiba City, past *Big Duna* (☎069/500-198). Run by Mgbul Abdalla from the Mzeina tribe. Basic huts and fish restaurant. ②.

Sultana Village, between Nuweiba City and the port (☎069/500-490, fax 500-491). Stone rooms with or without A/C on raised platforms with three beds. Shared showers. Restaurant. ⑤–⑥.

Sun Beach Camp, south of Nuweiba City, next to *Small Duna* (☎069/500-163). Similar setup with huts on the beach. ②.

Tropicana Nuweiba, between Nuweiba City and the port (☎069/500-056, fax 500-022). Comfortable four-star branch of *Tropicana* chain. ⑦.

DIVING CENTRES

Emperor Divers *Nakhil Inn* & *Tropicana Nuweiba* (☎069/500-056, fax 500-022, *info@emperordivers.com*). PADI.

Dive Point *Coral Hilton Resort* (☎069/520-320, fax 520-327). PADI.

Diving Camp Nuweiba *Helnan Nuweiba Hotel* (☎069/500-403, fax 500-260, *dcn@sinainet.com.eg*). PADI, CMAS.

Scuba Divers *La Sirene* (☎069/500-701, fax 500702, *scuba@gega.net*). SSI.

Diving, snorkelling and inland safaris

Aside from the **dolphin** (see box above), Nuweiba has less to offer underwater than other resorts, despite having several shallow **reefs** offshore, the best of which is the **Stone House** beyond the southern promontory. Though fine for **snorkelling**, they're not so great for **diving** unless you're still a novice, so the divers that come here usually travel to Ras Abu Galum (p.587) or dive sites north of Nuweiba (see p.593). These trips can be arranged by any of the four diving centres in Nuweiba: Dive Point has a jeep dive trip to Ras Mamleh for US$60, and a two-day trip to Ras Mamleh and Ras Abu Galum for US$195 including food and four dives. Diving Camp Nuweiba charges US$650 per person for a six-day camel, jeep and boat-diving package and they also rent out surf boards, pedaloes and canoes.

Jeep and camel safaris

Local Bedouin guides offer a wide range of **camel or jeep safaris** into the interior. Their duration depends on your destination and mode of transport; it usually takes two or three times as long by camel as it does by jeep. Most guides charge £E60–100 per person per day, (camel journeys are more expensive than jeep) which should include meals and the cost of registering the trip with the police. Drinking water may cost extra and be more expensive the further you get from shops, so it's wise to buy plenty to take along.

The nearest destinations are the palmy oasis of **Ain el-Furtaga** (which can be reached by regular car) and the colourful sandstone canyon of **Wadi Huweiyit** (by camel or 4WD). Slightly further north lies **Moyat el-Wishwashi**, a large rainwater catchment cistern hidden in a canyon between imposing boulders. All these sites can be reached by camel in a day. The most popular day excursion by jeep is to the **Coloured Canyon**, (about £E50 per person) via a trail from Ain el-Furtaga. Its name comes from the vivid striations on the steep walls of the canyon, which is sheltered from the wind and eerily silent. Having got there by 4WD, you can hike through the canyon in either direction. Other destinations include **Wadi Ghazala**, with its dunes and acacia groves where gazelles may be glimpsed; **Ain Umm Ahmed**, whose deep torrent fed by snow on the highest peaks of the Sinai shrinks to a stream as the seasons advance; and the oasis of **Ain Khudra**, supposedly the Biblical Hazeroth, where Miriam was stricken with leprosy for criticizing Moses.

A recommended guide is Hassan Hamid at *Sun Beach Camp* (☎069/500-889), who takes groups of up to six people by jeep to Ain Khudra, Ain el-Furtaga and the Coloured Canyon (£E50 per person excluding food), and also offers the same itinerary by camel (£E80 per person including food). At *Nakhil Inn* camel trips are available at the same rate, but jeep safaris cost a little less (£E40 per person for 6–8 people). Other **guides** can be contacted at a kiosk near the highway at Ras al-Shaitun, 10km up the coast, which is the starting point for many excursions.

Eating, nightlife and other practicalities

Although Tarabeen has a number of passable beach-side cafes and restaurants, Nuweiba City offers the widest choice of **places to eat**. Low-budget travellers gravitate towards *Dr Shishkabab* and other restaurants dotted around the bazaar area of Nuweiba city. The only place in Nuweiba City licensed to sell alcohol is the upmarket restaurant in the *Helnan*. The Mall contains a **bakery** and and a **supermarket** (daily 8am–4pm & 6–10.30pm), and there's a couple of stalls selling fresh fruit near *Dr Shishkabab*. **Nightlife** boils down to a disco in the *Helnan* (£E15 admission), or playing guitars, drums or backgammon and getting stoned at Tarabeen. The *White Palace* camp (☎069/500-010) in Tarabeen also claims to have a disco twice a week.

Restaurants

Bedouin Fish Restaurant, Nuweiba City, opposite *Helnan* (☎069/500-082). Basic meals, offers group discounts.

Blue Bus, Tarabeen. Camp and restaurant serving reasonable fish, pasta and pizza dishes. Nice position on the beach.

Carmina, Tarabeen. One of the best camps and cafés in Tarabeen behind the *Blue Bus*. Lemon juice with vanilla recommended.

Cleopatra, Nuweiba City, opposite *Helnan*. Undistinguished place, but worth considering for coffee and *sheeshas*.

Dr Shishkabab, Nuweiba City (☎069/500-273). Sandwiches (£E5–8), meat and vegetarian (£E8) dishes. Daily 7am–1am.

Habiba, Nuweiba City just past El-Waha. Well-prepared food at this camp's buffet restaurant on the beach, which gets very busy at lunchtimes serving tourists on day trips from Sharm. Daily 11am–midnight.

Han Kang, Nuweiba City, opposite *Helnan* (☎069/500-970). Excellent Chinese-Korean restaurant; daily 11am–2pm & 6–10pm.

Pizzina, new commercial centre near the bazaar in Nuweiba City (☎069/500-608). Eat in or take-away pizza at reasonable prices.

Listings

Banks and exchange At the bank in the *Helnan* (daily except Fri 9am–1pm & 6–9pm). Further afield there are banks in the port area and at the *Hilton*.

Bicycle rental From *Sim Sim* camp in Tarabeen or from the *Helnan*.

Doctor There is a doctor on call at the *Helnan*. (The hospital in Nuweiba is poorly equipped, so head for Sharm or Israel if you're seriously ill).

Film & processing Focus Photo Express (daily 10am–10pm). Sells slide and Advantix film.

Internet Café At *Habiba* camp (daily 10am–10pm; £E60 per hour).

Pharmacy Gasser, near *Dr Shishkabab*. (daily 10am–10pm; ☎069/500-605).

Police Located near the Town Council (☎069/500-242); the tourist police office is beside the parking lot outside the *Helnan*; both are open 24 hours.

Post office North of the mall (daily except Fri 8am–3pm); has EMS.

Telephone office North of the mall (open 24 hours), has international phones which take phonecards. For local calls there is a stall with phones near *Dr Shishkabab* that also sells international newspapers.

Moving on

Although there is supposed to be a bus station in **Nuweiba City**, the de facto terminal is the parking lot outside the *Helnan* hotel campground. **Buses** run from here to Dahab (1hr; £E10), Na'ama Bay (3hr; £E20) and Sharm el-Sheikh (3hr; £E15), leaving daily at 6.30am and 3.30pm; services to Taba depart at 5.30am and 11.30am (1hr; £E10).

Of the two buses to Cairo, the 10am service (8hr; £E55) runs via St Catherine's Monastery, while the 2.30pm service (£E60) travels further north across the interior of the peninsula via Nekhl. There is sometimes a 5pm Cairo bus which has a better chance of having seats. Buses to Cairo also leave from Nuweiba Port; these have no fixed schedule and leave when they're full. They're not that nice either, but they might save you from being at the mercy of the taxi drivers waiting outside.

As **Tarabeen**'s popularity has grown, **service taxis** have started hanging around to pick up passengers bound for Taba, Dahab, Sharm el-Sheikh or St Catherine's. Prices are negotiable, so bargain hard.

Boats to Aqaba in Jordan

The only reason to visit Nuweiba's Port (☎069/520-216) is to catch a **boat to Aqaba** in Jordan; either an ordinary ferry or the high-speed catamaran. Whichever one you opt for, it's advisable to turn up at the Port two hours before the scheduled departure time.

The **ferry** leaves every day at noon (supposedly) and takes 3–5 hours, depending on the weather. Foreigners must buy a first-class **ticket** (US$32 one-way), and can *only* pay in US dollars. During Ramadan or the *Hadj* season, it's a definite advantage to have access to the first-class lounge, as the boat is crowded with Egyptian workers returning home, or pilgrims bound for Mecca. The ferry also carries **vehicles** (US$100). Tickets are sold inside the Port's entrance; you'll need to show your passport to go through the gates, and once inside you're not allowed to leave. Foreigners are assigned an official to guide them through customs and immigration and onto the boat. Don't be surprised if it leaves much later than scheduled. On boarding you'll be asked to hand over your passport, which will be returned at Aqaba customs, or, if you go searching for it, on the boat.

The **catamaran** also operates daily, departing at 3pm and takes about an hour. **Tickets** (US$42 one-way) are sold at the *Coral Hilton Resort*. The vessel is far more comfortable than the ferry, but it doesn't carry cars. Formalities at Nuweiba's Port are identical to those for the ferry.

Jordanian visas (valid for one month) are issued on board the ferry and catamaran, or immediately after disembarkation. Things go quicker if you've already obtained one in Cairo, but British, Canadian, US, Australian and New Zealand citizens shouldn't have any trouble getting one on the spot. Visa charges vary according to nationality; for Australians it's free, British citizens pay US$35, New Zealanders US$20, US citizens US$48, while Canadians have to cough up US$60. If there are five or more of you travelling, you can ask for a **group visa**, which is free of charge for a minimum four-night stay. It is no longer a problem if your passport shows **evidence of a visit to Israel**, though this will still preclude entry to Syria.

If you just want to visit Petra and return, you can book trips through *Habiba* camp (☎069/500-770).

Between Nuweiba and Taba

The 70km of coastline **between Nuweiba and Taba** (the border crossing into Israel) used to harbour several low-key resorts that are reckoned by some to be the nicest in Sinai. They're still there, but they've been joined by plenty of new holiday villages and a massive new tourist development called **Taba Heights**. The nicer places are still signposted from the highway and may be visible depending on the terrain. **Buses** can drop you at any point along the way if you ask the driver. Just bear in mind that there are no **banks** until Taba, nor anywhere to buy **food** except the resorts' restaurants, which are usually quite pricey.

The first spot worth noting is **MAAGANA BEACH**, whose southern end – called **Lami Beach** – begins 8km from Tarabeen. Though its reefs are quite shallow and unimpressive, the beach itself is nice, with public showers and toilets and striking rock formations. There's a **campground** with huts (②) and a cafeteria frequented by Bedouin who run **camel and jeep trips** to Wadi Huweiyit (see p.597) and other sites. Two kilometres further on lies the picturesque headland of **RAS AL-SHAITUN** (Devil's Head), where the **reef** drops off sharply to the north, making it ideal for beach diving. *Castle Beach* resort (☎012/3174754; ④) has **beach bungalows** with verandahs, a good restaurant, and a shop selling souvenirs. There is a house reef for divers, and you can **rent camels** and guides for excursions to Moyat el-Wishwashi (see previous page). Guides hang out on the beach and at a kiosk beside the highway. Note that **fishing** is forbidden at both sites.

Another 8km up the coast is the more upmarket beach resort of **BAWAKI** (☎069/500-470, fax 500-471; ⑤–⑦), boasting A/C rooms with hot showers and a few triple-bed huts (⑤). It has a restaurant, bar and pool, and may soon have a diving centre; **horse-riding** costs £E40 an hour. Breakfast is included in the price of accommodation, but other meals are expensive.

Basata

The trendiest resort is **BASATA** (Arabic for "Simplicity"), by the headland of Ras el-Burqa. Created by the German-educated Sherif el-Ghamrawy, it is Egypt's most eco-friendly resort, with its own greenhouse, generator, bakery and desalination plant. Organic waste is fed to Basata's donkeys, goats, pigeons and ducks, or used to fertilize the fruit and vegetables. The huts are made entirely from natural materials; empty Baraka bottles are shredded and sent back to the company for recycling, and children can earn treats by collecting cigarette butts from the beach. Alcohol, drugs, television and loud music are forbidden lest they spoil the ambience, which is family-oriented with a New Age ethos. There's a communal vegetarian or fish dinner each night, and guests may help themselves in the kitchen and bakery: write down what you've taken and pay when you leave. You can store your own food in the fridge.

Such is Basata's popularity that it's advisable to **reserve ahead** (☎ & fax 069/500-481; ③–④). There are sixteen huts, some of them mud-brick, or you can pitch a tent on the beach. Guests can sign up for **inland safaris** (£E70 per person per day by jeep, £E90 by camel) or rent **snorkelling** gear (£E20), but divers aren't welcome. You'll either feel at home with Basata's New Agers, or find them unbearably cliquey.

Aquasun, Bir Swair and on to Taba

Five kilometres after Basata comes **AQUASUN** (☎069/530-391, fax 530-390; ⑦), a less eco-conscious mixture of rooms with or without A/C and bathrooms. Though you might be allowed to camp here, it's not encouraged. The quiet sandy beach has a lovely **reef**, and is a very pleasant place to do a PADI open water course (US$330) with the resident dive centre. Guests can also make **jeep or camel trips** to Wadi Quseib and other destinations. A mile or so further on is the oddly named *Sallyland* (☎069/530-380, fax 530-381; ⑤), a two-star hotel of A/C rooms of little note except that it has one of the few bars in the area.

Next to *Sallyland* is **BIR SWAIR**, a Bedouin settlement that has spawned a new wave of beach camps. The nicest camp here is *Friends*, with basic but comfortable huts by one of Sinai's nicest beaches, as well as friendly staff and atmosphere (②).

Travellers with their own car and scuba gear can explore several wonderful **reefs** within walking distance of the highway, notably **El-Muqeibila**, 25km before Taba. Ten kilometres north is another great spot for beach-diving called the **Sun Pool**, which begins with a gentle slope and then plunges as it nears the **Fjord**, a beautiful inlet in the hills by the shore. It's here that one finds **SALIMA** (☎069/530-130; ④), a few rooms with communal showers, behind a nice café overlooking the Fjord.

TABA HEIGHTS DEVELOPMENT

A new development just south of Taba covering 4.5 million square metres of land and with 5km of beach, Taba Heights is set to change the topography of the Sinai when it becomes fully operational in late 2000. Part of the so-called "Red Sea Riviera", this huge resort complex is based around a "village", which features a casino, watersports and diving centre, restaurants, bars, cafés, shops and bazaars and a medical clinic. If successful, it will draw thousands of tourists to this area of Sinai for the first time, using the Taba international airport instead of the airport in Sharm el-Sheikh. Among the places already open are the following:

Sea Star Resort Taba (☎02/582-8141, fax 581-9977, *seastar@link.com.eg*). Opened in April 2000, featuring 171 rooms overlooking the Gulf of Aqaba. A/C rooms, satellite TV, children's facilities, travel agency and shopping arcade. ⑥–⑦.

Hyatt Regency Acacia (☎02/402-7178, fax 401-2833). Huge five-star hotel with 426 rooms with balconies, A/C, disabled rooms, 6 restaurants and bars, shops, 3 pools, private beach, kids' club, health centre, tennis courts, shuttle-bus and car rental. ⑧.

Intercontinental (☎02/366-1041, fax 366-1043). 480 A/C rooms with satellite TV, 4 restaurants and bars, shops, laundry, health club, tennis and squash, 4 pools and an aqua-centre. ⑧.

Pharaoh's Island

Seven kilometres before Taba you'll sight **Pharaoh's Island** (*Gezirat Faraun*), known to Israelis as "Coral Island". Its barren rocks are crowned by the renovated ruins of a **Crusader fort** built in 1115 to levy taxes on Arab merchants while ostensibly protecting pilgrims travelling between Jerusalem and St Catherine's Monastery. The fort was subsequently captured by Salah al-Din but abandoned by the Arabs in 1183. Being only 250m offshore, it can be admired just as well from the mainland if you'd rather not pay £E10 for the boat ride (leaves from the *Salah al-Din* hotel, see below) and another £E10 to tour the fort, which retains several towers and passageways and a large cistern. There's also an expensive cafeteria that only opens when lots of tourists are present. Actually, the main reason to come is to dive or snorkel in the maze of **reefs** off the northeastern tip of the island, which draw boatloads of visitors from Eilat and Aqaba. As the currents are strong and the reefs labyrinthine, it's best to be accompanied by a guide. This can be arranged at the *Salah al-Din* **hotel** (☎069/530-340, fax 530-343, *mstc@ritsec3.com.eg*; ⑦) by the road on the mainland opposite the island (children under twelve stay free). The price includes breakfast.

Taba – and crossing the border

TABA is in the throes of development, with cafés, travel agencies and shops springing up on the Egyptian side, which is dominated by the deluxe *Hilton Taba Hotel* (☎ & fax 069/530-140; ⑧). It took ten years of bitter negotiations before international arbitration finally returned this disputed border enclave to Egypt in 1989. Hitherto, Israel had claimed that Taba lay outside the jurisdiction of the Camp David Accords, and then demanded US$60 million compensation for its investment in tourist facilities.

The **border** is open 24 hours, but as almost all transport and businesses in Israel shut down over *shabbat*, you'd be foolish to cross after mid-morning on Friday or any time on Saturday. The whole process can take up to two hours, and travellers must walk across a no-man's land between the Egyptian and Israeli checkpoints. There's an **exit tax** of £E2 payable on leaving Egypt. The Israelis issue free three-month **visas** to EU, US, Australian and New Zealand citizens. From the checkpoint you can catch a shared taxi or a #15 bus into Eilat. **Coming from Israel** there is a NIS67 exit tax and a £E17 entry tax into Egypt. **Buses** from Taba run daily to **Nuweiba** (6.30am, 9am, 2pm & 3pm; £E10), **Dahab** and **Sharm el-Sheikh** (3pm; £E10–15), **Cairo** (8am, 10am & 2pm; £E65–70) and **Suez** (7am; £E30). You can also get an A/C minibus operated by Europcar from the *Hilton* to Nuweiba (£E35) and Dahab (£E70) at 6.30am, 9.30am, 11.30am, 1pm & 5pm, while **service taxis** charge whatever they can get away with. Try and aim for per person rates of: Tarabeen £E30, Nuweiba £E30, Dahab £E50, Sharm £E75.

Eilat: some notes

Israel's number one holiday resort, **EILAT** combines reefs and beaches with upfront hedonism and hustle. Thieving is rife and sleeping on the beaches can be risky, so it's advisable to find a proper bed (almost impossible during Passover and other major Jewish holidays). There are lots of **hostels** near the bus station. **Buses to Jerusalem** leave at 7am, 10am, 2pm and 5pm; on Fridays the last is at 2pm. Unless you've reserved a seat you'll probably have to stand in the aisle.

THE INTERIOR

The **interior of Sinai** is a baking wilderness of jagged rocks, drifting sand and wind-scoured gravel pans, awesome in its desolation. Yet life flourishes around its isolated springs and water holes, or whenever rain falls, renewing the vegetation across vast tracts of semi-desert. Hinterland settlements bestride medieval pilgrimage routes, which the Turks transformed from camel tracks into dirt roads, then the Egyptians and Israelis improved and fought over. Both sides also built and bombed the airstrips which the MFO now use to monitor the Sinai's demilitarized zones.

As a result, the only readily accessible part is **St Catherine's Monastery**, **Mount Sinai** and **Feiran Oasis**, although some other, smaller oases can be reached by jeep or camel from the Aqaba coast or St Catherine's (see below). That said, most buses from Cairo to Nuweiba traverse the **Plateau of El-Tih** (The Wanderings) via **Nekhl** and the **Mitla Pass**, allowing you to see something of the peninsula's interior. However, because of the unexploded ordnance lying around, independent motoring is officially restricted outside the St Catherine's–Feiran Oasis area.

Inland safaris and treks

Though most tourists are initially attracted by Sinai's beaches and reefs, even a brief trip into the interior should prove a memorable experience that'll whet your appetite for more.

Inland safaris range from half-day excursions by jeep or camel to fully fledged treks lasting up to two weeks. Travelling **by jeep** is obviously faster and makes little or no demands on your physique, but tends to distance you from the landscape and at the worst can reduce the experience to a mere outing. This is rarely the case if you travel **by camel**, which feels totally in keeping with the terrain. If you've never ridden a camel before, try a half-day excursion before committing yourself to a longer trip. Even a few hours in the saddle can leave you with aches in muscles that you never knew existed. It's easy to get the hang of steering: pull firmly and gradually on the nose rope to change direction; a camel should stop if you turn its head to face sideways. Couching the animal – this entails thrusting one's face close to its muzzle and growling "*kkhhurr, kkhhurr*" – is best left to the Bedouin guides. See "Camels" in Basics chapter for advice on posture.

Safaris can be organized at any of the resorts on the Aqaba coast; you'll find details and prices listed under each resort. For those with more time and stamina, a third option is to go **trekking on foot,** which is the most rewarding way to experience remote areas. Treks can be arranged at the village of St Catherine's or at certain points along the roads into the interior, such as Sheikh Hamid – and also through some of the Bedouin who run trips from the coastal resorts. The list of destinations below is by no means all-inclusive, but should give an idea of what's on offer. Some places are described elsewhere in this chapter; others are not.

Practicalities depend on one's destination and mode of travel. Day excursions from the coast can be made on a Sinai-only visa, but to travel for any longer or explore the High Mountain Region beyond the immediate vicinity of St Catherine's Monastery and Mount Sinai you must have a proper **Egyptian visa**. To climb mountains you must also have a **permit** from the police, which can be obtained by your Bedouin guide. It is illegal – and highly risky – to go trekking without a guide. To help you select destinations and plot routes, buy the 1:250,000 *Sinai Map of Attractions* published by the Israeli firm Tzofit, which is sold at the main resorts on the coast. Other things to **bring** are listed in the "High Mountain Region and Feiran Oasis" section (p.602).

Finally, **respect the landscape** and leave it unspoiled. Bring plastic bags to remove your rubbish when you go and burn any toilet paper left behind. Gathering firewood should be left to your guide, and gardens should never be entered without permission from the owners.

Safari destinations

The following are all keyed to the map on p.554.

Ain el-Furtaga 16km from Nuweiba by road. Palmy oasis at the crossroads of trails to the Coloured Canyon, Wadi Ghazala and Ain Khudra Oasis.

Ain Khudra Oasis One of the loveliest oases in Sinai. Reached by hiking from the St Catherine's road, with help from local Bedouin, or from the south by 4WD.

Ain Kid Oasis 14km off the road between Sharm el-Sheikh and Dahab; reached via Wadi Kid, a red-walled canyon where a spring appears in rainy years. The oasis has a fresh-water well.

Ain Umm Ahmed Another beautiful oasis, accessible by 4WD or camel from Bir es-Sawa. Can serve as a base for climbing expeditions to Ras el-Qalb (see below).

Arched Canyon Sinuous gorge that's only accessible on foot; drop-off and pick-up by 4WD from Ain el-Furtaga or Bir es-Sawa.

Bir es-Sawra Small oasis with a spring issuing from a cave, beside the El-Thammed road.

Blue Valley 5km from St Catherine's. Canyon painted blue by a Belgian artist.

Coloured Canyon North of Ain el-Furtaga. Two rainbow-hued canyons, great for walking or rock-climbing (no water). One of the most popular day trips from Nuweiba.

El-Haduda The biggest sand dune in eastern Sinai, reached from Sheikh Hamid (see below).

Feiran Oasis Over 12,000 palm trees, monastic remains, and access to Jebel Serbal. Wadi Feiran may have been the route taken by the Israelites to reach Mount Sinai.

Forest of Pillars Unique natural phenomenon on the cliffs of Jebel el-Tih, to the east of Sarabit el-Khadim (see below). Access by 4WD or camel only; guide essential.

Jebel Sabah A 2280m peak from which Saudi Arabia and mainland Egypt are visible on clear days. Experienced climbers only, with abundant food and water. Permit required.

Jebel Serbal Near Feiran Oasis. One of the loveliest mountains in Sinai, with ruined chapels lining the trail to the summit (2070m). No climbing skills needed, but guide and permit required.

Jebel Umm Shaumar The second highest peak in Sinai, whose summit (2854m) affords a view of the entire southern horn of the peninsula. Experienced climbers only. Permit required.

Nuwamis Prehistoric site with 5550-year-old graves and inscriptions. Reached on foot (2hr 30min) from Sheikh Hamid, by appointment only.

Ras el-Qalb Isolated mountain (999m) associated in Bedouin folklore with the monster Ula. For climbers only; no water. Permit required.

Sarabit el-Khadim Hilltop temple overlooking the Gulf of Suez, with ancient turquoise mines and inscriptions in the surrounding valleys. Access by 4WD, then on foot.

Sheikh Hamid Bedouin settlement on the road to St Catherine's, 7km from the Dahab–Nuweiba road. Starting point for walking or camel treks to Ain Khudra, Nuwamis, El-Haduda, and remoter destinations (up to two weeks).

Wadi Ghazala Links Ain el-Furtaga and Ain Khudra Oasis. Acacia groves, dunes and gazelles.

Wadi Huweiyit North of Nuweiba. Colourful canyon with typical desert flora; easy hiking.

Wadi Mandar 40km north of Sharm el-Sheikh. Bedouin camel races occur here on January 1.

Wadi Naseb Running down from Mount Catherine towards Dahab, the verdant upper reaches of the wadi are inhabited by Bedouin. 4WD essential.

St Catherine's Monastery and Mount Sinai

Venerated by Christians, Jews and Muslims as the site of God's revelation of the Ten Commandments, **Mount Sinai** overlooks the valley where Moses is said to have heard the Lord speaking from a burning bush.

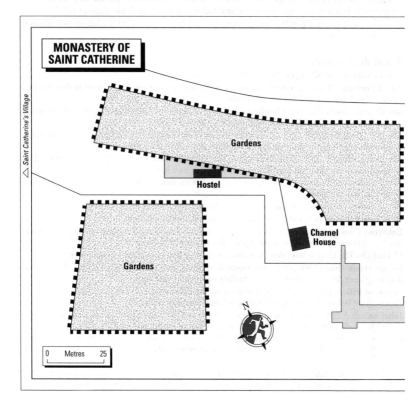

The bush is now enshrined in **St Catherine's Monastery**, nestling in a valley at the foot of the Mount, surrounded by high walls and lush gardens. As tourists have followed pilgrims in ever greater numbers the sacred mount has witnessed unseemly quarrels over sleeping space, and the monastery itself shows signs of strain. Yet for most travellers it remains a compelling visit, while other seldom visited peaks offer equally magnificent views if you're prepared to make the effort to reach them.

Getting there – and moving on

Despite its isolated location, St Catherine's is one of the most accessible parts of South Sinai. You can visit on **organized tours** from Na'ama Bay, Nuweiba, Cairo, Hurghada or Eilat, or you can make your own way by bus, car or *service* taxi.

The only drawback to **buses** are their variable schedules. When last heard, you could reach St Catherine's directly from Cairo (8hr; £E55) on a bus leaving the Sinai Terminal at 9am, though it's cheaper to travel to Suez and get a bus from there at 2pm (6hr; £E25) – both are routed via Feiran Oasis. Services from the Aqaba resorts follow a road skirting the Jebel Gunna, which turns off the highway between Dahab and Nuweiba; they start from Sharm (7.30am), stopping at Na'ama (soon afterwards), Dahab (9.30am), Nuweiba (10.30am) and Taba (10am). Ask to be dropped at the turn-off for the Monastery, 1.5km before St Catherine's village. The village's restaurants are pick-up points for people **leaving** by bus; most depart between noon and 1pm, except for the Suez bus, which goes at 6am.

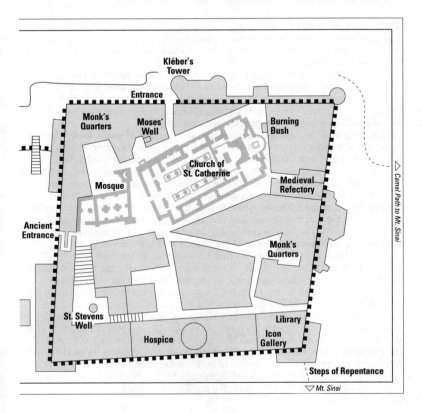

For a group of travellers, another option is to engage a **service taxi** at Suez, Dahab, Nuweiba or Taba and split the cost. Taxis usually run in the morning and afternoon if enough customers are interested, raising their fares once the last bus has left. The same goes for taxis leaving St Catherine's, which run to Dahab and other places, depending on demand.

The Monastery of St Catherine

The **Monastery of St Catherine** is a Greek Orthodox – rather than Coptic – foundation. Its origins date back to 337 AD, when the Byzantine **Empress Helena** ordered the construction of a chapel around the putative **Burning Bush**, already a focus for hermits and pilgrimages. During the sixth century, the site's vulnerability to raiders persuaded Emperor Justinian to finance a fortified enclosure and basilica, and to supply two hundred guards – half of them Greeks or Slavs – from whom the Jebeliya Bedouin claim descent.

Although the Prophet Mohammed is said to have guaranteed the monastery's protection after the Muslim conquest, the number of monks gradually dwindled until the "discovery" of St Catherine's relics (see p.603), which ensured a stream of pilgrims and bequests during the period of Crusader domination (1099–1270). Since then, it has had cycles of expansion and decline, on occasion being totally deserted. There are currently 22 monks, most of whom came here from the monasteries of Mount Athos in Greece.

Visiting the monastery

The monastery is **open** to visitors from 9.30am till noon; it's closed on Fridays, Sundays and on all Greek Orthodox holidays. There is no admission charge, but visitors must be modestly dressed.

You enter through a small gate in the northern wall near **Kléber's Tower** (named after the Napoleonic general who ordered its reconstruction) rather than the main portal facing west, which has a funnel for pouring boiling oil onto attackers. Built of granite, 10–15m high and 2–3m thick, St Catherine's **walls** are essentially unchanged since Stephanos Ailisios designed them in the sixth century.

Emerging from the passage, a right turn takes you past **Moses's Well**, where the then-fugitive from Egypt met Zipporah, one of Jethro's seven daughters, whom he married at the age of forty. Walking the other way and around the corner, you'll see a thorny evergreen bush outgrowing an enclosure. This is the transplanted descendant of the **Burning Bush** whence God spoke to Moses: "Come now therefore, and I will send thee unto Pharaoh, that thou mayest bring forth my people the children of Israel out of Egypt" (Exodus 3:10). Sceptics may be swayed by the news that it's the only bush of its kind in the entire peninsula, and that all attempts to grow cuttings from it elsewhere have failed. The Bush was moved to its present site when Helena's chapel was built over its roots, behind the apse of the Church of St Catherine.

A granite basilica, **St Catherine's Church** was erected by Justinian between 542 and 551; the walls and pillars and the cedar-wood doors between the narthex and nave are all original. Its twelve pillars – representing the months of the year and hung with icons of the saints venerated during each one – have ornately carved capitals, loaded with symbolism. At the far end, a lavishly carved and gilded iconostasis rises towards a superb mosaic depicting Jesus flanked by Moses and Elijah, with Peter, John and James kneeling below – unfortunately it's roped off and hard to see behind the ornate chandeliers and censers suspended from the coffered, eighteenth-century ceiling. Behind the iconostasis is the **Chapel of the Burning Bush**, only viewable by special dispensation. The narthex displays a selection of the monastery's vast collection of **icons**, running the gamut of Byzantine styles and techniques, from encaustic wax to tempera. The church's **bell** is rung 33 times to rouse the monks before dawn.

Other parts of the monastery are often closed to laypersons. Amongst them are an eleventh-century **mosque**, added to placate Muslim rulers; a **library** of over 3000 manuscripts and 5000 books, surpassed only by the Vatican's; and a **refectory** with Gothic arches and Byzantine murals. You can usually enter the **charnel house**, however, heaped with monks' skeletons; the cemetery itself is small, so corpses have to be disinterred after a year and moved into the ossuary. The cadaver in vestments is Stephanos, a sixth-century guardian of one of the routes to the Mount.

St Catherine's Village

While the monastery and Mount Sinai are the focus of interest, most of the facilities of use to tourists are in the **village of St Catherine**, 3km away. Shared taxis provide **transport** between the two, charging £E5. The village's main square acts as the bus station, since the road terminates there. On one side is an arcade containing a **bank** (Sun–Thurs 8.30am–2pm & 6–9pm), several supermarkets and restaurants; on the other side are the **tourist police** and a small **hospital**. In the vicinity of the mosque are a **post office** and **telephone exchange**.

There's not much difference between the **restaurants** (6am–10pm), which do simple meals of chicken and rice or spaghetti Bolognese – the *Panorama* also runs to soup and pizzas. A **bakery** opposite the mosque sells pitta bread.

If you're planning to do any trekking in the High Mountain Region, ask locals to point you towards **El-Milga**, uphill past the main square, where you'll find **Sheikh Musa** (☎069/771-004, ext 457), the chief of the Bedouin guides who lead expeditions. For more details, see "The High Mountain Region and Feiran Oasis" p.602, and p.596.

Accommodation

Many travellers leave their packs in the monastery's storeroom (£E2) and ascend the camel path to **sleep out on Mount Sinai**. Most people on tours arrive in the early hours to climb the mountain and **catch the sunrise** before descending again. With night-time temperatures around 10°C during summer and near-zero over winter (when frosts and snow aren't uncommon) a sleeping bag is essential if you plan to spend the night, unless you want to rent blankets on the summit. With so many people wanting to sleep out, there is often little room at the summit, and you may have to sleep further down the mountain at Elijah's Hollow (see below) and complete the journey before sunrise.

If you just need a roof over your head, the best option is the 150-bed **hostel** at the monastery (see below). Most other accommodation is a considerable distance from St Catherine's, though most arrange transport.

Daniela Village, in St Catherine's village (☎ & fax 069/470-379). A/C rooms with baths; restaurant, cafeteria and bar (the only one in town). ⑥.

Green Lodge, near the start of the road to Wadi Feiran, 6km from the monastery (☎ & fax 069/470-080). Dorm beds (£E21 per person) and tents with cots. Provides transport to and from the monastery, if you contact their office next to the post office in El-Milga. ②.

Katherine Plaza, just outside the village (☎069/470-289). Smart four-star place with A/C rooms, restaurant and bar. ⑦.

Monastery Hostel (☎069/470-350, fax 470-343). Beds in dorms (£E35 per person) or triple rooms with showers (£E40 per person); simple meals included. The gates are locked at 10pm.

Morgana Land Village, 200m from *Zeitouna Camp* (see below) (☎069/470-404, fax 470-331). Dorm beds (£E25), or large rooms with showers; there's also a restaurant. ④.

St Catherine Tourist Village, by the main road, 500m from the monastery (☎069/470-324, fax 470-323). The smartest hotel in the area, with comfortable A/C apartments; breakfast and dinner included. ⑦.

Zeitouna Camp, on the Nuweiba road, 5km from the monastery (£E5 per person by taxi) (☎069/470-409). Tents with cots and stone huts, communal showers plus a restaurant. ②–③.

Ascending Mount Sinai

Whilst some archeologists question whether **Mount Sinai** was really the Biblical mountain where Moses received the Ten Commandments, it's hard not to agree with John Lloyd Stephens that "among all the stupendous works of Nature, not a place can be selected more fitting for the exhibition of Almighty power". A craggy, sheer-faced massif of grey and red granite "like a vengeful dagger that was dipped in blood many ages ago", its loftiest peak rises 2285m above sea level. Strictly speaking, it's only this that the Bedouin call *Jebel Musa* (Mount Moses), though the name is commonly applied to the whole massif. Some Biblical scholars reckon that Moses proclaimed the Commandments from Ras Safsafa, at the opposite end of the ridge, which overlooks a wide valley where the Israelites could have camped.

Walking to the summit

Neither of the two **routes to the summit** requires a guide, but you shouldn't attempt the walk at night without a torch, and certainly not during winter – accidents are not uncommon.

The longer but easier route is via the switchback **camel path**, starting 50m behind the monastery. You can rent a camel for most of the ascent (£E40; £E15 at midday) but it's really worth the effort of walking (3hr). Don't be misled by the peak with a conspicuous chapel, which is not Mount Sinai. You can stock up on water at the monastery shop before setting off; there are refreshment stalls along the way but their prices are higher. You can also rent blankets and mattresses for the night for £E5–10.

Beyond the cleft below the summit, the path is joined by the other route, known as the *Sikket Saiyidna Musa* (Path of Our Lord Moses) or **Steps of Repentance**. Hewn by a penitent monk, the 3750 steps make a much steeper ascent from the monastery (1hr 30min), which is hell on the leg muscles. Some of the steps are a metre high.

At present, the only building on the summit is a small **chapel** sited near the cave where God sheltered Moses: "I will put thee in a cleft of the rock, and will cover thee with my hand while I pass over" (Exodus 33:22); the view over scores of arid peaks is breathtaking, particularly at sunset.

Many people ascend by the camel path and descend by the steps. Start your ascent around 5pm (earlier during winter) to avoid the worst of the heat and arrive in time to watch the spellbinding sunset. With a torch, you could also climb the camel path (but not the steps) by night, though not during winter. Descending the steps you'll enter a depression containing a 500-year-old cypress tree, known as the Plain of Cypresses or **Elijah's Hollow**, where pilgrims pray and sing. Here Elijah heard God's voice (I Kings 19:9–18) and hid from Jezebel, being fed by ravens. One of the two chapels is dedicated to him, the other to his successor, Elisha.

The High Mountain Region and Feiran Oasis

The area around St Catherine's is sometimes termed the **High Mountain Region**, as it contains numerous peaks over 2000 metres (6500 feet). Snow frequently covers the ground in winter and flash-floods can occur at any time of the year. The scenery is fantastic, with phalanxes of serrated peaks looming above wadis full of tumbled boulders and wiry fruit trees; springs that are mere trickles in summer turn into waterfalls over winter. This harsh but beguiling land is the stamping ground of the Jebeliya and Aulad Said tribes, some of whom act as guides for **treks** on foot or by camel; with a few exceptions, the terrain is too rough for vehicles, even with 4WD. The trekking season runs from March to October. By law, foreigners are forbidden to embark on such expeditions without a Bedouin guide.

The main **starting point** for treks is the village of El-Milga near St Catherine's (see p.600), where Sheikh Musa will get things organized. He'll take your passport, register it with the police, purchase food and water, and work out all the details of the expedition. It costs £E55 per day to rent a Bedouin guide – who are generally helpful and reliable – plus £E30 per day for each camel. Even if you're going to walk, you'll need a camel to carry your baggage; surplus gear can be left at the sheikh's house. The ideal number of trekkers is three to five people; larger groups travel more slowly. You'll need comfortable hiking boots, warm clothes, a sleeping bag, sunglasses, sunscreen, lip-salve, bug repellent and toilet paper. Though Sheikh Musa can provide eating utensils, you'll need to bring water purification tablets unless you're willing to drink from springs. To make sense of the landscape, it's essential to have a good map of South Sinai (see p.596) and a compass. Depending on your destination, you may also need a ten-metre-long rope (not necessary for the two hikes detailed below). Always take away any trash and burn used toilet paper when you leave.

Mount Catherine, Blue Valley and other walks

Egypt's highest peak, **Mount Catherine** (*Jebel Katerina*; 2642m) lies roughly 6km south of Mount Sinai, and can be reached on foot in five to six hours. The path starts behind the village and runs up the Wadi el-Leja on Mount Sinai's western flank, past the deserted Convent of the Forty and a Bedouin hamlet. Shortly afterwards the trail forks, the lower path winding off up a rubble-strewn canyon, Shagg Musa, which it eventually quits to ascend Mount Catherine – a straightforward but exhausting climb. On the summit are a chapel with water, a meteorological station and two rooms for pilgrims to stay overnight. The **panoramic view** encompasses most of the peninsula, from Hammam Faroun and the Wilderness of the Wanderings to the Arabian mountains beyond the Gulf of Aqaba.

According to tradition, it was on this peak that priests found the remains of **St Catherine** during the ninth or tenth century. Believers maintain that she was born in 294 AD in Alexandria of a noble family, converted to Christianity and subsequently lambasted Emperor Maxentius for idolatry, confounding fifty philosophers who tried to shake her faith. Following an attempt to break her on a spiked wheel (hence Catherine Wheels), which shattered at her touch, Maxentius had her beheaded; her remains were transported to Sinai by angels. Others doubt that she ever existed and regard her cult as an invention of Western Catholicism, validated by "the land of her supposed sufferings" because of medieval France's demand for "holy oil" and other relics.

If climbing Mount Catherine seems too ambitious, consider visiting the **Blue Valley**, 5km southeast of the intersection of the roads to St Catherine's, Nuweiba and Feiran Oasis. The canyon's name owes to a Belgian who painted its rocks a deep blue in emulation of the Bulgarian artist Christo, who hung drapes across the Grand Canyon and wrapped up the Reichstag in Berlin. Hikes can be arranged through Sheikh Musa, while the Bedouin guides who hang out at Sheikh Hamid near the junction with the coastal highway offer longer camel trips.

Longer treks

The two **four-day treks** outlined below give an idea of what can be done; some other possibilities are mentioned under "Feiran Oasis" (see below).

Starting off in El-Milga, the **first trek** begins by taking the path through the **Abu Giffa Pass** down into Wadi Tubug, passing walled gardens en route to Wadi Shagg, where you'll find Byzantine ruins and huge boulders. From there you proceed to a grove of olive trees reputedly planted by the founder of the Jebeliya tribe, where you spend the night. The next day you follow the trail through Wadi Gibal and climb one of two peaks offering magnificent views, before descending to Farash Rummana, a camping spot with showers. On the third day you strike north through a canyon to the water holes of Galt al-Azraq, pushing on to camp out at Farsh Umm Sila or Farsh Tuweita. The final day begins with an easy hike down towards Wadi Tinya, before climbing Jebel Abbas Pasha (2383m), named after the paranoid ruler who built a palace there (now in ruins). Having retrieved your gear at the foot of the mountain, you follow a path down through the Zuweitun and Tubug valleys, back to Abu Giffa and El-Milga.

The **second trek** starts at **Abu Sila** village, 3km from El-Milga, where there are some rock inscriptions. You'll probably camp out near the sweetwater spring of Bustan el-Birka. Day two involves descending into Wadi Nugra, below Jebel el-Banat, where you can relax and bathe in pools fed by a twenty-metre-high waterfall. You then press on along the path through Wadi Gharba to the tomb of Sheikh Awad, where the Aulad Gundi tribe holds an annual feast in his honour. Having spent the night here, you have a choice of three routes to Farsh Abu Tuweita, the final night's camping spot. On the fourth day you follow the same route as the final leg of the other hike, visiting Abbas Pasha's ruined palace before returning to El-Milga.

Feiran Oasis

It's thought that the ancient Israelites reached Mount Sinai by the same route that buses coming from the west use today, via Wadi Feiran and Wadi el-Sheikh. Travelling this road in the other direction, you might glimpse the **Tomb of Nabi Salah** near the **Watiyyah Pass**, where Bedouin converge for an annual **moulid** on the Prophet Mohammed's birthday. Celebrants smear themselves with "lucky" tomb dust, sacrifice sheep, race camels, bury their dead and pray, before enacting a rodeo and feasting on roast camel stuffed with sheep. Beyond the pass lies El-Tafra, a small and dismal oasis village.

Roughly 60km from St Catherine's the road passes a huge walled garden marking the start of **FEIRAN OASIS**. A twisting, granite-walled valley of palms and tamarisks, the oasis belongs to all the tribes of the *Tawarah*, who have houses and wells here. (Elsewhere, inter-tribal law permits the grazing of animals and pitching of tents on any land, but not the cutting of wood or building of stone houses.) Feiran was the earliest Christian stronghold in the Sinai, with its own bishop and **convent**, ruined during the seventh century but now rebuilt. More anciently, this was supposedly the *Rephidim* of the Amalakites, who denied its wells to the thirsty Israelites, causing them to curse Moses until he smote the Rock of Horeb with his staff, and water gushed forth. Refreshed, they joined battle with the Amalakites the next day, inspired by the sight of Moses standing on a hilltop, believed to have been the conical one that the Bedouin call **Jebel el-Tannuh**, with ruined chapels lining the track to its summit (1hr).

Other **hiking** possibilities in the area include **Jebel el-Banat** (1510m), further north, and the highly challenging ascent of **Jebel Serbal** (2070m), south of the oasis. This is approached via the rugged Wadi Aleyat, with a few springs at its upper end. From here you can either follow a goat track up a steep, boulder-strewn ravine called Abu Hamad (5hr), or take the longer but less precipitous *Sikket er-Reshshah* (Path of the Sweaty) to the summit. From the main peak on the ridge there's a wonderful view of the oasis, countless mountains and wadis, with a narrow ledge jutting over a 1200m precipice. As for finding a guide, make arrangements in El-Milga; a *service* taxi to Feiran costs £E70 for a group. Although Feiran Oasis lacks any tourist **accommodation**, you could probably camp out somewhere in the palm groves with local consent.

En route to the coast, **motorists** might consider detouring north to the turquoise mines of Jebel Abu Alaqa and the rock-hewn temple at Sarabit el-Khadim (see p.565).

The Wilderness of the Wanderings

Separating the granite peaks of South Sinai from the sandy wastes of the north is a huge tableland of gravel plains and fissured limestone, riven by wadis: the **Wilderness of the Wanderings** (*Badiet el-Tih*). Life exists in this desert thanks to sporadic rainfall between mid-October and mid-April; two or three downpours are enough to send yellow torrents surging down the wadis, rejuvenating the hardy vegetation that supports wildlife and refilling the cisterns that irrigate groves of palms and tamarisks. During Byzantine times, these cisterns sustained dozens of villages along the Sinai–Negev border; nowadays, the largest irrigated gardens are in Wadi Feiran and Wadi el-Arish.

Crossing the Wilderness via Nekhl and the Mitla Pass

The shortest route between Cairo and Nuweiba (470km) crosses the great Wilderness via Nekhl and the Mitla Pass, more or less following the old *Darb el-Hadi* pilgrimage trail from Suez to Aqaba. By day the heat-hazed plateau is stupefyingly monotonous and it's hard not to fall asleep, which would mean missing a glimpse of several historic locations.

The road from Nuweiba heads north to El-Thammed before cutting west across Wadi el-Arish. **NEKHL**, at the heart of the peninsula, features a **derelict castle** built by Sultan al-Ghuri in 1516 and a big MFO observation post. South of one of the wadi's many tributaries lies **Qalat el-Gundi** (Fortress of the Soldier), a **ruined fort** built by Salah al-Din, which can also be reached by a track from Ras Sudr, on the Gulf of Suez. The fort stands atop a small mountain about one hour's climb from the road; be extremely careful when ascending the path, as there's a sheer drop on either side.

Moving west, the road descends through the 480-metre-high **Mitla Pass**, one of three cleavages in the central plateau. When Ralph Bagnold attempted this route from Cairo by Model-T Ford in the early 1920s, it was choked with "yellow undulating cushions" of sand that buried the wire-mesh road laid by the British during World War I. The outcome of three Arab-Israeli conflicts was arguably determined at the Mitla Pass in some of the bloodiest **tank battles** in history. During the war of 1956, an Israeli parachute battalion seized and held the road until the arrival of armoured columns from El-Thammed, which dominated the interior. Having deployed their tanks in expectation of a similar strategy, the Egyptians were wrongfooted during the 1967 War, when the Israelis advanced from Abu Ageila (in the northeast), captured the passes and then systematically annihilated their encircled foes, leaving the roadside littered with charred remains. In the October War of 1973, Egyptian forces failed to exploit their breakthrough along the Bar-Lev Line by rapidly seizing the Mitla and Giddi passes; many blamed their subsequent defeat on the cautiousness of the Commander-in-Chief, General Ismail.

NORTHERN SINAI

While jagged mountains dominate the gulf coasts and interior of the peninsula, **northern Sinai** is awash with sand: pale dunes rising from coastal salt marshes and lagoons to meet gravel plains and wadis far inland. A succession of water holes along the coastal strip between Egypt and Palestine has made this *Via Maris* the favoured route for trade and invasions since late pharaonic times. However, few of the settlements have ever amounted to much, nor deserve a visit nowadays. Although Egyptians have begun flocking to the palmy beaches at **El-Arish**, most foreigners just zip through on direct buses between Cairo and Tel Aviv or Jerusalem, crossing the border near the divided town of **Rafah**.

Some **buses** now run to El-Arish, although from most places you will still be reliant on *service* taxis. In Cairo buses leave from the Turgoman terminal (6 daily; 5hr;

BEDOUIN CULTURE

Although the provision of schools, medical posts and water tanks has enticed many **Bedouin** to forsake nomadic lives, others still roam the desert with their flocks. From the El-Arish road you can glimpse black-garbed women in veils or leather masks spangled with coins, girls in peacock robes with hennaed tresses, aloof boys and men, or a black tent pitched in the desert. **Women** are responsible for weaving the goat-hair *beit shaar* ("house of hair") and striking, packing, unloading and erecting them whenever the family moves on; in Bedouin divorces the husband gets the domestic animals while the woman keeps the tent. The colour of the cross-stitched embroidery on a woman's robe and hood indicates whether she's married (red) or not (blue).

The Bedouin are keen observers of the Sinai's furtive **wildlife**. Hares and foxes can lead them to water holes; desert sandgrouse, gazelles and the rare mountain ibex (*bedan*) make good hunting; and flocks must be guarded against the depredations of the jackal (*taaleb*), wolf (*dib*) and hyena (*dhaba*). The last has a mythological counterpart, the *dhabia*, believed to have the power to mesmerize solitary travellers into entering its lair. Other creatures imbued with supernatural significance are the dreaded horned viper, known as *Abu Jenabiya* (Father of Going Sideways), and the fox – personifying wisdom and cunning – who is a favourite character in children's tales.

Plants are even more important to the Bedouin, who feed their camels on a prickly tribulus called *ghraghada*, and make extensive use of **herbal medicine**. Among the many remedies, *rabla* is an aromatic flower made into an essential oil that's used as a general pick-me-up; while *handl* seeds are ground into a paste, cooked in olive oil and applied in a bandage to aching joints, or mixed with garlic to treat snake or scorpion bites.

Storytelling holds a special place in Bedouin culture, where poetic imagery and Koranic rhetoric sprang naturally from the lips of shepherds exposed to a rich oral heritage since childhood. When food is lacking for guests, hospitality can still be rendered in words: "Had I known that you would honour me by walking this way, I should have strewn the path between your house and mine with mint and rose petals!". Although professional reciters of Arabic poetry are now rare, most Bedouin can reel off folk tales, which usually begin with the phrase "*Kan ma kan . . .*" (There was, there was not).

Conversation is the expected reward for Bedouin **hospitality**, which traditionally stretched to three days, each named after a stage in the ritual: *salaam* (greeting), *ta'aam* (eating) and *kelaam* (speaking). Before the rising of the morning star on the fourth day, hosts helped their guests prepare for departure; those who lingered beyond the drying of the dew were as welcome "as the spotted snake". Honour can now be satisfied by three servings of tea or coffee, and it's no longer mandatory to slaughter an animal.

£E12–15); in Ismailiya, you can get a bus at the main terminal (6 daily; 3hr; £E10) or alternatively a *service* taxi (£E6). *Service* taxis also leave from Qantara on the east bank of the Suez Canal (2hr 30min; £E6). There are EgyptAir **flights** from Cairo to El-Arish (Thurs & Sun; 1hr; US$109 one-way) during summer only.

With no north–south transport across the Sinai peninsula, it's only possible to travel **between the Mediterranean and Aqaba coasts** via Cairo and Suez. It's quickest to do this by **service taxi**, changing at Ismailiya and then again at Suez (or vice versa).

The road from Suez to El-Arish

Roughly 40km along the road to El-Arish you pass a signposted turn-off for **PELUSIUM**, a fortress town that guarded Egypt's eastern border for many centuries, named after the Pelusiac branch of the Nile that once watered its surroundings. Many stories are attached to what the Bible records as the "Strength of Egypt". The Assyrian king

Sennacherib lost 185,000 soldiers after swarms of rats ate their bows and quivers, while the army of Cambyses is said to have induced Pelusium's garrison here to surrender without a fight by driving cats (the sacred animal of the goddess Bastet) before them. Here the Roman general Pompey was murdered on the orders of Ptolemy XII, and the Crusader king Baldwin I died of potamine poisoning after eating putrid fish.

Although the Pelusiac branch of the Nile started to dry up in the third century AD, the city remained inhabited well into the Islamic era, before being abandoned to the sands. In recent years, moves to bring 400,000 *feddans* of land under cultivation by digging the **Al-Salaam Canal** through this region have spurred a rash of **excavations** to recover archeological evidence before it is destroyed. The sites range from Qantara by the Suez Canal to Tell el-Mahraf near El-Arish. At Pelusium, they have uncovered parts of the pharaonic town and a **Roman amphitheatre** that can now be visited by tourists (daily 9am–5pm) – though since you need a car to get there, it seldom receives visitors.

Notwithstanding this, the dominant impression of the road to El-Arish is of a string of **new towns** consisting of huge apartment buildings, and named after hitherto insignificant villages based around wells. Whereas nineteenth-century guidebooks compared the merits of vital watering holes like **Bir el-Abd** ("brackish water and some telegraph-men's huts") and **Mazar** ("it is better not to camp near the well on account of the camel ticks"), modern travellers can drive past without a qualm. Between these towns lie ramshackle villages where the local Bedouin are being induced to settle (see box), interspersed by golden **sand dunes** up to 50m high and 200m long.

El-Arish

Originally a Roman garrison town named *Rhinocolorum* ("Noses Cut Off") after the fate of dissidents exiled there, **EL-ARISH** has experienced more than its fair share of invasions. Happily the latest one is peaceful and largely welcomed: Egyptian tourists attracted by the palm-shaded beaches and bracing rollers. But Westerners have been slow to follow, which is why the tourist poster advertising El-Arish superimposes their images on the beach.

Whether through cause or effect, El-Arish is more **conservative** than the Aqaba coast resorts, with restrictions on booze and dress and a relatively subdued nightlife. However, for a group of travellers into renting a beach apartment and providing their own entertainment, El-Arish could be the place. Its most attractive feature is a mass of **palm groves** on the outskirts, which are unfortunately being whittled away as more and more holiday villas are built. Otherwise, the town is undistinguished and rarely makes news – the last instance being in 1995, when two mass graves of Egyptian POWs shot by the Israelis in the 1967 war were found in the desert, causing outrage in Egypt and shrugs in Israel.

Arrival and accommodation

From a visitor's standpoint there are really only two streets in town. Arriving from the west, you'll cruise along **Sharia Fouad Zakry** – parallel to the beach – until it swings inland and downhill to become **Sharia 23rd July**. This eventually turns into a **souk** of wooden-shuttered stores that look like a set from a Wild West movie, and terminates in **Midan Baladiya**, with its raucous mosque and fuming **bus station**. Minibuses (50pt) and *service* taxis (50–75pt) constantly shuttle between the souk and the beach, sparing you the 2–3km walk and stopping at any point along the way.

Accommodation

Outside of the July–September season there shouldn't be any problem **finding somewhere to stay**. New places are springing up every year, mostly aimed at middle-class

MEDITERRANEAN SEA

Chalets Sireen
Moonlight Hotel
Greenland Beach Hotel
SHARIA FOUAD ZAKRY
Egoth Oberoi
Semiramis El-Arish Hotel
Sinai Beach Hotel
Police Station & Hospital
SHARIA EL-GEISH
Sinai Sun Hotel
Museum & Zoo
SHARIA 23RD JULY
Safa Hotel
EgyptAir
Bank
Airport
MIDAN BALADIYA
Bus & Taxi Station
N
EL-ARISH

Egyptians. Only if you're in a group, or you don't feel happy without A/C and mod cons, is it worth booking ahead.

Chalets Sireen, Sharia Fouad Zakry (☎068/351-420, fax 352-519). Four-person chalets with kitchen, dining room, bathroom. ⑤.

Egoth Oberoi, across from the beach on Sharia Faoud Zakry (☎068/351-321, fax 352-352). Luxurious singles, doubles and triples; a nightclub, pool and tennis courts for guests only. The only bar in El-Arish. £E25 to use beach and pool for outside guests. ⑧.

Greenland Beach Hotel, Sharia Fouad Zakry (☎068/340-601). Rooms with fans, balconies and baths and sea views. No meals except in summer. ③.

Moonlight (☎068/341-362). An appealing beachside location, and the rooms are being gradually upgraded to en-suite chalets. ③.

Safa Hotel, Sharia 23rd July (☎068/353-798). Friendly staff, reasonable rooms with showers and fans. Roof restaurant with nice views. Laundry service. ②.

Semiramis El-Arish, Sharia Fouad Zakry (☎068/344-166, fax 344-168). Singles and doubles far from the beach, and Med-facing suites for a lot more. ⑦–⑧.

Sinai Beach, Sharia Fouad Zakry (☎068/341-713). Doubles and triples with private bathrooms and A/C. Some with balconies overlooking the sea. ⑤–⑥.

Sinai Sun, Sharia 23rd July (☎ & fax 068/341-855). Decent rooms of all sizes with balconies, bathrooms, A/C and TV. ④.

The beach and town

Despite the huts and chalets lining several kilometres of **beach**, you can still find uncrowded stretches shaded by palm trees, the odd wrecked anti-aircraft gun adding a surreal touch. With cooler, rougher seas than the Aqaba coastline, and no reefs, El-Arish's beach is better for bracing dips and idle sunbathing than snorkelling or diving (there's no dive shop, anyway). Foreigners often get invited to join family gatherings and for solo women travellers this can be a good way to avoid hassle from lecherous youths. Visitors are exhorted to stay off the beach after dark and dress modestly when in town – rules enforced by the police.

For a town of 40,000 inhabitants, El-Arish offers few sights or entertainments. In the summer the *Oberoi* has a nightclub with live music and bellydancers. On Thursdays year-round a **Bedouin market** sells fruit, vegetables and other paraphernalia including Bedouin handicrafts; these are also available in the tourist shops such as Elotaify Leather Shop on Sharia 23rd July (☎068/353-311), or El-Khalily Bazaar (☎068/350-359) on Fouad Zakry St. The only other attraction is a **Sinai Heritage Museum**, just past the UN post along the coastal road to Rafah (catch a bus or *service* taxi). The museum is open daily (summer 8am–8pm; winter 10am–6pm; £E4) and contains mostly stuffed wildlife and Bedouin handicrafts. Next door is a small and miserable **zoo** (same hours).

Eating, nightlife and other practicalities

The cheapest places to eat are the *fuul* and *taamiya* joints around Midan Baladiya or the simple **restaurants** along Sharia 23rd July. *Aziz* (below the *El-Salaam Hotel*, beside Midan Baladiya) and *Sammar* (300m up the road) do good *kofta* and salad, or chicken and chips, at reasonable rates. On the beach try *Basata*, past the *Oberoi*, for good seafood. The only places serving **alcohol** are the disco – where you're limited to Stella – and the well-stocked but expensive bar in the *Egoth Oberoi*. If desperate for hard liquor, you could take a *service* taxi to the border and use the duty-free shop outside Egyptian customs and immigration.

Smoking *sheeshas* over backgammon in a café on Sharia 23rd July is usually all that El-Arish can offer in the way of **nightlife** – and that's an exclusively male pursuit. Otherwise, the outdoor restaurant opposite the *Egoth Oberoi,* an unmarked dance hall on the beach nearer town and a lifeless disco on Sharia 23rd July occasionally host entertainers during high season.

The **tourist police** (☎068/341-016) and a useless **information** kiosk (daily except Fri 8am–2pm & 7–10pm) can be found on Fouad Zakry, just before the beach; the main **police** station (☎122) and **hospital** (☎068/340-010) lie east along Sharia el-Geish, which forks off inland. There is a better equipped **Mubarak Military Hospital** (☎068/324-018) near the North Sinai Governate in Dahiya. Pharmacy Fouad (Sun-Thurs 8am-midnight, Fri 8am-1.30pm & 5pm) on 23rd July can recommend a doctor. One block further north and across the road, a side street leads to a **bank**, **post office** (daily except Fri 8am–2pm) and 24-hour **telephone exchange** (international calls possible, but no card-phones), and the EgyptAir office.

Moving on

Direct buses run from the terminal beside Midan Baladiya to Cairo (£E12–15) and Ismailiya (£E10); minibus **service taxis** also run to **Ismailiya** (£E6) and **Cairo** (£E12). Over summer, there are **flights** to Cairo (Thurs & Sun) and an international service to Sharjah in the United Arab Emirates – contact EgyptAir for details.

Crossing the border into Israel

Most tourists **heading for Israel** via northern Sinai travel directly from Cairo to Tel Aviv or Jerusalem on special buses that run straight to the **Rafah border crossing**, 41km past El-Arish. Alternatively, you can catch a *service* taxi to El Arish from Cairo (£E12) and another from El Arish to the border at Rafah (£E5). From here the #362 bus (NIS35) leaves three times daily for Tel Aviv (the last one is at 2.30pm). The border is open 24 hours, although banks and other facilities on the Israeli side close down over *shabbat*. Your baggage will be X-rayed by the Egyptians before you reboard the bus and trundle across a no-man's land to the Israeli checkpoint, where you'll be quizzed by security police who'll refuse entry to anyone with insufficient funds, but otherwise issue a visa free of charge to most nationalities. After everyone has been processed you board another bus and continue your journey via a highway that deliberately skirts the Gaza Strip.

There is a £E18 **exit tax** on leaving Egypt. Although no taxes are levied on entering Israel, people **coming from Israel** are charged a NIS105 (US$26) plus NIS3 commission exit tax and a £E7 entry tax into Egypt. You should expect delays, since all buses bound for Cairo travel in a convoy with a police escort. Don't believe any tour guide who says there's a "convoy charge" – it's just a ruse to get money from passengers. Tour operators may also ask you for US$30 or US$35 for your Israeli departure tax, when it is actually US$26.

Visiting Rafah and the Gaza Strip

On the off-chance that you're interested enough to visit, entry to Gaza is relatively simple, though if you tell the Israeli authorities at the border you are going there, they will give you a one-month visa instead of three. After passport control you take a bus (NIS10) to the Palestinian border. Here you can take a *service* taxi to **Gaza City** (NIS20–30) or **Khan Yunis**. You can save money by taking the border *service* to **Rafah** (NIS4) and then a regular *service* to Gaza City (NIS4), but this adds around 30min to the journey.

CHAPTER EIGHT

THE RED SEA COAST AND EASTERN DESERT

For 1250 kilometres, from Suez to the Sudanese border, turquoise waves lap rocky headlands and windswept beaches along a coastline separated from the Nile Valley by the arid hills and mountains of the **Eastern Desert**. Like Sinai, the region's infertility and sparse population belie its mineral wealth and strategic location, and there are further points in common in the wildlife, Bedouin nomads and long monastic tradition. Tourism, too, is developing along similar lines, with holiday villages proliferating along the coast, and dive boats ranging down the Red Sea as far south as Eritrea.

An *entrepôt* since ancient times, the **Red Sea Coast** was once a microcosm of half the world, as Muslim pilgrims from as far away as Central Asia sailed to Arabia from its ports. Though piracy and slaving ceased towards the end of the nineteenth century, smuggling still drew adventurers like Henri de Monfried long after the Suez Canal had sapped the vitality of the Red Sea ports. Decades later, the coastline assumed new significance with the discovery of oil, and its vulnerability to Israeli commando raids, which led to large areas being mined – one reason why tourism didn't arrive until the 1980s.

While Cairenes appreciate the beaches at **Ain Sukhna**, south of Suez, the real lure consists of fabulous island reefs off the coast of **Hurghada** – a booming, bold and brash resort town – and the less touristic settlements of **Port Safaga**, **El-Quseir** and **Mersa Allam** to the south. Pending completion of an international airport at Mersa Allam, access to points further south remains difficult unless you have your own transport, although this looks likely to change, with the coast south of Quseir now subject to ambitious development. Dive companies are establishing supply bases for their dive boats along the southern coastline, opening up "virgin" reefs in the south to divers, whose only option previously was a long journey by sea from Hurghada or Sharm el-Sheikh in the Sinai.

ACCOMMODATION PRICE CODES

Throughout the guide, hotels and pensions are graded on a scale of ① to ⑨, indicating the price (including tax) of the **cheapest double room** in each establishment in high season (for places that offer **dorm beds**, rates per person are given in £E). Please note that most hotels in categories ⑧ and ⑨ quote rates in US$, but will accept payment in £E. For a full explanation of the following categories, see p.46. The price bands to which these codes refer are as follows:

① under £E20/US$7	④ £E45–65/US$15–20	⑦ £E150–300/US$50–100
② £E20–30/US$7–10	⑤ £E65–100/US$20–35	⑧ US$100–200/£E300–600
③ £E30–45/US$10–15	⑥ £E100–150/US$35–50	⑨ US$200/£E600 upwards

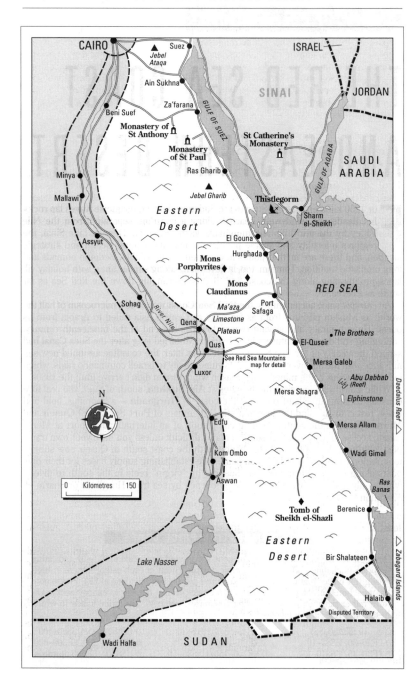

Crossing the Eastern Desert by bus gives little idea of its spectacular highlands. Apparently devoid of life, the granite ranges and limestone wadis harbour ancient temples and quarries, gazelles and ibexes, and Bedouin. While you might not have the inclination, stamina or money for long excursions into the interior, thousands of Copts visit the **Red Sea monasteries**, and further south, amid the **Red Sea Mountains**, truckloads of dervishes converge on **Wadi Humaysara** for the **Moulid of Al-Shazli**. If totally off-the-beaten-track destinations are your thing, the Eastern Desert has more to offer than at first appears.

The Red Sea Monasteries

Secreted amidst the arid Red Sea Hills, Egypt's oldest **monasteries** – dedicated to **St Paul** and **St Anthony** – trace their origins back to the infancy of Christian monasticism, observing rituals that have scarcely changed over sixteen centuries. This tangible link with the primitive church gives them a special resonance for believers, but you don't have to be religious to appreciate their tranquil atmosphere and imposing setting – there's also scope for **bird-watching** in the vicinity.

WARNING – MINEFIELDS

Large areas of Red Sea coastline and many wadis are still mined. Any area with barbed-wire fencing (however rusty) is suspect. Don't wander off public beaches or into the desert without a guide.

Transport, tours and accommodation

Though neither monastery is directly accessible by public transport, they can still be reached in several ways. The main thing to realize is that a quick visit is impossible, and no one is in any hurry once you get there. If you feel OK about travelling with devout believers, it's best to join the **pilgrim tours** arranged from Cairo by the Coptic Patriarchate (22 Sharia Ramses, Abbassiya; ☎02/960-025), or the *YMCA* (27 Sharia al-Gumhorriya; ☎02/917-360), which dispatches a minibus every week. Coptic churches in Luxor or Hurghada may also run tours on a non-profit basis.

Commercial **tours** from Cairo or Hurghada are another possibility. Misr Travel does a tour from Hurghada to both monasteries for US$55 per person; other agencies charge less but visit only one. Depending on your starting point and number, it could work out cheaper to negotiate a **rented taxi**. A six- to eight-hour excursion should cost about £E240 from Suez, £E340 from Cairo or Hurghada; taxis from Za'farana might do a four- to five-hour jaunt for around £E150. An overnight stay for your driver adds at least £E80 more. To drive from one monastery to the other (82km) takes about ninety minutes.

The cheapest method combines **public transport, hitching and walking**. Outside of the hottest months, this shouldn't be dangerous providing you bring ample water and minimal luggage. Any bus from Cairo or Suez to Hurghada can drop you at the **turn-off for St Paul's Monastery**, 26km south of Za'farana, which is recognizable by its plastic-roofed bus shelter. Young Copts alight here, confident of hitching to the monastery, 13km uphill, for there's a fair amount of traffic along the well-paved road. If pilgrims visiting both sites don't offer you a lift, St Anthony's Monastery can be approached via *service* taxis running between Beni Suef and Za'farana. From the signposted turn-off 33km west of Za'farana, it's 15km uphill to the monastery, with some hitching prospects.

To **stay** at the monasteries' guesthouses, you *must* have written permission from their "residence" in Cairo (26 El-Kenisa El Morcosia St Kolet Beck, Cairo; ☎02/590-6025) and the offer is open only to religious groups. Accommodation is in basic dormitories or family rooms. Both monasteries have cafeterias and St Paul's has a shop selling basic foodstuffs, but you might want to bring extra food. Respect conventions on dress and behaviour; smoking and drinking alcohol are forbidden.

The Monastery of St Anthony

West of Za'farana a wide valley cleaves the Galala Plateau and sets the road on course for the Nile, 168km away. Called **Wadi Arraba**, its name derives from the carts that once delivered provisions to the monastery, though legend attributes it to the pharaoh's chariots that pursued the Israelites towards the Red Sea. Turning off the road and south into the hills, it's possible to spot the monastery sited beneath a dramatic ridge of cliffs. If in doubt, ask anyone you encounter to point you towards *Deir Amba Antonyos* or *Deir Qaddis Antwan*.

Lofty walls with an interior catwalk surround the **Monastery of St Anthony** (daily 9am–5pm; closed during Lent and Christmas), whose lanes of two-storey dwellings, churches, mills and gardens of vines, olive and palms basically amount to a village. Formerly self-sufficient, the community now gets most of its food either from Cairo or its own farm near Beni Suef, but remains dependent on water from its **spring**, where Arab legend has it that Miriam, sister of Moses, bathed during the Exodus.

An English-speaking monk will give you a partial tour of the monastery, which varies with each visitor; don't expect to see everything. Highlights include the **keep**, a soot-blackened **bakery** and a **library** of over 1700 manuscripts. The oldest of the five **churches** – featuring thirteenth-century murals and graffiti – is dedicated to the monastery's namesake, who may be buried underneath it. During Lent (when the gates are locked and deliveries are winched over the walls), monks celebrate the liturgy in the twelve-domed Church of St Luke, dating from 1776. Some of the churches date from the early 20th century and there are new ones under construction. There is a well-stocked bookshop which sells books about the monastery and the Coptic Church in Egypt, as well as souvenirs and postcards. At the time of writing, a small museum detailing the monastery's history was set to open beside the bookshop.

All of these buildings are recent compared to the monastery's foundation, shortly after Anthony's death in 356. A sojourn by St John the Short (whose body was later stolen by other monks) is all that's recorded of its early **history**, but an influx of

---

SAINT ANTHONY

The life of **St Anthony** (251–356) coincided with a sea-change in Christianity's position. When Anthony was orphaned at the age of eighteen, he placed his sister in a convent, sold his possessions and became a hermit. Christians at the time faced growing persecution – the "Era of Martyrs" from which the Coptic calendar is dated – but the transformation of Christianity into a state religion in 313 caused many believers to view the church as tainted by worldliness and foreign influences, and the hermit's life as a purer alternative. Admirers pursued Anthony ever deeper into the wilderness, camping out beneath Mount Qalah, where he dwelt in a cave until his death at the age of 105.

Icons depict the saint clothed in animal skins, barefoot and white-bearded, with an escort of lions. A century later, the Greek scholar Athanasius recounted his privations and visions in that prototypical work of Christian hagiography, the *Life of Anthony*, basis for the depictions of Anthony in the Wilderness throughout the next millennium of Coptic and Western art.

refugees from Wadi Natrun, and then Melkite monks, occurred during the sixth and seventh centuries. Subsequently pillaged by Bedouin and razed by Nasr al-Dawla, the monastery was restored during the twelfth century by Coptic monks, from whose ranks several Ethiopian bishops were elected. After a murderous revolt by the monastery servants, it was reoccupied by Coptic, Syrian and Ethiopian monks.

Today's 65 permanent brethren are university graduates and ex-professionals – not unlike the kind of people drawn to monasticism in the fourth century AD. A typical day at the monastery begins at 4am, with two hours of prayer and hymns followed by communion and mass, all before breakfast. Despite the hard conditions, applications are increasing every year. The expansion of the guesthouse to accommodate up to three hundred people is a fair indication of the resurgence of interest in asceticism amongst Egypt's Coptic community.

St Anthony's Cave

Early morning or late afternoon is the best time to ascend to **St Anthony's Cave** (*maghara*), 2km from, and 276m above, the monastery (bring water). After passing a sculpture of St Anthony carved into the mountain rock, you'll face 1200 steps (45min) up to the cave, but the stunning views from 680m above the Red Sea reward your effort. Technicolour wadis and massifs spill down into the azure gulf, with Sinai's mountains rising beyond. The cave where Anthony spent his last 25 years contains medieval graffiti and modern *tilbas*: scraps of paper bearing supplications inscribed with "Remember, Lord, your servant", which pilgrims stick into cracks in the rock. **Birdlife** – hoopoes, desert larks, ravens, blue rock thrushes and pied wagtails – is surprisingly abundant, and you might glimpse shy **gazelles** in the early morning.

The Monastery of St Paul

The **Monastery of St Paul** (daily 9am–5pm; closed during Lent and Christmas) has always been overshadowed by St Anthony's. Its titular founder (not to be confused with the apostle Paul) was only sixteen when he fled Alexandria to escape Emperor Decius's persecutions, making him the earliest known hermit. Shortly before his death in 348, Paul was visited by Anthony and begged him to bring the robe of Pope Athanasius, for Paul to be buried in. Anthony departed to fetch this, but on the way back had a vision of Paul's soul being carried up to heaven by angels, and arrived to find him dead. While Anthony was wondering what to do, two lions appeared and dug a grave for the body, so Anthony shrouded it in the robe and took Paul's tunic of palm leaves as a gift for the pope, who subsequently wore it at Christmas, Epiphany and Easter.

The monastery (called *Deir Amba Bula* or *Deir Mari Bolus*) was a form of posthumous homage by Paul's followers: its turreted walls are built around the cave where he lived for decades. To a large extent, its fortunes have followed those of its more prestigious neighbour. In 1484 all its monks were slain by the Bedouin, who occupied St Paul's for eighty years; rebuilt by Patriarch Gabriel VII, it was again destroyed near the end of the sixteenth century.

The monastery is smaller than St Anthony's and a little more primitive-looking. In its main **Church of St Paul**, the murals, too, are less fluid – though better preserved thanks to gung-ho restoration. A monk will show you round the chapels and identify their icons: notice the angel of the furnace with Shadrach, Meshach and Abednego, and the ostrich eggs hung from the ceiling – a symbol of the Resurrection. The southern sanctuary of the larger **Church of St Michael** contains a gilded icon of the head of John the Baptist on a dish. When Bedouin raided the monastery, its monks retreated into the five-storey **keep**, supplied with spring water by a hidden canal. Nowadays this is not enough to sustain the seventy-odd monks and their guests, so water is brought in from outside.

There is a small shop selling supplies and a reasonably priced cafeteria just outside the monastery grounds.

Ain Sukhna

Without private transport or a firm intention to visit the Red Sea monasteries (see p.613), it's hardly worth stopping **between Suez and Hurghada**. Except for the first 30km, chewed up by tanks in the October War, the road is excellent and most of the blind corners are over by the time drivers get accustomed to speeding on the straights. Traffic is increasing, however, particularly trucks and heavy vehicles, because of major construction projects on the coast road. Heading south past the oil-refineries and natural gas refineries that appear at intervals all along the coast, you'll see parched highlands rising inland. The **Jebel Ataqa** is the northernmost range in the Eastern Desert and an old Bedouin smuggling route by which hashish reached Cairo; Henri de Monfried sent his cargo this way.

Roughly 50km south of Suez, a series of beaches and coves marks **AIN SUKHNA**, where middle-class Cairenes come to picnic at weekends. Ain Sukhna's name derives from the **hot springs** (35°C) that originate in the Jebel Ataqa, but it's the sea that attracts people. Dark patches offshore indicate **coral reefs**, ideal for snorkelling; while rusty barbed-wire fences delineate areas sown with land mines (beneath the cliffs).

EL-GOUNA

Approximately 22km north of Hurghada lies the vast tourist resort of **El-Gouna**. Built on a series of islands linked by purpose-built bridges and canals, it covers 17,000 square kilometres of land, supports 10,000 staff and includes a hospital, four power plants, an international airport and several factories. There are currently eight hotels ranging from three- to five-star, (with a further seven scheduled to open by 2004), several clusters of private villas and two shopping centres. The infrastructure includes a brewery that makes Sakkara and Löwenbrau beer, a winery producing Obelisque wine, a cheese factory making mozzarella, a state-of-the-art hospital and decompression chamber (☎065/549-709), plus an 18-hole golf course and a casino. The main shopping centre has an open-air cinema, cafés, restaurants, bars, nightclubs, a school, banks, two travel agencies, a museum, aquarium and a post office. There are dive centres attached to four of the hotels, and if you're still looking for something to do you can fly a micro-light plane, go horse-riding, go-karting, and play tennis or squash.

The resort is already popular with the Egyptian jetset, although its Western clientele is not quite as well-heeled, being more of a middle-class package-tour crowd. Most people stay closeted within the resort's confines; however, a minibus runs throughout the day between El-Gouna and Hurghada (£E10–30), or else you'll have to rely on taxis (£E50–100).

El-Gouna's **accommodation** comprises properties with typical four- and five-star amenities; most also offer para-sailing, water skiing and windsurfing facilities. The following is a selection of places that are already fully operational.

Steigenberger Golf Resort (☎065/580-140, fax 580-149, *El-gouna@steigenberger.de*). German-owned plush hotel. ⑨.

Sheraton Miramar (☎ & fax 065/545-608, *Sheraton_Miramar_Egypt@sheraton.com*). Built on nine islands. 338 A/C rooms with terrace and sea view, satellite TV and in-room safe. Five swimming pools and a dive centre. ⑨.

Sonesta Paradiso Hotel (☎065/547-951, fax 547-933). A/C rooms with bath, balcony or patio overlooking sea, pool or gardens, satellite TV. Has three swimming pools, a dive centre and a 2km stretch of beach. ⑨.

Sultan Bey Swiss Inn Hotel (☎065/545-600, fax 545-601). A/C rooms with balcony views of lagoon, satellite TV. ⑨.

There are paying **beaches** (£E20–40) in front of the *Ain Sukhna* and *Mena Oasis* hotels; other stretches are free. If you haven't got a car, Ain Sukhna is best reached by **bus from Suez** (see p.538; last bus back 3.30pm). The *Mena Oasis* (☎069/290-850 or 290-855; half-board only ⑦), *Ain Sukhna* (☎069/328-488 or 325-562; ⑥), *Palmera* (☎069/410-816 or 410-817; ⑦) and *Portrait* (☎069/325-560; ⑨) attract plenty of affluent Egyptians, but hardly any foreigners. There are several resorts in the area offering luxury accommodation, water sports and in some cases golf. *El Ein Bay* (☎02/347-0827, fax 02/332-0672) even claims to offer its guests skiing on a simulated piste.

Further south, the beach at **Za'farana** has only one resort, the rather grandly named *Windsor Za'farana* (☎0195/100-191, fax 100-190; half-board only ⑨) approximately 10km south of the town. The *Sahara Inn* motel, a little further on near the petrol station is a cheaper option (no phone, no A/C; ⑤). Its cafeteria is a good place to ask around for a lift to the monasteries. The next bus stop is at **Ras Gharib**, an oil town buffeted year-round by winds, whose sole hotel, the *Al-Alem*, is usually full – the place holds little appeal, except perhaps to mountaineers interested in tackling **Jebel Gharib** (1757m). Another 145km and you are in Hurghada.

Hurghada (Ghardaka)

In the course of two decades, **HURGHADA** has been transformed from a humble fishing village of a few hundred souls into a booming town of 50,000 people, drawn here from all over Egypt by the lure of making money. This phenomenal growth is almost entirely due to **tourism**, which accounts for 95 percent of the local economy. Yet it's worth taking Hurghada's claims to be a seaside resort with a handful of salt. Unlike Sinai, where soft sand and gorgeous reefs are within easy reach and women can bathe unhassled, Hurghada's public beaches are distant or uninviting, while the best marine life is far offshore. If you're not into diving or discos, it's hard to find much to like about Hurghada – though you have to admire its commercial gusto; many of the townsfolk come from Luxor's west bank, where tourism has been a way of life for generations.

While package tourists laze in their resorts, independent travellers often feel hard done by. Paying for boat trips and private beaches is unavoidable if you're to enjoy Hurghada's assets, and although conditions for diving, windsurfing and deep-sea fishing are great, the **cost** is high, with real bargains limited to accommodation. Nor will you save much by self-catering; everything in the shops is more expensive than in Cairo or the Nile Valley. As tour groups come all year round, there's no "off" season for

---

RUSSIANS IN HURGHADA

The biggest change to Hurghada's tourist scene in the last decade has been the huge influx of **Russian tourists**. Their arrival in 1994 was greeted with joy by hoteliers, whose occupancy rates had plummeted following terrorist attacks in the Nile Valley. Being inured to chaos and inflation back home, the Russians weren't deterred by bomb scares and proved to be big spenders. Sadly, however, cultural differences soon soured things, and many locals now regard them all as drunks or whores, while the Russians reciprocate with equal contempt. It doesn't help that some of the Russians really *are* mafiosi or prostitutes (the latter ply their trade in hotels as "personal assistants") – nor that the Egyptians are irked by the lack of a common language in which to hustle them.

Aside from filling up the holiday villages, the Russians haven't had much effect on other tourists – except perhaps for the bewilderment when they first see restaurant signs advertising *borsch* and *pelmeni*. As the Russians generally have little interest in diving (being content to make descents in the *Sindbad Submarine* (see p.629), or snorkelling trips to Giftun Island), not much mixing occurs, except in Hurghada's discos.

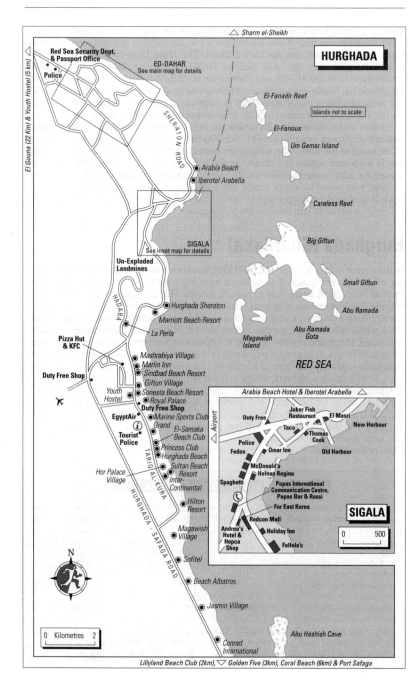

△ Sharm el-Sheikh

HURGHADA

Red Sea Security Dept. & Passport Office

Police

El Gouna (22 Km) & Youth Hostel (5 km)

ED-DAHAR
See main map for details

El-Fanadir Reef

Islands not to scale

SHERATON ROAD

El-Fanous

Um Gamar Island

Arabia Beach
Iberotel Arabella

Careless Reef

SIGALA
See inset map for details

Big Giftun

Un-Exploded
Landmines

HADABA

Small Giftun

Hurghada Sheraton
Marriott Beach Resort
La Perla

Abu Ramada

Pizza Hut
& KFC

Abu Ramada
Gota

Magawish
Island

Duty Free Shop

RED SEA

Mashrabiya Village
Marlin Inn
Sindbad Beach Resort
Giftun Village
Sonesta Beach Resort
Royal Palace
Duty Free Shop

Youth
Hostel

EgyptAir

Marine Sports Club
Grand El-Samaka
Beach Club
Princess Club
Hurghada Beach
Sultan Beach
Resort
Inter-
Continental

Tourist
Police

TARIQ AL-KURA

Hor Palace
Village

Arabia Beach Hotel & Iberotel Arabella △

Airport

Duty Free

Joker Fish
Restaurant

El Masri

New Harbour

Taco

Police
Fedex

Thomas
Cook

Omar Inn

Old Harbour

McDonald's
Helnan Regina

Spaghetti

Papas International
Communication Centre,
Papas Bar & Rossi

Far East Korea

Redcon Mall

Andrea's
Hotel &
Hepca
Shop

Holiday Inn

Felfela's

SIGALA

0   500

Hilton
Resort

Magawish
Village

HURGHADA · SAFAGA ROAD

Sofitel

Beach Albatros

N

Jasmin Village

Abu Hashish Cave

0   Kilometres   2

Conrad
International

Lillyland Beach Club (2km), ▽ Golden Five (3km), Coral Beach (6km) & Port Safaga holiday villages, whose **peak times** are the European Christmas and Easter holidays and the Russian vacation period of August and September. Low-budget hotels are most in demand over winter, when templed-out backpackers flood in from the Nile Valley en route to Sinai.

The town itself is a hotchpotch of utilitarian structures, garish hotels and gaudy boutiques, but Egyptians love its wide boulevards and sea breezes, the spaciousness and "Benetton **ambience**". Nowhere else in Egypt are shorts de rigueur and holiday romances so easy. Russians (see box p.617) have added fresh spice to its already cosmopolitan mix of Italians, Germans, French, Brits, Aussies and Japanese, whose hedonistic potential is grasped by Saudi princes, for whom Hurghada is only two hours away by private jet. For Westerners, however, the chief lure remains underwater: a score of coral islands and reefs within a few hours' reach by boat, and many other amazing dive sites that can be visited on liveaboards.

Approaches to Hurghada

Hurghada's multiplicity of **approaches** makes it more accessible than its location suggests. Vehicles go flat out along the coastal highway and desert roads, but a full tank of petrol is essential – there are few pumps en route. Some of the desert routes from the Nile are described in more detail later on.

● **From Alexandria** Superjet (£E75) and Upper Egypt (£E60) both have one bus daily to Hurghada. EgyptAir fly on Monday and Friday (8.45am; 2hr; US$176) via Sharm el-Sheikh.

● **From Cairo** Twice daily EgyptAir **flights** (1hr; US$131 one-way) need to be booked several days ahead over winter. There are eight **buses** daily from the Ahmed Helmi or Turgoman terminals, three of them A/C Superjets (£E47–60), the others Upper Egypt (£E45). During the morning there may also be **service taxis** to Hurghada (£E40) from the Ahmed Helmi depot.

● **From Suez** The 410km from Suez can be covered in five hours by **service taxi** (£E25 per person), or at a less perilous speed by one of the eleven daily **buses** (£E21–26), most with A/C. *Service* taxis leave from just outside the Arba'in Terminal, while buses to Hurghada leave from Bus Station No. 2, near the train station. You should be able to get a bus ticket at an hour's notice, except during the *Hadj* season or major Muslim festivals.

● **From Sinai** Suez can serve for connections if you can't afford direct transport from Sinai (see p.538). Early bookings are advised for EgyptAir **flights** to Hurghada from Sharm el-Sheikh (currently departing Mon 3.30am, Sat 6am & Sun 11.30pm; US$96). At time of writing the airport at St Catherine's Monastery was closed except to private charter planes, but may reopen to scheduled flights in 2001. The ninety-minute journey across the Gulf of Suez by **catamaran** (Mon, Tues, Thurs & Sat departures at 6pm; US$33/£E115, cars £E250) can be booked in Sharm el-Sheikh through Travco (☎069/661-111); it's not worth saving US$6 to travel on the much slower and unreliable **ferry**. Schedules vary according to the season and the catamaran is liable to be out of service for several weeks in the late spring for maintenance. Catamaran bookings can also be made through Travco in Cairo (daily 9am–5pm; ☎02/342-0488), Luxor (daily 9am–3pm & 7–9pm; ☎095/383-811, fax 374 845) and Aswan (daily 9am–3pm & 7–9pm; ☎097/316-393, fax 315 960) – a more reliable option for advance bookings than the hotels in any of these cities.

● **From the Nile Valley** During winter, hordes of travellers come from Luxor, whence there are five daily **buses** (4hr; £E20) via Qena and Safaga. Alternatively, take a *service* taxi to Qena, walk to another taxi depot and catch a *service* on to Hurghada (4hr; £E15).

There are three buses a day from Aswan (8hr; £E35) via Safaga, while a few *service* taxis cross the desert between Beni Suef and Za'farana, or Qift and El-Quseir. Weekly EgyptAir **flights** from Luxor (Wed 12.30am; US$55) should be booked as far ahead as possible.

Orientation

Despite being even more strung out than Alexandria – stretching for nearly 40km down the coast – Hurghada is easily divisible into three zones, whose salient features are mapped on p.618 and p.622.

The **town** proper – known as **Ed-Dahar** (The Harbour) – is separated from the coast by a barren rock massif, so you rarely glimpse the sea. Coming in from the north, its evolution is apparent as administrative buildings give way to hotels, shops, and a maze of mud-brick homes at the feet of Jebel el-Afish. Its amorphous downtown embraces the bazaar quarter and – typical of any thriving tourist centre – a flourishing and nameless strip of restaurants, shops and hotels, which spreads from Sharia Abdel Aziz Mustafa to the Aquarium on the Corniche and whose main landmark is The Market mall alongside the vast *Three Corners Empire Hotel*. The main thoroughfare is **Tariq en-Nasr** (aka El-Nasre Way), whose busiest stretch lies between the bus station and the telephone exchange (known as the *centraal*), which acts as a terminus for local public transport.

From Ed-Dahar, two main roads run 2–4km south to **Sigala** (pronounced "Si-*gala*"), which contains the modern **port** of Hurghada and a mass of restaurants and hotels, squeezed in wherever the terrain allows. Beyond Sigala is nothing but desert and an endless array of **coastal holiday villages** and construction sites, linked by slip-roads to the Hurghada–Safaga road and dignified with the name of **New Hurghada**. This extends more than 30km south of Sigala and there seems nothing to prevent it from ultimately linking up with the resorts at Port Safaga, 50km south.

Arrival, information and transport

Most independent travellers **arrive** in Ed-Dahar at the **bus station** on the southern edge of the downtown area, though coming by Superjet from Cairo you'll be dropped at a nondescript terminal 1km north, while *service* taxis from the Nile Valley wind up at the **taxi station** midway between them. If you're planning to stay in Ed-Dahar it should be possible to find accommodation within walking distance of any of these points.

People arriving by boat from Sinai will disembark at the Old or New **harbour** in Sigala, whence you could walk to several mid-range places or catch a taxi to anywhere in Ed-Dahar for £E10. Each day, forty to fifty plane-loads of package tourists fly into the **airport** off the Hurghada–Safaga road, and are whisked off to their resorts in buses; arriving independently, a taxi into Ed-Dahar costs £E15.

Hurghada's gleaming new **tourist information** centre is located in New Hurghada (daily except Fri 8am–2pm; ☎065/444-420) next to the tourist police and opposite the *Grand Hotel*. Large and airy with helpful staff, it is let down by the lack of practical information, or even a decent map of Hurghada. Much more useful is the *Hurghada Bulletin*, a free monthly magazine with a listings guide and area map; it's available in bars, cafés and most budget hotels. Also worth checking out is *Red Sea Today*, a pocket-sized guide published quarterly by *Egypt Today*. It costs £E5 in tourist bazaars, but you might be able to pick up a free copy from its distributors DHL, based in the Redcon Mall in Sigala. In all events, private agencies, hotels, dive centres and individual fixers are ready to help – for a price. Any information you get given in Hurghada must be regarded as suspect, since everyone earns a commission on whatever you can be induced to spend. Normally this doesn't matter too much – except when they steer you towards dodgy, potentially lethal dive centres.

Transport

While **walking** is fine for getting around Ed-Dahar, transport is needed to reach Sigala or anywhere further south. Locals rely on **private minibuses**, which run from the *centraal* telephone exchange on Tariq en-Nasr out to Sigala (50pt), the *Sheraton* (£E1) and as far south as the *Jasmin Village* (£E5), 21km away. Running from 7am to 11pm, at virtually one-minute intervals for most of the day, they can be flagged down at any point along their route.

Alternatively, **private taxis** are happy to oblige. Expect to pay £E5–10 for a ride in Ed-Dahar, £E10 to Sigala or the *Sheraton*, and £E15–30 to the holiday villages further out. The cost is bound to increase once the last minibus has gone – long before the discos close. Should you need to rent a taxi for the day, £E120 seems to be the going rate for five or six hours, assuming that you don't drive any further than Port Safaga.

Some tourists scoot around on rented **bicycles**, which are OK in town if you can handle the traffic but are not up to trips down the coastal highway, which is often buffeted by strong crosswinds. There are lots of places around the bazaar renting bikes for £E10–20 per day; rates in Sigala are slightly higher. To really get around you could rent a car. Local **car rental** firms have lower prices than the bigger firms, but their deals tend to be for limited mileage on poorly maintained cars.

If you're into posing, El Hanouf, in front of the *Marriott*, and Seti First Travel near *Shedwan Beach* both rent out US Hummers, with drivers, for expeditions into the desert.

Accommodation

Much of Hurghada consists of **hotels and holiday villages**; at the time of writing there were well over 100 in operation and more in the pipeline, with demand so high at the moment that most villages boast occupancy rates of 80–100 percent. If you're coming here to go diving, a **package deal** makes a lot of sense, as you'll pay a lot less than you would otherwise, and without having to do the rounds of the dive centres. Hotels catering to **independent travellers** get £E150 commission for each guest that they sign up for a diving course, so signing on should also improve your chances of negotiating a cut in the price of a room. As in Luxor and Aswan, many hotels make more on trips and commissions than on rooms – not to mention other transactions, at places with a liberal attitude toward selling dope.

Arriving at Hurghada's bus station, you'll be mobbed by **hotel touts**, offering free transport to their establishment (see above). In the event of having to pay, £E10 is absolute tops for a ride to anywhere in Ed-Dahar – which is where most visitors stay if they haven't booked into a holiday village beyond Sigala. If you're bent on locating a hotel on your own, bear in mind that few streets are named, and there are effectively no house numbers.

Hurghada's **water** has to be piped from the Nile Valley, so depending on your hotel's storage capacity it might be cut off for several hours a day. Profligate consumption means that others go short. Foreigners who live here strongly advise against **drinking** the tap water, and if the thought of cooling down by standing under the sprinklers that irrigate the gardens of some of the upmarket hotels appeals, think again: this (barely) treated sewage is largely responsible for the stink that blankets the town.

Downtown Ed-Dahar

Most **low-budget places** cluster around the bazaar or the "strip" of cafés and shops between Sharia Abdel Aziz Mustafa and the Corniche, while **mid-range hotels** are sited off the main road near the Esh-Shahid Mosque and the coastal **holiday villages**. Many new places are currently being built on the lower slopes of Jebel el-Afish, above

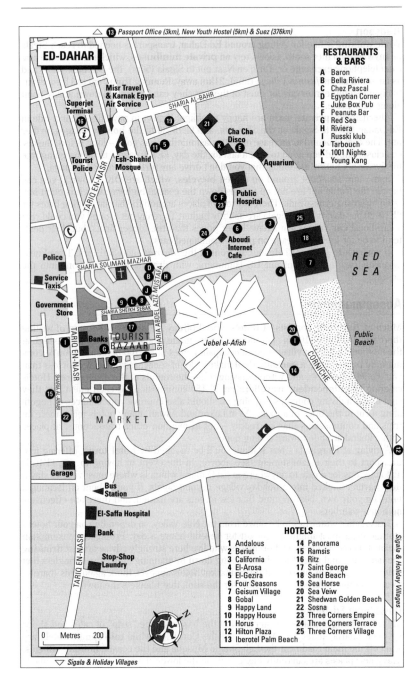

△ ⑬ Passport Office (3km), New Youth Hostel (5km) & Suez (376km)

ED-DAHAR

Misr Travel
& Karnak Egypt
Air Service

Superjet
Terminal
⑯
(i)

Tourist
Police

SHARIA AL-BAHR

Esh-Shahid
Mosque

⑲

㉑

Cha Cha
Disco

K

E

Aquarium

TARIQ EN-NASR

⑪ ⑤

C F
㉓

Public
Hospital

RED
SEA

Police

SHARIA SOLIMAN MAZHAR

Service
Taxis

Government
Store

D
B
H

J

⑨ ⑧
L
SHARIA SHEIKH SEBAK

⑰

Banks

TOURIST
BAZAAR

G

A

Jebel el-Afish

SHARIA ABDEL AZIZ MUSTAFA

⑮

㉒

MARKET

TARIQ EN-NASR

SHARIA AL-ARAB

⑩

Garage

Bus
Station

El-Saffa Hospital

Bank

Stop-Shop
Laundry

TARIQ EN-NASR

㉔

①

Aboudi
Internet
Cafe

⑥

③

④

㉕

⑱

⑦

⑳
(i)

⑭

CORNICHE

Public
Beach

②

Sigala & Holiday Villages

RESTAURANTS
& BARS

A Baron
B Bella Riviera
C Chez Pascal
D Egyptian Corner
E Juke Box Pub
F Peanuts Bar
G Red Sea
H Riviera
I Russki klub
J Tarbouch
K 1001 Nights
L Young Kang

HOTELS

1	Andalous	14	Panorama
2	Beriut	15	Ramsis
3	California	16	Ritz
4	El-Arosa	17	Saint George
5	El-Gezira	18	Sand Beach
6	Four Seasons	19	Sea Horse
7	Geisum Village	20	Sea Veiw
8	Gobal	21	Shedwan Golden Beach
9	Happy Land	22	Sosna
10	Happy House	23	Three Corners Empire
11	Horus	24	Three Corners Terrace
12	Hilton Plaza	25	Three Corners Village
13	Iberotel Palm Beach		

▽ Sigala & Holiday Villages

0   Metres   200

the public beach; the first ones to open will have large rooms and sea views, but will also suffer from the continuing noisy construction work all around. The mostly empty public beach is scheduled to undergo a form of privatization by the end of 1999 which will mean a higher entrance fee, but also the introduction of cafés, bazaars, palm trees and umbrellas and hopefully a better atmosphere.

In general hotels are not as "luxury" as they claim to be – a good guide would be to subtract one star from their rating. All of the following places are marked on the map opposite. Breakfast is included unless stated otherwise, and you can generally count on hot water.

Andalous, on the strip (☎ & fax 065/548-602). Smart, carpeted A/C rooms with bedside lamps and private bathrooms. A good option in this price bracket. ④.

California, at the Corniche end of the strip (☎065/549-101, fax 548-414). Cleanish, cramped rooms, a few with baths; exotic murals adorn the corridors. You can sleep on the roof, which has a sea view. Breakfast is not included. ②.

El-Arosa, on the Corniche (☎ & fax 065/549-190). Nice, clean A/C rooms with baths; indoor pool and music bar. Guests can use the beach at the *Geisum Village*, across the road. ⑥.

El-Gezirah, off Sharia al-Bahr (☎065/547-785, fax 548-708). Spacious A/C rooms with TV. Bar, restaurant and disco, plus free use of the pool and disco at the *Sand Beach*. Mainly German, Dutch and Russian groups. ⑨.

Four Seasons, near the Corniche end of the strip (☎065/549-882, fax 545-456). Simple, cleanish rooms, all with baths, balconies and partial sea views; a few have A/C (£E5 extra). ②–③.

Geisum Village, on the Corniche (☎065/546-692, fax 547-994). Three-star complex of A/C rooms, all with TV, phone and fridge. Pool, diving centre and smallish beach. Largely German and French clientele. ⑥.

Gobal, Sharia Sheikh Sebak (☎065/546-623). Slightly shabby rooms with shared bathrooms, in the noisy, funky tourist bazaar. Mostly used by Egyptians. ②.

Happy House, between the Ed-Dahar Mosque and Tariq en-Nasr (☎065/549-420). Small, friendly low-budget hotel of long standing. Clean rooms with fans; one hot shower; kitchen. ①.

Happy Land, Sharia Sheikh Sebak (☎065/547-373). Similar to the *Gobal*, but the rooms here have private bath. On the downside, it's within earshot of a mosque. ②.

Hilton Plaza, south end of the Corniche (☎065/549-745, fax 547-597). Massive but isolated five-star resort perched on an arid hill between Ed-Dahar and Sigala; if you're going to stay here, you probably won't bother leaving its confines. ⑨.

Horus, off Sharia al-Bahr (☎065/549-801, fax 549-806). Three-star pile with garish atrium but nice A/C rooms, all with satellite TV and fridge. Rooftop sundeck and pool; residents-only disco. Mainly used by Russian, Polish, Dutch and French groups. ⑤.

Iberotel Palm Beach, Corniche Road 6km north of Hurghada (☎065/549-840, fax 549-849). Large out-of-town resort with 295 double rooms and evening folklore shows. ⑧.

Panorama, off the Corniche (☎065/547-890, fax 548-890). Simple, breezy A/C rooms with baths and soft beds. Billiards; dismal bar and disco. Half-board only over Christmas. ⑤.

Ramsis, Sharia al-Arabi (☎065/549-632). Nice, colourful, clean hotel with shared or private bathrooms. ④.

Ritz, near the tourist office (☎065/547-031, fax 543-845). Chic and clean, but fairly remote from the action. All rooms with private baths, A/C or fans. Bar and restaurant. Mostly Russian guests. ④.

St George, off Sharia Sheikh Sebak (☎065/548-246). Clean, semi-carpeted rooms (some with baths) in a noisy backstreet in the bazaar. Same prices year round. Mainly used by Copts. ②.

Sand Beach, on the Corniche (☎065/547-992, fax 547-822). Four-star holiday village with three pools, a beach and diving centre, billiards room and disco. Popular with Russians. ⑥–⑦.

Sea Horse, off Sharia al-Bahr (☎065/547-016, fax 548-704). Comfortable rooms with private baths, A/C and balconies. Restaurant, bar, disco, billiards, backyard pool and sea views. Residents can use this beach, or the one at the *New Sea Horse*, by *Hilton Plaza*. ⑥.

Sea View, on the Corniche (☎065/545-959, fax 546-779). Modern, clean A/C rooms with baths and satellite TV. Tiny swimming pool. Seafood restaurant and free use of the *Sea Horse*'s beach for residents. ⑤.

Shedwan Golden Beach, on the Corniche (☎065/547-007, fax 548-045). Three-star holiday village with flash reception and plainer A/C rooms. Pool, beach, diving and windsurfing centres. Rates are negotiable but they start pretty high. ⑧.

Sosna, off Tariq en-Nasr (☎065/546-647). Clean, carpeted rooms with fans and bedside lamps; private bathrooms are optional. Mainly used by Egyptians. Liberal atmosphere. ②.

Three Corners Empire, off the Corniche (☎065/549-200/9, fax 549-212, *info@threecorners.com*). Sister hotel to the *Three Corners Village* and the *Three Corners Terrace* next door. Home to *Peanuts Bar*, but the main draw with the *Three Corners* properties is the beach available to all their guests. ⑤.

Three Corners Terrace, (☎065/546-618, fax 548-617). Smaller, slightly cheaper than the *Empire* but still well managed. ⑤.

Three Corners Village, on the Corniche (☎065/547-816, fax 547-514). A less opulent version of the *Sand Beach*, but the rooms are a shade cheaper. ⑥.

Sigala

Despite a relatively good choice of places to eat, it's hard to see why anyone would want to stay in Sigala, since there are better mid-range options in Ed-Dahar and ritzier holiday villages in New Hurghada. However, if everywhere else is full, you could try the following options:

Andrea's, (☎065/442-251, fax 443-388). Pleasant Italian-owned place near *Papa's Bar* and home of the HEPCA shop (see p.626). A/C rooms, three bars and a swimming pool. Popular with young English, German and French tourists. £E5 to use *Sheraton* beach. ⑥.

Arabia Beach, 800m north of the new harbour (☎065/548-790, fax 548-796). Mega-holiday village that's seen better days. A/C bungalows with TV, fridge, phone and piped music; the place also boasts three pools and a marina. Popular with Gulf Arabs. ⑦.

Helnan Regina, (☎065/442-275, fax 442-276, *cenres@helnan.com*). On the beach with three pools and a jetty. A/C rooms and chalets. ⑦.

Holiday Inn, (☎065/445-086, fax 445-085). A beachfront five-star complex, up to usual *Holiday Inn* standards. ⑧.

Iberotel Arabella, next to the Arabia (☎065/545-086, fax 545-090). One of the nicer-looking four-star hotels with A/C rooms, satellite TV, two large pools, extensive sports facilities and popular *Kalaboush* disco. Half-board only. ⑥.

New Hurghada

New Hurghada is the name given to the array of **holiday villages** that have proliferated for 30km south along the coast. Each is fully self-contained, so there's zero incentive to leave the complex. Though geared to package tourists, they'll take independent travellers if trade is slack. Where the clientele is mainly from certain countries, you could feel at a disadvantage if you don't speak the right language. Unless stated otherwise, all of the holiday villages are A/C, with a pool, diving centre, beach and disco. We've calculated their distance from town starting from the bus station in Ed-Dahar; for their exact locations, see the map on p.622.

Beach Albatros, 20.5km (☎065/446-571, fax 446-570). An indoor heated pool and jacuzzi head the roll-call of amenities at this gleaming white complex, chiefly patronized by Swiss. ⑧.

Conrad International, 22km (☎065/443-250, fax 443-258). Five-star resort with an onyx-floored lobby and an outsized pool; largely German guests but also English. Half-board only. ⑧.

Coral Beach, 28km (☎065/447-162, fax 443-577). Stylish rooms with satellite TV and minibar. Two pools, tennis, squash and horse-riding. Large beach with reef. Mainly caters to Italians. ⑧.

El-Samaka Beach Club, 16km (☎065/446-532, fax 442-227). Bungalows (A/C midday and evenings only) with a small beach and windsurfing lagoon; no pool. Used by German and Russian tour groups. ⑥.

Giftun Village, 14km (☎065/442-665, fax 442-666). Spanish-style chalets with fans, fronting a good beach and windsurfing lagoon. Half-board. ⑦.

Golden Five, 25km (☎065/446-306). A Vegas-style combination of theme park and hotel complex, with daily shows, a replica Egyptian village and a cable-car lift. ⑧.

Grand Hotel, 16km (☎065/447-485, fax 443-750). Spacious resort with a large sandy beach. Diving and windsurfing centres; no disco. Mostly used by Italians and Germans. ⑧.

Hilton Resort, 17km (☎065/442-116, fax 442-113). The same five-star rating as its sister *Plaza* hotel, but a bit older and less pricey. ⑧.

Hor Palace Village, 16km (☎065/443-710, fax 442-603). Unfortunate name, but pleasant enough A/C rooms with usual mod cons. ⑥.

Hurghada Beach, 16km (☎ & fax 065/443-710). A bit old-fashioned and shabby compared to other tourist villages. Excellent windsurfing lagoon; reef 400m offshore. Mostly used by Russians. ⑦.

Inter-Continental, 17km (☎065/446-911, fax 446-910). Opulent complex of rooms with bath, bidet, satellite TV and sea views. Very large marina. One of the better luxury hotels. ⑧.

Jasmin Village, 21km (☎065/446-442, fax 446-441). Simple rooms with satellite TV and fridge. Small beach with reef and windsurfing lagoons. Playground, zoo and aviary. Disabled access. Half-board only. ⑦.

La Perla, 2km south of Sigala (☎065/443-281, fax 443-280). Pleasant enough and well-managed; has A/C rooms and a swimming pool. A bit far from the action and the beach, but still popular with English groups. ⑥.

Lillyland Beach Club, 24km (☎065/446-424, fax 446-426). Exclusively Italian resort, with a large pool and an offshore reef. All the rooms have kitchens and satellite TV. Rates include half-board. ⑧.

Magawish Village, 19km (☎065/442-621, fax 442-759). A former *Club Med*, with a big beach and good sports facilities, especially for windsurfing, plus a children's playground. Rates include half-board. ⑦.

Marine Sports Club, 16km (☎065/444-861, fax 442-646). Good value A/C rooms with TV and fridge. Popular with Egyptian sport fishermen. ⑥.

Marlin Inn, 13km (☎065/443-791, fax 443-790). A well-run place with a smallish pool and beach, separated by phalanxes of rooms. Half-board only. ⑧.

Marriott Beach Resort, 11km (☎065/446-950, fax 446-970). Five-star complex with a large pool and a small sandy beach; marina and residents-only disco. ⑧.

Mashrabiya Village, 13km (☎065/443-332, fax 443-344). Quasi-Moorish resort with a small beach, popular with French, Russians and Germans. Rooms, villas and suites. Half-board only. ⑦.

Royal Palace Hotel, 15km (☎065/443-660, fax 443-665). Beachfront pile with A/C rooms and satellite TV. Pool and watersports. Home to *Aquascope* (see p.629). ⑦–⑧.

Princess Club, 16km (☎065/443-100, fax 443-109). Spacious A/C rooms with satellite TV and fridge; the three-storey villas are equipped for self-catering. Small pool and windsurfing lagoon. Also rents villas across the road on a timeshare basis. ⑥.

Sheraton, 11km (☎065/442-000, fax 444-443). Large 1960s five-star hotel, with a yacht marina, two very nice beaches and a small offshore reef. The first luxury hotel in Hurghada. Half-board only. ⑧.

Sindbad Beach Resort, 13km (☎065/443-261, fax 443-267). Efficiently managed and family-oriented four-star complex with lots of nightlife and a huge waterchute on the beach. Home to *Sindbad Submarine* (see p.629). Half-board only. ⑦–⑧.

Sofitel, 20km (☎065/447-261, fax 442-260). Classy pseudo-Moorish complex with a glacial welcome; undoubtedly the snobbiest hotel in Hurghada. Used by Hayes & Jarvis tours. Half-board only. ⑧.

Sonesta Beach Resort, 14km (☎065/443-664, fax 441-665). Small pool and decent-sized beach. Used by Italians, Germans and tour company Kuoni. ⑧.

Camping, hostelling and apartment rental

With rooms so cheap in Ed-Dahar, saving money hardly justifies the hassle of **camping**. Would-be campers must first obtain a permission request form from the small security office behind the Esh-Shahid Mosque and then take it together with their passport to another office over the road (both open daily 8am–noon & 8–9pm). You then have to find a vacant spot to the north of Ed-Dahar or south of Sigala – which is easier said than done. All in all, it's not worth the effort.

A more feasible option is Hurghada's shiny new **youth hostel** (☎065/544-989; £E18.50), on the beach 5km north of town, next to the Marine Institute of Oceanic Studies. It has separate blocks for men and women, containing spartan rooms with fans, bunk beds, and clean shared bathrooms. Non-HI members pay £E1 extra. Hurghada's other hostel (☎065/441-173; £E18.50) is a bit run down, but is more centrally located, opposite the *Royal Palace Hotel*. Both hostels have a three-day maximum stay.

If you're hoping to stay and work, **renting an apartment** may make sense. Most rentals are arranged through diving centres or hotels that employ foreigners, but if you put the word out, prospective landlords – and housemates – should come forward. It's also worth checking the classifieds in the *Hurghada Bulletin*. Expect to pay about £E800 per month (excluding bills) for a two-bedroom apartment near the beach, and about £E600 in the amorphous Amal district, between Ed-Dahar and Sigala.

Diving

It is **diving** that really put Hurghada on the map, kick-starting tourism along the Red Sea Coast. The marine life here is broadly similar to that found off the coast of Sinai (see p.562), but the topography favours island corals over coastal reefs, with sharks, giant moray eels and manta rays in its deeper, rougher waters. The tide here is more dramatic too; it drops by up to five metres from high to low tide, compared with a one-metre change in Sinai. Many islands have sheer-sided coral *ergs* (pillars) that are fantastic for drift diving, while others are shallow enough for snorkelling. There are about ten islands within day-trip range and over a score of sites that can be visited on extended dive safaris, or "liveaboards".

As ever, dive **tourism** is its own worst enemy: once-rich coral and shellfish grounds have been devastated by the sheer weight of visitors. Hurghada welcomes hordes of tourists each week, and waiting for them are over one thousand tour boats. Anchoring on the reefs does irreparable damage to fragile corals, and those closest to the port have been hit especially hard. The problem is being tackled by **HEPCA** (Hurghada Environmental Protection and Conservation Association), which is installing mooring buoys and trying to raise ecological awareness – but few of the local dive centres show much interest. Tourists can help by favouring centres that belong to HEPCA and display a certificate from the Egyptian Underwater Sports Federation – and by refusing to buy marine curios like clamshells (whose export is illegal) or stuffed sharks. You can make a difference simply by minimizing your own impact upon the dive sites you visit; don't touch the coral, don't remove anything from the sea bed, don't throw anything in the water (particularly cigarette butts) and don't feed the fish.

Your life may depend on **choosing the right diving centre**; some outfits are dangerously incompetent (leaving divers marooned at sea or lost in caves, in two notorious cases). Always check that the instructor is qualified, with valid ID and insurance, not merely photocopies. Many are freelancers who frequently change jobs, so even the best centres sometimes get bad ones (or vice versa). As a rule of thumb, however, it is safer to dive with the large outfits attached to holiday villages than with backstreet operators taking clients sent by low-budget hotels (whose recommendations *can't* be trusted). See the box opposite for a list of reliable dive centres.

The **courses** on offer are similar to those in Sinai. A four- or five-day PADI openwater course costs US$280–350 (including certificate); a two-day advanced course US$190–250. Beginners can expect to pay US$45–60 for an introductory lecture followed by two supervised dives. Scuba equipment is included in the price of courses, but otherwise costs extra (US$20–25); renting snorkelling gear is far cheaper (£E10–20 a day). The average rate for a day's **boat diving** is US$40–60; most trips comprise two dives, separated by lunch which is normally included in the price. Never hand over cash to someone on the street who promises to arrange a trip; book through a dive centre, where you can complain if things go wrong. You'll need to sign up and surrender your passport the night before; check that details are correctly noted, since wrongly documented passengers may be prevented from boarding.

While day trips can be arranged at short notice through any centre, it is better to book trips on **liveaboards** in advance, from home (see Basics chapter for tour operators that deal with these). Individuals who try to get one in Hurghada risk missing out,

DIVING CENTRES

Of the one-hundred-odd centres currently operating, the only ones subject to monitoring are those affiliated to HEPCA, which are listed below. We'd advise that in general you should **avoid** those that aren't members of HEPCA. Should you have specific marine safety or environmental concerns, contact HEPCA at P.O. Box 144, Hurghada, Red Sea, Egypt (☎065/446-674, fax 445-035, *hepca@hepca.org*), or alternatively advise the EEAA Ranger (☎065/549 632), in front of the public beach in Ed-Dahar.

Aquanaut, *Shedwan Village* (☎065/549-891, fax 547-045).

Aquarius Diving Club, *Iberotel Palm Beach* (☎065/549-840, fax 548-849).

Blue Brothers Diving Centre, (☎065/547-934, fax 547-933).

Blue Water Diving Center, *Arabia Beach Hotel* (☎065/548-790, fax 548-796, *info@blue-water-dive.com*).

Dive Inn Diving Center, *Melia Pharaoh* (☎065/446-720, fax 446-724).

Diver's International, (☎065/547-745, fax 547-597).

Divers Lodge, *Inter-Continental* (☎065/446-911, fax 446-910).

Dive Point, *Coral Beach* (☎065/447-162, fax 442-019, *hurghada@dive-point.com*).

Diving World, *Hurghada Sheraton* (☎065/442-000, fax 443-333).

Easy Diver, *Three Corners Village* (☎065/548-816, fax 547-514, *easydive@intouch.com*).

El-Samaka, *El-Samaka Beach Hotel* (☎ & fax 065/446-543).

Emperor Divers, *Hilton Resort* (☎065/442-119, fax 442-113) and *Princess Club*. (☎065/443-100, fax 443-109, *info.hurghada@emperordivers.com*).

James & Mac, *Giftun Village* (☎065/442-665, fax 442-300, *info@james-mac.com*).

Jasmin Diving Center, *Jasmin Village* (☎065/446-455, fax 446-441, *jasmindc@intouch.com*).

Pro Sea Team, *Conrad International* (☎065/443-250, fax 443-258, *diving@pros-eateam.com*).

Ocean Red, *Beach Albatros* (☎ & fax 065/546-280).

Orca, *Geisum Villlage* (☎065/548-048).

Sea Horse, *New Sea Horse* (☎ & fax 065/547-621).

Sea World, *Holiday Inn* (☎065/445-080, fax 445-085).

Sub Aqua, *Sofitel* (☎065/442-473).

Subex, downtown, off the Corniche (☎065/547-593, fax 547-471).

unless they can muster a group of at least six people to make it worth the captain's effort. As in Sinai, the cost depends on the amenities of the vessel and the quality of the meals provided; expect to pay at least US$100 per person per day. Most safaris last for one or two weeks, though boats going as far south as Yemen or Eritrea can be at sea for a month. Even if you're only going to Giftun Island, check that the boat has a radio, lifejackets, oxygen and a first-aid kit. Many of the dive boats lack **safety equipment**. In case of emergency, there are decompression chambers in the Hurghada area: in El-Gouna's new hospital (see p.632); the Mubarak Naval Hyperbaric & Emergency Medical Centre, near the old harbour; and at *Magawish Village*.

Dive sites

Most sites within day-trip range are to the east and northeast of Hurghada. Inexperienced divers should be wary of the northerly reefs, where the currents are strongest. While many liveaboards go as far north as Ras Mohammed, sites to the south are regarded as more prestigious. Though mentioned under other towns, they are only accessible via Hurghada, or on package holidays based outside Safaga or El-Quseir. All of the following are within day-trip range unless stated otherwise.

Abu Hashish Cave An underwater cave in the reef, once used as a dope smugglers' cache.

Abu Ramada Three coral blocks covered in psychedelic-hued soft corals, off Giftun Island.

Abu Ramada Gota (aka "Aquarium"") Amazing standing *ergs* and 1500-year-old stony corals, with a profusion of bannerfish, sweetlips and spotted groupers.

Brothers Several *ergs* emerging from the deeps of the Red Sea, 80km northeast of El-Quseir. A popular liveaboard destination, now open only to boats with permits.

Careless Reef (aka "Carless") Two *ergs* atop a plateau with a phenomenal drop-off and gardens of table and soft corals, frequented by whitetip reef sharks and moray eels, which can be seen fighting and mating by day. Only accessible in calm weather.

El-Fanadir Beautiful reef slope and large table corals, to the north of Sigala.

El-Fanous Coral gardens just off Big Giftun Island, good for snorkelling as well as diving.

Giftun Island Most of the reefs on the Big and Small Giftun have been ruined by years of dive boats dropping their anchors onto the coral, and are now mostly visited by craft packed with snorkellers (£E30–40 per person; £E90 overnight; equipment and food included). If you want to go on one of the less crowded boats used by divers, it'll cost £E5–10 extra. Two notable spots are the Small Giftun Drift (fine reef wall and lovely fan corals), and the Stone Beach on the northeast side of Big Giftun.

Shadwan Island Halfway to Sinai, so out of day-trip range. Sheer walls and deep trenches attract reef and oceanic sharks. Its lighthouse was of keen interest to de Monfried, when he navigated his boat through these waters in the early 1920s, with 600 kilos of hashish secreted in its hold.

Thistlegorm Sunken cargo ship full of jeeps, found by Jacques Cousteau off the coast of Sinai. A very popular four-day safari, albeit cheaper to make from Na'ama Bay (see p.573).

Umm Gamar Island Sheer walls and caves, brilliant for drift diving. You can swim through a cave filled with thousands of silvery glassfish.

Zabagard Island Deep reefs teeming with oceanic fish and corals, 100km southeast of Berenice. A favourite long-haul destination, only open to boats with permits.

Beaches, pools and watersports

While diving is the main activity (see above), Hurghada presents itself as an all-round beach resort – a claim that's quite true, but not so great as it sounds. After years of grousing by visitors, the **public beach** (daily 8am–sunset; £E1) is at last to be transformed, from a wasteland where no foreign tourist would be seen dead, to a tidy shore lined with shops and cafes. However, to sunbathe without unwanted attention, there's really no alternative but to go for **private beaches**. In Ed-Dahar, the *Shedwan, Three Corners, Geisum* and *Sand Beach* open their beaches to outsiders for £E25 (you can also use the pools at the *Shedwan* and *Sand Beach*). Interlopers who slip past security usually get caught on the beach because they lack the distinctive bathing mats that are issued to residents and paying guests.

Further down the coast is the cheaper option of *Shellghada Beach*, just north of the *Sheraton*, where £E10 buys a day on the sand, volleyball and use of their fresh-water showers. Eat at the restaurant and there is no entry charge. *El Saqiaa Restaurant and Beach* near the harbour offers the same deal and has a larger beach than *Shellghada*. The *Sheraton* itself has two beaches: you can sneak into the smaller Beach A via the marina, although the proximity of boats means the water here is always dirty; the larger Beach B is for residents only. Other holiday villages allow outsiders to use their beaches and **swimming pools** for a charge that ranges from £E35 at the *El-Samaka* to £E60 at the *Magawish* (which has the nicest beach). Admission policies may change, so phone ahead to avoid a wasted journey. Small coral reefs offshore from the *Shedwan Golden Beach, Jasmin Village, Coral Beach* and *Lillyland* offer a taste of the colourful array of fish and corals further out to sea. Buying beach or camping gear in Hurghada can be expensive; the central Government Store has a good selection at low fixed prices.

Powerful gusts make Hurghada a great place for **windsurfing**, especially the beaches at the *Magawish* and *Hurghada Beach*. Several holiday villages have lagoons and centres where you can rent boards and wetsuits, and some places offer windsurfing instruction. Happy Surf has branches at *Three Corners* (☎065/547-816) the *Sofitel* (☎065/447-261) and *Magawish* (☎065/446-450); Pro Center is based at *Jasmin Village* (☎065/446-450) and Habri/Friendly Surfing Center (☎065/443-710) is at the *Hurghada Beach Resort*. The *Arabia Tourist Village* has facilities for **paragliding** and **water-skiing**. If you book one or two days ahead, *Marine Sports Club* (☎065/444-861/2/3) can arrange **deep-sea fishing** day trips for £E400 per boat (6–8 people) including equipment. For a few hours' **snorkelling**, try Prince Sea Trips (☎065/549-882) at the *Four Seasons* in Ed-Dahar. Run by friendly Bedouin brothers who grew up in Hurghada, they charge just £E30 if you book with them direct, rather than the £E50–60 charged by most of the operators and commissioned agents around town.

The Aquarium, Sindbad Submarine and Aquascope

If you want a glimpse of the Red Sea's wonders without getting wet, visit the newly-renovated **Red Sea Aquarium** (daily 9am–11pm; £E10, camera £E5) on the Corniche. Its tanks are labelled in English, with diagrams of where to find each species on the reef. You can learn to recognize wrasses, triggerfish, sailfintangs, angelfish and many other types, but it's sad to see them in such cramped conditions when you know that millions of others are swimming freely not far away.

Alternatively, there's the much-hyped **Sindbad Submarine** (US$50, kids $25), which can convey you to depths of 22m in comfort. Disappointingly, however, the trip is more of a photo-opportunity than anything else. Half the time is spent getting to and from the sub's mooring offshore from the *Sindbad Beach Resort*, and after submerging a diver swims alongside trailing bait to attract wrasses, groupers and parrotfish past the portholes. You'd do better to go on an introductory dive – but if the sub still appeals, bookings can be made at the *Sindbad* (☎065/444-688) or other holiday villages.

Another window on the underwater world is open to you on board **Aquascope** ($40), a sort of new-age glass-bottom boat. The two-hour trip leaves from the *Royal Palace Hotel* (☎065/446-906) and includes a fifty-minute tour of the coral reefs. A more traditional glass-bottom boat experience can be had on the **Red Sea Dolphin** (10am & 3pm; 2hr; US$39 including drinks), which is based at the *Inter-Continental*.

Eating and drinking

Hurghada is good for **eating out**, with a wider choice of cuisine than anywhere else in Egypt but Cairo or Alexandria. Besides the places listed below there are dozens of restaurants in holiday villages, mostly upmarket and with **music** in the evenings. The *Aladdin Restaurant* in the *Sindbad Beach Resort* deserves an honourable mention for its *oud* player. It is also home to the only Russian restaurant and bar in Hurghada. For cheaper meals, check out the many (sometimes nameless) places in Ed-Dahar and Sigala, where new ones are opening every week. **Opening hours** are generally mid-morning until 11pm or midnight (maybe later in high season), though the choice of food dwindles after 10pm. Almost everywhere adds 10–12 percent in **service taxes** to the bill – at some holiday villages they bump things up by as much as 21 percent.

If you're keen on saving money it's worth tracking down some **street stalls**. There are two good *fuul* and *felafel* stands on the street running south of, and parallel to, Sharia Sheikh Sebak; juice bars and nut stalls are scattered around the bazaar, and there are *kushari* stands near the bus station. In Sigala, there's a pair of *felafel* stands on Sigala Square near the police station, and a place with refrigerated carcasses outside that does tasty kebab, *kofta* and pizzas. Don't miss the two excellent cake shops inside The Market mall, on the strip. For the less adventurous there are the ubiquitous *Pizza Hut* and *KFC* opposite *Sindbad Beach Resort*, and *McDonald's* in downtown Sigala.

Unless stated otherwise, all of the places listed below are in Ed-Dahar; most places close around 11pm–midnight, and nearly all are shown on the maps on p.618 and p.622.

Abo Khadega, in Sigala. Small workers' café where you can get a tasty meal of soup, rice, salad, beans and grilled meat for £E6.

Baron, in the bazaar. A small, simple local eatery serving chicken, beans, bread and salad for £E5.

Bella Riviera, opposite *Shakespears Hotel*. Friendly café serving tasty lentil soup, spaghetti Bolognese, lasagne and salads at low prices. No alcohol.

Chez Pascal, in *Three Corners Empire* shopping centre. Belgian-managed pizza (£E12–20) and steak (£E30) restaurant, which offers good food and service in a soothing atmosphere. Sells alcohol.

Egyptian Corner, near the *Bella Riviera*. A few tables in a garden, good for a *fuul*, tomato and feta cheese breakfast (£E5), chicken with rice and salad (£E7), or *tajine* (£E8). No alcohol.

El-Masri, near the *Joker*. Offers kebabs, traditional Egyptian food and chicken at very reasonable prices (around £E10).

Joker, near the police station in Sigala square. Excellent seafood restaurant with generous portions at very good prices (£E10–15). Try the calamari soup. Recommended.

Far East Korea, Redcon Mall, Sigala (☎065/445-207). Good value Chinese-Korean restaurant with friendly staff, also offers takeaway.

Felfela's, (☎065/442-410) Sigala, between *Holiday Inn* and *Sheraton*. Branch of the famous Cairo restaurant chain serving decent Egyptian food at reasonable rates. Lots of space, nice atmosphere and great view of the harbour. Sells beer. Good for vegetarians. Does takeaway.

Mahyma, Giftun Island. A bar and restaurant for tourists visiting the island, open till 10pm. As you might expect, not terribly cheap and a limited menu. Pizza £E18, Stella £E10, coffee £E5.

Omar Inn, (☎065/446-166) Sigala, opposite the *Golf* hotel. Strictly speaking a coffee shop, but serves pizza, seafood, snacks and fruit juice. Good place for people watching. Does take-away.

Red Sea, in the bazaar, off Tariq en-Nasr. One of Hurghada's classiest seafood places, with a rooftop garden and A/C downstairs. Main dishes cost £E20–50. Sells alcohol; takes most credit cards.

Rossi's, opposite the Aquafun waterpark, Sigala. Popular Italian joint with standard pizza, pasta and ice cream options.

Scruples, on Tariq en-Nasr and the Corniche. Two branches of an A/C steak house serving pub food and booze at moderately expensive rates with bouts of Oriental dancing. The same firm runs *Scruples Billiardeni*, a pool hall on the corner of Sharia Abdel Aziz Mustafa.

Spaghetti, near *McDonald's* in Sigala. Newish seafood restaurant with large outdoor seating area. Good value and popular with families.

Taco, in Sigala, near *McDonald's*, and also one in Ed-Dahar. Popular fast-food outlet, famous for its *shawarma*.

Tarboush, Sharia Abdel Aziz Mustafa. Small, simple pizzeria, with about fifteen not so different-tasting varieties (£E8–18) on the menu. No alcohol.

Young Kang, Sharia Sheikh Sebak. Reasonable Chinese-Korean restaurant, with fair-sized portions at moderate prices. Sells beer.

Drinking

As you'd expect in a major resort, lots of **drinking** goes on in discos, restaurants and hotels – though the number of actual bars isn't that large. Most restaurants don't sell alcohol during Ramadan and before 1pm on Fridays, but holiday villages are exempt from these restrictions. There are **duty-free shops** in the AKA mall near the *Royal Palace* in New Hurghada, or next to the *Ambassador Hotel* on the road to the airport. Egyptian beer and wine can be bought to take away at the *1001 Nights* (see below). If your taste for intoxicants runs in other directions, be warned that Hurghada is less of a smoking town than Luxor or Dahab – which isn't surprising given that *bango* costs at least £E50 a *talga*. The following **bars** are open till midnight.

Juke Box Pub, next to *Shedwan* on the Corniche in Ed-Dahar. Tacky bar but has good views from its rooftop beer garden. Serves food and you might be subjected to an oriental belly-dance show.

Papa's Bar, next to *Rossi's* in Sigala. Hurghada's most popular bar for foreigners, mainly because it's Dutch-run and full of diving instructors.

Peanuts Bar, in the *Three Corners* mall, on the strip. A lively hang-out, packed with tourists and peanuts. Serves Stella (£E8.50), draught Bitburger (£E18) and cocktails (£E12–22).

1001 Nights, in the *Shedwan Golden Beach* on the Corniche. Late night café-cum-bar serving the cheapest Stella in town (£E7.50); take it away for £E7 a bottle. Omar Khayyum wine is £E27 – stick to the red and rosé versions, and avoid the white altogether. Obelisque is a good bet if available.

Nightlife

Hurghada has some of the liveliest **nightlife** in mainland Egypt, as hotels strive to outdo each other's discos and floorshows – but none are wild raves and the music is strictly mainstream. Posh places baulk at shorts or trainers; smart casual **dress** is universally acceptable. Most discos set a **minimum charge** per person, sometimes paid up front in return for a card that gets punched whenever you buy a drink – don't lose it. Drinks **prices** vary from £E8 to £E14 for a Stella, Sakkara Gold or Meister, £E20–25 for an imported beer or a cocktail. Few discos get going before 11pm, and while most are advertised as staying open till 4am, they may close earlier if things are quiet.

Discos wax and wane in popularity, with the most popular hangout at present being the *Kalaboush* in the *Iberotel Arabella*, a lively place full of young Egyptian guys and their Russian girlfriends. Other favourites are in holiday villages; the *Dome* (10pm-4am) at the *Inter-Continental* has the best dance floor but restricts admission to mixed couples (in theory, anyway), whereas the discos at the *Sand Beach*, *Princess Club* and *Sindbad Beach Resort* put on Russian shows (see below) to pull in males. Although £E20 minimum charge is standard almost everywhere, the *Giftun Village* settles for £E15, while the discos in the *Sofitel* and *Sheraton* are free of charge, but don't have a show.

Discos aside, the main entertainments are bellydancing and Russian shows – unless you count the cringe-inducing "Animation Teams" at some tourist villages. **Russian shows** were pioneered in Hurghada, the novelty of pale-skinned Slav women in skimpy costumes soon proving to be a hit elsewhere, to the chagrin of Egyptian **bellydancers**. If this is your thing, the main venue is *Elf Leila Wa Leila* (*1001 Nights*), situated on the southern outskirts of Hurghada. Tickets including transport can be bought at most hotels, even the budget ones; (US$15–18 including dinner, 8–10.30pm; $10 with soft drinks only, 8.30–10.30pm). Slightly less exotic and less expensive is the **bowling alley** at the *Sindbad Beach Resort* (☎065/442-944).

Listings

American Express Supposedly has an agent beside the garage on Tariq en-Nasr, but they'll only report stolen cards, and don't seem interested in expanding their range of services.

Banks Of the two close together on Tariq en-Nasr, the Banque Misr (daily 9am–9pm) has an ATM outside and gives cash advances on Visa and MasterCard, while the National Bank of Egypt (Sun–Thurs 8.30am–2pm & 6–9pm, Fri 9–11am & 2–5pm) takes travellers' cheques. Money transfers can be arranged through Federal Express or Thomas Cook (see below).

Books and newspapers The Red Sea Bookshop on Tariq en-Nasr, near the bus station, and *Abdoui's Internet Café and Bookshop* at the Corniche end of the strip, have the best selection.

Car rental CRC Rent-a-Car (☎065/442-116), next to Thomas Cook in Sigala, is one of the cheapest national companies and charges US$45 per day for a Peugeot 106. Limo 1, at the *Inter-Continental* (☎065/446-903, fax 446-931) has Mazdas from $29 per day or a 4WD Lada Niva at $45. Hertz (☎065/442-884), opposite EgyptAir in New Hurghada, tends to have older cars, while Budget (☎065/442-261) at the *Sofitel* and *Marriott* has some of the newest ones, and is the only company to offer unlimited mileage with a three-day package. Other companies worth considering are Europcar (☎065/443-660) based at the *Royal Palace*; Avis (☎065/447-400) which has a good range of 4WD's; and Thrifty at the *Melia Pharoah* (☎065/446-723) and *Conrad International* (☎065/443-250).

Federal Express In Sigala (daily 8am–6pm; ☎065/442-444). Costly, fast and reliable worldwide express mail service. Can also wire money.

Hospitals The general hospital in Ed-Dahar (☎065/546-814) and the private El-Saffa on El-Nasr St, (☎065/546-965) have improved but the best medical treatment is available at the private hospital in El-Gouna (☎549-709 ext. 2201/2; emergencies ext. 2200), or El-Salam hospital (☎065/548-790) in *Arabia Village Hotel*. Less serious complaints can be treated by physicians on call at holiday villages, or check the listings in the *Hurghada Bulletin*. Diving emergencies can be dealt with either at El-Gouna Hospital or Hurghada's new Naval Hyperbaric & Emergency Medical Centre (☎065/549-525 or 544-195) near the harbour.

Internet cafés These are sprouting up in Hurghada and there should be one within walking distance of your hotel. *Papa's* (daily 10am–midnight; ☎065/445-230, *papasicc@red-sea.com*; £E16 per hr), next to *Papa's Bar* in Sigala also offers international phone and fax services at competitive rates; *Aboudi Internet Café*, just along from the *Four Seasons* (daily 10am–midnight; ☎065/547-089, *kassem@hurghada.ie-eg.com*; £E25 per hr), also has an Internet phone service and can do scanning and printing.

Laundry Stop-Shop (daily 8am–8pm; ☎065/446-609), off Tariq en-Nasr, 300m south of the bus station, charges 50pt–£E4 an item. Most hotels can have your washing sent out for £E2–8 per piece.

Passport office Entrance on the left side of the prominently signposted Red Sea Security Department building, 2km past the Esh-Shahid Mosque (Sun–Thurs 8am–2pm; ☎065/446-727).

Permits It's hard to obtain permits to travel south beyond Mersa Allam if you want to stay overnight. Put your case to the most senior English-speaking officer you can find at the Red Sea Security Department (*not* the passport office) and hope that he'll set the ball rolling. Don't be surprised if you're treated with suspicion and given the runaround for days.

Pharmacies There are several on Sharia Abdel Aziz Mustafa and Tariq en-Nasr. You can also find pharmacies outside the hospitals. Good Luck Bazaar, in the arcade outside the *Sand Beach*, sells imported condoms.

Police The Ed-Dahar office (☎122) is on Tariq en-Nasr, out towards the passport office; the branch in Sigala (☎065/442-485) is near the main intersection. Little or no English is spoken at either; both are open 24 hours. Visitors might be disturbed to overhear suspects being beaten up on the premises.

Post office On Tariq al-Nasr, 200m north of the bus station (daily except Fri 8am–2pm). Has direct-dial phones and Express Mail Service.

Telephone calls Direct-dial phones in the 24-hour *centraal* on Tariq al-Nasr, and at several points on the street; phonecards are sold at the *centraal*. If you're prepared to pay premium rates, many hotels and shops in the bazaar advertise international lines that may result in speedier connections. A new *centraal* is due to open in Sigala, just south of *McDonald's*.

Thomas Cook In Sigala (daily 9am–2pm & 6–9pm; ☎ & fax 065/443-500). Offers all usual services including Moneygrams, and also handles MasterCard emergencies.

Tourist police Next to the tourist office in Ed-Dahar (24hr; ☎065/546-765).

Working Distinctly feasible if you have diving qualifications (Divemaster upwards) or foreign languages (especially Japanese or Russian). Hotels and dive centres need people to work at reception or drum up clients. Ask other foreigners working here which firms are dodgy, and don't hand over your passport lightly – the biggest sharks aren't found in the Red Sea. *Do not invest any money in Hurghada.*

Moving on

Scores of travel agencies offer **excursions** to Luxor, Sinai or Cairo as day trips or overnight packages. Terms and prices vary, so shop around. Among the contenders it's worth mentioning Misr Travel (daily 8.30am–10pm; ☎065/548-715) for its day trips to the **Red Sea Monasteries** (US$55), **Mons Claudianus** (US$42) and **Wadi Hammamat** (US$25, $30 with barbecue). Other long-established and experienced agents in Hurghada include: Abu Noub Travel (☎065/442-843), Spring Tours (☎065/548-151), Travco (☎065/442-231) and Eastmar (☎065/444-581). As well as local trips, they handle tours to Cairo (two days; US$135), and day-trips to Luxor (6am–11pm; US$75), and to Sinai by catamaran, including taking in St Catherine's Monastery and Dahab (US$155).

Moving on by regular transport, you've the usual choice between buses, *service* taxis and the odd flight, plus a sea link across the Gulf of Suez to Sharm el-Sheikh in Sinai.

Buses

For travel by **bus** to Cairo and Luxor, it's a good idea to buy your tickets in advance from the main bus station (☎065/547-582). There are five A/C buses daily to Cairo (10am, 1pm, 5pm, 11pm & 12.30am; 6–8hr; £E45). Suez is served by a dozen buses daily (9.30am–1am; 5–8hr; £E25) and tickets are sold on the bus. Buses to Luxor (12.30pm, 1am & 2am; 5hr; £E20) are routed via Safaga and Qena; those to Aswan (9.30am, 10.30pm, 11pm, 11.30pm; 8hr; £E30–35) also go via Safaga, which is also accessible by buses bound for El-Quseir (5am & midnight; 2hr; £E10–12) and Mersa Allam (4hr; £E20). Other buses travel to Safaga hourly (7am–2am; £E8). Buses to Assyut (£E14) and Sohag (£E12) in Middle Egypt run frequently but are unlikely to have A/C.

Besides the above, A/C **Superjet** buses with toilets and "in-flight" snacks and movies depart three times a day for Cairo (12pm, 2.30pm & 6pm; £E52) from the Superjet ticket office (☎065/546-768) near the Esh-Shahid Mosque, which serves as the terminal; the 2.30pm bus carries on to Alexandria (£E75). There is also a daily Superjet bus to Sharm el-Sheikh, via Suez (11.30pm; £E55). Buy tickets in advance to be sure of a seat.

Taxis

Mornings are the best time to catch seven-seater **service taxis** to Suez (5hr; £E20), Cairo (6–7hr; £E30), Port Safaga (45min; £E5) or El-Quseir (1hr 30min; £E8). Whatever the time of day, you shouldn't have to wait more than half an hour for a *service* to Qena (4hr; £E10), whence other taxis run on to Luxor (see p.292). Don't believe anyone who says there's a "convoy charge" for foreigners. Groups of travellers can consider taking their own **taxi** all the way to Sharm el-Sheikh (about £E700) – which is one way to avoid a tedious interlude at Suez (see p.538). Plenty of taxis are prepared to take tourists to Luxor; £E180 for seven people is a fair price.

Flights

If you've got the money and book early, EgyptAir **flights** are the quickest way of reaching several major destinations (all the following prices are for one-way tickets). There are at least two daily to **Cairo** (8.45am & 6.45pm; US$115) with more laid on at weekends and public holidays. Likewise the flights to **Sharm el-Sheikh** (Mon 2.15am & 10.40am, Fri 10.40am, Sat 3.15am, Sun 2.15am; US$96) are often boosted if they are busy. The 10.40am flights on Monday and Friday both continue to **Alexandria** (US$176). There is also a weekly flight to **Luxor** (Wed 12.30am; US$55). You don't have to trek out to EgyptAir (☎065/447-503) in New Hurghada to make bookings, as everything can be handled by a subsidiary in town, Karnak EgyptAir (☎065/547-893); both are open daily 8am–8pm. The **airport** is 15km south of Ed-Dahar, off the Hurghada–Safaga road (£E15 by taxi).

By sea

Links with Sinai have been transformed by the introduction of a **high-speed catamaran** that cuts the journey to Sharm el-Sheikh to ninety minutes – as opposed to five or six hours by the old ferry, and 12–18 hours overland. The **catamaran** runs four times a week to Sharm (Mon & Tues 5am, Thurs & Sat 8.30am; US$33, £E115, cars £E250). It's worth bearing in mind that the catamaran may be out of service for several weeks in the late spring. Bookings can also be made ahead of time through Sherif

Tours at the _Sand Beach_ (☎065/545-147) or El-Shaymaa Sea Trips (☎065/546-907), in front of the _Gobal_.

The Red Sea Mountains

Inland of Hurghada the barren plains erupt into the **Red Sea Mountains**, which follow the coast southwards towards Ethiopia. This geologically primitive range of granite, porphyry and breccia contains Egypt's highest mountains outside Sinai, rearing up to 2187m (over 7000ft) above sea level. During winter, peaks exceeding 1500m draw moisture from rising masses of air, while in summertime they precipitate brief, localized storms accompanied by violent lightning and flash floods. Hardy desert plants flourish in their wake, providing grazing for feral ruminants and the flocks of a few thousand nomads. Roaming their vast tribal lands, these Bedouin are perfectly at home in the wilderness – unlike isolated groups of miners and soldiers, who feel almost as exiled as the slaves who quarried here in ancient times.

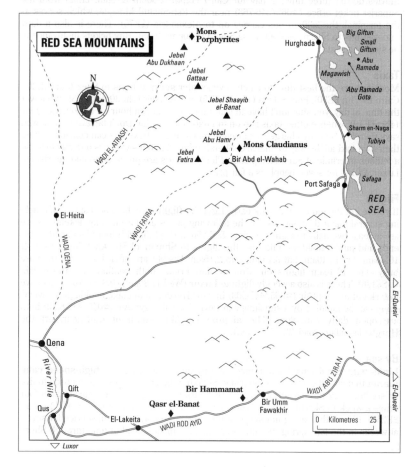

Exploring the mountains

Short of befriending some Bedouin and tagging along with them, the Red Sea Mountains are most easily accessible via **day excursions from Hurghada**. The basic scenario is a half-day camel or jeep safari, timed for sundown if you want to have a barbecue with Bedouin entertainments, which will set you back around US$35. Prince Safari Trips (☎065/549-882), at the *Four Seasons* hotel, offers a sunset "safari" (£E60), which entails a half-hour journey by Landcruiser to a Bedouin village for a camel ride, followed by tea and some Bedouin music. If you haven't been to the desert before, this can be a good introduction to the Bedouin and the majestic landscape they live in – old desert hands can probably give it a miss. It also runs longer desert camping trips (£E180 per person per day, minimum five people) for the more adventurous.

The following accounts go somewhat further, to give an idea of what the mountains hold in store for travellers with the determination to embark on a trek through the region. The government is currently trying to promote **adventure tourism** in the Eastern Desert, so the opportunities for organized treks or mountain-climbing are improving. So far, the only company to offer extensive trips is the excellent Geographic Adventures (5 Abbas Helmy St, Heliopolis, Cairo; ☎ & fax 02/418-4821, *geo-adv@intouch.com*), run by safari experts Walid Ramadan and Sherif Abu Pasha.

As far as Europeans are concerned, the Red Sea Mountains were first climbed in the 1920s and 30s, and have hardly been scaled since; as Sinai becomes increasingly commercialized, this may become the next wilderness to attract tourists.

Two Roman quarries

Twenty kilometres north of Hurghada, a piste quits the highway and climbs inland towards **Jebel Abu Dukhaan**, the 1161-metre-high "Mountain of Smoke". Anciently known as **Mons Porphyrites**, this was the Roman Empire's main source of fine red porphyry, used for columns and ornamentation. Blocks were dragged 150km to the Nile, or by a shorter route to the coast, whence they were shipped to far-flung sites such as Baalbek or Constantinople.

Roundabout the extensive quarries lies a **ruined town** of rough-hewn buildings with two large cisterns and an unfinished Ionic temple. Rock hyraxes (a kind of large rodent) lived in dens around Jebel Abu Dukhaan until all its trees were cut down for fuel. From the ruins, the piste follows Wadi el-Atrash and Wadi Qena down to the Nile Valley.

Mons Claudianus

Although **Mons Claudianus** is only 50km distant from Mons Porphyrites as the crow flies, lofty massifs necessitate more roundabout approaches. Coming from Hurghada, you need to follow a piste that starts between the port and Magawish Village. There are also two routes off the Port Safaga–Qena road: a well-surfaced one, 41km from the coast, and a longer, rougher piste nearer Qena.

Under the emperors Trajan and Hadrian, the pale, black-flecked granite quarried at Mons Claudianus was used to construct the Pantheon and Trajan's Forum in Rome. Around the **quarries**, beneath Jebel Fatira and Jebel Abu Hamr, you'll find numerous unformed capitals and abandoned columns. Wadi Fatira contains a cracked, 200-tonne monster, dubbed the **"Mother of Columns"** by the Arabs, while in the quarries of Hydreuma lies a giant unfinished **sarcophagus**. There's also a sizeable ruined town, **Fons Trajanus**.

Mountains and water sources

Between the two quarries rise the highest mountains in the Eastern Desert: Jebel Gattaar and Jebel Shaayib el-Banat.

> ### THE MA'AZA BEDOUIN, GAZELLES AND IBEXES
>
> From St Anthony's Monastery to the Qift–El-Quseir road, 90,000 square kilometres of highland form the stamping ground of the **Ma'aza** (Goat) tribe of **Bedouin**, who migrated here from Arabia in the 1700s. As their name suggests, goats form the basis of their livelihood, although gathering plants and hunting are also important. Herbalists buy wormwood, henbane, argel and ben-tree seeds from the nomads, while hunters from the Gulf Emirates used to rent them as guides until the Ma'aza grew disgusted with their wanton slaughter of Barbary sheep (now almost extinct), ibexes and gazelles.
>
> Traditionally the Ma'aza only hunt with dogs, rocks and knives, sprinting after their quarry. Whereas **gazelles** are regarded as everyday food, ibex meat is prized because it supposedly enables them to run up mountains without tiring. The sound of rutting **ibexes** locking horns in September attracts the foul **botfly**, which squirts its larvae into their mouths and nostrils. Smashing dead branches with rocks makes the same noise – something to remember should you camp out in these mountains, as botfly can also live as parasites in humans.

Jebel Gattaar and Jebel Shaayib el-Banat

Jebel Gattaar (1963m) is esteemed by the Bedouin for its permanent springs and comparatively abundant vegetation. Umm Yasar and other wadis draining from Gattaar contain hundreds of acacia and ben trees, a remnant of once-extensive forests that were ravaged by charcoaling. As late as the 1880s, E.A. Floyer found Wadi Gattaar "thickly studded with big mimosa trees, some twenty and thirty feet high", whose reckless felling compelled the Bedouin to cut down live acacias for fodder when drought struck in the 1950s.

Further south, the loftier **Jebel Shaayib el-Banat** (2187m) rises to a summit that the geographer and mountaineer George Murray likened to a "monstrous webbed hand of seven smoothed fingers". The highest mountain in mainland Egypt, its peak was first climbed by Murray in 1922. In Bedouin folklore, Shaayib harbours a "Tree of Light" whose leaves can cure blindness; the world's only other one is believed to be in Lebanon.

Wadi Naggaat and the Ma'aza Limestone Plateau

Early Christian hermits made their home in **Wadi Naggaat**, between Jebel Abu Dukhaan and Jebel Shaayib. *Naggaat* means "dripping place", a Bedouin term applied to a particular type of water source that falls from cliffs to irrigate maidenhair ferns, reeds and mosses, and fills pools where ibexes and people drink.

But with only four *naggaat* in the Eastern Desert and not enough rope to plumb the fifty-metre-deep well of Bir Gattaar, the Bedouin must also use surface springs and gravel seeps. These are far more common in the granite Red Sea Mountains than on the **Ma'aza Limestone Plateau** that separates the range from the Nile Valley; one reason why Bedouin dislike this "Place of Strayings". Its mysterious **Bir Shaitan** (Pool of Satan) is popularly believed to be replenished by Nile water via an underground passage but is actually dependent on rainfall; the shade from the overhanging rocks prevents evaporation.

South of Hurghada

Down the coast from Hurghada, the stream of holiday resorts becomes less dense until two belated spurts of development on the outskirts of **Port Safaga** (58km) and **El-Quseir** (a further 85km). At first sight Safaga is a total dump, but it has some charms and is within boat range of some stunning offshore reefs, while El-Quseir retains a sleepy charm unlike anywhere else on the Red Sea. From both points, connections with the Nile Valley are assured, via roads that cut across the Eastern Desert following old camel routes.

Further south, communications become tenuous and bureaucratic obstacles loom as you head **towards the Sudanese border**. From Shalateen onwards, you need military permission to proceed further south, or into the mountains. Though tourism has long been forbidden in what is still a militarily sensitive area, the authorities are now seeking to promote it, and access should become easier within a few years. Meanwhile, the allure of the far south depends on its reefs, which can only be reached by dive boats operating out of Hurghada, Safaga and El-Quseir.

The highway initially runs several kilometres inland before regaining the coast. About 40 km after Hurghada and 18km before Safaga, a signpost indicates the turn-off for **SHARM EN-NAGA** a wide bay where *Sharm En-Naga Camp* (☎010/151-3615; ④–⑤) has 26 pastel-coloured tents furnished with beds and wardrobes. The tents also have 24-hour electricity and the site has hot water showers. The main attraction here is the **beach-diving**, and day-trippers from Hurghada (£E80–100 return in a minibus) often come here to use the beach (£E15). If you have your own transport, Sharm En-Naga makes an excellent alternative to overcrowded Hurghada.

The luxury development of **Soma Bay** (2km further on from Sharm En-Naga) boasts, among other things, an 18-hole golf course. There are several hotels offering similar facilities, of which the *Sheraton Soma Bay* (☎065/545-845 or 545-915, fax 545-885; ⑨) is the most appealing.

Port Safaga and the road to Qena

Once known for the restorative health properties of its sandy beaches, **PORT SAFA-GA** (*Bur Safaga*) now amounts to very little. Coming in from the north you pass a slip-road curving off to six holiday villages on a headland, which cater to groups on diving holidays. The town begins 3km later and consists of a single windswept avenue running straight on past concrete boxes with bold signs proclaiming their function, until the bus station and a final mosque, 4km south. Silos and cranes identify the port, which runs alongside (but out of bounds) for most of this distance. Safaga's only attraction is the **reefs** to the north, and if you're not going to see them, there's no much reason to hang around. As buses and taxis travelling between Hurghada and Luxor use the desert highway that turns off at Safaga, passengers can see all there is to see as they drive through town.

Accommodation

In Safaga itself, accommodation is limited to several overpriced **hotels** near the beach, a cheaper budget hotel on the main road and a couple of very cheap but basic places near the port. A better option is to stay out of town at one of the places recommended below, all of which are 3–5km north of town unless otherwise stated; minibuses (£E1) run as far out as the *Shams Safaga*, the most distant of the resort complexes.

Cleopatra, opposite EgyptAir, in town (☎065/253-926). Clean carpeted rooms with baths, off dingy corridors. Caters mainly to Egyptians. ③.

Coralia, on the coast between the port and the town (☎065/253-821). Smart upmarket hotel, though far away from the rest of the tourist villages. ⑧.

El-Ezz, near the port entrance and bus station (☎065/252-312). Basic rooms, mostly used by arrivals at the port rather than foreign travellers. No breakfast. ①.

Holiday Inn Resort, (☎065/252-823). Safaga's most stylish tourist village, with an outsized pool and fine sea views; rooms have A/C, fridge and satellite TV. Happy hour 8–10pm for cocktails in the *Windsurf Bar*. ⑧.

Lotus Bay Resort & Gardens, (☎065/252-443, fax 251-042). Also called *Lotus Bay Club Villas*. Spacious array of villas in a nice garden; the rooms have all mod cons. Caters to Italians and Swiss. Rates include half-board. ⑤.

Maka, near the Bank of Alexandria and port entrance (☎065/253-814). Basic, semi-finished concrete box with shared bathrooms and iffy hot water. No breakfast. ①.

Menaville Village, (☎065/251-760, fax 251-764). A decent place that's less flashy than the others, and reasonably priced near the bottom of the price band. Mainly Swiss, Italian and French clientele. ⑤.

Safaga Hotel & Marina, in town (☎065/251-133, fax 252-670). Built for business clientele before tourism came to Safaga, it mainly caters for German and Dutch holidaymakers. ⑥.

Safaga Paradise, (☎065/251-633, fax 251-630). The first tourist village in Safaga has had a much needed refit, and improvements are ongoing. Has its own diving centre. Half-board only. ⑦.

Shams Safaga, (☎065/251-781, fax 251-780). Has a private reef and better sports facilities and children's playground than the others. Used by British tour groups. Half-board only. ⑦.

Sun Beach, next to the *Lotus Bay Resort* (☎065/252-658, fax 252-699). Chalets on the beach with a choice of A/C or fans, or you can bring your own tent (£E10–20 per person) and use the showers and café. Used as a stop-off by overland adventure groups, it's also home to Orca dive centre. Rates for chalets include half-board. ⑤–⑦.

Diving and snorkelling

It can be hard to just turn up and get a boat to the reefs. Boats and instructors at the main **diving centres** are fully committed to groups – though they can fit in extra people with a few days notice. As a guide, expect to pay around US$300 for an open-water course; two boat dives, not including equipment, costs US$40. If you have your own equipment, a cheaper way is to take a snorkelling **day trip** to Tubiya Island, organized by *Sun Beach* for £E30 per person with lunch.

The main diving grounds lie 6–8km offshore from the holiday villages, between Safaga Island and Ras Abu Soma. **Tubiya Island** is ringed with corals only just off its beach, while dive boats drop their clients directly over the sunken **North and South Fairway Reefs** or the twin pairs of sites known as **Tubiya Kebir**, **Tubiya Soraya**, **Gamul Soraya** and **Gamul Kebir**. Other sites include the **Seven Pillars** off Ras Abu Soma, and the **Panorama Reef** and **Shark Point**, 10km east of Safaga Island. Most of them are notable for their coral pillars and strong currents.

Among the big fish prevalent in these waters are **hammerhead sharks**, reputedly an aggressive species. Research suggests that they track their victims with two forms of biological sensor. At long range and when closing in on its kill, the hammerhead senses vibrations in the water, but in the final seconds it tunes into electromagnetic fields "bounced" off its target. It was hammerheads that caused many of the fatalities of Egypt's greatest maritime disaster, in December 1992, when a ferry returning from Jeddah hit a reef only miles offshore and 480 of the 650 passengers perished during seven hours in the water.

DIVING CENTRES

Barakuda, *Lotus Bay Club Villas* (☎065/252-443, fax 251-042) and *Menaville* (☎065/446-950, fax 446-970).

Ducks, *Holiday Inn Resort* (☎065/252-821, fax 02/578-3585).

Dune, 200m behind *Safaga Marina* (☎065/253-075).

Orca, *Sun Beach* (☎065/252-658).

Paradise, *Safaga Paradise Village* (☎065/251-635, fax 251-630).

Shams Safaga, *Shams Safaga* (☎065/251-782, fax 251-780).

Volkert, *Safaga Paradise* (☎065/251-633, fax 251-630).

Other practicalities – and leaving Safaga

Such facilities as there are are all on Safaga's main drag, starting with the **police** station and **EgyptAir**, 200m south of the City Council, followed by a **hospital** 500m on. There's a **petrol station** beyond the next turn-off, across the main road from the Bank of Alexandria; further south on the other side are Banque Misr and the National Bank of Egypt, and a **telephone exchange**. Tourists staying at the holiday villages can more conveniently **change money** at banks inside *Safaga Marina* and the *Shams Safaga* or the Banque du Caire in the shopping arcade near the *Safaga Paradise*. The arcade also has a Fuji photographic shop, while a bit further on, beside the *Holiday Inn* there is another arcade where you can find a Duty Free shop. There are several cafés offering sandwiches or *shawarmas* on the main drag, but their turnover can be low so it's not a great option. The holiday villages are a better bet for food and the only place to get alcoholic drinks.

When **leaving** becomes imperative, cast about at the bus station near the port first and then look for *service* taxis at the depot 500m north. There should be about nine **buses** daily to Hurghada (6am–11.30pm; £E15) and Suez (£E20–35), seven to Cairo (6am–11.30pm; £E25–50), a dozen to Qena (8am–midnight; £E6–8), two direct buses to Luxor (9.45am, 10.45am; £E10–15) – and two to Aswan (leaving from the port at 4am, and the bus station at 1.30am; £E45). Sticking to the Red Sea Coast, two buses a day (6am and 4pm; £E6) run down to El-Quseir, while a third (at 2.30am) carries on to Halaib, near the Sudanese border. **Service taxis** run in between buses to Hurghada or Qena and charge similar rates to the buses but it can take a long time to muster enough passengers for El-Quseir.

The road to Qena and off to the quarries

Safaga is primarily a commercial port for shipping out phosphates and importing US grain sent as food aid. The reopening of a long-abandoned freight railway has ended a windfall for the Ma'aza Bedouin, who used to feed their flocks on grain spilt along **the desert road to Qena** (161km). However, elders still spend their final years here: the pickings are good and they get to meet everybody. It's a harsh landscape of fissured rocks and canyons, with a beautiful dune cascading down the hillside shortly before you pass a small cafeteria, 85km from Qena. There are no petrol stations en route, but passengers can refresh themselves at wayside stands planted with trees, irrigated by the pipeline that conveys water from the Nile to Safaga and Hurghada.

Those with 4WD vehicles might consider two routes leading off **towards Mons Claudianus** (see p.635). The turn-off west of Safaga gets there in 25km via Bir Abd el-Wahab, whereas the rougher piste outside Qena follows its eponymous wadi to El-Heita before forking right up Wadi el-Atrash towards Jebel Abu Dukhaan (roughly 150km).

El-Quseir and the route to Qift

EL-QUSEIR, 85km from Safaga, is likewise into phosphates extraction, but has fewer inhabitants and more appeal. In pharaonic times, it was from here that boats sailed to the "Land of Punt" (thought to be Yemen or Somalia), as depicted in reliefs within Hatshepsut's temple at Deir el-Bahri. The Romans knew it as *Leukos Limen* (White Harbour), while under Arab rule El-Quseir was the largest port on the Red Sea until the tenth century, and remained a major transit point for pilgrims until the 1840s, when Flaubert caught its last flickers of exoticism. Crude pearl-fishers' *pirogues* resembling dug-out tree trunks shared the harbour with graceful Arab *dhows*, whose outsize sterns and high prows mimicked calligraphic flourishes, while Arabs and Africans jostled with Tartars from Bukhara and Crimea.

Today, El-Quseir is a sleepy place that seems mostly unaffected by tourism, despite the presence of three holiday villages on its outskirts. The town retains a charm all of its own, and locals are happy to help with directions if you get lost – not that it's necessary, as you'll soon find everything. The main **orientation** point is a traffic roundabout where *service* taxis drop and wait for passengers, near a Co-op garage and the *Sea Princess Hotel*.

The road bearing off to the right leads to a small **harbour** where you can watch men building boats on the beach, or stroll past shuttered and balconied houses to reach a **mosque** dating back to the thirteenth century, and a **quarantine hospital** built to screen pilgrims in the nineteenth century. This prison-like edifice is easily mistaken for the **fort** built by Mohammed Ali, whose crumbling walls enclose a watchtower and an execution chamber. It was originally an induction camp for some of the 20,000 Sudanese who were conscripted by the pasha and trained by European mercenaries in the hope of forging a modern army, but foiled his plans by sickening and dying en masse. The fort stands beside Sharia el-Gumhorriya, 200m uphill from the traffic roundabout, past a few fruit and vegetable stalls that are joined by other vendors on Fridays, when Ma'aza and Ababda Bedouin flock into town for the weekly **market**.

Practicalities

Accommodation is limited to one rather shabby hotel in the centre and three holiday villages outside town. The central *Sea Princess* (☎065/332-880; ②) is an odd little hotel decorated with film posters and vintage banknotes, whose friendly staff and clean bathrooms just fail to make the rabbit-hutch rooms tolerable. If you have money to spend, you're better off heading 1.5km south of town (25min walk) to the *Fanadir* (☎065/331-414, fax 331-415; ⑦), a modest holiday village of A/C chalets and triple-person "villas", with a smallish pool, a dive centre and little shade, whose rates include half-board. Its Nubian-style architecture is aped on a grander scale by the *Mövenpick* (☎065/332-100, fax 332-128; ⑧), a vast five-star resort 5km north of town (£E15–20 by taxi) with every facility imaginable, whose guests seldom leave its confines. Next door, the brand new four-star *Flamenco Beach Resort* (☎065/332-802, fax 332-801; ⑦), painted a garish pink, seems representative of hotel development to come.

Aside from **eating** at the holiday villages, you're reliant on whatever materializes at two nameless cafés by the roundabout: soup, *fuul*, rice or chicken, if you're lucky – if not, just tea. A nicer place to pass time is the vine-shaded café overlooking the beach, which has *sheeshas* and backgammon. Alcohol and **nightlife** are confined to the holiday villages, which sometimes feature a bellydancer; non-residents may attend at the management's discretion.

The same goes for watersports, with **diving centres** deferring to guests, who may object to outside divers tagging along on sea trips. If you want to dive here, it's best to get a package deal from the start. Although the Quei and Wizr **reefs** are closer, the best sites are the **Brothers**, east of El-Quseir, and the **Elphinestone** and **Abu Dabbab** reefs, down towards Mersa Allam. Access to the Brothers is currently only possible on board a few safari boats that leave from Hurghada.

El-Quseir has few facilities. There's a **bank** on Sharia el-Gumhorriya, beyond the fort, while the road that turns right at this point leads to an old-fashioned **telephone exchange**. **Buses** leave from the unmarked bus stop just down from the *Sea Princess Hotel*, on the road to the harbour; tickets are bought on the bus. There are two A/C buses daily to **Cairo** (7.45pm & 11pm; 10hr; £E55) and two non-A/C (5am & 8pm; 10hr; £E30); all four services stop at Safaga and Hurghada. Heading south, there are two buses daily to **Shalateen** via the coastal route (4hr; 2.30am, £E30; 7.30am, £20). There are six buses daily that head inland to **Qena**, three of which (11.30am, 1.30pm & 2.30pm; 2hr; £E8–10) also carry on to Shalateen. **Service taxis** depart from 50m south of the *Sea Princess Hotel*, bound for Cairo (£E40), Hurghada (£E8), Safaga (£E5),

Mersa Allam (£E10) and Qena (£E15). Another alternative is to get a group together to hire a **minibus** and driver from one of the tourist agencies in town. Koshar Tourist Services (☎065/331-666, fax 331-695) will take up to eleven people to Cairo (£E600), Hurghada (£E150), Safaga (£E100), Qena (£E250), Mersa Allam (£E150), Berenice (£E300) or Shalateen (£E500).

The desert road to Qift

The modern road from **El-Quseir to Qift** (216km) follows the earliest known route across the Eastern Desert, partially explored by the V Dynasty but not fully established until Ramses IV's time (1164–1157 BC), when wells were dug at intervals. In those days, the main attraction was the hard, dark breccia – used for statues and sarcophagi – found in **Wadi Hammamat**, roughly midway between El-Quseir and Qift. When Flaubert travelled this way by camel, it was necessary to drink from an earthy source "reached by sliding under a rock", while other parties "breasted ahead" over sand dunes in a haze of dust, "as though they were wading through clouds". Nowadays the hardships and romance have gone, and vehicles rarely stop at the great well of **Bir Hammamat**, dug by eight thousand men for Ramses IV; nor at **Bir Umm Fawakhir** (92km from El-Quseir), where ancient mines specified on an Egyptian survey map of c.1400 BC have recently been reopened.

Roughly 100km further on from Bir Umm Fawakhir, you might glimpse the sizeable ruins of **Qasr el-Banat** (Fortress of the Maidens), scratched with Greek, Coptic and Sinaitic characters, and formerly reputed to be haunted. Nowadays, the only way-station as such is **El-Lakeita**, a tiny oasis-village whose cistern bears a faint inscription from the reign of Tiberius Claudius.

For Bedouin, the road marks the boundary between **Ma'aza** tribal land and **Ababda** territory. Though traditional rivals, they may graze and water their flocks on each other's preserves should their own land be drought-stricken. Tribal politics are conditioned by the harsh environment and long memories; the names of wells and landmarks are often historically specific. For example, Bir Umm Howeitat, near the Umm Rus gold mine inland of Mersa Umbarak, is named after the Saudi Bedouin who harried the Ma'aza in their original homeland and later in Sinai.

To Mersa Allam and the Moulid of Al-Shazli

MERSA ALLAM, 132km beyond El-Quseir, marks the southernmost point realistically of interest to divers and holidaymakers, as **military permission** is required to visit the region towards the border with Sudan. Pending completion of Mersa Allam's international airport, access is in any case difficult, and if you do manage to get this far, accommodation is sparse and fairly expensive. That said, this stretch of the coast road offers some of the most amazing landscape and desert in Egypt. As the road heads southwards to the Sudanese border the seemingly endless coastline is almost completely empty except for the occasional mangrove, herd of grazing camels or cluster of tanks left by the military.

Unsurprisingly the southern Red Sea coast is growing in popularity with travellers and divers, but tourist infrastructure is far from developed. Divers should be aware that as yet, there is no decompression chamber this far south; the nearest one is in Hurghada. There is no telephone system in place either, so bookings are made through head offices in Cairo. *Shams Safaga* and *Red Sea Diving Safari* do have satellite phones for emergencies (US$5 per min).

Since 1999, several new tourist developments have popped up on the coastal road south of Quseir, but they are unlikely to be on their own for long. The first resort, 20km south of Quseir, is the *Utopia* (no phone, half-board only; ⑧), an upmarket four-star place with A/C rooms, swimming pool and diving centre. A further 9km down the road you will find *Mangrove Bay Resort* (☎02/348-6748, fax 360-5458; half-board only ⑦), a slightly cheaper tourist village. Both feature beautiful white sandy beaches with access to the 20km of coral reefs offshore.

If you have your own transport, you might head further south to the five-star *Kahramana* (☎02/360-5987, fax 349-9327; ⑨), whose stunning architecture is set against beautiful and empty sandy beaches. It doesn't have its own reef, but the hotel's diving centre is run by *Red Sea Diving Safari* (see below), which caters to divers with boat trips to nearby reefs.

Eighteen kilometres north of Mersa Allam, at **Mersa Shagra**, is *Red Sea Diving Safari* (☎02/337-1833, fax 349-4219, *redseasaf@hotmail.com*). This stunningly situated beachside resort offers a variety of environmentally-friendly accommodation, ranging from tents on the beach (⑦) to rather smart huts (⑦), both with shared bath facilities, and more luxurious en-suite chalets (⑨). Rates include all meals and unlimited soft-drinks (beer is available at US$3 a bottle).

The town of **MERSA ALLAM** itself is undistinguished, consisting of a large army base and some government buildings grafted onto a fishing port. You can change *service* **taxis** en route between the Red Sea coast and the Nile Valley town of Edfu, 230km inland, or use the Mersa Allam–Edfu road to visit the annual Moulid of *Al-Shazli* at Wadi Humaysara. Though rarely marked on maps, this site is widely known and more accessible than you'd imagine – the main problem is whether you'll be allowed through the checkpoints, even with a permit.

A new dive-resort venture has recently begun taking guests on day-trips to local reefs offshore, as well as to **Abu Dabab, Elphinstone** and **Fury Shoal** reefs on overnight excursions. *Shams Alam Hotel and Beach Resort* (☎02/417-0046, fax 417-0158; half-board only; ⑦) is situated 50km south of Mersa Allam, and is – for now at least – the most southerly hotel on the Red Sea coast.

The Moulid of Abul Hassan al-Shazli

Outside Egypt, **Abul Hassan al-Shazli** (who died in 1258) is known as Al-Shadhili, hence the name of his Sufi order, the *Shadhiliyya*. According to believers, Al-Shazli asked God to let him die in a place where nobody had ever sinned, and the Prophet Mohammed buried him high in the mountains at **Wadi Humaysara**. The remoteness of his grave has never deterred pilgrims, for whom the journey has become much easier since a local entrepreneur built a road to the site as a gift. It turns off the Edfu road at the tomb of another Sufi sheikh, Salim, which pilgrim trucks circle three times to avoid incurring his jealousy, before driving on to Wadi Humaysara (100km).

Al-Shazli's **moulid** starts ten days before the Muslim feast of *Eid al-Adha* and reaches its climax the day before the *Eid*. Sixty thousand Sufis from all over Egypt gather to perform *zikrs* outside his tomb, and hundreds of tents and snack stalls are pitched for the occasion. Arranging a ride there will require much palaver, but you shouldn't have any problem identifying the pilgrim trucks, festooned with banners and loudspeakers.

The far south: Berenice to the Sudanese border

A further 145km south is the town of **BERENICE**, named after the wife of Ptolemy II, on whose instigation a trading port was established here in 275 BC. Abandoned during the fifth century AD, the site was excavated in 1818 by Belzoni, who found a Temple of Semiramis and other ruins. Nowadays, Berenice amounts to a few characterless buildings clustered together in a windswept bay, with little to interest tourists except a Bedouin museum apparently instigated by the wife of the Belgian ambassador to Egypt.

With tourism increasingly being encouraged, however, the hinterland of Berenice has several would-be attractions. For climbers, there is the challenge of Egypt's "most aggressive peaks", **Jebel Farayid** (whose highest point was reached by Murray in 1925) and the **Berenice Bodkin** – the largest rock needle in the whole of North Africa and the Middle East. Here, too, are the ancient **Emerald Mines of Wadi Sakait**, worked from pharaonic to Roman times and under the khalifs; Mohammed Ali had them reopened, but few gems remained to be found and the mines were soon abandoned. Nearby is a small Ptolemaic rock temple, dedicated to Isis and Serapis.

The reasons why this area has long been off limits are geopolitical. Following the Iranian Revolution, the **Ras Banas air base** was earmarked for use by the US Rapid Deployment Force and war games were held in the Eastern Desert, simulating an Allied response to an Iranian attack on the Saudi oil fields. Such manoeuvres waned after Iran was embroiled in war by Iraq, and the US "forward base" withdrew to Diego Garcia – so that when Iraq invaded Kuwait in 1990, the only unit available for immediate airlift into Saudi Arabia was a single battalion of Egyptian commandos.

More recently, the **far south** has been a bone of contention between Egypt and Sudan, whose common border was arbitrarily set by the British in 1899 on the basis of the 22nd parallel. After independence, both agreed that this was unfair on the Bishari nomads whose tribal grounds straddled the border, so a slice of Egyptian territory was placed under Sudanese administration – a compromise that worked fine until Sudan granted a Canadian oil company offshore exploration rights, and Egypt responded by sending in troops to reassert its sovereignty. Since 1992, the region from **Bir Shalateen** down to **Halaib** has been under military rule, and Egypt has launched a crash programme of "development" to cement its hold on this previously neglected, potentially oil-rich region.

In May 1999, some restrictions were lifted and tourists can now travel at least as far as **Shalateen**. As yet there is no tourist accommodation in the area, and official permissions must be obtained from police in Berenice or Shalateen if you wish to camp. An alternative is to arrange a trip with Geographic Adventures (see p.635). The area is still a very sensitive military zone and anyone not obtaining permissions is likely to be treated with extreme suspicion.

PART THREE

THE

CONTEXTS

THE HISTORICAL FRAMEWORK

The present borders of Egypt are almost identical to those in pharaonic times; territories such as Sinai and Nubia being essentially marginal to the heartland of the Nile Valley and its Delta, where Egyptian civilization emerged some five thousand years ago. The historical continuity is staggering: the pharaonic era alone lasted thirty centuries before being appropriated by Greek and Roman emperors.

Egypt's significance in the ancient world was paramount, and the country has never been far from the frontline of world history. Although neither Christianity nor Islam was born in Egypt, both are stamped with its influence. In modern times, when the Arab world sought to rid itself of European masters, Egypt was at the forefront of the anti-colonial struggle, while its peace treaty with Israel altered the geopolitics of the Middle East.

UNCERTAINTIES . . .

Any attempt to précis this vast span of history inevitably runs the risk of obscuring social dynamics and ordinary people amid a roll call of dynasties and great men and women. While the continuity of so many aspects of Egyptian life supports this conservative view, dramatic watersheds and subtle fluxes are also a feature of Egyptian history. Nor are the facts graven in stone. Egyptology is riddled with uncertainties, not least in its chronology of dynasties and kings.

In recent years, **chronology** has been a hotly debated issue in the world of Egyptology, whose established dating system has been under attack by two writers advancing utterly dissimilar theories. Their arguments deserve to be read in full, but can be summarized as follows.

In *A Test of Time*, **David Rohl** examines the "Four Pillars" of synchronicity between ancient Egyptian and Biblical history and judges only one to be impeccable. Anomalies such as the royal burials at Tanis and Deir el-Bahri, Israelite chariots on the Ashkelon Wall at Karnak, and evidence of their sojourn at Avaris call for a revision of the chronology of the Third Intermediate Period, with knock-on effects on earlier times. Rohl's **New Chronology** puts the Exodus in the XIII rather than the XIX Dynasty, and makes Akhenaten a contemporary of David and Saul; further ramifications are still being worked out for his doctoral thesis.

Unlike Rohl, **Anthony West** is not a professional Egyptologist, and his *Serpent in the Sky* – propounding that the Egyptian temples embody the legacy of an older, greater civilization dating back to Atlantis – was laughed off until two geologists agreed that the erosion in the bedrock of the Sphinx shows that it was created at least 2600 years earlier than had hitherto been assumed. Egyptologists failed to refute their evidence in a showdown at the 1992 conference of the American Association for the Advancement of Science, but have since taken comfort from a study by the Getty Institute, which concludes that the erosion proves nothing of the kind.

As both debates are unresolved, we've stuck to the **established chronology**, which even mainstream Egyptologists acknowledge as having margins of error. These are up to a hundred years in the period around 3000 BC, seventy-five years around 2000 BC, and between ten and fifteen years around 1000 BC. From 500 BC onwards, dates are fairly precise until the Ptolemaic era, when the chronology gets hazy, only firming up again in Roman times.

THE BEGINNINGS

Stone tools from the gravel beds of Upper Egypt attest to the presence of **hunter-gathering hominids** in the area over 250,000 years ago, when the Sahara was a savannah that supported zebras, elephants and other game. Drastic climatic changes late in the **Paleolithic** era (c.25,000 BC) caused widespread **desertification**, which compelled the nomadic tribes to settle around the **Nile and the oases**. While most still lived by hunting and fishing, a primitive pastoral and agricultural life emerged even before cereal cultivation, sheep and goat herding filtered through from the Near East (c.7000 BC).

During the **Neolithic** era, Middle Egypt and the Delta had **settled communities** that cultivated wheat and flax, herded flocks and wove linen. Although some reverted to a nomadic lifestyle after the rains of the Neolithic era checked the process of desertification, others remained to develop into agricultural societies.

PRE-DYNASTIC EGYPT

Notwithstanding the Delta's exposure to Levantine and Aegean influences, the impetus for development came from southern Egypt, where archeologists have identified three main cultures. The earliest is known as the **Badarian**, after the village of El-Badari where Brunton carried out excavations in the 1920s. The Badarians were farmers, hunters and miners; they made fine pottery, carved bone and ivory, and traded for turquoise and wood.

The **Naqada I** period, from about 4000 BC onwards, was characterized by larger settlements and a distinctive style of pottery: burnished red-clay ware with black rims or white zoomorphic decorations. Clay and ivory figurines show Naqada menfolk sporting beards and penis shields, raising a possible ethnic connection with their Libyan neighbours. More extraordinary are the narrow-necked vases carved from basalt, which can't be reproduced by twentieth-century technology, but were supposedly made by the Stone Age Naqada I culture.

In the conventional scheme of things, graves from the **Naqada II** period contain copper tools and glazed beads that signify advances in technology, and extraneous materials such as lapis lazuli, indicating trade with Asia. The graves themselves evolved from simple pits into painted tombs lined with mats and wood, and, later still, brick. The development of extensive irrigation systems (c.3300 BC) boosted productivity and promoted links between communities.

THE TWO LANDS

By this time, the communities of Upper and Lower Egypt existed in two loose **confederations**. As power coalesced around Naqada in the south and Behdet in the Delta, each confederation became identified with a chief deity and a symbol of statehood: Seth and the White Crown with **Upper Egypt**, Horus and the Red Crown with the **Delta**.

Later, each acquired a new capital (Hierakonpolis and Buto, respectively) and strove for domination over the entire region. The eventual triumph of the southern kingdom resulted in the **unification of the Two Lands** (c.3100 BC) under the quasi-mythical ruler **Menes** (aka Narmer), and the start of Egypt's Dynastic period.

THE ARCHAIC PERIOD (c.3100–2686 BC)

The **Early Dynastic** or **Archaic Period** was the formative epoch of Egyptian civilization. Its beginnings are a mix of history and myth, relating to the foundation – supposedly by Menes – of the city of **Memphis**, located at the junction between Upper and Lower Egypt: the first imperial city on earth.

From this base, Djer and Den, the third and fifth kings of the **I Dynasty** (c.3100–2890 BC), attempted to bring Sinai under Egyptian control. Writing, painting and architecture became increasingly sophisticated, while royal tombs at Saqqara and Abydos developed into complex *mastabas*.

Equally indicative of future trends was the dissolution of the unified kingdom as centralized authority waned towards the end of the dynasty. Although this was restored by **Raneb** (or Hotepsekhemwy), founder of a new line of rulers, regional disputes persisted throughout the **II Dynasty** (c.2890–2686 BC).

These disputes probably inspired the **contendings of Seth and Horus**, a major theme in Egyptian mythology. The Stele of Peribsen shows a temple facade surmounted by the figure of Seth, rather than Horus, the traditional symbol of kings. However, the rivalry between the two regions and their respective deities appears to have been resolved under **Khasekhem**, the last king of the dynasty – paving the way for an era of assurance.

THE OLD KINGDOM (c.2686–2181 BC)

During the **Old Kingdom** – which began with the **III Dynasty** (c. 2686–2613 BC) – advances in technology and developments in culture raised Egypt to an unprecedented level of civilization.

The main figure of the III Dynasty was **King Zoser** (or Djoser), whose architect, **Imhotep**, built the first **Step Pyramid** at Saqqara in the 27th century BC. The pyramid's conception and construction were a landmark and later generations deified Imhotep as the ultimate sage. On the economic and political front, the III Dynasty also sent expeditions into Sinai, to seek turquoise and copper and subjugate the local Bedouin.

Pyramid-building and expansionism were likewise pursued during the **IV Dynasty** (c.2613–2494 BC). The Dynasty's first king, **Snofru** (aka Sneferu), raised two pyramids at Dahshur, and made incursions into Nubia and Libya. His successors, **Cheops** (Khufu), **Chephren** (Khafre) and **Mycerinus** (Menkaure), erected the **Pyramids of Giza**, expanded trade relations with the Near East, and developed mining activities in Nubia, where a copper-smelting factory was established at the Second Cataract. Though Snofru's line expired with the death of **Shepseskaf**, his widow Queen **Khentkawes** is believed to have married a high priest to produce an heir.

A debt to the priesthood of **Heliopolis** may explain the increased **worship of Re** during the **V Dynasty** (c.2494–2345 BC), whose rulers styled themselves "son of Re" and built elaborate sun temples at Abu Ghurab. Their pyramids at Abu Sir and Saqqara were smaller than those of the previous dynasty but more finely worked. It was **Unas**, the last pharaoh of the dynasty, who introduced religious texts into his pyramid: descriptions of the underworld and afterlife that subsequently inspired the *Book of the Dead*. Meanwhile, the tombs of nobles grew larger and further away from the royal pyramids, suggesting that their independence was increasing.

This trend continued during the **VI Dynasty** (c.2345–2181 BC) when nobles were buried in their own **nomes** (provinces). While punitive expeditions carried the pharaoh's banner deep into Nubia, Libya and Palestine, domestic power ebbed to the *nomarchs*, reaching the point of no return under **Pepi II** (aka Neferkare), whose death heralded the **end of the Old Kingdom**.

THE FIRST INTERMEDIATE PERIOD (c.2181–2050 BC)

After Pepi's death, decades of provincial rivalry and chaos ensued, with petty dynasties claiming the mantle of the Old Kingdom. The Greek historian Manetho records seventy rulers during the brief **VII Dynasty** (c.2181–2173), while an unknown number of kings vainly asserted their claims from Memphis during the **VIII Dynasty** (c.2173–2160).

When rains failed over the Ethiopian highlands, famine struck Egypt, exacerbating civil disorder. Weak principalities sought powerful allies such as **Heracleopolis**, the dominant city of the Twentieth Nome, whose ruler, **Achthoes**, gained control of Middle Egypt, assumed the throne name Meryibre, and founded the **IX Dynasty** (c.2160–2130).

Whereas most of the north came under the control of the IX and **X Dynasty** (c.2130–2040) kings of Heracleopolis, Upper Egypt was contested by the rulers of Edfu and Thebes. After vanquishing his rival, the Theban ruler Inyotef Sehertowy tried to extend his power beyond Upper Egypt, founding the **XI Dynasty** (c.2133–1991 BC). The struggle between north and south was only finally resolved by **Nebhepetre Mentuhotpe II**, who reunited the whole country under one authority, establishing the Middle Kingdom in 2050 BC.

THE MIDDLE KINGDOM (c.2050–1786 BC)

During Mentuhotpe's fifty-year reign the mines and trade routes were reopened; incursions into Libya, Nubia and Sinai resumed; and arts and crafts flourished again. His successors, Mentuhotpe III and IV, were most notable for their expeditions to the Land of Punt. Inscriptions from Wadi Hammamat name the vizier in charge of the second expedition as **Amenemhat** (or Ammenemes), who subsequently founded the **XII Dynasty** (c.1991–1786 BC).

Amenemhat returned the capital to Memphis and safeguarded the Nile Delta from raiders by constructing the Walls of the Prince, a fortified *cordon sanitaire*. Northern Nubia was annexed, and trade extended further into Palestine and Syria.

Under Amenemhat's son, **Senusert I** (aka Sesostris I), the administrative capital was transferred to the **Fayoum**, where massive waterworks were undertaken. Amenemhat II curbed the power of the nomarchs, while Senusert III may have abolished the office completely. These kings also built **the last pyramids**, at Lahun, El-Lisht and Hawara, where the final pyramid was erected by Amenemhat III, alongside the Labyrinth described by Herodotus.

According to Rohl's New Chronology, it was **Amenemhat III** who took **Joseph** as his vizier and let the **Israelites** settle in the Delta (c.1662 BC). Graves at Avaris suggest a large Semitic population stricken by calamities, akin to the Biblical account of the events leading up to the **Exodus**, which Rohl assigns to the reign of the XIII Dynasty pharaoh **Dudimose** (c.1447 BC). Both these dates are utterly at variance with the conventional chronology, which places the Exodus two centuries later, during the New Kingdom.

However, there is no disagreement that the late XII Dynasty was a **troubled time**, with the Nile flooding at record levels, bringing poor harvests and famine in its wake. The faces of the statues of pharaohs of this era are uniquely stern and careworn. Whether or not Egypt was also smitten by plagues and disrupted by an exodus from the Delta, it was obviously in poor shape to resist an invasion.

THE SECOND INTERMEDIATE PERIOD (c.1786–1567 BC)

Under the XIII Dynasty Egypt slid into an era of disorder that archeologists term the **Second Intermediate Period**, when the pharaohs lost control of Nubia and the Delta. The historian Manetho records that "peoples of an obscure race" overran the Delta in the reign of Dudimose, and went on to capture Memphis. Known to posterity as the **Hyksos** or "Shepherd Kings", they ruled from the Delta city of **Avaris**, maintaining links with Palestine, Crete and Persia. Although Egyptian chronicles describe their rule as anarchic, evidence such as the *Rhind Mathematical Papyrus* suggests that the Hyksos fostered native culture, took Egyptian names and ruled as pharaohs. The Hyksos may

also have introduced the horse to Egypt – though its use was limited to hauling chariots.

From 1650 BC onwards, Hyksos rule was challenged by the **XVII Dynasty** of Theban kings, who claimed all of Egypt. The balance of power shifted back and forth, with Nubia allied to whichever state recognized its independence. Eventually, the Theban ruler Wadikheperre Kamose besieged Avaris, and his successor **Ahmosis** finally expelled the Hyksos from Egypt in 1567 BC, ushering in a new era.

THE NEW KINGDOM (c.1567–1085 BC)

The **XVIII Dynasty** (c.1567–1320 BC) founded by Ahmosis inaugurated the **New Kingdom**, a period of stability, wealth and expansion, whose rulers include some of the most famous names in Egyptian history. During this era **Nubia** was brought under Egyptian control, yielding gold, ivory, ebony, gems and, most importantly, slaves. The professional armies of the pharaohs also invaded the Near East, Syria and Palestine, establishing colonies governed by Egyptian viceroys or local satraps. One result was an influx of immigrants into Egypt, bringing new customs, ideas and technology.

The effects are evident at **Thebes**, capital of the New Kingdom, where a spate of temples and tombs symbolize the pre-eminence of the god **Amun** and the power of the pharaohs. While **Tuthmosis I** (c.1525–1512 BC) built the first tomb in the Valley of the Kings, his daughter **Hatshepsut** raised the great mortuary temple of Deir el-Bahri, ruling as pharaoh (c.1503–1482 BC) despite her stepson's claim on the throne. Having belatedly assumed power, **Tuthmosis III** embarked on imperial conquests, extending Egyptian power beyond the Fourth Cataract in Nubia, and across the Euphrates to the boundaries of the Hittite empire. His successor **Amenophis II** (c.1459–1425 BC) penetrated deeper into Nubia, and **Tuthmosis IV** (c.1425–1417 BC) further strengthened the empire by marrying a princess of Mitanni, a state bordering the Hittites.

The zenith of Egyptian power coincided with the reign of **Amenophis III** (c.1417–1379 BC). With the empire secure and prosperity at home, the king devoted himself to the arts and the construction of great edifices such as Luxor Temple. During the same period, a hitherto minor aspect of the sun-god was increasingly venerated in royal circles: the **cult of Aten**, which the pharaoh's son would subsequently enshrine above all others.

THE AMARNA REVOLUTION

By changing his name from Amenophis IV to **Akhenaten** and founding a new capital at Tell el-Amarna, the young king underlined his commitment to a new **monotheistic religion** that challenged the existing priesthood and bureaucracy. Since the story of Akhenaten and **Nefertiti** is related in detail on p.268, it suffices to say that the **Amarna revolution** barely outlasted his reign (c.1379–1362 BC) and that of his mysterious successor, **Smenkhkare**, who died the following year.

The boy king **Tutankhamun** (1361–1352 BC) was easily persuaded to abjure Aten's cult and return the capital to Thebes, heralding a **Theban counter-revolution** that continued under **Ay** and **Horemheb**. Though Horemheb (c.1348–1320 BC) effectively restored the *status quo ante*, his lack of royal blood and, more importantly, an heir, brought the XVIII Dynasty to a close.

THE XIX DYNASTY

The **XIX Dynasty** (c.1320–1200 BC) began with the reign of Horemheb's vizier, **Ramses I** (c.1320–1318 BC), whose family was to produce several warrior-kings who would recapture territories lost under Akhenaten. **Seti I** (c.1318–1304 BC) reasserted pharaonic authority in Nubia, Palestine and the Near East, and began a magnificent temple at Abydos. His son **Ramses II** (c.1304–1237 BC) completed the temple and the reconquest of Asia Minor, commemorating his dubious victory at Qadesh with numerous reliefs, but later concluding a treaty with the Hittites. At home, Ramses usurped temples and statues built by others, and raised his own monumental edifices – notably the Ramesseum at Thebes and the sun temples at Abu Simbel.

His son **Merneptah** (c.1236–1217 BC) faced invasions by the "Sea Peoples" from the north and Libyans from the west, but eventually defeated the latter at Pi-yer in the western Delta. He is also popularly believed to be the pharaoh of the **Exodus**, though the only known pharaonic reference to the Israelites describes an Egyptian victory against these "nomads". The XIX Dynasty expired with **Seti II** (c.1210 BC), to be followed by a decade without a ruling dynasty.

THE XX DYNASTY

The **XX Dynasty** (c.1200–1085 BC), begun by Sethnakhte, was the last of the New Kingdom. His successor **Ramses III** (c.1198–1166 BC) repulsed three great invasions by the Libyans and Sea Peoples, and built the vast temple-cum-pleasure palace of **Medinet Habu**. But strikes by workmen at the royal necropolis and an assassination attempt within the king's harem presaged problems to come. Under the eight kings who followed (all called Ramses), Egypt lost the remains of its Asiatic empire, and thieves plundered the necropolis. **Ramses XI** (c.1114–1085 BC) withdrew to his residence in the Delta, delegating control of Upper Egypt to **Herihor**, high priest of Amun, and Lower Egypt to Vizier **Smendes**.

THE THIRD INTERMEDIATE PERIOD (c.1069–664 BC)

This division was consolidated under the **XXI Dynasty** (c.1069–945 BC), the successors of Herihor and Smendes ruling their respective halves of Egypt from **Thebes** and **Tanis**. The two ruling houses (both designated as the XXI Dynasty) seem to have coexisted in harmony, with the Theban priest-kings acknowledging the Tanite pharaohs' superiority. Towards the end of this era, a powerful new dynasty of **Libyan** extraction was founded by **Shoshenk I**. This **XXII Dynasty** (c.945–715 BC) ruled Egypt from Bubastis in the Delta until a rival line seized power in Upper Egypt, precipitating **civil war** between the Bubastite monarchs and the Theban **XXIII Dynasty** (818–720 BC), which was further complicated by a brief **XXIV Dynasty** (727–715 BC) of Ethiopian kings.

The lifespan of these four dynasties – termed the **Third Intermediate Period** (TIP) – is one of the murkiest eras of Egyptian history, yet crucial to the New Chronology hypothesis, as the accepted dates for the New Kingdom hinge on the length of the TIP. Rohl contends that the XXI and XXII Dynasties overlapped for generations, and that the duration of the TIP should therefore be reduced accordingly – with knock-on effects down the line.

THE NUBIAN KINGS

Egypt's prolonged instability was finally brought to an end by foreign intervention. The Nubian king Piankhi advanced as far north as Memphis, while his brother **Shabaka** went on to conquer the Delta and reunite the Two Lands. The **XXV Dynasty** of **Nubian kings** (c.747–656 BC) was marked by a revival of artistic and cultural life, and renewed devotion to Amun (as evinced by reliefs at Karnak and Luxor).

By the reign of **Tanutamun**, however, Egypt was menaced by the **Assyrians**, who occupied Memphis and then sacked Thebes, whereupon Tanutamun fled to Nubia. According to Rohl, the **sack of Thebes** in 664 BC is the only one of the "Four Pillars" of synchronicity that can be relied upon to link the histories of ancient Egypt and the Near East, being attested by many different sources.

THE LATE PERIOD (c.664–332 BC)

Years before the sack of Thebes, a new family of rulers began emerging in the Delta, which paid tribute to the Assyrians until they withdrew from Egypt to defend their empire from the Babylonians, leaving a vacuum that was filled by **Psammetichus I**, the fourth ruler of the **XXVI Dynasty** (664–525 BC). Known as the Saïte Dynasty after its capital at **Saïs** in the Delta, this was the last great age of pharaonic civilization, harking back to the glories of the Old Kingdom in art and architecture, but also adopting new technologies and allowing colonies of Greek merchants at Naucratis, and Jewish mercenaries at Elephantine.

Necho II (610–595 BC) defeated Josiah, King of Judah, at Megiddo, but was routed by the Babylonians. He is also credited with starting to build a canal to link the Nile with the Red Sea. Though **Psammetichus II** (595–589 BC) enjoyed several victories, his successor **Apries** was overthrown following defeat in Cyrenacia, the throne passing to **Amasis** "the Drunkard", who relied on Greek allies to stave off the Persian empire.

PERSIAN RULE

The **Persian invasion** of 525 BC began an era of rule by foreigners that essentially lasted until Nasser eventually overthrew Egypt's monarchy in 1952.

Mindful of the Assyrians' mistake, the Persian emperors **Cambyses** and **Darius I** kept a tight grip on Egypt. Besides completing Necho's canal and founding a new city near Memphis, called **Babylon-in-Egypt** (today's

"Old Cairo"), they built and restored temples to enhance their legitimacy. But **rebellions** against Xerxes and Artaxerxes testified to Egyptian hatred of this foreign **XXVII Dynasty** (c.525–404 BC).

Ousted by Amyrtaeus, sole ruler of the XXVII Dynasty, the Persians constantly assailed the native rulers that followed. Though **Nectanebo I** of the **XXX Dynasty** (c.380–343 BC) managed to repulse them with Greek help, his successor's campaign in Phoenicia failed. Finally, bereft of allies, **Nectanebo II** (360–343 BC) was crushingly defeated by Artaxerxes III, and fled to Nubia. Egypt remained under Persian control until 332 BC, when their entire empire succumbed to **Alexander the Great**.

THE PTOLEMIES

Alexander's stay in Egypt was brief, though long enough for him to adopt local customs. He offered sacrifices to the gods of Memphis and visited Amun's temple at Siwa, reorganized the country's administration, installing himself as pharaoh, and founded the coastal city of **Alexandria**; he then went off to conquer what remained of the known world. Upon his death in 323 BC, Alexander's Macedonian generals divided the empire, Ptolemy becoming ruler of Egypt and establishing the **Ptolemaic Dynasty** in 332.

Under Ptolemy I, **Greek** became the official language and Hellenistic ideas had a profound effect on Egyptian art, religion and technology. Although Greek deities were also introduced, the Ptolemies cultivated the Egyptian gods and ruled much like Egyptian pharaohs, erecting great cult temples such as Edfu and Kom Ombo. They also opened new ports, established the great Library of Alexandria and had Hebrew scriptures translated into Greek by Jewish rabbis. The first synagogue in Egypt was founded at Leontopolis in the Delta.

It was dynastic disputes that led to the loss of Ptolemaic control. **Roman intervention** in Egypt grew until, under Ptolemy XII Auletes (80–51 BC), Egypt was almost totally dependent on Rome. **Julius Caesar** attacked Egypt in 54 BC, taking Alexandria by force.

The most famous queen of Egypt, **Cleopatra VII** (51–30 BC) was also the last of the Ptolemies. Under the protection of Julius Caesar – by whom she bore a son, Caesarion – Cleopatra managed to prolong her family's rule.

After Caesar's death, she formed a similar alliance with **Mark Antony** to preserve Egyptian independence. Their joint fleets, however, suffered disaster against **Octavian** at the Battle of Actium, and both committed suicide rather than face captivity. Subsequently Egypt was reduced to the status of a province of the Roman Empire (30 BC).

ROMAN RULE AND THE RISE OF CHRISTIANITY

The **Roman emperors**, like the Ptolemies, adopted many of the Egyptian cults, building such monuments as Trajan's kiosk at Philae, and temples at Dendara and Esna. Their main interest in the new colony, however, lay in its potential as grain supplier to Rome. With this end constantly in mind, trade routes were ensured by Roman garrisons at Alexandria, Babylon (Old Cairo) and Syene (Aswan). In terms of culture, language and administration, **Hellenistic influence** barely diminished and Alexandria continued to thrive as an important centre of Greek and Hebrew learning.

Although the **Holy Family's flight to Egypt** from Palestine cannot be proven, Egypt's Jewish colonies would have been a natural place of refuge, and several sites remain associated with the episode. According to Coptic tradition, **Christianity** was brought to Egypt by **St Mark**, who arrived in the time of Nero. Mark converted many to the new underground faith, founding the Patriarchate of Alexandria in 61 AD.

Politically, the most significant ruler was **Trajan** (98–117), who reopened Necho's Red Sea Canal. Trade flourished with the export of glass, linen, papyrus and precious stones. But the *fellaheen* were growing increasingly discontented with heavy taxation and forced recruitment into the Roman army.

THE COPTS

First-century Egypt was fertile ground for the spread of Christianity. The religion of the old gods had lost its credibility over the millennia of political manipulations and disasters, while the population – Egyptians and Jews alike – was becoming increasingly anti-Roman and nationalistic in its outlook. The core of Christianity, too, had a resonance in ancient traditions, with its emphasis on resurrection, divine judgement and the cult of the great mother.

Inevitably, as Egypt's Christians – who became known as **Copts** – grew in political confidence, there was conflict with the Roman authorities. In 202, **persecutions** began, reaching their height under **Diocletian** (284–305), when thousands of Coptic Christians were massacred. Copts date their calendar from the massacres in 284.

The legalization of Christianity and its adoption as the imperial religion by **Constantine** in 313 did little to help the Copts. The Roman leaders, from their new capital at **Byzantium**, embraced an orthodox faith that differed fundamentally from that of their Egyptian co-religionists – and persecutions continued. An attempt to reconcile differences at the **Council of Nicaea** (325) failed and the split had become irrevocable by the time it was formalized at the **Council of Chalcedon** (451), following which the Copts established their own completely separate Patriarchate at Alexandria.

The same period also saw the emergence of **monasticism**, which took root in the Egyptian deserts. The monasteries of St Catherine in the Sinai, those of Wadi Natrun and Sohag, and St Anthony's and St Paul's in the Red Sea Hills, all originated in these years.

THE COMING OF ISLAM

Apart from a brief invasion in 616, Egypt remained under **Byzantine rule** until the **advance of Islam** in the seventh century. Led by the Prophet Mohammed's successor, Abu Bakr, the Muslim armies defeated the Byzantine army in 636. General **Amr Ibn al-As** then advanced towards Babylon-in-Egypt, which surrendered after a brief siege, to be followed by Heliopolis (640) and finally the imperial capital of Alexandria (642).

Amr built his capital, **Fustat**, north of the fortress town of Babylon-in-Egypt, in what is today Old Cairo. However, Egypt was merely a province in the vast Islamic empire that was governed from Damascus and Baghdad. As in Roman times, Egypt's primary role was as a bread basket for the empire.

Arabization and Islamicization was a gradual and uneven process, with intermittent periods of religious toleration and discrimination. Much depended on the character of the khalifs, and their own power struggles, whose impact was felt throughout the Islamic empire.

In 750, the empire's ruling **Umayyad** dynasty was defeated by the armies of Abu al-Abbas (a descendant of Abu Bakr) and an **Abbasid** khalifate came to power in Baghdad, administering Egypt, along with its other territories, for the next two centuries.

THE TULUNIDS (868–905) AND IKHSHIDIDS (935–969)

In 868, **Ahmed Ibn Tulun**, sent to administer Egypt on behalf of Khalif al-Mu'tazz, declared the territory independent. He and his successors, the **Tulunids**, ruled for 37 years, during which time economic stability and order were restored. Like previous rulers, Ibn Tulun built a new capital city, **Al-Qitai**, whose vast mosque still remains. The dynasty did not long outlive him, however. His spendthrift son, Khomaruya, was assassinated, as were his heirs, and by 905 Abbasid rule was reimposed.

Egypt remained under the direct control of Baghdad until 935, when Mohammed Ibn Tughj was appointed governor and granted the title *Ikhshid* (ruler or king) by the khalif. Like the Tulunids, the **Ikhshidid dynasty** functioned virtually independently of the khalifate. Severe taxation, though, led to popular discontent, and the death in 965 of Tughj's second son, Ali, combined with famine, drought and political instability, opened the way for an invasion of the **Shi'a Fatimids** from Tunisia.

THE FATIMID ERA (969–1171)

The early **Fatimid khalifs** ruled half the Muslim world, with Egypt forming the central portion of an empire that included North Africa, Sicily, Syria and western Arabia. **Gohar**, commander of the khalifal forces, built the city of **Al-Qahira** (the Triumphant) as a new capital in 969, its walls containing opulent palaces and the prestigious mosque-university of Al-Azhar. **Khalif al-Muizz** installed himself in the city and from there ruled the empire. Trade with India, Africa and Europe expanded, the burdensome tax system was abolished, and a vast multi-racial army that included Europeans, Berbers, Sudanese and Turks was formed.

Whereas Al-Muizz and his successor Al-Aziz were efficient and tolerant rulers, under whom Egypt's economy prospered and the arts flourished, the third khalif – **Al-Hakim** (996–1021) – was a mad and capricious despot. His laws outraged the population, while his support of Byzantine against Latin Christians, and destruction of the Church of the Holy Sepulchre in Jerusalem, later provided a pretext for the First Crusade. His mysterious disappearance (see p.124) was taken by his followers – he championed Shi'a against Sunni Islam – as proof of messianic stature.

By the long reign of Al-Hakim's grandson, **Al-Mostansir** (1035–94), decay had set in. The empire was largely controlled by army commanders, administration was chaotic and famine added to the troubles. A series of governors imposed control over the army and restored peace and prosperity to Egypt for a further hundred years, but the loss of Syria to the Seljuk Turks, and new forces in Europe, left the empire increasingly vulnerable.

The **First Crusade** (1097–99), and those that followed, were motivated as much by the desire to acquire estates as to restore Christian dominance to the Holy Land. Egypt, however, was not attacked until 1167, by which time the Crusader kingdom held the former Fatimid coastal area of Palestine. Outraged at the fraternization between Franks and Fatimids, the Seljuk Sultan, Nur al-Din, sent an expedition to Cairo to repel them. The sultan's deputy, Shirkoh, occupied Upper Egypt, while his nephew, Salah al-Din al-Ayyubi – known to Europe as Saladin – took possession of Alexandria.

THE AYYUBIDS (1171–1250)

On the death of the last Fatimid khalif in 1171, **Salah al-Din** became ruler of Egypt. To this day he remains a hero in the Arab world, a ruler renowned for his personal modesty, generosity, culture and political acumen. Having no pretensions to religious leadership, Salah al-Din chose for himself the secular title of *Al-Sultan* (the power) rather than that of khalif, giving his family's name – Ayyub – to the dynasty that succeeded him. Of his 24-year reign, he spent only eight years in Cairo, the rest being spent in **liberating Crusader-held territory**. By 1183, Syria had been won back and in 1187 Jerusalem was recaptured.

In Cairo, Salah al-Din built a fortress – today's Citadel – and expanded the Fatimid walls to enclose the city. In order to propagate Sunni orthodoxy, he also introduced the Seljuk institution of the **madrassa** or teaching mosque, thus turning Cairo into a great centre of learning. Hospitals were endowed, too, and the pharaonic canal at Fayoum was reopened.

Following his peaceful death in Damascus in 1193, Salah al-Din's eastern territories fragmented into principalities, though Egypt remained united under the Ayyubids. His nephew, **Al-Kamil** (1218–38), repulsed the Fifth Crusade. The last of the dynasty, **Ayyub** (1240–49), built up a formidable army of Turkish-speaking Qipchak slaves from the Black Sea region, and he himself married a slave girl, **Shagar al-Durr** (Tree of Pearls).

It was Shagar al-Durr who took power following Ayyub's death, ruling openly as sultana until the Abbasid khalifs insisted that she take a husband, quoting the Prophet's words: "Woe to the nations ruled by women." Jealous of her power and warned by astrologers that he would die at a woman's hands, her husband, Aybak, planned to take a second wife, whereupon she had him murdered. She herself was assassinated soon afterwards, but her henchman, **Beybars the Crossbowman**, clawed his way to power, inaugurating the Mamluke era.

THE MAMLUKES (1250–1517)

Beybars was a commander among the foreign troops – the Mamlukes – on whom the later Ayyubids depended. Following his accession, **Mamluke amirs** (military leaders) retained control of Egypt for the next three centuries, each sultan intriguing his way up the ranks to assume the throne by *coup d'état* or assassination.

BAHRI MAMLUKES (1250–1382)

The **Bahri** (River) **Mamlukes**, named after their garrison by the Nile and predominantly Turkic, formed the first of these military dynasties. The dynasty was founded by **Qalaoun**, who poisoned Beybars's heirs to inherit the throne. He sponsored numerous buildings in Cairo, and established relations as far afield as Ceylon and East Africa, concluding treaties with the Hapsburg Emperor Rudolph and other European princes. His son, **Khalil**, forced the remaining Crusaders from their stronghold in Acre in 1291.

Qalaoun's son **Mohammed al-Nasir** (1294–1340) was another great builder and power-broker. He concluded treaties with the

Mongols, after defeating them in Syria, and strengthened political and trade ties with Europe. After his death a series of weak relatives were barely able to hold the throne in the face of conflicts between rival Mamluke factions.

BURGI MAMLUKES (1382–1517)

In 1382 the sultanate was seized by **Barquq**, one of the Circassian **Burgi** (Tower) **Mamlukes** from the garrison below the Citadel. To finance his campaigns against the **Mongols**, who by 1387 were on the borders of Syria, he had to impose punitive taxes that beggared the economy.

Hardships were exacerbated by famine and plague during the reign of his son, **Farag** (1399–1405), and it was only under Sultan **Barsbey** (1422–37) that Egypt regained some of its power. Barsbey established friendly relations with the new power in the north, the Ottoman Turks, and expanded trade in the Indian Ocean. But although the next hundred years saw relative peace and security, the Egyptian economy remained shaky.

The country experienced a brief revival under the rule of **Qaitbey** (1468–1495), though his lavish building programme imposed a huge burden. The 46th, and penultimate sultan, **Qansuh al-Ghuri** (1501–16), suffered the loss of customary revenues after Vasco da Gama discovered the Cape of Good Hope, dealing a crippling blow to Egypt's spice trade monopoly. Worse was to come, as the **Ottoman Turks** consolidated their northern empire, defeating the Shi'ite Persians and then attacking Mamluke territory in northern Syria. In 1516, Al-Ghuri was killed in battle and his successor, Tumanbey, was executed in Cairo by the Ottomans in 1517.

OTTOMAN EGYPT (1517–1789)

Even after the Turkish conquest, the Mamlukes remained powerful figures, running the administration of what was now a province of the vast Ottoman Empire. Government was provided by a series of **pashas**, career officials trained in Istanbul. As long as taxes were received, the Ottomans interfered little with Egyptian affairs and Cairo retained its importance as a religious, if not cultural or commercial, centre.

The Mamluke army continued to grow with the import of Caucasian slaves and by the end of the sixteenth century had become powerful enough to depose a pasha, although the

Ottomans still held overall control. The growing power of the highest rank of the military corps – **the Beys** – posed a challenge to that of the pashas. Their arbitrary taxes, profligate ways and internal rivalry dominated events.

Meanwhile, economic decline, accelerated by changes in European shipping routes, and an outbreak of plague in 1719, left the country in a sorry shape. The French traveller Volney, visiting around 1784, described a depopulated country, whose capital was crumbling and surrounded by mounds of rubbish.

FRENCH OCCUPATION 1798–1802

At the end of the eighteenth century, Egypt became a pawn in the struggle for power between France and Britain. **Napoleon** saw Egypt as a means to disrupt British commerce and eventually overthrow their rule in India. In 1798, his fleet landed at Alexandria, where he issued a proclamation that began with the Islamic *bismillah* ("In the name of God . . ."); stated his aim of liberating Egypt from the "riffraff of slaves"; and concluded that he respected Allah, his Prophet and the Koran more than the Mamlukes did.

Although Napoleon routed the Mamlukes at Imbaba and occupied Cairo, he left his fleet exposed at Abu Qir Bay, where it was attacked and destroyed by the British under Nelson. With his grand vision in tatters, and facing a declaration of war from the Ottoman sultan, Napoleon returned secretly to France. General Kléber, whom he left in charge, had a victory over the Ottomans, but was then assassinated. When his successor, General Menou, took charge, declared his conversion to Islam, and proclaimed Egypt a **French protectorate**, the British invaded from Abu Qir and occupied Alexandria. Combined Ottoman-British forces then took Damietta and Cairo, and the French were forced to surrender. Under the Capitulation Agreement, the archeological treasures gathered by Napoleon's savants were surrendered to Britain – which is why the **Rosetta Stone** ended up in the British Museum rather than the Louvre.

MOHAMMED ALI AND HIS HEIRS (1805–92)

After the expulsion of the French a power struggle ensued, which was won by **Mohammed Ali**, an officer in the Albanian Corps of the Ottoman forces. Widely regarded as the founder of modern Egypt, his dynasty was to change Egypt more radically than any ruler since Salah al-Din.

The Ottomans confirmed Mohammed Ali as **Pasha** in 1805, whereupon he proceeded to decapitate – literally and figuratively – what remained of the Mamluke power structure. The first time was on the occasion of his accession, where he tricked them into a coup attempt; six years later, he dispensed with the rest of the Mamluke leadership, inviting 470 Beys to a feast at the Citadel and slaughtering the lot.

Though nominally a vassal of the Ottoman sultan, Mohammed Ali's control was absolute. He confiscated private land for his own use and set about modernizing Egypt with European expertise, building railways, factories and canals. Meanwhile, his son Ibrahim led a murderous campaign to subjugate northern **Sudan**, of which the only positive result was the introduction of a special kind of **cotton** – henceforth Egypt's major cash crop.

When Mohammed Ali died insane in 1849, his power greatly reduced after disastrous adventurism in Greece and Syria, he was succeeded by **Abbas** (1848–54), who closed the country's factories and schools and opened Egypt to free trade, thus delaying the country's industrial development for the next century.

Abbas's successor, **Said Pasha** (1854–63), granted a concession to a French engineer, **Ferdinand de Lesseps**, to build the **Suez Canal**. The project was completed in 1869, by which time **Khedive Ismail** (1863–79) was in power. An ambitious and enlightened ruler, Ismail transformed Cairo, spending lavishly on modernization. However, exorbitant interest rates had to be paid on loans from European lenders. Egyptian indebtedness spiralled and, to stave off bankruptcy, Ismail sold his Suez Canal shares to the British government in 1875.

He was deposed and succeeded by his son **Tewfiq** (1879–92), whose own financial control was limited by the French and British, to the disgust of patriotic Egyptians. A group of army officers forced him to make power-sharing concessions and to appoint their leader, **Ahmed Orabi**, as Minister of War. France and Britain responded by sending in the gunboats, shelling Alexandria and landing an army at Ismailiya, which subsequently routed Orabi's forces at Tell el-Kebir and restored Tewfiq as a puppet ruler under British control.

BRITISH OCCUPATION ... AND NATIONALISM

Britain's stated intention was to set Egyptian affairs in order and then withdraw, but its interests dictated a more active and permanent involvement. From 1883 to 1907, Egypt was controlled by the British Consul-General, Sir Evelyn Baring, later **Lord Cromer**, who coined the term "Veiled Protectorate" to describe the relationship between the two countries.

The emergence of the **Mahdi** in Sudan accelerated the trend towards direct British involvement in military and civil affairs. Sudan was nominally an Egyptian khedival possession – a status quo which the British, ostensibly, moved to protect. However, Britain was clearly pursuing its own interests, and dominating Egyptian government to the extent of replacing its key officials with British colonial personnel. Egyptian resentment at this usurpation of authority found expression both under Tewfiq's son, **Abbas II**, who came to power in 1892, and in a nationalist movement led by a young lawyer, **Mustafa Kamil**. To ameliorate the situation, the British made a series of reforms and allowed Orabi to return from exile in Ceylon.

Economically, however, Egypt was effectively a colony, with Britain supplying all the country's manufactured goods, and in turn encouraging Egyptian dependence on cotton exports. In order to grow cotton, the *fellaheen* had to take out loans; when prices fell, many were forced to sell up to large landowners.

TOWARDS INDEPENDENCE

Politically, things came to a head when Turkey entered **World War I** on the side of Germany, in November 1916. Egypt was still nominally a province of the Ottoman Empire, so to protect its interests – the Suez Canal and free passage to the East – Britain declared Egypt a protectorate. By 1917, **Fouad**, the sixth son of Ismail, was khedive of Egypt, with Sir Reginald Wingate its High Commissioner.

The **nationalist movement** flourished under wartime conditions. In 1918, its leader, **Sa'ad Zaghloul**, presented the High Commissioner with a demand for autonomy, which was rejected. The request to send a del-

egation (*Wafd*) to London led to Zaghloul's arrest and deportation to Malta, a decision rescinded after nationwide anti-British riots. In 1922 Britain abolished the protectorate and recognized Egypt as an independent state, but kept control of the legal system, communications, defence and the Suez Canal. In March 1922, Fouad assumed the title of king.

The years between independence and World War II saw a struggle for power between the king, the British and the nationalist **Wafd Party**. Backed by the masses, the Wafd won landslide elections, but King Fouad retained power and the backing of the British. His son, **King Farouk**, succeeded him to the throne in 1935 and a year later signed a twenty-year **Anglo-Egyptian treaty**, which ended British occupation but empowered British forces to remain in the Suez Canal Zone. In 1937, Egypt joined the League of Nations, but the outbreak of World War II halted its move to complete independence.

WORLD WAR II

During **World War II**, Egypt served a vital strategic role as a British base in the Middle East. The Wafd leadership went along with support for the Allies – on the tacit understanding that full independence would be granted after the war – keeping internal tensions controlled. Cairo itself, however, became an extraordinary centre of international power-broking, with its British political-military command and exiled Balkan royals and governments.

Rommel's **Afrika Korps** came within 111 kilometres of Alexandria, but was repulsed by the **Eighth Army** under General Montgomery at the **Battle of El-Alamein** in October 1942. Thereafter the tide of war turned in the Western Desert Campaign and the Allies continued to advance across North Africa, through Libya and Tunisia.

POST-WAR MANOEUVRINGS

On **conclusion of the war**, the Wafd demanded the evacuation of British troops and unification with Sudan – in opposition to British plans for the latter's self-government. Popular resentment was expressed in anti-British riots and strikes, supported by the **Muslim Brotherhood**, which led to clashes with British troops. In January 1947, British troops were evacuated from Alexandria and the Canal Zone.

Following the declaration of the state of **Israel** in May 1948, Egypt joined Iraq, Syria and Jordan in a military invasion. The defeat of the Arab forces was followed by a UN-organized treaty in February 1949 that left the coastal **Gaza Strip** of Palestine under Egyptian administration. Many of the Egyptian officers who fought in this war were left disgusted by the incompetence and corruption of their superiors: it was from the officers' ranks that many of the leading lights of the 1952 Revolution were to emerge.

THE 1952 REVOLUTION

For the time being, the country experimented with democracy, holding its first **elections** in ten years. The Wafd won a majority and formed a government with Nahas Pasha as prime minister. A course for crisis was set, as the **Suez Canal** – which the British still controlled – loomed increasingly large. In 1952, Nahas was dismissed by King Farouk after abrogating the 1936 Treaty with Britain, and the army was sent out onto the streets to quell anti-British protests.

Reaction was swift. On July 23, 1952, a group of conspiratorial **Free Officers** seized power and forced the **abdication of King Farouk**. General Naguib, the official leader of the group, was made commander of the armed forces and became prime minister, but real power lay in the hands of the nine officers of the **Revolutionary Command Council** (RCC), foremost amongst whom was Colonel **Gamal Abdel Nasser**.

Under RCC direction, the constitution was revoked, political parties dissolved, the monarchy abolished and Egypt declared a **republic** (July 26, 1953). Meanwhile, a struggle for power was taking place behind the scenes, as Naguib attempted to step beyond his figurehead status and moderate the revolutionary impulses of the RCC. After being implicated in an attempt on Nasser's life at Alexandria in 1954, Naguib was placed under house arrest. Nasser became acting head of state and in June 1956 was confirmed as president.

THE NASSER ERA (1956–70)

President Nasser dominated Egypt and the Arab world until his death in 1970, his ideology of Arab nationalism and socialism making him supremely popular with the masses (if not always their governments) from Iraq to Morocco. Under his leadership, Egypt was at the forefront of **anti-colonialism**, lending support to liberation struggles in Algeria, sub-Saharan Africa and other regions. Nasser also helped to set up the **Non-Aligned Movement** with Yugoslavia, India and Indonesia in 1955.

DIPLOMACY AND WAR

Nasser's most urgent priority, from the start, was to assert Egyptian control over the **Suez Canal**. In 1954 he reached agreement for the withdrawal of British troops from the Canal Zone, though the canal's management and profits were to remain in foreign hands. At the same time he was seeking credits from the World Bank to finance construction of the Aswan High Dam, and for weapons to rearm Egyptian forces, depleted from the 1948 war.

When the Soviet Union offered to supply the latter, the United States vetoed loans for the dam. Committed to the Aswan plan, Nasser had little alternative but to **nationalize the Suez Canal**, in order to secure revenue. This he did in July 1956.

His action was regarded by the West, and especially by Britain, as a threat to vital interests, and an unholy alliance was formed to combat the "Arab Hitler". Britain and France concluded a secret agreement with Israel, whose **invasion of Sinai** in October 1956 was to provide the pretext for their own military intervention. Following massive bombardment of the zone, and British paratroop landings in Port Said, the United States stepped in to impose a solution, threatening to destabilize the British economy unless their forces were withdrawn. The American motivation was to keep Britain and France from gaining control of the Middle East, and the Arabs from moving en masse into the Soviet camp. In the event, the canal was reopened under full Egyptian control and Nasser emerged from the **Suez Crisis** as a champion of Arab nationalism.

On a wave of **pan-Arabist** sentiment, Egypt and Syria united to form the **United Arab Republic** (UAR) in 1958: an unworkable arrangement that foundered within three years. Nasser also intervened in the **Yemen civil war**, supporting the revolutionary faction, to the extent of authorizing the use of poison gas against royalist forces. On a broader political front, he moved closer to the Soviet Union, accepting technical and military assistance on a massive scale, to help build the Aswan Dam and to counter an increasingly well-armed, US-supplied Israel. Meeting in Cairo in 1964, the **Arab League** set aside funds for the formation of the **Palestine Liberation Organization**.

War was again on the horizon. When Israel threatened to invade Syria in 1967, Nasser sent Egyptian forces into Sinai, ordered UN monitors to withdraw, and blockaded the Tiran Straits, cutting shipping to the Israeli port of Eilat. Israel responded with a pre-emptive strike, destroying the Egyptian air force on the ground and seizing the entire Sinai. This **Six Day War** resulted in permanent Israeli occupation of Sinai and the Gaza Strip, the West Bank and the Golan Heights. It was a shattering defeat for the Arabs, and Nasser in particular, who proffered his resignation to the public, only resuming the presidency after vast demonstrations of support on the streets.

The Six Day War had no official resolution, merely subsiding into a **War of Attrition**, which was to drag on for the next two years. From their positions in Sinai, Israeli forces bombarded Egypt's Canal cities and even Cairo and Middle Egypt suffered bombing raids. Egypt, meanwhile, was rearming with Soviet assistance and struggling to deal with millions of refugees from the Canal Zone and the newly occupied Gaza Strip.

PROGRESS AND REPRESSION

Amid the political drama of Suez and the wars with Israel, it is easy to overlook the **social achievements** of the Nasser era. One of the first acts of the Revolutionary Command Council was to break up the old feudal estates, transferring **land** to the *fellaheen*. As a result of the **Aswan Dam**, the amount of land under cultivation increased by fifteen percent – exceeding Egypt's population growth for the first time. The Dam's electricity also powered a huge new **industrial base**, which was established virtually from scratch.

Similarly radical progress was made in the fields of **education and health care**. The number of pupils in school doubled, and included both sexes for the first time. As a result of a huge programme of local health centres, and the doubling of the number of doctors, average life expectancy rose from 43 to 52 years.

The downside of Nasser's socialism was a heavily bureaucratic, often Soviet-modelled system. Political life was stifled by the merging of all parties into the **Arab Socialist Union** (**ASU**). Opponents of the regime were not tolerated: censorship, torture, show trials and political internment were widespread.

Nevertheless, **Nasser's death** – from a heart attack – in September 1970 came as a profound shock to the whole Arab world. His funeral procession in Cairo was the largest the country has ever seen.

EGYPT UNDER SADAT (1970–81)

Nasser's successor was his vice president, **Anwar Sadat**, whom the ASU hierarchy confirmed as president in October 1970. His role was to reform an Egypt demoralized by defeat in the 1967 war, economic stagnation and austerity. His first significant act was to announce a **"corrective revolution"**, reversing the policy of centralized economic control, and expelling over a thousand Soviet advisors.

Again, however, social and economic affairs were overshadowed by military developments. In concert with Syria and Jordan, Egypt launched a new campaign against Israel. On October 6, 1973, Egyptian forces crossed the Suez Canal, storming the "invincible" Bar-Lev Line to enter Israeli-occupied Sinai. This **October War** (aka 10th Ramadan/Yom Kippur War) ultimately turned against the Arabs, but enhanced their bargaining position and dealt a blow to Israeli self-confidence. In addition, Egypt regained a strip of territory to the east of the Suez Canal.

THE OPEN DOOR POLICY

After the war, extensive changes took place in Egypt. An amnesty was granted to political prisoners, press censorship was lifted and some political parties, including the Muslim Brotherhood, were allowed. Equally important was Sadat's economic policy of *infitah* or **"open door"**, designed to encourage private and foreign investment and to reduce the role of the state in the economy.

Helped by Gulf Arab investments – a reward for the October War – and stimulated by the reconstruction of the Canal cities, the economy boomed. However, the benefits were distributed totally unevenly. While the number of millionaires rose from 500 to 17,000 between 1975 and 1981, and an affluent middle class developed, the condition of the urban poor and peasants worsened. Some five million families subsisted on less than US$30 a month, and one and a half million Egyptians migrated to work in the Gulf states.

In 1977, when the International Monetary Fund insisted on the removal of subsidies on basic foodstuffs, there were nationwide **food riots**. Sadat saw the crunch coming and needed a major injection of Western capital.

CAMP DAVID AND AFTERWARDS

In 1977 Sadat went to Jerusalem, the first Arab leader to visit Israel. This dramatic step, accompanied by a total realignment of Egyptian foreign policy towards the United States, has been explained in two ways. One theory holds that it was solely motivated by the desire for US investment; the other, by Israel's acquisition of nuclear weapons, which rendered impossible a military solution in the region.

Under the resulting, US-sponsored **Camp David Agreement** of 1978, Egypt recognized Israel's right to exist and Israel agreed to withdraw from Sinai. This independent peace treaty, which failed to resolve the Palestinian issue, outraged Arab opinion. Meeting in Baghdad, the Arab League Council decided to withdraw their ambassadors to Egypt, sever economic and political links, and transfer the League's headquarters from Cairo to Tunis.

At home, Sadat encouraged the rise of Islamic political forces to counter leftist influences. But as the Muslim Brotherhood grew stronger and protested against the economic slump and Camp David, Sadat clamped down, with wholesale arrests of critics. In this charged atmosphere, **Sadat's assassination** by Islamic militants in October 1981 was not altogether surprising.

THE 1980S, 1990S AND BEYOND: MUBARAK'S EGYPT

Sadat's policies have for the most part been continued, with rather more caution, by his successor **Hosni Mubarak**, who took office in 1981 and remains in power at the time of writing. While sheer survival counts for something, the country's situation is as precarious as it was in the early 1970s, when the writer Naguib Mahfouz likened Egypt to a group of drowning men struggling to reach the water's surface.

THE ECONOMY

The **economy** was left in dire straits at the end of the Sadat era, and its root problems seem intractable. Less than three percent of Egypt's land is useable for agriculture, while the **population** rises by a million every nine months (it currently stands at around 64 million). Since the mid-1980s, Egypt has had to import half the food it needs, and its **national debt** has reached over US$50 billion. Without **US aid** (Egypt is the second largest recipient, after Israel), the economy would collapse. It is this economic situation that has led the government to inaugurate such schemes as the Toshka Irrigation Project, which aims to make 500,000 acres of desert fertile by irrigating it with water pumped from Lake Nasser (see p.407).

Domestic revenues, such as they are, depend on a narrow base, which is highly vulnerable to the political climate: remittances from Egyptians working abroad, crude oil production, tolls on shipping through the Suez Canal, and tourism. All of these were badly hit by the **Gulf War** of 1990–91, which led to over a million refugees returning from Kuwait and Iraq and wiped out the tourist industry for a year. The government's staunch support for US action against Iraq was rewarded by the writing-off of US$7 billion in debts, further military and economic aid, and the promise of contracts and jobs for Egyptians in the Gulf states, once the Palestinans formerly employed there had been expelled. However, prospects had hardly begun to improve when terrorist attacks on **tourists** exposed another aspect of the economy's vulnerablity.

The net result is that, for the majority of Egyptians, **living standards** are no higher than in Nasser's time, and the need for housing, jobs and land is greater than ever. Discontent is also aroused by widespread **corruption**. Governors are allowed to enrich themselves before being moved on to another province, and crooked contractors get away with erecting buildings that collapse during earthquakes. Popular belief has it that corruption extends to the very highest levels of government.

Nevertheless, in the past five years Egypt has seen massive **new investment**, both from foreign and domestic sources. The gap between

Egypt's rich and poor remains the same, but the **IMF** now rates Egypt as a genuine emerging market.

DOMESTIC POLITICS AND FOREIGN AFFAIRS

Mubarak's cautious liberalization of the media and parliamentary politics has given a democratic gloss to an authoritarian system, essentially unchanged since Nasser's time. In September 1999, a national referendum asked "Do you want Mubarak to continue as president?". The result – which saw Mubarak endorsed for a fourth six-year term – surprised no-one, and mutterings about a more democratic election process were predictably subdued. Although a diverse press is tolerated, the government retains – and exercises – the right of **censorship**, banning reports on human rights violations and confiscating "atheist works" at the Cairo Book Fair.

As the third president to have emerged from the armed forces, Mubarak is even more beholden to them than his predecessors. Ex-military and police officers hold top jobs in civilian life, and **internal security** is a constant preoccupation. According to Amnesty International, torture is widely used to extract information, or simply as a punishment. Military courts have sentenced over 100 convicted bombers to hang, and a similar number have been shot while "resisting arrest" – with no end in sight to the war between Islamic radicals and the state. Unable to tackle the root causes of discontent,

the Egyptian government blames it on **subversion** by Iran or Sudan – which has certainly occurred. There's little doubt that the Sudanese regime played a key role in the attempt to kill Mubarak during his visit to Ethiopia in June 1995.

Mubarak's **foreign policy** involves a delicate balancing of priorities. He has maintained a "cold peace" with Israel, while managing to restore ties with other Arab states, which in 1990 re-admitted Egypt to the Arab League, whose headquarters have since returned to Cairo. But links with the US remain paramount, with both governments regarding Iran as the chief threat to their interests in the region, now that Iraq's power has been reduced. Although this was affirmed at the Sharm el-Sheikh Summit in 1996, any pretence of unity over the Middle East peace process was subsequently dashed by the Israeli massacre of refugees at Qana and the election of a conservative Likud government in Israel, opposed to trading land for peace.

The 1999 election of Ehud Barak may see the return of a more moderate stance in Israel, but Egypt remains impaled on the **contradictions** of its relationship with America, Israel and the Arab world. Mindful of what happened to Sadat, US policy-makers fear to pin all their hopes on Mubarak – who has now survived three assassination attempts, the most recent being in September 1999 – and have hedged their bets by establishing contact with the domestic opposition.

ISLAM

It's difficult to get any grasp of Egypt without first knowing something of Islam. What follows is a very basic background: some theory, some history and an idea of Egypt's place in the modern Islamic world.

BEGINNINGS: PRACTICE AND BELIEF

Islam was a new religion born of the wreckage of the Greco-Roman world around the south of the Mediterranean. Its founder, a merchant named **Mohammed** from the wealthy city of Mecca (now in Saudi Arabia), was chosen as God's Prophet; in about 609 AD, he began to hear divine messages, which were later transcribed into the **Koran**, Islam's holy book. This was the same God worshipped by Jews and Christians – Jesus is one of the minor prophets in Islam – but Muslims claim He had been misunderstood by both earlier religions.

The distinctive feature of this new faith was directness – a reaction to the increasing complexity of established religions and an obvious attraction. In Islam there is no intermediary between man and God (**Allah**) in the form of an institutionalized priesthood or complicated liturgy; and worship, in the form of prayer, is a direct and personal communication with God. Believers face five essential requirements, the so-called **"Pillars of Faith"**: prayer five times daily, the pilgrimage (*Hadj*) to Mecca, the Ramadan fast, a religious levy, and – most fundamental of all – the acceptance that "There is

no God but Allah and Mohammed is His Prophet".

THE PILLARS OF FAITH

The Pillars of Faith are still central to Muslim life, articulating and informing daily existence. Ritual **prayers** are the most visible. Bearing in mind that the Islamic day begins at sunset, the five daily times are sunset, after dark, dawn, noon and afternoon. Prayers can be performed anywhere, but preferably in a mosque. In the past, and even today in some places, a muezzin (prayer crier) would climb his minaret each time and summon the faithful.

Nowadays, the call is likely to be pre-recorded; even so, this most distinctive of Islamic sounds has a beauty all of its own, especially when neighbouring muezzins are audible simultaneously. Their message is simplicity itself: "God is most great (*Allahu Akbar*). I testify that there is no God but Allah. I testify that Mohammed is His Prophet. Come to prayer, come to security. God is great." Another phrase is added in the morning: "Prayer is better than sleep."

Prayers are preceded by ritual washing and are spoken with the feet bare. Facing Mecca (the direction indicated in a mosque by the *mihrab* or niche), the worshipper recites the *Fathah*, the first chapter of the Koran: "Praise be to God, Lord of the worlds, the Compassionate, the Merciful, King of the Day of Judgement. Only thee do we worship and thine aid do we seek. Guide us on the straight path, the path of those on whom thou hast bestowed thy grace, not the path of those who incur thine anger nor of those who go astray." The same words are then repeated twice in the prostrate position, with some interjections of *Allahu Akbar*. It is a highly ritualized procedure, the prostrate position symbolic of the worshipper's role as servant (Islam literally means "submission"), and the sight of thousands of people going through the same motions simultaneously in a mosque is a powerful one. On Islam's holy day, Friday, all believers are expected to attend prayers in their local grand mosque. Here the whole community comes together in worship led by an *imam*, who may also deliver the *khutba*, or sermon.

Ramadan is the name of the ninth month in the lunar Islamic calendar, the month in which the Koran was revealed to Mohammed. For the whole of the month, believers must obey a rigorous fast (the custom was originally modelled on Jewish and Christian practice), forsaking all forms of consumption between sunrise and sundown; this includes food, drink, cigarettes and any form of sexual contact. Only a few categories of people are exempted: travellers, children, pregnant women and warriors engaged in a *jihad*, or holy struggle. Given the climates in which many Muslims live, the fast is a formidable undertaking, but in practice it becomes a time of intense celebration.

The pilgrimage, or **Hadj**, to Mecca is an annual event, with millions flocking to Mohammed's birthplace from all over the world. Here they go through several days of rituals, the central one being a sevenfold circumambulation of the Ka'ba, before kissing a black stone set in its wall. Islam requires that all believers go on a *Hadj* as often as is practically possible, but for the poor it may well be a once-in-a-lifetime occasion, and is sometimes replaced by a series of visits to lesser, local shrines – in Egypt, for instance, to the mosques of Saiyida Zeinab or El-Hussein in Cairo.

Based on these central articles, the new Islamic faith proved to be inspirational. Mohammed's own Arab nation was soon converted, and the Arabs then proceeded to carry their religion far and wide in an extraordinarily rapid territorial expansion.

DEVELOPMENT IN EGYPT

Islam's **arrival in Egypt**, in 640, coincided with widespread native resentment of Byzantine rule and its particular version of Christianity. By promising to respect Egyptian Christians and Jews as "people of the Book", the Muslim leader **Amr** got acquiescence, if not immediate support, from the population, in the wake of the Arab conquest. For many Egyptians who had found Christianity a more valid religion than the old pagan, polytheistic theology, Islam must have seemed a logical simplification, capturing the essence of human relationships with an all-powerful god.

Early on, the spread of Islam was accompanied by a somewhat bizarre conflict of interest. The Arabs wished to spread the faith, yet their administration depended on finance raised by a poll tax levied on non-Muslims. A balance was maintained for a while, but towards the end of the ninth century, rulers began to use the tax as a punitive measure, alongside a series of repressive acts directed against the Christian

and Jewish faiths. Khalif al-Hakim, in particular, embarked on a programme of destroying churches and synagogues. However, it was not until the eleventh century that Cairo attained a **Muslim majority**, and not until the thirteenth century for Egypt as a whole.

The original Arab dynasties of Egypt subscribed to **Sunni Islam** – the more "orthodox" branch of the religion, dominant then, as now, in most parts of the Arab world. However, the Fatimid dynasty, which took control of Egypt in 969, signalled a shift to **Shi'ite** Islam, which was to continue (among the rulers, at least) until late in the twelfth century. Under the Ayyubid dynasty that followed, Egypt reverted, permanently as it turned out, to Sunni adherence, with orthodoxy propagated through the new institution of the **madrassa** – a theological college attached to a mosque.

Orthodoxy, by its very nature, has to be an urban-based tradition. Learned men – lawyers, Koranic scholars and others – could only congregate in the cities where, gathered together and known collectively as the **ulema**, they regulated the faith. In Sunni Islam, the *ulema* divide into four schools (*madhahib*): *Hanbali*, *Maliki*, *Hanafi* and *Shafi'i* – the last two of which predominate in Egypt. The *ulema* of Cairo's great **Mosque of Al-Azhar** is regarded as the ultimate theological authority by most Sunnis outside of the Gulf Arab states.

SHEIKHS AND SUFIS

Alongside this formal religious establishment, Egypt also developed a **popular religious culture**, manifested in the veneration of sheikhs and the formation of Sufi brotherhoods – both of which remain important today.

Sheikhs are basically local holy men: people who developed reputations for sanctity and learning. There is no set process for their sanctification in Islam – only acclamation – so the names change with the locality. Similar to sheikhs are individuals revered simply as **saiyid** (lord) or **saiyida** (lady), often due to their direct decent from the Prophet's line. Important Egyptian examples include Saiyid el-Hussein, Mohammed's grandson and the son of Ali, and the Prophet's granddaughters, Saiyida Zeinab and Saiyida Nafisa.

Although the Koran explicitly prohibits monasticism and isolation from the community, Islam soon developed religious orders dedicated to asceticism and a mystical experience of God. Collectively known as the **Sufis**, these groups generally coalesced around a charismatic teacher, from whom they derived their name. The largest of these brotherhoods (*tariqas*) in Egypt are the **Rifai**, the **Ahmediya** and the **Shadhiliyya** – who can be seen at moulids ("saint's day" festivals) parading with their distinctive banners.

TOWARDS CRISIS

With all its different forms, Islam permeates almost every aspect of Egyptian society. Unlike Christianity (or at least Protestant Christianity), which has accepted the separation of church and state, Islam sees no such distinction. Civil law was provided by the *sharia*, the religious law contained in the Koran, and intellectual life by the *madrassas* and Al-Azhar university.

The religious basis of Arab study and intellectual life did not prevent its **scholars and scientists** from producing work that was hundreds of years ahead of contemporary "Dark Age" Europe. The medical treatises of Ibn Sina (known in Europe as Avicenna) and the piped water and sewage systems of Fustat are just two Egyptian examples. Arab work in developing and transmitting Greco-Roman culture was also vital to the whole development of the European Renaissance.

By this time, however, the Islamic world was beginning to move away from the West. The **Crusades** were one enduring influence towards division. Another was the Islamic authorities themselves, who were increasingly suspicious (like the Western church) of any challenge and actively discouraging of innovation. At first it did not matter in political terms that Islamic culture became static. But by the end of the eighteenth century, Europe was ready to take advantage. Napoleon's expedition to Egypt in 1798 marked the beginning of a century in which virtually every Islamic country came under the control of a **European power**.

Islam cannot, of course, be held solely responsible for the Muslim world's material decline. But because it influences every part of its believers' lives, and because East–West rivalry had always been viewed in primarily religious terms, the nineteenth and twentieth centuries saw something of a **crisis in religious confidence**. Why had Islam's former power now passed to infidel foreigners?

THE ISLAMIST RESPONSE

Reactions and answers veered between two extremes. There were those who felt that Islam should try to incorporate some of the West's secularism and materialism; on the other side, there were movements holding that Islam should turn its back on the West, purify itself of all corrupt additions and thus rediscover its former power.

The earliest exponent of the latter view was the **Muslim Brotherhood** (*Ikhwan el-Muslimeen*), founded in Ismailiya by **Hassan el-Banna** in 1928. The Brotherhood preached a moral renewal of Islam, established a network of schools and training centres, and set up clandestine paramilitary groups. It was aimed as much against the corrupt feudal and khedival institutions as Western imperialism.

Within fifteen years, the Brotherhood had spread through Egypt and spawned offshoots through the Middle East. Its terrorist activities prompted a violent state response, with its banning by King Farouk, whose bodyguards assassinated El-Banna in 1949.

After Egyptian independence, and the Revolution of 1952, the legitimized Brotherhood rapidly became disillusioned with Nasser's secular nationalism. In 1954, two Brothers attempted to assassinate him during a public meeting in Alexandria. Mass arrests followed and the Brotherhood went underground again, not surfacing in public until the Sadat era, when the government regarded it as a useful counterweight to the left.

By this time the Brotherhood had moderated its strategy, if not its aims, and its tacit cooperation with the state led to the emergence of more radical groups. One such group, *Al-Taqfir w'al-Higrah* (Repentance and Holy Flight), gained notoriety for attacking boutiques and nightclubs in Cairo during the food riots of 1977. Another faction, established within Egypt's Military Academy, planned a *coup d'état* but was nipped in the bud. Most famous – and effective – was the organization known as **Al-Jihad** (Holy Struggle), which assassinated Sadat and attempted to launch a revolution in Assyut in 1981.

Under Mubarak, the mainstream Islamic opposition was allowed to establish clinics and schools for the poor, achieving a greater influence over cultural life. During the late 1980s, **Gamaat Islamiya** (Islamic Societies) captured the professional unions, and thousands of

Egyptians put their savings into Islamic investment houses, which offered higher returns than ordinary banks. When these went bankrupt amid accusations of fraud, the Islamic movement's credibility was badly dented, but its prompt distribution of aid after the 1991 Cairo earthquake redeemed its reputation amongst the urban poor.

Meanwhile, the struggle with Islamic militants spread far beyond Middle Egypt, as bombings and shootings provoked mass arrests and torture, answered by further acts of **terrorism**. In May 1992, gunmen massacred thirteen Christian farmers at Sanabu, heightening fears of sectarian conflict. Two months later, the liberal writer **Farag Fouda** was assassinated for daring to mock the "unenlightened groups of darkness" (*Gamaat Islamiya*) and debate ideas in public with Islamic fundamentalists. Subsequent attacks on tourists, culminating in the 1997 massacre of 58 foreigners, made headlines abroad and crippled a crucial source of revenue. In other ways, however, the authorities deferred to the Islamist agenda, by jailing 300 Egyptians for the "crime" of converting to Christianity, and ruling that a Cairo professor found "guilty" of apostasy must separate from his wife. As recently as January 2000, nineteen Copts and two Muslims were killed in clashes at El-Qusiya.

Although the government accuses Iran and Sudan of fomenting terrorism, more profound causes lie in Egypt and the wider world. Egypt's stagnant economy breeds despair, and its corrupt elite provokes anger. The appeal of Islam as a radical solution gains strength from its historic stature – by returning to the "pure" Islam of the Prophet, it is argued, Muslims can reunite and pursue their destiny, free of the arbitrary nation-states and parasitical regimes bequeathed by imperialism. It also derives from the widening **gulf between Muslim and Western perceptions** of world events. Having swallowed decades of Western indulgence towards Israeli violence, contrasted with a crushing response to Iraq's invasion of Kuwait, the war in Bosnia was seen by most Muslims as one of Christian genocide, abetted by the Western powers.

This shared outrage masks two **conflicts within the Islamic world**. One is between visions of society: whether secular or Islamic principles should predominate, and to what extent a creed formulated in the seventh century is relevant to today's needs. The other is less universal than geopolitical, as Iran and Egypt vie for hegemony over the Persian Gulf and the wider Arab world, each reckoning the other's gains as a setback.

MONUMENTAL CHRONOLOGY

*The chronology below is designed for general reference of monuments and dynasties or rulers. For simplicity, only the **major figures of each dynasty** or era are listed; likewise the monuments and artefacts.*

*The following **abbreviations** are used: EAM (Egyptian Antiquities Museum in Cairo), IAM (Islamic Arts Museum in Cairo) and BM (British Museum in London).*

c.250,000 BC	**Hunter-gathering hominids** roam the savannahs.	Stone tools have been discovered in gravel beds of Upper Egypt and Nubia.
c.25,000 BC	**Late Paleolithic** era. Onset of desertification.	Ostrich eggs and flints have been found beneath dunes of Great Sand Sea.

PRE-DYNASTIC EGYPT

c.5000 BC	**Badarian culture**.	Pottery, jewellery and ivory excavated at village of El-Badari in Upper Egypt.
c.4000 BC	**Naqada I culture**.	Burnished pottery and granite mace heads have been found near Qus in Upper Egypt.

ARCHAIC PERIOD (c.3100–2686 BC)

c.3100 BC	**Unification of the Two Lands** (Upper and Lower Egypt) by **Menes**.	Foundation of Memphis; Palette of Narmer (EAM); Stele of Peribsen (BM).

OLD KINGDOM (c.2686–2181 BC)

2686–2613 BC	**III Dynasty** *Zoser; Sekhemkhet; Huni.*	Step Pyramid and Unfinished Pyramid built at Saqqara; Collapsed Pyramid at Maidum.
2613–2494 BC	**IV Dynasty** *Snofru; Cheops; Chephren; Mycerinus.*	Bent Pyramid at Dahshur; Great Pyramids of Giza.
2494–2345 BC	**V Dynasty** *Userkaf; Sahure; Neferefre; Nyuserre; Unas.*	Sun Temples and Pyramids at Abu Sir; several further pyramids at Saqqara.
2345–2181 BC	**VI Dynasty** *Teti; Pepi I; Pepi II.*	More pyramids at Saqqara.

FIRST INTERMEDIATE PERIOD (c.2181–2050 BC)

2181–2160 BC	**VII and VIII Dynasties**. Period of anarchy and fragmentation of power.	
2160–2130 BC	**IX Dynasty** *Achthoes.*	Capital at Heracleopolis, near Beni Suef.
2130–2040 BC	**X Dynasty**	
2133–1991 BC	**XI Dynasty** *Inyotef Sehertowy. Nebhepetre Mentuhotpe II reunites Two Lands in 2050 BC.*	Ruined mortuary temple at Deir el-Bahri; Mentuhotpe's statue (EAM).

MIDDLE KINGDOM (c.2050–1786 BC)

1991–1786 BC	**XII Dynasty** *Amenemhat I; Senusert I and II;* *Amenemhat III.*	Pyramids at Lahun, Lisht and Hawara; rock tombs at Beni Hassan and Aswan; site of Medinet Ma'adi.

SECOND INTERMEDIATE PERIOD (c.1786–1567 BC)

1786–1603 BC	**XIII and XIV Dynasties**	
1674–1567 BC	**XV (Hyksos) Dynasty** *Khyam; Apophis I and II.*	Capital at Avaris in the Delta (with Minoan frescoes); *Rhind Mathematical* *Papyrus* (BM).
1684–1567 BC	**XVI and XVII Dynasty.** Expulsion of the Hyksos by Ahmosis.	Tombs at Qarat Hilwah.

NEW KINGDOM (c.1567–1085 BC)

1567–1320 BC	**XVIII Dynasty**. Two Lands reunited; period of imperial expansion.*Ahmosis;* *Amenophis I; Tuthmosis I and II;* *Hatshepsut; Tuthmosis III; Amenophis II* *and III; Akhenaten; Smenkhkare;* *Tutankhamun; Ay; Horemheb.*	Temple of Deir el-Bahri; site of Tell el- Amarna; royal tombs in the Valleys of the Kings and Queens at Thebes; Luxor and Karnak temples; Tutankhamun's gold (EAM).
1320–1200 BC	**XIX Dynasty** *Ramses I; Seti I; Ramses II; Merneptah;* *Seti II.*	Serapeum at Saqqara; temples at Abydos and Abu Simbel; Ramesseum and royal tombs at Thebes.
1200–1085 BC	**XX Dynasty** *Sethnakhte; Ramses III (and eight other* *minor and hopeless Ramses).*	Temple of Medinet Habu and further royal tombs at Thebes.

THIRD INTERMEDIATE PERIOD (c.1069–664 BC)

1085–945 BC	**XXI Dynasty**. Authority divided between Tanis and Thebes. *Smendes; Herihor; Psusennes I and II.*	Capital at Tanis; Treasure of Tanis (EAM); *Book of the Dead* (BM).
945–715 BC	**XXII Dynasty** *Shoshenk; Osorkon.*	Ruins at Tanis; Shoshenk's relief at Karnak.
818–715 BC	**XXIII and XXIV Dynasties**	
747–656 BC	**XXV (Nubian) Dynasty** *Piankhi; Shabaka; Taharqa; Tanutamun.*	Reliefs at Luxor; Kiosk of Taharqa at Karnak; statue of Amenirdis (EAM).

LATE PERIOD (664–332 BC)

664–525 BC	**XXVI (Saïte) Dynasty** *Psammetichus I; Necho II;* *Psammetichus II; Apries; Amasis.*	Ruins of Naucratis; steles at Ismailiya.
525–404 BC	**XXVII (Persian) Dynasty**. Persian invasion. *Cambyses; Darius I; Xerxes;* *Artaxerxes I.*	Temple of Hibis at Kharga Oasis; com- pletion of Nile–Red Sea canal; founda- tion of Babylon-in-Egypt (Cairo).

404–380 BC	**XXVIII and XXIX Dynasties**. *Amyrtaeus.*	Temple of El-Ghweeta, Kharga Oasis.
380–343 BC	**XXX Dynasty** *Nectanebo I and II.*	Additions to Philae and Karnak; ruined temple of Amun at Siwa Oasis.

PTOLEMAIC ERA (332–30 BC)

332–30 BC	**Alexander the Great** takes power, the first of **fourteen Ptolemies** to rule Egypt, the line expiring with **Cleopatra VII** (51–30BC). Influx of Hellenistic and Judaistic influence; extensive trade with Mediterranean world; foundation of **Alexandria**.	Construction (or modification) of temples of Edfu, Esna, Kom Ombo, Dendara and Philae; catacombs in Alexandria; Sanctuary of Amun at Siwa Oasis; ruins of Karanis and Qasr Qaroun in the Fayoum.

ROMAN AND BYZANTINE PERIOD (30 BC–640 AD)

30 BC	Octavian (Augustus) annexes Egypt to the **Roman Empire**.	Tomb of Kitnes and Temple of Dush in Kharga Oasis.
45 **AD**	St Mark brings **Christianity** to Egypt.	Muzawaka Tombs in Dakhla Oasis.
249–305	**Persecution of Coptic Christians** under Decius and Diocletian.	"Pompey's Pillar" at Alexandria.
313	Edict of Milan **legalizes Christianity**.	Foundation of monasteries of Wadi Natrun, St Anthony, St Paul and St Catherine.
395	Partition of Roman Empire into East and West; Egypt falls under Eastern, **Byzantine**, sphere.	Necropolis of El-Bagawat at Kharga Oasis.
451	Council of Chalcedon leads to **expulsion of Copts from Orthodox Church**.	Numerous objects in Coptic Museum (Cairo).

ARAB DYNASTIES (640–1517)

640–642	**Arab conquest** of Egypt; **introduction of Islam**.	Mosque of Amr and ruins of Fustat in Cairo.
661–750	Egypt forms part of **Umayyad Khalifate**, ruled from the dynasty's capital at Damascus.	Ceramics and pottery (IAM).
750–935	**Abbasids** depose Umayyads and form new dynasty, ruling from Baghdad. In 870 Egypt's governor, **Ibn Tulun**, declares independence, founding a dynasty which rules until 905.	Mosque of Ibn Tulun in Cairo.
935–969	**Ikhshidid dynasty** takes power in Egypt.	
969–1171	**Shi'ite Fatimid dynasty** conquers Egypt and seizes the Islamic Khalifate, which it rules from Cairo.	Mosques of Al-Azhar, Al-Hakim and Al-Aqmar, Mausoleum of Imam Al-Shafi'i, and various fortified gates, in Cairo.
1171–1250	**Salah al-Din** founds **Ayyubid dynasty** and liberates land conquered by the Crusaders. Egypt returns to **Sunni Islam**. Intrigues of **Shagar al-Durr** open the way to **Mamluke** takeover.	Madrassa-Mausoleum of Al-Silah Ayyub in Cairo; ruins of Shali in Siwa Oasis. Mausoleum of Shagar al-Durr in Cairo.

MAMLUKE DYNASTIES (1250–1517)

1250–1382 **Bahri Mamlukes**.
Qalaoun; Khalil; Mohammed al-Nasir.

In Cairo: Qalaoun's Maristan-Mausoleum-Madrassa, Mosques of Al-Nasir, House of Uthman Katkhuda, and Qasr Bashtak.

1382–1517 **Burgi Mamlukes**
Barquq; Farag; Barsbey; Qaitbey;
Qansuh al-Ghuri.

In Cairo: Barquq's Mausoleum, Madrassa and Khanqah of Barsbey, Mosque of Qaitbey, and the Ghuriya. Also, Fort Qaitbey in Alexandria.

OTTOMAN PERIOD (1517–1798)

1517   **Selim the Grim conquers Egypt**. For the next three centuries the country is ruled as an Ottoman province from Constantinople.

In Cairo: Mosques of Suleyman al-Silahdar and Suleyman Pasha; Sabil-Kuttab of Abd al-Rahman Katkhuda. Terbana Mosque in Alex.

1798–1802 French occupation of Egypt. Capitulation Agreement of 1802 leaves British in effective control of the country.

Treasures shipped off to Louvre/British Museum. European graffiti left on numerous temples.

PASHAS, KHEDIVES AND KINGS (1805–1952)

1805   **Mohammed Ali** seizes power and begins a programme of ruthless **modernization**.

Mohammed Ali Mosque in Cairo; Ras el-Tin Palace and Mahmudiya Canal in Alexandria.

Belzoni, Mariette and others pioneer digs at pharaonic sites in the Nile Valley and Delta.

1848–54 Reign of **Abbas I**.
1854–63 Reign of **Said Pasha**.

Suez Canal begun.

1863–79 Reign of **Khedive Ismail**.

Completion of Suez Canal; Central Cairo boulevards constructed.

1879–92 Reign of **Khedive Tewfiq**. British crush the **Orabi Revolt** (1882–83). Tewfiq reinstated as a puppet ruler under British control.

Howard Carter discovers Tutankhamun's tomb at Thebes (1922) at the tail end of a period of intensive excavations throughout Egypt.

1935–52 Reign of **King Farouk**; during World War II Egypt stays under British control.

1952–53 Farouk overthrown by Free Officers. **Egypt declared a republic**.

Construction of Midan Tahrir in Cairo.

MODERN EGYPT (1952–)

1956   **Nasser** becomes President; **Suez Crisis**.

1967   **Six Day War** with Israel.

Major industrialization programme, and construction of schools, hospitals and public housing. Massive damage to Canal cities during Six Day War.

1970   **Nasser dies** and is succeeded as president by **Sadat**.

High Dam at Aswan completed (1970).

1973   **October War** with Israel.

1977–78	Food Riots. Sadat's trip to Jerusalem leads to **Camp David** agreement.	Mohandiseen district of Cairo built, along with hundreds of new hotels, shops, etc. First line of Cairo metro completed.
1981	**Assassination of Sadat**. Presidency assumed by **Mubarak**.	
1990	**Gulf War**.	
1992	**Cairo earthquake**	Many buildings damaged in Cairo, but the second metro line is pushed to completion.
1994	**Underwater finds at Alexandria**.	Divers and archeologists begin exploration of possible site of the ruins of the ancient Lighthouse of Pharos in the harbour at Alexandria.
1996	**Valley of the Mummies**.	Egypt's largest cache of mummies is discovered by accident in Bahariya, in the Western Desert.
1997	**Shooting of tourists in Luxor**	58 foreigners killed by Islamic fundamentalists at Hatshepsut's Temple, near Luxor.

MUSIC

As with other cultural spheres, Egypt's musical traditions date back to pharaonic times, though the primary influences are Arab and Islamic. Given Egypt's status in the Arab world, it is no surprise that Cairo is the centre of the Arab recording industry – a dominance partly acquired by the collapse of its rivals in the Lebanon, Libya and Kuwait. Egypt's sixty-four million population makes it the most important market for Arab music, and the amazingly high proportion of youth (over thirty million Egyptians are under 25) has ensured a big demand for contemporary sounds.

The different types of folk or popular music you come across vary greatly with the region and environment: Cairo, the Nile Valley, the Delta and the desert all have their own characteristic sounds, rhythms and instruments. Often their songs reflect the rituals of everyday life: weddings, moulids, harvest festivals, old stories of village life or triumphs. What follows is the briefest of introductions to the various major forms.

RELIGIOUS MUSIC

During Ramadan and other major festivals you'll encounter **religious music** – renditions of **Koranic verses**, or praises to Allah, teased out in any number of ways.

Performers may be **munshids** – professional reciters who move from one festival to another – or simply the **muezzin** or **imam** of the local mosque. In everyday religious life, all muezzins have their individual styles of phrasing, which are sometimes jealously guarded. In a celebrated court case in the 1980s an Egyptian judge ruled that no copyright existed on any expression of the Koran, since God himself created it.

Recitals at **moulids** are often more participation than performance, with dozens of Sufi devotees chanting and swaying to the accompaniment of a drum. These recitals, known as **zikrs**, can last for days.

CLASSICAL ARAB MUSIC

Antecedents of **classical Arabic music** can be traced back to the **Bedouin** reciters and singers of the Arabian peninsula, but also to the more refined **court music** of the great khalifal cities of Baghdad and Damascus, and Ottoman Constantinople.

During the last century, the form has been characterized by oriental scales, passionate rhetoric, bravura soloists, massed orchestras and male choirs. The most famous twentieth-century exponent was **Umm Kalthoum** (aka Oum Khalsoum); until her death in 1975, she was the most popular singer in the Arab world. Her career coincided with the advent of long-distance broadcasting and she was essentially the first Arab music star. In Egypt, she was a national institution, known as "The Mother of Egypt" and accorded a weekly concert on radio (and, later, TV). Although she is still widely played today, the genre itself has become ossified and its admirers tend to be amongst the older generation.

REGIONAL/ETHNIC MUSIC

SAIYIDI

The music of Upper Egypt – known, like its people, as **Saiyidi** – has a characteristic rhythm, which horses are trained to dance to. It is based upon two instruments: the *nahrasan*, a two-sided drum hung over the chest and beaten with sticks; and the *mismar saiyidi*, a kind of wooden trumpet. Performances often involve monologues, ripe with puns and wit. One of the famous names of the genre, **Omar Gharzawi**, is known for his rebuttals of the stereotyped image of stupid, hot-headed Saiyidis. **Shoukoukou**, who died several years ago, has

EGYPTIAN MUSIC: A CASSETTOGRAPHY

Cassettes are the medium for almost all recorded Egyptian music. Introduced in the early 1970s, they have proved robust, cheap and very easy to copy – piracy is such a problem that it has its own special police division in Cairo. Outlets are street-corner kiosks, small shops and market stalls, most of which tend to specialize in either *Shaabi* or *Al-Jeel*, or the old oriental musics, traditional and modern. There are no charts as such, though you will soon know when a song is the city's "number one". If it's big, producers can expect to sell up to a million copies.

The following is a highly **selective list of artists and cassettes** to start you off in Cairo cassette browsing. In Britain or North America, you can find a limited range of records, too – mostly Umm Kalthoum and the like, though with a few more contemporary releases on "world music" labels. By far the most compelling of these is David Lodge's brilliant **Yalla: Hitlist Egypt** collection (Mango/Island, 1990), which devotes a side each to *Shaabi* and *Al-Jeel*.

RELIGIOUS MUSIC
Sheikh Mohammed el-Hosni *Doa Khetm el-Koran il-Karim*. Highly emotional.

CLASSICAL ARABIC MUSIC
Umm Kalthoum *Al-Atalaal* and *Enta Omri*. Two of her greatest live recordings – among dozens of releases.

SAIYIDI MUSIC
Ahmed Ismail and Sohar Magdy. Anything by this duo is worth acquiring.

AL-JEEL MUSIC
Ehab Tawfek *Maraheel*. Promising New Wave newcomer.

Mohammed Foad *Shams* or *Kamanana*. Poppy love songs.

NUBIAN MUSIC
Khedr *Ya Sahabba*. Sung in an obscure Nubian dialect – and popular mainly among Nubians.

BEDOUIN MUSIC
You won't find cassettes in Cairo but may strike lucky in Sinai or Mersa Matrouh.

SHAABI MUSIC
Ahmed Adaweer *Al-Tareek* or *Adaweat*. The father of it all at his best.

Magdy Shabeeni *Hasanahan*. Big on social comment and aggressive rhythms.

Hassan el-Asmar *Mish Hasheebak*. Classic *Shaabi* lyrics of hard urban life.

---

a special instrument (a joke clapping doll, sold at festivals) named after him. On a more official standing is *Rais* ("Boss") **Met'al al-l'nawi**, often chosen by the government to represent Egypt at foreign music festivals.

FELLAHI
The northern counterpart to Saiyidi music, found in the Delta, is known as **fellahi** (peasant) music. It is generally softer, with a fondness for the *matsoum* (one and a half) rhythm, and use of instruments like the *rababa*, a two-stringed viol, and the *mismar*, a kind of oboe.

SAWAHEELI
Found along the Mediterranean coast and in the Canal Zone, **Sawaheeli** music is characterized by the use of a banjo-like stringed instrument, the *simseemeya*. Another form, specific to Alexandria, also features the accor-dion, the result of the city's Greek and Turkish influences.

BEDOUIN
There are two kinds of **Bedouin** music: one found in the Western Desert, towards Libya, the other in the Eastern Desert and Sinai. Both have songs recounting old intrigues, activities and stories to a strong rhythmic accompaniment. This has been a major influence on *Al-Jeel* music (see below).

NUBIAN
Performed in its own language, in the southern reaches of the Nile Valley, **Nubian** music has more African than Arab roots. It relies a lot on hand-clapping and the *duf*, a kind of tambourine. More urbanized versions – found in Aswan or Khartoum – have opted for brass sections and female choruses.

URBAN MUSIC

In Cairo and other cities, rural traditions have mixed with the more elite classical styles, and adapted to reflect urban preoccupations and the faster pace of life. Over the last couple of decades, this **urban music** has come to reject the melodrama, ornate melodies and scales of classical Arab music, while its lyrics express the concerns of the more freewheeling post-Nasser years. By the mid-1980s, two main types of music had developed: **Shaabi** and **al-Jeel**.

SHAABI

Shaabi ("people") music was born in the working-class quarters of Cairo, where millions of second- and third-generation rural migrants live. It blends the traditional form of the *mawal* (plaintive vocal improvisations) with a driving beat. Its lyrics are often raunchy or satirical, politically and socially provocative. You will never hear this music via the media. It is not so much banned as beneath the contempt of the middle classes and "respectable society", who see its rudeness and social criticism as coming from another Egypt. It is to be heard, however, at weddings and parties throughout working-class Cairo and at some of the nightclubs along Pyramids Road.

The original *Shaabi* singer was **Ahmed Adaweer**, who, from 1971 on, introduced the idea of street language and subsequently broke every rule in the book. He was basically a punk, and the youth of the backstreets loved him. Later exponents introduced elements of rap and disco into the *Shaabi* sound, rather in the manner of Algerian *Raï* music.

AL-JEEL

Al-Jeel means "the generation" and is the latest post-*Shaabi* sound. It takes disco elements a step further, using drum tracks and synthesized backing, and mixes these with Nubian and Bedouin rhythms. The latter came in large part through the influence of Libyan musicians, who had fled to Cairo in the late 1970s after Gaddafi's "cultural revolution", where he clamped down on Western musical influences.

Al-Jeel lyrics, in contrast to *Shaabi*, are usually about love or the country and rarely stray into sensitive areas. Singers and musicians, too, are less crucial than the arrangers and producers who put the songs and cassettes together. Nevertheless, performances remain a focus for discontented youth, echoing the West's 1960s idea that rock music was radical or even revolutionary.

BOOKS

Most of the books listed below are in print; those that are out of print (o/p) should be easy to track down in secondhand bookstores. Books that are only published in Egypt are most easily available in Cairo; we have identified these by giving the publisher's name after the book title (the American University in Cairo Press is abbreviated to AUC).

TRAVEL

GENERAL

Karl Baedeker, *Egypt: Handbook for Travellers* (o/p). The classic guidebook, used by generations of tourists from the 1870s until World War II. Of the numerous editions, the 1929 revision – which includes the discovery of Tutankhamun's tomb – is the one to hunt for in secondhand bookshops (it sells for about £100/US$160; a facsimile edition, published in the 1980s, is also out of print but can often be found for £20/US$30 or so).

Robert Curzon, *Visits to Monasteries in the Levant* (E. Mellen). Famed account, by a man later made Viceroy of Egypt, of youthful adventurings in Egypt, Palestine and Greece in the 1830s. Several chapters deal with Egyptian monasteries, where Curzon got the monks drunk and stole their antiquarian manuscripts.

Amelia Edwards, *A Thousand Miles up the Nile* (Darf). Verbose, patronizing classic from the mid-nineteenth century. All books on Egypt have their Amelia quotes – the *Rough Guide* included.

Gustave Flaubert, *Flaubert in Egypt* (Penguin). A romp through the brothels, baths and sites by the future author of *Madame Bovary*, who cared little for monuments but delighted in Egyptian foibles and vices. Skilfully edited by Francis Steegmuller.

E.M. Forster, *Alexandria: A History and a Guide* (o/p UK). A foreword by Lawrence Durrell and stylishly erudite notations by Michael Haag enhance Forster's 1922 guidebook. Forster's companion piece was *Pharos and Pharillon* (o/p), a diverse collection of essays on Alexandrian life.

Amitav Ghosh, *In an Antique Land* (Granta). Wry tales of contemporary life in a Delta village, interspersed with snippets of historical research which are far less absorbing.

Douglas Kennedy, *Beyond the Pyramids* (Abacus). A dour, Paul Theroux-ish jaunt around Egypt in the late 1980s; the Alex and Assyut sections stand out.

E.W. Lane, *Manners and Customs of the Modern Egyptians* (East-West). Facsimile edition of this encyclopedic study of life in Mohammed Ali's Cairo, first published in 1836. Highly browsable.

Deborah Manley, *The Nile: A Traveller's Anthology* (o/p). A good anthology to go for: nicely illustrated and with selections gathered from some very obscure sources.

Bimbashi McPherson, *The Man Who Loved Egypt* (o/p). Edited letters of a paternalist British administrator, interesting for the light they cast on Cairo in the early twentieth century (when he headed the secret police).

Henri de Monfreid, *Hashish* (o/p). A latter day swashbuckler who followed a spell in Djibouti jail by smuggling hash on the Red Sea during the 1920s. The second half relates his dealings with the Suez underworld.

Jan Morris, *Destinations* (o/p). This collection of essays includes an interesting if overblown piece on Cairo.

Murray's, *Handbook for Travellers in Egypt* (o/p). A worthy rival to Baedeker, likewise replete with footnotes, engravings and colonial attitudes. Later editions distinguished by their coverage of Sinai sell for around £30/US$50.

Gerard de Nerval, *Journey to the Orient*. Stoned on hash, De Nerval thrilled to Mohammed Ali's Egypt; splendour and squalor, eroticism and cruelty – the Orientalist fantasy that still colours perceptions today. A wacky read.

Florence Nightingale, *Letters from Egypt* (Parkway). A stuffier view of Egypt, by a 29-

year-old Englishwoman who had yet to make herself famous in the Crimean War. Illustrated with paintings and drawings by David Roberts, Edward Lear and other artists of the period.

Christopher Pick, *Egypt: A Traveller's Anthology* (J. Murray). Mixed bag of observers from the eighteenth and nineteenth centuries, including Disraeli, Mark Twain, Vita Sackville-West, Flaubert, E.M. Forster and Freya Stark.

Charlie Pye-Smith, *The Other Nile* (o/p). Witty and insightful account of a tour in the early 1980s, interwoven with recollections of trips into Sudan and Ethiopia, before coups and famine made them inaccessible.

Paul William Roberts, *River in the Desert*. Chiefly interesting for its eyewitness account of a *zaar* (exorcism) and a chapter on the Kushmaan Bedouin of the Eastern Desert.

Stanley Stewart, *Old Serpent Nile: A Journey to the Source* (Flamingo). Stewart managed to travel from the Nile Delta to the Mountains of the Moon in Uganda in the late 1980s, and relates his adventures in spare, taut prose.

CAIRO

James Aldridge, *Cairo* (o/p). Highly readable history of the city from ancient times until the mid-1960s, including several fine maps and photographs. Only found in secondhand bookshops.

Artemis Cooper, *Cairo in the War* (o/p). Excellent account of a febrile era, with vignettes of Evelyn Waugh, Olivia Manning and other post-war luminaries.

Trevor Mostyn, *Egypt's Belle Epoque: Cairo 1869–1952* (o/p). Expat highlife and diplomatic intrigue, from the time of Ismail to the revolution that overthrew King Farouk.

Richard Parker, *Islamic Monuments of Cairo: A Practical Guide* (AUC). Excellent and detailed handbook to the monuments and history of seventh- to nineteenth-century Cairo.

Desmond Stewart, *Great Cairo, Mother of the World* (AUC). Entertaining and erudite history of the city, from pharaonic times through to the Nasser era. Available in Cairo.

THE DESERT

Michael Asher, *In Search of the Forty Days Road*; *Impossible Journey* (o/p). Only peripherally related to Egypt, but well worth reading.

Asher's camel journeys, in the Sudanese desert and from Mauritania to the Nile, evoke all the hardships and magic of the desert.

R.A. Bagnold, *Libyan Sands: Travels in a Dead World* (M. Haag). One of a band of motorized explorers of the Libyan Desert during the 1920s and 30s, Bagnold later wrote the seminal work on dune-formation, *The Physics of Blown Sand and Desert Dunes* – a book continuously in print since 1939 and used by NASA to interpret satellite photos of Mars. *Libyan Sands*, despite the restrained prose, is compelling boy's own stuff, and the sheer range of journeys – to all the oases, Jebel Uwaynat, the Great Sand Sea and the Forty Days Road – makes it a bible for desert buffs.

Burton Bernstein, *Sinai: The Great and Terrible Wilderness* (o/p). Mixture of travel writing and history, describing Sinai on the eve of its handover to Egypt in 1979. Dated but still the best book on the region.

Ahmed Fakhry, *The Oases of Egypt* (AUC; 2 vols.). Fakhry's unfinished trilogy is still the last word on the Western Desert Oases. Volume I, covering Siwa, is fascinating; Volume II, on Bahariya and Farafra, is heavier going, while Fakhry's death in 1973 aborted the volume on Dakhla and Kharga. Volume I has been republished in paperback; Volume II remains out of print, but can be found in Cairo bookshops.

George Murray, *Dare Me to the Desert* (o/p). Despite its awful title, this is an interesting account of Murray's climbing expeditions in the Red Sea Mountains during the 1920s and 30s.

Cassandra Vivian, *Islands of the Blest: A Guide to the Oases and Western Desert of Egypt* (International Publications). The best guide available on the subject, covering all of the oases in minute detail, including sites far off the beaten track. Illustrated with drawings and colour photos, plus an excellent set of maps. An updated second edition is due out in 2000. Sold in Cairo. Highly recommended.

ANCIENT HISTORY

GENERAL WORKS

Martin Bernal, *Black Athena* (Vintage). These dense, provocative works assert the "Africanness" of ancient Egyptian civilization and its contribution to Greek and Roman culture. The first two volumes (1987 and 1991) show a formidable breadth of enquiry, though Egyptologists and Classicists nit-pick holes everywhere.

Margaret Bunson, *Encyclopedia of Ancient Egypt* (Facts on File). Over 1500 entries, with useful subject indexes, charts and chronologies – though not as comprehensive as the *British Museum Dictionary of Ancient Egypt* (see below).

Mark Collier & Bill Manley, *How to Read Egyptian Hieroglyphics: A step-by-step guide to teach yourself* (British Museum Press). Just what the title says – and an unexpected best-seller, thanks to its clarity and the exciting sense of knowledge that it confers.

Peter France, *The Rape of Egypt* (o/p). Interesting background on the characters and personalities of the early "archeologists", and a no-holds-barred indictment of imperialist looting.

Nicholas Grimal, *A History of Ancient Egypt* (Blackwell). The first detailed, reign-by-reign account since Gardiner's *Egypt of the Pharaohs* (1961), which synthesizes a mass of recent revisions, particularly chronological.

George Hart, *A Dictionary of Egyptian Gods and Goddesses* (Routledge). Indispensable guide to the deities and myths of ancient Egypt, profusely illustrated with line drawings. Hart's *Egyptian Myths* is equally informative, covering similar ground.

T.G.H. James, *An Introduction to Ancient Egypt* (o/p); *Egypt: The Living Past*; *Ancient Egypt: The Land and its Legacy*; *Egyptian Painting*; *Egyptian Sculpture*. James was the keeper of the Egyptian Antiquities department of the British Museum until the mid-1980s. His *Introduction* is a serious text for beginners; *The Land and its Legacy* and *The Living Past* are coffee-table books, good for pre-visit reading; while the *Painting* and *Sculpture* volumes are accessibly written and lavishly illustrated.

Jaromir Malek, *The Cat in Ancient Egypt* (British Museum Press). A charming monograph with delightful illustrations.

Geoffrey T. Martin, *The Hidden Tombs of Memphis* (Thames & Hudson). A detailed account of recent discoveries at Memphis, most notably the Tomb of Maya, a contemporary of Tutankhamun.

Dimitri Meeks & Christine Favard-Meeks, *Daily Life of the Egyptian Gods* (J. Murray). Scholarly study of the rituals and beliefs surrounding the gods; a TV spin-off focused on the more salacious bits.

Richard Parkinson, *Voices from Ancient Egypt: An Anthology of Middle Kingdom Writings* (o/p UK; University of Oklahoma). All kinds of literature, from spells and curses to state propaganda. The material for once brings to life people rather than monuments.

Stephen Quirke & Jeffrey Spencer (ed.), *The British Museum Book of Ancient Egypt* (British Museum Press). A good general survey, lavishly illustrated with material from the museum's Egyptian collection.

Gay Robins, *Women in Ancient Egypt* (British Museum Press). Interesting study of a subject largely ignored until a decade ago, focusing on queens and priestesses, fertility rituals and much else.

David Rohl, *A Test of Time: The Bible – From Myth to History* (Arrow). Stimulating argument for revising the chronology of ancient Egyptian and Bibical history, illustrated with scores of photos, plans and charts. Highly recommended.

Ian Shaw and Paul Nicholson, *British Museum Dictionary of Ancient Egypt* (British Museum Press). Richly illustrated, coffee-table-sized dictionary, especially good for site plans and assessments of recent discoveries.

John Taylor, *Egypt and Nubia* (British Museum Press). Covers the history of Nubia from 4000 BC to the dawning of the Christian era, focusing on ancient Nubian art and relations with Egypt.

Jean Vercoutter, *The Search for Ancient Egypt* (Thames & Hudson). Pocket-sized account of Egypt's "discovery" by foreigners, packed with drawings, photos and engravings.

John Anthony West, *Serpent in the Sky: The High Wisdom of Ancient Egypt* (Quest); *The Traveler's Key to Ancient Egypt: A Guide to the Sacred Places of Ancient Egypt* (Quest). West's New Age interpretation – postulating a connection with the mythical civilization of High Atlantis – has been greeted with derision by mainstream Egyptologists. *The Traveler's Key* is a lively on-site guide that makes fewer demands on one's credulity.

Karl-Theodore Zauzich, *Discovering Egyptian Hieroglyphs: A Practical Guide*. Profusely illustrated guide to the subject, revealing how to read hieroglyphs and their symbolic nuances.

PYRAMIDOLOGY

Guillemette Andreu, *Egypt in the Age of the Pyramids* (Murray). Nicely illustrated study of the pyramids' evolution in the context of Egyptian life and culture, by a French Egyptologist.

Robert Bauval, *The Orion Mystery* (Mandarin). Postulates that the Giza Pyramids corresponded to the three stars in Orion's Belt as it was in 10,500 BC. Archeologists are unconvinced, but at least the theory isn't as preposterous as Hancock's extrapolations (see below).

I.E.S. Edwards, *The Pyramids of Egypt* (Penguin). Lavishly illustrated, closely argued survey of all the major pyramids, recently updated to take account of new discoveries and theories, though Mendelssohn (see below) is conspicuously absent.

Graham Hancock, *Fingerprints of the Gods* (Mandarin); *The Message of the Sphinx*; *The Mars Mystery* (Heinemann); *Heaven's Mirror* (Penguin). Picking up where Bauval left off, Hancock asserts that the Egyptian and Pre-Columbian pyramids, Angkor Wat temple and the stone figures of Easter Island were all created by a lost civilization propagated by Martians. Bestselling codswallop.

Peter Hodges, *How the Pyramids were Built* (Arris & Phillips). As a professional stonemason, Hodges has practical experience rather than academic qualifications, on his side. An easy read, and quite persuasive.

Britta Le Va and Salima Ikram, *Egyptian Pyramids* (Zeitouna). Slim booklet of evocative sepia photos and brief accounts of the major pyramids. Available in Cairo.

Kurt Mendelssohn, *The Riddle of the Pyramids* (o/p). An attempt to resolve the enigma of the Maidum and Dahshur pyramids, which postulates a "pyramid production line" and caused a stir in the world of Egyptology during the 1980s.

THE AMARNA PERIOD/TUTANKHAMUN

Cyril Aldred, *Akhenaten, King of Egypt* (Thames & Hudson). Conventional account of the Amarna period by one of Britain's leading post-war Egyptologists.

Christiane Desroches-Noblecourt, *Tutankhamen: Life and Death of a Pharaoh* (Penguin). Brilliantly illustrated, detailed study of all aspects of the boy pharaoh and his times.

Thomas Hoving, *Tutankhamun: the Untold Story* (o/p). Lifts the lid on archeological backbiting and the tomb thefts by Carter and Carnarvon.

Nicholas Reeves and John H. Taylor, *Howard Carter Before Tutankhamun* (British Museum Press). Original photographs and drawings and first-hand accounts of excavations bring the irascible Carter to life.

Julia Samson, *Nefertiti and Cleopatra* (Rubicon). Fascinating account of Egypt's most famous queens, by the Petrie Museum's expert on Amarna civilization. Samson concludes that Smenkhkare, Akhenaten's mysterious successor, was actually Nefertiti; her coverage of Cleopatra is rather less controversial.

Philipp Vandenberg, *The Curse of the Pharaohs* (o/p); *Nefertiti*. Sensationalism masquerading as Egyptology. Thought- (and chuckle-) provoking, providing you suspend critical faculties.

PTOLEMAIC, ROMAN AND COPTIC EGYPT

Alan Bowman, *Egypt After the Pharaohs* (British Museum Press). Scholarly, nicely illustrated study of an often overlooked period.

Lucy Hughes-Hallet, *Cleopatra: Histories, Dreams and Distortions* (Pimlico). Arresting deconstruction analysis of Cleopatra in history and myth down through the ages.

Otto Meinardus, *Monks and Monasteries of the Egyptian Desert* (AUC). A rather turgid history and guide to Egypt's Coptic monasteries.

Barbara Watterson, *Coptic Egypt* (Scott Academic Press). Covers Coptic history and culture from ancient times to the present.

MEDIEVAL AND MODERN HISTORY

THE CRUSADES

Amin Maalouf, *The Crusades through Arab Eyes* (Al Saqi Books). Lebanese writer and journalist Maalouf has used the writings of contemporary Arab chroniclers of the Crusades to retrace two centuries of Middle Eastern history. His conclusion is that present-day relations between the Arab world and the West are still marked by the battle that ended seven centuries ago.

Steven Runciman, *A History of the Crusades* (Penguin). Highly readable three-volume narrative, laced with anecdote and scandal. Runciman's hero is Salah al-Din, rather than Richard the Lionheart, who is depicted (like most of the other traditional Western good guys) in all his murderous ferocity.

COLONIAL ERA

George Annesley, *The Rise of Modern Egypt* (Pentland). A readable survey of the period from Napoleon's invasion to the Suez Crisis, marred by Annesley's colonialist attitudes.

Corelli Barnett, *The Desert Generals* (Cassell Military). An iconoclastic study that concludes that Montgomery was a less assured general than his predecessors, let alone Rommel. Still, he did win the North African campaign.

George Greenfield, *Chasing the Beast* (R. Cohen, US). Evocative memoirs of the Western Desert campaign, by a Cambridge graduate who joined the infantry.

Peter Mansfield, *The British in Egypt* (o/p). Interesting account of how Egypt passed from being the "veiled protectorate" to an outright imperial possession. Mansfield is also author of *The Arabs* (Penguin), a clear, perceptive and wide-ranging introduction to the Arab world from the arrival of Islam to the 1970s.

Barrie Pitt, *The Crucible of War* (o/p). Blow-by-blow account of the Battle of El-Alamein.

Anthony Sattin, *Lifting the Veil: British Society in Egypt 1768–1956* (o/p). A fascinating slice of social history, charting the rise and fall of British tourists and expatriates in Egypt. Classic photographs, too.

POST-INDEPENDENCE

A.J. Barker, *Arab-Israeli Wars* (o/p). An illustrated account of the 1948, 1956, 1967 and 1973 wars, by a military historian. Photographs (and sympathies) come largely from the Israeli side.

Raymond William Baker, *Sadat and After* (J. B. Tauris). Heavyweight but fascinating critique of Egyptian society from six different perspectives, including those of the Muslim Brotherhood, Nasserists, Marxists and Osman Ahmed Osman, each presented sympathetically. A *tour de horizon* of contemporary Egyptian political thought.

Nemat Guenena, *The "Jihad". An "Islamic Alternative" in Egypt* (Cairo Papers Vol. 9, Summer 1986). As the quotation marks imply, a cautious academic investigation into the beliefs and social profile of Egypt's leading radical fundamentalist group. Available in Cairo.

Mohammed Heikal, *Cutting the Lion's Tail*; *The Road to Ramadan*; *The Autumn of Fury* (all o/p, though most libraries will turn up one or another). These three books cover, respectively, the Suez Crisis, the 1973 War, and Sadat's rise and fall. As a confidante of Nasser's since the Revolution, one-time editor of *Al-Ahram* and Minister of Information, Heikal provides a genuine inside view.

David Hirst and Irene Beeson, *Sadat* (o/p). Revealing political biography of the man whom Kissinger described as "the greatest since Bismarck", but which stops short of his assassination.

Derek Hopwood, *Egypt: Politics and Society 1945–90* (Routledge). Accessible and useful survey of the modern era, now in its third edition.

Human Rights Watch, *Hostage-Taking and Intimidation by Security Forces*; *Violations of Freedom of Religious Belief and Expression of the Christian minority*. Two sobering reports of human rights abuses in contemporary Egypt.

Anwar Sadat, *In Search of Identity* (Buccaneer). An anodyne, ghosted autobiography that reveals less about the character of Egypt's assassinated president than either Heikal or Hirst and Beeson.

Robert St John, *The Boss* (o/p). Racy, anecdotal biography of Nasser, written a decade before his death. Interesting, albeit dated since its publication in 1960.

ANTHROPOLOGY, SOCIOLOGY AND FEMINISM

Nayra Atiya (ed.), *Khul-Khaal: Five Egyptian Women tell their Stories* (Syracuse University Press, US). Gripping biographical accounts by women from diverse backgrounds, revealing much about contemporary Egyptian life. Essential reading.

Nicholas Biegman, *Egypt's Side-Shows*. Engaging colour photos of moulids, weddings and other rituals of Egyptian life. For a slightly academic treatment of the former, see Biegman's *Egypt – Moulids, Saints and Sufis*.

R. Critchfield, *Shahhat: An Egyptian* (AUC). A wonderful book, based on several years' resident research with the Nile Valley *fellaheen*, across the river from Luxor. Moving, amusing and shocking, by turn.

Joseph Hobbs, *Bedouin Life in the Egyptian Wilderness*. Fascinating, albeit academic account of the Khushmaan clan of Ma'aza Bedouin living in the Jebel Galala of the Eastern Desert.

Rana Kabbani, *Egypt's Myths of Orient* (o/p). An easier read than Edward Said's heavyweight *Orientalism*, this book unravels the erotic fantasies and myths which Western travellers, painters and poets built up about the East. Starting with the Crusades and continuing on through the Victorians, Kabbani shows how the East was portrayed as sexually voracious and thus intellectually and morally inferior.

Smadar Lavie, *The Poetics of Military Occupation: Mzeina Allegories of Bedouin Identity Under Israeli and Egyptian Rule* (University of California Press, US). Interesting study of the Bedouin tribe most affected by the changes in Sinai under both regimes, by an Israeli anthropologist.

Lila Abu Lughod, *Veiled Sentiments: Honour and Poetry in a Bedouin Society* (University of California Press, US). Another anthropological study, devoted to the Awlad Ali tribe of the Western Desert.

Nawal el-Saadawi, *The Hidden Face of Eve* (Zed). Egypt's best-known woman writer, Saadawi has been in conflict with the Egyptian authorities most of her life. This is her major polemic, covering a wide range of topics – sexual aggression, female circumcision, prostitution, divorce and sexual relationships.

Huda Shaarawi, *Harem Years: Memoirs of an Egyptian Feminist 1879–1924* (Virago). A unique document from the last generation of upperclass Egyptian women, who spent their childhood and married life in the segregated world of the harem.

ISLAM

A.J. Arberry (trans.), *The Koran*. This translation by Oxford University Press is the best English-language version of Islam's holy book, whose revelations and prose style form the basis of the Muslim faith and Arab literature. Arberry's scholarship is also evident in *Sufism: An Account of the Mystics of Islam* and *The Koran Interpreted*.

Titus Burckhardt, *Art of Islam: Language and Meaning* (o/p). Superbly illustrated, intellectually penetrating overview of Islamic art and architecture.

H.A.R. Gibb, *Islam* (in the US: *Studies on the Civilization of Islam*) (o/p). Concise exposition of the historical development and nature of Islam.

WILDLIFE

Bertel Bruun, *Common Birds of Egypt* (AUC). Slim illustrated guide, ideal for bird-watching your way around the country.

Eric Hanauer, *The Egyptian Red Sea – A Diver's Guide* (o/p). A comprehensive guide to the reefs and fish, and where to find them.

Richard Hoath, *Natural Selections: A Year of Egypt's Wildlife* (AUC). Enlightening and charming study of Egypt's birds, land and sea creatures, illustrated with the author's drawings.

EGYPTIAN FICTION

André Aciman, *Out of Egypt: A Memoir* (Harvill). Wry, affectionate tale of a flamboyant Jewish family who emigrated to Alex at the turn of the century and left three generations later. Aciman himself came of age in Italy and France.

Salwa Bakr, *The Golden Chariot* (Garnet). Absorbing novel set in a women's prison near Cairo, seen through the eyes of an Alexandrian aristocrat jailed for murder. The inmates' stories represent a microcosm of women's oppression in contemporary Egypt.

André Chedid, *The Sixth Day; From Sleep Unbound* (Swallow). Another émigré author, whose metaphor-laden plots and clinical prose are not exactly beach reading.

Gamal al-Ghitani, *Incidents in Zafraani Alley* (Egyptian Book Organization – only available in

Egypt); *Zayni Barakat. Incidents* is a highly accessible, darkly humorous read, which could be interpreted as a satire on state paranoia and credulous fundamentalism. Its ending is confused by the fact that the page order has been scrambled in the English-language edition. *Zayni Barakat* is a convoluted, elliptical drama set in the last years of Mamluke rule, which reached a wider audience at home when it was adapted for Egyptian television in 1994.

Nabil Naoum Gorgy, *The Slave's Dream and Other Stories* (Quartet). The amorality of man and nature is the main theme of this collection of tales, apparently influenced by Borges and Bowles.

Gamil Attiyah Ibrahim, *Down to the Sea* (Quartet). Stumbling translation mars what is by all accounts – in the original – a fascinating exploration of life in Cairo's Cities of the Dead.

Yusuf Idris, *The Cheapest Nights*; *Rings of Burnished Brass* (P. Owen). Two superb collections by Egypt's finest writer of short stories, who died in 1991. Uncompromisingly direct, yet ironic.

Naguib Mahfouz, *Adrift on the Nile*; *Arabian Days and Nights*; *Miramar*; *Midaq Alley*; *Palace Walk*; *Palace of Desires*; *Sugar Street*; *The Thief and the Dogs*; *Respected Sir*; *The Search*; *Wedding Song*; *The Beggar*; *The Beginning and the End*; *Autumn Quail*. Awarded the Nobel Literature Prize in 1989, Mahfouz is the Grand Old Man of Egyptian letters. His novels have a rather nineteenth-century feel, reminiscent in plot and characterization of Balzac or Victor Hugo; most are set in Cairo or Alexandria. Favoured themes include the discrepancy between ideology and human problems, hypocrisy and injustice, and taking personal responsibility.

Alifa Rifaat, *Distant View of a Minaret* (Heinemann). A well-known writer in her fifties expresses her revolt against male domination and suggests solutions within the orthodox Koranic framework.

Nawal el-Saadawi, *Woman at Point Zero* (Zed); *The Fall of the Imam* (Minerva); *God Dies by the Nile* (Zed); and others. Saadawi's novels are informed by her work as a doctor and psychiatrist in Cairo, and by her feminist and socialist beliefs; they range through subjects virtually taboo in Egypt. *Point Zero*, her best, is a power-

ful and moving story of a woman condemned to death for killing a pimp. You will find very few of her books on sale in Egypt, though *The Fall of the Imam* is the only one officially banned.

Adhaf Soueif, *Aisha*; *In the Eye of the Sun* (Bloomsbury). Born in Cairo and educated in Egypt and England, Soueif's semi-autobiographical first book was acclaimed for its sensibility. *In the Eye of the Sun* is a 790-page novel exploring love and destiny in the Middle East during the 1960s and 70s.

Bahaa Taher, *Aunt Safiyya and the Monastery* (University of California Press, US). Beautifully crafted novella set in a village in Upper Egypt, where the imperatives of a vendetta are challenged by a Muslim farmer and a Coptic monk. Taher's lapidary prose is sensitively translated by Barbara Romaîne.

ANTHOLOGIES

Margot Badran and Miriam Cooke (eds.), *Opening the Gates: a Century of Arab Feminist Writing* (Virago). Mix of fiction and polemic, including a fair number of Egyptian contributors.

Marylin Booth (ed./trans.), *My Grandmother's Cactus: Stories by Egyptian Women* (Quartet). Short stories by the latest generation of women writers, including Radwa Ashour, Salwa Bakr, Etidal Osman, Neamet el-Biheiri, Ibtihal Salem and Sahar Tawfiq.

Inea Bushnaq, *Arab Folktales* (Pantheon). Great collection of folk stories from across the Arab world, including many from Egypt, with interesting thematic pieces putting them in context. Highly recommended.

W.M. Hutchins (ed./trans.), *Egyptian Tales and Short Stories of the 1970s & 80s* (AUC). Includes various stories by Nawal el-Saadawi, Amira Nowaira, Gamal al-Ghitani and Fouad Higazy.

POETRY, BIOGRAPHY AND CRITICISM

C.P. Cavafy, *Collected Poems*. Elegiac evocations of the Alexandrian myth by the city's most famous poet. An excerpt from *The City* appears under "Alexandria" in this book.

Tawfiq al-Hakim, *The Prison of Life* (AUC). An autobiographical essay by one of the formative figures of modern Egyptian literature, covering the first thirty years of Al-Hakim's life.

Jane Lagoudis Pinchin, *Alexandria Still: Forster, Durrell and Cavafy* (AUC). Studies the influence of the city and its three most famous writers on one another. Rather dry, and strictly for people seriously into these writers.

FOREIGN FICTION

Noel Barber, *A Woman of Cairo*. Ill-starred love and destiny amongst the Brits and Westernized Egyptians of King Farouk's Cairo, interwoven with historical events and characters. From that perspective, a good insight into those times.

Gillian Bradshaw, *The Beacon at Alexandria* (o/p). A woman learns medicine in secret, disguises herself as a man and practises it in sectarian strife-ridden Alexandria, and later in barbarian-haunted Thrace.

Moyra Caldecott, *Daughter of Amun* (Bladud). Romanticized account of the rise and fall of Queen Hatshepsut.

Agatha Christie, *Death Comes at the End*; *Death on the Nile* (Collins). The latter is a classic piece of skullduggery solved by Hercules Poirot aboard a Nile cruiser, which Christie wrote while staying at the *Old Cataract Hotel* in Aswan. *Death Comes at the End* is a lamer effort, set around Luxor and the Valley of the Kings.

Robin Cook, *Sphinx* (o/p). A humdrum thriller about a secret tomb in the Valley of the Kings.

Len Deighton, *City of Gold*. A hard-boiled thriller set in 1941, when vital information was being leaked to Rommel. Follet's *The Key to Rebecca* (see below) concerns a later phase in the war, involving another spy.

Lawrence Durrell, *The Alexandria Quartet* (Faber). Endless sexual and metaphysical ramblings, occasionally relieved by a dollop of Alex atmosphere, from one of the century's most overrated writers.

Daniel Easterman, *Name of the Beast* (o/p). If you can swallow the notion of the Antichrist masterminding an Islamic fundamentalist coup, this fantasy-thriller grips from the beginning. The ending is a letdown, however.

Ken Follet, *The Key to Rebecca* (Pan). Fast-paced thriller based on the true story of a German spy, Eppler, who operated in Cairo during 1942. Follet exercises artistic licence when describing the outcome, but the bellydancer

Sonia, and Sadat's involvement, are largely faithful to history.

Anton Gill, *City of the Horizon* (Bloomsbury). The first volume of Gill's trilogy pits the scribe Huy against conspirators as Tutankhamun is enthroned and Horemheb amasses power. The story continues in *City of Dreams* (Bloomsbury); the final part, *City of the Dead* (Bloomsbury), is yet to be published.

Robert Irwin, *The Arabian Nightmare* (Dedalus). Brilliant, paranoid fantasy set in the Cairo of Sultan Qaitbey, where a Christian spy contracts the affliction of the title. As his madness deepens, reality and illusion spiral inwards like an opium-drugged walk through a *medina* of the mind.

Christian Jacques, *Ramses the Great*; *The Battle of Kadesh* (Simon & Schuster) et al. This over-hyped series of historical novels makes Jeffrey Archer seem like Scott Fitzgerald. Not worth reading, never mind buying.

Robert Liddell, *Unreal City* (P. Owen); *The Rivers of Babylon* (P. Owen). Two ironic novels of expat life, the first set in wartime Alexandria, the second in Cairo prior to the Suez Crisis.

Penelope Lively, *Oleander, Jacaranda* (Penguin). Fond memories of growing up in Cairo in the 1930s–40s, by a British novelist whose childhood perceptions were often at odds with those of her adult contemporaries.

Norman Mailer, *Ancient Evenings* (Abacus). Set in the reign of Ramses II like Jacques' stories, but far more prolix, tedious and rambling. Only enlivened by its sex scenes.

Olivia Manning, *The Levant Trilogy* (Penguin). The second half of this six-volume blockbuster of love 'n' war finds the Pringles in Egypt, where Harriet mopes and Guy is as crass as ever.

Michael Pearce, *The Mamur Zapt and the Donkey-vous*; *The Mamur Zapt and the Girl in the Nile*; *The Mamur Zapt and the Men Behind*; *The Mamur Zapt and the Return of the Carpet*; *The Mamur Zapt and the Spoils of Egypt.*. A series of cracking yarns set in Khedival Egypt, featuring the chief of Cairo's secret police.

William Smethurst, *Sinai* (Headline). Political skullduggery, ancient history and the paranormal keep you hooked and baffled till the end. Mostly set in Sinai, so an ideal read for the beach at Dahab.

JOURNALS

Journal of Egyptian Archeology; Egyptian Archeology. Published by the Egyptian Exploration Society, the *Journal* is the world's leading forum for all matters Egyptological: all the new theories and discoveries get printed here first. *Egyptian Archeology* magazine, illustrated and with a popular slant, is also published by the Society. Membership of the society costs £30 or £40 per annum (depending on whether you wish to receive one or both publications). For details contact: The Secretary, Egyptian Exploration Society, 3 Doughty Mews, London WC1N 2PG (☎020/7242-1880, fax 020/7404-6118).

LANGUAGE

Egyptians are well used to tourists who speak only their own language, but an attempt to tackle at least a few words in Arabic is invariably greeted with great delight and encouragement, and as often as not the exclamation "You speak Arabic better than I do!". Whatever else you do, at least make an effort to learn the Arabic numerals and polite greetings.

Although most educated and urban Egyptians will have been taught some English and are only too happy to practise it on you, a little Arabic is a big help in the more remote areas. French may also come in handy in some cities, such as Alexandria, where Greek is also spoken by older folk; German, too, is increasingly understood in tourist-related spheres.

EGYPTIAN ARABIC

Although Arabic is the common and official language of 23 countries, the spoken dialect of each can vary considerably. Egyptian Arabic, however, because of the country's vast film, television and music industry, is the most widely understood in the Arab world.

PRONUNCIATION

Transliteration from Arabic script into English presents some pronunciation problems, since some letters have no equivalents. The phonetic guide below should help: everything is pronounced.

ai	as in eye	ey/ay	as in day
aa	as in bad but lengthened	ee	as in feet
'a	as when asked to say ah by the doctor	kh	as in Scottish loch
a'	a glottal stop as in bottle	gh	like the French r (back of the throat)

Note that **double consonants** should always be pronounced separately.

BASICS

Yes	*aiwa (or) na'am*	Come in, please	*itfaddal (m) / itfaddali (f)*
No	*la*		*(to m/f)*
Thank you	*shukran*	Excuse me	*an iznak (m) / 'an iznik (f)*
You're welcome	*afwan*	Sorry	*aasif (m) / asfa (f)*
Please (to m/f)	*min fadlak (m) / fadlik (f)*	God willing	*inshallah*

GREETINGS AND FAREWELLS

Welcome/hello	*ahlan w-sahlan*	(response –	*masa' in-nur*
(response)	*ahlan bik (m) / biki (f) /*	evening of light)	
	bikum (pl)	How are you (m/f) ?	*izzayak (m) / izzayik (f)*
Hello (formal)	*assalaamu aleikum*	I (m/f) am fine,	*qwayyis (m) / qwayyisa*
(response)	*wa-aleikum assalaam*	Thanks be to God	*(f) il-hamdu lilla*
Greetings	*sa'eeda*	Good night	*tisbah (m) / tisbahi (f)*
Nice to meet you	*fursa sa'eeda*		*'ala kheer*
Good morning	*sabah il-kheer*	And to you (m/f)	*wenta (m) / wenti (f)bi-*
(morning of goodness)		*kheer*	
(response – morning	*sabah in-nur*	Goodbye	*ma'a salaama*
of light)			
Good evening (evening	*masa' il-kheer*		
of goodness)			

Continues over

EGYPTIAN ARABIC (continued)

QUESTIONS AND DIRECTIONS

What is your (m/f) name?	ismak (m) / ismik (f) ey?	. . . the airport?	. . . il-mataar?
My name is . . .	ismi . . .	. . . the toilet?	. . . il-twalet?
Do you (m/f) speak Arabic?	titkallim (m) / titkallimi (f) 'Arabi?	. . . a restaurant?	. . . mat'am?
English?	ingleezi?	Left/right/straight ahead	shimaal/yimeen/alatool
French?	fransawi?	Near/far	areeb/ba'eed
I speak English	ana batkallim ingleezi	Here/there	hinna/hinnak
I don't speak Arabic	ana ma-batkallimsh 'arabi	When does the bus leave?	il-autobees yissafir imta?
I understand (a little)	ana fahem (shwaiya)	When does the train leave?	il-atr yissafir imta?
I don't understand	ana mish fahem	. . . arrive?	. . . yoosal?
What's that in English?	ya'ani ey bil-ingleezi?	What time (is it)?	issa'a kam?
Where is Hotel . . . ?	feyn funduk il . . . ?	First/last/next	il-awil/il-akhir/et-tani
. . . the bus station?	. . . mahattat il-autobees?	Nothing	wallahagga
. . . the train station?	. . . mahattat il-atr?	Not yet	lissa

REQUESTS AND SHOPPING

Do you (m/f) have . . . ?	fi 'andak (m) / 'andik (f) . . . ?	(but)	(wa-laakin)
. . . cigarette(s)	. . . sigara/sagayir	bigger/smaller	akbar/asghar
. . . matches	. . . kibreet	How much (is it)?	bi-kam (da)?
. . . newspaper	. . . gurnal	It's too expensive	da ghaali awi
I (m/f) want something . . .	ayyiz (m) / ayyza (f) haga . . .	big	kebir awi
. . . else	. . . tanya	small	sughayyar awi
. . . better than this	. . . ahsan min da	That's fine	maashi
. . . cheaper	. . arkhas min da	There is/is there?	fi/fi?
. . . like this	. . . zay da	This/that	di/da
		I (m/f) don't want . . .	mish ayyiz (m)/ayyza (f) . . .

ACCOMMODATION

Do you (m/f) have a room?	fi 'andak (m) / 'andik (f) ouda?	. . . hot water?	mayya sukhna?
I (m/f) would like to see the rooms	ayyiz/ayyza ashuf il-owad	. . . a shower?	. . . doush?
		. . . a balcony?	. . . balcona?
Can I see the rooms?	mumkin ashuf il-owad?	. . . air conditioning?	. . . takyeef hawa?
		. . . a telephone?	. . . telifoon?
Is there . . . ?	fi . . . ?	How much is the bill?	. . . kam il-hisab?

REACTIONS AND SMALL TALK

I (m/f) don't understand	ana mish fahem (m) / fahma (f)	It's not your business	mish shorlak
I (m/f) don't know	ana mish 'arif (m) / 'arfa (f)	Don't touch me!	sibni le wadi!
I (m/f) am tired/ unwell	ana ta'aban (m) / ta'abana (f)	Let's go	yalla
		Slowly	baranah
I (m/f) am hungry	ana gawa'an (m) / gawa'ana (f)	Enough! Finished!	khalas
		Never mind	maalesh
I (m/f) am thirsty	ana 'atshaan (m) / 'atshaana (f)	It doesn't matter	mush muhim
		There's no problem	ma feesh mushkila
I (m/f) am (not) married	ana (mish) mitgawwiz (m) / mitgawwiza (f)	It's not possible	mish mumkin

CALENDAR

day	*youm*	later	*bahdeen*
night	*leyla*	Saturday	*youm is-sabt*
week	*usbu'a*	Sunday	*youm il-ahad*
month	*shahr*	Monday	*youm il-itnayn*
year	*sana*	Tuesday	*youm it-talaata*
today	*innaharda*	Wednesday	*youm il-arb'a*
tomorrow	*bukkra*	Thursday	*youm il-khamees*
yesterday	*imbaarih*	Friday	*youm il-gum'a*

MONEY

Where's the bank?	*feyn il-bank?*	Egyptian pound	*giney*
I (m/f) want to	*ayyiz/ayyza aghayyar . . .*	half pound	*nuss giney*
change . . .		quarter pound	*robah giney*
. . . money	*. . . floos*	piaster	*irsh*
. . . British pounds	*. . . ginay sterlini*	2 piastres	*irshayn*
. . . US dollars	*. . . dolar amrikani*	5 piastres	*khamsa irsh*
. . . travellers' cheques	*. . . shikaat siyahiyya*		

NUMBERS AND FRACTIONS

0	*sifr*	11	*hidarsha*	30	*talaateen*	500	*khamsa miyya*
1	*wahid*	12	*itnarsha*	40	*arb'aeen*	1000	*alf*
2	*itnayn*	13	*talatarsha*	50	*khamseen*	2000	*alfayn*
3	*talaata*	14	*arb'atarsha*	60	*sitteen*	3000	*talaat alaaf*
4	*arb'a*	15	*khamastarsha*	70	*sab'aeen*	4000	*arb'at alaaf*
5	*khamsa*	16	*sittarsha*	80	*tamaneen*	1/2	*nous*
6	*sitta*	17	*sab'atarsha*	90	*tis'een*	1/4	*robah*
7	*sab'a*	18	*tamantarsha*	100	*miyya*	1/8	*tumna*
8	*tamanya*	19	*tis'atarsha*	150	*miyya wa-khamseen*		
9	*tes'a*	20	*ashreen*				
10	*ashara*	21	*wahid wa-l 'ashreen*	200	*mitayn*		
				300	*talaata miyya*		

NUMERALS

١	1	١٠	10	١٩	19	٨٠	80
٢	2	١١	11	٢٠	20	٩٠	90
٣	3	١٢	12	٢١	21	١٠٠	100
٤	4	١٣	13	٢٢	22	٢٠٠	200
٥	5	١٤	14	٣٠	30	٣٠٠	300
٦	6	١٥	15	٤٠	40	٤٠٠	400
٧	7	١٦	16	٥٠	50	١٠٠٠	1000
٨	8	١٧	17	٦٠	60		
٩	9	١٨	18	٧٠	70		

GLOSSARY OF EGYPTIAN TERMS

This is a glossary of basic Egyptian terms in everyday use, plus Islamic and architectural terms; for pharaonic symbols and terms used in temple architecture, see p.255 and p.288. Common alternative spellings are given in brackets.

ABLAQ Striped. An effect achieved by painting, or laying courses of different coloured masonry (the costlier method); usually white with red or buff. A Bahri Mamluke innovation, possibly derived from the Roman technique of *opus mixtum* – an alternation of stone and brickwork.

ABU "Father of"; a term of respect.

AIN (AYN, EIN) Spring.

AMIR (EMIR) Commander, prince.

BAB Gate or door, as in the medieval city walls.

BAHR River, sea, canal.

BAKSHEESH Alms or tips.

BALADI Local, rural or countrified.

BARAKA Blessing.

BEIT House. Segregated public and private quarters, the *malqaf*, *maq'ad* and *mashrabiya* are typical features of old Cairene mansions.

BEY (BAY) Lord or noble; an Ottoman title.

BIR (BEER) Well.

BIRKA (BIRQA, BIRKET) Lake.

BURG (BORG) Tower.

CADI (QADI) Judge.

CALECHE Horse-drawn carriage.

CORNICHE Seafront or riverfront promenade.

DARB Path or way; can apply to alleyways or thoroughfares.

DEIR Monastery or convent.

FELAHEEN (sing. FELAH) Peasant farmers who work their own land or as sharecroppers for wealthier farmers.

FELUCCA Nile sailing boat.

FINIAL Ornamental crown of a dome or minaret, often topped by an Islamic crescent.

GALABIYYA Loose flowing robe worn by men.

GEZIRA Island.

GHIRD (GHARD) Sand dune.

GOM'A Large congregational mosque, as opposed to a *masguid*.

HADJ (HAJ) Pilgrimage to Mecca.

HAGG/HAGGA One who has visited Mecca.

HAIKAL Sanctuary of a Coptic church.

HAMMAM Turkish bathhouse.

HANTOUR Horse-drawn carriage.

HARAMLIK Literally the "forbidden" area; ie women's or private apartments in a house or palace.

ITYHPHALLIC Decorous term for a god with an erection; Min, Amun and Osiris were often depicted thus by the ancient Egyptians.

JEBEL (GEBEL, GABAL, etc) Hill or mountain.

KHALIF Successor to the Prophet Mohammed and spiritual and political leader of the Muslim empire. A struggle over this office caused the Sunni–Shia schism of 656 AD. Most khalifs ruled from Baghdad or Damascus and delegated control of imperial provinces like Egypt.

KHALIG Gulf or canal.

KHAN Place where goods were made, stored and sold, which also provided accommodation for travellers and merchants, like a *wikala*. It's from *khan* that we get the word caravanserai.

KHANQAH Sufi hostel, analagous to a monastery.

KHEDIVE Viceroy.

KOM Mound of rubble and earth covering an ancient settlement.

KUBRI Bridge.

KUFIC The earliest style of Arabic script; Foliate *kufic* was a more elaborate form, superseded by *naskhi* script.

KUTTAB Koranic school, usually for boys or orphans.

LIWAN Arcade or vaulted space off a courtyard, commonly found in mosques and *madrassas*. Originally, the term meant a sitting room opening onto a covered court.

MADRASSA Literally a "place of study" but generally used to designate theological schools.

Each *madrassa* propagates a particular rite of Islamic jurisprudence.

MAHWAGI Local laundryman or woman.

MALQAF Wind scoop for directing cool breezes into houses; in Egypt, they always face north.

MAQ'AD Arch-fronted "sitting place" on the second floor of old Cairene houses, overlooking the courtyard.

MARISTAN The medieval term for a public hospital.

MASHRABIYA An alcove in lattice windows where jars of water can be cooled by the wind; and by extension, the projecting balcony and screened window itself, which enabled women to watch streetlife or the *salamlik* without being observed. Although flat latticework partitions are strictly termed *mashrafiya*, *mashrabiya* loosely covers both types of work.

MASGUID A small local mosque, as opposed to a *gom'a*.

MASR (MISR, MUSR) Popular name for Egypt, and Cairo.

MASTABA Stone or mud-brick benches at the entrance to buildings. Mohammed Ali had them removed to reduce idling and speed up the traffic.

MERLONS Indentations and raised portions along a parapet. Fatimid merlons were angular; Mamluke ones crested, trilobed (like a fleur-de-lys) or in fancier leaf patterns.

MIDA'A Fountain for the ritual ablutions that precede prayer, located in a mosque's vestibule or courtyard.

MIDAN Open space or square; originally, most were polo grounds.

MIHRAB Niche indicating the direction of Mecca, to which all Muslims pray.

MINARET Tower from which the call to prayer is given; derived from *minara*, the Arabic word for "beacon" or "lighthouse".

MINBAR Pulpit from which an address to the Friday congregation is given. Often superbly inlaid or carved in variegated marble or wood.

MIT Village.

MOSQUE A simple enclosure facing Mecca in its original form, the mosque acquired minarets, *riwaqs*, *madrassas* and mausolea as it was developed by successive dynasties. Large congregational mosques are called *gom'a*; smaller,

local "places of prostration" are known as *masguid* – a very old distinction. Very small mosques, often associated with Sufi orders or fundamentalist groups, are known as *zawiyas*.

MOULID Popular festival marking an event in the Koran or the birthday of a Muslim saint. The term also applies to the name-days of Coptic saints.

MUEZZIN A prayer-crier (who nowadays is more likely to broadcast by loudspeaker than climb up and shout from the minaret).

MUNSHID Professional reciter of Koranic verses and praises to Allah.

MURQANAS Stalactites, pendants or honeycomb ornamentation of portals, domes or squinches.

MUSTACHFA The modern Egyptian term for a public hospital.

NASKHI Form of Arabic script with joined-up letters, introduced by the Ayyubids.

PASHA (PACHA) Ruler – a lord or prince. Nowadays, a respectful term of address for anyone in authority, pronounced "basha".

QALA Fortress, citadel.

QARAT Peak, ridge.

QASR Palace, fortress, mansion.

QIBLA The direction in which Muslims pray, ie the wall where the *mihrab* is located.

QUBBA Dome, and by extension any domed tomb.

RAS Cape, headland, peak.

RIWAQ Arcaded aisle around a mosque's *sahn*, originally used as residential quarters for theological students; ordinary folk may also take naps here.

SABIL Public fountain or water cistern. During the nineteenth century it was often combined with a Koranic school to make a *SABIL-KUTTAB*.

SAHN Central courtyard of a mosque, frequently surrounded by *riwaqs* or *liwans*.

SALAMLIK The "greeting" area of a house; ie the public and men's apartments.

SANCTUARY The *liwan* incorporating the *qibla* wall.

SOFFITS Undersides of arches, often decorated with stripes (*ablaq*) or formalized plant designs (an Ottoman motif).

SQUINCH An arch spanning the right angle formed by two walls, so as to support a dome.

SHARIA Street (literally "way"). Also laws based on Koranic precepts, which Muslim fundamentalists wish to see applied in Egypt.

SHARM Bay.

SUFIS Islamic mystics who seek to attain union with Allah through trance-inducing *zikrs* and dances. Whirling Dervishes belong to one of the Sufi sects.

TABUT A cenotaph or grave marker, sometimes embellished with a "hat" indicating the deceased's rank.

TARIQA Sufi order or brotherhood.

TELL Another word for **KOM** (see above).

THULUTH Script whose vertical strokes are three times larger than its horizontal ones; *Thuluth* literally means '"third".

WADI Valley or watercourse (usually dry).

WAQF The endowment of some religious, educational or charitable institution in perpetuity. In Egypt, thousands of such bequests are overseen by the Ministry of Awaqf.

WAHAH Oasis.

WIKALA Bonded warehouse with rooms for merchants upstairs. Here they bought trading licences from the *Muhtasib*, and haggled over sales in the courtyard. *Okel* is another term for a *wikala*.

ZAAR Exorcism.

ZAWIYA Originally a *khanqah* centred around a particular sheikh or Sufi order (*tariqa*), but nowadays used to mean a very small mosque.

ZIKR Marathon session of chanting and swaying, intended to induce communion with Allah.

ZIYADA Outer courtyard separating early mosques from their surroundings; literally "an addition".

ZUQAQ Narrow cul-de-sac, from the Turkish word for "street".

INDEX

Stay in touch with us!

ROUGH*NEWS* is Rough Guides' free newsletter.
In four issues a year we give you news, travel
issues, music reviews, readers' letters and the
latest dispatches from authors on the road.

I would like to receive ROUGH*NEWS*: please put me on your free mailing list.

NAME . . . .

ADDRESS . . . .

Please clip or photocopy and send to: Rough Guides, 62–70 Shorts Gardens, London WC2H 9AB,
England or Rough Guides, 375 Hudson Street, New York, NY 10014, USA.

ROUGH GUIDES: Travel

Amsterdam
Andalucia
Australia

Austria
Bali & Lombok
Barcelona
Belgium &
  Luxembourg
Belize
Berlin
Brazil
Britain
Brittany &
  Normandy
Bulgaria
California
Canada
Central America
Chile
China
Corfu & the
  Ionian Islands
Corsica
Costa Rica
Crete
Croatia
Cyprus
Czech & Slovak
  Republics
Dodecanese &
  the East Aegean

Dominican
  Republic
Ecuador
Egypt
England
Europe
Florida
France
French Hotels &
  Restaurants
  1999
Germany
Goa
Greece
Greek Islands
Guatemala
Hawaii
Holland
Hong Kong &
  Macau
Hungary
India
Indonesia
Ireland
Israel & the
  Palestinian
  Territories
Italy
Jamaica
Japan
Jordan

Kenya
Lake District
Laos
London
Los Angeles
Malaysia,
  Singapore &
  Brunei
Mallorca &
  Menorca
Maya World
Mexico
Morocco
Moscow
Nepal
New England
New York
New Zealand
Norway
Pacific
  Northwest
Paris
Peru
Poland
Portugal
Prague
Provence & the
  Côte d'Azur
The Pyrenees
Rhodes & the
  Dodecanese

Romania
St Petersburg
San Francisco
Sardinia
Scandinavia
Scotland
Scottish
  highlands and
  Islands
Sicily
Singapore
South Africa
South India
Southwest USA
Spain
Sweden
Syria

Thailand
Trinidad &
  Tobago
Tunisia
Turkey
Tuscany &
  Umbria
USA
Venice
Vienna
Vietnam
Wales
Washington DC
West Africa
Zimbabwe &
  Botswana

AVAILABLE AT ALL GOOD BOOKSHOPS

ROUGH GUIDES: Mini Guides, Travel Specials and Phrasebooks

MINI GUIDES
Antigua
Bangkok
Barbados
Big Island of
  Hawaii
Boston
Brussels
Budapest

Dublin
Edinburgh
Florence
Honolulu
Jerusalem
Lisbon
London
  Restaurants
Madrid
Maui
Melbourne
New Orleans
Rome
Seattle
St Lucia

Sydney
Tokyo
Toronto

TRAVEL SPECIALS
First–Time Asia
First–Time
  Europe
Women Travel

PHRASEBOOKS
Czech
Dutch

Egyptian Arabic
European
French
German
Greek
Hindi & Urdu
Hungarian
Indonesian
Italian
Japanese

Mandarin
  Chinese
Mexican
  Spanish
Polish
Portuguese
Russian
Spanish
Swahili
Thai
Turkish
Vietnamese

AVAILABLE AT ALL GOOD BOOKSHOPS

ROUGH GUIDES:
Reference and Music CDs

REFERENCE

Classical Music
Classical:
  100 Essential CDs
Drum'n'bass
House Music
Jazz
Music USA

Opera
Opera:
  100 Essential CDs
Reggae
Reggae:
  100 Essential CDs
Rock
Rock:
  100 Essential CDs
Techno
World Music
World Music:
  100 Essential CDs
English Football
European Football

Internet
Millennium

ROUGH GUIDE MUSIC CDs

Music of the
  Andes
Australian
  Aboriginal
Brazilian Music
Cajun & Zydeco

Classic Jazz
Music of
  Colombia
Cuban Music
Eastern Europe

Music of Egypt
English Roots
  Music
Flamenco
India & Pakistan
Irish Music
Music of Japan
Kenya & Tanzania
Native American
North African
Music of Portugal

Reggae
Salsa
Scottish Music
South African
  Music
Music of Spain
Tango
Tex-Mex
West African
  Music
World Music
World Music Vol 2
Music of
  Zimbabwe

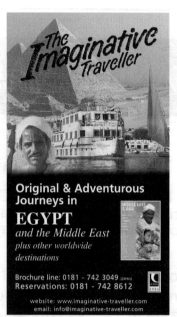
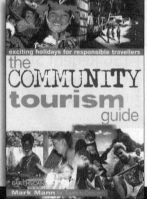